Emery
A327727
B1-16

NORTH AMERICAN
FILM AND VIDEO DIRECTORY

NORTH AMERICAN FILM AND VIDEO DIRECTORY

A Guide to Media Collections and Services

Compiled by Olga S. Weber

With the assistance of Deirdre Boyle, Consultant

R. R. BOWKER COMPANY
A Xerox Publishing Company
New York & London, 1976

Published by R. R. Bowker Co. (A Xerox Publishing Company)
1180 Avenue of the Americas, New York, N.Y. 10036

Copyright © 1976 by Xerox Corporation

All rights reserved. Reproduction of this book, in whole or in part,
without written permission of the publisher is prohibited.
International Standard Book Number: 0-8352-0883-4
International Standard Serial Number: 0362-7802
Library of Congress Catalog Card Number: 76-26748
Printed and bound in the United States of America

The R. R. Bowker Company has used its best efforts to include the
information submitted, but has no legal responsibility for
accidental omissions or errors in these listings.

027.9
W375n
cop. 3

CONTENTS

CONTENTS

PREFACE

This is the first edition of the *North American Film and Video Directory: A Guide to Media Collections and Services*. It is both a revision and extension of the pioneer *Directory of Film Libraries in North America*, published by the Film Library Information Council in 1971, in that in addition to updating data on film and other media services, information has been expanded to include institutions offering video services and/or maintaining video tape collections. Our coverage of film and video services extends to public, academic, archival, and special libraries; no attempt has been made to gather similar information for elementary or secondary schools.

We feel this survey of libraries and media centers involved in the use of AV materials and related services will be frequently consulted for interlibrary loan information, for directing patrons to other sources, for consultation in collection development, and in the preparation of budget and grant proposals. You, the reader, will undoubtedly find many other ways to utilize the information contained in these pages.

Though a number of libraries and media centers did not respond to our questionnaire, in spite of repeated requests for information (see page ix), we are pleased to have been able to capture much information in a neglected area of documentation. Your comments, corrections, and additions will be welcomed in helping to identify the universe of institutions offering film and video services, thus assuring a greater coverage in the next edition and a more comprehensive volume.

We appreciate greatly the support and cooperation of the Film Library Information Council, the Educational Film Library Association, and the Public Library Association/Audio-Visual Committee of ALA, and are pleased to have the following prefatory comments from each appear in this first edition.

From the Film Library Information Council (FLIC)
by William Sloan, Editor, *Film Library Quarterly*

The *North American Film and Video Directory* has its genesis in the *Directory of Film Libraries in North America* published by the Film Library Information Council. FLIC is the national organization of film librarians in public libraries in North America. The Directory was conceived in the late 1960s and was the project of Joan Clark Wilkinson, who served for some years as the president of FLIC. She was for many years the New York State Audio-Visual Consultant to public libraries in the state, working in the Division of Library Development of the State Education Department. In carrying out her work, she was in constant touch with librarians throughout the United States. It was this personal correspondence file that formed the basis for a card file which in turn was the foundation of the FLIC Directory. Using these files, FLIC surveyed public libraries and universities throughout the United States and Canada concerning their film staff and film holdings. In this way the entries for the directory were completed.

However, financing the printing of the directory presented a problem. Fortunately, one of the FLIC directors, Octavio Noda, who was the chief of the film services at the Suburban Library System in Illinois, discovered that one of his film borrowers was a retired printer, and had a printing press in his basement. Using the services of his friendly printer, Mr. Noda was able to supervise the production of the directory for little more than the cost of materials. In 1971 the work was completed, and FLIC began issuing the directory to libraries and film distributors throughout North America. Both Mrs. Joan Clark Wilkinson and Octavio Noda later left public library film work, and the Film Library Information Council turned its directory materials over to the American Library Association and the R. R. Bowker Company in order to help make it possible to bring out an updated version.

From the Educational Film Library Association (EFLA)
by Nadine Covert, Executive Director

The Educational Film Library Association is a national membership association, founded in 1943, to serve as a clearinghouse for information about 16mm film utilization, selection, evaluation, production, and distribution. Members include public library film departments, university and college film collections, school media centers, museums, religious organizations, government, business, and other community agencies that utilize films; film distribution companies and service agencies; and individual librarians, teachers, filmmakers, writers.

EFLA activities and services include a film evaluation program with results published ten times a year; a quarterly magazine, *Sightlines*; publication of annotated film lists on a variety of subjects and pamphlets on film evaluation, utilization, selection; sponsorship of the annual American Film Festival; presentation of workshops on topics of interest to members; a library open to the public; mail and telephone information and referral services for members.

EFLA is interested in cooperating with other organizations serving the educational film field and we are pleased to have been a part of this joint project.

From the Public Library Association/Audio-Visual Committee
by Laura Murray, Metro Toronto Library Board, Canada, and Chairperson, PLA/AV Committee

This publication was made possible by the close and cooperative efforts of several associations working with

Bowker to produce this much-awaited directory. One of these groups is the PLA/AV Committee of ALA which was formed to focus attention on bringing better AV materials-services to the public library user. Members of these associations assisted in developing the questionnaire, promoting prompt returns, and checking information received.

In particular, special thanks are given to the following: Nadine Covert (Exec. Director, Educational Film Library Association, N.Y.), Helen Cyr (Enoch Pratt Free Library, Baltimore, Md.), Pat Del Mar (Long Beach Public Library, Calif.), Leon Drolet (Suburban Audiovisual Service, Burr Ridge, Ill.), Jacqueline Ek (Indianapolis-Marion County Public Library, Ind.), Larry Freeman (Greenville County Library, S.C.), Stephen Harvey (Geauga County Public Library, Chardon, Ohio), Carolyn Hauck (Enoch Pratt Free Library, Baltimore, Md.), Patricia Hogan (North Suburban Library System, Wheeling, Ill.), George Holloway (Free Library of Philadelphia, Pa.), Mary Helen Karpinski (Memphis & Shelby City Public Library, Tenn.), David Leamon (Tulsa City-County Library, Okla.), Jim Limbacher (Henry Ford Centennial Library, Dearborn, Mich.), Myra Nadler (Palos Verdes Library District, Calif.), Penny Northern (Kansas City Public Library, Mo.), Euclid Peltier (Boston Public Library, Mass., and Pres., Film Library Information Council), Diane Purtill (Chicago Public Library, Ill.), Donald J. Sager (Columbus Public Library, Ohio), Darlene Weston (Minneapolis, Public Library, Minn.).

Acknowledgments

Many have given of their time and effort in the compilation of this directory, but first and foremost, I personally thank all who responded to our questionnaires and who provided the information necessary to the successful completion of this work. A special thanks to Patricia G. Schuman, former Bowker editor, who enlisted and obtained the support of the PLA/AV Committee of ALA, EFLA, and FLIC in endorsing this project and urging the cooperation of their members. This has given me the opportunity and pleasure of working with such ever-helpful, always encouraging, persons as Nadine Covert of EFLA, Bill Sloan and Ed Peltier of FLIC, and Laura Murray and her hard-working PLA/AV Committee. I am especially grateful to Deirdre Boyle, who served as consultant in the preliminary stages in the development and design of questionnaires, and who was always able and available to interpret the technical data submitted.

Of the many other individuals who participated in the compilation of this work, a particular note of gratitude must be sounded for Stephen Calvert and Valerie Saint-Rossy, who, with Julia Raymunt of Bowker's Editing Department, shaped the raw material of the questionnaires into a logical and standardized format and handled the flow of copy to the compositor, always meeting the ever-present deadline.

OLGA S. WEBER

HOW TO USE THIS BOOK

The gathering of information for a new directory is never an easy task. The success of the compilation depends mainly on the cooperation and willingness of the questionnaire recipient to carve out of his busy day the time needed to thoughtfully respond to the queries asked.

Our mailing list was developed from those entries in the *American Library Directory* which indicated libraries with films, the *Directory of Film Libraries in North America*, and various video source lists and museum lists. Two questionnaires were designed and printed, one for film services and one for video services. The first mailing of questionnaires was made in October 1975 with a follow-up mailing the following month. In the Spring of 1976, a third mailing was made to nonrespondents, each questionnaire accompanied by a special letter from a PLA/AV Committee member within his geographically assigned area urging recipients to respond. Through such cooperation and combined effort, we are able to present in this first edition documentation of the film and video services offered by 1,273 libraries and media centers.

General Arrangement

Entries have been arranged geographically by state (or province) and city, and under each town or city alphabetically by name. Each has been classified by a symbol. All public libraries have been identified in the margin with the key "P." University, college, and junior college libraries carry the key "C." The key "A" identifies archival libraries such as museums and gallery collections, or those with noncirculating film collections. Special libraries (key "S") include those of hospitals, business firms, video centers, foundations and associations, state government agencies, state libraries, and the libraries or media centers of specialized colleges. For other abbreviations used throughout the book, see the list following this section.

Each entry contains the name and address of the library or media center, postal zip code, telephone number, year in which film service was established, and the name and title of the person in charge of film services. Figures given for the number of audiovisual staff, including the breakdown by number of professional, clerical, and technical staff, are full-time equivalent approximations. Methods of selection of new films for purchase are indicated in the *Film Sel* statement. *Holdings* identifies a library's collection of films, either in a subject area or type of film, and the percentage in each area of the total collection. Libraries which indicated equal holdings in all subject areas were noted in the entry as maintaining a general collection of films, while those which showed holdings of 20 percent or more within a certain subject area or type of film have also been indexed in the Special Collections section in the backmatter.

In the paragraph **Free-Loan Film Serv** information on the free-loan film service provided by the library is noted.

Eligibility requirements for individuals and organizations permitted to use this free service are given. *Restrictions* apply to geographical restrictions for individuals and institutions. Further restrictions as to use of borrowed films, e.g., fund-raising, classroom use, are so noted, as is free-loan policy in terms of availability to researchers and scholars for on-site viewing, borrowing by mail, and length of loan period. *Total Yr Film Loan* figures given are for the year as of July 1975 unless otherwise designated.

In **Film Rental Serv**, the same statements of eligibility for individuals and organizations and geographical restrictions are given about the rental service provided by the library. Policy concerning length of rental period is noted. *Total Yr Film Booking* figures are for the year as of July 1975 unless otherwise designated. Additionally, information on the sale or the production of films or other media appears in this portion of the entry.

Film Collection gives figures as to the size of collections. The total number of the film collection, both 16mm and 8mm, is given in terms of the number of titles (t) and the number of prints (p), e.g., 100t/250p. Where the number of titles equals the number of prints, the figure will appear, for example, as 100t/p. An approximation of the number of titles acquired annually is given. Collection figures representing both titles and prints are broken down into holdings of 16mm, 8mm reel to reel, 8mm cartridge, S8mm reel to reel, and S8mm cartridge, and are noted as circulating or noncirculating collections. Information on publications, such as catalogs and supplements, their price and frequency, is given in this paragraph as well as data on other materials published which pertain to the collection.

In **Other Film Serv**, information is given on the various means by which libraries obtain films, other than by purchase, and the ways in which these are used by the library, e.g., film fairs/festivals. [It was brought to our attention, too late for corrections to be made, that the name of the Consortium of University Film Centers appears in several entries as a coop loan system from which films were obtained. The CUFC does not loan films; it is a group dedicated to cooperative planning to promote and improve the use of films in education, and is involved in research and information exchange to insure optimal standards of service and distribution. The required adjustments will be made in our next edition.] The availability of a permanent viewing facility to the community, either by rental or free use, is indicated. Types of film equipment available for loan or rental, and the quantity of equipment owned, is noted. In some instances, where a responding library did not indicate either rental or loan, only the figures for equipment owned are shown.

Other Media Collections gives information on AV holdings other than film or video, such as *audio*, discs (33⅓ rpm, 45rpm, 78rpm), tape (cassette, cartridge, reel to reel); *filmstrips*, sound and silent (exclusive of sets), sound and silent sets; and *slides*, single and sets. Here titles have been designated "t" while copies appear as "c."

The total library budget for all materials, print and nonprint, is given in **Budget & Expenditures** with the fiscal year in parentheses. When reported on the questionnaire, further information such as total FY film budget or total AV materials budget appears. Where no figures other than the total library budget are given, we have used the statement "No separate AV budget." Information on *membership* in well-known national media groups such as AECT, AFI, ALA, CUFC, EFLA, and FLIC, as well as in state and regional organizations, will be found in this paragraph in the entry.

The **Video** information in an entry includes the year in which video services were established, as well as the number of full-time (f-t) or part-time (p-t) staff and technicians. The reasons for using video are given in *Video Use*, and the availability of video services, either on demand or by appointment, is noted.

The number and various types of video equipment owned and available either for in-house use only or for loan are designated in the paragraph **Video Equipment/Facilities**. Policy on the length of the equipment loan period is stated, as well as the training of individuals in the use of video equipment. Noted, also, are those centers with tape duplication service.

Video Tape Loan/Rental/Sale Serv gives information on the type of service provided, and the loan or rental eligibility of individuals and groups, and geographical restrictions. Policy on the use of tapes, borrowing by mail, and loan period is also given.

In **Video Collection**, the methods of obtaining tapes or maintaining a collection are given. The types of tape used or played, e.g., ½", ¼", 1", 2" reel to reel, ½" cartridge, or ¾" cassette, the sources for tapes, and the method of tape selection are described. The size of a video tape collection is indicated in terms of tape used/played, black-and-white or color, and figures given to represent number of video tape titles (t) and number of copies (c).

The organization of the tape collection, e.g., Dewey Decimal, as well as information on special collections, is also noted. Described in this paragraph also are *other video services* offered, such as programming or taping of other media, and published materials on video, such as catalogs and supplements.

In **Cable & CCTV**, data indicates whether or not a community is now served by a cable television system (or soon will be) and if the institution reporting receives its services. The involvement of the institution in the system in terms of production of programs for cablecasting, advisory or administrative role in the cable system operation, etc., is described. Also noted is whether or not a closed circuit television system exists within the institution, the number of monitors comprising the system, and programming sources used.

The backmatter of the directory contains two indexes: One, Index of Libraries, is an alphabetical index to all entry names with city and state. Those libraries/centers which provide video services have been designated with an asterisk. The other, Index of Special Collections, is an alphabetical arrangement by subject, film category, or private collection of those library/center collections which were 20 percent or more of the total collection. The library name, city, and state appears under each appropriate heading.

Also forming part of the backmatter is the section on Film Circuits and Cooperatives. Each entry gives information reported on name, address, telephone number of the group, the name of the person in charge, film holdings, membership total, membership criteria and audience served, initial membership fee, yearly assessment, budget, frequency of general and preview-selection committee meetings and where held, and publications.

An Addendum has been included for those centers heard from after page makeup had been completed for their geographical area. Included here also are libraries who are members of a film circuit or cooperative about whom we received information in soliciting data for the Film Circuits and Cooperatives section but which arrived too late for inclusion in their appropriate state pages.

ABBREVIATIONS

ALA   American Library Association
AV   audiovisual
approx   approximate(ly)
Assn   Association
Asst   Assistant
Ave   Avenue

b&w   black & white
Blvd   Boulevard

c   copy(ies)
c.   circa
CCTV   Closed Circuit Television
CUFC   Consortium of University Film Centers
circ   circulating
cl   clerical
col   color
coop   cooperative
Coord   Coordinator

Dept   Department
Dir   Director

E   East
EFLA   Educational Film Library Association
Est   Established
excl   excluding, exclusive
ext   extension

FY   Fiscal Year
f-t   full-time
FLIC   Film Library Information Council

geog   geographical

hr   hour

IMC   Instructional Media Center
indiv   individual(s)

Jr   Junior

LC   Library of Congress

LRC   Learning Resources Center
Lab   Laboratory

Mgr   Manager
misc   miscellaneous

N   North
noncirc   noncirculating

org   organization

p   print(s)
p-t   part-time
paraprof   paraprofessional
prof   professional
Pubns   Publications

Rd   Road
reel   reel to reel

S   South
SE   Southeast
SEG   Special Effects Generator
sel   selection
Serv   Service(s)
Spec   Special
Sr   Senior
St   Street
Superv   Supervisor
suppl   supplement

t   title(s)
TV   television
tech   technician
technol   technology
Tel   Telephone

W   West
wk   week

Yr   Year

UNITED STATES

Alabama

Andalusia

P- ANDALUSIA PUBLIC LIBRARY, 212 S 3 Notch St, 36420. *Tel:* (205) 222-6612. *Film Serv Est:* 1972. *In Charge:* Margaret West, Dir. *AV Staff:* 1 (2cl, 1 tech). *Film Sel:* committee preview.
Free-Loan Film Serv *Eligibility:* educational inst, civic & religious groups, indiv with library cards, prof groups. *Restrictions:* for indiv, interlibrary loan, only in Covington County; for inst, none. Available to researchers/scholars for on-site viewing. May borrow by mail. *Loan Period:* 2 days. *Total Yr Film Loan:* 357.
Other Film Serv Rent film from distributors for patrons, obtain film from coop loan system (Ala. Coop Film Circuit), obtain film from other libraries, film fairs/festivals, library film programs. Permanent viewing facility available free to community. *Equipment:* lend 16mm sound projector, lend 8mm reel projector, lend projection screens.
Budget & Expenditures No separate budget. *Member:* Ala. Library Assn, Ala. Instructional Media Assn.

Auburn

S- AUBURN UNIVERSITY, Coop Extension Serv, B-12 Extension Hall, 36830. *Tel:* (205) 826-4972. *In Charge:* Elbert Williams, Visuals Editor. *AV Staff:* 7 (3 prof, 1 cl, 3 tech). *Film Sel:* committee preview. *Holdings:* agriculture 65%, career education 5%, consumer affairs 5%, engineering 5%, science 10%, women 10%.
Free-Loan Film Serv *Eligibility:* staff & students, educational inst, civic & religious groups. *Restrictions:* for indiv, only in state. Available to researchers/scholars for on-site viewing. May borrow by mail. *Loan Period:* 30 days. Produce films. Produce slides, tapes, posters, transparencies.
Film Collection 200t/300p. Approx 15t acquired annually. *Pubns:* catalog, every 2 yr; suppl, no set policy.
Budget & Expenditures No separate budget.

Decatur

P- WHEELER BASIN REGIONAL LIBRARY, Box 1766, 35601. *Tel:* (205) 353-2993. *Film Serv Est:* 1972. *In Charge:* Deborah Clearman. *AV Staff:* 1. *Film Sel:* committee preview, catalogs.
Free-Loan Film Serv *Eligibility:* adults with library cards. *Restrictions:* for indiv, only in Morgan & Limestone counties; 25¢ maintenance fee for loan of 16mm films; 8mm films loaned free. Available to researchers/scholars for on-site viewing. May borrow by mail. *Loan Period:* 1 day. *Total Yr Film Loan:* 1064.
Film Collection 137t/p. Approx 1 (16mm), 10-15 (8mm)t acquired annually. *Circ:* 16mm, 8t/p; 8mm reel, 129t/p.
Other Film Serv Obtain film from coop loan system (Ala. Coop Film Circuit), obtain film from other libraries, library film programs. *Equipment:* rent 16mm sound projector (1), rent 8mm reel projector (1), lend projection tables & stands, lend projection screens (2), lend audio cassette tape recorder (1).

Budget & Expenditures Total library budget $25,550 (FY 7/1/74-7/1/75). Total FY film budget $500. *Member:* ALA, Ala. Library Assn.

Fayette

C- BREWER STATE JUNIOR COLLEGE, Learning Resources Center, 35555. *Tel:* (205) 932-3221, ext 227. *Film Serv Est:* 1970. *In Charge:* Evelyn Olive, Media Specialist. *AV Staff:* 1½ (1 prof, ¼ cl). *Film Sel:* faculty/staff recommendations, chief film librarian's decision. *Holdings:* social sciences 60%.
Free-Loan Film Serv *Eligibility:* staff & students, educational inst, civic, religious, & prof groups. *Restrictions:* for indiv & inst, only in state. Cannot use for fund-raising. May not borrow by mail. *Loan Period:* 3 days.
Film Collection 96t/p. Approx 10-12t acquired annually. *Circ:* 16mm, 69t/p; S8mm cartridge, 27t/p. *Pubns:* catalog, annual.
Other Film Serv Rent film from distributors for patrons, obtain film from coop loan system, obtain film from other libraries, film reference serv. Permanent viewing facility available for rent to community.
Other Media Collections *Audio:* disc, 33⅓rpm, 211t/c; tape, cassette, 287t/c. *Filmstrips:* sound, 153t/c; silent, 37t/c; *Slides:* single, 1000t/c; sets, 11t/c.
Budget & Expenditures Total library budget $18,857 (FY 10/1/74-10/1/75). Total FY film budget $6315. *Member:* ALA, Ala. Library Assn, Ala. Jr College Library Assn.

Livingston

C- LIVINGSTON UNIVERSITY, College of Education, Media Center, 35470. *Tel:* (205) 652-9661, ext 223. *Film Serv Est:* 1968. *In Charge:* Martha Fluker, Dir. *AV Staff:* 3 (1 prof, 1 cl, 1 tech). *Film Sel:* faculty/staff recommendations.
Free-Loan Film Serv *Eligibility:* staff & students, educational inst. *Restrictions:* for indiv & inst, only in Sumter County. Cannot transmit electronically. Available to researchers/scholars for on-site viewing. May not borrow by mail. *Loan Period:* 3 days.
Film Collection 567t/550p. Approx 35t acquired annually. *Circ:* 16mm, 567t/550p.
Other Film Serv Permanent viewing facility.
Video Serv *Est:* 1968. *In Charge:* Martha Fluker, Dir. *Video Staff:* 3 f-t, 1 tech. *Video Use:* documentation of community/school events, in-service training, as art form, teacher training. Video serv available on demand. Produce video tapes. Have production studio/space.
Video Equipment/Facilities *In-House Use Only:* recording/playback decks (11), ½″ b&w, Sony AV 3600, Craig 6401, Craig 6407; monitor (11), b&w, Sony, Craig, GE; tripods (11); audio tape recorders (33). Provide training in use of equipment to students.
Video Tape Loan/Rental/Sale Serv *Serv Provided:* occasionally swap with other inst. *Loan Eligibility:* staff & stu-

Livingston (cont'd)

dents, civic groups, religious groups. *Restrictions:* for indiv, only in Sumter County. Cannot duplicate, air without permission.

Video Collection Maintained by purchase, own production, exchange/swap. Use/play ½″ reel to reel. *Special Collections:* in-house training tapes.

Cable & CCTV Receive serv of cable TV system.

Maxwell Air Force Base

C- AIR UNIVERSITY, AV Library, 3825th Academic Serv Group, 36112. *Tel:* (205) 293-2208. *Film Serv Est:* 1952. *In Charge:* Dewey L. Glass, Chief. *AV Staff:* 5 (1 prof, 2 cl, 2 tech). *Film Sel:* committee preview, faculty/staff recommendations, chief film librarian's decision. *Holdings:* commercial 10%; military 90%.

Free-Loan Film Serv *Eligibility:* staff & students. *Restrictions:* for indiv, interlibrary loan, only in region; for inst, only in region. Available to researchers/scholars for on-site viewing. May not borrow by mail. *Loan Period:* 5 days. *Total Yr Film Loan:* 12,000.

Film Collection 2025t/2525p. Approx 100t acquired annually. *Circ:* 16mm, 2000t/2500p; 8mm reel, 25t/p. *Pubns:* catalog, every 3 yr; suppl, monthly.

Other Film Serv Obtain film from other libraries, film reference serv. Permanent viewing facility available. *Equipment:* lend 16mm sound projector (50), lend 8mm cartridge projector (3), lend 8mm reel projector (2), lend projection tables & stands (10), lend projection screens (20).

Other Media Collections *Audio:* disc, 33⅓rpm, 100t/c; tape, cassette, 30t/c; tape, reel, 50t/c. *Filmstrips:* sound, 100t/c; silent, 75t/c; silent sets, 50t/c. *Slides:* single, 10,000t/c.

Budget & Expenditures Total FY film budget $3500.

Mobile

C- S. D. BISHOP STATE JUNIOR COLLEGE, Library, 351 N Broad St, 36603. *Tel:* (205) 433-7476, ext 49. *In Charge:* Robert L. Parker, Dir, Library Serv.

Film Collection 164t/p. *Circ:* 16mm, 99t/p; 8mm cartridge, 64t/p; S8mm reel, 1t/p.

Other Film Serv Permanent viewing facility available for rent to community. *Equipment:* 16mm camera (1), 16mm sound projector (3), 8mm cartridge projector (8), 8mm reel projector (8), projection tables & stands (6), projection screens (12).

Other Media Collections *Audio:* disc, 33⅓rpm, 340t/344c; disc, 78rpm, 5t/1c; tape, cassette, 160t/165c; tape, reel, 190t/c. *Filmstrips:* sound sets, 118t/c; silent sets, 150t/c. *Slides:* single, 156t/c.

Video Serv *Est:* 1972. *In Charge:* Robert L. Parker, Dir, Library Serv. *Video Staff:* 4 f-t, 2 p-t. *Video Use:* practical video/TV training courses. Video serv available by appointment. Produce video tapes. Have production studio/space.

Video Equipment/Facilities *In-House Use Only:* portapak (1), b&w, Sony AC3400; monitor (1), b&w, Sony; tripods (1); audio tape recorders (1). Provide training in use of equipment to faculty.

Video Tape Loan/Rental/Sale Serv *Serv Provided:* free loan. *Loan Eligibility:* staff & students. *Restrictions:* May not borrow by mail.

Video Collection Maintained by own production. Tapes organized in numerical order.

Cable & CCTV Will have CCTV in inst. *Programming Sources:* tapes produced by students.

P- MOBILE PUBLIC LIBRARY, Contemporary Media Center, 701 Government St, 36602. *Tel:* (205) 433-0483, ext 41. *Film Serv Est:* 1972. *In Charge:* Mary D. Toulmin, Head. *AV Staff:* 3 (1 prof, 1 cl, 1 tech). *Film Sel:* committee preview.

Free-Loan Film Serv *Eligibility:* staff, educational inst, civic groups, religious groups, indiv with library cards, prof groups. *Restrictions:* for indiv & inst, only in city & in Mobile County cities without film libraries. Cannot use for fund-raising, transmit electronically. May not borrow by mail. *Loan Period:* 2 days. *Total Yr Film Loan:* 2633.

Film Collection 72t/p. Approx 18t (+35/circuit) acquired annually. *Circ:* 16mm, 72t/p, 8mm reel 200t/p. *Pubns:* catalog, annual; suppl, no set policy.

Other Film Serv Obtain film from coop loan system (Ala. Public Library System), film reference serv, library film programs. Permanent viewing facility available.

Other Media Collections *Audio:* disc, 33⅓rpm, 4000t/7000c; tape, cassette, 800t/5000c. *Filmstrips:* sound sets, 120t/202c. *Slides:* single, 12,118t; sets, 25t.

Budget & Expenditures Total library budget $230,157 (FY 10/1/74-10/1/75). Total FY film budget $5000. *Member:* ALA, EFLA, FLIC, Ala. Library Assn.

Video Serv *Est:* 1975. *In Charge:* Mary D. Toulmin. *Video Staff:* 1 p-t. *Video Use:* documentation of community/school events, to increase community's library use, in-service training. Video serv available on demand. Produce video tapes. Have production studio/space.

Video Equipment/Facilities *In-House Use Only:* recording deck (5), col, Sony; studio camera (2), b&w/col, Sony, AKAI; monitor (5), Sony; lighting (45); microphones (3); tripods (1); audio tape recorders (2); dissolve unit (1). Have portable viewing installations: receivers & players on carts. Provide training in use of equipment to professionals.

Video Collection Maintained by purchase, own production. Use/play ¾″ cassette. *Sources:* commercial distributors, community productions, exchange. *Tape Sel:* preview. Tapes organized by title. *Collection, Color:* ¾″ cassette, 25t/50c. *Pubns:* catalog.

Cable & CCTV Receive serv of cable TV system. Inform public about cable system serv & facilities.

C- UNIVERSITY OF SOUTH ALABAMA, Instructional Media Dept, 307 University Blvd, 36688. *Tel:* (205) 460-7029. *Film Serv Est:* 1969. *In Charge:* Joaquin M. Holloway, Jr., Supervisor of Instructional Media. *AV Staff:* 2 (1 prof, 1 cl). *Film Sel:* committee preview, faculty/staff recommendations. *Holdings:* animated films 10%, dance 5%, fine arts 20%, science 50%, social sciences 30%, women 5%.

Film Rental Serv *Eligibility:* no restrictions. *Restrictions:* only in city. Cannot use for fund-raising, transmit electronically. *Rental Period:* 1 day.

Film Collection 308t. *Circ:* 16mm, 280t; S8mm reel, 28t. *Pubns:* catalog, every 2 yr ($1); suppl (free).

Other Film Serv Library film programs. Permanent viewing facility available free to community. *Equipment:* rent 16mm sound projector (7), rent S8mm cartridge projector (1), rent projection tables & stands (20), rent projection screens (20), 35mm projectors (10), overhead projectors (2), opaque projector (1).

Other Media Collections *Audio:* disc, 33⅓rpm, 473t; tape, cassette, 50t; tape, reel, 84t. *Filmstrips:* sound, 90t; silent sets, 71t. *Slides:* single, 58t; sets, 20t.

Budget & Expenditures Total library budget $5000 (FY 10/1/74-10/1/75). Total FY film budget $3500. *Member:* AECT, ALA.

Video Serv *In Charge:* Joaquin M. Holloway, Jr. *Video Staff:* 1 f-t. Video serv available by appointment. Produce video tapes. Will have production studio/space & separate control room.

Video Equipment/Facilities Have permanent & portable viewing installations.

Video Collection Maintained by purchase, own production. Use/play ½″ reel to reel, ½″ cartridge, ¾″ cassette. *Sources:* commercial distributors. Tapes organized by title. *Collection, Color:* ¾″ cassette, 6t/c. *Collection, B&W:* ¾″ cassette, 18t/c.

Cable & CCTV Have CCTV in inst. *Programming Sources:* over-the-air commercial & public broadcasting, tapes produced by inst, tapes produced professionally.

Montgomery

P- ALABAMA PUBLIC LIBRARY SERVICE, 155 Administrative Bldg, 36104. *Tel:* (205) 832-5743. *Film Serv Est:* 1964. *In*

Charge: Mrs. Jananne P. Wilson, AV Librarian. *AV Staff:* 1 (1 prof, 2 cl). *Film Sel:* staff recommendations, chief film librarian's decision, published reviews. *Holdings:* children's films 80%.

Free-Loan Film Serv *Eligibility:* public libraries. *Restrictions:* for indiv, interlibrary loan, only in state; for inst, only in state. Cannot use for fund-raising, transmit electronically. Available to researchers/scholars for on-site viewing. May borrow by mail. *Loan Period:* 1 day. *Total Yr Film Loan:* 2217.

Film Collection 246t/256p. *Circ:* 16mm, 246t/256p. *Pubns:* catalog, every 2 yr; suppl, in yr catalog not published. Published Bicentennial AV List.

Other Film Serv Obtain film from coop loan system (Ala. Coop Film Circuit), film reference serv, library film programs. *Equipment:* projection tables & stands (6), 35mm filmstrip projector, slide projector, record player, cassette player.

Other Media Collections *Filmstrips:* sound, 20c; silent, 100c; sound sets, 50c; silent sets, 50c. *Slides:* sets, 18c.

Budget & Expenditures Total film budget $5400 (FY 7/1/74-7/1/75). *Member:* Ala. Library Assn, Southeastern Library Assn.

Selma

C- GEORGE C. WALLACE STATE COMMUNITY COLLEGE, Box 1049, 36701. *Tel:* (205) 875-2634, ext 55. *Film Serv Est:* 1971. *In Charge:* William C. Buchanan, Dir of Learning Resources. *AV Staff:* 1 (1 prof). *Film Sel:* faculty/staff recommendations, chief film librarian's decision.

Film Collection 10t. Approx 50t acquired annually. *Noncirc:* 16mm, 10t/p.

Other Film Serv Rent film from distributors for patrons. Permanent viewing facility available. *Equipment:* S8mm camera (4), 16mm sound projector (3), projection tables & stands (4), projection screens (2).

Other Media Collections *Audio:* disc, 33⅓rpm, 192c; tape, cassette, 372c; tape, reel, 2c. *Filmstrips:* silent, 177c; sound sets, 4c. *Slides:* single, 689c.

Budget & Expenditures Total library budget $12,625 (FY 10/1/74-10/1/75). Total FY film budget $2500.

Video Serv *Est:* 1971. *In Charge:* William C. Buchanan, Dir of Learning Resources. *Video Staff:* 1 f-t. *Video Use:* documentation of community/school events, in-service training, playback only of professionally produced tapes. Video serv available by appointment. Produce video tapes. Have production studio/space.

Video Equipment/Facilities *In-House Use Only:* recording deck (1), col, Sony; playback deck (1), col; studio camera (1), col, Sony; monitor (1), col; microphones (1); tripods (1).

Video Collection Maintained by purchase, own production. Use/play ½" reel to reel. *Tape Sel:* faculty/staff recommendations, catalogs. *Special Collections:* in-house training tapes. Tapes organized by subject. *Collection, Color:* ½" reel, 44t/c.

Troy

C- TROY STATE UNIVERSITY, Library, AV Dept, 36081. *Tel:* (205) 566-3000, ext 441. *In Charge:* Hubert L. Conner, Coord of AV Serv. *AV Staff:* 7 (1 prof, 16 tech). *Film Sel:* committee preview, faculty/staff recommendations, chief film librarian's decision.

Free-Loan Film Serv *Eligibility:* staff & students. *Restrictions:* Cannot use for fund-raising, transmit electronically. Available to researchers/scholars for on-site viewing. May not borrow by mail. *Loan Period:* 3 days.

Film Collection 1000t/p. Approx 15-20t acquired annually. *Circ:* 16mm, 600t/p; 8mm cartridge, 100t/p; S8mm cartridge, 300t/p.

Other Film Serv Rent film from distributors for patrons, obtain film from other libraries, projection serv for classrooms.

Equipment: lend 16mm sound projector, lend 8mm cartridge projector, lend 8mm reel projector, lend S8mm cartridge projector, lend S8mm reel projector, lend projection tables & stands, lend projection screens, overhead, opaque, slide, & filmstrip projectors, tape recorders, record players.

Other Media Collections *Audio:* disc (total), 3100t/c; tape, 650t/c. *Filmstrips:* sound, 1020t/c; silent, 1730t/c. *Slides:* sets, 124t/c. *Member:* ALA.

Tuscaloosa

P- FRIEDMAN LIBRARY, 1305 24 Ave, 35401. *In Charge:* Annette Watters, Adult Serv Librarian. *AV Staff:* ¾ (½ prof, ¼ cl). *Film Sel:* committee preview, published reviews.

Free-Loan Film Serv *Eligibility:* indiv with library cards for 8mm films, group showings for 16mm films & filmstrips. *Restrictions:* for indiv & inst, only in Tuscaloosa County. Film is for non-theatrical use with free admission. Film must be cleared for TV use. May not borrow by mail. *Loan Period:* 1 day.

Film Collection 204t. Approx 20t acquired annually. *Circ:* 8mm reel, 204t/p. Publish annotated bibliographies.

Other Film Serv Obtain film from coop loan system (Ala. Coop Film Circuit, Mobile Public Library). *Equipment:* lend 16mm sound projector (1), lend projection screens (1), lend filmstrip projectors (2).

Other Media Collections *Audio:* disc, 33⅓rpm, 4383c. *Filmstrips:* sound, 257c; silent sets, 1c. *Slides:* single, 649c.

Budget & Expenditures Total library budget $53,637 (FY 10/1/74-10/1/75). Total FY film budget $1500.

Video Serv *In Charge:* Annette Watters, Adult Serv Librarian. *Video Staff:* 2 p-t. *Video Use:* to increase community's library use. Produce video tapes for local cablecasting.

Video Collection Maintained by own production. Use/play ½" b&w reel to reel. Tapes are erased & reused.

Cable & CCTV Receive serv of cable TV system. Produce programs for cablecasting.

University

C- UNIVERSITY OF ALABAMA, Educational Media, Box 1991, 35486. *Tel:* (205) 348-6081. *Video Serv Est:* 1955. *In Charge:* Dr. Joel S. Whitman, Dir. *Video Staff:* 4 f-t, 9 p-t, 2 tech. *Video Use:* documentation of community/school events, in-service training, practical video/TV training courses, playback only of professionally produced tapes, as art form. Video serv available on demand. Produce video tapes. Have production studio/space & separate control room.

Video Equipment/Facilities Have portable viewing installation. *Equipment Loan Period:* loan is dependent upon duration of specific need. Provide training in use of equipment to faculty & students. Have tape duplication serv.

Video Tape Loan/Rental/Sale Serv *Serv Provided:* free loan, swap with other inst, sale. *Loan Eligibility:* staff & students, prof groups, such as ETV Network & others, such as state agencies, local school district. *Restrictions:* for inst, standing approved agreements. Cannot use for fund-raising. *Total Yr Tape Loan:* 60.

Video Collection Maintained by own production. Use/play ½", 1", 2" reel to reel, ¾" cassette. *Member:* ACDHE (only for training). Tapes organized by subject, producer. *Other Video Serv:* programming, taping of other media, production workshops.

Cable & CCTV Receive serv of cable TV system. Produce programs for cablecasting. Serve as production facility for others. Run cable programs for special audiences. Have advisory/administrative role in cable system operation. Have CCTV in inst. *Programming Sources:* over-the-air commercial & public broadcasting, tapes produced by inst, tapes produced professionally, ETV Network.

Alaska

Anchorage

P- ANCHORAGE PUBLIC LIBRARIES, Z.J. Loussac Public Library, 427 F St, 99501. *Tel:* (907) 272-2538. *Film Serv Est:* 1975. *AV Staff:* ½ cl. *Film Sel:* committee preview. *Holdings:* children's films 33%, experimental films 33%, feature films 33%.

Free-Loan Film Serv *Eligibility:* educational inst, civic & religious groups. *Restrictions:* for indiv & inst, only in city. Cannot use for fund-raising, transmit electronically. Available to researchers/scholars for on-site viewing. May not borrow by mail.

Film Collection 35t. *Circ:* 16mm, 35t.

Other Film Serv Obtain film from other libraries, film fairs/festivals, library film programs.

Other Media Collections *Audio:* disc, 33⅓rpm, 1000t/1050c; tape, cassette, 250t; tape, cartridge, 50t.

Budget & Expenditures Total library budget $100,000 (FY 1/1/75-1/1/76). Total FY film budget $11,400. *Member:* Alaska Library Assn.

Fairbanks

P- FAIRBANKS NORTH STAR BOROUGH, Library, 901 First Ave, 99701. *Tel:* (907) 452-5179. *Film Serv Est:* 1971. *In Charge:* James Hotchkiss, Extension & AV Coord. *AV Staff:* 2. *Film Sel:* preview, faculty/staff recommendations. *Holdings:* children's films 50%, miscellaneous 50%.

Free-Loan Film Serv *Eligibility:* indiv with library cards. *Restrictions:* for indiv, interlibrary loan, only in state; for inst, only in state. Cannot transmit electronically. Available to researchers/scholars for on-site viewing. May borrow by mail. *Loan Period:* 3 days. *Total Yr Film Loan:* 1000 (16mm), 1450 (8mm).

Film Collection 400t/450p. Approx 25-30(8mm)t acquired annually. *Circ:* 16mm, 150t/p; 8mm reel, 150t/175p; S8mm reel, 100t/125p. Will publish annual catalog & suppl.

Other Film Serv Obtain film from coop loan system (Pacific NW Bibliographic Center), obtain film from other libraries. *Equipment:* lend S8mm camera (1), 16mm sound projector (4), 8mm reel projector (3), S8mm reel projector (3), projection screens (2).

Other Media Collections *Audio:* disc, 33⅓rpm, 1300t/c; tape, cassette, 275t/c. *Filmstrips:* sound sets, 55t/c; silent sets, 25t/c. *Slides:* sets, 28t/c.

Budget & Expenditures Total library budget $43,536 (FY 7/1/74-7/1/75). Total FY film budget $3000. *Member:* Alaska Library Assn.

Video Serv *Est:* 1972. *In Charge:* James Hotchkiss, Extension & AV Coordinator. *Video Staff:* 2 f-t. *Video Use:* documentation of community/school events, community video access. Video serv available on demand. Produce video tapes.

Video Equipment/Facilities *For Loan:* portapak (1), ½", b&w, Sony AV3400; recording/playback deck (1), ¾", col, Sony VO1600; monitor (1), col, Sony; microphones (2); tripods (1); audio tape recorders (1). Have portable viewing installation. *Equipment Loan Period:* 3 days. Provide training in use of equipment to patrons & students.

Video Tape Loan/Rental/Sale Serv *Serv Provided:* free loan. *Loan Eligibility:* civic groups, religious groups, indiv with library cards, prof groups. *Restrictions:* for indiv & inst, only in borough. Cannot air without permission. May not borrow by mail.

Video Collection Maintained by purchase, own production. Use/play ½" reel to reel, ¾" cassette. *Sources:* community productions. *Collection, Color:* ½" reel, 2t/c; ¾" cassette, 1t/c. *Collection, B&W:* ½" reel, 57t/c. *Other Video Serv:* production workshops.

C- UNIVERSITY OF ALASKA, Elmer E. Rasmuson Library, Media Serv Film Library, Box 95203, 99701. *Tel:* (907) 479-7023. *In Charge:* Pat Ercolin, Head. *AV Staff:* 10 (2 prof, 1 cl, 7 tech) *Film Sel:* faculty/staff recommendations. *Holdings:* Northern & Arctic studies.

Free-Loan Film Serv *Eligibility:* staff & students of university & its branches. *Restrictions:* for indiv, only in state. Cannot use for fund-raising, transmit electronically. Available to researchers/scholars for on-site viewing. May borrow by mail. *Loan Period:* 3 days; bush flights, 6 weeks.

Film Rental Serv *Eligibility:* no restrictions. *Restrictions:* only in state. Cannot use for fund-raising, transmit electronically, violate copyright. *Rental Period:* 3 days; bush flights, 6 weeks. Sell films. Produce films. Produce ¾" U-matic.

Film Collection 2150t/2200p. *Circ:* 16mm, 1950t/2000p. *Noncirc:* 16mm, 200t. *Pubns:* catalog, annual (staff & students, free; others, $3); suppl, in yr catalog not published.

Other Film Serv Rent film from distributors for patrons, obtain film from coop loan system, obtain film from other libraries, film reference serv. Permanent viewing facility available. *Equipment:* lend S8mm camera, lend/rent 16mm sound projector, lend 8mm cartridge projector, lend/rent 8mm reel projector, lend/rent S8mm reel projector, lend/rent projection tables & stands, lend/rent projection screens.

Other Media Collections *Audio:* disc, 33⅓rpm, 2000 hrs.

Budget & Expenditures Total FY (1975-76) film budget $27,550.

Video Serv *Est:* 1970. *In Charge:* R. A. Emmert, Dir of Production. *Video Staff:* 1 f-t, 1 p-t. *Video Use:* documentation of community/school events, to increase community's library use, in-service training. Video serv available on demand. Produce video tapes. Have production studio/space & separate control room.

Video Equipment/Facilities *In-House Use Only:* recording deck (14), ½" Sony; playback deck (1), ¾" col, Sony; editing deck (2), col, Sony 3656, Sony 2850; studio camera (4),⅔" b&w, Sony 3200; SEG (1), Sony; additional camera lenses (4); lighting (8); microphones (6); tripods (4); audio tape recorders (1). *For Loan:* portapak (6), ½" b&w, Sony; monitor (12), Sony. Have portable viewing installation. *Equipment Loan Period:* no set policy. Provide training in use of equipment to faculty & classes. Have tape duplication serv.

Video Tape Loan/Rental/Sale Serv *Serv Provided:* free loan. *Loan Eligibility:* staff & students. *Restrictions:* for indiv, only in state (equipment, only in city). Cannot use for fund-raising, duplicate, air without permission. May borrow by mail. *Loan Period:* 7 days; bush, 2 weeks.

Video Collection Maintained by purchase, own production, exchange/swap. Use/play ½" reel to reel, ¾" cassette. *Sources:* commercial distributors. *Tape Sel:* preview, faculty/staff recommendations. *Special Collections:* films in video format, state documentaries. Tapes organized by Dewey Decimal. *Collection, Color:* ¾" cassette, 15t. *Collection, B&W:* ½" reel, 5t. *Other Video Serv:* programming, taping of other media, production workshops, custom production, equipment purchase reference. *Pubns:* catalog.

Juneau

S- ALASKA STATE LIBRARY, Film Library, Juneau Center, Pouch G, 99811. *Tel:* (907) 465-2916. *Film Serv Est:* 1974. *In Charge:* Peggy J. Cummings, Librarian. *AV Staff:* 6 (1 prof, 2 paraprof, 2 cl, 1 tech). *Film Sel:* committee preview, staff recommendations.

Free-Loan Film Serv *Eligibility:* staff & students, educational inst, civic & religious groups, indiv with library cards, prof groups. *Restrictions:* for indiv & inst, interlibrary loan, only in state. Cannot use for fund-raising, transmit electronically. Available to researchers/scholars for on-site viwing. May borrow by mail. *Loan Period:* varies. *Total Yr Film Loan:* 3000.

Film Collection 1200t/1800p; Anchorage Center, 4500t/7500p. *Circ:* 16mm, 5700t/9300p. *Pubns:* catalog, as needed; suppl, no set policy.
Other Film Serv Permanent viewing facility available. *Member:* ALA, Alaska Library Assn, Pacific NW Library Assn.

S- ALASKA STATE MUSEUM, Pouch FM, 99801. *Tel:* (907) 586-1221. *Video Serv Est:* 1972. *In Charge:* Dan L. Monroe, Education & Media Specialist. *Video Staff:* several p-t. *Video Use:* documentation of community/school events, in-service training. Video serv available on request within state. Produce video tapes. Have production studio/space.
Video Equipment/Facilities *In-House Use & Loan to State Agencies:* portapak (2), ½″, b&w, Sony 3400; recording playback deck (1), ½″, b&w, Sony 3600; editing deck (1), ½″,
b&w, Sony 3650; monitor (2), b&w, Sony; SEG (1), Shintron 360; additional camera lenses (5); microphones; tripods (2); audio tape recorders. Have permanent viewing installation. Provide training in use of equipment to faculty & public, on limited basis.
Video Tape Loan/Rental/Sale Serv *Serv Provided:* free loan, swap with other inst. *Loan Eligibility:* educational inst. *Restrictions:* for inst, only in state. May borrow by mail. *Loan Period:* varies.
Video Collection Maintained by own production. Use/play ½″ reel to reel, ¾″ cassette. *Member:* UNET. *Special Collections:* training tapes, multimedia learning programs. *Collection, B&W:* ½″ reel, 15t/20c; ¾″ cassette, 15t/20c. *Other Video Serv:* production workshops.
Cable & CCTV Produce programs for cablecasting.

Arizona

Douglas

C- COCHISE COLLEGE, Learning Resource Center, 85607. *Tel:* (602) 364-3451. *In Charge:* C. A. Lincer, AV Dir. *Video Staff:* 3 f-t, 15 p-t, 1 tech. *Video Use:* documentation of community/school events, in-service training, practical video training courses, video lecture retrieval. Video serv available on demand. Produce video tapes.
    Video Equipment/Facilities *In-House Use Only:* porta-pak (1), ½", b&w, Sony 3400; recording deck (5), ½", b&w/col, Sony 3600, 3650, 8600; studio camera (4), ½", b&w, Sony 3200, 3250; microphones (10); tripods (5). Have permanent viewing installation (preview room). *Equipment Loan Period:* 1 day, for playback only. Provide training in use of equipment to faculty & students.
    Video Collection Maintained by purchase, rental, own production. Use/play ½" reel to reel. *Sources:* commercial distributors. *Tape Sel:* preview, faculty/staff recommendations. *Special Collections:* in-house training tapes. Tapes organized by LC classification. *Collection, B&W:* ½" reel, 50t. *Other Video Serv:* production workshops.

Phoenix

P- PHOENIX PUBLIC LIBRARY, AV Serv, 12 E McDowell Rd, 85004. *Tel:* (602) 262-7359. *Film Serv Est:* 1974. *In Charge:* Irene Stevens, AV Librarian. *AV Staff:* 2 (1 prof, 1 tech). *Film Sel:* committee preview, staff recommendations.
    Free-Loan Film Serv *Eligibility:* civic & religious groups, & others, such as branch libraries. *Restrictions:* for inst, only in city. Cannot use for fund-raising, transmit electronically, borrow for classroom use. May not borrow by mail. *Loan Period:* 1-5 days. *Total Yr Film Loan:* 7546.
    Film Collection 61t/p. Approx 40-50t acquired annually. *Noncirc:* 16mm, 60t/p; S8mm reel, 1t/p. Publish film lists for library agencies.
    Other Film Serv Obtain film from coop loan system (State Library Extension Serv), film reference serv, library film programs. Permanent viewing facility available for rent to community. *Equipment:* 16mm sound projector (9), 8mm/S8mm cartridge/reel projector (1), projection tables & stands (10), projection screens (8), sound filmstrip projectors (7), carousel slide projectors (2).
    Other Media Collections *Audio:* disc, 33⅓rpm, 10,000t/4000c; tape, cassette, 121t. *Filmstrips:* sound, 122t.
    Budget & Expenditures Total library budget $650,500 (FY 7/1/74-7/1/75). Total FY film budget $8520. *Member:* AECT, ALA, EFLA, Ariz. State Library Assn, AV Education Assn.

Tempe

A- ARIZONA DEPT OF LIBRARY, ARCHIVES, & PUBLIC RECORDS, AV Section, Library Extension Serv, 2219 S 48 St, Suite D, 85282. *Tel:* (602) 271-5841. *In Charge:* Richard Parent, AV Consultant. *AV Staff:* 4 (1 prof, 1½ cl, 1½ tech). *Film Sel:* preview, chief film librarian's decision. *Holdings:* Arizona & Arizona Indians.
    Free-Loan Film Serv *Eligibility:* civic, religious, & prof groups, & non-profit org, except educational inst. *Restrictions:* for indiv & inst, only in state. Cannot transmit electronically, borrow for classroom use, use as part of a business. Available to researchers/scholars for on-site viewing. May borrow by mail. *Loan Period:* varies. *Total Yr Film Loan:* 19,929.
    Film Collection 1233t/1330p. Approx 145t acquired annually. *Circ:* 16mm, 1223t/1330p. *Pubns:* catalog, every 3 yr; suppl, in yrs catalog not published. Publish AV Newsletter 3 times a yr.
    Other Film Serv Film reference serv. Permanent viewing facility available.

    Other Media Collections *Filmstrips:* sound, 10t/c; silent, 15t/c. *Slides:* single, 2700c.
    Budget & Expenditures Total library budget $30,000 (FY 7/1/74-7/1/75). Total FY film budget $25,000. *Member:* AECT, ALA, EFLA, FLIC, Ariz. State Library Assn, Ariz. Assn for AV Education.

S- ARIZONA STATE UNIVERSITY, Central Arizona Film Coop, 85281. *Tel:* (602) 965-7564. *Film Serv Est:* 1945. *In Charge:* Warren Fry, Dir AV Serv. *AV Staff:* 18 (6 prof, 6 cl, 6 tech). *Film Sel:* faculty/public school recommendations.
    Film Rental Serv *Eligibility:* educational org, civic groups, patrons/public. *Restrictions:* only in U.S. Cannot use for fund-raising, transmit electronically. *Rental Period:* 3 days. *Total Yr Film Booking:* 56,000. Produce multimedia slide programs.
    Film Collection 6000t/10,000p. Approx 200t acquired annually. *Circ:* 16mm, 6000t/10,000p. *Pubns:* catalog, every 2 yr ($3); suppl, in yr catalog not published.
    Other Film Serv Obtain film from other libraries. Permanent viewing facility.
    Budget & Expenditures Total library budget $300,000 (FY 7/1/75-7/1/76). Total FY film budget $100,000.

Tsaile

C- NAVAJO COMMUNITY COLLEGE, Moses Donner Film Collection, 86556. *Tel:* (602) 724-3311, ext 233. *Film Serv Est:* 1973. *In Charge:* Marvin E. Pollard, Jr., AV Librarian. *AV Staff:* 2 (1 prof, 1 tech). *Film Sel:* committee preview, chief film librarian's decision. *Holdings:* Indians of North & South America.
    Free-Loan Film Serv *Eligibility:* only educational inst, prof groups, & other org on Navajo Indian reservations & groups which aid Navajos. *Restrictions:* Cannot use for fund-raising. Available to researchers/scholars for on-site viewing. May not borrow by mail. *Loan Period:* 3 days. *Total Yr Film Loan:* 75.
    Film Collection 161t. Approx 5-10t acquired annually. *Circ:* 16mm, 161t. *Pubns:* catalog, every 2 yr ($2); suppl, no set policy.
    Other Film Serv Rent film from distributors for patrons, film fairs/festivals. Permanent viewing facility available. *Equipment:* lend 16mm sound projector.
    Budget & Expenditures Total library budget $30,000 (FY 7/1/74-7/1/75). Total FY film budget $5000.

Tucson

P- TUCSON PUBLIC LIBRARY, Box 5547, 85703. *Tel:* (602) 791-4391. *Film Serv Est:* 1966. *In Charge:* Janet Lombard, Fine Arts Librarian.
    Free-Loan Film Serv *Eligibility:* civic groups, religious groups, indiv, non-profit org. *Restrictions:* for indiv & org, only in Pima County. Cannot use for fund-raising, transmit electronically, borrow for classroom use, charge admission for viewing. May not borrow by mail. *Loan Period:* 1 day. *Total Yr Film Loan:* 2281. Contract with Univ of Ariz. permits borrowing approx 6500p for reloan. Another 1200p comes from the Ariz. State Library Ext Serv for reloan to nonprofit orgs only. Each agency has own catalog with periodic supplements. No Film Collection maintained.
    Other Film Serv Obtain film from other libraries.
    Other Media Collections *Audio:* disc, 33⅓rpm, 30,600c; tape, cassette, 3300c. *Filmstrips:* sound, 760c; silent, 22c; sound sets, 2c.
    Budget & Expenditures Total library budget $375,115 (FY 7/1/74-7/1/75). Total FY film budget $1500. *Member:* Ariz. State Library Assn, SW Library Assn, INTAMEL.
    Video Serv *Est:* 1974. *In Charge:* Helen Scott. *Video Staff:* 1 p-t. *Video Use:* documentation of community/school events, to

increase community's library use, in-service training. Video serv available on demand (1 branch), by appointment (2 branches). Produce video tapes.

Video Equipment/Facilities *For Loan:* recording deck (2), ¾″, col, Sony V1800; playback deck (3), ¾″, col, Sony V1000, JVC CP5000V; studio camera (2), col, Sony 3210 DX, 3260; monitor (18), b&w/col, Sony; SEG (1), Sony SEG 1A; microphones (5); tripods (2); audio tape recorders (1). *Loan Eligibility:* on a limited basis to other city depts & local inst which helped develop tape collection. Have permanent & portable viewing installations. *Equipment Loan Period:* no set policy. Provide training in use of equipment to faculty, other city depts, video club members. Have tape duplication serv.

Video Tape Loan/Rental/Sale Serv *Serv Provided:* swap with other inst. *Restrictions:* Cannot use for fund-raising, duplicate or air without permission.

Video Collection Maintained by purchase, own production, exchange/swap. Use/play ¾″ cassette. *Sources:* commercial distributors, community productions, exchange (Ariz. Center for Experiments with TV, Tucson Medical Center, Pima Community College, Ariz. State Library, Tucson school districts). *Tape Sel:* preview, published reviews. Tapes organized by Dewey Decimal. *Collection, Color:* ¾″ cassette, 60t. *Collection, B&W:* ¾″ cassette, 51t. *Other Video Serv:* programming, production workshops for staff & other city depts, young adult video club for high school students.

Cable & CCTV Have CCTV in inst, with 18 monitors. *Programming Sources:* tapes produced by inst, tapes produced professionally, tapes produced by community groups & indiv.

C- **UNIVERSITY OF ARIZONA**, Bureau of AV Serv, Bldg No. 78, 85721. *Tel:* (602) 884-3852. *Film Serv Est:* 1919. *In Charge:* Clarence E. Eddleblute, Dir. *AV Staff:* 44 (7 prof, 15 cl, 22 tech). *Film Sel:* faculty/staff recommendations, chief film librarian's decision. *Holdings:* general collection, fine arts 18%, science 22%, social sciences 20%, teacher education 9%.

Free-Loan Film Serv *Eligibility:* staff of university. *Restrictions:* for indiv, none; for inst, only for classes & official university business. Cannot use for fund-raising, transmit electronically. Available to researchers/scholars for on-site viewing. May not borrow by mail. *Loan Period:* 2 days. *Total Yr Film Loan:* 8055.

Film Rental Serv *Eligibility:* educational org, civic groups, patrons/public. *Restrictions:* only in U.S. Cannot use for fund-raising, transmit electronically, charge admission for viewing. *Rental Period:* 2 days. *Total Yr Film Booking:* 13,675. Sell films. Produce audio recordings, graphics, photographs.

Film Collection 5200t/6700p. Approx 200t acquired annually. *Circ:* 16mm, 5200t/6700p. *Noncirc:* 16mm, 1500t/p. *Pubns:* catalog, every 3 yr; suppl, 3 times a yr.

Other Film Serv Rent film from distributors for patrons, obtain film from coop loan system (CUFC), obtain film from other libraries, film reference serv, film fairs/festivals. Permanent viewing facility available. *Equipment:* rent 16mm sound projector (88), rent 8mm cartridge projector (1), rent S8mm cartridge projector (2), rent 8/S8mm reel projector (17), rent projection tables & stands (23), rent projection screens (64), overhead projectors (73), opaque projectors (8), cassette recorders (25), reel recorders (45), p. a. systems (4).

Budget & Expenditures Total library budget $84,000 (FY 7/1/74-7/1/75). *Member:* AECT, AFI, CUFC, EFLA, Tucson AV Assn, Educational Products Information Exchange, American Federation of Film Libraries, Educational Communications Inc.

Arkansas

Arkadelphia

C- ONACHITA BAPTIST UNIVERSITY, Riley Library, 71925. *Tel:* (501) 246-4531, ext 254. *Film Serv Est:* 1967. *In Charge:* Kim M. Patterson, AV Coord. *AV Staff:* 5 (1 prof, 1 cl, 3 tech). *Film Sel:* committee preview, faculty/staff recommendations, chief film librarian's decision.

Film Collection 175t/p. Approx 30t acquired annually. *Noncirc:* 16mm, 25t/p; S8mm cartridge, 150t/p. *Pubns:* catalog, every 2 yr; suppl, monthly.

Other Film Serv Rent film from distributors for patrons, obtain film from Ark. Dept of Education, obtain film from other libraries, film reference serv. Permanent viewing facility available for rent to community. *Equipment:* lend S8mm camera, 16mm camera, 16mm sound projector, 8mm cartridge projector, 8mm reel projector, S8mm cartridge projector, S8mm reel projector, projection tables & stands, projection screens, tape recorders, lend record players.

Other Media Collections *Audio:* disc, 33⅓rpm, 600c; tape, cassette, 175c; tape, reel, 285c. *Filmstrips:* sound, 435c; silent, 215c. *Slides:* single, 1200c.

Budget & Expenditures No separate budget.

Video Serv *Est:* 1970. *In Charge:* Kim M. Patterson, AV Coord. *Video Staff:* 1 f-t, 9 p-t. *Video Use:* in-service training, practical video/TV training courses, playback only of professionally produced tapes. Video serv available by appointment. Produce video tapes. Have production studio/space & separate control room.

Video Equipment/Facilities *In-House Use Only:* portapak (1), ½", b&w, Sony; recording deck (5), ½", ¾", b&w/col, Sony, Panasonic, JVC; playback deck (1), ¾", col, JVC; studio camera (2), b&w, RCA; monitor (30), b&w/col; SEG (1), Sony; lighting (2); microphones (24); audio tape recorders (23). *For Loan:* audio tape recorders (23). Have permanent & portable viewing installations. *Equipment Loan Period:* no set policy. Provide training in use of equipment to faculty & student teachers. Have tape duplication serv.

Video Collection Maintained by purchase, rental, own production. Use/play ½" reel to reel, ¾" cassette. *Sources:* commercial distributors. *Tape Sel:* faculty/staff recommendations. *Special Collections:* in-house training tapes. Tapes organized by accession number. *Collection, B&W:* ½" reel, 87t/c; ¾" cassette, 20t/c. *Other Video Serv:* taping of other media.

Cable & CCTV Have CCTV in inst, with 100 monitors. *Programming Sources:* over-the-air commercial & public broadcasting, tapes produced by inst, tapes produced professionally.

Fort Smith

C- WESTARK COMMUNITY COLLEGE, Holt Library, Box 3649, 72901. *Tel:* (501) 785-4241, ext 252. *Film Serv Est:* 1974. *In Charge:* S. Jack Gorham, Media Specialist. *AV Staff:* 1 (1 prof, ½ cl). *Film Sel:* faculty/staff recommendations. *Holdings:* fine arts 5%, medicine 25%, psychology 10%, science 60%.

Free-Loan Film Serv *Eligibility:* staff & students, educational inst, civic & religious groups, prof groups & others, such as Whirlpool, Rheem. *Restrictions:* for indiv & inst, none. Cannot use for fund-raising, transmit electronically. Available to researchers/scholars for on-site viewing. May borrow by mail. *Loan Period:* 7 days. *Total Yr Film Loan:* 9.

Film Rental Serv *Eligibility:* no restrictions. *Restrictions:* none. Cannot use for fund-raising, transmit electronically. *Rental Period:* 7 days. *Total Yr Film Booking:* 9.

Film Collection 144t/59p. Approx 5-10t acquired annually. *Circ:* 16mm, 25t/12p; 8mm cartridge, 50t/26p; S8mm cartridge, 69t/21p.

Other Film Serv Rent film from distributors for patrons, obtain film from other libraries. *Equipment:* lend 16mm sound projector (13), lend 8mm cartridge projector (25), lend S8mm

cartridge projector (2), lend projection tables & stands (20), lend projection screens (50).

Other Media Collections *Audio:* disc, 33⅓rpm, 1500t/c; disc, 45rpm, 1t/c; disc, 78rpm, 49t/c; tape, cassette, 476t/c; tape, cartridge, 25t/c; tape, reel, 456t/c. *Filmstrips:* sound, 19t/c; silent, 198t/c; sound sets, 5t/c; silent sets, 25t/c. *Slides:* single, 1217t/c; sets, 12t/c.

Budget & Expenditures No separate budget. *Member:* ALA, Ark. Library Assn, SW Library Assn.

Video Serv *Est:* 1974. *In Charge:* S. Jack Gorham, Media Specialist. *Video Staff:* 1 f-t, 1p-t. *Video Use:* documentation of community/school events, in-service training, playback only of professionally produced tapes. Video serv available by appointment. Produce video tapes.

Video Equipment/Facilities *For Loan:* recording deck (1), ¾", col, Sony; playback deck (1), ¾", col, Sony; studio camera (1), b&w, Sony; monitor (1), col, Sony; microphones (1); tripods (1). *Equipment Loan Period:* no set policy. Provide training in use of equipment. Have audio tape duplication serv.

Video Tape Loan/Rental/Sale Serv *Serv Provided:* free loan. *Loan Eligibility:* staff & students, educational inst, civic & religious groups, & others, such as Whirlpool, Rheem, & GE. *Restrictions:* for indiv & inst, none. Cannot use for fund-raising. May borrow by mail. *Loan Period:* 7 days.

Video Collection Maintained by purchase, rental, own production. Use/play ¾" cassette. *Sources:* commercial distributors. *Tape Sel:* preview, faculty/staff recommendations. *Special Collections:* in-house training tapes, films in video format. Tapes organized by subject. *Collection, B&W:* ¾" cassette, 1t/c.

Helena

C- PHILLIPS COUNTY COMMUNITY COLLEGE, AV Dept, Box 785, 72342. *Tel:* (501) 338-6496, ext 47. *Film Serv Est:* 1971. *In Charge:* Parker Gunn, AV Technician. *AV Staff:* 1 prof. *Film Sel:* faculty/staff recommendations, chief film librarian's decision.

Free-Loan Film Serv *Eligibility:* staff, educational inst, civic & religious groups. *Restrictions:* for indiv, interlibrary loan. Cannot use for fund-raising, transmit electronically. Available to researchers/scholars for on-site viewing. May borrow by mail. Produce S8mm films & slides.

Film Collection 59t. *Circ:* 16mm, 8t; S8mm cartridge, 50t. *Noncirc:* 16mm, 1t/p.

Other Film Serv Rent film from distributors for patrons, obtain film from coop loan system (State AV Dept, Ark. Jr College Consortium), obtain film from other libraries. *Equipment:* lend S8mm camera (4), 16mm sound projector (6), 8mm reel projector (1), S8mm cartridge projector (8), S8mm reel projector (2), projection tables & stands (20), projection screens (8).

Other Media Collections *Audio:* disc, 33⅓rpm, 800t; disc, 45rpm, 1t; tape, cassette, 200t; tape, reel, 50t. *Filmstrips:* sound, 20t; silent, 150t; sound sets, 30t; silent sets, 5t. *Slides:* single, 2000t.

Budget & Expenditures Total library budget $2525 (FY 9/1/74-9/1/75). Total FY film budget $1125.

Video Serv *Est:* 1971. *In Charge:* Parker Gunn, AV Technician. *Video Staff:* 1 f-t. *Video Use:* documentation of community/school events, in-service training. Video serv available by appointment. Produce video tapes & filmstrips.

Video Equipment/Facilities *In-House Use Only:* monitor (1), Sony; additional camera lenses (2); microphones (10); tripods (4); audio tape recorders (20). *For Loan:* recording deck (1), ½", b&w, Sony AV2000. Have permanent viewing installation. *Equipment Loan Period:* no set policy. Provide training in use of equipment. Have audio tape duplication serv.

Video Tape Loan/Rental/Sale Serv *Serv Provided:* free loan. *Loan Eligibility:* staff & students, educational inst, civic & religious groups, prof groups. *Restrictions:* for indiv, interlibrary loan, only in Phillips County; for inst, none. Cannot use for fund-raising. May borrow by mail.

Video Collection Maintained by own production. Use/play ½" reel to reel. *Sources:* community productions.

Paragould

P- NORTHEAST ARKANSAS REGIONAL LIBRARY, 120 N 12 St, 72450. *Tel:* (501) 236-8761. *In Charge:* Kathleen Sharp, Dir. *Film Sel:* staff recommendations, chief film librarian's decision. *Holdings:* children's films.

Free-Loan Film Serv *Eligibility:* civic & religious groups. *Restrictions:* for indiv & inst, only in Greene County. Cannot use for fund-raising, borrow for classroom use. May not borrow by mail. *Loan Period:* 7 days.

Film Collection 105t. Approx 5t acquired annually. *Circ:* 8mm reel, 105t/p.

Other Film Serv Obtain film from Ark. Dept of Education. *Equipment:* rent 16mm sound projector (1).

Other Media Collections *Audio:* disc, 33⅓rpm, 600t; disc, 45rpm, 50t; disc, 78rpm, 50t; tape, cassette, 132t. *Filmstrips:* sound, 10t; sound sets, 30t. *Slides:* sets, 2t.

Budget & Expenditures No separate budget. *Member:* ALA, Ark. Library Assn.

California

Alameda

P- ALAMEDA FREE LIBRARY, 1433 Oak St, 94501. *Tel:* (415) 522-3578. *Film Serv Est:* 1966. *In Charge:* Carl Hamilton, City Librarian. *AV Staff:* .05. *Film Sel:* chief film librarian's decision. *Holdings:* children's films 10%.
    Free-Loan Film Serv *Eligibility:* indiv with library cards & Calif. driver's license. *Restrictions:* for inst, only in Alameda & Contra Costa counties. Available to researchers/scholars for on-site viewing. May not borrow by mail. *Loan Period:* 2 days. *Total Yr Film Loan:* 364.
    Film Collection 195t. Approx 30t acquired annually. *Circ:* 16mm, 5t; S8mm cartridge, 131t; 60 S8mm loops. *Pubns:* catalog, every 2 yrs.
    Other Film Serv Library film programs. *Equipment:* rent 16mm sound projector (4), S8mm cartridge projector (4), silent loop projector (4), lend projection screens (4).
    Other Media Collections *Audio:* disc, 33⅓rpm, 7383t; tape, cassette, 72t. *Filmstrips:* sound sets, 24t; silent sets, 30t. *Slides:* sets, 1t.
    Budget & Expenditures Total library budget $58,125 (FY 7/74-7/75). Total FY film budget $2500. *Member:* Calif. Library Assn.

Altadena

P- ALTADENA LIBRARY DISTRICT, 600 E Mariposa, 91001. *Tel:* (213) 798-0833. *In Charge:* Carole Smith, Head of Circulation. *AV Staff:* 1 cl. *Film Sel:* chief film librarian's decision.
    Free-Loan Film Serv *Eligibility:* indiv with library cards. *Restrictions:* for indiv, only in city. Cannot use for fund-raising. Available to researchers/scholars for on-site viewing. May not borrow by mail. *Loan Period:* 2 days. *Total Yr Film Loan:* 3554.
    Film Collection 78t. Approx 3t acquired annually. *Circ:* 16mm, 40p; 8mm reel, 30p; S8mm reel, 8p. *Pubns:* Publish monthly film list.
    Other Film Serv Obtain film from coop loan system (Public Library Film Circuit), obtain film from other libraries, library film programs. Permanent viewing facility available to community. *Equipment:* lend 16mm sound projector (1).
    Budget & Expenditures Total library budget $54,815 (FY 7/74-7/75). Total FY film budget $400. *Member:* ALA, Calif. Library Assn.

Anaheim

P- ANAHEIM PUBLIC LIBRARY, 500 W Broadway, 92805. *Tel:* (714) 533-5227, ext 264. *Film Serv Est:* 1973. *In Charge:* Trudy Rothschild, Library Asst. *AV Staff:* 1. *Film Sel:* committee preview. *Holdings:* children's films 20%.
    Free-Loan Film Serv *Eligibility:* indiv with library cards. *Restrictions:* for indiv, interlibrary loan; for inst, only in Orange County. Cannot use for fund-raising, transmit electronically. May not borrow by mail. *Loan Period:* 1 day. ½ *Yr Film Loan:* 2054.
    Film Collection 185t/p. Approx 18-20t acquired annually. *Circ:* 16mm, 185t. *Noncirc:* S8mm cartridge, 6t. *Pubns:* catalog, annual (25¢). Publish bimonthly annotated list of films in rotating packet.
    Other Film Serv Obtain film from coop loan system (Santiago Library System), obtain film from other libraries, film reference serv, library film programs.
    Other Media Collections *Audio:* disc, 33⅓rpm, 5300c. *Filmstrips:* silent, 26t/c; sound sets, 9t/c.
    Budget & Expenditures Total library budget $170,000 (FY 7/1/74-7/1/75). Total FY film budget $5000. *Member:* EFLA, Calif. State Library System.

Aptos

C- CABRILLO COLLEGE, Individualized Learning Center, 6500 Soquel Drive, 95003. *Tel:* (408) 425-6296. *Film Serv Est:* 1959. *In Charge:* Dr. John R. Hinton, Dean, Instructional Serv. *AV Staff:* 10½ (2½ prof, 5 cl, 3 tech). *Film Sel:* faculty/staff recommendations.
    Free-Loan Film Serv *Eligibility:* staff, students enrolled in inst, local educational inst, & others, such as local governmental agencies. *Restrictions:* for campus use only. May not borrow by mail. *Loan Period:* 1 day. *Total Yr Film Loan:* 300.
    Film Collection 100t/p. Approx 5-10t acquired annually. *Circ:* 16mm, 100t/p. *Pubns:* catalog, annual.
    Other Film Serv Permanent viewing facility. *Equipment:* lend (campus use only) 16mm sound projector (34), 8mm cartridge projector (2), 8mm reel projector (1), S8mm cartridge projector (1), S8mm reel projector (1), projection tables & stands (50), projection screens (50).
    Other Media Collections *Audio:* disc, 33⅓rpm, 100t; tape, cassette, 5000t; tape, reel, 500t. *Filmstrips:* silent, 20t; sound sets, 400t. *Slides:* single, 10,000t; sets, 50t.
    Budget & Expenditures Total library budget $200,000 (FY 7/1/74-7/1/75). Total FY film budget $11,000. *Member:* AECT.
    Video Serv *Est:* 1962. *Video Staff:* 10½ f-t, 1½ p-t, 3 tech. *Video Use:* documentation of community/school events, in-service training, practical video/TV training courses, playback only of professionally produced tapes. Video serv available on demand. Produce video tapes.
    Video Equipment/Facilities *In-House Use Only:* portapak (2), ½" b&w, Sony & JVC; recording deck (7), ½" & ¾" b&w/col; playback deck (7), ½" & ¾" b&w/col; editing deck (2), ½" & ¾" b&w/col; studio camera (3), b&w/col, Panasonic; monitor (15), b&w/col; SEG (1), b&w; additional camera lenses (2); microphones (4); tripods (4); audio tape recorders (100). Have permanent & portable viewing installations. *Equipment Loan Period:* no set policy. Provide training in use of equipment to faculty & students.
    Video Tape Loan/Rental/Sale Serv *Serv Provided:* free loan, swap with other inst. *Loan Eligibility:* staff & students, educational inst, local governmental agencies such as police/fire depts. *Restrictions:* only in college serv district. May not borrow by mail. *Total Yr Tape Loan:* 900.
    Video Collection Maintained by purchase, rental, own production, exchange/swap. Use/play ½" reel to reel, ¾" cassette. *Sources:* commercial distributors, community productions *Member:* Bay Area Calif. Comm. College TV Consortium. *Tape Sel:* preview, faculty/staff recommendations. *Special Collections:* instructional programs. *Collection, Color:* ¾" cassette, 250t. *Collection, B&W:* ½" reel, 150t. *Other Video Serv:* taping of other media. *Pubns:* catalog. Publish materials on video (computer managed library list).
    Cable & CCTV Receive serv of cable TV system. Produce programs for cablecasting (limited). Have CCTV in inst, with 15 monitors. *Programming Sources:* over-the-air commercial & public broadcasting, tapes produced by inst, rentals, tapes produced professionally.

Arcadia

P- ARCADIA PUBLIC LIBRARY, AV Dept, 20 W Duarte Rd, 91006. *Tel:* (213) 446-7111, ext 32. *Film Serv Est:* 1958. *In Charge:* Virginia A. May, AV Supervisor. *AV Staff:* 3½ (2½ cl, 1 tech). *Film Sel:* published reviews.
    Free-Loan Film Serv *Eligibility:* indiv with library cards. *Restrictions:* for indiv, only in city. Cannot use for fund-raising, transmit electronically. May not borrow by mail. *Loan Period:* 1 day. *Total Yr Film Loan:* 11,709.
    Film Collection 225t/230p. Approx 12-18t acquired annually. *Circ:* 8mm reel, 279t; S8mm reel, 104t. *Pubns:* catalog, every 2 yrs. suppl, in yr catalog not published.

Other Film Serv Obtain film from coop loan system (Film Council Circuit Comm), film reference serv, library film programs. Permanent viewing facility available for rent to community. *Equipment:* rent 16mm sound projector (5).

Other Media Collections *Audio:* disc, 33⅓rpm, 3800t; tape, cassette, 564t.

Budget & Expenditures Total library budget $80,000 (FY 7/1/74-7/1/75). Total FY film budget $5400. *Member:* EFLA, FLIC, Calif. Library Assn.

Azusa

P- AZUSA PUBLIC LIBRARY, 729 N. Dalton, 91702. *Tel:* (213) 334-0338. *Film Serv Est:* 1964. *In Charge:* Elsie Vandale, AV Supervisor. *AV Staff:* 2 (1 prof, 1 cl). *Film Sel:* committee preview, staff recommendations.

Free-Loan Film Serv *Eligibility:* indiv with library cards. *Restrictions:* for indiv, none. Cannot use for fund-raising, transmit electronically. May not borrow by mail. *Loan Period:* 1 day. *Total Yr Film Loan:* 6575.

Film Collection 200t/p. Approx 10t acquired annually. *Circ:* 16mm, 200t; 8mm reel, 128t. *Pubns:* catalog, every 2 yrs; suppl, no set policy. Publish flyers.

Other Film Serv Obtain film from coop loan system (PLFC, MCLS, FCA, APIA), obtain film from other libraries, film reference serv, library film programs. Permanent viewing facility. *Equipment:* rent 16mm sound projector (3), 8mm reel projector (2), S8mm reel projector (2), projection screen (1).

Other Media Collections *Audio:* disc, 33⅓rpm, 4000c; tape, cassette, 350c.

Budget & Expenditures No separate budget. *Member:* Calif. Library Assn.

C- CITRUS COLLEGE, Hayden Memorial Library, 18824 E Foothill, 91702. *Tel:* (213) 335-0521, ext 290. *Video Serv Est:* 1969. *In Charge:* Aline Crowley Wisdom, Dir Library Servs. *Video Staff:* 2 p-t, 1 tech. *Video Use:* documentation of community/school events, playback only of professionally produced tapes. Video serv available by appointment. Produce video tapes. Have production studio/space.

Video Equipment/Facilities *In-House Use Only:* playback deck (8), b&w/col; editing deck (1), b&w; studio camera (1), b&w; monitor (12), b&w/col; synthesizer (1); additional camera lenses (5); lighting (2); microphones (4); tripods (4); audio tape recorders (2). Have portable viewing installation. Provide training in use of equipment to students.

Video Tape Loan/Rental/Sale Serv *Serv Provided:* free loan. *Loan Eligibility:* staff. *Restrictions:* May not borrow by mail.

Video Collection Maintained by own production. Use/play ½″ reel to reel, ¾″ cassette. *Sources:* community productions. *Tape Sel:* faculty/staff recommendations. *Special Collections:* in-house training tapes. Tapes organized by subject. *Collection, Color:* ¾″ cassette, 112t/c. *Collection, B&W:* ½″ reel, 170t/c. *Other Video Serv:* taping of other media.

Cable & CCTV Have CCTV in inst, with 4 monitors. *Programming Sources:* tapes produced by inst.

Bakersfield

C- CALIFORNIA STATE COLLEGE BAKERSFIELD, AV Center, 9001 Stockdale Hwy, 93309. *Tel:* (805) 833-2391. *Film Serv Est:* 1970. *In Charge:* Dr Richard Graves, AV Coord. *AV Staff:* 4½ (1 prof, 1 cl, 2½ tech). *Film Sel:* faculty/staff recommendations. *Holdings:* black studies 10%, experimental films 5%, feature films 1%, fine arts 20%, Indian education, science 30%, teacher education 30%.

Film Collection 200t. Approx 10t acquired annually. *Circ:* 16mm, 195t; 8mm cartridge, 10t; S8mm reel, 200t; S8mm cartridge, 5t. *Noncirc:* 16mm, 5t.

Other Film Serv Rent film from distributors for patrons, obtain film from coop loan system (county) obtain film from other libraries, film reference serv. Permanent viewing facility.

Other Media Collections *Audio:* disc, 33⅓rpm, 1055t; tape, cassette, cartridge, reel, 798t. *Filmstrips:* silent, 198t; sound sets, 12t; silent sets, 8t.

Budget & Expenditures Total library budget $12,000 (FY 6/30/74-6/30/75). Total FY film budget $8000. *Member:* AECT.

Video Serv *Est:* 1970. *Video Staff:* 3 f-t, 1 p-t, 2 tech. *Video Use:* documentation of community/school events, in-service training. Video serv available on demand. Produce video tapes. Have production studio/space & separate control room.

Video Equipment/Facilities *In-House Use Only:* porta-pak (4), ¼″ & ½″ b&w/col, AKAI & Panasonic; recording deck (6), ½″ b&w/col, Sony & Panasonic; playback deck (4), ¾″ b&w/col, Sony & Panasonic; editing deck (1), ½″ col, Panasonic; studio camera (3), b&w, Panasonic; monitor (3), b&w/col, SEG (2); additional camera lenses (5); microphones (20); tripods (5); audio tape recorders (3). Have permanent viewing installation. *Equipment Loan Period:* no set policy. Provide training in use of equipment to students. Have tape duplication serv.

Video Tape Loan/Rental/Sale Serv *Serv Provided:* free loan. *Loan Eligibility:* staff, students enrolled in inst. *Restrictions:* Cannot use for fund-raising, duplicate, air without permission. Campus use only. May not borrow by mail.

Video Collection Maintained by purchase, own production. Use/play ½″, ¼″ reel to reel, ¾″ cassette. *Sources:* commercial distributors. *Tape Sel:* preview, faculty/staff recommendations, catalogs. *Special Collections:* in-house training tapes, films in video format. *Collection, Color:* ¼″ reel, 3t; ¾″ cassette, 14t. *Collection, B&W:* ½″ reel, 75t.

Cable & CCTV Have CCTV in inst, with 15 monitors. *Programming Sources:* tapes produced professionally.

P- KERN COUNTY LIBRARY SYSTEM, 1315 Truxtun Ave, 93301. *Tel:* (805) 861-2137. *In Charge:* Louann Uhler, AV Librarian. *AV Staff:* 2.4. *Film Sel:* committee preview.

Free-Loan Film Serv *Eligibility:* for public use. *Restrictions:* for inst & indiv, only in Kern County. Cannot transmit electronically, borrow for classroom use. May not borrow by mail. *Loan Period:* 1 day. *Total Yr Film Loan:* 11,521.

Film Collection 600t/929p. Approx 150t acquired annually. *Circ:* 16mm, 241p; 8mm & S8mm reel, 643p; S8mm cartridge, 55p. *Pubns:* publish film lists.

Other Film Serv Library film programs. Permanent viewing facility.

Budget & Expenditures Total library budget $298,053 (FY 7/1/74-8/31/75). Total FY film budget $8000. *Member:* EFLA, Calif. Library Assn.

Video Serv *Est:* 1973. *Video Staff:* 1 p-t. *Video Use:* documentation of community/school events, to increase community's library use, community video access, in-service training. Video serv available by appointment. Produce video tapes.

Video Equipment/Facilities *In-House Use Only:* porta-pak (1), ½″ b&w, Sony 3400; playback deck (1), ½″ b&w, Sony 3600; editing deck (1), ½″ b&w, Sony 3650; monitor (2), b&w, Sony CVM-112; SEG (1), Sony; lighting (3); microphones (3); tripods (2); audio tape recorders. Have portable viewing installation. *Equipment Loan Period:* no set policy. Provide training in use of equipment to staff.

Video Tape Loan/Rental/Sale Serv *Serv Provided:* swap with other inst. *Loan Eligibility:* org members, staff, libraries. *Restrictions:* for inst, none. Cannot use for fund-raising, air without permission. May borrow by mail. *Loan Period:* 14 days.

Video Collection Maintained by own production, exchange/swap. Use/play ½″ reel to reel. Tapes organized by subject. *Collection, B&W:* ½″ reel, 57t/c. *Other Video Serv:* programming.

Cable & CCTV Produce programs for cablecasting. Have advisory/administrative role in cable system operation through Video Access Board of Dir.

Berkeley

A- UNIVERSITY OF CALIFORNIA ART MUSEUM, Pacific Film Archive, 2625 Durant Ave, 94720. *Tel:* (415) 642-1412. *Film Serv Est:* 1967. *In Charge:* Tom Luddy, Film Cur.

Berkeley (cont'd)

Film Sel: donation. *Holdings:* animated films 15%, black studies 1%, children's films 1%, experimental films 15%, feature films 40%, fine arts 5%.

Film Collection 3000t/p. Approx 100t acquired annually.

Other Film Serv Rent film from distributors for patrons, film reference serv. Permanent viewing facility available for rent to community.

C- UNIVERSITY OF CALIFORNIA, Berkeley Campus, Rm 9, Dwinelle Hall, 94720. *Tel:* (415) 642-2536. *Video Serv Est:* 1959. *In Charge:* Peter C. Kerner, Instructional TV Coord. *Video Staff:* 14 f-t, 9 p-t, 5 tech. *Video Use:* in-service training, practical video/TV training courses, playback only of professionally produced tapes, as art form, broadcast courses. Video serv available on demand. Produce video tapes. Have production studio/space & separate control room.

Video Equipment/Facilities *In-House Use Only:* portapak (3), ½″ b&w/col, Sony 8400; recording deck (4), ½″ b&w, Sony 3650; playback deck (20), ¾″ col, Sony 1200; studio camera (2), 2″ b&w/col, Ampex; monitor (3), 1″ b&w, Ampex; SEG (2); keyer; additional camera lenses; lighting; microphones; tripods; audio tape recorders. *For Loan:* portapak (3), ½″ b&w/col, Sony 8400; playback deck (20), ¾″ col, Sony 1200. Have permanent viewing installation. *Equipment Loan Period:* no set policy. Provide training in use of equipment to faculty, staff & teaching assistants. Have tape duplication serv.

Video Tape Loan/Rental/Sale Serv *Serv Provided:* free loan, swap with other inst, sale. *Loan Eligibility:* only within system. *Restrictions:* Cannot duplicate, air without permission. May not borrow by mail.

Video Collection Maintained by purchase, own production, exchange/swap. Use/play ½″, 1″, 2″ reel to reel, ¾″ cassette. *Sources:* exchange with other educational institutions. *Tape Sel:* preview, faculty/staff recommendations. *Special Collections:* video as art. Tapes organized by subject. *Collection, Color:* ¾″ cassette, 240t. *Collection, B&W:* ½″ reel, 400t; 1″ reel, 200t; 2″ reel, 300t. *Pubns:* U.C. Union catalog 1974.

Cable & CCTV Have advisory/administrative role in cable system operation. Have CCTV in inst, with 150 monitors. *Programming Sources:* tapes produced by inst, tapes produced professionally, live distribution of course materials.

C- UNIVERSITY OF CALIFORNIA, Extension Media Center, 2223 Fulton St, 94720. *Tel:* (415) 642-0460. *Film Serv Est:* 1915. *In Charge:* C. Cameron Macauley, Dir. *AV Staff:* 24½ (4 prof, 17½ cl, 3 tech). *Film Sel:* committee preview, faculty/staff recommendations.

Film Rental Serv *Eligibility:* no restrictions. *Restrictions:* only in U.S. & territories. Cannot use for fund-raising, transmit electronically. *Rental Period:* 1 day. *Total Yr Film Booking:* 33,529. Sell films. Produce audiotapes.

Film Collection 3605t/8332p. *Pubns:* catalog, every 2 yrs; suppl, every 6 months. Publish study guides, books, brochures.

Other Film Serv Film reference serv. Permanent viewing facility available for previews only. *Equipment:* rent 16mm sound projector, S8mm reel projector, projection tables & stands, projection screens.

Other Media Collections *Audio:* disc, 33⅓rpm, 1t; tape, cassette, 283t; tape, reel, 283t.

Budget & Expenditures Total media center budget $847,500 (FY 7/1/74-7/1/75). No separate AV budget. *Member:* AECT, CUFC, EFLA.

Beverly Hills

P- BEVERLY HILLS PUBLIC LIBRARY, 444 N Rexford Drive, 90210. *Tel:* (213) 274-7044, ext 31. *Film Serv Est:* 1972. *In Charge:* Mona Schroeder, AV Librarian. *AV Staff:* 2 (½ prof, ½ cl, 1 tech). *Film Sel:* committee preview, staff recommendations, chief film librarian's decision. *Holdings:* animated films 24%.

Free-Loan Film Serv *Eligibility:* indiv with library cards. *Restrictions:* for indiv & inst, only in city. Cannot use for fund-raising, transmit electronically. May not borrow by mail. *Loan Period:* 1 day. *Total Yr Film Loan:* 1541.

Film Collection 117t/p. *Circ:* 16mm, 73t/p; S8mm reel, 24t/p. *Noncirc:* 16mm, 20t/p. *Pubns:* catalog, annual; suppl, no set policy. Publish publicity flyers.

Other Film Serv Obtain film from coop loan system (Public Library Film Circuit), obtain film from other libraries, film reference serv, library film programs. Permanent viewing facility available to community.

Other Media Collections *Audio:* disc, 33⅓rpm, 2322t/100c; tape, cassette, 703t/30c; tape, reel, 68t/p. *Slides:* single, 2242t/c.

Budget & Expenditures Total library budget $98,900 (FY 7/1/74-7/1/75). Total FY film budget $881. *Member:* ALA, Public Library Film Circuit.

Carlsbad

S- CARLSBAD CITY LIBRARY, 1250 Elm Ave, 92008. *Tel:* (714) 729-7933. *In Charge:* Joseph Skymba, AV Dept Head. *AV Staff:* 2 (1 prof, 1 cl, 1 tech). *Film Sel:* chief film librarian's decision. *Holdings:* children's films 22%, experimental films 20%, feature films 18%, fine arts 10%.

Free-Loan Film Serv *Eligibility:* staff & students, educational inst, civic groups, religious groups, indiv with library cards, prof groups, & others, such as sports groups. *Restrictions:* for indiv, interlibrary loan, only in San Diego County; for inst, only in city. Cannot borrow for classroom use. May not borrow by mail. *Loan Period:* 1 day. *Total Yr Film Loan:* 55. Produce S8 sound & silent films.

Film Collection 97t/p. Approx 15t acquired annually. *Circ:* 16mm, 61t/p; 8mm reel, 3t. *Noncirc:* S8mm cartridge, 36t/p. *Pubns:* catalog, as needed; suppl, no set policy.

Other Film Serv Obtain film from coop loan system (Serra Regional Library System AV Center, San Diego), obtain film from other libraries, film fairs/festivals, library film programs. Permanent viewing facility available to community. *Equipment:* lend 16mm camera (1), 16mm sound projector (2), projection screens (1).

Other Media Collections *Audio:* disc, 33⅓rpm, 2379t/c; tape, cassette, 1284t/c. *Filmstrips:* sound, 36t/c; silent 12t/c. *Slides:* single, 200t.

Budget & Expenditures Total library budget $12,000 (FY 7/1/73-7/1/74). Total FY film budget $2800.

Video Serv *Video Staff:* 2 f-t, 1 p-t, 1 tech. *Video Use:* documentation of community/school events, in-service training, as art form, interviews. Video serv available on demand. Produce video tapes.

Video Equipment/Facilities *In-House Use Only:* portapak (1), ½″ b&w, Panasonic; monitor (1), 22″ b&w, Magnavox; microphones (2); tripods (1). Have portable viewing installation. *Equipment Loan Period:* no set policy. Provide training in use of equipment to AV personnel.

Video Tape Loan/Rental/Sale Serv *Eligibility:* staff. *Restrictions:* Cannot duplicate, air without permission. May not borrow by mail. *Loan Period:* 1 day.

Video Collection Maintained by own production. Use/play ½″ reel to reel. *Sources:* community productions. Tapes organized by subject. *Collection, B&W:* ½″ reel, 46t/c.

Cerritos

P- CITY OF CERRITOS PUBLIC LIBRARY, AV Serv, 18025 Bloomfield Ave, 90701. *Tel:* (213) 924-5775. *Film Serv Est:* 1972. *In Charge:* Iris Ruiz, AV Librarian. *AV Staff:* 3 (1 prof, 1 cl, 1 tech). *Film Sel:* committee preview, staff recommendations, chief film librarian's decision, published reviews. *Holdings:* animated films 25%, children's films 23%, sports 12%.

Free-Loan Film Serv *Eligibility:* indiv with library cards. *Restrictions:* for indiv, interlibrary loan. Cannot use for fund-raising, transmit electronically. Available to researchers/scholars for on-site viewing. *Loan Period:* 1 day.

Film Collection *Circ:* 16mm, 126t/p. *Pubns:* catalog, annual; suppl.
Other Film Serv Obtain film from coop loan system (Metropolitan Cooperative Library System), obtain film from other libraries, film reference serv, library film programs. Permanent viewing facility available for rent to community. *Equipment:* lend 16mm sound projector (8), S8mm reel projector (3), projection screens (2). *Member:* EFLA, MCLS, Calif. Library Assn.

Chula Vista

P- CHULA VISTA PUBLIC LIBRARY, AV Dept, 365 F St, 92010. *Tel:* (714) 427-4234. *Film Serv Est:* 1969. *In Charge:* Nora McMartin, AV Librarian. *AV Staff:* 5 (1 prof, 2 cl, 2 tech). *Film Sel:* committee preview.
Free-Loan Film Serv *Eligibility:* civic groups, religious groups, indiv with library cards, prof groups. *Restrictions:* for indiv, interlibrary loan, members of Serra Regional Library System; for inst, only members of SRLS. Cannot use for fund-raising, transmit electronically, borrow by mail. May not borrow by mail. *Loan Period:* 1 day. *Total Yr Film Loan:* 2,461.
Film Collection 78t/p. *Circ:* 16mm, 78t/p. *Pubns:* catalog, suppl, no set policy. Publish materials pertaining to collection.
Other Film Serv Obtain film from coop loan system (Serra Regional Library System), film reference serv, library film programs. Permanent viewing facility. *Equipment:* lend 16mm sound projector (3), projection screens (2).
Other Media Collections *Audio:* disc, 33⅓rpm, 5000t; tape, cassette, 2000t. *Filmstrips:* sound, 20t.
Budget & Expenditures Total library budget $100,000 (FY 7/1/75-7/1/76). No separate AV budget. *Member:* EFLA, Calif. Library Assn.
Video Serv *Est:* 1976. *Video Staff:* 4 f-t, 2 p-t, 2 tech. *Video Use:* to increase community's library use, in-service training. Have production studio/space.
Video Equipment/Facilities *In-House Use Only:* recording deck (1), ¾", VTR Sony; studio camera (1); keyer (1), ¾"; lighting (5); audio tape recorders (1). Have portable viewing installation. Provide training in use of equipment to staff.
Video Tape Loan/Rental/Sale Serv *Loan Eligibility:* staff. *Restrictions:* for in-house use only. Cannot use for fund-raising, duplicate, air without permission. May not borrow by mail. *Member:* CVRP/Calif.
Cable & CCTV Receive serv of cable TV system. Have CCTV in inst, with 7 monitors. *Programming Sources:* over-the-air commercial & public broadcasting, tapes produced professionally, tapes produced by community groups & indiv.

Commerce

P- CITY OF COMMERCE PUBLIC LIBRARY, 5655 Jillson St, 90040. *Tel:* (213) 722-6660. *In Charge:* James N. Church.
Free-Loan Film Serv *Eligibility:* indiv with library cards. *Restrictions:* interlibrary loan, members of MCLS. Available to researchers/scholars for on-site viewing. May not borrow by mail. *Loan Period:* 1 day.
Film Collection 113t/p. *Circ:* 16mm, 78t/p; 8mm reel, 7t/p; S8mm reel, 28t/p. *Pubns:* catalog, as needed.
Other Film Serv Obtain film from coop loan system (S. Calif. Film Circuit). Permanent viewing facility. *Equipment:* lend 16mm sound projector (1), 8mm reel projector (1), S8mm reel projector (1), projection screens.

Dominguez Hills

C- CALIFORNIA STATE COLLEGE, Dominguez Hills, Library, AV Services, 1000 E Victoria St, 90747. *Tel:* (213) 323-2475. *Film Serv Est:* 1966. *In Charge:* David Hudson, Dir, AV Serv. *AV Staff:* 8½ (1 prof, 2 cl, 4 tech). *Film Sel:* committee preview, faculty/staff recommendations, chief film librarian's decision.
Free-Loan Film Serv *Eligibility:* staff & students, educational inst, civic groups. *Restrictions:* for indiv, only in city, only in Calif. State Inter-Library System; for inst, only in city. Cannot use for fund-raising, transmit electronically. Available to researchers/scholars for on-site viewing. *Loan Period:* 1 day. *Total Yr Film Loan:* 11,391.
Film Collection 1000t/1140p. *Circ:* 16mm, 1000t/1140p; S8mm cartridge, 161t/p. *Pubns:* catalog, every 2 yrs; suppl, in yr catalog not published. Publish annual report.
Other Film Serv Rent film from distributors for patrons, obtain film from other libraries, film reference serv. Permanent viewing facility available to community.
Other Media Collections *Audio:* disc, 33⅓rpm, 2440c; tape, cassette, 582c; tape, reel, 348c. *Filmstrips:* sound sets, 198c. *Slides:* single, 6600c.
Budget & Expenditures Total FY film budget $24,000 (7/1/74-7/1/75). *Member:* AECT, Calif. State College film exchange.

El Cajon

C- GROSSMONT COLLEGE, Instructional Media Center, 8800 Grossmont College Ave, 92020. *Tel:* (714) 465-1700, ext 330. *Film Serv Est:* 1965. *In Charge:* R. Ingalls, Instructional Media Coord. *AV Staff:* 10 (1 prof, 2 cl, 7 tech). *Film Sel:* faculty/staff recommendations, chief film librarian's decision. *Holdings:* animated films 10%, black studies 10%, career education 15%, experimental films 10%, social sciences 20%.
Free-Loan Film Serv *Eligibility:* org members. *Restrictions:* only on campus.
Film Collection 250t/p. Approx 20t acquired annually. *Circ:* 16mm, 250t. *Pubns:* catalog; suppl, in yr catalog not published.
Other Film Serv Rent film from distributors for patrons, obtain film from coop loan system (County Consortium). Permanent viewing facility. *Equipment:* rent S8mm camera (20), 16mm sound projector (100), 8mm cartridge projector (10), 8mm reel projector (8), S8mm cartridge projector (3), S8mm reel projector (5), projection tables & stands (200), projection screens (50).
Other Media Collections *Audio:* disc, 33⅓rpm, 700c; tape, cassette, 2000c; tape, reel, 700c.
Budget & Expenditures Total library budget $600,000. Film purchase $15,000.
Video Serv *Est:* 1969. *Video Staff:* 10 f-t, 40 p-t, 4 tech. *Video Use:* in-service training, practical video/TV training courses, playback only of professionally produced tapes, as art form, auto-tutorial instruction. Video serv available on demand. Produce video tapes. Have production studio/space.
Video Equipment/Facilities *In-House Use Only:* recording deck (3), col, Sony VP1800; editing deck (17), col, Sony VP1200. *For Loan:* portapak (1), ½" b&w, Sony 3400. Have permanent viewing installation. Provide training in use of equipment to faculty & students.
Video Tape Loan/Rental/Sale Serv *Serv Provided:* free loan, swap with other inst. *Loan Eligibility:* staff & students. *Restrictions:* for campus use only. Cannot use for fund-raising, duplicate, air without permission. May borrow by mail.
Video Collection Maintained by purchase, own production. Use/play ¾" cassette. *Sources:* commercial distributors. *Member:* San Diego County Consortium. *Tape Sel:* preview, faculty/staff recommendations, commercial TV showings. *Special Collections:* in-house training tapes, films in video format. Tapes organized by accession number. *Collection, Color:* ¾" cassette, 300t/c. *Collection, B&W:* ¾" cassette, 200t/c. *Other Video Serv:* taping of other media, production workshops.
Cable & CCTV Have CCTV in inst, with 50 monitors. *Programming Sources:* over-the-air commercial & public broadcasting, tapes produced by inst, tapes produced professionally.

Escondido

P- ESCONDIDO PUBLIC LIBRARY, 239 S Kalmin St, 92025. *Tel:* (714) 745-2217. *In Charge:* Ramona Rodger, AV Librarian. *AV Staff:* 1 prof. *Film Sel:* committee preview, chief film librarian's decision. *Holdings:* animals 10%, animated

Escondido (cont'd)

films 17%, bicentennial 6%, children's films 60%, comedy 24%, discussion 6%, fine arts 10%, Indians 7%, travel 10%, women 5%.

Free-Loan Film Serv *Eligibility:* indiv with library cards. *Restrictions:* for indiv, only in San Diego County. Cannot use for fund-raising, transmit electronically. May not borrow by mail. *Loan Period:* 1-4 days. *Total Yr Film Loan:* 5708.

Film Collection 279t/p. Approx 36t acquired annually. *Circ:* 16mm, 139t/p; 8mm reel, 100t/p; S8mm reel, 40t/p. *Pubns:* catalog, annual; suppl, no set policy.

Other Film Serv Obtain film from coop loan system (Serra Regional Library System), film reference serv, library film programs. Permanent viewing facility. *Equipment:* lend/rent S8mm camera, lend 16mm sound projector (1), S8mm cartridge projector (3).

Other Media Collections *Audio:* disc, 33⅓rpm, 1300c.

Budget & Expenditures Total library budget $63,500 (FY 7/1/74-7/1/75). Total FY film budget $7,000. *Member:* ALA, Calif. Library Assn.

Eureka

C- COLLEGE OF THE REDWOODS, AV Servs, 95501. *Tel:* (707) 443-8411, ext 334. *Film Serv Est:* 1965. *In Charge:* William F. Scoble, Asst. Librarian, AV Servs. *AV Staff:* 5 (1 prof, 1 cl, 3 tech). *Film Sel:* faculty/staff recommendations.

Free-Loan Film Serv *Eligibility:* staff & students, civic groups. *Restrictions:* for indiv & inst, only in Humboldt County. Cannot use for fund-raising. Available to researchers/scholars for on-site viewing. May borrow by mail. *Loan Period:* 14 days.

Film Collection 16t/p. Approx 3t acquired annually. *Circ:* 16mm, 16t/p. *Pubns:* catalog, annual.

Other Film Serv Rent film from distributors for patrons, obtain film from coop loan system (North State Coop System), obtain film from other libraries, film reference serv. *Equipment:* lend S8mm camera (3), 16mm camera (2), 16mm sound projector (27), S8mm cartridge projector (7), S8mm reel projector (2), projection tables & stands (4), projection screens (5), splicers (2).

Budget & Expenditures No separate budget. *Member:* Calif. Jr College Assn.

Video Serv *Est:* 1972. *In Charge:* Gerald E. Brogan, Dean, Library & Media Servs. *Video Staff:* 1 f-t, 6 p-t, 1 tech. *Video Use:* documentation of community/school events, in-service training, practical video/TV training courses. Video serv available by appointment. Produce video tapes. Have production studio/space & separate control room.

Video Equipment/Facilities *In-House Use Only:* portapak (1), ½" col, Sony AV8400; recording deck (2), ¾" col, Panasonic AV2125; playback deck (2), 1" col, IVC800, 870; studio camera (3), b&w/col, IVC90, Sony, Blonder-Tongue; monitor (2), col, GE & Zenith; SEG (1), Sound Genesis; keyer (1), additional camera lenses (1); microphones (8); tripods (3); audio tape recorders (2). *For Loan:* portapak (2), ½" b&w, Sony AV3400; recording deck (1), ¾" col, Sony VO1800; lighting (2); audio cassette recorders (5). Have permanent viewing installation. *Equipment Loan Period:* 1 day. Provide training in use of equipment to faculty & students. Have tape duplication serv.

Video Tape Loan/Rental/Sale Serv *Serv Provided:* free loan. *Loan Eligibility:* staff & students, educational inst, civic groups, prof groups, such as County Medical, Legal & history societies. *Restrictions:* for indiv & inst, only in Humboldt County. Cannot use for fund-raising, air without permission. May not borrow by mail. *Loan Period:* 7 days.

Video Collection Maintained by purchase, own production. Use/play ½", 1" reel to reel, ¾" cassette. *Tape Sel:* faculty/staff recommendations. Tapes organized by subject, title. *Other Video Serv:* reference serv, taping of other media.

Cable & CCTV Have CCTV in inst, with 14 monitors. *Programming Sources:* over-the-air commercial & public broadcasting, tapes produced by inst, tapes produced professionally.

Fairfield

P- SOLANO COUNTY LIBRARY, 744 Empire St, 94533. *Tel:* (707) 429-6450. *In Charge:* D. Barnewitz, AV Librarian. *AV Staff:* 3 (1 prof, 2 tech). *Film Sel:* committee preview, published reviews.

Free-Loan Film Serv *Eligibility:* indiv with library cards. *Restrictions:* for indiv & inst only in Solano County. May not borrow by mail.

Film Collection 235t/p. Approx 10t acquired annually. *Circ:* 16mm, 146t; 8mm reel & cartridge, S8mm reel & cartridge, 89t. Publish film list.

Other Film Serv Obtain film from coop loan system (North Bay Coop Library System), library film programs. Permanent viewing facility. *Equipment:* lend 16mm sound projector (7), S8mm cartridge projector (1), S8mm reel projector (2), projection screens (7), opaque projector (1).

Other Media Collections *Audio:* disc, 33⅓rpm, 6858c; tape, cartridge, 221c. *Filmstrips:* sound & silent, 117c.

Budget & Expenditures Total library budget $134,927 (FY 7/1/74-7/1/75). *Member:* AECT, AFI, ALA, CUFC, EFLA, FLIC, Calif. Library Assn, N. Calif. Library Film Circuit.

Glendale

P- GLENDALE PUBLIC LIBRARY, 222 E Harvard St, 91205. *Tel:* (213) 956-2033. *Film Serv Est:* 1953. *In Charge:* Marie Fish, Adult Librarian. *AV Staff:* 3½ (1 prof, 2 cl, ½ tech). *Film Sel:* chief film librarian's decision.

Free-Loan Film Serv *Eligibility:* indiv with library cards; members of Metropolitan Coop Library System. *Restrictions:* for indiv, only in city. Cannot use for fund-raising, transmit electronically. May not borrow by mail. *Loan Period:* 1 day. *Total Yr Film Loan:* 13,624.

Film Collection 465t/467p. Approx 35t acquired annually. *Circ:* 16mm, 374t/376p; 8mm reel, 89t/p; S8mm reel, 2t/p. *Pubns:* catalog, every 3 yrs (25¢); suppl, in yr catalog not published.

Other Film Serv Obtain film from coop loan system (MCLS), film reference serv, library film programs. Permanent viewing facility available for rent to community.

Other Media Collections *Audio:* disc, 33⅓rpm, 20,000t; 78rpm, 1000c; tape, cassette, 400c. *Slides:* 55t/c.

Budget & Expenditures Total library budget $153,900 (FY 7/1/74-7/1/75). Total FY film budget $9100. *Member:* EFLA, FLIC, Calif. Library Assn.

Hayward

P- ALAMEDA COUNTY LIBRARY SYSTEM, 22777 Main St, 94541. *Tel:* (415) 881-6376. *Film Serv Est:* 1975. *In Charge:* Luanne Gilbert, AV Coord. *AV Staff:* 2 (1 prof, 1 cl). *Film Sel:* committee preview. *Holdings:* management training/business 3%.

Free-Loan Film Serv *Eligibility:* indiv over 18 yrs with library cards. *Restrictions:* for indiv, none. Cannot use for fund-raising, transmit electronically, borrow for classroom use. May not borrow by mail. *Loan Period:* 1 day.

Film Collection 405t/407p. Approx 100t acquired annually. *Circ:* 16mm, 405t/407p; 8mm & S8mm reel, 500p. *Noncirc:* 16mm, 3t/p. *Pubns:* catalog, annual; suppl, no set policy.

Other Film Serv Film reference serv, library film programs.

Other Media Collections *Audio:* disc, 33⅓rpm, 13,936c. *Filmstrips:* sound, 165c.

Budget & Expenditures Total library budget $500,000 (FY 7/1/74-7/1/75). Total FY film budget $32,000. *Member:* ALA, EFLA, FLIC, Calif. Library Assn.

C- CHABOT COLLEGE, Media Servs, 25555 Hesperian Blvd, 94544. *Tel:* (415) 782-3000, ext 266. *Film Serv Est:* 1961. *In Charge:* Ed Quinnell, Media Resources Librarian. *AV Staff:* 11 (2 prof, 2 cl, 7 tech). *Film Sel:* faculty/staff recommendations, chief film librarian's decision, published reviews. *Holdings:* animated films 1%, business 6%, experimental films 1%, humanities 3%, language arts 8%, law 1%, medicine 6%, science 35%, social sciences 35%, teacher education 1%.

Free-Loan Film Serv *Eligibility:* staff. *Restrictions:* for indiv, on campus. Available to researchers/scholars for on-site viewing. May not borrow by mail. *Loan Period:* 1 day.

Film Collection 150t/p. *Circ:* 16mm, 150t/p; 8mm cartridge, 50t/p; S8mm cartridge, 2000t/p. Publish film lists, bibliographies.

Other Film Serv Obtain film from coop loan system (Community College Consortium, Alameda County Film Consortium), obtain film from other libraries, film reference serv. Permanent viewing facility. *Equipment:* lend S8mm camera (1), 16mm camera (1), 16mm sound projector (50), 8mm cartridge projector (2), 8mm reel projector (1), S8mm cartridge projector (2), S8mm reel projector (1), projection screens (6).

Other Media Collections *Audio:* disc, 33⅓rpm, 10,000t/c; tape, cassette, 2000t/c; tape, reel, 8000t/c. *Filmstrips:* sound, 1400t/c; silent, 1200t/c. *Slides:* single, 10,000c; sets, 2000c.

Budget & Expenditures Total library budget $60,460 (FY 7/1/74-7/1/75). Total FY film budget $13,000. *Member:* AECT, CSLA, CTA, CAEMAT.

Video Serv *In Charge:* Don Mayo, Asst Dean, Learning Resources. *Video Staff:* 2 f-t, 3 p-t, 3 tech. *Video Use:* documentation of community/school events, community video access, in-service training, practical video/TV training courses, as art form. Video serv available on demand. Produce video tapes. Have production studio/space & separate control room.

Video Equipment/Facilities *In-House Use Only:* portapak (2), ½" b&w/col, Sony, JVC; recording deck (14), 1", ½", ¾" b&w/col, Ampex, Sony, JVC; studio camera (6), b&w/col, Dage, JVC; SEG (1), 3M 672; lighting (25); microphones (10); tripods (9); audio tape recorders (2). Have permanent viewing installations. Provide training in use of equipment to faculty, students & staff.

Video Tape Loan/Rental/Sale Serv *Serv Provided:* free loan, swap with other inst. *Loan Eligibility:* org members, staff, students enrolled in inst, educational inst. *Restrictions:* only community colleges in GT 70. Cannot use for fund-raising, duplicate, air without permission.

Video Collection Maintained by purchase, own production, exchange/swap. Use/play ½", 1", reel to reel, ¾" cassette. *Sources:* commercial distributors. *Member:* GT 70 & Bay Area Consortium. *Tape Sel:* preview, faculty/staff recommendations. Tapes organized by subject.

Cable & CCTV Receive serv of cable TV system. Produce programs for cablecasting. Have CCTV in inst, with 120 monitors, 5 channels. *Programming Sources:* over-the-air commercial & public braodcasting, tapes produced by inst, tapes produced professionally, tapes produced by community groups & indiv.

Huntington Beach

P- HUNTINGTON BEACH LIBRARY, 7111 Talbert, 92647. *Tel:* (714) 842-4481, ext 26. *Film Serv Est:* 1965. *In Charge:* Linda Strauss. *AV Staff:* 17 (1 prof, 5½ cl, 1½ tech). *Film Sel:* committee preview, staff recommendations, chief film librarian's decision.

Film Rental Serv *Eligibility:* patrons/public, within library/school coop. *Restrictions:* only in Orange County. Cannot use for fund-raising, transmit electronically. *Rental Period:* 1 day. *Total Yr Film Booking:* 55,673.

Film Collection 1300t/1600p. Approx 25-50t acquired annually. *Circ:* 16mm, 1300t/1600p; 8mm reel, 45t/54p; 8mm cartridge, 167t/p; S8mm reel, 135t/153p; S8mm cartridge, 40t/p. *Noncirc:* 8mm reel, 22t/26p; 8mm cartridge, 35t/p; S8mm reel, 70t/79p; S8mm cartridge, 8t/p. *Pubns:* catalog, every 2 yrs ($2); suppl, in yr catalog not published (50¢). Publish media catalog.

Other Film Serv Obtain film from coop loan system (Santiago Library System), obtain film from other libraries, film reference serv, library film programs. Permanent viewing facility available to community. *Equipment:* rent 16mm sound

projector (8), 8mm cartridge projector (1), 8mm reel projector (6), S8mm cartridge projector (4), lend/rent S8mm reel projector (1), projection screens (5), audio equipment, filmstrip projectors.

Other Media Collections *Audio:* disc, 33⅓rpm, 2500t/3000c; tape, cassette, 450t/600c. *Filmstrips:* silent, 50t/c. *Slides:* single, 200t/c; sets, 10t.

Budget & Expenditures Total library budget $982,086 (FY 7/1/74-7/1/75). Total FY film budget $27,300. *Member:* AECT, EFLA, Calif. Library Assn, Public Library film circuit.

Video Serv *Est:* 1975. *Video Staff:* 14 f-t, 5 p-t, 1½ tech. *Video Use:* to increase community's library use, practical video/TV training courses, class instruction. Video serv available on demand.

Video Equipment/Facilities *In-House Use Only:* portapak (4), JVC CR6000n, Sony VD 1600; monitor (3), col, Unimedia UMT 1203; SEG (2), Sony 7830 UM; audio tape recorders (14). *For Loan:* microphones (2). Have permanent viewing installation. Provide training in use of equipment.

Video Tape Loan/Rental/Sale Serv *Serv Provided:* free loan, swap with other inst. *Loan Eligibility:* indiv with library cards. *Restrictions:* inst & indiv, equipment use within library. May borrow tapes by mail.

Video Collection Maintained by exchange/swap. Use/play ¾" cassette. *Sources:* community productions. *Tape Sel:* by availability. Tapes organized by title. *Collection, Color:* 5t/25c. *Collection, B&W:* 5c. *Other Video Serv:* production workshops.

Cable & CCTV Have CCTV in inst, with 5 monitors.

Inglewood

A- NORTHROP UNIVERSITY, American Hall of Aviation History, 1155 W Arbor Vitae St, 90306. *Tel:* (213) 670-6339. *Film Serv Est:* 1975. *In Charge:* J. Grant Morey, Asst to Pres—University Affairs. *AV Staff:* 2 (1 prof, 1 cl.) *Film Sel:* chief film librarian's decision.

Film Rental Serv *Eligibility:* no restrictions. *Restrictions:* none. Cannot duplicate. *Rental Period:* 7 days. Sell films. Produce slide presentations on aviation.

Film Collection 151t/p. *Pubns:* catalog, as needed; suppl, no set policy.

Other Media Collections *Audio:* tape, cassette, 1c. *Slides:* single, 1000c; sets, 3c.

Lodi

P- LODI PUBLIC LIBRARY, 49-99 Coop Library System Film Circuit, 305 W Pine, 95240. *Tel:* (209) 369-6823. *Film Serv Est:* 1965. *In Charge:* Ruth Miller, Library Clerk. *AV Staff:* ½ cl. *Film Sel:* committee preview.

Free-Loan Film Serv *Eligibility:* indiv with library cards. *Restrictions:* for indiv & inst only in 49-99 System area. Cannot use for fund-raising. Available to researchers/scholars for on-site viewing. May not borrow by mail. *Loan Period:* 1 day. *Total Yr Film Loan:* 2504.

Film Collection 600t/p. *Circ:* 16mm, 600t/p. *Pubns:* catalog, annual; suppl, no set policy.

Other Film Serv Obtain film from coop loan system (49-99 Coop Loan System). Permanent viewing facility available to community. *Equipment:* lend 16mm sound projector (2).

Other Media Collections *Audio:* disc, 33⅓rpm, 3470t/c. *Filmstrips:* silent, 200t/c; sound sets, 10t/c.

Budget & Expenditures Total library budget $31,000 (FY 7/1/74-7/1/75). Total FY film budget $900.

Long Beach

C- CALIFORNIA STATE UNIVERSITY, Long Beach Library, 90840. *Tel:* (213) 498-4028. *Video Serv Est:* 1973. *In Charge:* Henry J. DuBois, Media Resources Librarian. *Video Staff:* 3 f-t, 8 p-t. *Video Use:* documentation of community/school events, playback only of professionally produced tapes. Video serv available on demand. Have permanent viewing installations. *Equipment Loan Period:* no set policy.

Long Beach (cont'd)

Video Tape Loan/Rental/Sale Serv *Serv Provided:* free loan. *Loan Eligibility:* staff, students enrolled in inst. *Restrictions:* for indiv, only in Library, for inst, only through Inter-Library Loan Serv. Cannot duplicate. May borrow by mail. *Loan Period:* 30 days. *Total Yr Tape Loan:* 17,435.

Video Collection Maintained by purchase, own production. Use/play ½″ reel to reel, ¾″ cassette. *Sources:* commercial distributors. *Tape Sel:* preview, faculty/staff recommendations, gallery previews, published reviews, catalogs. *Special Collections:* in-house training tapes, video as art, films in video format. Tapes organized by subject, title, author. *Collection, Color:* ¾″ cassette, 304t. *Collection, B&W:* ½″ reel, 183t. *Other Video Serv:* reference serv. *Pubns:* catalog.

S- **LONG BEACH MUSEUM OF ART**, 2300 E Ocean Blvd, 90803. *Tel:* (213) 439-2119. *In Charge:* David Ross, Deputy Dir TV/Film. *Video Staff:* 3 f-t. *Video Use:* as art form.

Video Equipment/Facilities *In-House Use Only:* portapak (1), ½″ b&w, Sony; recording deck (1), ¾″ b&w, Sony; monitor (2), b&w, Triniton, GBC-ITC. Have permanent viewing installations. Have tape duplication serv.

Video Tape Loan/Rental/Sale Serv *Serv Provided:* free loan, swap with other inst. *Loan Eligibility:* Long Branch Library, artists. *Restrictions:* for inst, only in city. May not borrow by mail.

Video Collection Use/play ¾″ cassette. *Sources:* exchange (with museums & artists). *Tape Sel:* preview. *Special Collections:* video as art. Tapes organized by name of artist. *Pubns:* publish exhibition catalogs.

Cable & CCTV Have CCTV in inst, with 1 monitor.

P- **LONG BEACH PUBLIC LIBRARY**, Film Service, Ocean and Pacific, 90802. *Tel:* (213) 597-3341. *Film Serv Est:* 1948. *In Charge:* Patricia F. Del Mar, Film Librarian. *AV Staff:* 3 (1 prof, 2 cl). *Film Sel:* committee preview, staff recommendations, chief film librarian's decision, published reviews.

Free-Loan Film Serv *Eligibility:* org members, civic groups, indiv with library cards. *Restrictions:* for indiv & inst, only in city. Cannot use for fund-raising, transmit electronically. May not borrow by mail. *Loan Period:* 1 day. *Total Yr Film Loan:* 15,627.

Film Rental Serv *Eligibility:* educational org, civic groups, patrons/public. *Restrictions:* none. Cannot use for fund-raising, transmit electronically. *Rental Period:* 1 day. *Total Yr Film Booking:* 15,627.

Film Collection 950t/945p. Approx 15-20t acquired annually. *Circ:* 16mm, 950t/945p. *Noncirc:* 16mm, 5t. *Pubns:* catalog, every 3 yrs ($2); suppl, annually.

Other Film Serv Film reference serv, film fairs/festivals, library film programs. Permanent viewing facility available to community.

Other Media Collections *Audio:* disc, 33⅓rpm, 18,761c; tape, cassette, cartridge, reel, 305c. *Filmstrips:* sound, 55c.

Budget & Expenditures Total library budget $10,000 (FY 7/1/74-7/1/75). Total FY film budget $5000. *Member:* AECT, AFI, ALA, EFLA, FLIC, Calif. Library Assn, Special Libraries Assn.

Video Serv *Est:* 1973. *In Charge:* Susan Possner, Community Servs Librarian. *Video Use:* to increase community's library use, in-service training. Video serv available on demand. Produce video tapes.

Video Equipment/Facilities *In-House Use Only:* portapak (1), ½″ b&w, Sony 3400; recording deck (3), ½″ & ¾″ b&w, Sony 3400, 3650, VD 1800; playback deck (3), editing deck (1), ½″ b&w, Sony 3650; studio camera (1), ½″ b&w, Sony 3400; microphones (1); tripods (1); audio tape recorders (1). *For Loan:* portapak (1), ½″ b&w, Sony 3400; recording deck (3), ½″ & ¾″ b&w, Sony 3400, 3650, VD 1800; playback deck (3), b&w, editing deck (1), ½″ b&w, Sony 3650; studio camera (1), ½″ b&w, Sony 3400; Have portable viewing installation. *Equipment Loan Period:* no set policy.

Video Tape Loan/Rental/Sale Serv *Serv Provided:* free loan. *Loan Eligibility:* staff & students, other city depts.

Video Collection Maintained by purchase, own production. Use/play ½″, reel to reel, ¾″ cassette. *Sources:* commercial distributors. *Special Collections:* in-house training tapes, promotional. *Collection, B&W:* ½″ reel, 6t/c; ¼″ reel, 1t/c.

Los Angeles

S- **CHILDRENS HOSPITAL**—University Affiliated Program, 4650 Sunset Blvd, 90027. *Tel:* (213) 660-2450, ext 2781, 2789. *Video Serv Est:* 1969. *In Charge:* Neil Goldstein, Asst Tech Training Dir. *Video Staff:* 1 f-t. *Video Use:* community video access, in-service training, pracical video/TV training courses, playback only of professionally produced tapes. Video serv available on demand. Produce video tapes. Have production studio/space & separate control room.

Video Equipment/Facilities *In-House Use Only:* studio camera (3), 1″, ⅔″ b&w; monitor (25), b&w/col, Ampex, Sony; SEG (3), Sony; lighting (6); microphones (20); tripods (8); audio tape recorders (18). *For Loan:* portapak (4), ½″, 1″ b&w/col, Sony; recording deck (10), ½″, ¾″ b&w/col, Ampex, Sony; editing deck (1), ¾″ col, Sony; studio camera (3), 1″, ⅔″ b&w; monitor (25), b&w/col, Ampex, Sony; lighting (6); microphones (20); tripods (8); audio tape recorders (18). Have permanent & portable viewing installations. Provide training in use of equipment to faculty & students. Have tape duplication serv.

Video Tape Loan/Rental/Sale Serv *Serv Provided:* free loan, swap with other inst, rental, sale. *Loan/Rental Eligibility:* staff & students, educational inst, civic groups, indiv with library cards. May not borrow by mail. *Loan Period:* 7 days.

Video Collection Maintained by purchase, own production, exchange/swap. Use/play ½″, 1″, reel to reel, ¾″ cassette. *Sources:* commercial distributors, exchange. *Tape Sel:* preview, faculty/staff recommendations. Tapes organized by AVAF numbering system. *Collection, Color:* ½″ reel, 5t; ¾″ cassette, 5t. *Collection, B&W:* ½″ reel, 500t; 1″ reel, 60t. *Other Video Serv:* programming, taping of other media, production workshops. *Pubns:* publish materials on video.

Cable & CCTV Will produce programs for cablecasting. Inform public about cable system serv & facilities. Serve as production facility for others. Have CCTV in inst, with 15 monitors. *Programming Sources:* tapes produced by inst.

S- **HIPPOVIDEO: THE FOUNDATION FOR MULTIMEDIA AND THE ARTS**, 1290 Wilshire Blvd, 90017. *Tel:* (213) 482-4848, 4747. *Video Serv Est:* 1973. *Video Use:* as art form. Produce video tapes. Have production studio/space & separate control room.

Video Equipment/Facilities *In-House Use Only:* portapak (1), ½″ b&w, Sony; recording deck (2), ½″ b&w, Sony 3650; monitor (7), b&w/col, Sony, Shibaden; SEG (1), Sony; additional camera lenses; lighting; microphones; tripods; audio tape recorders (1); special switchers. Have permanent viewing installation.

Video Tape Loan/Rental/Sale Serv *Serv Provided:* free loan. *Loan Eligibility:* TV stations, art groups. *Restrictions:* none.

Video Collection Maintained by own production. Use/play ½″ reel to reel. *Sources:* produce own. Tapes organized by project. *Other Video Serv:* production workshops, mixed media.

Cable & CCTV Have CCTV in inst, with 7 monitors.

P- **LOS ANGELES CITY PUBLIC LIBRARY**, AV Dept, 630 W Fifth St, 90071. *Tel:* (213) 626-7461, ext 267. *Film Serv Est:* 1951. *In Charge:* Wm. J. Speed, Principal Librarian. *AV Staff:* 14½ (2 prof, 10 cl, 2½ tech). *Film Sel:* chief film librarian's decision.

Free-Loan Film Serv *Eligibility:* civic groups, religious groups, indiv with library cards, prof groups. *Restrictions:* none. Cannot borrow for classroom use. Available to researchers/scholars for on-site viewing. May not borrow by mail. *Loan Period:* 1 day.

Film Collection 2600t/p. Approx 150-200t acquired annually. *Pubns:* catalog, every 2 yrs; suppl, in yr catalog not published (50¢).

Other Film Serv Film reference serv, library film programs.

Other Media Collections *Audio:* disc, 33⅓rpm, 35,000t; tape, cassette, 6000t. *Filmstrips:* sound, 300t/c. *Slides:* sets, 25t/c.

Budget & Expenditures Total library budget $2,061,032 (FY 7/1/74-7/1/75). Total FY film budget $44,000. *Member:* AECT, AFI, EFLA, FLIC, Calif. Library Assn.

P- LOS ANGELES COUNTY PUBLIC LIBRARY, AV Serv, 320 W Temple St, 90012. *Tel:* (213) 974-6548. *Film Serv Est:* 1960. *In Charge:* Joyce Sumbi, AV Coord. *AV Staff:* 47 (18 prof, 29 cl). *Film Sel:* AV Coord, film librarians.

Free-Loan Film Serv *Restrictions:* for indiv & inst only in Los Angeles County. Cannot use for fund-raising, transmit electronically, borrow for classroom use. Available to researchers/scholars for on-site viewing. May not borrow by mail. *Loan Period:* 3 days. *Total Yr Film Loan:* 70,632.

Film Collection 1923t/3055p. *Circ:* 16mm, 1923t/3055p; 8mm reel, 85t/132p; S8mm reel, 90t/140p. *Noncirc:* S8mm cartridge, 5t/p. *Pubns:* catalog, as needed; suppl, in yr catalog not published.

Other Film Serv Library film programs. Permanent viewing facility available for rent to community. *Equipment:* lend S8mm camera (1), 16mm sound projector (73), S8mm cartridge projector (2), S8mm reel projector (2), projection tables & stands (33), projection screens (73).

Other Media Collections *Audio:* disc, 33⅓rpm, 9000t/55,043c; tape, cassette, 1400t/5635c; tape, reel, 75t/c. *Filmstrips:* sound, 9t/c.

Budget & Expenditures Total FY film budget $71,000 (FY 7/1/74-7/1/75). *Member:* AFI, ALA, EFLA, FLIC, Calif. Library Assn.

C- LOS ANGELES TRADE-TECHNICAL COLLEGE, 400 W Washington, 90015. *Tel:* (213) 746-0800, ext 446. *Film Serv Est:* 1971. *In Charge:* E. W. Mason, AV Librarian. *AV Staff:* 1 prof. *Film Sel:* faculty/staff recommendations.

Film Collection 359t. *Circ:* 16mm, 359t. *Pubns:* catalog, as needed.

Other Film Serv Rent film from distributors for patrons, obtain film from other libraries, film fairs/festivals.

Other Media Collections *Audio:* tape, cassette, 325t. *Filmstrips:* sound & silent, single, 383t/c; sets, 18t/c.

Budget & Expenditures Total library budget $97,900 (FY 7/1/74-7/1/75). Total FY film budget $36,500. *Member:* Calif. Library Assn.

S- NATAS-UCLA, TV Library, Theater Arts Dept, UCLA, 90024. *Tel:* (213) 825-4480. *Video Serv Est:* 1965. *In Charge:* Ruth Schwartz, Dir. *Video Staff:* 1 f-t, 3 p-t. *Video Use:* playback only of professionally produced tapes. Video serv available by appointment.

Video Equipment/Facilities *In-House Use Only:* portapak (1); moviola flatbed. Have portable viewing installation.

Video Tape Loan/Rental/Sale Serv *Serv Provided:* free loan. *Loan Eligibility:* staff.

Video Collection Maintained by donation. Use/play ½″, 1″, 2″ reel to reel, ½″ cartridge, ¾″ cassette. *Sources:* commercial distributors. Tapes organized by subject. *Collection:* 2″ reel, 150t/c; ½″ cartridge, 50t/c; ¾″ cassette, 200t/c. *Other Video Serv:* reference serv, taping of other media. *Pubns:* catalog.

C- UNIVERSITY OF CALIFORNIA, UCLA MEDIA CENTER, Instructional Media Library, 8 Royce Hall, 405 Hilgard Ave, 90024. *Tel:* (213) 825-0755. *In Charge:* Helga Milewski, Supervisor. *AV Staff:* 3 (2 prof, 1 tech). *Film Sel:* committee preview, faculty/staff recommendations, chief film librarian's decision.

Free-Loan Film Serv *Eligibility:* staff. Available to researchers/scholars for on-site viewing. May not borrow by mail.

Film Rental Serv *Eligibility:* no restrictions. *Restrictions:* only in U.S. & territories & Canada. *Rental Period:* 3 days. Sell films. Produce films.

Film Collection 1700t/2000p. Approx 15-40t acquired annually. *Pubns:* catalog, every 3 yrs ($2.50); suppl, no set policy.

Other Film Serv Rent film from distributors for patrons, obtain film from other libraries, film reference serv. Permanent viewing facility.

Budget & Expenditures No separate budget. *Member:* CUFC, EFLA, FLIC.

C- UNIVERSITY OF SOUTHERN CALIFORNIA, Norris Medical Library, Health Science Campus, 2025 Zonal Ave, 90033. *Tel:* (213) 226-2409. *Film Serv Est:* 1974. *In Charge:* Tony R. Kwak, Media Specialist. *AV Staff:* 3 (1 prof, 1½ cl). *Film Sel:* faculty/staff recommendations, chief film librarian's decision, published reviews. *Holdings:* medicine 100%.

Free-Loan Film Serv *Eligibility:* faculty, staff & students. *Restrictions:* none. Cannot use for fund-raising, transmit electronically, borrow for classroom use. Available to researchers/scholars for on-site viewing. May not borrow by mail.

Film Collection 16t/p. *Noncirc:* 16mm, 6t; 8mm reel, 1t; 8mm cartridge, 7t; S8mm cartridge, 2t. *Pubns:* catalog, as needed; suppl, no set policy. Publish media newsletter, subject bibliographies.

Other Film Serv Film reference serv, library film programs. Permanent viewing facility.

Other Media Collections *Audio:* disc, 33⅓rpm, 4t; tape, cassette, 93t. *Filmstrips:* sound sets, 2t. *Slides:* sets, 92t.

Budget & Expenditures Total library budget $502,802 (FY 7/1/74-7/1/75). *Member:* ALA, MLA, HESCA, ASIS, SLA.

Video Serv *Est:* 1974. *Video Staff:* 2 f-t, 1 p-t. *Video Use:* instruction. Video serv available on demand.

Video Equipment/Facilities *In-House Use Only:* playback deck (3), ¾″ col, Sony 1000, 1200. Have permanent viewing installation. Provide training in use of equipment to library users.

Video Tape Loan/Rental/Sale Serv *Serv Provided:* free loan. *Loan Eligibility:* staff & students, faculty. *Restrictions:* on-site use only. Cannot use for fund-raising, duplicate, air without permission. May not borrow by mail.

Video Collection Maintained by purchase. Use/play ¾″ cassette. *Sources:* commercial distributors, parent inst productions. *Tape Sel:* preview, faculty/staff recommendations, published reviews, catalogs. *Special Collections:* in-house training tapes. Tapes organized by LC, Natl Library of Medicine. *Collection, Color:* ¾″ cassette, 150t/c. *Other Video Serv:* reference serv. *Pubns:* catalog. Publish bimonthly media newsletter, subject bibliographies.

Modesto

P- STANISLAUS COUNTY FREE LIBRARY, 1500 Eye St, 95354. *Tel:* (209) 526-6826. *In Charge:* Helene Kosher, Art & AV Librarian. *AV Staff:* 4 cl. *Film Sel:* committee preview. *Holdings:* agriculture 2%, animated films 16.7%, black studies 3%, career education .6%, children's films 17%, consumer affairs .6%, dance 1%, engineering .6%, experimental films 3.6%, feature films 9.8%, fine arts 11.4%, industrial arts .3%, medicine 1%, science 13%, social sciences 16.7%, women 2.6%.

Free-Loan Film Serv *Eligibility:* library staff, indiv with library cards. *Restrictions:* for indiv, in County 49-99 Co-op Library System. Cannot use for fund-raising. Available to researchers/scholars for on-site viewing. May not borrow by mail. *Loan Period:* 1-3 days.

Film Collection 304t/305p. Approx 20-40t acquired annually. *Circ:* 16mm, 219t/292p; 8mm reel cartridge, S8mm reel, 222t/226p; S8mm cartridge, 31t/p. *Noncirc:* 16mm, 13t/p. *Pubns:* catalog, annual (50¢); suppl, no set policy. Publish materials pertaining to collection. Publish film lists.

Other Film Serv Obtain film from coop loan system (49-99 Cooperative Library System), obtain film from other libraries, film reference serv, library film programs. Permanent viewing facility available for rent to community. *Equipment:* rent 16mm sound projector (10), projection screens (5), filmstrip/slide projector (1).

Modesto (cont'd)

Other Media Collections *Audio:* disc, 33⅓rpm, 13,865c; tape, cassette, 3,885c.

Budget & Expenditures Total library budget $290,559 (FY 7/1/74-7/1/75). Total FY film budget $22,641. *Member:* ALA, EFLA, Calif. Library Assn.

Video Serv *Est:* 1972. *Video Use:* community video access, in-service training. Video serv available by appointment. Produce video tapes.

Video Equipment/Facilities *In-House Use Only:* recording deck (1), ½" b&w, Sony 3600; editing deck (1), ½" b&w, Sony 3650; keyer (1), audio tape recorders (4). *For Loan:* portapak (2), ½" b&w, Sony 3400; monitor (2), ½" b&w, Sony; microphones (2); tripods (1). *Equipment Loan Period:* 3 days. Provide training in use of equipment to staff & students.

Video Tape Loan/Rental/Sale Serv *Serv Provided:* free loan. *Loan Eligibility:* staff & students, community adults. *Restrictions:* for indiv, only in Stanislaus County. Cannot use for fund-raising, duplicate, air without permission. May borrow by mail. *Total Yr Tape Loan:* 23.

Video Collection Maintained by own production. Use/play ½" reel to reel. *Sources:* community & staff productions. *Tape Sel:* library committee. Tapes organized by title. *Collection, B&W:* ½" reel, 40t/c. *Other Video Serv:* production workshops.

Cable & CCTV Receive serv of cable TV system.

Montebello

P- LOS ANGELES COUNTY PUBLIC LIBRARY, Rio Hondo Regional Library, 1550 W Beverly Blvd, 90640. *Tel:* (213) 722-6551. *Film Serv Est:* 1966. *In Charge:* Charlene Parks, AV Librarian. *AV Staff:* 3 (1 prof, 2 cl). *Film Sel:* committee preview, chief film librarian's decision. *Holdings:* Spanish language 5%.

Free-Loan Film Serv *Eligibility:* indiv with library cards. *Restrictions:* for indiv & inst, only in Los Angeles County. Cannot use for fund-raising, borrow for classroom use. Available to researchers/scholars for on-site viewing. May not borrow by mail. *Loan Period:* 1 day. *Total Yr Film Loan:* 6342.

Film Collection 450t/p. Approx 5t acquired annually. *Circ:* 16mm, 450 t/p. *Pubns:* catalog, annual; suppl, no set policy.

Other Film Serv Film reference serv, library film programs. Permanent viewing facility available for rent to community.

Other Media Collections *Audio:* disc, 33⅓rpm, 2000t/c; tape, cassette, 300t/c.

Budget & Expenditures Total FY film budget $1000 (FY 6/74-6/75). *Member:* Calif. Library Assn, AV Chapter.

Monterey Park

P- BRUGGEMEYER MEMORIAL LIBRARY, 318 South Romona Ave, 91754. *Tel:* (213) 573-1411, ext 24. *In Charge:* Dustin Miller, AV Librarian. *AV Staff:* 3 (1 prof, 2 cl). *Film Sel:* staff recommendations, chief film librarian's decision.

Film Rental Serv *Eligibility:* patrons/public, over 18 yrs with library card. Cannot use for fund-raising, transmit electronically. *Rental Rate:* 50¢ per title per day. *Total Yr Film Booking:* 2140.

Film Collection 75t/330p. *Circ:* 16mm, 75t/p; 8mm reel, 180t/p; S8mm reel, 75t/p. *Pubns:* catalog, annual.

Other Film Serv Obtain film from coop loan system (Film Council, Public Library Film Circuit), obtain film from other libraries, film reference serv, film fairs/festivals, library film programs. Permanent viewing facility available for rent to community. *Equipment:* rent 16mm sound projector (2), 8mm reel projector (1).

Other Media Collections *Audio:* disc, 33⅓rpm, 2500t/c; tape, cassette, 300t/c. *Filmstrips:* sound, 55t/c; silent, 64t/c.

Budget & Expenditures Total library budget $4430 (FY 7/1/74-7/1/75). No separate AV budget. *Member:* PLFC, FCA.

Napa

P- NAPA CITY-COUNTY LIBRARY, Film Dept, 1150 Division St, 94558. *Tel:* (707) 255-2091. *Film Serv Est:* 1960. *In Charge:* Karla Jones, AV Librarian. *AV Staff:* 3 cl. *Film Sel:* committee preview.

Free-Loan Film Serv *Eligibility:* civic groups, religious groups, indiv with library cards. *Restrictions:* for residents in North Bay Co-op Library System. May not borrow by mail. *Loan Period:* 1 day. *Total Yr Film Loan:* 11,244.

Film Collection 579t/607p. Approx 30t acquired annually. *Circ:* 16mm, 379t/397p; 8mm reel, 200t/210p. *Pubns:* catalog, as needed; suppl, no set policy. Publish monthly list of circuit films available.

Other Film Serv Obtain film from coop loan system (North Bay Coop Library System), obtain film from other libraries, film reference serv, library film programs. *Equipment:* lend 16mm sound projector (4), projection screens (3).

Other Media Collections *Audio:* disc, 33⅓rpm, 1717c; tape, cassette, 31c. *Filmstrips:* silent, 213c. *Slides:* sets, 1c.

Budget & Expenditures Total library budget $80,000 (FY 7/1/74-7/1/75). Total FY film budget $5300. *Member:* ALA, Calif. Library Assn.

National City

P- NATIONAL CITY PUBLIC LIBRARY, 200 E 12 St, 92050. *Tel:* (714) 477-5131. *Film Serv Est:* 1972. *In Charge:* Rebecca J. Reed, Library Tech. *Film Sel:* chief film librarian's decision. *Holdings:* animated films 43%, children's films 85%, classic comedy 35%, social sciences 14%.

Free-Loan Film Serv *Eligibility:* civic groups, religious groups, indiv with library cards, hospitals, convalescent homes. *Restrictions:* for indiv, over 18 yrs, interlibrary loan. Cannot use for fund-raising, transmit electronically, borrow for classroom use. Available to researchers/scholars for on-site viewing. May not borrow by mail. *Loan Period:* 1 day. *Total Yr Film Loan:* 1713.

Film Collection 104t/p. Approx 25t acquired annually. *Circ:* 16mm, 14t/p; 8mm reel, 48t/p; S8mm reel, 36t/p. *Noncirc:* S8mm cartridge, 6t. *Pubns:* catalog, as needed; suppl, no set policy. Publish flyer.

Other Film Serv Obtain film from coop loan system (Serra Regional Library System), obtain film from other libraries, library film programs. Permanent viewing facility. *Equipment:* lend 16mm sound projector (2), 8mm reel projector (1), S8mm cartridge projector (1), S8mm reel projector (1), projection tables & stands (1), projection screens (1).

Other Media Collections *Audio:* disc, 33⅓rpm, 2172c; tape, cassette, 519c; tape, cartridge, 277c; tape, reel, 9c. *Filmstrips:* sound, 19t/p; silent sets, 2c. *Slides:* single, 112c.

Budget & Expenditures Total library budget $33,853 (FY 7/1/74-7/1/75). Total FY film budget $2523. *Member:* ALA, EFLA, Calif. Library Assn.

Newport Beach

P- NEWPORT BEACH PUBLIC LIBRARY, 2005 Dover Drive, 92660. *Tel:* (714) 640-2141. *Film Serv Est:* 1969. *In Charge:* Walter James McGraw Jr, AV Librarian. *AV Staff:* 2½ (1 prof, 1½ cl). *Film Sel:* committee preview, chief film librarian's decision.

Free-Loan Film Serv *Eligibility:* indiv with library cards. *Restrictions:* for indiv, only in Santiago County; for inst, none. Cannot transmit electronically, borrow for classroom use. May borrow by mail. *Loan Period:* 1 day. *Total Yr Film Loan:* 5769.

Film Collection 83t/165p. Approx 2t acquired annually. *Circ:* 16mm, 83t/85p. *Noncirc:* S8mm cartridge, 80t/p. *Pubns:* catalog, annual; suppl, no set policy. Publish bimonthly film list.

Other Film Serv Obtain film from coop loan system (Santiago Library System), film reference serv, library film programs. *Equipment:* rent 16mm sound projector (3), lend S8mm cartridge projector (2).

Other Media Collections *Audio:* tape, cassette, 30c. *Slides:* single, 260c.

Budget & Expenditures No separate budget. *Member:* Calif. Library Assn.

Video Serv *Est:* 1972. *Video Staff:* 2 f-t, 1 p-t. *Video Use:* documentation of community/school events, to increase community's library use, in-service training. Video serv available by appointment. Produce video tapes.

Video Equipment/Facilities *In-House Use Only:* recording deck (1), b&w/col, Sony VO1600; SEG (1), Sony; audio tape recorders (1).

Video Collection Maintained by own production. Use/play ¾" cassette. *Sources:* commercial distributors. *Tape Sel:* preview, catalogs. *Special Collections:* in-house training tapes. Tapes organized by subject. *Collection, Color:* ¾" cassette, 2t/c. *Other Video Serv:* reference serv. *Pubns:* catalog.

Cable & CCTV Inform public about cable system serv & facilities.

Oakland

A- THE OAKLAND MUSEUM, 1000 Oak St, 94707. *Tel:* (415) 273-3401, ext 3931. *In Charge:* T Heyman, Sr Cur. *AV Staff:* 3 (2 prof, 1 cl, 2 tech). *Holdings:* black studies, fine arts.

Free-Loan Film Serv Available to researchers/scholars for on-site viewing. May not borrow by mail.

Film Collection 20t/p.

Other Film Serv Rent film from distributors for patrons, obtain film from other libraries, film fairs/festivals.

Other Media Collections *Audio:* tape, cassette, 10c; tape, reel, 10c. *Slides:* single, 10,000c.

Budget & Expenditures Total FY film budget $2000.

Video Serv *Est:* 1975. *In Charge:* L. Thomas Frye, Cur. *Video Staff:* 1 tech. *Video Use:* documentation of community/school events, as art form, record historical material. Video Serv available to staff only. Produce video tapes. Have production studio/space.

Video Equipment/Facilities *In-House Use Only:* portapak (1), ¾" col, Sony 3800; recording deck (1), ¾" col, Sony 2850; playback deck (2), ¾" col, JVC 5000, Sony 1200; editing deck (1), ¾" col, Sony 2850; studio camera (1), col, Sony; monitor (5), col, Sony; lighting (5); microphones (3); audio tape recorders (2). Have portable viewing installation.

Video Tape Loan/Rental/Sale Serv *Serv Provided:* free loan. *Loan Eligibility:* educational inst, civic groups, prof groups, such as museum affiliates. *Restrictions:* for inst, none. Cannot use for fund-raising, duplicate.

Video Collection Maintained by own production. Use/play ¾" cassette. *Sources:* in-house production. Tapes organized by subject.

Cable & CCTV Will receive serv of cable TV system.

P- OAKLAND PUBLIC LIBRARY, 125 14 St, 94612. *Tel:* (415) 273-3567. *Film Serv Est:* 1961. *In Charge:* Richard Colvig, Fine Arts Librarian. *AV Staff:* 3 (1 prof, 1 cl, 1 tech). *Film Sel:* chief film librarian's decision, published reviews, ALA Booklist.

Free-Loan Film Serv *Eligibility:* indiv with library cards over 18 yrs. *Restrictions:* for indiv, only in East Bay County. May not borrow by mail. *Loan Period:* 1 day. *Total Yr Film Loan:* 13,290.

Film Collection 270t/285p. Approx 25t acquired annually. *Circ:* 16mm, 270t/285p. *Pubns:* catalog, annual.

Other Film Serv Obtain film from coop loan system (Berkeley/Oakland Serv System, E Bay Coop, N Calif. Library Film Circuit), film reference serv, library film programs.

Other Media Collections *Audio:* disc, 33⅓rpm, 3000t/4000c; tape, cassette, 500t/c.

Budget & Expenditures Total library budget $286,500 (FY 7/74-7/75). Total FY film budget $9000. *Member:* ALA, Calif. Library Assn.

Oceanside

P- OCEANSIDE PUBLIC LIBRARY, 615 4th St, 92054. *Tel:* (714) 433-9011. *In Charge:* Donna Banos, AV Librarian. *AV Staff:* 2½ (1 prof, ½ cl, 1 tech). *Film Sel:* committee preview, chief film librarian's decision.

Free-Loan Film Serv *Eligibility:* educational inst, civic groups, religious groups, indiv with library cards, prof groups. *Restrictions:* only in San Diego & Imperial Counties, Serra Regional Library System. Cannot use for fund-raising, transmit electronically. May not borrow by mail. *Loan Period:* 1 day. *Total Yr Film Loan:* 4231.

Film Collection 332t/336p. *Circ:* 16mm, 101t; 8mm reel, 67t; S8mm reel, 105t; S8mm cartridge, 63t. *Pubns:* catalog, as needed; suppl, no set policy.

Other Film Serv Obtain film from coop loan system (Serra Regional Library System), obtain film from other libraries, film reference serv, library film programs. Permanent viewing facility available to community. *Equipment:* rent 16mm sound projector (1), 8mm reel projector (1), S8mm cartridge projector (3), S8mm reel projector (1), projection screens (1), phonograph (1).

Other Media Collections *Audio:* disc, 33⅓rpm, 1744c; tape, cassette, 408c. *Filmstrips:* sound, 3c.

Budget & Expenditures Total library budget $87,416. Total FY film budget $9881. *Member:* ALA, Calif. Library Assn.

Ontario

P- ONTARIO CITY LIBRARY, 215 E C St, 91764. *Tel:* (714) 984-2758, ext 32. *Film Serv Est:* 1965. *In Charge:* Carl A Barthelette, Head, AV Servs. *AV Staff:* 2½ (1 prof, 1 cl). *Film Sel:* committee preview, chief film librarian's decision.

Free-Loan Film Serv *Eligibility:* indiv with library cards. *Restrictions:* for inst, libraries by interlibrary loan. Cannot use for fund-raising, borrow for classroom use. Available to researchers/scholars for on-site viewing. May borrow by mail. *Loan Period:* 1 day.

Film Collection 550t/572p. Approx 70t acquired annually. *Circ:* 16mm, 450t/454p; S8mm reel, 43t/p; S8mm cartridge, 65t/75p.

Other Film Serv Obtain film from coop loan system (Inland Library System), library film programs. *Equipment:* lend 16mm sound projector (1), lend S8mm cartridge projector (1).

Other Media Collections *Audio:* disc, 33⅓rpm, 4808c; tape, cassette, 1131c. *Filmstrips:* sound, 70c. *Slides:* sets, 12c.

Budget & Expenditures Total library budget $155,055 (FY 7/1/74-7/1/75). Total FY film budget $5000.

Orland

P- ORLAND FREE LIBRARY, 333 Mill St, 95963. *Tel:* (916) 865-3465. *Film Serv Est:* 1971. *In Charge:* Lorrayne I. Foltz, AV Librarian. *AV Staff:* 1. *Film Sel:* staff recommendations. *Holdings:* old time movies.

Free-Loan Film Serv *Eligibility:* educational inst, civic groups, religious groups, indiv with library cards. *Restrictions:* for indiv, interlibrary loan, N. State Cooperative Library System. *Loan Period:* 1-5 days. *Total Yr Film Loan:* 784.

Film Collection 32t/p. Approx 5-10t acquired annually. *Circ:* 16mm, 5t/p.

Other Film Serv Obtain film from coop loan system, (N. State Cooperative Library System), obtain film from other libraries, library film programs. *Equipment:* 16mm sound projector (1), projection tables & stands (1), projection screens (1).

Other Media Collections *Audio:* tape, cassette, 252t/190c; tape, reel, 1t.

Budget & Expenditures Total library budget $10,500 (FY 7/1/74-7/1/75). No separate AV budget.

Oroville

C- BUTTE COMMUNITY COLLEGE DISTRICT, Butte College Library, Box 183A, Route No. 1, 95965. *Tel:* (916) 895-2430. *Film Serv Est:* 1966. *In Charge:* R. Ellsworth, Media Coord. *AV Staff:* 4 (1 prof, 2 cl). *Film Sel:* faculty/staff recommendations. *Holdings:* agriculture, black studies, fine arts, industrial arts, science, social sciences.

Film Rental Serv *Eligibility:* film cooperatives only.

Film Collection 400t/p. Approx 50t acquired annually. *Circ:* 16mm, 400t/p. *Pubns:* catalog, annual.

Other Film Serv Rent film from distributors for patrons, obtain film from coop loan system (North/State Cooperative), obtain film from other libraries, film reference serv. Permanent viewing facility.

Other Media Collections *Audio:* disc, 33⅓rpm, 700t/c; tape, cassette, 300t/c. *Filmstrips:* sound sets, 15t/c; silent sets, 25t/c. *Slides:* sets, 20t/c.

Video Serv *Est:* 1975. *In Charge:* Robert Ellsworth, Media Coord. *Video Staff:* 4 f-t, 1 tech. *Video Use:* documentation of community/school events, to increase community's library use, community video access, in-service training, practical video/TV training courses. Video serv available by appointment. Produce video tapes. Have production studio/space & separate control room.

Video Equipment/Facilities *In-House Use Only:* porta-pak (1), ½" b&w, Sony; recording deck (4), ¾" & 1" col, Panasonic & IVC; playback deck (6), ¾" col, Panasonic; editing deck (1), 1" col, IVC; studio camera (3), b&w/col, Shibaden & Sony; monitor (9), b&w/col, Unimedia & Zenith; SEG (1), 3M; lighting (10); microphones (2); tripods (3); audio tape recorders (50). Have permanent viewing installation. *Equipment Loan Period:* no set policy. Provide training in use of equipment to faculty & students.

Video Tape Loan/Rental/Sale Serv *Serv Provided:* free loan. *Loan Eligibility:* org members.

Video Collection Maintained by purchase, rental, own production. Use/play ½", 1" reel to reel, ¾" cassette. *Sources:* commercial distributors. *Tape Sel:* preview, faculty/staff recommendations, catalogs. Tapes organized by subject. *Collection, Color:* 1" reel, 15t; ¾" cassette, 50t.

Cable & CCTV Produce programs for cablecasting.

Palm Desert

C- COLLEGE OF THE DESERT, 43500 Monterey Ave, 92260. *Tel:* (714) 346-8041, ext 282. *Film Serv Est:* 1965. *In Charge:* Wendell Ford, Coord, AV & Broadcast Serv Center. *AV Staff:* 3 (1 prof, 1 cl, 1 tech). *Film Sel:* faculty/staff recommendations.

Film Collection 5t/8p. Approx 1t acquired annually.

Other Film Serv Rent film from distributors for patrons, obtain film from other libraries, film reference serv. Permanent viewing facility available for rent to community.

Budget & Expenditures Total library budget $10,000 (FY 7/1/74-7/1/75). *Member:* CCMA, CAEMAT, CCTAC.

Video Serv *Est:* 1965. *Video Staff:* 3 f-t. *Video Use:* classroom instruction. Video serv available by appointment. Produce video tapes. Have production studio/space & separate control room.

Video Equipment/Facilities *In-House Use Only:* porta-pak, b&w/col; recording/playback deck (4), 1", 2", IVC, Ampex; studio camera (8), Telemation, Sarkes; SEG (1); keyer (1); lighting, microphones. Have permanent viewing installation. Provide training in use of equipment to faculty & students. Have tape duplication serv.

Video Tape Loan/Rental/Sale Serv *Serv Provided:* swap with other inst.

Video Collection Maintained by purchase, rental, own production, exchange/swap. Use/play ½", 1", 2" reel to reel, ¾" cassette. *Sources:* commercial distributors, galleries, community productions, exchange. *Tape Sel:* preview, faculty/staff recommendations, gallery previews, published reviews, catalogs. *Special Collections:* in-house training tapes, films in video format. Tapes organized by alphabetical & numerical order. *Collection:*

½" reel, 1" reel, 2" reel, ½" cartridge, ¾" cassette. *Other Video Serv:* programming, reference serv, taping of other media, production workshops.

Cable & CCTV Receive serv of cable TV system. Produce programs for cablecasting. Inform public about cable system serv & facilities. Run cable programs for special audiences. Have CCTV in inst, with 200 monitors. *Programming Sources:* over-the-air commercial & public broadcasting, tapes produced by inst, tapes produced professionally, tapes produced by community groups & indiv, rental of tapes.

Palo Alto

P- PALO ALTO CITY LIBRARY, 1213 Newell Rd, 94303. *Tel:* (415) 329-2436. *Film Serv Est:* 1974. *Film Sel:* committee preview.

Free-Loan Film Serv *Eligibility:* indiv with library cards. *Restrictions:* only in city. Cannot use for fund-raising. May not borrow by mail. *Loan Period:* 1 day.

Film Collection 460t/p. Approx 10-20t acquired annually.

Other Film Serv Obtain film from coop loan system (Santa Clara County Library), obtain film from other libraries for library sponsored programs only, library film programs.

Other Media Collections *Audio:* disc, 33⅓rpm, 2235c; tape, cassette, 381c; tape, reel 10c.

Budget & Expenditures Total library budget $185,650 (FY 7/1/75-7/1/76). Total FY film budget $4500. *Member:* ALA, Calif. Library Assn.

Palos Verdes Peninsula

P- PALOS VERDES LIBRARY DISTRICT, AV Dept, 650 Deep Valley Drive, 90274. *Tel:* (213) 377-9584, ext 38, 39. *Film Serv Est:* 1970. *In Charge:* Myra Nadler, Supervisor. *AV Staff:* 5 (1 prof, 4 cl/tech). *Film Sel:* committee preview, staff recommendations, chief film librarian's decision. *Holdings:* animated films 25%, black studies 1%, children's films 20%, consumer affairs 1%, dance 1%, ecology 15%, engineering 2%, experimental films 2%, feature films 2%, fine arts 10%, science 10%, social sciences 10%, travel/entertainment 3%.

Free-Loan Film Serv *Eligibility:* indiv with library cards. *Restrictions:* for indiv, none; for inst, none. Available to researchers/scholars for on-site viewing. May not borrow by mail. *Loan Period:* 1 day. *Total Yr Film Loan:* 1461.

Film Collection 320t/340p. Approx 30t acquired annually. *Circ:* 16mm, 320t/340p; 8mm reel, 420t/437p; S8mm reel, 100t/p. *Pubns:* catalog, every 2 yr ($2); suppl, as needed. Publish film annotation highlight sheets; press releases for in-house showings.

Other Film Serv Rent film from distributors for patrons, obtain film from coop loan system (Metropolitan Cooperative Library System), obtain film from other libraries, film reference serv, film fairs/festivals, library film programs, community planning & film programming. Permanent viewing facility available free to community. *Equipment:* lend 16mm sound projector (4), 8mm reel projector (2), S8mm reel projector (2), carousel slide projector (1).

Other Media Collections *Audio:* disc, 33⅓rpm, 9500t/18,000c; tape, cassette, 400t/500c. *Filmstrips:* sound, 60t/c. *Slides:* single, 50t/c; sets, 9t/c.

Budget & Expenditures Total library budget $202,500 (FY 7/1/74-7/1/75). Total FY film budget $9500. *Member:* ALA, EFLA, FLIC, Calif. Library Assn.

Pleasant Hill

P- CONTRA COSTA COUNTY LIBRARY, 1750 Oak Park Blvd, 94523. *Tel:* (415) 937-4100, ext 274. *Film Serv Est:* 1973. *In Charge:* Helene J. Kosher, AV Coord. *AV Staff:* 1 prof. *Film Sel:* committee preview. *Holdings:* agriculture 1%, animated films 8%, black studies 2%, children's films 25%, dance 1%, experimental films 3%, feature films 11%, fine arts 12%, industrial arts 1%, law 1%, medicine 1%, science

9%, social sciences 15%, sports & games 5%, teacher education 2%, women 3%.

Free-Loan Film Serv *Eligibility:* civic groups, religious groups, prof groups, such as library staff/branch programming. *Restrictions:* for groups, only in Contra Costa County. Cannot use for fund-raising, transmit electronically, borrow for classroom use. Available to researchers/scholars for on-site viewing. May not borrow by mail. Films must be reserved in advance. *Loan Period:* noon to 5 p.m. following day.

Film Collection 113t/p. *Circ:* 16mm, 113t/p; 8mm & S8mm reel, 420t/426p; 8mm cartridge, 6t/p; S8mm cartridge, 28t/p. *Pubns:* catalog, as needed; suppl, no set policy. Publish materials pertaining to collection. Publish filmographics & subject lists.

Other Film Serv Obtain film from coop loan system (East Bay Cooperative), film reference serv, film fairs/festivals, library film programs. *Equipment:* lend (interbranch only) S8mm camera (4), lend/16mm sound projector (11), lend (interbranch only) 8mm reel/S8mm duals projector (6), S8mm cartridge projector (2), S8mm reel projector (3), projection screens (2).

Other Media Collections *Audio:* disc, 33⅓rpm, 1654t/c; tape, cassette, 495t/c. *Filmstrips:* sound sets, 18t/c; silent sets, 3t/c. *Slides:* sets, 8t/c.

Budget & Expenditures Total library budget $470,017 (FY 7/1/74-7/1/75). Total FY film budget $5000. *Member:* ALA, EFLA, Calif. Library Assn.

Video Serv *Est:* 1975. *In Charge:* Helene Kosher, AV Coord. *Video Use:* community video access, as information tool to add to library resources. Video serv available on demand. Produce video tapes.

Video Equipment/Facilities *In-House Use Only:* recording deck (1), ½" b&w, Sony AV3650; playback deck (2), ¾" col, Sony VO1600 & 1800; studio camera (2), b&w, Sony; SEG (1), Sony SEG 1; microphones (3); tripods (3); audio tape recorders (11). *For Loan:* portapak (2), ½" b&w, Sony AV8400; monitor (13), 9-Sony CVM115, 4-RCA Lyceum. Have portable viewing installation (monitor & player on cart with headphone sets). *Equipment Loan Period:* noon to 5 p.m. following day. Provide training in use of equipment to members of non-profit groups or organizations & library staff. Have tape duplication serv.

Video Tape Loan/Rental/Sale Serv *Loan Eligibility:* civic groups, religious groups, prof groups, such as library staff & county agency personnel, & others, such as library branches for programs. *Restrictions:* for indiv & inst, only in Contra Costa County. Cannot use for fund-raising, duplicate, air without permission. May not borrow by mail.

Video Collection Maintained by purchase, own production. Use/play ½" reel to reel, ¾" cassette. *Sources:* commercial distributors, community productions. *Member:* California Video Resource Project, San Francisco. *Tape Sel:* preview. Tapes organized by title. *Collection, Color:* ¾" cassette, 26t. *Collection, B&W:* ½" reel, 5t. *Other Video Serv:* programming, taping of other media, production workshops.

Cable & CCTV Receive serv of cable TV system (7 branches). Produce programs for cablecasting. Serve as production facility for others. Run cable programs for special audiences.

Pomona

P- POMONA PUBLIC LIBRARY, AV Division, Box 2271, 91766. *Tel:* (714) 620-2014. *In Charge:* Gregory B. Shapton, AV Supervisor. *AV Staff:* 4.6 (2 prof, .9 cl, 1.8 tech). *Film Sel:* committee preview.

Film Rental Serv *Eligibility:* patrons/public. *Restrictions:* only in Los Angeles, San Bernardino, Riverside & Orange counties. Cannot use for fund-raising, transmit electronically. *Rental Period:* 1 day. *Total Yr Film Booking:* 25,217.

Film Collection 875t/p. Approx 180t acquired annually. *Circ:* 16mm, 728t; 8mm reel, 51t; S8mm reel, 94. *Pubns:* catalog, every 2 yr ($2); 2 or 3 suppls, published between catalogs ($.25). Publish filmographies on specialized and/or interesting topics; promotional flyers & art work for library film showings.

Other Film Serv Obtain film from coop loan system (Public Library Film Circuit), obtain film from other libraries, film reference serv, film fairs/festivals, library film programs.

Other Media Collections *Audio:* disc 33⅓rpm, 4000t; tape, cassette, 1300t/c. *Slides:* sets, 5t.

Budget & Expenditures Total library budget $134,312 (FY 7/1/74-7/1/75). Total FY film budget $12,000. *Member:* EFLA, Calif. Library Assn.

Porterville

P- PORTERVILLE PUBLIC LIBRARY, 41 W Thurman, 93257. *Tel:* (209) 784-0177. *In Charge:* Brenda Avery, Library Assistant. *AV Staff:* 1. *Film Sel:* staff recommendations, published reviews.

Free-Loan Film Serv *Eligibility:* civic groups, religious groups, indiv with library cards. *Restrictions:* for indiv, only in city; for inst, only in city. Cannot use for fund-raising, transmit electronically. May not borrow by mail. *Loan Period:* 1-14 days. *Total Yr Film Loan:* 1401.

Film Collection 150t/p. Approx 10-15t acquired annually. *Circ:* 16mm, 14t/p; 8mm reel, 133t/p; S8mm reel, 11t/p.

Other Film Serv Obtain film from other libraries, library film programs. Permanent viewing facility. *Equipment:* lend 16mm sound projector (1), projection screens (2).

Other Media Collections *Audio:* disc, 33⅓rpm, 2595t/c; disc, 45rpm, 8t/c; tape, cassette, 101t/c. *Filmstrips:* sound sets, 1t/c. *Slides:* sets, 56t/c.

Budget & Expenditures Total library budget $25,000 (FY 7/1/74-7/1/75). No separate AV budget.

Redding

C- SHASTA COLLEGE, Instructional Media Center, 96001. *Tel:* (916) 241-3523, ext 215. *Film Serv Est:* 1966. *In Charge:* John Bertrand, Coord. *AV Staff:* 15 (1 prof, 4 cl, 10 tech). *Film Sel:* faculty/staff recommendations, chief film librarian's decision.

Free-Loan Film Serv *Eligibility:* staff & students. *Restrictions:* available to researchers/scholars for on-site viewing. May not borrow by mail. *Total Yr Film Loan:* 1200.

Film Collection 300t/p. Approx 10-20t acquired annually. *Circ:* 16mm, 300t/p; S8mm cartridge, 50t/p. *Pubns:* catalog, every 2 yrs; suppl, in yr catalog not published.

Other Film Serv Rent film from distributors for patrons, obtain film from coop loan system (North Valley Coop, N Calif. Higher Educational Council, County Schools Office), obtain film from other libraries.

Other Media Collections *Audio:* disc, 33⅓rpm, 1500t; tape, cassette, 1000t. *Filmstrips:* silent, 200t; sound sets, 150t.

Budget & Expenditures Total library budget $10,000 (FY 7/74-7/75). Total FY film budget $7000. *Member:* AECT, EFLA.

Video Serv *Est:* 1968. *In Charge:* John Bertrand, Coord. *Video Staff:* 1 f-t, 1 tech. *Video Use:* documentation of community/school events, in-service training, practical video/TV training courses, playback only of professionally produced tapes. Video serv available by appointment. Produce video tapes. Have production studio/space & separate control room.

Video Equipment/Facilities *In-House Use Only:* portapak (3), ½" b&w, Sony 3400, Panasonic 3080; recording deck (2), ¾" col, Sony 1600; playback deck (5), ¾" col, Sony 1000; editing deck (2), ½", 1" col, Sony 210, 8650; studio camera (3), Sony 3200; monitor (4), col, Sony; SEG (1), Sony SEG-1; additional camera lenses (2). Have permanent viewing installation. *Equipment Loan Period:* no set policy. Provide training in use of equipment to faculty & students.

Video Tape Loan/Rental/Sale Serv *Serv Provided:* free loan, swap with other inst. *Loan Eligibility:* staff. *Restrictions:* cannot duplicate. May not borrow by mail.

Video Collection Maintained by purchase, own production, exchange/swap. Use/play ½", 1" reel to reel, ¾" cassette. *Sources:* commercial distributors. *Tape Sel:* preview, faculty/staff recommendations. Tapes organized by subject. *Collection, Color:* ½" reel, 170t; ¾" cassette, 320t. *Collection, B&W:* ½" reel, 60t; 1" reel, 80t. *Other Video Serv:* production workshops.

Cable & CCTV Have CCTV in inst, with 20 monitors. *Programming Sources:* over-the-air commercial & public broadcasting, tapes produced by inst, tapes produced professionally, tapes produced by community groups & indiv.

Redding (cont'd)

P- SHASTA COUNTY LIBRARY, 1855 Shasta St, 96001. *Tel:* (916) 246-5756, ext 4. *Film Serv Est:* 1952. *In Charge:* Maxine Goddard, Library Assistant. *AV Staff:* 1 cl. *Film Sel:* committee preview, staff recommendations. *Holdings:* children's films 75%.

Free-Loan Film Serv *Eligibility:* educational inst, civic groups, religious groups, indiv with library cards, prof groups. *Restrictions:* for indiv, only in Shasta County; for inst, only in Shasta County. Cannot use for fund-raising, transmit electronically. May not borrow by mail. *Loan Period:* 1 day. *Total Yr Film Loan:* 1027.

Film Collection 100t/p. *Circ:* 16mm, 100t/p. *Pubns:* catalog, as needed.

Other Film Serv Obtain film from coop loan system (N Calif. Library Film Circuit, N State Cooperative Library System), obtain film from other libraries, library film programs. Permanent viewing facility available for rent to community.

Budget & Expenditures No separate budget.

Redlands

P- A.K. SMILEY PUBLIC LIBRARY, Box 751, 92373. *Tel:* (714) 793-2201. *Film Serv Est:* 1966. *In Charge:* Barbara Courson, Library Asst. *AV Staff:* 2 (3 prof, 1 tech).

Free-Loan Film Serv *Eligibility:* adults. *Restrictions:* for indiv, none. Cannot use for fund-raising, transmit electronically. May not borrow by mail. *Loan Period:* 1 day.

Film Collection 105t/p. Approx 10t acquired annually. *Circ:* 16mm, 1t/p; 8mm reel, 85t/p; S8mm reel, 20t/p. *Pubns:* Use monthly packet sheets provided by film circuit.

Other Film Serv Rent film from distributors for special programs in the library, coop loan system (Film Council Film Circuit). Permanent viewing facility.

Other Media Collections *Audio:* disc, 33⅓rpm, 1962t/2002c; tape, cassette, 523t/528c.

Budget & Expenditures Total library budget $30,000 (FY 7/1/74-7/1/75). Total FY film budget $1400.

Redondo

P- REDONDO BEACH PUBLIC LIBRARY, 309 Esplanade, 90277. *Tel:* (213) 376-8723. *Film Serv Est:* 1967. *In Charge:* Rosemary S. Taylor, AV Librarian. *AV Staff:* 3 (1 prof, 1 cl, 1 tech). *Film Sel:* committee preview.

Free-Loan Film Serv *Eligibility:* indiv with library cards. *Restrictions:* for indiv, interlibrary loan. Cannot use for fund-raising. Available to researchers/scholars for on-site viewing. May not borrow by mail. *Loan Period:* 1 day. *Total Yr Film Loan:* 4098.

Film Collection 146t/p. Approx 5t acquired annually. *Circ:* 16mm, 50t; 8mm reel, 10t; S8mm reel, 9t; S8mm cartridge, 75t. *Pubns:* catalog, as needed. Publish monthly list of circuit 16mm, 8mm & S8mm reel to reel & S8mm cartridge films.

Other Film Serv Obtain film from coop loan system (Metropolitan Coop Library System, Public Library Film Circuit), obtain film from other libraries, film reference serv, library film programs. *Equipment:* lend 16mm sound projector (2), S8mm cartridge projector (3).

Other Media Collections *Audio:* disc, 33⅓rpm, 3011t.

Budget & Expenditures Total library budget $34,885 (FY 7/1/74-7/1/75). Total FY film budget $1050. *Member:* FLIC, Calif. Library Assn.

Redwood

P- REDWOOD CITY PUBLIC LIBRARY, AV Center, 881 Jefferson Ave, 94063. *Tel:* (415) 369-3739. *Film Serv Est:* 1974. *In Charge:* Mrs. Betty L. James, AV Librarian. *AV Staff:* 2½ (1 prof, 1½ cl). *Film Sel:* chief film librarian's decision.

Free-Loan Film Serv *Eligibility:* indiv with library cards. *Restrictions:* cannot use for fund-raising, transmit electronically. Available to researchers/scholars for on-site viewing.

May not borrow by mail. *Loan Period:* 1-7 days. *Total Yr Film Loan:* 5746.

Film Collection 210t. Approx 125t acquired annually. *Circ:* 16mm, 60t; 8mm reel, 110t; S8mm reel, 40t. *Pubns:* publish monthly lists of circuit films.

Other Film Serv Obtain film from coop loan system (Peninsula Library System), on-demand showings when library is open. Permanent viewing facility available for rent to community. *Equipment:* S8mm camera (2), 16mm sound projector (2), S8mm cartridge projector (2), S8mm reel projector (2), projection tables & stands (3), projection screens (3).

Other Media Collections *Audio:* disc, 33⅓rpm, 4000t/6000c.

Budget & Expenditures Total library budget $107,000 (FY 7/1/74-7/1/75). Total FY film budget $13,500. *Member:* ALA, Calif. Library Assn.

Richmond

P- RICHMOND PUBLIC LIBRARY, Civic Center Plaza, 94804. *Tel:* (415) 234-6632. *Video Serv Est:* 1973. *In Charge:* Brenda Motomura, Supervisor. *Video Staff:* 2 p-t. *Video Use:* documentation of community/school events, to increase community's library use, community video access, in-service training, practical video/TV training courses. Video serv available by appointment. Produce video tapes.

Video Equipment/Facilities *In-House Use Only:* portapak (1), ½″ b&w, Sony 3400; playback deck (1), ½″ b&w, Sony 3600; monitor (1), b&w, Sony. Have portable viewing installations. Provide training in use of equipment to staff & community members.

Video Collection Maintained by own production. Use/play ½″ reel to reel. *Collection, B&W:* ½″ reel, 8t/c.

Riverside

C- CALIFORNIA BAPTIST COLLEGE, Annie Gabriel Library, 8432 Magnolia Ave, 92504. *Tel:* (714) 689-5771, ext 17. *Video Serv Est:* 1973. *In Charge:* Janette B. Cutsinger, Library Dir. *Video Staff:* 1 p-t. *Video Use:* classroom activities. Video serv available by appointment. Produce video tapes.

Video Equipment/Facilities *In-House Use Only:* recording deck (1), ½″ b&w, Panasonic NV 309; playback deck (1), ½″ b&w, Panasonic NV 309; studio camera (1), Panasonic 340P; monitor (1), Panasonic AN236V; microphones (1); tripods (1). Have portable viewing installations. *Equipment Loan Period:* no set policy. Provide training in use of equipment to a few select people.

Video Tape Loan/Rental/Sale Serv *Loan/Rental Eligibility:* staff.

Rocklin

C- SIERRA COLLEGE LIBRARY, 5000 Rocklin Rd, 95677. *Tel:* (916) 624-3333, ext 257. *Film Serv Est:* 1968. *In Charge:* W. R. Pierce, Librarian. *AV Staff:* 2 (½ prof, ½ cl, 1 tech). *Film Sel:* committee preview. *Holdings:* feature films 25%.

Free-Loan Film Serv *Eligibility:* staff & students, groups, such as public libraries. *Restrictions:* for inst, community college district. Cannot use for fund-raising, transmit electronically. Available to researchers/scholars for on-site viewing. May not borrow by mail.

Film Collection 546t/p. Approx 30t acquired annually. *Circ:* 16mm, 228t/p; 8mm reel, 149t/p; S8mm reel, 169t/p. *Pubns:* catalog, as needed; suppl pages annually.

Other Film Serv Rent film from distributors for patrons, obtain film from coop loan system (Mountain Valley Library System), obtain film from other libraries, film reference serv, film fairs/festivals, library film programs. Permanent viewing facility. *Equipment:* lend S8mm camera (2), 16mm sound projector (24), 8mm reel projector (3), S8mm reel projector (2), projection tables & stands (29), projection screens (4).

Other Media Collections *Audio:* disc, 33⅓rpm, 2514t/ tape, cassette, 2750t/c. *Filmstrips:* silent, 84t/c; sound set 253t/c. *Slides:* sets, 115t/c.

Budget & Expenditures Total library budget $48,450 (FY 7/1/74-7/1/75). Total FY film budget $4500. *Member:* ALA, Calif. Library Assn, CAEMAT.

Video Serv *Est:* 1975-6. *In Charge:* W. R. Pierce, Librarian. *Video Use:* documentation of community/school events, to increase community's library use, playback only of professionally produced tapes. Video serv available on demand. Produce video tapes. Have production studio/space & separate control room.

Video Equipment/Facilities *In-House Use Only:* portapak (1), ½" b&w, Sony. *For Loan:* portapak (1), ½" b&w, Sony. Have permanent viewing installations. Provide training in use of equipment to faculty & students. Have tape duplication serv.

Video Tape Loan/Rental/Sale Serv *Serv Provided:* free loan. *Loan Eligibility:* staff & students, public libraries. *Restrictions:* for inst, community college district. Cannot use for fundraising, duplicate, air without permission. May borrow by mail.

Video Collection Maintained by purchase, rental, own production, exchange/swap. Use/play ¾" cassette. *Sources:* commercial distributors. *Tape Sel:* preview, faculty/staff recommendations. Tapes organized by Dewey Decimal.

Rosemead

P- ROSEMEAD PUBLIC LIBRARY (Part of the L.A. County System) 8800 Valley Blvd., 91770. *Tel:* (213) 573-8681. *Film Serv Est:* 1968. *In Charge:* Vilalia E. Aguerd, Librarian. *AV Staff:* 6 (1 prof, 5 cl). *Film Sel:* committee preview, staff recommendations. *Holdings:* animated films 15%, children's films 60%, feature films 2%.

Free-Loan Film Serv *Eligibility:* civic groups, religious groups, indiv with library cards. *Restrictions:* for indiv, only in Los Angeles County; for inst, only in Los Angeles County. Cannot transmit electronically. Available to researchers/scholars for on-site viewing. May not borrow by mail. *Loan Period:* 2 days. *Total Yr Film Loan:* 850 per month.

Film Collection 306t. Approx 10t acquire annually. *Pubns:* catalog, every 2 yr; suppl, no set policy.

Other Film Serv Library film programs. Permanent viewing facility.

Other Media Collections *Audio:* disc, 33⅓rpm, 3271t; tape, cassette, 90t.

Budget & Expenditures Total library budget $2500 (FY 7/75-7/76). Total FY film budget $700. *Member:* Calif. Library Assn.

Sacramento

C- CALIFORNIA STATE UNIVERSITY, SACTO, Center for Instructional Media, 6000 J St, 95819. *Tel:* (916) 454-6397. *In Charge:* Dr. Robert Jarecke, Dir. *AV Staff:* 22 (4 cl). *Film Sel:* faculty/staff recommendations.

Free-Loan Film Serv *Eligibility:* staff & students, educational inst. *Restrictions:* for indiv, only in Sacramento County; for inst, only in Sacramento County. May not borrow by mail. *Total Yr Film Loan:* 300.

Film Collection 964t/1055p. Approx 78t acquired annually. *Pubns:* catalog, every 2 yr; suppl, every semester.

Other Film Serv Film reference serv, film fairs/festivals. Permanent viewing facility. *Equipment:* lend S8mm camera, 16mm camera, 16mm sound projector, 8mm cartridge projector, 8mm reel projector, S8mm cartridge projector, S8mm reel projector, projection tables & stands, projection screens. *Member:* AECT, Calif. Library Assn, CAEMAT, NEA, NAEB, PDK.

C- COSUMNES RIVER COLLEGE, 8401 Center Parkway, 95823. *Tel:* (916) 421-1000, ext 257.

Video Serv *Est:* 1973. *Video Staff:* 2 f-t, 1 p-t, 3 tech. *Video Use:* documentation of community/school events, community

video access, in-service training, practical video/TV training courses. Video serv available on demand & by appointment. Produce video tapes. Have production studio/space & separate control room.

Video Equipment/Facilities *In-House Use Only:* portapak (3), ½" b&w, Sony; recording deck (3), 1" col, IVC; playback deck (16), ¾" col, JVC; editing deck (1), 1" col, IVC; studio camera (4), col, Shibaden; monitor (16), col, JVC; SEG (1), JVC; keyer (2), additional camera lenses (3); lighting; microphones; tripods; audio tape recorders. Have permanent viewing installation. Provide training in use of equipment.

Video Collection Maintained by purchase, rental, own production, exchange/swap. Use/play ½", 1" reel to reel, ¾" cassette. *Sources:* commercial distributors, community productions, exchange (cooperatives in the area). *Tape Sel:* preview, faculty/staff recommendations, catalogs. *Special Collections:* in-house training tapes, films in video format. Tapes organized by subject & Library of Congress classification. *Collection, Color:* 1" reel, 150t/c; 2" reel, 36t/c; ¾" cassette, 150t/c. *Collection, B&W:* ½" reel, 8t/c.

Cable & CCTV Produce programs for cablecasting. Have CCTV in inst, with 16 monitors. *Programming Sources:* tapes produced by inst, tapes produced by community groups & indiv.

C- LOS RIOS COMMUNITY COLLEGE DISTRICT, Film Library, 2100 Arden Way, 95825. *Tel:* (916) 484-8011, ext 291. *Film Serv Est:* 1968. *In Charge:* Dr. Leadie Clark, Assistant Superintendent. *AV Staff:* 1 cl. *Film Sel:* committee preview, faculty/staff recommendations.

Film Collection 1200t. Approx 50t acquired annually. *Circ:* 16mm, 1200t. *Pubns:* catalog, every 5 yr; suppl, no set policy.

Other Film Serv Obtain film from coop loan system (Sacramento County Schools), obtain film from other libraries.

Budget & Expenditures Total library budget $50,000 (FY 7/1/74-7/1/75). Total FY film budget $35,000.

P- SACRAMENTO PUBLIC LIBRARY, 1930 T St, 95814. *Tel:* (916) 449-5651. *Film Serv Est:* 1956. *In Charge:* Kathryn Gunning, AV Librarian. *AV Staff:* 4 (1 prof, 3 cl). *Film Sel:* committee preview.

Free-Loan Film Serv *Eligibility:* educational inst, civic groups, rel\igous groups, indiv with library cards, prof groups. *Restrictions:* for indiv & inst, only in city; only in county; Mountain Valley Library System members. Cannot use for fund-raising, transmit electronically. Available to researchers/scholars for on-site viewing. May not borrow by mail. *Loan Period:* 2 days.

Film Collection 650t. *Circ:* 16mm, 650t. *Pubns:* catalog, annual; suppl, quarterly.

Other Film Serv Obtain film from coop loan system (Mountain Valley Library System), film reference serv, library film programs. Permanent viewing facility available to community.

Other Media Collections *Audio:* disc, 33⅓rpm, 5000t/c; tape, cassette, 200t/c. *Filmstrips:* sound sets, 200t/c.

Budget & Expenditures Total FY film budget $20,000. *Member:* ALA, EFLA, Calif. Library Assn.

Video Serv *Est:* 1974. *In Charge:* Kathryn Gunning. *Video Staff:* 1 f-t. *Video Use:* documentation of community events, to increase community's library use, in-service training. Video serv available on demand. Produce video tapes.

Video Equipment/Facilities *In-House Use Only:* portapak (1), ½" b&w/col, Panasonic 3085; recording deck (1), ¾" b&w/col, Panasonic; playback deck (1), ½" b&w, Sony 3600; editing deck (1), ½" b&w/col, Sony 8650; monitor (4), b&w, Sony; microphones (1); audio tape recorders (1). *Equipment Loan Period:* no set policy.

Video Collection Maintained by own production. Use/play ½" reel to reel, ¾" cassette. *Sources:* Cosumnes River College, Title I grant productions. *Collection, Color:* ¾" cassette, 45t/4c. *Collection, B&W:* ¾" cassette, 45t/4c.

Cable & CCTV Have CCTV in inst, with 4 monitors. *Programming Sources:* produced by inst, tapes produced by local Jr. College.

San Bernardino

P- SAN BERNARDINO PUBLIC LIBRARY, AV Division, 401 N Arrowhead Ave, 92405. *Tel:* (714) 889-0264 ext 32. *Film Serv Est:* 1966. *In Charge:* Robert A. Krasney, AV Coord. *AV Staff:* 6 (1 prof, 4 cl, 1 tech). *Film Sel:* chief film librarian's decision.

Free-Loan Film Serv *Eligibility:* indiv with library cards. *Restrictions:* for indiv, only in city; for inst, only in city. Cannot transmit electronically. Available to researchers/scholars for on-site viewing. *Loan Period:* 1 day. *Total Yr Film Loan:* 2700.

Film Collection 258t/262p. Approx 12-15t acquired annually. *Circ:* 16mm, 258t/262p; 8mm-S8mm reel, 16t/p; 8mm cartridge, 44t/p. *Pubns:* catalog, annual; suppl, quarterly as needed. Publish catalogs for all AV material we have or have access to.

Other Film Serv Obtain film from coop loan system (Inland Library System, Southern Calif. Film Circuit), obtain film from other libraries, film reference serv, library film programs, rental of feature films. Permanent viewing facility available to community. *Equipment:* lend 16mm sound projector (1), 8mm reel projector (2), S8mm cartridge projector (2), cassette recorder.

Other Media Collections *Audio:* disc, 33⅓rpm, 3500t/4500c; tape, reel, 267t/c.

Budget & Expenditures Total library budget $530,000 (FY 7/1/74-7/1/75). Total FY film budget $10,725. *Member:* ALA, EFLA.

San Diego

P- SAN DIEGO COUNTY LIBRARY, 5555 Overland, 92123. *Tel:* (714) 565-5106. *Film Serv Est:* 1970. *In Charge:* David Davis, AV Coord. *AV Staff:* 8 (1 prof, 6 cl, 1 tech). *Film Sel:* chief film librarian's decision, published reviews.

Free-Loan Film Serv *Eligibility:* civic groups, religious groups, indiv with library cards, prof groups except teachers. *Restrictions:* for indiv, only in San Diego County; for inst, only in San Diego County. Cannot use for fund-raising, transmit electronically, borrow for classroom use. *Loan Period:* 1 day. *Total Yr Film Loan:* 6409.

Film Collection 467t/p. *Pubns:* catalog, as needed; suppl, no set policy.

Other Film Serv Obtain film from coop loan system (Serra Regional Library System), obtain film from other libraries, film reference serv, library film programs. *Equipment:* S8mm camera (1), 16mm sound projector (12), projection screens (12).

Other Media Collections *Audio:* tape, cassette, 2000c.

Video Serv *Est:* 1975. *In Charge:* David Davis. *Video Staff:* 8 f-t, 1 tech. *Video Use:* documentation of community/school events, to increase community's library use, community video access, in-service training, playback of professionally produced tapes, as art form. Video serv available on demand. Produce video tapes.

Video Equipment/Facilities *In-House Use Only:* porta-pak (1), ½" b&w, Sony; recording deck (2), ½", ¾" b&w/col, Sony, JVC; playback deck (3), ½", ¾" b&w/col, Panasonic, Sony; monitor (4), b&w/col, Sony, Panasonic; microphones (5); tripods (2); audio tape recorders (2). Have permanent & portable viewing installations. Provide training in use of equipment to staff.

Video Collection Maintained by purchase, own production. Use/play ½" reel to reel, ¾" cassette. *Sources:* commercial distributors, community productions. *Tape Sel:* preview, published reviews. *Special Collections:* in-house training tapes, video as art, films in video format. Tapes organized by subject. *Collection, B&W:* ½" reel, 30t. *Other Video Serv:* programming, taping of other media. *Pubns:* catalog.

Cable & CCTV Receive serv of cable TV system. Have CCTV in inst, wit 4 monitors. *Programming Sources:* over-the-air commercial & public broadcasting, tapes produced by inst, tapes produced professionally, tapes produced by community groups & indiv.

P- SERRA COOPERATIVE LIBRARY SYSTEM, 5555 Overland Ave, 92123. *Tel:* (714) 278-8090. *Film Serv Est:* 1971. *In*

Charge: Peter Ahlstrom, System Coord. *AV Staff:* 3 (1 cl, 2 tech). *Film Sel:* committee preview.

Free-Loan Film Serv *Eligibility:* indiv with library cards, member libraries, community groups. *Restrictions:* indiv & inst, only in Serra System (13 members). Cannot use for fund-raising, transmit electronically, borrow for classroom use. May not borrow by mail. *Loan Period:* 1 day. *Total Yr Film Loan:* 6800.

Film Collection 642t/717p. *Circ:* 16mm, 400t/475p; S8mm cartridge, 242t/p. *Pubns:* catalog, as needed; suppl, no set policy.

Other Film Serv Obtain film from other libraries, film reference serv, film fairs/festivals, advise on equipment & films.

Budget & Expenditures Total library budget $104,452 (FY 7/1/74-7/1/75). Total FY film budget $39,308.

Video Serv Act as resource of information to member libraries. Video serv available on demand. Produce video tapes.

Video Equipment/Facilities *In-House Use Only:* porta-pak (1), ½" b&w, Sony AV3400; recording deck (1), ½" b&w, Panasonic 3020; playback deck (1), ½" b&w, Panasonic VTR3010; monitor (2), b&w, Panasonic TR513, Panasonic TR195V; microphones (1); tripods (1); audio tape recorders (2); carts (1).

Video Tape Loan/Rental/Sale Serv *Serv Provided:* swap with other inst. *Loan Eligibility:* org members. May not borrow by mail.

Video Collection Maintained by own production. Use/play ½" reel to reel. *Other Video Serv:* reference serv, keep equipment in repair, see to distribution of equipment to members.

C- UNITED STATES INTERNATIONAL UNIVERSITY, Walter Library—Learning Resources Center, 10455 Pomerado Rd, 92131. *Tel:* (714) 271-4300, ext 215. *Film Serv Est:* 1967. *In Charge:* Kathleen M. Whetstone, Coord. *AV Staff:* 1 (1 prof). *Film Sel:* committee preview, faculty/staff recommendations. *Holdings:* dance 13%, human behavior 37%.

Film Collection 40t. *Noncirc:* 16mm, 40t.

Other Film Serv Rent film from distributors for patrons.

Other Media Collections *Audio:* disc, 45rpm, 381t; tape, cartridge, 1500t. *Filmstrips:* sound-silent, 400t; sound sets, 235t/20c; silent sets, 713t. *Slides:* single, 2000t; sets, 35t.

Video Serv *Est:* 1973. *In Charge:* John Campbell, Media Servs Coord. *Video Staff:* ½ f-t, ¼ p-t. *Video Use:* documentation of community/ school events, in-service training, as art form. Video serv available by appointment. Produce video tapes.

Video Equipment/Facilities *In-House Use Only:* porta-pak (2), ½", Sony; recording deck (1), ¾", Sony VD1800; editing deck (1), ½" b&w, Sony 3650; studio camera (2), ½" b&w, Sony AVC 3250. Provide training in use of equipment to faculty & students.

Video Tape Loan/Rental/Sale Serv *Loan/Rental Eligibility:* staff & students, educational inst. *Restrictions:* for indiv & inst, none. May borrow by mail.

Video Collection Maintained by own production. Use/play ½" reel to reel, ¾" cassette. *Sources:* commercial distributors. *Tape Sel:* faculty/staff recommendations, catalogs. Tapes organized by Library of Congress. *Collection, B&W:* ½" reel, 21t; ¾" cassette, 10t. *Other Video Serv:* production workshops. *Pubns:* catalog.

San Francisco

C- GOLDEN GATE UNIVERSITY, 536 Mission, 94105. *Tel:* (415) 391-7800, ext 275. *In Charge:* John Ballard. *AV Staff:* 1 cl. *Film Sel:* chief film librarian's decision. *Holdings:* business 100%.

Film Collection 25t/p. Approx 3-4t acquired annually. *Noncirc:* 16mm, 25t/p.

Other Media Collections *Audio:* disc, 33⅓rpm, 1075t/c; disc, tape, cassette, 400t/c. *Filmstrips:* sound, 100t/c. *Slides:* single, 3100t/c.

S- INSIGHT EXCHANGE, Box 42584, 94101. *Tel:* (415) 621-2713. *Video Serv Est:* 1973. *In Charge:* Rose Meden, Video Dir. *Video Use:* disseminate information to people working for personal/political change. Video serv available on demand & by appointment.

Video Tape Loan/Rental/Sale Serv *Serv Provided:* free loan, rental, sale. *Loan/Rental Eligibility:* community org, women's groups. *Restrictions:* for indiv & inst, USA only. Cannot duplicate, air without permission. May borrow by mail. *Total Yr Tape Loan:* 50. *Other Video Serv:* programming. *Pubns:* catalog.

S- MUSEUM OF CONCEPTUAL ART (MOCA), 75 Third St, 94103. *Tel:* (415) 495-3193. *Video Serv Est:* 1970. *In Charge:* Tom Marioni, Dir. *Video Staff:* 5 f-t. *Video Use:* documentation of events, as art form. Video serv available by appointment. Produce video tapes. Have production studio/space & separate control room.

Video Equipment/Facilities *In-House Use Only:* portapak (2); recording deck (1); playback deck (1); studio camera (1); monitor (1); microphones (1); tripods (1); audio tape recorders (1). Have portable viewing installation.

Video Collection Maintained by own production. Use/play ½″, ¼″ reel to reel. *Sources:* commercial distributors. *Collection, B&W:* ½″ reel, 1t/c.

Cable & CCTV Receive serv of cable TV system. Produce programs for cablecasting.

S- OPTIC NERVE, 141 Tenth St, 94103. *Tel:* (415) 861-4385. *Video Serv Est:* 1972. *In Charge:* John Rogers, Pres. *Video Staff:* 6 f-t. *Video Use:* produce documentaries, do social work. Video serv available by appointment. Produce video tapes. Have production studio/space & separate control room.

Video Equipment/Facilities *In-House Use Only:* portapak (3), ½″ & ¾″ b&w/col, Sony AVC 3400, 3800; playback deck (2), Sony 3650; editing deck (1), Sony 8650. Inst has capabilities for b&w/col cassette production. Have portable viewing installation. *Equipment Loan Period:* have tape duplication serv.

Video Tape Loan/Rental/Sale Serv *Serv Provided:* swap with other inst, rental, sale. *Loan/Rental Eligibility:* no restrictions. *Restrictions:* for indiv & inst, none. Cannot duplicate, air without permission. May borrow by mail. *Loan Period:* flexible.

Video Collection Maintained by exchange/swap. Use/play ½″ reel to reel. *Sources:* community productions. *Tape Sel:* direct contact w/community groups. Tapes organized by subject. *Other Video Serv:* programming, taping of other media, production workshops.

P- SAN FRANCISCO PUBLIC LIBRARY, Civic Center, 94102. *Tel:* (415) 558-4514. *Film Serv Est:* 1970. *In Charge:* Anne Kincaid & Effie Lee Morris, Coords. *AV Staff:* 1 (1 tech). *Film Sel:* committee preview, staff recommendations.

Film Collection 491t/p. *Noncirc:* 16mm, 302t.

Other Film Serv Library film programs.

Video Serv *Est:* 1974. *In Charge:* Roberto Esteves, Dir. *Video Staff:* 4 f-t, 1 p-t, 1 tech. *Video Use:* documentation of community/school events, to increase community's library use, in-service training, as art form. Video serv available only to Calif. libraries. Produce video tapes.

Video Equipment/Facilities *In-House Use Only:* portapak (2), ½″ col, Sony 8400; recording deck (1), ½″ b&w, Sony 3600; editing deck (2), ½″ b&w/col, Sony 3650, 8650; studio camera (1), b&w, Sony AVC3200; additional camera lenses (1); lighting (3); microphones (5); tripods (3); audio tape recorders (1). Have permanent viewing installations. *Equipment Loan Period:* no set policy. Provide training in use of equipment to staff & production volunteers. Have tape duplication serv.

Video Tape Loan/Rental/Sale Serv *Serv Provided:* rental, sale. *Rental Eligibility:* municipal agencies & some Calif. Libraries. *Restrictions:* for inst, only municipal agencies & Calif. libraries eligible for LSCA funding. Cannot use for fund-raising, duplicate, air without permission. May not borrow by mail.

Video Collection Maintained by purchase, own production. Use/play ½″ reel to reel, ¾″ cassette. *Sources:* commercial distributors, galleries, community productions. *Tape Sel:* pre-

view, gallery previews, published reviews. Tapes organized by title. *Collection, Color:* ¾″ cassette, 34t/c. *Collection, B&W:* ½″ reel, 23t/c. *Other Video Serv:* programming, production workshops. *Pubns:* catalog & suppl. Publish materials on video. Publish *CVRP Patch Panel.*

Cable & CCTV Produce programs for cablecasting. Inform public about cable system serv & facilities. Have advisory/administrative role in cable system operation. Have CCTV in inst, with 2 monitors. *Programming Sources:* over-the-air commercial & public broadcasting, tapes produced by inst, tapes produced professionally, tapes produced by community groups & indiv.

C- SAN FRANCISCO STATE UNIVERSITY, AV Center, 1600 Holloway Ave, 94132. *Tel:* (415) 469-1492. *Film Serv Est:* c. 1940. *In Charge:* Dr. Francis X. Moakley, Dir. *AV Staff:* (5 prof, 3 cl, 11 tech). *Film Sel:* faculty/staff recommendations. *Holdings:* animated films 5%, black studies 5%, experimental films 8%, feature films 4%, women 4%.

Film Collection 1400t/p. Approx 50t acquired annually. *Noncirc:* 16mm, 1400t/p; 8mm reel, 20t/p; 8mm cartridge, 170t/p. *Pubns:* catalog, every 3 yrs; suppl, no set policy.

Other Film Serv Rent film from distributors for patrons, film reference serv.

Other Media Collections *Audio:* tape, cassette, 800c. *Filmstrips:* sound sets, 70c; silent sets, 150c. *Slides:* sets, 11c.

Budget & Expenditures Total library budget $430,000 (FY 7/1/74-7/1/75). Total FY film budget $12,000. *Member:* AECT, AFI, EFLA, CAEMAT, UFA, HFC, SAVC.

San Jose

P- SAN JOSE PUBLIC LIBRARY, Media Center, 180 W. San Carlos, 95113. *Tel:* (408) 287-2788, ext 4876. *In Charge:* Anne Slater, Media Center Librarian. *AV Staff:* 7 (1 prof, 2 cl, 4 tech). *Film Sel:* committee preview, staff recommendations, chief film librarian's decision. *Holdings:* animated films 15%, children's films 10%.

Free-Loan Film Serv *Eligibility:* indiv with library cards. *Restrictions:* for indiv, only in Santa Clara County. Cannot use for fund-raising, transmit electronically. Available to researchers/scholars for on-site viewing. May not borrow by mail. *Loan Period:* 1 day. *Total Yr Film Loan:* 16,769.

Film Collection 900t/p. Approx 80-100t acquired annually. *Circ:* 16mm, 890t/p; 8mm reel, 40t/p. *Noncirc:* 16mm, 10t/p. *Pubns:* catalog, every 2 yrs ($.50); suppl, as needed.

Other Film Serv Obtain film from coop loan system (San Jose University & San Jose Unified School District, S. Bay Area Coop Network), obtain film from other libraries, film reference serv, film fairs/festivals, library film programs. Permanent viewing facility available free to community. *Equipment:* lend/rent 16mm sound projector (9), projection tables & stands (2), projection screens (2).

Other Media Collections *Audio:* disc, 33⅓rpm, 30,000t; tape, cassette, 800t; tape, cartridge, 200t. *Filmstrips:* sound, 25t/c; sound sets, 3t/c; silent sets, 6 t/c. *Slides:* sets, 150t/c.

Budget & Expenditures Total library budget $311,600 (FY 7/1/74-7/1/75). Total FY film budget $19,000. *Member:* ALA, EFLA, Calif. Library Assn.

Video Serv *Est:* 1975. *In Charge:* Michael Ferrero, TV Production Specialist. *Video Staff:* 2 f-t, 1 p-t. *Video Use:* to increase community's library use, community video access. Video serv available by appointment. Produce video tapes. Have production studio/space.

Video Equipment/Facilities *In-House Use Only:* portapak (1), ¼″ b&w, Sony-AV3400; editing deck (2), ½″ col, Panasonic 3130; studio camera (2), col, Sony; microphones (1); audio tape recorders (1). Have portable viewing installation.

Video Tape Loan/Rental/Sale Serv *Serv Provided:* swap with other inst. *Loan Eligibility:* members of S. Bay Coop Library System. *Restrictions:* for inst, only members of S. Bay Coop Library System. May not borrow by mail.

Video Collection Maintained by own production. Use/play ½″ reel to reel. Tapes organized by numerical system.

Cable & CCTV Produce programs for cablecasting. *Programming Sources:* tapes produced by inst.

San Jose (cont'd)

C- SAN JOSE STATE UNIVERSITY, ITV Center, 95192. *Tel:* (408) 277-2529. *Video Serv Est:* 1955. *In Charge:* Bob Reynolds, ITV Production Supervisor. *Video Staff:* 3 f-t, 2 p-t. *Video Use:* in-service training, practical video/TV training courses, as art form. Video serv available on demand & by appointment. Produce video tapes. Have production studio/space & separate control room.

Video Equipment/Facilities *In-House Use Only:* recording/playback/editing decks (20), b&w; studio camera (7); monitors (50); SEG (3); additional camera lenses. *For Loan:* portapak (20), ½″ b&w, Sony, Panasonic. *Loan Period:* 24 hr portapak loan (no weekends). Provide training in use of equipment to faculty & students. Have tape duplication serv.

Video Tape Loan/Rental/Sale Serv *Serv Provided:* swap with other inst, sale. *Loan Eligibility:* staff & students. *Restrictions:* for indiv, none; for inst, none. May not borrow by mail.

Video Collection Maintained by own production. Use/play ½″, 1″, 2″ reel to reel, ¾″ cassette. *Tape Sel:* faculty/staff recommendations. Tapes organized by subject. *Collection, B&W:* ½″ reel, 200t; 2″ reel, 250t. *Other Video Serv:* programming, taping of other media, production workshops. *Pubns:* catalog.

Cable & CCTV Receive serv of cable TV system. Produce programs for cablecasting. Serve as production facility for others. Have CCTV in inst, with 300 monitors. *Programming Sources:* over-the-air commercial & public broadcasting, tapes produced by inst, tapes produced professionally.

P- SANTA CLARA COUNTY LIBRARY, 1095 N. Seventh St, 95112. *Tel:* (415) 293-2326. *In Charge:* Janice Yee, Supervising Librarian. *Film Sel:* committee preview, chief film librarian's decision.

Free-Loan Film Serv *Eligibility:* indiv with library cards. *Restrictions:* cannot use for fund-raising, transmit electronically. May not borrow by mail. *Loan Period:* 1 day. *Total Yr Film Loan:* 30,127.

Film Collection 1239p. Approx 40-50t acquired annually. *Circ:* 16mm, 559t/569p; 8mm cartridge, 365p; S8mm cartridge, 305p.

Other Film Serv Film reference serv, library film programs. *Equipment:* lend 16mm sound projector (1).

Other Media Collections *Audio:* disc, 33⅓rpm, 20,829c.

Budget & Expenditures Total library budget $494,940 (FY 7/1/74-7/1/75). Total FY film budget $20,000. *Member:* ALA, EFLA, Calif. Library Assn.

San Mateo

C- COLLEGE OF SAN MATEO, Learning Resources Center, 1700 W. Hillsdale Blvd, 94402. *Tel:* (415) 574-6103. *Film Serv Est:* 1964. *In Charge:* Dr. Ronald F. Trugman, Dir. *AV Staff:* 20 (10 prof, 5 cl, 5 tech). *Film Sel:* committee preview, faculty/staff recommendations, chief film librarian's decision. *Holdings:* animated films 10%, black studies 10%, career education 10%, experimental films 10%, fine arts 10%, industrial arts 10%, science 10%, social sciences 10%, teacher education 10%, women 10%.

Free-Loan Film Serv *Eligibility:* org members, staff. *Restrictions:* for indiv, none; for inst, none. Cannot use for fund-raising, transmit electronically. Available to researchers/scholars for on-site viewing. May not borrow by mail. *Loan Period:* 5 days. *Total Yr Film Loan:* 10,000.

Film Collection 500t/700p. Approx 50t acquired annually. *Circ:* 16mm, 500t/700p; S8mm cartridge, 100t/p. *Pubns:* catalog, every 3 yrs; suppl, in yr catalog not published.

Other Film Serv Rent film from distributors for patrons, obtain film from coop loan system (San Mateo County), obtain film from other libraries, film reference serv, film fairs/festivals, library film programs. Permanent viewing facility. *Equipment:* lend S8mm camera (10), 16mm camera (1), 16mm sound projector (30), 8mm cartridge projector (10), 8mm reel projector (10), S8mm cartridge projector (10), S8mm reel projector (10), projection tables & stands (10), projection screens (20).

Other Media Collections *Audio:* disc, 33⅓rpm, 3000c; tape, cassette, 1000c; tape, reel, 2000c. *Filmstrips:* sound, 200c; silent, 300c; sound sets, 500c. *Slides:* single, 5000c.

Budget & Expenditures Total library budget $50,000 (FY 7/74-7/75). Total FY film budget $10,000. *Member:* AECT, AFI, ALA, EFLA, Calif. Library Assn, Community College Media Assn, Calif. Assn for Media & Tech, Learning Resources Assn of Calif. Community Colleges.

Video Serv *Est:* 1964. *In Charge:* Dr. Ronald F. Trugman, Dir. *Video Staff:* 10 f-t, 12 p-t, 2 tech. *Video Use:* documentation of community/school events, to increase community's library use, community video access, in-service training, practical video/TV training courses, playback only of professionally produced tapes, as art form. Video serv available on demand & by appointment. Produce video tapes. Have production studio/space & separate control room.

Video Equipment/Facilities *In-House Use Only:* recording deck (3), ¾″ col, Sony; monitor (15), b&w/col, RCA; SEG (1), Sony; keyer (1), Sony. *For Loan:* portapak (3), ½″ b&w Sony; playback deck (3), ¾″ col, Sony; studio camera (2), ½″ b&w, Sony. Have permanent viewing installation. Provide training in use of equipment to faculty & students.

Video Tape Loan/Rental/Sale Serv *Serv Provided:* free loan, swap with other inst. *Loan/Rental Eligibility:* staff. *Restrictions:* for indiv, only in San Mateo County; for inst, only in San Mateo County. Cannot use for fund-raising, duplicate, air without permission. May not borrow by mail. *Total Yr Tape Loan:* 753.

Video Collection Maintained by purchase, rental, own production, exchange/swap. Use/play ½″ reel to reel, ¾″ cassette. *Member:* Bay Area TV Consortium. *Tape Sel:* preview, faculty/staff recommendations, published reviews, catalogs. *Special Collections:* in-house training tapes, video as art, films in video format. Tapes organized by subject. *Collection, Color:* ½″ reel, 25t; ¾″ cassette, 185t. *Collection, B&W:* ½″ reel, 70t. *Other Video Serv:* programming, reference serv, taping of other media, production workshops. *Pubns:* catalog & suppl.

Cable & CCTV Receive serv of cable TV system. Produce programs for cablecasting. Inform public about cable system serv & facilities. Serve as production facility for others. Run cable programs for special audiences. Have advisory/administrative role in cable system operation. Have CCTV in inst, with 250 monitors. *Programming Sources:* over-the-air commercial & public broadcasting, tapes produced by inst, tapes produced professionally, tapes produced by community groups & indiv.

P- SAN MATEO PUBLIC LIBRARY—CENTRAL, 55 W. Third Ave, 94402. *Tel:* (415) 574-6950, ext 29. *Film Serv Est:* 1968. *In Charge:* Rosalie Devlin, Assistant Head Librarian. *AV Staff:* 4 (3 cl, 1 tech). *Film Sel:* committee preview. *Holdings:* humanities 12%.

Free-Loan Film Serv *Eligibility:* indiv with library cards, others, such as convalescent homes. *Restrictions:* for indiv, interlibrary loan; for inst, only in San Mateo County. May not borrow by mail. *Loan Period:* 1 day. *Total Yr Film Loan:* 5028.

Film Collection 180t/p. Approx 5-10t acquired annually. *Circ:* 16mm, 180t/p; 8mm reel, 140t/p; S8mm reel, 40t/p. *Pubns:* catalog, every 2 yrs; suppl, in yr catalog not published. Publish monthly sheets.

Other Film Serv Obtain film from coop loan system (Peninsula Library System), obtain film from other libraries, library film programs. *Equipment:* 8mm reel projector (3).

Other Media Collections *Audio:* disc, 33⅓rpm, 7000t; tape, cassette, 60t/c. *Slides:* single, 1000t; sets, 500t.

Budget & Expenditures Total library budget $3500 (FY 7/1/74-7/1/75). Total FY film budget $3000. *Member:* Northern Calif. Library System.

Santa Ana

P- SANTA ANA PUBLIC LIBRARY, Film Service, 26 Civic Center Plaza, 92701. *Tel:* (714) 834-4077. *Film Serv Est:* 1968. *In Charge:* Ann Wyatt, Library Assistant. *AV Staff:* 5½ (1 prof, 4½ cl). *Film Sel:* committee preview.

Free-Loan Film Serv *Eligibility:* org members, civic groups. *Restrictions:* for indiv, library employees only, for inst, only in city. Cannot use for fund-raising, transmit electronically. May borrow by mail. *Loan Period:* 1 day. *Total Yr Film Loan:* 8482.

Film Rental Serv *Eligibility:* patrons of Santiago Library System. *Restrictions:* cannot use for fund-raising, transmit electronically. *Rental Period:* 1 day. *Total Yr Film Booking:* 8482. Produce videotapes.

Film Collection 205t/206p. Approx 2t acquired annually. *Circ:* 16mm, 103t/p; 8mm reel, 52t/p; S8mm reel, 51t/p. *Pubns:* catalog. Publish monthly list of 16mm films.

Other Film Serv Obtain monthly approx 100 16mm & 6 S8mm films from coop loan system (Santiago Library System, Film Council Circuit Commission). Permanent viewing facility available free to community. *Equipment:* rent 16mm sound projector (3), 8mm reel projector (1), S8mm cartridge projector (1), S8mm reel projector (1), projection screens (1).

Other Media Collections *Audio:* disc, 33⅓ rpm, 6655c; tape, cassette, 1267c.

Budget & Expenditures Total library budget $128,070 (FY 7/1/74-7/1/75). Total FY film budget $2077. *Member:* ALA, Calif. Library Assn.

Santa Clara

S- UNIVERSITY OF SANTA CLARA, de Saisset Art Gallery & Museum, University of Santa Clara, 95053. *Tel:* (408) 984-4528. *Video Serv Est:* 1970. *In Charge:* George Bolling, Video Curator. *Video Staff:* 2 f-t. *Video Use:* as art form. Video serv available by appointment. Produce video tapes. Have production studio/space.

Video Equipment/Facilities *In-House Use Only:* portapak (1), ½″ b&w, Sony AV3400; recording deck (1), ½″ col, Sony AV8600; playback deck (1), ¾″ col, Sony VP1200; editing deck (1), ½″ col, Sony AV8650; studio camera (1). Have permanent viewing installation. *Equipment Loan Period:* no set policy.

Video Collection Maintained by purchase, rental, own production. Use/play ½″ reel to reel, ¾″ cassette. *Sources:* galleries, artists. *Tape Sel:* preview, catalogs. *Special Collections:* video as art. Tapes organized by Dewey Decimal. *Collection, Color:* ½″ reel, 20t/c; 1″ reel, 4t/c; ¾″ cassette, 10t/c. *Collection, B&W:* ½″ reel, 88t/c; 1″ reel, 10t/c; ¾″ cassette, 6t/c. *Other Video Serv:* reference serv. *Pubns:* catalog & suppl.

Santa Cruz

C- UNIVERSITY OF CALIFORNIA, SANTA CRUZ, Office of Instructional Serv, UCSC, 95064. *Tel:* (408) 429-2324. *Film Serv Est:* 1965. *In Charge:* David Kirk, Film Archivist. *Film Sel:* committee preview, faculty/staff recommendations. *Holdings:* animated films 15%, black studies 5%, children's films 5%, dance 3%, experimental films 25%, feature films 25%, fine arts 10%, science 9%, women 3%.

Free-Loan Film Serv *Eligibility:* org members & staff. *Restrictions:* for indiv & inst, UCSC only. Cannot use for fund-raising. Available to researchers/scholars for on-site viewing. May not borrow by mail. *Loan Period:* 3 days. *Total Yr Film Loan:* 716.

Film Collection Approx 10-15t acquired annually. *Circ:* 16mm, 289t/p; 8mm reel, 35 t/p; 8mm cartridge, 6t/p; S8mm reel, 21t/p; S8mm cartridge, 35t/p. *Pubns:* catalog, every 2 yrs ($1); suppl, in yr catalog not published.

Other Film Serv Film reference serv, library film programs. Permanent viewing facility. *Equipment:* lend/rent S8mm camera (6), 16mm camera (3), 16mm sound projector (47), 8mm cartridge projector (1), 8mm reel projector (2), S8mm cartridge projector (2), S8mm reel projector (10), projection tables & stands (30), projection screens (20).

Other Media Collections *Audio:* disc, 33⅓ rpm, 102t/c; tape, reel, 2632t/c. *Filmstrips:* silent, 2t/c; sound sets, 4t/c.

Budget & Expenditures No separate budget. *Member:* AECT.

Video Serv *Est:* 1966. *In Charge:* Thomas J. Karwin, Coord. *Video Staff:* 2 f-t, 6 p-t, 2 tech. *Video Use:* documentation

of community/school events, to increase community's library use, in-service training, practical video/TV training courses, college instruction. Video serv available by appointment. Produce video tapes. Have production studio/space & separate control room.

Video Equipment/Facilities *In-House Use Only:* portapak (7), b&w, Sony EIAJ-1; recording deck (5), b&w, Sony EIAJ-1. Have permanent & portable viewing installations. *Equipment Loan Period:* 3 days. Provide training in use of equipment to faculty & students. Have tape duplication serv.

Video Tape Loan/Rental/Sale Serv *Loan Eligibility:* staff & students. *Restrictions:* Cannot use for fund-raising, duplicate, air without permission. May not borrow by mail.

Video Collection Maintained by purchase, own production, exchange/swap. Use/play ½″, 1″, 2″ reel to reel, ¾″ cassette. *Tape Sel:* preview, faculty/staff recommendations, catalogs. Tapes organized by title. *Collection, Color:* ¾″ cassette, 3t/c. *Collection, B&W:* ½″ reel, 70t/c; ¾″ cassette, 47t/c. *Other Video Serv:* reference serv, production workshops. *Pubns:* catalog & suppl.

Cable & CCTV Produce programs for cablecasting. Inform public about cable system serv & facilities. Have advisory/administrative role in cable system operation. Have CCTV in inst, with 50 monitors. *Programming Sources:* over-the-air commercial & public broadcasting, tapes produced by inst, tapes produced professionally, tapes produced by community groups & indiv, on-campus programming.

Santa Maria

P- SANTA MARIA PUBLIC LIBRARY, 420 S. Broadway, 93454. *Tel:* (805) 925-0994. *Film Serv Est:* 1965. *In Charge:* Lillian Christmas, Library Assistant. *AV Staff:* ½ (½ tech). *Film Sel:* committee preview.

Free-Loan Film Serv *Eligibility:* educational inst, civic groups, religious groups, indiv with library cards. *Restrictions:* for indiv, interlibrary loan. Cannot use for fund-raising, transmit electronically. May borrow by mail. *Loan Period:* 1 day. *Total Yr Film Loan:* 3220.

Film Collection 348t/p. Approx 6t acquired annually. *Circ:* 16mm, 23t/p; 8mm cartridge, 25t/p. *Pubns:* catalog, annual; suppl, in yr catalog not published.

Other Film Serv Rent film from distributors for patrons, obtain film from coop loan system (Black Gold Cooperative Library System). Permanent viewing facility.

Other Media Collections *Audio:* disc, 33⅓ rpm, 45rpm, 78rpm, 4821t/c; tape, cassette, 256t/c.

Budget & Expenditures Total library budget $42,950 (FY 7/1/74-7/1/75). Total FY film budget $700.

Santa Monica

C- SANTA MONICA COLLEGE, Instructional Materials Center, 16mm Film Library, 1815 Pearl St, 90405. *Tel:* (213) 392-4911, ext 296, 326. *Film Serv Est:* prior to 1950. *In Charge:* Mrs. Tish Aaron, Dir. *AV Staff:* 4 (3 prof, 1 cl/tech). *Film Sel:* committee preview, faculty/staff recommendations, chief film librarian's decision.

Free-Loan Film Serv *Eligibility:* org members, staff. *Restrictions:* for indiv & inst, on campus. Cannot use for fund-raising, transmit electronically. Available to researchers/scholars for on-site viewing. May not borrow by mail. *Loan Period:* 1 day. *Total Yr Film Loan:* 750.

Film Collection 240t/p. Approx 20t acquired annually. *Circ:* 16mm, 271t/p. *Pubns:* catalog, annual; suppl, monthly.

Other Film Serv Film reference serv. *Equipment:* lend 16mm sound projector (54), 8mm cartridge projector (5), 8mm reel projector (15), S8mm cartridge projector (3), S8mm reel projector (15), projection tables & stands (75), projection screens (30).

Budget & Expenditures Total FY film budget $25,000.

Video Serv *Est:* 1969. *In Charge:* Tish Aaron, Dir. *Video Staff:* 3 f-t, 6 p-t, 2 tech. *Video Use:* in-service training, practical video/TV training courses. Video serv available by appoint-

Santa Monica (cont'd)

ment. Produce video tapes. Have production studio/space & separate control room.

Video Equipment/Facilities *In-House Use Only:* portapak (7), ½″ b&w/col, Panasonic 3085; recording deck (12), ½″, ¾″, 1″ b&w/col, JVC, Panasonic, Bell & Howell; editing deck (4), ½″ col, Panasonic 3130; studio camera (2), col, Panasonic; monitor (14), b&w/col, Sony, Electrohome; SEG (1), additional camera lenses; lighting (16); microphones (13); tripods (5); audio tape recorders (61). *For Loan:* playback deck (22), JVC; monitor (22), b&w/col, Sony, Electrohome; audio tape recorders (94). Have permanent & portable viewing installations. *Equipment Loan Period:* 1 day. Provide training in use of equipment to faculty & students.

Video Tape Loan/Rental/Sale Serv *Loan Eligibility:* org members, staff, students enrolled in inst. *Restrictions:* cannot use for fund-raising, duplicate, air without permission. May not borrow by mail.

Video Collection Maintained by own production. Use/play ½″ reel to reel, ¾″ cassette. Tapes organized by title. *Collection, Color:* ¾″ cassette, 400t/c. *Collection, B&W:* ¾″ cassette, 150t/c. *Other Video Serv:* taping of other media. *Pubns:* catalog & suppl.

Cable & CCTV Receive serv of cable TV system. Have CCTV in inst, with 4 monitors. *Programming Sources:* tapes produced by inst.

Santa Rosa

C- SANTA ROSA JR. COLLEGE, Plover Library, 1501 Mendocino Ave, 95401. *Tel:* (707) 527-4261. *Film Serv Est:* 1972. *In Charge:* Howard Shipman, AV Coord. *AV Staff:* 7 (1 prof, 2 cl, 4 tech). *Film Sel:* committee preview, faculty/staff recommendations.

Free-Loan Film Serv *Eligibility:* staff, community groups. *Restrictions:* for indiv, only in city; for inst, only in city. Cannot use for fund-raising. Available to researchers/scholars for on-site viewing. May not borrow by mail. *Loan Period:* 3 days. *Total Yr Film Loan:* 2200.

Film Collection 161t/p. Approx 5-12t acquired annually. *Circ:* 16mm, 160t/161p. *Pubns:* catalog, annual.

Other Film Serv Obtain film from other libraries. Permanent viewing facility available for rent to community. *Equipment:* lend 16mm sound projector (67), 8mm reel projector (6), S8mm reel projector (2), projection tables & stands (70), projection screens (30).

Other Media Collections *Audio:* disc, 33⅓rpm, 2500t/2100c; disc, 45rpm, 100t/c; tape, cassette, 1600t/2100c; tape, reel, 2200t/2400c. *Filmstrips:* sound sets, 22t/c. *Slides:* sets, 12t/c.

Budget & Expenditures Total library budget $41,600 (FY 7/1/74-7/1/75). Total FY film budget $9000. *Member:* CAEMAT.

Video Serv *Est:* 1971. *In Charge:* Howard Shipman. *Video Staff:* 7 f-t, 4 tech. *Video Use:* documentation of community/school events, in-service training, playback only of professionally produced tapes, as art form. Video serv available on demand & by appointment. Produce video tapes. Have production studio/space & separate control room.

Video Equipment/Facilities *In-House Use Only:* recording deck (6), col, Sony; playback deck (12), col, Sony; editing deck (1), col, Sony; studio camera (2), b&w, Sony; monitor (28), Sony, col; SEG (1); additional camera lenses (2); lighting (10); microphones (8); tripods (2); audio tape recorders (50). Have permanent viewing installation. *Equipment Loan Period:* 1-3 days. Provide training in use of equipment to faculty & students. Have tape duplication serv.

Video Tape Loan/Rental/Sale Serv *Serv Provided:* free loan, swap with other inst. *Loan/Rental Eligibility:* staff, community groups. *Restrictions:* for indiv, only in city. Cannot use for fund-raising. May not borrow by mail.

Video Collection Maintained by purchase, own production, exchange/swap. Use/play ½″ reel to reel, ¾″ cassette. *Sources:* commercial distributors. *Tape Sel:* preview. Tapes

organized by acquisition no. *Collection, Color:* ¾″ cassette, 1200t/c. *Collection, B&W:* ½″ reel, 400t/c; ¾″ cassette, 100t/c.

Cable & CCTV Receive serv of cable TV system. Run cable programs for special audiences. Have CCTV in inst, with 20 monitors. *Programming Sources:* over-the-air commercial & public broadcasting, tapes produced by inst, tapes produced professionally.

Stanford

A- HOOVER INSTITUTION, Archives, 94305. *Tel:* (415) 497-0603. *Video Serv Est:* 1973. *In Charge:* George Marotta, Public Affairs Coord. *Video Staff:* 1 p-t. *Video Use:* scholarly reference & research. Video serv available on demand.

Video Equipment/Facilities *In-House Use Only:* playback deck (1), b&w, Sony. Have portable viewing installation.

Video Tape Loan/Rental/Sale Serv *Serv Provided:* swap with other inst, rental. *Loan/Rental Eligibility:* any bona fide scholar. *Restrictions:* cannot duplicate. May borrow by mail from Vanderbilt University, Nashville, Tenn. *Total Yr Tape Loan:* 20.

Video Collection Use/play ¾″ cassette. *Sources:* Vanderbilt University. *Member:* Vanderbilt TV News Archives. *Tape Sel:* catalogs, indexes published by Vanderbilt University. Tapes organized at Vanderbilt: 3 major networks by date. *Pubns:* catalog & suppl.

C- STANFORD UNIVERSITY, Meyer Film Service, Stanford University Libraries, 94305. *Tel:* (415) 497-1380. *Film Serv Est:* 1956. *In Charge:* Renee Eggleston, Office Assistant. *AV Staff:* ¾ (1 cl). *Film Sel:* faculty/staff recommendations, librarian's decision.

Free-Loan Film Serv *Eligibility:* staff & students, prof groups affiliated with Stanford. *Restrictions:* cannot use for fund-raising, transmit electronically. May not borrow by mail. *Loan Period:* 1 day. *Total Yr Film Loan:* 64.

Film Collection *Circ:* 16mm, 40t/p.

Other Film Serv Rent film from distributors for patrons, obtain film from other libraries.

Other Media Collections *Audio:* disc, 33⅓rpm, 4337t/500c; tape, cassette, 201t/c; tape, reel, 411t/c.

Budget & Expenditures No separate budget. *Member:* EFLA.

Stockton

P- 49-99 COOPERATIVE LIBRARY SYSTEM, 605 N Eldorado St, 95202. *Tel:* (209) 944-8362. *Film Serv Est:* 1965. *In Charge:* Kathryn Page, AV Librarian. *AV Staff:* 4 (1 prof, 1½ cl, 1½ tech). *Film Sel:* committee preview, staff recommendations, published reviews. *Holdings:* animated films 15%, black studies 5%, children's films 15%, feature films 7½%, fine arts 15%, science 15%, social sciences 20%, women 3%.

Free-Loan Film Serv *Eligibility:* staff, educational inst, civic groups, religious groups, indiv with library cards. *Restrictions:* for indiv & inst, only in 7-county system (San Joaquin, Stanislaus, Amador, Calaveras, Tuolumne, Merced Counties & Lodi Public Library). Cannot charge admission. Available to researchers/scholars for on-site viewing. May borrow by mail. *Loan Period:* 1 day. *Total Yr Film Loan:* 51,793.

Film Collection 602t/p. Approx 40-60t acquired annually. *Circ:* 16mm, 558t/p. *Noncirc:* 16mm, 44t/p. Publish materials pertaining to collection. Publish film list monthly.

Other Film Serv Obtain film from coop loan system, film reference serv, library film programs. Permanent viewing facility available to community.

Other Media Collections *Filmstrips:* sound, 24t/96c; sound sets, 42t/168c.

Budget & Expenditures Total FY (7/1/74-7/1/75) film budget $20,000 ($10,000 from member library fees plus $10,000 from P.L.S.C.A. Fund).

Susanville

C- LASSEN COLLEGE, Learning Resources Center, Box 3000, 96130. *Tel:* (916) 257-6181, ext 42. *Film Serv Est:* 1971. *In Charge:* Russell Rose, Dir, Learning Resources. *AV Staff:* 6 (1 prof, 3 cl, 2 tech). *Film Sel:* faculty/staff recommendations. *Holdings:* agriculture 9%, industrial arts 10%, science 40%, social sciences 40%, women 1%.

Free-Loan Film Serv *Eligibility:* staff & students, educational inst, & others, such as public schools within county & public agencies. *Restrictions:* for indiv, only in our county; for inst, only in our county. Cannot use for fund-raising, transmit electronically. Available to researchers/scholars for on-site viewing. May borrow by mail. *Loan Period:* 1 day. *Total Yr Film Loan:* 1500.

Film Collection 190t/p. Approx 50-60t acquired annually. *Circ:* 16mm, 190t/p; S8mm cartridge, 200t/p. *Pubns:* catalog, annual; suppl, published quarterly.

Other Film Serv Rent film from distributors for patrons, obtain film from coop loan system (Northeastern Calif. Higher Education Council). *Equipment:* lend 16mm sound projector (15), 8mm reel projector (20), S8mm cartridge projector (20), S8mm reel projector (2), projection tables & stands (30), projection screens (25).

Other Media Collections *Audio:* disc, 33⅓rpm, 50t/c; tape, cassette, 200t/c; tape, reel, 40t/c. *Filmstrips:* sound, 50t/c; silent, 50t/c. *Slides:* single, 4500t/c; sets, 500t/c.

Budget & Expenditures Total library budget $45,000 (FY 7/1/74-7/1/75). No separate AV budget. *Member:* AECT, Northern Calif. Higher Education Council.

Video Serv *Est:* 1975. *Video Staff:* 6 f-t, 11 p-t. *Video Use:* documentation of community/school events, to increase community's library use, in-service training, as art form. Video serv available on demand. Produce video tapes.

Video Equipment/Facilities *In-House Use Only:* recording deck (1), ¾″ col, Panasonic; studio camera (1), b&w; JVC; audio tape recorders (4). *For Loan:* playback deck (3), ¾″ col, Panasonic. Have portable viewing installation. *Equipment Loan Period:* no set policy. Provide training in use of equipment to faculty. Have tape duplication serv.

Video Tape Loan/Rental/Sale Serv *Serv Provided:* free loan, swap with other inst. *Loan/Rental Eligibility:* org members, staff, educational inst, indiv with library cards. *Restrictions:* for indiv, interlibrary loan; for inst, other colleges in Northeastern Calif. Cannot air without permission. May borrow by mail. *Loan Period:* 14 days.

Video Collection Maintained by purchase, rental, own production, exchange/swap. Use/play ¾″ cassette. *Sources:* commercial distributors, community productions, exchange. *Tape Sel:* preview, faculty/staff recommendations. Tapes organized by Dewey Decimal. *Collection, Color:* ¾″ cassette, 150t/c. *Other Video Serv:* programming, taping of other media. *Pubns:* catalog.

Cable & CCTV Receive serv of cable TV system. Produce programs for cablecasting. Inform public about cable system serv & facilities. Serve as production facility for others. Run cable programs for special audiences. Have CCTV in inst, with 10 monitors. *Programming Sources:* over-the-air commercial & public broadcasting, tapes produced by inst, tapes produced professionally, tapes produced by community groups & indiv.

Valencia

C- CALIFORNIA INSTITUTE OF THE ARTS, 24700 McBean Pkwy, 91355. *Tel:* (805) 255-1050, ext 234. *Video Serv Est:* 1975. *In Charge:* Margie Hanft, Film Librarian. *Video Staff:* 1 f-t, 3 p-t. *Video Use:* documentation of community/school events, practical video/TV training courses, as art form. Video serv available on demand. Produce video tapes. Have production studio/space & separate control room.

Video Equipment/Facilities *In-House Use Only:* playback deck (1), col, Sony U-Matic VP-1000. Provide training in use of equipment to faculty & students.

Video Collection Maintained by own production. Use/play ¾″ cassette. *Tape Sel:* preview. *Special Collections:* in-house training tapes, video as art. Tapes organized by subject. *Collection, B&W:* ¾″ cassette, 10t/c (in preparation).

Cable & CCTV Receive serv of cable TV system.

Venice

S- WESTSIDE VIDEO COLLECTIVE, 26 Westminster Ave, 90291. *Tel:* (213) 396-2365. *Video Serv Est:* 1970. *In Charge:* Collective Directorship. *Video Staff:* 5 f-t, 8 p-t, 4 tech. *Video Use:* documentation of community/school events, community video access, in-service training, practical video/TV training courses, as art form. Video serv available by appointment. Produce video tapes. Have production studio/space.

Video Equipment/Facilities *In-House Use Only:* portapak (3), ½″, ¾″ b&w/col, Sony & Panasonic; recording deck (3), ½″, ¾″ b&w/col, Sony & Panasonic; playback deck (3); editing deck (2), ½″ col, Sony & Panasonic; studio camera (1), b&w, Sony; monitor (5), b&w/col, Sony & Panasonic; additional camera lenses (4); lighting (5); microphones (5); tripods (4); audio tape recorders (5). *For Loan:* portapak (3), ½″, ¾″ b&w/col, Sony & Panasonic; recording deck (3), ½″, ¾″ b&w/col, Sony & Panasonic; playback deck (3); editing deck (2), ½″ col, Sony & Panasonic; monitor (5), b&w/col, Sony & Panasonic. Have portable viewing installation. Provide training in use of equipment to faculty, students, public, community, business organizations. Have tape duplication serv.

Video Tape Loan/Rental/Sale Serv *Serv Provided:* rental, sale. *Rental Eligibility:* staff & students enrolled in inst. *Restrictions:* for indiv, none; for inst, none.

Video Collection Maintained by own production. Use/play ½″ reel to reel, ¾″ cassette. Tapes organized by subject. *Collection, Color:* ½″ reel, 7t/2c; ¾″ cassette, 7t/2c. *Collection, B&W:* ½″ reel, 3t/2c; ¾″ cassette, 3t/2c. *Other Video Serv:* reference serv, production workshops, consultation, documentation, exhibition.

Cable & CCTV Receive serv of cable TV system. Produce programs for cablecasting. Inform public about cable system serv & facilities. Serve as production facility for others.

Whittier

P- WHITTIER PUBLIC LIBRARY, 7344 S. Washington Ave, 90602. *Tel:* (213) 698-8181, ext 8. *Film Serv Est:* 1956. *In Charge:* Rebecca Susan Castillo, Library Asst II. *AV Staff:* 2½. *Film Sel:* committee & indiv previews.

Free-Loan Film Serv *Eligibility:* indiv with library cards. *Restrictions:* for indiv, only in city; for inst, only in city. Cannot use for fund-raising. May not borrow by mail.

Film Rental Serv *Eligibility:* patrons/public, over 18 yrs old. Cannot use for fund-raising. *Rental Period:* 1 day. *Total Yr Film Booking:* 24,296.

Film Collection 380t/385p. Approx 10-15t acquired annually. *Circ:* 16mm, 276t/277p; 8mm reel, 68t/70p; S8mm reel, 36t/38p. *Pubns:* catalog, annual ($1); suppl, no set policy.

Other Film Serv Obtain film from coop loan system (Metropolitan Coop Library System, Southern Calif. Film Circuit), obtain film from other libraries, library film programs.

Other Media Collections *Audio:* disc, 33⅓rpm, 3102t/3120c; tape, cassette, 165t/c; tape, reel, 2t/c.

Budget & Expenditures Total library budget $78,327 (FY 7/1/74-7/1/75). Total FY film budget $2420. *Member:* ALA, EFLA, Calif. Library Assn.

Willows

P- WILLOWS PUBLIC LIBRARY, 201 N. Lassen St, 95988. *Tel:* (916) 934-5156. *Film Serv Est:* 1969. *In Charge:* Bonnie Arbogast, City Librarian. *AV Staff:* 1 (1 cl). *Film Sel:* committee preview.

Free-Loan Film Serv *Eligibility:* educational inst, civic groups, religious groups, indiv with library cards, prof groups.

Willows (cont'd)
Restrictions: for indiv & inst, only in system area of 11 counties. Cannot use for fund-raising, transmit electronically. May borrow by mail. *Loan Period:* 1-7 days. *Total Yr Film Loan:* 1000.

Other Film Serv Obtain film from coop loan system (Northern Calif. Library Film Circuit).

Other Media Collections *Audio:* tape, cassette, 1900c.

Budget & Expenditures No separate budget. *Member:* ALA, Calif. Library Assn.

Yorba Linda

P- YORBA LINDA DISTRICT LIBRARY, 18262 Lemon Dr, 92686. *Tel:* (714) 528-7039, ext 6. *Film Serv Est:* 1962. *In Charge:* Helen Holmberg, AV Librarian. *AV Staff:* 3 (1 prof, 1 cl, 1 tech). *Film Sel:* committee preview, chief film librarian's decision.

Free-Loan Film Serv *Eligibility:* educational inst, civic groups, religious groups, indiv with library cards, prof groups, such as serv organizations. *Restrictions:* for indiv, interlibrary loan; for inst, none. Cannot use for fund-raising. Available to researchers/scholars for on-site viewing. May not borrow by mail. *Loan Period:* 1 day.

Film Collection 136t. Approx 25t acquired annually. *Pubns:* catalog, annual; suppl, monthly. Publish materials pertaining to collection. Publish flyers & lists.

Other Film Serv Obtain film from coop loan system (Santiago & Public Library Film Circuit), obtain film from other libraries, film fairs/festivals, library film programs. Permanent viewing facility available for rent to community. *Equipment:* lend 16mm sound projector (5), 8mm reel projector (1), S8mm cartridge projector (1), S8mm reel projector (1), projection screens (1).

Other Media Collections *Audio:* disc, 33⅓rpm, 5582t; tape, cassette, 275t.

Budget & Expenditures Total library budget $42,000 (FY 7/1/74-7/1/75). Total FY film budget $7500. *Member:* ALA, Calif. Library Assn.

Video Serv *Est:* 1962. *Video Staff:* 3 f-t. *Video Use:* documentation of community/school events, to increase community's library use, in-service training. Video serv available on demand. Produce video tapes.

Video Equipment/Facilities *In-House Use Only:* recording deck (1), b&w, Sony; playback deck (1), b&w, Sony; studio camera (1), b&w, Sony; tripods (1). Have portable viewing installation. *Equipment Loan Period:* limited no. of days.

Video Tape Loan/Rental/Sale Serv *Loan Eligibility:* org members, staff & students, educational inst. *Restrictions:* for indiv, only in city; for inst, only in city. May not borrow by mail.

Video Collection Maintained by own production. Use/play ½" reel to reel, ½" cartridge. *Sources:* commercial distributors. *Special Collections:* in-house training tapes. Tapes organized by subject.

Colorado

Alamosa

C- ADAMS STATE COLLEGE, Learning Resource Center, 81102. *Tel:* (303) 589-7781. *In Charge:* Don Moeny, AV Technician. *AV Staff:* 1 prof. *Film Sel:* committee preview, faculty/staff recommendations, chief film librarian's decision. *Holdings:* agriculture, animated films, black studies, career education, children's films, consumer affairs, fine arts, industrial arts, law, medicine, science, social sciences, teacher education, women.
   Free-Loan Film Serv *Eligibility:* staff & students, educational inst, civic groups, indiv with library cards, prof groups, such as Chamber of Commerce, medical & teachers assn. *Restrictions:* for indiv & inst, only in state. Cannot use for fundraising, transmit electronically. Available to researchers/scholars for on-site viewing. May borrow by mail. *Loan Period:* 7 days. *Total Yr Film Loan:* 3400.
   Film Collection 1450t/1500p. Approx 150t acquired annually. *Circ:* 16mm, 1250t/1300p; S8mm cartridge, 200t/p. *Pubns:* catalog, every 3 yr; suppl, no set policy.
   Other Film Serv Obtain film from coop loan system (Colo. State Library Film Serv), obtain film from other libraries, film reference serv. Permanent viewing facility available for rent to community. *Equipment:* lend 16mm sound projector (3), 8mm reel projector (1), S8mm cartridge projector (3), S8mm reel projector (1), projection tables & stands (7), projection screens (13).
   Other Media Collections *Audio:* disc, 33⅓rpm, 1275c; disc, 78rpm, 100c; tape, cassette, 675c; tape, reel, 150c. *Filmstrips:* sound, 150c; silent, 150c. *Slides:* sets, 100c.
   Budget & Expenditures No separate budget. *Member:* AECT, ALA, Colo. AV Assn.
   Video Serv *In Charge:* Don Moeny, AV Technician. *Video Staff:* 1 f-t, 1 p-t.
   Cable & CCTV Receive serv of cable TV system. Produce programs for cablecasting.

Aspen

P- PITKIN COUNTY LIBRARY, 120 E Main St, 81611. *Tel:* (303) 925-7124.
   Free-Loan Film Serv Use free serv of Colo. State Library Film Serv. *Restrictions:* for indiv, interlibrary loan. Cannot use for fund-raising. *Loan Period:* 7 days.
   Other Film Serv *Equipment:* lend 16mm sound projector, lend 8mm reel projector.

Aurora

P- AURORA PUBLIC LIBRARY, 1298 Peoria, 80011. *Tel:* (303) 364-9358. *In Charge:* D. Chayne, AV Librarian.
   Other Film Serv Obtain film from coop loan system (Colo. State Library). Permanent viewing facility available for rent to community.
   Other Media Collections *Audio:* disc, 33⅓rpm, 1895t; tape, cassette, 257t; tape, reel, 11t. *Filmstrips:* sound, 20t; silent, 160t. *Slides:* single, 3641t.
   Budget & Expenditures Total library budget $46,000 (FY 1/1/75-1/1/76). No separate AV budget. *Member:* Colo. State Library Assn.

Boulder

C- UNIVERSITY OF COLORADO, Film Library, Educational Media Center, Stadium Bldg, 80309. *Tel:* (303) 492-7341. *Film Serv Est:* 1923. *In Charge:* Robert W. Bruns, Supervisor. *AV Staff:* 8 (2 prof, 3 cl, 3 tech). *Film Sel:* committee preview, faculty/staff recommendations, chief film librarian's decision.
   Film Rental Serv *Eligibility:* no restrictions. *Restrictions:* only in U.S. Cannot transmit electronically, reloan. *Rental Period:* 3 days. *Total Yr Film Booking:* 23,500. Sell films. Produce films.
   Film Collection 5200t/6000p. Approx 60t acquired annually. *Circ:* 16mm, 5000t, 5800p. *Noncirc:* 16mm, 200t/p. *Pubns:* catalog, every 2 yr ($2); suppl, in yr catalog not published. Publish flyers for new titles & titles for sale.
   Other Film Serv Rent film from distributors for patrons, obtain film from other libraries, film reference serv. Permanent viewing facility available.
   Budget & Expenditures Total library budget $25,700 (FY 7/1/74-7/1/75). Total FY film budget $25,700. *Member:* AECT, CUFC, EFLA.

Colorado Springs

P- PIKES PEAK REGIONAL LIBRARY DISTRICT, Box 1579, 80901. *Tel:* (303) 636-3948, ext 46. *Film Serv Est:* 1963. *In Charge:* M. K. Carlson, Librarian I. *AV Staff:* 1 prof. *Film Sel:* chief film librarian's decision.
   Free-Loan Film Serv *Eligibility:* indiv with library cards. *Restrictions:* for indiv, Plains & Peaks Library System. *Loan Period:* 7 days. *Total Yr Film Loan:* 2537.
   Film Collection 322t. Approx 32t acquired annually. *Circ:* 8mm reel, 272t; S8mm reel, 50t.
   Other Film Serv Rent film from distributors for patrons, obtain film from coop loan system (Colo. State Library), library film programs.
   Other Media Collections *Audio:* disc, 33⅓rpm, 4340t/865c. *Filmstrips:* sound, 15t; silent, 692t; sound sets, 9t; silent sets, 5t. *Slides:* single 309t.
   Budget & Expenditures Total library budget $220,760 (FY 1/1/74-1/1/75). Total FY film budget $450. *Member:* ALA, Colo. Library Assn.

Crested Butte

S- ACE SPACE COMPANY, (SPACECO), Box 183, 81224. *Tel:* (303) 349-6506. *Video Serv Est:* 1972. *In Charge:* Dana Atchley, Dir. *Video Staff:* 1 f-t. *Video Use:* documentation of community/school events, community video access, as art form. Video serv available to North American inst which elect to have company in residence for 1 day or more. Produce video tapes. Have production studio/space & separate control room.
   Video Equipment/Facilities *For Loan with operator only:* portapak (1), ¾", b&w/col, Sony AV3000; recording/playback deck (1), ¾", b&w/col, Sony AV1800; monitor (1), col, Sony Trinitron; lighting (5); microphones (6); tripods (1); audio tape recorders (3); color camera (1); audio mixer (1). Have portable viewing installation. *Equipment Loan Period:* no set policy. Provide training in use of equipment to students & inst.
   Video Tape Loan/Rental/Sale Serv *Serv Provided:* swap with other inst, rental, sale. *Loan/Rental Eligibility:* educational inst, prof groups. *Restrictions:* for inst, none. Cannot duplicate.
   Video Collection Maintained by own production, exchange/swap. Use/play ½" reel to reel, ¾" cassette. *Sources:* community productions, exchange. *Tape Sel:* preview, recommendations. *Collection, B&W:* ½" reel, 15t; ¾" cassette, 6t. *Other Video Serv:* production workshops.
   Cable & CCTV Serve as production facility for others.

Denver

S- COLORADO STATE LIBRARY, Film Serv, 1362 Lincoln St, 80203. *Tel:* (303) 892-2171. *Film Serv Est:* 1955. *In Charge:* Robyn Foreman, Film Librarian. *AV Staff:* 3 (1 prof, 1 cl, 1

Denver (cont'd)

tech). *Film Sel:* staff recommendations, chief film librarian's decision, published reviews. *Holdings:* public library programs.

Free-Loan Film Serv *Eligibility through local libraries:* staff & students, educational inst, civic & religious groups, indiv with library cards, prof groups, & others. *Restrictions:* for indiv & inst, only in state. Cannot transmit electronically, charge admission for viewing. May borrow by mail. *Loan Period:* 5 days. *Total Yr Film Loan:* 12,000.

Film Collection 746t/967p. Approx 150t acquired annually. *Circ:* 16mm, 700t. *Noncirc:* 16mm, 46t. *Pubns:* catalog, annual; suppl, 6 months after catalog. Publish articles in Colo. State Library Newsletter.

Other Film Serv Film reference serv.

Budget & Expenditures Total library budget $65,000 (FY 7/1/74-7/1/75). *Member:* EFLA.

C- **COMMUNITY COLLEGE OF DENVER, NORTH CAMPUS,** Learning Materials Center, 1001 E 62 Ave, 80216. *Tel:* (303) 287-3311, ext 231. *Film Serv Est:* 1968. *In Charge:* Clark Wong, Dir. *Film Sel:* faculty/staff recommendations.

Film Collection 187t. *Circ:* S8mm cartridge, 187t.

Other Film Serv Rent film from distributors for patrons, obtain film from other libraries. *Equipment:* lend 16mm sound projector (11), 8mm cartridge projector (17), 8mm reel projector (2), projection tables & stands (16), projection screens (44).

Other Media Collections *Audio:* disc, 33⅓rpm, 959t; tape, cassette, 356t; tape, reel, 20t. *Filmstrips:* sound, 774t; silent, 495t. *Slides:* single, 8537t; sets, 212t.

Budget & Expenditures Total library budget $134,622 (FY 7/1/74-7/1/75). Total FY film budget $107.52. *Member:* AECT, Colo. Library Assn.

Video Serv *Est:* 1972. *In Charge:* Clark Wong, Dir. *Video Staff:* 1 f-t, 3 p-t, 1 tech. *Video Use:* documentation of community/school events, in-service training, playback only of professionally produced tapes, local educational productions. Video serv available on demand. Produce video tapes.

Video Equipment/Facilities *In-House Use Only:* portapak (2), b&w, Sony; recording deck (6), b&w/col, Sony, JVC; playback deck (4), b&w/col, Sony, JVC; editing deck (2), col, JVC; studio camera (3), b&w/col, Sony, JVC; monitor (14), b&w/col, Sony, JVC; SEG (1), Sony; additional camera lenses (2); lighting (9); microphones (8); tripods (4); audio tape recorders (16). Have permanent & portable viewing installations. *Equipment Loan Period:* 1 day. Provide training in use of equipment to faculty. Have tape duplication serv.

Video Tape Loan/Rental/Sale Serv *Serv Provided:* free loan. *Loan Eligibility:* staff & students, educational inst, civic & religious groups. *Restrictions:* for indiv, only in city; for inst, only in Denver metropolitan area. Cannot use for fund-raising, duplicate, air without permission. May not borrow by mail.

Video Collection Maintained by purchase, rental, own production. Use/play ½″ reel to reel, ¾″ cassette. *Sources:* commercial distributors. *Tape Sel:* faculty/staff recommendations, published reviews. Tapes organized by symbol & accession number. *Collection, Color:* ½″ reel, 2t; ¾″ cassette, 217t. *Collection, B&W:* ½″ reel, 49t; ¾″ cassette, 6t. *Pubns:* catalog.

Cable & CCTV Have CCTV in inst, with 2 monitors. *Programming Sources:* tapes produced professionally.

P- **DENVER PUBLIC LIBRARY,** Film Center, 1357 Broadway, 80203. *Tel:* (303) 573-5152, ext 228. *Film Serv Est:* 1963. *In Charge:* Lana M. Papesh, Head of Film Center. *AV Staff:* 6 (5 cl, 1 library asst). *Film Sel:* committee preview.

Free-Loan Film Serv *Eligibility:* org members. Cannot use for fund-raising. May not borrow by mail. *Loan Period:* 1 day. *Total Yr Film Loan:* 3600 (prior to 1976, when film service was eliminated from city budget; Film Center is attempting to become self-supporting by charging $4 service fee).

Film Rental Serv *Eligibility:* no restrictions. *Restrictions:* 8-county metropolitan area. Cannot use for fund-raising, transmit electronically. *Rental Period:* 1 day. *Total Yr Film Booking:* 22,652.

Film Collection 1000t/1050p. Approx 100t acquired annually. *Circ:* 16mm, 1000t/1050p. *Pubns:* catalog, annual ($1.00); suppl, 6 mos after annual catalog.

Other Film Serv Film reference serv, library film programs, obtain films from State Library. Permanent viewing facility available for rent to community.

Other Media Collections *Audio:* disc, 33⅓rpm, 2000t/3000c; tape, cassette, 274t/c. *Filmstrips:* sound. *Slides:* single.

Budget & Expenditures Total FY film budget $22,750. *Member:* AECT, ALA, EFLA, FLIC.

Video Serv *Est:* 1973. *In Charge:* John Ward, Materials Sel Offr & Nancy Casey, Asst Publ Inf Offr. *Video Staff:* 2 f-t. Materials Selection deals with purchase of video tapes for patron use; PIO deals with in-house production. *Video Use:* in-service training. Video tapes available on demand; production scheduled by priority. Produce video tapes. Have production studio/space & separate control room (annex in auditorium).

Video Equipment/Facilities *In-House Use Only:* recording deck (2), ½″, ¾″ col, Panasonic 3110, NV-2120; editing deck (1), ½″ col, Panasonic 3110; SEG (1), Panasonic VY-922; microphones (3); tripods (6); audio tape recorders (2). Have video viewing installation.

Video Tape Loan/Rental/Sale Serv *Serv Provided:* swap with other inst. *Loan Eligibility:* org members. All patrons may view patron tapes free of charge in library.

Video Collection Maintained by own production. Use/play ¾″ cassette. *Tape Sel:* preview, faculty/staff recommendations, published reviews, catalogs. *Special Collections:* as requested by departments & branches. Tapes organized by subject. *Collection, B&W:* ¾″ cassette, 256t.

Durango

C- **FORT LEWIS COLLEGE,** AV Center, College Heights, 81301. *Tel:* (303) 247-7417. *Film Serv Est:* 1968. *In Charge:* Ross Worley, AV Tech. *AV Staff:* 2 (1 prof, 1 cl). *Film Sel:* faculty/staff recommendations.

Free-Loan Film Serv *Eligibility:* staff & students, educational inst, civic groups, religious groups. *Restrictions:* none. Available to researchers/scholars for on-site viewing. May not borrow by mail. *Loan Period:* 3 days. *Total Yr Film Loan:* 2281.

Film Collection 502t/p. Approx 25t acquired annually. *Circ:* 16mm, 486t/p; 8mm reel, 4t/p; S8mm cartridge 12t/p. *Pubns:* catalog, every 3 yrs or as needed; supplement, in yr catalog not published.

Other Film Serv Obtain film from coop loan system (Colorado State Library) & from other libraries, film reference serv. Permanent viewing facility.

Other Media Collections *Audio:* disc, 33⅓rpm, 2100t/c; tape, cassette, 56t/c; tape, reel, 157t/c.

Video Serv *Est:* 1969. *Video Staff:* 1 f-t. *Video Use:* documentation of community/school events, playback only of professionally produced tapes, classroom instruction in athletics, PE, speech, theater & education to record techniques, faults, physical behavior of students. Video serv available by appointment. Produce videotapes.

Video Equipment/Facilities *In-House Use Only:* portapak (1), b&w, Sony DVK 2400; recording deck (4), ½″, b&w, Sony AV 3400; playback deck (2), b&w, Sony CV 2200; editing deck (1), b&w, Sony AV 5000A; studio camera; monitor; SEG; audio tape recorders (3). Have portable viewing installations. Provide training in use of equipment.

Video Collection Maintain by purchase, own production. Use/play ½″ reel to reel. *Sources:* commercial distributors. *Tape Sel:* faculty/staff recommendations, catalogs. Tapes organized by accession order on shelf, LC cataloging system. *Collection, B&W:* ½″ reel, 20t/c. *Pubns:* catalog.

C- **LORETTO HEIGHTS COLLEGE,** May Bonfils Library, 3001 S Federal Blvd, 80236. *Tel:* (303) 936-8441, ext 287. *Film Serv Est:* 1972. *In Charge:* Dan Mancini, Educational Media Dir. *AV Staff:* 2 (2 prof, 2 cl). *Film Sel:* faculty/staff recommendations, chief film librarian's decision.

Film Collection 8t. *Noncirc:* 8mm reel, 8t.

Other Film Serv Permanent viewing facility available for rent to community. *Equipment:* rent 16mm sound projector, 8mm cartridge projector, 8mm reel projector, S8mm cartridge projector, S8mm reel projector.

Other Media Collections *Audio:* disc, 33⅓rpm, 740t/c; tape, cassette, 310t/c; tape, reel, 273t/c. *Filmstrips:* sound, 40t/c; silent, 27t/c. *Slides:* single, 25t/c. *Member:* AECT.

Video Serv *Est:* 1974. *In Charge:* Dan Mancini, Educational Media Dir. *Video Staff:* 2 f-t, 3 p-t. *Video Use:* documentation of community/school events, in-service training, playback only of professionally produced tapes. Video serv available by appointment. Produce video tapes. Have production studio/space.

Video Equipment/Facilities *For Loan to Students Only:* portapak (2), ½", b&w, Sony AV3400; recording deck (1), ½", b&w/col, Sony AV3650; playback deck (1), ¾", col, Sony VO1800; recording/editing deck (1), ½", col, Sony 8650; studio camera (2), b&w, Sony, Panasonic; monitor (5); SEG (1), Shintron 366; lighting (3); microphones (2); tripods (4); audio tape recorders (5); cassette tape recorders (4); audio mixer (1). Have portable viewing installation. *Equipment Loan Period:* 1-3 days. Provide training in use of equipment to faculty & students. Have tape duplication serv.

Video Tape Loan/Rental/Sale Serv *Serv Provided:* free loan, swap with other inst, rental. *Loan/Rental Eligibility:* staff & students. *Restrictions:* only in city. Cannot duplicate, air without permission. May not borrow by mail.

Video Collection Maintained by purchase, own production, exchange/swap. Use/play ½" reel to reel, ¾" cassette. *Sources:* commercial distributors. *Tape Sel:* preview, faculty/staff recommendations. Tapes organized by subject. *Collection, Color:* ½" reel; ¾" cassette. *Collection, B&W:* ½" reel, 50t.

Cable & CCTV Have CCTV in inst, with 1 monitor. *Programming Sources:* over-the-air commercial & public broadcasting, tapes produced by inst, tapes produced professionally, tapes produced by community groups & indiv.

Grand Junction

C- MESA COLLEGE, Media Center, Box 2647, 81501. *Tel:* (303) 248-1315. *In Charge:* Charles Hendrickson, Dir. *AV Staff:* 3 (1 prof, 1 cl, 1 tech). *Film Sel:* faculty/staff recommendations, published reviews. *Holdings:* agriculture 1%, consumer affairs 1%, engineering 1%, fine arts 1%, law 5%, nursing 3%, nutrition 3%, science 2%, screen news digest 84%, social sciences 5%.

Free-Loan Film Serv *Eligibility:* staff & students, civic groups. *Restrictions:* for indiv & inst, only in city. Available to researchers/scholars for on-site viewing. May not borrow by mail. *Loan Period:* 5 days. *Total Yr Film Loan:* 14.

Film Collection 88t/p. Approx 3-5t acquired annually. *Circ:* 16mm, 88t/p.

Other Film Serv Rent film from distributors for patrons, obtain film from coop loan system (Mountain Plains Film Library), obtain film from other libraries. *Equipment:* lend/rent S8mm camera (2), lend 16mm camera (1), lend/rent 16mm sound projector (18), 8mm reel projector (3), rent S8mm cartridge projector (2), S8mm reel projector (2), projection tables & stands (32), lend/rent projection screens (12).

Other Media Collections *Audio:* disc, 33⅓rpm, 500t; tape, cassette, 200t. *Filmstrips:* sound, 20t; silent, 40t; sound sets, 50t. *Slides:* single, 10,000t; sets, 20t.

Budget & Expenditures Total library budget $65,486 (FY 7/1/75-7/1/76). No separate AV budget. *Member:* AECT, Colo. Educational Media Assn.

Video Serv *In Charge:* Charles Hendrickson, Dir. *Video Staff:* 3 f-t, 1 tech. *Video Use:* documentation of community/school events, playback of professionally produced tapes, self-evaluation. Video serv available by appointment. Produce video tapes. Have production studio/space & separate control room.

Video Equipment/Facilities *In-House Use Only:* portapak (2), ½", b&w, JVC 4500; recording deck (1), ¾", col, JVC 6100U; playback deck (2), ¾", col, JVC5000; studio camera (3),

b&w, Concord; monitor (5), b&w, Micro Studio; SEG (1), Micro Studio; lighting (25); microphones (4); tripods (2); audio tape recorders (1); turntable (1). Have permanent & portable viewing installations. Provide training in use of equipment only to own serv personnel. Have audio tape duplication serv.

Video Tape Loan/Rental/Sale Serv *Serv Provided:* free loan. *Loan Eligibility:* org members, staff & students. *Restrictions:* cannot use for fund-raising, duplicate, air without permission. May not borrow by mail.

Video Collection Maintained by purchase, rental, own production. Use/play ¾" cassette. *Sources:* commercial distributors, community productions, exchange (Colo. State University). *Tape Sel:* faculty/staff recommendations, catalogs. *Special Collections:* supplemental instruction. Tapes organized by subject. *Collection, Color:* ¾" cassette, 20t. *Collection, B&W:* ¾" cassette, 100t. *Other Video Serv:* playback of prerecorded material. *Pubns:* catalog.

Cable & CCTV Receive serv of cable TV system. Have CCTV in inst, with 6 monitors. *Programming Sources:* tapes produced by inst, tapes produced professionally, tapes produced by community groups & indiv.

Greeley

C- AIMS COMMUNITY COLLEGE, Box 69, 80631. *Tel:* (303) 353-8008, ext 226, 227. *In Charge:* Linda Piper, Coord of Materials Acquisition & Distribution.

Free-Loan Film Serv *Eligibility:* staff & students, community. *Restrictions:* for indiv, High Plains Public Library system. Cannot use for fund-raising, transmit electronically. Available to researchers/scholars for on-site viewing. May not borrow by mail. *Loan Period:* 3 days. *Total Yr Film Loan:* 20. Produce films.

Film Collection 50t/p. *Pubns:* catalog, annual; suppl.

Other Film Serv Rent film from distributors for patrons, obtain film from coop loan system (High Plains film circuit), obtain film from other libraries, film fairs/festivals. Permanent viewing facility available.

Other Media Collections *Audio:* disc, 33⅓rpm, 300t/400c; tape, cassette, 700t/900c. *Filmstrips:* sound sets, 80t/100c; silent sets, 20t/c. *Slides:* 15t/20c.

Budget & Expenditures Total library budget $40,000 (FY 7/1/74-7/1/75). Total FY film budget $8000. *Member:* Colo. Library Assn, Assn of Colo. Community College Learning Resources Centers, Colo. Assn of School Librarians, Colo. AV Assn, Mountain Plains Library Assn.

Video Serv *Est:* 1974. *In Charge:* Daniel Templeton, Coord. *Video Staff:* 3 f-t, 2 p-t. *Video Use:* to increase community's library use, community video access, in-service training, practical video/TV training courses, playback only of professionally produced tapes. Video serv available on demand. Produce video tapes. Have production studio/space & separate control room.

Video Equipment/Facilities *In-House Use Only:* recording deck (1), ½", b&w/col, Panasonic 3130; playback deck (1), ½", b&w/col, Sony; editing deck (1), ½", b&w/col; studio camera (3), b&w, Panasonic; monitors; SEG (1), Panasonic; additional camera lenses (4); lighting (1); microphones (4); tripods (6); audio tape recorders (20). *For Loan:* portapak (1), ½" b&w, Sony 3400. Have permanent viewing installation. *Equipment Loan Period:* 1 day. Provide training in use of equipment to faculty, students, community. Have tape duplication serv.

Video Tape Loan/Rental/Sale Serv *Loan Eligibility (Equipment):* staff & students, civic & religious groups. *Restrictions:* for indiv & inst, only in Weld County. May not borrow by mail.

Video Collection Maintained by purchase, own production. Use/play ½" reel to reel, ¾" cassette. *Sources:* community productions. *Tape Sel:* preview, faculty/staff recommendations. Tapes organized by LC classification. *Other Video Serv:* taping of other media, production workshops.

Cable & CCTV Have CCTV in inst, with 25 monitors. *Programming Sources:* over-the-air commercial & public broadcasting, tapes produced by inst, tapes produced professionally.

Gunnison

C- WESTERN STATE COLLEGE, Savage Library, 81230. *Tel:* (303) 943-2053. *Film Serv Est:* 1965. *Film Sel:* faculty/staff recommendations.

Free-Loan Film Serv *Eligibility:* staff & students. *Restrictions:* for indiv & inst, only in state. Available to researchers/scholars for on-site viewing. May not borrow by mail. *Loan Period:* 1 semester (faculty). *Total Yr Film Loan:* 145.

Film Collection 65t/p. Approx 10-12t acquired annually. *Circ:* 16mm, 55t/p; S8mm cartridge, 10t/p.

Other Film Serv Rent film from distributors for patrons, obtain film from coop loan system (Colo. State Library), obtain film from other libraries. Permanent viewing facility available.

Other Media Collections *Audio:* disc, 33⅓rpm, 1800t/1900c; tape, cassette, 100t/c; tape, reel, 25t/c. *Filmstrips:* sound, 100t/c; sound sets, 25t/c.

Budget & Expenditures Total library budget $100,000 (FY 7/1/74-7/1/75). Total FY film budget $3000. *Member:* ALA, Colo. Library Assn, Mountain Plains Library Assn.

Littleton

P- EDWIN BEMIS PUBLIC LIBRARY, 6014 S Datura, 80120. *Tel:* (303) 794-4229. *In Charge:* Phyllis Larison. *AV Staff:* 1 prof. *Film Sel:* chief film librarian's decision.

Free-Loan Film Serv *Eligibility:* indiv with library cards. *Restrictions:* for indiv, only in metropolitan Denver. Available to researchers/scholars for on-site viewing. May not borrow by mail. *Loan Period:* 7 days.

Film Collection 147t/148p. Approx 30t acquired annually. *Circ:* 8mm cartridge, 57t/p; S8mm cartridge, 90t/p. *Pubns:* catalog, annual.

Other Film Serv Obtain film from coop loan system (Central Colo. Library System), obtain film from other libraries. Permanent viewing facility available for rent to community.

Other Media Collections *Audio:* disc, 33⅓rpm, 1474t; tape, cassette, 488t.

Budget & Expenditures Total library budget $50,000 (FY 1/1/75-1/1/76). Total FY film budget $800. *Member:* ALA, Colo. State Library Assn.

Connecticut

Bridgeport

P- BRIDGEPORT PUBLIC LIBRARY, 925 Broad St, 06604. *Tel:* (203) 576-7401. *Film Serv Est:* 1968. *In Charge:* Bernadette Baldino, Film Librarian. *AV Staff:* 2 (1 cl, 1 tech). *Film Sel:* committee preview, staff recommendations.

Free-Loan Film Serv *Eligibility:* staff & students, educational inst, civic & religious groups, indiv with library cards. *Restrictions:* for indiv & inst, only in city. Cannot transmit electronically. Available to researchers/scholars for on-site viewing. May not borrow by mail. *Loan Period:* 3 days. *Total Yr Film Loan:* 500.

Film Collection 300t. Approx 50t acquired annually. *Circ:* 16mm, 200t; 8mm reel, 95t; S8mm reel, 5t. *Pubns:* catalog, every 2 yr (25¢); suppl, in yr catalog not published.

Other Film Serv Obtain film from coop loan system (Conn. State Library Film Dept, Fairfield County Feature Film Circuit), film reference serv, library film programs. Permanent viewing facility available. *Equipment:* 16mm sound projector (6), projection tables & stands (6), projection screens (9).

Other Media Collections *Audio:* disc, 33⅓rpm, 3000t. *Filmstrips:* sound sets, 176t; silent sets, 4t.

Budget & Expenditures Total film budget $8500 (FY 7/1/74-7/1/75). *Member:* Conn. Library Assn.

Video Serv *Est:* 1972. *In Charge:* Bernadette Baldino, Film Librarian. *Video Staff:* 1 f-t, 1 tech. *Video Use:* documentation of community/school events, to increase community's library use, in-service training, practical video/TV training courses. Video serv available on demand. Produce video tapes. Have production studio/space.

Video Equipment/Facilities *In-House Use Only:* portapak (1), ½", b&w, Panasonic NV3082; recording/playback deck (1), ½", b&w, Panasonic NV3020; editing deck (1), ½", b&w, Panasonic NV3130; monitor (2), b&w, Panasonic TR910VN, TR195V; microphones (3); tripods (1); audio tape recorders (2). *Equipment Loan Period:* no set policy. Provide training in use of equipment to library staff & interested community members. Have tape duplication serv.

Video Tape Loan/Rental/Sale Serv *Serv Provided:* free loan, swap with other inst. *Loan Eligibility:* staff & students, educational inst, civic & religious groups. *Restrictions:* for indiv & inst, only in city. Cannot duplicate. May not borrow by mail. *Loan Period:* 3 days.

Video Collection Maintained by own production. Use/play ½" reel to reel. Tapes organized by subject. *Collection, B&W:* ½" reel, 75t. *Other Video Serv:* programming.

Bristol

P- BRISTOL PUBLIC LIBRARY, 5 High St, 06010. *Tel:* (203) 582-9505, ext 24. *Film Serv Est:* 1973. *In Charge:* Thomas J. Hartnett, Business & Tech/Film Librarian. *AV Staff:* ½ prof, ½ cl. *Film Sel:* committee preview.

Free-Loan Film Serv *Eligibility:* indiv with library cards. *Restrictions:* for indiv & inst, none. Cannot use for fund-raising, transmit electronically. May not borrow by mail. *Loan Period:* 3 days. *Total Yr Film Loan:* 331.

Film Collection 150t/c. Approx 50t acquired annually. *Circ:* 16mm, 150t/p. *Pubns:* catalog, annual; suppl, no set policy.

Other Film Serv Obtain film from coop loan systems (Town & Gown, State Film Serv), film reference serv, library film programs. Permanent viewing facility available. *Equipment:* 16mm camera (1).

Budget & Expenditures Total library budget $1800 (FY 7/1/74-7/1/75). Total FY film budget $1800. *Member:* EFLA.

Danbury

P- DANBURY PUBLIC LIBRARY, Box 1111, 170 Main St, 06810. *Tel:* (203) 792-0260. *Video Serv Est:* 1974. *In Charge:*

William P. Morton, Dir of Video. *Video Staff:* 2 f-t, 2 p-t. *Video Use:* documentation of community/school events, to increase community's library use, in-service training, practical video/TV training courses, as art form, cablecasting. Video serv available by appointment. Produce video tapes. Have production studio/space.

Video Equipment/Facilities *In-House Use Only:* portapak (2), ½", b&w, Panasonic 3085; recording deck (1), ½", b&w, Panasonic 3020; editing deck (1), ½", col, Panasonic 3130; studio camera (3), ½", b&w, Panasonic 341P; monitor (3), b&w, Sony CVM 950; SEG (1), Panasonic 545P; additional camera lenses (4); lighting (2); microphones (10); tripods (4); audio tape recorders (1); modulator (1). Have permanent viewing installation. Provide training in use of equipment to faculty & community groups.

Video Tape Loan/Rental/Sale Serv *Serv Provided:* free loan, swap with other inst. *Loan Eligibility:* staff, educational inst, civic & religious groups, prof groups, such as lawyers, doctors. *Restrictions:* for indiv, must be linked to inst or group use in state; for inst, only in state. Cannot use for fund-raising, duplicate, air without permission. May borrow by mail. *Loan Period:* varies. *Total Yr Tape Loan:* 5.

Video Collection Maintained by own production, exchange/swap. Use/play ½" reel to reel, ½" cartridge, ¾" cassette. *Sources:* commerical distributors, community productions, exchange (State Library). *Tape Sel:* preview. *Special Collections:* video as art, community-produced tapes. Tapes organized by subject. *Collection, B&W:* ½" reel, 30t/50c; ½" cartridge, 5t/c. *Other Video Serv:* programming, production workshops.

Cable & CCTV Receive serv of cable TV system. Produce programs for cablecasting. Serve as production facility for others. Run cable programs for special audiences. Have advisory/administrative role in cable system operation. Produce mayoral reports weekly & municipal information programs daily. Have CCTV in inst, with 2 monitors. *Programming Sources:* tapes produced by inst, tapes produced by community groups & indiv, community message wheel.

C- WESTERN CONNECTICUT STATE COLLEGE, AV-TV Center, 181 White St, 06810. *Tel:* (203) 792-1400, ext 307. *Video Serv Est:* 1965. *In Charge:* George J. Theisen, Dir. *Video Staff:* 4 f-t, 6 p-t. *Video Use:* documentation of community/school events, community video access, in-service training, practical video/TV training courses. Video serv available on demand. Produce video tapes. Have production studio/space & separate control room.

Video Equipment/Facilities *In-House Use Only:* portapak (2), b&w, Sony 3400; recording deck (10), ½", ¾", 1", b&w/col, various models; editing deck (3), 1", col, Ampex 7800; studio camera (5), b&w/col, Fairchild; monitor (many); SEG (2), Panasonic, Shintron; keyer (2), Panasonic, Shintron; additional camera lenses (many); lighting; microphones (many); tripods (many); audio tape recorders (many). Have permanent viewing installation. *Equipment Loan Period:* 3 days; dept loan, 1 semester. Provide training in use of equipment to faculty, students, community groups. Have tape duplication serv.

Video Tape Loan/Rental/Sale Serv *Serv Provided:* free loan, swap with other inst. *Loan Eligibility:* staff & students, educational inst, civic groups, prof groups, by special request. *Restrictions:* for indiv & inst, requests handled individually. Cannot use for fund-raising, duplicate, air without permission. May not borrow by mail. *Total Yr Tape Loan:* 25.

Video Collection Maintained by rental, own production, exchange/swap. Use/play ½", 1" reel to reel, ¾" cassette. *Sources:* community productions. *Tape Sel:* faculty/staff recommendations. *Special Collections:* in-house training tapes, video as art. Tapes organized by subject. *Collection, Color:* ½" reel, 30t; ¾" cassette, 10t. *Collection, B&W:* ½" reel, 50t; 1" reel, 100t. *Other Video Serv:* production workshops.

Danbury (cont'd)

Cable & CCTV Receive serv of cable TV system. Produce programs for cablecasting. Inform public about cable system serv & facilities. Serve as production facility for others. Have advisory/administrative role in cable system operation. Member of Cable Council for Educational Access Channel.

Derby

S- VALLEY CABLE VISION, Connecticut Community Video Serv, 9 11 St, 06418. *Tel:* (203) 735-9975. *Video Serv Est:* 1972. *In Charge:* William J. Shanahan, Jr., Programming Dir. *Video Staff:* 1 p-t. *Video Use:* documentation of community/school events, as art form. Video serv available by appointment. Produce video tapes. Have production studio/ space & separate control room.
   Video Equipment/Facilities *In-House Use Only:* portapak (1), ½″, b&w, Sony 3400; recording deck (1), ¾″, col, JVC6000U; playback deck (1), ¾″, col, JVC5000U; editing deck (2), ½″, b&w/col, Shibaden 510, 520; studio camera (2), 1″, b&w, Shibaden FP100; monitor (6), b&w, Sony, Shibaden; SEG (1), Telemet; keyer (1), Telemet; lighting (8); microphones (6); tripods (3); time base corrector (1). Have permanent & portable viewing installations. Provide training in use of equipment to anyone in cable franchise area. Have tape duplication serv.
   Video Tape Loan/Rental/Sale Serv *Serv Provided:* swap, with other inst, rental, sale. *Rental Eligibility:* staff & students, educational inst, civic groups. *Restrictions:* for indiv, only in Valley Cable Vision franchise area; for inst, none. Cannot use for fund-raising, duplicate. May borrow by mail. *Loan Period:* by arrangement. *Total Yr Tape Loan:* 5.
   Video Collection Maintained by own production. Use/play ½″ reel to reel, ¾″ cassette. *Sources:* community productions. *Member:* Educational Video Exchange. *Tape Sel:* preview. Tapes organized by production date. *Collection, B&W:* ½″ reel, 7t. *Other Video Serv:* programming.
   Cable & CCTV Receive serv of cable TV system. Produce programs for cablecasting. Inform public about cable system serv & facilities. Serve as production facility for others. Run cable programs for special audiences. Have advisory/administrative role in cable system operation. Have CCTV in inst, with 3 monitors. *Programming Sources:* tapes produced by inst, tapes produced by community groups & indiv.

Farmington

C- TUNXIS COMMUNITY COLLEGE, Learning Resources Lab, Rtes 6 & 177, 06032. *Tel:* (203) 677-7701, ext 34. *Film Serv Est:* 1972. *In Charge:* A. G. Miele, Coord AV Serv. *AV Staff:* 2 (1 prof, ½ cl, ½ tech). *Film Sel:* faculty/staff recommendations.
   Free-Loan Film Serv *Eligibility:* org members. Available to researchers/scholars for on-site viewing. May not borrow by mail. *Loan Period:* 1 day.
   Film Collection 75t. Approx 10t acquired annually. *Pubns:* catalog, annual. Publish newsletter.
   Other Film Serv Rent film from distributors for patrons, obtain film from coop loan system. Permanent viewing facility available. *Equipment:* lend S8mm camera, 16mm camera, 16mm sound projector, 8mm cartridge projector, 8mm reel projector, S8mm cartridge projector, S8mm reel projector, projection tables & stands, projection screens. *Member:* Conn. AV Educational Assn.

Greenwich

P- GREENWICH LIBRARY, 101 W Putnam Ave, 06830. *Tel:* (203) 869-4700. *Film Serv Est:* 1949. *In Charge:* Wayne Campbell, Film Serv Coord. *AV Staff:* 4½ (1½ prof, 1 cl, 2 tech). *Film Sel:* chief film librarian's decision. *Holdings:* animated films 9%, black studies 1.5%, children's films 25%, dance 1.5 %, experimental films 3%, feature films 22%, fine arts 8%, history 8%, humor 8%, science 2.3%, social sciences 4%, miscellaneous 7.7%.

Free-Loan Film Serv *Eligibility:* educational inst, civic & religious groups, indiv with library cards. *Restrictions:* for indiv & inst, only in city except Fairfield County libraries. Cannot use for fund-raising, transmit electronically. Cannot show feature films outside city. Available to researchers/scholars for on-site viewing. May not borrow by mail. *Loan Period:* 36 hours.
   Film Collection 800t/850p. Approx 30t acquired annually. *Circ:* 16mm, 800t/850p. *Noncirc:* 16mm, 30t/p. *Pubns:* catalog, every 2 yr ($1); suppl, in yr catalog not published. Publish monthly calendar suppl.
   Other Film Serv Obtain film from coop loan system (Conn. Film Circuit), obtain film from other libraries, film reference serv, library film programs. Permanent viewing facility available free to community. *Equipment:* rent 16mm sound projectors (12), rent projection screens (2).
   Other Media Collections *Audio:* disc, 33⅓rpm, 9225t, circ; tape, cassette, 292t.
   Budget & Expenditures Total library budget $152,333 (FY 7/1/74-7/1/75). Total FY film budget $16,966. *Member:* AFI, ALA, EFLA, FLIC, Conn. Library Assn.
   Video Serv *Est:* 1973. *In Charge:* Wayne Campbell, Film Serv Coord. *Video Staff:* 1 f-t. *Video Use:* documentation of community/school events, to increase community's library use, as art form. Video serv available on demand for video cartridge viewing, by appointment for equipment use & training. Produce video tapes.
   Video Equipment/Facilities *In-House Use Only:* playback deck (2), ½″, col, Panasonic; editing deck (1), ½″, col, Panasonic 3130; monitor (2), Panasonic, Hitachi. *For Loan:* portapak (1), ½″, b&w, Panasonic 3082; microphones (1); tripods (1). Have permanent & portable viewing installations. *Equipment Loan Period:* no set policy. Provide training in use of equipment to community.
   Video Tape Loan/Rental/Sale Serv *Serv Provided:* free loan, swap with other inst. *Loan Eligibility:* civic groups, indiv with library cards. *Restrictions:* for indiv & inst, only in city. May borrow by mail. *Loan Period:* to be arranged.
   Video Collection Maintained by purchase, own production. Use/play ½″ reel to reel, ½″ cartridge. *Sources:* commercial distributors, community productions, exchange. *Special Collections:* video as art, films in video format. Tapes organized by title. *Collection, Color:* ½″ cartridge, 10t/c. *Collection, B&W:* ½″ cartridge, 40t/c. *Other Video Serv:* reference serv, production workshops. Publish Greenwich Video Newsletter.

Hamden

P- HAMDEN PUBLIC LIBRARY, Miller Memorial Library, 2914 Dixwell Ave, 06518. *Tel:* (203) 288-4052. *Film Serv Est:* 1975. *In Charge:* Lew Daniels, Media Coord. *AV Staff:* 1 prof. *Film Sel:* committee preview.
   Free-Loan Film Serv *Eligibility:* educational inst, civic & religious groups, indiv with library cards. *Restrictions:* for indiv, only in city & 2 neighboring towns; for inst, only in city. Non-residents may borrow for $5 annual fee. Cannot use for fund-raising. Available to researchers/scholars for on-site viewing. May not borrow by mail. *Loan Period:* 1 day. *Total Yr Film Loan:* 3972.
   Film Collection 400t/p. Approx 30t acquired annually. *Circ:* 16mm, 400t/p. *Pubns:* catalog, as needed; suppl, no set policy. Publish materials pertaining to collection.
   Other Film Serv Obtain film from coop loan system (State Library, Conn. Film Circuit), obtain film from other libraries, library film programs. *Equipment:* lend 16mm sound projectors (2), lend projection screens (2).
   Other Media Collections *Audio:* disc, 33⅓rpm, 1300t/c.
   Budget & Expenditures Total library budget $47,505 (FY 7/1/74-7/1/75). *Member:* Conn. Library Assn.
   Video Serv *In Charge:* Lew Daniels, Media Coord. *Video Use:* documentation of community/school events, playback only of professionally produced tapes. Produce video tapes.
   Video Collection Maintained by own production. Use/play ½″, 1″ reel to reel. *Sources:* exchange (State Library).

Cable & CCTV Have advisory/administrative role in city's cable system operation.

Hartford

P- HARTFORD PUBLIC LIBRARY, 500 Main St, 06103. *Tel:* (203) 525-9121, ext 72. *Film Serv Est:* 1963. *In Charge:* Ruby Bieth, Administrative Assistant, Art, Music & Recreation Dept. *Film Sel:* committee preview. *Holdings:* animated films, black studies, children's films, dance, experimental films, fine arts.
Free-Loan Film Serv *Eligibility:* indiv with library cards. *Restrictions:* for indiv & inst, only in city. Cannot use for fund-raising, transmit electronically. May not borrow by mail. *Loan Period:* 1 day. *Total Yr Film Loan:* 10,071.
Film Collection *Circ:* 16mm, 230t; 8mm reel, 100t; S8mm reel, 60t. *Pubns:* catalog, as needed (50¢); suppl, no set policy.
Other Film Serv Obtain film from coop loan system, film reference serv, library film programs. Permanent viewing facility available. *Equipment:* lend to branch libraries: 16mm sound projectors (3), 8mm reel projector (1), projection tables & stands (2), projection screens (6).
Other Media Collections *Audio:* disc, 33⅓rpm, 6090t/c; disc, 78 rpm, 120t/c. *Member:* EFLA, FLIC.

Manchester

C- MANCHESTER COMMUNITY COLLEGE, AV Center, 60 Bidwell St, 06040. *Tel:* (203) 646-4900, ext 220. *Film Serv Est:* 1966. *In Charge:* J. Scheideman, Dir AV Serv. *AV Staff:* 2 prof, 1 cl, 1 tech. *Film Sel:* faculty/staff recommendations. *Holdings:* black studies 3%, career education 30%, experimental films 2%, feature films 10%, science 5%, social sciences 40%, teacher education 10%.
Free-Loan Film Serv *Eligibility:* recognized inst in Manchester area. *Restrictions:* cannot use for fund-raising, transmit electronically. Available to researchers/scholars for on-site viewing. May not borrow by mail. *Loan Period:* 1 day. *Total Yr Film Loan:* 10.
Film Collection 142t/150p. *Circ:* 16mm, 117t/125p; S8mm reel, 25t/p. *Pubns:* catalog, as needed; suppl, no set policy.
Other Film Serv Rent film from distributors for patrons, obtain film from other libraries. Permanent viewing facility available. *Equipment:* S8mm camera (5), 16mm camera (1), 16mm sound projector (13), S8mm cartridge projector (10), S8mm reel projector (1), projection tables & stands (15), projection screens (2).
Other Media Collections *Filmstrips:* sound, 152t/c; silent, 110t/c.
Budget & Expenditures Total film budget $2400 (FY 7/1/74-7/1/75). *Member:* AECT, Conn. AV Educational Assn.
Video Serv *Est:* 1968. *In Charge:* J. Scheideman, Dir AV Serv. *Video Staff:* 2 f-t, 3 p-t, 1 tech. *Video Use:* documentation of community/school events, practical video/TV training courses, playback only of professionally produced tapes. Video serv available on demand. Produce video tapes. Have production studio/space & separate control room.
Video Equipment/Facilities *In-House Use Only:* recording deck (5), ½", b&w, Sony 3500; playback deck (3), ½", b&w, Panasonic 3010; studio camera (2), b&w, IVC; monitor (12), b&w, Sony; SEG (1); keyer (1); lighting (10); microphones (5); tripods (2); audio tape recorders (2); turntables. *For Loan:* portapak (1), ½", b&w, Sony. Provide training in use of equipment to faculty & students.
Video Tape Loan/Rental/Sale Serv *Serv Provided:* free loan. *Loan Eligibility:* staff. *Restrictions:* for indiv, only in campus classrooms. Cannot use for fund-raising, duplicate, air without permission. May not borrow by mail.
Video Collection Maintained by own production. Use/play ½" reel to reel. Tapes organized by subject. *Collection, B&W:* ½" reel, 50t. *Other Video Serv:* production workshops.
Cable & CCTV Inform public about community's cable system serv & facilities.

Middletown

P- RUSSELL LIBRARY, 119 Broad St, 06457. *Tel:* (203) 347-2528, ext 22. *Film Serv Est:* 1948. *In Charge:* Linda Rusczek, Film Librarian. *AV Staff:* 4 (1 prof, 2 cl, 1 tech). *Film Sel:* chief film librarian's decision.
Film Rental Serv *Eligibility:* no restrictions. *Restrictions:* walk-in serv only. Cannot use for fund-raising, transmit electronically. *Rental Rate:* annual membership fee. *Rental Period:* 1-7 days. *Total Yr Film Booking:* 25,000.
Film Collection 942t/p. Approx 50-60t acquired annually. *Circ:* 16mm, 815t/p; 8mm cartridge, 120t/p; S8mm cartridge, 2t/p. *Noncirc:* 16mm, 5t/p. *Pubns:* catalog, every 3 yr ($1); suppl, in yrs catalog not published.
Other Film Serv Obtain film from coop loan system (Conn. Film Circuit), obtain film from other libraries, film reference serv, film fairs/festivals, library film programs. *Equipment:* rent 16mm sound projectors (2), rent projection screens (2).
Other Media Collections *Audio:* disc, 33⅓rpm, 4861t/c; tape, cassette, 27t/c. *Filmstrips:* silent, 40t/c. *Slides:* sets, 1t/c.
Budget & Expenditures Total library budget $294,300 (FY 7/1/74-7/1/75). Total FY film budget $7398. *Member:* ALA, EFLA, FLIC, Conn. Library Assn, New England Library Assn.

C- WESLEYAN UNIVERSITY, Saudak-Omnibus Collection, Art Dept, 06457. *Tel:* (203) 347-9411, ext 253. *Film Serv Est:* 1975. *In Charge:* James Steffensen, Cur. *AV Staff:* 1 (⅓ prof, ⅓ cl, ⅓ tech). *Film Sel:* gifts. *Holdings:* TV program "Omnibus" (12 yr of weekly programs) transferred to 16mm film. Also the Elia Kazan Collection of his personal papers (housed in Olin Library) and of his personal 16mm prints of his films (under the supervision of John Frazer, Professor of Art).
Free-Loan Film Serv *Eligibility:* staff & students, indiv scholars upon application. *Restrictions:* for indiv & inst, only on campus. Cannot use for fund-raising, transmit electronically. Available to researchers/scholars for on-site viewing. May not borrow by mail. Sell films.
Film Collection 400t/800p. *Noncirc:* 16mm, 400t/800p. *Pubns:* list of holdings in preparation.
Other Film Serv Obtain film from coop loan system (Univ. Film Study Center). Permanent viewing facility available for rent to community.
Other Media Collections *Slides:* single, 100,000t/c (Art History).

New London

C- CONNECTICUT COLLEGE, Library, Afro-American Resources Center, Mohegan Ave, 06320. *Tel:* (203) 442-5391, ext 212. *Film Serv Est:* 1973. *In Charge:* Carrie Evento, Circulation Librarian. *Film Sel:* faculty/staff recommendations. *Holdings:* black studies 67%, science 25%, teacher education 8%.
Free-Loan Film Serv *Eligibility:* staff & students, educational inst, civic & religious groups. *Restrictions:* for indiv & inst, southeastern Conn. May not borrow by mail. *Total Yr Film Loan:* 300.
Film Collection 59t/p. Approx 4t acquired annually. *Circ:* 16mm, 39t/p. *Noncirc:* 16mm, 20t/p. *Pubns:* catalog, as needed; suppl, no set policy.
Other Media Collections *Audio:* disc, 33⅓rpm, 3525t. *Filmstrips:* sound sets, 35t/c; silent sets, 1t/c.
Budget & Expenditures Total library budget $109,000 (FY 7/1/74-7/1/75). No separate AV budget. *Member:* ALA, Conn. Library Assn, SE Conn. Library Assn.

Seymour

P- SEYMOUR PUBLIC LIBRARY, 46 Church St, 06483. *Tel:* (203) 888-3903. *Member:* Film Coop of Conn.

South Windsor

P- SOUTH WINDSOR PUBLIC LIBRARY, 993 Sullivan Ave, 06074. *Tel:* (203) 644-1542. *In Charge:* Wm. Clayton Massey, Library Dir. *AV Staff:* 1 prof. *Film Sel:* faculty/staff recommendations.
   Free-Loan Film Serv *Eligibility:* civic & religious groups, indiv with library cards. *Restrictions:* for indiv, interlibrary loan, only in city; for inst, only in city. Cannot use for fund-raising, transmit electronically. Cannot borrow films from Film Coop of Conn. for classroom use. Available to researchers/scholars for on-site viewing. May not borrow by mail. *Loan Period:* 1 day. *Total Yr Film Loan:* 93. Publish film lists on specific subjects.
   Other Film Serv Obtain film from coop loan system (Film Coop of Conn., Conn. State Library Film Serv). *Equipment:* lend 16mm camera (1), lend 16mm sound projectors (2), lend projection screens (1).
   Other Media Collections *Audio:* disc, 33⅓rpm, 2800t/c. *Filmstrips:* sound, 47t/c.
   Budget & Expenditures Total library budget $33,948 (FY 7/1/74-7/1/75). Total FY film budget $894. *Member:* Conn. Library Assn.

Stamford

P- THE FERGUSON LIBRARY, Film Serv, 96 Broad St, 06901. *Tel:* (203) 325-4354, ext 53, 54, 65. *Film Serv Est:* 1946. *In Charge:* W. G. Smith, Supervisor. *AV Staff:* 5½ (2 prof, 1½ cl, 1½ tech, 2 pages). *Film Sel:* committee preview, staff recommendations, chief film librarian's decision. *Holdings:* animated films 10%, black studies 5%, children's films 25%, feature films 5%, fine arts 5%, general entertainment 30%, golden oldies 10%, sports 10%, women 5%.
   Free-Loan Film Serv *Eligibility:* indiv with library cards. *Restrictions:* for indiv, only in city. Cannot use for fund-raising, transmit electronically. Available to researchers/scholars for on-site viewing. May not borrow by mail. *Loan Period:* 1 day. *Total Yr Film Loan:* 14,768.
   Film Rental Serv *Eligibility:* no restrictions. *Restrictions:* cannot use for fund-raising, transmit electronically, use in classrooms outside Stamford. *Rental Period:* 1 day.
   Film Collection 800t/810p. Approx 75t acquired annually. *Circ:* 16mm, 800t/810p. *Noncirc:* S8mm cartridge, 50t/p. *Pubns:* catalog, every 2 yr ($1); suppl, no set policy. Publish materials pertaining to collection.
   Other Film Serv Rent film from distributors for patrons, obtain film from coop loan system (Conn. Film Circuit, Fairfield County Film Circuit), obtain film from other libraries, film reference serv, film fairs/festivals, library film programs. Permanent viewing facility available free to community. *Equipment:* rent 16mm sound projector (3), rent projection screens (3).
   Other Media Collections *Audio:* disc, 33⅓rpm, 6000t/c; tape, cassette, 2500t/c.
   Budget & Expenditures Total library budget $177,650 (FY 7/1/74-7/1/75). Total FY film budget $14,500. *Member:* AFI, EFLA, FLIC, Conn. Library Assn.
   Video Serv *Est:* 1975. *In Charge:* Geraldine Sydney Ewart, Community Serv Librarian. *Video Staff:* 1 f-t, 1 p-t. *Video Use:* documentation of community/school events, to increase community's library use. Video serv available by appointment. Produce video tapes. Have production studio/space.
   Video Equipment/Facilities *In-House Use Only:* porta-pak (1), ½'', b&w, Sony 8400; editing deck (1), Sony 3650; monitor (2), b&w/col, Sony CVM950U, Panasonic CT911V; lighting (1); microphones (2); tripods (1); audio tape recorders (1). Have portable viewing installations. Provide training in use of equipment to faculty.
   Video Tape Loan/Rental/Sale Serv *Serv Provided:* free loan. *Loan Eligibility:* civic groups. *Restrictions:* for indiv & inst, only in city. Cannot use for fund-raising, duplicate, air without permission. May not borrow by mail.
   Video Collection Maintained by own production, exchange/swap. Use/play ½'' reel to reel. *Sources:* exchange.

Storrs

C- UNIVERSITY OF CONNECTICUT, Film Library, Center for Instructional Media & Technology, Box U-1, 06268. *Tel:* (203) 487-2530. *Film Sel:* faculty/staff recommendations, chief film librarian's decision. *Holdings:* consumer affairs 10%.
   Film Rental Serv *Eligibility:* no restrictions. *Restrictions:* only in U.S. Cannot transmit electronically. *Rental Period:* 5 days. *Total Yr Film Booking:* 17,000.
   Film Collection 5000t/5200p. Approx 300t acquired annually. *Circ:* 16mm, 5000t/5200p. *Pubns:* catalog, every 2 yr; suppl, no set policy. Publish newsletter.
   Other Film Serv Obtain film from coop loan system (CUFU), film reference serv, library film programs. Permanent viewing facility available. *Equipment:* lend 16mm camera, lend 16mm sound projector, lend projection tables & stands, lend projection screens.
   Budget & Expenditures Total library budget $500,000 (FY 7/1/74-7/1/75). Total FY film budget $10,000. *Member:* CUFC.
   Video Serv *Est:* 1974. *In Charge:* James C. Reynolds, Asst Prof of Education. *Video Staff:* 1 p-t. *Video Use:* in-service training, practical video/TV training courses, playback only of professionally produced tapes. Video serv available by appointment. Have production studio/space & separate control room.
   Video Equipment/Facilities *In-House Use Only:* porta-pak (2), ½'', b&w, Sony 3400; recording deck (1), ½'', b&w, Sony 3600; editing deck (1), ½'', b&w, Sony 3650; studio camera (3), b&w, Sony 3200DX; monitor (1), b&w, Sony CVM194; SEG (1), Sony TPPC1; lighting (8); microphones (3); tripods (3); audio tape recorders (1). Have portable viewing installation. Provide training in use of equipment to faculty & students. Have tape duplication serv.
   Video Tape Loan/Rental/Sale Serv *Serv Provided:* free loan. *Loan Eligibility:* staff & students. *Restrictions:* May not borrow by mail.
   Video Collection Maintained by own production. Use/play ½'' reel to reel.
   Cable & CCTV Have CCTV in inst. *Programming Sources:* over-the-air commercial & public broadcasting, tapes produced by inst, tapes produced by community groups & indiv.

Waterford

P- WATERFORD PUBLIC LIBRARY, Eastern Connecticut Film Circuit, 49 Rope Ferry Rd, 06385. *Tel:* (203) 443-0224. *Film Serv Est:* 1968. *In Charge:* Pat Williams, Children's Librarian. *Film Sel:* committee preview. *Holdings:* animated films 20%, children's films 30%, dance 2%, fine arts 20%, women 2%.
   Free-Loan Film Serv *Eligibility:* indiv with library cards, members of Eastern Conn. Film Circuit member libraries.
   Film Rental Serv *Eligibility:* patrons/public. *Restrictions:* only members of Eastern Conn. Film Circuit. Cannot use for fund-raising. *Rental Period:* 1 day. *Total Yr Film Booking:* 1849.
   Film Collection 182t/p. Approx 10-20t acquired annually. *Circ:* 16mm, 160t; 8mm reel, 10t; S8mm reel, 12t. *Pubns:* catalog, annual.
   Other Film Serv Obtain film from coop loan system (Russell Library, Middletown, Conn.; State Library), library film programs. Permanent viewing facility available free to community.
   Other Media Collections *Audio:* disc, 33⅓rpm, 2500t; tape, cassette, 100t. *Filmstrips:* sound sets, 60t/c; silent sets, 30t/c. *Slides:* sets, 5t/c.
   Budget & Expenditures Total library budget $15,000 (9/1/74-7/1/75). Total film budget $4000 (6/1/74-6/1/75). *Member:* ALA, EFLA, Conn. Library Assn.

West Hartford

P- NOAH WEBSTER MEMORIAL LIBRARY, Film Dept, 20 S Main St, 06107. *Tel:* (203) 236-4561, ext 341. *Film Serv Est:* 1957. *In Charge:* Elsie Tetlow, Film Coord. *AV Staff:* 2 (1 prof).

Free-Loan Film Serv *Eligibility:* educational inst, civic & religious groups, indiv with library cards. *Restrictions:* for indiv, only in city. Cannot use for fund-raising, borrow for classroom use. May not borrow by mail. *Loan Period:* 1 day. *Total Yr Film Loan:* 6549.

Film Collection 168t. *Circ:* 16mm, 168t. *Pubns:* catalog, every 3 yr; suppl, no set policy.

Other Film Serv Obtain film from coop loan system (State Library, Conn. Film Circuit).

Other Media Collections *Audio:* disc; tape.

Budget & Expenditures Total library film budget $4200 (FY 7/1/74-7/1/75). *Member:* EFLA, FLIC, Conn. Library Assn.

Westport

P- WESTPORT PUBLIC LIBRARY, Film Serv, Box 31, 06880. *Tel:* (203) 227-8411, ext 29. *Film Serv Est:* 1960. *In Charge:* Joanna Dougherty, Film Librarian. *AV Staff:* 3 (2 prof, 1 cl). *Film Sel:* committee preview, chief film librarian's decision.

Free-Loan Film Serv *Eligibility:* any city resident & anyone who works 20 hours per week in city. *Restrictions:* for indiv, only in city. Cannot transmit electronically, borrow for classroom use. Available to researchers/scholars for on-site viewing. May not borrow by mail. *Loan Period:* 1 day. *Total Yr Film Loan:* 4931.

Film Rental Serv *Eligibility:* no restrictions. *Restrictions:* only in state. Cannot use for fund-raising, transmit electronically. *Rental Period:* 1 day. *Total Yr Film Booking:* 4.

Film Collection 110t/p. Approx 10-25t acquired annually. *Circ:* 16mm, 100t/p; S8mm reel, 10t/p. *Pubns:* catalog, annual; suppl, no set policy. Publish monthly list of films available from Conn. Film Circuit.

Other Film Serv Rent film from distributors for patrons, obtain film from coop loan system (SW Conn. Library System), obtain film from other libraries, film reference serv, library film programs. Permanent viewing facility available. *Equipment:* rent 16mm sound projectors (3), rent projection screens (2).

Other Media Collections *Audio:* disc, 33⅓rpm, 2000c; tape, cassette, 550c.

Budget & Expenditures Total library budget $57,800 (FY (7/1/74-7/1/75). Total FY film budget $6200. *Member:* AFI, ALA, EFLA, FLIC, Conn. Library Assn, Conn. AV Education Assn.

Delaware

Georgetown

C- DELAWARE TECHNICAL & COMMUNITY COLLEGE, Southern Campus Library, Box 610, 19947. *Tel:* (302) 856-5438. *Film Serv Est:* 1971. *In Charge:* Helen Moynihan, Librarian. *AV Staff:* 1 (1 tech). *Film Sel:* committee preview, faculty/staff recommendations.
  Film Collection 50t. *Circ:* 16mm, 25t; 8mm reel, 15t; S8mm reel, 10t; *Pubns:* catalog; suppl.
  Budget & Expenditures Total library budget $7600. No separate AV budget. *Member:* AECT, ALA, Del. Library Assn, Del. Learning Resources Assn.
  Video Serv *Est:* 1973. *In Charge:* Ray Bouchard, AV Tech. *Video Staff:* 1 f-t, 1 tech. *Video Use:* documentation of community/school events, in-service training, instruction (classroom). Produce video tapes.
  Video Equipment/Facilities *In-House Use Only:* portapak (2), b&w, Sony; recording deck (2); playback deck (2); editing deck (1); studio camera (2); monitor (6); SEG (1); lighting; microphones; tripods; audio tape recorders. *Equipment Loan Period:* no set policy. Provide training in use of equipment to instructors.
  Video Tape Loan/Rental/Sale Serv *Serv Provided:* swap with other inst. *Loan Eligibility:* org members, staff & students.
  Video Collection Maintained by rental, own production. Use/play ½" reel to reel, ¾" cassette. *Sources:* community productions. *Tape Sel:* preview, faculty/staff recommendations, published reviews. Tapes organized by subject.
  Cable & CCTV Have CCTV in inst.

Newark

C- UNIVERSITY OF DELAWARE, College of Agricultural Sciences, 19711. *Tel:* (302) 738-2505. *Film Serv Est:* 1960. *In Charge:* Jerry Webb, Agric Editor. *AV Staff:* 3 prof, 2 cl. *Film Sel:* USDA. *Holdings:* agriculture 100%.
  Free-Loan Film Serv *Eligibility:* org members, staff, students enrolled in inst, educational inst, civic groups, & others, such as extension service. *Restrictions:* for indiv & inst, only in state. Cannot use for fund-raising, transmit electronically. May not borrow by mail.
  Film Collection 140t/p. Approx 2t acquired annually. *Circ:* 16mm, 140t/p. *Pubns:* catalog, every 3 yrs; suppl, no set policy.
  Other Film Serv Obtain film from coop loan system (Extension Service). *Equipment:* lend 16mm camera (1), 16mm sound projector (2), projection tables & stands (3), projection screens (5).

C- UNIVERSITY OF DELAWARE, Instructional Resources Center, 19711. *Tel:* (302) 738-2685. *Film Serv Est:* 1966. *In Charge:* Don Nelson, Dir. *AV Staff:* 21 (9 prof, 4 cl, 8 tech). *Film Sel:* faculty/staff recommendations.
  Free-Loan Film Serv *Eligibility:* staff. *Restrictions:* campus use only. May not borrow by mail. *Loan Period:* 3 days. *Total Yr Film Loan:* 2506.

Film Rental Serv *Eligibility:* no restrictions. *Restrictions:* only in state. *Rental Period:* 3 days. *Total Yr Film Booking:* 727. Sell films.
  Film Collection 1800t/p. Approx 25-30t acquired annually. *Circ:* 16mm, 1800t/p. *Pubns:* catalog, every 5 yrs ($2); suppl, no set policy.
  Other Film Serv Rent film from distributors for patrons, film reference serv. Permanent viewing facility. *Equipment:* lend/rent S8mm camera (6), 16mm camera (6), 16mm sound projector (230), 8mm cartridge projector (10), 8mm reel projector (10), S8mm cartridge projector (15), S8mm reel projector (15), projection tables & stands (50), projection screens (20).
  Budget & Expenditures Total library budget $8000 (FY 7/1/74-7/1/75). Total FY film budget $8000. *Member:* AECT, EFLA.
  Video Serv *Video Staff:* 1 f-t, 3 tech. *Video Use:* classroom instruction. Video serv available by appointment. Produce video tapes. Have production studio/space & separate control room.
  Video Equipment/Facilities *In-House Use Only:* portapak (1), cassette col, Sony DXC 1600, VO 3800; recording/playback deck (5), ½", ¾", 1" col, Sony 2850, IVC 870C, AV 8650; editing deck (2), ½", ¾" col, RM 400, VO 1800; studio camera (7), b&w/col, Plumbicon, Vidicon, Gates TE 201, IVC 92B, Sarkes Tarzian 2700L. Have permanent viewing installation. *Equipment Loan Period:* academic yr. Provide training in use of equipment to faculty & students.
  Video Tape Loan/Rental/Sale Serv *Serv Provided:* free loan, rental, sale. *Loan/Rental Eligibility:* staff, students enrolled in inst, faculty. *Restrictions:* for indiv, on campus; for inst, only in state. Cannot use for fund-raising, duplicate, air without permission. May borrow by mail. *Total Yr Tape Loan:* 6.
  Video Collection Maintained by purchase, own production. Use/play ½", 1" reel to reel, ¾" cassette. *Sources:* other universities, Great Plains ITU Library. *Collection, Color:* ¾" cassette, 14t/1c. *Other Video Serv:* production courses.
  Cable & CCTV Receive serv of cable TV system. Produce programs for cablecasting. Run cable programs for special audiences. Have advisory role in cable system operation. Have CCTV in inst, with 20 monitors. *Programming Sources:* tapes produced by inst.

Wilmington

P- WILMINGTON INSTITUTE LIBRARY, AV Serv, 10th and Market Sts, 19801. *Tel:* (302) 656-3131 ext 22. *Film Serv Est:* 1975. *In Charge:* David H. Burdash, Acting Dir. *AV Staff:* 1½ (½ prof, 1 tech). *Film Sel:* committee preview.
  Free-Loan Film Serv *Eligibility:* registered indiv. *Restrictions:* for indiv, only in state. Cannot use for fund-raising, charge admission. Available to researchers/scholars for on-site viewing. May not borrow by mail.
  Film Collection 950t/p. *Circ:* 16mm, 950t/p. *Pubns:* catalog, as needed ($1); suppl, no set policy.
  Other Film Serv Library film programs. *Member:* Del. Library Assn.

District of Columbia

Washington

S- AMERICAN SOCIETY OF ASSOCIATION EXECUTIVES, Information Central, 1101 16 St, NW, 20036. *Tel:* (202) 659-3333. *Film Serv Est:* 1965. *In Charge:* Elissa Matulis Myers, Dir Information Central. *AV Staff:* 2 (1 prof, 1 cl).
   Film Rental Serv *Eligibility:* no restrictions. *Restrictions:* none. *Rental Period:* varies. Produce films. Produce cassettes, slide-tape presentations.
   Film Collection 10t/30p. *Pubns:* catalog, annual. Publish promotional material.
   Other Film Serv Film reference serv.
   Other Media Collections *Audio:* tape, cassette, 150t. *Slides:* sets, 10t/11c.

S- FARM FILM FOUNDATION, 1425 H St, NW 20005. *Tel:* (202) 628-1321. *Film Serv Est:* 1946. *In Charge:* Edith T. Bennett, Exec VP. *AV Staff:* 8 (2 cl, 2 tech). *Holdings:* agriculture 100%.
   Free-Loan Film Serv *Eligibility:* educational inst, civic groups, religious groups, prof groups, such as agricultural orgs. *Restrictions:* none. Cannot use for fund-raising, transmit electronically. Available to researchers/scholars for on-site viewing. May borrow by mail. *Loan Period:* 3 days. *Total Yr Film Loan:* 22,159.
   Film Collection 71t/2075p. Approx 4-6t acquired annually. *Circ:* 16mm, 71t/2075p. *Pubns:* catalog, annual; suppl, no set policy. Publish flyers.
   Other Film Serv Film fairs/festivals. *Member:* AFI, University Film Assn, Wash DC Film Council.

S- FOLGER SHAKESPEARE LIBRARY, Film Archive, 201 E Capitol St SE, 20003. *Tel:* (202) 546-4800, ext 27. *Film Serv Est:* 1975. *In Charge:* Dr Phillip Knachel, Assoc Dir. *AV Staff:* 7 (3 prof, 3 cl, 1 tech). *Film Sel:* chief film librarian's decision. *Holdings:* Shakespeare 100%.
   Film Collection *Noncirc:* 16mm, 20t/p.
   Other Film Serv Film reference serv, film fairs/festivals. Permanent viewing facility.
   Other Media Collections *Slides:* sets, 10t/c.
   Budget & Expenditures Total FY film budget $26,000 (FY 7/1/75-7/1/76). *Member:* AFI, American Assn of Museums, Ind Research Library Assn.

C- HOWARD UNIVERSITY, Center for Learning Systems, Box 472 Howard University, 20059. *Tel:* (202) 636-6739, ext 6739. *Film Serv Est:* 1965. *In Charge:* Dr J. Edwin Foster, Dir. *AV Staff:* 7 (3 prof, 1 cl, 3 tech). *Film Sel:* faculty/staff recommendations. *Holdings:* black studies 5%, science 20%, social sciences 65%, teacher education 10%.
   Free-Loan Film Serv *Eligibility:* staff & students. *Restrictions:* campus use only. Cannot borrow for classroom use. May not borrow by mail. *Loan Period:* 1 day. *Total Yr Film Loan:* 100.
   Film Collection 300t/p. Approx 10t acquired annually. *Circ:* 16mm, 300t/p. *Pubns:* catalog, every 3 yrs. *Equipment:* lend 16mm sound projector (6), 8mm cartridge projector (2), projection tables & stands (10), projection screens (4).
   Budget & Expenditures Total library budget $6000 (FY 7/1/74-7/1/75). Total FY film budget $1000. *Member:* AECT.
   Video Serv *Est:* 1968. *Video Staff:* 4 f-t, 7 p-t, 7 tech. *Video Use:* documentation of community/school events, practical video/TV training courses. Video serv available on demand. Produce video tapes.
   Video Equipment/Facilities *In-House Use Only:* recording deck (1), 1" col, Sony; editing deck (1), b&w; monitor (8),

b&w, Setchell-Carl. *For Loan:* portapak (2), ½" b&w, Sony; microphones (5); tripods (2); audio tape recorders (10). *Equipment Loan Period:* no set policy. Provide training in use of equipment to students.
   Video Tape Loan/Rental/Sale Serv *Serv Provided:* free loan. *Loan Eligibility:* staff & students. *Restrictions:* for indiv, on campus. May not borrow by mail.
   Video Collection Use/play ½", 1" reel to reel. *Sources:* own production. *Tape Sel:* faculty/staff recommendations. *Special Collections:* in-house training tapes. Tapes organized by subject.
   Cable & CCTV Have CCTV in inst, with 8 monitors.

S- INSTITUTE FOR CROSS-CULTURAL RESEARCH, 4000 Albemarle St, NW, 20016. *Tel:* (202) 362-6668. *Film Serv Est:* 1965. *In Charge:* Theodore L Stoddard, Dir. *AV Staff:* 2 (1 prof, 1 cl). *Holdings:* social sciences 100%.
   Other Film Serv Obtain film from other libraries, library film programs. Permanent viewing facility. *Member:* Committee on Visual Anthropology.

P- THE LIBRARY OF CONGRESS, Motion Picture Section, Reference Dept, Prints & Photographs Div, 20540. *Tel:* (202) 426-5000. *Film Serv Est:* 1894. *In Charge:* Alan M. Fern, Chief, Prints & Photographs Div.
   Holdings *Copyright Deposit:* Films have been selected from copyright deposits since 1942—feature films & short subjects for entertainment; educational, scientific, religious, & business-sponsored films; & TV documentary, educational, & entertainment programs. *Historic Collections:* Motion pictures produced before 1915—3000 titles in the paper print collection, more than 350 in the George Kleine collection, 100 titles (some later than 1915) in the Mary Pickford collection, & several hundred titles in the American Film Institute collection. Other early films are in the collections of Louise Ernst, John Allen, & Gatewood Dunstan, among others. Viewing copies exist for most of the titles. *Major Studio Deposits:* Original motion picture preprint materials (negatives, master positives & work prints) from Columbia Pictures Corporation, Hal Roach Studios, Monogram Pictures, Paramount Pictures, RKO Radio Pictures, United Artists Corporation, & Warner Brothers. Titles include short subjects & features. Viewing copies exist for only a small portion of the titles. *Films Seized during World War II:* More than 5000 feature films, short subjects, documentaries, newsreels & educational films made in Nazi Germany & several hundred films made in Japan & Italy. Viewing copies available for many of the titles. *U.S. Government-Produced Films:* Limited collection; The National Archives & Records Service in Washington, D.C., is official repository for these films, as well as other Federal records.
   Free-Loan Film Serv The Motion Picture Section maintains the Library's film collections for scholarly study & research. Public projection, preview & loan services are not available. The Section Staff answers written & telephone inquiries about the holdings & makes appointments for the use of the reference facilities by individual scholars. Inquiries should be addressed to: Motion Picture Section, Library of Congress, Washington, D.C. 20540. The Section is open from 8:30 A.M. to 4:30 P.M. Monday through Friday & is located in the Annex Bldg, Rm 1046. The viewing facilities, which consist of several 16mm & 35mm viewing machines, may be used free of charge by serious researchers only; viewing times must be scheduled in advance. The facilities may not be used by high school students; undergraduate college students must provide a letter from their professor endorsing their project.

Washington (cont'd)

Film Collection Over 60,000 titles, or more than 200,000 reels. More than a thousand titles, including TV films & video tapes, are added each year through copyright deposit, purchase, gift, or exchange. Also include more than 300,000 stills. *Pubns:* at present there is no printed catalog describing the library's collection. Publishes cataloging information for films & related materials which are of general interest to libraries, schools, & individuals; the films are not necessarily added to the Library's collections. The data, produced by the Processing Department, are available in the form of the printed catalog card; a book catalog, *Library of Congress Catalog—Films and Other Materials for Projection,* issued quarterly & in annual cumulation, & appearing as volumes in the quinquennial cumulation of the Library's *National Union Catalog;* and as computer tapes produced monthly in a machine-readable cataloging (MARC) format. For sale by the Card Division, Library of Congress, Bldg 159, Navy Yard Annex, Washington, D.C. 20541. Prepares a semiannual *Catalog of Copyright Entries: Motion Pictures & Filmstrips* and five cumulative catalogs entitled *Motion Pictures,* which together cover copyright registrations for films for the years 1894-1969. Both for sale by the Superintendent of Documents, U.S. Government Printing Office, Washington, D.C. 20402.

Other Film Serv Reading room with extensive card file describing Library's motion picture holdings. Files include a shelflist, a dictionary catalog, a nitrate film file, a directors file, & chronological & production company files for silent films. Basic collection of reference books on cinema subjects, film distribution catalogs, yearbooks, reviews, & trade periodicals. Descriptive materials (pressbooks, plot synopses, continuities, dialogue scripts, stills, & posters) for motion pictures registered for copyright after 1912. Copies of film footage not restricted by copyright, by provisions of gift or transfer, or by physical condition may be ordered through the Section. The requester is responsible for a search, either in person or by mail, of Copyright Office records to determine the copyright status of specific works. Inquiries should be directed to: Register of Copyrights, Library of Congress, Washington, D.C. 20559. The Motion Picture Section creates & maintains a catalog of all films added to the Library's collections. A pilot project is under way to automate the cataloging information and eventually to replace the various card files maintained by the Section with a single data base, from which bibliographic information could be retrieved in a variety of ways.

Member International Federation of Film Archives (FIAF).

A- **MUSEUM OF AFRICAN ART,** Eliot Elisofon Archives, 316-18 A St, NE, 20002. *Tel:* (202) 546-7977. *Film Serv Est:* 1973. *In Charge:* Frederick Lamp, Archivist. *AV Staff:* 3. *Film Sel:* chief film librarian's decision. *Holdings:* dance 40%, fine arts 40%, social sciences 20%.

Film Rental Serv *Eligibility:* no restrictions. *Rental Period:* 14 days. Sell films. Produce films. Produce slide packages with cassette tapes.

Film Collection 45t/65p. Approx 5t acquired annually. *Circ:* 16mm, 1t/20p. *Noncirc:* 16mm, 44t/p.

Other Film Serv Film fairs/festivals. Permanent viewing facility available for rent to community. *Equipment:* 16mm sound projector (1), projection tables & stands (2), projection screens (1).

Other Media Collections *Audio:* disc, 33⅓rpm, 45t. *Filmstrips:* silent, 7t. *Slides:* single, 50,000c.

Budget & Expenditures No separate budget.

P- **NATIONAL AUDIOVISUAL CENTER (GSA),** 20409. *Tel:* (301) 763-7420. *Film Serv Est:* 1968. *In Charge:* J. McLean, Dir. *AV Staff:* 60 (15 prof, 20 cl, 25 tech). *Film Sel:* Federal productions. *Holdings:* science 80%, training films 20%.

Free-Loan Film Serv *Eligibility:* general public. *Restrictions:* only in U.S. Cannot use for fund-raising. *Loan Period:* 3 days.

Film Rental Serv *Eligibility:* public. *Restrictions:* only in U.S. Cannot use for fund-raising. *Rental Period:* 3 days. Sell films.

Film Collection 10,000t. Approx 500t acquired annually. *Pubns:* catalog, every 3 yrs; suppl, no set policy. Publish bibliographies.

Other Film Serv Film reference serv. *Member:* all Federal agencies.

P- **NATIONAL GALLERY OF ART,** Extension Service, Sixth St at Constitution Ave, 20565. *Tel:* (202) 737-4215, ext 292. *Film Serv Est:* 1962. *In Charge:* Frank Figgins, Mgr. *AV Staff:* 9 (1 prof, 4 cl, 4 tech). *Film Sel:* staff recommendations, films produced by & of the Gallery. *Holdings:* fine arts 100%.

Free-Loan Film Serv *Eligibility:* staff & students, educational inst, civic groups, religious groups, prof groups, open eligibility. *Restrictions:* for indiv, none; for inst, none. Cannot transmit electronically (special permission can be obtained for some selections). Available to researchers/scholars for on-site viewing. May borrow by mail. *Loan Period:* 3 days. *Total Yr Film Loan:* 4360.

Film Collection 32t/1725 p. Approx 5t acquired annually. *Circ:* 16mm, 32t/1725p. *Pubns:* catalog, annual; suppl, no set policy. Publish monthly calendar of events listing new programs.

Other Film Serv Film reference serv, slide lectures available—same program as films. Permanent viewing facility available.

Other Media Collections *Filmstrips:* silent sets, 2t/200c. *Slides:* sets, 43t/3675c.

Budget & Expenditures Total library budget $45,000 (FY 7/1/75-7/1/76). No separate AV budget.

S- **NATIONAL TRUST FOR HISTORIC PRESERVATION,** 740 Jackson Place NW, 20006. *Tel:* (202) 638-5200. *In Charge:* Cathie Wardell, Iconographer. *Film Sel:* committee preview.

Free-Loan Film Serv *Eligibility:* org members. *Restrictions:* only in U.S. & Canada. May borrow by mail. *Loan Period:* 5 days.

Film Rental Serv *Eligibility:* no restrictions, only in U.S. & Canada. *Rental Period:* 5 days. Produce films.

Film Collection 25t/p. Approx 2-3t acquired annually. *Circ:* 16mm, 25t. *Pubns:* catalog, as needed.

Other Film Serv Obtain film from National Collegiate Film & Video Competition. Permanent viewing facility available for rent to community. *Member:* EFLA.

S- **POPULATION REFERENCE BUREAU, INC.,** Population Education Film Library, 1754 N St NW, 20036. *Tel:* (202) 638-5500. *Film Serv Est:* 1975. *In Charge:* Judith R. Seltzer, Dir Population Educ. *AV Staff:* ½. *Film Sel:* staff recommendations. *Holdings:* population & environmental education 100%.

Film Rental Serv *Eligibility:* no restrictions. *Rental Period:* 7 days.

Film Collection 13t/p. *Circ:* 16mm, 13t/p. Publish film list.

Budget & Expenditures No separate budget.

S- **WASHINGTON COMMUNITY VIDEO CENTER,** Box 21068, 20009. *Tel:* (202) 462-6700. *Video Serv Est:* 1972. *In Charge:* Ray Popkin, Vickie Costello, Co-dirs. *Video Staff:* 6 f-t. *Video Use:* documentation of community/school events, community video access, in-service training, practical video/TV training courses, as art form. Video serv available by appointment. Produce video tapes. Have production studio/space & separate control room.

Video Equipment/Facilities *In-House Use Only:* portapak (3), ½" b&w, Panasonic 3082; recording deck (2), ½" b&w/col, Sony 8600, Panasonic 3120; editing deck (2), col, Panasonic 3130; studio camera (2), b&w, Panasonic 360; moni-

Washington (cont'd)

tor (4); SEG (1), Panasonic 545P; keyer (1); lighting (5); microphones (5); tripods (4). *For Loan:* portapak (3), ½″ b&w, Panasonic 3082; recording deck (2), ½″ b&w/col, Sony 8600, Panasonic 3120; editing deck (2), col, Panasonic 3130; studio camera (2), b&w, Panasonic 360; monitor (4); SEG (1), Panasonic 545P; keyer (1); lighting (5); microphones (5); tripods (4). Have portable viewing installation. *Equipment Loan Period:* no set policy. Provide training in use of equipment. Have tape duplication serv.

Video Tape Loan/Rental/Sale Serv   *Serv Provided:* free loan, swap with other inst, rental, sale. *Loan/Rental Eligibility:* org members, educational inst, civic groups, religious groups. *Restrictions:* none. May borrow by mail.

Video Collection   Maintained by own production, exchange/swap. Use/play ½″ reel to reel. *Sources:* galleries, community productions, exchange. *Tape Sel:* producer contact. *Collection, Color:* ½″ reel, 10t; ¾″ cassette, 3t. *Collection, B&W:* ½″ reel, 100t. *Other Video Serv:* programming, reference serv, taping of other media, production workshops. *Pubns:* Televisions magazine.

Cable & CCTV   Inform public about cable system serv & facilities.

Florida

Avon Park

S- DEPT OF HEALTH & REHABILITATION SERVS, STATE OF FLORIDA, Florida Alcoholism Treatment Center, 100 W College Dr, 33825. *Tel:* (813) 453-3151, ext 115, 193. *Film Serv Est:* 1960. *In Charge:* Joe G. Marguart, Dir of Continuing Education. *AV Staff:* 2½ (1 prof, 1 cl, ½ tech). *Film Sel:* committee preview, staff recommendations. *Holdings:* alcohol abuse 100%.

Free-Loan Film Serv *Eligibility:* educational inst, & others, such as community alcohol programs. *Restrictions:* for inst, only in state. Cannot use for fund-raising. Available to researchers/scholars for on-site viewing. May borrow by mail. *Loan Period:* 7 days. *Total Yr Film Loan:* 1000.

Film Collection 200t/350p. Approx 20t acquired annually. *Circ:* 16mm, 200t/350p. *Pubns:* catalog, as needed.

Other Film Serv Permanent viewing facility. *Equipment:* lend 16mm camera (6), projection screens (6).

Budget & Expenditures Total library budget $20,000 (FY 7/1/74-7/1/75). Total FY film budget $10,000.

Daytona Beach

P- VOLUSIA COUNTY PUBLIC LIBRARIES, City Island, 32014. *Tel:* (904) 252-8374. *Film Serv Est:* 1967. *In Charge:* James Bozeman, AV Librarian. *AV Staff:* 2 (1 prof, 1 cl). *Film Sel:* committee preview, staff recommendations, chief film librarian's decision, published reviews.

Free-Loan Film Serv *Eligibility:* indiv with library cards. *Restrictions:* only in Volusia County. Cannot use for fund-raising, transmit electronically, borrow for classroom use. *Loan Period:* 1 day. *Total Yr Film Loan:* 5358.

Film Collection 503t/p. Approx 30t acquired annually. *Circ:* 16mm, 390t/p; S8mm reel, 113t/p. *Pubns:* catalog, annual; suppl, no set policy.

Other Film Serv Rent film from distributors for patrons, obtain film from other libraries, film reference serv, library film programs. *Equipment:* lend 16mm sound projector (10), 8mm reel projector (3), S8mm reel projector (3), projection screens (12), overhead projector, slide projector, opaque projector, strip projector.

Other Media Collections *Audio:* tape, cassette, 200t/1000c. *Filmstrips:* sound, 52t; silent, 58t. *Slides:* single, 1149t.

Budget & Expenditures Total library budget $171,000 (FY 10/1/74-10/1/75). *Member:* ALA, FLIC, Fla. Library Assn.

Fort Lauderdale

C- BROWARD COMMUNITY COLLEGE, 3501 SW Davie Rd, 33314. *Tel:* (305) 581-8700, ext 293. *Film Serv Est:* 1968. *In Charge:* I. S. Call, Dir, Learning Resources. *AV Staff:* 13 (1 prof, 5 cl, 7 tech). *Film Sel:* committee preview, faculty/ staff recommendations. *Holdings:* English literature, fine arts 25%, science 25%, social sciences 25%.

Free-Loan Film Serv *Eligibility:* staff & students, educational inst, civic groups, religious groups. *Restrictions:* for inst, only in Broward County. Cannot use for fund-raising, transmit electronically. Available to researchers/scholars for on-site viewing. May borrow by mail. *Loan Period:* 7 days. *Total Yr Film Loan:* 6150, internal use only.

Film Collection 250t/p. Approx 10-15t acquired annually. *Pubns:* catalog, as needed; suppl, in yr catalog not published.

Other Film Serv Rent film from distributors for patrons. Permanent viewing facility. *Equipment:* lend for internal use only 16mm sound projector (50-60), S8mm reel projector (3), projection tables & stands (50-60), projection screens (50-60).

Other Media Collections *Audio:* disc, 33⅓rpm, 250c; tape, cassette, 1500c. *Filmstrips:* silent, 300c; sound sets, 200c.

Budget & Expenditures Total FY film budget $10,000 (FY 7/1/75-7/1/76). *Member:* AECT.

Video Serv *Video Staff:* 3 f-t, 1 tech. *Video Use:* documentation of community/school events, in-service training, as educational suppls. Video serv available on demand. Produce video tapes. Have production studio/space & separate control room.

Video Equipment/Facilities *In-House Use Only:* portapak (5), ½" col, Sony; recording deck (14), col, Sony/JVC; editing deck (2), col, Sony 2850; studio camera (2), col, Hitachi; SEG (1), Panasonic; lighting. *For Loan:* portapak (5), ½" col, Sony; audio tape recorders (200-300). Have permanent installation. *Equipment Loan Period:* provide training in use of equipment to students. Have tape duplication serv.

Video Tape Loan/Rental/Sale Serv *Serv Provided:* swap with other inst. *Loan Eligibility:* org members, staff & students, local educational inst, civic groups. *Restrictions:* for inst, only in southern Florida. Cannot use for fund-raising, duplicate, air without permission. May not borrow by mail. *Total Yr Tape Loan:* limited.

Video Collection Maintained by purchase, rental, own production, exchange/swap. Use/play ½", 1" reel to reel, ¾" cassette. *Sources:* commercial distributors. *Tape Sel:* preview, faculty/staff recommendations. Tapes organized by subject. *Collection, Color:* ½" reel, 50-100t/c; 1" reel, 100t/c; ¾" cassette, 100t/c. *Other Video Serv:* programming.

Cable & CCTV Have CCTV in inst, with 200 monitors. *Programming Sources:* over-the-air commercial & public broadcasting, tapes produced by inst, tapes produced professionally.

Gainesville

C- UNIVERSITY OF FLORIDA, Institute of Food and Agricultural Sciences, GO22 McCarty Hall, 32611. *Tel:* (904) 392-1771. *Film Sel:* faculty/staff recommendations. *Holdings:* agriculture 100%.

Free-Loan Film Serv *Eligibility:* prof groups, such as county agents, & others. *Restrictions:* for indiv & inst, only in state. Available to researchers/scholars for on-site viewing. May borrow by mail. *Loan Period:* 14 days. *Total Yr Film Loan:* 3000. Sell films. Produce films. Produce slides, tapes.

Film Collection 350t/400p. Approx 10-20t acquired annually. *Circ:* 16mm, 350t/400p. *Pubns:* catalog, every 3 yrs; suppl, no set policy. Publish flyers.

Other Film Serv *Equipment:* lend 16mm sound projector (8), S8mm cartridge projector (2), projection tables & stands (4), lend/rent projection screens (6).

Video Serv *Est:* 1975. *In Charge:* John W. Thorne, Jr (temporary). *Video Staff:* 1 f-t, 1 p-t. *Video Use:* in-service training. Video serv available by appointment. Produce video tapes. Have production studio/space.

Video Equipment/Facilities *In-House Use Only:* recording deck (1), ¾" reel col, Sony CV440; editing deck (1), ½" reel col, Concord; studio camera (1), col, Panasonic WV2100P; lighting (10); microphones (2). *For Loan:* portapak (1), ½" reel col, Sony AV-8400S; playback deck (2), ½" reel col, Sony VO-1800; monitor (2), 19" col, Panasonic; tripods (3); audio tape recorders (3). Have portable viewing installation. *Equipment Loan Period:* no set policy. Have tape duplication serv.

Video Tape Loan/Rental/Sale Serv *Serv Provided:* free loan. *Loan Eligibility:* staff. *Restrictions:* for indiv, only state staff; for inst, only in state. May borrow by mail. *Loan Period:* 21 days. *Total Yr Tape Loan:* 25.

Video Collection Maintained by own production. Use/ play ½" reel to reel, ½" cartridge, ¾" cartridge, ¾" cassette. *Sources:* own production only. Tapes organized by subject. *Collection, Color:* ½" reel, 15t/8c; 2" reel, 6t; ½" cartridge, 20t/6c; ¾" cassette, 21t/10c.

Cable & CCTV Have CCTV in inst, with monitors. *Programming Sources:* over-the-air commercial & public broadcasting.

Leesburg

C- LAKE-SUMTER COMMUNITY COLLEGE, Learning Resources Center, 32748. *Tel:* (904) 787-3747, ext 54. *Video Serv Est:* 1973. *In Charge:* W. Douglas Trabert, Coord, Inst Resources. *Video Staff:* 1 f-t, 2 p-t, 5 tech. *Video Use:* documentation of community/school events, playback only of professionally produced tapes, classroom instruction. Video serv available on demand.

Video Equipment/Facilities *In-House Use Only:* recording deck (2), ½″, ¾″ col, Panasonic; playback deck (4), ½″, ¾″ col, Panasonic; studio camera (2), b&w, Panasonic; monitor (4); keyer (1); additional camera lenses (1); microphones (7); tripods (3); audio tape recorders (16). Have permanent viewing installation. Provide training in use of equipment to student technicians.

Video Tape Loan/Rental/Sale Serv *Serv Provided:* swap with other inst.

Video Collection Maintained by purchase, rental, own production, exchange/swap. Use/play ½″ cartridge, ¾″ cassette. *Sources:* commercial distributors. *Tape Sel:* preview, faculty/staff recommendations. *Special Collections:* acquire for TV classes. *Collection, Color:* ½″ cartridge, 90t/c; ¾″ cassette, 40t/c. *Other Video Serv:* programming.

Marianna

C- CHIPOLA JR. COLLEGE, Learning Resources Center, 32446. *Tel:* (904) 482-4935, ext 138. *Film Serv Est:* 1962. *In Charge:* W. H. Stabler, Dir of L.R.C. *AV Staff:* 3 (1 prof, 1 cl, 1 tech). *Film Sel:* faculty/staff recommendations.

Free-Loan Film Serv *Eligibility:* org members, staff, students enrolled in inst, staff & students, educational inst, civic groups, religious groups, indiv with library cards, prof groups, such as forestry, medical. *Restrictions:* for indiv, only in city; for inst, only in County. Cannot use for fund-raising, transmit electronically. Available to researchers/scholars for on-site viewing. May not borrow by mail. *Loan Period:* 3 days. *Total Yr Film Loan:* 146.

Film Collection 279t/p. *Circ:* 16mm, 226t/p; 8mm reel, 26t/p; 8mm cartridge, 27t/p. *Pubns:* catalog, every 2 yrs.

Other Film Serv Rent film from distributors for patrons. Permanent viewing facility available for rent to community. *Equipment:* S8mm camera (2), 16mm sound projector (16), 8mm cartridge projector (6), 8mm reel projector (2), projection tables & stands (21), projection screens (2).

Other Media Collections *Audio:* disc, 33⅓ rpm, 1194t/c; tape, cassette, 800t/c; tape, reel, 100t/c. *Filmstrips:* sound, 299t/c; silent, 875t/c. *Slides:* single, 1025t/c.

Budget & Expenditures Total FY film budget $1000 (FY 7/1/74-7/1/75). *Member:* Fla. Assoc for Media in Educ.

Video Serv *Est:* 1970. *Video Staff:* 1 f-t, 1 p-t, 1 tech. *Video Use:* documentation of community/school events, playback only of professionally produced tapes. Video serv available on demand. Produce video tapes. Have production studio/space & separate control room.

Video Equipment/Facilities *In-House Use Only:* portapak (1), ½″ b&w, Riker; recording deck (2), ½″ b&w, Panasonic NV3020; editing deck (1), ½″ b&w, Panasonic NV3020; studio camera (2), ½″ b&w, Sony AVC 3210; monitor (19), b&w, GE; additional camera lenses (1); lighting; microphones (3); tripods (2); audio tape recorders (2). Have permanent viewing installation. Provide training in use of equipment to students.

Video Tape Loan/Rental/Sale Serv *Serv Provided:* free loan. *Loan Eligibility:* org members, staff, students enrolled in inst. *Restrictions:* for campus use only. Cannot use for fund-raising, duplicate, air without permission. May not borrow by mail. *Loan Period:* 1 day. *Total Yr Tape Loan:* 38.

Video Collection Maintained by purchase, rental, own production. Use/play ½″ reel to reel. *Member:* Fla. State Dept of Educ, Instructional TV Section. *Tape Sel:* preview, faculty/staff recommendations, catalogs. Tapes organized by title. *Collection, B&W:* ½″ reel, 10t/c.

Cable & CCTV Receive serv of cable TV system. Have CCTV in inst, with 19 monitors. *Programming Sources:* over-the-air commercial & public broadcasting, tapes produced by inst, tapes produced professionally.

Miami

C- INTERCOLLEGIATE VIDEO CLEARING HOUSE, Drawer 33000 R, 33133. *Video Serv Est:* 1974. *In Charge:* Dr. Barry J. Hersker, Dir. *Video Staff:* 5 p-t, 25 tech. *Video Use:* documentation of community/school events, to increase community's library use, in-service training. Produce video tapes. Have production studio/space & separate control room. Have tape duplication serv at Video City, Inc., North Miami.

Video Tape Loan/Rental/Sale Serv *Serv Provided:* swap with other inst, sale. *Restrictions:* cannot duplicate.

Video Collection Maintained by own production, exchange/swap. Use/play ¾″ cassette. *Sources:* commercial distributors, universities, government. *Tape Sel:* preview. *Special Collections:* college level educ. Tapes organized by subject. *Collection, Color:* ¾″ cassette, 55t/160c. *Collection, B&W:* 20t/60c. *Pubns:* publish materials on video. Publish newsletter & lists.

Cable & CCTV Have CCTV in inst, with 400 monitors. *Programming Sources:* tapes produced by inst.

P- MIAMI-DADE PUBLIC LIBRARY, 1 Biscayne Blvd, 33132. *Tel:* (305) 579-5001. *Film Serv Est:* 1954. *In Charge:* Michel Anguilano, Art, Music, AV Librarian. *AV Staff:* 3 (1 prof, 1 cl, 1 tech). *Film Sel:* committee preview, staff recommendations, chief film librarian's decision, published reviews.

Free-Loan Film Serv *Eligibility:* organizations of 20 or more members. *Restrictions:* only in Dade County. Cannot use for fund-raising, transmit electronically. May not borrow by mail. *Loan Period:* 3 days. *Total Yr Film Loan:* 9392.

Film Collection 1485t/2325p. *Circ:* 16mm, 1485t/2325p; 8mm reel, 138t/p. *Pubns:* catalog, every 2 yrs. Publish special subject lists.

Other Film Serv Permanent viewing facility.

Other Media Collections *Audio:* disc, 33⅓rpm, 25,000t. *Filmstrips:* silent, 260t.

Budget & Expenditures Total library budget $2,271,000 (FY 10/1/74-10/1/75). Total FY film budget $69,841. *Member:* ALA, EFLA, Fla. Library Assn.

Ocala

C- CENTRAL FLORIDA COMMUNITY COLLEGE, Box 1388, 32670. *Tel:* (904) 237-2111, ext 76-78.

Other Film Serv Rent film from distributors for patrons, obtain film from other libraries. *Equipment:* lend S8mm camera (1), 16mm sound projector (1), S8mm reel projector (1), projection screens (1).

Other Media Collections *Audio:* disc, 33⅓rpm, 2339t; tape, cassette, 399t; tape, reel, 235t. *Filmstrips:* sound, 324c; silent, 638c; sound sets, 300c. *Slides:* single, 9796c; sets, 40c.

Budget & Expenditures Total library budget $47,712 (FY 7/1/74-7/1/75). Total FY film budget $6106. *Member:* ALA, Fla. Library Assn.

Panama City

P- NORTHWEST REGIONAL LIBRARY SYSTEM, Bay County Public Library, 25 W Government St, 32401. *Tel:* (904) 785-3457. *In Charge:* Sarah Howell, Program Coord. *AV Staff:* ⅔ (⅓ prof, ⅓ cl).

Free-Loan Film Serv *Eligibility:* civic groups, religious groups, indiv with library cards, prof groups, such as ABE

Panama City (cont'd)
Centers, Art Assn. *Restrictions:* for indiv & inst, only in region. Cannot use for fund-raising, transmit electronically, borrow for classroom use. Available to researchers/scholars for on-site viewing. May not borrow by mail. *Loan Period:* 1 day. *Total Yr Film Loan:* 251.

Film Collection 57t/p. *Circ:* 16mm, 15t/p; 8mm reel, 42 t/p.

Other Film Serv Rent film from distributors for patrons, obtain film from free film sources, library film programs. Permanent viewing facility available to community. *Equipment:* lend 16mm sound projector (6), 8mm & S8mm cartridge projectors (5), projection screens (2).

Other Media Collections *Audio:* disc, 33⅓rpm, 2000t/c; tape, cassette, 364t/c. *Filmstrips:* sound sets, 5t/c.

Budget & Expenditures Total library budget $57,150. No separate AV budget. *Member:* ALA, Fla. Library Assn.

Cable & CCTV Receive serv of cable TV system.

Pensacola

P- WEST FLORIDA REGIONAL LIBRARY SYSTEM, HQS, Pensacola Public Library, 200 W Gregory St, 32504. *Tel:* (904) 438-5479. *Film Serv Est:* 1965. *In Charge:* Elaine Goley, Coord AV Servs. *AV Staff:* 2 (1 prof, 1 tech). *Film Sel:* chief film librarian's decision. *Holdings:* black studies 20%, children's films 40%.

Free-Loan Film Serv *Eligibility:* indiv with library cards. *Restrictions:* for indiv, only in Escambia & Santa Rosa Counties. Cannot use for fund-raising, transmit electronically. Available to researchers/scholars for on-site viewing. May not borrow by mail. *Loan Period:* 2 days. *Total Yr Film Loan:* 3000. Produce films for library use only.

Film Collection 100t/450p. Approx 5t acquired annually. *Circ:* 16mm, 100t/p; 8mm reel, 150t/350p. *Noncirc:* S8mm reel, S8mm cartridge, 1t/p. *Pubns:* catalog, annual; suppl, no set policy. Publish 8mm titles list.

Other Film Serv Film reference serv, library film programs. *Equipment:* lend 16mm sound projector (10), 8mm cartridge/reel projector (6), projection tables & stands (5), projection screens (10).

Other Media Collections *Audio:* disc, 33⅓rpm, 1500t/2000c. *Filmstrips:* silent, 229t/c. *Slides:* sets, 2t/c.

Budget & Expenditures Total library budget $50,000 (FY 10/75-10/76). Total FY film budget $2000. *Member:* ALA, Fla. Library Assn.

St. Petersburg

S- MUSEUM OF FINE ARTS, 255 Beach Dr NE, 33701. *Tel:* (813) 896-2667. *Film Serv Est:* 1965. *In Charge:* Curator of Educ. *Film Sel:* staff decision. *Holdings:* fine arts 100%.

Free-Loan Film Serv *Eligibility:* educational inst. *Restrictions:* for indiv, only in Pinellis County. Available to researchers/scholars for on-site viewing. May not borrow by mail. *Loan Period:* 3 days. *Total Yr Film Loan:* 1.

Film Collection 6t/p. *Circ:* 16mm, 6t/p. Publish school flyer.

Other Film Serv Film fairs/festivals. Permanent viewing facility. *Equipment:* lend S8mm camera (4), 16mm sound projector (2), S8mm reel projector (1), projection screens (2), 35mm slide projectors (2).

Other Media Collections *Audio:* disc, 33⅓rpm, 7t; tape, reel, 2t. *Filmstrips:* sound, 1t; silent, 1t. *Slides:* single, 4500t.

Budget & Expenditures Total library budget $2600 (FY 1/1/75-1/1/76). No separate AV budget.

Video Serv *Est:* 1965. *Video Staff:* 1 f-t. *Video Use:* community video access, in-service training, practical video/TV training courses, art education. Video serv available by appointment. Produce video tapes. Have production studio/space & separate control room.

Video Equipment/Facilities *In-House Use Only:* recording deck (1), ¾" Sony 3400; playback deck (1), ¾" Sony 3400; studio camera (1), Sony; monitor (1); microphones (8); tripods (1); audio tape recorders (2). Have portable viewing installation. Provide training in use of equipment.

Video Tape Loan/Rental/Sale Serv *Serv Provided:* free loan, swap with other inst. *Loan Eligibility:* org members, educational inst, civic groups, religious groups, other art museums. *Restrictions:* only in U.S. Cannot use for fundraising, duplicate, air without permission. May borrow by mail. *Loan Period:* 7 days. *Total Yr Tape Loan:* 3.

Video Collection Maintained by exchange/swap. Use/play ¾" cassette. *Sources:* museums. *Special Collections:* in-house training tapes. Tapes organized by subject. *Collection, Color:* ¾" cassette, 8t. *Collection, B&W:* ¾" cassette, 16t. *Pubns:* publish school brochure.

Cable & CCTV Have CCTV in inst, with 1 monitor. *Programming Sources:* tapes produced professionally, tapes produced by community groups & indiv.

C- TAMPA COLLEGE, 4950 34 St N, 33714. *Tel:* (813) 527-8464. *Film Serv Est:* 1975. *In Charge:* Hazel Wilson, Librarian. *AV Staff:* 1 prof. *Film Sel:* committee preview, faculty/staff recommendations, chief film librarian's decision.

Film Collection 4t/p.

Other Film Serv *Equipment:* rent 16mm sound projector (1), projection tables & stands, projection screens.

Other Media Collections *Audio:* disc, 78rpm, 50t/c; tape, cartridge, 5c; tape, reel, 75c.

Video Serv *Est:* 1975. *Video Staff:* 1 f-t. *Video Use:* classroom instruction. Video serv available on demand. Produce video tapes.

Video Equipment/Facilities *In-House Use Only:* studio camera (1), monitor (1), microphones (1); tripods (1); audio tape recorders (3). *Equipment Loan Period:* no set policy. Provide training in use of equipment to faculty.

Video Tape Loan/Rental/Sale Serv *Serv Provided:* swap with other inst. *Loan Eligibility:* staff.

Video Collection *Collection, B&W:* 2" reel, 100t.

Tallahassee

C- FLORIDA STATE UNIVERSITY, Instructional Media Center, Film Library, 32306. *Tel:* (904) 644-2820. *Film Serv Est:* 1955. *In Charge:* Dan Isaacs, Dir. *AV Staff:* 8 (2 prof, 6 cl). *Film Sel:* faculty/staff recommendations, chief film librarian's decision.

Film Rental Serv *Eligibility:* educational org, civic groups, patrons/public. *Restrictions:* in U.S. Cannot use for fund-raising, transmit electronically. Can be used only by indiv or group placing the original order. *Rental Period:* 2 days. *Total Yr Film Booking:* 10,350.

Film Collection 5200t. Approx 50-100t acquired annually. *Pubns:* catalog, every 2 yr ($3); suppl, in yr catalog not published (free).

Other Film Serv Rent film from distributors for patrons, obtain film from coop loan system, obtain film from other libraries, film reference serv. Permanent viewing facility. *Member:* CUFC.

P- LEON COUNTY PUBLIC LIBRARY, 127 N Monroe St, 32301. *Tel:* (904) 488-8716. *Film Serv Est:* 1970. *In Charge:* Paul Donovan, Dir. *AV Staff:* 2 cl. *Film Sel:* committee preview, chief film librarian's decision.

Free-Loan Film Serv *Eligibility:* indiv with library cards. *Restrictions:* for indiv, interlibrary loan. Cannot use for fundraising, transmit electronically. Available to researchers/scholars for on-site viewing. May borrow by mail. *Loan Period:* 1 day. *Total Yr Film Loan:* 9763.

Film Collection 325t/p. Approx 30-40t acquired annually. *Circ:* 16mm, 250t/p; 8mm reel, 60t/p; S8mm reel, 15t/p. *Pubns:* catalog, as needed; suppl, no set policy.

Other Film Serv Film fairs/festivals, library film programs. *Equipment:* lend 16mm sound projector (9), 8mm reel projector (3), S8mm reel projector (3), projection screens (6), slide projectors (3), filmstrip projectors (3), rear projection screen.

Other Media Collections *Audio:* disc, 33⅓rpm, 2500t/c; tape, cassette, 150t/c. *Filmstrips:* sound, 65t/c; silent, 30t/c. *Slides:* single, 1000t/c.

Budget & Expenditures Total library budget $69,000 (FY 10/1/74-10/1/75). Total FY film budget $9000. No separate budget. *Member:* ALA, Fla. Library Assn.

Video Serv *Est:* 1974. *Video Staff:* 2 f-t. *Video Use:* documentation of community/school events, to increase community's library use, community video access, in-service training, as art form. Video serv available by appointment. Produce video tapes.

Video Equipment/Facilities *In-House Use Only:* editing deck (1), col, Panasonic; monitor (1), b&w, Sony. *For Loan:* portapak (2), b&w, Panasonic; microphones; tripods; audio tape recorders. *Equipment Loan Period:* no set policy. Provide training in use of equipment. Have tape duplication serv.

Video Tape Loan/Rental/Sale Serv *Serv Provided:* free loan, swap with other inst. *Loan Eligibility:* indiv with library cards. *Restrictions:* for indiv, only in Leon-Jefferson County. Cannot use for fund-raising. May borrow by mail.

Video Collection Maintained by purchase, own production, exchange/swap. Use/play ½″ reel to reel, ¾″ cassette. *Sources:* community productions, exchange. *Other Video Serv:* programming, production workshops.

Cable & CCTV Will receive serv of cable TV system. Plan to produce programs for cablecasting, inform public about cable system serv & facilities, serve as production facility for others, run cable programs for special audiences.

C- TALLAHASSEE COMMUNITY COLLEGE LIBRARY, 444 Applegate Drive, 32304. *Tel:* (904) 576-5181. *Film Serv Est:* 1968. *In Charge:* Albert Sprodley, AV Coord. *AV Staff:* 3 (1 prof, 2 cl). *Film Sel:* faculty/staff recommendations.

Free-Loan Film Serv *Eligibility:* org members. Available to researchers/scholars for on-site viewing. May not borrow by mail.

Film Collection *Circ:* 16mm, 428t/p; 8mm cartridge, 302t/p. *Pubns:* catalog, as needed; suppl, no set policy.

Other Film Serv Rent film from distributors for patrons, obtain film from other libraries, library film programs. Permanent viewing facility.

Other Media Collections *Audio:* disc, 33⅓rpm, 1804t; tape, cassette, 2000t. *Filmstrips:* silent, 186t; silent sets, 316t. *Slides:* sets, 346t. *Member:* ALA, Fla. Library Assn.

Video Serv *Est:* 1972. *Video Staff:* 3 f-t. *Video Use:* documentation of community/school events, classroom instruction. Video serv available on demand. Produce video tapes.

Video Equipment/Facilities *In-House Use Only:* portapak (1), ½″ b&w, Sony 3400; recording deck (4), ½″, ¾″, 1″ b&w/col, Ampex, Sony; studio camera (3), b&w/col, Sony, Magnavox; monitor (11), b&w/col; SEG (1), SEG 1; microphones (4); tripods (2); audio tape recorders (56). Have permanent & portable viewing installations. *Equipment Loan Period:* no set policy. Provide training in use of equipment to faculty & AV staff. Have tape duplication serv.

Video Tape Loan/Rental/Sale Serv *Serv Provided:* free loan. *Loan/Rental Eligibility:* org members. May not borrow by mail.

Video Collection Maintained by purchase, rental, own production. *Sources:* commercial distributors. *Tape Sel:* faculty/staff recommendations. Tapes organized by accession number.

Tampa

C- HILLSBOROUGH COMMUNITY COLLEGE, AV-Film Servs, Box 22127, 33622. *Tel:* (813) 933-3730, ext 363. *Film Serv Est:* 1975. *In Charge:* Patricia Hauenstein, AV Tech II. *AV Staff:* 10½ (1 cl, 1 tech). *Film Sel:* preview, faculty/staff recommendations. *Holdings:* business 9%, English 7%, fine arts 12%, foods 12%, Lamaze natural childbirth method 7%, police science 14%, science 15%, social sciences 27%.

Free-Loan Film Serv *Eligibility:* staff, civic groups (rarely). *Restrictions:* instructors of our various collegiums. Cannot use for fund-raising, transmit electronically, borrow for classroom use. Available to researchers/scholars for on-site viewing. May not borrow by mail. *Loan Period:* 7 days. *Total Yr Film Loan:* approx 1200.

Film Rental Serv Produce slides, filmstrips, graphics, video tapes.

Film Collection 80t/p. Approx 20t acquired annually. *Pubns:* catalog, every 2 yrs (free); suppl, no set policy.

Other Film Serv Rent film from distributors for patrons, obtain film from other libraries, film fairs/festivals. Permanent viewing facility.

Budget & Expenditures Total library budget $106,000 (FY 7/1/75-7/1/76). Total FY film budget $17,000. *Member:* ALA, EFLA.

C- UNIVERSITY OF SOUTH FLORIDA, Film Library, 4202 Fowler, 33620. *Tel:* (813) 974-2341, ext 21, 22. *Film Serv Est:* 1965. *In Charge:* Kate Reynolds, Film Coord. *AV Staff:* 13 (4 prof, 4 cl, 5 tech). *Film Sel:* chief film librarian's decision. *Holdings:* animated films 2%, children's films 2%, experimental films 1%, feature films 2%.

Free-Loan Film Serv *Eligibility:* staff only. *Restrictions:* scheduled courses only. Cannot use for fund-raising, transmit electronically. Available to researchers/scholars for on-site viewing. May not borrow by mail. *Loan Period:* 1 day. *Total Yr Film Loan:* 10,000.

Film Rental Serv *Eligibility:* no restrictions. *Restrictions:* only in U.S. Cannot transmit electronically. *Rental Period:* 2 days. *Total Yr Film Booking:* 10,000. Sell films. Produce films.

Film Collection 3000t/3300p. Approx 75-100t acquired annually. *Circ:* 16mm, 2800t/3100p. *Noncirc:* 16mm, 200t/p. *Pubns:* catalog, every 2 yrs ($2); suppl, no set policy. Publish monthly film news bulletin.

Other Film Serv Rent film from distributors for patrons, obtain film from other libraries, film reference serv. Permanent viewing facility available to community. *Equipment:* rent S8mm camera (10), 16mm sound projector (60), 8mm cartridge projector (20), 8mm reel projector (5), S8mm cartridge projector (20), S8mm reel projector (10), projection tables & stands (50), projection screens (20).

Other Media Collections *Audio:* disc, 33⅓rpm, 9193 t/10,200c; tape, 1253t. *Slides:* single, 7332t; sets, 200t.

Budget & Expenditures Total library budget $832,000 (FY 7/1/74-7/1/75). Total FY film budget $10,000. *Member:* AECT, CUFC, EFLA, Fla. Library Assn.

C- UNIVERSITY OF SOUTH FLORIDA, Learning Laboratory, Div of Educ Resources, Fowler Ave, 33620. *Tel:* (518) 974-2341, ext 40. *Video Serv Est:* 1968. *In Charge:* Michele N. Heller, Supervisor. *Video Staff:* 2 tech. *Video Use:* documentation of community/school events, practical video/TV training courses, classroom instruction. Video serv available by appointment. Produce video tapes. Have production studio/space & separate control room.

Video Equipment/Facilities *In-House Use Only:* recording deck (20), ½″ b&w, Sony, Panasonic; playback deck (3), ¾″ Sony, JVC; editing deck (2), ½″ b&w, Panasonic; monitor (25), b&w/col, Sony, Panasonic; SEG (2), Panasonic; additional camera lenses (14); lighting (3); microphones (35); tripods (10); audio tape recorders (65). Have portable viewing installation. *Equipment Loan Period:* no set policy. Provide training in use of equipment to faculty & students. Have tape duplication serv.

Video Tape Loan/Rental/Sale Serv *Serv Provided:* free loan, swap with other inst, sale. *Loan Eligibility:* org members, staff, educational inst.

Video Collection Maintained by purchase, own production. Use/play ½″, 1″, 2″ reel to reel, ¾″ cassette. *Sources:* own TV station. *Tape Sel:* preview, faculty/staff recommendations, catalogs. Tapes organized by alpha-numeric. *Collection, Color:* ¾″ cassette, 59t/c. *Collection, B&W:* ½″ reel, 41t/c; 1″ reel, 403t/c. *Other Video Serv:* taping of other media, production workshops.

Cable & CCTV Have CCTV in inst, with 46 monitors. *Programming Sources:* over-the-air commercial & public broadcasting, tapes produced by inst.

Winter Haven

C- POLK COMMUNITY COLLEGE, 999 Ave H NE, 33880. *Tel:* (813) 294-7421, ext 305. *In Charge:* P. S. Miller, Dir, Learning Resources. *AV Staff:* 1 tech. *Film Sel:* faculty/staff recommendations, chief film librarian's decision.

Free-Loan Film Serv *Eligibility:* staff & students, civic groups. *Restrictions:* for campus use only. Available to researchers/scholars for on-site viewing. May not borrow by mail. *Loan Period:* 1 day. *Total Yr Film Loan:* 2924. Produce slides, tapes, transparencies.

Film Collection 609t. Approx 50t acquired annually. *Circ:* 16mm, 629t; 8mm reel, 174t. *Pubns:* catalog, annual. Publish preview notices.

Other Film Serv Rent film from distributors for patrons, obtain film from other libraries. Permanent viewing facility available to community.

Other Media Collections *Audio:* disc, 33⅓rpm, 45rpm, 78rpm, 797t; tape, cassette, 188t; tape, reel, 54t. *Filmstrips:* sound & silent, 324t.

Budget & Expenditures Total library budget $44,788 (FY 7/1/74-7/1/75). Total FY film budget $5000. Member: AECT, ALA, Fla. Library Assn, Fla. Assn for Media in Educ.

Video Serv *Est:* 1966. *Video Staff:* 1 f-t, 2 p-t tech. *Video Use:* playback only of professionally produced tapes, instruction. Produce video tapes. Have production studio/space.

Video Equipment/Facilities *In-House Use Only:* portapak (1); recording deck (8), b&w/col, Panasonic; playback deck (3), b&w/col, Panasonic; studio camera (5); monitor (4); SEG (1); lighting; tripods (5); audio tape recorders. Have portable viewing installation. *Equipment Loan Period:* no set policy. Provide training in use of equipment to faculty & students. Have tape duplication serv.

Video Tape Loan/Rental/Sale Serv *Serv Provided:* free loan. *Loan Eligibility:* staff. *Restrictions:* for instruction only. Cannot air without permission. May not borrow by mail.

Video Collection Maintained by purchase, rental, own production. Use/play ½", reel to reel, ½" cartridge, ¾" cassette. *Sources:* commercial distributors, consortium. *Member:* Fla. College TV Consortium. *Tape Sel:* preview, faculty/staff recommendations, gallery previews, published reviews, catalogs, consortium. Tapes organized by subject. *Collection, Color:* ½" cartridge, 3t. *Collection, B&W:* ½" reel, 20t.

Georgia

Albany

P- ALBANY DOUGHERTY PUBLIC LIBRARY—AV DEPT,
2215 Barnsdale Way, 31707. *Tel:* (912) 439-4310. *Film Serv
Est:* 1971. *In Charge:* David M. Piper, Media Specialist. *AV
Staff:* 2 (1 prof, 1 tech). *Film Sel:* committee preview, chief
film librarian's decision. *Holdings:* animated films 15%,
children's films 75%, social sciences 10%.

Free-Loan Film Serv *Eligibility:* educational inst, civic
groups, religious groups, indiv with library cards. *Restrictions:*
for indiv, only in County; for inst, only in state. Cannot use for
fund-raising. Available to researchers/scholars for on-site viewing. May borrow by mail. *Loan Period:* 3 days.

Film Collection 50t/p.

Other Film Serv Obtain film from coop loan system (Ga.
Dept of Education), obtain film from other libraries, film reference serv, library film programs. Permanent viewing facility.
Equipment: 16mm sound projector (5), 8mm cartridge projector
(1), 8mm reel projector (1), S8mm reel projector (1), projection
tables & stands (4), projection screens (7).

Other Media Collections *Audio:* disc, 33⅓ rpm, 800c; tape,
cassette, 50c; tape, reel, 100c. *Filmstrips:* sound, 23c; silent, 10c.
Slides: single, 1259c.

Budget & Expenditures Total library budget $100,000 (FY
7/1/74-7/1/75). Total FY film budget $1500.

Video Serv *Est:* 1974. *In Charge:* David Piper. *Video Staff:*
1 f-t, 1 p-t. *Video Use:* documentation of community/school
events, to increase community's library use, community video
access, in-service training. Video serv available by appointment. Produce video tapes. Have production studio/space.

Video Equipment/Facilities *In-House Use Only:* recording deck (1), ¾″ col, Sony VD 1600; studio camera (1), b&w, Sony
AVC 3210; monitor (2), col, Sony CKV121; lighting (1); microphones (2); tripods (1); audio tape recorders (5). *For Loan:* audio
tape recorders (5). Have portable viewing installation. Provide training in use of equipment to staff & patrons.

Video Tape Loan/Rental/Sale Serv *Serv Provided:* free
loan. *Loan Eligibility:* indiv with library cards. *Restrictions:* for
indiv, only in County; for inst, depends on situation. Cannot use
for fund-raising, air without permission. May not borrow by
mail. *Total Yr Tape Loan:* 20.

Video Collection Maintained by own production. Use/
play ¾″ cassette. *Sources:* community productions. *Tape Sel:*
preview, published reviews, catalogs. Tapes organized by subject. *Collection, B&W:* ¾″ cassette, 20t. *Other Video Serv:* production workshops.

Cable & CCTV Receive serv of cable TV system.

Americus

P- LAKE BLACKSHEAR REGIONAL LIBRARY SYSTEM,
111 S Jackson St, 31709. *Tel:* (912) 924-6144. *Film Serv Est:*
1966. *In Charge:* Eunice S. Lee, AV Coord. *AV Staff:* 1½ (1
prof, ½ cl). *Film Sel:* staff recommendations.

Free-Loan Film Serv *Eligibility:* indiv with library cards.
Restrictions: for indiv, only in our four county region; for
inst, only in our four county region. Cannot use for fund-
raising. Available to researchers/scholars for on-site viewing.
May borrow by mail. *Loan Period:* specific show dates. *Total Yr
Film Loan:* 796.

Film Collection 211t/p. Approx 2/t acquired annually.
Circ: 16mm, 22t/p; 8mm reel, 175t/p; S8mm reel, 14t/p.

Other Film Serv Obtain film from coop loan system (S. Ga.
Library Assn, Ga. State Film Library), obtain film from other
libraries, film reference serv, library film programs. Permanent
viewing facility available for free to community. *Equipment:*
lend 16mm sound projector (5), 8mm reel projector (4), S8mm
reel projector (1), projection tables & stands (2), projection
screens (8).

Other Media Collections *Audio:* disc, 33⅓ rpm, 1236t;
tape, cassette, 686t. *Filmstrips:* sound, 497t; sound sets, 152t.
Slides: single, 1201t.

Budget & Expenditures Total library budget $46,888.52
(FY 7/1/74-7/1/75). No separate AV budget. *Member:* ALA, Ga.
Library Assn, Southeastern Library Assn.

Atlanta

P- STATE DEPT OF EDUCATION, Atlanta Film Library,
1066 Sylvan Rd SW, 30310. *Tel:* (404) 656-2421. *Film Serv
Est:* 1947. *In Charge:* Ben W. Hulsey, Film Library Mgr.
AV Staff: 23 (1 prof, 4 cl, 2 tech). *Film Sel:* committee
preview, faculty/staff recommendations.

Free-Loan Film Serv *Eligibility:* educational inst. *Restrictions:* for inst, only in state. Educational inst required to pay $70
annual registration fee to defray postage costs. Cannot use for
fund-raising, transmit electronically. May borrow by mail. *Loan
Period:* 2 days. *Total Yr Film Loan:* 211,000.

Film Collection 4200t/40,000p. Approx 50-100t acquired
annually. *Circ:* 16mm, 4200t/40,000p. *Pubns:* catalog, every 4
yrs; suppl, in yr catalog not published.

Other Media Collections *Audio:* tape, cassette, 6000c.

Budget & Expenditures Total library budget $500,000 (FY
7/1/74-7/1/75). No separate AV budget. *Member:* AECT.

Augusta

P- AUGUSTA REGIONAL LIBRARY, AV Dept, 902 Greene
St, 30902. *Tel:* (404) 724-1871, ext 26. *Film Serv Est:* 1956. *In
Charge:* Gary Swint, Head, AV Dept. *AV Staff:* 3 (1 prof, 2
cl). *Film Sel:* committee preview, chief film librarian's
decision.

Free-Loan Film Serv *Eligibility:* educational inst, civic
groups, religious groups, indiv with library cards. *Restrictions:*
for indiv, members of the Burke, Columbia, Glascock, Lincoln &
Richmond Counties Regional Library System; for inst, members
of the Burke, Columbia, Glascock, Lincoln & Richmond Counties Regional Library System, not loaned to public elementary
schools. Cannot use for fund-raising. Available to research-
ers/scholars for on-site viewing. May not borrow by mail. *Loan
Period:* 1 day, longer for outlying Counties. *Total Yr Film Loan:*
11,478.

Film Collection 273t/p. Approx 41t acquired annually.
Circ: 16mm, 273t/p; 8mm reel, 150t/p. *Pubns:* catalog, annual;
suppl, no set policy. Publish annotation list.

Other Film Serv Rent film from distributors for patrons,
obtain film from coop loan system (Public Library Film Service),
film reference serv, library film programs, also a Talking Book
Center for blind & physically handicapped, c. 4000 TB's. *Equipment:* lend projection screens (2), filmstrip projectors (7),
cassette players (4), slide projectors (3).

Other Media Collections *Audio:* disc, 33⅓ rpm, 6400t;
tape, cassette, 700t. *Filmstrips:* 1113t. *Slides:* single, 900t.

Budget & Expenditures Total library budget $111,000 (FY
7/1/74-7/1/75). Total FY film budget $9000.

Brunswick

P- BRUNSWICK-GLYNN COUNTY REGIONAL LIBRARY,
1608 Newcastle St, 31520. *Tel:* (912) 265-6232. *Film Serv
Est:* 1963. *In Charge:* Harriette C. Hammond, Dir. *AV
Staff:* 1 (1 prof). *Film Sel:* committee preview. *Holdings:*
animated films 10%, children's films 40%, comedy 20%,
safety 10%, travel 20%.

Free-Loan Film Serv *Eligibility:* educational inst, civic
groups, religious groups, prof groups. *Restrictions:* for indiv &
inst, only in our seven county library system. May borrow by
mail. *Loan Period:* 2-5 days. *Total Yr Film Loan:* 570.

Brunswick (cont'd)

Film Collection 62t/p. Approx 10t acquired annually.

Other Film Serv *Equipment:* lend S8mm camera (1), 16mm sound projector (4), tape recorders (2), record players (4), cassette players (3), filmstrip projectors, opaque projectors (11), overhead projectors (1).

Other Media Collections *Audio:* disc, 33⅓rpm, 1200t; tape, cassette, 275t. *Filmstrips:* sound & silent, 1600t. *Slides:* sets, 9c.

Budget & Expenditures Total library budget $39,337.10 (FY 7/1/74-7/1/75). Total FY film budget $1000. *Member:* ALA, Ga. Library Assn, SELA.

Video Serv *Est:* 1976. *In Charge:* Elizabeth Rountree, Dir. Building under construction.

Cochran

C- MIDDLE GEORGIA COLLEGE, Roberts Memorial Library, 31014. *Tel:* (912) 934-6221, ext 271. *Film Serv Est:* 1961. *In Charge:* Steven A. Baughman, Assistant Librarian. *AV Staff:* 1 (1 prof). *Film Sel:* faculty/staff recommendations, chief film librarian's decision.

Film Collection 409t/p. Approx 15t acquired annually. *Circ:* 16mm, 409t/p; 8mm reel, 136t/p; 8mm cartridge, 136t/p; S8mm reel, 136t/p. *Pubns:* catalog, every 3 yr (for faculty use only).

Other Film Serv Obtain film from coop loan system (Ga. State Films—Statesboro, Central Ga. Associated Libraries).

Other Media Collections *Audio:* disc, 33⅓rpm, 45rpm, & 78rpm, 2101t/c; tape, cassette, cartridge, & reel, 960t/c. *Filmstrips:* sound, silent, sound sets, & silent sets, 1157t/c. *Slides:* single, & sets, 6356t/c.

Budget & Expenditures Total library budget $41,904.52 (FY 7/1/74-7/1/75). No separate AV budget. *Member:* ALA, Ga. Library Assn.

Video Serv *Est:* 1961. *In Charge:* Steven Baughman, Assistant Librarian. *Video Staff:* 1 f-t, 1 p-t. *Video Use:* in-service training. Have portable viewing installation. Provide training in use of equipment to students. Have cassette tape duplication serv.

Video Tape Loan/Rental/Sale Serv *Loan Eligibility:* org members, staff. *Member:* Central Ga. Associated Libraries. *Tape Sel:* faculty/staff recommendations.

Cable & CCTV Receive serv of cable TV system.

Decatur

C- DEKALB COMMUNITY COLLEGE—SOUTH CAMPUS, Learning Resources Center, 3251 Panthersville Rd, 30034. *Tel:* (404) 243-3860, ext 11. *Film Serv Est:* 1972. *In Charge:* Robert R. Clark, Media Specialist. *AV Staff:* 3 (1 prof, 2 cl). *Film Sel:* committee preview, faculty/staff recommendations.

Film Collection 30t/p. Approx 15t acquired annually. *Circ:* 16mm, 30t/p. *Pubns:* catalog, annual; suppl, no set policy.

Other Film Serv Rent film from distributors for patrons, obtain film from coop loan system, obtain film from other libraries, film reference serv. *Equipment:* lend 16mm sound projector (5), 8mm cartridge projector (1), 8mm reel projector (1), S8mm cartridge projector (1), projection tables & stands (15), projection screens (8).

Other Media Collections *Audio:* disc, 33⅓ rpm, 250t; tape, cassette, 211t. *Filmstrips:* sound sets, 76t; silent sets, 3t. *Slides:* sets, 128t.

Budget & Expenditures Total library budget $60,000 (FY 7/1/74-7/1/75). *Member:* AECT, ALA, Ga. Library Assn.

Video Serv *Est:* 1972. *In Charge:* Robert Clark, Media Specialist. *Video Staff:* 3 f-t. *Video Use:* documentation of community/school events, in-service training, playback only of professionally produced tapes. Video serv available on demand & by appointment. Produce video tapes.

Video Equipment/Facilities *In-House Use Only:* studio camera (1), col, Magnavox VC 400; monitor (12), col, Zenith, Sony; synthesizer; microphones; audio tape recorders (20). *For*

Loan: portapak (1), ½″ b&w, Sony 3400; monitor (12), col, Zenith, Sony; audio tape recorders (20). Have permanent viewing installation. Provide training in use of equipment to faculty & students. Have cassette tape duplication serv.

Video Tape Loan/Rental/Sale Serv *Loan Eligibility:* org members, staff & students.

Video Collection Maintained by purchase, rental, own production, exchange/swap. Use/play ¾″ cassette. *Sources:* commercial distributors, exchange. *Tape Sel:* preview, faculty/staff recommendations, gallery previews, published reviews, catalogs. *Special Collections:* in-house training tapes, films in video format. Tapes organized by Library of Congress. *Other Video Serv:* taping of other media, production workshops.

Cable & CCTV Have CCTV in inst, with 4 monitors. *Programming Sources:* tapes produced by inst, tapes produced professionally.

P- DEKALB LIBRARY SYSTEM, Headquarters and Processing Center, 3560 Kensington Rd, 30032. *Film Serv Est:* 1975. *In Charge:* Louise Trotti, Dir.

Free-Loan Film Serv *Eligibility:* staff.

Film Collection 200t. *Noncirc:* 16mm, 200t.

Milledgeville

C- GEORGIA COLLEGE, Ina Dillard Russell Library, Hancock St, 31061. *Tel:* (912) 453-4047. *Video Serv Est:* 1972. *In Charge:* R. J. Richardson, Head of Public Servs. *Video Staff:* 1 f-t, 1 p-t. *Video Use:* in-service training. Video serv available primarily for Library & Education Dept use. Produce video tapes.

Video Equipment/Facilities *In-House Use Only:* portapak (1), ½″ b&w, Sony 3400; recording deck, studio camera (1), b&w, Sony 3650; monitor (4), b&w/col, Sony, Panasonic; microphones (3); tripods (2); audio tape recorders (2), videocassette player/recorder (1). *Equipment Loan Period:* no set policy. Provide training in use of equipment to faculty & students.

Video Tape Loan/Rental/Sale Serv *Loan Eligibility:* staff & students. *Restrictions:* May not borrow by mail.

Video Collection Maintained by own production. Use/play ½″ reel to reel, ¾″ cassette. *Sources:* those made on campus. Tapes organized by subject. *Collection, Color:* ½″ reel, 3t/c; ¾″ cassette, 3t/c. *Collection, B&W:* ½″ reel, 3t/c; ¾″ cassette, 3t/c. *Other Video Serv:* production workshops.

Cable & CCTV Receive serv of cable TV system.

C- GEORGIA COLLEGE, Learning Resources Center, 31061. *Tel:* (912) 453-5016. *In Charge:* Mary Louise Mortensen, Head, Media Servs. *AV Staff:* 1 (1 prof). *Film Sel:* faculty/staff recommendations.

Free-Loan Film Serv *Eligibility:* staff & students.

Other Film Serv Rent film from distributors for patrons, obtain film from coop loan system (Ga. Dept of Education, Central Ga. Assn of Libraries). *Equipment:* lend 16mm sound projector (5), cartridge projector (2), projection tables & stands (7), projection screens (2).

Other Media Collections *Audio:* disc, 33⅓rpm, 1105t; tape, cassette, 545t; tape, reel, 180t. *Filmstrips:* sound, silent, sound sets, & silent sets, 411t. *Slides:* single, & sets, 3988t.

Budget & Expenditures No separate budget. *Member:* ALA, Ga. Library Assn.

Rome

C- FLOYD JUNIOR COLLEGE, Library, Box 1864, 30161. *Tel:* (404) 231-6318. *Film Serv Est:* 1971. *In Charge:* Cathy Spencer, AV Librarian. *AV Staff:* 3 (1 prof, 2 tech). *Film Sel:* faculty/staff recommendations.

Free-Loan Film Serv *Eligibility:* staff & students, educational inst, civic groups, religious groups, prof groups, such as law enforcement officers. *Restrictions:* for indiv, only in Floyd County; for inst, only in Floyd County. Available to researchers/scholars for on-site viewing. May not borrow by mail. *Loan Period:* 2 days.

Film Collection *Circ:* 16mm, 140t/p; S8mm cartridge, 26t/p.

Other Film Serv Permanent viewing facility. *Equipment:* lend S8mm camera (1), 16mm sound projector (4), 8mm cartridge projector (1), 8mm reel projector (1), S8mm cartridge projector (1), S8mm reel projector (1).

Other Media Collections *Audio:* disc, 33⅓ rpm, 421t/716c; tape, cassette, 1146c. *Slides:* single, 4184c. *Member:* AECT, ALA.

Video Serv *Est:* 1972. *In Charge:* Cathy Spencer. *Video Staff:* 3 f-t, 2 tech. *Video Use:* documentation of community/school events, to increase community's library use, community video access, in-service training. Video serv available by appointment. Produce video tapes. Have production studio/space & separate control room.

Video Equipment/Facilities *In-House Use Only:* recording/playback deck (3), ½″ col, Panasonic NV-3120; editing deck (1), ½″ col, Panasonic NV-3130; studio camera (2), col, Panasonic WV-2100P; monitor (1), col, Panasonic CT25; SEG (1), Panasonic WJ5000P; lighting (1); microphones (5); tripods (2); audio tape recorders (1), videocassette (1), ¾″ col, Panasonic NV2125; videocartridge (5), ½″ col, Panasonic NV5110. *For Loan:* portapak (1), ½″ col, Panasonic NV3082; recording/playback deck (3), ½″ col, Panasonic NV-3120. Have permanent viewing installation. *Equipment Loan Period:* 1-7 days. Provide training in use of equipment to faculty & students.

Video Tape Loan/Rental/Sale Serv *Loan Eligibility:* staff & students, educational inst, civic groups, religious groups. *Restrictions:* for indiv, only in Floyd County; for inst, only in Floyd County. May not borrow by mail.

Video Collection Maintained by purchase, own production. Use/play ½″ reel to reel, ¾″ cassette. *Sources:* various divisions of the college. *Tape Sel:* faculty/staff recommendations. *Special Collections:* in-house training tapes. Tapes organized by Library of Congress classification. *Other Video Serv:* programming, taping of other media.

Cable & CCTV Produce programs for cablecasting. Serve as production facility for others. Run cable programs for special audiences. Have CCTV in inst, with 9 monitors. *Programming Sources:* over-the-air commercial & public broadcasting, tapes produced by inst, tapes produced professionally.

P- TRI-COUNTY REGIONAL LIBRARY, AV Dept, Box 277, 30161. *Tel:* (404) 235-5561, ext 10. *In Charge:* Elizabeth Mulder, AV Librarian. *AV Staff:* 6 (2 prof, 2 cl, 2 tech). *Film Sel:* committee preview, published reviews. *Holdings:* crime & juvenile delinquency 30%, drug abuse 20%.

Free-Loan Film Serv *Eligibility:* indiv with library cards. *Restrictions:* for indiv, none; for inst, none. Available to researchers/scholars for on-site viewing. May borrow by mail. *Total Yr Film Loan:* 1004.

Film Collection 230t. Approx 5t acquired annually. *Circ:* 16mm, 53t; 8mm reel, 137t. *Pubns:* catalog, as needed; suppl, no set policy.

Other Film Serv Obtain film from coop loan system (Ga. State Dept of Education AV Servs), obtain film from other libraries, library film programs, obtain from business, government & service groups. Permanent viewing facility available for free to community. *Equipment:* lend S8mm camera, 16mm sound projector (3), 8mm reel projector (1), projection screens (8).

Other Media Collections *Audio:* disc, 33⅓ rpm, 6601t/5040c; tape, cartridge, 234t. *Filmstrips:* silent, 2844t. *Slides:* 2151t.

Budget & Expenditures Total library budget $462,023 (FY 7/1/74-7/1/75). Total FY film budget $5000. *Member:* ALA, FLIC, Ga. Library Assn, SELA.

Video Serv *In Charge:* Elizabeth Mulder, AV Librarian. *Video Use:* documentation of community/school events, to increase community's library use, in-service training, production of daily program for cable TV. Video serv available by appointment. Produce video tapes. Have production studio/space & separate control room.

Video Equipment/Facilities *In-House Use Only:* editing deck (1), ½″ b&w, Sony AV3650. *For Loan:* portapak (1), ½″ b&w, Sony AV8400; recording deck (2), ¾″ col, Sony 1600 & 1800; editing deck (1), ½″ b&w, Sony AV3650; studio camera (2), b&w/col, Sony 5000 & 1200; monitor (2), b&w/col, Sony CVM112; SEG, Unimedia SMY-12P; lighting (1); microphones (2); tripods (3); audio tape recorders (6). Have portable viewing installation. *Equipment Loan Period:* no set policy. Provide training in use of equipment to staff.

Video Tape Loan/Rental/Sale Serv *Serv Provided:* free loan, swap with other inst. *Loan Eligibility:* all considered by Video Committee. *Restrictions:* for indiv, none; for inst, none. Cannot air without permission. May borrow by mail. *Loan Period:* time needed.

Video Collection Maintained by own production, exchange/swap. Tapes organized by subject. *Collection, Color:* ¾″ cassette, 75t/105c. *Other Video Serv:* daily program via local cable channel.

Cable & CCTV Receive serv of cable TV system. Produce programs for cablecasting.

Valdosta

P- SOUTH GEORGIA REGIONAL LIBRARY, 300 Woodrow Wilson Drive, 31601. *Tel:* (912) 244-0202; 242-2410. *Film Serv Est:* 1950. *In Charge:* Augusta Deahins, Admin. Assistant. *Film Sel:* committee preview. *Holdings:* career education 50%, children's films 50%.

Free-Loan Film Serv *Eligibility:* all. *Restrictions:* for indiv, only in our counties; for inst, only in our counties. Cannot use for fund-raising, transmit electronically, borrow for classroom use. Available to researchers/scholars for on-site viewing. May not borrow by mail. *Loan Period:* 1 day. *Total Yr Film Loan:* 93.

Film Collection 35t.

Other Film Serv Obtain film from coop loan system (Ga. State Dept; South Ga. Associated Libraries), library film programs. Permanent viewing facility. *Equipment:* lend 16mm sound projector (4), projection screens (2). *Member:* Ga. Library Assn.

Hawaii

Honolulu

C- CHAMINADE COLLEGE OF HONOLULU, Instructional Media Center, 96816. *Tel:* (808) 732-1471, ext 146. *Video Serv Est:* 1970. *In Charge:* Jean Rene Des Roches, AV Dir. *Video Staff:* 1 f-t, 3 p-t, 2 tech. *Video Use:* documentation of community/school events, community video access, in-service training, playback only of professionally produced tapes. Video serv available on demand. Produce video tapes. Have production studio/space & separate control room.

Video Equipment/Facilities *In-House Use Only:* recording deck (3), ½″ col, Sony AV-8600; playback deck, ¾″ col, Sony VO-1800; editing deck (1), ½″ col, Sony AV-8650; studio camera (2), b&w, Sony AVC-4600; monitor (3), Sony & RCA; SEG (1), Sony; additional camera lenses (2); lighting (3); microphones (3); tripods (3); audio tape recorders (2). Have permanent & portable viewing installations. *Equipment Loan Period:* no set policy. Provide training in use of equipment to faculty & students. Have tape duplication serv.

Video Tape Loan/Rental/Sale Serv *Serv Provided:* free loan, swap with other inst, rental. *Loan/Rental Eligibility:* educational inst. *Restrictions:* for indiv, only in city; for inst, only in city. May not borrow by mail. *Total Yr Tape Loan:* 129.

Video Collection Maintained by purchase, rental, own production, exchange/swap. Use/play ½″ reel to reel, ¾″ cassette. *Sources:* commercial distributors. *Tape Sel:* preview. *Special Collections:* in-house training tapes, films in video format. Tapes organized by subject. *Collection, Color:* ½″ reel, 30t/c; ¾″ cassette, 60t/c. *Collection, B&W:* ½″ reel, 20t/c. *Other Video Serv:* programming, reference serv, production workshops.

Cable & CCTV Produce programs for cablecasting. Inform public about cable system serv & facilities. Serv as production facility for others. Run cable programs for special audiences. Have advisory/administrative role in cable system operation as programming consultant. Have CCTV in inst, with 15 monitors. *Programming Sources:* over-the-air commercial & public broadcasting, tapes produced by inst, tapes produced professionally, tapes produced by community groups & indiv.

P- DEPARTMENT OF EDUCATION, OFFICE OF LIBRARY SERVS, Technical Assistance Center, 1270 Queen Emma St, Room 708, 96813. *Tel:* (808) 548-6250. *Video Serv Est:* 1973. *In Charge:* Robert M. F. Yee, Prog Spec/Asst Administrator. *Video Staff:* 2 f-t, 2 p-t, 1 tech. *Video Use:* educational, information and reference. Video serv available upon 2-week request. Produce video tapes.

Video Equipment/Facilities *In-House Use Only:* recording deck (3), ½″ & ¾″ col, Sony 1600, 1800, Panasonic NV3010; playback deck (1), ¾″ col, Sony VP1000; editing deck (1), ½″ col, Panasonic NV3030; studio camera (1), col, Panasonic VP2100P; monitor (4), col, Sony; audio tape recorders (1). *For Loan:* portapak (1), ½″ b&w, Panasonic NV3080. Have permanent viewing installation. *Equipment Loan Period:* 7 days. Provide training in use of equipment to faculty, students, and librarians. Have tape duplication serv.

Video Tape Loan/Rental/Sale Serv *Serv Provided:* free loan. *Loan Eligibility:* org members. *Restrictions:* for indiv, interlibrary loan (in-house only), only in state; for inst, only in state. Cannot use for fund-raising, duplicate, air without permission. May borrow by mail. *Loan Period:* 7 days.

Video Collection Maintained by purchase, own production, exchange/swap. Use/play ½″, 1″ reel to reel, ¾″ cassette. *Sources:* commercial distributors, community productions. *Tape Sel:* preview, faculty/staff recommendations, published reviews, catalogs. *Special Collections:* in-house training tapes, video as art, films in video format, educational, information and recreational use. Tapes organized by title or series. *Collection, Color:* ¾″ cassette, 200t/300c. *Collection, B&W:* ½″ reel, 25t/30c. *Other*

Video Serv: production workshops. *Pubns:* catalog. Publish holdings list.

Cable & CCTV Receive serv of cable TV system. Have advisory/administrative role in cable system operation through 2 community libraries.

P- HAWAII STATE DEPARTMENT OF EDUCATION, LIBRARY BRANCH, AV Unit, 478 S King St, 96813. *Tel:* (808) 548-5913. *Film Serv Est:* 1950. *In Charge:* Mary Lu T. Kipilii, AV Librarian. *AV Staff:* 4 (1 prof, 1 cl, 1 tech). *Film Sel:* committee preview.

Free-Loan Film Serv *Eligibility:* educational inst, civic groups, religious groups, indiv with library cards, prof groups. *Restrictions:* for indiv & inst, only in state. Cannot use for fund-raising, transmit electronically. May borrow by mail, neighbor island residents only. *Loan Period:* 4 days. *Total Yr Film Loan:* 27,671.

Film Collection 1220t/1429p. Approx 100t acquired annually. *Circ:* 16mm, 1220t/1429p. *Pubns:* catalog, as needed ($2); suppl, in yr catalog not published. Publish annotated film lists on specific subjects.

Other Film Serv Film reference serv, library film programs. Permanent viewing facility available for staff only. *Equipment:* lend (only to state agencies in the Civic Center complex) 16mm sound projector (2), S8mm cartridge projector (1), projection carts (2), projection screens (9).

Other Media Collections *Audio:* disc, 33⅓ rpm, 13,408c; tape, cassette, 505c. *Filmstrips:* silent, 15t/20c; sound sets, 75t/c; silent sets, 25t/c. *Slides:* sets, 5t/8c.

Budget & Expenditures Total library budget $213,122 (FY 7/1/74-7/1/75). Total FY film budget $21,000. *Member:* EFLA.

S- HONOLULU ACADEMY OF ARTS, AV Center, 900 S Beretania St, 96814. *Tel:* (808) 538-3693, ext 52. *Film Serv Est:* 1971. *In Charge:* Brone Jameikis, Keeper. *AV Staff:* 2 (2 prof). *Film Sel:* staff recommendations. *Holdings:* art, children's films 30%.

Free-Loan Film Serv *Eligibility:* educational inst, civic groups, religious groups. *Restrictions:* for inst, only in state. Cannot use for fund-raising, transmit electronically. Available to researchers/scholars for on-site viewing. May borrow by mail. *Loan Period:* 3 days.

Film Rental Serv *Total Yr Film Booking:* 210. Produce films. Produce slide-cassettes.

Film Collection 100t/100p. Approx 15t acquired annually. *Circ:* 16mm, 100t/100p. *Pubns:* publish list of film holdings.

Other Film Serv Film fairs/festivals. Permanent viewing facility. *Equipment:* lend Sound-O-Matic cassette player with slide-cassettes (6).

Other Media Collections *Audio:* tape, cassette, 20t/40c. *Filmstrips:* sound, 5t/5c. *Slides:* single, 35,600t/35,600c; sets, 12t/14c.

Budget & Expenditures No separate AV budget.

C- UNIVERSITY OF HAWAII, Instructional Resources Serv Center, 1733 Donaghho Rd, 96822. *Tel:* (808) 948-8075. *Video Serv Est:* 1965. *In Charge:* Dr. Paul Snipes, Dir. *Video Staff:* 8 f-t, 14 p-t, 3 tech. *Video Use:* in-service training, practical video/TV training courses, microteaching. Video serv available by appointment. Produce video tapes. Have production studio/space.

Video Equipment/Facilities *In-House Use Only:* recording deck (2), ½″, ¾″ b&w/col, Sony 8650, 1600; playback deck (1), ¾″ col, Sony 1400; editing deck (1), ½″ col, Sony 8650; studio camera (4), b&w, Ampex, Telemation; monitor (12), 23″ b&w, Setchel-Carlson; SEG (1), Telemation; additional camera lenses (2); lighting (4); microphones (6); audio tape recorders (3). *For Loan:* portapak (1), ½″ b&w, Sony 3400. Have permanent viewing installation. *Equipment Loan Period:* overnight. Provide training in use of equipment to faculty & employees.

Video Tape Loan/Rental/Sale Serv *Loan Eligibility:* staff. *Restrictions:* for indiv & inst, none. Cannot use for fund-raising. May not borrow by mail.

Video Collection Maintained by own production. Use/play ½″ reel to reel, ¾″ cassette. *Sources:* own productions. *Tape Sel:* preview. *Collection, B&W:* ½″ reel, 20t/c; ¾″ cassette, 14t. *Pubns:* catalog.

Cable & CCTV Have CCTV in inst, with 12 monitors. *Programming Sources:* tapes produced by inst.

C- UNIVERSITY OF HAWAII LIBRARY, AV Servs, 2425 Campus Rd, 96822. *Tel:* (808) 948-8009. *Film Serv Est:* 1970. *In Charge:* Don R. Huddleston, Head, AV Servs. *AV Staff:* 3 (1 prof, 1 cl). *Film Sel:* faculty/staff recommendations.

Free-Loan Film Serv *Eligibility:* staff & students, educational inst. *Restrictions:* for indiv, only in state; for inst, only in state. Cannot use for fund-raising. Available to researchers/scholars for on-site viewing. May borrow by mail. *Loan Period:* 3 days. *Total Yr Film Loan:* 14,009.

Film Rental Serv *Restrictions:* only in state. *Rental Rate:* flat handling charge. *Rental Period:* 3 days. *Total Yr Film Booking:* 1496.

Film Collection 1800t/2100p. Approx 50t acquired annually. *Circ:* 16mm, 1800t/2100p. *Pubns:* catalog, every 4 yr ($1.35); suppl, every 2 yr (free).

Other Film Serv Obtain film from coop loan system (Univ. of Hawaii and state library), obtain film from other libraries. Permanent viewing facility (1 room). *Equipment:* lend 8mm cartridge projector, 8mm reel projector, projection tables & stands, projection screens.

Other Media Collections *Audio:* disc, 33⅓ rpm, 1000c; 45rpm, 150c; tape, cassette, 500c; cartridge, 300c; reel, 500c. *Filmstrips:* sound sets, 50c; silent sets, 200c. *Slides:* single, 67c.

Budget & Expenditures Total library expenditures $925,857 (FY 7/1/74-7/1/75). Total FY film budget $30,000. *Member:* AECT.

Laie

C- BRIGHAM YOUNG UNIVERSITY—HAWAII CAMPUS, Learning Resource Center, 55-2201 Kulanui, 96762. *Tel:* (808) 293-9211, ext 216. *Film Serv Est:* 1955. *In Charge:* Rex Frandsen, Coord. *AV Staff:* 9 (1 prof, 3 cl, 5 tech). *Film Sel:* committee preview, faculty/staff recommendations.

Film Rental Serv *Eligibility:* educational org, civic groups, patrons/public. *Restrictions:* some titles for campus use only. *Rental Period:* as scheduled. *Total Yr Film Booking:* 200.

Film Collection 810t. Approx 25t acquired annually. *Circ:* 16mm, 780t/p. *Noncirc:* 16mm, 20t/p; S8mm reel, 50t/p. *Pubns:* catalog, every 2 yr.

Other Film Serv Rent film from distributors for patrons, obtain film from other libraries, film reference serv. *Equipment:* rent 16mm sound projector (10), rent 8mm cartridge projector (2), rent 8mm reel projector (2), rent S8mm cartridge projector (2), rent projection tables & stands (2), rent projection screens (5).

Other Media Collections *Audio:* disc, 33⅓ rpm, 700t/c; disc, 78rpm, 100t/c; tape, cassette, 300t/c. *Filmstrips:* sound sets, 380t/c; silent sets, 40t/c. *Slides:* single, 8000t/c.

Budget & Expenditures Total library budget $90,000 (FY 9/74-9/75). Total FY film budget $20,000. *Member:* AECT, ALA.

Video Serv *Est:* 1973. *Video Staff:* 3 f-t, 2 tech. *Video Use:* community video access, in-service training, practical video/TV training courses, as art form, educational instruction. Video serv available on demand or by appointment. Produce video tapes. Have production studio/space & separate control room.

Video Equipment/Facilities *In-House Use Only:* portapak (2), ½″ b&w, Sony; recording deck (3), ¾″ col, Sony; playback deck (2), ¾″ b&w/col, Sony; editing deck (1), ¾″ col, Sony; studio camera (2), b&w/col, Sony, Ampex; monitor (8), b&w/col, Sony, RCA; SEG (1), Telemation; keyer (1), Telemation; lighting (19); microphones (7); tripods (3); audio tape recorders (10). *For Loan:* audio tape recorders (10). Have permanent & portable viewing installations. *Equipment Loan Period:* no set policy. Provide training in use of equipment to faculty & students. Have tape duplication serv.

Video Tape Loan/Rental/Sale Serv *Serv Provided:* swap with other inst, rental. *Loan/Rental Eligibility:* staff & students, educational inst. *Restrictions:* for indiv, interlibrary loan.

Video Collection Maintained by purchase, rental, own production, exchange/swap. Use/play ½″ reel to reel, ¾″ cassette. *Sources:* commercial distributors, community productions, exchange. *Tape Sel:* preview. *Collection, Color:* ¾″ cassette, 140t/c. *Collection, B&W:* ½″ reel, 45t/c. *Other Video Serv:* programming, taping of other media.

Cable & CCTV Inform public about cable system serv & facilities. Have CCTV in inst, with 6 monitors. *Programming Sources:* over-the-air commercial & public broadcasting, tapes produced by inst, tapes produced professionally, tapes produced by community groups & indiv.

Lihue

C- UNIVERSITY OF HAWAII, Kauai Community College Learning Resources Center, R.R. 1, Box 216, 96766. *Tel:* (808) 245-6741. *Film Sel:* faculty/staff recommendations.

Free-Loan Film Serv *Eligibility:* staff & students, educational inst. *Restrictions:* for indiv, only in Kauai County; for inst, only in state. Cannot use for fund-raising. Available to researchers/scholars for on-site viewing. May not borrow by mail. *Loan Period:* 1 day.

Film Collection *Pubns:* catalog, as needed; suppl, no set policy.

Other Film Serv Obtain film from coop loan system (Hawaii Community Colleges).

Other Media Collections *Audio:* disc, 33⅓ rpm, 1037t/1037c; tape, cassette, 1456t/1456c. *Slides:* single, 7316t/7316c.

Budget & Expenditures Total library budget $35,435 (FY 7/1/74-7/1/75). *Member:* ALA, Hawaii Library Assn.

Video Serv Produce video tapes.

Video Equipment/Facilities *In-House Use Only:* portapak (1), ½″ b&w, Sony; recording deck (2), ¾″ col, Sony VP 1000; playback deck (2), ¾″ col, Sony VO1800; editing deck (1), ½″ col, Sony AV8650; microphones (4); tripods (4); audio tape recorders (40). Have permanent viewing installation. *Equipment Loan Period:* year-to-year to instructional staff. Provide training in use of equipment to faculty & students. Have tape duplication serv.

Video Tape Loan/Rental/Sale Serv *Serv Provided:* swap with other inst. *Loan Eligibility:* staff & students. *Restrictions:* only in our county; for inst, only in our county. Cannot use for fund-raising. May not borrow by mail.

Video Collection Maintained by purchase, own production, exchange/swap. Use/play ¾″ cassette. Tapes organized by Library of Congress system.

Cable & CCTV Receive serv of cable TV system. Have CCTV in inst, with 4 monitors.

Idaho

Boise

P- IDAHO STATE LIBRARY, 325 W State St, 83702. *Tel:* (208) 384-2150, ext 29. *Film Serv Est:* 1963. *In Charge:* Gaye Walter, Film Librarian. *AV Staff:* 1 (1 prof). *Film Sel:* committee preview, faculty/staff recommendations, chief film librarian's decision. *Holdings:* children's films 10%, library science 1%.

Free-Loan Film Serv *Eligibility:* public libraries for their sponsored programs. *Restrictions:* for inst, only in state. Cannot use for fund-raising. Available to researchers/scholars for on-site viewing. May borrow by mail. *Loan Period:* 1 day. *Total Yr Film Loan:* 5716.

Film Rental Serv *Eligibility:* no restrictions. *Restrictions:* only in state. Cannot use for fund-raising. *Rental Period:* 1 day. *Total Yr Film Booking:* 5716.

Film Collection 1110t/1126p. Approx 80t acquired annually. *Circ:* 16mm, 1110t/1126p. *Pubns:* catalog, as needed ($2); suppl, no set policy ($.50).

Other Film Serv Film reference serv, library film programs. Permanent viewing facility.

Other Media Collections *Audio:* disc, 33⅓rpm, 2000t/c; cassette, 100t/c. Full Library of Congress depository for blind & handicapped—about 16,000 discs.

Budget & Expenditures Total library budget $55,800 (FY 7/1/74-7/1/75). Total FY film budget $20,000. *Member:* ALA, Idaho Library Assn.

Moscow

C- UNIVERSITY OF IDAHO, AV Center, 83843. *Tel:* (208) 885-6411. *Film Serv Est:* 1947. *In Charge:* L. Lind, Dir. *AV Staff:* 8 (1 prof, 2 cl, 5 tech). *Film Sel:* committee preview, faculty/staff recommendations.

Free-Loan Film Serv *Eligibility:* staff. *Restrictions:* for indiv, only in city. Cannot use for fund-raising, transmit electronically. Available to researchers/scholars for on-site viewing. May borrow by mail. *Loan Period:* 5 days. *Total Yr Film Loan:* 1560.

Film Rental Serv *Eligibility:* no restrictions. *Restrictions:* none. *Rental Period:* 5 days. *Total Yr Film Booking:* 3500.

Film Collection 1890t/2000p. Approx 30t acquired annually. *Circ:* 16mm, 1280t/1230p; 8mm reel, 22t/12p; 8mm cartridge, 38t/38p; S8mm reel, 29t/13p; S8mm cartridge, 18t/18p. *Pubns:* catalog, every 2 yr; suppl, in yr catalog not published.

Other Film Serv Rent film from distributors for patrons, obtain film from other libraries, film reference serv. Permanent viewing facility available for rent to community. *Equipment:* lend S8mm camera, 16mm sound projector, 8mm cartridge projector, 8mm reel projector, S8mm cartridge projector, S8mm reel projector, projection tables & stands, projection screens.

Other Media Collections *Audio:* disc, 33⅓ rpm, 50c; tape, cassette, 150c; tape, reel, 100c. *Filmstrips:* sound, 310c; silent, 500c; sound sets, 280c; silent sets, 445c. *Slides:* single, 600c; sets, 50c.

Budget & Expenditures Total library budget $70,000 (FY 7/1/74-7/1/75). Total FY film budget $8,000. *Member:* AECT, CUFC.

Video Serv *Est:* 1975. *In Charge:* C. Barnes, AV Technician. *Video Staff:* 4 f-t, 11 p-t, 2 tech. *Video Use:* documentation of community/school events, in-service training, practical video/TV training courses. Video serv available by appointment. Produce video tapes.

Video Equipment/Facilities *In-House Use Only:* portapak (2), ½" b&w, Sony; recording deck (3), ½" b&w/col, Sony; playback deck (3), ¾" col, Sony; monitor (4), col, Sony. *For Loan:* audio tape recorders (55). *Equipment Loan Period:* 3 days. Provide training in use of equipment to faculty & technicians. Have tape duplication serv.

Video Tape Loan/Rental/Sale Serv *Serv Provided:* free loan, swap with other inst, rental, sale. *Loan/Rental Eligibility:* staff & students, educational inst. *Restrictions:* for indiv, only in city; for inst, only in state. Cannot use for fund-raising, duplicate, air without permission. May borrow by mail. *Loan Period:* 5 days. *Total Yr Tape Loan:* 25.

Video Collection Maintained by purchase, own production, exchange/swap. Use/play ½" reel to reel, ¾" cassette. *Sources:* commercial distributors, community productions, exchange. *Tape Sel:* preview, faculty/staff recommendations. *Special Collections:* in-house training tapes, video as art, films in video format. Tapes organized by subject. *Other Video Serv:* programming, reference serv, taping of other media. *Pubns:* catalog.

Cable & CCTV Receive serv of cable TV system. Produce programs for cablecasting. Inform public about cable system serv & facilities. Serve as production facility for others. Run cable programs for special audiences. Have CCTV in inst, with 100 monitors. *Programming Sources:* tapes produced by inst, tapes produced professionally, tapes produced by community groups & indiv.

Pocatello

C- IDAHO STATE UNIVERSITY, Box 8111, 83209. *Tel:* (208) 236-2857. *Video Serv Est:* 1965. *In Charge:* Richard Warth, CCTV Mgr. *Video Staff:* 2 f-t, 3 p-t, 1 tech. *Video Use:* inservice training, practical video/TV training courses, playback only of professionally produced tapes, as art form. Video serv available on demand. Produce video tapes. Have production studio/space & separate control room.

Video Equipment/Facilities *In-House Use Only:* recording deck (6), ½", 1", 2" b&w/col; studio camera (4), b&w/col; monitor (15); SEG (1); additional camera lenses (4); lighting (25); microphones (10); tripods (6); audio tape recorders (5). *For Loan:* playback deck (1), ¾". Provide training in use of equipment to students. Have tape duplication serv.

Video Tape Loan/Rental/Sale Serv *Serv Provided:* free loan, swap with other inst. *Loan/Rental Eligibility:* staff & students, educational inst, civic groups, religious groups, prof groups. *Restrictions:* for indiv, only in city; for inst, none. Cannot air without permission. May borrow by mail.

Video Collection Maintained by own production, exchange/swap. Use/play ½", 1", 2" reel to reel, ¾" cassette. *Sources:* commercial distributors. *Tape Sel:* faculty/staff recommendations, catalogs. *Other Video Serv:* programming, reference serv.

Cable & CCTV Have CCTV in inst, with 25 monitors. *Programming Sources:* over-the-air commercial & public broadcasting, tapes produced by inst, tapes produced professionally, tapes produced by community groups & indiv.

C- IDAHO STATE UNIVERSITY, AV Servs, Box 8064, 83209. *Tel:* (208) 236-2355 or 2112. *Film Serv Est:* 1938. *In Charge:* Jay H. Dickinson, Dir. *AV Staff:* 4 (2 prof, 1 cl, 1 tech). *Film Sel:* faculty/staff recommendations, chief film librarian's decision. *Holdings:* O.W.I. Films 2%, News Magazine of the Screen (8/55-5/58) 2%.

Free-Loan Film Serv *Eligibility:* staff. *Restrictions:* only on campus except for continuing education classes. Available to researchers/scholars for on-site viewing. May not borrow by mail. *Loan Period:* length of a class period. *Total Yr Film Loan:* 2791.

Film Rental Serv *Eligibility:* no restrictions. *Restrictions:* none. Cannot use for fund-raising, transmit electronically. *Rental Period:* 1-4 days. *Total Yr Film Booking:* 1830. Produce slides, tapes, overhead transparencies, posters.

Film Collection 1800t/2200p. Approx 110t acquired annually. *Circ:* 16mm, 1700t/2088p. *Noncirc:* 16mm, 100t/112p.

Pubns: catalog, every 2 yr; suppl, no set policy. Publish monthly newsletter.

Other Film Serv Obtain film from coop loan system (Consortium of University Film Centers), obtain film from other libraries, film reference serv. Permanent viewing facility available. *Equipment:* lend/rent 16mm sound projector (20), 8mm cartridge projector (1), S8mm cartridge projector (1), projection tables & stands (8), projection screens (12), overhead projectors & carousel slide projectors.

Other Media Collections *Audio:* disc, 33⅓ rpm, 146t/146c; tape, cassette, 184t/184c; tape, reel, 56t/56c. *Filmstrips:* sound sets, 50t/50c.

Budget & Expenditures Total library budget $52,626 (FY 7/1/74-7/1/75). Total FY film budget $18,656. *Member:* AECT, CUFC, Idaho Educational Media Assn.

P- **POCATELLO PUBLIC LIBRARY,** 812 E Clark, 83201. *Tel:* (208) 232-1263. *Video Serv Est:* 1974. *In Charge:* Paul Tamminen, Head, Adult & Community Servs Division. *Video Staff:* 2 f-t. *Video Use:* documentation of community/school events, to increase community's library use, community video access, in-service training. Video serv currently available by appointment. On demand in future. Produce video tapes. Have production studio/space.

Video Equipment/Facilities *In-House Use Only:* portapak (1), ½″ b&w/col, Sony AV 8400C; editing deck (1), ½″ col, Sony AV 8650; monitor (2), col, Sony CVM 1720; lighting (1); audio tape recorders (2). *For Loan:* portapak (1), ½″ b&w/col, Sony AV8400C; monitor (1), b&w, Zenith; audio tape recorders (2). *Equipment Loan Period:* no set policy. Provide training in use of equipment to faculty, students & community. Have tape duplication serv.

Video Tape Loan/Rental/Sale Serv *Serv Provided:* free loan, swap with other inst. *Loan Eligibility:* staff & students, educational inst, civic groups, religious groups, prof groups. *Restrictions:* May borrow by mail. *Loan Period:* not yet determined.

Video Collection Maintained by own production, exchange/swap. Use/play ½″ reel to reel, ¾″ cassette. *Sources:* community productions, exchange. *Tape Sel:* catalogs. *Special Collections:* none. Tapes organized by subject. *Collection, Color:* ½″ reel, 2t/c. *Collection, B&W:* ½″ reel, 15t. *Other Video Serv:* programming, production workshops. *Pubns:* publish information/promotional brochures.

Cable & CCTV Receive serv of cable TV system. Produce programs for cablecasting. Inform public about cable system serv & facilities. Serve as production facility for others. Run cable programs for special audiences. Have advisory/administrative role in cable system operation (library staff actively supports Citizens Cable Committee).

Illinois

Burr Ridge

P- NORTH SUBURBAN LIBRARY SYSTEM & SUBURBAN LIBRARY SYSTEM, Suburban AV Servs, 125 Tower Dr, 60521. *Tel:* (312) 325-7450. *Film Serv Est:* 1967. *In Charge:* Leon L. Drolet, Jr, Dir. *AV Staff:* 17 (2 prof, 14 cl, 1 tech). *Film Sel:* chief film librarian's decision. *Holdings:* agriculture 1%, animated films 15%, black studies 5%, children's films 20%, consumer affairs 1%, dance 10%, experimental films 5%, feature films 20%, fine arts 20%, industrial arts 1%, law 1%, medicine 1%, science 5%, social sciences 10%, women 1%.

    Free-Loan Film Serv *Eligibility:* indiv with library cards. *Restrictions:* for indiv & inst, only in state (but ALA material throughout U.S.). Cannot use for fund-raising, transmit electronically, borrow for classroom use. Available to researchers/scholars for on-site viewing. May not borrow by mail. *Loan Period:* 6-9 days. *Total Yr Film Loan:* 64,530.

    Film Collection 2750t/3650p. Approx 420t acquired annually. *Circ:* 16mm, 2750t/3650p. *Pubns:* catalog, annual ($2.25); suppl, as needed.

    Other Film Serv Obtain film from other libraries, film reference serv, film fairs/festivals, library film programs, feature film rental. Permanent viewing facility. *Equipment:* lend 16mm sound projector (8), 8mm reel projector (1), S8mm reel projector (1), projection screens (6).

    Other Media Collections *Audio:* disc, 33⅓rpm, 7500t/8300c; tape, cassette, 150t/150c.

    Budget & Expenditures Total library budget $198,000 (FY 7/1/74-7/1/75). Total FY film budget $192,000. *Member:* ALA, EFLA, FLIC.

Carterville

P- SHAWNEE LIBRARY SYSTEM, RR 2, Box 136A, 62918. *Tel:* (618) 985-3711. *Film Serv Est:* 1968. *In Charge:* Marilyn Gulley, Clerk Typist I. *AV Staff:* 1½ cl. *Film Sel:* staff recommendations.

    Free-Loan Film Serv *Eligibility:* area public library outlets. *Restrictions:* for indiv, none; for inst, none. Cannot use for fund-raising, transmit electronically. Available to researchers/scholars for on-site viewing. May borrow by mail. *Loan Period:* 1 day. *Total Yr Film Loan:* 9108.

    Film Collection 425t. Approx 60t acquired annually. *Circ:* 16mm, 425t/450p. *Pubns:* catalog, every 2 yrs; suppl, in yr catalog not published.

    Other Media Collections *Audio:* disc, 33⅓rpm, 3000t/5000c; tape, cassette, 1000t/1500c.

    Budget & Expenditures Total library budget $120,000 (FY 7/1/74-7/1/75). Total FY film budget $20,000.

Champaign

P- CHAMPAIGN PUBLIC LIBRARY, AV Loan Center, 306 W Church St, 61820. *Tel:* (217) 356-7243, ext 23. *Film Serv Est:* 1970. *In Charge:* Janet Otto, Section Head. *AV Staff:* 3 cl. *Film Sel:* committee preview. *Holdings:* animated films, children's films, feature films, silent film classics.

    Free-Loan Film Serv *Eligibility:* indiv with library cards. *Restrictions:* for indiv, interlibrary loan. Cannot use for fund-raising. May not borrow by mail. *Loan Period:* 1 day. *Total Yr Film Loan:* 10,700.

    Film Rental Serv *Eligibility:* no restrictions. *Restrictions:* none. *Rental Period:* 7 days. *Total Yr Film Booking:* 4000.

    Film Collection 300t/300p. Approx 50-100t acquired annually. *Circ:* 8mm reel, 100t/100p; S8mm reel, 200t/200p. *Pubns:* catalog, as needed.

    Other Film Serv Obtain film from coop loan system (Lincoln Trails Library System), library film programs. Permanent

viewing facility available to community. *Equipment:* rent 16mm sound projector (6), 8mm reel projector (5), S8mm reel projector (2), projection stands (4), projection screens (4).

    Other Media Collections *Audio:* disc 33⅓ rpm, 5000t/5000c. *Filmstrips:* sound sets, 59t/59c.

    Budget & Expenditures Total library budget $100,000 (FY 7/1/74-7/1/75). Total FY film budget $2000. *Member:* Ill. State Library Assn.

P- LINCOLN TRAIL LIBRARIES SYSTEM, Box 3471 C.F., 61820. *Tel:* (217) 352-0047. *Film Serv Est:* 1968. *In Charge:* Charles D. Dawson, AV Consultant. *AV Staff:* 4½ (1 prof, 1½ cl, 2 tech). *Film Sel:* joint decision of executive director and AV consultant.

    Free-Loan Film Serv *Eligibility:* indiv with library cards. *Restrictions:* for indiv, none. Cannot use for fund-raising, transmit electronically. May borrow by mail. *Loan Period:* 1-3 days. *Total Yr Film Loan:* 23,884.

    Film Collection 1227t/1391p. Approx 150t acquired annually. *Circ:* 16mm, 1227t/1391p. *Pubns:* catalog, every 3 yrs; suppl, no set policy.

    Other Film Serv Obtain film from coop loan system, obtain film from other libraries, film reference serv, film fairs/festivals, library film programs. *Equipment:* lend 16mm sound projector (5), lend projection screens (4).

    Other Media Collections *Audio:* disc, 33⅓ rpm, 3000t/3100c. *Filmstrips:* sound sets, 128t/128c.

    Budget & Expenditures Total library budget $70,000 (FY 7/1/74-7/1/75). Total FY film budget $60,000. *Member:* EFLA, Ill. Library Assn.

C- UNIVERSITY OF ILLINOIS, Visual Aids Service, 1325 S Oak St, 61820. *Tel:* (217) 333-1362. *Film Serv Est:* 1936. *In Charge:* Thomas H. Boardman, Dir. *AV Staff:* 41 (4 prof, 18 cl, 19 tech). *Film Sel:* faculty/staff recommendations, chief film librarian's decision. *Holdings:* general collection. All curriculum areas.

    Free-Loan Film Serv *Eligibility:* staff & students, education inst, civic groups, religious groups.

    Film Rental Serv *Eligibility:* no restrictions. *Restrictions:* only in continental U.S. Cannot use for fund-raising, transmit electronically. *Rental Period:* 2 days. *Total Yr Film Booking:* 150,000.

    Film Collection 12,000t/27,000p. Approx 910t acquired annually. *Circ:* 16mm, 12,000t/27,000p. *Pubns:* catalog, every 3 yrs ($5); suppl, in yr catalog not published.

    Other Film Serv Obtain film from other libraries, film reference serv.

    Budget & Expenditures Total library budget $506,004 (FY 7/1/74-7/1/75). Total FY film budget $506,004. *Member:* AECT, CUFC, EFLA.

Charleston

C- EASTERN ILLINOIS UNIVERSITY, Booth Library, 61920. *Tel:* (217) 581-5433. *Video Serv Est:* 1973. *In Charge:* Paladugu V. Rao, Head, Information Systems Dept. *Video Staff:* 7 f-t, 1 p-t. *Video Use:* support the educational process of the university. Video serv available on demand & by appointment.

    Video Equipment/Facilities *In-House Use Only:* recording deck (1), col, Sony VO 1600; playback deck (1), col, Sony; monitor (2), col, Sony; video projector, screen & tuner. Provide training in use of equipment to staff & student assistants.

    Video Tape/Loan /Rental/Sale Serv *Loan Eligibility:* org members, staff, students enrolled in inst.

    Video Collection Maintained by purchase, rental. Use/play ¾" cassette. *Sources:* tapes prepared by AV dept. *Tape Sel:* faculty/staff recommendations, catalogs. Tapes organized by

LC or reserve number. *Collection, Color:* ¾″ cassette, 30t. *Collection, B&W:* ¾″ cassette, 60t. *Other Video Serv:* catalog.

Cable & CCTV Receive serv of cable TV system.

Chicago

C- CENTER CINEMA CO-OP, c/o School of the Art Institute, Michigan Ave at Adams St, 60602. *Tel:* (312) 236-1519. *Film Serv Est:* 1968. *In Charge:* Barbara Scharres, Mgr. *Holdings:* experimental films 100%.

Film Rental Serv *Eligibility:* no restrictions. *Restrictions:* only in U.S. Cannot use for fund-raising, transmit electronically. *Rental Period:* films rent by showing & must be returned immediately after last showing for which they were booked.

Film Collection 375/390p. Approx 10-15t acquired annually. *Pubns:* catalog, as needed; suppl, no set policy.

P- CHICAGO PUBLIC LIBRARY, AV Center, 60602. *Tel:* (312) 269-2910. *In Charge:* Diane Purtill, Head, AV Center. *AV Staff:* 15 (5 prof, 10 cl). *Film Sel:* committee preview.

Free-Loan Film Serv *Eligibility:* educational inst, civic groups, religious groups, prof groups, and businesses. *Restrictions:* for inst, only in city. Cannot use for fund-raising, transmit electronically, cannot be duplicated or video taped. May not borrow by mail. *Loan Period:* 3 days.

Film Collection 1903t/2503p. Approx 225t acquired annually. *Circ:* 16mm, 1903t/2503p; 8mm reel, 141t/198p; S8mm reel, 68t/209p; S8mm cartridge, 50t/50p. *Pubns:* catalog, as needed ($2); suppl, bi-monthly.

Other Film Serv Library film programs.

Other Media Collections *Audio:* tape, cassette, 414t/414c. *Filmstrips:* silent, 723t/1052c. *Slides:* single, 12,458t/12,468c.

Budget & Expenditures No separate budget. *Member:* AFI, ALA, EFLA, FLIC, Ill. Library Assn.

C- CHICAGO STATE UNIVERSITY, Div Of Learning Resources, Douglas Library, 95 St at King Dr, 60628. *Tel:* (312) 995-2211. *Film Serv Est:* 1950. *In Charge:* Dr. Serene Onesto, Head, D.L.R. *AV Staff:* 8 (2 prof, 2 cl, 4 tech). *Film Sel:* committee preview, faculty/staff recommendations, chief film librarian's decision. *Holdings:* teacher education 50%.

Free-Loan Film Serv *Eligibility:* staff, students enrolled in inst, prof groups, occasionally other institutions. *Restrictions:* for indiv, none. Available to researchers/scholars for on-site viewing. May not borrow by mail. *Loan Period:* 1 day. *Total Yr Film Loan:* 860.

Film Rental Serv *Eligibility:* educational org. *Restrictions:* written request from AV director or administrator of borrowing institution. *Rental Rate:* $5. *Rental Period:* 1 day. *Total Yr Film Booking:* 4. Produce sound filmstrip programs.

Film Collection 830t/834p. Approx 50-75t acquired annually. *Circ:* 16mm, 536t/536p; 8mm reel, 298t/298p. *Pubns:* catalog, annual; suppl, no set policy.

Other Film Serv Obtain film from coop loan system (Chicago Metropolitan Higher Ed. Council), other libraries, film reference serv. Permanent viewing facility.

Other Media Collections *Audio:* disc, total, 3972c; tape, cassette, cartridge, & reel, 1538c. *Filmstrips:* sound & silent, 4416c; sound & silent sets, 72c. *Slides:* single 1867c; sets, 100c.

Budget & Expenditures Total library budget $225,000 (FY 7/1/74-7/1/75). Total FY film budget $39,700. *Member:* AECT, EFLA, IAVA, Ill. Library Assn.

Video Serv *Est:* 1960. *In Charge:* Thomas Newman, Head, Media Tech. Serv. *Video Staff:* 3 f-t, 3 p-t. *Video Use:* documentation of community/school events, in-service training, practical video/TV training courses. Video serv available by appointment. Produce video tapes. Have production studio/space & separate control room.

Video Equipment/Facilities *In-House Use Only:* portapak (14), b&w, Sony; recording deck (14), b&w/col, Sony; studio camera (8), b&w/col, Sony; SEG (1), IUC. *For Loan:* portapak (14), b&w, Sony; recording deck (14), b&w/col, Sony. Have

permanent viewing installation. *Equipment Loan Period:* no set policy. Provide training in use of equipment.

Video Tape Loan Serv *Serv Provided:* free loan, swap with other inst. *Loan Eligibility:* staff & students, educational inst. *Restrictions:* for indiv, none; for inst, none. May not borrow by mail. *Loan Period:* 7 days. *Total Yr Tape Loan:* 10.

Video Collection Maintained by purchase, rental, own production, exchange/swap. Use/play 1″ reel to reel, ¾″ cassette. *Sources:* commercial distributors, community productions, exchange. *Tape Sel:* preview, faculty/staff recommendations. *Special Collections:* in-house training tapes. Tapes organized by subject.

S- COMMUNICATIONS FOR CHANGE, 22 W Erie, 60610. *Tel:* (312) 565-1785. *Video Serv Est:* 1972. *In Charge:* Tedwilliam Theodore, Dir. *Video Staff:* 3 f-t, 1 p-t. *Video Use:* documentation of community/school events, in-service training, video intervention. Produce video tapes.

Video Equipment/Facilities *In-House Use Only:* portapak (1), b&w, Panasonic; recording deck (3), b&w/col, Panasonic; playback deck (1), b&w, Panasonic; editing deck (1), col, Panasonic; studio camera (1), b&w, Panasonic; monitor (5), b&w, Panasonic; additional camera lenses; lighting; microphones; tripods; audio tape recorders. Have permanent & portable viewing installations. *Equipment Loan Period:* provide training in use of equipment. Have tape duplication serv.

Video Tape Loan/Rental/Sale Serv *Serv Provided:* swap with other inst. *Loan Eligibility:* educational inst, civic groups, religious groups.

Video Collection Maintain tapes by own production. Use/play ½″ reel to reel. *Sources:* community productions. Tapes organized by subject. *Collection, B&W:* ½″ reel, 30t. *Other Video Serv:* production workshops.

S- HORSFIELD/BLUMENTHAL INTERVIEWS, 1263 Paulina, 60622. *Tel:* (312) 227-0121. *Video Serv Est:* 1973. *In Charge:* Kate Horsfield, Lyn Blumenthal, Co-Presidents. *Video Staff:* 2 f-t, 1 p-t, 1 tech. *Video Use:* documentation of community/school events, to increase community's library use, as art form. Video serv available on demand & by appointment. Produce video tapes. Have production studio/space.

Video Equipment/Facilities *In-House Use Only:* portapak (1), ½″ b&w, Panasonic; recording deck (1), ½″ b&w, Panasonic; playback deck, ¾″, Panasonic; editing deck (1), ½″ b&w; monitor (2), Shibaden; SEG (3), Sony; keyer (1), Ampex; additional camera lenses (4); microphones (2); tripods (3); audio tape recorders (1). Have portable viewing installation.

Video Tape Loan/Rental/Sale Serv *Serv Provided:* swap with other inst, rental. *Loan/Rental Eligibility:* org members, staff & students.

Video Collection Maintained by purchase, rental, own production, exchange/swap. Use/play ½″ reel to reel, ¾″ cassette. *Sources:* galleries, community productions, exchange (Art Institute Data Bank). *Tape Sel:* preview. *Special Collections:* video as art, video interview tapes of artists. Tapes organized by subject. *Collection, B&W:* ½″ reel, 35t/70c; ¾″ cassette, 35t/70c. *Other Video Serv:* reference serv, taping of other media. *Pubns:* catalog

C- THE LOOP COLLEGE (City Colleges of Chicago), 64 E Lake St, 60601. *Tel:* (312) 269-8017. *Film Serv Est:* 1963. *In Charge:* J. William Locke, AV Dir. *AV Staff:* 3 (1 prof, 2 tech). *Film Sel:* faculty/staff recommendations.

Free-Loan Film Serv *Eligibility:* staff. *Restrictions:* for indiv, none; for inst, none.

Film Collection 600t/600p. Approx 19t acquired annually. *Pubns:* catalog, every 2 yrs.

Other Film Serv Rent film from distributors for patrons, obtain film from coop loan system (Chicago Public Library).

Other Media Collections *Audio:* disc, 33⅓ rpm, 2000t/2300c; tape, cassette, 200c; tape, reel, 7000c. *Filmstrips:* total 341t. *Slides:* single, 8000t.

Chicago (cont'd)

Budget & Expenditures Total library budget $43,000 (FY 7/1/74-7/1/75). Total FY film budget $4700. *Member:* AECT, ALA, EFLA.

Video Serv *Est:* 1964. *In Charge:* J. William Locke, Dir. *Video Staff:* 1 f-t, 8 p-t, 2 tech. *Video Use:* documentation of community/school events. Video serv available by appointment for college-related activities only. Produce video tapes. Have production studio/space.

Video Equipment/Facilities *In-House Use Only:* portapak (1), ¾" col, Sony; recording deck (2), ¾" col, Sony; playback deck (4), ¾" col, Sony; studio camera (1), col, Sony. Have permanent viewing installation. *Equipment Loan Period:* 1 hr. Provide training in use of equipment to faculty & students.

Video Tape Loan/Rental/Sale Serv *Loan Eligibility:* staff.

Video Collection Maintained by purchase, rental, own production. Use/play ¾" cassette. *Sources:* commercial distributors. *Tape Sel:* faculty/staff recommendations. Tapes organized by subject. *Collection, Color:* ¾" cassette, 300c.

Cable & CCTV Have CCTV in inst, with 6 monitors. *Programming Sources:* tapes produced by inst, tapes produced professionally, tapes produced by community groups & indiv.

C- **LOYOLA UNIVERSITY OF CHICAGO**, 6525 N Sheridan, 60626. *Tel:* (312) 274-3000. *Film Serv Est:* 1949. *In Charge:* Mary McGrath, Circulation Librarian. *Film Sel:* faculty/staff recommendations. *Holdings:* children's films, feature films, fine arts, medicine, science, social sciences, teacher education.

Free-Loan Film Serv *Eligibility:* staff. *Restrictions:* for indiv, none; for inst, none. Available to researchers/scholars for on-site viewing. May not borrow by mail. *Loan Period:* no time limitations.

Film Collection 600t/600p. Approx 7t acquired annually. *Circ:* 16mm, 600t/600p. Permanent viewing facility. *Equipment:* lend S8mm camera (2), 16mm camera (2), 16mm sound projector (10), 8mm reel projector (1), S8mm reel projector (6), projection tables & stands (12), projection screens (11).

Other Media Collections *Audio:* disc, 5000t/5000c; tape, 1000t/c. *Filmstrips:* sound, 1140t total. *Slides:* single, 6500t.

Budget & Expenditures Total library budget $481,892 (FY 7/1/74-7/1/75). Total FY film budget $3000. *Member:* ALA, Ill. State Library Assn.

C- **MAYFAIR COLLEGE** (City Colleges of Chicago), Library, 4626 N Knox Ave, 60630. *Tel:* (312) 286-1323, ext 67. *Film Serv Est:* 1960. *In Charge:* Sally Anderson, AV Librarian. *AV Staff:* 3 (1 prof, 1 cl, 1 tech). *Film Sel:* committee preview, faculty/staff recommendations, chief film librarian's decision, published reviews.

Free-Loan Film Serv *Eligibility:* staff & students. May not borrow by mail. *Loan Period:* class period. *Total Yr Film Loan:* 1007.

Film Collection 236t/237p. Approx 30t acquired annually. *Circ:* 16mm, 236t/237p; S8mm cartridge, 600t. *Pubns:* catalog, annual; suppl, monthly.

Other Film Serv Rent film from distributors for patrons, obtain film from coop loan system (Illinois Regional Library Council), obtain film from other libraries. Permanent viewing facility. *Equipment:* lend S8mm camera (1), 16mm camera (1), 16mm sound projector (14), 8mm cartridge projector (1), 8mm reel projector (1), S8mm cartridge projector (7), S8mm reel projector (1), projection tables & stands (24), projection screens (12).

Other Media Collections *Audio:* disc, 33⅓ rpm, 1900t/2000c; disc, 45rpm, 50t/240c; tape, cassette, 100t/2000c; tape, reel, 20t/500c. *Filmstrips:* silent, 122c. *Slides:* single, 1000t/1000c; sets, 4t/145c.

Budget & Expenditures Total library budget $212,250 (FY 7/1/74-7/1/75). Total FY film budget $10,000. *Member:* AECT, ALA, FLIC.

C- **NORTH PARK COLLEGE**, Wallgren Library, 5125 N Spaulding, 60625. *Tel:* (312) 583-2700, ext 353. *Film Serv*

Est: 1965. *In Charge:* Charles Peterson, Dir, Instructional Media. *AV Staff:* 5 (2 cl, 15 tech). *Film Sel:* faculty/staff recommendations.

Free-Loan Film Serv *Eligibility:* org members, students enrolled in inst. *Restrictions:* for indiv, campus; for inst, campus. Available to researchers/scholars for on-site viewing. May not borrow by mail. Produce slides.

Film Collection 30t. Approx 3t acquired annually. *Circ:* 16mm, 25t/25p. *Noncirc:* 16mm, 3t/20p. *Pubns:* catalog, as needed; suppl, no set policy.

Other Film Serv Rent film from distributors for patrons, film reference serv, film fairs/festivals. Permanent viewing facility available for rent to community. *Equipment:* lend/rent 16mm sound projector (6), lend/rent 8mm reel projector (1), lend/rent projection tables & stands, lend/rent projection screens.

Other Media Collections *Audio:* disc, 33⅓ rpm, 3000t; tape, cassette, 400t; tape, reel, 100t. *Filmstrips:* sound, 6t; silent, 100t; sound sets, 8t. *Slides:* single, 1000t; sets, 10t.

Budget & Expenditures Total library budget $47,822 (FY 7/1/74-7/1/75). Total FY film budget $1900.

Video Serv *Est:* 1972. *In Charge:* Charles Peterson, Dir. *Video Staff:* 1 f-t, 3 tech. *Video Use:* in-service training, playback only of professionally produced tapes. Video serv available by appointment. Produce video tapes.

Video Equipment/Facilities *In-House Use Only:* portapak (1), R-R b&w, Sony; recording deck (2), R-R b&w, Sony; playback deck, col, JVC; monitor (2), b&w, Sony; audio tape recorders (3). Have portable viewing installation. *Equipment Loan Period:* no set policy. Provide training in use of equipment to students. Have tape duplication serv.

Video Tape Loan/Rental/Sale Serv *Serv Provided:* free loan. *Loan Eligibility:* staff & students. *Restrictions:* for indiv, only on campus. May not borrow by mail.

Video Collection Maintained by rental, own production. Use/play ½" reel to reel, ¾" cassette. *Collection, Color:* ¾" cassette, 10t.

S- **POLISH MUSEUM OF AMERICA**, 984 N Milwaukee Ave, 60622. *Tel:* (312) 384-3352. *Film Serv Est:* 1968. *AV Staff:* 1 (1 cl). *Film Sel:* chief film librarian's decision. *Holdings:* Poles and their culture.

Free-Loan Film Serv *Eligibility:* educational inst, civic groups, religious groups, prof groups. *Restrictions:* for inst, only in U.S. Cannot use for fund-raising. May borrow by mail. *Loan Period:* 7 days.

Film Rental Serv *Eligibility:* educational org, civic groups. *Restrictions:* only in U.S. & territories. Cannot use for fund-raising.

Film Collection 50t/50p. *Circ:* 16mm, 50t.

Other Media Collections *Audio:* 78rpm, 150t. *Slides:* single, 250t.

Budget & Expenditures Total library budget $12,000.

Video Serv *Est:* 1968. *Video Staff:* 1 f-t. *Video Use:* documentation of community events, as art form. Video serv available by appointment. Have portable viewing installation.

Video Collection Maintained by exchange/swap.

C- **ROOSEVELT UNIVERSITY**, AV & Television, 430 S Michigan Blvd, 60605. *Tel:* (312) 341-3650. *Film Serv Est:* 1950. *In Charge:* Randall E. Jackson, Dir. *AV Staff:* 1½ (1 prof, ½ cl). *Film Sel:* faculty/staff recommendations, chief film librarian's decision.

Film Collection 293t/293p. *Noncirc:* 16mm, 293t/293p. *Pubns:* catalog, as needed; suppl, as needed.

Other Film Serv Rent film from distributors for patrons, obtain film from other libraries, film reference serv. *Member:* AECT, ALA, EFLA.

Video Serv *Est:* 1968. *In Charge:* Randall E. Jackson, Dir. *Video Staff:* ½ p-t, 1 tech. *Video Use:* to increase community's library use, in-service training, practical video/TV training courses. Video serv available by appointment. Produce video tapes. Have production studio/space & separate control room.

Video Equipment/Facilities *In-House Use Only:* portapak (3), ½" b&w, Shibaden; recording deck, ½" b&w, Shibaden;

playback deck (3), 1″ b&w/col, Shibaden, IVC; editing deck, ½″ col, Ampex; studio camera (3), b&w, Panasonic; monitor, Shibaden; SEG; keyer (1), Dynair; additional camera lenses; lighting; microphones; tripods; audio tape recorders. Have portable viewing installation. *Equipment Loan Period:* no set policy. Provide training in use of equipment to faculty & students. Have tape duplication serv.

Video Tape Loan/Rental/Sale Serv *Serv Provided:* swap with other inst.

Video Collection Maintained by purchase, rental, own production, exchange/swap. Use/play ½″, 1″, reel to reel. *Tape Sel:* preview, faculty/staff recommendations. *Special Collections:* in-house training tapes. *Other Video Serv:* production workshops.

Cable & CCTV Have CCTV in inst, with 8 monitors. *Programming Sources:* tapes produced by inst.

C- SCHOOL OF THE ART INSTITUTE OF CHICAGO, Film Center Study Collection, Michigan Ave at Adams St, 60602. *Tel:* (312) 443-3733. *Film Serv Est:* 1972. *In Charge:* Camille J. Cook, Dir, Film Center. *AV Staff:* 4 (2 prof, 1 cl, 1 tech). *Film Sel:* committee preview, faculty/staff recommendations, chief film librarian's decision, published reviews. *Holdings:* experimental films 80%.

Free-Loan Film Serv *Eligibility:* instructional staff, educational inst, prof groups, such as Art Institute associate groups. *Restrictions:* on-site only. Cannot use for fund-raising, transmit electronically, borrow for classroom use outside Art Institute. Available to researchers/scholars for on-site viewing. May not borrow by mail. *Loan Period:* on-site screenings only.

Film Collection 248t/270p. *Noncirc:* 16mm, 248t/270p; 8mm reel, 2t/p; S8mm reel, 1t/p; S8mm cartridge, 3t/p. *Pubns:* publish list of current collection in Film Center Annual Report.

Other Film Serv Obtain film from coop loan system (Assn of Specialized Film Exhibitors), film reference serv, film fairs/festivals, film exhibitions within museum. Permanent viewing facility.

Budget & Expenditures No separate budget. $10,000 matching grant from Natl Endowment for the Arts Museum Purchase Plan 1974-75 enabled purchase of $20,000 in experimental film. *Member:* Film Study Committee (Chicago), Union of Independent Colleges of Art.

C- SOUTHWEST COLLEGE, Learning Resource Center, 7500 Spulaski, 60652. *Tel:* (312) 735-3000, ext 224. *Film Serv Est:* 1968. *In Charge:* Dr. Inez McCord, Dir. *AV Staff:* 3 (1 prof, 1 cl, 1 tech). *Film Sel:* committee preview, faculty/staff recommendations, chief film librarian's decision. *Holdings:* architecture, drama, engineering, fine arts, science, social sciences, speech, teacher education.

Free-Loan Film Serv *Eligibility:* staff & students, civic groups. *Restrictions:* for indiv, only in community area; for inst, only in community area. Cannot use for fund-raising, transmit electronically. Available to researchers/scholars for on-site viewing. May not borrow by mail. *Loan Period:* class period.

Film Collection 400t/400p. *Pubns:* catalog, as needed; suppl, annually.

Other Film Serv Rent film from distributors for patrons, obtain film from other libraries. Permanent viewing facility available to community. *Equipment:* lend 16mm sound projector (20), lend 8mm reel projector.

Other Media Collections *Audio:* disc, 33⅓ rpm, 1500t/1500c; tape, cassette, 118c; tape, reel, 5c. *Filmstrips:* sound, 115t/115c; silent, 292t/298c; sound sets, 16t/16c. *Slides:* single, 15,786t/15,786c.

Budget & Expenditures Total library budget $25,000 (FY 7/1/74-7/1/75). No separate budget. *Member:* AECT, ALA.

Video Serv *Est:* 1968. *In Charge:* Dr. Inez McCord, Dir. *Video Staff:* 2 f-t, 10p-t, 1 tech. *Video Use:* documentation of community/school events, playback only of professionally produced tapes, production of classroom tapes. Video serv available on demand & by appointment. Produce video tapes.

Video Equipment/Facilities *In-House Use Only:* portapak (2); recording deck (2), Sony; playback deck (4), col, Sony, U-Matic; editing deck (1); studio camera (2); monitor (3), Magna-vox; microphones; tripods (6). *Equipment Loan Period:* no set policy. Provide training in use of equipment to faculty & students.

Video Tape Loan/Rental/Sale Serv *Serv Provided:* free loan. *Loan Eligibility:* staff & students, civic groups. *Restrictions:* for indiv, only in our school. Cannot use for fund-raising, duplicate, air without permission. May not borrow by mail.

Video Collection Maintained by purchase, own production. Use/play ½″ reel to reel, ¾″ cassette. *Sources:* commercial distributors. *Tape Sel:* preview, faculty/staff recommendations, published reviews, catalogs. Tapes organized by title.

Decatur

P- ROLLING PRAIRIE LIBRARIES, 345 W Eldorado, 62522. *Tel:* (217) 429-2586. *Film Serv Est:* 1966. *In Charge:* Larry Pepper, AV Coord. *AV Staff:* 3½ (1 prof, 2½ cl). *Film Sel:* chief film librarian's decision.

Free-Loan Film Serv *Eligibility:* indiv with library cards. *Restrictions:* none. Cannot use for fund-raising, transmit electronically. Available to researchers/scholars for on-site viewing. May borrow by mail. *Loan Period:* 1 day. *Total Yr Film Loan:* 18,344.

Film Collection 920t/1050p. Approx 200-300t acquired annually. *Circ:* 16mm, 920t/1050p. *Pubns:* catalog, annual; suppl, in yr catalog not published.

Other Film Serv Obtain film from coop loan system; obtain film from other libraries, film reference serv, library film programs. *Equipment:* lend 16mm sound projector (1), lend projection tables & stands (1), lend projection screens (2).

Other Media Collections *Audio:* disc, 33⅓ rpm & tape cassettes, 2225 total.

Budget & Expenditures Total library budget $130,000 (FY 7/1/74-7/1/75). Total FY film budget $39,000. *Member:* ALA, EFLA, Ill. Library Assn.

Dekalb

C- NORTHERN ILLINOIS UNIVERSITY EDUCATIONAL FILM LIBRARY, Media Distribution Dept, 60115. *Tel:* (815) 753-0171, ext 43. *Film Serv Est:* 1959. *In Charge:* G. L. Silverstein, Head, Media Distribution Dept. *AV Staff:* 11 (1 prof, 7 cl, 3 tech). *Film Sel:* faculty/staff recommendations, dept head's decision. *Holdings:* teacher education.

Free-Loan Film Serv *Eligibility:* staff & students. *Restrictions:* for indiv, University use only. *Loan Period:* 1 day. *Total Yr Film Loan:* 14,000.

Film Rental Serv *Restrictions:* only in U.S. & territories. Cannot use for fund-raising, transmit electronically. *Rental Period:* 1-5 days. *Total Yr Film Booking:* 17,500. Sell films. Produce films.

Film Collection 3200t/4000p. Approx 100t acquired annually. *Circ:* 16mm, 2825t/3625p. *Noncirc:* 16mm, 375t/375p. *Pubns:* catalog, every 3 yrs; suppl, no set policy.

Other Film Serv Rent film from distributors for patrons, obtain film from other libraries, film reference serv. Permanent viewing facility. *Equipment:* rent S8mm camera, rent 16mm sound projector, rent 8mm cartridge projector, rent 8mm reel projector, rent S8mm reel projector, rent projection tables & stands, rent projection screens, rent video & audio recorder, overhead projector, carousel slide projector.

Budget & Expenditures Total library budget $94,000 (FY 7/1/74-7/1/75). Total FY film budget $72,000. *Member:* CUFC.

Elk Grove Village

P- ELK GROVE VILLAGE PUBLIC LIBRARY, 101 Kennedy Blvd, 60007. *Tel:* (312) 439-0447. *Film Serv Est:* 1969. *In Charge:* Mark West, Librarian IV. *AV Staff:* 1 (1 prof). *Film Sel:* chief film librarian's decision.

Free-Loan Film Serv *Eligibility:* indiv with library cards. *Restrictions:* for indiv, only in city; for inst, only members of North Suburban Library System. May not borrow by mail. *Loan Period:* 7 days. *Total Yr Film Loan:* 994.

Elk Grove Village (cont'd)

Film Collection 200t/220p. Approx 35t acquired annually. *Circ:* 8mm reel, 75t/80p; S8mm reel, 125t/140p.

Other Film Serv Obtain film from coop loan system (North Suburban Library System AV Service), obtain film from other libraries, film fairs/festivals, library film programs. *Equipment:* lend 16mm sound projector (1).

Other Media Collections *Audio:* disc, 33⅓ rpm, 1300t/1400c; tape, cassette, 425t/450c.

Budget & Expenditures Total library budget $45,000 (FY 5/1/74-5/1/75). Total FY film budget $500. *Member:* ALA.

Evanston

P- EVANSTON PUBLIC LIBRARY, Film Department, 1703 Orrington Ave, 60201. *Tel:* (312) GR5-6700, ext 58. *Film Serv Est:* 1948. *AV Staff:* 3 (1 prof, 1 cl, 1 tech). *Film Sel:* committee preview, staff recommendations, published reviews.

Film Rental Serv *Eligibility:* patrons/public. *Restrictions:* only in city. Cannot use for fund-raising, transmit electronically. *Rental Period:* 2 days. *Total Yr Film Booking:* 6091.

Film Collection 315t/p. *Circ:* 16mm, 315t/322p; 8mm reel, 119t/p; S8mm reel, 61t/p. *Pubns:* catalog, every 4 yrs; suppl, as needed.

Other Film Serv Obtain film from coop loan system (North Suburban Library System). Permanent viewing facility available for rent to community. *Equipment:* rent 16mm sound projector (4), rent 8mm cartridge projector (1), rent projection screens (3), rent slide projectors, cassette player, opaque projector & slide-filmstrip projector.

Other Media Collections *Audio:* disc, 33⅓ rpm, 4543t/4543c. *Slides:* single, 5081t/5081c.

Budget & Expenditures Total library budget $113,000 (FY 1/1/75-1/1/76). Total FY film budget $6000. *Member:* ALA, EFLA, Ill. Library Assn.

C- NORTHWESTERN UNIVERSITY, Film Library, Box 1665, 60204. *Tel:* (312) 869-0602. *Film Serv Est:* 1965. *In Charge:* Bernice Gregorio, Dir. *Film Sel:* chief film librarian's decision. *Holdings:* animated films, drama in education, experimental films, social sciences, speech pathology, teacher education.

Film Rental Serv *Eligibility:* no restrictions. *Restrictions:* only in U.S. & territories, one screening per fee. Sell films. Produce films.

Film Collection 50t/75p. Approx 2-6t acquired annually. *Circ:* 16mm, 50t/60p. *Pubns:* catalog, every 2 yrs; suppl, as needed.

Other Film Serv Obtain film from coop loan system (Consortium of University Film Centers). *Member:* CUFC.

Franklin Park

P- FRANKLIN PARK PUBLIC LIBRARY DISTRICT, 9618 Franklin Ave, 60131. *Tel:* (312) 455-6016. *Film Serv Est:* 1963.

Free-Loan Film Serv *Eligibility:* indiv with library cards. *Restrictions:* for indiv, only in our library district; for inst, only in our library district. Cannot use for fund-raising, transmit electronically, borrow for classroom use. May not borrow by mail. *Loan Period:* 16mm, 1 day; 8mm, 7 days.

Film Collection *Circ:* 8mm reel, 123t.

Other Film Serv Obtain film from coop loan system (Dupage Lib System; Suburban AV Service). *Equipment:* lend 16mm sound projector (1), lend 8mm reel projector (2), lend S8mm reel projector.

Other Media Collections *Audio:* disc, 33⅓ rpm, 1692t.

Budget & Expenditures Total library budget $71,500 (FY 7/1/75-7/1/76). No separate AV budget. *Member:* ALA, Ill. Library Assn.

Freeport

P- FREEPORT PUBLIC LIBRARY, 314 W Stephenson St, 61032. *Tel:* (815) 232-7187. *Film Serv Est:* 1975. *In Charge:* John Locascio, Librarian. *Film Sel:* chief film librarian's decision. *Holdings:* animated films 13%, biography, drama, documentary, feature films 11%, history.

Free-Loan Film Serv *Eligibility:* indiv with library cards. *Restrictions:* for indiv, members of Northern Illinois Library System. Available to researchers/scholars for on-site viewing. May not borrow by mail. *Loan Period:* 7 days.

Film Collection 107t/107p. *Circ:* 8mm reel, 2t/2p; S8mm reel, 105t/105p.

Other Film Serv Obtain film from coop loan system (Northern Illinois Library System). *Member:* ALA, Ill. Library Assn.

Glen Ellyn

C- COLLEGE OF DUPAGE, Learning Resources Center, Lambert Rd & 22 St, 60137. *Tel:* (312) 858-2800, ext 383. *Film Serv Est:* 1967. *AV Staff:* 6 (2 prof, 3 cl, 1 tech). *Film Sel:* faculty/staff recommendations, chief film librarian's decision. *Holdings:* animated films 3%, black studies 1%, career education 3%, consumer affairs 4%, engineering 3%, experimental films 5%, feature films 3%, fine arts 22%, industrial arts 9%, law 1%, science 15%, social sciences 25%, teacher education 3%, women 2%.

Free-Loan Film Serv *Eligibility:* staff & students. Cannot use for fund-raising, transmit electronically. Available to researchers/scholars for on-site viewing. May not borrow by mail. *Loan Period:* hourly basis. *Total Yr Film Loan:* 19,000. Sell films. Produce films. Produce video, slides, audio.

Film Collection 500t/654p. Approx 30-40t acquired annually. *Circ:* 16mm, 500t/654p; S8mm cartridge, 300t/500p. *Pubns:* catalog, every 2 yrs; suppl, in yr catalog not published.

Other Film Serv Rent film from distributors for patrons, obtain film from coop loan system (Northern Ill. Learning Resources Coop), obtain film from other libraries, film reference serv, library film programs. Permanent viewing facility. *Equipment:* lend S8mm camera (15), lend 16mm sound projector (65), lend 8mm cartridge projector (3), lend 8mm reel projector (10), lend S8mm cartridge projector (8), lend S8mm reel projector (12), lend projection tables & stands (166), lend projection screens (60).

Other Media Collections *Audio:* disc, 33⅓ rpm, 4650c; tape, cassette, cartridge & reel, 4025. *Filmstrips:* total 2054c. *Slides:* single, 42,214c; sets, 899c.

Budget & Expenditures Total library budget $150,000 (FY 7/1/75-7/1/76). Total FY film budget $40,000. *Member:* AECT, ALA, Ill. Library Assn.

Video Serv *Est:* 1972. *In Charge:* Ted Sodergren, TV Production Consultant. *Video Staff:* 3 f-t, 4 p-t, 1 tech. *Video Use:* documentation of community/school events, to increase community's library use, in-service training, playback only of professionally produced tapes, as art form, instructional tool. Video serv available on demand & by appointment. Produce video tapes. Have production studio/space & separate control room. Have permanent & portable viewing installations. *Equipment Loan Period:* hourly basis. Provide training in use of equipment to faculty & students. Have tape duplication serv.

Video Tape Loan/Rental/Sale Serv *Serv Provided:* free loan, swap with other inst, sale. *Loan Eligibility:* staff & students, educational inst. *Restrictions:* for indiv, interlibrary loan; for inst, only Community College Cooperative. Cannot use for fund-raising, duplicate, air without permission. Restrictions dependent upon release agreement or copyright. May borrow by mail.

Video Collection Maintained by purchase, rental, own production, exchange/swap. Use/play ½" reel to reel, ¾" cassette. *Sources:* commercial distributors, exchange (Northern Ill. Learning Resource Coop). *Member:* Northern Ill. Learning Resources Coop. *Tape Sel:* preview, faculty/staff recommendations, published reviews. *Special Collections:* in-house training tapes, films in video format. Tapes organized by subject, LC classification. *Collection, Color:* ¾″ cassette, 120t. *Other Video Serv:* programming, taping of other media, production workshops. *Pubns:* catalog.

Glenview

P- GLENVIEW PUBLIC LIBRARY, 1930 Glenview Rd, 60025. *Tel:* (312) 724-5200. *Film Serv Est:* 1959. *In Charge:* Katherine Lindeman, Adult Servs Chief. *Film Sel:* published reviews. *Holdings:* animated films, children's films, feature films, fine arts.
Free-Loan Film Serv *Eligibility:* civic groups, religious groups, indiv with library cards. *Restrictions:* for indiv, interlibrary loan; for inst, none. Available to researchers/scholars for on-site viewing. May borrow by mail. *Loan Period:* 7 days.
Film Collection 310t/314p. Approx 50t acquired annually. *Circ:* 16mm, 4t/4p; 8mm reel, 296t/300p; S8mm reel, 10t/10p. *Pubns:* catalog, every 2 yrs.
Other Film Serv Obtain film from coop loan system (SAVS), library film programs. Permanent viewing facility available for rent to community. *Equipment:* rent 16mm sound projector (6), rent 8mm reel projector (2), rent S8mm reel projector (2), rent projection screens (1), lend cassette players (9), lend filmstrip projector (4).
Other Media Collections *Audio:* disc, 33⅓ rpm, 2911t/3088c; tape, cassette, 750t/766c. *Filmstrips:* sound, 179t/179c. *Slides:* single, 2843t/2843c; sets, 68t/68c.
Budget & Expenditures Total library budget $56,000 (FY 5/1/74-5/1/75). Total FY film budget $1300. *Member:* ALA, Ill. Library Assn.

Harvey

P- HARVEY PUBLIC LIBRARY, 155 St & Turlington Ave, 60426. *Tel:* (312) 331-0757. *In Charge:* Cheryl Flanagin, AV Specialist. *AV Staff:* 2 (1 prof, 1 cl). *Film Sel:* chief film librarian's decision, published reviews.
Free-Loan Film Serv *Eligibility:* indiv with library cards. *Restrictions:* for indiv, interlibrary loan. Cannot use for fund-raising, borrow for classroom use. May not borrow by mail. *Loan Period:* 7 days. *Total Yr Film Loan:* 1020.
Film Collection 450t/450p. Approx 35-50t acquired annually. *Circ:* 8mm reel, 450t/450p.
Other Film Serv Obtain film from coop loan system (Suburban AV Service), obtain film from other libraries, library film programs. Permanent viewing facility available free to nonprofit groups.
Other Media Collections *Audio:* disc, 33⅓ rpm, 800t; tape, cassette, 450t.
Budget & Expenditures Total library budget $27,000 (FY 5/1/75-5/1/76). Total FY film budget $300. *Member:* ALA, Ill. Library Assn.

Joliet

P- BUR OAK LIBRARY SYSTEM, AV Services, 150 N Ottawa, 60431. *Tel:* (815) 726-5394, ext 33. *Film Serv Est:* 1968. *In Charge:* Carl Adams, AV Librarian. *AV Staff:* 2 (1 prof, 1 cl). *Film Sel:* staff recommendations, chief film librarian's decision. *Holdings:* cartoons 2%, Christmas 2%, comedy 90%, history 2%, horror 2%, westerns 2%.
Free-Loan Film Serv *Eligibility:* indiv with library cards. *Restrictions:* for indiv, Bur Oak Lib System area. Cannot use for fund-raising. Available to researchers/scholars for on-site viewing. May borrow by mail. *Loan Period:* determined by local member library.
Film Rental Serv *Eligibility:* patrons/public. Cannot use for fund-raising, 60 day advance booking limit on schools. *Rental Period:* 1 day. *Total Yr Film Booking:* 1200.
Film Collection 672t/673p. *Circ:* 16mm, 22t/23p; 8mm reel, 400t/400p; S8mm reel, 200t/200p; S8mm cartridge, 50t/50p. *Pubns:* catalog, as needed.
Other Film Serv Obtain film from coop loan system (Lincoln Trails Lib System), obtain film from other libraries, library

film programs. *Equipment:* lend 16mm sound projector (4), lend 8mm reel projector (14), lend S8mm cartridge projector (4), lend S8mm reel projector, lend projection tables & stands (1), lend projection screens (4), lend sound filmstrip projector (2), lend slide projector (3).
Other Media Collections *Audio:* disc, 33⅓ rpm, 2700t/2848c; tape, cassette, 910t/915c; tape, cartridge, 800t/800c. *Filmstrips:* sound, 148t/148c. *Slides:* sets, 21t/42c.
Budget & Expenditures Total library budget $58,000 (FY 7/1/75-7/1/76). Total FY film budget $1500. *Member:* ALA, Ill. Library Assn, Ill. AV Assn.

C- JOLIET JUNIOR COLLEGE, Learning Resources Center, 1216 Houbolt Ave, 60436. *Tel:* (815) 729-9020, ext 282. *Film Serv Est:* 1966. *In Charge:* M. Schumaker, Public Serv Libn. *AV Staff:* 4 (1 prof, 1 cl, 2 tech). *Film Sel:* faculty/staff recommendations, published reviews.
Free-Loan Film Serv *Eligibility:* students enrolled in inst, staff & students. *Restrictions:* campus use only. Cannot use for fund-raising, transmit electronically, borrow for classroom use. *Loan Period:* 3 days.
Film Collection 260t/260p. *Circ:* 16mm, 260t/260p.
Other Film Serv Rent film from distributors for patrons, obtain film from other libraries. Permanent viewing facility.
Other Media Collections *Audio:* disc, 33⅓ rpm, 1500t; tape, cassette, 2500t..
Budget & Expenditures Total library budget $59,440 (FY 7/75-7/76). Total FY film budget $6400. *Member:* Ill. Lib Assn.
Video Serv *Est:* 1972. *In Charge:* Paul Goldman, Associate Dir. *Video Staff:* 4 f-t, 5 p-t, 2 tech. *Video Use:* documentation of community/school events, in-service training, practical video/TV training courses. Video serv available by appointment. Produce video tapes. Have production studio/space & separate control room.
Video Equipment/Facilities *In-House Use Only:* portapak (1), ½″ b&w, Sony; recording deck (14), ½″ b&w, Sony; editing deck (2), 1″ b&w, Sony; studio camera (3), b&w, Panasonic; monitor (20), b&w, Telemation; SEG (1); lighting; microphones; tripods; audio tape recorders. Have portable viewing installation. *Equipment Loan Period:* 1-3 days. Provide training in use of equipment to faculty.
Video Tape Loan/Rental/Sale Serv *Serv Provided:* swap with other inst. *Loan Eligibility:* staff & students. *Restrictions:* for indiv, campus only. Cannot use for fund-raising, duplicate, air without permission. May not borrow by mail.
Video Collection Maintained by purchase, own production, exchange/swap. Use/play ½″, 1″ reel to reel, ¾″ cassette. *Member:* NILRC. *Tape Sel:* preview, faculty/staff recommendations, catalogs. *Collection, B&W:* ½″ reel, 60t; ¾″ cassette, 40t/20c. *Other Video Serv:* taping of other media, production workshops.
Cable & CCTV Receive serv of cable TV system. Produce programs for cablecasting. Have CCTV in inst, with 25 monitors. *Programming Sources:* over-the-air commercial & public broadcasting, tapes produced by inst, tapes produced professionally.

Lombard

P- HELEN M. PLUM MEMORIAL LIBRARY, 110 W Maple St, 60148. *Tel:* (312) 627-0316. *Film Serv Est:* 1970. *In Charge:* James Taylor. *Film Sel:* chief film librarian's decision.
Free-Loan Film Serv *Eligibility:* indiv with library cards, 8mm & S8mm through own collection & DuPage Lib System; 16mm through Suburban AV Serv. *Restrictions:* for indiv, only in city. Cannot borrow for classroom use. Available to researchers/scholars for on-site viewing. May borrow by mail. *Loan Period:* 7 days. *Total Yr Film Loan:* 3340.
Film Rental Serv *Eligibility:* civic groups, patrons/public. *Restrictions:* only in city. *Rental Period:* 1-7 days.
Film Collection 250t/250p. Approx 100t acquired annually. *Circ:* 8mm reel, 230t; S8mm cartridge, 20t.
Other Film Serv Obtain film from coop loan system (Suburban AV System, DuPage Lib System). Permanent viewing facility. *Equipment:* rent 16mm sound projector (2), 8mm car-

Lombard (cont'd)
tridge projector (1), projection tables & stands (1), projection screens (2), lend/rent Technicolor 1000 8mm sound projectors (2).

Other Media Collections *Audio:* disc, 33⅓rpm, 1948c; tape, cassette, 13t/13c. *Filmstrips:* total 258t.

Budget & Expenditures Total library budget $289,800 (FY 6/1/74-6/1/75). Total FY film budget $2000.

Macomb

C- WESTERN ILLINOIS UNIVERSITY, Media Center, 61455. *Tel:* (309) 298-1880. *In Charge:* M. H. Hassan, Dir. *AV Staff:* 6 (1 prof, 3 cl, 2 tech). *Film Sel:* committee preview, faculty/staff recommendations, chief film librarian's decision. *Holdings:* agriculture, animated films, black studies, career education, children's films, consumer affairs, dance, experimental films, fine arts, industrial arts, law, science, social sciences, teacher education.

Free-Loan Film Serv *Eligibility:* staff & students, educational inst, civic groups, religious groups. *Restrictions:* for indiv, only in state; for inst, only in state. Cannot use for fund-raising, transmit electronically. Available to researchers/scholars for on-site viewing. May borrow by mail. *Loan Period:* 2 days. *Total Yr Film Loan:* 4135.

Film Rental Serv *Eligibility:* no restrictions. *Restrictions:* only in state. Cannot use for fund-raising, transmit electronically. *Rental Period:* 2 days. *Total Yr Film Booking:* 538. Produce films. Produce slides, overhead transparencies, audio tape.

Film Collection 1800t. Approx 150t acquired annually. *Pubns:* catalog, every 2 yrs ($3); suppl, as needed.

Other Film Serv Rent film from distributors for patrons, obtain film from other libraries, film reference serv. Permanent viewing facility. *Equipment:* lend/rent S8mm camera, 16mm sound projector, 8mm cartridge projector, 8mm reel projector, S8mm cartridge projector, S8mm reel projector, projection tables & stands, projection screens, & other AV equipment.

Other Media Collections *Audio:* disc, 33⅓rpm, 1700t; tape, total 800t. *Filmstrips:* sound, 100t; silent, 283t. *Slides:* sets, 25t.

Budget & Expenditures Total film budget $55,000 (FY 7/1/74-7/1/75). *Member:* AECT, EFLA.

Moline

C- BLACK HAWK COLLEGE, 6600 34 Ave, 61265. *Tel:* (309) 796-1311, ext 345. *Video Serv Est:* 1968. *In Charge:* Robert Fletcher, Dir of ETV. *Video Staff:* 5 f-t, 4 p-t, 2 tech. *Video Use:* documentation of community/school events, to increase community's library use, community video access, in-service training, practical video/TV training courses, as sales tool, as art form. Video serv available on demand & by appointment. Produce video tapes. Have production studio/space & separate control room.

Video Equipment/Facilities *In-House Use Only:* portapak (2), ½" & ¾" b&w/col, Sony; recording deck (12), 2", 1½", ¾" b&w/col, Ampex, RCA, Sony, Panasonic; studio camera (4), b&w/col, Norelco; monitor (85), col, RCA, Sony; SEG (2), Magnavox; keyer (2); lighting (30); microphones (10); audio tape recorders (20). Have permanent viewing installation. *Equipment Loan Period:* no set policy. Provide training in use of equipment to students. Have tape duplication serv.

Video Tape Loan/Rental/Sale Serv *Serv Provided:* swap with other inst, rental. *Loan/Rental Eligibility:* staff & students.

Video Collection Maintained by purchase, rental, own production. Use/play ½", 1", 2" reel to reel, ¾" cassette. *Tape Sel:* preview, faculty/staff recommendations, catalogs. *Special Collections:* in-house training tapes, films in video format. *Collection, Color:* ½" reel, 15t/15c; 1" reel, 100t/100c; ¾" cassette, 220t/220c. *Collection, B&W:* 1" reel, 10t/10c; 2" reel, 298t/298c; ¾" cassette, 100t/100c. *Other Video Serv:* programming, production workshops. *Pubns:* catalog.

Cable & CCTV Receive serv of cable TV system. Produce programs for cablecasting. Inform public about cable system

serv & facilities. Serve as production facility for others. Have CCTV in inst, with 75 monitors. *Programming Sources:* tapes produced by inst, tapes produced professionally.

Monmouth

P- WESTERN ILLINOIS LIBRARY SYSTEM, AV Dept, 58 West Side Square, 61462. *Tel:* (309) 734-7141. *Film Serv Est:* 1960. *In Charge:* James Whitehead, Asst Dir, AV Dept. *AV Staff:* 2½ (1 prof, 1 cl, 2 tech). *Film Sel:* staff recommendations.

Free-Loan Film Serv *Eligibility:* educational inst, civic groups, religious groups, indiv with library cards, prof groups, such as serv organizations, & others, such as patrons of member libraries. *Restrictions:* for indiv & inst, library system's geographic area. Cannot use for fund-raising. Available to researchers/scholars for on-site viewing. May borrow by mail. *Loan Period:* 3 days. *Total Yr Film Loan:* 8452.

Film Collection 1017t/1061p. Approx 115t acquired annually. *Circ:* 1017t/1061p. *Pubns:* catalog, annual ($5.00); suppl, bimonthly.

Other Film Serv Obtain film from coop loan system (Ill. State Library), obtain film from other libraries. Permanent viewing facility. *Equipment:* 16mm sound projector (2).

Other Media Collections *Filmstrips:* sound, 37t/37c. *Slides:* sets, 42t/42c.

Budget & Expenditures Total library budget $76,564.21 (FY 7/1/1974-7/1/1975). Total FY film budget $14,300.

Mount Prospect

P- MOUNT PROSPECT PUBLIC LIBRARY, 14 East Busse Ave, 60056. *Tel:* (312) 253-5675. *Film Serv Est:* 1969. *In Charge:* Sharon Grieger, Adult Servs Librarian. *AV Staff:* 3 (1 prof, 1 cl, 1 tech). *Film Sel:* published reviews.

Free-Loan Film Serv *Eligibility:* indiv with library cards. *Restrictions:* for indiv, only in city; for inst, only in city. Cannot use for fund-raising, borrow for classroom use. May not borrow by mail. *Total Yr Film Loan:* 9395.

Film Collection 790t/820p. Approx 50t acquired annually. *Circ:* 8mm reel, 465t/485p; S8mm reel, 327t/335p. *Pubns:* catalog, as needed; suppl, no set policy.

Other Film Serv Obtain film from coop loan system (Suburban AV Service). *Equipment:* lend 16mm sound projector (1), 8mm reel projector (2), S8mm reel projector (1), projection screens (1), Look & Listen Kit, slide projector.

Other Media Collections *Audio:* disc, 33⅓ rpm, 2508t; tape, cassette, 461t. *Filmstrips:* silent, 9t. *Slides:* single, 782t; sets, 1t.

Budget & Expenditures Total library budget $53,750 (FY 5/1/74-5/1/75). Total FY film budget $2500. *Member:* Ill. Library Assn.

Normal

C- ILLINOIS STATE UNIVERSITY, Educational Media Service Center, Media Services Learning Lab, Rm 109, 61761. *Tel:* (309) 436-5461, ext 26. *Film Serv Est:* 1953. *In Charge:* Celia Mitrione, Coord, Learning Lab. *AV Staff:* 8 (1 prof, 6 cl, 1 tech). *Film Sel:* committee preview, faculty/staff recommendations. *Holdings:* agriculture 1.7%, black studies .4%, career education .4%, children's films .8%, consumer affairs 1%, dance 1%, fine arts 10%, industrial arts 3%, science 18%, social sciences 38%, teacher education 25%.

Free-Loan Film Serv *Eligibility:* staff & students. *Restrictions:* for indiv, none; for inst, none. Cannot use for fund-raising, transmit electronically. Available to researchers/scholars for on-site viewing. May not borrow by mail. *Loan Period:* 2 days. *Total Yr Film Loan:* 3645. Produce films. Produce video tapes.

Film Collection 469t/469p. Approx 10t acquired annually. *Circ:* 16mm, 469t. *Pubns:* catalog, every 3 yrs; suppl, in yr catalog not published.

Other Film Serv Rent film from distributors for patrons. Permanent viewing facility.

Other Media Collections *Audio:* disc, 33⅓ rpm, 119t; tape, cassette, 539t/690c. *Filmstrips:* silent, 1139t; sound sets, 121t; silent sets, 37t.

Budget & Expenditures Total library budget $40,500 (FY 7/1/74-7/1/75). Total FY film budget $33,000 film rental, $7400 16mm film purchase.

C- ILLINOIS STATE UNIVERSITY, Media Services TV Library, 61761. *Tel:* (309) 436-5461, ext 47. *Video Serv Est:* 1965. *In Charge:* Kim H. Krisco, Production Coord. *Video Staff:* 5 f-t, 10 p-t, 2 tech. *Video Use:* documentation of community/school events, community video access, in-service training, practical video/TV training courses, as art form, university instructional TV. Video serv available on demand & by appointment. Produce video tapes. Have production studio/space & separate control room.

Video Equipment/Facilities *In-House Use Only:* recording deck (6), ¾" col, Sony 2850, 1800; playback deck (1), ¾" col, Sony; editing deck (2), ¾" col, Sony; studio camera (3), 1" b&w, Ampex; monitor (24), 9"-15" b&w, Conrac, SC; SEG (1), Visual; additional camera lenses (3); lighting (26); microphones (12); tripods (3); audio tape recorders (4), character generator (1). Have permanent & portable viewing installations. *Equipment Loan Period:* no set policy. Provide training in use of equipment to faculty & students. Have tape duplication serv.

Video Tape Loan/Rental/Sale Serv *Serv Provided:* swap with other inst. *Loan Eligibility:* staff & students, educational inst, civic groups. *Restrictions:* for indiv, none; for inst, none. Cannot duplicate, air without permission. May borrow by mail.

Video Collection Maintained by own production, exchange/swap. Use/play ½", 1", 2" reel to reel, ¾" cassette. *Tape Sel:* preview, faculty/staff recommendations, catalogs. *Special Collections:* produce instructional series. Tapes organized by subject. *Collection, Color:* ¾" cassette, 20t. *Collection, B&W:* 1" reel, 90t; ¾" cassette, 240t. *Other Video Serv:* programming, production workshops. *Pubns:* catalog.

Cable & CCTV Produce programs for cablecasting. Serve as production facility for others. Have advisory role in selection, from requests of programming to be produced and/or distributed via local CATV. Have CCTV in inst, with 250 monitors. *Programming Sources:* tapes produced by inst.

Oak Lawn

P- OAK LAWN PUBLIC LIBRARY, 9444 S Cook Ave, 60453. *Tel:* (312) 422-4990. *Film Serv Est:* 1966. *In Charge:* Pauline Thomas, Adult Servs. *Film Sel:* chief film librarian's decision. *Holdings:* animated films, feature films.

Free-Loan Film Serv *Eligibility:* indiv with adult library cards. *Restrictions:* for indiv, only in city. Available to researchers/scholars for on-site viewing. May not borrow by mail. *Loan Period:* 3 weeks.

Film Collection Approx 20t acquired annually. *Circ:* 8mm reel, 127t. *Noncirc:* 8mm cartridge, 28t. *Pubns:* catalog.

Other Film Serv Obtain film from coop loan system (Suburban AV Service).

Other Media Collections *Audio:* disc, 33⅓ rpm, 2330t/2330c; tape, cassette, 290t/290c.

Budget & Expenditures Total library budget $612,490 (FY 1/1/74-1/1/75). Total FY AV budget $20,000. *Member:* ALA, Ill. Library Assn.

Ottawa

P- STARVED ROCK LIBRARY SYSTEM, Hitt & Swanson Sts, 61350. *Tel:* (815) 434-7537. *Film Serv Est:* 1969. *In Charge:* Mary T. Howe, System Dir. *AV Staff:* 2 (1 prof, 1 cl). *Film Sel:* committee preview.

Free-Loan Film Serv *Eligibility:* public library members of the system who in turn loan to registered patrons. *Restrictions:* for inst, only libraries in system area. Cannot borrow for classroom use. Available to researchers/scholars for on-site viewing. May borrow by mail. *Loan Period:* 7 days. *Total Yr Film Loan:* 357.

Film Rental Serv *Eligibility:* patrons or library members of system. *Restrictions:* only in region (6 Ill. counties). *Rental Period:* 1 day. *Total Yr Film Booking:* 695.

Film Collection 470t/470p. *Circ:* 16mm, 10t/10p; 8mm cartridge, 395t/395p; S8mm cartridge, 75t/75p.

Other Film Serv Obtain film from coop loan system (Suburban AV Service), film reference serv, library film programs. *Equipment:* lend 16mm sound projector (1), lend 8mm cartridge projector (4), lend 8mm reel projector (2), lend projection screens (1).

Other Media Collections *Audio:* discs & tapes, total 717c. *Filmstrips:* total 100c. *Slides:* total 225c.

Budget & Expenditures Total library budget $63,000 (FY 7/1/74-7/1/75). Total FY film budget $5000. *Member:* ALA, Ill. Library Assn.

Palatine

C- HARPER COLLEGE, 60067. *Tel:* (312) 397-3000, ext 261. *AV Staff:* 1 (1 cl). *Film Sel:* committee preview, faculty/staff recommendations. *Holdings:* business 25%, social sciences 30%.

Free-Loan Film Serv *Eligibility:* staff & students, educational inst, civic groups, prof groups. *Restrictions:* for indiv, only in NW Cook County; for inst, only in NW Cook County. Cannot use for fund-raising. Available to researchers/scholars for on-site viewing. May not borrow by mail. *Loan Period:* 5 days. *Total Yr Film Loan:* 816.

Film Collection 1300t. Approx 100-150t acquired annually. *Circ:* 16mm, 853t; 8mm cartridge, 459t. Publish listing of films.

Other Film Serv Rent film from distributors for patrons, obtain film from coop loan system (NILRC, School Dist 214, Suburban AV System), obtain film from other libraries, film reference serv. Permanent viewing facility.

Other Media Collections *Audio:* discs, total 2407t; tapes, total 2744. *Filmstrips:* silent, 1816t. *Slides:* single, 31,480t.

Budget & Expenditures Total library budget $153,450 (FY 7/1/74-7/1/75). No separate budget. *Member:* AECT, ALA, State Library Information Network.

Video Serv *Video Staff:* 1 tech. *Video Use:* instruction. Video serv available on demand & by appointment. Produce video tapes. Have production studio/space & separate control room.

Video Equipment/Facilities *In-House Use Only:* portapak (1), b&w, Sony; recording deck (10), b&w/col, Umatic; playback deck (2), col, Sony; editing deck (1), 1" col; studio camera (2), b&w, Ampex; SEG (1), Alma; additional camera lenses; lighting; microphones; tripods; audio tape recorders, time base corrector. Have permanent & portable viewing installations. *Equipment Loan Period:* no set policy. Provide training in use of equipment to faculty & students. Have tape duplication serv.

Video Tape Loan/Rental/Sale Serv *Serv Provided:* swap with other inst. *Loan Eligibility:* staff & students, educational inst, civic groups, prof groups. *Restrictions:* for indiv, only in community; for inst, only in community. Cannot use for fund-raising, air without permission.

Video Collection Maintained by purchase, own production, exchange/swap. Use/play ½", 1" reel to reel, ¾" cassette. *Sources:* exchange with other libraries, produce own. *Member:* NILRC. *Tape Sel:* preview, faculty/staff recommendations. *Special Collections:* instruction. Tapes organized by subject. *Collection, Color:* 1" reel, 370t. *Other Video Serv:* production workshops. *Pubns:* catalog & list of tapes.

Cable & CCTV Have CCTV in inst. *Programming Sources:* over-the-air commercial & public broadcasting, tapes produced by inst, tapes produced by community groups, indiv, & other colleges.

Park Forest South

C- GOVERNORS STATE UNIVERSITY, Learning Resources
Center, Steunkel Rd, 60466. *Tel:* (312) 534-5000, ext 2325.
Film Serv Est: 1970. *In Charge:* Donna Barber/Mary
Schellhorn, Media Librarians. *AV Staff:* 6 (2 prof, 3 cl, 1
tech). *Film Sel:* faculty/staff recommendations, chief film
librarian's decision. *Holdings:* alcoholism 5%.
   Free-Loan Film Serv *Eligibility:* staff & students. Cannot
use for fund-raising, transmit electronically. Available to re-
searchers/scholars for on-site viewing. May not borrow by mail.
Loan Period: 3 days. *Total Yr Film Loan:* 2941.
   Film Collection 950t. *Circ:* 16mm, 850t/950p. Permanent
viewing facility. *Member:* AECT, ALA, EFLA, IAVA.
   Video Serv *Est:* 1970. *Video Use:* documentation of commu-
nity/school events, instruction. Video serv available by appointment. Produce video tapes. Have production studio/space
& separate control room.
   Video Equipment/Facilities *In-House Use Only:* playback deck (15), col, Sony; monitor (15), b&w, Sony. Have permanent viewing installation.
   Video Tape Loan/Rental/Sale Serv *Serv Provided:* free
loan. *Loan Eligibility:* staff & students.
   Video Collection Maintained by purchase, own production. Use/play ¾" cassette. *Sources:* commercial distributors.
Tape Sel: preview, faculty/staff recommendations, catalogs.
Tapes organized by LC system.

Peoria

P- ILLINOIS VALLEY LIBRARY SYSTEM, Film Service, 107
N E Monroe, 61602. *Tel:* (309) 672-8877. *Film Serv Est:*
1949. *In Charge:* Dennis M. Huslig, Nonprint Media Consultant. *AV Staff:* 5 (1 prof, 2 cl, 2 tech). *Film Sel:* committee preview, chief film librarian's decision.
   Free-Loan Film Serv *Eligibility:* org members, civic
groups, religious groups, indiv with library cards. *Restrictions:*
for indiv, system boundaries & cooperating systems; for inst,
system boundaries & cooperating systems. Cannot use for fund-
raising, transmit electronically. Available to researchers/
scholars for on-site viewing. May borrow by mail. *Loan
Period:* 1 day.
   Film Rental Serv *Restrictions:* school districts within
system boundaries. Cannot use for fund-raising, transmit electronically. *Rental Period:* 1 day.
   Film Collection 1500t/1656p. Approx 40t acquired annually. *Circ:* 16mm, 1500t/1656p; 8mm reel, 126t/126p; S8mm reel,
40t/40p. *Pubns:* catalog, as needed ($1); suppl, as needed.
   Other Film Serv Rent film from distributors for patrons,
obtain film from coop loan system (Lincoln Trails, Rolling
Prairie Library System), film reference serv, library film programs. Permanent viewing facility available for rent to community. *Equipment:* lend 16mm sound projector (2).
   Other Media Collections *Filmstrips:* sound, 34t; silent,
307t; sound sets, 56t; silent sets, 56t. *Slides:* sets, 190t. *Member:*
ALA, EFLA, FLIC, Ill. Library Assn.

Quincy

P- QUINCY PUBLIC LIBRARY, Mississippi Valley Film Cooperative, 526 Jersey, 62301. *Tel:* (217) 222-0298. *Film Serv
Est:* 1962. *In Charge:* Scott Parsons, Film Librarian/Ex-
ecutive Secretary. *AV Staff:* 3 (3 cl). *Film Sel:* chief film
librarian's decision.
   Free-Loan Film Serv *Eligibility:* indiv with library cards.
Restrictions: for indiv, interlibrary loan; for inst, none. Cannot
transmit electronically. Available to researchers/scholars for
on-site viewing. May borrow by mail. *Loan Period:* 1 day.
   Film Collection 740t/750p. Approx 40t acquired annually.
Circ: 16mm, 740t/750p; 8mm reel, 255t/255p; S8mm reel,
14t/14p. Publish title lists.
   Other Film Serv Obtain film from coop loan system, film
reference serv, library film programs. Permanent viewing facility available for rent to community.

   Other Media Collections *Audio:* disc, 33⅓ rpm, 3717t; disc,
45rpm, 3717t. *Filmstrips:* sound, 222t.
   Budget & Expenditures Total FY film budget $39,080 (FY
3/1/74-3/1/75). *Member:* EFLA, FLIC.

River Forest

C- CONCORDIA TEACHERS COLLEGE, Klinck Memorial
Library, 7400 Augusta, 60305. *Tel:* (312) 771-8300, ext 447.
In Charge: Henry Latzke, Dir, Library Servs. *AV Staff:* 3 (2
prof, 1 cl). *Film Sel:* faculty/staff recommendations. *Holdings:* fine arts 2%, science 71%, social sciences 5%, teacher
education 22%.
   Free-Loan Film Serv *Eligibility:* staff & students. *Restrictions:* for indiv, only in city; for inst, only in city. May not
borrow by mail.
   Film Rental Serv *Eligibility:* educational org. *Restrictions:*
none.
   Film Collection 240t. Approx 7t acquired annually. *Circ:*
16mm, 100t/100p; 8mm cartridge, 59t/59p; S8mm cartridge,
81t/81p.
   Other Film Serv Rent film from distributors for patrons,
obtain film from coop loan system (LIBRAS, Suburban Library
System), obtain film from other libraries, film reference serv,
film fairs/festivals. Permanent viewing facility. *Equipment:*
lend S8mm camera, 16mm camera, 16mm sound projector, 8mm
cartridge projector, 8mm reel projector, S8mm cartridge projector, S8mm reel projector, projection tables & stands, projection
screens.
   Other Media Collections *Audio:* disc, 33⅓ rpm, 234t; disc,
45rpm, 5t; disc, 78rpm, 21t; tape, cassette, 58t; tape, reel, 83t.
Filmstrips: sound, 337t; silent, 737t; sound sets, 53t; silent sets,
1t. *Slides:* single, 6636t/6636c; sets, 21t.
   Budget & Expenditures Total library budget $43,207 (FY
7/1/74-7/1/75). No separate AV budget. *Member:* AECT, ALA,
EFLA, Ill. Library Assn.
   Video Serv *Est:* 1963. *In Charge:* Richard Richter, Director
of Television. *Video Staff:* 1 f-t. *Video Use:* practical video/TV
training courses, evaluation feedback in courses. Video serv
available by appointment. Produce video tapes. Have production studio/space & separate control room.
   Video Equipment/Facilities *In-House Use Only:* portapak (1), b&w; recording deck (2), b&w, Shibaden, Concord;
editing deck (2), col, Panasonic; studio camera (5), Shibaden;
monitor (8), b&w/col, Concord, Magnavox; SEG (2), Shibaden,
Viscount; keyer (1), Viscount; additional camera lenses (3);
lighting (11); microphones (6); tripods (5); audio tape recorders
(3), system sync gen. Have permanent viewing installation.
Equipment Loan Period: no set policy. Provide training in use of
equipment to faculty & students.
   Video Tape Loan/Rental/Sale Serv *Serv Provided:* free
loan, swap with other inst. *Loan Eligibility:* staff & students.
May not borrow by mail.
   Video Collection Maintained by own production. Use/
play ½" reel to reel. Tapes organized by subject. *Collection,
B&W:* ½" reel, 215t/215c.
   Cable & CCTV Have CCTV in inst, with 15 monitors.
Programming Sources: tapes produced by inst.

Rockford

P- NORTHERN ILLINOIS LIBRARY SYSTEM, 215 N Wyman,
61101. *Tel:* (815) 965-6731, ext 69. *Film Serv Est:* 1966. *In
Charge:* David Erickson, AV Consultant. *AV Staff:* 14 (2
prof, 8 cl, 4 tech). *Film Sel:* committee preview.
   Free-Loan Film Serv *Eligibility:* educational inst, civic
groups, religious groups, indiv with library cards, prof groups.
Restrictions: for indiv, only our system & systems with reciprocal borrowing agreements. Cannot use for fund-raising, transmit electronically. Available to researchers/scholars for on-site
viewing. May borrow by mail. *Loan Period:* 1-8 days. *Total Yr
Film Loan:* 31,000.

Film Rental Serv *Eligibility:* educational org. Cannot use for fund-raising, transmit electronically. *Rental Period:* 1-8 days.

Film Collection 1500t/1700p. Approx 100-200t acquired annually. *Circ:* 16mm, 1500t/1700p. *Pubns:* catalog, annual.

Other Film Serv Rent film from distributors for patrons, obtain film from coop loan system, obtain film from other libraries, film reference serv, film fairs/festivals, library film programs. Permanent viewing facility available for rent to community.

Other Media Collections *Audio:* disc, 33⅓rpm, 12,000t/16,000c; tape, cassette, 1500t; tape, reel, 1000t. *Filmstrips:* sound, 800t; silent, 1200t; sound sets, 200t. *Slides:* sets, 500t.

Budget & Expenditures Total library budget $25-30,000. No separate AV budget. *Member:* ALA, EFLA, Ill. Library Assn.

Schaumburg

P- SCHAUMBURG TOWNSHIP PUBLIC LIBRARY, 32 W Library Lane, 60172. *Tel:* (312) 885-3373. *Film Serv Est:* 1972. *In Charge:* Timothy Sullivan, AV Librarian. *AV Staff:* 5 (1 prof, 1 cl, 3 tech). *Film Sel:* chief film librarian's decision. *Holdings:* animated films 40%, feature films 60%.

Free-Loan Film Serv *Eligibility:* indiv with library cards. *Restrictions:* for indiv, only in township; for inst, only in township. Cannot use for fund-raising, transmit electronically, borrow for classroom use. Available to researchers/scholars for on-site viewing. May borrow by mail. *Loan Period:* 3 weeks.

Film Collection 375t/500p. Approx 30t acquired annually. *Circ:* 8mm reel, 250t; S8mm reel, 250t. *Pubns:* catalog, annual; suppl, no set policy.

Other Film Serv Obtain film from coop loan system (Suburban AV Service), obtain film from other libraries, film reference serv, film fairs/festivals, library film programs. Permanent viewing facility available for rent to community. *Equipment:* lend 16mm sound projector (4), 8mm reel projector (1), S8mm reel projector (1), projection screens (1).

Other Media Collections *Audio:* disc, 33⅓rpm, 3500t; tape, cassette, 1300t. *Slides:* single, 150t.

Budget & Expenditures Total library budget $90,000 (FY 3/1/74-3/1/75). Total FY film budget $500.

Smithton

P- KASKASKIA LIBRARY SYSTEM, 306 N Main St, 62298. *Tel:* (618) 235-4220. *Film Serv Est:* 1970. *In Charge:* Alayne Moore, AV Libn. *AV Staff:* 2½ (1 prof, 1 cl, ½ tech). *Film Sel:* committee preview, chief film librarian's decision.

Free-Loan Film Serv *Eligibility:* org members, educational inst, civic groups, religious groups, indiv with library cards, prof groups. *Restrictions:* for indiv, only in our system; for inst, only in our system, Lewis & Clark system & other systems in Ill. Cannot use for fund-raising, transmit electronically. May borrow by mail. *Loan Period:* 1 day. *Total Yr Film Loan:* 5928.

Film Collection 345t/571p. *Circ:* 16mm, 407t/408p; 8mm reel, 131t/156p. *Noncirc:* S8mm cartridge, 7t. *Pubns:* catalog, as needed; suppl, send out catalog cards as needed.

Other Film Serv Obtain film from coop loan system (Lewis & Clark Library System), obtain film from other libraries, film reference serv, library film programs. Permanent viewing facility. *Equipment:* lend 16mm sound projector (19), lend 8mm reel projector (9), lend projection screens (18), overhead projector (1), slide projector.

Other Media Collections *Audio:* disc, 33⅓rpm, 2237c; disc, 45rpm, 2237c; tape, cassette, 26t/41c. *Slides:* sets, 169t/236c.

Budget & Expenditures Total library budget $292,500 (FY 7/1/74-7/1/75). Total FY film budget $35,000. *Member:* ALA, EFLA, Ill. Library Assn.

Springfield

C- SANGAMON STATE UNIVERSITY, Shepherd Rd, 62708. *Tel:* (217) 786-6602. *AV Staff:* 10 (3 prof, 2 cl, 5 tech). *Film Sel:* faculty/staff recommendations.

Film Collection 50t/65p. Approx 10t acquired annually. *Circ:* 8mm reel, 10t/10p; S8mm reel, 10t/10p. *Noncirc:* 16mm, 50t/65p.

Other Film Serv Rent film from distributors for patrons, obtain film from other libraries, film reference serv, library film programs. Permanent viewing facility. *Equipment:* lend S8mm camera (12), lend 16mm camera (2), lend 16mm sound projector (2), lend 8mm cartridge projector (5), lend 8mm reel projector (2), lend S8mm reel projector (2), lend projection screens (2).

Other Media Collection *Audio:* disc, 33⅓rpm, 2000t; disc, 45rpm, 50t; tape, cassette, 50t; tape, reel, 20t. *Filmstrips:* sound, 80c; silent, 10c; sound sets, 20c; silent sets, 10c. *Slides:* single, 1000c; sets, 50c.

Budget & Expenditures Total library budget $235,000 (FY 7/1/75-7/1/76). Total FY film budget $28,000. *Member:* AECT.

Video Serv *Video Staff:* 10 f-t, 5 tech. *Video Use:* documentation of community/school events, in-service training, practical video/TV training courses, as art form. Video serv available on demand. Produce video tapes. Have production studio/space & separate control room.

Video Equipment/Facilities *For Loan:* portapak (5), ½" b&w, Sony; studio camera (2), b&w. Have portable viewing installation. Provide training in use of equipment to faculty & students. Have tape duplication serv.

Video Tape Loan/Rental/Sale Serv *Loan Eligibility:* staff & students. Cannot use for fund-raising, duplicate, air without permission. May not borrow by mail. *Total Yr Tape Loan:* 450.

Video Collection Maintained by purchase, own production. Use/play ½" reel to reel, ¾" cassette. *Tape Sel:* faculty/staff recommendations. Tapes organized by LC system. *Collection, Color:* ¾" cassette, 30t. *Collection, B&W:* ½" reel, 200t; ¾" cassette, 20t. *Other Video Serv:* reference serv, taping of other media, production workshops.

Cable & CCTV Will receive serv of cable TV system.

Streamwood

P- POPLAR CREEK PUBLIC LIBRARY DISTRICT, 20 W Streamwood Blvd, 60103. *Tel:* (312) 837-6800.

Film Rental Serv *Eligibility:* educational org, civic groups, patrons/public. *Restrictions:* only in our library district. Cannot use for classroom. *Rental Period:* 1 day.

Other Film Serv Obtain film from coop loan system (Suburban AV System). *Equipment:* rent S8mm camera (1), 16mm sound projector (2).

Other Media Collections *Audio:* disc, 33⅓rpm, 800c; tape, cassette, 118c.

Budget & Expenditures Total library budget $25,000 (FY 7/1/74-7/1/75). Total FY film budget $1500.

Sugar Grove

C- WAUBONSEE COMMUNITY COLLEGE, Learning Resources Center, Rt 47 at Harter Rd, 60554. *Tel:* (312) 466-4811, ext 318. *Video Serv Est:* 1974. *In Charge:* Gary W. Frazer, Dir, AV Servs. *Video Staff:* 4 f-t, 5 p-t, 2 tech. *Video Use:* documentation of community/school events, community video access, in-service training, practical video/TV training courses, playback only of professionally produced tapes, as art form. Video serv available by appointment. Produce video tapes. Have production studio/space & separate control room.

Video Equipment/Facilities *In-House Use Only:* portapak (2), ½" b&w, Sony; recording deck (7), ½" ¾" b&w/col, Sony; playback deck (12), ¾" col, Sony; editing deck (2), 1" col, Sony; studio camera (4), b&w, Sony, Shibaden; monitor (20), Sony; SEG (2), Sony, Shibaden; lighting (14); microphones (15); tripods (8); audio tape recorders (130). Have portable viewing

Sugar Grove (cont'd)
installation. Provide training in use of equipment to faculty & students. Have tape duplication serv.

Video Tape Loan/Rental/Sale Serv *Serv Provided:* swap with other inst. *Loan Eligibility:* org members, students enrolled in inst, educational inst, civic groups, prof groups, such as media or library organizations. *Restrictions:* for indiv, only in our college district. Cannot use for fund-raising, duplicate, air without permission. May not borrow by mail.

Video Collection Maintained by purchase, rental, own production exchange/swap. Use/play ½", 1" reel to reel, ¾" cassette. *Sources:* commercial distributors, exchange (Northern Ill. Learning Resources Coop). *Member:* Northern Ill. Learning Resources Coop. *Tape Sel:* preview, faculty/staff recommendations. *Special Collections:* instruction. Tapes organized by LC classification. *Collection, Color:* ¾" cassette, 75t. *Collection, B&W:* ½" reel, 45t; 1" reel, 30t; ¾" cassette, 13t. *Other Video Serv:* programming, taping of other media, production workshops.

Cable & CCTV Will receive serv of cable TV system. Produce programs for local cablecasting.

Urbana

C- UNIVERSITY OF ILLINOIS AT URBANA-CHAMPAIGN, Graduate School of Library Science, Learning Resources Laboratory, 61801. *Tel:* (217) 333-9890. *Film Serv Est:* 1970. *In Charge:* Jerome K. Miller. *AV Staff:* 1¾ (⅕ prof, 1½ cl). *Film Sel:* faculty/staff recommendations. *Holdings:* children's films, information retrieval, library science.

Free-Loan Film Serv *Eligibility:* staff & students. *Restrictions:* for indiv, none. Cannot use for fund-raising, transmit electronically. Available to researchers/scholars for on-site viewing. May not borrow by mail. *Loan Period:* flexible.

Film Collection *Circ:* 16mm, 104t/110p; 8mm cartridge, 2t/p; S8mm reel, 115t.

Other Film Serv Rent film from distributors for patrons, obtain film from coop loan system (Lincoln Trail), obtain film from other libraries, film reference serv. Permanent viewing facility. *Equipment:* lend S8mm camera (1), lend 16mm sound projector (3), lend 8mm cartridge projector (1), lend S8mm cartridge projector (1), lend projection tables & stands (5).

Video Serv *In Charge:* Jerome K. Miller. *Video Staff:* 6 p-t. *Video Use:* practical video/TV training courses. Video serv available on demand.

Video Equipment/Facilities *In-House Use Only:* editing deck (1), b&w, Sony; studio camera (1), b&w, Sony; monitor (2); lighting; microphones; tripods (1); audio tape recorders (6). Have portable viewing installation. *Equipment Loan Period:* 1 day, or over weekend. Provide training in use of equipment to students.

Video Tape Loan/Rental/Sale Serv *Serv Provided:* free loan. *Loan Eligibility:* staff & students. *Restrictions:* for indiv, none. Cannot use for fund-raising, duplicate, air without permission. May not borrow by mail.

Video Collection Maintained by purchase, rental, own production. Use/play ½" reel to reel. *Sources:* exchange (Florida State Univ Lib School). *Tape Sel:* faculty/staff recommendations, published reviews. Tapes organized numerically. *Collection, B&W:* ½" reel, 20t.

Cable & CCTV Will receive serv of cable TV system.

Indiana

Albion

P- NOBLE COUNTY PUBLIC LIBRARY, 109 N York St, 46701. *Tel:* (219) 636-7197. *Film Serv Est:* 1967. *In Charge:* Linda J. Shultz, Librarian. *AV Staff:* 1. *Film Sel:* staff recommendations.
   Free-Loan Film Serv *Eligibility:* indiv with library cards. *Restrictions:* for indiv, only in our taxing area. Available to researchers/scholars for on-site viewing. May not borrow by mail. *Loan Period:* 3 days. *Total Yr Film Loan:* 1664.
   Film Collection 9t/9p. Approx 1t acquired annually. *Circ:* 16mm, 9t/9p.
   Other Film Serv Obtain film from coop loan system (Indiana Library Film Circuit), firms listed in *Educator's Guide to Free Films. Equipment:* lend 16mm sound projector (1), lend projection screens (1).
   Other Media Collections *Audio:* disc, 33⅓ rpm, 160t; tape, cassette, 3t. *Filmstrips:* silent, 3t.
   Budget & Expenditures Total library budget $12,900 (FY 1/1/75-1/1/76). Total FY film budget $300. *Member:* Ind. Library Assn.

Anderson

P- ANDERSON-ANDERSON, STONY CREEK TOWNSHIP PUBLIC LIBRARY, AV Dept, 32 W 10 St, 46016. *Tel:* (317) 644-4421. *Film Serv Est:* 1971. *In Charge:* Patricia Lake, AV Libn. *AV Staff:* 2 (1 prof, 1 cl). *Film Sel:* chief film librarian's decision.
   Free-Loan Film Serv *Eligibility:* indiv with library cards. *Restrictions:* for indiv, only in our library dist; for inst, only in our library dist. Cannot use for fund-raising, transmit electronically, shown outside dist unless fee is paid. Available to researchers/scholars for on-site viewing. May not borrow by mail. *Loan Period:* 2 days. *Total Yr Film Loan:* 22,306.
   Film Rental Serv *Eligibility:* patrons/public, holders of nonresident cards. *Restrictions:* none. Cannot use for fund-raising. *Rental Period:* 2 days.
   Film Collection 900t/900p. Approx 20-40t acquired annually. *Circ:* 16mm, 900t/900p; 8mm reel, 175t/175p; S8mm reel, 125t/125p. *Pubns:* catalog, every 3 yrs; suppl, in yr catalog not published.
   Other Film Serv Obtain film from coop loan system (Ind. Library Film Circuit, Ind. State Library), film reference serv, library film programs. Permanent viewing facility available free to community. *Equipment:* lend 16mm sound projector (2).
   Other Media Collections *Audio:* disc, 33⅓rpm, 1550t; tape, cassette, 180t. *Filmstrips:* silent, 354t. *Slides:* sets, 130t.
   Budget & Expenditures Total library budget $138,000 (FY 1/1/75-1/1/76). Total FY film budget $13,500. *Member:* EFLA, Ind. Library Assn, Ind. Film Council.

Auburn

P- ECKHART PUBLIC LIBRARY, 46706. *Tel:* (219) 925-2414. *In Charge:* Sirleine Smith. *Member:* Ind. Library Film Serv.

Bedford

P- BEDFORD PUBLIC LIBRARY, 1323 K St, 47421. *Tel:* (812) 275-6621. *In Charge:* Laura Johnson, Kristine Rinella. *Member:* Library Flicks Library Servs Authority.

Berne

P- BERNE PUBLIC LIBRARY, 166 Sprunger St, 46711. *Tel:* (219) 589-2809. *In Charge:* Daniel Talbott. *Member:* Ind. Library Film Serv.

Bloomington

C- INDIANA UNIVERSITY, Undergraduate Library, 10th & Jordan, 47401. *Tel:* (812) 337-9857. *Video Serv Est:* 1975. *In Charge:* Media Librarian (position open). *Video Staff:* 1 f-t, 12-15 p-t. *Video Use:* for playback only of professionally produced tapes, for curriculum supplement & continuing education. Video serv available on demand & by appointment.
   Video Equipment/Facilities *In-House Use Only:* recording deck (1), ¾" col, Sony; playback deck (5), ¾" col, 4 Sony, 1 JVC; Wollensak audio (14); Advent audio-stereo (16). *For Loan:* audio tape recorders (25). Have portable viewing installation. *Equipment Loan Period:* in-house for video, length of tape; audio, in-house or 2 days. Provide training in use of equipment to student assistants & users.
   Video Tape Loan/Rental/Sale Serv *Equipment Loan Eligibility:* staff & students, any patron who comes in to the library. *Restrictions:* in-house only.
   Video Collection Maintained by purchase. Use/play ¾" cassette. *Sources:* commercial distributors, local production by other depts of university. *Tape Sel:* preview, faculty/staff recommendations, published reviews. Tapes organized by accession number. *Collection, Color:* ¾" cassette, 95t. *Collection, B&W:* ¾" cassette, 55t.
   Cable & CCTV Have CCTV in inst. *Programming Sources:* tapes produced by inst, live lectures.

S- INSTITUTE FOR SEX RESEARCH, Morrison 416, Indiana University, 47401. *Tel:* (812) 337-7686. *Film Serv Est:* 1970. *In Charge:* Paul H. Gebhard, Dir. *AV Staff:* 1. *Film Sel:* committee preview, chief film librarian's decision. *Holdings:* erotica & stag films 91.5%, medicine 1%, science 5%, social sciences 2%, women 0.5%.
   Film Rental Serv *Eligibility:* individuals with academic affiliation &/or scholarly credentials. *Restrictions:* none. Cannot use for fund-raising, may only be used for scholarly research or limited medical/sex education purposes. *Rental Period:* depends on time requested. *Total Yr Film Booking:* 85.
   Film Collection 1900t. *Noncirc:* 16mm, 350t/350p; 8mm reel, 1500t/1500p; S8mm reel, 50t/50p. Print annotated list of AV material. Permanent viewing facility.
   Other Media Collections *Audio:* disc, 33⅓rpm, 53t; disc, 45rpm, 9t; disc, 78rpm, 26t; tapes, 46t. *Slides:* single, 11,000t.
   Budget & Expenditures Total library budget $7600 (FY 7/1/74-7/1/75). Total FY film budget $1000.
   Video Serv *Est:* 1970. *In Charge:* Paul Gebhard, Dir. *Video Use:* scholarly research. Video serv available by application to Information Serv.
   Video Collection Maintained by gift contributions. Use/play 1" reel to reel, ¾" cassette. *Collection, Color:* ¾" cassette, 2t/2c. *Collection, B&W:* 1" reel, 1t/2c; ¾" cassette, 1t/1c.

P- MONROE COUNTY PUBLIC LIBRARY, 303 E Kirkwood, 47401. *Tel:* (812) 339-2271, ext 46. *In Charge:* Lee Guthrie, AV Libn. *AV Staff:* 3 (1 prof, 1 cl, 1 tech). *Film Sel:* committee preview, staff recommendations, chief film librarian's decision.
   Free-Loan Film Serv *Eligibility:* staff & students, educational inst, civic groups, religious groups, indiv with library cards, prof groups. *Restrictions:* for indiv, only in Monroe County, or those with library card from another county; for inst, only in Monroe County, or those with library cards from another county. Cannot use when admission is charged. Available to researchers/scholars for on-site viewing. May not borrow by mail. *Loan Period:* 1 day. *Total Yr Film Loan:* 3954.
   Film Collection Approx 20-25t acquired annually. *Circ:* 16mm, 168t/168p. *Pubns:* catalog, annual; suppl, no set policy.

Bloomington (cont'd)

Other Film Serv Obtain film from coop loan system (Ind. Lib Film Service, Canadian Travel Film Lib), library film programs. Permanent viewing facility available free to community. *Equipment:* lend 16mm sound projector (3), lend 8mm reel projector (3), lend S8mm reel projector (3), lend projection screens (2), lend filmstrip projector (1), lend cassette tape recorders (3).

Other Media Collections *Audio:* disc, 33⅓ rpm, 7000t. *Filmstrips:* sound, 50t/50c; silent, 10t/10c.

Budget & Expenditures Total library budget $10,000 (FY 1/1/74-1/1/75). Total FY film budget $5000. *Member:* ALA, EFLA, Ind. Library Assn.

Video Serv *Est:* 1973. *In Charge:* Lee Guthrie, Libn. *Video Staff:* 2 f-t, 1 p-t. *Video Use:* documentation of community/school events, to increase community's library use, community video access, in-service training, as art form. Video serv available on demand & by appointment. Produce video tapes. Have production studio/space.

Video Equipment/Facilities *In-House Use Only:* portapak (4), ½" b&w, Sony AV3400, AVC3400; recording deck (4), ½", ¾" b&w/col; Sony AV3650, VO1800, AV8600, JVC CR6000U; playback deck (3), ¾" col; Sony VP1200, VP1000; editing deck (2), ½" col, Panasonic NV2130; studio camera (1) b&w, Panasonic WV361P; monitor (4), b&w/col; SEG (1), Panasonic; audio tape recorder (1). *For Loan:* portapak (4), ½" b&w, Sony AV3400, AVC3400; lighting (1); microphones (10); tripods (4). Have portable viewing installation. *Equipment Loan Period:* no set policy. Provide training in use of equipment to community & patrons. Have tape duplication serv.

Video Tape Loan/Rental/Sale Serv *Serv Provided:* free loan, swap with other inst. *Loan Eligibility:* staff & students, educational inst, civic groups, religious groups, indiv with library cards, prof groups. *Restrictions:* for indiv, only in Monroe County; for inst, only in Monroe County. Cannot duplicate. May borrow by mail.

Video Collection Maintained by own production. Use/play ½" reel to reel, ¾" cassette. Tapes organized alphabetically. *Collection, B&W:* ½" reel, 50t; ¾" cassette, 50t. *Other Video Serv:* production workshops.

Cable & CCTV Receive serv of cable TV system. Produce programs for cablecasting. Inform public about cable system serv & facilities. Serve as production facility for others. Run cable programs for special audiences. Have CCTV in inst, with 8 monitors. *Programming Sources:* tapes produced by inst, tapes produced professionally, tapes produced by community groups & indiv, & Public Television Library tapes for closed circuit only.

Bluffton

P- BLUFFTON-WELLS COUNTY PUBLIC LIBRARY, 22 W Washington, 46714. *Tel:* (219) 824-1612. *In Charge:* Ursula Kirchhoff. *Member:* Ind. Library Film Serv.

Bremen

P- BREMEN PUBLIC LIBRARY, 304 N Jackson St, 46506. *Tel:* (219) 546-2849. *In Charge:* Gwendolyn Berry. *Member:* Ind. Library Film Serv.

Columbus

S- VIDEO ACCESS CENTER—CHANNEL 7, Box 146, 47201. *Tel:* (812) 372-8784. *Video Serv Est:* 1972. *In Charge:* Virginia J. Rouse, Dir. *Video Staff:* 5 f-t, 2 p-t. *Video Use:* community video access. Video serv available on demand. Produce video tapes. Have production studio/space & separate control room.

Video Equipment/Facilities *In-House Use Only:* playback deck (1), ½" b&w, Sony AV3650, 8600, Panasonic TC3130; studio camera (2), b&w, Sony 3400; monitor (6), b&w/col; lighting (6); microphones (6); tripods (3); audio tape recorders (1). *For Loan:*

portapak (5), ½" b&w, Sony AV3400. Have permanent viewing installation. *Equipment Loan Period:* 1 day, or over weekend. Provide training to anyone over 16. Have tape duplication serv.

Video Tape Loan/Rental/Sale Serv *Serv Provided:* free loan, swap with other inst, sale. *Loan Eligibility:* civic groups, religious groups, indiv with certified training, prof groups, such as business & industries (for fee). *Restrictions:* for indiv, only in Bartholomew County; for inst, only in Bartholomew County. Cannot duplicate without permission. May borrow by mail. *Loan Period:* 7 days.

Video Collection Maintained by own production, exchange/swap. Use/play ½" reel to reel, ¾" cassette. *Sources:* commercial distributors. *Tape Sel:* preview. Tapes organized by Dewey Decimal. *Collection, B&W:* ½" reel, 300t/300c; ¾" cassette, 10t/10c. *Other Video Serv:* taping of other media, production workshops, contract production. *Pubns:* catalog.

Cable & CCTV Receive serv of cable TV system. Produce programs for cablecasting. Inform public about cable system serv & facilities. Serve as production facility for others. Run cable programs for special audiences.

Connersville

P- CONNERSVILLE PUBLIC LIBRARY, 828 Grand Ave, 47331. *Tel:* (317) 825-4681. *In Charge:* Frances Brookbank, Marilyn Robinson. *Member:* Library Flicks Library Servs Authority.

Crawfordsville

P- CRAWFORDSVILLE PUBLIC LIBRARY, 222 S Washington St, 47933. *Tel:* (317) 362-2242. *In Charge:* Mary Bishop. *Member:* Ind. Library Film Serv.

Culver

P- CULVER PUBLIC LIBRARY, 46511. *Tel:* (219) 842-2941. *In Charge:* Jane Scruggs. *Member:* Ind. Library Film Serv.

Decatur

P- DECATUR PUBLIC LIBRARY, 122 S Third St, 46733. *Tel:* (219) 724-2605. *In Charge:* Elizabeth Zerkel. *Member:* Ind. Library Film Serv.

East Chicago

P- EAST CHICAGO PUBLIC LIBRARY, 2401 E Columbus Dr, 46312. *Tel:* (219) 397-2453. *Film Serv Est:* 1959. *In Charge:* Lorraine Simon, Admin Asst. *AV Staff:* 1 (1 prof). *Film Sel:* committee preview. *Holdings:* black studies 5%, children's films 25%.

Free-Loan Film Serv *Eligibility:* indiv with library cards. *Restrictions:* for indiv, none. Cannot use for fund-raising, transmit electronically. Available to researchers/scholars for on-site viewing. May not borrow by mail. *Loan Period:* 1 day. *Total Yr Film Loan:* 10,736.

Film Collection 948t/969p. Approx 100t acquired annually. *Circ:* 16mm, 680t/691p; 8mm reel, 250t/260p; S8mm cartridge, 18t/18p. *Pubns:* catalog, as needed; suppl, in yr catalog not published.

Other Film Serv Library film programs. Permanent viewing facility available free to community. *Equipment:* lend 16mm sound projector (7), lend S8mm cartridge projector (2), lend S8mm reel projector (7).

Other Media Collections *Audio:* disc, 33⅓ rpm, 7553c; tape, cassette, 321c. *Filmstrips:* sound, 196c. *Member:* ALA, EFLA, Ind. Library Assn.

Elkhart

P- ELKHART PUBLIC LIBRARY, 300 S Second St, 46514. *Tel:* (219) 523-0878. *In Charge:* Ruth Kellogg. *Member:* Ind. Library Film Serv.

Evansville

P- EVANSVILLE PUBLIC LIBRARY & VANDERBURGH COUNTY PUBLIC LIBRARY, Art & Film Room, 22 SE Fifth St, 47708. *Tel:* (812) 425-2621. *Film Serv Est:* 1956. *In Charge:* Ann Williams, Film Libn. *AV Staff:* 2½ (2 cl, ½ tech). *Film Sel:* committee preview.

Free-Loan Film Serv *Eligibility:* civic groups, religious groups, indiv with library cards. *Restrictions:* for indiv, only in the 11 counties of Area Lib Serv; for inst, only in 10 surrounding counties. Cannot use for fund-raising, transmit electronically. Available to researchers/scholars for on-site viewing. May not borrow by mail. *Loan Period:* 1 day. *Total Yr Film Loan:* 8993.

Film Collection 880t/897p. *Circ:* 16mm, 410t/421p. all 8mm films, 465t/476p. *Pubns:* catalog, every 2 yrs; suppl, in yr catalog not published.

Other Film Serv Film reference serv, library film programs. Permanent viewing facility. *Equipment:* lend 16mm sound projector (1), lend projection screens (2).

Other Media Collections *Audio:* disc, 33⅓rpm, 8127c. *Slides:* single, 200c.

Budget & Expenditures Total library budget $120,000 (FY 1/1/75-1/1/76). Total FY film budget $10,000. *Member:* EFLA.

Fort Wayne

S- CONCORDIA THEOLOGICAL SEMINARY, Library, 6600 N Clinton, 46825. *Video Serv Est:* 1968. *In Charge:* Dale Hartmann, AV Dir. *Video Staff:* 1 f-t, 2 p-t, 8 tech. *Video Use:* documentation of community/school events, to increase community's library use, in-service training, practical video/TV training courses, educational use. Video serv available on demand & by appointment. Produce video tapes. Have production studio/space & separate control room.

Video Equipment/Facilities *In-House Use Only:* monitor (4), b&w, Sony, Admiral; SEG (1), Nasco. *For Loan:* portapak (1), ½″ b&w, Sony; recording deck (2), ½″ b&w, Sony; playback deck (2), ½″ b&w, Sony; editing deck (1), ½″ b&w, Sony; studio camera (3), b&w; additional camera lenses (3); microphones (2); tripods (3); audio tape recorders (46). Have portable viewing installation. *Equipment Loan Period:* flexible. Provide training in use of equipment to faculty, students, & communication class members.

Video Tape Loan/Rental/Sale Serv *Serv Provided:* swap with other inst. *Loan Eligibility:* staff & students. *Restrictions:* for indiv, interlibrary loan; for inst, none. May borrow by mail. *Loan Period:* 2 weeks.

Video Collection Maintained by rental, own production, exchange/swap. Use/play ½″ reel to reel. *Sources:* exchange. *Tape Sel:* faculty/staff recommendations. *Special Collections:* in-house training tapes. Tapes organized by subject. *Collection, Color:* ¾″ cassette, 1t/1c. *Collection, B&W:* ½″ reel, 58t. *Other Video Serv:* programming, taping of other media, production workshops.

P- PUBLIC LIBRARY OF FORT WAYNE AND ALLEN COUNTY, 900 Webster St, 46802. *Tel:* (219) 742-7241, ext 219. *Film Serv Est:* 1965. *In Charge:* Vera Crawford. *AV Staff:* 4. *Film Sel:* chief film librarian's decision.

Free-Loan Film Serv *Eligibility:* indiv with library cards. *Restrictions:* for indiv, only in our county & out-of-county subscription borrowers. Cannot transmit electronically. May not borrow by mail. *Loan Period:* 4 days. *Total Yr Film Loan:* 8102.

Film Collection 1500t/1600p. Approx 100t acquired annually. *Circ:* 16mm, 77t/77p; 8mm reel, 1041p; S8mm reel, 505p. *Pubns:* catalog, annual; suppl, no set policy.

Other Film Serv Library film programs. Permanent viewing facility available free to community.

Other Media Collections *Audio:* disc, 33⅓rpm, 18,000t; disc, 78rpm, 15,000t; tape, cassette, 240t. *Slides:* single, 30,000c.

Video Serv *Est:* 1973. *In Charge:* Steven Fortriede, Branch Supervisor. *Video Staff:* 1 f-t. *Video Use:* documentation of community/school events, to increase community's library use, community video access, playback over CATV of library produced tapes. Video serv available by appointment. Produce video tapes. *For Loan:* portapak (1), b&w, Sony AV3400; recording deck (1), col, Sony AV8600; editing deck (1), col, Panasonic NV3130; studio camera (2), b&w, Sony 3210,3260; monitor (5), b&w; SEG (1), Dyn-Air; additional camera lenses (5); lighting (1); microphones (6); tripods (3); audio tape recorders (1). Have portable viewing installation. *Equipment Loan Period:* no set policy. Provide training in use of equipment to those registered for our workshops. Have tape duplication serv.

Video Tape Loan/Rental/Sale Serv *Serv Provided:* free loan, swap with other inst. *Loan Eligibility:* indiv with library cards. *Restrictions:* for indiv, none; for inst, none. Cannot duplicate without permission. May borrow by mail. *Loan Period:* as required.

Video Collection Maintained by own production, exchange/swap. Use/play ½″ reel to reel. *Sources:* community productions, own production. *Tape Sel:* catalogs. Tapes organized alphabetically. *Collection, B&W:* ½″ reel, 50t. *Other Video Serv:* taping of other media, production workshops. *Pubns:* catalog.

Gary

P- GARY PUBLIC LIBRARY, 220 W Fifth Ave, 46402. *Tel:* (219) 886-2484, ext 52. *In Charge:* Larry Hamrell, Head, Arts and Recreation Dept. *AV Staff:* 4 (2 prof, 2 cl). *Film Sel:* chief film librarian's decision.

Free-Loan Film Serv *Eligibility:* educational inst, civic groups, religious groups, indiv with library cards, & any institution with a borrowing agreement. *Restrictions:* for indiv, only in city, anyone with nonresident library card; for inst, only in city. Cannot use for fund-raising, transmit electronically. Available to researchers/scholars for on-site viewing. May not borrow by mail. *Loan Period:* 1 day. *Total Yr Film Loan:* 9000.

Film Collection 1350t/1400p. Approx 80t acquired annually. *Circ:* 16mm, 1100t/1150p; 8mm reel, 100t/100p; S8mm reel, 170t/170p. *Pubns:* catalog, as needed; suppl, in yr catalog not published.

Other Film Serv Film reference serv, library film programs. Permanent viewing facility available free to community. *Equipment:* lend 16mm sound projector (10), lend 8mm reel projector (1), lend projection tables & stands, lend projection screens.

Other Media Collections *Audio:* disc, 33⅓rpm, 15,000t/22,000c; tape, reel, 60t/60c. *Filmstrips:* sound, 300t/400c; silent, 50t/50c. *Slides:* sets, 47t/47c.

Budget & Expenditures Total library budget $186,700 (FY 11/1/74-11/1/75). Total FY film budget $11,000. *Member:* AECT, ALA, EFLA, FLIC, Ind. Library Assn, Ind. Film Council.

Goshen

P- GOSHEN PUBLIC LIBRARY, 601 S Fifth St, 46526. *Tel:* (219) 533-9531. *In Charge:* Pauline Thompson. *Film Sel:* committee preview.

Free-Loan Film Serv *Eligibility:* indiv with adult library cards. *Restrictions:* for indiv, only in library district. *Loan Period:* 1 day. *Total Yr Film Loan:* 4100.

Film Collection 191t.

Other Film Serv Obtain film from coop loan system (Ind. Library Film Service), library film programs. *Equipment:* lend 16mm sound projector.

Other Media Collections *Audio:* disc, 33⅓rpm, 1400t. *Filmstrips:* silent, 187t. *Member:* Ind. Library Assn.

Hammond

P- HAMMOND PUBLIC LIBRARY, 564 State St, 46320. *Tel:* (219) 931-5100. *In Charge:* Marjorie Sohl. *Member:* Ind. Library Film Serv.

Huntington

C- HUNTINGTON COLLEGE, Loew Alumni Library, 2303 College Ave, 46750. *Tel:* (219) 356-6000, ext library 27, tv studio 45. *Video Serv Est:* 1970. *In Charge:* David L. Lloyd, Dir of TV. *Video Staff:* 4 p-t, 1 tech. *Video Use:* documentation of community/school events, in-service training, practical video/TV training courses. Video serv available by appointment. Produce video tapes. Have production studio/ space & separate control room.

Video Equipment/Facilities *In-House Use Only:* recording deck (1), ¾″ col, Sony 1800; editing deck (2), ½″ col, Sony 5000A; studio camera (2), b&w, Sony AVC4000A; monitor (7), 25″, 9″ b&w/col, Sony; SEG (1), Sony; additional camera lenses (3); lighting (5); microphones (6); tripods (3); audio tape recorders (1). Have permanent viewing installation. Provide training in use of equipment to faculty & students.

Video Tape Loan/Rental/Sale Serv *Serv Provided:* swap with other inst. *Loan Eligibility:* students enrolled in inst, civic groups, religious groups. *Restrictions:* for inst, only in city. May not borrow by mail. *Total Yr Tape Loan:* 5.

Video Collection Maintained by purchase, rental, own production, exchange/swap. Use/play ½″ reel to reel, ¾″ cassette. *Sources:* exchange (Netche). *Member:* Netche. *Tape Sel:* preview, faculty/staff recommendations, published reviews, catalogs. *Special Collections:* in-house training tapes, films in video format. Tapes organized by subject. *Collection, Color:* ½″ reel, 2t; ¾″ cassette, 10t. *Collection, B&W:* ½″ reel, 12t.

Cable & CCTV Have CCTV in inst. *Programming Sources:* over-the-air commercial & public broadcasting, tapes produced by inst, tapes produced professionally.

Indianapolis

S- CHRISTIAN CHURCH SERVICES, Office of Communication, AV Library, Box 1986, 46206. *Tel:* (317) 353-1491, ext 240. *In Charge:* Thomas P. Inabinett, Exec-Coordinate/Utilization. *AV Staff:* 3 (1 prof, 2 cl). *Film Sel:* committee preview, chief coordinator's decision. *Holdings:* animated films, biblical, black studies, career education, children's films, church, fine arts, religion, social sciences, teacher education, women.

P- INDIANA STATE LIBRARY, Extension Division, 140 N Senate Ave, 46204. *Tel:* (317) 633-5620. *Film Serv Est:* 1953. *In Charge:* Martha Roblee, Admin Libn. *AV Staff:* 0.3 (0.1 prof, 0.2 cl). *Film Sel:* committee preview. *Holdings:* gerontology 24%, library science 76%.

Free-Loan Film Serv *Eligibility:* educational inst, civic groups, prof groups, such as libraries & librarians. *Restrictions:* for indiv, interlibrary loan, only in state; for inst, only in state. Available to researchers/scholars for on-site viewing. May borrow by mail. *Loan Period:* 7 days. *Total Yr Film Loan :* 252.

Film Collection 82t/87p. Approx 3t acquired annually. *Circ:* 16mm, 82t/87p. *Pubns:* catalog, as needed.

Other Film Serv Obtain film from coop loan system (Central Ind. Area Library Serv Authority), film reference serv. *Equipment:* lend 16mm sound projector (1), lend projection tables & stands (1), lend projection screens (1).

Other Media Collections *Audio:* disc, 33⅓ rpm, 5t/5c; disc, 78rpm, 7t/7c; tape, cassette, 5t/5c. *Filmstrips:* sound, 30t/35c; silent, 28t/28c; sound sets, 5t/5c. *Slides:* single, 540t/540c; sets, 4t/4c.

Budget & Expenditures Total library budget $125,000 (FY 7/1/74-7/1/75). No separate budget. *Member:* ALA, Ind. Library Assn.

Video Serv *Est:* 1974. *In Charge:* M. J. Smith, Information Editor & Sue Bell, Oral History Libn. *Video Staff:* 2 p-t. *Video Use:* documentation of community/school events, oral history files. Video serv available on demand. Produce video tapes. Have production studio/space.

Video Equipment/Facilities *In-House Use Only:* portapak (1), ½″ b&w, Sony; recording deck (1), col, Sony; playback deck (1), col, Sony; editing deck (1), ½″ col, Panasonic; studio camera (1), b&w, Sony; monitor (3), b&w, Sony, Motorola; SEG (1), Sony; microphones (3); tripods (2); audio tape recorders (2), mike mixer (1). Have portable viewing installation. Provide training in use of equipment to staff.

Video Tape Loan/Rental/Sale Serv *Serv Provided:* free loan, swap with other inst. *Loan Eligibility:* org members (equipment), public libraries (tapes). *Restrictions:* for inst, only in state. Cannot duplicate without permission.

Video Collection Use/play ½″ reel to reel, ¾″ cassette. *Tape Sel:* preview. *Special Collections:* oral history.

C- INDIANA VOCATIONAL TECHNICAL COLLEGE, Learning Resources Center, 1315 E Washington St, 46202. *Tel:* (317) 635-6100, ext 28, 41 or 52. *Film Serv Est:* 1973. *In Charge:* Diana Yu Swenson, Libn. *AV Staff:* 3 (1 prof, 3 cl). *Film Sel:* faculty/staff recommendations. *Holdings:* architecture, career education 4%, communications, computer programming, consumer affairs .1%, electronics, engineering 6%, industrial management, library aide, marketing, medicine 14%, science 2%, social sciences 2%, trade & technical.

Free-Loan Film Serv *Eligibility:* staff & students, educational inst, prof groups, such as American Soc of Training Directors. *Restrictions:* for indiv, none; for inst, none. Available to researchers/scholars for on-site viewing. May not borrow by mail. *Loan Period:* 1 day, or on special request. *Total Yr Film Loan:* 204.

Film Collection 130t/130p. Approx 10-20t acquired annually. *Circ:* 16mm, 50t/50p; S8mm cartridge, 94t/94p. Publish monthly list of new materials.

Other Film Serv Rent film from distributors for patrons, obtain film from coop loan system (Central Ind. Library Services Authority), obtain film from other libraries. *Equipment:* lend 16mm sound projector (13), lend 8mm cartridge projector, lend S8mm cartridge projector (4), lend projection tables & stands, lend projection screens (3).

Other Media Collections *Audio:* tape, cassette, 150t. *Filmstrips:* sound sets, 150t; silent sets, 59t. *Slides:* sets, 12t. *Member:* AECT, ALA.

Video Serv *Est:* 1973. *In Charge:* Beverly S. Simone, Div Chmn, Learning Resources. *Video Staff:* 2 f-t, 2 p-t, 1 tech. *Video Use:* in-service training, playback of professionally produced tapes, production of instructional materials. Video serv available on demand & by appointment. Produce video tapes. Have production studio/space.

Video Equipment/Facilities *In-House Use Only:* recording deck (1), ½″ col, Sony; editing deck (1), ½″ col, Sony; studio camera (2), col, Panasonic; monitor (1), Sony; SEG (1), Shintron; lighting (1); microphones (4); tripods (3); cassette recorders. *For Loan:* portapak (1), ½″ col, JVC; playback deck (2), ¾″ col, JVC; audio tape recorders (157). Have portable viewing installation. *Equipment Loan Period:* no set policy. Provide training in use of equipment to Learning Resources staff. Have tape duplication serv.

Video Tape Loan/Rental/Sale Serv *Serv Provided:* free loan, swap with other inst. *Loan Eligibility:* staff & students, educational inst. *Restrictions:* for indiv, none; for inst, none. Cannot duplicate without permission. May not borrow by mail. *Total Yr Tape Loan:* 99.

Video Collection Maintained by purchase, own production, exchange/swap. Use/play ½″ reel to reel, ¾″ cassette. *Sources:* commercial distributors, in-house production. *Tape Sel:* preview, faculty/staff recommendations, published reviews. *Special Collections:* in-house training tapes, instruction in various program areas. Tapes organized by subject. *Collection, Color:* ¾″ cassette, 70t/70c. *Other Video Serv:* programming, taping of other media.

P- INDIANAPOLIS-MARION COUNTY PUBLIC LIBRARY, 40 E St Clair St, 46204. *Tel:* (317) 635-5662, ext 321, 322. *Film Serv Est:* 1951. *In Charge:* Jacqueline Ek, Head, Films Div. *AV Staff:* 9 (3 prof, 6 cl). *Film Sel:* staff preview, chief film librarian's decision.
Free-Loan Film Serv *Eligibility:* indiv with library cards. *Restrictions:* for indiv, only in Marion County, members of Central Ind. Area Lib Service. Cannot use for fund-raising, transmit electronically. May not borrow by mail. *Total Yr Film Loan:* 31,689.
Film Collection 2369t/3052p. Approx 200t acquired annually. *Circ:* 16mm, 1691t/1794p; 8mm reel, 678t/693p; S8mm reel, 565p. *Pubns:* catalog, every 2 yrs ($2); suppl in yr catalog not published.
Other Film Serv Obtain film from coop loan system (Central Ind. Area Lib Serv Authority), film reference serv, library film programs. Permanent viewing facility available for rent to community.
Other Media Collections *Audio:* disc, 33⅓rpm, 10,000t; tape, cassette, 4t/4c. *Filmstrips:* sound, 85t/86c; silent, 77t/77c.
Budget & Expenditures Total FY film budget $59,700. *Member:* Ind. Library Assn.

S- INDIANAPOLIS MUSEUM OF ART, Film Library, 1200 W 38 St, 46208. *Tel:* (317) 923-1331, ext 44. *Film Serv Est:* 1974. *In Charge:* John W. Claxton, Asst Cur for Media. *AV Staff:* 2 (2 prof). *Film Sel:* produced in-house. *Holdings:* fine arts 100%.
Film Rental Serv *Eligibility:* no restrictions. *Restrictions:* only in U.S. Cannot use for fund-raising. *Rental Period:* 1 day. *Total Yr Film Booking:* 50-70. Sell films. Produce films. Produce multi-image video tape.
Film Collection 6t/30p. *Circ:* 16mm, 6t/30p.
Other Film Serv Film fairs/festivals. Permanent viewing facility available for rent to community. *Member:* AECT.

S- NEW WORLD COMMUNICATIONS, INC., 920 Westfield Blvd, 46220. *Tel:* (317) 259-7611. *Video Serv Est:* 1972. *In Charge:* Steve Sweitzer & Michael Zaphirion, Co-Directors. *Video Staff:* 4 f-t, 2 p-t. *Video Use:* documentation of community/school events, community video access, practical video/TV training courses, as art form. Video serv available by appointment. Produce video tapes. Have production studio/space.
Video Equipment/Facilities *In-House Use Only:* portapak (1), ½" col, Sony; recording deck (11), ½" col, Panasonic; editing deck (1), ½" col, Panasonic; studio camera (2), b&w, Panasonic; monitor (8), b&w/col, Sony; SEG (1), Panasonic; keyer (1), Shintion; audio tape recorders (2). *For Loan:* portapak (4), b&w, Sony; playback deck (1), ½" b&w, Panasonic; monitor (8), b&w/col, Sony; lighting (3); microphones (7); tripods (5); audio tape recorders (2). Have portable viewing installation. *Equipment Loan Period:* 3 days. Provide training in use of equipment to faculty, students, & individuals requesting it. Have tape duplication serv.
Video Tape Loan/Rental/Sale Serv *Serv Provided:* free loan, swap with other inst, rental, sale. *Loan/Rental Eligibility:* educational inst, civic groups, religious groups, prof groups, such as museums & arts organizations & others, such as individuals who have completed a day-long workshop. *Restrictions:* for indiv, only in city; for inst, none. Cannot use for fund-raising, duplicate, air without permission. May not borrow by mail. *Loan Period:* 7 days. *Total Yr Tape Loan:* 15.
Video Collection Maintained by own production, exchange/swap. Use/play ½" reel to reel. *Sources:* community productions. *Tape Sel:* preview. *Special Collections:* video as art, films in video format. Tapes organized by subject. *Collection, Color:* ½" reel, 4t/3c. *Collection, B&W:* ½" reel, 5t/2c. *Other Video Serv:* programming, production workshops, consultation, system design. Publish workshop instruction manual.
Cable & CCTV Produce programs for cablecasting. Inform public about cable system serv & facilities. Serve as production facility for others.

Film Rental Serv *Eligibility:* no restrictions. *Restrictions:* none. Cannot use for fund-raising (under some circumstances), transmit electronically. *Rental Period:* 1 day. Produce sound filmstrips. *Pubns:* catalog, every 3 yrs; suppl, as needed.
Other Film Serv Obtain film from coop loan system (Religious Film Libraries), workshops & training programs. Permanent viewing facility. *Member:* AECT, EFLA, Ind. Film Council.

Jeffersonville

P- JEFFERSONVILLE TOWNSHIP PUBLIC LIBRARY, Box 548, 47130. *Tel:* (812) 282-7765. *In Charge:* Lawrence W. Sullivan, Head of Circulation. *AV Staff:* ⅗ (⅖ cl, ⅕ tech). *Film Sel:* committee preview.
Free-Loan Film Serv *Eligibility:* indiv with library cards. *Restrictions:* for indiv, only in library dist. Cannot use for fund-raising. Available to researchers/scholars for on-site viewing. May not borrow by mail. *Loan Period:* 1 day. *Total Yr Film Loan:* 663.
Film Collection 611t/611p. Approx 25t acquired annually. *Circ:* 16mm, 107t/107p; 8mm reel, 490t/490p; S8mm reel, 14t/14p. *Pubns:* catalog, annual; suppl, no set policy.
Other Film Serv Library film programs. Permanent viewing facility available free to community.
Other Media Collections *Audio:* disc, 33⅓rpm, 2646t/2646c.
Budget & Expenditures Total library budget $42,731 (FY 1/1/75-1/1/76). Total FY film budget $2000. *Member:* ALA, Ind. Library Assn.

Kendallville

P- KENDALLVILLE PUBLIC LIBRARY, W Rush St, 46755. *Tel:* (219) 347-3554. *Film Serv Est:* 1958. *In Charge:* Linda Herendeen, Asst Libn. *AV Staff:* 1. *Holdings:* children's films 100%.
Free-Loan Film Serv *Eligibility:* indiv with library cards. *Restrictions:* for indiv, only in our tax area. May not borrow by mail. *Loan Period:* 1 day.
Film Collection 17t/17p. Approx 1t acquired annually. *Circ:* 16mm, 17t/17p.
Other Film Serv Obtain film from coop loan system (Ind. Library Film Service), library film programs. Permanent viewing facility available free to community. *Equipment:* lend 16mm sound projector (2), lend projection tables & stands (1), lend projection screens (2).
Other Media Collections *Audio:* disc, 33⅓rpm, 2050c; tape, cassette, 54c. *Filmstrips:* sound, 39c; silent, 38c. *Slides:* single, 34c.
Budget & Expenditures No separate AV budget. *Member:* Ind. Library Film Serv.

Kokomo

P- KOKOMO PUBLIC LIBRARY, 220 N Union, 46901. *Tel:* (317) 457-5558. *Film Serv Est:* 1958. *In Charge:* Jerry M. Henry, AV Coord. *AV Staff:* 2 (1 prof, 1 cl). *Film Sel:* chief film librarian's decision.
Free-Loan Film *Eligibility:* staff & students, educational inst, civic groups, religious groups, indiv with library cards, prof groups. *Restrictions:* for indiv, only in city & township; for inst, only in city & township. Available to researchers/scholars for on-site viewing. May not borrow by mail. *Loan Period:* 48 hours. *Total Yr Film Loan:* 4053.
Film Collection 220t/220p. *Circ:* 16mm, 220t/220p; 8mm reel, 144t/144p. *Pubns:* catalog, annual.
Other Film Serv Obtain film from coop loan system (Ind. Library Film Circuit, Ind. Festival Films). Permanent viewing facility available for rent to community.
Other Media Collections *Audio:* disc, 33⅓rpm, 6514t; tape, cassette, 215t. *Filmstrips:* silent, 282t.
Budget & Expenditures Total library budget $99,547.50 (FY 1/1/75-1/1/76). Total FY film budget $5500.

La Porte

P- LA PORTE PUBLIC LIBRARY, 904 Indiana Ave, 46350. *Tel:* (219) 362-2467. *In Charge:* Lois M. Harrell, Film Libn. *AV Staff:* 1½ (1 prof, ½ tech). *Film Sel:* staff recommendations, previews. *Holdings:* agriculture 1%, animated films 10%, children's films 15%, comedies, fine arts 3%, industrial arts 1%, social sciences 10%, sports, travel.

Free-Loan Film Serv *Eligibility:* educational inst, civic groups, religious groups, indiv with library cards, & others, such as nursing homes. *Restrictions:* for indiv, only in La Porte County; for inst, only in La Porte County. Cannot use for fund-raising. *Loan Period:* 1 day.

Film Collection 124t/125p. Approx 10t acquired annually. *Circ:* 16mm, 124t/125p. *Pubns:* catalog, every 2 yrs; suppl, as needed.

Other Film Serv Rent film from distributors for patrons, obtain film from coop loan system (Ind. Library Film Serv, Modern, ACI), obtain film from other libraries, film reference serv, film fairs/festivals, library film programs. Permanent viewing facility. *Equipment:* lend 16mm sound projector (3), lend/rent 8mm reel projector (2), lend projection tables & stands (1), lend projection screens (1).

Budget & Expenditures Total library budget $27,000 (FY 1/1/75-1/1/76). No separate AV budget. *Member:* ALA, Ind. Library Assn.

Liberty

P- UNION COUNTY PUBLIC LIBRARY, 2 E Seminary, 47353. *Tel:* (317) 458-5355. *In Charge:* Mary Frautschi, Joe Sawyer. *Member:* Library Flicks Library Servs Authority.

Ligonier

P- LIGONIER PUBLIC LIBRARY, 300 S Main, 46767. *Tel:* (219) 894-4511. *In Charge:* Marvina Blanchard, Jerry Nesbitt. *Member:* Library Flicks Library Servs Authority.

Logansport

P- CASS COUNTY PUBLIC LIBRARY, 616 E Broadway, 46947. *Tel:* (219) 753-3435. *In Charge:* Philip Shih. *Member:* Ind. Library Film Serv.

Madison

P- JEFFERSON COUNTY PUBLIC LIBRARY, 420 W Main St, 47250. *Tel:* (812) 265-2745. *In Charge:* Don Johnson. *Member:* Ind. Library Film Serv.

Marion

P- MARION PUBLIC LIBRARY, 105 W Sixth St, 46952. *Tel:* (317) 664-7942. *In Charge:* Sue Israel. *Member:* Ind. Library Film Serv.

Merrillville

P- LAKE COUNTY PUBLIC LIBRARY, AV Services, 1919 W Lincoln Highway, 46410. *Tel:* (219) 769-3541, ext 44. *Film Serv Est:* 1965. *In Charge:* Dorothy Maud, Head, AV Serv. *AV Staff:* 5 (1 prof, 4 cl). *Film Sel:* committee preview.

Free-Loan Film Serv *Eligibility:* indiv with library cards. *Restrictions:* for indiv, only in library district. Cannot use for fund-raising, transmit electronically. Available to researchers/scholars for on-site viewing. May not borrow by mail. *Loan Period:* 1-2 days. *Total Yr Film Loan:* 22,141.

Film Collection 720p. Approx 90-100t acquired annually. *Circ:* 16mm, 720p; 8mm reel, 185p. *Pubns:* catalog, annual; suppl, annually.

Other Film Serv Film reference serv, library film programs. Permanent viewing facility.

Budget & Expenditures Total FY film budget $16,000.

Michigan City

P- MICHIGAN CITY PUBLIC LIBRARY, Eighth & Spring St, 46360. *Tel:* (219) 879-8363. *In Charge:* Don Daniels. *Member:* Ind. Library Film Serv.

Mishawaka

P- MISHAWAKA PUBLIC LIBRARY, 209 Lincoln Way E, 46544. *Tel:* (219) 259-5277. *Film Serv Est:* 1967. *In Charge:* Kitty Bush, Film Libn. *AV Staff:* 1 (1 tech). *Film Sel:* committee preview, staff recommendations, chief film librarian's decision. *Holdings:* animated films 6%, children's films 26%, consumer affairs 9%, holiday 21%, social sciences 5%, travel 33%.

Free-Loan Film Serv *Eligibility:* educational inst, civic groups, religious groups, indiv with adult library cards. *Restrictions:* for indiv, only in St Joseph County; for inst, only in St Joseph County. Available to researchers/scholars for on-site viewing. May not borrow by mail. *Loan Period:* 3 days. *Total Yr Film Loan:* 1192.

Film Collection 79t/79p. Approx 1-5t acquired annually. *Circ:* 16mm, 79t/79p. *Pubns:* catalog, annual.

Other Film Serv Obtain film from coop loan system (Ind. Library Film Service), film fairs/festivals. Permanent viewing facility available for rent to community. *Equipment:* lend 16mm sound projector (1).

Other Media Collections *Audio:* disc, 33⅓rpm, 1727t/1727c. *Filmstrips:* silent, 443t; sound sets, 159t. *Slides:* single, 1683t.

Budget & Expenditures Total library budget $60,000 (FY 1/1/75-1/1/76). Total FY film budget $922.90. *Member:* ALA, Ind. Library Assn.

Muncie

P- MUNCIE PUBLIC LIBRARY, AV Center, 209 N Walnut, 47305. *Tel:* (317) 288-1411. *Film Serv Est:* 1955. *In Charge:* Patricia Schaefer, AV Libn. *AV Staff:* 4 (1 prof, 2 cl, 1 tech). *Film Sel:* chief film librarian's decision.

Free-Loan Film Serv *Eligibility:* indiv with library cards. *Restrictions:* for indiv, only in city. Cannot use for fund-raising, transmit electronically. May not borrow by mail. *Loan Period:* 3 days. *Total Yr Film Loan:* 12,173.

Film Collection 649t/650p. Approx 50t acquired annually. *Circ:* 16mm, 649t/650p; 8mm reel, 230t/230p. *Pubns:* catalog, every 3 yrs; suppl, in yr catalog not published.

Other Film Serv Obtain film from coop loan system (Ind. Library Film Service), library film programs.

Other Media Collections *Audio:* disc, 33⅓rpm, 7000t; disc, 78rpm, 400t; tape, cassette, 30t. *Filmstrips:* silent, 180t. *Slides:* sets, 227t.

Budget & Expenditures Total library budget $115,000 (FY 1/1/75-1/1/76). Total FY film budget $18,500. *Member:* AECT, ALA, EFLA, FLIC, Ind. Library Assn, Music Library Assn, Ind. Film Council.

New Albany

P- NEW ALBANY-FLOYD COUNTY PUBLIC LIBRARY, 180 W Spring St, 47150. *Tel:* (812) 944-8464. *In Charge:* Leonard Felkey, Ann M. Wunderlich. *Member:* Library Flicks Library Servs Authority.

New Castle

P- HENRY COUNTY PUBLIC LIBRARY, 296 S 15th St, 47362. *Tel:* (317) 529-0362. *In Charge:* Robert Tooley. *Member:* Ind. Library Film Serv.

North Vernon

P- JENNINGS COUNTY PUBLIC LIBRARY, 143 E Walnut St, 47265. *Tel:* (812) 346-2091. *In Charge:* Marjorie Woods. *Member:* Ind. Library Film Serv.

Peru

P- PERU PUBLIC LIBRARY, 102 E Main St, 46970. *Tel:* (317) 473-3069. *In Charge:* Charles Wagner. *Member:* Ind. Library Film Serv.

Plymouth

P- PLYMOUTH PUBLIC LIBRARY, 201 N Center St, 46563. *Tel:* (219) 936-2324. *Film Serv Est:* 1960. *In Charge:* Lillian Sherwood, AV Coord. *AV Staff:* 1. *Film Sel:* committee preview, staff recommendations, chief film librarian's decision. *Holdings:* feature films 57%, medicine 14%, science 3%, social sciences 23%, sports 3%.

Free-Loan Film Serv *Eligibility:* staff & students, educational inst, civic groups, religious groups, indiv with library cards, prof groups. *Restrictions:* for indiv, only in city & 2 townships; for inst, only in city, & those with out-of-township library cards. May not borrow by mail. *Loan Period:* 1 day. *Total Yr Film Loan:* 1233.

Film Collection 35t/35p. Approx 5-10t acquired annually. *Circ:* 16mm, 35t/35p. *Pubns:* catalog, as needed.

Other Film Serv Obtain film from coop loan system (Ind. Library Film Circuit), film reference serv, library film programs. Permanent viewing facility available free to community. *Equipment:* lend 16mm sound projector (1), lend projection screens (1).

Other Media Collections *Audio:* disc, 33⅓ rpm, 886t; tape, cassette, 29t. *Slides:* single, 26t; sets, 278t.

Budget & Expenditures Total library budget $14,685 (FY 1/1/74-1/1/75). Total FY film budget $1672. *Member:* ALA, Ind. Library Assn, Ind. Film Council.

Richmond

S- EARLHAM COLLEGE, Great Lakes Colleges Assn Center for East Asian Studies, East Asian AV Library, 47374. *Tel:* (317) 962-6561, ext 324. *Film Serv Est:* 1973. *In Charge:* Diana Battista, Assoc Dir. *AV Staff:* 1. *Film Sel:* committee preview, faculty/staff recommendations. *Holdings:* East Asia 100%.

Film Rental Serv *Eligibility:* no restrictions. *Restrictions:* none. Cannot use for fund-raising. *Rental Period:* varies. *Total Yr Film Booking:* 284. Produce video tape ½" reel to reel, ¾" video cassette.

Film Collection 66t/70p. *Circ:* 16mm, 66t/70p. *Noncirc:* 16mm, 3t/3p. *Pubns:* catalog, annual; suppl, no set policy.

Other Film Serv Obtain film from coop loan system (Great Lakes Colleges Assn, Oberlin College Lib Media Service), film reference serv.

Other Media Collections *Audio:* tape, cassette, 14t/14c; tape, reel, 2t/2c. *Filmstrips:* silent, 30t/30c; sound sets, 2t/2c. *Slides:* single, 200t/200c; sets, 8t/8c.

Budget & Expenditures No separate budget.

Video Serv *Est:* 1967. *In Charge:* John W. Schuerman, Dir, AV Serv. *Video Staff:* 3 f-t, 1 p-t, 1 tech. *Video Use:* as art form, produce own tapes. Video serv available by appointment. Produce video tapes.

Video Equipment/Facilities *In-House Use Only:* recording deck (3), ½" b&w/col, Panasonic; playback deck (1), ¾", Panasonic; editing deck (1), ½", Panasonic; studio camera (1), Panasonic; monitor (4), b&w/col; SEG (1), Panasonic; microphones; tripods (1); audio tape recorders. Have portable viewing installation. Provide training in use of equipment to faculty & students. Have tape duplication serv.

Video Tape Loan/Rental/Sale Serv *Serv Provided:* rental. *Loan/Rental Eligibility:* no restrictions. *Restrictions:* for indiv, none; for inst, none. Cannot use for fund-raising, dupli-

cate. May borrow by mail. *Loan Period:* varies with user. *Total Yr Tape Loan:* 10.

Video Collection Maintained by purchase, own production. Use/play ½" reel to reel, ¾" cassette. *Sources:* exchange (various educational institutions). *Tape Sel:* preview, faculty/staff recommendations. *Special Collections:* East Asian related subject matter. Tapes organized by subject. *Collection, Color:* ½" reel, 7t; ¾" cassette, 2t/4c. *Collection, B&W:* ¾" cassette, 6t/12c. *Pubns:* catalog.

Cable & CCTV Receive serv of cable TV system.

Rochester

P- FULTON COUNTY PUBLIC LIBRARY, 802 Jefferson St, 46975. *Tel:* (219) 223-2713. *In Charge:* Betty Becker, Claire Zehner. *Member:* Library Flicks Library Servs Authority.

Scottsburg

P- SCOTT COUNTY PUBLIC LIBRARY, 108 S Main St, 47170. *Tel:* (812) 752-2751. *Film Serv Est:* 1955. *In Charge:* Kathryn D. Nicholas, Libn. *AV Staff:* 1. *Film Sel:* committee preview, published reviews. *Holdings:* holidays.

Free-Loan Film Serv *Eligibility:* indiv with library cards. *Restrictions:* for indiv, only in Scott County; for inst, only in Scott County. May not borrow by mail. *Loan Period:* 3 days. *Total Yr Film Loan:* 1818.

Film Collection 66t/66p. Approx 2-3t acquired annually. *Circ:* 16mm, 66t/66p.

Other Film Serv Obtain film from coop loan system (Ind. Library Film Serv), library film programs. *Equipment:* lend 16mm sound projector (1), lend projection screens (1).

Other Media Collections *Audio:* disc, 33⅓ rpm, 715t/578c. *Filmstrips:* silent, 27t/27c.

Budget & Expenditures Total library budget $10,000 (FY 1/1/75-1/1/76). Total FY film budget $1155.

Seymour

P- SEYMOUR PUBLIC LIBRARY, Second & Walnut St, 47247. *Tel:* (812) 522-3412. *In Charge:* Helen Neal. *Member:* Ind. Library Film Serv.

South Bend

P- SOUTH BEND PUBLIC LIBRARY, Film Service, 122 W Wayne St, 46601. *Tel:* (219) 288-4413, ext 55, 56. *Film Serv Est:* 1967. *In Charge:* James R. Meyers, Film Libn. *AV Staff:* 3½ (1 prof, 2½ cl). *Film Sel:* committee preview, chief film librarian's decision.

Free-Loan Film Serv *Eligibility:* indiv with library cards. *Restrictions:* for indiv, none; for inst, none. Cannot use for fund-raising, transmit electronically. Available to researchers/scholars for on-site viewing. May not borrow by mail. *Loan Period:* 1 day. *Total Yr Film Loan:* 11,000.

Film Collection 400t/408p. Approx 40-50t acquired annually. *Circ:* 16mm, 400t/408p; 8mm reel, 150t/152p; S8mm reel, 76t/76p. *Pubns:* catalog, every 2 yrs; suppl, no set policy.

Other Film Serv Obtain film from coop loan system (Ind. Library Film Serv), film reference serv, film fairs/festivals, library film programs. Permanent viewing facility available for rent to community. *Equipment:* lend 16mm sound projector (5), lend 8mm reel projector (2), lend S8mm reel projector (2), lend projection tables & stands (3), lend projection screens (3).

Other Media Collections *Audio:* disc, 33⅓ rpm, 6132c. *Filmstrips:* sound, 10t; silent, 25t. *Slides:* single, 3350t; sets, 100t.

Budget & Expenditures Total library budget $150,000 (FY 1/1/75-1/1/76). Total FY film budget $17,500. *Member:* EFLA, FLIC.

Terre Haute

C- INDIANA STATE UNIVERSITY, AV Center—Film Library, Stalker Hall, Room 10, 47809. *Tel:* (812) 232-6311, ext 5681, 5682. *Film Serv Est:* 1953. *In Charge:* C. Wesley Lambert, Dir, AV Center. *AV Staff:* 20 (13 prof, 7 cl, 11 tech). *Film Sel:* faculty/staff recommendations. *Holdings:* driver education.

Free-Loan Film Serv *Eligibility:* staff & students. *Restrictions:* for indiv, none; for inst, none. Cannot transmit electronically. Available to researchers/scholars for on-site viewing. May not borrow by mail. *Loan Period:* varies with need. *Total Yr Film Loan:* 9543.

Film Rental Serv *Eligibility:* no restrictions. *Restrictions:* only in Indiana & surrounding states. Cannot transmit electronically. *Rental Period:* 4 days. *Total Yr Film Booking:* 1474. Sell films. Produce 16mm films. Produce slides, tape, sound filmstrips.

Film Collection 1750t/1927p. Approx 80-100t acquired annually. *Circ:* 16mm, 1750t/1927p. *Noncirc:* 16mm, 310t/310p. *Pubns:* catalog, every 5 yrs; suppl, no set policy.

Other Film Serv Rent film from distributors for patrons, obtain film from coop loan system (CUFC), obtain film from other libraries, film reference serv. *Equipment:* lend S8mm camera (7), lend 16mm camera (2), lend 16mm sound projector (152), lend 8mm cartridge projector (24), lend 8mm reel projector (12), lend S8mm cartridge projector (38), lend S8mm reel projector (10), lend projection tables & stands (275), lend projection screens (425), lend silent 16mm motion analysis projector (6).

Other Media Collections *Audio:* disc, total 48t. *Filmstrips:* silent, 227t; sound sets, 273t; silent sets, 411t. *Slides:* sets, 84t. *Member:* AECT, CUFC, EFLA, IAECT, PP of A, CINE, UFA, IFC.

P- VIGO COUNTY PUBLIC LIBRARY, 222 N Seventh St, 47807. *Tel:* (812) 232-5041, ext 36. *Film Serv Est:* 1953. *In Charge:* Ann Newman, Librn, AV Serv Div. *AV Staff:* 3 (1 prof, 1 cl, 1 tech). *Film Sel:* chief film librarian's decision, published reviews. *Holdings:* entertainment 18%.

Free-Loan Film Serv *Eligibility:* indiv with adult library cards. *Restrictions:* for indiv, only in Vigo County; for inst, only in Vigo County. Available to researchers/scholars for on-site viewing. May not borrow by mail. *Loan Period:* 2 days or weekend.

Film Collection 750t/750p. Approx 25-35t acquired annually. *Circ:* 16mm, 750t; 8mm reel, 400t; S8mm reel, 200t. *Pubns:* catalog, annual; suppl, no set policy.

Other Film Serv Obtain film from coop loan system (Ind. Library Film Serv), film reference serv, film fairs/festivals, library film programs. Permanent viewing facility available free to community. *Equipment:* lend 16mm sound projector (14), lend 8mm reel projector, lend S8mm reel projector (7), lend projection screens (8).

Other Media Collections *Audio:* tape, cassette, 300t/100c. *Filmstrips:* silent, 75t; sound sets, 20t. *Slides:* sets, 100t.

Budget & Expenditures Total FY film budget $16,000. *Member:* AECT, ALA, EFLA, FLIC, Ind. Library Assn, Ind. Film Council.

Video Serv *Est:* 1972. *In Charge:* Betty Dodson, Mediamobile Libn. *Video Staff:* 3 f-t, 1 tech. *Video Use:* documentation of community events, to increase community's library use, inservice training. Video serv available by appointment. Produce video tapes.

Video Equipment/Facilities *For Loan:* portapak (1), ½" b&w, Sony 3400; recording deck (1), b&w, Sony 3650; playback deck (1), ½" b&w, Sony 3650; monitor (3), b&w; additional camera lenses (1); microphones (3); tripods (1); audio tape recorders (4). *Equipment Loan Period:* 2 days. Provide training in use of equipment to representatives of nonprofit community groups.

Video Tape Loan/Rental/Sale Serv *Serv Provided:* free loan. *Loan Eligibility:* staff, civic groups, religious groups. *Restrictions:* for indiv, only in Vigo County; for inst, only in Vigo County. Cannot use for fund-raising. May not borrow by mail. *Loan Period:* 2 days.

Video Collection Maintained by own production. Use/play ½" reel to reel. *Sources:* community productions. *Special Collections:* in-house training tapes. Tapes organized by subject. *Collection, B&W:* ½" reel, 59t. *Other Video Serv:* programming.

Tipton

P- TIPTON COUNTY PUBLIC LIBRARY, 127 E Madison, 47390. *Tel:* (317) 675-2526. *In Charge:* Grace Chen, Donna Ekstrom. *Member:* Library Flicks Library Servs Authority.

Upland

C- TAYLOR UNIVERSITY, Learning Resource Center, Liberal Arts Building, 46989. *Tel:* (317) 998-2751, ext 254. *Film Serv Est:* 1967. *In Charge:* Gerald Hodson, Dir. *AV Staff:* 6 (3 prof, 3 cl). *Film Sel:* faculty/staff recommendations. *Holdings:* animated films 10%, black studies 10%, children's films 10%, experimental films 10%, feature films 10%, fine arts 10%, law 10%, science 10%, social sciences 10%, teacher education 10%.

Free-Loan Film Serv *Eligibility:* staff & students. May not borrow by mail. *Loan Period:* 7 days. Produce films. Produce video, overhead transparencies, filmstrips, tapes, slides, loops, photo visuals.

Film Collection 50t/50p. Approx 10t acquired annually.

Other Film Serv Rent film from distributors for patrons, obtain film from coop loan system (Christian College Consortium), obtain film from other libraries. *Equipment:* lend S8mm camera (3), 16mm camera (2), 16mm sound projector (12), 8mm cartridge projector (3), 8mm reel projector (3), S8mm cartridge projector (1), S8mm reel projector (3), projection tables & stands (16), projection screens (22).

Budget & Expenditures Total library budget $125,000 (FY 7/1/75-7/1/76). Total FY film budget $1000. *Member:* AECT.

Valparaiso

P- VALPARAISO PUBLIC LIBRARY, 107 Jefferson St, 46383. *Tel:* (219) 462-0524. *In Charge:* Wake Kanney. *Member:* Ind. Library Film Serv.

Vincennes

P- VINCENNES PUBLIC LIBRARY, 502 N Seventh St, 47591. *Tel:* (812) 882-6007. *In Charge:* Maxine Batman. *Member:* Ind. Library Film Serv.

Wabash

P- WABASH CARNEGIE PUBLIC LIBRARY, 188 W Hill, 46992. *Tel:* (219) 563-2972. *In Charge:* Bob Beauchamp, Linda Robertson. *Member:* Library Flicks Library Servs Authority.

West Lafayette

C- PURDUE UNIVERSITY, AV Center, Stewart Center, 47907. *Tel:* (317) 749-6202. *Film Serv Est:* 1950. *In Charge:* C. E. Snow, Film Libn. *AV Staff:* 27 (6 prof, 9 cl). *Film Sel:* faculty/staff recommendations, assistant film librarian's decision. *Holdings:* agriculture 5%, engineering 10%, experimental films 10%, medicine 5%, science 20%, social sciences 40%, teacher education 10%.

Film Rental Serv *Eligibility:* no restrictions. *Restrictions:* only in U.S. Cannot use for fund-raising. *Rental Period:* 2 days. *Total Yr Film Booking:* 10,000. Sell films. Produce films. Produce slide sets.

Film Collection 4500t/5000p. Approx 120t acquired annually. *Circ:* 16mm, 4500t/5000p. *Pubns:* catalog, every 2 yrs.

Other Film Serv Rent film from distributors for patrons, obtain film from other libraries, film reference serv. Permanent viewing facility available free to community. *Equipment:* 16mm sound projector (30), 8mm cartridge projector (2), S8mm cartridge projector (2), projection tables & stands (50), projection screens (30), overhead projector (25).

Other Media Collections *Audio:* disc, 33⅓ rpm, 200t/200c; tape, cassette, 3400t/4400c; tape, reel, 2500t/2500c. *Filmstrips:* sound sets, 400t/400c; silent sets, 100t/100c. *Slides:* sets, 1100t/1100c.

Budget & Expenditures Total library budget $10,000 (FY 6/1/74-6/1/75). No separate AV budget. *Member:* AECT, CUFC, EFLA.

Video Serv *Est:* 1954. *In Charge:* James S. Miles, Dir. *Video Use:* wide range of instructional application. Video serv available on basis of request. Produce video tapes. Have production studio/space & separate control room.

Video Equipment/Facilities *In-House Use Only:* recording deck (5), 2″ b&w, Ampex; playback deck (2), 1″ col, Ampex; editing deck (2), ¾″ col, JVC; studio camera (2), col, Shibaden. Have viewing installation (CCTV to 130 rooms in 15 buildings; 3 channels). Provide training in use of equipment to faculty & staff in acquiring department. Have tape duplication serv.

Video Tape Loan/Rental/Sale Serv *Serv Provided:* swap with other inst, rental, sale. *Rental Eligibility:* educational inst. *Restrictions:* for inst, none. Cannot use for fund-raising, duplicate, air without permission. May borrow by mail. *Loan Period:* varies.

Video Collection Maintained by purchase, rental, own production, exchange/swap. Use/play ½″, ¼″, 1″, 2″ reel to reel, ¾″ cassette. *Tape Sel:* preview, faculty/staff recommendations. Tapes organized by subject.

Cable & CCTV Receive serv of cable TV system. Produce programs for cablecasting. Have CCTV in inst, with 50 monitors. *Programming Sources:* tapes produced by inst.

Winamac

P- PULASKI COUNTY PUBLIC LIBRARY, 121 S Riverside Dr, 46996. *Tel:* (219) 946-3432. *In Charge:* Sarah Baker. *Member:* Ind. Library Film Serv.

Iowa

Bettendorf

C- SCOTT COMMUNITY COLLEGE LIBRARY, Belmont Rd, 52722. *Tel:* (319) 359-7531, ext 214. *Video Serv Est:* 1974. *In Charge:* William Alexander, Media Technician. *Video Staff:* 4 f-t, 1 p-t, 2 tech. *Video Use:* in-service training. Video serv available on demand. Produce video tapes. Have production studio/space & separate control room.

   Video Equipment/Facilities *In-House Only:* portapak (2), ½″ b&w, Shibaden; recording deck (2), ½″, ¾″ b&w/col, Shibaden, Sony; playback deck (1), ¾″ col, Sony; studio camera (3), b&w, Shibaden, Sony; monitor (3), b&w/col, Shibaden, Sony; SEG (1), Nasco; additional camera lenses (2); lighting (10); microphones (3); tripods (3); audio tape recorders. Have portable viewing installation. Have limited tape duplication serv.

   Video Collection Maintained by rental, own production. Use/play ½″ reel to reel, ¾″ cassette. *Sources:* commercial distributors. *Tape Sel:* faculty/staff recommendations. *Special Collections:* in-house training tapes. Tapes organized by subject. *Collection, Color:* ¾″ cassette, 8t. *Collection, B&W:* ½″ reel, 15t.

   Cable & CCTV Will receive serv of cable TV system.

Cedar Falls

P- CEDAR FALLS PUBLIC LIBRARY, 524 Parkade, 50613. *Tel:* (319) 266-2629. *Film Serv Est:* 1971. *In Charge:* Neal Johnson, Dir. *AV Staff:* 1 (1 prof). *Film Sel:* chief film librarian's decision. *Holdings:* children's films 10%, ecology 90%.

   Video Serv *Est:* 1974. *Video Staff:* 1 p-t. *Video Use:* to increase community's library use. Video serv available by appointment.

   Video Equipment/Facilities *In-House Use Only:* recording deck (1), col, Sony VO1600; playback deck (1), col, Sony VP1200; studio camera (1), b&w, Sony; monitor (2), col, RCA; microphones (1); tripods (1); audio tape recorders (30).

   Video Collection Maintained by purchase, rental. Use/play ¾″ cassette. *Sources:* commercial distributors. *Tape Sel:* preview, faculty/staff recommendations, published reviews, catalogs. *Collection, Color:* ¾″ cassette, 15t/1c. *Other Video Serv:* programming.

C- UNIVERSITY OF NORTHERN IOWA, Office of Television and Audio Services, 50613. *Tel:* (319) 273-6292. *Video Serv Est:* 1970. *In Charge:* Joseph Marchesani, Coord, TV & Audio Servs. *Video Staff:* 2 f-t, 25 p-t. *Video Use:* documentation of community/school events, practical video/TV training courses. Video serv available by appointment. Produce video tapes. Have production studio/space & separate control room.

   Video Equipment/Facilities *In-House Use Only:* portapak (2), ½″ b&w, Sony AV3400; recording deck (29), ½″, ¾″, 1″ b&w/col, Sony, IVC; editing deck (5), ½″, 1″ b&w/col, Sony, IVC; studio camera (6), 1″ b&w/col, Ampex; monitor (140), b&w/col, RCA, Sony; SEG (4), Sony; lighting (51); microphones (20); tripods (7); audio tape recorders (11). *For Loan:* portapak (1), ½″ b&w, Sony; recording deck (17), ½″, ¾″, 1″ b&w/col, Sony; monitor (17), b&w/col, Sony, RCA; SEG (1), Sony; additional camera lenses (17); microphones (8); tripods (2). Have permanent viewing installation. *Equipment Loan Period:* no set policy. Provide training in use of equipment to faculty & students. Have tape duplication serv.

   Video Tape Loan/Rental/Sale Serv *Serv Provided:* free loan. *Loan Eligibility:* staff. *Restrictions:* for indiv, only in city. Cannot use for fund-raising, duplicate, air without permission. May not borrow by mail.

   Video Collection Maintain tapes by own production. Use/play ½″, 1″ reel to reel, ¾″ cassette. Tapes organized by subject. *Collection, B&W:* ½″ reel, 500t; 1″ reel, 3t; ¾″ cassette, 100t. *Other Video Serv:* programming, production workshops.

Cedar Rapids

P- CEDAR RAPIDS PUBLIC LIBRARY, 428 Third Ave SE, 52403. *Tel:* (319) 398-5128. *In Charge:* Doris J. Wilcox, AV Specialist. *AV Staff:* 2 (2 cl). *Film Sel:* library director's decision. *Holdings:* children's films 50%, social sciences 50%.

   Free-Loan Film Serv *Eligibility:* civic groups, religious groups. *Restrictions:* for indiv, only in city; for inst, only in city. Cannot use for fund-raising, transmit electronically. Available to researchers/scholars for on-site viewing. May not borrow by mail. *Loan Period:* 2-3 days. *Total Yr Film Loan:* 18.

   Film Collection 404t. *Circ:* 16mm, 4t; 8mm reel, 200t; S8mm reel, 200t.

   Other Film Serv Obtain film from coop loan system (Iowa State Library), library film programs, search service. *Equipment:* lend 16mm sound projector (3), 8mm reel projector (1), S8mm reel projector (1), projection screens (1), slide projector (1).

   Other Media Collections *Audio:* disc, 78rpm, 600t; tape, cassette, 2500t; tape, cartridge, 700t. *Filmstrips:* sound sets, 24t. *Slides:* sets, 25t.

   Video Serv *Est:* 1974. *In Charge:* Doris J. Wilcox, AV Specialist. *Video Staff:* 2 f-t. *Video Use:* to increase community's library use, playback only of professionally produced tapes. Video serv available on demand. Produce video tapes.

   Video Equipment/Facilities *In-House Use Only:* recording deck (1), b&w, Sony TC270; playback deck (2), col, JVC; monitor (1), col, Sony; microphones (1); tripods (1); audio tape recorders (6). *For Loan:* monitor (1), b&w, Sony; audio tape recorders (7). *Equipment Loan Period:* no set policy. Provide training in use of equipment to borrowers if requested. *Loan Eligibility:* org members, civic groups, religious groups, prof groups, such as Social Services. *Restrictions:* only in city.

   Video Collection Maintained by purchase, own production. Use/play ½″ reel to reel, ¾″ cassette. *Sources:* commercial distributors, own production. *Tape Sel:* published reviews, catalogs. Tapes organized numerically by title. *Collection, Color:* ¾″ cassette, 65t/1c. *Collection, B&W:* ½″ reel, 1t.

Clinton

C- CLINTON COMMUNITY COLLEGE, Learning Res Center, 1000 Lincoln Blvd, 52732. *Tel:* (319) 242-6841. *Video Serv Est:* 1975. *In Charge:* Mike Simpson, AV Coordinator. *Video Staff:* 1 f-t, 1 p-t. *Video Use:* documentation of community/school events, practical video/TV training courses, playback only of professionally produced tapes. Video serv available by appointment. Produce video tapes. Have production studio/space. Have portable viewing installation.

   Video Collection Maintained by own production. Use/play ½″ reel to reel, ¾″ cassette. *Tape Sel:* preview.

   Cable & CCTV Receive serv of cable TV system. Have CCTV in inst, with 4 monitors. *Programming Sources:* tapes produced professionally.

P- CLINTON PUBLIC LIBRARY, 306 8th Ave S, 52732. *Tel:* (319) 242-8441.

   Free-Loan Film Serv *Eligibility:* civic groups, religious groups, indiv with library cards. *Restrictions:* for indiv, only in city or East Central System card holders; for inst, only in city. Cannot use for fund-raising. *Loan Period:* 7 days. *Total Yr Film Loan:* 1454.

   Film Collection 168t. *Circ:* S8mm reel, 168t. Have catalogs of 16mm films available from other coop loan systems.

Other Film Serv Obtain film from coop loan system (East Central Regional System, State Library Commission of Iowa, Quad City-Scott County Film Coop). *Equipment:* lend 16mm sound projector (2), lend S8mm reel projector (2).

Budget & Expenditures Total library budget $60,000 (FY 1/1/74-1/1/75). Total FY AV budget $5700. *Member:* Iowa Library Assn.

Council Bluff

C- IOWA WESTERN COMMUNITY COLLEGE, Herbert Hoover Media Center, 2700 College Rd, 51501. *Tel:* (712) 328-3831, ext 267. *Video Serv Est:* 1974. *In Charge:* Roger H Barry, Media Specialist. *Video Staff:* 2 f-t, 2 p-t. *Video Use:* in-service training. Video serv available on demand. Produce video tapes. Have production studio/space & separate control room.

Video Equipment/Facilities *In-House Use Only:* portapak (2), ½″ b&w, Panasonic; recording deck (3), ½″, ¾″ col, Panasonic; playback deck (2), ¾″ col, Sony; editing deck (1), ¾″ col, Sony; studio camera (2), b&w; monitor (2); SEG (1); additional camera lenses (2); microphones (4); tripods (5). Provide training in use of equipment to faculty. Have tape duplication serv.

Video Tape Loan/Rental/Sale Serv *Serv Provided:* free loan. *Loan Eligibility:* org members. May borrow by mail. *Loan Period:* 7 days. *Total Yr Tape Loan:* 5.

Video Collection Maintained by purchase, own production. Use/play ½″ reel to reel, ¾″ cassette. *Sources:* commercial distributors. *Tape Sel:* preview. *Special Collections:* video as art, films in video format. *Collection, Color:* ¾″ cassette, 2t/1c. *Collection, B&W:* ½″ reel, 30t/2c; ¾″ cassette, 50t/1c. *Other Video Serv:* programming, taping of other media, production workshops.

Creston

C- SOUTHWESTERN COMMUNITY COLLEGE, Learning Resource Center, 1501 W Townline, 50801. *Tel:* (515) 782-7081, ext 224. *Video Serv Est:* 1970. *In Charge:* D. Rieck, Dir, Learning Resource Center. *Video Staff:* 1 p-t, 1 tech. *Video Use:* documentation of community/school events, in-service training, practical video/TV training courses. Video serv available by appointment. Produce video tapes. Have production studio/space.

Video Equipment/Facilities *In-House Use Only:* portapak (1), ½″ b&w, Sony 3400; recording deck (2), ½″ b&w/col, Panasonic; studio camera (4), b&w, Panasonic; monitor (12), b&w/col; SEG (1), Panasonic; lighting (12); microphones (8); tripods (6); audio tape recorders (45). Have permanent viewing installation. Provide training in use of equipment to faculty, students or anyone requesting.

Video Collection Maintained by purchase, own production. Use/play ½″ reel to reel. *Sources:* commercial distributors. *Tape Sel:* preview. *Special Collections:* in-house training tapes. Tapes organized by acquisition number. *Collection, Color:* ½″ reel, 25t. *Collection, B&W:* ½″ reel, 50t. *Pubns:* catalog.

Cable & CCTV Receive serv of cable TV system. Produce programs for cablecasting. Have CCTV in inst, with 55 monitors. *Programming Sources:* over-the-air commercial & public broadcasting, tapes produced by inst, tapes produced professionally, tapes produced by community groups & indiv.

Des Moines

P- DES MOINES PUBLIC LIBRARY, Film Department, 100 Locust, 50309. *Tel:* (515) 283-4238. *Film Serv Est:* 1974. *In Charge:* Bob Boese, Library Consultant and AV Specialist. *AV Staff:* ½ prof.

Free-Loan Film Serv *Eligibility:* indiv with library cards. *Restrictions:* for indiv, only in state; for inst, only in state. Cannot borrow for classroom use. Available to researchers/scholars for on-site viewing. May borrow by mail. *Loan Period:* 1-7 days. *Total Yr Film Loan:* 300.

Film Collection 25t. *Circ:* 16mm, 25t/25p.

Other Film Serv Obtain film from coop loan system (Films for Iowa Library Media Service), obtain film from other libraries, library film programs. *Equipment:* lend 16mm sound projector (7).

Other Media Collections *Audio:* disc, 33⅓ rpm, 2000t/2000c; tape, cassette, 1000t/1200c.

Budget & Expenditures Total library budget $10,000 (FY 7/1/75-7/1/76). Total FY film budget $2000. *Member:* ALA, Iowa Library Assn, Iowa Educational Media Assn.

Fort Dodge

P- FORT DODGE PUBLIC LIBRARY, 50501. *Tel:* (515) 573-8681. *Film Serv Est:* 1960. *In Charge:* George P. Hynes, Dir. *AV Staff:* 1. *Film Sel:* staff recommendations, chief film librarian's decision. *Holdings:* agriculture 3%, animated films 5%, black studies 2%, children's films 3%, consumer affairs 3%, feature films 5%, fine arts 2%, science 2%, social sciences 72%, women 3%.

Free-Loan Film Serv *Eligibility:* indiv with library cards. *Restrictions:* for indiv, only in our county; for inst, only in city & county. Available to researchers/scholars for on-site viewing. May borrow by mail. *Loan Period:* 1 day. *Total Yr Film Loan:* 1500.

Film Collection *Circ:* 16mm, 100t; 8mm reel, 250t.

Other Film Serv Rent film from distributors for patrons, obtain film from coop loan system (Iowa State Film Coop, Iowa Film Media, Inc.), obtain film from other libraries. *Equipment:* rent 16mm sound projector (2), rent 8mm reel projector (4), rent projection screens (2).

Other Media Collections *Audio:* disc, 33⅓ rpm, 2287t; tape, cassette, 421t.

Budget & Expenditures Total library budget $22,200 (FY 1/1/75-1/1/76). Total FY film budget $2000.

Fort Madison

P- CATTERMOLE MEMORIAL LIBRARY, 614 Seventh St, 52627. *Tel:* (319) 372-5721. *Film Serv Est:* 1970. *In Charge:* Wayne Hanway, Dir. *Film Sel:* chief film librarian's decision.

Free-Loan Film Serv *Eligibility:* educational inst, civic groups, religious groups, indiv with library cards, prof groups. *Restrictions:* for indiv, no interlibrary loan; for inst, no interlibrary loan. Cannot use for fund-raising. Available to researchers/scholars for on-site viewing. May not borrow by mail. *Loan Period:* 7 days.

Film Collection 136t/140p. Approx 20-25t acquired annually. *Circ:* 16mm, 4t/4p; 8mm reel, 74t/74p; S8mm reel, 58t/60p.

Other Film Serv Obtain film from coop loan system (Mississippi Valley Film Coop), library film programs. *Equipment:* lend 16mm sound projector (2), 8mm reel projector (8), S8mm reel projector (8), projection screens (1).

Other Media Collections *Audio:* disc, 33⅓ rpm, 528t; tape, cassette, 193t.

Budget & Expenditures Total library budget $33,907 (FY 1/1/74-1/1/75). Total FY film budget $1500. *Member:* ALA, Iowa Library Assn.

Iowa City

P- IOWA CITY PUBLIC LIBRARY, 307 E College, 52240. *Tel:* (319) 354-1264. *Film Serv Est:* 1968. *In Charge:* Lolly Eggers, Dir. *Film Sel:* chief film librarian's decision.

Free-Loan Film Serv *Eligibility:* indiv with library cards, & others, such as public libraries. *Restrictions:* for indiv, interlibrary loan. Cannot use for fund-raising. May borrow 8mm by mail. *Loan Period:* 1-7 days.

Film Collection 255t. *Circ:* 16mm, 22t/22p; 8mm reel, 255t/255p. *Pubns:* catalog, as needed; suppl, no set policy.

Other Film Serv Obtain film from coop loan system (Iowa Library Commission, Films for Iowa Libraries Inc), obtain film

Iowa City (cont'd)
from other libraries, film reference serv, library film programs. Permanent viewing facility available free to community.
Other Media Collections *Audio:* disc, 33⅓ rpm, 3256c; tape, cassette, 102c.
Budget & Expenditures Total library budget $59,500 (FY 7/1/75-7/1/76). Total FY film budget $3317. *Member:* ALA, Iowa Library Assn.

C- UNIVERSITY OF IOWA, Media Library—AV Center, C-5 East Hall, 52242. *Tel:* (319) 353-5885. *Film Serv Est:* 1914. *In Charge:* Jan W. Cureton, Dir. *AV Staff:* 10 (1 prof, 5 cl, 4 tech). *Film Sel:* faculty/staff recommendations. *Holdings:* business administration, children's films, consumer affairs, engineering, fine arts, law, medicine, science, social sciences, teacher education.
Free-Loan Film Serv *Eligibility:* staff & students. *Restrictions:* for indiv, only on campus. Cannot use for fund-raising, transmit electronically. Available to researchers/scholars for on-site viewing. May not borrow by mail. *Loan Period:* 3 days. *Total Yr Film Loan:* 10,542.
Film Rental Serv *Eligibility:* no restrictions. *Restrictions:* only in U.S. Cannot use for fund-raising, transmit or reproduce electronically. *Rental Period:* 3 days. *Total Yr Film Booking:* 33,928. Sell films. Produce films.
Film Collection 4667t/7000p. Approx 150-250t acquired annually. *Circ:* 16mm, 4677t/7000p. *Noncirc:* 16mm, 2000t/5000p. *Pubns:* catalog, every 2 yrs; suppl, in yr catalog not published.
Other Film Serv Rent film from distributors for faculty & patrons, obtain film from coop loan system (Consortium of University Film Centers, Iowa Higher Education Instructional Resources Council), film reference serv. Permanent viewing facility. *Equipment:* lend/rent S8mm camera (2), 16mm camera (1), 16mm sound projector (81), 8mm cartridge projector (14), 8mm reel projector (26), S8mm cartridge projector (3), projection tables & stands (20), projection screens (25), tape players, slide & over head projectors.
Budget & Expenditures Total library budget $228,050 (FY 7/1/74-7/1/75). Total FY film budget $78,875. *Member:* AECT, CUFC, EFLA.

C- UNIVERSITY OF IOWA, Television Unit, E 215 East Hall, 52242. *Tel:* (319) 353-5885. *Video Serv Est:* 1975. *In Charge:* Daniel G. Lind, TV Coord. *Video Staff:* 2 f-t, 2 p-t, 2 tech. *Video Use:* in-service training, as art form, classroom instruction. Video serv available by appointment. Produce video tapes. Have production studio/space & separate control room.
Video Equipment/Facilities *In-House Use Only:* recording deck (3), ¾″ b&w/col, Panasonic, Sony; editing deck (3), ½″, ¾″ col, Panasonic, Sony; studio camera (3), b&w, Panasonic, Shibaden; monitor (3), b&w/col, Panasonic, Sony; SEG (1), Panasonic; lighting; microphones (7); tripods (3); audio tape recorders (1). *For Loan:* portapak (5), ½″ b&w, Panasonic NV3082; recording deck (3), ¾″ b&w/col, Panasonic, Sony, IVC; playback deck (1), ¾″ col, Sony; monitor (3), b&w/col, Panasonic, Sony; tripods (3). Have permanent viewing installation. *Equipment Loan Period:* short term only. Provide training in use of equipment to anyone. Have tape duplication serv.
Video Tape Loan/Rental/Sale Serv *Serv Provided:* swap with other inst. *Loan Eligibility:* staff & students, civic groups, religious groups, anyone connected with the university. *Restrictions:* for indiv, only in state; for inst, only in state. Cannot use for fund-raising, duplicate, air without permission.
Video Collection Maintained by own production. Use/play ½″, 1″ reel to reel, ¾″ cassette. *Sources:* exchange (Great Plains, NICEM). *Tape Sel:* preview. *Other Video Serv:* production workshops.

Iowa Falls

C- ELLSWORTH COMMUNITY COLLEGE, Learning Resource Center, 1100 College, 50126. *Tel:* (515) 648-4611, ext 33. *Film Serv Est:* 1971. *In Charge:* Mary Weeks, Dir, Learning Resource Center. *AV Staff:* 2½ (1 prof, 1½ cl). *Film Sel:* faculty/staff recommendations, chief film librarian's decision, published reviews. *Holdings:* career education, medicine, psychology 90%, science.
Free-Loan Film Serv *Eligibility:* staff & students, educational inst, civic groups, prof groups. *Restrictions:* for indiv, none; for inst, none. Available to researchers/scholars for on-site viewing. May borrow by mail. *Loan Period:* 7 days. *Total Yr Film Loan:* 1.
Film Collection 207t/207p. Approx 4-5t acquired annually. *Circ:* 16mm, 17t; 8mm cartridge, 24t; S8mm cartridge, 166t.
Other Film Serv Obtain film from coop loan system (Iowa Higher Education Instructional Resource Council). *Equipment:* lend S8mm camera, lend 16mm sound projector, lend 8mm cartridge projector, lend 8mm reel projector, lend S8mm cartridge projector, lend S8mm reel projector, lend projection screens.
Other Media Collections *Audio:* disc, 33⅓ rpm, 1107t/12c; tape, cassette, 351t/57c; tape, reel, 60t/2c. *Filmstrips:* sound, 326t. *Slides:* single, 5667t.
Budget & Expenditures No separate budget.
Video Serv *Est:* 1971. *In Charge:* Eldon Rahmiller, Media Specialist. *Video Staff:* 1 f-t, 1 p-t. *Video Use:* documentation of community/school events, playback only of professionally produced tapes, evaluation & delayed use of commercial broadcast. Video serv available on demand. Produce video tapes.
Video Equipment/Facilities *For Loan:* portapak (1), ½″ b&w, Panasonic; recording deck (2), ½″ b&w, Panasonic; monitor (2), Panasonic; additional camera lenses (3); microphones (2); tripods (1). Have portable viewing installation. *Equipment Loan Period:* no set policy. Provide training in use of equipment to faculty & workshop students. Have tape duplication serv.
Video Tape Loan/Rental/Sale Serv *Serv Provided:* swap with other inst. *Loan Eligibility:* staff & students, civic groups. *Other Video Serv:* taping of other media.

Mason City

P- NORTH CENTRAL REGIONAL LIBRARY/NORTH IOWA LIBRARY EXTENSION, INC., 225 Second St SE, 50401. *Tel:* (515) 423-1101. *In Charge:* Jean Fairbanks. *AV Staff:* 1. *Film Sel:* committee preview.
Free-Loan Film Serv *Eligibility:* any individual or organization. *Restrictions:* for indiv, interlibrary loan, only in our 13 county region; for inst, only in 13 county region. Cannot use for fund-raising, transmit electronically. May borrow by mail. *Loan Period:* 1-5 days. *Total Yr Film Loan:* 2498.
Film Collection 57t/57p. *Circ:* 16mm, 57t/57p; 8mm cartridge, 260t/260p; S8mm cartridge, 12t/12p. *Pubns:* catalog, as needed.
Other Film Serv Obtain film from coop loan system (Films for Iowa Library Media Services, Inc). *Equipment:* rent 16mm sound projector (2), rent 8mm reel projector (2), lend projection screens, rent cassette players, filmstrip viewers & projectors.
Other Media Collections *Audio:* tape, cassette, 150t. *Filmstrips:* sound sets, 25t/25c.

Mount Pleasant

C- IOWA WESLEYAN COLLEGE, Chadwick Library, AV Dept, 52641. *Tel:* (319) 385-8021, ext 327. *In Charge:* Robert Bensmiller, Dir. AV. *AV Staff:* 1 (1 prof, 1 cl, 1 tech). *Film Sel:* committee preview, faculty/staff recommendations.
Other Film Serv Obtain film from coop loan system (Iowa Collegiate Consortia, Iowa-Missouri/Illinois. Consortia), obtain film from other libraries. Permanent viewing facility available for rent to community.
Other Media Collections *Audio:* disc, 33⅓ rpm, 1100t/1100c; disc, 45rpm, 20t/20c; tape, cassette, 100t/100c; tape, reel, 120t/120c. *Filmstrips:* sound, 326t/326c; silent, 420t/420c; sound sets, 41t/c. *Slides:* single, 220t/220c; sets, 18t/18c.

Budget & Expenditures Total library budget $3200 (FY 7/1/74-7/1/75). No separate AV budget. *Member:* Iowa Library Intercollegiate Teletype Exchange.

Video Serv *Est:* 1968. *In Charge:* Robert Bensmiller, Dir, AV. *Video Staff:* 1 f-t, 1 p-t, 1 tech. *Video Use:* documentation of community/school events, to increase community's library use, in-service training, practical video/TV training courses. Video serv available by appointment. Produce video tapes. Have production studio/space & separate control room.

Video Equipment/Facilities *In-House Use Only:* portapak (1), ½″ b&w, Sony 3400; recording deck (1), ½″ b&w, Sony 3600; playback deck (1), ½″ b&w, Sony 3600; editing deck (1), ½″ b&w, Shibiton; studio camera (3), b&w, Sony; SEG (2), Sony; keyer (1), Sony; additional camera lenses (3); lighting (10); microphones (21); tripods (5); audio tape recorders (12). Have permanent & portable viewing installations. Provide training in use of equipment to faculty & students. Have tape duplication serv.

Video Tape Loan/Rental/Sale Serv *Serv Provided:* free loan, swap with other inst, rental. *Loan/Rental Eligibility:* org members & staff. Cannot air without permission. May borrow by mail. *Loan Period:* 5 days. *Total Yr Tape Loan:* 3.

Video Collection Maintained by purchase, own production. Use/play ½″ reel to reel, ¾″ cassette. *Sources:* commercial distributors. *Tape Sel:* preview, catalogs. *Special Collections:* films in video format. Tapes organized by subject. *Other Video Serv:* programming, taping of other media, production workshops.

Cable & CCTV Receive serv of cable TV system. Produce programs for cablecasting. Serve as production facility for others. Have advisory/administrative role in cable system operation. Have CCTV in inst, with 9 monitors. *Programming Sources:* over-the-air commercial & public broadcasting, tapes produced by inst, tapes produced professionally.

Muscatine

C- MUSCATINE COMMUNITY COLLEGE, 152 Colorado St, 52761. *Tel:* (319) 263-8250, ext 50. *Video Serv Est:* 1974. *In Charge:* Thomas Hanifan, Dir, Learning Resources. *Video Use:* documentation of community/school events, playback only of professionally produced tapes. Video serv available on demand. Produce video tapes. Have production studio/space & separate control room.

Video Equipment/Facilities *In-House Use Only:* SEG (1), Sony; microphones (3). *For Loan:* portapak (1), ½″ b&w, Sony; recording deck (4), b&w/col, Sony; studio camera (2), b&w, Sony; monitor (4), b&w/col, Sony; tripods (2). Have permanent viewing installation. *Equipment Loan Period:* no set policy. Provide training in use of equipment to faculty & students. Have tape duplication serv.

Video Tape Loan/Rental/Sale Serv *Serv Provided:* free loan, swap with other inst. *Loan Eligibility:* org members, educational inst, civic groups. *Restrictions:* for indiv, none; for inst, none. May not borrow by mail.

Video Collection Maintained by own production. Use/play ½″ reel to reel, ¾″ cassette. *Sources:* exchange (area colleges & high school centers). *Tape Sel:* faculty/staff recommendations. Tapes organized alphabetically. *Collection, B&W:* ½″ reel, 20t; ¾″ cassette, 35t.

Cable & CCTV Receive serv of cable TV system.

Sioux Center

P- SIOUX CENTER PUBLIC LIBRARY, 327 First Ave NE, 51250. *Tel:* (712) 722-2138. *Film Serv Est:* 1970. *In Charge:* Mrs. Steve C. Siebersma, Librarian.

Free-Loan Film Serv *Eligibility:* anyone requesting. *Restrictions:* for indiv, none. May borrow by mail. *Loan Period:* varies with need. *Total Yr Film Loan:* 200.

Film Collection 50t/50p. *Circ:* 8mm reel, 50t.

Other Film Serv Rent film from distributors for patrons, obtain film from coop loan system (Iowa State Library, Northwest Regional Library), library film programs. Permanent viewing facility available for rent to community. *Equipment:* lend 16mm sound projector.

Other Media Collections *Audio:* disc, 33⅓ rpm, 739t. *Slides:* sets, 12t.

Budget & Expenditures Total library budget $25,000 (FY 1/1/74-1/1/75). No separate AV budget. *Member:* ALA, Iowa Library Assn.

Sioux City

P- SIOUX CITY PUBLIC LIBRARY, Siouxland Film Service, 6 & Jackson, 51105. *Tel:* (712) 279-6179. *Film Serv Est:* 1973. *In Charge:* Edward Whitaker, Asst Dir. *AV Staff:* 3 (1 prof, 2 cl). *Film Sel:* chief film librarian's decision.

Free-Loan Film Serv *Eligibility:* educational inst, civic groups, religious groups, indiv with library cards, prof groups. *Restrictions:* for inst, interlibrary loan, only in state; for indiv, only in state. Cannot use for fund-raising, transmit electronically. Available to researchers/scholars for on-site viewing. May borrow by mail. *Loan Period:* 5 days. *Total Yr Film Loan:* 2218.

Film Collection 244t. *Circ:* 16mm, 244t. *Pubns:* catalog, as needed; suppl, no set policy.

Other Film Serv Obtain film from coop loan system (State Library Commission of Iowa), film reference serv, film fairs/festivals, library film programs. *Equipment:* S8mm camera (1), 16mm sound projector (6), projection screens (6).

Other Media Collections *Audio:* disc, 33⅓ rpm, 8000t; tape, cassette, 500t.

Budget & Expenditures Total library budget $80,000 (FY 7/1/74-7/1/75). Total FY film budget $11,000. *Member:* ALA, Iowa Library Assn.

Video Serv *Est:* 1974. *In Charge:* Janice Gray, Information Aide. *Video Staff:* 1 p-t. *Video Use:* in-service training. Video serv available to staff on demand. Produce video tapes.

Video Equipment/Facilities *In-House Use Only:* portapak (1), b&w, Concord; recording deck (1), b&w, Concord; playback deck (1), b&w, Concord; additional camera lenses (1); microphones (1). Have portable viewing installation.

Video Collection Maintained by own production.

Waterloo

C- HAWKEYE INSTITUTE OF TECHNOLOGY, Learning Resources Center, Box 8015, 50704. *Tel:* (319) 296-2320, ext 237, 238. *Film Serv Est:* 1970. *In Charge:* Deborah Dahlby, Media Technician. *AV Staff:* 2 (1 prof, 1 tech). *Film Sel:* committee preview, faculty/staff recommendations.

Free-Loan Film Serv *Eligibility:* staff & students, educational inst, civic groups, religious groups. *Restrictions:* for indiv, interlibrary loan; for inst, none. Available to researchers/scholars for on-site viewing. May borrow by mail. *Loan Period:* 3 days.

Film Collection 96t/96p. Approx 10t acquired annually. *Circ:* 16mm, 34t/34p; S8mm cartridge, 62t/62p.

Other Film Serv Obtain film from other libraries. *Equipment:* 16mm sound projector (4), 8mm cartridge projector (1), 8mm reel projector (1), S8mm cartridge projector (1), S8mm reel projector (4), projection tables & stands (10), projection screens (10).

Other Media Collections *Audio:* disc, 33⅓ rpm, 357t/357c; tape, cassette, 486t/486c. *Filmstrips:* sound sets, 662t/662c. *Slides:* single, 14,129t/14,129c.

Budget & Expenditures Total library budget $34,000 (FY 7/1/74-7/1/75). Total FY film budget $3000. *Member:* ALA.

Video Serv *Est:* 1972. *In Charge:* William Andrews. *Video Staff:* 1 f-t. *Video Use:* documentation of community/school events, in-service training. Video serv available only to instruc-

Waterloo (cont'd)

tion personnel. Produce video tapes. Have production studio/space.

Video Equipment/Facilities   *In-House Use Only:* porta-pak (1), ½ b&w, Sony; recording deck (2), ½″, ¾″ b&w/col, Sony; playback deck (2), ¾″ col, Sony; tripods (3).

Video Collection   Maintained by purchase, rental, own production. Use/play ½″ reel to reel, ¾″ cassette. *Sources:* commercial distributors. *Tape Sel:* preview, faculty/staff recommendations, published reviews. Tapes organized by Dewey Decimal. *Collection, Color:* ¾″ cassette, 40t/40c.

Kansas

Abilene

A- NATIONAL ARCHIVES AND RECORDS SERVICE, Dwight D. Eisenhower Library, 67410. *Tel:* (913) 263-4751. *Film Serv Est:* 1961. *In Charge:* Dr. John E. Wickman, Dir. *AV Staff:* 3 (1 prof, 1 cl, 1 tech).

Free-Loan Film Serv Available to researchers/scholars for on-site viewing.

Film Collection 489t. Approx 5t acquired annually.

Other Film Serv Film reference serv. Permanent viewing facility.

Other Media Collections *Audio:* disc, 33⅓ rpm, 450c; tape, reel, 2500c.

Emporia

C- EMPORIA KANSAS STATE COLLEGE, Instructional Media Center, 1200 Commercial, 66801. *Tel:* (316) 343-1200, ext 477. *Film Serv Est:* 1952. *In Charge:* Leslie R. Marks, Dir. *AV Staff:* 3 (1 cl, 2 tech). *Film Sel:* committee preview. *Holdings:* career education 10%, consumer affairs 5%, fine arts 3%, industrial arts 10%, law 2%, science 20%, social sciences 25%, teacher education 25%.

Free-Loan Film Serv *Eligibility:* org members, Emporia school district. *Restrictions:* none. May not borrow by mail. *Loan Period:* 3 days.

Film Collection 2000t/p. Approx 37t acquired annually.

Other Film Serv Rent film from distributors for patrons, obtain film from other libraries. Permanent viewing facility. *Equipment:* lend 16mm sound projector (20), 8mm cartridge projector (2), 8mm reel projector (4), S8mm cartridge projector (2), S8mm reel projector (2).

Other Media Collections *Audio:* tape, cassette, 49t; tape, reel, 530t. *Filmstrips:* silent, 3000c; sound sets, 223c. *Slides:* single, 100c.

Budget & Expenditures Total FY film budget $10,000. *Member:* AECT, AFI, EFLA, FLIC.

Video Serv *Est:* 1960. *In Charge:* Dr. Loren Pennington. *Video Staff:* 1 f-t, 3 p-t, 1 tech. Video serv available by appointment. Produce video tapes. Have production studio/space & separate control room.

Video Equipment/Facilities *In-House Use Only:* portapak (1), ½″ b&w, Sony 3400; recording deck (3), Sony; editing deck (1), ½″ b&w/col, Sony 8650; studio camera (6), b&w, Sony 3200; monitor (15), b&w/col, Sony Conrac; SEG (3), Seg & Sony; keyer; additional camera lenses; lighting (5); microphones (25); tripods (3); audio tape recorders (3). Have portable viewing installation. Provide training in use of equipment to students. Have tape duplication serv.

Video Collection Maintained by own production. Use/play ½″ reel to reel. Tapes organized by subject. *Collection, B&W:* ½″ reel, 300t/c.

Cable & CCTV Receive serv of cable TV system. Produce programs for cablecasting. Have CCTV in inst. *Programming Sources:* tapes produced by inst.

Great Bend

C- BARTON COUNTY COMMUNITY COLLEGE, LIBRARY, 67530. *Tel:* (316) 792-2701, ext 29. *Film Sel:* committee preview, faculty/staff recommendations.

Film Collection 25t/p. Approx 2t acquired annually. *Member:* MPLA, Kans. State Library Assn.

Video Serv *Video Use:* documentation of community/school events, in-service training, practical video/TV training courses, playback only of professionally produced tapes. Video serv available by appointment. Produce video tapes. Have production studio/space. Have permanent & portable viewing installations. *Equipment Loan Period:* no set policy. Provide training in use of equipment.

Video Tape Loan/Rental/Sale Serv *Serv Provided:* free loan. *Loan/Rental Eligibility:* staff & students. *Restrictions:* for indiv & inst only in Barton County. Cannot air without permission. May not borrow by mail.

Video Collection Maintained by purchase, own production. Use/play ½″, 1″ reel to reel. *Tape Sel:* preview, faculty/staff recommendations. *Special Collections:* in-house training tapes, video as art. Tapes organized by subject.

Cable & CCTV Receive serv of cable TV system. Produce programs for cablecasting. Inform public about cable system serv & facilities. Have CCTV in inst, with 15 monitors. *Programming Sources:* tapes produced by inst, tapes produced professionally.

Hesston

C- HESSTON COLLEGE, Mary Miller Library, 67062. *Tel:* (316) 327-4221, ext 242, 530. *Film Serv Est:* 1973. *In Charge:* Joe Nostetler, AV Dir. *AV Staff:* 1 (1 prof, 1 cl, 4 tech).

Free-Loan Film Serv *Eligibility:* campus use only.

Film Collection *Circ:* 16mm, 3t; S8mm reel, 72t.

Other Media Collections *Audio:* disc, 33⅓ rpm, 254t/400c; tape, cassette, 100c; tape, cartridge, 34c; tape, reel, 21c. *Filmstrips:* sound, 33c; sound sets, 22c. *Slides:* sets, 17c.

Budget & Expenditures Total library budget $11,000 (FY 7/74-7/75). No separate AV budget. *Member:* AECT, ALA.

Video Serv *Est:* 1973. *Video Staff:* 4 p-t. *Video Use:* documentation of community/school events, practical video/TV training courses, playback only of professionally produced tapes. Video serv available by appointment. Produce video tapes. Have production studio/space. Have portable viewing installation. *Equipment Loan Period:* 21 days. Provide training in use of equipment to faculty & students.

Video Tape Loan/Rental/Sale Serv *Serv Provided:* free loan. *Loan Eligibility:* no restrictions. Cannot use for fundraising. May not borrow by mail.

Video Collection Maintained by purchase, own production. Use/play ¾″ cassette. *Sources:* commercial distributors. *Tape Sel:* faculty/staff recommendations, published reviews, catalogs. Tapes organized by Dewey Decimal. *Collection, Color:* ¾″ cassette, 58t. *Other Video Serv:* taping of other media, production workshops.

Highland

C- HIGHLAND COMMUNITY JR COLLEGE LIBRARY, 66035. *Tel:* (913) 442-3317. *Film Serv Est:* 1967. *In Charge:* Kathleen Gaye Shattuck, Library Dir. *AV Staff:* 2 (1 prof, ½ cl, ½ tech). *Film Sel:* faculty/staff recommendations, chief film librarian's decision. *Holdings:* science 90%.

Free-Loan Film Serv *Eligibility:* staff & students, educational inst, civic groups, religious groups, indiv with library cards. *Restrictions:* for indiv, only in Doniphan County; for inst, only in NE Kansas. Available to researchers/scholars for on-site viewing. May not borrow by mail.

Film Collection 97t/p. Approx 2t acquired annually. *Circ:* 16mm, 17t; 8mm reel, 80t.

Other Film Serv Obtain film from other libraries. *Equipment:* lend 16mm sound projector (5), 8mm cartridge projector (1).

Other Media Collections *Audio:* disc, 78rpm, 1212t; tape, cassette, 254t; tape, reel, 159t. *Filmstrips:* sound, 255t; silent, 60t. *Slides:* single, 900t.

Budget & Expenditures Total library budget $12,000 (FY 7/1/74-7/1/75). *Member:* ALA, Mid-America Interlibrary Serv.

Hutchinson

C- HUTCHINSON COMMUNITY JR COLLEGE, J. F. Kennedy Library, 1300 N Plum St, 67501. *Tel:* (316) 663-5781, ext 125. *Film Serv Est:* 1969. *AV Staff:* 2 (1 prof, 1 tech). *Film Sel:* faculty/staff recommendations.
Film Collection 150t/p. Approx 5t acquired annually. *Circ:* 16mm, 118t; S8mm cartridge, 33t.
Other Film Serv Rent film from distributors for patrons, obtain film from other libraries. Permanent viewing facility.
Other Media Collections *Audio:* disc, 33⅓ rpm, 800t; tape, cassette, 2500t; tape, cartridge, 80t; tape, reel, 200t. *Filmstrips:* silent, 120c. *Slides:* single, 15,000c; sets, 100c.
Budget & Expenditures Total library budget $23,600 (FY 6/30/74-6/30/75). Total FY film budget $1500. *Member:* AECT, ALA, KSAS, Kans. Library Assn.

P- HUTCHINSON PUBLIC LIBRARY, 901 N Main, 67501. *Tel:* (316) 663-5441.
Other Film Serv Obtain film from coop loan system (S Central Kansas Library System). Permanent viewing facility available to community. *Equipment:* lend 16mm sound projector (2), projection screens (1).
Other Media Collections *Audio:* disc, 33⅓ rpm, 4000t; tape, cassette, 150t. *Filmstrips:* sound sets, 250t; silent sets, 25t.
Budget & Expenditures Total library budget $37,500 (FY 1/1/75-1/1/76). No separate AV budget. *Member:* ALA, Kans. Library Assn.

Lawrence

C- UNIVERSITY OF KANSAS, Film Serv, 746 Massachusetts St, 66044. *Tel:* (913) 864-3352. *Film Serv Est:* 1912. *In Charge:* Breck Marion, Dir. *AV Staff:* 8 (1 prof, 5 cl, 2 tech). *Film Sel:* faculty/staff recommendations, chief film librarian's decision.
Free-Loan Film Serv *Eligibility:* anyone. *Restrictions:* only in U.S. Cannot use for fund-raising, transmit electronically. Available to researchers/scholars for on-site viewing. May borrow by mail. *Loan Period:* 5 days. *Total Yr Film Loan:* 250.
Film Rental Serv *Eligibility:* no restrictions. *Restrictions:* only in U.S. Cannot use for fund-raising, transmit electronically. *Rental Period:* 5 days. Sell films. Produce films.
Film Collection 4500t/7000p. Approx 300t acquired annually. *Circ:* 16mm, 4500t/7000p. *Noncirc:* 16mm, 500t/p. *Pubns:* catalog, every 3 yrs; suppl, in yr catalog not published. Publish flyers & subject lists.
Other Film Serv Rent film from distributors for patrons, film reference serv. Permanent viewing facility.
Budget & Expenditures Total library budget $40,000 (FY 7/1/73-7/1/74). *Member:* AECT, CUFC, EFLA.

Sterling

C- STERLING COLLEGE, Kelsey Library, 67579. *Tel:* (316) 278-2173, ext 233. *Film Serv Est:* 1965. *In Charge:* Viola Rhoades, Reference Librarian. *Film Sel:* faculty/staff recommendations.
Free-Loan Film Serv *Eligibility:* staff & students, educational inst, civic groups, religious groups. *Restrictions:* for indiv, only in Rice County; for inst, none. Cannot transmit electronically. Available to researchers/scholars for on-site viewing. May borrow by mail. *Loan Period:* 7 days. *Total Yr Film Loan:* 15.
Other Film Serv Obtain film from coop loan system (Assoc Colleges of Central Kansas).
Other Media Collections *Audio:* disc, 33⅓ rpm, 3007c; tape, cassette, 295c. *Filmstrips:* sound sets, 1140c. *Slides:* sets, 861c.
Budget & Expenditures Total library budget $19,000 (FY 7/1/74-7/1/75). Total FY film budget $1025. *Member:* ALA, Kans. Library Assn.

Topeka

P- TOPEKA PUBLIC LIBRARY, 1515 W Tenth, 66604. *Tel:* (913) 233-2040, ext 31. *In Charge:* Larry D. Peters. *AV Staff:* 4. *Film Sel:* faculty/staff recommendations, dep't head's decision, donations. *Holdings:* animated films 4%, black studies 2%, children's films 14%, dance 3%, experimental films 15%, fine arts 35%, holidays 7%, Kansas 6%, science 10%, social sciences 28%, sports 3%.
Free-Loan Film Serv *Eligibility:* staff & students, educational inst, civic groups, religious groups, indiv with library cards, prof groups, such as Menninger foundation, & others, such as youth organizations. *Restrictions:* for indiv & inst, only in NE Kans. Library system. Cannot use for fund-raising, transmit electronically. May not borrow by mail. *Loan Period:* 1 days. *Total Yr Film Loan:* 160.
Film Collection 205t/206p. *Circ:* 16mm, 205t/206p; 8mm reel, 55t/p; S8mm reel, 44t/p. *Pubns:* catalog, as needed; suppl, no set policy.
Other Film Serv Film fairs/festivals, library film programs. Permanent viewing facility available to community. *Equipment:* lend 16mm sound projector (1), 8mm reel projector (1), S8mm reel projector (1), projection screens (1), slide projector (2), filmstrip projector (1).
Other Media Collections *Audio:* disc, 33⅓ rpm, 5000t/c; disc, 78rpm, 200t/c; tape, cassette, 150t/c; tape, reel, 50t/c. *Filmstrips:* silent, 200t/c; sound sets, 50t/c. *Slides:* single, 10,000t/c; sets, 70c.
Budget & Expenditures Total FY film budget $3500 (FY 1/1/74-1/1/75). *Member:* ALA, Kans. Library Assn.

Wichita

C- FRIENDS UNIVERSITY, Media Center, 2100 University, 67213. *Tel:* (316) 263-9131, ext 238. *Film Serv Est:* 1971. *In Charge:* Jerry M Keen, Media Center Supervisor. *AV Staff:* 3 (1 prof). *Film Sel:* faculty/staff recommendations. *Holdings:* teacher education 100%.
Free-Loan Film Serv *Eligibility:* staff, students enrolled in inst. Available to researchers/scholars for on-site viewing. May not borrow by mail.
Film Collection 80t/p. *Circ:* 16mm, 30t/p; S8mm cartridge, 50t/p. *Equipment:* lend S8mm camera (1), 16mm sound projector (3), S8mm cartridge projector (4), projection screens.
Other Media Collections *Audio:* disc, 33⅓ rpm, 2000c; tape, cassette, 200c; tape, reel, 100c. *Member:* AECT.
Video Serv *Est:* 1972. *Video Staff:* 2 f-t, 1 p-t. *Video Use:* in-service training, practical video/TV training courses. Video serv available by appointment. Produce video tapes. Have production studio/space.
Video Equipment/Facilities *In-House Use Only:* recording deck (2), b&w, EIAS-1, Sony 3600, 3650; studio camera (2), b&w, Concord; monitor (2), b&w, Dage Bell; additional camera lenses (2); microphones; audio tape recorders (5). *For Loan:* portapak (1), b&w, EIAS-1, Sony 3400. Have permanent & portable viewing installations. *Equipment Loan Period:* no set policy. Provide training in use of equipment to students.
Video Tape Loan/Rental/Sale Serv *Serv Provided:* free loan, rental. *Loan/Rental Eligibility:* staff, students enrolled in inst.
Video Collection Maintained by purchase, rental, own production. Use/play ½″ reel to reel. *Tape Sel:* preview. Tapes organized by LC number.
Cable & CCTV Have CCTV in inst, with 9 monitors. *Programming Sources:* over-the-air commercial & public broadcasting, tapes produced by inst, tapes produced professionally.

P- STATE AV CENTER, 223 S Main, 67202. *Tel:* (316) 265-5281, ext 49 or 76. *Film Serv Est:* 1970. *In Charge:* Sondra B. Koontz, State Film Librarian. *AV Staff:* 4 (1 prof, 2 cl, 1 tech). *Film Sel:* committee preview, faculty/staff recommendations, chief film librarian's decision.
Film Rental Serv *Eligibility:* state insts, educational org, civic groups, patrons/public, religious groups. *Restrictions:* only in state. Cannot use for fund-raising, transmit electronically,

duplicate, use in public schools. *Rental Period:* 7 days. *Total Yr Film Booking:* 11,753.

Film Collection 1400t/1500p. Approx 150t acquired annually. *Circ:* 16mm, 1400t/1500p. *Pubns:* catalog, annual. Publish monthly newsletter.

Other Film Serv Film reference serv, film fairs/festivals, library film programs, workshops. *Equipment:* rent 16mm sound projector (4), lend/rent projection tables & stands (3), projection screens (4), filmstrip projectors (2), opaque projector, slide projector, overhead projector.

Budget & Expenditures Total FY film budget $84,500 (FY 1/1/74-1/1/75). *Member:* AECT, ALA, EFLA, FLIC, Kans. Library Assn.

Kentucky

Berea

C- BEREA COLLEGE, AV Serv, CPO 2349, Berea College Station, 40403. *Tel:* (606) 986-9341, ext 419, 518. *In Charge:* Louise Gibson, Dir, AV Serv. *AV Staff:* 1 (1 prof, ½ cl, 5 tech). *Film Sel:* faculty/staff recommendations. *Holdings:* Appalachia 12%, medicine 25%.

Film Collection 290t/p. Approx 5-10t acquired annually. *Noncirc:* 16mm, 130t/p; S8mm cartridge, 160t/p.

Other Film Serv Rent film from distributors for patrons, obtain film from other libraries. *Equipment:* lend/rent S8mm camera, 16mm camera, 16mm sound projector, 8mm cartridge projector, 8mm reel projector, S8mm cartridge projector, S8mm reel projector, projection tables & stands, projection screens.

Budget & Expenditures Total nonprint library budget $16,700 (FY 7/1/74-7/1/75). Total FY film budget $1700. *Member:* AECT.

Video Serv *Est:* 1968. *In Charge:* Louise Gibson, Dir, AV Serv. *Video Staff:* 1 p-t. *Video Use:* documentation of community/school events, in-service training. Video serv available by appointment. Produce video tapes. Have production studio/space & separate control room.

Video Equipment/Facilities *In-House Use Only:* recording deck (3), ½", b&w/col, Sony 3650, 8600, 8650; playback deck (1), ¾", col, Sony 1200; editing deck (2), ½", b&w/col, Sony 3650, 8650; studio camera (5), b&w, Sony 3210, Panasonic Telemation; monitor (6), b&w/col, Sony, Magnavox; SEG (1), Sony; lighting (6); microphones (3); tripods (5). *For Loan:* portapak (3), ½", b&w, Panasonic, Sony; audio tape recorders (8). Have portable viewing installation. *Equipment Loan Period:* 7-30 days. Provide training in use of equipment to faculty & students.

Video Collection Maintained by purchase, rental, own production. Use/play ½" reel to reel, ¾" cassette. *Collection:* ¾" cassette, 34t.

Cable & CCTV Receive serv of cable TV system. Have CCTV in inst, with 11 monitors. *Programming Sources:* tapes produced professionally.

Bowling Green

P- BOWLING GREEN PUBLIC LIBRARY, 1225 State St, 42274. *Tel:* (502) 781-4882. *Film Serv Est:* 1971. *In Charge:* William F. Bolte, Head Librarian. *Film Sel:* State Library.

Free-Loan Film Serv *Eligibility:* staff, civic & religious groups, prof groups, such as Comprehensive Care. *Restrictions:* for inst, only in Warren County. Cannot use for fund-raising, borrow for classroom use. May borrow by mail. *Loan Period:* 2 days. *Total Yr Film Loan:* 100.

Film Collection 10t/p. *Circ:* S8mm reel, 10t/p.

Other Film Serv Obtain film from coop loan system (Ky. Dept of Library & Archives, Barren River District Library of Ky.). *Equipment:* lend 16mm sound projector (2), lend S8mm reel projector (1), lend projection tables & stands, lend projection screens.

Other Media Collections *Audio:* disc, 33⅓ rpm, 1000t; tape, cassette, 60t. *Filmstrips:* sound, 50t; silent, 20t. *Slides:* sets, 12t.

Budget & Expenditures Total library budget $30,000 (FY 7/1/74-7/1/75). No separate AV budget. *Member:* Ky. Library Assn.

C- WESTERN KENTUCKY UNIVERSITY, Third District Film Library—Div of Media Servs, AV Serv Center, 101 College of Education Bldg, 42101. *Tel:* (502) 745-3752. *Film Serv Est:* 1961. *In Charge:* Fithian S. Faries, Dir, AV Serv Center. *AV Staff:* 2 prof, 3 cl. *Film Sel:* committee preview, faculty/staff recommendations.

Free-Loan Film Serv *Eligibility:* org members, staff & students. *Restrictions:* for inst, only members of Third District Film Library. Cannot use for fund-raising, transmit electroni-

cally. Available to researchers/scholars for on-site viewing. May not borrow by mail. *Loan Period:* 3 days. *Total Yr Film Loan:* 35,000. Sell films. Produce films. Produce slide sets, filmstrips, video tapes.

Film Collection 5000t/5500p. Approx 300t acquired annually. *Circ:* 16mm, 5000t. *Pubns:* catalog, every 2 yr; suppl, in yr catalog not published. Publish brochures.

Other Film Serv Rent film from distributors for faculty, obtain film from other libraries, film reference serv, film fairs/festivals. Permanent viewing facility. *Equipment:* lend S8mm camera (1), 16mm camera (1), 16mm sound projector (64), 8mm cartridge projector (20), 8mm reel projector (5), projection tables & stands, projection screens.

Other Media Collections *Audio:* disc, 4876t (total); tape, 3697t (total).

Budget & Expenditures Total library budget $385,209 (FY 7/1/74-7/1/75). Totay FY film budget $20,000. *Member:* AECT, KLA.

C- WESTERN KENTUCKY UNIVERSITY, Video Tape Library— Div of Media Servs, TV Center—Academic Complex, 42101. *Tel:* (502) 745-2153. *In Charge:* Dr. Charles Anderson, Dir, Media Servs. *Video Staff:* 7 f-t, 2 tech. *Video Use:* documentation of community/school events, to increase community's library use, in-service training, practical video/TV training courses, classroom instruction. Video serv available on demand & by appointment. Produce video tapes. Have production studio/space & separate control room.

Video Equipment/Facilities *In-House Use Only:* editing deck (2), ¾" col, Sony 2825; studio camera (1), 1" col, Hitadii 1000. *For Loan:* recording deck (5), ¾" col, Sony 1800; playback deck (19), ¾" col, Sony 1200; studio camera (1), 1" col, Hitadii 1000; monitor (80), 21" b&w/col, GE, Sony. Have permanent & portable viewing installations. Provide training in use of equipment. Have tape duplication serv.

Video Tape Loan/Rental/Sale Serv *Serv Provided:* free loan, sale. *Loan Eligibility:* staff, educational inst, prof groups, such as AECT, KAVA. *Restrictions:* for indiv & inst, only in state. Cannot use for fund-raising, duplicate, air without permission. May borrow by mail. *Loan Period:* 7 days. *Total Yr Tape Loan:* 75.

Video Collection Maintained by purchase, rental, own production, exchange/swap. Use/play ½", 2" reel to reel, ¾" cassette. *Sources:* commercial distributors, exchange. *Tape Sel:* faculty/staff recommendations. Tapes organized by subject. *Collection, Color:* 2" reel, 240t/c; ¾" cassette, 510t/c. *Other Video Serv:* programming, reference serv, taping of other media, production workshops. *Pubns:* catalog. Publish brochures on selected tapes.

Cable & CCTV Have CCTV in inst. *Programming Sources:* over-the-air commercial & public broadcasting, tapes produced by inst, tapes produced professionally.

Campbellsville

C- CAMPBELLSVILLE COLLEGE, 42718. *Tel:* (502) 465-8158, ext 26. *In Charge:* Bette Davis, Media Technician. *AV Staff:* 1 cl, 1 tech. *Film Sel:* faculty/staff recommendations.

Free-Loan Film Serv *Eligibility:* staff & students, civic & religious groups. *Restrictions:* for indiv, only in county. Available to researchers/scholars for on-site viewing.

Film Collection 28t. *Circ:* S8mm reel, 28t.

Other Film Serv Library film programs. *Equipment:* rent 16mm sound projectors (2), projection screens (2).

Other Media Collections *Audio:* disc, 33⅓ rpm, 676t; tape, cassette, 480t. *Filmstrips:* silent, 287t.

Budget & Expenditures Total library budget $14,700 (FY 7/1/75-7/1/76). Total FY film budget $900. *Member:* ALA, Ky. Library Assn, SE Library Assn.

Video Serv *In Charge:* Bette Davis, Media Technician. *Video Use:* documentation of community/school events, in-service training. Video serv available on demand. Produce video tapes.

Video Equipment/Facilities *In-House Use Only:* recording deck (1), ½", b&w, Shibaden SV510U; studio camera (1), b&w, Shibaden FP71U; monitor (2); microphones (2); tripods (1); audio tape recorders (6).

Video Collection Maintained by own production. Use/play ½" reel to reel. *Collection, B&W:* ½" reel, 22t.

Elizabethtown

C- ELIZABETHTOWN COMMUNITY COLLEGE, 42701. *Tel:* (502) 769-2371, ext 286. *In Charge:* M. Maurice Utley, Supervisor, Academic Support Serv. *AV Staff:* 2 (1 prof, 1 tech). *Film Sel:* faculty/staff recommendations.

Free-Loan Film Serv *Eligibility:* staff & students. *Restrictions:* cannot use for fund-raising.

Film Collection 23t. Approx 2t acquired annually.

Video Serv *Est:* 1972. *In Charge:* M. Maurice Utley, Supervisor, Academic Support Serv. *Video Staff:* 2 f-t. *Video Use:* documentation of school events, playback only of professionally produced tapes. Video serv available by appointment. Produce video tapes. Have small production studio/space & separate control room.

Video Equipment/Facilities *In-House Use Only:* recording playback deck (2), col, Panasonic, Concord; studio camera (3); monitor (2), b&w; SEG (1); microphones (6).

Video Collection Maintained by purchase, own production. Use/play ½" reel to reel, ½" cartridge. *Tape Sel:* University of Ky. Tapes organized by subject.

Cable & CCTV Have CCTV in inst, with 22 monitors. *Programming Sources:* tapes produced by inst, tapes produced professionally, tapes produced by community groups & indiv.

Fort Mitchell

C- THOMAS MORE COLLEGE, AV Center, Box 85, 41017. *Tel:* (606) 341-5800, ext 59. *Film Serv Est:* 1947. *In Charge:* Jeanne Pike, AV Dir. *AV Staff:* 3 (1 prof, 2 cl, 1 tech). *Film Sel:* committee preview, faculty/staff recommendations, chief film librarian's decision.

Free-Loan Film Serv *Eligibility:* staff & students, civic & religious groups. *Restrictions:* for indiv & inst, none. Available to researchers/scholars for on-site viewing. May borrow by mail. *Loan Period:* 7 days. *Total Yr Film Loan:* 3214.

Film Rental Serv *Eligibility:* no restrictions. *Restrictions:* only in region (Ky., Ohio, Ind., Tenn.). *Rental Period:* 7 days.

Film Collection 800t/p. *Circ:* 16mm, 800t/p. *Pubns:* catalog, as needed ($1); suppl, no set policy.

Other Film Serv Obtain film from other libraries.

Other Media Collections *Audio:* tape, reel, 700t. *Filmstrips:* sound, 200t; silent, 4000t; sound sets, 90t.

Budget & Expenditures No separate budget. *Member:* AECT.

Frankfort

S- KENTUCKY DEPT OF LIBRARY & ARCHIVES, Box 537, Berry Hill, 40601. *Tel:* (502) 564-7910. *Film Serv Est:* 1965. *In Charge:* Linda Stith, AV Librarian. *AV Staff:* 4 (1 prof, 3 cl). *Film Sel:* preview, chief film librarian's decision, published reviews.

Free-Loan Film Serv *Eligibility:* civic & religious groups, indiv with library cards, & others, such as public libraries, state employees. *Restrictions:* for indiv & inst, only in state. Cannot use for fund-raising, transmit electronically, borrow for classroom use. Available to researchers/scholars for on-site viewing. May borrow by mail. *Loan Period:* varies. *Total Yr Film Loan:* 20,382.

Film Collection 1700t/1900p. Approx 300t acquired annually. *Circ:* 16mm, 1700t/1900p. *Pubns:* catalog, as needed; suppl, no set policy.

Other Film Serv Film reference serv, library film programs. Permanent viewing facility available. *Equipment:* lend 16mm sound projector (1), projection screens.

Budget & Expenditures Total library budget $78,000 (FY 7/1/74-7/1/75). Total FY film budget $50,000. *Member:* EFLA, Ky. AV Assn.

Golden Pond

S- TENNESSEE VALLEY AUTHORITY, Land Between the Lakes, 42231. *Tel:* (502) 924-5602, ext 245. *In Charge:* L. Darryl Armstrong, Reports Editor. *AV Staff:* 2 (2 prof, 1 cl, 2 tech). *Film Sel:* staff recommendations. *Holdings:* feature films 75%.

Free-Loan Film Serv *Eligibility:* educational inst, civic groups, prof groups. *Restrictions:* for indiv & inst, none. Cannot use for fund-raising. Available to researchers/scholars for on-site viewing. May borrow by mail. *Loan Period:* 7 days.

Film Collection 14t/50p. Approx 4t acquired annually. *Circ:* 16mm, 14t/50p.

Other Film Serv Obtain film from other libraries, film reference serv. Permanent viewing facility available.

Video Serv *Est:* 1973. *In Charge:* L. Darryl Armstrong, Reports Editor. *Video Staff:* 2 f-t. *Video Use:* documentation, public serv. Video serv available by appointment.

Video Tape Loan/Rental/Sale Serv *Serv Provided:* free loan. *Loan Eligibility:* news media. *Restrictions:* cannot use for fund-raising. May borrow by mail. *Loan Period:* 7 days. *Total Yr Tape Loan:* 25.

Video Collection Maintained by own production. Use/play 2" reel to reel. *Special Collections:* in-house training tapes, public serv. Tapes organized by subject. *Collection, Color:* 2" reel, 4t/25c.

Henderson

C- HENDERSON COMMUNITY COLLEGE, Hwy 605, 42420. *Tel:* (502) 827-1867. *In Charge:* Wendell Hisce, Librarian. *AV Staff:* 1 (1 prof, 1 tech). *Film Sel:* committee preview, faculty/staff recommendations, chief film librarian's decision. *Holdings:* medicine 40%, science 60%.

Free-Loan Film Serv *Eligibility:* staff & students, educational inst, civic & religious groups, indiv with library cards, prof groups. *Restrictions:* for indiv & inst, none. Available to researchers/scholars for on-site viewing. May not borrow by mail. *Loan Period:* 14 days. *Total Yr Film Loan:* 16.

Film Rental Serv *Eligibility:* University of Ky. staff. *Rental Period:* 5 days. *Total Yr Film Booking:* 130. Produce slides, audiotape, sound filmstrips, overheads.

Film Collection 99t/p. Approx 8t acquired annually. *Circ:* S8mm reel, 99t/p.

Other Film Serv Rent film from distributors for patrons, obtain film from coop loan system (University of Ky.), film fairs/festivals. *Equipment:* lend 16mm sound projectors (7), lend S8mm cartridge projector (5), lend S8mm reel projector (3), lend projection screens (3).

Other Media Collections *Audio:* disc, 33⅓ rpm, 765c; tape, cassette, 94c. *Filmstrips:* sound, 54t/c; silent, 1t. *Slides:* sets, 35t/c.

Budget & Expenditures Total library budget $10,000 (FY 7/1/74-7/1/75). No separate AV budget. *Member:* AECT, ALA, Ky. Library Assn.

Video Serv *Est:* 1973. *In Charge:* Wendell Hisce, Dir of Learning Resources. *Video Staff:* 1 f-t, 1 p-t. *Video Use:* documentation of community/school events, community video access, delayed broadcast to classrooms. Video serv available by appointment. Produce video tapes. Have production studio/space & separate control room.

Video Equipment/Facilities *In-House Use Only:* portapak (1), ½" b&w, Panasonic; recording deck (2), ½" b&w, Panasonic 3020, Sony 3650; studio camera (2), b&w, Sony; monitor (5), b&w, Avcom, Ampex; SEG (1); additional camera lenses; lighting; microphones; tripods.

Video Collection Maintained by purchase, own production. Use/play ½" reel to reel. *Sources:* University of Ky. Tapes

Henderson (cont'd)

organized by subject. *Collection, B&W:* ½″ reel, 70t/c. *Other Video Serv:* programming.

Cable & CCTV Receive serv of cable TV system. Produce programs for cablecasting. Run cable programs for special audiences. Have CCTV in inst, with 20 monitors. *Programming Sources:* over-the-air commercial & public broadcasting, tapes produced by inst, tapes produced professionally.

Jackson

C- LEES JUNIOR COLLEGE, 601 Jefferson St, 41339. *Tel:* (606) 666-7521, ext 75. *Video Serv Est:* 1971. *In Charge:* Terry C. Blosser, Dir of Media. *Video Staff:* 1 f-t. *Video Use:* documentation of community/school events, community video access, in-service training, practical video/TV training courses. Video serv available on demand. Produce video tapes. Have production studio/space & separate control room.

Video Equipment/Facilities *In-House Use Only:* portapak (1), ½″, b&w, Sony 3400; recording/playback deck (2), ½″, b&w/col, Sony 5000; editing deck (2), ½″, b&w/col; studio camera (3), b&w/col, GBC, Sony; monitor (12), col; SEG (1); lighting; microphones (3); tripods (2); audio tape recorders (2). Provide training in use of equipment to faculty & students. Have tape duplication serv.

Video Collection Maintained by own production. Use/play ½″ reel to reel. *Tape Sel:* preview, published reviews, catalogs. Tapes organized by subject. *Collection, Color:* ½″ reel, 45t/c. *Collection, B&W:* ½″ reel, 20t/c. *Other Video Serv:* taping of other media, production workshops.

Cable & CCTV Will receive serv of cable TV system in 1976. Have CCTV in inst, with 12 monitors. *Programming Sources:* over-the-air commercial & public braodcasting, tapes produced by inst, tapes produced by community groups & indiv.

Lexington

S- UNIVERSITY OF KENTUCKY, Law Library, 40506. *Tel:* (606) 257-1981. *Video Serv Est:* 1973. *In Charge:* Susan H. Waller, Law Media Librarian. *Video Staff:* 1 f-t, 1 p-t. *Video Use:* documentation of community/school events, to increase community's library use, in-service training. Video serv available by appointment. Produce video tapes. Have production studio/space & separate control room.

Video Equipment/Facilities *In-House Use Only:* recording deck (2), ½″, b&w, Sony 3600, 3650; studio camera (2), b&w, Panasonic 360P; monitor (4), b&w/col, Sony CVM9204, CKV191; SEG (1), Panasonic VY922; additional camera lenses (2); microphones (5); tripods (4); audio tape recorders (3); videocassette recorder (1). *For Loan:* portapak (2), ½″, b&w, Sony 3400. Have portable viewing installation. *Equipment Loan Period:* no set policy. Provide training in use of equipment. Have tape duplication serv.

Video Tape Loan/Rental/Sale Serv *Serv Provided:* free loan, swap with other inst, rental. *Loan Eligibility:* staff & students, educational inst, prof groups, such as bar assn. *Restrictions:* for indiv & inst, 80 mile radius. Cannot air without permission. May borrow by mail. *Loan Period:* 14 days. *Total Yr Tape Loan:* 15.

Video Collection Maintained by own production. Use/play ½″ reel to reel, ¾″ cassette. Tapes organized by subject. *Collection, B&W:* ½″ reel, 97t/c; ¾″ cassette, 42t/c. *Pubns:* catalog.

London

C- SUE BENNETT COLLEGE, Learning Resource Center, 40741. *Tel:* (606) 864-6770. *Film Sel:* committee preview.

Other Film Serv Rent film from distributors for patrons, obtain film from other libraries. Permanent viewing facility available for rent to community. *Equipment:* lend/rent 16mm sound projector (3), lend/rent projection tables & stands, lend/rent projection screens, tape recorders, overhead & opaque projectors.

Other Media Collections *Audio:* disc, 78rpm, 750t; tape, cassette, 450t/500c; tape, reel, 50t. *Filmstrips:* sound, 25t; silent, 75t. *Slides:* single, 1500t.

Video Serv *Est:* In planning stage. *In Charge:* Virginia Baker. *Video Staff:* 1 f-t, 6 p-t. *Video Use:* documentation of community/school events, classroom suppl. Video serv available on demand. Will produce video tapes.

Cable & CCTV Will receive serv of CCTV system.

Louisville

C- BELLARMINE COLLEGE, Library, Newburg Rd, 40205. *Tel:* (502) 452-8411. *Video Serv Est:* 1969. *In Charge:* Joan E. Wettig, AV Librarian. *Video Staff:* 1 f-t. *Video Use:* documentation of community/school events, in-service training, speech classes. Video serv available by appointment. Produce video tapes. Have production studio/space & separate control room.

Video Equipment/Facilities *In-House Use Only:* recording/playback deck (6), b&w, Sony 2000, 2600, 3400, 3450; editing deck (6), b&w, GE, Sony; additional camera lenses (2); microphones (6); tripods (6); aduio tape recorders (22). Have viewing installation. Provide training in use of equipment to faculty & students. Have audio tape duplication serv.

Video Tape Loan/Rental/Sale Serv *Serv Provided:* swap with other inst.

Video Collection Maintained by own production, exchange/swap. Use/play ½″ reel to reel.

Morehead

C- JOHNSON CAMDEN LIBRARY, Material Center, 40351. *Tel:* (606) 783-2251, ext 26. *Film Serv Est:* 1965. *In Charge:* Albert Evans, Assistant Librarian. *AV Staff:* 4 (2 prof, 2 cl). *Film Sel:* faculty/staff recommendations.

Free-Loan Film Serv *Eligibility:* staff & students, educational inst, civic & religious groups, indiv with library cards. *Restrictions:* for indiv, interlibrary loan, only in state; for inst, none. Cannot transmit electronically. Available to researchers/scholars for on-site viewing. May borrow by mail. *Loan Period:* 3 days.

Film Collection 633t. Approx 25-30t acquired annually. *Circ:* 16mm, 330t; 8mm cartridge, 37t; S8mm cartridge, 266t. *Pubns:* catalog, annual; suppl, no set policy.

Other Film Serv Library film programs. *Equipment:* lend S8mm camera (2), lend 8mm cartridge projector (2), lend projection tables & stands (2), lend projection screens (4), cassette tape players (10), filmstrip projectors (8).

Other Media Collections *Audio:* disc, 33⅓ rpm, 6200t; disc, 45rpm, 750t; tape, cassette, 2450t; tape, reel, 170t. *Filmstrips:* 5200t. *Slides:* sets, 372t.

Budget & Expenditures Total library budget $179,000 (FY 7/1/74-7/1/75). No separate AV budget. *Member:* AECT, ALA, EFLA, Ky. Library Assn.

Murray

C- MURRAY STATE UNIVERSITY, 42071. *Video Serv Est:* 1965. *In Charge:* Ray Mofield, General Manager. *Video Staff:* 2 f-t, 2 p-t, 2 tech. Video serv available by appointment. Produce video tapes. Have production studio/space & separate control room.

Video Equipment/Facilities *In-House Use Only:* recording deck (1); playback deck (1); editing deck (1); studio camera (4), b&w/col, RCA; monitor (1); SEG (1); keyer (1); additional camera lenses (2); lighting (1); microphones (10); tripods (2); audio tape recorders (2). Have permanent viewing installation. Provide training in use of equipment to students.

Video Tape Loan/Rental/Sale Serv *Serv Provided:* free loan, swap with other inst. *Loan Eligibility:* staff & students, educational inst, prof groups. *Restrictions:* for indiv, only in Calloway County. May not borrow by mail.

Video Collection Use/play ½″, 1″, 2″ reel to reel.

Cable & CCTV Receive serv of cable TV system. Produce programs for cablecasting. Run cable programs for special audiences. Have CCTV in inst, with 50 monitors. *Programming Sources:* over-the-air commercial & public broadcasting, tapes produced professionally.

Pippa Passes

Ç- ALICE LLOYD COLLEGE, Learning Resources Center, 41844. *In Charge:* Bennie L. Moore, Dir. *AV Staff:* 1½ (1 prof, 1 cl). *Film Sel:* faculty/staff recommendations. *Holdings:* Appalachia.

Free-Loan Film Serv *Eligibility:* staff & students, educational inst, civic & religious groups, prof groups. *Restrictions:* for indiv, none. Available to researchers/scholars for on-site viewing.

Film Collection 125t. *Circ:* 16mm, 20t; 8mm cartridge, 20t; S8mm reel, 85t.

Other Film Serv Rent film from distributors for patrons. *Equipment:* lend S8mm camera (4), lend 16mm sound projector (3), lend 8mm cartridge projector (2), lend 8mm reel projector (1), lend S8mm cartridge projector (6), lend S8mm reel projector (6), lend projection tables & stands (10), lend projection screens (12).

Other Media Collections *Filmstrips:* silent, 420t/c; sound sets, 85t/c. *Slides:* single, 2000t; sets, 10t.

Budget & Expenditures Total library budget $20,000. Total film budget $4000.

Video Serv *Est:* 1973. *In Charge:* Bennie L. Moore, Dir. *Video Staff:* 1 f-t, 3 p-t. *Video Use:* documentation of community/school events, to increase community's library use, community video access, in-service training, as sales tool, as art form, documentation of area's traditional culture. Video serv available on demand. Produce video tapes.

Video Equipment/Facilities *In-House Use Only:* microphones (6); tripods (3); audio tape recorders (20). *For Loan:* portapak (2), ½″, b&w, Sony 3400; recording deck (2), ½″, b&w, Sony; studio camera (2), b&w, Sony; monitor (4), b&w, Sony; SEG (1), SEG-1. *Equipment Loan Period:* no set policy. Provide training in use of equipment to general public. Have tape duplication serv.

Video Tape Loan/Rental/Sale Serv *Serv Provided:* free loan, swap with other inst. *Loan Eligibility:* staff & students, educational inst, civic & religious groups, prof groups. *Restrictions:* for indiv & inst, none. Cannot air without permission. May borrow by mail.

Video Collection Maintained by purchase, own production. Use/play ½″ reel to reel. *Tape Sel:* preview, faculty/staff recommendations. *Special Collections:* in-house training tapes, films in video format, Appalachian subjects. Tapes organized by subject. *Collection, B&W:* ½″ reel, 50t. *Other Video Serv:* taping of other media, production workshops.

Cable & CCTV Produce programs for cablecasting.

Prestonburg

C- PRESTONSBURG COMMUNITY COLLEGE, Library, 41653. *Tel:* (606) 886-3863, ext 288.

Film Collection 45t. Approx 5t acquired annually. *Circ:* S8mm cartridge, 45t.

Other Film Serv Obtain film from coop loan system (University of Ky. Film Library), obtain film from other libraries. Permanent viewing facility available for rent to community. *Equipment:* lend 8mm reel projector (1), S8mm cartridge projector (10), S8mm reel projector (1), projection tables & stands (12), projection screens (6), slide projectors (6), filmstrip projectors (3).

Other Media Collections *Audio:* disc, 33⅓ rpm, 1450t; tape, cassette, 325t; tape, reel, 410t. *Filmstrips:* silent, 110t; sound sets, 280t; silent sets, 35t. *Slides:* single, 6200t.

Budget & Expenditures Total library budget $14,460 (FY 7/1/74-7/1/75). No separate AV budget. *Member:* Ky. Library Assn, SE Library Assn, Ky. AV Assn.

Cable & CCTV Receive serv of cable TV system. Have CCTV in inst, with 20 monitors. *Programming Sources:* over-the-air commercial & public broadcasting.

Wilmore

C- ASBURY COLLEGE, Morrison-Kenyon Library, 40390. *Tel:* (606) 858-3402, ext 246. *In Charge:* Gari Lidh, AV Assistant. *AV Staff:* 1 (1 prof, 5 tech). *Film Sel:* faculty/staff recommendations, chief film librarian's decision. *Holdings:* Christian education 50%, fine arts 50%.

Free-Loan Film Serv *Eligibility:* staff & students, educational inst, civic & religious groups. *Restrictions:* for indiv & inst, none. Cannot use for fund-raising, transmit electronically. Available to researchers/scholars for on-site viewing. May not borrow by mail. *Loan Period:* 3 days.

Film Rental Serv *Eligibility:* no restrictions. *Restrictions:* none. Cannot use for fund-raising, transmit electronically. *Rental Period:* 3 days. *Total Yr Film Booking:* 36. Produce cassette tapes.

Film Collection 17t/25p. *Circ:* 16mm, 2t/10p. *Noncirc:* 16mm, 15t/p.

Other Film Serv Rent film from distributors for patrons, film reference serv. *Equipment:* lend/rent 16mm sound projector (5), lend projection tables & stands (3), lend projection screens (2 of 27).

Other Media Collections *Audio:* tape, cassette, 250t/c; tape, reel, 200t/c. *Filmstrips:* silent, 200t/c. *Slides:* sets, 20t/c.

Budget & Expenditures Total film rental budget $2500 (FY 6/1/74-6/1/75).

Video Serv *Est:* 1976. *In Charge:* Gari Lidh, AV Assistant. *Video Staff:* 1 f-t, 5 p-t. *Video Use:* in-service training. Video serv available by appointment. Produce video tapes. Have production studio/space.

Video Equipment/Facilities *In-House Use Only:* portapak (2), b&w, Sony; recording deck (2); playback deck (2); studio camera (2); monitor (2). Have portable viewing installation. Provide training in use of equipment to faculty. Have tape duplication serv.

Video Collection Maintain by purchase, own production. Use/play ½″ reel to reel. *Sources:* commercial distributors. *Tape Sel:* faculty/staff recommendations. *Other Video Serv:* programming, taping of other media.

Louisiana

Baton Rouge

S- LOUISIANA STATE LIBRARY FILMS & RECORDINGS DEPT, Box 131, 70821. *Tel:* (504) 389-5538. *Film Serv Est:* 1949. *In Charge:* Mrs. Dell D. Scholz, Dept Head. *AV Staff:* 5 (1 prof, 4 cl). *Film Sel:* staff recommendations, chief film librarian's decision. *Holdings:* animated films 3%, black studies 3%, children's films 14%, fine arts 4%, science 3%.

Free-Loan Film Serv *Eligibility:* all groups & org. *Restrictions:* only in state. Cannot use for fund-raising, transmit electronically, borrow for classroom use. May borrow by mail. *Loan Period:* 1 day. *Total Yr Film Loan:* 20,904.

Film Collection 1019t/1581p. Approx 220t acquired annually. *Circ:* 16mm, 1019t/1581p. *Pubns:* catalog, as needed; suppl, no set policy. Publish subject list.

Other Film Serv Film reference serv, library film programs. Permanent viewing facility available to community.

Other Media Collections *Audio:* disc, 33⅓ rpm, 4498t; tape, cassette, 2t.

Budget & Expenditures Total library budget $213,764 (FY 7/1/74-7/1/75). Total FY film budget $43,503. *Member:* ALA, EFLA, FLIC, La. Library Assn.

Hammond

C- SOUTHEASTERN LOUISIANA UNIVERSITY, School Film Library, 70401. *Tel:* (504) 549-2128. *Film Serv Est:* 1950. *In Charge:* Dr. F. Landon Greaves, Head Librarian. *AV Staff:* 1 cl. *Film Sel:* La. State Dept of Educ.

Free-Loan Film Serv *Eligibility:* staff & students, area elementary & secondary schools. *Restrictions:* for indiv, only in 9 parishes of SE La. Available to researchers/scholars for on-site viewing. May borrow by mail. *Loan Period:* 7 days. *Total Yr Film Loan:* 6672.

Film Collection 1500t/500p. *Circ:* 16mm, 1500t/500p. *Pubns:* catalog, annual; suppl, no set policy.

Other Film Serv *Equipment:* lend 16mm sound projector (2).

Houma

P- TERREBONNE PARISH LIBRARY, Box 510, 70360. *Tel:* (504) 872-3264. *Film Sel:* faculty/staff recommendations, chief librarian's decision.

Free-Loan Film Serv *Eligibility:* indiv with library cards. *Restrictions:* for indiv & inst, none. Cannot use for fund-raising, transmit electronically, borrow for classroom use. Available to researchers/scholars for on-site viewing. May not borrow by mail. *Total Yr Film Loan:* 15.

Film Collection 4t/5p. Approx 1t acquired annually. *Circ:* 16mm, 4t/5p. *Noncirc:* 16mm, 4t/5p.

Other Film Serv Obtain film from coop loan system (Bayouland Pilot Library System), obtain film from other libraries, library film programs. *Equipment:* lend 16mm sound projector (4), 8mm reel projector (1), projection screens (3), filmstrip projectors (5), cassette players (5).

Other Media Collections *Audio:* disc, 78rpm, 2000t. *Filmstrips:* sound, 73t; silent, 26t; sound sets, 1t. *Slides:* sets, 6t.

Budget & Expenditures Total library budget $64,500 (FY 1/1/75-1/1/76). Total FY film budget $4000.

Lafayette

P- UNIVERSITY OF SOUTHWESTERN LOUISIANA, Regional Film Library, Box 396—U.S.L. Station, 70501. *Tel:* (318) 233-3850, ext 244. *In Charge:* Charles A. Bernard, AV Consultant. *AV Staff:* 2 (1 prof, 2 cl). *Film Sel:* La. State Dept of Educ.

Free-Loan Film Serv *Eligibility:* educational inst, civic groups, religious groups. *Restrictions:* for indiv, only in state. Cannot use for fund-raising. May borrow by mail. *Loan Period:* 5 days. *Total Yr Film Loan:* 6267.

Film Collection 1500t/1922p. *Pubns:* catalog, as needed; suppl.

Other Film Serv Permanent viewing facility.

Lake Charles

P- CALCASIEU PARISH PUBLIC LIBRARY, Downtown Branch, Box 2857, 411 Pujo St, 70601. *Tel:* (318) 433-1045, ext 9. *Film Serv Est:* 1957. *In Charge:* Dorothy Love, AV Dept Head. *AV Staff:* 2 (1 cl, 1 tech). *Film Sel:* previews, chief film librarian's decision. *Holdings:* animated films 5%, black studies 3%, children's films 55%, dance 2%, feature films 2%, fine arts 5%, medicine 3%, science 5%, social sciences 15%, teacher education 5%.

Free-Loan Film Serv *Eligibility:* indiv with library cards. *Restrictions:* for indiv & inst only in Calcasieu Parish. Cannot use for fund-raising, borrow for classroom use. Available to researchers/scholars for on-site viewing. May borrow by mail. *Loan Period:* 1 day. *Total Yr Film Loan:* 3908.

Film Collection 433t/435p. Approx 50t acquired annually. *Circ:* 16mm, 433t/435p. *Pubns:* catalog, every 2 yrs; suppl, in yr catalog not published.

Other Film Serv Permanent viewing facility. *Equipment:* lend 16mm sound projector (2), 8mm reel projector (1), projection tables & stands (1), lend/rent projection screens (2).

Other Media Collections *Audio:* disc, 33⅓ rpm, 5128t/c. *Slides:* sets, 4c.

Budget & Expenditures Total library budget $47,500 (FY 1/75-1/76). No separate AV budget. *Member:* La. Library Assn.

C- McNEESE STATE UNIVERSITY, Regional Film Library, 70601. *Tel:* (318) 477-2520, ext 267. *In Charge:* Gloria L. Cotten, Film Librarian. *AV Staff:* 1. *Film Sel:* State Dept of Educ, AV Supervisor.

Free-Loan Film Serv *Eligibility:* staff & students, educational inst, civic groups, religious groups. *Restrictions:* only in Calcasieu, Cameron, Allen, Beauregard, Jefferson Davis Parishes. Cannot use for fund-raising, transmit electronically. Available to researchers/scholars for on-site viewing. May borrow by mail. *Loan Period:* 3 days. ½ *Yr Film Loan:* 2978.

Film Collection 1977p. *Circ:* 16mm, 1977p. *Pubns:* catalog, as needed; suppl, no set policy.

Budget & Expenditures No separate budget. *Member:* La. State Dept of Educ regional film libraries.

Video Serv *In Charge:* Dr. Elmer H. Wagner, ext 261. *Video Staff:* 2 f-t, 1 tech. *Video Use:* in-service training, practical video/TV training courses, playback only of professionally produced tapes. Video serv available by appointment. Produce video tapes. Have production studio/space & separate control room.

Video Equipment/Facilities *In-House Use Only:* recording/playback decks (5), 1″, ½″ b&w/col, IVC800, Sony AV5000, JVC; studio camera (4), b&w, Plombicon, Norelco; monitor (6), b&w, CONRAC; SEG (1), Telemotion; keyer (1), Telemotion; synthesizer (1); additional camera lenses; lighting; microphones (10); tripods (4); audio control multiplexer. Have permanent viewing installation. *Equipment Loan Period:* provide training in use of equipment to students.

Video Tape Loan/Rental/Sale Serv *Serv Provided:* free loan, swap with other inst. *Loan Eligibility:* campus use only.

Video Collection Maintained by purchase, rental, own production. Use/play ½″, 1″ reel to reel, ¾″ cassette. *Sources:* educational producers. *Tape Sel:* preview, faculty/staff recommendations. *Special Collections:* in-house training tapes, education. Tapes organized by subject. *Collection, Color:* ¾″ cassette, 50t/c. *Other Video Serv:* production workshops.

Cable & CCTV Receive serv of cable TV system. Produce programs for cablecasting. Inform public about cable system serv & facilities. Run cable programs for special audiences. Have CCTV in inst, with 40 monitors. *Programming Sources:* over-the-air commercial & public broadcasting, tapes produced by inst, tapes produced professionally.

New Orleans

C- NEW ORLEANS BAPTIST THEOLOGICAL SEMINARY LIBRARY, 4110 Seminary Place, 70126. *Tel:* (504) 282-4455, ext 289, 279. *Film Serv Est:* 1953. *In Charge:* C. William Eidenire, Circulation-Reference Librarian. *AV Staff:* 1 tech. *Film Sel:* faculty/staff recommendations, published reviews. *Holdings:* theology, religion 100%.
Film Collection 207t/p. Approx 5t acquired annually. *Non-circ:* 16mm, 207t/p.
Other Media Collections *Audio:* disc, 33⅓ rpm, 1426t/1783c; tape, cassette, 2566t/3207c; tape, reel, 640t/800c. *Filmstrips:* silent 703t/c. *Slides:* single, 1494t/c.
Budget & Expenditures Total AV materials budget $8000. No separate budget.
Video Serv *Est:* 1969. *Video Staff:* 1 f-t, 1 p-t. *Video Use:* instructional aid. Video serv available on demand & by appointment. Produce video tapes, Have production studio/space & separate control room.
Video Equipment/Facilities *In-House Use Only;* recording deck (3), b&w/col, Sony, Ampex; playback deck (3), b&w/col, Sony; studio camera (2), b&w, Sony, Ampex; monitor (3), b&w/col, Sony; microphones (3); tripods (3); audio tape recorders (2). Have portable viewing installation. *Equipment Loan Period:* no set policy. Provide training in use of equipment to faculty & students. Have tape duplication serv.
Video Tape Loan/Rental/Sale Serv *Serv Provided:* free loan. *Loan Eligibility:* instructional staff only. *Restrictions:* may not borrow by mail.
Video Collection Maintained by purchase, rental, own production. Use/play ½″, 1″ reel to reel, ¾″ cassette. *Tape Sel:* faculty/staff recommendations, published reviews. *Special Collections:* in-house training tapes. Tapes organized by subject. *Collection, Color:* ¾″ cassette, 11t/c.
Cable & CCTV Have CCTV in inst.

A- NEW ORLEANS MUSEUM OF ART, Box 19123, 70179. *Tel:* (504) 488-2631, ext 47. *In Charge:* David C. Swoyer, Asst Curator of Educ. *AV Staff:* 1 prof. *Film Sel:* committee preview. *Holdings:* children's films 20%, fine arts 100%.
Film Collection 50t/p. Approx 5t acquired annually. *Non-circ:* 16mm, 50t/c.
Other Film Serv Rent film from distributors for patrons, obtain film from other libraries, film fairs/festivals, library film programs. Permanent viewing facility.
Budget & Expenditures No separate budget. *Member:* AECT, AFI, EFLA, Special Library Assn, ARLIS/NA.
Video Serv *Est:* 1971. *Video Staff:* 1 f-t, 1 p-t. *Video Use:* documentation of community/school events, in-service training, for exhibits. Video serv available on demand. Produce video tapes.
Video Equipment/Facilities *In-House Use Only:* portapak (1), ½″ b&w, Sony, AVC 3400; recording deck (1), ¾″ b&w/col, Sony TV122DC; playback deck (1), ¾″ b&w/col, Victor Co of Japan CR6100U; monitor (1), b&w/col, Sony; lighting (3); microphones (3); tripods (2); audio tape recorders (5). Have portable viewing installation. Provide training in use of equipment to staff & volunteers.
Video Tape Loan/Rental/Sale Serv *Serv Provided:* free loan. *Loan Eligibility:* prof groups, such as museums. *Restrictions:* none. May borrow by mail.
Video Collection Maintained by own production. Use/play ½″ reel to reel, ¾″ cassette. *Sources:* own production. *Special Collections:* in-house training tapes. Tapes organized by production date. *Collection, Color:* ¾″ cassette, 20t/1c. *Collection, B&W:* ½″ reel, 25t/1c.

P- NEW ORLEANS PUBLIC LIBRARY, 219 Loyola Ave, 70140. *Tel:* (601) 586-4936. *In Charge:* Marilyn Wilkins, Head, Art & Music Div. *AV Staff:* 5 prof, 2 cl. *Film Sel:* chief film librarian's decision.
Free-Loan Film Serv *Eligibility:* indiv with library cards. *Restrictions:* for indiv & inst only in city. May not borrow by mail. *Loan Period:* 21 days. *Total Yr Film Loan:* 3429.
Film Rental Serv *Restrictions:* only in state. Cannot transmit electronically. *Rental Rate:* 50¢. *Rental Period:* 1 day.
Film Collection 1000t/p. *Pubns:* catalog, as needed; suppl, no set policy.
Other Film Serv Obtain film from coop loan system (La. State Library). Permanent viewing facility available to community. *Equipment:* lend 8mm reel projector (1), projection tables & stands, projection screens.
Video Serv *Est:* 1973. *In Charge;* Ann E. Gaumeyer. *Video Staff:* 1 f-t, 2 tech. *Video Use:* documentation of community/school events, to increase community's library use, in-service training, as art form. Video serv available by appointment. Produce video tapes. Have production studio/space.
Video Equipment/Facilities *In-House Use Only:* portapak (1), b&w, Sony; recording deck (1), b&w, Javelin; editing deck (1), b&w Sony; studio camera (1), b&w, JVC; monitor (3), b&w, Sony; additional camera lenses (1); microphones (2); tripods (1); audio tape recorders (1). Have portable viewing installation. *Equipment Loan Period:* no set policy. Provide training in use of equipment to library personnel. Have tape duplication serv.
Video Tape Loan/Rental/Sale Serv *Serv Provided:* free loan, swap with other inst. *Loan Eligibility:* staff & students, educational inst, civic groups, religious groups, indiv with library cards. *Restrictions:* none. May borrow by mail. *Total Yr Tape Loan:* 4.
Video Collection Maintained by own production, exchange/swap. Use/play ½″ reel to reel, ¾″ cassette. *Sources:* community productions, exchange. *Tape Sel:* preview, faculty/staff recommendations. Tapes organized by subject. *Collection, B&W:* ½″ reel, 10t; ¾″ cassette, 2t.

P- NEW ORLEANS VIDEO ACCESS CENTER (NOVAC), 1020 St Andrew St, 70130. *Tel:* (504) 524-8626. *Video Serv Est:* 1973. *In Charge:* Stevenson Palfi, Executive Dir. *Video Staff:* 10 f-t. *Video Use:* documentation of community/school events, community video access, in-service training, practical video/TV training courses, as art form, welfare servs. Video serv available on demand. Produce video tapes.
Video Equipment/Facilities *In-House Use Only:* playback deck (1), ½″ b&w, Sony 3600; editing deck (1), ½″ b&w, Sony 3650; studio camera (2), ½″ b&w, Sony. *For Loan:* portapak (2), ½″ b&w, Sony 3400; recording deck (2), ½″ b&w, Sony 3400; monitor (3), b&w, Sony, Concord; lighting (3); microphones (3); tripods (2); audio tpae recorders (2); microphone mixer (1), cables. Have portable viewing installation. *Equipment Loan Period:* 4 days. Provide training in use of equipment. Have tape duplication serv.
Video Tape Loan/Rental/Sale Serv *Serv Provided:* free loan, swap with other inst, sale. *Loan Eligibility:* staff & students, educational inst, civic groups, religious groups, indiv with library cards, prof groups, & others. *Restrictions:* for indiv & inst only in city. Cannot duplicate or air without permission. May not borrow by mail.
Video Collection Maintained by own production, exchange/swap. Use/play ½″ reel to reel. *Sources:* community productions. *Tape Sel:* preview, staff recommendations. Tapes organized by own system. *Collection, B&W:* ½″ reel, 75t. *Other Video Serv:* programming, reference serv, taping of other media, production workshops. *Pubns:* publish monthly newsletter.
Cable & CCTV Inform public about cable system serv & facilities.

C- UNIVERSITY OF NEW ORLEANS, AV Center, Lake Front, 70122. *Tel:* (504) 288-3161, ext 285. *Film Serv Est:* 1967. *In Charge:* Dr. Lane E. Bonham, Dir. *AV Staff:* 5 (3 prof, 2 cl, 3 tech). *Film Sel:* faculty/staff recommendations.

New Orleans (cont'd)

Free-Loan Film Serv *Restrictions:* only New Orleans area.

Film Collection 375t/p. *Pubns:* catalog, every 3 yrs; suppl, in yr catalog not published.

Other Film Serv Rent film from distributors, obtain film from coop loan system (Orleans Parish film library. Permanent viewing facility. *Member:* EFLA.

Video Serv *Est:* 1969. *In Charge:* Ralph Hogan, Video Engineer. *Video Staff:* 3 tech. *Video Use:* documentation of community/school events, in-service training. Video serv available by appointment. Produce video tapes. Have production studio/space & separate control room.

Video Equipment/Facilities *In-House Use Only:* recording deck (4), 1″ b&w/col, Ampex, Sony; studio camera (2), b&w, Telemation; monitor (12), 12″-24″ b&w/col, Telemation, Sony; SEG (1), Telemation; keyer (11), lighting; microphones; audio tape recorders (1), videocassettes (2). Have permanent viewing installation. Provide training in use of equipment to students. Have tape duplication serv.

Video Tape Loan/Rental/Sale Serv *Serv Provided:* free loan. *Loan Eligibility:* staff, students enrolled in inst. Cannot air without permission.

Video Collection Maintained by own production. Use/play 1″ reel to reel, ¾″ cassette. *Sources:* own production. *Special Collections:* in-house training tapes, classroom instruction. Tapes organized by alpha-numeric. *Collection, Color:* ¾″ cassette, 20t/c. *Collection, Color:* ¾″ cassette, 20t/c. *Collection, B&W:* 1″ reel, 150t/c. *Other Video Serv:* reference serv.

Cable & CCTV Have CCTV in inst, with 10 monitors. *Programming Sources:* tapes produced professionally.

C- XAVIER UNIVERSITY LIBRARY, Palmetto & Pine Sts, 70125. *Tel:* (504) 486-7411, ext 320. *Film Serv Est:* 1968. *In Charge:* Bryant, S.B.S., Asst Librarian—Media Specialist. *AV Staff:* 2 prof. *Film Sel:* committee preview, faculty/staff recommendations.

Free-Loan Film Serv *Eligibility:* staff & students, educational inst, civic groups, religious groups. *Restrictions:* for indiv, interlibrary loan; for inst, only in city. Cannot use for fund-raising, transmit electronically. Available to researchers/scholars for on-site viewing. May borrow by mail. *Loan Period:* 3 days. *Total Yr Film Loan:* 15. Produce slides, tapes, transparencies.

Film Collection 105t/p. Approx 1t acquired annually. *Noncirc:* 16mm, 90t/p; 8mm reel, 15t/p. *Pubns:* film list every 6 months.

Other Film Serv Obtain film from coop loan system (Orleans Parish Public School, Library), film fairs/festivals. Permanent viewing facility. *Equipment:* lend 16mm sound projector (2), 8mm cartridge projector (1), projection tables & stands (2), projection screens (2).

Other Media Collections *Audio:* disc, 33⅓ rpm, 3390t/4872c; tape, cassette, 626t/c; tape, cartridge, 43t/c; tape, reel, 198t/c. *Filmstrips:* sound, 421t/c; silent, 350t/c; sound sets, 25t/c; silent sets, 20t/c. *Slides:* single, 11t/c; sets, 33t/c.

Budget & Expenditures Total library budget $35,000 (FY 8/1/74-8/1/75). Total FY film budget $1000. *Member:* ALA, Dominican College, Loyola University.

Video Serv *Est:* 1968. *Video Staff:* 2 f-t. *Video Use:* to increase community's library use, classroom instruction. Video serv available on demand.

Video Equipment/Facilities *In-House Use Only:* recording deck (1), Sony; playback deck (1), Sony; monitor (1), Zenith; audio tape recorders (1). Have portable viewing installation. *Equipment Loan Period:* no set policy. Provide training in use of equipment to students.

Video Tape Loan/Rental/Sale Serv *Serv Provided:* free loan, swap with other inst. *Loan Eligibility:* staff & students, educational inst, divic groups, religious groups. *Restrictions:* for indiv, interlibrary loan; for inst, only in city. Cannot use for fund-raising, duplicate, air without permission. May borrow by mail. *Loan Period:* 5 days.

Video Collection Maintained by purchase. Use/play ¾″ cassette. *Sources:* university depts. *Member:* Loyola Univ, Dominican College. *Tape Sel:* preview, faculty/staff recommendations, published reviews. *Special Collections:* films in video format. Tapes organized by subject. *Collection, Color:* ¾″ cassette, 13t/c.

Maine

Augusta

P- MAINE STATE LIBRARY, Cultural Bldg, 04330. *Tel:* (207) 289-3561. *Member:* North County Library Film Coop.

C- UNIVERSITY OF MAINE, 04330. *Tel:* (207) 622-7131, ext 201, 202. *Film Serv Est:* 1965. *In Charge:* Bruce Bierce, Dir AV Serv. *AV Staff:* 2 (1 prof, 1 tech). *Film Sel:* faculty/staff recommendations, chief film librarian's decision.

Free-Loan Film Serv *Eligibility:* staff & students, educational inst, civic & religious groups. *Restrictions:* for indiv & inst, only in state. Cannot use for fund-raising. Available to researchers/scholars for on-site viewing. May borrow by mail. *Loan Period:* 1-7 days. Produce films. Produce slides, transparencies.

Film Collection 252t/p. *Circ:* 16mm, 50t/p; S8mm cartridge, 202t/p.

Other Film Serv Rent film from distributors for patrons, obtain film from coop loan system (University of Maine), obtain film from other libraries, film reference serv. Permanent viewing facility available for rent to community. *Equipment:* lend S8mm camera, 8mm cartridge projector, 8mm reel projector, S8mm cartridge projector, S8mm reel projector, projection tables & stands, projection screens.

Other Media Collections *Audio:* disc, 33⅓ rpm, 1115t/c; tape, cassette, 705t/c; tape, cartridge, 2t/c; tape, reel, 1248t/c. *Filmstrips:* sound, 78t/c; silent, 145t/c. *Slides:* single, 3846t/c; sets, 38t/c.

Budget & Expenditures Total library budget $18,335 (FY 7/1/74-7/1/75). No separate AV budget. *Member:* ALA, Maine Library Assn, NE College Librarians, Assn of College & Research Libraries.

Video Serv *Est:* 1972. *In Charge:* Bruce Bierce, Dir, AV Serv. *Video Staff:* 2 f-t. *Video Use:* documentation of community/school events, in-service training, practical video/TV training courses, as art form. Video serv available on demand. Produce video tapes. Have production studio/space & separate control room.

Video Equipment/Facilities *In-House Use Only:* playback deck (1), U-Matic col, Sony; editing deck (1), U-Matic col, Sony; keyer (1). *For Loan:* portapak (2), ½" b&w, Sony; recording deck (1), ½" b&w, Sony; playback deck (1), U-Matic col, Sony; monitor (2), b&w, Sony; SEG (4), Sony; additional camera lenses; microphones; tripods; audio tape recorders (35). Have permanent & portable viewing installations. *Equipment Loan Period:* no set policy. Provide training in use of equipment to faculty, students, community groups.

Video Tape Loan/Rental/Sale Serv *Serv Provided:* free loan, swap with other inst. *Loan Eligibility:* staff & students, educational inst, civic & religious groups, prof groups, such as State Police. *Restrictions:* for indiv & inst, only in Kennebec County. Cannot use for fund-raising. May borrow by mail. *Loan Period:* varies.

Video Collection Maintained by purchase, own production, exchange/swap. Use/play ½" reel to reel, ¾" cassette. *Tape Sel:* preview, faculty/staff recommendations. Tapes organized by subject. *Collection, Color:* ¾" cassette, 105t. *Collection, B&W:* ½" reel, 23t. *Other Video Serv:* taping of other media, production workshops.

Cable & CCTV Produce programs for cablecasting. Have CCTV in inst, with 8 monitors. *Programming Sources:* tapes produced by inst, tapes produced professionally, tapes produced by community groups & indiv.

Orono

C- UNIVERSITY OF MAINE, Film Rental Library, 14 Shibles Hall, 04473. *Tel:* (207) 581-7541. *Film Serv Est:* 1925. *In Charge:* John Henderson, Manager. *AV Staff:* 2 (2 prof, 4

cl, 2 tech). *Film Sel:* faculty/staff recommendations, published reviews. *Holdings:* agriculture 20%, animated films 10%, black studies 1%, career education 3%, children's films 5%, consumer affairs 2%, dance 1%, engineering 1%, experimental films 3%, feature films 1%, fine arts 2%, fish & game 3%, industrial arts 5%, law 3%, medicine 1%, public health 3%, science 10%, social sciences 20%, teacher education 5%, women 1%.

Film Rental Serv *Eligibility:* no restrictions. *Restrictions:* only in NE region. Cannot use for fund-raising, transmit electronically. *Rental Period:* 2 days. *Total Yr Film Booking:* 14,200.

Film Collection 3500t/4000p. Approx 500t acquired annually. *Circ:* 16mm, 3480t/3980p. *Noncirc:* 16mm, 20t/p. *Pubns:* catalog, every 2 yrs; suppl, in yr catalog not published. Publish promotional materials.

Other Film Serv Rent film from distributors for patrons, obtain film from other libraries, film reference serv, film fairs/festivals, library film programs. Permanent viewing facility available.

Budget & Expenditures Total library budget $16,500 (FY 7/1/74-7/1/75). Total FY film budget $16,500. *Member:* CUFC, EFLA, Maine Educational Media Assn.

Portland

P- PORTLAND PUBLIC LIBRARY, 619 Congress St, 04101. *Tel:* (207) 773-4761. *Film Serv Est:* 1972. *In Charge:* Shirley Barry, Secretary. *AV Staff:* 1 (1 prof, 1 cl). *Film Sel:* committee preview. *Holdings:* children's films 100%.

Free-Loan Film Serv *Eligibility:* civic & religious groups. *Restrictions:* for inst, only in greater Portland. Cannot use for fund-raising, transmit electronically, borrow for classroom use. May not borrow by mail. *Loan Period:* 3 days. *Total Yr Film Loan:* 865.

Film Collection 9t/p. *Circ:* 16mm, 9t/p.

Other Film Serv Obtain film from coop loan system (Prime Regional Resource Center, N Country Libraries Film Coop), library film programs. *Equipment:* S8mm camera (1), 16mm sound projector (4), S8mm reel projector (1), projection screens (4).

Other Media Collections *Audio:* disc, 33⅓ rpm, 3746c; tape, cassette, 72c.

Budget & Expenditures Total library budget $639,434 (FY 1/1/74-1/1/75). *Member:* ALA, FLIC, Maine Library Assn.

Waterville

C- COLBY COLLEGE, Miller Library, 04901. *Tel:* (207) 873-1131, ext 209, 237. *Film Serv Est:* 1971. *In Charge:* D. Lea Girardin, AV Libn. *AV Staff:* 1 prof, 5 student workers. *Film Sel:* committee preview, faculty/staff recommendations, chief film librarian's decision. *Holdings:* experimental films 20%, feature films 80%.

Free-Loan Film Serv *Eligibility:* staff & students. *Restrictions:* cannot use for fund-raising, transmit electronically. Available to researchers/scholars for on-site viewing. May not borrow by mail.

Film Collection 18t/p. Approx 3t acquired annually.

Other Film Serv Rent film from distributors for patrons, obtain film from other libraries, film reference serv, film fairs/festivals. Permanent viewing facility available for rent to community. *Equipment:* lend S8mm camera (3), 16mm camera (2), 16mm sound projector (4), 8mm cartridge projector (1), 8mm reel projector (3), S8mm reel projector (4), projection tables & stands (2), projection screens (6).

Other Media Collections *Audio:* disc, 33⅓ rpm, 400c; tape, cassette, 200c; tape, reel, 30c. *Filmstrips:* sound, 4c; silent, 20c.

Waterville (cont'd)

Budget & Expenditures Total library budget $121,650. (FY 6/30/74-6/30/75). Total FY film budget $2500. *Member:* ALA, Me. Library Assn.

Video Serv *Est:* 1972. *Video Staff:* 1 f-t, 5 p-t. *Video Use:* documentation of community/school events, practical training of individual students. Video serv available on demand (with training). Produce video tapes. Have production studio/space.

Video Equipment/Facilities *In-House Use Only:* porta-pak (1), ½" b&w, Sony; recording deck (1), ½" col, Panasonic; studio camera (1), b&w, Diamond; SEG (1), Panasonic. *For Loan:* portapak (1), ½" b&w, Panasonic. Have video viewing installation. *Equipment Loan Period:* 1 day. Provide training in use of equipment to faculty & students.

Video Tape Loan/Rental/Sale Serv *Serv Provided:* free loan, swap with other inst. *Loan Eligibility:* staff & students, educational inst, civic groups, prof groups, such as Civil Liberties Union & others, such as special summer programs. *Restrictions:* for indiv, only in county; for inst, none (for tapes). May borrow by mail. *Loan Period:* 7 days.

Video Collection Maintain by purchase, own production. Use/play ½" reel to reel, ¾" cassette. *Sources:* commercial distributors, community productions. *Tape Sel:* preview, faculty/staff recommendations, catalogs. *Special Collections:* support certain subject areas. *Collection, Color:* ½" reel, 30t/c. *Collection, B&W:* ½" reel, 20t/c. *Other Video Serv:* taping of other media.

Maryland

Baltimore

C- COMMUNITY COLLEGE OF BALTIMORE, Bard Library, 2901 Liberty Heights Ave, 21215. *AV Staff:* 7 (4 prof, 2 cl, 1 tech).

Other Film Serv *Equipment:* 16mm sound projector (10), 8mm cartridge projector (10), 8mm reel projector (2), S8mm cartridge projector (5), S8mm reel projector (2), projection tables & stands (30), projection screens (100).

Other Media Collections *Audio:* disc, 33⅓ rpm, 2900t; disc, 45rpm, 25t; disc, 78rpm, 75t; tape, cassette, 200t; tape, reel, 26t. *Filmstrips:* silent, 5t. *Slides:* single, 910t.

Budget & Expenditures Total library budget $100,000 (FY 7/1/74-7/1/75). No separate AV budget. *Member:* AECT, ALA.

Video Serv *Video Use:* documentation of community/school events, in-service training, practical video/TV training courses, instructional program. Video serv available by appointment.

Video Equipment/Facilities *In-House Use Only:* portapak (2), ½″, b&w, Sony; recording deck (3), b&w/col; playback deck (3), b&w/col; editing deck (1), b&w/col; studio camera (4), b&w/col; monitor (30), b&w/col; SEG (1); additional camera lenses (1); lighting (2); microphones (10); tripods (3); audio tape recorders (30). Have permanent & portable viewing installations. *Equipment Loan Period:* no set policy. Provide training in use of equipment to faculty & students.

Video Collection Maintained by own production. Use/play ½″ reel to reel. Tapes organized by subject. *Collection, B&W:* ½″ reel, 50t/c. *Other Video Serv:* taping of other media.

Cable & CCTV Have CCTV in inst, with 25 monitors. *Programming Sources:* tapes produced by inst.

C- DUNDALK COMMUNITY COLLEGE, Learning Resources Center, 7200 Sollers Point Rd, 21222. *Tel:* (301) 282-6700, ext 310, 311, 312. *Film Serv Est:* 1971. *In Charge:* Tish Cavaleri, Media Resource Specialist. *AV Staff:* 2½ (1 prof, 1½ cl). *Film Sel:* committee preview, faculty/staff recommendations, chief film librarian's decision.

Free-Loan Film Serv *Eligibility:* staff & students, educational inst, & others, by special arrangement. *Restrictions:* for indiv & inst, only in Baltimore County. *Total Yr Film Loan:* 900.

Film Collection 196t/198p. Approx 75t acquired annually. *Circ:* 16mm, 148t/150p; S8mm cartridge, 48t/p.

Other Film Serv Rent film from distributors for instructors, obtain film from coop loan system (Baltimore County Community Colleges), obtain film from other libraries, film reference serv, film fairs/festivals, library film programs. Permanent viewing facility available. *Equipment:* lend to faculty only: 16mm sound projector (12), S8mm cartridge projector (5), S8mm reel projector (20), projection tables & stands (40), projection screens (100), slide & sound filmstrip projectors (9).

Other Media Collections *Audio:* disc, 33⅓ rpm, 411t; tape, cassette, 285t; tape, reel, 50t. *Filmstrips:* sound, 130t; silent, 29t; sound sets, 3t. *Slides:* sets, 50t.

Budget & Expenditures Total film budget $9000 (FY 7/1/74-7/1/75).

Video Serv *Est:* 1973. *In Charge:* Bill Harrison, Production Coord. *Video Staff:* 1 f-t, 1 tech. *Video Use:* documentation of community/school events, in-service training, practical video/TV training courses, playback only of professionally produced tapes. Video serv available on demand. Produce video tapes. Will have production studio/space.

Video Equipment/Facilities *In-House Use Only:* playback deck (7), ½″, ¾″ b&w/col, JVC; editing deck (1), ¾″, col, JVC; studio camera (3), b&w/col, Panasonic; monitor (6); SEG (1), Panasonic; additional camera lenses (2); lighting (1); microphones (6); audio tape recorders (1). *For Loan:* portapak (3), ½″, b&w, Sony, Sanyo; recording deck (6), ½″, ¾″, b&w/col, Sony, Panasonic. Have permanent & portable viewing installations.

Equipment Loan Period: no set policy. Provide training in use of equipment.

Video Tape Loan/Rental/Sale Serv *Serv Provided:* free loan, swap with other inst. *Loan Eligibility:* staff & students, educational inst, prof groups. May borrow by mail. *Loan Period:* 3 days. *Total Yr Tape Loan:* 90.

Video Collection Maintained by purchase, rental, own production, exchange/swap. Use/play ½″ reel to reel, ½″ cartridge, ¾″ cassette. *Sources:* commercial distributors, exchange. *Tape Sel:* preview, faculty/staff recommendations, published reviews, catalogs. *Special Collections:* in-house training tapes, films in video format. Tapes organized by LC classification. *Collection, Color:* ¾″ cassette, 40t. *Collection, B&W:* ¾″ cassette, 10t. *Other Video Serv:* taping of other media, production workshops.

Cable & CCTV Have CCTV in inst, with 10 monitors. *Programming Sources:* over-the-air commercial & public broadcasting, tapes produced by inst, tapes produced professionally.

A- FORT McHENRY NATIONAL MONUMENT & HISTORIC SHRINE, End of E Fort Ave, 21230. *Tel:* (301) 962-4290. *In Charge:* Paul E. Plamann, Historian.

Free-Loan Film Serv *Eligibility:* educational inst, civic & religious groups, prof groups. *Restrictions:* for indiv & inst, none. Available to researchers/scholars for on-site viewing. May borrow by mail. *Loan Period:* 5 days. *Total Yr Film Loan:* 12.

Film Collection 12t/20p. *Circ:* 16mm, 1t/3p. *Noncirc:* 16mm, 11t/17p.

Other Film Serv Permanent viewing facility available free to community.

Budget & Expenditures No separate budget.

C- LOYOLA-NOTRE DAME LIBRARY, 200 Winston Ave, 21212. *Tel:* (301) 532-8787. *Film Serv Est:* 1973. *In Charge:* Barry Pierce, AV Specialist. *AV Staff:* 3 (1 prof, 2 cl). *Film Sel:* committee preview, faculty/staff recommendations, chief film librarian's decision.

Free-Loan Film Serv *Eligibility:* staff. Available to researchers/scholars for on-site viewing. May not borrow by mail. *Loan Period:* 7 days. *Total Yr Film Loan:* 25.

Film Collection 42t/42p. Approx 6t acquired annually. *Circ:* 16mm, 42t/42p.

Other Film Serv Obtain film from other libraries, film reference serv. Permanent viewing facility. *Equipment:* 16mm sound projector (3), S8mm cartridge projector (1), S8mm reel projector (1), projection tables (2).

Other Media Collections *Audio:* disc, 33⅓ rpm, 1900t/2100c; tape, cassette, 70t/90c; tape, reel, 240t/240c. *Filmstrips:* silent, 215t/215c; sound sets, 5t/5c. *Slides:* single, 5300t/5300c; sets, 10t/10c.

Budget & Expenditures Total library budget $100,000 (FY 7/1/74-7/1/75).

Video Serv *Est:* 1973. *In Charge:* Barry Pierce, AV Specialist. *Video Staff:* 2 f-t, 3 p-t. *Video Use:* playback only of professionally produced tapes. Video serv available by appointment. Produce video tapes.

Video Equipment/Facilities *In-House Use Only:* recording deck (2), ½″, ¾″ U col, Panasonic 3130, JVC 6300; playback deck (4), ½″ EIAV col, Panasonic 3040; monitor (5), 25″, 12″ col, Magnavox IC5950, Panasonic CT25V; audio tape recorders (3). Have permanent viewing installation. Have tape duplication serv.

Video Tape Loan/Rental/Sale Serv *Serv Provided:* free loan. *Loan Eligibility:* staff. May not borrow by mail. *Loan Period:* 7 days. *Total Yr Tape Loan:* 15.

Video Collection Maintained by purchase, own production. Use/play ½″ reel to reel, ¾″ cassette. *Sources:* provided by instructor. *Tape Sel:* preview, faculty/staff recommendations. Tapes organized by subject. *Collection, Color:* ½″ reel, 8t/8c; ¾″

Baltimore (cont'd)
cassette, 2t/2c. *Collection, B&W:* ½″ reel, 9t/9c. *Other Video Serv:* reference serv. *Pubns:* catalog.

Cable & CCTV Have CCTV in inst, with 5 monitors and 6 receivers. *Programming Sources:* over-the-air commercial & public broadcasting, tapes produced professionally.

S- MARYLAND ACADEMY OF SCIENCES, 601 Light St, 21230. *Tel:* (301) 685-2370. *Video Serv Est:* 1976. *In Charge:* Theodore Manekin, Communications Specialist—Media. *Video Staff:* 2 f-t. *Video Use:* education, exhibitions. Video serv available by appointment. Produce video tapes. Have production studio/space.

Video Equipment/Facilities *In-House Use Only:* recording deck (1), ¾″, col, Sony 1800; playback deck (1), ¾″, col, Sony 1200; studio camera (1), col, Sony 1600; monitor (2), b&w/col, GBC 900, Conrac 21; video projector (1). Have permanent viewing installation. Have tape duplication serv.

Video Tape Loan/Rental/Sale Serv Not yet established.

Video Collection Maintained by own production, exchange/swap. Use/play ¾″ cassette. *Sources:* TV stations. *Tape Sel:* preview. *Special Collections:* in-house training tapes, education, exhibitions. Tapes organized by subject. *Collection, Color:* ¾″ cassette, 5t.

Cable & CCTV Will have CCTV in inst, with 5-10 monitors. *Programming Sources:* tapes produced by inst, tapes produced professionally.

College Park

C- UNIVERSITY OF MARYLAND, Undergraduate Library, 20742. *Tel:* (301) 454-4723. *Video Serv Est:* 1973. *In Charge:* Lynne E. Bradley, Acting Head of Nonprint Serv. *Video Staff:* 4 f-t, 14 p-t, 2 tech. *Video Use:* playback only of professionally & locally produced tapes. Video serv available on demand. Have control room.

Video Equipment/Facilities *In-House Use Only:* recording deck (2), ¾″, col; playback deck (18), ¾″, col, Sony 1000; modified U-matic playback units for "dial access system" use (8). Have viewing installation. Provide training in use of equipment to faculty & students.

Video Tape Loan/Rental/Sale Serv *Serv Provided:* free loan. *Loan Eligibility:* staff & students. *Restrictions:* cannot duplicate. May not borrow by mail. *Loan Period:* during library hours only.

Video Collection Maintained by purchase. Use/play ¾″ cassette. *Sources:* commercial distributors. *Tape Sel:* preview, faculty/staff recommendations, catalogs. *Special Collections:* in-house training tapes, video as art, films in video format. Tapes organized by LC classification. *Collection, Color:* ¾″ cassette, 900t/c. *Other Video Serv:* reference serv.

Cable & CCTV Have CCTV in inst, with 20 monitors. *Programming Sources:* tapes produced by inst.

Columbia

C- HOWARD COMMUNITY COLLEGE, Little Patuxent Pkwy, 21044. *Tel:* (301) 730-8000, ext 60. *Film Serv Est:* 1970. *In Charge:* Ruth Wales, Head Librarian. *Film Sel:* faculty/staff recommendations, published reviews.

Free-Loan Film Serv *Eligibility:* org members, staff, students enrolled in inst. *Restrictions:* for indiv, interlibrary loan, for inst, only in county. May not borrow by mail. *Loan Period:* 1 day. *Total Yr Film Loan:* 60.

Film Collection 80t/80p. Approx 10-15t acquired annually. *Circ:* 16mm, 80t. *Pubns:* catalog, as needed; suppl, no set policy.

Other Film Serv Rent film from distributors for patrons, obtain film from coop loan system, obtain film from other libraries. Permanent viewing facility.

Budget & Expenditures Total library budget $220,241 (FY 7/1/75-7/1/76). Total FY film budget $2500. *Member:* AECT, ALA.

Video Serv *Est:* 1970. *In Charge:* Quent Kardos, AV Coord. *Video Use:* instruction. Video serv available on demand. Produce video tapes. Have production studio/space & separate control room.

Video Equipment/Facilities *In-House Use Only:* recording deck (9), 1″ IVC, EIAJ #1, U-matic col, IVC 800a, Sony 8600, 1600, JVC 6100; playback deck (3), U-matic col, Sony 2000, JVC 5000; editing deck (1), EIAJ #1, U-matic b&w/col, Sony 3650, JVC 5000; studio camera (6), b&w, Panasonic 341-P, Sony 3200; monitor (4), b&w, Sony, Panasonic; SEG (2), Sony SEG 1,2; additional camera lenses (1); microphones (7); tripods (7); audio tape recorders (4); turntable (1); color camera (1). *For Loan:* portapak (2), EIAJ #1 b&w, Sony 3400; playback deck (5), U-matic col, Sony 1000. Have portable viewing installation. *Equipment Loan Period:* no set policy. Provide training in use of equipment to faculty. Have tape duplication serv.

Video Tape Loan/Rental/Sale Serv *Serv Provided:* free loan, swap with other inst. *Loan Eligibility:* org members, staff & students. *Restrictions:* for indiv, interlibrary loan; for inst, only in county. Cannot air without permission. May not borrow by mail. *Loan Period:* 1 day.

Video Collection Maintained by purchase, rental, own production. Use/play ½″ cartridge, ¾″ cassette. *Sources:* commercial distributors. *Tape Sel:* preview, faculty/staff recommendations, published reviews, catalogs. Tapes organized by Library of Congress system. *Other Video Serv:* programming, taping of other media.

Cable & CCTV *Programming Sources:* over-the-air commercial & public broadcasting, tapes produced by inst, tapes produced professionally.

Frederick

C- FREDERICK COMMUNITY COLLEGE, Learning Resource Center, Educational Media Dept, O'Possumtown Pike, 21701. *Tel:* (301) 662-0101, ext 218. *Film Serv Est:* 1969. *In Charge:* C. David Hamby, Asst Dir. *AV Staff:* 2 (1 prof, 1 tech). *Film Sel:* faculty/staff recommendations.

Film Collection 201t/p. *Circ:* 16mm, 1t/p; 8mm cartridge, 64t/p; S8mm cartridge, 136t/p.

Other Film Serv Obtain film from coop loan system (Frederick Board of Education), obtain film from other libraries. *Equipment:* lend S8mm camera (2), lend projection screens (8).

Other Media Collections *Audio:* disc, 33⅓ rpm, 479t/484c; tape, cassette, 641t/650c; tape, reel, 228t/c. *Filmstrips:* sound, 106t/109c; silent, 175t/180c; sound sets, 45t/47c; silent sets, 8t/c. *Slides:* sets, 76t/c.

Budget & Expenditures No separate budget. *Member:* AECT.

Video Serv *Est:* 1969. *In Charge:* C. David Hamby. *Video Staff:* 2 f-t, 3 p-t, 1 tech. *Video Use:* to increase community's library use, practical video/TV training courses, program production. Video serv available on demand. Produce video tapes. Have production studio/space.

Video Equipment/Facilities *In-House Use Only:* portapak (1), b&w, Sony; recording deck (5), b&w/col, Sony 1600, 3600, 3650; monitor (8), b&w/col, Sony, RCA, Sears; SEG (1), Sony; lighting (3); microphones (2); tripods (2). Have portable viewing installation. Provide training in use of equipment to faculty.

Video Tape Loan/Rental/Sale Serv *Serv Provided:* free loan. *Loan Eligibility:* staff & students, educational inst. *Restrictions:* may not borrow by mail.

Video Collection Maintained by own production. Use/play ½″ reel to reel, ¾″ cassette. *Sources:* community productions. *Tape Sel:* faculty/staff recommendations. Tapes organized by subject. *Collection, Color:* ¾″ cassette, 140t. *Collection, B&W:* ½″ reel, 30t.

Cable & CCTV Produce programs for cablecasting. *Programming Sources:* tapes produced by inst.

Hagerstown

S- WASHINGTON COUNTY MUSEUM OF FINE ARTS, Library, Box 423, 21740. *Tel:* (301) 739-5727. *Film Serv Est:*

1950. *In Charge:* Susan Friend, Research Asst. *AV Staff:* 2 (1 cl, 2 tech). *Film Sel:* staff recommendations, published reviews. *Holdings:* fine arts 100%.

Free-Loan Film Serv *Eligibility:* staff & students, educational inst, civic & religious groups, indiv with library cards, prof groups. *Restrictions:* for indiv & inst, none. Cannot use for fund-raising, transmit electronically. May borrow by mail. *Loan Period:* 14 days.

Film Collection 12t. *Circ:* 16mm, 12t. *Pubns:* catalog, every 2 yr; suppl, no set policy.

Budget & Expenditures Total library budget $250 (FY 7/1/74-7/1/75). No separate AV budget.

P- WESTERN MARYLAND PUBLIC LIBRARIES, 100 S Potomac St, 21740. *Tel:* (301) 739-3250, ext 43. *Film Serv Est:* 1970. *In Charge:* Lawrence K. Springer, Film Librarian. *AV Staff:* 1 tech. *Film Sel:* chief film librarian's decision.

Free-Loan Film Serv *Eligibility:* educational inst, civic & religious groups, & others. *Restrictions:* for indiv & inst, only in Washington, Allegany, & Garrett counties. Cannot transmit electronically. May borrow by mail. *Loan Period:* varies.

Film Collection 1060t/1067p. Approx 50t acquired annually. *Circ:* 16mm, 460t/467p; 8mm reel, 300t/p; S8mm reel, 300t/p. *Pubns:* catalog, annual; suppl, no set policy. Publish materials pertaining to collection.

Other Film Serv Obtain film from coop loan system (Enoch Pratt Free Library), library film programs. Permanent viewing facility available. *Equipment:* lend 16mm sound projector, 8mm reel projector, S8mm reel projector, projection screens.

Budget & Expenditures Total library budget $127,000 (FY 7/1/75-7/1/76). Total FY film budget $15,910.

Hyattsville

P- PRINCE GEORGE'S COUNTY MEMORIAL LIBRARY, AV Serv, 6532 Adelphi Rd, 20782. *Tel:* (301) 699-3500, ext 251, 252. *Film Serv Est:* 1946. *In Charge:* Kent A. Moore, Coord of AV Serv. *AV Staff:* 7 (1 prof, 3 cl, 3 tech). *Film Sel:* chief film librarian's decision. *Holdings:* experimental films 5%, feature films 15%.

Free-Loan Film Serv *Eligibility:* indiv with library cards. *Restrictions:* for indiv, only in state. Cannot use for fundraising, transmit electronically, borrow for classroom use. May not borrow by mail. *Loan Period:* 1 day. *Total Yr Film Loan:* 30,273.

Film Collection 1575t/1775p. Approx 150t acquired annually. *Circ:* 16mm, 1575t/1775p. *Pubns:* catalog, annual ($1); suppl, quarterly.

Other Film Serv Obtain film from other libraries, film reference serv, library film programs. Permanent viewing facility available free to community.

Other Media Collections *Audio:* disc, 33⅓ rpm, 17,253t/63,736c. *Filmstrips:* silent, 724t/c.

Budget & Expenditures Total library budget $591,897 (FY 7/1/74-7/1/75). Total FY film budget $43,000. *Member:* ALA, EFLA, Md. Library Assn.

Video Serv *Est:* 1967. *In Charge:* Mary A. Hall, Assistant Dir, Public Serv. *Video Use:* documentation of community/school events, in-service training. Video serv available on demand. Produce video tapes.

Video Equipment/Facilities *In-House Use Only:* portapak (1), b&w, Sony 3400; recording playback deck (2), b&w, Sony 2200, 3600; editing deck (1), b&w, Sony 3650; studio camera (2), b&w, Sony; monitor (2), b&w, Sony 192U; lighting (4); microphones (3); tripods (2).

Video Collection Maintained by own production. Use/play ½″ reel to reel. *Collection, B&W:* ½″ reel, 50t/c.

Largo

C- PRINCE GEORGE'S COMMUNITY COLLEGE, Learning Resources Center, 301 Largo Rd, 20870. *Tel:* (301) 336-6000, ext 457. *Film Serv Est:* 1966. *In Charge:* Charmaine Yochim, Head, Acquisition & Tech Serv. *AV Staff:* 1 (1

prof, 1 cl). *Film Sel:* committee preview, faculty/staff recommendations, chief film librarian's decision.

Free-Loan Film Serv *Eligibility:* staff & students. *Restrictions:* May not borrow by mail. *Total Yr Film Loan:* 7035.

Film Collection 375t/385p. Approx 50-75t acquired annually. *Noncirc:* 16mm, 375t/385p. *Pubns:* catalog, every 2 yr; suppl, in yr catalog not published.

Other Film Serv Rent film from distributors for patrons, obtain film from coop loan system, obtain film from other libraries, film reference serv, library film programs. Permanent viewing facility available.

Other Media Collections *Audio:* disc, 33⅓ rpm, 3800t/4000c; tape, cassette, 800t/1200c. *Filmstrips:* 1000t/1250c. *Slides:* single, 15,500t; sets, 245t.

Budget & Expenditures Total library budget $85,000 (FY 7/1/74-7/1/75). Total FY AV budget $30,700. *Member:* AECT, ALA, EFLA, Md. Library Assn.

Video Serv *Est:* 1972. *In Charge:* Alan Mickelson, Media Specialist. *Video Staff:* 2 f-t, 5 p-t, 2 tech. *Video Use:* in-service training, practical video/TV training courses, playback of professionally produced tapes, classroom use. Video serv available on demand. Produce video tapes. Have production studio/space & separate control room.

Video Equipment/Facilities *In-House Use Only:* portapak (4), ½″, b&w, Sony; recording deck (4), ¾″, col, Sony 1200, 1600; playback deck (23), ¾″, col, Sony; studio camera (5), b&w/col, Panasonic; monitor (10), b&w/col; SEG (1), Panasonic; lighting; microphones (9); tripods (5); audio tape recorders (1). Have permanent viewing installation(s). Provide training in use of equipment to faculty & students.

Video Tape Loan/Rental/Sale Serv *Serv Provided:* free loan, swap with other inst. *Loan Eligibility:* staff & students. *Restrictions:* for indiv, only classroom use. Cannot duplicate. May not borrow by mail.

Video Collection Maintained by purchase, rental, own production, exchange/swap. Use/play ¾″ cassette. *Sources:* commercial distributors. *Tape Sel:* preview, faculty/staff recommendations, published reviews. *Special Collections:* films in video format, instructional materials. Tapes organized by LC classification. *Collection, Color:* ¾″ cassette, 370t/450c. *Other Video Serv:* reference serv, taping of other media, production workshops. *Pubns:* catalog.

Northeast

C- CECIL COMMUNITY COLLEGE, Learning Resources Center, RD 1, Box 57, 21901. *Tel:* (301) 287-6060. *Film Serv Est:* 1974. *In Charge:* Harry G. Jennings, Dir. *AV Staff:* 2. *Film Sel:* faculty/staff recommendations.

Film Collection 28t/p. *Circ:* 16mm, 28t/p.

Other Film Serv Rent film from distributors for patrons, obtain film from coop loan system, obtain film from other libraries. Permanent viewing facility available. *Equipment:* lend 16mm sound projector, 8mm reel projector, S8mm cartridge projector, projection tables & stands, projection screens.

Other Media Collections *Audio:* disc, 33⅓ rpm, 350c; tape, cassette, 2000c. *Filmstrips:* sound sets, 32c. *Slides:* single, 800c.

Budget & Expenditures Total library budget $60,000 (FY 7/1/74-7/1/75). Total FY film budget $200. *Member:* AECT.

Video Serv *Est:* 1974. *In Charge:* Harry G. Jennings, Dir of Learning Resources. *Video Staff:* 2 f-t, 4 p-t. *Video Use:* documentation of community/school events, community video access, in-service training, practical video/TV training courses, playback only of professionally produced tapes, as art form, instruction. Video serv available on demand. Produce video tapes.

Video Equipment/Facilities *In-House Use Only:* playback deck (1), JVC; monitor (10), col, RCA. *For Loan:* portapak (2), ½″, b&w, Panasonic 3085; recording deck (1), ½″, b&w, Panasonic; additional camera lenses (2); lighting (1); microphones; tripods; audio tape recorders. Have permanent & portable viewing installations. *Equipment Loan Period:* no set policy. Provide training in use of equipment to faculty.

Video Tape Loan/Rental/Sale Serv *Serv Provided:* free loan, swap with other inst. *Loan Eligibility:* staff & students,

Northeast (cont'd)
educational inst, civic groups, indiv with library cards. *Restrictions:* for indiv, only in Cecil County; for inst, none. Cannot use for fund-raising, duplicate, air without permission. May borrow by mail. *Loan Period:* 7 days. *Total Yr Tape Loan:* 84.

Video Collection Maintained by purchase, rental, own production. Use/play ½" reel to reel, ¾" cassette. *Sources:* commercial distributors. *Tape Sel:* preview. Tapes organized by LC classification. *Collection, Color:* ¾" cassette, 53t. *Collection, B&W:* ½" reel, 42t/c. *Pubns:* catalog. Publish newsletter.

Cable & CCTV Have CCTV in inst, with 10 monitors. *Programming Sources:* over-the-air commercial & public broadcasting, tapes produced by inst, tapes produced professionally.

Oakland

P- RUTH ENLOW LIBRARY OF GARRETT COUNTY, 6 N Second St, 21550. *Tel:* (301) 334-3996. *Film Serv Est:* 1960. *AV Staff:* ⅛ (1 cl).

Free-Loan Film Serv *Eligibility:* educational inst, civic & religious groups, indiv with library cards, prof groups, such as County Health Dept. *Restrictions:* for indiv & inst, none. Cannot use for fund-raising. May not borrow by mail. *Loan Period:* 1-7 days. *Total Yr Film Loan:* 1714.

Film Collection 2t/p. Approx 1t acquired annually. *Circ:* 16mm, 2t/p.

Other Film Serv Obtain film from coop loan system (Enoch Pratt Free Library), obtain film from other libraries, library film programs. *Equipment:* lend 16mm sound projector (4), 8mm reel projector (5), projection screens (2), filmstrip & slide projectors (6).

Other Media Collections *Audio:* disc, 33⅓ rpm, 1000t/1126c; tape, cassette, 350t/c. *Filmstrips:* sound sets, 73c.

Budget & Expenditures Total library budget $23,000 (FY 7/1/74-7/1/75). Total FY film budget $700.

Rockville

P- MONTGOMERY COUNTY PUBLIC LIBRARIES, Suburban Washington Film Serv, 99 Maryland Ave, 20850. *Tel:* (301) 424-7227. *Film Serv Est:* 1953. *In Charge:* Martha Spencer, Film Librarian. *AV Staff:* 6 (1 prof, 5 cl). *Film Sel:* committee preview, chief film librarian's decision.

Free-Loan Film Serv *Eligibility:* educational inst, civic & religious groups, indiv with library cards, & others, such as nursing homes. *Restrictions:* for indiv, interlibrary loan; for inst, only in state & Alexandria, Arlington, & Fairfax counties, Va. Cannot use for fund-raising, transmit electronically, borrow for classroom use. Available to researchers/scholars for on-site viewing. May not borrow by mail. *Loan Period:* 1 day. *Total Yr Film Loan:* 30,550.

Film Collection 3300t/4300p. Approx 200t acquired annually. *Circ:* 16mm, 3300t/4300p. *Pubns:* catalog, annual; suppl, (50¢).

Other Film Serv Obtain film from other libraries, film reference serv, film fairs/festivals, library film programs. Permanent viewing facility available. *Equipment:* rent 16mm sound projector (12).

Other Media Collections *Audio:* disc, 33⅓ rpm, 42,630c.

Budget & Expenditures Total library budget $701,150 (FY 7/1/75-7/1/76). Total FY film budget $24,000. *Member:* AECT, AFI, ALA, EFLA, FLIC, Md. Library Assn, Washington Film Council.

Video Serv *Est:* 1954. *In Charge:* Martha Spencer, Film Librarian. *Video Staff:* 4 f-t, 3 p-t. *Video Use:* reference. Video serv available on demand. Produce video tapes. Have production studio/space & separate control room.

Video Equipment/Facilities Have portable viewing installation.

Video Collection Maintained by purchase. Use/play ¾" cassette. *Sources:* commercial distributors. *Tape Sel:* preview. *Special Collections:* reference.

St. Mary's City

C- ST. MARY'S COLLEGE OF MARYLAND, Library, 20686. *Tel:* (301) 994-1600, ext 305. *Film Serv Est:* 1970. *In Charge:* John Hayes, AV Librarian. *AV Staff:* 1 (1 prof). *Film Sel:* faculty/staff recommendations.

Free-Loan Film Serv *Eligibility:* staff & students, prof groups, such as local historical society. *Restrictions:* for indiv, only in St. Mary's County; for inst, only in St. Mary's County. Available to researchers/scholars for on-site viewing. May not borrow by mail. *Loan Period:* 1 day.

Film Collection 33t/33p. Approx 1t acquired annually. *Circ:* 16mm, 33t/33p; S8mm reel, 3t/3p. Permanent viewing facility available free to community. *Equipment:* lend S8mm camera (1), 16mm sound projector (12), S8mm reel projector (1), projection tables & stands (15), projection screens (4).

Other Media Collections *Audio:* disc, 33⅓ rpm, 1319t; tape, cassette, 257t; tape, reel, 56t. *Filmstrips:* sound, 415t. *Slide:* single, 4549t.

Budget & Expenditures Total library budget $122,640 (FY 7/1/74-7/1/75). Of total library budget, AV film rental 5%. No separate AV budget. *Member:* ALA, Md. Library Assn.

Video Serv *Est:* 1970. *In Charge:* John Hayes, AV Librarian. *Video Use:* in-service training, practical video/TV training courses, education. Video serv available by appointment. Produce video tapes. Have production studio/space & separate control room.

Video Equipment/Facilities *In-House Use Only:* recording deck (4), b&w, Sony AV3600, 3650, 3200; studio camera (4), mobile b&w, Sony AVC3200; monitor (4), b&w, Sony CVM 2211A, CVM 9200; SEG (2), Sony SEG 1; additional camera lenses (4); microphones (6); tripods (2). *For Loan:* portapak (2), R-to-R b&w, Sony 3400; lighting (4); audio tape recorders (1). Have permanent & portable viewing installations. *Equipment Loan Period:* 1 day. Provide training in use of equipment to faculty, students & staff.

Video Tape Loan/Rental/Sale Serv *Loan Eligibility:* staff & students, civic groups, religious groups, prof groups, such as local historical society. *Restrictions:* for indiv, only in St. Mary's County; for inst, only in St. Mary's County. May not borrow by mail.

Video Collection Maintained by rental. Use/play ½" reel. *Sources:* commercial distributors. *Tape Sel:* faculty/staff recommendations. *Special Collections:* video as art, instruction. Tapes organized by Lib of Congress number. *Other Video Serv:* production workshops.

Stevenson

C- VILLA JULIE COLLEGE, Library, Greenspring Valley Rd, 21153. *Tel:* (301) 486-7348, ext 35. *Film Serv Est:* 1971. *In Charge:* Helene Jeng, Head Librarian. *AV Staff:* (1 prof, 1 tech). *Film Sel:* staff recommendations. *Holdings:* psychology.

Free-Loan Film Serv *Eligibility:* staff & students. *Restrictions:* for indiv, none. Available to researchers/scholars for on-site viewing. May not borrow by mail. *Loan Period:* 1 day. *Total Yr Film Loan:* 1.

Film Collection 8t.

Other Film Serv Permanent viewing facility available for rent to community. *Equipment:* 16mm camera (3), 8mm cartridge projector (1), projection tables & stands (2), projection screens (1).

Video Serv *Est:* 1971. *Video Use:* documentation of school events, in-service training. Video serv available on demand. Produce video tapes. Have production studio/space.

Video Equipment/Facilities *In-House Use Only:* studio camera (1), b&w, Panasonic; monitor (1), b&w, Panasonic; microphones (1); tripods (1); audio tape recorders (1).

Video Collection Maintained by exchange/swap. Use/play ½" reel to reel. *Collection, B&W:* ½" reel, 2t.

Cable & CCTV Have CCTV in inst, with 1 monitor. *Programming Sources:* tapes produced by inst.

Massachusetts

Amherst

C- HAMPSHIRE COLLEGE, Harold F. Johnson Library Center, 01002. *Tel:* (413) 542-4700. *Video Serv Est:* 1970. *In Charge:* Richard Muller, Dir of Educational Technol. *Video Staff:* 10 f-t, 3 tech. *Video Use:* documentation of community/school events, to increase community's library use, community video access, in-service training, practical video/TV training courses, as art form. Video serv available by appointment. Produce video tapes. Have production studio/space & separate control room.

Video Equipment/Facilities *In-House Use Only:* recording deck (1), ½″ b&w, Sony 3600; playback deck (1), ½″ b&w, Sony 3650; editing deck (1), 1″ b&w, Sony EV310; studio camera (1), 1″ b&w, Sony EV320; monitor (1), 1″ b&w, Sony; SEG (1); lighting (2); microphones; tripods; audio tape recorders. *For Loan:* portapak (4), ½″ b&w, Sony 3400; recording deck (2), ½″ b&w, Sony 3600; SEG (2); additional camera lenses (3); Panasonic; microphones; tripods; audio tape recorders. Have permanent & portable viewing installations. *Equipment Loan Period:* 2 days. Provide training in use of equipment to faculty & students. Have tape duplication serv.

Video Tape Loan/Rental/Sale Serv *Serv Provided:* free loan, swap with other inst, rental, sale. *Loan/Rental Eligibility:* staff & students, educational inst. *Restrictions:* none. Cannot use for fund-raising, duplicate, air without permission. May not borrow by mail.

Video Collection Maintained by purchase, rental, own production, exchange/swap. Use/play ½″, 1″ reel to reel, ¾″ cassette. *Sources:* community productions, exchange (local Five-College groups). *Tape Sel:* preview, faculty/staff recommendations, catalogs. *Special Collections:* in-house training tapes, video as art, films in video format. Tapes organized by title. *Collection, B&W:* ½″ reel, 30t; 1″ reel, 50t; ¾″ cassette, 5t. *Other Video Serv:* programming, reference serv, taping of other media, production workshops. *Pubns:* publish materials on video.

Cable & CCTV Receive serv of cable TV system. Produce programs for cablecasting. Inform public about cable system serv & facilities. Serve as production facility for others. Run cable programs for special audiences. Have advisory/administrative role in cable system operation. Some students/faculty involved with local Cable Advisory Committee. Have CCTV in inst, with 80 monitors. *Programming Sources:* over-the-air commercial & public broadcasting, tapes produced by inst, tapes produced professionally, tapes produced by community groups & indiv.

Auburn

P- AUBURN PUBLIC LIBRARY, 369 Southbridge St, 01501. *Tel:* (617) 832-2081. *Film Serv Est:* 1971. *In Charge:* Virginia Powers. *AV Staff:* 1. *Film Sel:* chief film librarian's decision.

Free-Loan Film Serv *Eligibility:* civic groups, religious groups, indiv with library cards. *Restrictions:* for indiv, only in state. Cannot use for fund-raising. Available to researchers/scholars for on-site viewing. *Loan Period:* 7 days.

Film Collection Approx 10-15t acquired annually. *Circ:* 8mm reel, 110t/p. *Noncirc:* 16mm, 1t/p. *Pubns:* catalog, as needed.

Other Film Serv Obtain film from coop loan system. *Equipment:* lend 16mm sound projector (1), 8mm reel projector (1), S8mm reel projector (1).

Other Media Collections *Audio:* disc, 33⅓ rpm, 1800t/100c; tape, cassette, 40t/c. *Filmstrips:* sound sets, 50t/c.

Budget & Expenditures Total library budget $20,000 (FY 7/1/74-7/1/75). Total FY film budget $100. *Member:* Central Mass. Regional Library System.

Video Serv *Est:* 1974. *In Charge:* Ruth Morin. *Video Staff:* 1 p-t. *Video Use:* documentation of community/school events, to increase community's library use, community video access, in-service training. Video serv available by appointment. Produce video tapes. Have production studio/space.

Video Equipment/Facilities *In-House Use Only:* recording deck (1), ½″ b&w, Sony 3600; editing deck (1), b&w, Sony 3650; monitor (1), 1″ col. *For Loan:* portapak (1), ½″ b&w/col, Sony 3400/8400; monitor (1), 8″, b&w; additional camera lenses (1); lighting (1); microphones (3); tripods (2); audio tape recorders (1). Have portable viewing installation. *Equipment Loan Period:* no set policy. Provide training in use of equipment to faculty & students. Have tape duplication serv.

Video Tape Loan/Rental/Sale Serv *Serv Provided:* free loan, swap with other inst. *Loan Eligibility:* civic groups, religious groups, indiv with library cards. *Restrictions:* for indiv, only in city; for inst, only in city. Cannot use for fund-raising. May borrow by mail.

Video Collection Maintained by own production, exchange/swap. Use/play ½″ reel to reel, ¾″ cassette. *Sources:* community productions, exchange. *Collection:* ½″ reel; ¾″ cassette. *Other Video Serv:* programming.

Cable & CCTV Produce programs for cablecasting. Serve as production facility for others.

Boston

P- BOSTON PUBLIC LIBRARY, AV Center, Copley Square, 02117. *Tel:* (617) 536-5400, ext 209. *Film Serv Est:* 1947. *In Charge:* Euclid J. Peltier, Coord of AV Serv. *AV Staff:* 15 (4 prof, 6 cl, 5 tech). *Film Sel:* committee preview, staff recommendations.

Free-Loan Film Serv *Eligibility:* educational inst (except classrooms), civic groups, religious groups, prof groups. *Restrictions:* for inst, free-loan through interlibrary loan, only in city and eastern part of state. Cannot use for fund-raising, transmit electronically, borrow for classroom use. Available to researchers/scholars for on-site viewing. May borrow by mail. *Loan Period:* 3 days.

Film Collection 3600/5500p. Approx 400t acquired annually. *Circ:* 16mm, 3600t/5000p; S8mm cartridge, 300t/400p. *Noncirc:* 16mm, 300t. *Pubns:* catalog, every 4 yrs ($7.50); suppl, ($1); approx quarterly. Publish materials pertaining to collection. Publish special subject lists, program lists.

Other Film Serv Film reference serv, film fairs/festivals, library film programs. Permanent viewing facility available to community. *Equipment:* lend to other libraries only S8mm camera (1), 16mm camera (1), 16mm sound projector (15), 8mm reel projector (1), S8mm cartridge projector (6), S8mm reel projector (1), projection tables & stands (12), projection screens (15).

Other Media Collections *Audio:* disc, 33⅓ rpm, 196,787c; cassette, 14,352c. *Filmstrips:* sound sets, 577c. *Slides:* single 14,352c.

Budget & Expenditures No separate budget. *Member:* ALA, EFLA, FLIC, MLA, NELA (New England Library Assn).

Video Serv *Est:* 1973. *Video Staff:* 4 f-t, 3 tech. *Video Use:* in-service training. Video serv available by appointment. Produce video tapes. Have production studio/space.

Video Equipment/Facilities *In-House Use Only:* portapak (1), ½″ b&w, Sony; recording deck (2), ½″ b&w, Sony; playback deck (2), ½″ b&w, Sony; studio camera (1), ½″ b&w, Sony; microphones (3); tripods (2); audio tape recorders (6). Have portable viewing installation. *Equipment Loan Period:* 7 days. Provide training in use of equipment to staff & public librarian.

Video Tape Loan/Rental/Sale Serv Loan policy anticipated in future. *Loan Eligibility:* org members, staff, prof groups, such as librarians. *Restrictions:* public libraries in regional system only.

Video Collection Maintained by own production. Use/play ½″ reel to reel, ¾″ cassette. *Sources:* commercial distributors. *Tape Sel:* faculty/staff recommendations, catalogs. *Special*

Boston (cont'd)
Collections: in-house training tapes. *Collection, B&W:* ½″ reel, 30t; ¾″ cassette, 30t.
    Cable & CCTV Will receive serv of cable TV system.

S- MASS. DEPT OF EDUCATION, Bureau of Library Ext, 648 Beacon St, 02215. *Tel:* (617) 536-4030, ext 39, 267-9400, ext 9. *In Charge:* Mary Litterest. *AV Staff:* 4 (3 prof, 1 tech). *Film Sel:* award winning films. *Holdings:* children's films, library science and technol (promotional).
    Free-Loan Film Serv *Eligibility:* staff & students, educational inst, civic groups, prof groups, such as library organizations. *Restrictions:* for indiv, only in state; for inst, only in state. Available to researchers/scholars for on-site viewing. May borrow by mail. *Loan Period:* 2 weeks. *Total Yr Film Loan:* approx 10.
    Film Collection Partially cataloged: 19t/24p approx. *Pubns:* publish newsletter, acquisitions lists.
    Other Film Serv Permanent viewing facility. *Equipment:* lend 16mm sound projector (2). *Member:* AECT, AFI, ALA, CUFC, EFLA, FLIC, MEMA, NEEMA.
    Video Serv *Est:* 1975. *In Charge:* John LeBaron, Education Specialist. *Video Staff:* 4 f-t, 2 tech. *Video Use:* documentation of community/school events, to increase community's library use, community video access, in-service training, practical video/TV training courses, to promote interlibrary cooperation. Video serv available on demand. Produce video tapes. Have production studio/space & separate control room.
    Video Equipment/Facilities *In-House Use Only:* recording deck (3), ½″ & ¾″ col, Panasonic 3130, JVC; playback deck (3), ½″ & ¾″ col, Panasonic 3130, JVC; editing deck (2), ½″ col, Panasonic 3130; studio camera Panasonic, Concord; monitor (6), b&w/col; SEG (1); lighting (3); microphones (6); tripods (6). *For Loan:* portapak (4), ½″ b&w, Panasonic WV3085; monitor (6), b&w/col; microphones (6); tripods (6). Have portable viewing installation. *Equipment Loan Period:* 1 month. Provide training in use of equipment to faculty & students, librarians, & school media specialists. Have tape duplication serv. Patrons supply own tape.
    Video Tape Loan/Rental/Sale Serv *Serv Provided:* free loan planned, swap with other inst. *Loan Eligibility:* educational inst. *Restrictions:* for inst, only in state. Cannot air without permission, cannot be used for commercial purposes. May not borrow by mail.
    Video Collection In planning stages: own production, exchange/swap. Use/play ½″ reel to reel, ¾″ cassette. *Sources:* commercial distributors, community productions, exchange (plan state clearinghouse for locally produced tapes). *Tape Sel:* to be determined. *Special Collections:* local tapes, unrestricted topics. *Other Video Serv:* programming, production workshops, curriculum development. *Pubns:* publish materials on video. Publish bibliographies & occasional papers.

A- MUSEUM OF FINE ARTS, Boston, 465 Huntington Ave, 02115. *Tel:* (617) 267-9300, ext 305. *In Charge:* Deac Rossell, Museum Film Coord. *AV Staff:* 4 (4 prof, 1 cl, 2 tech). *Film Sel:* chief film librarian's decision. *Holdings:* fine arts 90%.
    Film Collection 50p. Approx 12t acquired annually. *Noncirc:* 16mm, 50t/p. *Pubns:* publish materials pertaining to collection. Publish film notes for all exhibition programs.
    Other Film Serv Rent film from distributors for patrons, obtain film from other libraries, film reference serv, film fairs/festivals, major historical & contemporary retrospectives and year-round exhibition program complementing the Museum's contemporary art program. Permanent viewing facility.
    Other Media Collections *Slides:* single 11,000t.
    Budget & Expenditures (FY 7/1/74-7/1/75). No separate budget. *Member:* Assn of Specialized Film Exhibitors.

Bridgewater

C- BRIDGEWATER STATE COLLEGE, 02324. *Tel:* (617) 697-8321, ext 311, 312. *Film Serv Est:* 1952. *In Charge:* Dr. Henry Rosen, Chairman, Instruc Media Dept. *AV Staff:* 6

(6 prof, 2 cl, 2 tech). *Holdings:* animated films 5%, career education 10%, children's films 40%, consumer affairs 5%, fine arts 5%, industrial arts 5%, science 10%, social sciences 5%, teacher education 10%.
    Free-Loan Film Serv *Eligibility:* staff & students, educational inst. *Restrictions:* for indiv, only in state; for inst, only in state. Available to researchers/scholars for on-site viewing. May not borrow by mail. *Loan Period:* 5 days.
    Film Collection 1200t. *Circ:* 16mm, 800t; 8mm reel, 50t; 8mm cartridge, 50t; S8mm reel, 150t; S8mm cartridge, 50t. *Noncirc:* 16mm, 100t. *Pubns:* catalog, every 2 yrs (free); suppl, no set policy.
    Other Film Serv Permanent viewing facility.
    Other Media Collections *Audio:* disc, 33⅓ rpm, 3000t; disc, 78rpm, 250t; tape, cassette, 1000t; reel, 3000t. *Filmstrips:* sound, 1500t; silent, 4500t; sound sets, 250t; silent sets, 255t. *Slides:* single, 10,000t; sets, 450t.
    Budget & Expenditures Total library budget $10,000 (FY 7/1/74-7/1/75). Total FY film budget $2500. No separate AV budget. *Member:* AECT, EFLA, Mass. Film Coop.
    Video Serv *Est:* 1965. *Video Staff:* 6 f-t, 8 p-t, 2 tech. *Video Use:* documentation of community/school events, in-service training, practical video/TV training courses. Video serv available on demand. Produce video tapes. Have production studio/space.
    Video Equipment/Facilities *In-House Use Only:* portapak (2), b&w, Sony; recording deck (18), b&w/col, IVC, Sony; playback deck (18), b&w/col, IVC, Sony; studio camera (4), monitor (60), SEG (2); additional camera lenses (4); lighting (6); microphones (28); tripods (6); audio tape recorders (50). *For Loan:* monitor (60); lighting (6); tripods (6); audio tape recorders (50). Have permanent & portable viewing installations. *Equipment Loan Period:* 1 day. Provide training in use of equipment to faculty.
    Video Tape Loan/Rental/Sale Serv *Serv Provided:* swap with other inst. *Loan Eligibility:* staff & students, educational inst. *Restrictions:* for indiv, only in state; for inst, only in state. Cannot use for fund-raising. May not borrow by mail.
    Video Collection Maintained by purchase, rental, own production, exchange/swap. Use/play ½″, 1″ reel to reel, ¾″ cassette. *Sources:* commercial distributors, community productions, exchange. *Tape Sel:* preview, faculty/staff recommendations. *Special Collections:* in-house training tapes, films in video format. Tapes organized by subject. *Collection, Color:* ½″ reel, 125t; 1″ reel, 75t; ¾″ cassette, 10t. *Other Video Serv:* production workshops. *Pubns:* publish materials on video as part of media catalog.
    Cable & CCTV Have CCTV in inst, with 60 monitors. *Programming Sources:* tapes produced by inst, tapes produced professionally.

Cambridge

C- HARVARD GRADUATE SCHOOL OF EDUCATION, Monroe Gutman Library, 02138. *Tel:* (617) 495-4228. *Film Serv Est:* before 1968. *In Charge:* Joseph Blatt, Media Spec. *AV Staff:* 2 prof. *Film Sel:* committee preview, faculty/staff recommendations. *Holdings:* children's films 20%, experimental films 10%, social sciences 70%.
    Free-Loan Film Serv *Eligibility:* staff & students. *Restrictions:* cannot use for fund-raising. Available to researchers/scholars for on-site viewing. May not borrow by mail. *Loan Period:* 2 days.
    Film Collection 250t/265p. Approx 10t acquired annually. *Circ:* 16mm, 150t/160p. *Noncirc:* 16mm, 100t/105p. *Pubns:* catalog, as needed; suppl, no set policy.
    Other Film Serv Rent film from distributors for patrons, film reference serv. Permanent viewing facility.
    Video Serv *Est:* 1968. *Video Staff:* 2 f-t. *Video Use:* documentation of community/school events, in-service training, practical video/TV training courses, playback only of professionally produced tapes. Video serv available by arrangement only to staff and students of Harvard Graduate School of Education. Produce video tapes. Have production studio/space & separate control room.

Video Equipment/Facilities *In-House Use Only:* porta-pak (4); recording deck (4); editing deck (2); studio camera (3); monitor (10); SEG (1); additional camera lenses (3); lighting; microphones (20); tripods (5); audio tape recorders (15). Have permanent viewing installation. *Equipment Loan Period:* no set policy, but short-term loan only. Provide training in use of equipment to faculty & students.

Video Tape Loan/Rental/Sale Serv *Loan Eligibility:* staff & students only. *Restrictions:* cannot use for fund-raising, air without permission. May not borrow by mail.

Video Collection Maintained by own production. Use/play ½″ reel to reel, ¾″ cassette. *Other Video Serv:* reference serv.

Cable & CCTV Have CCTV in inst, with 30 monitors. *Programming Sources:* tapes produced by inst, tapes produced professionally.

S- URBAN PLANNING AID, Media Project-Video, 639 Massachusetts Ave, 02139. *Tel:* (617) 661-9220. *Video Serv Est:* 1971. *In Charge:* Bob Matorin, Dir, Video. *Video Use:* documentation of community/school events, community video access, practical video/TV training courses. Video serv available by appointment. Produce video tapes.

Video Equipment/Facilities *In-House Use Only:* porta-pak (1), ½″ b&w, Sony 3400; recording deck (1), ½″ b&w, Sony 3600; studio camera (1), ½″ b&w, Sony 3650; monitor (2), b&w, Sony; microphones; tripods; audio tape recorders. Have permanent & portable viewing installations. *Equipment Loan Period:* 1 day. Provide training in use of equipment to community groups with video needs. Have tape duplication serv.

Video Tape Loan/Rental/Sale Serv *Serv Provided:* free loan, swap with other inst. *Loan Eligibility:* low-income community groups, non-profit groups. *Restrictions:* for indiv & inst, none. Only for non-profit, educational purposes. May borrow by mail.

Video Collection Maintained by own production, exchange/swap. Use/play ½″ reel to reel. *Sources:* community productions. *Other Video Serv:* programming, production workshops. *Pubns:* catalog & cable book.

Cable & CCTV Receive serv of cable TV system. Produce programs for cablecasting. Inform public about cable system serv & facilities. Serve as production facility for others.

Chelmsford

P- ADAMS LIBRARY, Boston Rd, 01824. *Tel:* (617) 256-5521. *Film Serv Est:* 1971. *In Charge:* Linda Webb, Dept Head, Fine Arts & Music. *AV Staff:* 2. *Film Sel:* chief film librarian's decision. *Holdings:* animated films 10%, children's films 10%, comedy, sports, travel.

Free-Loan Film Serv *Eligibility:* indiv with library cards. *Restrictions:* for indiv, interlibrary loan; for inst, none. Cannot transmit electronically. Available to researchers/scholars for on-site viewing. May not borrow by mail. *Loan Period:* 7 days. *Total Yr Film Loan:* 1585.

Film Collection 300t/p. Approx 150t acquired annually. *Circ:* 8mm cartridge, 200t/p; S8mm cartridge, 100t/p. *Pubns:* publish materials pertaining to collection. Publish title listing.

Other Film Serv Obtain film from coop loan system (Mass.-Eastern Region Library System). *Equipment:* S8mm camera (1), 16mm sound projector (1), projection screen (1).

Other Media Collections *Audio:* disc, 33⅓ rpm, 4500t.

Budget & Expenditures Total film budget $1500 (FY 7/1/74-7/1/75). *Member:* Mass. Library Assn.

Video Serv *Est:* 1975. *In Charge:* Susan Schleigh, Assistant Dir. *Video Staff:* 1 p-t. *Video Use:* documentation of community/school events, to increase community's library use, community video access, entertainment & education. Video serv available on demand. Produce video tapes. Have production studio.

Video Equipment/Facilities *In-House Use Only:* porta-pak (1), ½″ b&w/col, Sony; recording deck (1), ¾″ col, Sony VO1800; playback deck (2), ½″ b&w, ¾″ col, Sony VP1200, Panasonic 3010; editing deck (1), ½″ b&w/col, Panasonic 3130;

monitor (3), 2 b&w/1 col, 2 Hitachi, 1 Sony Trinitron; additional camera lenses (3); microphones (3); tripods (1); audio tape recorders (1). Have permanent viewing installation.

Video Tape Loan/Rental/Sale Serv *Serv Provided:* swap with other inst.

Video Collection Maintained by own production, exchange/swap. Use/play ½″ reel to reel, ¾″ cassette. *Sources:* exchange (other schools/libraries by arrangement). *Collection, Color:* ¾″ cassette, 5t/c. *Collection, B&W:* ½″ reel, 6t/c; ¾″ cassette, 9t/c. *Pubns:* catalog, materials on video, titles list.

Framingham

P- FRAMINGHAM PUBLIC LIBRARY, 929 Worcester Rd, 01701. *Tel:* (617) 872-7432. *Video Serv Est:* 1974. *In Charge:* Lillian C. Giuliano, Assistant Dir. *Video Staff:* 8 p-t. *Video Use:* documentation of community/school events, to increase community's library use, community video access. Video serv available on demand. Produce video tapes. Have production studio/space.

Video Equipment/Facilities *In-House Use Only:* porta-pak (1), ½″ b&w, Sony 3600; recording deck (1), ½″ col, Panasonic NV3130; monitor (2), b&w, Panasonic 8″, Shibaden 23″; tripods (2); audio tape recorders (1), mixer. *For Loan:* portapak (1), ½″ b&w, Sony 3400; playback deck (1), ½″ b&w; monitor (2), b&w, Sony 194U; microphones (2). Have portable viewing installation. *Equipment Loan Period:* no set policy. Provide training in use of equipment to staff & community groups.

Video Tape Loan/Rental/Sale Serv *Serv Provided:* free loan, swap with other inst. *Loan Eligibility:* staff, civic groups, religious groups, prof groups, such as libraries and other groups in subregion. *Restrictions:* for indiv, none; for inst, only in city and subregion. Cannot air without permission. May borrow by mail. *Loan Period:* flexible.

Video Collection Maintained by own production, exchange/swap. Use/play ½″ reel to reel. *Sources:* community productions. *Collection, B&W:* ½″ reel, 20t. *Other Video Serv:* production workshops.

Cable & CCTV Exploring community cable TV system. *Member:* citizen's advisory committee.

Gardner

C- MOUNT WACHUSETT COMMUNITY COLLEGE, Green St, 01440. *Tel:* (617) 632-6600, ext 149. *Film Serv Est:* 1970. *In Charge:* Frank K. Hirons, Dir of Media. *AV Staff:* 6 (2 tech). *Film Sel:* faculty/staff recommendations. *Holdings:* career education 10%, consumer affairs 21%, fine arts 9%, science 70%, social sciences 10%.

Free-Loan Film Serv *Eligibility:* staff & students, civic groups, religious groups. *Restrictions:* available to researchers/scholars for on-site viewing. May not borrow by mail.

Film Collection 150t/p. *Circ:* 16mm, 150t/p.

Other Film Serv Rent film from distributors for patrons, film reference serv. Permanent viewing facility available to community. *Equipment:* lend S8mm camera (2), 16mm camera (1), 16mm sound projector (1), 8mm reel projector (1), S8mm cartridge projector (2), S8mm reel projector (2), projection tables & stands (2), projection screens (2).

Other Media Collections *Audio:* disc, 33⅓ rpm, 300t/c. *Filmstrips:* sound, 30t/c. *Member:* AECT.

Video Serv *Est:* 1970. *Video Staff:* 6 f-t, 2 tech. *Video Use:* documentation of community/school events, to increase community's library use, community video access, in-service training, practical video/TV training courses, playback only of professionally produced tapes, as art form. Video serv available on demand. Produce video tapes. Have production studio/space & separate control room.

Video Equipment/Facilities *In-House Use & For Loan:* portapak (5), ½″ 3 b&w/2 col, Panasonic; recording deck (8), ½″-1″ col, Panasonic 3130, IVC 700, 760, 820; editing deck (6), ½″-1″ b&w, Panasonic 3130; studio camera (6), b&w, IVC 760, 870, Panasonic CEI; SEG (3), keyer (2); lighting (3); microphones (15); tripods (3); audio tape recorders (16); color production

Gardner (cont'd)

studios (2), 1″. Have permanent & portable viewing installations. *Equipment Loan Period:* no set policy. Provide training in use of equipment. Have tape duplication serv.

Video Tape Loan/Rental/Sale Serv *Serv Provided:* free loan, swap with other inst. *Loan Eligibility:* staff & students, educational inst, prof groups, such as consortium. *Restrictions:* for indiv & inst, various campuses of our college, consortium. May not borrow by mail.

Video Collection Maintained by purchase, own production. Use/play 1″ reel to reel, ¾″ cassette. *Sources:* commercial distributors, community productions. *Member:* Community College. *Tape Sel:* preview, faculty/staff recommendations, catalogs. *Special Collections:* in-house training tapes, films in video format. Tapes organized by subject. *Collection, Color:* ½″ reel, 60t/c; 1″ reel, 40t/c; ¾″ cassette, 70t/c. *Collection, B&W:* 1″ reel, 80t/c.

Cable & CCTV Receive serv of cable TV system. Produce programs for cablecasting. Inform public about cable system serv & facilities. Run cable programs for special audiences. Have CCTV in inst, with 25 monitors. *Programming Sources:* over-the-air commercial & public broadcasting, tapes produced by inst, tapes produced professionally, tapes produced by community groups & indiv.

Haverhill

P- HAVERHILL PUBLIC LIBRARY, 99 Main St, 01830. *Tel:* (617) 373-1586, ext 9. *Video Serv Est:* 1973. *In Charge:* James L. Sheldon, Coord of Documentation. *Video Staff:* 2 f-t, 3 p-t. *Video Use:* documentation of community events, to increase community's library use, community video access, in-service training, playback only of professionally produced tapes, as art form. Video serv available on demand. Produce video tapes. Have production studio/space & separate control room.

Video Equipment/Facilities *In-House Use Only:* editing deck (1), ½″ col, Pan NV 3130; SEG (1); audio tape recorders (2). *For Loan:* portapak (2), ½″ b&w/col, Sony AV8400; recording deck (1), ½″ b&w, Sony AV3400; studio camera (1), b&w, Sony AVC 3120DX; monitor (8), 6 b&w, 2 col; lighting (8); microphones (6); tripods (4). Have permanent & portable viewing installations. *Equipment Loan Period:* no set policy. Provide training in use of equipment to students. Have tape duplication serv.

Video Tape Loan/Rental/Sale Serv *Serv Provided:* free loan, swap with other inst. *Loan Eligibility:* staff & students, educational inst, civic groups, religious groups, indiv with library cards, prof groups, such as Community Action, Spanish Center, hospital, & others, such as Rotary, realtors, Women's City Club. *Restrictions:* for indiv & inst, only in city. Equipment must be used for nonprofit purposes only. May borrow by mail. *Loan Period:* as needed. *Total Yr Tape Loan:* 55.

Video Collection Maintained by own production, exchange/swap. Use/play ½″ reel to reel. *Sources:* community productions, exchange. *Tape Sel:* faculty/staff recommendations, published reviews, catalogs. *Special Collections:* community serv & information. Tapes organized by title. *Collection, Color:* ½″ reel, 3t/1c. *Collection, B&W:* ½″ reel, 101t/1c. *Other Video Serv:* programming, production workshops. *Pubns:* publish bibliography of video/cable print materials, video/cable/libraries policy statements & information.

Cable & CCTV Receive serv of cable TV system. Produce programs for cablecasting. Inform public about cable system serv & facilities. Serve as production facility for others. Have advisory/administrative role in cable system operation. Member of cable advisory committee. Have CCTV in inst, with 3 monitors. *Programming Sources:* over-the-air commercial & public broadcasting, tapes produced by inst, tapes produced by community groups & indiv.

New Bedford

P- NEW BEDFORD FREE PUBLIC LIBRARY, Box C-902, 02741. *Tel:* (617) 999-6291. *Film Serv Est:* 1974. *In Charge:*

Peter S. Barney, AV Section Head. *Film Sel:* staff recommendations, chief film librarian's decision. *Holdings:* children's films 50%, feature films 30%, short subjects 20%.

Free-Loan Film Serv *Eligibility:* civic groups, religious groups, indiv with library cards, & others, such as our subregional libraries. *Restrictions:* for indiv, only in city; for inst, in our subregion.

Film Collection 200t/p. Approx 50t acquired annually. *Circ:* 16mm, 30t; 8mm reel, 150t; S8mm reel, 20t; S8mm cartridge, 21t; *Noncirc:* 16mm, 20t. *Pubns:* suppl, no set policy.

Other Film Serv Rent film from distributors for patrons, obtain film from coop loan system (Interlibrary loan from Boston Public Library), obtain film from other libraries, library film programs. *Equipment:* lend 16mm sound projector (1), projection screen (1).

Other Media Collections *Audio:* disc, 33⅓ rpm, 5000t; tape, cassette, 1500t.

Budget & Expenditures Total FY film budget $1300 (FY 7/1/74-7/1/75). *Member:* ALA, FLIC, Eastern Mass. Library Assn.

Video Serv *Est:* 1975. *Video Staff:* 1 p-t. *Video Use:* documentation of community/school events, practical video/TV training courses. Video serv available by appointment. Produce video tapes. Have production studio/space & separate control room.

Video Equipment/Facilities *In-House Use Only:* portapak (1), b&w, Panasonic; recording deck (1), b&w, Panasonic; playback deck (1), b&w, Panasonic; monitor (1), b&w, Panasonic; tripod (1). Have permanent viewing installation. *Equipment Loan Period:* no set policy. Provide training in use of equipment to students.

Video Collection Use/play ½″ reel to reel.

Newton

P- NEWTON FREE LIBRARY, 414 Centre St, 02158. *Tel:* (617) 523-0064. *Film Serv Est:* 1965. *In Charge:* Virginia A. Tashjian, Library Dir.

Free-Loan Film Serv Via Boston Public Library film collection. *Eligibility:* civic groups, religious groups, prof groups, such as Assn of Nurses. *Restrictions:* for inst, only in city. Cannot use for fund-raising, transmit electronically, borrow for classroom use.

Other Film Serv Obtain film from coop loan system (Boston Public Library), library film programs. Permanent viewing facility.

Budget & Expenditures No separate budget. *Member:* ALA, EFLA, Mass. Library Assn.

Northampton

P- FORBES LIBRARY, Media Center, 20 West St, 01060. *Tel:* (413) 584-8550. *Film Serv Est:* 1971. *In Charge:* Glenda L. Henerey, Media Librarian. *AV Staff:* 2 (1 prof, ½ cl, 1 tech). *Film Sel:* chief film librarian's decision.

Free-Loan Film Serv *Eligibility:* educational inst, civic groups, religious groups, prof groups, such as hospitals, nursing homes. *Restrictions:* for inst, only in city. Cannot use for fund-raising, transmit electronically, borrow for classroom use. Available to researchers/scholars for on-site viewing. May not borrow by mail. *Loan Period:* 3 days. *Total Yr Film Loan:* 1298.

Film Rental Serv *Eligibility:* no restrictions, educational org, civic groups, religious groups, nursing homes, hospitals. *Restrictions:* only in region (W Mass.). Cannot use for fund-raising, transmit electronically, no classroom use. *Rental Period:* 3 days. *Total Yr Film Booking:* 325.

Film Collection 308t/p. Approx 50t acquired annually. *Circ:* S8mm reel, 308t/p. *Pubns:* catalog, as needed (free); suppl, no set policy (free).

Other Film Serv Obtain film from coop loan system (Western Regional Public Library System, Five College Interlibrary Loan System), library film programs. Permanent viewing facility. *Equipment:* lend/rent 16mm sound projector (2), S8mm reel projector (6), projection screens, tape recorders, filmstrip projectors, slide projectors, overhead projectors.

Other Media Collections *Audio:* tape, cassette, 503t. *Filmstrips:* silent, 69t; sound sets, 118t. *Slides:* sets, 64t.

Budget & Expenditures Total library budget $46,871, excl salaries & operating budget (FY 7/1/74-7/1/75). Total FY film budget $2000. *Member:* AECT.

South Hadley

P- SOUTH HADLEY LIBRARY SYSTEM, Bardwell St, 01075. *Tel:* (413) 532-1241. *Video Serv Est:* 1972. *In Charge:* Constance Clancy, Dir. *Video Use:* documentation of community/school events, community video access, in-service training, practical video/TV training courses. Video serv available by appointment. Produce video tapes. Have production studio/space.

Video Equipment/Facilities *In-House Use Only:* portapak (1), ½″ b&w, Sony VO3800; recording deck (1), ¾″ col, Sony VO1800; editing deck (1), ½″ b&w, Sony 3650; studio camera (2), b&w, Sony AVC3210DX, Panasonic WV361P; monitor (2), 17″ col, Sony CKU, CVM; character generator (1); mounted quad monitor (1), Sony. *For Loan:* portapak (4), ½″ b&w, Sony AVC3400; recording deck (1), ½″ b&w, Sony AV3600; playback deck (1), ¾″ col, Sony VP1200; monitor (5), 9, 11″ b&w, Sony CYM; lighting (1); microphones (5); audio tape recorders (7), dolly (6). Have portable viewing installation. *Equipment Loan Period:* 1 day unless other arrangements approved. Provide training in use of equipment to adults in workshops; young adults in Camera Club. Have tape duplication serv.

Video Tape Loan/Rental/Sale Serv *Serv Provided:* free loan, swap with other inst. *Loan Eligibility:* org members, staff, students enrolled in inst, staff & students, educational inst, civic groups, religious groups, indiv with library cards & training, & others, such as anyone trained in library workshop. *Restrictions:* for indiv, & inst, none. May not borrow by mail. *Loan Period:* 7 days.

Video Collection Maintained by purchase, own production, exchange/swap. Use/play ½″ reel to reel, ½″ cartridge, ¾″ cassette. *Sources:* community productions, exchange (Western Regional Public Library System). *Tape Sel:* preview, published reviews. Tapes organized by Dewey Decimal. *Other Video Serv:* programming, production workshops.

Cable & CCTV Receive serv of cable TV system. Produce programs for cablecasting. Inform public about cable system serv & facilities. Serve as production facility for others. Run cable programs for special audiences. Have advisory/administrative role in cable system operation. Member of town Cable Committee.

Stoneham

P- STONEHAM PUBLIC LIBRARY, 431 Main St, 02180. *Tel:* (617) 438-1324. *Film Serv Est:* 1968. *In Charge:* Jean Palmer, Assistant Librarian. *AV Staff:* 1½ (1 prof, ½ cl). *Film Sel:* chief film librarian's decision, published reviews. *Holdings:* children's films 57%.

Free-Loan Film Serv *Eligibility:* civic groups, religious groups, indiv with library cards. *Restrictions:* for indiv, only in state; for inst, only in state. Cannot use for fund-raising, transmit electronically. Available to researchers/scholars for on-site viewing. May borrow by mail. *Loan Period:* 3 days. *Total Yr Film Loan:* 302.

Film Collection 24t/p. Approx 5t acquired annually. *Circ:* 16mm, 24t. *Pubns:* catalog, annual (free); suppl, no set policy (free).

Other Film Serv Rent film from distributors for patrons, obtain film from coop loan system (Mass. Dept of Education, Mass. Film Coop), obtain film from other libraries, film reference serv, library film programs. Permanent viewing facility available to community.

Other Media Collections *Audio:* disc, 33⅓ rpm, 1989t; tape, cassette, 169t. *Slides:* single, 105t.

Budget & Expenditures Total library budget $30,900 (FY 7/1/74-7/1/75). No separate AV budget. *Member:* ALA, Mass. Library Assn.

Waltham

S- JOHN F. KENNEDY LIBRARY, Presidential Archives, 380 Trapelo Rd, 02154. *Tel:* (617) 223-7250. *Film Serv Est:* 1963. *In Charge:* Allan B. Goodrich, AV Archivist. *AV Staff:* 3 (2½ prof). *Holdings:* spec collection on life and career of John F. Kennedy.

Film Rental Serv *Eligibility:* no restrictions. *Restrictions:* none. Cannot use for fund-raising, transmit electronically. *Rental Period:* 3 days or 1 week. Sell films.

Film Collection 3,000,000 feet.

Other Media Collections *Audio:* disc, 33⅓ rpm, 2000t; disc, 45rpm, 700t; disc, 78rpm, 20t; tape, cassette, 300t; tape, reel, 1500t.

Budget & Expenditures Total library budget $560,000 (FY 7/1/74-7/1/75). No separate AV budget.

Weymouth

P- TUFTS LIBRARY, 46 Broad St, 02190. *Tel:* (617) 337-1402. *In Charge:* Scott C. Phillips. *AV Staff:* 1. *Holdings:* children's films 90-95%.

Free-Loan Film Serv *Eligibility:* educational inst, civic groups, indiv with library cards. *Restrictions:* for indiv, only in city; for inst, only in city. 16mm films restricted to inst use only. May not borrow by mail. *Loan Period:* 1 day. 8mm films circulate for 1 week.

Film Collection 28t/p. Approx 2-3t acquired annually. *Circ:* 16mm, 28t/p; 8mm reel, 56t/p. *Pubns:* publish titles list of 16mm films for inst use; print titles list of 8mm films for indiv use.

Other Film Serv Obtain film from coop loan system (Mass. Library Film Coop), library film programs. Permanent viewing facility available for rent to community. *Equipment:* lend 16mm sound projector (4), 8mm reel projector (1), projection screens (2), filmstrip/slide projectors.

Other Media Collections *Audio:* disc, 33⅓ rpm, 2325t; tape, reel, 290t/c. *Filmstrips:* silent sets, 80t/c.

Budget & Expenditures No separate AV budget. *Member:* ALA, Mass. Library Assn.

Worcester

P- CENTRAL MASS. REGIONAL LIBRARY SYSTEM, Film Library, Salem Square, 01608. *Tel:* (617) 752-3751, ext 52. *Film Serv Est:* 1963. *In Charge:* James Izatt, AV Coord. *AV Staff:* 2 prof, 3 cl. *Film Sel:* committee preview, staff recommendations.

Free-Loan Film Serv *Eligibility:* educational inst, civic groups, religious groups, indiv with library cards. *Restrictions:* for indiv, interlibrary loan, only in Worcester County; for inst, only in Worcester County. Cannot use for fund-raising, transmit electronically. Available to researchers/scholars for on-site viewing. May borrow by mail. *Loan Period:* 1 day. *Total Yr Film Loan:* 16,708.

Film Collection 2000t/2250p. Approx 200-250t acquired annually. *Circ:* 16mm, 2000t/2250p; S8mm cartridge, 65t. *Pubns:* catalog, as needed ($3); suppl, in yr catalog not published. Publish materials pertaining to collection. Publish special subject film lists, such as human rights.

Other Film Serv Obtain film from coop loan system (Canadian Travel Film Library/Assn Sterling), obtain film from other libraries, film reference serv, film fairs/festivals, library film programs. Permanent viewing facility available free to community. *Equipment:* lend S8mm camera (1), 16mm sound projector (30), 8mm cartridge projector (2), 8mm reel projector (8), S8mm cartridge projector (6), S8mm reel projector (8), projection screens (10), 35mm slide projectors (9), 35mm filmstrip viewers (18), 35 mm filmstrip projectors (7).

Worcester (cont'd)

Other Media Collections   *Audio:* disc, 33⅓ rpm, 9560t/7339c; tape, 1338t. *Filmstrips:* sound, 26t. *Slides:* single, 342t.

Budget & Expenditures   No separate budget. *Member:* AFI, ALA, EFLA, FLIC, Mass. Library Assn, New England Library Assn.

Video Serv   *Est:* 1972. *In Charge:* David Lavaliee, Video Tech. *Tel:* (617) 752-3751, ext 34. *Video Staff:* 1 f-t, 1 tech. *Video Use:* documentation of community/school events, to increase community's library use, community video access, in-service training. Video serv available by appointment. Have production studio/space.

Video Equipment/Facilities   *In-House Use Only:* recording deck (2), ½" b&w, Sony AV3600; editing deck (1), ½" b&w, Sony AV3650; studio camera (2), ½" b&w, Sony AVC 3200; SEG (2), Sony SEG-1, SEG-2; additional camera lenses (2); lighting (4); microphones (3); audio tape recorders (10). *For Loan:* portapak (3), ½" b&w, Sony AV3400/AVC 3400; playback deck (5), ½" b&w, Panasonic NV3010; monitor (5) b&w, Sony; tripods (3). Have permanent viewing installation. *Equipment Loan Period:* 1 day. Weekly by spec arrangement. Provide training in use of equipment to librarians & representatives of community groups. Have tape duplication serv if customer provides blank tape.

Video Tape Loan/Rental/Sale Serv   *Serv Provided:* free loan, swap with other inst. *Loan Eligibility:* org members, staff, students enrolled in inst, staff & students, educational inst, civic groups, religious groups, indiv with library cards who represent nonprofit making, civic groups & have received our video training. *Restrictions:* for indiv, only in Worcester County; for inst, only in Worcester County. Cannot air without permission. May borrow by mail. *Loan Period:* 1 day. 2-3 weeks for interlibrary loan by arrangement.

Video Collection   Maintained by own production, exchange/swap. Use/play ½" reel to reel, ½" cartridge. *Sources:* community productions, exchange. *Tape Sel:* not yet involved in large-scale purchase of video-cartridges or tapes. Plan ½" cartridge purchasing in future. Cataloging in process. *Other Video Serv:* programming, reference serv, production workshops. *Pubns:* catalog.

Cable & CCTV   Produce programs for cablecasting. Inform public about cable system serv & facilities. Serve as production facility for others. Run cable programs for special audiences.

Michigan

Adrian

P- ADRIAN PUBLIC LIBRARY, E Church St, 49221. *Tel:* (313) 263-2161, ext 277. *In Charge:* Jule Fosbender. *Member:* Mich. Library Film Circuit, Inc.

Allegan

P- ALLEGAN PUBLIC LIBRARY, 331 Hubbard St, 49010. *Tel:* (616) 673-4625. *Film Serv Est:* 1967. *In Charge:* Claudia Ross, Asst Librarian. *AV Staff:* 2 (1 prof, 1 cl). *Film Sel:* staff recommendations, chief film librarian's decision, published reviews.

Free-Loan Film Serv *Eligibility:* educational inst, civic groups, religious groups, indiv with library cards. *Restrictions:* for indiv, interlibrary loan; for inst, only in area served by Library. May not borrow by mail. *Loan Period:* 1 day. *Total Yr Film Loan:* 494.

Film Collection 5t/p.

Other Film Serv Obtain film from coop loan system (Kalamazoo Area Library System, KETAL, Mich. Library Film Circuit).

Budget & Expenditures Total library budget $45,473 (FY 7/1/74-7/1/75). Total FY film budget $675. *Member:* ALA, MFLA, Mich. Library Assn.

Alma

C- ALMA COLLEGE, Monteith Library, 48801. *Tel:* (517) 463-2141, ext 457. *In Charge:* Debra Oyler, AV Supervisor. *AV Staff:* 1 prof. *Film Sel:* faculty/staff recommendations.

Free-Loan Film Serv *Eligibility:* staff & students, & others. *Restrictions:* for indiv & inst, only in city. Available to researchers/scholars for on-site viewing. May borrow by mail.

Film Collection 92t/p. Approx 1-2t acquired annually. *Circ:* 16mm, 42t/p; 8mm cartridge, 20t/p; S8mm cartridge, 27t/p.

Other Film Serv Rent film from distributors for patrons, obtain film from coop loan system (Mich. Library Consortium), obtain film from other libraries. Permanent viewing facility available for rent to community. *Equipment:* lend 16mm sound projector (8), 8mm reel projector (1), S8mm cartridge projector (2), S8mm reel projector (1), projection tables & stands (10), projection screens (4).

Other Media Collections *Audio:* disc, 33⅓ rpm, 701t/c; tape, cassette, 38t/c; tape, reel, 31t/c. *Filmstrips:* silent, 259t/c; sound sets, 27t/c. *Slides:* sets, 26t/c.

Budget & Expenditures Total library budget $107,884 (FY 7/1/75-7/1/76). No separate AV budget. *Member:* ALA.

Video Serv *Video Staff:* 1 f-t. *Video Use:* documentation of community/school events, playback only of professionally produced tapes. Video serv available by appointment. Produce video tapes.

Video Equipment/Facilities *In-House Use Only:* synthesizer (1). *For Loan:* recording deck (1), ½" b&w, Sony; playback deck (1), ½" b&w, Sony; studio camera (1); monitor (1); microphones (3); tripods (1); audio tape recorders (6). *Equipment Loan Period:* no set policy. Provide training in use of equipment to faculty & students.

Video Tape Loan/Rental/Sale Serv *Serv Provided:* free loan. *Loan Eligibility:* staff & students, civic groups, religious groups. *Restrictions:* for indiv & inst, only in city.

Video Collection Maintained by own production. Use/play ½" reel to reel. *Sources:* own production. Tapes organized by acquisition number. *Collection, B&W:* ½" reel, 32t/c. *Other Video Serv:* taping of other media. *Pubns:* catalog.

Ann Arbor

S- CERBERUS, INC, 75 Barton Dr, 48105. *Tel:* (313) 994-3226. *Video Serv Est:* 1972. *In Charge:* David Miller, Pres. *Video Use:* documentation of community/school events, community video access, practical video/TV training courses, as art form. Video serv available by special appointment. Produce video tapes. Have production studio/space.

Video Equipment/Facilities *In-House Use Only:* portapak (1), ½" b&w/col, Sony 8400; recording deck (1), ½" b&w/col, Sony 8600; editing deck (1), ½" b&w/col, Sony 8650; monitor (1), col, Sony Trinitron. *For Loan:* portapak (1), ½" b&w/col, Sony 8400; recording deck (1), ½" b&w/col, Sony 8600; editing deck (1), ½" b&w/col, Sony 8650. Have portable viewing installations. *Equipment Loan Period:* no set policy. Provide training in use of equipment to indiv interested in video for community serv or as an art form.

Video Tape Loan/Rental/Sale Serv *Serv Provided:* free loan, swap with other inst. *Loan Eligibility:* staff & students, indiv. *Restrictions:* for indiv & inst, none. May borrow by mail. *Total Yr Tape Loan:* 30.

Video Collection Maintained by own production, exchange/swap. Use/play ½" reel to reel, ¾" cassette. *Sources:* community productions, exchange (Midwest Video Bicycle). *Member:* Midwest Video Bicycle. *Tape Sel:* preview, faculty/staff recommendations, catalogs. *Special Collections:* video as art. Tapes organized by subject. *Collection, Color:* ½" reel, 10t/c; ¾" cassette, 5t/c. *Collection, B&W:* ½" reel, 60t/c. *Other Video Serv:* programming, reference serv, taping of other media, production workshops, live video performances.

Cable & CCTV Receive serv of cable TV system. Produce programs for cablecasting. Inform public about cable system serv & facilities. Serve as production facility for others.

P- MEDIA ACCESS CENTER, 204 S Fourth Ave, 48105. *Video Serv Est:* 1973. *In Charge:* George de Pue, Dir. *Video Staff:* 4 p-t. *Video Use:* documentation of community/school events, community video access, community production training. Video serv available by appointment. Produce video tapes. Have production studio/space.

Video Equipment/Facilities *For Loan:* portapak (1), ½" b&w, Sony; recording deck (2); playback deck (2); editing deck (1); studio camera (1); monitor (5); SEG (1); keyer (1); synthesizer (1); additional camera lenses (3); microphones (10); tripods (3); audio tape recorders (4). Have portable viewing installation. Provide training in use of equipment to Washtenaw County residents. Have tape duplication serv.

Video Tape Loan/Rental/Sale Serv *Serv Provided:* free loan, swap with other inst, sale. *Loan Eligibility:* educational inst, civic groups, religious groups, indiv. *Restrictions:* for indiv, only in Washtenaw County; for inst, none. Cannot duplicate, air without permission. May borrow by mail.

Video Collection Maintained by rental, own production, exchange/swap. Use/play ¼" reel to reel. *Sources:* community productions, exchange. *Tape Sel:* preview, faculty/staff recommendations. Tapes organized by subject. *Collection, B&W:* ¼" reel, 300t/310c. *Other Video Serv:* programming, production workshops.

Cable & CCTV Receive serv of cable TV system. Produce programs for cablecasting. Inform public about cable system serv & facilities. Serve as production facility for others. Run cable programs for special audiences. Have advisory/administrative role in cable system operation. Have CCTV in inst, with 3 monitors. *Programming Sources:* over-the-air commercial & public broadcasting, tapes produced by inst, tapes produced by community groups & indiv, exchange.

C- UNIVERSITY OF MICHIGAN, AV Education Center, 416 S Fourth St, 48109. *Tel:* (313) 764-5360. *Film Serv Est:* 1938. *In Charge:* Ford Lemler, Dir. *AV Staff:* 26 (9 prof, 12 cl, 5

Ann Arbor (cont'd)

tech). *Film Sel:* preview, faculty/staff recommendations, chief film librarian's decision. *Holdings:* animated films 4%, black studies 3%, career education 2%, children's films 30%, consumer affairs 1%, dance .5%, engineering 1%, experimental films .25%, film studies 3%, fine arts 5%, gerontology 1%, industrial arts 1%, literature 27%, medicine 1%, science 8%, social sciences 25%, women 3%.

Free-Loan Film Serv *Eligibility:* classroom use only. *Restrictions:* only on University of Mich. campuses. Cannot transmit electronically. May not borrow by mail. *Loan Period:* 1 day. *Total Yr Film Loan:* 24,000.

Film Rental Serv *Eligibility:* no restrictions. *Restrictions:* only in U.S. Cannot use for fund-raising, transmit electronically. *Rental Period:* 3 days. *Total Yr Film Booking:* 85,000. Sell films. Produce films. Produce filmstrips.

Film Collection 7000t/12,000p. Approx 200-300t acquired annually. *Circ:* 16mm, 7000t/17,000p. *Pubns:* catalog, annual, every 3 yrs; suppl, approx once a yr. Publish subject lists, newsletter.

Other Film Serv Film reference serv, library film programs. Permanent viewing facility available for rent to community. *Equipment:* rent 16mm sound projector (30), 8mm reel projector (5), projection screens (5).

Budget & Expenditures Total library budget $350,000 (FY 7/1/74-7/1/75). Total FY film budget $300,000. *Member:* CUFC, EFLA.

C- UNIVERSITY OF MICHIGAN, School of Dentistry, 3066 Dentistry, 48109. *Tel:* (313) 763-0205. *Video Serv Est:* 1970. *In Charge:* Stewart L. White, Media Manager. *Video Staff:* 10 f-t, 2 p-t, 6 tech. *Video Use:* in-service training, practical video/TV training courses, classroom instruction. Video serv available on demand. Produce video tapes. Have production studio/space & separate control room.

Video Equipment/Facilities *In-House Use Only:* recording deck (21), ½", ¾", 1" col, RCA, Sony, IVC, JVC; playback deck (51), ½", ¾", 1" col, RCA, Sony, JVC, IVC; editing deck (6), ½", 1" col, RCA, IVC, Sony; studio camera (3), col, Philips plumbicon; SEG (3); keyer (2); lighting; microphones. Have permanent & portable viewing installations. Provide training in use of equipment to staff & students. Have tape duplication serv.

Video Tape Loan/Rental/Sale Serv *Serv Provided:* swap with other inst, rental, sale. *Loan/Rental Eligibility:* staff & students, accredited health science schools. *Restrictions:* for inst, none. Cannot use for fund-raising, duplicate, air without permission. May borrow by mail. *Loan Period:* 14 days.

Video Collection Maintained by own production, exchange/swap. Use/play ½", 1", 2" reel to reel, ¾" cassette. *Sources:* health science schools. *Tape Sel:* preview, faculty/staff recommendations, catalogs. *Special Collections:* in-house training tapes. Tapes organized alphabetically. *Collection, Color:* ½" reel, 3t/c; 1" reel, 30t/c; 2" reel, 800t/c; ¾" cassette, 500t/c. *Pubns:* catalog.

Cable & CCTV Have CCTV in inst, with over 100 monitors. *Programming Sources:* tapes produced by inst.

S- UNIVERSITY OF MICHIGAN, TV Center, 400 Fourth St, 48103. *Tel:* (313) 764-8298, ext 24. *Video Serv Est:* 1958. *In Charge:* Thomas B. Coates, TV Dir. *Video Staff:* 34 f-t, 6 tech. *Video Use:* as instructional tool. Video serv available by appointment. Produce video tapes.

Video Equipment/Facilities *In-House Use Only:* portapak (1), ½" b&w, Sony AV3400; editing deck (2), ½" b&w, Sony. *For Loan:* portapak (1), ½" b&w, Sony AV3400; recording deck (6), ½" b&w, Sony AV3650; studio camera (3), ½" b&w, AVC 3210, Sony; monitor (11), ½" b&w, Sony; SEG (1), ½" Sony; videocassette recorders, players, monitors. Have portable viewing installation. *Equipment Loan Period:* per day. Provide training in use of equipment to faculty & students. Have tape duplication serv. Cannot use for fund-raising, duplicate, air without permission.

Video Collection Maintained by rental, own production. Use/play ½", 2" reel to reel, ¾" cassette. *Sources:* own produc-

tion only. *Other Video Serv:* programming, production workshops. *Pubns:* catalog.

C- UNIVERSITY OF MICHIGAN, Undergraduate Library, 48109. *Tel:* (313) 764-1275. *Video Serv Est:* 1975. *In Charge:* Barbara MacAlpine, Sight & Sound Center Librarian. *Video Staff:* 2 f-t, 15 p-t. *Video Use:* to increase community's library use, community video access, classroom instruction. Video serv available on demand.

Video Equipment/Facilities *In-House Use Only:* playback deck (9), ¾" col, Sony VP1200; monitor (9), col, Sony. Have permanent & portable viewing installations. Provide training in use of equipment to students.

Video Tape Loan/Rental/Sale Serv *Serv Provided:* free loan. *Loan Eligibility:* staff & students. *Restrictions:* for inst, only in city. Cannot use for fund-raising, duplicate, air without permission. May not borrow by mail.

Video Collection Maintained by purchase, own production. Use/play ¾" cassette. *Sources:* commercial distributors. *Tape Sel:* preview, faculty/staff recommendations, published reviews, catalogs. Tapes organized numerically. *Collection, Color:* ¾" cassette, 43t/c. *Collection, B&W:* ¾" cassette, 17t/c. *Pubns:* publish promotional letters to faculty.

P- WASHTENAW COUNTY LIBRARY, AV Dept, 4133 Washtenaw Ave, 48107. *Tel:* (313) 971-6056. *In Charge:* Debra Sapsfora, Tech. *AV Staff:* 2¼ (2 cl, ¼ tech). *Film Sel:* committee preview.

Free-Loan Film Serv *Eligibility:* indiv with library cards. *Restrictions:* for indiv, only in Washtenaw & Livingston Counties. Cannot use for fund-raising, transmit electronically, borrow for classroom use. Available to researchers/scholars for on-site viewing. May not borrow by mail. *Loan Period:* 1 day. *Total Yr Film Loan:* 11,456.

Film Collection 703t/p. Approx 30t acquired annually. *Circ:* 16mm, 435t/p; 8mm reel, 268t/p. *Pubns:* catalog, annual. Publish flyers.

Other Film Serv Obtain film from coop loan system (Mich. Library Film Circuit, SE Mich. Regional Film Library). *Equipment:* lend 16mm sound projector (18), 8mm reel projector (10), projection screens.

Budget & Expenditures Total library budget $83,030 (FY 1/1/75-1/1/76). Total FY film budget $18,854. *Member:* AECT, AFI, ALA, CUFC, EFLA, FLIC, Monroe County Library.

Battle Creek

P- WILLARD LIBRARY, 7 W Van Buren, 49016. *Tel:* (616) 968-8166. *Film Serv Est:* 1956 (16mm), 1970 (8mm). *In Charge:* Dorothea Butts—8mm, AV Dept Head; Aulene Chapin—16mm, Reference Dept Head. *AV Staff:* 2 (½ prof, 1 cl, ½ tech). *Film Sel:* preview, chief film librarian & Library Dir decision.

Free-Loan Film Serv *Eligibility:* libraries in Willard Library System. *Restrictions:* interlibrary loan. Available to researchers/scholars for on-site viewing. *Loan Period:* 7 days. *Total Yr Film Loan:* 8mm, 3606.

Film Rental Serv *Eligibility:* patrons/public, with library cards, libraries, public schools. *Restrictions:* only in Willard Library system, Battle Creek Public Schools. *Rental Period:* 2 days. *Total Yr Film Booking:* 16mm, 1686.

Film Collection 650t/p. Approx 120t acquired annually. *Circ:* 16mm, 250t/p; 8mm reel, 300t/p; S8mm reel, 100t/p. *Pubns:* catalog, annual; suppl, no set policy.

Other Film Serv Rent film from distributors for patrons, obtain film from coop loan system (Mich. Library Film Circuit). Permanent viewing facility available to community.

Other Media Collections *Audio:* disc, 33⅓ rpm, 2500c; tape, cassette, 450c. *Slides:* sets, 2c.

Budget & Expenditures Total library budget $512,500 (FY 7/1/74-7/1/75). Total FY film budget $7200. No separate budget. *Member:* ALA, Mich. Library Assn.

Video Serv *Est:* 1974. *In Charge:* Marianne Upston, Community TV Center Dir. *Video Staff:* 2 f-t, 2 p-t. *Video Use:*

documentation of community/school events, to increase community's library use, community video access, practical video/TV training courses, as art form. Video serv available by appointment. Produce video tapes.

Video Equipment/Facilities *In-House Use Only:* recording deck (1), ½″ col, Sony 8400; editing deck (1), ½″ col, Sony 8650; audio tape recorders (1), cassette recorders (2); cassette players (4). *For Loan:* portapak (3), ½″ b&w, Sony 3400; playback deck (1), ½″ b&w, Shibaden 510; SEG (2), Sony CVM 10; additional camera lenses (1); lighting (1); microphones (4); tripods (3); audio tape recorders (1). Have permanent & portable viewing installations. *Equipment Loan Period:* 3 days. Provide training in use of equipment to library patrons over 18 yrs. Have tape duplication serv.

Video Tape Loan/Rental/Sale Serv *Serv Provided:* free loan, swap with other inst. *Loan Eligibility:* educational inst, indiv with library cards. Cannot use for fund-raising, duplicate, air without permission. May not borrow by mail.

Video Collection Maintained by purchase, own production, exchange/swap. Use/play ½″ reel to reel, ¾″ cassette. *Sources:* commercial distributors, community productions, exchange. *Tape Sel:* faculty/staff recommendations, published reviews, catalogs. *Collection, Color:* ¾″ cassette, 53t. *Collection, B&W:* ¾″ cassette, 47t. *Other Video Serv:* taping of other media, production workshops. *Pubns:* catalog of materials, manual on portapak operation.

Cable & CCTV Produce programs for cablecasting. Inform public about cable system serv & facilities. Serve as production facility for others. Run cable programs for special audiences.

Bay City

P- BAY COUNTY LIBRARY SYSTEM, 708 Center St, 48706. *Tel:* (517) 893-9566. *In Charge:* Linda Heemstra. *Member:* Michigan Library Film Circuit, Inc.

Benton Harbor

P- LIBRARY SYSTEM OF SOUTHWEST MICHIGAN, 213 E Wall St, 49022. *Tel:* (616) 926-6139. *In Charge:* Carolyn Sutter. *Member:* Mich. Library Film Circuit, Inc.

Berrien Springs

C- ANDREWS UNIVERSITY, James White Library—Teaching Materials Center, Andrews Station, 49104. *Tel:* (616) 471-3272. *In Charge:* Richard K. Powell, Dir TMC. *AV Staff:* 2½ (1 prof, 1½ cl). *Film Sel:* faculty/staff recommendations.

Free-Loan Film Serv *Eligibility:* staff & students, local organizations. *Restrictions:* none. Available to researchers/scholars for on-site viewing. *Loan Period:* 7 days. *Total Yr Film Loan:* 100.

Film Collection 20t/p. *Circ:* 16mm, 20t/p; 8mm reel, 10t/p; S8mm reel, 10t/p. Will publish catalog.

Other Film Serv Film reference serv. Permanent viewing facility available to community.

Other Media Collections *Audio:* disc, 33⅓ rpm, 934c; disc, 45rpm, 40c; disc, 78rpm, 50c; tape, cassette, 864c; tape, cartridge, 18c; tape, reel, 410c. *Filmstrips:* sound, 687c; silent, 2410c. *Slides:* sets, 224c. Overhead transparencies: 2109.

Budget & Expenditures Total library budget $120,000 (FY 7/1/74-7/1/75). *Member:* AECT, CEFP, OCLC, Mich. Assn for Media in Education.

Birmingham

P- BALDWIN PUBLIC LIBRARY, 351 Martin, 48012. *Film Serv Est:* 1970.

Free-Loan Film Serv *Eligibility:* indiv with library cards. *Restrictions:* only in service area. *Loan Period:* 1 day. *Total Yr Film Loan:* 310.

Other Film Serv Rent film from distributors for patrons, obtain film from other libraries, film reference serv, library film programs.

Budget & Expenditures Total library budget $47,337 (FY 7/1/74-7/1/75). No separate AV budget. *Member:* Mich. Library Film Circuit.

Bloomfield Hills

P- BLOOMFIELD TOWNSHIP PUBLIC LIBRARY, 1099 Lone Pine Rd, 48013. *Tel:* (313) 642-5800. *Film Serv Est:* 1970. *In Charge:* A. Michael Deller, Community Relations Coord. *AV Staff:* ¼ prof, ⅛ cl. *Film Sel:* committee preview, staff recommendations, published reviews, ALA previews.

Free-Loan Film Serv *Eligibility:* indiv with library cards, & others, such as nursing homes. *Restrictions:* for indiv & inst; only in city. Cannot use for fund-raising, transmit electronically. Available to researchers/scholars for on-site viewing. May not borrow by mail. *Loan Period:* 2 days. *Total Yr Film Loan:* 552.

Film Collection 132t/138p. Approx 10t acquired annually. *Circ:* 8mm reel, 60t/62p; S8mm reel, 72t/74p.

Other Film Serv Obtain film from coop loan system (Mich. Library Film Circuit), obtain film from other libraries, library film programs. Permanent viewing facility available for rent to community.

Other Media Collections *Audio:* disc, 33⅓ rpm, 3768t/c; tape, cassette, 895t/c; tape, cartridge, 24t/c; tape, reel, 149t/c.

Budget & Expenditures Total library budget $60,786 (FY 4/1/74-4/1/75). Total FY film budget $500. *Member:* ALA, Mich. Library Assn.

C- CRANBROOK ACADEMY OF ART, 500 Lone Pine Rd, 48013. *Tel:* (313) 645-3311. *Video Serv Est:* 1975. *In Charge:* John Peterson, Museum Dir. *Video Use:* community video access, practical video/TV training courses, as art form, education. Video serv available by appointment. Produce video tapes. Have production studio/space.

Video Equipment/Facilities *In-House Use Only:* recording deck (1), ¾″ col, Sony 1600; playback deck (1), ½″ b&w, Sony; editing deck (1), b&w, Sony 3650; studio camera (1), b&w, Sony; monitor (4), b&w/col, Sony; microphones (4); tripods (2); audio tape recorders (2). *For Loan:* portapak (3), ½″ b&w, Sony, Rover II. Have portable viewing installation. *Equipment Loan Period:* no set policy. Provide training in use of equipment to faculty & students.

Video Tape Loan/Rental/Sale Serv *Serv Provided:* free loan, swap with other inst. *Loan Eligibility:* org members, staff & students.

Video Collection Maintained by purchase, rental, own production, exchange/swap. Use/play ½″ reel to reel, ¾″ cassette. *Sources:* commercial distributors, galleries, community productions, exchange. *Tape Sel:* preview, faculty/staff recommendations, gallery previews. *Special Collections:* in-house training tapes, video as art. *Collection, Color:* ¾″ cassette, 8t. *Collection, B&W:* ½″ reel, 5t/c. *Other Video Serv:* production workshops.

Brighton

P- BRIGHTON PUBLIC LIBRARY, 202 W Main St, 48116. *Tel:* (313) 229-6571. *In Charge:* Dorothy Derorest. *Member:* Mich. Library Film Circuit, Inc.

Cadillac

P- MID-MICHIGAN LIBRARY LEAGUE, Cadillac-Wexford Public Library, Box 614, 49601. *Tel:* (616) 775-6541. *In Charge:* Donald Best. *Member:* Mich. Library Film Circuit, Inc.

Cassopolis

P- CASS COUNTY LIBRARY, 161-163 N Broadway, 49031. *Tel:* (616) 445-8155. *In Charge:* Linda Hilton. *Member:* Mich. Library Film Circuit, Inc.

Cheboygan

P- CHEBOYGAN PUBLIC LIBRARY, Ball St, 49721. *Tel:* (616) 627-2381. *Member:* Mich. Library Film Circuit, Inc.

Dearborn

P- DEARBORN DEPT OF LIBRARIES, Henry Ford Centennial Library, AV Division, 16301 Michigan Ave, 48124. *Tel:* (313) 271-1000, ext 27. *Film Serv Est:* 1948. *In Charge:* James L. Limbacher, AV Librarian. *AV Staff:* 9 (3 prof, 6 cl, 1 tech). *Film Sel:* committee preview. *Holdings:* feature films 25%.

Film Rental Serv *Eligibility:* no restrictions. *Restrictions:* none. Cannot use for fund-raising, transmit electronically. *Rental Period:* 3 days. *Total Yr Film Booking:* 21,127.

Film Collection 3800t/3820p. Approx 150t acquired annually. *Circ:* 16mm, 3265t/3285p; 8mm reel, 534t/536p. *Pubns:* publish program flyers, special lists.

Other Film Serv Film reference serv, film fairs/festivals, library film programs. Permanent viewing facility available for rent to community.

Other Media Collections *Audio:* disc, 33⅓ rpm, 18,422t; tape, cassette, 1173t.

Budget & Expenditures Total library budget $209,400 (FY 7/1/75-7/1/76). Total FY film budget $33,000. *Member:* AECT, AFI, ALA, EFLA, FLIC, Mich. Library Assn, Metropolitan Detroit AV Assn.

Decatur

P- VAN BUREN COUNTY LIBRARY, Webster Memorial Library, 200 Phelps St, 49045. *Tel:* (616) 423-4771. *In Charge:* Patricia Olsen. *Member:* Mich. Library Film Circuit, Inc.

Detroit

P- DETROIT PUBLIC LIBRARY, Film Dept, 5201 Woodward Ave, 48226. *Tel:* (313) 833-1495. *Film Serv Est:* 1948. *In Charge:* Robert Garen, Chief. *AV Staff:* 10 (3 prof, 6 cl, 2 tech). *Film Sel:* committee preview.

Free-Loan Film Serv *Eligibility:* anyone. *Restrictions:* only in city. Cannot use for fund-raising, transmit electronically. May not borrow by mail. *Loan Period:* 3 days. *Total Yr Film Loan:* 26,339.

Film Collection 2000t/p. *Pubns:* catalog, annual ($1.50); suppl. Publish materials pertaining to collection.

Other Film Serv Library film programs. Permanent viewing facility.

Budget & Expenditures Total library budget $30,000 (FY 7/74-7/75). No separate AV budget. *Member:* ALA, EFLA, Mich. Library Assn.

C- MERCY COLLEGE OF DETROIT, Learning Resource Center, 8200 W Outer Drive, 48126. *Tel:* (313) KE-1-7820, ext 387, 388. *Film Serv Est:* 1970. *In Charge:* Diana Balint, Media Librarian. *AV Staff:* 2 (1 prof, 1 cl). *Film Sel:* faculty/staff recommendations. *Holdings:* science 50%.

Free-Loan Film Serv *Eligibility:* staff. *Restrictions:* for campus use only. Available to researchers/scholars for on-site viewing. May not borrow by mail. *Total Yr Film Loan:* 25. Produce slides, filmstrips, cassette, reel tapes.

Film Collection 20t/p. Approx 1-3t acquired annually. *Circ:* 16mm, 20t/p. *Pubns:* catalog, annual; suppl, in yr catalog not published.

Other Film Serv Rent film from distributors for patrons, obtain film from other libraries, film reference serv. Permanent viewing facility. *Equipment:* lend 16mm sound projector (6), 8mm cartridge projector (4), 8mm reel projector (1), S8mm cartridge projector (4), projection screens (16), filmstrip, slide & overhead projectors.

Other Media Collections *Audio:* disc, 33⅓ rpm, 1345t/c; disc, 45rpm, 63t/c; disc, 78rpm, 29t/c; tape, cassette, 463t/c;

tape, reel, 197t/c. *Filmstrips:* silent, 1892t/c; sound sets, 1645t/c. *Slides:* sets, 94t/c.

Budget & Expenditures Total library budget $3290 (FY 7/75-7/76). Total FY film budget $3000.

Video Serv *Est:* 1970. *In Charge:* Anthony Semanik, Acting Dir LRC. *Video Staff:* 1 p-t. *Video Use:* documentation of community/school events, in-service training, practical video/TV training courses, playback only of professionally produced tapes, production of instructional programs. Video serv available by appointment. Produce video tapes. Have production studio/space.

Video Equipment/Facilities *In-House Use Only:* portapak (1), EIAJ-1 b&w, Sony 3400; recording deck (1), EIAJ-1 b&w, Sony 3600; editing deck (1), EIAJ-1 b&w, Sony 3650; studio camera (1), b&w, Sony 3200; monitor (2), b&w, Admiral 22"; lighting (4); microphones (4); tripods (2); audio tape recorders (1), audio mixer (1). Have portable viewing installation. Provide training in use of equipment to staff & students.

Video Tape Loan/Rental/Sale Serv *Serv Provided:* free loan. *Loan Eligibility:* org members, staff, students enrolled in inst. *Restrictions:* for campus use only. Cannot air without permission. May not borrow by mail.

Video Collection Maintained by purchase, rental, own production. Use/play ½" reel to reel. *Sources:* commercial distributors, educational institutions. *Tape Sel:* preview, faculty/staff recommendations, catalogs. Tapes organized by subject, LC. *Collection, B&W:* ½" reel, 20t/c.

C- UNIVERSITY OF DETROIT, 4001 W McNichols, 48221. *Tel:* (313) 927-1075.

Film Serv Film reference serv. Permanent viewing facility. *Equipment:* lend in-house only, 16mm sound projector (5), projection tables & stands (3), projection screens (4).

Other Media Collections *Audio:* disc, 33⅓ rpm; disc, 45rpm, 1500t/c; tape, cassette, 38t. *Filmstrips:* sound sets, 230t; silent sets, 3200t. *Slides:* single, 2500t. *Member:* ALA, Mich. Library Assn.

Video Serv *Est:* 1975. *In Charge:* Margaret Auer, Librarian. *Video Staff:* 3 f-t, 1 tech. *Video Use:* playback only of professionally produced tapes. Video serv available by appointment.

Video Equipment/Facilities *In-House Use Only:* recording deck (1), b&w, Sony 3600; playback deck (1), b&w, Sony 3600; studio camera (1), b&w; monitor (1), b&w, Sony; tripods (1). Have portable viewing installation. *Equipment Loan Period:* class period. Provide training in use of equipment to faculty.

Video Tape Loan/Rental/Sale Serv *Loan Eligibility:* instructional staff only. *Restrictions:* for campus use only. May not borrow by mail.

Video Collection Use/play ½" reel to reel.

C- WAYNE STATE UNIVERSITY, Instructional Materials Library, 5448 Cass, 48202. *Tel:* (313) 577-1980. *Film Serv Est:* 1960. *In Charge:* T. W. Roberts, Dir. *AV Staff:* 33 (4 prof, 7 cl, 22 tech). *Film Sel:* faculty/staff recommendations.

Film Rental Serv *Eligibility:* no restrictions. *Restrictions:* none. Cannot use for fund-raising, transmit electronically without permission. *Rental Period:* 3 days. *Total Yr Film Booking:* 10,000. Sell films. Produce films. Produce filmstrips.

Film Collection 3500t/5000p. *Circ:* 16mm, 3500t/5000p. *Pubns:* catalog, as needed ($2); suppl, no set policy.

Other Film Serv Obtain film from other libraries. Permanent viewing facility. *Equipment:* rent 16mm sound projector, 8mm cartridge projectors, 8mm reel projectors, S8mm cartridge projectors, S8mm reel projectors, projection tables & stands, projection screens, AV equipment, VTR.

Budget & Expenditures No separate budget. *Member:* AECT, CUFC, EFLA.

Dowagiac

P- DOWAGIAC PUBLIC LIBRARY, 211 Commercial St, 49047. *Tel:* (616) 782-5630. *In Charge:* Gary Bailey. *Member:* Mich. Library Film Circuit, Inc.

Farmington

P- FARMINGTON DISTRICT LIBRARY, 32737 W 12 Mile Rd, 48024. *Tel:* (313) 477-1313. *In Charge:* Mary Mitchell. *Member:* Mich. Library Film Circuit, Inc.

Flint

P- FLINT PUBLIC LIBRARY, 1026 E Kearsley St, 48502. *Tel:* (313) 232-7111. *In Charge:* William Vickrey, M.L.F.C. Inspection. *Member:* Mich. Library Film Circuit, Inc.

Fremont

P- FREMONT PUBLIC LIBRARY, 2 E Main St, 49412. *Tel:* (616) 924-3480. *Film Serv Est:* 1971. *In Charge:* Sherrie Anderson, Children's Librarian. *Holdings:* children's films 100%.
Free-Loan Film Serv *Eligibility:* indiv with library cards. *Restrictions:* for indiv & inst, only in Newaygo County. Available to researchers/scholars for on-site viewing. *Loan Period:* 1 day. *Total Yr Film Loan:* 3.
Film Collection 7t/p. Approx 3t acquired annually. *Circ:* 16mm, 7t/p.
Other Film Serv Obtain film from coop loan system (Mich. Library Film Circuit), obtain film from other libraries, library film programs. *Equipment:* lend 16mm sound projector (1), projection screens (1), slide projector, filmstrip projector.
Other Media Collections *Audio:* disc, 33⅓ rpm, 1266t; tape, cassette, 46t. *Filmstrips:* sound, 10t. *Slides:* sets, 30t.
Budget & Expenditures Total library budget $13,686 (FY 7/1/74-7/1/75). Total FY film budget $400. *Member:* ALA, Newaygo County Library Assn, Mich. State Library Assn.

Grand Rapids

C- CALVIN COLLEGE, AV Dept, 49506. *Tel:* (616) 949-4000, ext 2834. *Film Serv Est:* 1948. *In Charge:* Dr. John L. De Beer, AV Servs Dir. *AV Staff:* 4 (1 cl, 1 tech). *Film Sel:* faculty/staff recommendations. *Holdings:* black studies 5%, career education 5%, engineering 5%, fine arts 5%, industrial arts 1%, science 5%, social sciences 2%, teacher education 72%.
Film Collection *Noncirc:* 16mm, 250t/p.
Other Film Serv Rent film from distributors for patrons, obtain film from coop loan system (University of Mich.). Permanent viewing facility. *Equipment:* campus use only; S8mm camera (3), 16mm sound projector (22), 8mm reel projector (3), projection tables & stands (15), projection screens (58).
Budget & Expenditures Total library budget $12,900 (FY 8/1/74-8/1/75).
Video Serv *Est:* 1966. *Video Staff:* 3 f-t, 4 p-t, 1 tech. *Video Use:* documentation of community/school events. Video serv available by appointment. Produce video tapes. Have production studio/space & separate control room.
Video Equipment/Facilities *In-House Use Only:* portapak (2), ½" b&w, Sony 2000; playback deck (7), b&w, Sony; editing deck (1), b&w, Sony; studio camera (5), b&w, Sony; monitor (8), b&w, Sony; additional camera lenses (3); lighting (4); microphones (8); tripods (6); audio tape recorders (28). Have permanent viewing installation. *Equipment Loan Period:* 3-7 days. Provide training in use of equipment to students.
Video Tape Loan/Rental/Sale Serv *Serv Provided:* free loan, swap with other inst. *Loan/Rental Eligibility:* staff. *Restrictions:* for campus use only. Cannot use for fund-raising, air without permission. May not borrow by mail.
Video Collection Maintained by own production. Use/play ½" reel to reel. *Tape Sel:* catalogs. *Special Collections:* in-house training tapes. Tapes organized by subject. *Collection, B&W:* ½" reel, 55t/c. *Other Video Serv:* taping of other media.

C- GRAND RAPIDS JUNIOR COLLEGE, 143 Bostwick, NE, 49502. *Tel:* (616) 456-4876. *In Charge:* John A. Lelly, Dir Library Servs. *AV Staff:* 2½ (1½ prof, 1 cl). *Film Sel:* faculty/staff recommendations. *Holdings:* fine arts 30%, science 35%, social sciences 35%.
Film Collection 125t. Approx 5-20t acquired annually.

Other Film Serv Rent film from distributors for patrons, obtain film from coop loan system (Grand Rapids Board of Educ), public library. Permanent viewing facility.
Other Media Collections *Audio:* disc, 33⅓ rpm, 300t; tape, cassette, 300t.
Video Serv *Est:* 1972. *Video Staff:* 2 f-t, 2 p-t. *Video Use:* in-service training, as art form, classroom instruction. Video serv available by appointment. Produce video tapes. Have production studio/space.
Video Equipment/Facilities *In-House Use Only:* portapak (2), b&w; recording deck (4), b&w/col; editing deck (1), col; studio camera (3), b&w; monitor (3), col; SEG (1), b&w; lighting; microphones; tripods (3); audio tape recorders (50). Have permanent viewing installation. Provide training in use of equipment to faculty & students.
Video Tape Loan/Rental/Sale Serv *Serv Provided:* free loan. *Loan Eligibility:* org members. *Restrictions:* for campus use only.
Video Collection Maintained by own production. Use/play 1" reel to reel, ¾" cassette. Tapes organized by subject.

P- GRAND RAPIDS PUBLIC LIBRARY, Library Plaza, 49502. *Tel:* (616) 456-4400. *Video Serv Est:* 1975. *In Charge:* James Searn, Media Specialist. *Video Staff:* 1 f-t, 3 p-t, ½ tech. *Video Use:* documentation of community/school events, to increase community's library use, community video access, in-service training, practical video/TV training courses, as art form. Video serv available on demand. Produce video tapes. Have production studio/space & separate control room.
Video Equipment/Facilities *In-House Use Only:* portapak (2), ½" b&w, Sony AV3400; recording deck (1), ½" b&w, Sony; playback deck (1), ½" b&w, Panasonic; editing deck (1), ½" col, Sony AV8650; studio camera (1), ⅔" b&w, Shibaden F-71; monitor (10), b&w/col; SEG (1), Panasonic; additional camera lenses (6); lighting (1); microphones (12); tripods (2); audio tape recorders (12). *For Loan:* portapak (2), ½" b&w, Sony AV3400; recording deck (1), ½" b&w, Sony; playback deck (1), ½" b&w, Panasonic; SEG (1), Panasonic; additional camera lenses (6); lighting (1); microphones (12); tripods (2); audio tape recorders (12). Have permanent & portable viewing installations. *Equipment Loan Period:* 2 days. Provide training in use of equipment to staff & public. Have tape duplication serv.
Video Tape Loan/Rental/Sale Serv *Serv Provided:* free loan, swap with other inst, rental. *Loan/Rental Eligibility:* civic groups, religious groups, indiv with library cards, & others, such as political groups. *Restrictions:* only in city. Cannot use for fund-raising, duplicate, air without permission. May borrow by mail.
Video Collection Maintained by purchase, own production, exchange/swap. Use/play ½" reel to reel, ¾" cassette. *Sources:* commercial distributors, galleries, community productions, exchange with public library systems. *Tape Sel:* preview, faculty/staff recommendations, catalogs. *Special Collections:* video as art, women, alcoholism. Tapes organized by subject. *Collection, Color:* ¾" cassette, 10t/c. *Collection, B&W:* ½" reel, 50t/c. *Other Video Serv:* programming, reference serv, production workshops.
Cable & CCTV Receive serv of cable TV system. Produce programs for cablecasting. Inform public about cable system serv & facilities. Serve as production facility for others. Run cable programs for special audiences. Have advisory/administrative role in cable system operation. Have CCTV in inst, with 7 monitors. *Programming Sources:* over-the-air commercial & public broadcasting, tapes produced by inst, tapes produced by community groups & indiv.

P- KENT COUNTY LIBRARY, 775 Ball Ave NE, 49504. *Tel:* (616) 456-4450. *In Charge:* Joyce Pleune. *Member:* Mich. Library Film Circuit, Inc.

Grosse Pointe

P- GROSSE POINT PUBLIC LIBRARY, 10 Kercheval Ave, 48236. *Tel:* (313) 884-2200. *In Charge:* William Peters. *Member:* Mich. Library Film Circuit, Inc.

Hancock

C- SUOMI COLLEGE LIBRARY, 49930. *Tel:* (906) 482-5300, ext 70. *Film Serv Est:* 1968. *In Charge:* Janet A. Dalquist, Librarian. *AV Staff:* 1 prof, ½ cl. *Film Sel:* committee preview, faculty/staff recommendations. *Holdings:* fine arts 25%, physical education 30%, social sciences 25%.
　Film Rental Serv *Eligibility:* civic groups, patrons/public, churches. *Restrictions:* only in Mich. Northern Peninsula, Wisc. Cannot use for fund-raising, transmit electronically. *Rental Period:* 7 days.
　Film Collection *Circ:* 16mm, 37t.
　Other Film Serv Obtain film from coop loan system (Mich. Library Consortium). *Equipment:* lend 16mm sound projector (4), 8mm reel projector (1), projection tables & stands (1), projection screens (5).
　Other Media Collections *Audio:* disc, 33⅓ rpm, 846t/c; tape, cassette, 250t/c. *Filmstrips:* sound, 273t/c; sound sets, 254t/c. *Slides:* single, 2600t; sets, 17t.
　Budget & Expenditures Total library budget $18,500 (FY 7/74-7/75). Total FY film budget $1500. *Member:* ALA, Mich. Library Consortium.

Hartland

P- CROMAINE PUBLIC LIBRARY, 3688 N Hartland Rd, 48029. *Tel:* (313) 632-7485. *In Charge:* Ann Zick. *Member:* Mich. Library Film Circuit, Inc.

Hazel Park

P- HAZEL PARK MEMORIAL LIBRARY, 123 E Nine Mile Rd, 48030. *Tel:* (313) 542-0940. *Film Serv Est:* 1974. *In Charge:* G. R. Allen, Librarian. *Film Sel:* faculty/staff recommendations, patron suggestions. *Holdings:* animated films 7%, classic comedies 67%.
　Free-Loan Film Serv *Eligibility:* indiv with library cards. *Restrictions:* for interlibrary loan. Cannot use for fund-raising. Available to researchers/scholars for on-site viewing. May not borrow by mail. *Loan Period:* 7 days. *Total Yr Film Loan:* 341.
　Film Collection S8mm reel, 60t/62p.
　Other Film Serv Obtain film from coop loan system (Wayne Oakland Federal Library System). Permanent viewing facility. *Equipment:* rent 16mm sound projector, S8mm reel projector, projection screens.
　Other Media Collections *Audio:* disc, 33⅓ rpm, 400t. *Filmstrips:* 490t/c. *Slides:* sets, 2t.
　Budget & Expenditures Total library budget $16,403 (FY 7/1/74-7/1/75). Total FY film budget $1266.

Hillsdale

P- MITCHELL PUBLIC LIBRARY, 22 N Manning St, 49242. *Tel:* (517) 437-2581. *Film Serv Est:* 1973. *In Charge:* James G. Jaeger, Head Librarian.
　Film Rental Serv *Eligibility:* patrons/public. *Restrictions:* only in region. *Rental Period:* 7 days. *Total Yr Film Booking:* 76.
　Film Collection 200t. *Pubns:* catalog, annual; suppl.
　Other Film Serv Rent film from distributors for patrons, obtain film from coop loan system (Willard Library System). *Equipment:* rent 16mm sound projector (2), projection screens (1), filmstrip projector (1).
　Other Media Collections *Audio:* disc, 300c; tape, cassette, 60c. *Filmstrips:* 200c; sound sets, 6t/c.
　Budget & Expenditures Total library budget $10,000. No separate AV budget.

Holland

P- HERRICK PUBLIC LIBRARY, 300 River Ave, 49423. *Tel:* (616) 392-3114. *Film Serv Est:* 1961. *In Charge:* Robert L. Sherwood, AV Dir. *AV Staff:* 3 (1 prof, 2 cl). *Film Sel:* chief film librarian's decision, published reviews.

　Film Rental Serv *Eligibility:* no restrictions. *Restrictions:* only in city & surrounding townships. Cannot use for fund-raising, transmit electronically. *Rental Period:* 1 day.
　Film Collection 200t/p. Approx 12-15t acquired annually. *Pubns:* catalog, annual; suppl, twice a yr. Publish materials pertaining to collection.
　Other Film Serv Obtain film from coop loan system (Mich. Library film circuit), film reference serv, library film programs. Permanent viewing facility available to community.
　Other Media Collections *Audio:* disc, 33⅓ rpm, 3994c; tape, cassette, 307c. *Filmstrips:* sound 376c.
　Budget & Expenditures Total library budget $41,604 (FY 7/74-7/75). Total FY film budget $3500. *Member:* ALA, EFLA, FLIC, Mich. Library Assn.

Iron Mountain

P- MID-PENINSULA LIBRARY FEDERATION, Film Dept, 401 Iron Mountain St, 49801. *Tel:* (906) 774-3005. *Film Serv Est:* 1973. *In Charge:* Barbara Jauquet, Asst Dir. *Film Sel:* committee preview, faculty/chief film librarian's decision.
　Free-Loan Film Serv *Eligibility:* member libraries only. *Restrictions:* cannot borrow for classroom use, charge admission. Available to researchers/scholars for on-site viewing. May borrow by mail. *Loan Period:* 3 days. *Total Yr Film Loan:* 2074.
　Film Collection *Circ:* 16mm, 418t/431p. *Pubns:* catalog, as needed; suppl, no set policy.
　Other Film Serv Obtain film from coop loan system (Mich. Library Film Circuit). Permanent viewing facility available to community.
　Other Media Collections *Audio:* disc, 33⅓ rpm, 884t. *Filmstrips:* silent, 6t/c.
　Budget & Expenditures Total library budget $10,000 (FY 7/1/74-7/1/75).

Jackson

P- JACKSON COUNTY LIBRARY, Media Dept, 1400 N West Ave, 49202. *Tel:* (517) 782-0357. *Film Serv Est:* 1949. *In Charge:* Luciann M. Leraul, Media Librarian. *AV Staff:* 2 (1 prof, 1 cl). *Film Sel:* committee preview, faculty/staff recommendations, chief film librarian's decision.
　Free-Loan Film Serv *Eligibility:* indiv with library cards. *Restrictions:* only in Jackson County. Cannot use for fund-raising, transmit electronically. May not borrow by mail. *Loan Period:* 3 days. *Total Yr Film Loan:* 2877.
　Film Collection Approx 30t acquired annually. *Circ:* 16mm, 290t/348p. *Pubns:* catalog, every 2 yrs; suppl, twice a yr.
　Other Film Serv Obtain film from coop loan system (Mich. Library Film Circuit, Regional Film Library), obtain film from other libraries. *Equipment:* lend 16mm sound projector (7), projection screens (4).
　Other Media Collections *Audio:* disc, 33⅓ rpm, 958t; tape, reel, 4t/8c. *Filmstrips:* sound, 3469t/c. *Slides:* sets, 28t/c.
　Budget & Expenditures Total library budget $314,400 (FY 1/1/75-1/1/76). Total FY film budget $10,000. *Member:* EFLA, FLIC, Mich. Assn for Media in Education, Detroit Area Film Teachers.

P- JACKSON PUBLIC LIBRARY, 244 W Michigan Ave, 49201. *Tel:* (517) 782-0319. *Film Serv Est:* 1950. *AV Staff:* 3 (1 prof, 2 cl). *Film Sel:* committee preview. *Holdings:* animated films 15%, children's films 25%, entertainment 65%, feature films 5%, fine arts 10%, social sciences 5%.
　Free-Loan Film Serv *Eligibility:* anyone. *Restrictions:* only in Jackson County, Central Mich. Library System. Available to researchers/scholars for on-site viewing. *Loan Period:* 1 day. *Total Yr Film Loan:* 5660.
　Film Collection Approx 15t acquired annually. *Circ:* 16mm, 100t/p. *Pubns:* catalog, annual; suppl, no set policy.
　Other Film Serv Obtain film from coop loan system (Mich. Library Film Circuit), film reference serv, library film programs. Permanent viewing facility. *Equipment:* lend 16mm sound projector (2), projection screens (2).

Kalamazoo

C- KALAMAZOO COLLEGE, 1200 Academy St, 49001. *Tel:* (616) 383-8400. *In Charge:* Lisa Godfrey, Dir Instructional Serv. *AV Staff:* 3 (1 prof, 2 tech).
Other Film Serv Rent film from distributors for patrons, obtain film from other libraries, film reference serv. *Equipment:* lend S8mm camera (2), 16mm sound projector (7), 8mm reel projector (1), S8mm reel projector (2), lend/rent projection tables & stands, projection screens.
Other Media Collections *Audio:* tape, cassette, 400t. *Member:* AECT.
Video Serv *Video Use:* in-service training, playback only of professionally produced tapes, as art form. Video serv available on demand.
Video Collection Maintained by rental. Use/play ½″ reel to reel.
Cable & CCTV Receive serv of cable TV system.

S- KALAMAZOO NATURE CENTER, 7000 N Westnedge, 49007. *Tel:* (616) 381-1575, ext 28. *Film Serv Est:* 1966. *In Charge:* Jan Duffield, Appt Sec. *AV Staff:* ¾ (½ prof, ½ cl, ½ tech). *Film Sel:* faculty/staff recommendations. *Holdings:* environment 85%, natural history 15%.
Film Rental Serv *Eligibility:* no restrictions. *Restrictions:* none. *Rental Period:* 1 day. *Total Yr Film Booking:* 50. Sell films. Produce films. Produce slide/tapes, filmstrips.
Film Collection Approx 1t acquired annually. *Circ:* 16mm, 6t/12p. *Pubns:* catalog, every 2 yrs.
Other Film Serv Obtain film from coop loan system (KE-TAL, Western Mich. University), film reference serv, library film programs. Permanent viewing facility available for rent to community.
Other Media Collections *Audio:* tape, reel, 6t. *Filmstrips:* sound, 2t/2c; sound sets, 3t/1c; *Slides:* sets, 25/1c.
Budget & Expenditures Total library budget $1500 (FY 9/1/74-9/1/75). *Member:* Special Libraries Assn.

P- KALAMAZOO PUBLIC LIBRARY, AV Section, 315 S Rose St, 49006. *Tel:* (616) 342-9837, ext 46. *Film Serv Est:* 1929. *In Charge:* Mary Doud, AV Librarian. *AV Staff:* 4½ (1½ prof, 2½ cl, 1 tech). *Film Sel:* AV librarian & committee preview.
Free-Loan Film Serv *Eligibility:* indiv with library cards. *Restrictions:* only in city. Cannot use for fund-raising, transmit electronically, for limited classroom use only. Available to researchers/scholars for on-site viewing. May not borrow by mail. *Loan Period:* 1½ days.
Film Collection 280t/286p. Approx 2t acquired annually. *Circ:* 16mm, 280t/286p; S8mm reel, 350t/p. Publish title list with synopses.
Other Film Serv Obtain film from coop loan system (Mich. Library Film Circuit), film reference serv, library film programs. Permanent viewing facility available to community. *Equipment:* rent 16mm sound projector (4), 8mm reel projector (1), S8mm reel projector (1), projection screens (3).
Other Media Collections *Audio:* disc, 33⅓ rpm, 4500c; tape, reel, 29c. *Filmstrips:* silent, 156t. *Slides:* single, 7112t.
Budget & Expenditures Total library budget $92,936 (FY 7/1/74-7/1/75). *Member:* EFLA, FLIC, Regional Film Library SW Mich.

C- WESTERN MICHIGAN UNIVERSITY, AV Center, 49008. *Tel:* (616) 383-1620. *In Charge:* James Robinson, Manager. *AV Staff:* 5 (2 prof, 3 cl). *Film Sel:* faculty/staff recommendations.
Free-Loan Film Serv *Eligibility:* staff & students. *Restrictions:* for indiv, none. Cannot use for fund-raising, transmit electronically. Available to researchers/scholars for on-site viewing. May not borrow by mail. *Loan Period:* 3 days. *Total Yr Film Loan:* 10,000.
Film Rental Serv *Eligibility:* no restrictions. *Restrictions:* only in Kalamazoo County. Cannot use for fund-raising, transmit electronically. *Rental Period:* 3 days. Produce films.

Film Collection Approx 10-20t acquired annually. *Circ:* 16mm, 1700t/1800p. *Pubns:* catalog, every 3 yrs ($1); suppl, no set policy. Permanent viewing facility. *Member:* AECT.
Video Serv *Est:* 1961. *In Charge:* Frank R. Jamison, Mgr TV Servs. *Video Staff:* 6 f-t, 21 p-t, 4 tech. *Video Use:* in-service training, practical video/TV training courses, as art form, classroom instruction. Video serv available by appointment. Produce video tapes. Have production studio/space & separate control room.
Video Equipment/Facilities *In-House Use Only:* porta-pak (2), EIAJ b&w, Sony; recording deck (8), ½″, 1″, 2″ b&w/col, Ampex, Sony; editing deck (3), ½″, 1″, 2″ b&w/col, Ampex, Sony; studio camera (8), b&w, Marconi; monitor (110), b&w/col; SEG (4); keyer (2); synthesizer (1); additional camera lenses (5); lighting; microphones. *For Loan:* portapak (6), EIAJ b&w, Sony; recording deck (34), ½″, 1″, 2″ b&w/col, Ampex, Sony; SEG (2); keyer (2); additional camera lenses (3); lighting; microphones. Have permanent viewing installation. *Equipment Loan Period:* no set policy. Provide training in use of equipment to faculty, staff & students. Have tape duplication serv.
Video Tape Loan/Rental/Sale Serv *Serv Provided:* free loan, swap with other inst, rental, sale. *Loan/Rental Eligibility:* staff. *Restrictions:* for campus use only. Cannot duplicate. May borrow by mail.
Video Collection Maintained by purchase, rental, own production, exchange/swap. Use/play ½″, 1″, 2″ reel to reel, ¾″ cassette. *Tape Sel:* preview, faculty/staff recommendations. Tapes organized by number. *Other Video Serv:* programming, taping of other media, production workshops. *Pubns:* catalog.
Cable & CCTV Receive serv of cable TV system. Produce programs for cablecasting. Inform public about cable system serv & facilities. Have CCTV in inst, with 100 monitors. *Programming Sources:* tapes produced by inst, tapes produced professionally.

Lansing

P- LANSING PUBLIC LIBRARY, 401 S Capitol Ave, 48914. *Tel:* (517) 485-2257, ext 61. *Film Serv Est:* 1964. *In Charge:* Neil F. Gatton, Film Librarian. *AV Staff:* 1 cl, ½ tech. *Film Sel:* committee preview, published reviews.
Free-Loan Film Serv *Eligibility:* indiv with library cards. *Restrictions:* none. Cannot use for fund-raising, transmit electronically. May not borrow by mail. *Loan Period:* 2 days.
Film Collection Approx 30t acquired annually. *Circ:* 16mm, 300t/p. *Pubns:* catalog, annual; suppl, no set policy. Publish film list, program notices.
Other Film Serv Obtain film from coop loan system (Mich. Library Film Circuit), film reference serv, library film programs. Permanent viewing facility available for rent to community.
Other Media Collections *Audio:* disc, 33⅓ rpm, 2500c; tape, cassette, 696c; tape, cartridge, 25c.
Budget & Expenditures Total film budget $12,000 (FY 7/1/74-7/1/75). *Member:* ALA, EFLA, FLIC, Mich. Library Assn.

Madison Heights

P- MADISON HEIGHTS PUBLIC LIBRARY, 240 W Thirteen Mile Rd, 48071. *Tel:* (313) 588-1200. *Film Serv Est:* 1972. *In Charge:* M. St. Amour, City Librarian. *AV Staff:* ½. *Film Sel:* faculty/staff recommendations, chief film librarian's decision, published reviews. *Holdings:* children's films 50%.
Free-Loan Film Serv *Eligibility:* civic groups, religious groups, indiv with library cards. *Restrictions:* for indiv, interlibrary loan, only in city; for inst, only in city. Cannot use for fund-raising, borrow for classroom use. Available to researchers/scholars for on-site viewing. May not borrow by mail. *Loan Period:* 1-7 days.
Film Collection 500t/p. Approx 50t acquired annually. *Circ:* 8mm reel, 425t/p; S8mm reel, 10t/p. *Noncirc:* 16mm, 15t/p. *Pubns:* catalog, as needed; suppl, no set policy. Publish film list.

Madison Heights (cont'd)

Other Film Serv Obtain film from coop loan system (Wayne County Federated Library System), library film programs. Permanent viewing facility available for rent to community. *Equipment:* lend 16mm sound projector (2), 8mm reel projector (1).

Other Media Collections *Audio:* disc, 33⅓ rpm, 500t; tape, cassette, 385t. *Filmstrips:* silent, 500t. *Slides:* sets, 15t.

Budget & Expenditures Total library budget $150,000 (FY 7/74-7/75). Total FY film budget $3000. *Member:* ALA, Mich. Library Assn.

Marquette

P- PETER WHITE PUBLIC LIBRARY, 217 N Front St, 48955. *Tel:* (906) 228-9510. *In Charge:* Ruth Kell. *Member:* Mich. Library Film Circuit, Inc.

Mason

P- INGHAM COUNTY LIBRARY, 145 W Ash St, 48854. *Tel:* (517) 677-3081. *In Charge:* J. Smith. *Member:* Mich. Library Film Circuit.

Monroe

P- MONROE COUNTY LIBRARY SYSTEM, AV Center, 3700 S Custer Rd, 48161. *Tel:* (313) 241-5277, ext 23. *Film Serv Est:* 1948. *In Charge:* Barbara Bradley, AV Circulation Head. *AV Staff:* 4.15 (1.4 prof, 2.75 cl, 1 tech). *Film Sel:* committee preview, staff recommendations, chief film librarian's decision, published reviews.

Free-Loan Film Serv *Eligibility:* staff & students, educational inst, civic groups, religious groups, indiv with library cards, prof groups, such as medical societies, & others, such as libraries. *Restrictions:* for indiv, only in Monroe County; for inst, only in Raisin Valley Library System. Cannot use for fund-raising, transmit electronically, borrow for classroom use. Available to researchers/scholars for on-site viewing. May borrow by mail. *Loan Period:* indiv, overnight; inst, 7 days plus. *Total Yr Film Loan:* 7246.

Film Rental Serv *Eligibility:* educational org, civic groups, patrons/public. *Restrictions:* none. *Rental Period:* as needed. *Total Yr Film Booking:* 7246. Sell films. Produce films. Produce filmstrips, slide-tape sets, audio cassettes.

Film Collection Approx 50-60t acquired annually. *Circ:* 16mm, 1220t/1225p; 8mm reel, 50t/p; S8mm reel, 105t/p; S8mm cartridge, 600t/650p. *Pubns:* catalog, as needed ($2); suppl, no set policy. Publish flyers.

Other Film Serv Obtain film from coop loan system (Southeast Mich. Regional Film Library), obtain film from other libraries. Permanent viewing facility available to community. *Equipment:* lend S8mm camera (1), rent 16mm sound projector (17), 8mm cartridge projector (1), 8mm reel projector (3), S8mm cartridge projector (17), S8mm reel projector (3), lend projection tables & stands (2), lend projection screens (16), rent PA system, audio tape recorders (20).

Other Media Collections *Audio:* disc, 33⅓ rpm, 6124c; tape, cassette, 870c; tape, reel, 50c. *Filmstrips:* sound, 652c; silent, 1895c; sound sets, 44c; silent sets, 35c. *Slides:* single, 2000c; sets, 50c.

Budget & Expenditures Total library budget $31,000 (FY 1/1/75-1/1/76). Total FY film budget $12,500. *Member:* AECT, ALA, EFLA, FLIC, Mich. Library Assn, Mich. Assn Media Educators, National AV Assn.

P- RAISIN VALLEY LIBRARY SYSTEM, SE, Michigan Regional Film Library, 3700 S Custer Rd, 48161. *Tel:* (313) 241-5277. *Film Serv Est:* 1975. *In Charge:* Mary Daume, Dir. *AV Staff:* 1½ (1 prof, ½ cl). *Film Sel:* committee preview.

Free-Loan Film Serv *Eligibility:* public libraries in SE Mich. May borrow by mail. *Loan Period:* 7 days.

Film Collection *Circ:* 16mm, 250t. *Pubns:* catalog, annual; suppl, no set policy. Publish flyers.

Budget & Expenditures Total library budget $90,000 (FY 7/75-7/76).

Muskegon

P- HACKLEY PUBLIC LIBRARY, 316 W Webster Ave, 49440. *Tel:* (616) 722-7276. *In Charge:* Clifford Wightman. *Member:* Mich. Library Film Circuit, Inc.

Niles

P- NILES PUBLIC LIBRARY, 610 W Main St, 49120. *Tel:* (616) 683-8545. *In Charge:* Anne Frese. *Member:* Mich. Library Film Circuit, Inc.

Otsego

P- OTSEGO DISTRICT PUBLIC LIBRARY, 219 S Farmer St, 49078. *Tel:* (616) 694-9690. *Film Serv Est:* 1970. *In Charge:* Klair H. Bates, Librarian. *AV Staff:* 1 (2 cl). *Film Sel:* faculty/staff recommendations, published reviews. *Holdings:* adult comedy 31%, animated films 24%, children's films 18%, dance 3%, feature films 6%, science 9%, social sciences 9%.

Free-Loan Film Serv *Eligibility:* educational inst, civic groups, religious groups, indiv with library cards. *Restrictions:* only in school district. Cannot use for fund-raising, transmit electronically. Available to researchers/scholars for on-site viewing. May not borrow by mail. *Loan Period:* 1 day. *Total Yr Film Loan:* 1152.

Film Collection 34t/p. Approx 5t acquired annually. *Circ:* 16mm, 23t; 8mm reel, 5t; S8mm reel, 6t. *Pubns:* catalog, as needed; suppl, no set policy.

Other Film Serv Obtain film from coop loan system (Kalamazoo Area Library System, Mich. Library Film Circuit), library film programs. Permanent viewing facility available to community. *Equipment:* lend 16mm sound projector (2), 8mm reel projector (1), S8mm reel projector (1), projection tables & stands (1), projection screens (1), cassette recorder (1), slide projector (1), filmstrip/tape viewer (1).

Other Media Collections *Audio:* tape, cassette, 15t/c. *Filmstrips:* sound sets, 6t/c.

Budget & Expenditures Total library budget $40,256 (FY 7/1/74-7/1/75). Total FY film budget $2364. *Member:* ALA, Mich. Library Assn.

Petoskey

P- PETOSKEY PUBLIC LIBRARY, 451 E Mitchell St, 49770. *Tel:* (616) 347-4200. *Member:* Mich. Library Film Circuit, Inc.

Port Huron

P- BLUE WATER LIBRARY FEDERATION, St. Clair County Library, 210 McMorran Blvd, 48060. *Tel:* (313) 985-6173. *Film Serv Est:* 1955. *In Charge:* Harry P. Wu, Dir. *AV Staff:* 2 prof. *Film Sel:* committee preview, faculty/staff recommendations. *Holdings:* agriculture .8%, animated films 9.7%, black studies .68%, children's films 11.4%, dance .3%, feature films 3%, fine arts 1.4%, industrial arts 1.4%, law .4%, science 7.6%, social sciences 11.9%, travel 15%, women .1%.

Film Rental Serv *Eligibility:* educational org, civic groups, patrons/public. *Restrictions:* only in Blue Water Federation area (Huron, Lapeer, Macomb, St. Clair & Sanilac counties). Cannot use for fund-raising, transmit electronically. *Rental Period:* 1 day. *Total Yr Film Booking:* 3345. Sell films. Produce slides, transparencies, cassettes, laminated posters.

Film Collection Approx 40-70t acquired annually. *Circ:* 16mm, 730t/740p; 8mm reel, 89t; S8mm reel, 144t. *Pubns:* catalog, annual; suppl, as needed. Publish flyers.

Other Film Serv   Rent film from distributors for patrons, obtain film from coop loan system (Mich. Library Film Circuit, E Mich. Film Region), film reference serv, library film programs. Permanent viewing facility available for rent to community. *Equipment:* rent 16mm sound projector (4), 8mm reel projector (16), S8mm reel projector (1), projection screens (6), slide projector (1), overhead projector (1), filmstrip projector (2).

Other Media Collections   *Audio:* disc, 33⅓ rpm, 2460t/3000c; tape, reel, 2t. *Filmstrips:* silent, 1588t/1700c; sound sets, 6t. *Slides:* sets, 15t.

Budget & Expenditures   Total library budget $91,510 (FY 1/1/74-1/1/75). Total FY film budget $14,540. *Member:* ALA, Mich. Library Assn.

C- ST. CLAIR COUNTY COMMUNITY COLLEGE, Learning Resources Center, 323 Erie St, 48060. *Tel:* (313) 984-3881, ext 278, 313. *Video Serv Est:* 1970. *In Charge:* Donna R. Williams, Telecommunications Coord. *Video Staff:* 1 p-t. *Video Use:* documentation of community/school events, community video access, practical video/TV training courses, playback only of professionally produced tapes. Video serv available on demand. Produce video tapes. Have production studio/space & separate control room.

Video Equipment/Facilities   *In-House Use Only:* recording deck (4), ½", 1", 1 cassette col, IVC, Sony, Wollensak; editing deck (1); studio camera (3), b&w, Panasonic; SEG (1), Shintron; lighting (2); audio tape recorders (1). *For Loan:* microphones (5); audio tape recorders (1). Have portable viewing installation. Provide training in use of equipment to students. Have tape duplication serv.

Video Tape Loan/Rental/Sale Serv   *Serv Provided:* free loan campus use only. *Loan Eligibility:* org members, staff & students, civic groups, religious groups, prof groups. *Restrictions:* for community college district only. Cannot use for fund-raising, duplicate. May not borrow by mail.

Video Collection   Maintained by rental, own production. Use/play ½", 1" reel to reel, ¾" cassette. *Sources:* community productions. *Tape Sel:* preview, faculty/staff recommendations. *Special Collections:* in-house training tapes, films in video format. Tapes organized by subject. *Collection, Color:* 1" reel, 2t; ¾" cassette, 50t. *Collection, B&W:* 1" reel, 20t/c. *Other Video Serv:* programming, taping of other media, production workshops.

Cable & CCTV   Receive serv of cable TV system. Run cable programs for special audiences. Have CCTV in inst, with 5 monitors. *Programming Sources:* over-the-air commercial & public broadcasting, tapes produced by inst, tapes produced professionally.

Portage

P- PORTAGE PUBLIC LIBRARY, Box 37, 49081. *Tel:* (616) 327-6725. *Film Serv Est:* 1968. *AV Staff:* 1½ (1 prof). *Film Sel:* AV Specialist preview.

Free-Loan Film Serv   *Eligibility:* educational inst, civic groups, religious groups, indiv with library cards, prof groups. *Restrictions:* for inst, none. Cannot use for fund-raising, transmit electronically. Available to researchers/scholars for on-site viewing. May not borrow by mail. *Loan Period:* 1 day. *Total Yr Film Loan:* 997.

Film Collection   197t. *Circ:* 16mm, 27t; 8mm reel, 170t. *Pubns:* catalog, annual; suppl, no set policy.

Other Film Serv   Rent film from distributors for patrons, obtain film from coop loan system (KETAL, Mich. Library Film Circuit), obtain film from other libraries, film fairs/festivals, library film programs. Permanent viewing facility available for rent to community. *Equipment:* lend 16mm sound projector (4), 8mm reel projector (4), S8mm reel projector (4), projection screens, slide projector (1), overhead projector (1), cassette players (5).

Other Media Collections   *Audio:* disc, 33⅓ rpm, 500c; tape, cassette, 120c.

Budget & Expenditures   Total library budget $17,500 (FY 7/1/75-7/1/76). Total FY film budget $2500. *Member:* ALA, Mich. Library Assn, Kalamazoo Area Library System.

Rochester

C- OAKLAND UNIVERSITY, AV Center, 120 Varner Hall, 48063. *Tel:* (313) 377-2461. *Film Serv Est:* 1974. *In Charge:* Thomas Lyons, AV Dir. *AV Staff:* 10 (3 prof, 2 cl, 5 tech). *Holdings:* fine arts 6%, science 19%, social sciences 55%, teacher education 20%.

Film Rental Serv   *Eligibility:* educational org. *Restrictions:* only in state. Cannot transmit electronically. *Rental Period:* 3 days. *Total Yr Film Booking:* 200. Produce sound/slide tapes, video tapes.

Film Collection   *Circ:* 16mm, 41t/p. *Pubns:* catalog, every 2 yrs.

Other Film Serv   Rent film from distributors for patrons, film reference serv. Permanent viewing facility available for rent to community. *Equipment:* rent 16mm sound projector (15), 8mm reel projector (4), S8mm cartridge projector (1), S8mm reel projector (1), projection tables & stands (20), projection screens (10).

Other Media Collections   *Audio:* disc, 33⅓ rpm, 5750t; tape, reel, 1194t.

Budget & Expenditures   Total library budget $110,000 (FY 7/1/74-7/1/75). *Member:* AECT, EFLA, MSIT, NSPI, MAME, Mich. Library Assn.

Video Serv   *In Charge:* Daniel Brown, TV Engineer. *Video Staff:* 2 f-t, 2½ p-t, 2 tech. *Video Use:* documentation of community/school events, in-service training, practical video/TV training courses. Video serv available by arrangement. Produce video tapes. Have production studio/space & separate control room.

Video Equipment/Facilities   *In-House Use Only:* portapak (1), ½" b&w, Sony; recording deck (1), ½" b&w, Sony 3600; playback deck (3), ½" b&w, Sony 3600, 3650; editing deck (2), ½" b&w, Sony 3650; studio camera (2), b&w, IVC 40MV; monitor (25), b&w, Sony; SEG (1), Ball Brothers; keyer (1), Ball Brothers; additional camera lenses (5); lighting (20); microphones (50); tripods (6); audio tape recorders (7). Have permanent viewing installation. *Equipment Loan Period:* 1-7 days. Provide training in use of equipment to faculty & AV techs. Have tape duplication serv.

Video Tape Loan/Rental/Sale Serv   *Serv Provided:* free loan. *Loan Eligibility:* staff & students, educational inst. *Restrictions:* for indiv, interlibrary loan; for inst, only in state. Cannot duplicate, air without permission. May borrow by mail. *Loan Period:* 3 days. *Total Yr Tape Loan:* 20.

Video Collection   Maintained by purchase, own production. Use/play ½", 2" reel to reel, ¾" cassette. *Tape Sel:* preview, faculty/staff recommendations, published reviews. *Collection, Color:* ¾" cassette, 23t/30c. *Collection, B&W:* ½" reel, 20t/c; ¾" cassette, 54t/c. *Other Video Serv:* production workshops. Publish materials on video.

St. Joseph

P- MAUD PRESTON PALENSKIE MEMORIAL LIBRARY, 500 Market St, 49085. *Tel:* (616) 983-7167. *In Charge:* Mayme Bachteal. *Member:* Mich. Library Film Circuit, Inc.

Sault Ste. Marie

P- EASTERN PENINSULA LIBRARY SYSTEM, Armory Place, 49783. *Tel:* (906) 632-9331. *In Charge:* Joseph Marconi. *Member:* Mich. Library Film Circuit, Inc.

C- LAKE SUPERIOR STATE COLLEGE, Library, 49783. *Tel:* (906) 635-5893, ext 403. *Film Serv Est:* 1971. *In Charge:* Ronald G. Level, AV Coord. *AV Staff:* 2 (1 prof, 1 tech). *Film Sel:* committee preview, faculty/staff recommendations.

Film Collection   100t/p. Approx 5t acquired annually. *Noncirc:* 16mm, 100t/p; S8mm reel, 35t/p.

Other Film Serv   Rent film from distributors for patrons. Permanent viewing facility.

Sault Ste. Marie (cont'd)
Other Media Collections *Audio:* disc, 78rpm, 629t/c. *Filmstrips:* sound sets, 124t/c. *Slides:* sets, 84t/c.

Budget & Expenditures Total library budget $78,748 (FY 7/1/74-7/1/75). No separate AV budget.

Video Serv *Est:* 1971. *Video Staff:* 1 f-t, 1 tech. *Video Use:* documentation of community/school events, in-service training, playback only of professionally produced tapes. Video serv available on demand. Produce video tapes. Have production studio/space.

Video Equipment/Facilities *In-House Use Only:* portapak (1), ½" b&w, Panasonic; recording deck (1), ½" b&w, Panasonic; playback deck (2), ½" b&w, Panasonic; editing deck (1), ½" col, Panasonic; studio camera (2), b&w, Panasonic; monitor (8), b&w/col, Sony; SEG (1), Panasonic; lighting (1 set); microphones (6); tripods (2); cassette recorders (2); cassette players (2). *For Rent:* recording deck (1), ½" b&w, Panasonic; playback deck (2), ½" b&w, Panasonic; studio camera (2), b&w, Panasonic; monitor (8), b&w/col, Sony; microphones (6); tripods (2); cassette recorders (2); cassette players (2). Have permanent viewing installation. *Equipment Rental Period:* no set policy. Provide training in use of equipment to faculty, students & renters. Have tape duplication serv. *Rental Eligibility:* org members, staff & students.

Video Collection Maintained by purchase, own production. Use/play ½" reel to reel, ¾" cassette. *Tape Sel:* preview, faculty/staff recommendations.

Cable & CCTV Receive serv of cable TV system.

Sturgis

P- STURGIS PUBLIC LIBRARY, N Nottana at West St, 49091. *Tel:* (616) 651-7907. *Film Serv Est:* 1965. *In Charge:* F. Taube, AV Libn. *AV Staff:* 1 prof. *Film Sel:* staff recommendations, published reviews.

Free-Loan Film Serv *Eligibility:* indiv with library cards. *Restrictions:* none. *Loan Period:* 7 days.

Film Collection 154t/p. Approx 20t acquired annually. *Circ:* 16mm, 4t; 8mm reel, 150t.

Other Film Serv Obtain film from coop loan system, obtain film from other libraries, library film programs. Permanent viewing facility available to community.

Other Media Collections *Filmstrips:* sound, 5t; sound sets, 5t.

Budget & Expenditures Total library budget $300. No separate AV budget. *Member:* ALA, Willard Library System, Mich. Library Assn.

Traverse City

P- TRAVERSE CITY PUBLIC LIBRARY, 322 Sixth St, 49684. *Tel:* (616) 947-3850. *In Charge:* Robert Olney. *Member:* Mich. Library Film Circuit, Inc.

Troy

P- TROY PUBLIC LIBRARY, AV Servs, 510 W Big Beaver Rd, 48084. *Tel:* (313) 689-5665, ext 27, 26, 22. *Film Serv Est:* 1972. *In Charge:* Marguerite Hart, AV Librarian. *AV Staff:* 3 (1 prof, 1 cl, 1 tech). *Film Sel:* chief film librarian's decision, published reviews.

Film Rental Serv *Eligibility:* educational org, civic groups, patrons/public. *Restrictions:* none. Cannot use for fund-raising, transmit electronically. *Rental Period:* 1 day.

Film Collection 280t/p. Approx 50-60t acquired annually. *Circ:* 16mm, 160t/p; 8mm 120t/p. Publish bibliographies. Will publish catalog.

Other Film Serv Obtain film from coop loan system (Wayne Oakland Federated Library System), film reference serv, library film programs. Permanent viewing facility available for rent to community. *Equipment:* 16mm sound projector (2), projection tables & stands (2), projection screens (2).

Other Media Collections *Audio:* disc, 33⅓ rpm, 1330t; tape, cassette, 1978t. *Filmstrips:* sound, 523t; silent, 36t.

Budget & Expenditures Total library budget $125,840 (FY 7/1/74-7/1/75). Total FY film budget $26,000. *Member:* ALA, EFLA, Mich. Library Assn.

University Center

C- SAGINAW VALLEY STATE COLLEGE, Media Servs Dept/ Learning Resources Center, 2250 Pierce Rd, 48710. *Tel:* (517) 793-9800, ext 244. *Film Serv Est:* 1972. *In Charge:* Dorothy Horwath, Media Servs Librarian. *AV Staff:* 1¾ (1 prof, ¾ tech). *Film Sel:* faculty/staff recommendations.

Film Collection Approx 3t acquired annually. *Circ:* 16mm, 65t/p.

Other Film Serv Rent film from distributors for patrons, obtain film from other libraries. Permanent viewing facility.

Other Media Collections *Audio:* disc, 33⅓ rpm, 1320t; tape, reel, 1690t/1800c. *Filmstrips:* silent, 50t; sound sets, 7t. *Slides:* single, 3640t; sets, 8t. *Member:* AECT, ALA, EFLA.

Warren

P- WARREN PUBLIC LIBRARY, Miller Branch Library, 4700 E 13 Mile Rd, 48092. *Tel:* (313) 751-5370. *In Charge:* Mrs. D. Gerstner, Supervisory Librarian. *AV Staff:* 7. *Film Sel:* staff recommendations.

Free-Loan Film Serv *Eligibility:* staff & students, educational inst, civic groups, religious groups, indiv with library cards. *Restrictions:* for indiv & inst, only in Macomb County. May not borrow by mail. *Loan Period:* 7 days. *Total Yr Film Loan:* 883.

Film Collection 386t. Publish list of holdings.

Other Film Serv Obtain film from coop loan system (Macomb County Public Library). *Equipment:* lend 16mm sound projector (1), 8mm reel projector (1), S8mm reel projector (1), projection screens (1).

Other Media Collections *Audio:* disc, 33⅓ rpm, 1317t; tape, cartridge, 652t.

Budget & Expenditures Total library budget $708,473 (FY 7/1/75-7/1/76). No separate AV budget. *Member:* ALA, Mich. Library Assn.

Wayne

P- WATERFORD TOWNSHIP PUBLIC LIBRARY, Wayne-Oakland Federated Library System, 33030 VanBorn Rd, 48184. *Tel:* (313) 722-8000. *Film Serv Est:* 1968.

Free-Loan Film Serv *Eligibility:* civic groups, religious groups, indiv with library cards. *Restrictions:* for indiv, only in Township & service area. May borrow by mail. *Loan Period:* 1 day. *Total Yr Film Loan:* 125.

Film Collection Approx 5t acquired annually. *Circ:* 8mm reel & cartridge, 20t.

Other Media Collections *Audio:* disc, 33⅓ rpm, 681c; tape, cassette, 161c. *Filmstrips:* silent sets, 51c. *Slides:* single, 93c.

Budget & Expenditures Total library budget $11,500. No separate AV budget.

Ypsilanti

C- EASTERN MICHIGAN UNIVERSITY, Media Servs, 112 Library, 48197. *Tel:* (313) 487-2220. *Film Serv Est:* 1948. *In Charge:* Verne W. Weber, Media Servs Head. *AV Staff:* 19 (9 prof, 5 cl, 5 tech). *Film Sel:* faculty/staff recommendations.

Free-Loan Film Serv *Eligibility:* staff & students. *Restrictions:* for indiv, none. Cannot use for fund-raising. May not borrow by mail. *Total Yr Film Loan:* 4700. Sell films. Produce films.

Film Collection 1000t. Approx 20-60t acquired annually. *Circ:* 16mm, 1000t; 8mm cartridge, 300t; S8mm cartridge, 100t. *Pubns:* catalog, every 5 yrs.

Other Film Serv Rent film from distributors for patrons. Permanent viewing facility. *Equipment:* lend S8mm camera,

16mm camera, 16mm sound projector, 8mm cartridge projector, 8mm reel projector, S8mm cartridge projector, S8mm reel projector, projection tables & stands, projection screens.

Other Media Collections *Audio:* disc, 33⅓ rpm, 3400t; tape, cassette, 1600t. *Filmstrips:* 9000t.

Budget & Expenditures Total FY film budget $12,000 (FY 6/30/75-6/30/76). *Member:* AECT, AFI, DAFT.

Video Serv *Est:* 1960. *Video Staff:* 19 f-t, 25 p-t, 5 tech. *Video Use:* documentation of community/school events, community video access, in-service training, practical video/TV training courses, as art form. Video serv available on demand. Produce video tapes. Have production studio/space & separate control room.

Video Equipment/Facilities *In-House Use Only:* portapak (5), ½" b&w, Sony 3400; recording deck (20), ½" b&w, Sony 2400, 2600, 3600; playback deck (2), ¾" col, Sony 1600, 1800; editing deck (4), ½", 1" b&w/col, Sony, IVC; studio camera (4), b&w, RCA, Ampex, Tel; monitor (300), 23" b&w, RCA, MAG; SEG (2), VITAL, RCA; lighting (40); microphones (30); tripods (15); audio tape recorders (8). Have permanent viewing installation. Provide training in use of equipment to faculty, students & staff. Have tape duplication serv.

Video Tape Loan/Rental/Sale Serv *Serv Provided:* free loan. *Loan Eligibility:* org members, staff, students enrolled in inst, & others, such as community groups. Cannot duplicate, air without permission. May borrow by mail.

Video Collection Maintained by own production. Use/ play ½", 1", 2" reel to reel, ¾" cassette. *Tape Sel:* faculty/staff recommendations. *Special Collections:* in-house training tapes. Tapes organized by subject. *Collection, Color:* ½" reel, 20t; 1" reel, 100t; ¾" cassette, 115t. *Collection, B&W:* ½" reel, 780t; 1" reel, 400t; 2" reel, 500t; ¾" cassette, 40t. *Other Video Serv:* programming, production workshops.

Cable & CCTV Produce programs for cablecasting. Have CCTV in inst, with 300 monitors. *Programming Sources:* over-the-air commercial & public broadcasting, tapes produced by inst, tapes produced professionally.

Minnesota

Albert Lea

P- ALBERT LEA PUBLIC LIBRARY, 211 E Clark St, 56007. *Tel:* (507) 373-8862. *Film Serv Est:* 1969. *In Charge:* Gail Evenson, Film Clerk. *AV Staff:* 1 cl. *Film Sel:* published reviews.

Free-Loan Film Serv *Eligibility:* educational inst, civic groups, religious groups, prof groups. *Restrictions:* for inst, only in our county. Cannot borrow for classroom or individual home use. Available to researchers/scholars for on-site viewing. May borrow by mail. *Loan Period:* 1 day. *Total Yr Film Loan:* 1009.

Film Collection 75t/p. *Circ:* 8mm reel, 75t/p.

Other Film Serv Obtain film from coop loan system (Minn. Library Film Circuit), obtain film from other libraries. Permanent viewing facility available for rent to community. *Equipment:* lend 16mm sound projector (1), Dual S8mm reel projector (1), projection screens (1).

Budget & Expenditures Total library budget $12,905 (FY 1/1/74-1/1/75). Total FY film budget $900. *Member:* Minn. Library Assn.

Alexandria

P- ALEXANDRIA PUBLIC LIBRARY, Seventh & Fillmore St, 56308. *Tel:* (612) 763-4640. *Member:* Minn. Library Film Circuit.

Austin

P- AUSTIN-MOWER COUNTY LIBRARY, 201 Second Ave NW, 55912. *Tel:* (507) 433-2391. *Member:* Minn. Library Film Circuit.

Bemidji

P- BEMIDJI PUBLIC LIBRARY, 602 Beltrami Ave, 56601. *Tel:* (218) 751-3963.

Free-Loan Film Serv *Eligibility:* indiv with library cards. *Restrictions:* for indiv, only in our county & Cass, Crowwing & Wadena. Cannot use for fund-raising. Available to researchers/scholars for on-site viewing. May not borrow by mail. *Loan Period:* 7 days.

Other Film Serv Obtain film from coop loan system (Minn. Circulating Film System). *Equipment:* lend 16mm sound projector (1).

Other Media Collections *Filmstrips:* silent, 30t.

Blaine

P- ANOKA COUNTY LIBRARY, 707 Highway 10, 55434. *Tel:* (612) 784-1100. *Member:* Minn. Library Film Circuit.

Brainerd

C- BRAINERD COMMUNITY COLLEGE, College Dr, 56401. *Tel:* (218) 829-4771. *In Charge:* Stephen Bibus, AV Aide. *AV Staff:* 2 (2 cl).

Other Film Serv Rent film from distributors for faculty, obtain film from other libraries, film reference serv. Permanent viewing facility available for rent to community. *Equipment:* lend S8mm camera (1), 16mm sound projector (4), 8mm reel projector (1), S8mm reel projector (1), projection tables & stands (4), projection screens (10).

Other Media Collections *Audio:* disc, 33⅓ rpm, 300t/c; tape, cassette, 10t/c; tape, reel, 10t/c. *Filmstrips:* sound sets, 100c. *Slides:* sets, 5c.

Video Serv *Est:* 1975. *Video Staff:* 2 f-t. *Video Use:* documentation of community/school events. Video serv available on demand. Produce video tapes.

Video Equipment/Facilities *In-House Use Only:* recording deck (1), ¾″ col, Sony VO-1800; studio camera (1), b&w, Shibaden; monitor (2), b&w/col, Sony KV-1711, Setchell Carlson; microphones (4); tripods (1); tuner timer (1). *For Loan:* audio tape recorders (15). Have portable viewing installation. Provide training in use of equipment to anyone who needs it.

Video Tape Loan/Rental/Sale Serv *Serv Provided:* swap with other inst. *Loan Eligibility:* staff & students, educational inst, civic groups, religious groups, indiv with library cards. *Restrictions:* for indiv, only in our county; for inst, only in our county. Cannot use for fund-raising, air without permission. May borrow by mail. *Loan Period:* as long as needed. *Total Yr Tape Loan:* 2.

Video Collection Maintained by own production. Use/play ¾″ cassette. *Sources:* community productions. *Collection, B&W:* ¾″ cassette, 15t/c. *Other Video Serv:* reference serv.

Burnsville

P- DAKOTA COUNTY LIBRARY SYSTEM, 1101 W County Road 42, 55337. *Tel:* (612) 435-8111. *Member:* Minn. Library Film Circuit.

Cambridge

P- EAST CENTRAL REGIONAL LIBRARY, 244 S Birch St, 55008. *Tel:* (612) 689-1901. *Film Serv Est:* 1960. *In Charge:* Alzina Stone, Film Clerk.

Free-Loan Film Serv *Eligibility:* educational inst, civic groups, religious groups, indiv with library cards, prof groups. *Restrictions:* for indiv, only in our six-county region; for inst, in six-county region. May borrow by mail. *Loan Period:* 1 day.

Film Collection 4t/p. *Pubns:* catalog, annual.

Other Film Serv Obtain film from coop loan system (Minn. Library Film Circuit), library film programs. *Equipment:* lend 16mm sound projector (6), projection screens.

Other Media Collections *Audio:* disc, 33⅓ rpm, 3314c; tape, cassette, 107c. *Filmstrips:* silent, 858c; silent sets, 73c. *Slides:* sets, 47t/c.

Budget & Expenditures Total library budget $47,400 (FY 7/1/74-7/1/75). Total FY film budget $1800. *Member:* ALA, Minn. Library Assn.

Chaska

P- CARVER COUNTY LIBRARY, 314 Walnut St, 55318. *Tel:* (612) 448-2782. *Member:* Minn. Library Film Circuit.

Coon Rapids

C- ANOKA-RAMSEY COMMUNITY COLLEGE, 11200 Mississippi Blvd, 55433. *Tel:* (612) 427-2600, ext 251. *Film Serv Est:* 1967. *In Charge:* Cress Gackle, AV Dir. *AV Staff:* 2 (2 prof). *Film Sel:* faculty/staff recommendations.

Free-Loan Film Serv *Eligibility:* staff & students, community groups. *Restrictions:* for indiv, none; for inst, only in city. Cannot use for fund-raising, transmit electronically, borrow for classroom use. Available to researchers/scholars for on-site viewing. May not borrow by mail. *Loan Period:* 1 day.

Film Collection 160t. Approx 10t acquired annually. *Circ:* 16mm, 40t; S8mm cartridge, 135p. *Noncirc:* 16mm, 1t. *Pubns:* catalog, annual.

Other Film Serv Obtain film from coop loan system (Metro Film Coop). *Equipment:* lend S8mm camera (1), 16mm camera (1), 16mm sound projector (12), 8mm cartridge projector (13), 8mm reel projector (2), S8mm cartridge projector (12), S8mm reel projector (2).

Other Media Collections *Audio:* disc, 200c; tape, 400c. *Filmstrips:* sound, 326c; sound sets, 7c. *Slides:* single, 12c.

Budget & Expenditures Total library budget $23,000. Total FY film budget $3700 (incl rentals).

Video Serv *Est:* 1967. *Video Staff:* 2 f-t, 8 p-t, 2 tech. *Video Use:* documentation of community/school events, to increase community's library use, community video access, in-service training. Video serv available by appointment. Produce video tapes. Have production studio/space & separate control room.

Video Equipment/Facilities *In-House Use Only:* portapak (1), ½" b&w/col, Panasonic 3082; recording deck (5), ½" b&w/col, Panasonic 3600, 3120; editing deck (1), ½" col, Panasonic 1120; studio camera (1), col, Shibaden 1000A; monitor (8); SEG (1); additional camera lenses; lighting; microphones; tripods; audio tape recorders. *For Loan:* portapak (1), ½" b&w/col, Panasonic 3082. Have portable viewing installation. Provide training in use of equipment to faculty & students. Have tape duplication serv.

Video Tape Loan/Rental/Sale Serv *Serv Provided:* free loan, swap with other inst. *Loan Eligibility:* staff & students, educational inst, civic groups, prof groups. *Restrictions:* for indiv, none; for inst, none. May not borrow by mail.

Video Collection Maintained by purchase, own production, exchange/swap. Use/play ½" reel to reel, ½" cartridge, ¾" cassette. *Sources:* commercial distributors. Tapes organized by Dewey Decimal. *Collection, Color:* ½" reel, 175t; ½" cartridge, 10t/c; ¾" cassette, 10t/c. *Collection, B&W:* ½" reel, 25t. *Other Video Serv:* production workshops on demand.

Duluth

P- DULUTH PUBLIC LIBRARY, 101 W Second St, 55802. *Tel:* (218) 722-5803. *Film Serv Est:* 1966. *In Charge:* Paul Roen, Library Asst II. *AV Staff:* 2 (1 cl, 1 tech). *Film Sel:* committee preview.

Free-Loan Film Serv *Eligibility:* civic groups, religious groups, indiv with library cards, prof groups. *Restrictions:* for indiv, only in 7-county Arrowhead Library System; for inst, only in state. Cannot transmit electronically, borrow for classroom use. May borrow by mail. *Loan Period:* 1-7 days.

Film Collection 139t/p. Approx 6t acquired annually. *Circ:* 8mm reel, 123t/p. *Noncirc:* 16mm, 16t/p.

Other Film Serv Rent film from distributors for patrons, obtain film from coop loan system (Minn. Library Film Circuit), film reference serv, library film programs. *Equipment:* rent 16mm sound projector (1), 8mm reel projector (1), projection screens (2).

Other Media Collections *Audio:* disc, 33⅓rpm, 2721c; tape, cassette, 1415c. *Filmstrips:* sound, silent, sound sets, silent sets, 267c. *Slides:* single, 898c.

Budget & Expenditures Total library budget $120,000 (FY 1/1/74-1/1/75). Total FY film budget $8569. No separate budget. *Member:* ALA, Minn. Library Assn.

Video Serv *Est:* 1974. *In Charge:* Jeanette Smith. *Video Use:* to increase community's library use, in-service training. Video serv available by appointment. Produce video tapes.

Video Equipment/Facilities *In-House Use Only:* recording deck (1), b&w, Panasonic; editing deck (1), b&w; studio camera (1), b&w; monitor (2); microphones (3); tripods (1); audio tape recorders (1).

Video Collection Maintained by own production. Use/play ½" reel to reel.

Cable & CCTV Produce programs for cablecasting.

Fairmont

P- MARTIN COUNTY LIBRARY, 110 N Park St, 56031. *Tel:* (507) 238-4207. *Member:* Minn. Library Film Circuit.

Faribault

P- FARIBAULT (BUCKHAM MEMORIAL LIBRARY), Division & Central St, 55021. *Tel:* (507) 334-5635. *Member:* Minn. Library Film Circuit.

Fergus Falls

P- FERGUS FALLS PUBLIC LIBRARY, 125 N Union, 56537. *Tel:* (218) 739-9387. *Member:* Minn. Library Film Circuit.

Fridley

P- ANOKA COUNTY LIBRARY, Fridley Branch Library, 410 Mississippi St, 55421. *Tel:* (612) 571-1934. *In Charge:* Mark Scott, Media Spec. *AV Staff:* 1 prof. *Film Sel:* staff recommendations, chief film librarian's decision, published reviews.

Free-Loan Film Serv *Eligibility:* indiv with library cards. *Restrictions:* for indiv, none; interlibrary loan, only in city; only in state; only in our 7-county area; for inst, only in our 7-county area. Available to researchers/scholars for on-site viewing. May borrow by mail. *Loan Period:* 1 day. *Total Yr Film Loan:* 4286.

Film Collection 85t/p. *Circ:* 16mm, 85t/p; 8mm reel, 8mm cartridge, S8mm reel, & S8mm cartridge, 450t/p. *Pubns:* publish announcements of film showings.

Other Film Serv Obtain film from coop loan system (Minn. Film Library Circuit), obtain film from other libraries, film reference serv, library film programs. Permanent viewing facility available free to community. *Equipment:* rent 16mm sound projector (5), 8mm/S8mm reel projector (7), projection screens (2), cassette player (5), slide projector/sync (1) reel to reel tape player (1), portapak (1).

Other Media Collections *Audio:* disc, 33⅓rpm, 4387t; tape, cassette, 139t. *Filmstrips:* sound sets, 8t/c. *Slides:* sets, 2t/c. *Member:* ALA, Minn. Library Assn.

Video Serv *Est:* 1975. *Video Use:* to increase community's library use, community video access, in-service training, as art form. Video serv available on demand & by appointment. Produce video tapes. Have production studio/space.

Video Equipment/Facilities *In-House Use Only:* monitor (1), col, Sony; microphones (2); tripods (1); audio tape recorders (1); amplifier (1); modulator (1). *For Loan:* portapak (1), ½" b&w, Sony 8400; microphones (1); tripods (1); audio tape recorders (1). Have portable viewing installation(s). *Equipment Loan Period:* 1 day. Provide training in use of equipment to anyone.

Video Tape Loan/Rental/Sale Serv *Serv Provided:* free loan, swap with other inst. *Loan Eligibility:* indiv with library cards. *Restrictions:* for indiv, only in Anoka County; for inst only in Anoka County. Cannot duplicate, air without permission.

Video Collection Maintained by own production, exchange/swap. Use/play ½" reel to reel. *Sources:* community productions, exchange (Minneapolis & St Paul). *Tape Sel:* preview, staff recommendations, catalogs, Anoka County communications workshop. *Collection, B&W:* ½" reel, 10t/c. *Other Video Serv:* programming, production workshops. *Pubns:* publish portapak flyer.

Cable & CCTV Receive serv of cable TV system. Produce programs for cablecasting. Inform public about cable system serv & facilities. Serve as production facility for others. Have advisory/administrative role in cable system operation. Have CCTV in inst, with 1 monitor. *Programming Sources:* tapes produced by inst, tapes produced by community groups & indiv.

Hibbing

P- HIBBING PUBLIC LIBRARY, 2020 E Fifth Ave, 55746. *Tel:* (218) 262-1038. *Member:* Minn. Library Film Circuit.

Inver Grove Heights

C- INVER HILLS COMMUNITY COLLEGE, Learning Resources Center, 8445 College Trail, 55075. *Tel:* (612) 455-9621, ext 58. *Film Serv Est:* 1970. *In Charge:* Wes Lines, AV Dir. *AV Staff:* 3 (1 prof, 1 tech). *Film Sel:* committee preview, faculty/staff recommendations, chief film librarian's decision. *Holdings:* feature films 10%, science 50%, social sciences 30%.

Inver Grove Heights (cont'd)

Free-Loan Film Serv *Eligibility:* staff & students, Twin Cities Metro Area State Community Colleges. *Restrictions:* for inst, only in city, including Minneapolis. Available to researchers/scholars for on-site viewing. May not borrow by mail.

Film Collection *Circ:* 16mm, 42t; S8mm cartridge, 375t. *Pubns:* catalog, annual.

Other Film Serv Rent film from distributors for patrons, obtain film from coop loan system (Metro Area State Community Colleges), obtain film from other libraries, library film programs. *Equipment:* lend S8mm camera (1), 16mm camera (1), 16mm sound projector (6), S8mm cartridge projector (6), S8mm reel projector (3), projection screens (4).

Other Media Collections *Audio:* disc, 33⅓ rpm, 1400t; tape, cassette, cartridge, & reel, 1700t. *Filmstrips:* sound & silent, 82t; sound sets, 40t. *Slides:* single, 10,000t; sets, 50t.

Budget & Expenditures Total library budget $26,600 (FY 7/1/74-7/1/75). Total FY film budget $1150.

Video Serv *Est:* 1970. *In Charge:* Wes Lines, AV Dir. *Video Staff:* 3 f-t, 1 tech. *Video Use:* documentation of community/school events, in-service training, playback only of professionally produced tapes. Video serv available by appointment. Produce video tapes. Have production studio/space.

Video Equipment/Facilities *In-House Use Only:* portapak (1), ½″ b&w, Sony; recording/playback deck (1), ½″ b&w, Concord; editing deck (1), ½″ col, Concord; studio camera (2), b&w, Sony, Concord; monitor (5), b&w/col, RCA, Sony, Concord; microphones; tripods (3); audio tape recorders. Provide training in use of equipment to faculty & students.

Video Tape Loan/Rental/Sale Serv *Serv Provided:* swap with other inst. *Loan Eligibility:* staff & students, educational inst. *Restrictions:* for indiv, none; for inst, only in city. May not borrow by mail.

Video Collection Maintained by own production, exchange/swap. Use/play ½″ reel to reel. *Tape Sel:* faculty/staff recommendations. Tapes organized by subject. *Collection, Color/B&W:* ½″ reel, 350t.

Lake Elmo

P- WASHINGTON COUNTY LIBRARY, 3459 Lake Elmo Ave N, 55042. *Tel:* (612) 777-8143. *Member:* Minn. Library Film Circuit.

Mankato

C- MANKATO STATE UNIVERSITY, Educational Resource Center, M.S.U., 101 Memorial Library, 56001. *Tel:* (507) 389-1913, 2019. *Film Serv Est:* 1966-67. *In Charge:* David W. Allan, Coord. *AV Staff:* 6 (3 prof, 3 cl). *Film Sel:* faculty/staff recommendations, chief film librarian's decision, published reviews. *Holdings:* agriculture 3%, animated films 6%, black studies 12%, career education 5%, children's films 10%, consumer affairs 5%, dance 5%, engineering 1%, experimental films 5%, feature films 1%, fine arts 2%, industrial arts 5%, law 1%, medicine 2%, psychology 10%, science 3%, social sciences 15%, teacher education 6%, women 3%.

Free-Loan Film Serv *Eligibility:* staff & students. *Restrictions:* for indiv, interlibrary loan. Cannot use for fund-raising, transmit electronically. Available to researchers/scholars for on-site viewing. May not borrow by mail. *Loan Period:* 3 days. *Total Yr Film Loan:* 6764.

Film Collection 1490t/1719p. Approx 15-20t acquired annually. *Circ:* 16mm, 1490t/1719p; 8mm reel, 2t/6p; 8mm cartridge, 660t/675p; S8mm cartridge, 4t/10p. *Pubns:* microfiche catalog, quarterly ($.50). Publish materials pertaining to collection.

Other Film Serv Rent film from distributors for patrons, obtain film from coop loan system (Educational Regional Film Library), obtain film from other libraries, film reference serv, library film programs. Permanent viewing facility. *Equipment:* lend 16mm sound projector (43), 8mm cartridge projector (19), 8mm reel projector (4), S8mm cartridge projector (20), S8mm reel projector (3), projection tables & stands (50), projection screens, 2″ x 2″ slide, filmstrip, overhead & opaque projectors.

Other Media Collections *Audio:* disc, 33⅓ rpm, 45rpm, 78rpm, 800t/875c; tape, cassette, cartridge, & reel, 905t/1065c. *Filmstrips:* sound, & silent, 800-1000t/c, sound sets, 66t/c; silent sets, 200t/c. *Slides:* sets, 1500-2000t/c.

Budget & Expenditures Total library budget $200,000 (FY 7/74-7/75). Total FY film budget $3500. *Member:* AECT, ALA, EFLA, Minn. Library Assn.

Video Serv *Est:* 1963-4. *In Charge:* David Allan. *Video Staff:* 6 f-t, 2 tech. *Video Use:* in-service training, practical video/TV training courses. Video serv available on demand & by appointment. Produce video tapes. Have production studio/space & separate control room.

Video Equipment/Facilities *In-House Use Only:* recording deck (4), ½″, ¾″ b&w/col, Panasonic 3130 & 2120; editing deck (2), ½″ b&w/col, Panasonic 3130; studio camera (3), b&w, Concord R 2L-5, Panasonic WV341P; SEG (1), Concord; lighting (7); microphones (7); tripods (5). *For Loan:* portapak (2), ½″ b&w, Sony 2400, Panasonic 3085; recording deck (14), ½″, 1″ b&w/col, Ampex 5000/5100 & 7500, Sony 2200 & 3600; playback deck (3), ¾″ b&w/col, Sony 1000, Panasonic 2110M; studio camera (6), b&w, Panasonic WV341P; monitor (36) b&w/col, Panasonic CT-25V, TR-513 V & CT-98V, Setchel 19P65, 9M902 & 2100 SD, RCA CF 315 W; Tripods (8); audio tape recorders cassette (184) & reel (37). Have portable viewing installation. *Equipment Loan Period:* 2 days. Provide training in use of equipment to anyone. Have tape duplication serv.

Video Tape Loan/Rental/Sale Serv *Serv Provided:* free loan, swap with other inst. *Loan Eligibility:* staff & students, some educational inst, civic groups, religious groups, prof groups. *Restrictions:* for indiv, only in city & county; for inst, only in city & county. Cannot duplicate, air without permission. May not borrow by mail.

Video Collection Maintained by purchase, rental, own production, exchange/swap. Use/play ½″, 1″, 2″ reel to reel, ¾″ cassette. *Sources:* commercial distributors, exchange (other state universities in Minn.). *Tape Sel:* preview, faculty/staff recommendations. Tapes organized by title. *Collection, Color:* ½″ reel, 50t/c; ¾″ cassette, 65t/c. *Collection, B&W:* ½″ reel, 180t/c; ¾″ cassette, 20t/c. *Other Video Serv:* programming, production workshops. *Pubns:* catalog & suppl.

Cable & CCTV Receive serv of cable TV system. Produce programs for cablecasting. Run cable programs for special audiences. Have CCTV in inst. *Programming Sources:* tapes produced by inst, tapes produced professionally, tapes produced by community groups & indiv.

P- MINNESOTA VALLEY REGIONAL LIBRARY, 120 S Broad St, 56001. *Tel:* (507) 387-3431. *Member:* Minn. Library Film Circuit.

P- TRAVERSE DES SIOUX REGIONAL LIBRARY, 516 S Broad St, 56001. *Tel:* (507) 387-6169. *Member:* Minn. Library Film Circuit.

Marshall

P- MARSHALL LYON COUNTY LIBRARY, 301 W Lyon St, 56258. *Tel:* (507) 532-2046. *Member:* Minn. Library Film Circuit.

C- SOUTHWEST STATE UNIVERSITY, Instructional Resources Center, 56258. *Tel:* (507) 537-7210. *Film Serv Est:* 1969. *In Charge:* Frank Shindo, Coord. *AV Staff:* ½ (1 prof). *Film Sel:* faculty/staff recommendations.

Free-Loan Film Serv *Eligibility:* staff & students. *Restrictions:* cannot use for fund-raising. Available to researchers/scholars for on-site viewing. May not borrow by mail. *Total Yr Film Loan:* 1000.

Film Collection 750t/764p. Approx 80t acquired annually. *Noncirc:* 16mm, 750t/p; 8mm cartridge, 30t/p; S8mm reel, 50t/p; S8mm cartridge, 800t/p.

Other Film Serv Obtain film from other libraries, film reference serv. Permanent viewing facility available for rent to community. *Equipment:* lend (to university community only) 16mm sound projector (25), 8mm cartridge projector (2), 8mm reel projector (4), S8mm cartridge projector (12), S8mm reel projector (2), projection tables & stands (20), projection screens (8).

Other Media Collections *Audio:* disc, 33⅓rpm, 6000t; tape, cassette, 1000t; tape, reel, 2000t. *Filmstrips:* sound & silent, 800t; sound sets & silent sets, 500t. *Slides:* single, 10,000t; sets, 58t.

Budget & Expenditures Total library budget $97,000 (FY 7/1/74-7/1/75). No separate AV budget. *Member:* AECT, ALA, Minn. Library Assn, AVCAM.

Video Serv *Est:* 1968. *In Charge:* Soren Munkhof. *Video Staff:* 4 f-t, 2 tech. *Video Use:* in-service training, practical video/TV training courses, playback only of professionally produced tapes. Video serv available by appointment. Produce video tapes. Have production studio/space & separate control room.

Video Equipment/Facilities *In-House Use Only:* portapak (14), ½" b&w, Sony 3400; recording deck (7), 1" b&w, Ampex 5100, 7000, 7800; playback deck (34), ½" b&w, Sony 3600, Panasonic; editing deck (4), ½", 1" b&w, RCA, Sony; studio camera (14), b&w, Sony, Panasonic, Shibaden; monitor (30), b&w, RCA, Shibaden, Sony; SEG (1), Shibaden; additional camera lenses (6); lighting (30); microphones (28); tripods (14); audio tape recorders (110); Sync Generator (4). Have permanent & portable viewing installations. Provide training in use of equipment to faculty & students. Have tape duplication serv.

Video Collection Maintained by purchase, own production. Use/play ½", 1" reel to reel, ¾" cassette. *Tape Sel:* preview, published reviews. *Collection, B&W:* ½" reel, 60t; 1" reel, 289t; ¾" cassette, 124t. *Other Video Serv:* programming, taping of other media, production workshops.

Cable & CCTV Receive serv of cable TV system. Produce programs for cablecasting. Have CCTV in inst, with 11 monitors. *Programming Sources:* over-the-air commercial & public broadcasting, tapes produced by inst, tapes produced professionally.

Minneapolis

C- MINNEAPOLIS COLLEGE OF ART & DESIGN LIBRARY, 200 E 25 St, 55404. *Tel:* (612) 874-0300, ext 291-2. *Video Serv Est:* 1974. *In Charge:* George de Stefano, Dir. *Video Staff:* 2 f-t, 1 p-t, 1 tech. *Video Use:* documentation of community/school events, to increase community's library use, practical video/TV training courses, playback only of professionally produced tapes, as art form, degree program. Video serv available on demand & by appointment. Produce video tapes. Have production studio/space & separate control room.

Video Equipment/Facilities *In-House Use Only:* recording deck (5), ½", ¾", 1" b&w, Sony 3400 & 3650, Ampex 5800; playback deck (2), ¼" col, Wollensack; editing deck (2), ¼", 1" col, Ampex 5800, Sony VO1600; studio camera (4), Shibaden, Magnavox; monitor (26), b&w/col; SEG (1); lighting (12); microphones (6); tripods (2); audio tape recorders (1). *For Loan:* portapak (3), b&w, Sony 3400; recording deck (5), ½", ¾", 1" b&w, Ampex 5800, Sony 3400, 3650, VO1600. Have permanent & portable viewing installations. *Equipment Loan Period:* 1 day. Provide training in use of equipment to faculty & students. Have tape duplication serv.

Video Tape Loan/Rental/Sale Serv *Serv Provided:* swap with other inst. *Loan Eligibility:* org members, staff & students. *Restrictions:* for inst, none. Cannot use for fundraising, duplicate. May not borrow by mail.

Video Collection Maintained by own production. Use/play ½", ¼", 1" reel to reel, ¾" cassette. *Sources:* commercial distributors, galleries, visiting artist program. *Tape Sel:* preview, faculty/staff recommendations, gallery previews. *Special Collections:* in-house training tapes, video as art, films in video format. Tapes organized by Dewey Decimal, subject & succession number. *Collection, Color:* 1" reel & ¾" cassette, 250t/c. *Collection, B&W:* ½" reel, 60t/c. *Other Video Serv:* programming, taping of other media, production workshops. *Pubns:* catalog & suppl.

Cable & CCTV Produce programs for cablecasting. Run cable programs for special audiences. Have CCTV in inst, with 24 monitors. *Programming Sources:* tapes produced by inst.

S- MINNEAPOLIS INSTITUTE OF ARTS, AV Center, 2400 Third Ave S, 55404. *Tel:* (612) 874-3196. *Video Serv Est:* 1975. *In Charge:* Jerry Downes, AV Supervisor. *Video Staff:* 3 f-t. *Video Use:* documentation of museum events, as art form, educational device in galleries. Archival video serv available. Produce video tapes. Have production studio/space.

Video Equipment/Facilities *In-House Use Only:* portapak (1), ½" col, Sony; playback deck (2), 1" col, Sony; monitor (2), col, Sony. Have portable viewing installation.

Video Tape Loan/Rental/Sale Serv *Serv Provided:* swap with other inst. *Loan Eligibility:* staff. *Restrictions:* may not borrow by mail.

Video Collection Maintained by purchase, rental, own production. Use/play 1" cassette. *Sources:* commercial distributors. *Tape Sel:* preview, faculty/staff recommendations, published reviews, catalogs, gifts. *Special Collections:* video as art, films in video format. *Other Video Serv:* taping of other media.

Cable & CCTV Produce programs for cablecasting. *Programming Sources:* tapes produced by inst, tapes produced professionally, tapes produced by community groups & indiv.

C- UNIVERSITY OF MINNESOTA, AV Library Serv, 3300 University Ave, SE, 55414. *Tel:* (612) 373-3810. *In Charge:* Dr. W. D. Philipson, Dir.

Film Rental Serv *Eligibility:* no restrictions. *Restrictions:* in all states except Hawaii. Cannot use for fund-raising, transmit electronically. *Rental Period:* 1-5 days. Sell films. Produce films. Produce video tapes, audio tapes, filmstrip & slide sets, games, print material.

Film Collection 9300t/21,000p. Approx 550t acquired annually. *Circ:* 16mm, 9300t/21,000. *Noncirc:* 16mm, 1300t/1450p. *Pubns:* catalog, every 2 yrs; suppl, in yr catalog not published ($4.50). Publish materials pertaining to collection. Publish bibliographies.

Other Film Serv Rent film from distributors for patrons, obtain film from coop loan system (Consortium of University Film Centers), obtain film from other libraries, film reference serv, film fairs/festivals, library film programs. Permanent viewing facility available to community. *Equipment:* rent 16mm sound projector, 8mm cartridge projector, 8mm reel projector, S8mm cartridge projector, S8mm reel projector, projection tables & stands, projection screens.

Budget & Expenditures Total AV library budget $120,000 (FY 7/1/74-7/1/75). Total FY film budget $128,000. *Member:* AECT, ALA, CUFC, EFLA, AVCOM.

C- UNIVERSITY STUDENT TELECOMMUNICATIONS CORP, University—Community Video, Rarig Center, University of Minn, 55455. *Tel:* (612) 376-3333. *Video Serv Est:* 1972. *In Charge:* Stephen Kulczycki, Manager. *Video Staff:* 6 f-t, 4 p-t, 1 tech. *Video Use:* documentation of community/school events, community video access, practical video/TV training courses, video documentaries. Video serv available on demand & by appointment. Produce video tapes. Have production studio/space.

Video Equipment/Facilities *In-House Use Only:* portapak (2), col, Sony 3400 & 8400; editing deck (2), col, Sony 8650; studio camera (3); monitor (9); SEG (1); additional camera lenses (6); lighting; microphones (15); tripods (6); audio tape recorders (3). *For Loan:* portapak (9), b&w, Sony 3400 & 8400; editing deck (3), col, Panasonic 3130. Have portable viewing installations. *Equipment Loan Period:* 1 day. Provide training in use of equipment to anyone. Have tape duplication serv.

Video Tape Loan/Rental/Sale Serv *Serv Provided:* free loan, swap with other inst, rental, sale. *Loan/Rental Eligibility:* staff & students, educational inst, civic groups, indiv with library cards. *Restrictions:* for indiv, none; for inst, none. Cannot air without permission. May borrow by mail. *Loan Period:* 7 days. *Total Yr Tape Loan:* 150.

Video Collection Maintained by own production. Use/play ½", 1", 2" reel to reel, ¾" cassette. *Sources:* commercial

Minneapolis (cont'd)
distributors, community productions, exchange. *Tape Sel:* preview, published reviews, catalogs. Tapes organized by subject. *Collection, Color:* ½″ reel, 100t/c; 1″ reel, 5t/c. *Collection, B&W:* ½″ reel, 100t/c. *Other Video Serv:* programming, reference serv, production workshops. *Pubns:* catalog & suppl. Publish materials on video.

A- WALKER ART CENTER, Film Study Collection, Vineland Pl, 55403. *Tel:* (612) 377-7500. *Film Serv Est:* 1973. *In Charge:* Melinda Ward, Film Coord. *AV Staff:* 4 (1 prof, 1 cl, 2 tech). *Film Sel:* chief film librarian's decision. *Holdings:* experimental films 50%, fine arts 20%.
   Free-Loan Film Serv *Restrictions:* cannot use for fund-raising, transmit electronically. Available to researchers/scholars & the general public for on-site viewing only.
   Film Collection 50t/p. Approx 20t acquired annually. *Non-circ:* 16mm, 50t/p.
   Other Film Serv Permanent viewing facility available for rent to community.
   Budget & Expenditures No separate budget. *Member:* AFI.
   Video Serv *Est:* 1970. *In Charge:* Charles Helm, AV Tech. *Tel:* (612) 377-7500, ext 29. *Video Staff:* 1 f-t, 1 p-t. *Video Use:* documentation of museum events, playback only of professionally produced tapes, as art form. Video serv available on demand, by appointment. Produce video tapes. Have production studio/space.
   Video Equipment/Facilities *In-House Use Only:* portapak (1), ½″ b&w, Sony Rover; recording deck (2), ½″ & ¾″ b&w/col, Sony 3650, Wollensak cassette; playback deck (2), ¾″ col, Wollensak cassette; monitor (4), 3 b&w/1 col, 2-25″, 1-19″, 1-17″; lighting; microphones; tripods (1); audio tape recorders (3). Have portable viewing installation. Provide training in use of equipment to staff.
   Video Tape Loan/Rental/Sale Serv *Serv Provided:* swap with other inst, rental, sale. *Rental Eligibility:* educational inst, prof groups, such as other art museums. *Restrictions:* cannot use for fund-raising, duplicate, air without permission. May borrow by mail. *Rental Period:* flexible.
   Video Collection Maintained by purchase, rental, own production, exchange/swap. Use/play ½″ reel to reel, ¾″ cassette. *Sources:* commercial distributors, galleries, exchange. *Tape Sel:* staff recommendations, catalogs. *Special Collections:* video as art, performing arts & exhibition archives. Tapes organized by subject. *Collection, Color:* ¾″ cassette, 1t/6c. *Collection, B&W:* ½″ reel, 4t/8c. *Other Video Serv:* taping of other media.

Montevideo

P- CHIPPEWA COUNTY LIBRARY, 224 S First St, 56265. *Tel:* (612) 269-6501. *Member:* Minn. Library Film Circuit.

Moorhead

P- LAKE AGASSIZ REGIONAL LIBRARY, 115 S Sixth St, 56560. *Tel:* (218) 233-7594. *Member:* Minn. Library Film Circuit.

Owatonna

P- OWATONNA PUBLIC LIBRARY, 105 N Elm St, 55060. *Tel:* (507) 451-4660. *Member:* Minn. Library Film Circuit.

Pine River

P- KITCHIGAMI REGIONAL LIBRARY, 56474. *Tel:* (218) 587-2171. *Member:* Minn. Library Film Circuit.

Red Wing

P- RED WING PUBLIC LIBRARY, 225 Broadway, 55066. *Tel:* (512) 388-2884. *Film Serv Est:* 1975. *In Charge:* Roger

Sween, Dir. *AV Staff:* 6. *Film Sel:* Minn. Libraries Film Circuit, SELCO Film Circuit.
   Free-Loan Film Serv *Eligibility:* indiv with library cards 18 yrs or older. *Restrictions:* for indiv & inst with library cards, only in Goodhue County. Cannot use for fund-raising, transmit electronically, borrow for classroom use. Available to researchers/scholars for on-site viewing. May borrow by mail. *Loan Period:* 2 days.
   Film Collection 9t. *Circ:* 8mm reel, 9t. *Pubns:* catalog, annual (free).
   Other Film Serv Obtain film from coop loan system (Minn. Libraries Film Circuit). Permanent viewing facility available to community. *Equipment:* rent 16mm sound projector (2), S8mm reel projector (1).
   Budget & Expenditures Total library budget $21,275 (FY 1/1/75-1/1/76). Total FY film budget $800.
   Video Serv *Est:* 1975. *Video Staff:* 6 f-t, 2 p-t. *Video Use:* for Winona College courses. Video serv available on demand.
   Video Equipment/Facilities *In-House Use Only:* audio tape recorders (3); television sets (3). Have portable viewing installation. *Equipment Loan Period:* do not loan equipment. Provide training in use of equipment.
   Video Tape Loan/Rental/Sale Serv *Loan/Rental Eligibility:* staff & students, & others. *Restrictions:* in-house use only. May not borrow by mail.
   Video Collection *Sources:* exchange (Winona State College). *Tape Sel:* college courses. Tapes organized by subject.

Rochester

P- ROCHESTER PUBLIC LIBRARY, Broadway at First St, SE, 55901. *Tel:* (507) 288-9070, ext 36. *Film Serv Est:* 1962. *In Charge:* Chris N. Holm, Film Librarian. *AV Staff:* 1 (½ cl, ½ tech). *Film Sel:* committee preview.
   Free-Loan Film Serv *Eligibility:* indiv with library cards. *Restrictions:* for indiv & inst, only in Olmstead County. Cannot use for fund-raising, transmit electronically. May not borrow by mail. *Loan Period:* 1 day. *Total Yr Film Loan:* 6492.
   Film Collection 180t/p. Approx 25t acquired annually. *Circ:* 16mm, 182t/p; 8mm reel, 54t/p; S8mm cartridge, 91t/p. *Pubns:* catalog, annual ($0.25); suppl, no set policy (free). Publish listing of new films in monthly newsletter.
   Other Film Serv Obtain film from coop loan system (Minn. Library Film Circuit), film fairs/festivals, library film programs. Permanent viewing facility available for rent to community.
   Other Media Collections *Audio:* disc, 33⅓ rpm, 4400t; tape, cassette, 160t; tape, cartridge, 150t.
   Budget & Expenditures Total library budget $60,000 (FY 1/1/74-1/1/75). Total FY film budget $6910. *Member:* ALA, Minn. State Library Assn.

P- SOUTHEASTERN LIBRARIES COOPERATING (SELCO), Holiday Inn Arcade (Downtown), 55901. *Tel:* (507) 288-5513. *Member:* Minn. Library Film Circuit.

St. Cloud

P- GREAT RIVER REGIONAL LIBRARY, 125 Fifth Ave S, 56301. *Tel:* (612) 251-7282. *Member:* Minn. Library Film Circuit.

St. James

P- WATONWAN COUNTY LIBRARY, 56081. *Tel:* (507) 379-3791. *Member:* Minn. Library Film Circuit.

St. Joseph

C- COLLEGE OF ST BENEDICT LIBRARY, 56374. *Tel:* (612) 363-4515. *Film Serv Est:* 1972. *In Charge:* Norma Dickaw, Dir Educational Media. *AV Staff:* 3 (2 prof, 1 cl). *Film Sel:* committee preview, faculty/staff recommendations. *Holdings:* animated films 14%, fine arts 8%, physical education

2%, religion 13%, science 8%, social sciences 33%, teacher education 11%, women 2%.

Free-Loan Film Serv *Eligibility:* staff & students. Available to researchers/scholars for on-site viewing. May not borrow by mail.

Film Collection Approx 5t acquired annually. *Circ:* 16mm, 40t. *Pubns:* catalog, annual.

Other Film Serv Rent film from distributors for patrons, obtain film from other libraries. *Equipment:* lend for campus use only: S8mm camera (4), 16mm sound projector (12), 8mm reel projector (3), S8mm cartridge projector (1), S8mm reel projector (3), projection tables & stands (25), projection screens (20).

Other Media Collections *Audio:* disc, 33⅓ rpm, 45rpm, 78rpm, 336c; tape, cassette, 397c; tape, reel, 96c. *Filmstrips:* silent, 212c; sound sets, 188c. *Slides:* sets, 150c.

Budget & Expenditures Total library budget $52,254 (FY 7/1/74-7/1/75). No separate AV budget. *Member:* AECT, ALA.

Video Serv *Est:* 1973. *Video Staff:* 3 f-t, 7 p-t. *Video Use:* documentation of community/school events, to increase community's library use, in-service training, playback only of professionally produced tapes. Video serv available on demand. Produce video tapes.

Video Equipment/Facilities *In-House Use Only:* portapak (3), ½" b&w, Sony, Videocorder; recording deck (2), ½" b&w, Sony 3600; playback deck (4), ¾" col, JVC 2-6000, 6300; studio camera (2), col, Sony VCM2000; monitor (3), b&w, Sony 192U; microphone; tripods (3); audio tape recorders (1). Have portable viewing installation. Provide training in use of equipment to faculty & students.

Video Tape Loan/Rental/Sale Serv *Serv Provided:* swap with other inst. *Loan Eligibility:* staff & students. *Restrictions:* may not borrow by mail.

Video Collection Maintained by purchase, rental, own production, exchange/swap. Use/play ½" reel to reel, ¾" cassette. *Sources:* commercial distributors, exchange (VA Hospital, St. Cloud, St. Cloud State University). *Tape Sel:* preview. Tapes organized by Library of Congress system. *Collection, B&W:* ½" reel, 35t. *Pubns:* catalog.

St. Paul

C- COLLEGE OF ST. THOMAS, AV Center, 55105. *Tel:* (612) 647-5267. *Film Serv Est:* 1950. *In Charge:* Harry Webb, Dir. *AV Staff:* 8 (7 prof, 1 cl). *Film Sel:* faculty/staff recommendations.

Free-Loan Film Serv *Eligibility:* org members. *Restrictions:* for indiv, none. Cannot transmit electronically. Available to researchers/scholars for on-site viewing. May borrow by mail. Produce films, slides & other graphic formats.

Film Collection *Noncirc:* 16mm, 200t/p; 8mm reel, 150 t/p.

Other Film Serv Rent film from distributors for patrons, obtain film from coop loan system, obtain film from other libraries, film reference serv, film fairs/festivals. Permanent viewing facility available for rent to community. *Equipment:* lend (to institution only) S8mm camera (3), 16mm camera (2), 16mm sound projector (20), 8mm cartridge projector (1), 8mm reel projector (2), S8mm reel projector (8), projection tables & stands (200), projection screens (200).

Other Media Collections *Audio:* tape, cassette, 1000c; tape, reel, 3000c.

Budget & Expenditures Total library budget $10,000 (FY 7/1/74-7/1/75). Total FY film budget $4000. *Member:* AECT.

Video Serv *Est:* 1970. *Video Staff:* 1 f-t, 5 p-t. *Video Use:* documentation of community/school events, in-service training, practical video/TV training courses, as art form. Video serv available on demand. Produce video tapes. Have production studio/space & separate control room.

Video Equipment/Facilities *For Loan:* portapak (6), 1" & ½" b&w, col, Sony; editing deck (1), 1" b&w; studio camera (4), b&w; monitor (20), b&w; SEG (1), b&w; additional camera lenses; lighting; microphones; tripods (8). Have permanent & portable viewing installations. *Equipment Loan Period:* no set policy. Provide training in use of equipment to faculty & students. Have tape duplication serv.

Video Tape Loan/Rental/Sale Serv *Serv Provided:* swap with other inst. *Loan Eligibility:* staff, educational inst. *Restrictions:* for indiv, none; for inst, only in consortium. May not borrow by mail.

Video Collection Maintained by purchase, rental, own production, exchange/swap. Use/play ½", 1", 2" reel to reel. *Sources:* commercial distributors, exchange. *Member:* Minn. Inter-Institute TV. *Tape Sel:* preview, faculty/staff recommendations, catalogs. Tapes organized by subject. *Collection, B&W:* ½" reel, 50t; 1" reel, 60t; 2" reel, 30t. *Other Video Serv:* production workshops.

Cable & CCTV Have CCTV in inst, with 12 monitors. *Programming Sources:* over-the-air commercial & public broadcasting, tapes produced by inst, tapes produced professionally, tapes produced by community groups & indiv.

P- DAKOTA-SCOTT REGIONAL LIBRARY, 40 E Emerson Ave, 55189. *Tel:* (612) 372-6558. *Film Serv Est:* 1947. *In Charge:* Marlea Warren, Dept Head. *AV Staff:* 8.6 (2 prof, 3.6 cl, 3 tech). *Film Sel:* chief film librarian's decision, published reviews. *Holdings:* agriculture 1%, arts & humanities 40%, black studies 6%, children's films 30%, consumer affairs 2%, dance 3%, experimental films 5%, fine arts 25%, law 1%, science 5%, social sciences 20%, women 2%.

Free-Loan Film Serv *Eligibility:* special inner-city programs. *Restrictions:* for inst, only in city. May not borrow by mail. *Loan Period:* 2 days. *Total Yr Film Loan:* 16,167.

Film Collection 2094t/2401p. Approx 300t acquired annually. *Circ:* 16mm, 2094t/2401p. *Pubns:* catalog, every 3 yrs ($2); suppl, annually ($.50). Publish occasional film lists.

Other Film Serv Obtain film from coop loan system (Metropolitan Library Serv Agency), film reference serv, library film programs. Permanent viewing facility available for rent to community. *Equipment:* rent 16mm sound projector (5), projection screens (4), slide projector (2), filmstrip projector (1).

Other Media Collections *Audio:* disc, 33⅓ rpm, 45rpm & 78rpm, 42,243c; tape, cassette, cartridge & reel, 3487c. *Filmstrips:* sound, 100c; silent, 1840c. *Slides:* single, 37,827.

Budget & Expenditures Total library budget $659,305 (FY 1/1/75-1/1/76). Total FY film budget $31,000. *Member:* AECT, EFLA.

C- HAMLINE UNIVERSITY, Bush Memorial, 1536 Hewitt Ave, 55104. *Tel:* (612) 641-2380. *Video Serv Est:* 1969. *In Charge:* Robert A. Bauman, Dir Instructional Serv. *Video Staff:* 3 f-t, 15 p-t, 1 tech. *Video Use:* in-service training, practical video/TV training courses, classroom instruction. Video serv available on demand on campus only. Produce video tapes. Have production studio/space & separate control room.

Video Equipment/Facilities *In-House Use Only:* portapak (1), b&w, Sony; recording deck (3), b&w; editing deck (2), b&w, Shibaden; studio camera (3); monitor (6); SEG (1); keyer (1); additional camera lenses (3); lighting; microphones; tripods; audio tape recorders (15). Have permanent viewing installation. Provide training in use of equipment to faculty & students.

Video Tape Loan/Rental/Sale Serv *Loan Eligibility:* org members, students enrolled in inst.

Video Collection Maintained by purchase, rental, own production. Use/play ½" reel to reel, ¾" cassette. *Sources:* commercial distributors. *Tape Sel:* faculty/staff recommendations. Tapes organized numerically. *Collection, B&W:* ½" reel, 150t/c. *Other Video Serv:* production workshops.

P- RAMSEY COUNTY PUBLIC LIBRARY, 2180 Hamline Ave N, 55113. *Tel:* (612) 631-0494. *In Charge:* Margaret Koons, General Library Asst. *AV Staff:* 1½. *Film Sel:* chief film librarian's decision, published reviews, jobbers listings.

Free-Loan Film Serv *Eligibility:* members of Metropolitan Library Serv Agency. *Restrictions:* cannot use for fundraising. May borrow by mail. *Loan Period:* 2 days. *Total Yr Film Loan:* 325.

St. Paul (cont'd)

Film Collection 32t/p. Approx 2-4t acquired annually. *Circ:* 16mm, 32t/p; 8mm reel, 400t/800p; S8mm reel, 500t/1057p. *Pubns:* catalog, annual.

Other Film Serv Obtain film from coop loan system (Minn. Library Film Circuit, Metropolitan Library Serv Agency).

Other Media Collections *Audio:* disc, 33⅓ rpm & 45rpm, 5000t/12,222c; tape, cassette, 300c. *Slides:* sets, 1t/c.

Budget & Expenditures Total library budget $190,000 (FY 1/1/75-1/1/76). No separate AV budget. *Member:* Minn. Library Assn.

P- ST PAUL PUBLIC LIBRARY, Arts & Audio Visual Servs, 90 W Fourth St, 55102. *Tel:* (612) 224-3383, ext 40. *Film Serv Est:* 1953. *In Charge:* Margaret Doyle, Film Librarian. *AV Staff:* 1⅘ (1 prof, 1⅜ cl). *Film Sel:* chief film librarian's decision, published reviews.

Free-Loan Film Serv *Eligibility:* org members, staff, students enrolled in inst, staff & students, educational inst, civic groups, religious groups, indiv with library cards from Metropolitan Library Serv Agency. *Restrictions:* cannot use for fund-raising, transmit electronically. May not borrow by mail. *Total Yr Film Loan:* 10,822.

Film Collection 601t/674p. Approx 20-30t acquired annually. *Circ:* 16mm, 601t/674p; 8mm reel, 1439t. *Pubns:* catalog, every 3 yrs ($1); suppl, in yr catalog not published. Publish materials pertaining to collection.

Other Film Serv Obtain film from coop loan system (Metropolitan Library Serv Agency), film reference serv, library film programs. Permanent viewing facility. *Equipment:* 16mm sound projector (16), 8mm reel projector (1), dual 8mm/S8mm reel projector (5), projection tables & stands (11), projection screens (11), lend slide projectors (2), filmstrip projectors (2), slide/filmstrip projectors (2), opaque projector (1), overhead projector (1).

Other Media Collections *Audio:* disc, 33⅓ rpm, 17,118c; tape, cassette, 2608c. *Filmstrips:* sound, 26c; silent, 136c; sound sets, 7c. *Slides:* single, 14,762c.

Budget & Expenditures Total library budget $200,000 (FY 1/1/75-1/1/76). Total FY 16mm film budget $4700. *Member:* EFLA, FLIC.

P- ST PAUL PUBLIC LIBRARY, Video Communications Center, 1080 University Ave, 55104. *Tel:* (612) 645-7914. *Video Serv Est:* 1975. *In Charge:* Annette Salo, Librarian. *Video Staff:* 3 f-t. *Video Use:* documentation of community/school events, to increase community's library use, community video access, in-service training. Video serv available on demand. Produce video tapes. Have production studio/space.

Video Equipment/Facilities *In-House Use Only:* portapak (1), ½″ b&w, Panasonic 3085; recording deck (1), ½″ b&w, Panasonic 3020; editing deck (1), ½″ col, Panasonic 3130; monitor (3), b&w, Sony CVM 1720 & 19211, Setchell; additional camera lenses (1); lighting (1); microphones (4); tripods (2); audio tape recorders (1). *For Loan:* portapak (1), ½″ b&w, Panasonic 3085; monitor (1), b&w, Sony CVM-950; additional camera lenses (1); microphones (4); tripods (2). Have portable viewing installation. *Equipment Loan Period:* 1 day. Provide training in use of equipment to anyone. Have tape duplication serv.

Video Tape Loan/Rental/Sale Serv *Serv Provided:* free loan, swap with other inst. *Loan Eligibility:* staff & students, civic groups, religious groups, indiv with library cards. *Restrictions:* for indiv, only in city; for inst, only in city. Cannot use for fund-raising, duplicate, air without permission. May borrow by mail. *Loan Period:* 7 days. *Total Yr Tape Loan:* 18.

Video Collection Maintained by purchase, own production, exchange/swap. Use/play ½″ reel to reel, ¾″ cassette. *Sources:* commercial distributors, galleries, community productions, exchange. *Tape Sel:* preview, faculty/staff recommendations, published reviews, catalogs. *Special Collections:* in-house training tapes. Tapes organized by subject. *Collection, Color:* ¾″ cassette, 16t/c. *Collection, B&W:* ½″ reel, 58t/c. *Other Video Serv:* production workshops. *Pubns:* publish servs booklist, bibliography, video glossary.

C- UNIVERSITY OF MINNESOTA, AV Teaching Materials Library, 442 Coffey Hall, University of Minn., 55108. *Tel:* (612) 373-1252. *Film Serv Est:* 1940. *In Charge:* Don Breneman. *AV Staff:* 9 (3 prof, 4 cl, 2 tech). *Film Sel:* faculty/staff recommendations. *Holdings:* agriculture 60%, children's films 20%, consumer affairs 20%.

Film Rental Serv *Eligibility:* no restrictions. *Restrictions:* only in state. *Rental Period:* 1 day. *Total Yr Film Booking:* 5700. Produce films & slide sets.

Film Collection 650t/917p. Approx 50t acquired annually. *Circ:* 16mm, 650t/917p. *Pubns:* catalog, every 2 yrs; suppl, monthly.

Other Film Serv Rent film from distributors for patrons, obtain film from other libraries, film reference serv. Permanent viewing facility.

Other Media Collections *Slides:* sets, 550t/1534c. *Member:* AECT.

Shakopee

P- SCOTT COUNTY LIBRARY SYSTEM, 206 W Fourth St, 55379. *Tel:* (612) 445-2189. *Member:* Minn. Library Film Circuit.

Thief River Falls

P- N W REGIONAL LIBRARY, 56701. *Tel:* (218) 681-4325. *Member:* Minn. Library Film Circuit.

Virginia

P- ARROWHEAD REGIONAL LIBRARY SYSTEM, 701 Eleventh St, 55792. *Tel:* (218) 741-3840. *Member:* Minn. Library Film Circuit.

P- VIRGINIA PUBLIC LIBRARY, 215 Fifth Ave S, 55792. *Tel:* (218) 741-2260. *Member:* Minn. Library Film Circuit.

Waseca

P- LE SUEUR-WASECA REGIONAL LIBRARY, 56093. *Tel:* (507) 835-2910. *Member:* Minn. Library Film Circuit.

Willmar

P- CROW RIVER REGIONAL LIBRARY, 410 W Fifth St, 56201. *Tel:* (612) 235-3162. *Film Serv Est:* 1959. *In Charge:* Shirley Wicklund, Coord. *AV Staff:* ½ (2 prof, ¼ cl, ½ tech). *Film Sel:* committee preview, chief film librarian's decision, published reviews.

Free-Loan Film Serv *Eligibility:* educational inst, civic groups, religious groups, indiv with library cards. *Restrictions:* for indiv, only in 3 county regional system; for inst, only in 3 county regional system. Cannot use for fund-raising, transmit electronically. May borrow by mail. *Loan Period:* 1 day. *Total Yr Film Loan:* 2500.

Film Collection 100t. Approx 15-20t acquired annually. *Circ:* 16mm, 26t; 8mm reel, 40t/4p; S8mm reel, 40t/5p. *Pubns:* catalog, as needed; suppl, no set policy. Publish materials pertaining to collection. Publish special listings of holiday films.

Other Film Serv Obtain film from coop loan system (Minn. Library Film Circuit), obtain film from other libraries, library film programs. Permanent viewing facility available for rent to community. *Equipment:* rent 16mm sound projector (5), 8mm reel projector (2), projection screens (5).

Other Media Collections *Audio:* disc, 33⅓ rpm, 2500t; tape, cassette, 100t. *Filmstrips:* silent, 350t; sound sets, 150t.

Budget & Expenditures Total library budget $70,000 (FY 1/1/75-1/1/76). Total FY film budget $4000. *Member:* Minn. Library Assn.

Video Serv *Est:* 1973. *In Charge:* Katherine Matson. *Video Staff:* 2 p-t. *Video Use:* to increase community's library use. Video serv by appointment. Produce video tapes.

Video Equipment/Facilities *For Loan:* audio tape recorders (5). *Equipment Loan Period:* 1 day.

Video Tape Loan/Rental/Sale Serv *Loan/Rental Eligibility:* civic groups, religious groups, indiv with library cards, prof groups. *Restrictions:* for indiv & inst, in our 3-county regional system. Cannot use for fund-raising, duplicate, air without permission. May borrow by mail. *Loan Period:* 1 day.

Video Collection Maintained by own production. *Sources:* community productions. *Other Video Serv:* programming.

Cable & CCTV Produce programs for cablecasting. Inform public about cable system serv & facilities. Have advisory/administrative role in cable system operation.

Winona

P- WINONA PUBLIC LIBRARY, 151 W Fifth St, 55987. *Tel:* (507) 452-4582. *In Charge:* Virginia Keith, Library Aide. *AV Staff:* ¼ (¼ cl). *Film Sel:* state library film circuit.

Free-Loan Film Serv *Eligibility:* indiv with library cards. *Restrictions:* for indiv & inst, only in Winona County. Cannot charge for showing. May not borrow by mail. *Loan Period:* 1 day.

Other Film Serv Obtain film from coop loan system (Minn. Library Film Circuit), library film programs.

Other Media Collections *Audio:* tape, cassette, 238c.

Budget & Expenditures Total library budget $39,714 (FY 1/1/75-1/1/76). Total FY film budget $800. *Member:* ALA, Minn. Library Assn. CUFC, EFLA, FLIC.

Worthington

P- NOBLES COUNTY LIBRARY & INFORMATION CENTER, Box 1667, 56187. *Tel:* (507) 372-2981. *Member:* Minn. Library Film Circuit.

P- PLUM CREEK REGIONAL LIBRARY, c/o Nobles County Library, Box 1667, 56187. *Tel:* (507) 376-5803. *Member:* Minn. Library Film Circuit.

Mississippi

Corinth

P- NORTHEAST REGIONAL LIBRARY, 1023 Fillmore St, 38834. *Tel:* (601) 287-2441, ext 5. *Film Serv Est:* 1975. *In Charge:* Bruce Evans, Asst Dir Reference-Extension. *AV Staff:* 1 prof. *Film Sel:* committee preview.

Free-Loan Film Serv *Eligibility:* educational inst, civic groups, religious groups, & others, such as senior citizens' groups, nursing home programs. *Restrictions:* only within 5-county system. Cannot use for fund-raising, transmit electronically. Available to researchers/scholars for on-site viewing. May not borrow by mail. *Loan Period:* 5 days. *Total Yr Film Loan:* 16.

Film Collection 31t/p. Approx 10t acquired annually. *Circ:* 16mm, 12t; S8mm reel, 19t. Publish list.

Other Film Serv Rent film from distributors for patrons, obtain film from coop loan system (Miss. Library Commission), library film programs. Permanent viewing facility available to community.

Other Media Collections *Audio:* disc, 33⅓ rpm, 500t; tape, cassette, 54t/c. *Filmstrips:* sound, 24t/c; silent, 12t/c.

Budget & Expenditures Total library budget $45,000 (FY 10/74-10/75). Total FY film budget $2000. *Member:* Miss. Library Assn.

Hattiesburg

C- UNIVERSITY OF SOUTHERN MISSISSIPPI, S Miss. Educ Film Assn, Box 54 S Station, 39401. *Tel:* (601) 266-7304. *Film Serv Est:* 1949. *In Charge:* Bob Price, Dir Media Servs. *AV Staff:* 4 (½ prof, 3 cl, 1 tech). *Film Sel:* faculty/staff recommendations. *Holdings:* agriculture 5%, animated films 5%, black studies 5%, career education 20%, children's films 30%, engineering 7%, experimental films 2%, fine arts 10%, industrial arts 7%, medicine 5%, science 15%, social sciences 15%, teacher education 10%.

Free-Loan Film Serv *Eligibility:* org members. *Restrictions:* member schools only. Available to researchers/scholars for on-site viewing. May borrow by mail. *Loan Period:* 4 days.

Film Rental Serv *Eligibility:* educational org. *Restrictions:* only in state. *Rental Period:* 3 days. *Total Yr Film Booking:* 200.

Film Collection Approx 60t acquired annually. *Circ:* 16mm, 700t/2000p. *Pubns:* catalog, annual every 2 yrs; suppl, in yr catalog not published.

Other Film Serv Rent film from distributors for patrons, film reference serv. *Equipment:* lend/rent S8mm camera, 16mm camera, 16mm sound projector, 8mm cartridge projector, 8mm reel projector, S8mm cartridge projector, S8mm reel projector, projection tables & stands, projection screens.

Budget & Expenditures No separate AV budget. *Member:* AECT.

Video Serv *Est:* 1962. *Video Staff:* 2 f-t, 6 p-t. *Video Use:* documentation of community/school events, in-service training, practical video/TV training courses, playback only of professionally produced tapes. Video serv available on demand. Produce video tapes. Have production studio/space & separate control room.

Video Equipment/Facilities *In-House Use Only:* portapak (1), ½" b&w, Panasonic; recording deck (2), U-matic col, Sony VO-1600; playback deck (2), U-matic col, Sony VO-100; editing deck (1), ½" col, Panasonic; studio camera (1), col, Sony DVC-500; monitor (4), col, GE; SEG (2), GE; keyer (2); additional camera lenses (4); lighting (1); microphones (8); tripods (7); audio tape recorders (6), cameras, film chain. *For Loan:* portapak (1), ½" b&w, Panasonic; recording deck (2), U-matic col, Sony VO-16100; playback deck (2), U-matic col, Sony VO-100; editing deck (1), ½" col, Panasonic; studio camera (1), col, Sony DVC-500; monitor (4), col, GE; SEG (2), GE; keyer (2); additional camera lenses (4); lighting (1); microphones (8); tripods (7); audio tape recorders (6), cameras, film chain. Have permanent viewing installation. *Equipment Loan Period:* no set policy. Provide training in use of equipment. Have tape duplication serv.

Video Tape Loan/Rental/Sale Serv *Serv Provided:* free loan, swap with other inst. *Loan Eligibility:* staff & students. *Restrictions:* for campus use only. May not borrow by mail.

Video Collection Maintained by purchase, rental, own production, exchange/swap. Use/play ½" reel to reel, ¾" cassette. *Sources:* community productions, exchange. *Tape Sel:* preview, faculty/staff recommendations. *Special Collections:* in-house training tapes, films in video format. *Other Video Serv:* reference serv, taping of other media, dubbing.

Cable & CCTV Have CCTV in inst, with 20 monitors. *Programming Sources:* over-the-air commercial & public broadcasting, tapes produced by inst.

Itta Bena

C- MISSISSIPPI VALLEY STATE UNIVERSITY, James Herbert White Library, 38941. *Tel:* (601) 254-2321, ext 274, 275, 276. *In Charge:* Lula L. Taylor, Media Librarian. *AV Staff:* 1 prof. *Film Sel:* faculty/staff recommendations, published reviews.

Free-Loan Film Serv *Eligibility:* staff & students. *Restrictions:* for campus use only. *Loan Period:* 7 days. *Total Yr Film Loan:* 223.

Film Collection *Circ:* 16mm, 291t/293p; S8mm cartridge, 195t/p. Permanent viewing facility. *Equipment:* lend 16mm sound projector (3), S8mm cartridge projector (2), projection screens (3), slide projectors (2), filmstrip projectors (6).

Other Media Collections *Audio:* disc, 33⅓ rpm, 691t/696c; tape, cassette, 221t/c; tape, reel, 61t/c. *Slides:* sets, 1340t/1346c.

Budget & Expenditures No separate budget. *Member:* Miss. Library Assn.

Jackson

S- MISSISSIPPI LIBRARY COMMISSION, Box 3260, 39056. *Tel:* (601) 354-7211. *In Charge:* Gerald Buchanan, Asst Dir Library Operations.

Free-Loan Film Serv *Eligibility:* libraries, state employees. *Restrictions:* for inst, only in state. Cannot use for fund-raising, transmit electronically. Available to researchers/scholars for on-site viewing. May borrow by mail. *Loan Period:* 1-3 days. *Total Yr Film Loan:* 1735.

Film Collection Approx 25t acquired annually. *Circ:* 16mm, 225t/p. *Pubns:* catalog, as needed.

Budget & Expenditures Total library budget $150,000 (FY 7/1/74-7/1/75). Total FY film budget $10,000.

Mathiston

C- WOOD JUNIOR COLLEGE, Wood Memorial Library, Drawer C, 39752. *Tel:* (601) 263-5352. *Film Serv Est:* 1970. *In Charge:* Neuberry Brown, AV Supervisor. *Film Sel:* faculty/staff recommendations.

Free-Loan Film Serv *Eligibility:* staff & students, civic groups, religious groups. *Restrictions:* none. Available to researchers/scholars for on-site viewing. May not borrow by mail. *Loan Period:* 3 days.

Film Collection *Circ:* 16mm, 8t/p.

Other Film Serv Rent film from distributors for patrons. Permanent viewing facility available to community.

Other Media Collections *Audio:* disc, 33⅓ rpm, 774c; tape, cassette, 240c. *Filmstrips:* 700c. *Slides:* single, 3525c.

Budget & Expenditures Total library budget $8000 (FY 7/1/74-7/1/75). No separate AV budget. *Member:* SELA, Miss. Library Assn.

Prentiss

C- PRENTISS INSTITUTE JUNIOR COLLEGE, Ruby E. Stutts Lyells Library, Drawer C, 39474. *Tel:* (601) 792-5899. *Film Serv Est:* 1974. *In Charge:* Janice L. Lucas, Library/Media Dir. *AV Staff:* 1½ (1 prof). *Film Sel:* faculty/staff recommendations, chief film librarian's decision, published reviews.

Free-Loan Film Serv *Eligibility:* staff & students. *Restrictions:* for inst, only in city. Cannot borrow for classroom use. Available to researchers/scholars for on-site viewing. May not borrow by mail. *Loan Period:* 1 day. *Total Yr Film Loan:* 11.

Film Collection 100t/p. *Circ:* 16mm, 10t/p; 8mm reel, 100t/p. *Pubns:* publish lists for faculty.

Other Film Serv Rent film from distributors for patrons. Permanent viewing facility. *Equipment:* own 16mm sound projector (10), 8mm reel projector (6).

Other Media Collections *Audio:* tape, cassette, 75t/c; tape, cartridge, 100t/c; tape, reel, 10t/c. *Filmstrips:* silent, 100c; sound sets, 20c; silent sets, 5c.

Budget & Expenditures Total library budget $45,000 (FY 7/1/74-7/1/75). Total FY film budget $5000. *Member:* ALA, Miss. Library Assn, Southeastern Library Assn.

Video Serv *Est:* 1974. *Video Staff:* 1 f-t, 1 p-t. *Video Use:* documentation of community/school events, to increase community's library use, in-service training, playback only of professionally produced tapes. Video serv available by appointment. Produce video tapes. Have production studio/space.

Video Equipment/Facilities *In-House Use Only:* playback deck (1), ½″ b&w; editing deck (1), ½″ b&w. Have portable viewing installation. Provide training in use of equipment to students. Have tape duplication serv.

Video Tape Loan/Rental/Sale Serv *Serv Provided:* free loan. *Loan Eligibility:* org members. *Restrictions:* for campus use only. May not borrow by mail.

Video Collection Maintained by own production. Use/play ½″ cartridge. *Sources:* commercial distributors. *Tape Sel:* faculty/staff recommendations. Tapes not organized. *Collection, B&W:* ½″ cartridge, 8t/10c.

Cable & CCTV Have CCTV in inst, with 1 monitor. *Programming Sources:* tapes produced professionally, tapes produced by community groups & indiv.

Raymond

C- HINDS JUNIOR COLLEGE, 39154. *Tel:* (601) 857-5261, ext Lib 243, Media 294. *Film Serv Est:* 1974. *In Charge:* John Childress, Dir Media Servs. *AV Staff:* 5 (2 prof, 1 cl, 2 tech). *Film Sel:* faculty/staff recommendations, published reviews.

Film Collection Approx 50t acquired annually. *Circ:* 16mm, 150t. *Pubns:* catalog, annual.

Other Film Serv Rent film from distributors for patrons, obtain film from coop loan system, obtain film from other libraries. Permanent viewing facility available for rent to community.

Other Media Collections *Audio:* disc, 33⅓ rpm, 759t; tape, cassette, 2535t. *Filmstrips:* sound, 1293t. *Slides:* single, 20,862t; sets, 250t.

Budget & Expenditures Total library budget $82,602 (FY 7/1/75-7/1/76). Total FY film budget $10,000. *Member:* AECT, ALA, Miss. Library Assn, Southeastern Library Assn.

Video Serv *Est:* 1968. *Video Staff:* 3 f-t, 2 tech. *Video Use:* documentation of community/school events, in-service training, classroom instruction. Video serv available by appointment. Produce video tapes. Have production studio/space & separate control room.

Video Equipment/Facilities *In-House Use Only:* recording deck (7), ½″, ¾″ col, Sony; playback deck (5), ¾″ col, Sony; editing deck (1), 1″ col, IVC; studio camera (2), col, Sony; monitor (3), col, RCA, Sony; SEG (1), Dynac; additional camera lenses; lighting; microphones (20); tripods (3); audio tape recorders (100). Have permanent viewing installation. *Equipment Loan Period:* no set policy. Provide training in use of equipment to students & media personnel.

Video Tape Loan/Rental/Sale Serv *Serv Provided:* free loan, swap with other inst. *Loan Eligibility:* org members, civic groups, religious groups. *Restrictions:* for indiv, interlibrary loan; for inst, none. Cannot use for fund-raising. May not borrow by mail.

Video Collection Maintained by purchase, own production. Use/play ½″, 1″ reel to reel, ¾″ cassette. *Sources:* commercial distributors, community productions, exchange. *Tape Sel:* preview, faculty/staff recommendations. *Special Collections:* in-house training tapes. Tapes organized by subject. *Collection, Color:* ½″ reel, 400t; ¾″ cassette, 152t. *Collection, B&W:* ½″ reel, 55t.

Cable & CCTV Have CCTV in inst, with 50 monitors. *Programming Sources:* over-the-air commercial & public broadcasting, tapes produced by inst, tapes produced professionally, tapes produced by community groups & indiv.

Missouri

Bolivar

P- SOUTHWEST REGIONAL LIBRARY, 120 E Jackson, 65613. *Tel:* (417) 326-4531. *In Charge:* Frances Roberts, Libn. *Member:* Mo. Libraries Film Corp.

Cape Girardeau

P- CAPE GIRARDEAU PUBLIC LIBRARY, Courthouse Park, 63701. *Tel:* (314) 334-5279. *In Charge:* Martha Ann Maxwell, Libn. *Member:* Mo. Libraries Film Coop.

C- SOUTHEAST MISSOURI STATE UNIVERSITY, Eastern Mo. Film Company, 900 Normal Ave, 63701. *Tel:* (314) 334-8211, ext 232. *Film Serv Est:* 1959. *In Charge:* George W. Pendergrass Jr, Coord of Media Serv. *AV Staff:* 11 (1 prof, 9 cl, 2 tech). *Film Sel:* committee preview, faculty/staff recommendations.
Film Rental Serv *Eligibility:* no restrictions. *Restrictions:* only in region (Mo. and surrounding states). *Rental Period:* 3 days. *Total Yr Film Booking:* 22,040.
Film Collection 2800t. Approx 250t acquired annually. *Circ:* 16mm, 2800t. *Pubns:* catalog, as needed ($3.25). Publish newsletter. Permanent viewing facility. *Equipment:* rent S8mm camera (3), 16mm sound projector (15), 8mm cartridge projector (2), 8mm reel projector (3), S8mm cartridge projector, projection tables & stands (10), projection screens (10).
Other Media Collections *Audio:* disc, 33⅓ rpm, 379t; tape, cassette, 1359t; tape, reel 718t. *Filmstrips:* sound, 850t; silent, 1869t. *Slides:* sets, 107t/c.
Budget & Expenditures Total library budget $60,000 (FY 7/1/74-7/1/75). Total FY film budget $3500. *Member:* AECT, Mo. AECT.

Charleston

P- MISSISSIPPI COUNTY LIBRARY, N Main St, 63834. *Tel:* (314) 683-6748. *In Charge:* Betty Powell, Libn. *Member:* Mo. Libraries Film Coop.

Chillicothe

P- LIVINGSTON COUNTY LIBRARY, Locust & Clay Sts, 64601. *Tel:* (816) 646-0547. *In Charge:* Lillian Des Marias, Libn. *Member:* Mo. Libraries Film Coop.

Clinton

P- HENRY COUNTY LIBRARY, 64735. *Tel:* (816) 885-2612. *In Charge:* Olga M. Boyles. *Member:* Mo. Libraries Film Coop.

Columbia

C- UNIVERSITY OF MISSOURI-COLUMBIA, Academic Support Center, Film Library, 505 E Stewart Rd, 65201. *Tel:* (314) 882-3601. *In Charge:* John S. Fick, Asst Dir. *AV Staff:* 8 (1 prof, 4½ cl, 2½ tech). *Film Sel:* faculty/staff recommendations, chief film librarian's decision.
Free-Loan Film Serv *Eligibility:* org members, staff, university ext division throughout state. *Restrictions:* only in state. Cannot use for fund-raising, transmit electronically, for Univ of Mo. instructional uses only. Available to researchers/scholars for on-site viewing. May not borrow by mail. *Loan Period:* 2 or more days. *Total Yr Film Loan:* 5400.
Film Rental Serv *Eligibility:* no restrictions. *Restrictions:* only in U.S. Cannot transmit electronically, charge admission. *Rental Period:* 2 or more days. *Total Yr Film Booking:* 6600.

Film Collection 6000t/7000p. Approx. 250t acquired annually. *Circ:* 16mm, 6000t/7000p. *Pubns:* catalog, every 5 yr ($2.00); suppl, no set policy (free). Publish materials pertaining to collection.
Other Film Serv Obtain film from coop loan system (Consortium of University Film Centers), film reference serv. Permanent viewing facility. *Equipment:* lend/rent 16mm sound projector, 8mm reel projector, S8mm reel projector, projection screens, record players, video cassette playback units, Sony color TVs, lecterns, P.A. systems, audio tape recorders, overhead projectors, 35mm sound slide projectors, 2 x 2 & 3¼ x 4 slide projectors, 35mm filmstrip projectors, electric pointer, opaque projector. No separate budget. *Member:* AECT, CUFC.

Columbus

P- DANIEL BOONE REGIONAL LIBRARY, 100 W. Broadway, 65201. *Tel:* (314) 443-3161. *In Charge:* Gene Martin. *Member:* Mo. Libraries Film Coop.

Gallatin

P- DAVIESS COUNTY LIBRARY, 215 N Main, 64640. *Tel:* (816) 663-3222. *Film Serv Est:* 1954. *In Charge:* Hazel Gibbens, Asst Librarian. *AV Staff:* 1 (1 tech). *Holdings:* children's films, fine arts, travel.
Free-Loan Film Serv *Eligibility:* educational inst, civic & religious groups, indiv with library cards. *Restrictions:* for indiv, only adjoining county library patrons. Available to researchers/scholars for on-site viewing. *Loan Period:* 14 days. *Total Yr Film Loan:* 189.
Film Collection 80t. *Circ:* 16mm, 60t. 8mm reel, 22t. *Pubns:* publish newspaper notices and/or articles.
Other Film Serv *Equipment:* lend 16mm sound projector (2), 8mm cartridge projector (1), projection screens (2), slide projectors (3).
Other Media Collections *Audio:* discs, total 1077t; tape, cassette, 105t. *Filmstrips:* silent, 492t; sound sets, 127t. *Slides:* sets, 5t. *Member:* ALA, Mo. Library Assn.
Video Serv *Est:* 1970. *Video Staff:* 2 f-t, 4 p-t. *Video Use:* documentation of community/school events, to increase community's library use, as art form, entertainment. Video serv available by appointment.
Video Equipment/Facilities *In-House Use Only:* cassette recorders (3); cassette playbacks (10). Provide training in use of equipment to staff & patrons.
Video Tape Loan/Rental/Sale Serv *Serv Provided:* free loan, swap with other inst. *Loan Eligibility:* staff & students, indiv with library cards. *Restrictions:* for indiv, in other adjoining counties. May not borrow by mail.
Video Collection Maintained by purchase, own production. Use/play ¾" cassette. *Sources:* commercial distributors. *Tape Sel:* catalogs. *Collection:* ¾" cassette. Publish materials on video.

Harrisonville

P- CASS COUNTY LIBRARY, 64701. *Tel:* (816) 884-3483. *Member:* Mo. Libraries Film Coop.

Houston

P- TEXAS COUNTY LIBRARY, 65483. *Tel:* (417) 967-2258. *In Charge:* Louise Johnson. *Member:* Mo. Libraries Film Coop.

Independence

P- MID-CONTINENT PUBLIC LIBRARY, 15616 E 24 Highway, 64050. *Tel:* (816) 836-5200, ext. 47 & 49. *Film Serv Est:* 1956. *In Charge:* Mary MacPherson, Dept Head. *AV Staff:* 7 (7 cl). *Film Sel:* chief film librarian's decision. *Holdings:* state library films 10%.
  Free-Loan Film Serv *Eligibility:* civic & religious groups, indiv with library cards, prof groups, & others, such as Boy & Girl Scouts, FAA, day care centers, businesses. *Restrictions:* for indiv & inst, none; Cannot use for fund-raising, transmit electronically, borrow for classroom use. May not borrow by mail. *Loan Period:* 1 day (longer by arrangement). *Total Yr Film Loan:* 9774.
  Film Collection 1400t. Approx 100-125t acquired annually. *Circ:* 16mm, 1400t/1500p. *Pubns:* catalog, annual; suppl, as needed.
  Other Film Serv Administration of Mo. Libraries Film Coop, library film programs.
  Other Media Collections *Filmstrips:* 1400t.
  Budget & Expenditures Total FY film budget $20,000 (FY 1/74-1/75). (Fed funds for Mo. Libraries Film Coop $140,000). *Member:* EFLA, Mo. Library Assn.

A- NATIONAL ARCHIVES AND RECORDS SERV, Harry S. Truman Library, 64050. *Tel:* (816) 833-1400. *Film Serv Est:* 1957. *In Charge:* Benedict K. Zobrist, Dir. *AV Staff:* 2 (1 prof, 1 tech). *Film Sel:* faculty/staff recommendations. *Holdings:* Harry S. Truman and administration. Available to researchers/scholars for on-site viewing. May not borrow by mail.
  Film Collection 175t/175p. Approx 20t acquired annually. *Noncirc:* 16mm, 175t.
  Other Film Serv Obtain film from coop loan system (National Archives and Records Serv), obtain film from other libraries, library film programs. Permanent viewing facility. *Equipment:* (no loan or rental) 16mm sound projector (6), projection tables & stands (2), projection screens (3), 16mm editor, 16mm-35mm splicer.
  Other Media Collections *Audio:* disc, 33⅓rpm, 50t/50c; disc, 45rpm, 1t/1c; disc, 78rpm, 200t/200c; tape, reel, 500t/500c. *Filmstrips:* sound sets, 8t/8c. *Slides:* single, 2000t/2000c.

Ironton

A- OZARK REGIONAL LIBRARY, 63650. *Tel:* (314) 546-2615. *In Charge:* Gertrude Zimmer. *Member:* Mo. Libraries Film Coop.

Jefferson City

S- MISSOURI DIVISION OF HEALTH, Films & Literature Unit, 1407 Southwest Blvd, Box 570, 65101. *Tel:* (314) 751-4131. *Film Serv Est:* approx 1945. *In Charge:* Dorothy A. Duncan, Supervisor. *AV Staff:* 5 (5 cl). *Film Sel:* committee preview, faculty/staff recommendations. *Holdings:* health, guidance, safety.
  Free-Loan Film Serv *Eligibility:* any state resident. *Restrictions:* for inst, only in state. Cannot charge admission. Available to researchers/scholars for on-site viewing. May borrow by mail. *Loan Period:* flexible. *Total Yr Film Loan:* 20,986.
  Film Collection 781t/1850p. Approx 80-90t acquired annually. *Pubns:* catalog, every 3 yr; suppl, no set policy. Publish new film listings in house organ. *Equipment:* lend 16mm sound projector (3), projection tables & stands (2), projection screens (6), slide, filmstrip/record, overhead, opaque, tape recorder.
  Budget & Expenditures Total library budget $16,506 (FY 7/1/74-7/1/75). No separate AV budget.

P- THOMAS JEFFERSON LIBRARY SYSTEM, 210 Adams St, 65101. *Tel:* (314) 635-7256. *In Charge:* Doris J. Athy. *Member:* Mo. Libraries Film Coop.

Joplin

P- JOPLIN PUBLIC LIBRARY, 830 Wall St, 64801. *Tel:* (417) 623-7953. *In Charge:* Margaret Hager. *Member:* Mo. Libraries Film Coop.

Kahoka

P- NORTHEAST MISSOURI LIBRARY SERV, 207 W Chestnut, 63445. *Tel:* (816) 727-3262. *In Charge:* Margaretta G. Drury. *Member:* Mo. Libraries Film Coop.

Kansas City

P- KANSAS CITY PUBLIC LIBRARY, Film Dept, 311 E 12 St, 64106. *Tel:* (816) 221-2685, ext. 167. *Film Serv Est:* 1950. *In Charge:* Penny Northern, Head, Film Dept. *AV Staff:* 5 (4 cl, 1 tech). *Film Sel:* chief film librarian's decision.
  Free-Loan Film Serv *Eligibility:* indiv with library cards. *Restrictions:* for indiv, only in city. Cannot use for fund-raising, transmit electronically. Available to researchers/scholars for on-site viewing. May not borrow by mail. *Loan Period:* 2 days. *Total Yr Film Loan:* 20,351.
  Film Collection 1300t/1300p. Approx 46t acquired annually. *Circ:* 16mm, 1300t. *Pubns:* catalog, every 2 yr ($1.00); suppl, every 3 mo. Publish subject lists, programs, filmographies.
  Other Film Serv Film reference serv, film fairs/festivals, library film programs. Permanent viewing facility. *Equipment:* (no loan or rental) 16mm sound projector (4), projection tables & stands (4), projection screens (12).
  Budget & Expenditures Total library budget $289,984 (FY 7/1/74-7/1/75). Total FY film budget $14,636. *Member:* ALA, EFLA, FLIC, Mo. Library Assn.

Kennett

P- DUNKLIN COUNTY LIBRARY, 226 N Main, 63857. *Tel:* (314) 888-3561. *In Charge:* Benny D. Freeman. *Member:* Mo. Libraries Film Coop.

Lebanon

P- KINDERHOOK REGIONAL LIBRARY, 104 E Commercial, 65536. *Tel:* (417) 532-2148. *Member:* Mo. Libraries Film Coop.

Maryville

P- MARYVILLE PUBLIC LIBRARY, 64468. *Tel:* (816) 582-5281. *In Charge:* Leah Johnson. *Member:* Mo. Libraries Film Coop.

Mexico

P- MEXICO-AUDRAIN COUNTY LIBRARY, 305 W Jackson St, 65265. *Tel:* (314) 581-4939. *In Charge:* Eldon R. Burgess, Dir. *AV Staff:* 1 (1 cl, 1 tech). *Film Sel:* chief film librarian's decision. *Holdings:* children's films, 10%.
  Free-Loan Film Serv *Eligibility:* indiv with library cards. *Restrictions:* for indiv, in Audrain County; other counties via mutual agreement. May not borrow by mail. *Loan Period:* 7 days. *Total Yr Film Loan:* 1450.
  Film Rental Serv *Eligibility:* civic groups, patrons/public. *Restrictions:* in Audrain County.
  Other Film Serv Obtain film from coop loan system, library film programs. Permanent viewing facility available free to community. *Equipment:* lend 16mm sound projector, 8mm reel projector, S8mm reel projector, projection screens.
  Budget & Expenditures No separate budget. *Member:* ALA, Mo. State Library Assn.
  Video Serv *Est:* 1965. *Video Staff:* 1 f-t, 1 p-t. *Video Use:* to increase community's library use, community video access.

Mexico (cont'd)
Video serv available by appointment. Have permanent & portable viewing installations. *Equipment Loan Period:* set policy.

Video Tape Loan/Rental/Sale Serv *Loan Eligibility:* staff & students, educational inst, civic & religious groups, indiv with library cards, prof groups, such as hospital staffs. *Restrictions:* for inst, in city & in Audrain County; other counties by mutual agreement. May not borrow by mail.

Video Collection *Sources:* commercial distributors. *Tape Sel:* published reviews. *Other Video Serv:* programming.

Moberly

P-LITTLE DIXIE REGIONAL LIBRARY, 111 N. Fourth St, 65270. *Tel:* (816) 263-4426. *In Charge:* Valerie Macrander. *Member:* Mo. Libraries Film Coop.

Monett

P- BARRY-LAWRENCE REGIONAL LIBRARY, 503 Bond, 65708. *Tel:* (417) 235-6646. *Film Serv Est:* 1957. *In Charge:* David Doennig, Dir. *AV Staff:* 4 (2 cl, 2 tech). *Film Sel:* committee preview.

Free-Loan Film Serv *Eligibility:* educational inst, civic groups, religious groups, indiv with library cards. *Restrictions:* for indiv, Barry & Lawrence Counties. Cannot use for fund-raising, transmit electronically. Available to researchers/scholars for on-site viewing. May not borrow by mail. *Loan Period:* 1 day. *Total Yr Film Loan:* 3000.

Film Collection 25t. *Pubns:* catalog, annual.

Other Film Serv Obtain film from coop loan system (Mo. Libraries Film Coop), library film programs. Permanent viewing facility available for rent to community. *Equipment:* lend 16mm sound projector (8), projection tables & stands (5), projection screens (8).

Other Media Collections *Audio:* disc, 33⅓ rpm, 2400t/2400c; tape, cassette, 160t/160c. *Filmstrips:* silent, 3000t/3000; silent sets, 30t/30c. *Slides:* single, 150t/150c; sets, 10t/10c.

Budget & Expenditures Total library budget $26,825 (FY 7/1/74-7/1/75). Total FY film budget $3000.

Neosho

P- TOWN & COUNTRY REGIONAL LIBRARY, 403 S Jefferson, Box 581. *Tel:* (417) 451-4231. *In Charge:* Jack Wood. *Member:* Mo. Libraries Film Coop.

North Kansas City

P- NORTH KANSAS CITY PUBLIC LIBRARY, 715 E 23 Ave, 64116. *Tel:* (816) 221-3360. *In Charge:* Jacquelyn Hershewe. *Member:* Mo. Libraries Film Coop.

Ozark

P- CHRISTIAN COUNTY LIBRARY, 1005 N Fourth Ave, 65721. *Tel:* (417) 485-2432. *In Charge:* Marilyn Prosser. *Member:* Mo. Libraries Film Coop.

Poplar Bluff

C- THREE RIVERS COMMUNITY COLLEGE, 507 Vine St, 63901. *Tel:* (314) 785-7794, ext. 57. *In Charge:* Dr. Dale C. Talburt, Dir, Learning Resources. *AV Staff:* 5 (3 prof, 2 cl). *Film Sel:* faculty/staff recommendations, previews.

Free-Loan Film Serv *Eligibility:* staff & students, civic groups. *Restrictions:* for indiv & inst, college district. Cannot use for fund-raising. Available to researchers/scholars for on-site viewing. May not borrow by mail. *Loan Period:* 3 days. *Total Yr Film Loan:* 100. Produce S8mm films.

Film Collection 150t. *Circ:* 16mm, 20t/20p; S8mm reel, 130t/130p; *Pubns:* catalog, as needed; suppl, no set policy.

Other Film Serv Rent film from distributors for patrons, obtain film from other libraries, film reference serv. Permanent viewing facility. *Equipment:* lend S8mm camera (2), 16mm sound projector (8), S8mm cartridge projectors (6), S8mm reel projector (1), projection tables & stands (20), projection screen (5).

Other Media Collections *Audio:* disc, 33⅓ rpm, 173t; 45rpm, 27t; tape, cassette, 176t; tape, reel, 30t. *Filmstrips:* sound, 187t; silent, 111t; sound sets, 10t. *Slides:* single, 200t; sets, 42t.

Budget & Expenditures Total library budget $55,128 (FY 7/1/74-7/1/75). Total FY film budget $2346. *Member:* ALA, Mo. Library Assn, MAECT.

Video Serv *Video Use:* documentation of community/school events, in-service training. Video serv available on demand. Produce video tapes.

Video Equipment/Facilities *In-House Use Only:* recording deck (1), b&w/Sony 3600; studio camera (1), b&w, /Sony; monitor (2), b&w, lighting (3); microphones (3); tripod (1); audio tape recorders (3). *Equipment Loan Period:* no set policy. Provide training in use of equipment to faculty & student help.

Video Tape Loan/Rental/Sale Serv *Serv Provided:* swap with other inst. *Loan Eligibility:* staff & students. May not borrow by mail.

Video Collection Maintained by own production, exchange/swap. Use/play ½" reel to reel. Tapes organized by subject. *Other Video Serv:* taping of other media.

Cable & CCTV Receive serv of cable TV system.

Portageville

P- NEW MADRID COUNTY LIBRARY, 63873. *Tel:* (314) 379-3583. *In Charge:* Marshall Dial. *Member:* Mo. Libraries Film Coop.

Potosi

P- WASHINGTON COUNTY LIBRARY, 411 E High St. *Tel:* (314) 438-4691. *In Charge:* Donna Doughty. *Member:* Mo. Libraries Film Coop.

Princeton

P- MERCER COUNTY LIBRARY, 64673. *Tel:* (816) 748-3725. *In Charge:* Esther Shroyer. *Member:* Mo. Libraries Film Coop.

Richmond

P- RAY COUNTY LIBRARY, 64085. *Tel:* (816) 776-3291. *Film Serv Est:* 1965. *In Charge:* Virginia Corley, Librarian. *Film Sel:* chief film librarian's decision. *Holdings:* entertainment, holiday.

Free-Loan Film Serv *Eligibility:* educational inst, indiv with library cards, prof groups. *Restrictions:* for indiv & inst, only in Ray County. *Loan Period:* 1 day.

Film Collection 16t. Approx 1t acquired annually. *Circ:* 16mm, 8t/8p; 8mm reel, 8t.

Other Film Serv Obtain film from coop loan system (Mo. Libraries Film Coop), library film programs. *Equipment:* lend S8mm camera (1), 16mm sound projector (3), 8mm cartridge projector, 8mm reel projector, projection screens (2).

Budget & Expenditures Total library budget $12,000 (FY 1/1/74-1/1/75). No separate AV budget. *Member:* MSL.

Rock Port

P- ATCHISON COUNTY LIBRARY, 64482. *Tel:* (816) 744-5404. *In Charge:* Dorothy Proper. *Member:* Mo. Libraries Film Coop.

Rolla

P- ROLLA PUBLIC LIBRARY, 65401. *Tel:* (314) 364-2604. *In Charge:* Andrew Alexander. *Member:* Mo. Libraries Film Coop.

C- UNIVERSITY OF MISSOURI-ROLLA, G-5 Library, 65401. *Tel:* (314) 341-4385. *Video Serv Est:* 1970. *In Charge:* G. Schowengerdt, Dir of Learning Resources. *Video Staff:* 4 f-t, 3 p-t, 1 tech. *Video Use:* documentation of community/school events, in-service training, instruction. Video serv available by appointment. Produce video tapes. Have production studio/space & separate control room.
   Video Equipment/Facilities *In-House Use Only:* recording deck (6), ¾″, 1″ b&w/col, Ampex, IVC, Sony; playback deck (4), ¾″, 1″ col, IVC, Sony, JVC; studio camera (4), b&w/col, Ampex, GBC; monitor (8), b&w/col; SEG (1), col; keyer (1); additional camera lenses; lighting; microphones (10); tripods (3); audio tape recorders; receiver. *For Loan:* portapak (1), ½″ EIAJ b&w/Sony; recording deck (6), ¾″, 1″ b&w/col, Ampex, IVC, Sony; playback deck (4), ¾″, 1″ col, IVC, Sony, JVC; studio camera (4), b&w/col, Ampex, GBC; lighting. Have permanent & portable viewing installations. *Equipment Loan Period:* no set policy. Provide training in use of equipment to users. Have tape duplication serv.
   Video Tape Loan/Rental/Sale Serv *Serv Provided:* free loan, swap with other inst, rental, sale. *Loan/Rental Eligibility:* staff & students, educational inst, civic groups, prof groups. *Restrictions:* for indiv & inst, none. May borrow by mail. *Loan Period:* flexible.
   Video Collection Maintained by purchase, own production, exchange/swap. Use/play ½″, 1″ reel to reel, ¾″ cassette. *Sources:* business, industry. *Tape Sel:* preview, faculty/staff recommendations.
   Cable & CCTV Receive serv of cable TV system. Have CCTV in inst. *Programming Sources:* over-the-air commercial & public broadcasting, tapes produced by inst, tapes produced professionally & by community groups & indiv.

St. Charles

P- ST. CHARLES CITY-COUNTY LIBRARY, 1900 Merrill Dr, 63301. *Tel:* (314) 723-0232. *In Charge:* Betty Harrison. *Member:* Mo. Libraries Film Coop.

St. James

P- JAMES MEMORIAL LIBRARY, 300 W Scioto St, 65559. *Tel:* (314) 265-7211. *In Charge:* Betty L. Highes. *Member:* Mo. Libraries Film Coop.

St. Joseph

P- ROLLING HILLS CONSOLIDATED LIBRARY, 413 N Belt Highway, 64506. *Tel:* (816) 232-2029. *In Charge:* Daniel J. Bradbury. *Member:* Mo. Libraries Film Coop.

P- ST. JOSEPH PUBLIC LIBRARY, Tenth & Felix Sts, 64501. *Tel:* (816) 232-7729. *In Charge:* Isabel Evans. *Member:* Mo. Libraries Film Coop.

St. Louis

S- CONCORDIA SEMINARY, Library, 801 Demun Ave, 63105. *Tel:* (314) 721-5934 ext. 298. *In Charge:* W. L. Bielenberg, Dir of Library Serv. *AV Staff:* 1 (1 prof, ½ cl, 2 tech). *Holdings:* social sciences 75%, theology 25%.
   Free-Loan Film Serv *Eligibility:* staff & students. *Restrictions:* Available to researchers/scholars for on-site viewing. May not borrow by mail. *Total Yr Film Loan:* 6.
   Film Collection 21t. Approx 3t acquired annually. *Circ:* 16mm, 14t.
   Other Film Serv Rent film from distributors for patrons, obtain film from coop loan system (St. Louis Theological Consortium). Permanent viewing facility available for rent to community.
   Other Media Collections *Audio:* disc, 33⅓rpm, 1200t/1236c; tape, cassette, 3000t. *Filmstrips:* sound, 350t/350c; sound sets, 100t/100c. *Slides:* single, 1000t.
   Budget & Expenditures Total library budget $54,500 (FY 7/1/74-7/1/75). Total FY film budget $2000. *Member:* Mo. Library Assn, Amer Theological Library Assn.
   Video Serv *Est:* 1960. *Video Staff:* 1 f-t, 2 tech. *Video Use:* documentation of community/school events, instruction. Video serv available by appointment. Produce video tapes. Have production studio/space & separate control room.
   Video Equipment/Facilities *In-House Use Only:* recording deck (5), ½″ r-t-r, Panasonic EIAJ; playback deck (1), cart, Panasonic EIAJ; editing deck (2), ½″, Panasonic EIAJ; studio camera (6), b&w/col, Panasonic EIAJ; monitor (5), b&w/col, Panasonic EIAJ; SEG (1); keyer (1), col; additional camera lenses (1); lighting (12); microphones (22); tripods (6); audio tape recorders (16). Have permanent & portable viewing installations. Have tape duplication serv.
   Video Tape Loan/Rental/Sale Serv *Serv Provided:* free loan. *Loan Eligibility:* staff & students. Cannot use for fundraising, duplicate, air without permission. May not borrow by mail. *Total Yr Tape Loan:* 10.
   Video Collection Maintained by purchase, own production. Use/play ½″ reel to reel, ½″ cartridge. *Sources:* commercial distributors. *Tape Sel:* preview, faculty/staff recommendations, catalogs. *Special Collections:* films in video format. Tapes organized by accession order. *Collection, Color:* ½″ reel, 5t; ¾″ cassette, 5t/5c.
   Cable & CCTV *Programming Sources:* over-the-air commercial & public broadcasting, tapes produced by inst, tapes produced professionally.

C- ST. LOUIS COUNTY JUNIOR COLLEGE DISTRICT, 5801 Wilson Ave, 63110. *Tel:* (314) 644-6400, ext 312. *In Charge:* Michael Summers, Admin Assoc.
   Video Collection Maintained by purchase, rental. Use/play ½″, 1″, 2″ reel to reel, ¾″ cassette. *Tape Sel:* preview, faculty/staff recommendations.
   Note Institution serves as processing office for 3 colleges: Forest Park Community College, 5600 Oakland Ave, St. Louis, 63160 (Jackie Beulick); Florissant Valley Community College, 3400 Pershall Rd, Ferguson, 63135 (Charles Rock); Meramec Community College, 11333 Big Bend Blvd, Kirkwood, 63122 (Virginia Hagebush).

P- ST. LOUIS COUNTY LIBRARY, AV Dept, 1640 S Lindbergh Blvd, 63131. *Tel:* (314) 994-3300, ext. 30. *Film Serv Est:* 1952. *In Charge:* George R. Durnell, AV Supervisor. *AV Staff:* 10 (1 prof, 8 cl, 1 tech). *Film Sel:* chief film librarian's decision.
   Free-Loan Film Serv *Eligibility:* educational inst, civic & religious groups, prof groups, such as businesses. *Restrictions:* for indiv & inst, only in city and library district. Cannot use for fund-raising, transmit electronically. May not borrow by mail. *Loan Period:* 1 day. *Total Yr Film Loan:* 44,573.
   Film Collection Approx 75t acquired annually. *Circ:* 16mm, 1975t/2025p; 8mm cartridge, 250p. *Pubns:* catalog, every 4 yr ($1.00); suppl; in yr catalog not published ($.25).
   Other Film Serv Film reference serv, film fairs/festivals, library film programs. Permanent viewing facility.
   Other Media Collections *Audio:* disc, 33⅓rpm, 10,000t/32,347c; tape, cassette, 1387t/1387c. *Slides:* single, 9224t/9224c.
   Budget & Expenditures Total library budget $650,000 (FY 1/1/75-1/1/76). *Member:* ALA, Mo. Library Assn.

P- ST. LOUIS PUBLIC LIBRARY, Film Library Serv, 1624 Locust St, 63103. *Tel:* (314) 241-2288, ext. 236, 237. *Film Serv. Est:* 1948. *In Charge* Rita Broughton, Film Librarian. *AV Staff:* 6 (1 prof, 3 cl, 1 tech). *Film Sel:* chief film librarian's decision.
   Free-Loan Film Serv *Eligibility:* educational inst, civic & religious groups. *Restrictions:* for indiv & inst, only in city and

St. Louis (cont'd)
county library district. Cannot use for fund-raising, transmit electronically. May not borrow by mail. *Loan Period:* 1 day. *Total Yr Film Loan:* 24,981.

Film Collection 1800t. Approx 125-150t acquired annually. *Circ:* all. *Pubns:* catalog, as needed ($1); suppl, annual ($.25). Publish lists of new titles.

Budget & Expenditures Total library budget $32,842 (FY 4/74-4/76). Total FY film budget $32,500. *Member:* ALA, EFLA, FLIC, Mo. Library Assn.

Video Serv *Est:* 1972. *In Charge:* A. J. Lyons, Adult Education Coord. *Video Staff:* 1 p-t. *Video Use:* documentation of community/school events, to increase community's library use, community video access, in-service training, playback. Video serv available by appointment. Produce video tapes.

Video Equipment/Facilities *In-House Use Only:* portapak (1), ½" b&w, Sony 3400; editing deck (1), ½" b&w, Sony 3650; monitor (1), ½" b&w, Sony; microphones; audio tape recorders. Have viewing installation. Provide training in use of equipment to staff.

Video Tape Loan/Rental/Sale Serv *Serv Provided:* plan to swap with other inst. *Loan Eligibility:* org members, in special cases to community groups and schools. *Restrictions:* for indiv, only in city. May not borrow by mail.

Video Collection Maintained by own production. Use/play ½" reel to reel. *Collection, B&W:* ½" reel, 12t/12c. *Pubns:* Publish materials on AV and cable access TV.

Cable & CCTV Inform public about cable system serv & facilities.

Sedalia

P- BOONSLICK REGIONAL LIBRARY, Sixth & Lamine. *Tel:* (816) 826-6195. *In Charge:* Richard Parker. *Member:* Mo. Libraries Film Coop.

Trenton

P- GRUNDY COUNTY-JEWETT NORRIS LIBRARY, 1331 Main, 64683. *Tel:* (816) 359-3577. *Film Serv Est:* 1973. *Film Sel:* staff recommendations.

Free-Loan Film Serv *Eligibility:* indiv with library cards. *Restrictions:* for inst, only in county. Available to researchers/scholars for on-site viewing. May not borrow by mail. *Loan Period:* 1 day. *Total Yr Film Loan:* 500. *Pubns:* Publish materials pertaining to collection.

Other Film Serv Obtain film from coop loan system (Mo. Libraries Film Coop). Permanent viewing facility. *Equipment:* lend 16mm sound projector (3), projection tables & stands.

Other Media Collections *Filmstrips:* sound, 150t/1c. *Slides:* single, 1000c.

Budget & Expenditures Total library budget $7000. Total FY film budget $1000. *Member:* Mo. Library Assn.

Union

C- FOUR RIVERS FILM COOPERATIVE, Box 529, 63084. *Tel:* (314) 583-5193, ext. 44. *Film Serv Est:* 1974. *In Charge:* Paul Howard Jackson, Librarian. *AV Staff:* ¼ (⅛ prof). *Film Sel:* committee preview.

Free-Loan Film Serv *Eligibility:* educational inst which are coop members. *Restrictions:* for inst, coop members only. Available to researchers/scholars for on-site viewing. May not borrow by mail. *Loan Period:* 7 days. *Total Yr Film Loan:* 165.

Film Collection 135t/135p. *Circ:* 16mm, 135t/135p. *Pubns:* catalog, annual.

Budget & Expenditures Total library budget $9161 (FY 7/1/74-7/1/75). No separate AV budget. *Member:* ALA.

P- SCENIC REGIONAL LIBRARY, 11 S Washington, 63084. *Tel:* (314) 583-3224. *In Charge:* Sallie Henderson. *Member:* Mo. Libraries Film Coop.

Van Buren

P- CURRENT RIVER REGIONAL LIBRARY, AV Center, Box 309, 63965. *Tel:* (314) 323-4315, ext 4582. *Film Serv Est:* 1956. *In Charge:* Janice Keeney, Clerk. *AV Staff:* 1. *Film Sel:* chief film librarian's decision.

Free-Loan Film Serv *Eligibility:* educational inst, civic & religious groups. *Restrictions:* for indiv & inst, only in Carter, Ripley, Reynolds & Oregon Counties. Cannot use for fund-raising, transmit electronically. Available to researchers/scholars for on-site viewing. May borrow by mail. *Loan Period:* 3 days. *Total Yr Film Loan:* 612.

Film Collection 75t. *Pubns:* catalog, annual.

Other Film Serv Obtain film from coop loan system (Mo. Libraries Film Coop). *Equipment:* lend 16mm sound projector (11), projection screens (11), slide & filmstrip projectors (12), cassette players (10).

Other Media Collections *Audio:* disc, 33⅓, 45, 78rpm, 500t/500c; tape, cassette, 124t/124c. *Filmstrips:* silent, 607t; silent sets, 18t. *Slides:* sets, 12t. *Member:* Mo. Library Assn.

Video Serv *Video Staff:* 1 f-t. *Video Use:* community video access. Video serv available on demand & by appointment. *Equipment Loan Period:* 1-2 days. Provide training in use of equipment to staff and users.

Video Tape Loan/Rental/Sale Serv *Serv Provided:* free loan. *Loan Eligibility:* educational inst, civic & religious groups, indiv with library cards. *Restrictions:* for indiv & inst, only in Carter, Ripley, Reynolds & Oregon Counties. Cannot use for fund-raising, duplicate, air without permission. *Loan Period:* 14 days. *Tape Sel:* catalogs.

Warrensburg

C- CENTRAL MISSOURI STATE UNIVERSITY, AV Campus Serv, Library, Room 10, 64093. *Tel:* (816) 429-4142. *Film Serv Est:* 1948. *In Charge:* John Siebert, Dir, AV, Campus Serv. *AV Staff:* 2 (1 prof, 1 cl). *Film Sel:* faculty/staff recommendations.

Free-Loan Film Serv *Eligibility:* staff & students. *Restrictions:* for indiv, on campus only. May not borrow by mail. *Loan Period:* 1 day.

Film Collection 975t/975p. Approx 35t acquired annually. *Noncirc:* 16mm, 950t/950p; 8mm reel, 25t/25p. *Pubns:* catalog, every 2 yr; suppl, semiannual.

Other Film Serv Rent film from distributors for patrons, film reference serv. Permanent viewing facility. *Equipment:* S8mm camera (5), 16mm camera (3), 16mm sound projector (100), 8mm cartridge projector (25), 8mm reel projector (5), S8mm reel projector (2), projection tables & stands (50), projection screens (50).

Other Media Collections *Filmstrips:* 650t/650c.

Budget & Expenditures Total library budget $8000 (FY 7/1/74-7/1/75). Total FY film budget $8000.

P- TRAILS REGIONAL LIBRARY, Box 498, 64093. *Tel:* (816) 747-9177. *Film Serv Est:* 1958. *In Charge:* Esther Gilman, Regional Librarian. *AV Staff:* 1 (1 prof, ½ cl, ½ tech). *Film Sel:* coop members, not locally.

Free-Loan Film Serv *Eligibility:* educational inst (restricted), civic groups, religious groups, indiv with library cards. *Restrictions:* for indiv & inst, regional library service area (Johnson & Lafayette Counties). Cannot use for fund-raising, transmit electronically. *Loan Period:* 1 day. *Total Yr Film Loan:* 3904.

Film Collection *Pubns:* catalog, annual.

Other Film Serv Obtain film from coop loan system (Mo. Libraries Film Coop). *Equipment:* lend 16mm sound projector (5), projection tables & stands (4), projection screens (7). In 4 locations.

Budget & Expenditures Total library budget $61,200 (FY 1/1/75-1/1/76). Total FY film budget $4200 (coop fees, primarily). *Member:* ALA, FLIC, Mo. Library Assn.

Montana

Billings

P- BILLINGS PUBLIC LIBRARY, 59101. *Tel:* (406) 248-7392. *Film Serv Est:* 1968. *In Charge:* Virginia Ekstrom, Head, Circulation. *AV Staff:* 1 cl. *Film Sel:* staff recommendations, chief film librarian's decision. *Holdings:* American Indian, animated films 5%, children's films 20%, Christmas, comedy, documentary, experimental films 2%, feature films 2%, fine arts 2%, human relations, sports, the West.

Free-Loan Film Serv *Eligibility:* educational inst, civic groups, religious groups, community members. *Restrictions:* for indiv & inst, only in 3 adjacent counties. Cannot use for fund-raising, borrow for classroom use. Available to researchers/scholars for on-site viewing. May borrow by mail. *Loan Period:* 1 day, (longer for mail serv).

Film Collection 200t. Approx 50t acquired annually. *Circ:* 16mm, 200t/200p. *Pubns:* catalog, annual.

Other Film Serv Obtain film from coop loan system (Great Falls Public Library). Permanent viewing facility available for rent to community. *Equipment:* lend/rent 16mm camera, 16mm sound projector (2), lend projection screens.

Budget & Expenditures Total library budget $121,000 (FY 7/1/75-7/1/76). Total FY film budget $9000. *Member:* Mont. Library Assn.

Video Serv *Equipment Loan Period:* 1 day (longer for mail serv). Provide training in use of equipment to f-t page, special ed youths, desk clerks.

C- EASTERN MONTANA COLLEGE, Library (AV Circ), 59101. *Tel:* (406) 657-2320, ext 2329. *In Charge:* Edmund Arnold, Librarian. *AV Staff:* 2 (1 tech). *Film Sel:* faculty/staff recommendations.

Free-Loan Film Serv *Eligibility:* staff & students. *Restrictions:* for indiv & inst, none. Subject to college needs. Available to researchers/scholars for on-site viewing. May borrow by mail. *Loan Period:* 3 days.

Film Rental Serv *Eligibility:* no restrictions. *Restrictions:* none. Subject to college needs. *Rental Period:* 3 days.

Film Collection 50t.

Other Film Serv Rent film from distributors for patrons, obtain film from other libraries. Permanent viewing facility available for rent to community. *Equipment:* lend/rent 16mm sound projector, 8mm cartridge projector, 8mm reel projector, S8mm cartridge projector, projection tables & stands, projection screens.

Budget & Expenditures No separate budget. *Member:* AECT.

Video Serv *Video Staff:* 2 f-t, 1 p-t, 1 tech. *Video Use:* documentation of community/school events, community video access, in-service training, playback only of professionally produced tapes. Video serv available on demand and by appointment. Produce video tapes. Have production studio/space & separate control room.

Video Equipment/Facilities *In-House Use Only:* portapak, b&w; recording deck, b&w; playback deck , b&w; editing deck, b&w; studio camera, b&w; monitor, b&w; SEG; additional camera lenses; lighting; microphones; tripods; audio tape recorders. Have permanent & portable viewing installations. *Equipment Loan Period:* by the hour. Provide training in use of equipment to faculty & students. Have tape duplication serv.

Video Tape Loan/Rental/Serv *Serv Provided:* free loan, rental. *Loan/Rental Eligibility:* staff, students enrolled in inst, educational inst, civic & religious groups, prof groups, such as doctors, lawyers. *Restrictions:* for indiv & inst, none. Cannot use for fund-raising, duplicate, air without permission. May borrow by mail. *Loan Period:* 3 days.

Video Collection Maintained by rental, own production. Use/play ½″ reel to reel. *Sources:* commercial distributors. *Tape Sel:* faculty/staff recommendations, catalogs. Tapes organized by Dewey Decimal. *Other Video Serv:* programming.

Cable & CCTV Have CCTV in inst. *Programming Sources:* for overflow crowds for guest speakers.

Kalispell

C- FLATHEAD VALLEY COMMUNITY COLLEGE, Total Community Education Program, Box 1174, 59901. *Tel:* (406) 755-5222, ext 261, 264. *Video Serv Est:* 1973. *In Charge:* James R. Ludwig, Dir. *Video Staff:* 3 f-t, 1 p-t, 1 tech. *Video Use:* documentation of community/school events, community video access, in-service training, practical video/TV training courses, as art form, community outreach. Video serv available on demand and by appointment. Produce video tapes. Have production studio/space & separate control room.

Video Equipment/Facilities *In-House Use Only:* portapak (4), ½″ b&w/col, Sony 3400; recording/playback deck (4), ½″, ¾″ b&w/col, Sony 1200, 3650, 8650, 1800; editing deck (2), ½″ b&w/col, Sony 3650, 8650; studio camera (3), b&w, Sony 3200DX; monitor (5), b&w/col, Sony KV171; SEG (1), Sony; additional camera lenses; lighting (3); microphones (8); tripods (6); audio tape recorders (3). *For Loan:* portapak (4), ½″ b&w/col, Sony 3400. Have portable viewing installation. *Equipment Loan Period:* no set policy. Provide training in use of equipment to students. Have tape duplication serv.

Video Tape Loan/Rental Serv *Serv Provided:* free loan, swap with other inst, rental. *Loan/Rental Eligibility:* staff & students, educational inst, civic & religious groups, indiv with library cards, prof groups, such as educational organizations & others, such as American Indian groups, federal agencies. *Restrictions:* for indiv & inst, none. Cannot use for fund-raising, duplicate, air without permission. May borrow by mail. *Loan Period:* flexible.

Video Collection Maintained by own production, exchange/swap. Use/play ½″ reel to reel, ¾″ cassette. *Sources:* community productions, student productions. *Tape Sel:* preview, faculty/staff recommendations. Tapes organized by subject. *Collection, Color:* ¾″ cassette, 20t. *Collection, B&W:* ½″ reel, 75t. *Other Video Serv:* programming, reference serv, taping of other media, production workshops. *Pubns:* brochures.

Cable & CCTV Receive serv of cable TV system. Produce programs for cablecasting. Inform public about cable system serv & facilities. Serve as production facility for others. Run cable programs for special audiences. Have advisory/administrative role in cable system operation of community. Have CCTV in inst, with 6-8 monitors. *Programming Sources:* over-the-air commercial & public broadcasting, tapes produced by inst & by community groups & indiv.

Nebraska

Fairbury

P- SOUTHEAST COMMUNITY COLLEGE, Fairbury Campus, Fairbury Library/Media Center, 68352. *Tel:* (402) 729-6148, ext 26. *Video Serv Est:* 1972. *In Charge:* Shirley H. Lewis, Library/Media Dir. *Video Staff:* 2 f-t, 2 p-t. *Video Use:* documentation of community/school events, in-service training, playback only of professionally produced tapes. Video serv available by appointment. Produce video tapes. Have production studio/space & separate control room.

Video Equipment/Facilities *In-House Use & For Loan:* portapak (1), ½″ b&w, Sony; recording deck (2), ½″ b&w, Sony; studio camera (1), ½″ b&w, Sony 3650; microphones (2); audio tape recorders (7). Have portable viewing installation. *Equipment Loan Period:* no set policy. Provide training in use of equipment to students & library personnel. Have tape duplication serv.

Video Tape Loan/Rental/Sale Serv *Serv Provided:* swap with other inst. *Loan Eligibility:* staff & students, educational inst, civic & religious groups, business clubs. *Restrictions:* cannot duplicate, air without permission. May not borrow by mail. *Total Yr Tape Loan:* 3.

Video Collection Maintained by rental, own production, exchange/swap. Use/play ½″ reel to reel. *Sources:* commercial distributors. *Tape Sel:* faculty/staff recommendations, published reviews, catalogs. Tapes organized by subject. *Collection, B&W:* ½″ reel, 10t/c. *Other Video Serv:* reference serv, taping of other media. *Pubns:* catalog.

Cable & CCTV Receive serv of cable TV system. Inform public about cable system serv & facilities. Run cable programs for special audiences.

Holdrege

P- HOLDREGE PUBLIC LIBRARY SYSTEM, 604 E Ave, 68949. *Tel:* (308) 995-5722. *Film Serv Est:* 1974. *In Charge:* Jerry Koup, Dir. *AV Staff:* ½ (¼ prof, ¼ cl). *Film Sel:* chief film librarian's decision.

Free-Loan Film Serv *Eligibility:* indiv with library cards. *Restrictions:* for indiv, within six county region. Cannot use for fund-raising, transmit electronically. Available to researchers/scholars for on-site viewing. May borrow by mail. *Loan Period:* 3 days, longer by arrangement. *Total Yr Film Loan:* 331.

Film Collection 50t/p. Approx 10t acquired annually. *Circ:* 16mm, 10t/p; 8mm reel, 40t/p. *Pubns:* catalog, annual (free); suppl, annual, published six months after catalog.

Other Film Serv Obtain film from coop loan system (Neb. Film Serv, Lincoln). Permanent viewing facility available for rent to community. *Equipment:* lend 16mm sound projector (1), 8mm reel projector (1), S8mm reel projector (1), projection screens (3).

Other Media Collections *Audio:* disc, 33⅓rpm, 1200c; tape, cassette, 350c. *Filmstrips:* sound sets, 170c; silent sets, 10c. *Slides:* sets, 4c.

Budget & Expenditures Total library budget $30,110.60 (FY 7/1/74-7/1/75). Total FY film budget $1400. *Member:* ALA, Nebr. Library Assn, Nebr. Education Media Assn.

Lincoln

P- LINCOLN CITY LIBRARIES, Film Dept, 136 S 14 St, 68508. *Tel:* (402) 435-2146, ext 36. *Film Serv Est:* 1951. *In Charge:* Loreta Tiemann, Film Librarian. *AV Staff:* 4½ (1 prof, 3½ tech). *Film Sel:* chief film librarian's decision. *Holdings:* criminal justice 33%.

Free-Loan Film Serv *Eligibility:* indiv with library cards, prof groups, such as Nebr. Criminal Justice Agenices. *Restrictions:* for indiv, in Lancaster County or Nebr. criminal justice personnel. Cannot use for fund-raising, transmit electronically.

May borrow by mail. *Loan Period:* 1 day, but flexible as needed. *Total Yr Film Loan:* 20, 862.

Film Collection 1102t/1158p. Approx 140t acquired annually. *Circ:* 16mm, 1102t/1158p. *Pubns:* catalog, every 2 yrs (free); suppl, in yr catalog not published (free). Publish annual Criminal Justice Film Catalog.

Other Film Serv Obtain film from coop loan system, film reference serv. Permanent viewing facility available for rent to community at branch libraries. *Equipment:* rent 16mm sound projector (9), projection screens (5).

Other Media Collections *Filmstrips:* sound sets, 171t; silent sets, 498t. *Slides:* sets, 82t.

Budget & Expenditures Total library budget $197,465 (FY 9/1/74-9/1/75). Total FY film budget $15,000 (plus Fed LEAA $20,000 grant). *Member:* ALA, EFLA, FLIC, Nebr. Library Assn.

Video Serv Produce video tapes.

Video Equipment/Facilities *In-House Use Only:* portapak (1), ½″ b&w/col, Panasonic; recording deck (4), ½″ & ¾″ b&w/col, Sony 3600, Panasonic VCR; playback deck (2), col; monitor (5), Panasonic/Sony; lighting (3); microphones; tripods (1); audio tape recorders (2); portable camera, col, AKAI. Have portable viewing installation.

Video Collection Maintained by purchase, own production. Use/play ¾″ cassette. *Collection, Color:* ¾″ cassette, 26t/1c.

S- NEBRASKA LIBRARY COMMISSION, Film Dept, 1420 P St, 68508. *Tel:* (402) 471-2045, ext 38. *Film Serv Est:* 1974. *In Charge:* Paula Durling, Film Librarian. *AV Staff:* 2 (1 prof, ½ cl, ½ tech). *Film Sel:* preview, faculty/staff recommendations, chief film librarian's decision, published reviews.

Free-Loan Film Serv *Eligibility:* state residents with library cards, through interlibrary loan. Cannot use for fund-raising, transmit electronically, borrow for classroom use. May borrow by mail. *Loan Period:* varies. *Total Yr Film Loan:* 6000.

Film Collection 850t/910p. *Circ:* 16mm, 850t/910p. *Pubns:* catalog, annual (free); suppl, no set policy.

Budget & Expenditures No separate budget. *Member:* EFLA, Nebr. State Library Assn.

C- NEBRASKA WESLEYAN UNIVERSITY, Cochrane-Woods Library, 50 St. Paul, 68504. *Tel:* (402) 466-2371, ext 354.

Video Serv *Est:* 1968. *In Charge:* Lois W. Collings, ITV Coord. *Video Staff:* 2 f-t. *Video Use:* playback only of professionally produced tapes. Video serv available by appointment.

Video Equipment/Facilities *In-House Use Only:* portapak (1), b&w, Sony; recording deck (5), b&w/col, Sony; studio camera (2), b&w/col, Sony; monitor (18), portable b&w/col, RCA, Stachell, Carlson. *For Loan:* (campus use only) audio cassette recorders (28). Have viewing installation.

Video Collection Maintained by purchase, rental, own production, exchange/swap. Use/play ¾″ cassette. *Sources:* exchange (borrow from NETCHE library). *Member:* NETCHE (Nebr. Television Council for Higher Education, Inc). *Tape Sel:* faculty/staff recommendations. Tapes organized by title.

Cable & CCTV Receive serv of cable TV system. Have CCTV in inst. *Programming Sources:* over-the-air commercial & public broadcasting.

C- UNIVERSITY OF NEBRASKA, Instructional Media Center, 421 Nebraska Hall, 68588. *Tel:* (402) 472-2171. *Film Serv Est:* 1928. *In Charge:* Dr. James G. Buterbaugh, Dir. *AV Staff:* 28 (3 prof, 13 cl, 12 tech). *Film Sel:* committee preview, faculty/staff recommendations, chief film librarian's decision.

Free-Loan Film Serv *Restrictions:* for indiv & inst, only in state. Available to researchers/scholars for on-site viewing. May borrow by mail. *Loan Period:* 1-2 days. *Total Yr Film Loan:* 2000.

Film Rental Serv *Eligibility:* no restrictions. *Restrictions:* only in U.S. Cannot use for fund-raising, transmit electronically. *Rental Period:* 1-2 days. *Total Yr Film Booking:* 30,000. Produce films, slides & filmstrips.

Film Collection 8000t/5500p. Approx 1000t acquired annually. *Circ:* 16mm, 8000t/5500p. *Pubns:* catalog, every 3 yrs; suppl, annual (free). Publish materials pertaining to collection. Publish newsletters, selective indexes.

Other Film Serv Rent film from distributors for patrons, obtain film from other libraries, film reference serv, film fairs/festivals. Permanent viewing facility. *Equipment:* lend S8mm camera, 16mm sound projector, 8mm cartridge projector, 8mm reel projector, S8mm cartridge projector, S8mm reel projector, projection tables & stands, projection screens.

Other Media Collections *Audio:* tape, cartridge, 3000t. *Filmstrips:* sound, 600t; silent, 6000t.

Budget & Expenditures Total library budget $300,000 (FY 6/74-6/75). Total FY film budget $175,000. *Member:* AECT, CUFC, EFLA, NAVA (Nebr. Education Media Assn).

A- UNIVERSITY OF NEBRASKA, Sheldon Film Theater, Sheldon Memorial Art Gallery, 68588. *Tel:* (402) 472-2461. *In Charge:* Dan Ladely, Dir, Sheldon Film Theater. *Film Sel:* committee preview. *Holdings:* animated films 25%, children's films 25%, experimental films 25%, fine arts 75%.

Film Rental Serv *Eligibility:* no restrictions. *Restrictions:* none. *Rental Rate:* $100 per year. *Rental Period:* by screening. *Total Yr Film Booking:* 2.

Film Collection 22t/23p. *Circ:* 16mm, 1t/p. *Noncirc:* 16mm, 22t/p.

Other Film Serv Rent film from distributors for patrons, obtain film from coop loan system, obtain film from other libraries, film reference serv, film fairs/festivals, library film programs. Permanent viewing facility available for rent to community.

Budget & Expenditures Total library budget $40,000 (FY 7/1/74-7/1/75). Total FY film budget $40,000.

Milford

C- SOUTHEAST COMMUNITY COLLEGE, Milford Campus, Learning Resource Center, 68405. *Tel:* (402) 761-2131, ext 245. *Film Serv Est:* 1975. *In Charge:* Marilyn Lester, Dir, LRC. *AV Staff:* 2 (1 prof, 1 cl). *Film Sel:* committee preview, faculty/staff recommendations. *Holdings:* industrial arts 100%.

Film Collection 54t/p. Approx 5t acquired annually. *Pubns:* catalog, forthcoming.

Other Film Serv Obtain film from coop loan system (other SCC campuses at Lincoln & Fairbury). *Equipment:* lend S8mm camera (1), 16mm camera (1), 16mm sound projector (8), 8mm reel projector (1), S8mm reel projector (1), projection tables & stands (3), projection screens (6).

Other Media Collections *Audio:* disc, 33⅓ rpm, 6t; tape, cassette, 27t; tape, reel, 7t. *Slides:* single, 2500t.

Budget & Expenditures Total library budget $2000 (FY 7/1/74-7/1/75). No separate AV budget. *Member:* AECT, Nebr. Library Assn.

Video Serv *Est:* 1975. *Video Staff:* 1 f-t. *Video Use:* documentation of community/school events, in-service training, playback only of professionally produced tapes. Video serv available on demand. Produce video tapes. Have production studio/space & separate control room.

Video Equipment/Facilities *For Loan:* portapak (1), ½″ b&w, Sony; recording deck (1), ½″ b&w, Sony AV3600; studio camera (2), ½″ b&w, Sony; monitor (2), b&w, Sony; additional camera lenses (1); lighting (1); microphones (1); tripods (3); audio tape recorders (6). *Equipment Loan Period:* provide training in use of equipment to instructors.

Video Tape Loan/Rental/Sale Serv *Serv Provided:* free loan, swap with other inst. *Loan Eligibility:* staff & students, Nebraska residents. *Restrictions:* for indiv & inst, only in state. Cannot duplicate, air without permission. May borrow by mail. *Loan Period:* as needed.

Video Collection Maintained by rental, own production, exchange/swap. Use/play ½″ reel to reel. *Sources:* commercial distributors, exchange (with SCC campuses at Lincoln & Fairbury). *Tape Sel:* faculty/staff recommendations. Tapes organized by accession order. *Collection, B&W:* ½″ reel, 2t. *Other Video Serv:* taping of other media. *Pubns:* catalog.

Omaha

P- OMAHA PUBLIC LIBRARY, Film Dept, 1823 Harney, 68102. *Tel:* (402) 342-4766, ext 50. *Film Serv Est:* 1957. *In Charge:* Margaret B. Larsen. *AV Staff:* 3 (1 prof, 2 cl). *Film Sel:* committee preview.

Free-Loan Film Serv *Eligibility:* residents of Douglas County. *Restrictions:* for indiv & inst, only in Douglas County; annual subscription card for non-county residents. Cannot use for fund-raising, transmit electronically. Available to researchers/scholars for on-site viewing. May not borrow by mail. *Loan Period:* 1 day. *Total Yr Film Loan:* 12,112.

Film Collection 520t/525p. Approx 45-50t acquired annually. *Circ:* 8mm cartridge, 520t/525p. *Pubns:* catalog, annual (free); suppl, in yr catalog not published.

Other Film Serv Obtain film from other libraries, library film programs. Permanent viewing facility. *Equipment:* rent 16mm sound projector (3), projection screens.

Other Media Collections *Audio:* disc, 33⅓ rpm, 2000t/5500c.

Budget & Expenditures Total library budget $249,250 (FY 1/1/75-1/1/76). Total FY film budget $7850. *Member:* ALA, EFLA, Nebr. State Library Assn.

Scottsbluff

C- NEBRASKA WESTERN COLLEGE LIBRARY, 1601 E 27 St N E, 69361. *Tel:* (308) 635-3606, ext 35. *Film Serv Est:* 1970. *In Charge:* Kathlyn King Lundgren, Coord of AV Servs. *AV Staff:* 1 (1 prof, 1 cl). *Film Sel:* committee preview, faculty/staff recommendations, chief film librarian's decision.

Free-Loan Film Serv *Eligibility:* staff, educational inst, civic groups, prof groups, such as Rotary, Lions. *Restrictions:* for indiv & inst, only in city. Cannot use for fund-raising, transmit electronically. Faculty member must accompany film and equipment unless operator has been checked out on equipment. Available to researchers/scholars for on-site viewing. May not borrow by mail. *Loan Period:* as needed. *Total Yr Film Loan:* 583.

Film Collection 115t/p. *Circ:* 16mm, 115t/p; S8mm cartridge, 140t/p.

Other Film Serv Obtain film from coop loan system, obtain film from other libraries, film reference serv, library film programs. Permanent viewing facility. *Equipment:* lend 16mm sound projector (11), S8mm cartridge projector (8), projection tables & stands (23), projection screens (8).

Other Media Collections *Audio:* disc, 33⅓ rpm, 578t/c; tape, cassette, 506t/c. *Filmstrips:* silent, 40t/c; sound sets, 125t/c. *Slides:* sets, 55t/c; transparency sets, 15t/c.

Budget & Expenditures Total library budget $63,702 (FY 7/1/74-7/1/75). Total FY film budget $2935. *Member:* AECT, ALA, Nebr. State Library Assn, Mountain Plains Library Assn.

Video Serv *Est:* 1969. *Video Staff:* 1 f-t, 1 p-t. *Video Use:* documentation of community/school events, in-service training, for workshops, speech classes, student counseling, mental health program-counseling; also tape educational TV. Video serv available on demand. Produce video tapes. Have production studio/space.

Video Equipment/Facilities *In-House Use Only:* portapak (1), ½″ b&w, Sony DV 2400; studio camera (2), b&w, Sony & JVC-GS 2500; monitor (3), b&w; additional camera lenses (2); microphones (1); tripods (2); audio tape recorders (35); RF unit & TV switchbox. *Equipment Loan Period:* no set policy. Provide training in use of equipment to faculty & students. Have cassette tape duplication serv.

Scottsbluff (cont'd)

Video Tape Loan/Rental/Sale Serv　*Serv Provided:* free loan, swap with other inst. *Loan Eligibility:* staff & students, educational inst. *Restrictions:* for indiv, none; for inst, only in state. Cannot use for fund-raising, duplicate, air without permission. May borrow by mail. *Loan Period:* as needed.

Video Collection　Maintained by purchase, own production, exchange/swap. Use/play ½″ reel to reel. *Sources:* exchange (with other colleges), tape educational TV. *Tape Sel:* faculty/staff recommendations, published reviews. *Special Collections:* in-house training tapes. Tapes organized by LC system. *Other Video Serv:* taping of other media.

Nevada

Elko

P- ELKO COUNTY LIBRARY, 720 Court St, 89801. *Tel:* (702) 738-3066.
    Video Serv *Est:* 1974. *In Charge:* Hailie Gunn, Dir. *Video Staff:* 1 f-t, 1 p-t. *Video Use:* to increase community's library use. Video serv available by appointment. Have production studio/space.
    Video Equipment/Facilities Have permanent viewing installation. *Equipment Loan Period:* 3 days.
    Video Tape Loan/Rental/Sale Serv *Serv Provided:* free loan. *Loan Eligibility:* educational inst, civic groups, religious groups, prof groups. *Restrictions:* for indiv, no loan for individual home use; for inst, none. Cannot use for fund-raising, duplicate. May borrow by mail. *Loan Period:* 3 days.
    Video Collection Maintained by rental. Use/play ¾″ cassette. *Sources:* commercial distributors, exchange (University, Health Sciences Library, etc). *Member:* Nev. Media Circuit.
    Cable & CCTV Receive serv of cable TV system.

Las Vegas

P- CLARK COUNTY LIBRARY DISTRICT, 1401 E Flamingo Rd, 89109. *Tel:* (702) 733-7810, ext 03. *Film Serv Est:* 1974. *In Charge:* Lamar Marchese, Program Coord. *AV Staff:* 3 (1 prof, 1½ cl, ½ tech). *Film Sel:* committee preview.
    Free-Loan Film Serv *Eligibility:* educational inst, civic groups, religious groups, indiv with library cards, prof groups. *Restrictions:* for indiv & inst, Southern Nevada (Lincoln Nye, Esmerelda, Clark counties). Cannot use for fund-raising, transmit electronically. Available to researchers/scholars for on-site viewing. May borrow by mail. *Loan Period:* 1 day. *Total Yr Film Loan:* 3710.
    Film Collection 250t. *Circ:* 16mm, 175t; 8mm reel, 25t; S8mm reel, 50t. *Pubns:* catalog, every 2 yrs ($2-16mm, $1-8mm & S8mm); suppl, no set policy. Publish promotional brochure called "Coming Soon."
    Other Film Serv Obtain film from coop loan system (Nev. Library Media Coop), obtain film from other libraries, film reference serv, film fairs/festivals, library film programs. Permanent viewing facility available to community.
    Other Media Collections *Audio:* disc, 33⅓ rpm, 7500t; tape, cassette, 300t.
    Budget & Expenditures Total library budget $300,000. Total FY film budget $12,000. *Member:* ALA, EFLA, Nev. Library Assn.

Reno

P- WASHOE COUNTY LIBRARY, 3010 S Center, Box 2151, 89801. *Tel:* (702) 785-4190. *Film Serv Est:* 1974. *In Charge:* Wendy Muchmore, Coord. *AV Staff:* 2 prof. *Film Sel:* committee preview.
    Free-Loan Film Serv *Eligibility:* any school or organization needing films for entertainment or instruction. *Restrictions:* for indiv, interlibrary loan. Cannot use for fund-raising, transmit electronically; individuals may not borrow for home use. Available to researchers/scholars for on-site viewing. May borrow by mail. *Loan Period:* 3 days.
    Film Collection 320t. *Circ:* 16mm, 300t; 8mm reel, 20t.
    Other Film Serv Obtain film from coop loan system (Nev. Media Circuit). Permanent viewing facility available for use by community. *Equipment:* lend S8mm camera, 16mm camera, 16mm sound projector, S8mm cartridge projector, slide projector w/sound.
    Video Serv *Est:* 1975. *Video Use:* documentation of community/school events, to increase community's library use, community video access, in-service training, as art form. Video serv available on demand. Produce video tapes.
    Video Equipment/Facilities *In-House Use Only:* portapak (1), ½″ b&w, Panasonic NV3085; recording deck (1), col, Sony 8600; playback deck (1); studio camera (1), ¾″ col, JVC 5000; monitor (3), col, RCA Receiver, Monitor 968-W; keyer (1), Panasonic. Have portable viewing installation. *Equipment Loan Period:* no set policy.
    Video Tape Loan/Rental/Sale Serv Policy not yet established.
    Video Collection Not yet established.

New Hampshire

Chester

C- WHITE PINES COLLEGE LIBRARY, Box 278, 03036. *Tel:* (607) 887-4401. *In Charge:* Linda Feldman, Head Librarian. *AV Staff:* 2 (1 prof). *Film Sel:* faculty/staff recommendations, head film librarian's decision.
Free-Loan Film Serv *Eligibility:* org members & others. *Restrictions:* campus use only. May not borrow by mail.
Other Film Serv Obtain film from coop loan system (N.H. State Library).
Other Media Collections *Filmstrips:* 27t/c. *Slides:* single, 5t.
Budget & Expenditures Total library budget $3000 (FY 7/1/74-7/1/75). Total FY film budget $800. *Member:* N.H. Library Assn.

Concord

P- NEW HAMPSHIRE STATE LIBRARY, 20 Park St, 03301. *Tel:* (603) 271-2392. *Member:* North County Library Film Coop.

Durham

C- UNIVERSITY OF NEW HAMPSHIRE, Dept of Media Servs, 03909. *Tel:* (603) 862-2240. *Film Serv Est:* 1946. *In Charge:* John D. Bardwell, Dir. *AV Staff:* 17 (5 prof, 6 cl, 6 tech). *Film Sel:* faculty/staff recommendations, chief film librarian's decision.
Film Rental Serv *Eligibility:* no restrictions. *Restrictions:* only in region (New England states). Cannot use for fundraising, transmit electronically. *Rental Period:* 1 day. *Total Yr Film Booking:* 18,500. Sell films. Produce films. Produce slide/tapes, video tapes, overhead transparencies.
Film Collection Approx 200t acquired annually. *Circ:* 16mm, 3000t/3200p. *Pubns:* catalog, every 2 yrs; suppl, in yr catalog not published. Publish newsletters.
Other Film Serv Film reference serv. Permanent viewing facility.
Budget & Expenditures Total FY film budget $36,000 (FY 7/1/74-7/1/75). *Member:* AECT, CUFC.

Hanover

C- DARTMOUTH COLLEGE FILMS, Office of Instructional Servs & Educational Research, Fairbanks North Hall, 03755. *Tel:* (603) 646-2384. *Film Serv Est:* 1939. *In Charge:* J. B. Watson, Jr., Asst Dir. *AV Staff:* 15½ (5 prof, 3½ cl, 7 tech). *Film Sel:* faculty/staff recommendations. *Holdings:* black studies 1%, Dartmouth College 1%, engineering 1%, experimental films 1%, feature films 5%, fine arts 15%, industrial arts 5%, science 20%, social sciences 50%.
Film Rental Serv *Eligibility:* no restrictions. *Restrictions:* only in U.S. *Rental Period:* 1 day. Produce films.
Film Collection 650t/p. Approx 10-20t acquired annually. *Circ:* 16mm, 600t/650p. *Pubns:* catalog, as needed ($3); suppl, no set policy.
Other Film Serv Rent film from distributors for patrons, obtain film from coop loan system (Univ Film Study Center), from other libraries, film reference serv, campus film society. Permanent viewing facility available for rent to community. *Equipment:* rent S8mm camera (3), 16mm camera (5), 16mm sound projector (20), 8mm reel projector (2), S8mm reel projector (2), projection tables & stands (5), projection screens (10).
Other Media Collections *Filmstrips:* silent, 100t/c. *Slides:* sets, 5t/25c.
Budget & Expenditures Total library budget $25,000 (FY 7/1/75-7/1/76). Total FY film budget $8400. *Member:* AECT, AFI, EFLA, FLIC, Univ Film Assn, Amer Science Film Assn.

Manchester

P- CURRIER GALLERY OF ART, 192 Orange St, 03104. *Tel:* (603) 669-6144. *Film Serv Est:* 1973. *In Charge:* Marian Woodruff, Education Dir. *AV Staff:* 1 prof. *Film Sel:* chief film librarian's decision.
Free-Loan Film Serv *Eligibility:* educational inst, civic & religious groups. *Restrictions:* for indiv & inst, only in state. Available to researchers/scholars for on-site viewing. May borrow by mail. *Loan Period:* 7 days. *Total Yr Film Loan:* 8.
Film Collection 10t/2p. Approx 2t acquired annually. *Circ:* 16mm, 1t/p. *Noncirc:* 16mm, 9t/1p.
Other Film Serv Library film programs.

C- NEW HAMPSHIRE COLLEGE, H.A.B. Shapiro Memorial Library, 2500 River Rd, 03104. *Tel:* (603) 668-2211. *Video Serv Est:* 1971. *In Charge:* Richard J. Ball Jr., AV Servs Dir. *Video Staff:* 8 p-t. *Video Use:* documentation of community/school events, practical video/TV training courses, as art form, classroom instruction. Video serv available on demand. Produce video tapes. Have production studio/space & separate control room.
Video Equipment/Facilities *In-House Use Only:* portapak (4), ½" reel b&w, Sony AV 3400; recording deck (2), ½" col, Sony 3650; playback deck (1), ½" b&w, Panasonic; editing deck (2), ½" col, Panasonic; studio camera (4), b&w, Sony 8650; monitor (7), b&w/col, Panasonic; SEG (1), Panasonic; keyer (1), Craig 6105; synthesizer (2); additional camera lenses (2); lighting (15); microphones (10); tripods (7); audio tape recorders (20). *For Loan:* portapak (4), ½" reel b&w, Sony AV3400. Have portable viewing installation. *Equipment Loan Period:* no set policy. Provide training in use of equipment to students. Have tape duplication serv.
Video Tape Loan/Rental/Sale Serv *Serv Provided:* free loan, swap with other inst. *Loan Eligibility:* staff & students, educational inst, civic & religious groups. *Restrictions:* for inst, none. May borrow by mail.
Video Collection Maintained by purchase, rental, own production. Use/play ½" reel to reel. *Tape Sel:* preview, faculty/staff recommendations. Tapes organized alphabetically. *Collection, Color:* ½" reel, 50t. *Collection, B&W:* ½" reel, 100t. *Other Video Serv:* taping of other media, production workshops. *Pubns:* publish in-house lists.
Cable & CCTV Have CCTV in inst. *Programming Sources:* tapes produced by inst, tapes produced professionally, tapes produced by community groups & indiv.

Plymouth

C- PLYMOUTH STATE COLLEGE, Herbert H. Lamson Library, 03264. *Tel:* (603) 536-1550, ext 257. *Video Serv Est:* 1971. *In Charge:* Michael Flannery, Asst Librarian. *Video Staff:* 1 f-t, 2 tech. *Video Use:* documentation of community/school events, community video access, classroom instruction. Video serv available on demand. Produce video tapes. Have production studio/space & separate control room.
Video Equipment/Facilities *In-House Use Only:* playback deck (3), col, IVC. Have permanent viewing installation.
Video Collection Maintained by purchase, rental, own production. Use/play 1" reel to reel, ½" cartridge, ¾" cassette. Tapes organized by LC. *Collection, Color:* 1" reel, 12t. *Other Video Serv:* programming.
Cable & CCTV Provide serv of cable TV system. Produce programs for cablecasting. Inform public about cable system serv & facilities. Serve as production facility for others. Own & manage cable system operation. Have CCTV in inst, with 65 monitors. *Programming Sources:* over-the-air commercial & public broadcasting, tapes produced by inst.

New Jersey

Belleville

P- BELLVILLE PUBLIC LIBRARY, 221 Washington Ave, 07109. *Tel:* (201) 759-9200. *Member:* Garden State Library Film Circuit.

Bergenfield

P- BERGENFIELD FREE PUBLIC LIBRARY, 50 W Clinton Ave, 07621. *Tel:* (201) 384-2765. *Film Serv Est:* 1973. *AV Staff:* ¾ prof. *Film Sel:* chief film librarian's decision. *Holdings:* children's films.

Free-Loan Film Serv *Eligibility:* educational inst, civic groups, religious groups, indiv with library cards, & others, such as teachers, Federation members. *Restrictions:* for indiv, interlibrary loan; for inst, only in Bergen County. Cannot use for fund-raising. Available to researchers/scholars for on-site viewing. May not borrow by mail. *Loan Period:* 7 days. *Total Yr Film Loan:* 957.

Film Collection 200t. Approx 50t acquired annually. *Circ:* 8mm reel, 200t.

Other Film Serv Obtain film from other libraries, film reference serv, library film programs. Permanent viewing facility. *Equipment:* lend 16mm sound projector (1), 8mm reel projector (1), projection screens, filmstrip projectors (9).

Other Media Collections *Audio:* disc, 33⅓rpm, 600t; tape, cassette, 150t. *Filmstrips:* sound, 230t; silent, 30t. *Member:* ALA, N.J. Library Assn.

Berkeley Heights

P- BERKELEY HEIGHTS PUBLIC LIBRARY, 290 Plainfield Ave, 07922. *Tel:* (201) 464-9333. *Video Serv Est:* 1974. *In Charge:* Cecelia Pizzi, AV Librarian. *Video Staff:* 1 f-t. *Video Use:* documentation of community/school events, to increase community's library use. Video serv available by appointment. Produce video tapes. Have production studio/space & separate control room.

Video Equipment/Facilities *In-House Use Only:* portapak (1), ½″ b&w, Sony 3400; recording deck (1), ½″ b&w, Sony 3600; playback deck (1), ½″ b&w, Sony 3600; monitor (1); microphone (1); tripods (2); audio tape recorders (1). Staff tapes community programs; therefore, tapes can be shown/produced outside of library. Have portable viewing installation. *Equipment Loan Period:* no set policy. Have tape duplication serv at Plainfield Public Library.

Video Tape Loan/Rental/Sale Serv *Serv Provided:* free loan. *Loan/Rental Eligibility:* staff, & others, such as anyone who has access to playback equipment. Equipment is not loaned.

Video Collection Maintained by own production. Use/play ½″ reel to reel. *Sources:* community productions. *Special Collections:* community awareness & history. Tapes organized by subject. *Collection, B&W:* ½″ reel, 12t. *Other Video Serv:* programming.

Blackwood

C- CAMDEN COUNTY COLLEGE, Wolverton Learning Resources Center, Box 200, 08012. *Tel:* (201) 227-7200, ext 405. *In Charge:* Walter Dinteman, Media Specialist. *AV Staff:* 7 (2 prof, 3 cl, 2 tech). *Film Sel:* faculty/staff recommendations, recommendations of media specialists to faculty. *Holdings:* business management, film history, fine arts, science, social sciences.

Film Rental Serv *Eligibility:* staff & students for college classroom & independent student viewing only. *Restrictions:* only in Camden County. Produce films. Produce video cassettes, sound slide sets.

Film Collection *Circ:* 8mm cartridge, 50t/p; S8mm cartridge, 400t/450p. *Pubns:* publish listing of films cataloged with other media.

Other Film Serv Rent film from distributors for patrons. Permanent viewing facility.

Other Media Collections *Audio:* disc, 33⅓rpm, 2000t/2300c; tape, cassette, 2200t/2400c; tape, reel, 300t/c. *Filmstrips:* silent, 300t/c; sound sets, 1100t/1400c. *Slides:* single, 10,000t/c; sets, 300t/350c.

Budget & Expenditures No separate budget. *Member:* AECT, ALA, N.J. Library Assn.

Video Serv *Video Staff:* 2 f-t, 2 tech. *Video Use:* playback only of professionally produced tapes, instructional media. Video serv available by appointment. Produce video tapes. Have production studio/space & separate control room.

Video Equipment/Facilities *In-House Use Only:* recording deck (2), ¾″, ½″ b&w/col, Sony, G.E.; playback deck (4), ½″, ¾″ b&w/3 col; studio camera (2), b&w, G.E.; monitor (6), 3 b&w/3 col, Sony-Motorola; lighting (3); tripods (2). *For Loan:* microphones (12); audio tape recorders (50). Have portable viewing installation. Provide training in use of equipment to instructors & student assts.

Video Tape Loan/Rental/Sale Serv *Serv Provided:* free loan. *Loan Eligibility:* org members, staff. *Restrictions:* college use only. Cannot duplicate. May not borrow by mail. *Loan Period:* 5 days.

Video Collection Maintained by purchase. Use/play ½″ reel to reel, ¾″ cassette. *Sources:* commercial distributors. *Tape Sel:* preview, faculty/staff recommendations, published reviews, catalogs. *Special Collections:* films in video format, instructional media. Tapes organized by acquisition number. *Collection, Color:* ½″ reel, 50t/c. *Collection, B&W:* ½″ reel, 5t/c. *Other Video Serv:* programming. *Pubns:* catalog. Video information included in catalog of instructional media.

Bloomfield

C- BLOOMFIELD COLLEGE, AV Library, 07003. *Tel:* (201) 748-9000, ext 285. *Film Serv Est:* 1975. *In Charge:* Dr. Imre Gal, Head Librarian and Doris Severn, AV Librarian. *AV Staff:* 1½ (1 prof, 3 tech). *Film Sel:* committee preview, faculty/staff recommendations.

Film Collection *Pubns:* publish list of films rented & dates when they will be on campus in college newsletter for faculty information.

Other Film Serv Rent film from distributors for patrons, obtain film from coop loan system (Essex-Hudson Film Center), obtain film from other libraries, film reference serv. Films are shown as part of curriculum. Permanent viewing facility available for rent to community. *Equipment:* lend 16mm camera (1), 16mm sound projector (4), 8mm cartridge projector (1), projection tables & stands (7), slide projectors (2), sound filmstrip projectors (2), opaque projectors (2).

Other Media Collections *Audio:* disc, 33⅓rpm, 1100t/c; 78rpm, 244t/c; tape, reel, 110t/c. *Filmstrips:* sound sets, 8t/c. *Member:* AECT, ALA, N.J. Library Assn.

Video Serv *Est:* 1975. *Video Staff:* 1 f-t, 3 p-t, 3 tech. *Video Use:* documentation of community/school events, to increase community's library use, in-service training, practical video/TV training courses. Video serv available by appointment. Produce video tapes. Have production studio/space.

Video Equipment/Facilities *For Loan to College Only:* portapak (1), ½″ b&w, Sony 8400; recording deck (1), ½″ b&w, Sony 8400; SEG (2), Sony, 18″, JVC 12″; microphones (3); tripods (1); audio tape recorders (11) cassette, (1) stereo reel-to-reel. Have viewing installation. *Equipment Loan Period:* no set policy. Provide training in use of equipment to faculty & students.

Bloomfield (cont'd)

Video Tape Loan/Rental/Sale Serv *Loan Eligibility:* staff & students. *Restrictions:* college staff & students only. May not borrow by mail.

Video Collection Maintained by own production. Use/play ½" reel to reel. *Collection, B&W:* ½" reel, 24t/c. *Other Video Serv:* reference serv, taping of other media, production workshops. *Pubns:* catalog.

P- BLOOMFIELD PUBLIC LIBRARY, 90 Broad St, 07003. *Tel:* (201) 429-9292. *Member:* Garden State Library Film Circuit.

Bridgeton

P- CUMBERLAND COUNTY LIBRARY, 800 E Commerce St, 08302. *Tel:* (609) 455-0080. *Member:* Garden State Library Film Circuit.

Camden

P- CAMDEN COUNTY LIBRARY, Court House, 08101. *Tel:* (609) 964-8700. *Member:* Garden State Library Film Circuit.

P- CAMDEN PUBLIC LIBRARY, 616 Broadway, 08103. *Tel:* (609) 963-4807. *Member:* Garden State Library Film Circuit.

Cherry Hill

P- CHERRY HILL FREE PUBLIC LIBRARY, 1100 Kings Highway N, 08034. *Tel:* (609) 667-0300. *In Charge:* Bernice Ahquist, Dir. *AV Staff:* 1 prof, 2 cl. *Film Sel:* committee preview.

Free-Loan Film Serv *Eligibility:* indiv with library cards. *Restrictions:* for indiv, none. Cannot use for fund-raising. Available to researchers/scholars for on-site viewing. *Loan Period:* 1 day. *Total Yr Film Loan:* 2663 (16 mm).

Film Collection *Circ:* 8 mm 300t/p. *Pubns:* catalog, annual (free); suppl, no set policy. Publish monthly list of titles.

Other Film Serv Obtain film from coop loan system (Garden State Library Film Circuit), film reference serv, library film programs. Permanent viewing facility available to community.

Other Media Collections *Audio:* disc, 33⅓rpm, 978t/1542c; tape, cassette, 316t/341c.

Budget & Expenditures Total library budget $84,380 (FY 1/75-1/76). Total FY AV budget $8807. *Member:* ALA, Camden County Librarians Assn, Libraries Unlimited, N.J. Library Assn.

Convent Station

C- COLLEGE OF SAINT ELIZABETH, Mahoney Library, 07961. *Tel:* (201) 539-1600, ext 369. *In Charge:* Agnes Gregory Craig, Media Librarian. *AV Staff:* 1 prof.

Film Collection 11t. *Circ:* 16mm, 11t.

Other Film Serv Obtain film from other libraries, film reference serv. *Equipment:* lend S8mm camera (1), 16mm sound projector (4), projection screens (2).

Other Media Collections *Audio:* disc, 1167t; tape, cassette, 121t; tape, reel, 100t. *Filmstrips:* sound & silent sets, 215t. *Slides:* single, 553t.

Budget & Expenditures Total library budget $42,500 (FY 7/1/74-7/1/75). Total FY AV budget $3500. *Member:* AECT, ALA, N.J. State Library Assn.

Video Serv *Est:* 1974. *Video Use:* documentation of community/school events, in-service training. Video serv available by appointment.

Video Equipment/Facilities *In-House Use Only:* recording deck (1), ½" b&w, Sony 3600; studio camera (1), b&w,

Sony 10". Provide training in use of equipment to faculty & students.

Video Tape Loan/Rental/Sale Serv *Loan Eligibility:* staff & students. *Restrictions:* may not borrow by mail.

Video Collection Maintained by own production. Use/play ½" reel to reel. Tapes organized by subject. *Collection, B&W:* ½" reel, 2t.

Cable & CCTV Inform public about cable system serv & facilities. Have advisory/administrative role in cable system operation.

East Orange

P- EAST ORANGE PUBLIC LIBRARY, Essex-Hudson Regional Film Center, 21 S Arlington Ave, 07018. *Tel:* (201) 266-5625. *Film Serv Est:* 1973. *In Charge:* Ben Harrison, Film Librarian. *AV Staff:* 5½ (1 prof, 2½ cl, 2 tech). *Film Sel:* committee preview, chief film librarian's decision.

Free-Loan Film Serv *Eligibility:* indiv with library cards. *Restrictions:* for indiv, only in Essex & Hudson counties. Cannot use for fund-raising, transmit electronically. Films are borrowed from Film Center or any public library in Essex or Hudson counties. With some exceptions, daily delivery is made to the other libraries. *Loan Period:* 1 day. *Total Yr Film Loan:* 32,442.

Film Collection 903t/1024p. Approx 150t acquired annually. *Circ:* 16mm, 903t/1024p. *Pubns:* catalog, every 2 yrs ($1); suppl, in yr catalog not published (free).

Other Film Serv Film reference serv, library film programs. *Equipment:* rent 16mm sound projector (2).

Other Media Collections *Audio:* disc, 33⅓rpm, 5129t/8431c.

Budget & Expenditures Total library budget $103,346 (FY 1/1/74-1/1/75). Total FY film budget $111,683. *Member:* EFLA, FLIC.

C- UPSALA COLLEGE, Film Library, Prospect and Franklin Sts, 07019. *Tel:* (201) 266-7297. *Film Serv Est:* 1973. *In Charge:* Mark Gladstone, Media Librarian. *AV Staff:* 2 prof. *Film Sel:* faculty/staff recommendations, chief film librarian's decision. *Holdings:* feature films 88%, social sciences 12%.

Free-Loan Film Serv *Eligibility:* staff & students. *Restrictions:* for inst, only in city. *Loan Period:* 3 days. Produce 35mm transparencies, col & b&w prints, overhead transparencies, audio recordings.

Film Collection 50t/p. Approx 20t acquired annually. *Circ:* 16mm, 15t/p; S8mm reel, 35t/p. *Pubns:* publish news releases of holdings, Kardex visible file of AV holdings.

Other Film Serv Rent film from distributors for patrons, obtain film from other libraries. Permanent viewing facility. *Equipment:* lend 16mm sound projector (2), S8mm reel projector (1), projection tables & stands (5), projection screens (7).

Other Media Collections *Audio:* disc, 33⅓rpm, 4000t/c; tape, cassette, 400t/c; tape, reel, 50t/c. *Filmstrips:* silent, 30t/c; sound sets, 30t/28c; silent sets, 30t/1c. *Slides:* single, 600t/c.

Budget & Expenditures Total library budget $54,540 (FY 6/30/74-6/30/75). No separate AV budget. *Member:* ALA, EFLA.

Edison

C- MIDDLESEX COUNTY COLLEGE LIBRARY, Woodbridge Av, 08817. *Tel:* (201) 548-6000, ext 346. *Video Serv Est:* 1970. *In Charge:* Ed Ashley, Dir Learning Resources. *Video Staff:* 3 tech. *Video Use:* documentation of community/school events, practical video/TV training courses, playback only of professionally produced tapes, educational programs. Video serv available by appointment. Produce video tapes. Have production studio/space & separate control room.

Video Equipment/Facilities *In-House Use Only:* recording deck (6), ½", 1" b&w/col, Sony, IVC, AMP; studio camera (3), b&w/col, RCA; monitor (34); lighting (5); microphones (7);

tripods (4). *For Loan:* portapak (1), ½″ b&w, Sony; recording deck (6), ½″, 1″ b&w/col, Sony, IVC, AMP. Have permanent viewing installation. *Equipment Loan Period:* seldom loaned. Provide training in use of equipment to library media aides.

Video Tape Loan/Rental/Sale Serv *Serv Provided:* swap with other inst. *Loan Eligibility:* org members, staff, educational inst, such as state junior colleges. *Restrictions:* cannot use for fund-raising, air without permission. May borrow by mail. *Loan Period:* flexible.

Video Collection Maintained by purchase, rental, own production. Use/play ½″, 1″ reel to reel, ¾″ cassette. *Tape Sel:* preview, faculty/staff recommendations. *Special Collections:* educational programs. Tapes organized by accession order. *Collection, Color:* 1″ reel, 5t/c. *Collection, B&W:* ½″ reel, 40t/c; 1″ reel, 5t/c.

Cable & CCTV Serve as production facility for others. Have CCTV in inst, with 21 monitors. *Programming Sources:* over-the-air commercial & public broadcasting, tapes produced by inst.

Elizabeth

P- ELIZABETH PUBLIC LIBRARY, 11 S Broad St, 07202. *Tel:* (201) 354-6060. *In Charge:* Roman Zawycky. *Member:* N.J. Library Film Circuit.

Far Hills

S- UNITED STATES GOLF ASSN LIBRARY, Golf House, 07931. *Tel:* (201) 234-2300. *Film Serv Est:* 1962. *In Charge:* Janet Seagle, Librarian & Museum Cur. *AV Staff:* 1. *Holdings:* golf 100%.

Film Rental Serv *Eligibility:* no restrictions. *Restrictions:* only in U.S. & territories. Cannot transmit electronically. No TV or commercial use. *Rental Period:* 1 day. *Total Yr Film Booking:* 329. Sell films. Produce films.

Film Collection 30t/130p. Approx 1t acquired annually. *Circ:* 16mm, 30t/130p. *Noncirc:* 16mm, 72t/p. *Pubns:* catalog, annual (free); no set policy (free).

Freehold

P- MONMOUTH COUNTY LIBRARY, Monmouth County Regional Film Center, 25 Broad St, 07728. *Tel:* (201) 431-4000, ext 494. *Film Serv Est:* 1971. *In Charge:* Marie E. Cromwell, Dir. *AV Staff:* 4 (1 prof, 2 cl, 1 tech). *Film Sel:* committee preview, chief film librarian's decision.

Free-Loan Film Serv *Eligibility:* indiv with library cards. *Restrictions:* for indiv & inst, only in 4-county area. Cannot use for fund-raising, transmit electronically. Available to researchers/scholars for on-site viewing. May not borrow by mail. *Loan Period:* 3-7 days. *Total Yr Film Loan:* 12,500.

Film Collection 850t/900p. Approx 350-400t acquired annually. *Circ:* 16mm, 850t/900p. *Pubns:* catalog, annual ($1); suppl, no set policy (no extra charge if sold w/catalog.). Publish bookmarks, flyers, posters about general servs, occasional film bibliographies.

Other Film Serv Obtain film from other libraries, film reference serv, library film programs, organize seminars on use, programming & equipment of AV materials. Permanent viewing facility.

Budget & Expenditures Total library budget $144,500 (FY 4/1/74-4/1/75). Total FY film budget $75,000. *Member:* ALA, EFLA, N.J. Library Assn.

Glassboro

C- GLASSBORO STATE COLLEGE, Educational Media Center, Dept 20, 08028. *Tel:* (609) 445-6375. *Film Serv Est:* 1971. *In Charge:* Benjamin Fisher, Dir of Educational Media. *AV Staff:* 5 (2 prof, 2 cl, 1 tech). *Film Sel:* faculty/staff recommendations, published reviews, catalog descriptions, director's review.

Free-Loan Film Serv *Eligibility:* staff & students. *Restrictions:* for indiv, none. Cannot transmit electronically. Available to researchers/scholars for on-site viewing. May not borrow by mail. *Loan Period:* 5 days.

Film Collection 150t/p. Approx 15-20t acquired annually. *Circ:* 16mm, 150t/p. *Pubns:* catalog, as needed (free); suppl, no set policy (free).

Other Film Serv Rent film from distributors for patrons, obtain film from coop loan system (Tri-State Film Coop, N.J. AV Council), obtain film from other libraries. *Equipment:* lend S8mm camera (20), 16mm sound projector (35), 8mm cartridge projector (3), 8mm reel projector (2), S8mm cartridge projector (6), S8mm reel projector (15), projection tables & stands (6), projection screens (20-30).

Other Media Collections *Audio:* tape, reel, 125t.

Video Serv *Est:* 1970. *Video Staff:* 2 f-t, 2 p-t, 1 tech. *Video Use:* in-service training, practical video/TV training courses, as art form. Video serv available by appointment. Produce video tapes. Have production studio/space & separate control room.

Video Equipment/Facilities *In-House Use Only:* recording deck (1), 1½″ b&w, Ampex; playback deck (1), ¾″ col, Sony U-Matic; editing deck (1), ½″ b&w, Sony 3650; studio camera (3), b&w, Sony AVC-4600; monitors; SEG (1), ½″ Sony SEG-1; additional camera lenses; microphones; tripods; audio tape recorders. *For Loan:* portapak (1), ½″ b&w, Sony 3400; recording deck (6), ½″ b&w, Sony; SEG (1), ½″ Sony SEG-1. *Equipment Loan Period:* video equipment overnight, all other equipment 5 days. Provide training in use of equipment to faculty, students & administrators.

Video Tape Loan/Rental/Sale Serv *Loan Eligibility:* staff & students. *Restrictions:* for indiv, none. May borrow by mail.

Video Collection Maintained by rental, own production. Use/play ½″, 1″ reel to reel, ¾″ cassette. *Sources:* commercial distributors. *Tape Sel:* faculty/staff recommendations.

Gloucester City

P- GLOUCESTER CITY LIBRARY, 08030. *Tel:* (609) 456-4181. *Member:* Garden City Library Film Circuit.

Hackensack

P- JOHNSON FREE PUBLIC LIBRARY, Bergen-Passaic Regional Film Center, 275 Moore St, 07601. *Tel:* (201) 343-4169, ext 36. *Film Serv Est:* 1966. *In Charge:* Doris Newman, Film Librarian. *AV Staff:* 6 (1 prof, 3 cl, 2 tech). *Film Sel:* committee preview.

Free-Loan Film Serv *Eligibility:* educational inst, civic & religious groups, indiv with library cards, prof groups, such as AARP & others, such as YM/YWCA's, Boy/Girl Scouts, public libraries. *Restrictions:* for indiv & inst, only in Bergen & Passaic counties. Cannot use for fund-raising, transmit electronically. May not borrow by mail. *Loan Period:* 3 days. *Total Yr Film Loan:* 10,316 for first six months of 1975.

Film Collection 980t/1020p. Approx 265t acquired annually. *Circ:* 16mm, 980t/1020p. *Pubns:* catalog, as needed (free); suppl, no set policy (free).

Other Film Serv Obtain film from coop loan system (N.J. Regional Film Centers), film reference serv, library film programs.

Other Media Collections *Filmstrips:* sound, 350t.

Budget & Expenditures Total library budget $100,000 (FY 4/1/75-4/1/76). Total FY film budget $50,000. *Member:* EFLA, FLIC, N.J. Library Assn.

Hoboken

C- STEVENS INSTITUTE OF TECHNOLOGY, S. C. Williams Library, Castle Point Station, 07030. *Tel:* (201) 792-2700, ext 133. *Video Serv Est:* 1969. *In Charge:* Richard P. Widdicombe, Dir of Library. *Video Staff:* 8 p-t, 2 tech. *Video Use:* to increase community's library use, in-service train-

Hoboken (cont'd)

ing. Video serv available on demand. Produce video tapes. Have production studio/space & separate control room.

Video Equipment/Facilities *In-House Use Only:* recording deck (5), ¾", 1" b&w/col, Sony, JVC; editing deck (1), b&w, Sony; studio camera (3), b&w, GBC; monitor (16), b&w/col, RCA, Conrac; microphones (6); tripods (3); audio tape recorders (2), 1 cassette, 1 reel. *For Loan:* portapak (1), b&w, Sony. Have permanent & portable viewing installations. *Equipment Loan Period:* no set policy. Provide training in use of equipment to faculty & students. Have tape duplication serv.

Video Tape Loan/Rental/Sale Serv *Serv Provided:* free loan. *Loan Eligibility:* staff & students, educational inst, prof groups, such as IEEE, ASME, & others, such as local inst & corporations. *Restrictions:* for indiv & inst, none. Cannot duplicate, air without permission. May not borrow by mail.

Video Collection Maintained by own production. Use/play ¾" cassette. *Sources:* in-house productions. *Special Collections:* films in video format. Tapes organized by numerical log, with subject & author title cat. *Collection, Color:* ¾" cassette, 15t. *Collection, B&W:* 1" reel, 60t; ¾" cassette, 80t. *Pubns:* catalog.

Cable & CCTV Community receives serv of cable TV system. Have CCTV in inst, with 10 monitors. *Programming Sources:* tapes produced by inst.

Irvington

P- IRVINGTON PUBLIC LIBRARY, Civic Square, 07111. *Tel:* (201) 372-6400, ext 25. *Film Serv Est:* 1965. *In Charge:* James A. Thomas, Film Librarian. *AV Staff:* 1 (1 prof, 1 tech p-t). *Film Sel:* chief film librarian's decision. *Holdings:* children's films 40%, film classics 20%.

Free-Loan Film Serv *Eligibility:* indiv with library cards. *Restrictions:* cannot use for fund-raising, transmit electronically. Available to researchers/scholars for on-site viewing. May not borrow by mail. *Loan Period:* 1 day. *Total Yr Film Loan:* 2000.

Film Collection 120t/p. Approx 10t acquired annually. *Circ:* 16mm, 120t/p. *Pubns:* catalog, as needed (free).

Other Film Serv Obtain film from coop loan system (Garden State Library Film Circuit), obtain film from other libraries, library film programs. Permanent viewing facility available for rent to community. *Equipment:* lend 16mm sound projector (1), projection screens, filmstrip projector (1), opaque projector (1).

Other Media Collections *Audio:* disc, 33⅓rpm, 2100c. *Filmstrips:* silent, 40c. *Slides:* single, 1000c; sets, 50c.

Budget & Expenditures Total library budget $356,478 (FY 1/72-1/73). Total FY film budget $4466. *Member:* EFLA, FLIC.

Jersey City

P- JERSEY CITY PUBLIC LIBRARY, 678 Newark Ave, 07306. *Tel:* (201) 435-6262, ext 66. *Film Serv Est:* 1968. *In Charge:* Alfred Trattner, AV Librarian. *AV Staff:* 3 (1 prof, 1 cl, 1 tech). *Film Sel:* committee preview, staff recommendations.

Free-Loan Film Serv *Eligibility:* indiv with library cards. *Restrictions:* for inst, only in Hudson County. Cannot use for fund-raising, transmit electronically. May borrow by mail. *Loan Period:* 1 day. *Total Yr Film Loan:* 5500.

Film Collection 218t/245p. Approx 30t acquired annually. *Circ:* 16mm, 218t/245p; 8mm reel, 220t/p; S8mm reel, 28t/p. *Pubns:* catalog, annual; suppl, no set policy (free).

Other Film Serv Obtain film from coop loan system (N.J. Film Library Circuit), obtain film from other libraries, film reference serv, library film programs.

Other Media Collections *Audio:* disc, 33⅓ rpm, 5500t/6500c; tape, cassette, 185t. *Slides:* sets, 14t.

Budget & Expenditures Total library budget $160,000 (FY 1/75-1/76). Total FY film budget $8000. *Member:* AECT, ALA, EFLA, FLIC, N.J. Library Assn.

Video Serv *Est:* 1972. *Video Staff:* 2 f-t, 1 tech. *Video Use:* documentation of community/school events, community video

access, in-service training. Video serv available by appointment. Produce video tapes.

Video Equipment/Facilities *For Loan:* portapak (2), ½" b&w, Sony 3400; recording deck (1), ½" b&w, Sony 3650; microphones (2); tripods (2); audio tape recorders (6). Have portable viewing installation. *Equipment Loan Period:* no set policy. Provide training in use of equipment. Have tape duplication serv.

Video Tape Loan/Rental/Sale Serv *Serv Provided:* free loan, swap with other inst. *Loan Eligibility:* staff & students, civic & religious groups, indiv with library cards. *Restrictions:* for indiv, only in city; for public libraries, only in Hudson County. Cannot air without permission. May not borrow by mail. *Loan Period:* 2 days. *Total Yr Tape Loan:* 6.

Video Collection Maintained by own production, exchange/swap. Use/play ½" reel to reel, ½" cartridge, ¾" cassette. *Sources:* exchange (libraries & civic groups). *Tape Sel:* preview. Tapes organized by accession numbers & annotations. *Collection, B&W:* ½" reel, 76t/c. *Other Video Serv:* reference serv. *Pubns:* catalog. Publish materials on video.

C- JERSEY CITY STATE COLLEGE, Center for Media & Technol, 2039 Kennedy Blvd, 07305. *Tel:* (201) 547-3007. *Film Serv Est:* 1967. *In Charge:* Dr. John F. Egan, Dir. *AV Staff:* 15 (6 prof, 3 cl, 6 tech). *Film Sel:* faculty/staff recommendations, chief film librarian's decision. *Holdings:* animated films, career education, experimental films, fine arts, science, social sciences, teacher education, women.

Free-Loan Film Serv *Eligibility:* org members, staff & students. *Restrictions:* for indiv, none. Available to researchers/scholars for on-site viewing. May not borrow by mail. *Loan Period:* 3 days. *Total Yr Film Loan:* 3000.

Film Collection 420t/p. Approx 10-15t acquired annually. *Circ:* 16mm, 420t/p; S8mm cartridge, 25t/p. *Pubns:* catalog, every 2 yrs (free); suppl, no set policy (free).

Other Film Serv Obtain film from coop loan system, obtain film from other libraries. Permanent viewing facility. *Equipment:* lend S8mm camera (30), 16mm camera (15), 16mm sound projector (45), 8mm cartridge projector (10), 8mm reel projector (5), S8mm cartridge projector (20), S8mm reel projector (5), projection tables & stands (30), projection screens (100), all forms of TV equipment. Produce films & filmstrips.

Other Media Collections *Audio:* disc, 33⅓rpm, 3000t; tape, cassette, 500t; tape, reel, 4500t. *Filmstrips:* sound, 100t; silent, 450t.

Budget & Expenditures Total FY film budget $20,000 (FY 7/1/75-7/1/76). *Member:* AECT.

Video Serv *Est:* 1969. *Video Staff:* 4 f-t, 2 p-t, 2 tech. *Video Use:* documentation of community/school events, in-service training, practical video/TV training courses, playback only of professionally produced tapes, as art form. Video serv available by appointment. Produce video tapes. Have production studio/space & separate control room.

Video Equipment/Facilities *In-House Use Only:* recording deck (7), ½", 1" b&w/col, IVC; playback deck (2), ½", 3600 Sony; editing deck (2), ½", 3650 Sony; studio camera (9), 3 b&w/6 col, Sony; monitor; SEG; keyer; additional camera lenses; lighting; microphones; tripods; audio tape recorders. *For Loan:* portapak (15), ½" b&w, Sony 3400. Have permanent viewing installation. *Equipment Loan Period:* 3 days. Provide training in use of equipment to faculty & students. Have tape duplication serv.

Video Tape Loan/Rental/Sale Serv *Serv Provided:* free loan, swap with other inst. *Loan Eligibility:* org members, staff & students, educational inst. *Restrictions:* for indiv, none. Cannot air without permission. May not borrow by mail.

Video Collection Maintained by purchase, own production, exchange/swap. Use/play ½", 1" reel to reel, ¾" cassette. *Sources:* commercial distributors, community productions, exchange. *Tape Sel:* faculty/staff recommendations. *Special Collections:* in-house training tapes, video as art. Tapes organized by accession order. *Collection, Color:* ½" reel, 30t; 1" reel, 25t. *Collection, B&W:* ½" reel, 50t; 1" reel, 70t; ¾" cassette, 50t. *Other Video Serv:* production workshops.

Cable & CCTV Serve as production facility for others. Have CCTV in inst, with 10 monitors. *Programming Sources:* tapes produced by inst.

Lakewood

C- GEORGIAN COURT COLLEGE, 08701. *Tel:* (201) 364-2209. *In Charge:* Ruth Long, Librarian. *Film Sel:* faculty/staff recommendations.
   Film Collection 3t/p.
   Other Film Serv *Equipment:* lend 16mm sound projector (1), S8mm cartridge projector (1), projection screens (1). *Member:* ALA, N.J. Library Assn.
   Video Serv *Est:* 1974. *In Charge:* Jim Williams, Chairman, Education. *Tel:* (201) 364-2200, ext 40. *Video Staff:* 1 p-t. *Video Use:* documentation of community/school events, in-service training. Video serv available by appointment. Produce video tapes.
   Video Equipment/Facilities *In-House Use Only:* portapak (1), Sony. *Equipment Loan Period:* no set policy.
   Video Tape Loan/Rental/Sale Serv *Loan Eligibility:* org members, staff & students within college only. *Restrictions:* college students & personnel only. May not borrow by mail.
   Video Collection Maintained by own production. Use/ play ½″ reel to reel. *Sources:* commercial distributors. *Special Collections:* in-house training tapes. Tapes organized by subject.

Lincoln Park

P- LINCOLN PARK PUBLIC LIBRARY, 12 Boonton Turnpike, 07035. *Tel:* (201) 694-8283. *Video Serv Est:* 1973. *In Charge:* Naomi Birkenmeier, Dir. *Video Staff:* 2 p-t. *Video Use:* documentation of community/school events, to increase community's library use, community video access. Video serv available by appointment. Produce video tapes. Have production studio/space & separate control room.
   Video Equipment/Facilities *For Loan:* portapak (1), b&w, Sony; playback deck (1), b&w, Sony; microphones (2); tripods. Have portable viewing installation. *Equipment Loan Period:* 1 day. Provide training in use of equipment to students & adults.
   Video Tape Loan/Rental/Sale Serv *Serv Provided:* free loan, swap with other inst. *Loan Eligibility:* educational inst, civic & religious groups, indiv with library cards, prof groups, such as doctors, lawyers, etc. *Restrictions:* for indiv & inst, only in city. May borrow by mail. *Loan Period:* 7 days. *Total Yr Tape Loan:* 2.
   Video Collection Maintained by own production, exchange/swap. *Sources:* community productions, exchange (libraries). Tapes organized by subject. *Other Video Serv:* taping of other media.

Linden

P- LINDEN FREE PUBLIC LIBRARY, Film Dept, 31 E Henry St, 07036. *Tel:* (201) 486-3888, ext 23. *Film Serv Est:* 1970. *In Charge:* Robert Van Bergen, AV Coord. *AV Staff:* 3 (2 prof, 1 cl, 1 p-t tech). *Film Sel:* committee preview. *Holdings:* children's films 50%.
   Free-Loan Film Serv *Eligibility:* staff & students, educational inst, civic & religious groups, indiv over 18 with library cards, prof groups, such as business & professional women's clubs & others, such as Trailside Museum, senior citizens' organizations. *Restrictions:* for indiv, interlibrary loan; only in Union County; for inst, only in Union County. Cannot use for fund-raising. Available to researchers/scholars for on-site viewing. May not borrow by mail. *Loan Period:* 1 day, or by special arrangement. *Total Yr Film Loan:* 881.
   Film Collection 12 permanent & 30 rotating. Approx 12t acquired annually. *Circ:* 16mm, 79t/p. *Pubns:* catalog, as needed (free); suppl, no set policy (free). Publish news releases, posters, ads, annotated lists.

Other Film Serv Obtain film from coop loan system (Morris County Regional Film Center, Garden State Library Film Circuit), obtain film from other libraries, film reference serv, film fairs/festivals, library film programs. Permanent viewing facility available free to community.
   Other Media Collections *Audio:* disc, 33⅓ rpm, 3829t/4254c; tape, cassette, 165t/265c. *Filmstrips:* sound/silent 468t/477c. *Slides:* single, 736t/c.
   Budget & Expenditures Total library budget $74,248.79 (FY 1/1/75-1/1/76). Total FY film budget $6041.39. *Member:* EFLA, N.J. Library Assn.

Livingston

P- FREE PUBLIC LIBRARY OF LIVINGSTON, Memorial Park Drive, 07039. *Tel:* (201) 992-4600. *Film Serv Est:* 1974. *In Charge:* Raymond Simpson, Asst Dir. *AV Staff:* 1 (⅓ prof, ⅓ cl, ⅓ tech). *Film Sel:* committee preview. *Holdings:* children's films 85%.
   Free-Loan Film Serv *Eligibility:* indiv with library cards. *Loan Period:* 1 day. *Total Yr Film Loan:* 1952. Produce films.
   Film Collection *Circ:* 8mm reel, 188t/203p; S8mm reel, 97t/101p. *Noncirc:* 16mm, 28t/33p.
   Other Film Serv Obtain film from coop loan system (East Orange Area, Essex Hudson Film Circuit), library film programs. Permanent viewing facility available for rent to community. *Equipment:* 16mm sound projector (2), S8mm reel projector (1), projection tables & stands (2), projection screens (2).
   Other Media Collections *Audio:* disc, 33⅓ rpm, 1017t/1136c; tape, cassette, 47t/57c. *Filmstrips:* sound, 61t/65c.
   Budget & Expenditures Total library budget $52,000 (FY 1/1/75-1/1/76). No separate AV budget. *Member:* ALA, FLIC, N.J. Library Assn.
   Video Serv *Est:* 1975. *Video Staff:* 1 f-t. *Video Use:* documentation of community events. Produce video tapes.
   Video Equipment/Facilities *In-House Use Only:* portapak (1), b&w, Sony; recording deck (1), Sony; playback deck (1), Sony 3650; monitor (2), Sony 10″, Carlson 21″; lighting (1); tripods (1); audio tape recorders (1).
   Video Collection Maintained by own production. Use/play ½″ reel to reel.
   Cable & CCTV Will receive serv of cable TV system.

Lodi

C- FELICIAN COLLEGE, Felician Media Center, S Main St, 07644. *Tel:* (201) 778-1190, ext 36. *Film Serv Est:* 1970. *In Charge:* Sr. Mary Laura, Dir, Media Center. *AV Staff:* 3 (1 prof). *Film Sel:* faculty/staff recommendations.
   Film Collection *Circ:* 16mm, 21t.
   Other Film Serv Obtain film from coop loan system (N.J. Assn for Educational Communications & Technol), obtain film from other libraries, film reference serv. Permanent viewing facility available for rent to community. *Equipment:* S8mm camera (1), 16mm sound projector (3), 8mm cartridge projector (1), 8mm reel projector (1), S8mm cartridge projector (1), S8mm reel projector (30), projection screens (20).
   Other Media Collections *Audio:* disc, 33⅓ rpm, 10t; 45rpm, 74t; 78rpm, 100t; tape, cassette, 60t; tape, cartridge, 12t; tape, reel, 50t. *Filmstrips:* sound, 350t. *Slides:* single, 3136t.
   Budget & Expenditures Total library budget $1000 (FY 7/1/74-7/1/75). No separate AV budget. *Member:* AECT, ALA.
   Video Serv *Est:* 1973. *Video Staff:* 1 f-t, 2 p-t. *Video Use:* documentation of community/school events, in-service training, teacher & nurses training. Video serv available for college use only. Produce video tapes.
   Video Equipment/Facilities *In-House Use Only:* portapak (1), b&w; recording deck (2), b&w; playback deck (2), b&w; studio camera (1), b&w; monitor (2); microphones (2); tripods (2); audio tape recorders (2). Have portable viewing installation. Provide training in use of equipment to faculty.
   Video Tape Loan/Rental/Sale Serv *Serv Provided:* swap with other inst. *Loan Eligibility:* org members, staff.

Lodi (cont'd)

Video Collection Maintained by own production. Use/ play ½″ reel to reel, ¾″ cassette. *Tape Sel:* preview, faculty/ staff recommendations. *Special Collections:* in-house training tapes. Tapes organized by subject. *Collection, Color:* ½″ reel, 15t; ¾″ cassette, 36t. *Collection, B&W:* ½″ reel, 15t/; ¾″ cassette, 36t. *Other Video Serv:* taping of other media.

Madison

C- DREW UNIVERSITY, Media Resource Center, 07940. *Tel:* (201) 327-3000, ext 382. *Video Serv Est:* 1969. *In Charge:* Kurt W. Remmers, Dir, Media Resource Center. *Video Staff:* 2 f-t, 1 p-t, 1 tech. *Video Use:* documentation of community/school events, community video access, in-service training, as sales tool, playback only of professionally produced tapes. Video serv available on demand. Produce video tapes. Have production studio/space & separate control room.
   Video Equipment/Facilities *In-House Use & For Loan:* portapak (2), b&w, Sony; recording deck (9), 8 b&w/1 col, 3 Sony 1″, 5 Sony ½″, 1 Panasonic ¾″; playback deck (2), col; studio camera (3), b&w, Panasonic; monitor (25), b&w/col; SEG (1), b&w; keyer (1); additional camera lenses (7); lighting; microphones (10); tripods (5); audio tape recorders (5). Have portable viewing installation. *Equipment Loan Period:* 1 day. Provide training in use of equipment to students & community groups.
   Video Tape Loan/Rental/Sale Serv *Serv Provided:* swap with other inst, rental. *Loan/Rental Eligibility:* educational inst, prof groups, such as Morris County Council for Arts, & others, such as N.J. Shakespeare Festival. *Restrictions:* for indiv, interlibrary loan. for inst, none. Cannot duplicate. May borrow by mail. *Loan Period:* flexible. *Total Yr Tape Loan:* 20.
   Video Collection Maintained by purchase, rental, own production, exchange/swap. Use/play ½″, 1″ reel to reel, ¾″ cassette. *Sources:* commercial distributors, galleries, community productions, exchange. *Member:* N.J. Educational Media Consortium (part of N.J. AECT for Higher Education). *Tape Sel:* faculty/staff recommendations, published reviews. *Special Collections:* films in video format. *Collection, Color:* ½″ reel, 75t/c; ¾″ cassette, 10t/c. *Collection, B&W:* ½″ reel, 200t/c; 1″ reel, 20t/c. *Other Video Serv:* production workshops. *Pubns:* catalog.
   Cable & CCTV Will receive serv of cable TV system. Will produce programs for cablecasting. Inform public about cable system serv & facilities. Serve as production facility for others. Run cable programs for special audiences. Have advisory/administrative role in cable system operation. Have CCTV in inst, with 30 monitors. *Programming Sources:* over-the-air commercial & public broadcasting, tapes produced by inst, tapes produced professionally & by community groups & indiv.

Middlesex

P- MIDDLESEX PUBLIC LIBRARY, Mountain Ave, 08846. *Tel:* (201) 356-6602. *Film Serv Est:* 1972. *In Charge:* Flora S. Ingalls, Dir. *Film Sel:* Blackhawk & other catalogs. *Holdings:* silent films.
   Free-Loan Film Serv *Eligibility:* indiv with library cards. *Restrictions:* Federation library patrons only. Available to researchers/scholars for on-site viewing. May not borrow by mail. *Loan Period:* 7 days. *Total Yr Film Loan:* 1109.
   Film Collection 109t/p. Approx 10t acquired annually. *Circ:* 8mm-S8mm reel, 109t/p. *Pubns:* catalog, every 15 months (free).
   Other Film Serv Obtain film from coop loan system (Plainfield Area Library, N.J. Regional Center at Morris County, Raritan Valley Federation of Public Libraries). *Equipment:* lend S8mm camera (1), 16mm sound projector (1), rent 8mm reel projector (1), S8mm cartridge projector (1), S8mm reel projector (1), lend projection screen (1), slide projectors (2), overhead projector, filmstrip projector.
   Other Media Collections *Audio:* disc, 33⅓rpm, 1104t/1114c; tape, cassette, 157t/c. *Filmstrips:* sound sets, 43t/c.
   Budget & Expenditures Total library budget $18,875 (FY 1/1/75-1/1/76). Total FY film budget $250.

Video Serv *Est:* 1973. *In Charge:* Joan MacKinnon, Asst. Dir. *Video Use:* to increase community's library use, community video access, library reports. Video serv available by appointment. Produce video tapes.
   Video Equipment/Facilities *In-House Use Only:* monitor (1), b&w, Sony CVM-194. *For Loan:* portapak (1), ½″ b&w, Sony; recording deck/playback deck (1), b&w, Sony 3600; microphones (1); tripods (1); audio tape recorders (1), camera adaptor (1), power adaptor A.C. (1). Have portable viewing installation. *Equipment Loan Period:* no set policy. Provide training in use of equipment to interested community members.
   Video Tape Loan/Rental/Sale Serv *Serv Provided:* free loan, sale. *Loan Eligibility:* adults with library cards. *Restrictions:* for indiv, only in city. May not borrow by mail. *Loan Period:* flexible.
   Video Collection Maintained by own production. Use/ play ½″ reel to reel.

Montclair

P- MONTCLAIR PUBLIC LIBRARY, Film Dept, 50 S Fullerton Ave, 07042. *Tel:* (201) 744-0500. *Film Serv Est:* 1970. *In Charge:* John Skillin, Film Librarian. *AV Staff:* 1 prof, 1 p-t cl. *Film Sel:* preview, staff recommendations, chief film librarian's decision. *Holdings:* animated films 8%, black studies 2%, children's films 18%, dance 1%, experimental films 7%, feature films 7%, fine arts 3%, science 4%, silent film classics 12%, women 2%.
   Free-Loan Film Serv *Eligibility:* indiv with library cards. *Restrictions:* for indiv, only in city; for inst, only in Essex County. Cannot use for fund-raising. May not borrow by mail. *Loan Period:* 1 day. *Total Yr Film Loan:* 4335 (+2190 from Essex-Hudson).
   Film Collection Approx 15-20t acquired annually. *Circ:* 16mm, 185t/p. *Pubns:* catalog, every 2 yrs (free); suppl, in yr catalog not published (free). Publish program notes for regularly scheduled film showings.
   Other Film Serv Obtain film from coop loan system (Essex-Hudson Film Center), obtain film from other libraries, film reference serv, library film programs. Permanent viewing facility. *Equipment:* lend 16mm sound projector (3), 8mm reel projector (1), projection screen (1), slide projector, overhead projector, filmstrip projectors, cassette tape players.
   Other Media Collections *Audio:* disc, 33⅓rpm, 5400t/7500c; tape, cassette, 2500t/3000c. *Filmstrips:* sound sets, 175t/c. *Slides:* single, 2305t/c.
   Budget & Expenditures Total library budget $128,462 (FY 1/1/75-1/1/76). Total FY film budget $7525. *Member:* AFI, EFLA, FLIC.

Moorestown

P- MOORESTOWN PUBLIC LIBRARY, 111 W Second, 08057. *Tel:* (609) 234-0333. *Member:* Garden State Library Film Circuit.

Morristown

P- JOINT FREE PUBLIC LIBRARY OF MORRISTOWN TOWNSHIP, 1 Miller Rd, 07960. *Tel:* (201) 538-6161. *In Charge:* Christine Seltzer, AV Advisor. *Video Staff:* 1 p-t. *Video Use:* documentation of community/school events, to increase community's library use, community video access. Video serv available on demand. Produce video tapes.
   Video Equipment/Facilities *For Loan:* portapak (1), b&w, Panasonic NV-3085; microphones (1); tripods (1). Have portable viewing installation. *Equipment Loan Period:* 1-3 days. No long term loans.
   Video Tape Loan/Rental/Sale Serv *Serv Provided:* free loan, swap with other inst. *Loan Eligibility:* indiv with library cards, & others, such as local government & civic organizations. *Restrictions:* for indiv & inst, only in city. *Total Yr Tape Loan:* 10.

Video Collection Maintained by own production. Use/play ½″, 1″ reel to reel. *Sources:* own production. *Member:* Garden State Library Film Circuit. Tapes organized by subject. *Collection, B&W:* ½″ reel, 33t/c; 1″ reel, 16t/c. *Other Video Serv:* production workshops. *Pubns:* catalog.

Cable & CCTV Receive serv of cable TV system. Produce programs for cablecasting.

Mount Holly

P- BURLINGTON COUNTY LIBRARY, Film Dept, Woodlane Rd, 08060. *Tel:* (609) 267-9660, ext 17. *In Charge:* Sandra Howley, Media Serv Librarian. *AV Staff:* 5 (1 prof, 2 cl, 2 tech). *Film Sel:* committee preview, staff recommendations, chief film librarian's decision. *Holdings:* children's films 50%.

Free-Loan Film Serv *Eligibility:* indiv with library cards. Cannot use for fund-raising, transmit electronically. Available to researchers/scholars for on-site viewing. May not borrow by mail. *Loan Period:* 1 day.

Film Collection Approx 5-8t acquired annually. *Circ:* 16mm, 128t/p; 8mm reel, 75t/p. *Pubns:* catalog, annual (35¢).

Other Film Serv Obtain film from coop loan system (Garden State Library Film Circuit, Camden Regional Film Service), film reference serv, library film programs. Permanent viewing facility available for rent to community. *Equipment:* rent 16mm sound projector (4), 8mm reel projector (1), projection screen (1).

Other Media Collections *Audio:* disc, 33⅓rpm, 300t/350c; tape, cassette, 75t/86c; *Filmstrips:* sound, 200t; silent, 100t; sound sets, 100t; silent sets, 100t. *Slides:* sets, 30t.

Budget & Expenditures No separate budget. *Member:* EFLA, N.J. State Library Assn.

Video Serv *Est:* 1974. *Video Staff:* 1 f-t, 1 tech. *Video Use:* documentation of community events, to increase community's library use. Video serv available by appointment. Produce video tapes.

Video Equipment/Facilities *In-House Use Only:* studio camera (1), ½″ b&w/col, Panasonic; monitor (2), 21″, 7″ b&w, Panasonic; microphones (2); tripods (1). *For Loan:* portapak (2), ½″ b&w, Panasonic NV3082. *Equipment Loan Period:* no set policy. Provide training in use of equipment. Equipment owned equally by 4 county libraries: Burlington, Mt. Holly, Moorestown, Burlington City.

Video Tape Loan/Rental/Sale Serv *Serv Provided:* free loan. *Loan Eligibility:* civic & religious groups, & inst for specific use only. *Restrictions:* for inst, only in Burlington County. May not borrow by mail.

Video Collection Maintained by own production, exchange/swap. Use/play ½″ reel to reel. *Sources:* community productions.

New Brunswick

C- LIVINGSTON COLLEGE, RUTGERS UNIVERSITY, Urban Communications Teaching & Research Center, 08903. *Tel:* (201) 932-4103. *Video Serv Est:* 1971. *In Charge:* Barry Orton, Asst. Professor. *Video Staff:* 3 f-t, 3 p-t. *Video Use:* documentation of community/school events, practical video/TV training courses, as art form. Video serv available for college level courses or funded projects. Produce video tapes. Have production studio/space.

Video Equipment/Facilities *In-House Use Only:* portapak (8), ½″ b&w, Sony 3400; recording deck/playback deck (2), ½″ b&w, Sony 3600; editing deck (3), ½″ b&w, Sony 3650; monitor (7), b&w, Panasonic 3130; SEG (1), ½″, b&w; lighting; microphones; tripods; audio tape recorders. Have permanent viewing installation. *Equipment Loan Period:* no set policy. Provide training in use of equipment to faculty & students.

Video Tape Loan/Rental/Sale Serv *Serv Provided:* free loan, swap with other inst. *Loan Eligibility:* staff & students. *Restrictions:* for indiv & inst, none. Cannot use for fund-raising, duplicate, air without permission. May not borrow by mail.

Video Collection Maintained by own production, exchange/swap. Use/play ½″ reel to reel. *Sources:* exchange (UNET). *Tape Sel:* catalogs. Tapes organized by subject. *Collection, B&W:* ½″ reel, 200t. *Other Video Serv:* programming, production workshops. *Pubns:* catalog & suppl. Publish faculty articles, a statewide Cable & Video Information Project.

Cable & CCTV Produce programs for cablecasting. Inform public about cable system serv & facilities. Have CCTV in inst.

P- NEW BRUNSWICK FREE PUBLIC LIBRARY, 60 Livingston Ave, 08901. *Tel:* (201) 745-5337. *In Charge:* Joanne Hart. *Member:* N.J. Library Film Circuit.

C- RUTGERS UNIVERSITY, Alexander Library, AV Dept, 08901. *Tel:* (201) 932-7337. *Film Serv Est:* 1972. *In Charge:* Theodora T. Haynes, AV Librarian. *AV Staff:* 3 (1 prof, 2 cl). *Film Sel:* committee preview, faculty/staff recommendations, published reviews. *Holdings:* feature films 25%, social sciences 38%, women 5%.

Free-Loan Film Serv *Eligibility:* staff. *Restrictions:* some films are for campus use only; otherwise, all are available for any Rutgers-sponsored program. Cannot use for fund-raising, transmit electronically, duplicate. Available to researchers/scholars for on-site viewing. *Loan Period:* 1 day.

Film Collection 484t/486p. Approx 75t acquired annually. *Circ:* 16mm, 470t/472p; 8mm reel, 14t/p. *Pubns:* catalog & suppl, as needed (free).

Other Film Serv Film reference serv, library film programs. Permanent viewing facility.

Budget & Expenditures Total library budget $5,827,703 (FY 7/1/74-7/1/75). Total FY film budget $17,000. *Member:* ALA, EFLA.

New Providence

P- NEW PROVIDENCE MEMORIAL LIBRARY, 377 Elkwood Ave, 07974. *Tel:* (201) 665-0311. *Film Serv Est:* 1973. *In Charge:* Doris Lange, Senior Librarian. *AV Staff:* 3 (⅓ prof, ⅓ cl, ⅓ tech). *Film Sel:* library dir's decision. *Holdings:* feature films 100%, silent films.

Free-Loan Film Serv *Eligibility:* adult indiv with library cards. *Restrictions:* for indiv, only in Morris-Union county federation. *Loan Period:* 2 days. *Total Yr Film Loan:* 199.

Film Collection *Circ:* 8mm reel, 75-100t. *Equipment:* 16mm sound projector (1), 8mm reel projector (1), projection screen (1).

Other Media Collections *Audio:* disc, 45rpm, 650t; tape, cassette, 75t.

Budget & Expenditures Total library budget $14,000 (FY 1/75-1/76). No separate AV budget. *Member:* N.J. Library Assn.

Video Serv *Est:* 1973. *Video Staff:* 4 p-t, 2 tech. *Video Use:* documentation of community/school events, to increase community's library use. Video serv available as requested by inst if our staff is available. Produce video tapes.

Video Equipment/Facilities *In-House Use Only:* portapak (1), ½″ b&w, Panasonic; playback deck (1), ½″ b&w, Sony 3600; monitor (1), b&w, Sony CVM-194; microphones (1); tripods (1). Have portable viewing installation. *Equipment Loan Period:* no set policy. Provide training in use of equipment to staff.

Video Tape Loan/Rental/Sale Serv *Loan Eligibility:* org members. *Restrictions:* may not borrow by mail.

Video Collection Maintained by own production. Use/play ½″ reel to reel. *Sources:* commercial distributors, community productions. Some equipment & editing servs are pooled with the area library in Plainfield. Tapes organized by title. *Collection, B&W:* ½″ reel, 4t.

Newark

P- NEWARK PUBLIC LIBRARY, 5 Washington St, 07101. *Tel:* (201) 733-7763. *In Charge:* Irene Falk. *Member:* N.J. Library Film Circuit.

Newton

P- SUSSEX COUNTY LIBRARY, 07860. *Tel:* (201) 383-2321. *Member:* Garden State Library Film Circuit.

North Brunswick

P- NORTH BRUNSWICK FREE PUBLIC LIBRARY, 880 Hermann Rd, 08902. *Tel:* (201) 246-3545. *Film Serv Est:* 1972. *In Charge:* Carol Beyer, Reference Librarian. *Film Sel:* chief film librarian's decision.
  Free-Loan Film Serv *Eligibility:* indiv with library cards. *Restrictions:* for indiv, only in city. Cannot borrow for classroom use. May not borrow by mail. *Loan Period:* 1 day. *Total Yr Film Loan:* 603.
  Film Collection Approx 60-70t acquired annually. *Circ:* S8mm reel, 160t. *Pubns:* catalog, annual (free).
  Other Film Serv Obtain film from coop loan system (Monmouth County Film Circuit), obtain film from other libraries, film reference serv. *Equipment:* S8mm camera (2), 16mm sound projector (1), lend/rent projection tables & stands (1), projection screens (2).
  Other Media Collections *Audio:* disc, 33⅓ rpm, 1264t; tape, cassette, 305t. *Filmstrips:* sound, 114t.
  Budget & Expenditures Total library budget $32,000 (FY 1/1/75-1/1/76). Total FY film budget $1000.

Orange

P- ORANGE PUBLIC LIBRARY, 348 Main St, 07050. *Tel:* (201) 673-0153. *Member:* Garden State Library Film Circuit.

Paramus

S- BERGEN COMMUNITY MUSEUM, E. Ridgewood Ave, 07652. *Tel:* (201) 265-1248. *Video Serv Est:* 1975. *In Charge:* Nanci Kreidman. *Video Staff:* 1 f-t. *Video Use:* documentation of community/school events. Video serv available on demand. Produce video tapes. Provide training in use of equipment.
  Video Tape Loan/Rental/Sale Serv *Serv Provided:* free loan. *Loan Eligibility:* any interested indiv. *Restrictions:* for indiv & inst, none. May not borrow by mail.
  Video Collection Maintained by own production, exchange/swap. Use/play ½″ reel to reel. *Sources:* community productions, exchange. *Special Collections:* community development information. Tapes organized by subject. *Collection, B&W:* ½″ reel, 30t/c. *Other Video Serv:* taping of other media, production workshops. *Pubns:* publish materials on video periodically.
  Cable & CCTV Produce programs for cablecasting.

P- PARAMUS PUBLIC LIBRARY, E 116 Century Rd, 07652. *Tel:* (201) 265-1800. *In Charge:* R. M. Jones, Library Dir.
  Film Collection 150t. *Circ:* 8mm reel, 150t.
  Other Film Serv Obtain 16mm film from coop loan system (Johnson Public Library, State Film Center, Hackensack). *Equipment:* 16mm sound projector (1), 8mm reel projector (1), 35mm slide projector (1).
  Other Media Collections *Audio:* disc, 33⅓ rpm, 2000t; tape, cassette, 185t; tape, cartridge, 50t.
  Budget & Expenditures Total library budget $57,000. No separate AV budget.

Passaic

P- PASSAIC PUBLIC LIBRARY, Julius Forstmann Memorial, Gregory & Passaic Ave, 07055. *Tel:* (201) 779-0474. *In Charge:* David Bryant. *Member:* N.J. Library Film Circuit.

Paterson

C- PASSAIC COUNTY COMMUNITY COLLEGE, Learning Resources Center, 170 Paterson St, 07505. *Tel:* (201) 345-4863, ext 36. *Film Serv Est:* 1971. *In Charge:* André Côté, College Librarian. *AV Staff:* 9 (2 prof, 12 cl). *Film Sel:* committee preview, faculty/staff recommendations, chief film librarian's decision. *Holdings:* black studies 5%, medicine 40%.
  Film Collection 282t/p. Approx 10-20t acquired annually. *Circ:* 16mm, 29t/p; 8mm reel, 201t/p; S8mm reel, 52t/p. *Pubns:* catalog, annual (free); suppl, no set policy (free).
  Other Film Serv Rent from distributors for patrons, obtain film from coop loan system (Southern Passaic County Area Coordinating Council), obtain film from other libraries. Permanent viewing facility. *Equipment:* lend (for faculty use only), 16mm sound projector (7), 8mm cartridge projector (40), 8mm reel projector (1), S8mm cartridge projector (12), S8mm reel projector (6).
  Other Media Collections *Audio:* disc, 33⅓ rpm, 227c; tape, cassette, 214c. *Filmstrips:* sound, 332c; silent, 212c.
  Budget & Expenditures Total library budget $30,412 (FY 7/1/74-7/1/75). No separate AV budget. *Member:* ALA, N.J. AECT, N.J. Library Assn.

P- PATERSON PUBLIC LIBRARY, 250 Broadway, 07501. *Tel:* (201) 279-4200, ext 32. *Film Serv Est:* 1971. *In Charge:* Sylvia Jaroslaw, Superv Librarian, AV Dept. *AV Staff:* 8 (2 prof, 4 cl, 2 tech). *Film Sel:* committee preview, staff recommendations.
  Free-Loan Film Serv *Eligibility:* educational inst, civic & religious groups, indiv with library cards, prof such as teachers, nurses, policemen & librarians & others, such as social clubs & homes for the retarded. *Restrictions:* for indiv & inst, none. Cannot use for fund-raising, transmit electronically. May not borrow by mail. *Loan Period:* 1 day. *Total Yr Film Loan:* 4193.
  Film Collection 161t/163p. Approx 20t acquired annually. *Circ:* 16mm, 161t/163p. *Noncirc:* 16mm, 10t/p. *Pubns:* catalog, annual (free); suppl, in yr catalog not published no set policy (free).
  Other Film Serv Obtain film from coop loan system (N.J. Library Film Circuit, N.J. Regional Film Library Center), film reference serv, library film programs. Permanent viewing facility.
  Other Media Collections *Audio:* disc, 33⅓rpm, 7132t/7500c; tape, cassette, 100t/c. *Filmstrips:* sound, 162t. *Slides:* single, 500t.
  Budget & Expenditures Total library budget $140,000 (FY 1/1/75-1/1/76). Total FY film budget $6000. *Member:* ALA, EFLA, N.J. State Library Assn.

Phillipsburg

P- PHILLIPSUBRG PUBLIC LIBRARY, 200 Frost Ave, 08865. *Tel:* (800) 452-9182. *In Charge:* Nancy Smink. *Member:* N.J. Library Film Circuit.

Plainfield

P- PLAINFIELD PUBLIC LIBRARY, Plainfield Area Reference Center, Eighth St at Park Ave, 07060. *Tel:* (201) 757-1111. *Film Serv Est:* 1959. *In Charge:* John Hurley, AV Dept Head. *AV Staff:* 2½ (1 prof, ½ cl, 1 tech). *Film Sel:* chief film librarian's decision, published reviews.
  Free-Loan Film Serv *Eligibility:* indiv with library cards. *Restrictions:* for indiv, interlibrary loan; for libraries, only in reference area. Cannot use for fund-raising, transmit electronically. May not borrow by mail. *Loan Period:* 1 day. *Total Yr Film Loan:* 4602.
  Film Collection Approx 30t acquired annually. *Circ:* 16mm, 215t/222p. *Noncirc:* 16mm, 3t/p. *Pubns:* catalog, as needed (25¢); suppl (free).
  Other Film Serv Obtain film from coop loan system (Morris Regional Film Library), film fairs/festivals, library film

programs. Permanent viewing facility available for rent to community.

Other Media Collections *Audio:* disc, 33⅓ rpm, 1499t/1948c; tape, cassette, 228t/242c. *Filmstrips:* sound, 86t/147c. *Slides:* 3t/2598c.

Budget & Expenditures Total library budget $77,659 (FY 1/1/74-1/1/75. Total FY film budget $8000. *Member:* ALA, N.J. Library Assn.

Video Serv *Est:* 1973. *Video Staff:* 2 f-t. *Video Use:* documentation of community/school events, to increase community's library use, community video access, practical video/TV training courses. Video serv available by appointment. Produce video tapes. Have production studio/space.

Video Equipment/Facilities *In-House Use Only:* recording/playback deck (2), ½" reel b&w/col, Sony 3600, 8600; editing deck (1), ½" reel b&w, Sony 3650; studio camera (2), ½" b&w, GBC VF302; monitor (1), Sony; SEG (1), GBC-ITC; additional camera lenses (1); lighting (2); tripods (2); audio tape recorders (1). *For Loan:* portapak (3), ½" reel b&w/col, Sony 3400, 8400; monitor (2), Sony; lighting (3); microphones (8); tripods (3); microphone mixer (1). Have portable viewing installation. *Equipment Loan Period:* 1 day. Provide training in use of equipment to library members. Have tape duplication serv.

Video Tape Loan/Rental/Sale Serv *Serv Provided:* free loan. *Loan Eligibility:* indiv with library cards, libraries. *Restrictions:* cannot use for fund-raising, duplicate, air without permission. May not borrow by mail. *Total Yr Tape Loan:* 5.

Video Collection Maintained by own production. Use/play ½" reel to reel. *Sources:* community productions. *Member:* LIVE (Libraries In Video Education) Coop. Tapes organized by producer. *Collection, B&W:* ½" reel, 12t/20c. *Other Video Serv:* production workshops, editing & mixing for LIVE members.

Cable & CCTV Produce programs for cablecasting. Serve as production facility for others. Have advisory/administrative role in cable system operation.

Princeton

P- PRINCETON PUBLIC LIBRARY, 65 Witherspoon St, 08540. *Tel:* (609) 924-9529. *Film Serv Est:* 1962. *In Charge:* Therese Critchlow, AV Servs Librarian. *AV Staff:* 1 prof. *Film Sel:* staff preview.

Free-Loan Film Serv *Eligibility:* indiv with library cards. *Restrictions:* for indiv, none. Cannot use for fund-raising, transmit electronically. Available to researchers/scholars for on-site viewing. May not borrow by mail. *Loan Period:* 1 day. *Total Yr Film Loan:* 1874.

Film Collection 277t/283p. Approx 5-6t acquired annually. *Circ:* 16mm, 127t/128p; 8mm reel, 150t/155p. *Pubns:* catalog, annual (free); suppl, no set policy (free). Publish program flyers.

Other Film Serv Obtain film from coop loan system (N.J. Library Film Circuit & N.J. Regional Film Center), film reference serv. Permanent viewing facility available for rent to community. *Equipment:* 16mm sound projector (2), projection tables & stands (2), filmstrip projector (1), carousel slide projector (1), filmstrip/cassette player (1).

Other Media Collections *Audio:* tape, cassette, 342t/694c. *Filmstrips:* silent sets, 2000t.

Budget & Expenditures Total library budget $76,390. (FY 1/75-1/76). Total FY film budget $4000. *Member:* ALA, EFLA, FLIC, N.J. Library Assn.

Rahway

P- RAHWAY PUBLIC LIBRARY, 1175 St. Georges Ave, 07065. *Tel:* (201) 388-0761. *In Charge:* Carol Mirsky. *Member:* N.J. Library Film Circuit.

Ridgewood

P- RIDGEWOOD LIBRARY, 125 N Maple Ave, 07450. *Tel:* (201) 652-5200. *Film Serv Est:* 1970. *In Charge:* Miss M. Griffin,

AV Librarian. *AV Staff:* 4 (2 prof, 2 cl). *Film Sel:* committee preview, staff recommendations, published reviews.

Free-Loan Film Serv *Eligibility:* educational inst, civic & religious groups, prof groups. *Restrictions:* for inst, none. Cannot use for fund-raising, borrow for classroom use. Available to researchers/scholars for on-site viewing. May not borrow by mail. *Loan Period:* 1 day. *Total Yr Film Loan:* 2500.

Other Film Serv Obtain film from coop loan system (Hackensack Regional Film Center), obtain film from other libraries. Permanent viewing facility available to community. *Equipment:* lend 16mm sound projector (4).

Other Media Collections *Audio:* disc, 33⅓ rpm, 3500t/c; tape, cassette, 500t/1000c. *Filmstrips:* sound, 200t/c; silent, 100t/c; sound sets, 50t/c; silent sets, 50t/c. *Slides:* single, 100t/c.

Budget & Expenditures Total library budget $70,000 (FY 1/1/75-1/1/76). No separate AV budget. *Member:* ALA, N.J. State Library Assn.

Video Serv *Est:* 1976. *In Charge:* A. Van Slooten, AV Specialist. *Video Staff:* 35 f-t, 17 p-t. *Video Use:* to increase community's library use, community video access, as art form. Video serv available on demand.

Video Equipment/Facilities *In-House Use Only:* recording deck (1), ¾", Sony; playback deck (1), cassette, Sony; monitor (1), Sony; audio tape recorders (3). All owned by local library federation. Have portable viewing installation. Provide training in use of equipment to staff.

Video Tape Loan/Rental/Sale Serv *Serv Provided:* swap with other inst. *Restrictions:* may not borrow by mail.

Video Collection Owned by local library federation. Maintained by purchase. Use/play ¾" cassette. *Sources:* commercial distributors. *Tape Sel:* preview, published reviews, catalogs. Tapes organized by subject. *Collection, Color:* ¾" cassette, 25t/c.

Salem

P- SALEM FREE PUBLIC LIBRARY, 112 W Broadway, 08079. *Tel:* (609) 935-0526. *Film Serv Est:* 1970. *In Charge:* Pamela Pope, Jr Library Asst. *AV Staff:* 1 p-t clerk. *Film Sel:* catalogs. *Holdings:* children's films.

Free-Loan Film Serv *Eligibility:* civic groups, indiv with library cards, & others, such as day care centers, Boy Scouts. *Restrictions:* for indiv & inst, interlibrary loan, fee for nonresidents. Available to researchers/scholars for on-site viewing. May not borrow by mail. *Loan Period:* 1 day or weekend.

Film Collection *Circ:* 8mm reel, 74t.

Other Film Serv Obtain film from coop loan system (area or regional film library). *Equipment:* lend 16mm sound projector (1), 8mm reel projector (1), projection screens, filmstrip projectors (2).

Other Media Collections *Audio:* disc, 33⅓ rpm, 939t; tape, cassette, 17t. *Filmstrips:* silent, 398t; silent sets, 114t; *Slides:* sets, 26t.

Budget & Expenditures Total library budget $15,562.87 (FY 1/1/75-1/1/76). No separate AV budget. *Member:* ALA, N.J. Library Assn, S Jersey Libraries.

Sewell

C- GLOUCESTER COUNTY COLLEGE, Library-Media Center, Tanyard Rd, 08080. *Tel:* (609) 468-5000, ext 294. *Video Serv Est:* 1970. *In Charge:* Robert J. Haroutunian, AV Coord. *Video Staff:* 3 f-t, 3 p-t, 1 tech. *Video Use:* documentation of community/school events, in-service training, practical video/TV training courses. Video serv available by appointment. Produce video tapes. Have production studio/space.

Video Equipment/Facilities *In-House Use Only:* recording deck (3), ½", ¾" 1 b&w, 2 col, Panasonic, JVC; studio camera (2), b&w, Panasonic; monitor (5), 1 b&w/4 col, GE, Magnavox; microphones (6); tripods (3). *For Loan:* portapak (1), ½" b&w, Panasonic. Have permanent viewing installations. *Equipment Loan Period:* 7 days, renewable. Provide training in

Sewell (cont'd)
use of equipment to anyone who asks to borrow it. Have tape
duplication serv.

Video Tape Loan/Rental/Sale Serv *Serv Provided:* free
loan. *Loan Eligibility:* staff & students, educational inst, civic &
religious groups, prof groups, such as nursing assns. *Restrictions:* for indiv & inst, none. Cannot use for fund-raising,
duplicate. May borrow by mail. *Loan Period:* 7 days.

Video Collection Maintained by purchase, rental, own
production, exchange/swap. Use/play ½" reel to reel, ¾"
cassette. *Sources:* commercial distributors, community productions, exchange. *Member:* N.J. Educational Media Consortium.
Tape Sel: preview, faculty/staff recommendations. Tapes organized by subject. *Collection, Color:* ¾" cassette, 15t. *Collection,
B&W:* ½" reel, 30t. *Other Video Serv:* production workshops.

Somerville

P- SOMERSET COUNTY LIBRARY, Film Dept, County Administration Bldg, 08876. *Tel:* (201) 725-4700, ext 234, 235,
236. *Film Serv Est:* 1960. *In Charge:* Elizabeth G. MacConnell, AV Librarian. *AV Staff:* 2 (1 cl, 1 tech). *Film Sel:*
committee preview, staff recommendations, chief film librarian's decision.

Free-Loan Film Serv *Eligibility:* org members, educational inst, civic & religious groups, indiv with library cards,
prof groups. *Restrictions:* for indiv, none. Cannot use for fund-
raising, transmit electronically. Available to researchers/
scholars for on-site viewing. May not borrow by mail. *Loan
Period:* 1 day. *Total Film Loan:* 1495 (6 months).

Film Collection Approx 100t acquired annually. *Circ:*
16mm, 1585t/1600p. *Pubns:* catalog, annual. Publish flyers.

Other Film Serv Obtain film from coop loan system (Morris Regional Film Library, N.J. Library Film Circuit), film
reference serv, film fairs/festivals, library film programs.
Equipment: 16mm sound projector (2), lend projection screens
(2).

Other Media Collections *Audio:* disc, 33⅓ rpm, 2100t/c.
Filmstrips: sound, 50t/c.

Budget & Expenditures Total library budget $269,000 (FY
1/1/74-1/1/75). Total FY film budget $11,000. *Member:* ALA,
EFLA, N.J. Library Assn.

Video Serv *Est:* 1973. *Video Staff:* 1 f-t, 1 tech. *Video Use:*
documentation of community/school events, to increase community's library use, in-service training, practical video/TV
training courses. Video serv available on demand. Produce
video tapes.

Video Equipment/Facilities *In-House Use Only:* editing
deck (2), ½" reel b&w/col, Panasonic NV3130; monitor (1), ½"
reel col, Panasonic; audio tape recorders (1), bulk eraser (1), tool
kit. *For Loan:* portapak (2), ½" reel b&w, Panasonic; recording
deck (2), ½" reel b&w, Panasonic; playback deck (2), ½" reel
b&w, Panasonic 30/20NV; studio camera (1), ½" reel, b&w,
Panasonic WV341P; monitor (4), ½" reel b&w, Panasonic; additional camera lenses (2); lighting (2); microphones (2); tripods
(2); changer (2); adaptors (2); portable battery (1); switcher (1).
Have portable viewing installation. Provide training in use of
equipment. Have tape duplication serv.

Video Tape Loan/Rental/Sale Serv *Serv Provided:* free
loan, sale. *Loan Eligibility:* staff & students, indiv with library
cards. *Restrictions:* for indiv who have taken training course.
Cannot use for fund-raising. May not borrow by mail. *Total Yr
Tape Loan:* 5.

Video Collection Maintained by own production, ex-
change/swap. Use/play ½" reel to reel. *Sources:* community
productions. *Special Collections:* local, bicentennial. Tapes organized by title. *Collection, Color:* ½" reel, 1t. *Collection, B&W:*
½" reel, 12t. *Other Video Serv:* reference serv, production workshops. *Pubns:* catalog. Publish video instruction materials.

Cable & CCTV Will receive serv of cable TV system.

South Orange

C- SETON HALL UNIVERSITY, Educational Media Center,
400 S Orange Ave, 07079. *Tel:* (201) 762-9000, ext 219. *Film*

Serv Est: 1973. *In Charge:* Rosemary W. Skeele, Dir, EMC.
AV Staff: 4 (1 prof, 1 cl, 3 tech). *Film Sel:* faculty/staff
recommendations.

Free-Loan Film Serv *Eligiblity:* staff & students. *Restrictions:* Available to researchers/scholars for on-site viewing.
May not borrow by mail.

Film Collection Approx 6t acquired annually. *Noncirc:*
16mm, 14t/c. *Pubns:* catalog, every 2 yrs (free). Publish newsletter.

Other Film Serv *Equipment:* lend S8mm cameras, 16mm
cameras, 16mm sound projectors, 8mm cartridge projectors,
8mm reel projectors, S8mm cartridge projectors, S8mm reel
projectors, projection tables & stands, projection screens.

Other Media Collections *Audio:* disc, 33⅓ rpm, 100c; tape,
cassette, 100c; tape, reel, 25c. *Filmstrips:* silent, 200c; sound sets,
300c; silent sets, 150c. *Slides:* sets, 5c.

Budget & Expenditures Total nonprint library budget
$3000 (FY 7/1/74-7/1/75). *Member:* AECT.

Video Serv *Video Staff:* 1 f-t, 8 p-t, 1 tech. *Video Use:*
documentation of community/school events, in-service training, practical video/TV training courses, as art form. Video serv
available by appointment. Produce video tapes. Have production studio/space.

Video Equipment/Facilities *In-House Use Only:* editing
deck (1), ½" b&w, JVC; monitor (7), 6 b&w/col, 4 AD, 3 Sony;
lighting; tripods (4); audio tape recorders (60). *For Loan:* portapak (5), ½" b&w, Rover JVC; recording deck (3), ½", ¾" b&w,
Sony, Panasonic, JVC. Have portable viewing installation.
Equipment Loan Period: no overnight loans on video equipment. Provide training in use of equipment to faculty & students. Have tape duplication serv.

Video Tape Loan/Rental/Sale Serv *Loan Eligibility:*
staff & students. *Restrictions:* cannot use for fund-raising,
duplicate, air without permission. May not borrow by mail.

Video Collection Maintained by rental, own production.
Sources: commercial distributors, galleries. *Tape Sel:* preview,
faculty/staff recommendations. *Collection, B&W:* ½" reel, 10t/c;
¾" cassette, 5t/c. *Other Video Serv:* production workshops.

P- SOUTH ORANGE PUBLIC LIBRARY, 65 Scotland Rd,
07079. *Tel:* (201) 762-0230. *Film Serv Est:* 1966. *In Charge:*
Rosalie Cangialose, Asst Librarian. *AV Staff:* 1 (1 prof, 1
p-t tech). *Film Sel:* chief film librarian's decision. *Holdings:* children's films 50%, fine arts 10%.

Free-Loan Film Serv *Eligibility:* indiv with library cards.
Restrictions: for indiv & inst, only in city. Cannot use for fund-
raising. May not borrow by mail. *Loan Period:* 1 day. *Total Yr
Film Loan:* approx 300.

Film Collection Approx 2t acquired annually. *Circ:* 16mm,
14t/p. *Pubns:* catalog, annual (free). Publish flyers when new
films are added.

Other Film Serv Obtain film from coop loan system
(Garden State Library Film Circuit), library film programs.
Permanent viewing facility available for rent to community.

Other Media Collections *Audio:* disc, 33⅓ rpm, 1000t/c;
cassette, 88t/c. *Filmstrips:* sound, 94t/c; sound sets, 20t/c.

Budget & Expenditures Total FY film budget $2500 (FY
1/75-1/76). *Member:* ALA, EFLA, N.J. Library Assn.

Summit

P- FREE PUBLIC LIBRARY OF SUMMIT, 75 Maple St, 07922.
Tel: (201) 273-0350. *Video Serv Est:* 1972. *In Charge:* Jane
McClure, Dir. *Video Use:* documentation of communi-
ty/school events. Video serv available by appointment.
Produce video tapes. Have production studio/space.

Video Equipment/Facilities *In-House Use Only:* recording deck (1), ¼" b&w, Sony AV-3600; monitor (2), b&w, Sony
CVM194, Philco R-3626WA. *For Loan:* portapak (1), ¼" b&w,
Panasonic NV 3082/WV 3082; microphone (1); tripods (1);
undirectional microphone (1). Have portable viewing installation. *Equipment Loan Period:* no set policy.

Video Tape Loan/Rental/Sale Serv *Loan Eligibility:*
Summit Junior League video committee members. *Restrictions:*

for indiv, only in city; for inst, none. Cannot borrow equipment without permission of Library Dir. May not borrow by mail.

Toms River

P- OCEAN COUNTY LIBRARY, 15 Hooper Ave, 08753. *Tel:* (201) 349-6200. *Member:* Garden State Library Film Circuit.

Totowa Borough

P- DWIGHT D. EISENHOWER LIBRARY, 537 Totowa Rd, 07512. *Tel:* (201) 523-3265. *In Charge:* Mary T. Neil, Dir. *AV Staff:* ½ (cl).

Free-Loan Film Serv *Eligibility:* educational inst, civic groups, prof groups, such as Chamber of Commerce, teachers assn. *Restrictions:* cannot use for fund-raising, transmit electronically. *Loan Period:* 1 day.

Other Film Serv Obtain film from coop loan system (Hackensack Library), obtain film from other libraries, library film programs. Permanent viewing facility. *Equipment:* 16mm sound projector (1), projection screen (1).

Trenton

P- HAMILTON TOWNSHIP PUBLIC LIBRARY, Library Place at Municipal Dr, 08619. *Tel:* (609) 585-4623. *Film Serv Est:* 1975. *In Charge:* Deborah Murphy, Jr Librarian. *AV Staff:* 3 (2 prof, 1 tech). *Film Sel:* preview, staff recommendations, chief film librarian's decision, published reviews (Previews, Booklist). *Holdings:* animated films 60%, children's films 90%, comedy films 80%, holiday films 10%, science 5%.

Free-Loan Film Serv *Eligibility:* staff & students, civic & religious groups, indiv with library cards. *Restrictions:* for indiv, only in Trenton or Hamilton Township or outside subscription card holders. *Loan Period:* 1 day. *Total Yr Film Loan:* 102.

Film Collection 74t/p. Approx 6t acquired annually. *Circ:* 16mm, 74t/p. *Pubns:* catalog, annual (free); suppl, no set policy (free).

Other Film Serv Obtain film from coop loan system (N.J. Library Film Circuit, Monmouth County Film Circuit), obtain film from other libraries. *Equipment:* 16mm sound projector (3), projection screens (2).

Other Media Collections *Audio:* disc, 33⅓ rpm, 2170t.

Budget & Expenditures Total library budget $150,320 (FY 1/1/75-1/1/76). Total FY AV budget $6000.

C- MERCER COUNTY COMMUNITY COLLEGE, Film Library, Box B, 08690. *Tel:* (609) 586-4800, ext 479. *Film Serv Est:* 1967. *In Charge:* Marilyn Gilroy, AV Librarian. *AV Staff:* 2 (1 prof, 1 cl). *Film Sel:* faculty/staff recommendations, chief film librarian's decision. *Holdings:* agriculture 1%, animated films 3%, engineering 10%, experimental films 1%, feature films 2%, fine arts 50%, industrial arts 3%, law 1%, science 4%, social sciences 20%.

Free-Loan Film Serv *Eligibility:* staff & students. *Restrictions:* may not borrow by mail.

Film Collection *Circ:* 16mm, 620t/700p. *Pubns:* catalog, annual (free).

Other Film Serv Rent film from distributors for patrons. Permanent viewing facility available for rent to community.

Other Media Collections Are decentralized, not controlled or counted.

Budget & Expenditures Total library budget $10,000 (FY 9/12/74-6/30/75). No separate AV budget. *Member:* AECT, AFI, ALA, EFLA.

P- MERCER COUNTY LIBRARY, 41 Scotch Rd, 08628. *Tel:* (609) 882-2450. *Member:* Garden State Library Film Circuit.

P- TRENTON PUBLIC LIBRARY, 120 Academy St, Box 2448, 08607. *Tel:* (609) 392-7188. *In Charge:* Shirley Michael. *Member:* N.J. Library Film Circuit.

C- TRENTON STATE COLLEGE, Center for Media & Technol, Education Bldg 115, 08625. *Tel:* (609) 771-2491. *Film Serv Est:* 1958. *In Charge:* William R. Thomas, Asst Dir. *AV Staff:* 40 (3 prof, 3 cl, 7 tech). *Film Sel:* faculty/staff recommendations.

Free-Loan Film Serv *Eligibility:* staff & students. *Restrictions:* for indiv, none; not available to inst. Available to researchers/scholars for on-site viewing. May not borrow by mail. *Loan Period:* 1 day. *Total Yr Film Loan:* 2500. Produce slides, transparencies, TV.

Film Collection *Circ:* 16mm, 570t/575p; 8mm reel, cartridge & S8mm reel, cartridge, 600t/p. *Pubns:* catalog, as needed; suppl, no set policy.

Other Film Serv Film reference serv. Permanent viewing facility. *Equipment:* lend S8mm camera, 16mm sound projector, 8mm cartridge projector, 8mm reel projector, S8mm cartridge projector, S8mm reel projector, projection tables & stands, projection screens, slide, filmstrip, overhead, opaque projectors; cassette & reel recorders, record players, TV equipment.

Other Media Collections *Audio:* disc & tape (cassette, cartridge, reel). *Filmstrips:* sound & silent. *Slides:* single & sets. *Member:* AECT.

Video Serv *Est:* 1965. *Video Staff:* 10 f-t, 2 tech. *Video Use:* documentation of community/school events, in-service training, practical video/TV training courses. Video serv available by appointment. Produce video tapes. Have production studio/space & separate control room.

Video Equipment/Facilities *For Loan:* portapak, recording deck, playback deck, editing deck, studio camera, monitor, SEG, keyer, synthesizer, additional camera lenses, lighting, microphones, tripods, audio tape recorders. Have permanent viewing installation. *Equipment Loan Period:* 1 day. Provide training in use of equipment to faculty & students. Have tape duplication serv.

Video Tape Loan/Rental/Sale Serv *Serv Provided:* free loan, swap with other inst. *Loan Eligibility:* staff & students. *Restrictions:* none. May borrow by mail.

Video Collection Maintained by rental, own production, exchange/swap. Use/play ½″, ¼″, 1″ reel to reel, ½″ cartridge, ¾″ cassette. *Sources:* commercial distributors. *Tape Sel:* preview, faculty/staff recommendations, catalogs. *Special Collections:* in-house training tapes, general educational. Tapes organized by Dewey Decimal. *Other Video Serv:* reference serv, production workshops.

Cable & CCTV Have CCTV in inst. *Programming Sources:* over-the-air commercial & public broadcasting, tapes produced by inst, tapes produced professionally.

Vineland

C- CUMBERLAND COUNTY COLLEGE, Learning Resource Center, Box 517, 08360. *Tel:* (609) 691-8600. *AV Staff:* 1 prof. *Film Sel:* faculty/staff recommendations.

Free-Loan Film Serv *Eligibility:* staff. Available to researchers/scholars for on-site viewing. May not borrow by mail. *Loan Period:* unlimited.

Film Collection *Noncirc:* 16mm, 14t/p; S8mm cartridge, 134t/p.

Other Film Serv Rent film from distributors for patrons, obtain film from other libraries, film reference serv.

Other Media Collections *Audio:* disc, 33⅓ rpm, 1639c; tape, cassette, 249c. *Filmstrips:* silent sets, 107c. *Slides:* sets, 169c.

Budget & Expenditures Total FY film budget $3500 (FY 7/1/74-7/1/75). *Member:* AECT.

Video Serv *Est:* 1967. *In Charge:* R. King, Coord Media Servs. *Video Staff:* 1 p-t. *Video Use:* documentation of community/school events, in-service training, practical video/TV training courses. Video serv available by appointment. Produce video tapes. Have production studio/space.

Vineland (cont'd)

Video Equipment/Facilities *In-House Use Only:* portapak (1), ½" b&w, Sony 3600; recording deck (3), 1" b&w/col, Ampex 5800; studio camera (2), b&w, Telemation; monitor (3), b&w/col; additional camera lenses (1); lighting (4); microphones (4). Have permanent viewing installation. Provide training in use of equipment to students.

Video Tape Loan/Rental/Sale Serv *Serv Provided:* free loan, swap with other inst. *Loan Eligibility:* staff.

Video Collection Maintained by rental, own production, exchange/swap. Use/play ½", 1" reel to reel. *Tape Sel:* preview, faculty/staff recommendations. Tapes organized by production date. *Collection, B&W:* ½" reel, 45t/c; 1" reel, 90t/c. *Pubns:* catalog.

Cable & CCTV Produce programs for cablecasting.

P- VINELAND PUBLIC LIBRARY, Film Dept, 1058 E Landis Ave, 08360. *Tel:* (609) 696-1100. *Film Serv Est:* 1966. *In Charge:* Nancy Snyder, Film Librarian. *AV Staff:* 3 (2 prof, 1 tech). *Film Sel:* committee preview, chief film librarian's decision.

Free-Loan Film Serv *Eligibility:* indiv with library cards. *Restrictions:* for indiv & inst, none. Cannot use for fund-raising. Available to researchers/scholars for on-site viewing. May not borrow by mail. *Loan Period:* 1 day.

Film Collection 200t/p. Approx 30t acquired annually. *Circ:* 16mm, 200p; 8mm reel, 150p. *Pubns:* catalog, every 2 yrs (free); suppl, in yr catalog not published (free).

Other Film Serv Obtain film from coop loan system (Camden Regional Film Library, Garden State Library Film Circuit), film reference serv, library film programs. Permanent viewing facility available for rent to community. *Equipment:* rent 16mm sound projector (4).

Other Media Collections *Audio:* disc, 33⅓ rpm, 2800c; tape, cassette, 300c. *Filmstrips:* sound, 150t/p.

Budget & Expenditures Total library budget $50,000 (FY 1/1/74-1/1/75). Total FY film budget $5000. *Member:* ALA, EFLA, N.J. Library Assn.

Wayne

S- PASSAIC COUNTY AV AIDS COMMISSION, Passaic County Film Library, William Paterson College, 300 Pompton Rd, W16, 07470. *Tel:* (201) 279-8017, 881-2383. *Film Serv Est:* 1956. *In Charge:* Dr. Ernest Siegel, Dir. *Film Sel:* staff recommendations, chief film librarian's decision, published reviews (EFLA, Landers, Previews).

Free-Loan Film Serv *Eligibility:* org members. *Restrictions:* for indiv & inst, only in Passaic County participating school districts. Available to researchers/scholars for on-site viewing. May not borrow by mail. *Loan Period:* 5 days. *Total Yr Film Loan:* 18,408.

Film Collection 1400t/1500p. Approx 100t acquired annually. *Circ:* 16mm, 1000t/1100p. *Noncirc:* 16mm, 390t/400p. *Pubns:* catalog, annual (free).

Other Film Serv Obtain film from coop loan system (N.J. County AV Aids Commissions).

Budget & Expenditures Total film budget $20,000 (FY 9/1/74-6/30/75). *Member:* AECT, EFLA.

P- WAYNE PUBLIC LIBRARY, 475 Valley Rd, 07470. *Tel:* (201) 694-4272. *Film Serv Est:* 1973. *In Charge:* Joan Dicker, AV Librarian. *AV Staff:* 1½ (⅘ prof, ⅖ cl, ⅕ tech). *Film Sel:* chief film librarian's decision.

Free-Loan Film Serv *Eligibility:* indiv with library cards. *Restrictions:* for indiv, 18 yrs old; for inst, only in reference area. Cannot use for fund-raising, transmit electronically, borrow for classroom use. May not borrow by mail. *Loan Period:* 3 days for indiv, 7 days for other libraries.

Film Collection 145t/186p. *Circ:* 16mm, 30t/p; 8mm-S8mm reel, 145t/186p. *Pubns:* catalog, every 2 yrs (free); suppl, no set policy (free). Publish materials pertaining to collection. Publish press releases, calendar of programs.

Other Film Serv Obtain film from coop loan system (Bergen-Passaic Film Library). Permanent viewing facility.

Equipment: 16mm sound projector (4), 8mm reel projector (2), S8mm reel projector (2), projection tables & stands (2), projection screens (3).

Other Media Collections *Audio:* disc, 33⅓ rpm, 1603t; tape, cassette, 848t. *Filmstrips:* sound sets, 200t. *Slides:* sets, 6t.

Budget & Expenditures Total library budget $102,700. No separate AV budget. *Member:* ALA, EFLA, FLIC, Bergen/Passaic Film Center, N.J. Library Assn.

Whippany

C- MORRIS COUNTY FREE LIBRARY, Morris Regional Film Library, 30 E Hanover Ave, 07981. *Tel:* (201) 285-6116. *Film Serv Est:* 1948. *In Charge:* Thomas T. Elliott, Dir. *AV Staff:* 7 (1 prof, 3 cl, 2 tech). *Film Sel:* committee preview, faculty/staff recommendations, chief film librarian's decision.

Free-Loan Film Serv *Eligibility:* educational inst, civic & religious groups, indiv with library cards. *Restrictions:* for indiv & inst, only in our reference area. Cannot use for fund-raising, transmit electronically. Available to researchers/scholars for on-site viewing. May not borrow by mail. *Loan Period:* 1-2 days. *Total Yr Film Loan:* 12,800.

Film Collection 1100t/1200p. Approx 250-300t acquired annually. *Circ:* 16mm, 1100t/1200p; 8mm reel, 350t/p; S8mm reel, 250t/p. *Pubns:* catalog, every 2 yrs ($1); suppl, in yr catalog not published. Publish publicity materials.

Other Film Serv Library film programs. *Equipment:* lend 16mm sound projector (15), 8mm reel projector (1), projection screens (10).

Budget & Expenditures Total library budget $1,500,000 (FY Jan 1974-Dec 1975). Total FY film budget $200,000 (FY April 1974-March 1975). *Member:* AECT, ALA, EFLA, FLIC, N.J. Library Assn.

Video Serv *Est:* 1972. *Video Staff:* 1 f-t. *Video Use:* documentation of community/school events, community video access, in-service training. Video serv available by appointment. Produce video tapes.

Video Equipment/Facilities *In-House Use Only:* portapak (1), ½" b&w, Sony; recording deck (1), ½" b&w, Sony; playback deck (1), ½" b&w, Sony; editing deck (1), ½" b&w, Sony; studio camera (2), ½" b&w, GBC; monitor (3), 2 b&w/1 col, Sony; SEG (1), color, GBC; additional camera lenses (2); lighting (6); microphones (4); tripods (4); audio tape recorder. *For Loan:* portapak (2), ½" b&w, Sony. Have portable viewing installation. *Equipment Loan Period:* 1-2 days. Provide training in use of equipment to potential users. Have tape duplication serv.

Video Tape Loan/Rental/Sale Serv *Serv Provided:* free loan, swap with other inst. *Loan Eligibility:* org members, civic & religious groups. *Restrictions:* for indiv & inst, only in Morris County. Cannot use for fund-raising, air without permission. May not borrow by mail.

Video Collection Maintained by own production. Use/play ½" reel to reel. *Sources:* community productions. *Special Collections:* in-house training tapes, video as art. Tapes organized by subject. *Collection, B&W:* ½" reel, 40t/c. *Other Video Serv:* reference serv, production workshops.

Cable & CCTV Receive serv of cable TV system. Produce programs for cablecasting. Have advisory role in cable system operation. Have CCTV in inst, with 1 monitor. *Programming Sources:* tapes produced by inst.

Willingboro

P- WILLINGBORO PUBLIC LIBRARY, Salem Rd, 08046. *Tel:* (609) 877-6668. *Member:* Garden State Library Film Circuit.

Woodbridge

P- FREE PUBLIC LIBRARY OF WOODBRIDGE, George Frederick Plaza, 07095. *Tel:* (201) 634-4450. *Film Serv Est:* 1965. *In Charge:* William Spangler, Head, Film Dept. *AV Staff:* 3⅔ (1 prof, 1⅔ cl, 1 tech). *Film Sel:* 16mm by committee preview, 8mm by chief film librarian's decision. *Holdings:* fire fighting & prevention 3%, first aid 1%.

Free-Loan Film Serv *Eligibility:* indiv with library cards. *Restrictions:* for indiv & inst, none. Cannot use for fund-raising, transmit electronically. Available to researchers/scholars for on-site viewing. May not borrow by mail. *Loan Period:* 16mm, 1 day; S8mm, 7 days. *Total Yr Film Loan:* 9770.

Film Collection 1194p. Approx 220t acquired annually. *Circ:* 16mm, 568p; S8mm reel, 626p. *Pubns:* catalog, every 3 yrs ($0.50); suppl, no set policy (free).

Other Film Serv Obtain film from coop loan system (Monmouth County Library), film reference serv, library film programs. Permanent viewing facility available free to community. *Equipment:* lend 16mm sound projector (10), S8mm reel projector (15), projection screens (2), slide projectors (2), portapaks (2), sound filmstrip projectors (4).

Other Media Collections *Audio:* disc, 33⅓ rpm, 7134c; tape, cassette, 1591c. *Filmstrips:* sound, 185c; sound sets, 643c.

Budget & Expenditures Total library budget $165,000 (FY 1/1/75-1/1/76). Total FY film budget $15,400. *Member:* EFLA.

Video Serv *Est:* 1974. *In Charge:* Jeff Kesper, Librarian.

Video Staff: 2 p-t. *Video Use:* documentation of community/school events, to increase community's library use, community video access, in-service training. Video serv available by appointment. Produce video tapes.

Video Equipment/Facilities *In-House Use Only:* recording deck (1), ½" b&w, Panasonic; playback deck (1), ½" b&w, Panasonic; editing deck (1), ½" b&w, Sony-3650; studio camera (1), b&w, Panasonic WV391P; monitor (3), b&w, 2-Panasonic 2-COM-115, 1" 1-TR-195V; SEG (1), Panasonic. *For Loan:* portapak (3), ½" b&w, Panasonic NV-3082; lighting (1); microphones (3); tripods (1); mike mixer (1). *Equipment Loan Period:* 1 day. Provide training in use of equipment to indiv & inst. Have tape duplication serv.

Video Tape Loan/Rental/Sale Serv *Serv Provided:* free loan. *Loan Eligibility:* indiv with library cards. *Restrictions:* for indiv & inst, only in our reference area. Cannot use for fund-raising. May not borrow by mail. *Loan Period:* 1 day. *Total Yr Tape Loan:* 35.

Video Collection Maintained by own production. Use/play ½" reel to reel. Tapes organized by subject. *Collection, B&W:* ½" reel, 10t/c. *Other Video Serv:* production workshops.

New Mexico

Albuquerque

C- UNIVERSITY OF ALBUQUERQUE, Center for Learning & Information Resources, St. Joseph's Pl, 87124. *Tel:* (505) 243-9461, ext 230. *Film Serv Est:* 1972. *In Charge:* Eleanor Noble, Library Dir. *AV Staff:* 1 (1 tech). *Film Sel:* faculty/staff recommendations, chief film librarian's decision. *Holdings:* physical education.
    Free-Loan Film Serv *Eligibility:* staff. *Restrictions:* for indiv, interlibrary loan. Available to researchers/scholars for on-site viewing. May borrow by mail. *Loan Period:* 3 days.
    Film Collection 6t/p. Approx 2t acquired annually. *Circ:* 16mm, 6t.
    Other Film Serv Rent film from distributors for patrons, obtain film from coop loan system (Southwest Academic Lib Consortia) & from other libraries. Permanent viewing facility available for rent to community. *Equipment:* lend S8mm camera, 16mm camera, 16mm sound projector, 8mm cartridge projector, 8mm reel projector, S8mm cartridge projector, S8mm reel projector, projection tables & stands, projection screens.
    Budget & Expenditures Total library budget $51,735 (FY 7/1/74-7/1/75). Total FY film budget $1059.

C- UNIVERSITY OF NEW MEXICO, Health Sciences Library, North Campus, 87131. *Tel:* (505) 277-2311. *Video Serv Est:* 1969. *In Charge:* Mike Silva, Library Technical Asst. *Video Staff:* 20 f-t, 1 p-t. *Video Use:* playback only of professionally produced tapes. Video serv available on demand. Have permanent viewing installation.
    Video Tape Loan/Rental/Sale Serv *Serv Provided:* free loan. *Loan Eligibility:* staff & students, & others, such as health professionals in N.M., libraries of the South Central regional medical library program. *Restrictions:* for indiv, only in state; for inst, only in state or South Central region. May borrow by mail. *Loan Period:* 2 weeks. *Total Yr Tape Loan:* 320.
    Video Collection Maintained by purchase. Use/play ¾" cassette. *Sources:* commercial distributors. *Tape Sel:* faculty/staff recommendations. Tapes organized by National Library of Medicine classification. *Collection, Color:* ¾" cassette, 550t/c.

C- UNIVERSITY OF NEW MEXICO, Instructional Media Serv, 87131. *Tel:* (505) 277-6151. *Video Serv Est:* 1973. *In Charge:* Robert Kline, Director. *Video Staff:* 6 f-t, 4 tech. *Video Use:* teacher aid. Video serv available by appointment. Produce video tapes. Have production studio/space & separate control room.
    Video Equipment/Facilities *In-House Use Only:* portapak (5), ½" b&w, Sony 8450; recording deck (6), ¾" col, JVC 6100; playback deck (3), ¾" col, JVC 5000; editing deck (1), ½" b&w, Singer; studio camera (4), b&w/col, IVC, RCA; monitor (10), b&w, Conrac; SEG (1); keyer (1); lighting (8); microphones (4); tripods (4); audio tape recorders (2). Have permanent viewing installation. *Equipment Loan Period:* no set policy. Provide training in use of equipment to faculty & students. Have tape duplication serv.
    Video Collection Maintained by own production. Use/play ½", 1" reel to reel, ¾" cassette. *Sources:* commercial distributors. *Tape Sel:* catalogs.
    CCTV Have CCTV in inst, with 50 monitors. *Programming Sources:* tapes produced by inst.

Silver City

P- THE PUBLIC LIBRARY, 515 West College, 88061. *Tel:* (505) 538-3672. *Film Serv Est:* 1974. *In Charge:* Dottie Hill, Children's Librarian. *AV Staff:* 1. *Equipment:* 16mm sound projector (1), projection screens (1), silent & sound filmstrip projectors. Borrow or rent films.
    Other Media Collections *Audio:* disc, 20t. *Filmstrips:* sound, 3t/c; silent, 23t; sound sets, 2t.

C- WESTERN NEW MEXICO UNIVERSITY, Miller Library, 88061. *Tel:* (505) 538-6731. *In Charge:* James Essick, Librarian & AV Dir. *AV Staff:* 1 (1 cl). *Film Sel:* faculty/staff recommendations. *Holdings:* agriculture 1%, children's films 9%, law 19%, science 48%, social sciences 15%.
    Free-Loan Film Serv *Eligibility:* staff & students.
    Film Collection 300t/p. Approx 3t acquired annually. Permanent viewing facility.
    Video Serv *Est:* 1973. *Video Staff:* 1 f-t. *Video Use:* playback only of professionally produced tapes. Video serv available by appointment. Produce video tapes. Have production studio/space & separate control room.
    Video Equipment/Facilities *In-House Use Only:* recording deck (1), ½" b&w/col, Sony AV-3650, VO-1600; playback deck (1), b&w/col, Sony; editing deck (1), b&w/col, Sony AV-3650; studio camera (2); monitor (3), b&w, Sony; SEG (1), Sony; lighting (4); microphones (1); tripods (2); audio tape recorders (3). Have viewing installations. *Equipment Loan Period:* no set policy. Provide training in use of equipment to students.
    Video Collection Maintained by own production. Use/play ½" reel to reel, ¾" cassette. *Tape Sel:* faculty/staff recommendations. Tapes organized by subject. *Pubns:* catalog.
    Cable & CCTV Receive serv of cable TV system. Have CCTV in inst, with 3 monitors. *Programming Sources:* over-the-air commercial & public broadcasting, tapes produced by inst.

New York

Albany

S- NEW YORK STATE EDUCATION DEPARTMENT, Special Education Instructional Materials Center Film Library, 55 Elk St, Rm 117, 12234. *Tel:* (518) 474-2251. *Film Serv Est:* 1968. *In Charge:* Joan Miller, Associate, Instructional Materials for Handicapped. *AV Staff:* 6 (3 prof, 2 cl, 1 tech). *Film Sel:* committee preview, staff recommendations, chief film librarian's decision. *Holdings:* teacher education 100%.

Free-Loan Film Serv *Eligibility:* inst staff & students, educational inst, prof groups, such as educators of the handicapped & others, such as parents of handicapped children. *Restrictions:* for indiv, interlibrary loan, only in state (limited number loaned outside state); for inst, only in state (limited number loaned outside state). Available to researchers/scholars for on-site viewing. May borrow by mail. *Loan Period:* 14 days maximum. *Total Yr Film Loan:* 1016.

Film Collection 200t/206p. Approx 25-30t acquired annually. *Circ:* 16mm, 200t/206p. *Noncirc:* 16mm, 4t/12p. *Pubns:* catalog, annual; suppl, no set policy.

Other Film Serv Obtain film from coop loan system (Network of Learning Resource Centers), film reference serv. Permanent viewing facility.

Budget & Expenditures Total library budget $15,000 (FY 9/1/74-9/1/75). Total FY film budget $10,000. *Member:* AECT, N.Y. State Library Assn, ASIS, ASET.

Albertson

P- SHELTER ROCK PUBLIC LIBRARY, 165 Searingtown Rd, 11507. *Tel:* (516) 248-7363. *Film Serv Est:* 1971. *In Charge:* Helen Koslow, Librarian. *AV Staff:* 7 (1 prof, 2 cl, 4 tech). *Film Sel:* committee preview, chief film librarian's decision, published reviews, press releases.

Free-Loan Film Serv *Eligibility:* educational inst, civic groups, religious groups, indiv with library cards, & others, such as Girl Scouts, Senior Citizens. *Restrictions:* for indiv, only in Nassau County; for inst, only in Nassau County. Cannot use for fund-raising, transmit electronically, borrow for classroom use. *Loan Period:* 16mm 1 day, 8mm 7 days. *Total Yr Film Loan:* 6500.

Film Collection 83t. Approx 15t acquired annually. *Circ:* 16mm, 26t; 8mm reel, 42t; S8mm reel, 15t.

Other Film Serv Obtain film from coop loan system (Nassau Library Assn, Cooperative Film Circuit), film reference serv, film fairs/festivals, library film programs. Permanent viewing facility available for rent to community.

Other Media Collections *Audio:* disc, 33⅓ rpm, 2819t/3047c; tape, cassette, 736t. *Filmstrips:* sound, 83t/c.

Budget & Expenditures Total library budget $460,000 (FY 1/1/74-1/1/75). Total FY film budget $1600. *Member:* AFI, EFLA, Nassau County Library Assn.

Auburn

C- AUBURN COMMUNITY COLLEGE, Franklin St., 13021. *Tel:* (315) 252-0526. *Holdings:* behavioral sciences 23%, fine arts 10%, science 45%, social sciences 20%.

Free-Loan Film Serv *Eligibility:* staff & students, educational inst, civic & religious groups. *Restrictions:* for indiv & inst, only in Cayuga County. May borrow by mail. *Loan Period:* 1 day. *Total Yr Film Loan:* 3000. Produce slide-tape programs.

Film Collection 470t/p. Approx 1-20t acquired annually. *Circ:* 16mm, 470t/p. *Pubns:* publish list of holdings.

Other Film Serv Obtain film from other libraries, film reference serv.

Other Media Collections *Audio:* disc, 33⅓ rpm, 300c. *Filmstrips:* silent, 100c.

Budget & Expenditures No separate budget.

Bayside

C- QUEENSBOROUGH COMMUNITY COLLEGE, AV Media Servs, Springfield Blvd & 56th Ave, 11364. *Tel:* (212) 631-6271, 6296. *Film Serv Est:* 1959. *In Charge:* Allan Mirwis, Dir. *AV Staff:* 4 (1 prof, 1 cl, 2 tech). *Film Sel:* faculty/staff recommendations.

Free-Loan Film Serv *Eligibility:* staff & students, & colleges of the City University of N.Y. *Restrictions:* Available to researchers/scholars for on-site viewing. May not borrow by mail. *Loan Period:* negotiable.

Film Collection 314t/p. Approx 14t acquired annually. *Circ:* 16mm, 314t/p.

Other Film Serv Obtain film from coop loan system (City University of N.Y.), film reference serv. Permanent viewing facility available for rent to community.

Other Media Collections *Audio:* disc, 33⅓ rpm, 1984t/c; tape, cassette, 113t/c; tape, reel, 53t/c. *Filmstrips:* silent, 124t/c.

Budget & Expenditures No separate budget. *Member:* AECT.

Bellport

P- SUFFOLK COOPERATIVE LIBRARY SYSTEM, AV Dept, Box 187, 11713. *Tel:* (516) 286-1600, ext 63, 65. *Film Serv Est:* 1966. *In Charge:* Philip Levering, AV Consultant. *AV Staff:* 5 (1 prof, 4 cl). *Film Sel:* chief film librarian's decision.

Free-Loan Film Serv *Eligibility:* educational inst, civic groups, religious groups, indiv with library cards & others, such as hospitals & nursing homes. *Restrictions:* for indiv, only in Suffolk County; for inst, only in Suffolk County. Cannot use for fund-raising, transmit electronically (except with permission), borrow for classroom use. Available to researchers/scholars for on-site viewing. May not borrow by mail. *Loan Period:* 1 day. *Total Yr Film Loan:* 24,608.

Film Collection 1100t/1200p. Approx 60t acquired annually. *Circ:* 16mm, 1100t/1200p; S8mm reel, 25t/p; S8mm cartridge, 280t/340p. *Pubns:* catalog as needed; suppl, no set policy.

Other Film Serv Obtain film from coop loan system (N.Y. State Film Collection), obtain film from other libraries, film reference serv, library film programs. Permanent viewing facility. *Equipment:* lend 16mm sound projector (4), S8mm cartridge projector (6), S8mm reel projector (1), projection screens (1).

Budget & Expenditures Total library budget $75,000 (FY 1/1/75-1/1/76). Total FY film budget $25,000. *Member:* EFLA, FLIC, N.Y. Library Assn, Suffolk County Library Assn.

Binghamton

P- BINGHAMTON PUBLIC LIBRARY, 78 Exchange St, 13901. *Tel:* (607) 723-6457, ext 29. *Film Serv Est:* 1958. *In Charge:* George Schuter, Film Librarian. *AV Staff:* 3 (1 prof, 2 cl). *Film Sel:* chief film librarian's decision. *Holdings:* Canadian travel films.

Free-Loan Film Serv *Eligibility:* educational inst, civic groups, religious groups. *Restrictions:* for inst, only in Broome, Chenango, Otsego & Delaware Counties. Cannot use for fund-raising, transmit electronically, borrow for classroom use, home use, duplication. Available to researchers/scholars for on-site viewing. May not borrow by mail. *Loan Period:* 1 day or weekend.

Film Collection 880t. Approx 40-50t acquired annually. *Circ:* 16mm, 885t/889p; S8mm cartridge, 63t. *Pubns:* catalog, every 2-3 yrs ($1.50); suppl, no set policy.

Other Film Serv Obtain film from coop loan system (N.Y. State Film Library. Permanent viewing facility. *Equipment:* rent 16mm sound projector (1), S8mm cartridge projector (4).

Other Media Collections *Audio:* disc, 33⅓ rpm, 12,000t.

Binghamton (cont'd)
Budget & Expenditures   Total Library budget $86,000 (FY 1/1/74-1/1/75). Total FY film budget $8000.

Brooklyn

P- BROOKLYN PUBLIC LIBRARY, AV Division, 11238. *Tel:* (212) 636-3226. *Film Serv Est:* 1952. *In Charge:* Kenneth W. Axthelm, Div Chief. *AV Staff:* 8 (4 prof, 3 cl, 1 tech). *Film Sel:* committee preview. *Holdings:* general collection.
Free-Loan Film Serv   *Eligibility:* N.Y. City residents except schools. *Restrictions:* for indiv & inst, only in city. Cannot use for fund-raising, transmit electronically, borrow for classroom use. Available to researchers/scholars for on-site viewing. May not borrow by mail. *Loan Period:* 2 days. *Total Yr Film Loan:* 28,902.
Film Collection   1423t/1757p. Approx 100t acquired annually. *Circ:* 16mm, 1423t/1757p; 8mm cartridge, 306t/341p. *Pubns:* catalog, every 4 yrs ($1.50); suppl, annually.
Other Film Serv   Film reference serv, library film programs. Permanent viewing facility available for rent to community. *Equipment:* lend S8mm camera, 16mm sound projector, 8mm cartridge projector, S8mm reel projector, projection tables & stands, projection screens.
Other Media Collections   *Audio:* disc, 33⅓ rpm, 6539t/14,392c; tape, cassette, 167t/224c. *Filmstrips:* sound, 586t/632c.
Budget & Expenditures   Total FY film budget $50,000 (FY 7/74-7/75). *Member:* AFI, ALA, EFLA, FLIC.

C- CITY UNIVERSITY OF NEW YORK, N.Y. City Community College, 300 Jay St, 11201. *Tel:* (212) 643-5240. *In Charge:* Kenneth S. Kaplan, Librarian. *AV Staff:* 1. *Film Sel:* staff recommendations, published reviews & catalogs. *Holdings:* career education 50%, engineering & technology 10%, fine arts 5%, industrial arts 15%, medicine 10%, science 10%.
Film Collection   750t/770p. *Noncirc:* 8mm total 770t. Publish list of collection.
Other Film Serv   Obtain film from coop loan system (METRO, Academic Libraries of Brooklyn). Permanent viewing facility.
Other Media Collections   *Audio:* disc, 33⅓ rpm, 1350t/1416c; tape, cassette, 160t/174c. *Slides:* sets, 20t/c.
Budget & Expenditures   Total library budget $53,735 (FY 7/1/74-7/1/75). No separate AV budget. *Member:* ALA.
Video Serv   *Est:* 1975. *Video Use:* in-service training, playback only of professionally produced tapes. Video serv available on demand. Produce video tapes. Have production studio/space & separate control room.
Video Equipment/Facilities   *In-House Use Only:* recording deck (1), ½″, Panasonic; playback deck (1), Panasonic; monitor (1), col, Panasonic CT 300E. Have permanent viewing installation.
Video Collection   Maintained by own production. Use/play ½″ cartridge. *Sources:* commercial distributors.

C- KINGSBOROUGH COMMUNITY COLLEGE, Media Center, 2001 Oriental Blvd, 11235. *Tel:* (212) 769-9200, ext 371. *Film Serv Est:* 1967. *In Charge:* Jack Phillips, Ms. S. P. Schuster, Dir, Media Center, Media Librarian. *AV Staff:* 14 (5 prof, 3 cl, 2 tech). *Film Sel:* committee preview, faculty/staff recommendations, rented films which are evaluated in classrooms.
Free-Loan Film Serv   *Eligibility:* staff & students, educational inst within C.U.N.Y. *Restrictions:* for indiv, interlibrary loan, only in city; for inst, only in city. Cannot use for fund-raising, transmit electronically. Available to researchers/scholars for on-site viewing. May not borrow by mail. *Loan Period:* 1 day. Produce films. Produce video tape, audio tape, audio cassettes.
Film Collection   100t/p. Approx 10t acquired annually. *Circ:* 16mm, 80t/p. *Noncirc:* 16mm, 20t/p. *Pubns:* catalog, every 2 yrs, suppl, in yr catalog not published.

Other Film Serv   Rent film from distributors for patrons, obtain film from coop loan system (C.U.N.Y. Film Consortium), obtain film from other libraries, film reference serv, film fairs/festivals, classroom instructional film services. Permanent viewing facility. *Equipment:* lend S8mm camera, 16mm sound projector, 8mm cartridge projector, 8mm reel projector, S8mm cartridge projector, S8mm reel projector, projection tables & stands, projection screens, audio tape recorders, phonographs.
Other Media Collections   *Audio:* disc, 33⅓ rpm, 2000t; tape, cassette, 50t/c; tape, reel, 1200t. *Filmstrips:* sound, 100t/200c; silent, 75t/c.
Budget & Expenditures   Total FY film budget $8500. *Member:* AECT, EFLA, N.Y. SECA.
Video Serv   *Est:* 1972. *In Charge:* Dr. P. Utz, Producer-Dir. *Video Staff:* 2 f-t, 5 p-t. *Video Use:* documentation of community/school events, playback only of professionally produced tapes. Video serv available on demand & by appointment. Produce video tapes. Have production studio/space & separate control room.
Video Equipment/Facilities   *In-House Use Only:* portapak (3), ½″ b&w, Sony; recording deck (18), ½″ b&w, Sony; playback deck (15), ½″ b&w, Panasonic; editing deck (2), ½″, 1″ b&w, IVC, Panasonic; studio camera (4), b&w, Telemation; monitor (54), b&w, Panasonic, Sony; SEG (2), Sony, Dynair; keyer (1); additional camera lenses (6); lighting (14); microphones (12); tripods (10); audio tape recorders (2). Have permanent viewing installation. Provide training in use of equipment to faculty & students. Have tape duplication serv.
Video Tape Loan/Rental/Sale Serv   *Serv Provided:* swap with other inst. *Loan Eligibility:* staff & students.
Video Collection   Maintained by rental, own production. Use/play ½″, 1″ reel to reel. *Sources:* commercial distributors. Tapes organized by Dewey Decimal. *Collection, B&W:* ½″ reel, 700t/c; 1″ reel, 20t/c. *Other Video Serv:* reference serv. *Pubns:* catalog.

C- LONG ISLAND UNIVERSITY/THE BROOKLYN CENTER, Learning Center, 385 Flatbush Ave Ext, 11203. *Tel:* (212) 834-6036. *Video Serv Est:* 1975. *In Charge:* James Knowlton, Dir, Educational Communication. *Video Staff:* 1 f-t, 5 p-t, 2 tech. *Video Use:* documentation of community/school events, in-service training, classroom instruction & cuts tutoring. Video serv available on demand & by appointment. Produce video tapes. Have production studio/space & separate control room.
Video Equipment/Facilities   *In-House Use Only:* portapak (2), ¼″ b&w/col, AKAI; recording deck (1), ¾″ col, 3M; playback deck (1), 1″ b&w/col, Sony AV8600; editing deck (2), ¾″ col, 3M; studio camera (1), ¾″ col, 3M; monitor (4), b&w/col, Sony, AKAI; SEG (1), Sony; tripods (4). *For Loan:* portapak (2), ¼″ b&w/col, AKAI; recording deck (1), ¾″ col, 3M; playback deck (1), 1″ b&w/col, Sony AV8600; editing deck (2), ¾″ col, 3M; studio camera (1), ¾″ col, 3M; monitor (4), b&w/col, Sony, AKAI; SEG (1), Sony; tripods (4). Have permanent & portable viewing installations. *Equipment Loan Period:* no set policy. Provide training in use of equipment to students. Have tape duplication serv.
Video Tape Loan/Rental/Sale Serv   *Serv Provided:* swap with other inst. *Loan Eligibility:* staff & students. May not borrow by mail.
Video Collection   Maintained by own production. Use/play ½″, ¼″ reel to reel, ¾″ cassette. *Sources:* commercial distributors. *Tape Sel:* preview, faculty/staff recommendations. Tapes organized by subject. *Collection, Color:* ¾″ cassette, 100t. *Collection, B&W:* ¾″ cassette, 20t. *Other Video Serv:* taping of other media.

Buffalo

P- BUFFALO AND ERIE COUNTY PUBLIC LIBRARY, Film Dept, Lafayette Sq, 14203. *Tel:* (716) 856-7525, ext 222, 223. *Film Serv Est:* 1961. *In Charge:* Lydia M. Hoffmann, Head, Film Dept. *AV Staff:* 3½ (1 prof, 2½ cl). *Film Sel:* chief film librarian's decision, previews by specialists in respective fields.

Free-Loan Film Serv *Eligibility:* indiv with library cards who fill out film dept card. *Restrictions:* for indiv, only in Erie County; for inst, only in Erie County. Cannot use for fund-raising, transmit electronically, borrow for classroom use. May not borrow by mail. *Loan Period:* 1 day. *Total Yr Film Loan:* 22,977.
Film Collection 1274t/1450p. Approx 100-150t acquired annually. *Pubns:* catalog, every 3 yrs; suppl, no set policy.
Other Film Serv Obtain film from coop loan system (N.Y. State Auxiliary Film Library), film reference serv, film fairs/festivals, library film programs. Permanent viewing facility available for rent to community.
Budget & Expenditures Total library budget $19,700 (FY 1/1/75-1/1/76). Total FY film budget $18,000. *Member:* ALA, EFLA, FLIC, N.Y. Library Assn, Western N.Y. Educational Communications Council.
Video Serv *Est:* 1968. *In Charge:* William A. Miles, Asst. Deputy Dir. *Video Staff:* 9 f-t, 6 p-t. *Video Use:* documentation of community/school events, to increase community's library use, community video access, in-service training. Video serv available by appointment. Produce video tapes.
Video Equipment/Facilities *In-House Use Only:* portapak (2), ½" b&w, Sony 3400; recording deck (2), ½" b&w, Sony 3600; editing deck (1), ½" col, Panasonic; studio camera (1), ½" b&w, Sony 3210; monitor (8), b&w, Sony; SEG (1), Sony SEG; additional camera lenses (4); lighting (1); microphones (3); tripods (2). Provide training in use of equipment to staff & community.
Video Tape Loan/Rental/Sale Serv *Serv Provided:* swap with other inst. *Loan Eligibility:* org members.
Video Collection Maintained by purchase, own production, exchange/swap. Use/play ½", 1" reel to reel. *Sources:* commercial distributors. *Tape Sel:* preview, catalogs. *Special Collections:* in-house training tapes, films in video format. Tapes organized by subject. *Collection, B&W:* ½" reel, 75t/c; 1" reel, 20t/c. *Other Video Serv:* programming, taping of other media, production workshops.
Cable & CCTV Will receive serv of cable TV system.

C- STATE UNIVERSITY OF NEW YORK AT BUFFALO, Educational Communications Center, Media Library, 22 Foster Annex, 14214. *Tel:* (716) 831-2304. *Film Serv Est:* 1950. *In Charge:* William E. Goll, Media Library Supervisor. *AV Staff:* 6 (2 prof, 2 cl, 2 tech). *Film Sel:* faculty/staff recommendations.
Film Rental Serv *Eligibility:* no restrictions. *Restrictions:* only in U.S. Cannot transmit electronically. *Rental Period:* 3 days. *Total Yr Film Booking:* 6247.
Film Collection 1200t/1250p. Approx 50t acquired annually. *Circ:* 16mm, 1180t/1230p; 8mm reel, 2t/p; S8mm reel, 2t/p; S8mm cartridge, 15t/p. *Pubns:* catalog, every 2 yrs; suppl, in yr catalog not published.
Other Film Serv Rent film from distributors for patrons, obtain film from other libraries, film reference serv. Permanent viewing facility.
Other Media Collections *Audio:* disc, 33⅓ rpm, 300t/c; tape, reel, 150t/c. *Filmstrips:* sound, 25t/c; silent, 450t/c. *Slides:* sets, 140t/c.
Budget & Expenditures No separate budget. *Member:* EFLA, FLIC.

Cooperstown

S- NATIONAL BASEBALL HALL OF FAME & MUSEUM, INC., Library, 13326. *Tel:* (607) 547-9988. *Film Serv Est:* 1968. *In Charge:* John F. Redding, Librarian. *AV Staff:* 2 (2 tech). *Film Sel:* committee preview. *Holdings:* baseball 100%.
Free-Loan Film Serv *Eligibility:* org members. Available to researchers/scholars for on-site viewing. May borrow by mail.
Film Collection 209t/378p. *Pubns:* catalog, as needed.
Other Film Serv Film reference serv, library film programs. Permanent viewing facility.
Budget & Expenditures No separate budget.

Corning

S- CORNING MUSEUM OF GLASS, Centerway, 14830. *Tel:* (607) 937-5371, ext 2. *Film Sel:* staff recommendations. *Holdings:* glass.
Film Rental Serv *Eligibility:* no restrictions. *Restrictions:* only in U.S. Cannot use for fund-raising, transmit electronically. *Rental Period:* 7 days. *Total Yr Film Booking:* 100. Produce slides.
Film Collection 69t. Approx 5t acquired annually. *Pubns:* catalog, as needed.
Other Film Serv Permanent viewing facility available for rent to community.
Other Media Collections *Filmstrips:* sound, 2t/c. *Slides:* single, 500t/c.
Budget & Expenditures No separate budget. *Member:* ALA, N.Y. Library Assn, South Central Research Library Council.

P- SOUTHERN TIER LIBRARY SYSTEM, Civic Center Plaza, 14830. *Tel:* (607) 962-3141. *Film Serv Est:* 1961. *In Charge:* Genevieve Neu, Reference/Interloan Librarian. *AV Staff:* 4 p-t (2 prof, 1 cl, 1 tech). *Film Sel:* committee preview. *Holdings:* children's films 25%.
Free-Loan Film Serv *Eligibility:* civic groups, religious groups, & others, such as non-profit groups (not schools) within our 33 member libraries. *Restrictions:* for inst, only in Alleghany, Chemung, Schuyler, Steuben and Yates counties. Cannot borrow for classroom use. May borrow by mail. *Loan Period:* varies. *Total Yr Film Loan:* 1185.
Film Collection 265t/268p. Approx 25t acquired annually. *Circ:* 16mm, 265t/268p. *Pubns:* catalog, as needed; suppl, no set policy.
Other Film Serv Obtain film from coop loan system (N.Y. State Library, South Central Research Library Council), library film programs. Permanent viewing facility available free to community. *Equipment:* lend 16mm sound projector (5), projection screens (6).
Other Media Collections *Audio:* disc, 33⅓ rpm, 3084t/6226c; tape, cassette, 655c. *Filmstrips:* sound sets, 23c; silent sets, 3c. *Slides:* single, 8t/112c; sets, 3c.
Budget & Expenditures Total library budget $42,000 (FY 1/1/75-1/1/76). Total FY film budget $6000. *Member:* ALA, N.Y. Library Assn.

Cornwall-on-Hudson

P- CORNWALL PUBLIC LIBRARY, 24 Idlewild Ave, 12520. *Tel:* (914) 534-8282. *In Charge:* Leslie Weirman, Dir. *AV Staff:* 4 (4 cl). *Film Sel:* committee preview.
Free-Loan Film Serv *Eligibility:* org members, educational inst except public schools, civic & religious groups, indiv with library cards. *Restrictions:* for indiv & inst, only in our library system. Cannot use for fund-raising, transmit electronically, borrow for classroom use. Available to researchers/scholars for on-site viewing. May borrow by mail. *Loan Period:* 3 days. *Total Yr Film Loan:* 70.
Film Collection 859t.
Other Film Serv Obtain film from coop loan system (Ramapo Catskill Library System), film reference serv, film fairs/festivals, library film programs. *Equipment:* lend 16mm sound projector (1), projection screens, sound filmstrips projectors & cassette players.
Other Media Collections *Audio:* disc, 33⅓ rpm, 714t/c. *Filmstrips:* sound sets, 7t/c. *Member:* ALA, EFLA, N.Y. Library Assn.

Cortland

C- STATE UNIVERSITY COLLEGE AT CORTLAND, Sperry Learning Resources Center, Closed Circuit TV Dept, 13045. *Tel:* (607) 753-4117. *Video Serv Est:* 1967. *Video Staff:* 4 f-t, 1 tech. *Video Use:* instructional television. Video serv available by appointment. Produce video tapes. Have production studio/space & separate control room.

Cortland (cont'd)

Video Equipment/Facilities *In-House Use Only:* portapak (1), ½" b&w, Sony 3400; recording deck (3), ¾" b&w/col, Sony 1800; playback deck (1), ½" b&w/col, Sony 8600; editing deck (2), ¾" b&w/col, Sony 2850; studio camera (2), col, Sony DCX1200; monitor (2), col, Sony PVM9100; SEG (1), Shintron; lighting (20); microphones (15); editor (1). Have permanent viewing installation. Provide training in use of equipment to students in television program. Have tape duplication serv.

Video Tape Loan/Rental/Sale Serv *Serv Provided:* swap with other inst. *Loan Eligibility:* educational inst. *Restrictions:* for inst, none. Cannot air without permission.

Video Collection Maintained by own production, exchange/swap. Use/play ½" reel to reel, ¾" cassette. *Sources:* exchange (other SUNY colleges, N.Y. Network, State Education Dept). *Tape Sel:* preview, faculty/staff recommendations. Tapes organized by subject. *Collection, Color:* ¾" cassette, 30t/c. *Collection, B&W:* ½" reel, 60t/c; ¾" cassette, 40t/c. *Pubns:* catalog.

Cable & CCTV Will receive serv of cable TV system. Have CCTV in inst, with 120 monitors. *Programming Sources:* tapes produced by inst, tapes supplied by other institutions.

East Islip

P- EAST ISLIP PUBLIC LIBRARY, 381 E Main St, 11730. *Tel:* (516) 581-9200. *Film Serv Est:* 1967. *In Charge:* Gertrude Schweibish, Dir. *AV Staff:* ½ (½ prof). *Film Sel:* staff recommendations, published reviews, some previews. *Holdings:* children's films.

Free-Loan Film Serv *Eligibility:* indiv with library cards. *Restrictions:* for indiv, only in city. Cannot borrow for classroom use. Available to researchers/scholars for on-site viewing. May not borrow by mail. *Loan Period:* 6 days.

Film Collection 37t/p. *Circ:* 16mm, 8t/p; 8mm reel, 29t/p.

Other Film Serv Obtain film from coop loan system (Suffolk Cooperative Library System), library film programs. Permanent viewing facility available free to community. *Equipment:* lend S8mm camera (1), 16mm sound projector (2), S8mm cartridge projector (1), projection screens (1).

Other Media Collections *Audio:* disc, 33⅓ rpm, 2637t; disc, tape, cassette, 329t. *Slides:* single, 2200t.

Budget & Expenditures Total library budget $72,400 (FY 7/1/75-7/1/76). Total FY film budget $500. *Member:* ALA, N.Y. Library Assn, Suffolk County Library Assn.

Video Serv *Est:* 1973. *In Charge:* G. Schweibish, Dir. *Video Staff:* 1 p-t. *Video Use:* documentation of community events, to increase community's library use, community video access. Video serv available by appointment. Produce video tapes.

Video Equipment/Facilities *For Loan:* portapak (2), b&w, Panasonic NV3085, JVC PV4500; monitor (1), b&w, Hitachi P-43M; lighting (3); microphones (4); tripods (1); audio tape recorders (9). *Equipment Loan Period:* no set policy. Provide training in use of equipment to volunteers, senior citizens.

Video Collection Maintained by own production. Use/play ½" reel to reel, ¾" cassette. Tapes organized by subject. *Other Video Serv:* programming, production workshops.

Cable & CCTV Receive serv of cable TV system.

Elmira

C- ELMIRA COLLEGE, Gannett-Tripp Learning Center, 14901. *Tel:* (607) 734-3911, ext 287. *Film Serv Est:* 1950. *In Charge:* Beth Woodard, Reference, Media. *AV Staff:* 5 (2 prof, 1 cl, 2 tech). *Film Sel:* faculty/staff recommendations. *Holdings:* early childhood education.

Free-Loan Film Serv *Eligibility:* staff & students. *Restrictions:* for indiv, only through South Central Research Library Council. Cannot use for fund-raising, transmit electronically or reproduce. Available to researchers/scholars for on-site viewing. May not borrow by mail. *Loan Period:* 1 day. *Total Yr Film Loan:* 290. Produce video tapes.

Film Collection 160t/p. Approx 40t acquired annually. *Circ:* 16mm, 160t/p. *Pubns:* catalog, annual; suppl, monthly.

Other Film Serv Rent film from distributors for patrons, obtain film from coop loan system (South Central Research Library Council), obtain film from other libraries, film reference serv, film fairs/festivals. Permanent viewing facility available for rent to community. *Equipment:* lend S8mm camera (6), 16mm camera (4), 16mm sound projector (34), 8mm reel projector (1), S8mm cartridge projector (2), S8mm reel projector (2), projection tables & stands, projection screens.

Other Media Collections *Audio:* disc, 33⅓ rpm, 1700t; tape, cassette, 1500t. *Filmstrips:* sound sets, 500t. *Slides:* single, 10,000t.

Budget & Expenditures No separate budget. *Member:* ALA, N.Y. Library Assn.

Video Serv *Est:* 1973. *In Charge:* Ed Subkis, Production Coord. *Video Staff:* 5 f-t, 3 tech. *Video Use:* documentation of school events, in-service training, practical video/TV training courses, classroom use. Video serv available by appointment. Produce video tapes.

Video Equipment/Facilities *In-House Use Only:* playback deck (1), ½" b&w, Sony. *For Loan:* portapak (4), Sony AV3400, 2400; recording deck (4), ½" b&w, Sony; playback deck (1), ½" b&w, Sony 3650; studio camera (1); monitor (11), b&w, Sony, Motorola; additional camera lenses (4); microphones (70); tripods (4); audio tape recorders (67). Have permanent viewing installation. *Equipment Loan Period:* varies with need. Provide training in use of equipment to faculty & students.

Video Tape Loan/Rental/Sale Serv *Serv Provided:* free loan, swap with other inst. *Loan Eligibility:* staff & students. *Restrictions:* for indiv, interlibrary loan. Cannot use for fund-raising, duplicate, air without permission. May not borrow by mail. *Total Yr Tape Loan:* 50.

Video Collection Maintained by own production, exchange/swap. Use/play ½" reel to reel. *Sources:* community productions, exchange (Southern Central Research Library Council, N.Y. State Education Dept). *Member:* Southern Central Research Library Council. *Tape Sel:* faculty/staff recommendations. Tapes organized numerically. *Collection, B&W:* ½" reel, 45t/c. *Other Video Serv:* programming, reference serv.

Cable & CCTV Receive serv of cable TV system. Produce programs for cablecasting. Serve as production facility for others. Have CCTV in inst, with 24 monitors. *Programming Sources:* over-the-air commercial & public broadcasting, tapes produced by inst, tapes produced professionally, tapes produced by community groups & indiv.

Farmingdale

P- FARMINGDALE PUBLIC LIBRARY, Main St, 11735. *Tel:* (516) 249-9090. *Film Serv:* 1956. *In Charge:* Orrin B. Dow, Dir. *AV Staff:* 3 (1 prof, 1 cl, 1 tech). *Film Sel:* committee preview.

Free-Loan Film Serv *Eligibility:* indiv with library cards. *Restrictions:* for indiv, none. Available to researchers/scholars for on-site viewing. May not borrow by mail. *Loan Period:* 1 day. *Total Yr Film Loan:* 890.

Film Collection 68t/70p. Approx 10-15t acquired annually. *Circ:* 16mm, 68t/70p. *Pubns:* catalog, annual.

Other Film Serv Rent film from distributors for patrons, obtain film from coop loan system (Nassau Library System), obtain film from other libraries, film reference serv, film fairs/festivals, library film programs. Permanent viewing facility available for rent to community. *Equipment:* lend 16mm sound projector (5).

Other Media Collections *Audio:* disc, 33⅓ rpm, 2540c; tape, cassette, 650c.

Budget & Expenditures Total library budget $60,700 (FY 7/1/74-7/1/75). Total FY film budget $4000. *Member:* EFLA.

C- STATE UNIVERSITY OF NEW YORK, AGRICULTURAL & TECHNICAL COLLEGE, Thomas T. Greenley Hall Library, 11735. *Tel:* (516) 429-2222. *In Charge:* George Jacobus, Dir, Instructional Resources. *Video Staff:* 5 f-t. *Video Use:* practical video/TV training courses. Video serv available by appointment. Produce video tapes. Have production studio/space & separate control room.

Video Equipment/Facilities *In-House Use Only:* portapak (2), b&w, Sony Rover II; recording deck (4), ¾″, 1″ b&w; IVC870, 800, JVC 5000; playback deck (2), ¾″ col; studio camera (2), 1″ b&w, Ampex 927; monitor (9); SEG (1); additional camera lenses (4); lighting (45); microphones (6); tripods (6); audio tape recorders (15). Have permanent viewing installation. Provide training in use of equipment to faculty & students.

Video Collection Maintained by purchase, own production. Use/play ½″, 1″ reel to reel, ¾″ cassette. *Tape Sel:* preview, catalogs. Tapes organized by subject. *Collection, B&W:* ½″ reel, 6t/c; 1″ reel, 20t/c; ¾″ cassette, 50t/c. *Other Video Serv:* production workshops.

Cable & CCTV Have CCTV in inst.

Flushing

C- QUEENS COLLEGE, Portable Video Access, 65-30 Kissena Blvd, 11361. *Tel:* (212) 520-7408. *Video Serv Est:* 1971. *Video Staff:* 3 f-t, 1 tech. *Video Use:* documentation of community/school events, in-service training, practical video/TV training courses. Video serv available by appointment. Produce video tapes.

Video Equipment/Facilities *In-House Use Only:* editing deck (4), ½″ col, Panasonic 3130; monitor (4), b&w/col, Sony. *For Loan:* portapak (14), ½″ b&w/col, Sony AV8400, 3400; monitor (2), b&w/col, Sony; SEG (1), Adwar; lighting (5); microphones (15). Have permanent viewing installation. *Equipment Loan Period:* 2 days. Provide training in use of equipment to faculty & students. Have tape duplication serv.

Video Tape Loan/Rental/Sale Serv *Serv Provided:* free loan, swap with other inst, sale. *Loan Eligibility:* staff & students. *Restrictions:* for indiv, none. May not borrow by mail.

Video Collection Maintained by own production. Use/play ½″ reel to reel. *Other Video Serv:* production workshops. *Pubns:* catalog.

Cable & CCTV Will recieve serv of cable TV system. Inform public about cable system serv & facilities. Serve as production facility for others. Have CCTV in inst. *Programming Sources:* tapes produced by inst.

Freeport

P- FREEPORT MEMORIAL LIBRARY, S Ocean Ave & Merrick Rd, 11520. *Tel:* (516) 379-3274. *Film Serv Est:* 1959. *In Charge:* Gerald Nichols, Public Servs Librarian. *AV Staff:* 2 (1 prof, 1 cl, 3 tech). *Film Sel:* committee preview. *Holdings:* children's films 50%.

Free-Loan Film Serv *Eligibility:* educational inst. *Restrictions:* for inst, only in city. May not borrow by mail. *Loan Period:* 2 days. *Total Yr Film Loan:* 2374.

Film Rental Serv *Eligibility:* no restrictions. *Restrictions:* only in city. *Rental Period:* 2 days. *Total Yr Film Booking:* 2374.

Film Collection 475t/p. Approx 15t acquired annually. *Circ:* 16mm, 450t; S8mm reel, 25t. *Pubns:* catalog, every 2 yrs; suppl, no set policy.

Other Film Serv Rent film from distributors for patrons, obtain film from coop loan system (Nassau Library System), obtain film from other libraries, library film programs. *Equipment:* lend 16mm sound projector (3).

Budget & Expenditures Total library budget $529,360 (FY 6/1/74-6/1/75). Total FY film budget $2500. *Member:* EFLA.

Garden City

C- ADELPHI UNIVERSITY, Communications Dept, South Ave, 11530. *Tel:* (516) 294-8700, ext 7370. *Film Serv Est:* 1971. *In Charge:* Paul Pitcoff, Chairman. *AV Staff:* 2. *Film Sel:* produce own.

Film Rental Serv *Eligibility:* no restrictions. *Restrictions:* none. *Rental Period:* 5 days. Sell films. Produce films.

Other Film Serv Rent film from distributors for patrons. Permanent viewing facility. *Equipment:* lend/rent S8mm camera, 16mm camera, 16mm sound projector, 8mm reel projector, S8mm reel projector, projection tables & stands, projection screens.

Budget & Expenditures No separate budget.

Video Serv *Est:* 1972. *In Charge:* Leonard Price, Dir, Instructional Media. *Video Staff:* 2 f-t, 1 p-t, 1 tech. *Video Use:* documentation of community/school events, in-service training, practical video/TV training courses, playback only of professionally produced tapes, as art form. Video serv available by appointment. Produce video tapes. Have production studio/space & separate control room.

Video Equipment/Facilities *For Loan:* portapak (5), ½″ b&w, Sony AV3400; recording deck (7), ½″ b&w, Sony AV3600; playback deck (7), ½″ b&w, Sony; editing deck (2), ½″ b&w/col, Sony AV3650, 8650; studio camera (3), GBC; SEG (1). Have permanent & portable viewing installations. *Equipment Loan Period:* no set policy. Provide training in use of equipment to faculty & students. Have tape duplication serv.

Video Tape Loan/Rental/Sale Serv *Serv Provided:* free loan, swap with other inst, rental, sale. *Loan/Rental Eligibility:* staff & students, educational inst, civic groups, religious groups, prof groups. *Restrictions:* for indiv & inst, none. Cannot duplicate, air without permission. May borrow by mail. *Loan Period:* 7 days.

Video Collection Maintained by own production. Use/play ½″, 1″ reel to reel, ¾″ cassette. *Sources:* produce own. *Other Video Serv:* programming, taping of other media, production workshops.

Gloversville

P- GLOVERSVILLE FREE LIBRARY, 58 E Fulton St, 12078. *Tel:* (518) 725-2819. *Film Serv Est:* 1940. *In Charge:* Alyce Lanphere, Film Librarian. *AV Staff:* 1 (1 cl).

Free-Loan Film Serv *Eligibility:* civic groups, religious groups, indiv with library cards. *Restrictions:* for indiv, interlibrary loan; for inst, none. Cannot borrow for classroom use. *Loan Period:* 4-6 days. *Total Yr Film Loan:* 200.

Film Collection 96t/100p. *Circ:* 16mm, 96t.

Other Film Serv Obtain film from coop loan system (Mohawk Valley Library Assn), library film programs.

Other Meda Collections *Audio:* disc, 33⅓ rpm, 1400t; tape, cassette, 20t; tape, reel, 1t.

Budget & Expenditures Total library budget $13,000 (FY 1/1/75-1/1/76). No separate AV budget. *Member:* N.Y. Library Assn, Tryon Library Associates.

Hamburg

C- HILBERT COLLEGE, Learning Resource Center, 5200 S Park Ave, 14075. *Tel:* (716) 649-7900, ext 15/54. *Video Serv Est:* 1972. *In Charge:* Sister M. Tiburtia, Dir of LRC. *Video Staff:* 2 f-t, 4 p-t. *Video Use:* to increase community's library use. Video serv available by appointment. Produce video tapes.

Video Equipment/Facilities *In-House Use Only:* portapak (1), b&w, Sony; recording deck (1), b&w, Sony; playback deck (1), b&w, Sony; monitor (2), b&w, Emerson, RCA; tripods (1). Provide training in use of equipment to faculty & students.

Video Collection Maintained by purchase, own production. Use/play ½″ reel to reel.

Herkimer

C- HERKIMER COUNTY COMMUNITY COLLEGE, Instructional Resource Center, Reservoir Rd, 13350. *Tel:* (315) 866-0300, ext 56. *Film Serv Est:* 1968. *In Charge:* David A. Tiedemann, Assistant Librarian/Instructional Resources. *AV Staff:* 3 (1 prof, 1 cl, 1 tech). *Film Sel:* faculty/staff recommendations, college librarian's decision.

Free-Loan Film Serv *Eligibility:* staff. *Restrictions:* for indiv, only on campus. Cannot use for fund-raising, transmit electronically. Available to researchers/scholars for on-site viewing. May not borrow by mail. *Loan Period:* 7 days. *Total Yr Film Loan:* 699. Produce films. Produce audio, video, photographic, graphics.

Herkimer (cont'd)

Film Collection 237t/p. Approx 10-20t acquired annually. *Circ:* 16mm, 20t; S8mm cartridge, 217t. Publish listings in library publication.

Other Film Serv Rent film from distributors for patrons. Permanent viewing facility. *Equipment:* lend S8mm camera (1), 16mm camera (1), 16mm sound projector (13), S8mm cartridge projector (5), S8mm reel projector (1), projection tables & stands (20), projection screens (30).

Other Media Collections *Audio:* disc, 33⅓ rpm, 1018t/1200c; tape, cassette, 460t/550c; tape, reel, 216t/280c. *Filmstrips:* total 202t/240c. *Slides:* single, 215t/4000c.

Budget & Expenditures Total library budget $48,661 (FY 9/1/74-9/1/75). Total FY film budget $12,000. *Member:* AECT, ALA.

Video Serv *In Charge:* David A. Tiedemann, Assistant Librarian, Instructional Resources. *Video Use:* documentation of community/school events, playback only of professionally produced tapes. Video serv available by appointment. Produce video tapes. Have production studio/space & separate control room.

Video Equipment/Facilities *In-House Use Only:* recording & playback decks (2), ½", 1" b&w/col, Sony 3600, 8600, IVC825A; studio camera (2), b&w, DAGE 800; monitor (22), b&w/col; microphones (10); tripods (5); audio tape recorders (40). *For Loan:* portapak (3), ½" b&w, Sony AV3400; recording & playback decks (5), ½", 1" b&w/col, Sony, IVC; editing deck (4), ½" b&w/col, Sony 3650, Panasonic NV3130; SEG (1), Shintron; lighting (1); microphones (10); tripods (5); audio tape recorders (40), video projector (1). Have portable viewing installation. *Equipment Loan Period:* 2 weeks. Provide training in use of equipment to students.

Video Tape Loan/Rental/Sale Serv *Serv Provided:* free loan. *Loan Eligibility:* staff & students. *Restrictions:* for indiv, only in city. Cannot use for fund-raising, duplicate, air without permission. May not borrow by mail. *Loan Period:* 7 days.

Video Collection Maintained by purchase, rental, own production. Use/play ½", 1" reel to reel. *Sources:* commercial distributors, exchange (N.Y. State agencies). *Tape Sel:* preview, faculty/staff recommendations, published reviews, catalogs. Tapes organized by accession number. *Collection, Color:* ½" reel, 70t; 1" reel, 2t. *Collection, B&W:* ½" reel, 90t. *Other Video Serv:* taping of other media, production workshops. *Pubns:* listings of holdings in library bulletin.

Cable & CCTV Receive serv of cable TV system. Produce programs for cablecasting. Have CCTV in inst, with 10 monitors. *Programming Sources:* tapes produced professionally.

Hudson

C- COLUMBIA-GREENE COMMUNITY COLLEGE, Box 1000, 12534. *Tel:* (518) 828-4181, ext 62. *Video Serv Est:* 1973. *In Charge:* Tobe J. Carey, AV-TV Coord. *Video Staff:* 1 p-t. *Video Use:* documentation of community/school events, community video access, in-service training, practical video/TV training courses, as art form. Video serv available by appointment. Produce video tapes. Have production studio/space.

Video Equipment/Facilities *In-House Use Only:* portapak (2), ½" b&w/col, Sony 3400, 8400; recording deck (3), ½" b&w/col, Sony 3600, 3650, 8650; playback deck (1), ½" col, JVC; editing deck (1), ½" b&w/col, Sony; monitor (5), b&w/col, Sony, Panasonic, RCA; SEG (1), Anvel; lighting (1); microphones (7); tripods (3); audio tape recorders (3). *For Loan:* portapak (2), ½" b&w/col, Sony 3400, 8400; recording deck (3), ½" b&w/col, Sony 3600, 3650, 8650; playback deck (1), ½" col, JVC; editing deck (1), ½" b&w/col, Sony; monitor (5), b&w/col, Sony, Panasonic, RCA; SEG (1), Avtel; lighting (1); microphones (7); tripods (3); audio tape recorders (3). Have portable viewing installation. *Equipment Loan Period:* 2 days. Provide training in use of equipment to students. Have tape duplication serv.

Video Tape Loan/Rental/Sale Serv *Serv Provided:* free loan, swap with other inst. *Loan Eligibility:* staff & students, educational inst, with library cards, prof groups, such as media businesses. *Restrictions:* for indiv & inst, only in Columbia &

Greene Counties. Cannot use for fund-raising, duplicate, air without permission. May not borrow by mail. *Loan Period:* 7 days. *Total Yr Tape Loan:* 10.

Video Collection Maintained by own production, exchange/swap. Use/play ½" reel to reel. *Sources:* community productions, exchange, student production. Tapes organized by subject. *Collection, B&W:* ½" reel, 70t/c.

Cable & CCTV Will receive serv of cable TV system.

Huntington

S- INTER MEDIA ART CENTER INC., 81 Bay Ave, 11743. *Tel:* (516) 549-0939. *Video Serv Est:* 1974. *In Charge:* Michael Rothbard, Executive Dir. *Video Staff:* 3 f-t, 2 p-t, 1 tech. *Video Use:* community video access, as sales tool. Video serv available by appointment. Produce video tapes. Have production studio/space & separate control room.

Video Equipment/Facilities *In-House Use Only:* portapak (1), ½" b&w/col, Sony 8400; recording deck (3), ½", 1" b&w/col, Sony 3600, 8650; editing deck (2), b&w/col, Sony; studio camera (4), b&w/col, DXC 1600; monitor (3), b&w/col; Com 1720; keyer (2), Shintron, Panasonic; additional camera lenses (3); microphones (1); audio tape recorders (3). *For Loan:* portapak (5), ½" b&w/col, Sony 8400; recording deck (1), ½", 1" b&w/col, Sony 3600, 8650; editing deck (2), b&w/col, Sony; studio camera (4), b&w/col, DXC 1600; monitor (6), b&w/col, Com 1720; additional camera lenses (2); microphones (4); audio tape recorders (1). Have portable viewing installation. *Equipment Loan Period:* according to need. Provide training in use of equipment to any individual or group. Have tape duplication serv.

Video Tape Loan/Rental/Sale Serv *Serv Provided:* swap with other inst, rental. *Loan/Rental Eligibility:* org members, educational inst, & others, such as any nonprofit arts organization or individual artist. *Restrictions:* for indiv & inst, only in Nassau, Suffolk & Queens Counties. Cannot air without permission. May borrow by mail. *Loan Period:* 5 days.

Video Collection Maintained by own production. Use/play ½" reel to reel. *Sources:* own production, support independent producers who apply. *Tape Sel:* preview. *Special Collections:* video as art. *Other Video Serv:* programming, taping of other media, production workshops.

Cable & CCTV Will receive serv of cable TV system.

Ithaca

C- CORNELL UNIVERSITY, Listening Rooms, Uris Library, 14853. *Tel:* (607) 256-3342. *AV Staff:* 2 (1 prof). *Film Sel:* committee preview. *Holdings:* fine arts 75%. Produce sound/silent & small gauge video.

Film Collection 20t/25p. Approx 1t acquired annually. *Noncirc:* 16mm, 20t/25p.

Other Film Serv Film reference serv. *Equipment:* lend 16mm sound projector (1), 8mm cartridge projector (1).

Other Media Collections *Audio:* tape, total, 2500t/c. *Slides:* sets, 5t/c.

Budget & Expenditures No separate AV budget.

C- ITHACA COLLEGE, School of Communication, Performing Arts Bldg G24A, 14850. *Tel:* (607) 274-3242, ext 8. *Video Serv Est:* 1972. *In Charge:* Paul Smith, Dir TV Operations. *Video Staff:* 1 f-t, 2 p-t, 2 tech. *Video Use:* documentation of community/school events, to increase community's library use, practical video/TV training courses, playback only of professionally produced tapes. Video serv available by appointment. Produce video tapes. Have production studio/space & separate control room.

Video Equipment/Facilities Studio equipment includes IVC 960 (2); Ampex 7800C, 1100 (in MCR); time base correctors (2); film chain (2), b&w/col, IVC, Diamond; production switcher (4), Riker, various; audio control board (3); camera (5), b&w/col, GE, IVC, Telemation; record/playback deck (5), Ampex 5100, 7500, 7500C; portapak (1), EIAJ col, Sony. Note: The above equipment is shared by the Video Distribution Center, School of

Communication, and Instructional Resources Center. Have permanent & portable viewing installations. Provide training in use of equipment to faculty & students. Have tape duplication serv.

Video Tape Loan Serv *Serv Provided:* swap with other inst, sale. *Loan Eligibility:* org members, staff & students, educational inst, & others, such as area libraries, primary & secondary schools. *Restrictions:* for indiv, only in county; for inst, SUNY. Cannot use for fund-raising, duplicate, air without permission. May not borrow by mail.

Video Collection Maintained by own production, swap. Use/play ½″, 1″, 2″ reel to reel, ¾″ cassette. *Special Collections:* in-house training tapes. Tapes organized by in-house system. *Other Video Serv:* cable TV for community.

Cable & CCTV Receive serv of cable TV system. Produce programs for cablecasting. Inform public about cable system serv & facilities. Have CCTV in inst, with 20 monitors. *Programming Sources:* tapes produced by inst, free-loan films. CCTV systems of distribution are as follows: (1) in-house CCTV system for TVR faculty, (2) on-campus CCTV system serving 25 locations, (3) on-campus cut-out system on cable channel 6 interlocking with community cable system, (4) switchable head-end arrangement on cable channel 7 reaching all community members on Cerrache Cable System.

P- **TOMPKINS COUNTY PUBLIC LIBRARY**, 312 N Cayuga St, 14850. *Tel:* (607) 272-2782. *Video Serv Est:* 1976. *In Charge:* Lajos Mezgar, Dir. *Video Use:* documentation of community events, to increase community's library use. Video serv available by appointment. Produce video tapes.

Video Equipment/Facilities *In-House Use Only:* portapak (1), b&w, Sony AV3400, 8400; recording deck (3), col, Sony AV8650; editing deck, 1 col, Sony AV 8650; monitor (2), col, Sony; microphones (2); tripods (1). Have portable viewing installation. Provide training in use of equipment to library staff & volunteer help.

Video Tape Loan/Rental/Sale Serv *Serv Provided:* free loan. *Loan Eligibility:* org members & volunteer help. *Restrictions:* for indiv, only Tomkins County Library staff & Finger Lakes Library System staff. Cannot air without permission. May not borrow by mail.

Video Collection Maintained by rental, own production. Use/play ½″ reel to reel, ¾″ cassette. *Sources:* commercial distributors, community productions. *Tape Sel:* preview, published reviews. *Special Collections:* own productions & rentals. Tapes organized by subject. *Collection, B&W:* ¾″ cassette, 2t/c. *Other Video Serv:* programming.

Cable & CCTV Produce programs for cablecasting. Inform public about cable system serv & facilities.

Jamestown

P- **CHAUTAUQUA-CATTARAUGUS LIBRARY SYSTEM**, 106 W Fifth St, 14701. *Tel:* (716) 484-7135, ext 24. *Film Serv Est:* 1966. *In Charge:* Jean Haynes, Film Librarian. *AV Staff:* 2½ (1 prof, 1½ cl). *Film Sel:* chief film librarian's decision. *Holdings:* animated films, children's films, documentaries, experimental films, film as art, fine arts, social sciences.

Free-Loan Film Serv *Eligibility:* staff & students, civic groups, religious groups, indiv with library cards, prof groups. *Restrictions:* for indiv, interlibrary loan, only in Chautauqua & Cattaraugus counties; for inst, only in Chautauqua & Cattaraugus counties. Cannot use for fund-raising, transmit electronically, borrow for classroom (without a contract with school). Available to researchers/scholars for on-site viewing. May borrow by mail. *Loan Period:* 1-2 weeks. *Total Yr Film Loan:* 10,439.

Film Rental Serv *Eligibility:* educational org, schools & out-of-area institutions if they have contract. *Restrictions:* only in Chautauqua & Cattaraugus Counties & neighboring counties of N.Y. & Pa. Cannot use for fund-raising, transmit electronically. *Rental Period:* 1-2 weeks. *Total Yr Film Booking:* 941.

Film Collection 586t/p. Approx 50t acquired annually. *Circ:* 16mm, 586t/597p. *Pubns:* catalog, as needed; suppl, no set policy.

Other Film Serv Obtain film from coop loan system (Western N.Y. Library Resources, N.Y. State Special Serv Film), obtain film from other libraries, film reference serv, film fairs/festivals, library film programs. Permanent viewing facility available for rent to community. *Equipment:* lend 16mm sound projector (13), 8mm reel projector (3), S8mm reel projector (3), projection tables & stands (5), projection screens (5), loudspeakers, cassette recorders, filmstrip & slide projectors.

Budget & Expenditures Total library budget $40,576 (FY 1/1/74-1/1/75). Total FY film budget $16,420. *Member:* ALA, EFLA, FLIC, N.Y. Library Assn, N.Y. State Educational Communications, Western N.Y. Educational Communications.

Video Serv *Est:* 1975. *In Charge:* Jean Haynes, AV/Film Librarian. *Video Staff:* 2 f-t, 1 p-t. *Video Use:* documentation of community/school events, to increase community's library use, community video access, in-service training, practical video/TV training courses, playback only of professionally produced tapes, as art form. Video serv available by appointment. Produce video tapes. Have production studio/space.

Video Equipment/Facilities *For Loan:* portapak (1), b&w, Sony AVC 3450; recording deck (1), b&w, Sony AV 8400; playback deck (1), b&w, Sony AV 8400; editing deck (1), b&w, Sony AV 8650; monitor (1), b&w, Sony CVM 115; microphones (2); tripods (1); audio tape recorders (2). Have permanent viewing installation. *Equipment Loan Period:* no set policy. Provide training in use of equipment to students.

Video Tape Loan/Rental/Sale Serv *Serv Provided:* free loan, swap with other inst. *Loan Eligibility:* org members, prof groups. *Restrictions:* for indiv & inst, only in Chautauqua & Cattaraugus Counties. Cannot use for fund-raising, air without permission.

Video Collection Maintained by own production. Use/play ½″ reel to reel. *Sources:* galleries, community productions. *Collection, Color:* ½″ reel, 6t/c. *Collection, B&W:* ½″ reel, 6t/c. *Other Video Serv:* programming, reference serv, taping of other media, production workshops. *Pubns:* catalog.

Cable & CCTV Receive serv of cable TV system. Produce programs for cablecasting. Inform public about cable system serv & facilities. Serve as production facility for others. Actively promote local cable station.

Johnstown

C- **FULTON-MONTGOMERY COMMUNITY COLLEGE**, Route 67, 12095. *Tel:* (518) 762-4651, ext 396. *Film Serv Est:* 1968. *In Charge:* Eleanor Ferris, Administrator AV Serv. *AV Staff:* 3 (2 prof, 1 cl, 1 tech). *Film Sel:* committee preview, faculty/staff recommendations. *Holdings:* business 4%, dance 1%, physical education, 4%, science 85%, social sciences 10%.

Free-Loan Film Serv *Eligibility:* staff & students, educational inst, civic groups, religious groups, indiv with library cards. *Restrictions:* for indiv & inst, only in Fulton & Montgomery Counties. Cannot use for fund-raising. Available to researchers/scholars for on-site viewing. May not borrow by mail. *Loan Period:* 7 days. *Total Yr Film Loan:* 200.

Film Collection 600t/p. Approx 5-10t acquired annually. *Circ:* 16mm, 100t/p; 8mm cartridge, 500t/p. Publish media directory which includes film collection.

Other Film Serv Rent film from distributors for patrons, obtain film from coop loan system (Mohawk Assn of Colleges & Universities, N.Y. State Educational SUNY System), obtain film from other libraries, film reference serv. Permanent viewing facility. *Equipment:* lend S8mm camera (2), 16mm sound projector (16), 8mm cartridge projector (2), 8mm reel projector (4), S8mm cartridge projector (6), S8mm reel projector (4), projection tables & stands (60), projection screens (10).

Other Media Collections *Audio:* disc, 33⅓ rpm, 2000t; tape, cassette, 1000t; tape, reel, 800t. *Filmstrips:* sound, 480t; silent, 75t; sound sets, 20t; silent sets, 5t. *Slides:* single, 800t; sets, 5t.

Budget & Expenditures No separate AV budget. *Member:* ALA, N.Y. Library Assn, N.Y. State Educational Communications Assn.

Johnstown (cont'd)

Video Serv *Est:* 1971. *In Charge:* Carol Bollinger, Asst Dir, AV. *Video Staff:* 2 f-t, 1 tech. *Video Use:* documentation of community/school events, in-service training, practical video/ TV training courses, playback only of professionally produced tapes. Video serv available by appointment. Produce video tapes. Have production studio/space & separate control room.

Video Equipment/Facilities *In-House Use Only:* recording deck (2), b&w; playback deck (7), b&w/col, Sony, Panasonic; studio camera (4), b&w, Sony; monitor (8), GE, Sony; SEG (1), Sony; microphones (10); tripods (3); audio tape recorders (55). Have permanent viewing installation. Provide training in use of equipment to faculty & students.

Video Tape Loan/Rental/Sale Serv *Serv Provided:* free loan. *Loan Eligibility:* staff & students, civic groups. *Restrictions:* for indiv & inst, only on our campus. Cannot use for fund-raising, duplicate, air without permission. May not borrow by mail.

Video Collection Maintained by purchase, rental, own production. Use/play ½″ reel to reel, ¾″ cassette. *Sources:* commercial distributors. *Tape Sel:* preview, faculty/staff recommendations, published reviews, catalogs. *Special Collections:* in-house training tapes, films in video format. Tapes organized by subject. *Collection, Color:* ¾″ cassette, 20t/c. *Collection, B&W:* ½″ reel, 150t/c. *Other Video Serv:* reference serv. *Pubns:* catalog.

Cable & CCTV Have CCTV in inst, with 8 monitors. *Programming Sources:* over-the-air commercial & public broadcasting, tapes produced by inst, tapes produced professionally.

Lanesville

S- MEDIA CENTER IN LANESVILLE, N.Y., 12450. *Tel:* (914) 688-7084. *Video Serv Est:* 1969. *Video Staff:* 7 f-t. *Video Use:* documentation of community/school events, community video access, practical video/TV training courses, as art form. Video serv available by appointment. Produce video tapes. Have production studio/space & separate control room.

Video Equipment/Facilities *In-House Use Only:* portapak; recording deck; playback deck; editing deck; studio camera; monitor; SEG; keyer; additional camera lenses; lighting; microphones; tripods; audio tape recorders. Have permanent & portable viewing installations. *Equipment Loan Period:* no set policy. Provide training in use of equipment. Have tape duplication serv.

Video Tape Loan/Rental/Sale Serv *Serv Provided:* free loan, swap with other inst, rental, sale. *Loan/Rental Eligibility:* any individual or group. *Restrictions:* for indiv & inst, none. Cannot use for fund-raising, duplicate, air without permission. May not borrow by mail.

Video Collection Maintained by own production, exchange/swap. Use/play ½″, 1″ reel to reel, ¾″ cassette. *Sources:* community productions, exchange. *Tape Sel:* preview, contributions. *Special Collections:* circus, comedy, new ideas. Tapes organized by subject. *Other Video Serv:* programming, production workshops, production & technical assistance, systems design, performances & shows. *Pubns:* catalog. Publish *Spaghetti City Video Manual*, a book for the nontechnician.

Cable & CCTV Inform public about cable system serv & facilities. Serve as production facility for others. Run cable programs for special audiences in other communities. Have CCTV in inst, with 3 monitors. *Programming Sources:* tapes produced by inst & by community groups & indiv.

Lawrence

P- PENINSULA PUBLIC LIBRARY, 280 Central Ave, 11559. *Tel:* (516) 239-3262. *Film Serv Est:* 1966. *In Charge:* Martin Landweber, Film Librarian. *AV Staff:* 1 (1 prof, 1 cl). *Film Sel:* committee preview. *Holdings:* animated films 5%, children's films 75%, feature films 10%, social sciences 10%.

Free-Loan Film Serv *Eligibility:* educational inst, civic groups, religious groups, indiv with library cards, prof groups.

Restrictions: for indiv, only in library district; for inst, only in library district. Cannot use for fund-raising. May not borrow by mail. *Loan Period:* 3 days. *Total Yr Film Loan:* 1660.

Film Collection 185t/p. Approx 25t acquired annually. *Circ:* 16mm, 85t/p; 8mm reel, 100t/p.

Other Film Serv Obtain film from coop loan system (Cooperative Film Circuit of Nassau County, Nassau Library System), library film programs. Permanent viewing facility available for rent to community. *Equipment:* lend 16mm sound projector (1), filmstrip projectors (2).

Other Media Collections *Audio:* disc, 33⅓ rpm, 2123t/ 2232c; tape, cassette, 1101t/1146c. *Filmstrips:* sound, 37t/c; silent, 23t/c; sound sets, 9t/c; silent sets, 1t/c.

Budget & Expenditures No separate AV budget. *Member:* EFLA, FLIC.

Long Beach

P- LONG BEACH PUBLIC LIBRARY, 111 W Park Ave, 11561. *Tel:* (516) 432-7201. *Film Serv Est:* 1965. *In Charge:* Jana M. Jevnikar, AV Librarian. *AV Staff:* 2 (1 prof, 2 tech). *Film Sel:* chief film librarian's decision.

Free-Loan Film Serv *Eligibility:* civic groups, religious groups, indiv with library cards. *Restrictions:* for indiv, only in school district; for inst, only in school district. Cannot use for fund-raising, transmit electronically, borrow for classroom use. *Loan Period:* 1-3 days. *Total Yr Film Loan:* 806.

Film Collection 130t/p. Approx 4t acquired annually. *Circ:* 16mm, 43t/p; 8mm reel, 87t/p.

Other Film Serv Obtain film from coop loan system (Cooperative Film Circuit, Nassau Library System), library film programs. Permanent viewing facility available for rent to community. *Equipment:* rent 16mm sound projector (2), 8mm reel projector (1), S8mm reel projector (1), projection screens (1), film strip projector (1), slide projector (1).

Other Media Collections *Audio:* disc, 33⅓ rpm, 2500t/c; tape, cassette, 719t/c. *Filmstrips:* sound sets, 21t/c.

Budget & Expenditures Total library budget $84,885 (FY 7/1/74-7/1/75). Total FY film budget $1000.

Massapequa

P- MASSAPEQUA PUBLIC LIBRARY, 523 Central Ave, 11758. *Tel:* (516) 798-4607. *Film Serv Est:* 1960. *In Charge:* Barbara Simpson, Film Librarian. *AV Staff:* 1½ (1 prof, ½ cl, ½ tech). *Film Sel:* staff recommendations, chief film librarian's decision.

Free-Loan Film Serv *Eligibility:* educational inst, civic groups, religious groups, indiv with library cards. *Restrictions:* for indiv, none; for inst, only in library district. Cannot use for fund-raising, transmit electronically. May not borrow by mail. *Loan Period:* 3 days. *Total Yr Film Loan:* 585.

Film Collection 34t/p. Approx 6t acquired annually. *Circ:* 16mm, 34t/p. *Pubns:* catalog, annual.

Other Film Serv Obtain film from coop loan system (Nassau Film Cooperative System; Nassau Library System), obtain film from other libraries, library film programs. Permanent viewing facility available for rent to community. *Equipment:* rent 16mm sound projector (2), lend projection screens (2).

Other Media Collections *Audio:* disc, 33⅓ rpm, 2145t/2671c; tape, cassette, 250t/300c. *Filmstrips:* sound, 130t/c; silent, 22t/c.

Budget & Expenditures Total library budget $102,790 (FY 7/1/74-7/1/75). Total FY film budget $1000.

Middletown

P- RAMAPO CATSKILL LIBRARY SYSTEM, Box 866, 619 North St, 10940. *Tel:* (916) 343-4133. *Film Serv Est:* 1967. *In Charge:* Sheryl Freeman, Senior Clerk. *AV Staff:* 2-3 (2-3 cl). *Film Sel:* committee preview.

Free-Loan Film Serv *Eligibility:* civic groups, indiv with library cards, prof groups. *Restrictions:* for indiv, only in our library system; for inst, only in our library system. Cannot use for fund-raising, transmit electronically, borrow for classroom use. May not borrow by mail. *Loan Period:* 2 days. *Total Yr Film Loan:* 15,000.

Film Collection 850t/p. Approx 75-125t acquired annually. *Circ:* 16mm, 850t/p. *Pubns:* catalog, every 2 yrs; suppl, in yr catalog not published.

Other Film Serv Obtain film from coop loan system (N.Y. State Library), library film programs. Permanent viewing facility available for rent to community. *Equipment:* lend 16mm sound projector, projection tables & stands, projection screens, filmstrip projectors, viewers.

Budget & Expenditures Total FY film budget $30,000. *Member:* EFLA, N.Y. Library Assn.

New Rochelle

P- **WESTCHESTER LIBRARY SYSTEM,** c/o New Rochelle Public Library, 662 Main St, 10805. *Tel:* (914) 576-2728. *In Charge:* Charlotte Moslander Newman, Film Librarian. *AV Staff:* 4½ (1 prof, 3 cl, ½ tech). *Film Sel:* committee preview.

Free-Loan Film Serv *Eligibility:* indiv with library cards. *Restrictions:* for indiv, only in Westchester County. Cannot use for fund-raising, transmit electronically, borrow for classroom use. Available to researchers/scholars for on-site viewing. May borrow by system delivery. *Loan Period:* 2 days. *Total Yr Film Loan:* 8962.

Film Collection 678t/699p. Approx 36t acquired annually. *Circ:* 16mm, 678t/699p. *Pubns:* catalog, as needed ($2); suppl, 6 mos cumulative index ($2).

Other Film Serv Obtain film from other libraries, film reference serv. Permanent viewing facility available to community. *Equipment:* lend 16mm sound projector (5), projection tables & stands (5), projection screens (5).

Budget & Expenditures Total FY film budget $20,000. *Member:* ALA, EFLA, FLIC, N.Y. Library Assn.

New York

S- **ANGSTROM PRODUCTIONS, INC,** 295 7th Ave, 10001. *Tel:* (212) 255-3070. *In Charge:* Philip K. Perlman, Pres. *Video Use:* in-service training, as art form, documentaries. Video serv available on demand & by appointment. Produce video tapes. Have production studio/space.

Video Equipment/Facilities *For Rent:* portapak (1), b&w/col, Sony; recording deck (1); playback deck (1); editing deck (1); studio camera (5); monitor (4); keyer (1); microphones (5); tripods (5); audio tape recorders (3). Have portable viewing installation. Provide training in use of equipment.

Video Tape Loan/Rental/Sale Serv *Serv Provided:* rental, sale. *Loan/Rental Eligibility:* org members.

Video Collection Maintained by own production. Use/play ½″, 1″, 2″ reel to reel, ¾″ cassette. *Special Collections:* video as art, documentaries. *Collection, Color:* ½″ reel, 10t; 1″ reel, 3t; ¾″ cassette, 2t. *Collection, B&W:* ½″ reel, 15t; 1″ reel, 1t. *Other Video Serv:* production workshops, consultants. *Pubns:* publish materials on video.

C- **BARNARD COLLEGE,** Wollman Library, 117 St & Broadway, 10027. *Tel:* (212) 280-3846. *In Charge:* Catherine Meakin, Asst, Reference Library. *Video Staff:* 1 p-t, 2 tech. *Video Use:* documentation of community/school events, to increase community's library use, community video access, in-service training. Video serv available by appointment. Produce video tapes. Have production studio/space.

Video Equipment/Facilities *In-House Use Only:* recording deck (2), ½″ b&w, Sony AV3600; editing deck (1), ½″ col, Panasonic TC3130; studio camera (1), b&w, Panasonic WV341; monitor (2), 19″ col, Panasonic CT911V; microphones (1); tripods (2); audio tape recorders (2); reel cassette. *For Loan:* portapak (1), ½″ b&w, Sony AV3400; monitor (2), 19″ col, JVC 6201. Have portable viewing installation. Provide training in use of equipment to faculty & students.

Video Tape Loan/Rental/Sale Serv *Serv Provided:* free loan. *Loan/Rental Eligibility:* org members, staff & students. May not borrow by mail.

Video Collection Maintained by own production. Use/play ½″ reel to reel. *Sources:* commercial distributors. Tapes organized by subject. *Collection, B&W:* ½″ reel, 35t/c. *Other Video Serv:* taping of other media.

Cable & CCTV Receive serv of cable TV system. Run cable programs for special audiences.

S- **CASTELLI-SONNABEND TAPES & FILMS, INC,** 420 West Broadway, 10012. *Tel:* (212) 431-6279. *Video Serv Est:* 1972. *In Charge:* Joyce Nereaux, Dir. *Video Staff:* 2 f-t, 1 p-t, 1 tech. *Video Use:* as art form. Video serv available by appointment. Produce video tapes. Have production studio/space.

Video Equipment/Facilities *In-House Use Only:* portapak (1), ½″ b&w, Sony; recording deck (4), ½″, ¾″ b&w/col, Sony 3650, 1600; playback deck (2), ½″, ¾″ b&w/col, Sony 3600, 1000; studio camera (1), b&w, Sony. Have permanent & portable viewing installations. Have tape duplication serv.

Video Tape Loan/Rental/Sale Serv *Serv Provided:* rental, sale. *Rental Eligibility:* org members. *Restrictions:* for indiv, none. Cannot duplicate.

Video Collection Maintained by own production. Use/play ½″ reel to reel, ¾″ cassette. *Pubns:* catalog.

C- **CITY UNIVERSITY OF NEW YORK-BORO OF MANHATTAN COMMUNITY COLLEGE,** Dept of Instructional Resources Media Service, 136 W 52 St, 10019. *Tel:* (212) 262-3530. *Film Serv Est:* 1973. *In Charge:* Helen Matthews, Chairperson & Dean. *AV Staff:* 3½ (1 prof, ½ cl, 2 tech). *Film Sel:* faculty committee & individual preview, faculty/staff recommendations. Produce video production for documentation & instructional support.

Film Collection 45t/p. *Circ:* 16mm, 45t/p.

Other Film Serv Obtain film from other libraries, film reference serv.

Other Media Collections *Audio:* disc, 33⅓ rpm, 35t; tape, cassette, 100t; tape, reel, 100t. *Filmstrips:* sound, 10t/20c. *Slides:* single, 70t; sets, 2t.

Budget & Expenditures Total library budget $60,208 (FY 7/1/74-7/1/75). No separate budget. *Member:* METRO.

Video Serv *Video Staff:* 1 f-t, 1 p-t, 1 tech. *Video Use:* documentation of community/school events, to increase community's library use, in-service training, support instruction. Video serv available by appointment. Produce video tapes.

Video Equipment/Facilities *In-House Use Only:* portapak (2), ½″ b&w, Panasonic NV3082; recording deck (1), ½″ b&w, Sony AV3600; playback deck (1), ½″ b&w, Sony AV3650; editing deck (1), ½″ b&w, Sony; studio camera (2), ½″ b&w, Sony AVC3200; monitor (2), ½″ b&w/col, Panasonic; SEG (1), Sony SEG2; additional camera lenses (4); lighting (12); tripods (4); audio tape recorders (3). Provide training in use of equipment to staff & students. Have tape duplication serv.

Video Collection Maintained by purchase, rental, own production. Use/play ½″ reel to reel, ½″ cartridge. *Sources:* commercial distributors. *Tape Sel:* preview, faculty/staff recommendations, catalogs. *Special Collections:* in-house training tapes, Library Technology program. Tapes organized by subject. *Collection, B&W:* ½″ reel, 45t; 1″ reel, 20t; ½″ cartridge, 5t.

C- **COLUMBIA UNIVERSITY,** Health Sciences Library, 630 W 168 St, 10032. *Tel:* (212) 579-3694. *Video Serv Est:* 1974. *In Charge:* Merril Schindler, Media Services Librarian. *Video Staff:* 1 f-t. *Video Use:* in-service training, playback only of professionally produced tapes, medical education. Video serv available on demand.

Video Equipment/Facilities *In-House Use Only:* playback deck (6), ¾″ col, Sony; monitor (6), col, Sony. Have permanent viewing installation.

Video Tape Loan/Rental/Sale Serv *Serv Provided:* free loan. *Loan Eligibility:* staff & students, other medical libraries. *Restrictions:* for indiv & inst, interlibrary loan. Cannot use for

New York (cont'd)
fund-raising, duplicate, air without permission. May borrow by mail. *Loan Period:* 7 days. *Total Yr Tape Loan:* 6.

Video Collection Maintained by purchase. Use/play ¾″ cassette. *Sources:* commercial distributors. *Tape Sel:* preview, faculty/staff recommendations. *Special Collections:* undergraduate medical education. Tapes organized by subject. *Collection, Color:* ¾″ cassette, 275t/c. *Collection, B&W:* ¾″ cassette, 35t/c. *Pubns:* catalog & subject index (for in-house use).

S- ELECTRONIC ARTS INTERMIX, INC, 84 Fifth Ave, 10011. *Tel:* (212) 989-2316. *Video Serv Est:* 1971. *In Charge:* Howard Wise, President. *Video Staff:* 1 f-t, 1 tech. *Video Use:* as art form.

Video Equipment/Facilities *In-House Use Only:* recording deck (5), ½″, ¾″, 1″ b&w/col, Sony, JVC; editing deck (2), ½″, 1″ b&w/col, Sony; monitor (5), b&w/col, Sony; SEG (1), Panasonic; lighting (3). Have permanent viewing installation. Provide training to artists who wish to use editing facilities.

Video Tape Loan/Rental/Sale Serv *Serv Provided:* rental, sale. *Loan/Rental Eligibility:* artists & groups. Cannot use for fund-raising, duplicate, air without permission. *Loan Period:* varies.

Video Collection Maintained by rental. Use/play ¾″ cassette. *Sources:* independent artist/producers, WNET, WGBH, NCET. *Tape Sel:* preview. *Special Collections:* video as art. Tapes organized by artist, organization & group. *Collection, Color:* ¾″ cassette, 160t. *Other Video Serv:* programming, editing/post production facility available to qualified artists. *Pubns:* catalog & newsletters.

Cable & CCTV Will receive serv of cable TV system.

A- METROPOLITAN MUSEUM OF ART, Dept of Public Education, Fifth Ave & 82 St, 10028. *Tel:* (212) 879-5500, ext 392. *Film Serv Est:* 1960. *In Charge:* Gila Gevirtz, AV Specialist. *AV Staff:* 5 (1 prof, 4 tech). *Film Sel:* committee preview. *Holdings:* fine arts 100%.

Film Collection 450t/500p. Approx 25t acquired annually. *Noncirc:* 16mm, 450t/p.

Other Film Serv Film fairs/festivals, film programs, courses & seminars given at the museum. Permanent viewing facility.

Other Media Collections *Slides:* separate slide library of many thousands of slides.

Budget & Expenditures Total FY AV budget $8000. *Member:* N.Y. Film Council.

Video Serv *Video Use:* documentation of museum events, in-service training, playback of professionally produced tapes, as art form, as an educational resource in museum exhibitions. Video serv available on demand & by appointment. Produce video tapes. Have production studio/space.

Video Equipment/Facilities *In-House Use Only:* portapak (3), ½″ b&w, Sony; recording deck (7), ½″, 1″ b&w/col, Sony; playback deck (1), ¾″ col, Sony; editing deck (1), ½″ b&w, Sony; studio camera (1), col, Sony; monitor (10), b&w/col, Sony; lighting (1); microphones (2); tripods (2); audio tape recorders (2). Have permanent & portable viewing installations. Provide training in use of equipment to staff museum educators.

Video Tape Loan/Rental/Sale Serv *Serv Provided:* swap with other inst. *Loan Eligibility:* staff & students, prof groups, such as other museums. Cannot use for fund-raising, duplicate, air without permission.

Video Collection Maintained by purchase, own production. Use/play ½″ reel to reel, ¾″ cassette. *Sources:* commercial distributors, exchange (WNET, some film distributors). *Tape Sel:* preview, gallery previews. *Special Collections:* in-house training tapes, video as art, films in video format, art education. *Collection, Color:* ¾″ cassette, 6t/c. *Collection, B&W:* ½″ reel, 6t/c; ¾″ cassette, 6t/c. *Other Video Serv:* viewings of video tapings, seminars for staff & museum professionals.

A- THE MUSEUM OF MODERN ART, 11 W 53 St, 10019. *Tel:* (212) 956-6100. *Video Serv Est:* 1974. *In Charge:* Barbara J. London, Curatorial Assistant. *Video Staff:* 1 f-t. *Video Use:* as art form. Video serv available on demand.

Video Equipment/Facilities *In-House Use Only:* playback deck (1), col, Sony ¾″ U-Matic; monitor (2), col, Sony. Have permanent viewing installation.

Video Collection Maintained by purchase. Use/play ¾″ cassette. *Sources:* galleries. *Tape Sel:* staff recommendations, gallery previews, published reviews, catalogs. *Special Collections:* video as art. *Collection, Color:* ¾″ cassette, 4t/c. *Collection, B&W:* ¾″ cassette, 3t/c.

A- NEW YORK JAZZ MUSEUM, 55 W 63 St, 10023. *Tel:* (212) 765-2150. *Film Serv Est:* 1972. *In Charge:* Howard Fischer, Executive Dir. *AV Staff:* 1 (1 prof). *Film Sel:* staff recommendations. *Holdings:* jazz & blues music 100%.

Film Rental Serv *Eligibility:* no restrictions. *Restrictions:* none. *Rental Period:* flexible. Sell films. Produce films.

Other Film Serv Film reference serv. Permanent viewing facility available for rent to community.

Other Media Collections *Audio:* disc, 33⅓ rpm, 2500c; disc, 78rpm, 5000c; tape, total of 30 hrs. *Filmstrips:* total, 6c. *Slides:* total 300c.

Video Serv *Video Staff:* 1 f-t. Produce video tapes.

Video Tape Loan/Rental/Sale Serv *Serv Provided:* swap with other inst, rental. *Loan/Rental Eligibility:* any individual or group. *Restrictions:* for indiv & inst, none. Cannot duplicate. May not borrow by mail. *Loan Period:* flexible.

Video Collection Maintained by purchase, exchange/swap. *Tape Sel:* staff recommendations. *Special Collections:* jazz, blues, big bands.

A- THE NEW YORK PUBLIC LIBRARY, Jerome Robbins Archive, Dance Collection, 111 Amsterdam Ave, 10023. *Tel:* (212) 799-2200, ext 219. *Film Serv Est:* 1966. *In Charge:* Genevieve Oswald, Curator, Dance Collection. *AV Staff:* 3½ (2 prof, ½ cl, 1 tech). *Film Sel:* staff recommendations. *Holdings:* dance 100%.

Film Collection 1400t/2800p. Approx 125t acquired annually. *Noncirc:* 16mm, 1350t/2700p; 8mm reel, 20t/35p; S8mm reel, 30t/65c. *Pubns:* publish *The Dictionary Catalog of the Dance Collection* (G. K. Hall) which includes film & video & all other material in collection.

Other Film Serv Film reference serv, screening of films for study purposes in the collection. Permanent viewing facility.

Other Media Collections Tape, cassette, 100t/c; tape, reel, 655t/c. *Slides:* single, 4500t.

Budget & Expenditures Total library budget $1,245,000 (FY 7/1/74-1/1/75). No separate AV budget. *Member:* AFI, ALA, EFLA, Dance Films Assn, N.Y. Film Council.

Video Serv *Est:* 1971. *Video Staff:* 3 f-t, ½ p-t, 1 tech. *Video Use:* visual documentation of dance. Video serv available by appointment. Produce video tapes.

Video Equipment/Facilities *In-House Use Only:* editing deck (1), ½″ col, Sony AV5000A; monitor (1), col, Sony CVM 1220. Have portable viewing installation. Have tape duplication serv.

Video Collection Maintained by purchase, own production, exchange/swap. Use/play ½″ reel to reel, ¾″ cassette. *Sources:* commercial distributors, contributions. *Tape Sel:* preview, staff recommendations, gallery previews, published reviews, catalogs. *Special Collections:* tapes which record all aspects of dance. *Collection, Color:* ½″ reel, 125t; 1″ reel, 10t; 2″ reel, 25t; ¾″ cassette, 10t. *Collection, B&W:* ½″ reel, 50t. *Other Video Serv:* reference serv. *Pubns:* publish *The Dictionary Catalog of the Dance Collection.*

A- THE NEW YORK PUBLIC LIBRARY, Theatre on Film and Tape, Theatre Collection, 111 Amsterdam Ave, 10023. *Tel:* (212) 799-2200, ext 271. *Film Serv Est:* 1970. *In Charge:* Betty Corwin, Project Dir. *AV Staff:* 1 (½ prof, ½ tech). *Film Sel:* committee preview, staff recommendations, published reviews of theatrical productions. *Holdings:* theater 100%.

Film Collection 2t/4p. *Noncirc:* 16mm, 4t/4c.

Other Film Serv Film reference serv, screening of films for study purpose.

Budget & Expenditures Total library budget $1,245,000 (FY 7/1/74-7/1/75). No separate AV budget. *Member:* AFI, ALA, EFLA.

Video Serv *Video Staff:* 2 p-t, 1 tech. *Video Use:* documentation of theater productions & dialogues between professionals of the theater. Video serv available by appointment. Produce video tapes.

Video Equipment/Facilities *In-House Use Only:* recording deck (1), ½″ b&w, Sony; monitor (1), 12″ b&w, Panasonic; lighting (1). Have portable viewing installation.

Video Collection Maintained by purchase, own production. Use/play ½″ reel to reel. *Tape Sel:* staff recommendations, catalogs. *Special Collections:* tapes which document the theater. Tapes organized by accession number. *Collection, B&W:* ½″ reel, 62t/124c; 1″ reel, 40t/80c. *Other Video Serv:* reference serv.

C- **NEW YORK UNIVERSITY**, Alternative Media Center, School of the Arts, 144 Bleecker St, 10012. *Tel:* (212) 598-3338. *Video Serv Est:* 1971. *In Charge:* Red Burns, Executive Dir. *Video Staff:* 6 f-t. *Video Use:* documentation of community/school events, community video access, in-service training. Video serv available by appointment. Produce video tapes. Have production studio/space.

Video Equipment/Facilities *In-House Use Only:* portapak (1), ½″ b&w, Panasonic 3072; recording deck (1), ½″ b&w, Sony 3400; playback deck (2), ½″ b&w, Sony 3600; editing deck (1), ½″ b&w, Sony 3600; studio camera (1), ½″ col, Panasonic 3030; monitor (4), b&w, Sony; lighting (1); microphones (3); audio tape recorders (1). Have portable viewing installation. Provide training in use of equipment to students. Have tape duplication serv.

Video Tape Loan/Rental/Sale Serv *Serv Provided:* free loan, swap with other inst. *Loan Eligibility:* staff & students. *Restrictions:* for indiv, only in city; for inst, none. Cannot air without permission.

Video Collection Maintained by own production, exchange/swap. Use/play ½″ reel to reel, ¾″ cassette. *Sources:* community productions, through CATV apprenticeship program. *Tape Sel:* word of mouth. *Special Collections:* exchange basis. Tapes organized by producers, locality & time. *Collection, B&W:* ½″ reel, 300t. *Other Video Serv:* reference serv. *Pubns:* publish access workbooks & supplements.

Cable & CCTV Receive serv of cable TV system. Produce programs for cablecasting. Inform public about cable system serv & facilities. Run cable programs for special audiences. Have advisory/administrative role in cable system operation (consultancy: Manhattan Cable).

C- **NEW YORK UNIVERSITY**, Film Library, 26 Washington Pl, 10003. *Tel:* (212) 598-2250. *Film Serv Est:* 1940. *In Charge:* Daniel Lesser, Dir. *AV Staff:* 6 (2 prof, 3 cl, 1 tech). *Film Sel:* committee preview, faculty/staff recommendations. *Holdings:* behavioral science 30%, teacher education 50%.

Film Rental Serv *Eligibility:* educational org, civic groups, all bonafide groups, no rentals to individuals. *Restrictions:* only in U.S. Cannot transmit electronically or duplicate. *Rental Period:* 1 day. Sell films.

Film Collection 800-900t. *Circ:* 16mm, 800-900t/2200p. *Pubns:* catalog, every 4 yrs ($1); suppl, no set policy.

Other Film Serv Film reference serv, library film programs. Permanent viewing facility.

Budget & Expenditures No separate AV budget. *Member:* AECT, CUFC, EFLA.

C- **NEW YORK UNIVERSITY**, Institute of Film & TV, 40 E Seventh St, 10003. *Tel:* (212) 598-3366. *In Charge:* Vito Brunetti. *Video Staff:* 1 f-t, 1 p-t. *Video Use:* practical video/TV training courses. Video serv available on demand to students only.

Video Equipment/Facilities *In-House Use Only:* recording deck (1), ½″ col, Sony AV8600; playback deck (1), ½″ b&w, Sony; studio camera (2), b&w, Sony; video camera selector (1), b&w, Sony; additional camera lenses; lighting; microphones;

tripods; audio tape recorders. Have portable viewing installation. Provide training in use of equipment to students.

Video Collection Maintained by own production. *Special Collections:* in-house training tapes.

S- **THE RAINDANCE FOUNDATION INC.**, 51 Fifth Ave. *Tel:* (212) 675-3319. *Video Serv Est:* 1969. *In Charge:* I. Schneider, President. *Video Staff:* 2 f-t, 4 p-t, 1 tech. *Video Use:* as art form, information media. Video serv available on demand. Produce video tapes.

Video Equipment/Facilities *In-House Use Only:* portapak (2), ½″ b&w, Sony 3600, 3650; recording & playback deck (3), ½″ b&w/col, Sony 3600, 3650; editing deck (2), ½″ col, Sony 8650; monitor (4); additional camera lenses; lighting; microphones; tripods; audio tape recorders. Have portable viewing installation. Provide training in use of equipment to colleges.

Video Tape Loan/Rental/Sale Serv *Serv Provided:* rental, sale. *Rental Eligibility:* educational inst, any other groups.

Video Collection Maintained by own production. Use/play ½″ reel to reel, ¾″ cassette. *Sources:* own production. *Collection, Color:* ½″ reel, 30t/c. *Collection, B&W:* ½″ reel, 110t/120c. *Other Video Serv:* programming, taping of other media. Produced *Video Art: An Anthology* (Harcourt, 1976).

Cable & CCTV ·Receive serv of cable TV system.

S- **SOCIAL PSYCHIATRY RESEARCH INSTITUTE**, 150 E 69 St, 10021. *Tel:* (212) 628-4800. *Video Serv Est:* 1974. *In Charge:* Ari Kienund, President. *Video Staff:* 4 f-t, 4 p-t, 2 tech. *Video Use:* practical video/TV training courses, playback only of professionally produced tapes. Produce video tapes. Have production studio/space & separate control room.

Video Equipment/Facilities *In-House Use Only:* portapak; recording deck; playback deck; editing deck; studio camera; monitor; SEG; keyer; synthesizer; additional camera lenses; lighting; microphones; tripods; audio tape recorders. Have permanent & portable viewing installation.

Video Tape Loan/Rental/Sale Serv *Serv Provided:* rental, sale. *Rental Eligibility:* educational inst, prof groups, such as medical & nursing associations. Cannot air without permission. May borrow by mail. *Loan Period:* 30 days.

Video Collection Maintained by own production. Use/play ½″, 2″ reel to reel, ¾″ cassette. *Other Video Serv:* programming. *Pubns:* catalog.

Cable & CCTV Receive serv of cable TV system. Have CCTV in inst. *Programming Sources:* tapes produced by inst, tapes produced professionally.

C- **TEACHERS COLLEGE LIBRARY**, COLUMBIA UNIVERSITY, Box 12, 10027. *Tel:* (212) 678-3822. *Film Serv Est:* 1968. *In Charge:* Richard Allen, AV Supervisor. *AV Staff:* 5 (1 cl, 2 tech). *Film Sel:* faculty/staff recommendations. *Holdings:* black heritage (CBS series) 10%.

Free-Loan Film Serv *Eligibility:* staff. Available to researchers/scholars for on-site viewing. May not borrow by mail. *Total Yr Film Loan:* 1033.

Film Rental Serv *Eligibility:* educational org. *Restrictions:* none. Cannot use for fund-raising, transmit electronically. *Rental Period:* 1 day. *Total Yr Film Booking:* 60. Produce films. Produce any format for any piece of AV equipment.

Film Collection 529t/p. Approx 10-20t acquired annually. *Circ:* 16mm, 500t; 8mm cartridge, 60t; S8mm reel, 100t; S8mm cartridge, 100t. *Noncirc:* 16mm, 29t. *Pubns:* catalog, every 5 yrs ($2); suppl, no set policy.

Other Film Serv Rent film from distributors for patrons, obtain film from other libraries, film reference serv. Permanent viewing facility available for rent to community. *Equipment:* rent S8mm camera, 8mm cartridge projector, 8mm reel projector, S8mm cartridge projector, S8mm reel projector.

Other Media Collections *Audio:* disc, 33⅓ rpm, 3000t; tape, cassette, 400t; tape, reel, 100t. *Filmstrips:* total, 1000t. *Slides:* total, 3000t.

Budget & Expenditures Total library budget $82,000 (FY 9/1/74-9/1/75). Total FY film budget $11,400. *Member:* AECT.

New York (cont'd)

S- **WOMEN'S INTERART CENTER**, 549 W 52 St, 10019. *Tel:* (212) 246-6570. *Video Serv Est:* 1972. *In Charge:* Susan Milano, Video Coordinator. *Video Staff:* 5 f-t, 3 p-t. *Video Use:* documentation of community events, practical video/TV training courses, as art form, presentation. Produce video tapes. Have production space.

    Video Equipment/Facilities *In-House Use Only:* portapak (2), ½" b&w, Sony; playback deck (1), ½" b&w/col, Sony; editing deck (1), ½" b&w, Sony; monitor (5), b&w, Sony, Panasonic; lighting (3); microphones (5); tripods (1); microphone mixer (1), battery belt (1). Have permanent & portable viewing installations. Provide training in use of equipment to members of org.

    Video Tape Loan/Rental/Sale Serv *Serv Provided:* free loan, swap with other inst, rental, sale. *Loan/Rental Eligibility:* members of our video staff & students.

    Video Collection Maintained by purchase, rental, own production, exchange/swap. *Use/play* ½" reel to reel. *Tape Sel:* suggestions of women's org throughout country. *Other Video Serv:* taping of other media, production workshops. *Pubns:* catalog.

S- **YOUNG FILMAKERS INC**, Media Equipment Resource Center, 4 Rivington St, 10002. *Tel:* (212) 673-9363. *Video Serv Est:* 1971. *In Charge:* Jaime Caro, Dir. *Video Staff:* 4 f-t, 1 p-t. *Video Use:* community video access, in-service training, practical video/TV training courses, as art form. Video serv available on demand & by appointment. Produce video tapes. Have production studio/space & separate control room.

    Video Equipment/Facilities *In-House Use Only:* recording deck (2), ½", Sony 3400; editing deck (4), ½", 1" b&w/col, Sony, Panasonic,; studio camera (7); monitor; SEG (2), Panasonic, Sony; keyer (2), Shintron; additional camera lenses; lighting; microphones; tripods; audio tape recorders. *For Loan:* portapak (5), ½" b&w/col, Sony; SEG (2), Panasonic, Sony; keyer (2), Shintron. Have permanent & portable viewing installations. Have tape duplication serv.

    Video Tape Loan/Rental/Sale Serv *Serv Provided:* free loan, swap with other inst. *Loan Eligibility:* educational inst, civic groups, religious groups, prof groups, such as those in theater & dance & others, such as organizations engaged in non-profit artistic projects. *Restrictions:* for indiv & inst, only in state. May not borrow by mail.

Newark

P- **WAYNE COUNTY & ONTARIO COOPERATIVE LIBRARY SYSTEM**, Film Library, 503 W Union St, 14513. *Tel:* (315) 331-2143. *Film Serv Est:* 1959. *In Charge:* Alice S. Traister, AV Consultant. *AV Staff:* 2 (1 prof, 1 cl). *Film Sel:* committee preview, staff recommendations, chief film librarian's decision, community resource groups. *Holdings:* children's films 55%, fine arts 5%, travel 5%.

    Free-Loan Film Serv *Eligibility:* civic groups, religious groups, indiv with library cards, prof groups, & others, such as public & parochial schools with a contract. *Restrictions:* for indiv, only in Wayne & Ontario Counties; for inst, only in Wayne & Ontario Counties & adjoining county groups where local library card holder is responsible. Cannot use for fund-raising, transmit electronically. Available to researchers/scholars for on-site viewing. May not borrow by mail. *Loan Period:* 5 days. *Total Yr Film Loan:* 4185.

    Film Rental Serv *Eligibility:* educational org (elementary & secondary levels). *Restrictions:* only in Wayne & Ontario Counties. Cannot use for fund-raising, transmit electronically. *Rental Period:* 5 days. *Total Yr Film Booking:* 1567.

    Film Collection 400t/p. Approx 40t acquired annually. *Circ:* 16mm, 398t/p. *Pubns:* catalog, every 2 yrs; suppl, in yr catalog not published.

    Other Film Serv Obtain film from coop loan system (Rochester Public Library AV Dept), obtain film from other libraries, film reference serv, film fairs/festivals, library film programs. *Equipment:* rent 16mm sound projector (4), lend projection screens (4), rent 35mm slide projectors (2).

Other Media Collections *Audio:* disc, 33⅓ rpm, 1500t/2200c; tape, cassette, 200t/300c.

    Budget & Expenditures Total library budget $36,531 (FY 1/1/74-1/1/75). Total FY film budget $8000. *Member:* ALA, EFLA, N.Y. Library Assn.

    Video Serv *Est:* 1975. *Video Staff:* 1 p-t. *Video Use:* to increase community's library use, in-service training, as art form.

    Video Equipment/Facilities *In-House Use Only:* playback deck (1), col, Panasonic 2110M; audio tape recorders (2). Have portable viewing installation.

    Video Collection Maintained by exchange/swap. *Use/play* ¾" cassette. *Sources:* commercial distributors, exchange (Pioneer Library System). *Tape Sel:* staff recommendations. *Special Collections:* films in video format. Tapes organized by subject. *Collection, Color:* ¾" cassette, 35t/c.

Peekskill

S- **ROYAL VIDEOCASSETTE LIBRARY, INC**, Rd 3, Andre Lane, 10566. *Tel:* (914) 737-7011. *Film Serv Est:* 1972. *In Charge:* Benjamin Packer, Pres. *AV Staff:* 10 (8 prof, 1 cl, 1 tech). *Film Sel:* chief film librarian's decision. *Holdings:* agriculture, black studies, career education, consumer affairs, engineering, fine arts, industrial arts, medicine, science, social sciences, teacher education.

    Video Rental Serv *Eligibility:* no restrictions. *Restrictions:* none. *Rental Period:* 7 days. Sell & produce video cassettes.

    Video Collection 2000 programs. Approx 300 programs acquired annually. *Pubns:* catalog, every 2 yrs; suppl, no set policy.

    Other Video Serv Rent video cassettes from distributors for patrons. *Equipment:* rent video cassette player.

    Budget & Expenditures Total library budget $100,000. No separate AV budget.

Port Washington

P- **PORT WASHINGTON PUBLIC LIBRARY**, 245 Main St, 11050. *Tel:* (516) 883-4400, ext 59. *Video Serv Est:* 1971. *In Charge:* Kinney Littlefield, Head, Media Dept. *Video Staff:* 2 f-t. *Video Use:* documentation of community events, community video access, in-service training. Video serv available on demand & by appointment. Produce video tapes. Have production studio/space.

    Video Equipment/Facilities *In-House Use Only:* playback deck (1), ½" b&w, Sony. *For Loan:* portapak (1), ½" b&w, Sony 3400; recording deck (1), ½" b&w, Sony; editing deck (3), ½" b&w, Sony 3650. Have portable viewing installation. *Equipment Loan Period:* no set policy. Provide training in use of equipment.

    Video Tape Loan/Rental/Sale Serv *Serv Provided:* free loan, swap with other inst. *Loan Eligibility:* civic groups, religious groups, indiv with library cards, indiv in community. *Restrictions:* for indiv & inst, only in our county. May borrow by mail. *Loan Period:* varies.

    Video Collection Maintained by own production. *Use/play* ½" reel to reel. *Sources:* community productions. Tapes organized by subject. *Other Video Serv:* reference serv, production workshops. *Pubns:* catalog.

    Cable & CCTV Will receive serv of cable TV system.

Potsdam

C- **STATE UNIVERSITY OF NEW YORK COLLEGE AT POTSDAM**, Educational Communication Center, Kellas Hall, 13676. *Tel:* (315) 268-2981. *Film Serv Est:* 1971. *In Charge:* Alfred V. Roman, Dir, Educational Communications. *AV Staff:* 15 (14 prof, 1 cl, 14 tech). *Film Sel:* individual departments. *Holdings:* computer science 3%, dance 3%, fine arts 9%, history 4%, science 44%, social sciences 19%, teacher education 18%.

    Free-Loan Film Serv *Eligibility:* staff & students, educational inst, civic groups, prof groups. *Restrictions:* for indiv &

inst, none. Available to researchers/scholars for on-site viewing. May not borrow by mail. *Loan Period:* 2 weeks.

Film Collection 211t/p. *Circ:* 16mm, 211t/p. *Pubns:* catalog, as needed.

Other Film Serv Obtain film from coop loan system (Associated Colleges of St. Lawrence Valley), film reference serv, library film programs. Permanent viewing facility.

Budget & Expenditures No separate AV budget.

Video Serv *Est:* 1971. *Video Staff:* 15 f-t, 1 tech. *Video Use:* documentation of community/school events, practical video/TV training courses, production & televising of college-level instruction. Video serv available by appointment. Produce video tapes. Have production studio/space & separate control room.

Video Equipment/Facilities Professional television facility which includes quadrature tape recorders (2), two-inch helicals (4), one-inch machines (3), studio cameras (4), two cameras for student use, & a campus rf distribution/origination network. Have permanent viewing installation. Provide training in use of equipment to faculty & students. Have tape duplication serv.

Video Tape Loan/Rental/Sale Serv *Serv Provided:* free loan, swap with other inst, rental. *Loan/Rental Eligibility:* staff & students, educational inst, civic & religious groups. *Restrictions:* for indiv & inst, none. Cannot use for fund-raising, duplicate, air without permission. May not borrow by mail. *Total Yr Tape Loan:* 50.

Video Collection Maintained by own production, exchange/swap. Use/play ½″, ¼″, 1″, 2″ reel to reel, ½″ cartridge, ¾″ cassette. *Sources:* galleries, exchange, in-house production. *Tape Sel:* preview, faculty/staff recommendations, published reviews, catalogs. *Special Collections:* in-house training tapes. Tapes organized alphabetically. *Collection, Color:* ½″ reel, 10t; 1″ reel, 75t; 2″ reel, 700t; ¾″ cassette, 2t. *Other Video Serv:* programming, taping of other media, production workshops. *Pubns:* catalog. Publish materials on video.

Cable & CCTV Receive serv of cable TV system. Have microwave link with WNPE/WNPI. Have CCTV in inst, with 300 monitors. *Programming Sources:* over-the-air commercial & public broadcasting, tapes produced by inst, tapes produced professionally.

Poughkeepsie

P- MID-HUDSON LIBRARY SYSTEM, 103 Market St, 12601. *Tel:* (914) 471-6060. *Film Serv Est:* 1964. *In Charge:* Michael D. Miller, Dept Head, AV Serv. *AV Staff:* 5 (1 prof, 3 cl, 1 tech). *Film Sel:* chief film librarian's decision.

Free-Loan Film Serv *Eligibility:* civic groups, religious groups, indiv with library cards. *Restrictions:* for indiv, only in Putnam, Dutchess, Columbia, Greene & Ulster counties; for inst, only Putnam, Dutchess, Columbia, Greene & Ulster counties. Cannot use for fund-raising, transmit electronically, borrow for classroom use. Available to researchers/scholars for on-site viewing. May borrow by mail. *Loan Period:* varies. *Total Yr Film Loan:* 9384.

Film Collection 1139t/1179p. Approx 200t acquired annually. *Circ:* 16mm, 1139t/1179p; S8mm reel, 66t/110p; S8mm cartridge, 31t/p. *Pubns:* catalog, every 2 yrs ($1); suppl, no set policy.

Other Film Serv Obtain film from coop loan system (N.Y. State Film Collection), film reference serv, film fairs/festivals, library film programs. Permanent viewing facility. *Equipment:* lend 16mm sound projector (4), S8mm cartridge projector (2), S8mm reel projector (2), projection screens (4).

Other Media Collections *Audio:* disc, 33⅓ rpm, 1182t; tape, cassette, 1552t. *Filmstrips:* sound sets, 23t. *Slides:* single, 910t; sets, 6t/7c.

Budget & Expenditures Total library budget $61,182 (FY 1/1/75-1/1/76). Total FY film budget $25,000. *Member:* ALA, EFLA, FLIC, N.Y. Library Assn.

Video Serv *Est:* 1974. *Video Staff:* 1 f-t. *Video Use:* documentation of community events, to increase community's library use, community video access, in-service training, as art form. Video serv available through libraries on rotating basis. Produce video tapes.

Video Equipment/Facilities *For Loan:* recording deck (1), ¾″ col, JVC CR6000V; monitor (1), col, Sony KV1710. Have

portable viewing installation. *Equipment Loan Period:* 4 mos, member libraries only. Provide training in use of equipment to librarians & indiv in community.

Video Tape Loan/Rental/Sale Serv *Serv Provided:* free loan. *Loan Eligibility:* civic groups, religious groups, indiv with library cards. *Restrictions:* for indiv & inst, only in Putnam, Dutchess, Columbia, Greene & Ulster counties. Cannot use for fund-raising, duplicate, air without permission. May not borrow by mail.

Video Collection Maintained by purchase, own production. Use/play ¾″ cassette. *Sources:* commercial distributors, exchange (indiv artists, N.Y. State Council on the Arts). *Tape Sel:* preview. *Special Collections:* video as art. Tapes organized by subject & acquisition numbers. *Collection, Color:* ¾″ cassette, 44t. *Other Video Serv:* production workshops. *Pubns:* catalog.

Rochester

C- MONROE COMMUNITY COLLEGE, Television Center, Box 9720, 14623. *Tel:* (716) 442-9950, ext 726. *Video Serv Est:* 1961. *In Charge:* Eugene L. Edwards, Dir of Instructional Serv. *Video Staff:* 2 f-t, 1 p-t. *Video Use:* documentation of community/school events, in-service training, practical video/TV training courses, playback only of professionally produced tapes. Video serv available on demand & by appointment. Produce video tapes. Have production studio/space & separate control room.

Video Equipment/Facilities *In-House Use Only:* recording deck (1), b&w/col, Ampex; studio camera (7), Ampex, Conrac; monitor (35); microphones (20); audio tape recorders (14). Have permanent viewing installation. Provide training in use of equipment to AV technology students. Have tape duplication serv.

Video Tape Loan/Rental/Sale Serv *Serv Provided:* free loan, swap with other inst. *Loan Eligibility:* educational inst. *Restrictions:* for inst, only in city. Cannot use for fund-raising, duplicate, air without permission. May not borrow by mail.

Video Collection Maintained by purchase, own production, exchange/swap. Use/play ½″, 1″, 2″ reel to reel, ¾″ cassette. *Sources:* exchange (area colleges & universities). *Tape Sel:* preview, faculty/staff recommendations. Tapes organized by subject & numerically. *Collection, Color:* 1″ reel, 22t/c; 2″ reel, 10t/c. *Collection, B&W:* ½″ reel, 19t/c; 1″ reel, 278t/c; 2″ reel, 166t/c. *Other Video Serv:* programming, reference serv, taping of other media. *Pubns:* catalog.

Cable & CCTV Have CCTV in inst, with 108 monitors, 21 channels. *Programming Sources:* over-the-air commercial & public broadcasting, tapes produced by inst, tapes produced professionally, tapes produced by community groups & indiv.

P- ROCHESTER PUBLIC LIBRARY, Reynolds AV Dept, 115 South Ave, 14604. *Tel:* (716) 546-2260, ext 33, 34, 35. *Film Serv Est:* 1949. *In Charge:* Robert Barnes, Head. *AV Staff:* 10 (2 prof, 5 cl, 3 tech). *Film Sel:* committee preview, staff recommendations, chief film librarian's decision, published reviews.

Free-Loan Film Serv *Eligibility:* educational inst, civic groups, religious groups, indiv with library cards, prof groups, such as AAUW, labor groups & others, such as PTA's, Boy Scouts. *Restrictions:* for indiv, interlibrary loan; for inst, only in 5 counties of our service area. Cannot use for fund-raising, transmit electronically. Available to researchers/scholars for on-site viewing. May not borrow by mail. *Loan Period:* 3 days. *Total Yr Film Loan:* 34,671.

Film Collection 4000p. Approx 200t acquired annually. *Circ:* 16mm, 3500t; 8mm reel, 3300t; 8mm cartridge, 100t. *Pubns:* catalog, every 2 yrs ($7); suppl, quarterly ($.75).

Other Film Serv Film reference serv, film fairs/festivals, library film programs. Permanent viewing facility available for rent to community. *Equipment:* rent 16mm sound projector (10).

Budget & Expenditures No separate AV budget. *Member:* AECT, AFI, ALA, EFLA, N.Y. State Educational Commission.

Video Serv *Est:* 1972. *Video Staff:* 10 f-t, 6 p-t, 1 tech. *Video Use:* to increase community's library use, community video access, in-service training. Video serv available on demand & by appointment. Produce video tapes.

Rochester (cont'd)

Video Equipment/Facilities *In-House Use Only:* recording deck (1), ¾" col, Panasonic; playback deck (1), ¾" col, Panasonic. Have permanent & portable viewing installations. Provide training in use of equipment to library staff.

Video Collection Maintained by purchase. Use/play ¾" cassette. *Sources:* commercial distributors, community productions. *Tape Sel:* preview, staff recommendations, published reviews. Tapes organized by subject. *Collection, Color:* ½" reel, 10t/c; ¾" cassette, 50t/c. *Pubns:* catalog.

C- UNIVERSITY OF ROCHESTER, Center for Instructional Media, Morey Hall Rm 108, 14627. *Tel:* (716) 275-4014. *Video Serv Est:* 1972. *In Charge:* Nicholas A Cattat, Dir. *Video Staff:* 5 f-t, 10 p-t, 2 tech. *Video Use:* documentation of community/school events, in-service training, playback only of professionally produced tapes. Video serv available by appointment. Produce video tapes. Have production studio/space.

Video Equipment/Facilities *In-House Use Only:* portapak (3), b&w/col, Sony 3400; recording deck (1), 1" col, IVC 700; playback deck (1), 1" col, IVC 700; editing deck (1), 1" col, IVC 800; studio camera (2), b&w; monitor (6), b&w/col, Tectronic, Conrac; SEG (1), Dynair; synthesizer (1); additional camera lenses; lighting; microphones; tripods (4); audio tape recorders. *For Loan:* portapak (3), b&w/col, Sony 3400; lighting; microphones; tripods (4); audio tape recorders. Have permanent viewing installation. *Equipment Loan Period:* short term only. Provide training in use of equipment to faculty & students. Have tape duplication serv.

Video Tape Loan/Rental/Sale Serv *Serv Provided:* free loan, swap with other inst. *Loan Eligibility:* org members. *Restrictions:* for indiv, interlibrary loan. Cannot duplicate, air without permission. May not borrow by mail.

Video Collection Maintained by purchase, rental, own production. Use/play ½", 1", 2" reel to reel, ¾" cassette. *Sources:* commercial distributors, community productions, exchange. *Tape Sel:* preview, faculty/staff recommendations. Tapes organized by own code. *Collection, Color:* 2" reel, 60t. *Collection, B&W:* ½" reel, 70t; 2" reel, 25t.

Sanborn

C- NIAGARA COUNTY COMMUNITY COLLEGE, Library Learning Center, 3111 Saunders Settlement Rd, 14132. *Tel:* (716) 731-3271, ext 231. *Film Serv Est:* 1963. *In Charge:* Eleanor Seminara, Dir, Library Learning Center. *AV Staff:* 10 (4 prof, 2 cl, 4 tech). *Film Sel:* committee preview, faculty/staff recommendations, chief film librarian's decision.

Free-Loan Film Serv *Eligibility:* staff & students. *Restrictions:* for indiv, only in inst. Available to researchers/scholars for on-site viewing. May not borrow by mail. *Loan Period:* 1 day.

Film Collection 300p. *Circ:* 16mm, 300t; S8mm reel, 10t; S8mm cartridge, 250t. *Pubns:* catalog, as needed.

Other Film Serv Rent film from distributors for patrons, obtain film from coop loan system (public library), obtain film from other libraries, film reference serv, own production. Permanent viewing facility. *Equipment:* lend S8mm camera, 16mm sound projector, 8mm reel projector, S8mm cartridge projector, S8mm reel projector, projection tables & stands, projection screens. *Member:* AECT, AFI, ALA, EFLA, N.Y. Library Assn.

Video Serv *Est:* 1968. *Video Staff:* 8 f-t, 4 p-t, 4 tech. *Video Use:* documentation of community/school events, in-service training, practical video/TV training courses, playback only of professionally produced tapes, production of instructional tapes. Video serv available on demand & by appointment. Produce video tapes. Have production studio/space & separate control room.

Video Equipment/Facilities *In-House Use Only:* portapak (3), b&w; recording deck (9), ½", ¾", 1" col; playback deck (5), col; editing deck (2), 1" b&w/col, IVC, Ampex; studio camera

(2), ¾" col; monitor (40); SEG (1); keyer (1); lighting (10); microphones (4); tripods (3); audio tape recorders (1). Have permanent & portable viewing installations. Provide training in use of equipment to faculty & student help. Have tape duplication serv.

Video Tape Loan/Rental/Sale Serv *Serv Provided:* swap with other inst. *Loan Eligibility:* org members. *Restrictions:* for indiv, only in inst. May not borrow by mail.

Video Collection Maintained by purchase, rental, own production, exchange/swap. Use/play ½", 1" reel to reel, ¾" cassette. *Sources:* commercial distributors, exchange (N.Y. State Education Dept). *Tape Sel:* preview, faculty/staff recommendations, catalogs. Tapes organized by subject & accession number. *Collection, Color:* ¾" cassette, 125t/c. *Other Video Serv:* programming, reference serv, taping of other media, production workshops, credit & non-credit courses in video methods. *Pubns:* catalog. Publish handbook for students & faculty.

Cable & CCTV Receive serv of cable TV system. Have CCTV in inst, with 36 monitors. *Programming Sources:* over-the-air commercial & public broadcasting, tapes produced by inst, tapes produced professionally & by community groups & indiv.

Saratoga Springs

P- SOUTHERN ADIRONDACK LIBRARY SYSTEM, 22 Whitney Pl, 12866. *Tel:* (518) 584-7300. *Film Serv Est:* 1969. *In Charge:* Patricia Pratt, AV Librarian. *AV Staff:* 2 (1 prof, 1½ cl). *Film Sel:* committee preview.

Free-Loan Film Serv *Eligibility:* civic groups, religious groups, indiv with library cards, prof groups, such as mental health, correctional & nursing inst. *Restrictions:* for indiv, none; for inst, none. Cannot use for fund-raising, borrow for classroom use. Available to researchers/scholars for on-site viewing. May borrow by mail. *Loan Period:* 1-14 days. *Total Yr Film Loan:* 3668.

Film Collection 500t/505p. Approx 40t acquired annually. *Circ:* 16mm, 500t/505p. *Pubns:* catalog, every 2 yrs ($.50); suppl, no set policy.

Other Film Serv Rent film from distributors for patrons, obtain film from other library systems, film reference serv, film fairs/festivals, library film programs. Permanent viewing facility available to community. *Equipment:* lend 16mm sound projector (2), projection screens (1).

Other Media Collections *Audio:* tape, cassette, 200c.

Budget & Expenditures Total library budget $80,734 (FY 1/1/74-1/1/75). Total FY film budget $22,282. *Member:* ALA, EFLA, FLIC, N.Y. Library Assn.

Schenectady

P- MOHAWK VALLEY LIBRARY ASSOCIATION, 858 Duanesburg Rd, 12306. *Tel:* (518) 355-2010. *Film Serv Est:* 1967. *In Charge:* Anthony Messineo, Deputy Dir. *AV Staff:* 3 (2 prof, 3 cl). *Film Sel:* committee preview. *Holdings:* animated films, black studies, children's films, consumer affairs, dance, experimental films, feature films, fine arts, industrial arts, science, social sciences, women.

Free-Loan Film Serv *Eligibility:* civic & religious groups, indiv with library cards, neighboring library systems. *Restrictions:* for indiv & inst, only in our four county system. Cannot use for fund-raising, transmit electronically, borrow for classroom use. *Loan Period:* varies. *Total Yr Film Loan:* 5458.

Film Collection 500t/504p. Approx 30-40t acquired annually. *Circ:* 16mm, 500t/504p. *Pubns:* catalog, as needed ($1); suppl, as needed.

Other Film Serv Obtain film from other libraries & library systems, library film programs. Permanent viewing facility. *Equipment:* lend 16mm sound projector (4), projection screens (1).

Other Media Collections *Audio:* disc, 33⅓ rpm, 2507t/2808c. *Member:* ALA, EFLA, FLIC.

Sparkill

C- ST. THOMAS AQUINAS COLLEGE, Route 340, 10976. *Tel:* (914) 359-6400, ext 283. *Video Serv Est:* 1960. *In Charge:* Dorothea Anders, Media Librarian. *Video Staff:* 1 f-t. *Video Use:* documentation of community/school events, in-service training, practical video/TV training courses, student teaching evaluation. Video serv available by appointment. Produce video tapes. Have production studio/space.

Video Equipment/Facilities *In-House Use Only:* portapak (1), b&w, Sony Rover II, AV 3400; recording & playback deck (2), b&w/col, Sony Rover, 3600, Panasonic EV 3200; studio camera (1), b&w, Panasonic WV 370P; monitor (1), b&w, Panasonic AV 67P; additional camera lenses (1); microphones (2); tripods (2). Provide training in use of equipment to faculty & students.

Video Collection Maintained by own production. Use/play ½″, 1″ reel to reel. Tapes organized by Dewey Decimal. *Collection, B&W:* ½″ reel, 10t/c; 1″ reel, 5t/c. *Other Video Serv:* production workshops.

Cable & CCTV Have CCTV in inst, with 9 monitors.

Stony Brook

C- STATE UNIVERSITY OF NEW YORK AT STONY BROOK, Library, 11787. *Tel:* (516) 246-5654. *Film Serv Est:* 1970. *In Charge:* Connie Koppelman, Art & AV Librarian. *AV Staff:* 2 (1 cl, 1 tech). *Film Sel:* committee preview, faculty/staff recommendations.

Free-Loan Film Serv *Eligibility:* staff & students. May not borrow by mail. *Loan Period:* 2 days. *Total Yr Film Loan:* 250.

Film Collection 300t/p. *Circ:* 16mm, 285t/300p. *Pubns:* catalog, every 2 yrs, suppl, no set policy.

Other Film Serv Film reference serv, library film programs.

Budget & Expenditures Total library budget $650,000. No separate AV budget. *Member:* State University of N.Y. Library Assn.

Syracuse

S- EVERSON MUSEUM OF ART, 401 Harrison St, 13202. *Tel:* (315) 474-6064, ext 29. *Video Serv Est:* 1972. *In Charge:* Richard J. Simmons, Associate Curator Video. *Video Use:* community video access, as art form. Video serv available by appointment. Produce video tapes. Have production studio/space.

Video Equipment/Facilities *In-House Use Only:* portapak (1), ½″ b&w, Sony 3400; recording deck (2), ½″, ¾″ col, Panasonic 3130, JVC; playback deck (2), ½″, ¾″ col, Panasonic; editing deck (2), ½″, ¾″ col, Panasonic; studio camera (2), b&w, Panasonic; monitor (1), Panasonic; SEG (1), Shintron; microphones; tripods; audio tape recorders. *For Loan:* portapak (1), ½″ b&w, Sony. Have permanent viewing installation. *Equipment Loan Period:* 1 day.

Video Collection Maintained by purchase, rental, own production. Use/play ½″ reel to reel, ¾″ cassette. *Sources:* commercial distributors, galleries, artists contributions. *Member:* Long Beach Museum of Art. *Tape Sel:* preview, staff recommendations, gallery previews, published reviews, catalogs. *Special Collections:* in-house training tapes, video as art, films in video format. Tapes organized alphabetically by artist. *Collection, Color:* ½″ & ¾″ cassette, 300t. *Other Video Serv:* programming, reference serv, taping of other media. *Pubns:* catalog. Publish posters & pamphlets of upcoming museum exhibits.

Cable & CCTV Have CCTV in inst, with 1 monitor. *Programming Sources:* tapes produced by inst, tapes produced by community groups & indiv.

P- ONONDAGA COUNTY PUBLIC LIBRARY, AV Servs, 327 Montgomery St, 13202. *Tel:* (315) 422-0342. *Film Serv Est:* 1968. *In Charge:* Edgar G Sanford, Head, AV Serv. *AV Staff:* 3½ (2 prof, 1 cl, ½ tech). *Film Sel:* committee preview, chief film librarian's decision, community need.

Free-Loan Film Serv *Eligibility:* civic groups, religious groups, indiv with library cards, prof groups, such as businesses, hospitals, librarians & others, such as nursing homes, day care centers, library programs. *Restrictions:* for indiv, only in Onondaga County; for inst, only in Onondaga County. Cannot use for fund-raising, transmit electronically, borrow for classroom use. Available to researchers/scholars for on-site viewing. May not borrow by mail. *Loan Period:* 2-3 days. *Total Yr Film Loan:* 11,825. Produce b&w EIAJ video, 35mm slides.

Film Collection 620t/625p. Approx 50t acquired annually. *Circ:* 16mm, 620t/625p. *Pubns:* catalog, every 2 yrs ($1); suppl, in yr catalog not published.

Other Film Serv Obtain film from coop loan system (N.Y. State Film Collection), film reference serv, film fairs/festivals, library film programs. *Equipment:* lend 16mm sound projector (4), projection tables & stands (2), projection screens (2).

Budget & Expenditures Total library budget $68,000 (FY 1/1/75-1/1/76). Total FY film budget $20,000. *Member:* AECT, ALA, EFLA.

Video Serv *Est:* 1975. *Video Staff:* 1 f-t. *Video Use:* documentation of community events, to increase community's library use, in-service training. Video serv available by appointment. Produce video tapes.

Video Equipment/Facilities *In-House Use Only:* portapak (2), ½″ b&w, Sony AV 8400; editing deck (1), ½″ col, Sony AV 8650; monitor (2), 11″ b&w, Sony CVM 115; microphones (2). *For Loan:* portapak (2), ½″ b&w, Sony AV8400; monitor (2), 11″ b&w, Sony CVM115; microphones (2). Have portable viewing installation. *Equipment Loan Period:* no set policy. Provide training in use of equipment to all users & borrowers.

Video Collection Maintained by own production. Use/play ½″ reel to reel. *Sources:* community productions. *Tape Sel:* own productions & local events. Tapes organized by production data & shelf number. *Collection, B&W:* ½″ reel, 10t. *Other Video Serv:* production workshops.

C- SYRACUSE UNIVERSITY, Film Rental Center, 1455 E Colvin St, 13210. *Tel:* (315) 479-6631. *Film Serv Est:* 1935. *In Charge:* B. A. Weekes, Dir. *AV Staff:* 24 (3 prof, 15 cl, 9 tech). *Film Sel:* faculty/staff recommendations, chief film librarian's decision, school requests. *Holdings:* agriculture, animated films, black studies, career education, children's films, consumer affairs, dance, engineering, experimental films, feature films, fine arts, industrial arts, law, medicine, science, social sciences, teacher education, women.

Film Rental Serv *Eligibility:* educational org, civic groups, patrons/public. *Restrictions:* only in U.S. Cannot transmit electronically or duplicate. *Rental Period:* 2-3 days. *Total Yr Film Booking:* 70,000. Sell films. Produce films.

Film Collection 10,000t/15,000p. Approx 800-900t acquired annually. *Circ:* 16mm, 10,000t/15,000p. *Pubns:* catalog, every 2 yrs; suppl, no set policy.

Other Film Serv Rent film from distributors for patrons, obtain film from coop loan system (University Film Rental Centers), film reference serv, film fairs/festivals, library film programs. Permanent viewing facility. *Equipment:* lend 16mm sound projector (2). *Member:* AECT, EFLA, N.Y. State AV Assn.

Troy

C- HUDSON VALLEY COMMUNITY COLLEGE, Instructional Media Center, 80 Vandenburgh Ave, 12180. *Tel:* (518) 283-1100, ext 476. *Film Serv Est:* 1970. *In Charge:* Bernard G. Law, Assoc. Dir, Learning Resources Center-Media. *AV Staff:* 10 (2 prof, 1 cl, 7 tech). *Film Sel:* faculty/staff recommendations.

Free-Loan Film Serv *Eligibility:* staff & students, educational inst, prof groups, such as Rotary, Visiting Nurses. *Restrictions:* for inst, only Rensselaer, Albany, Saratoga & Columbia Counties. Cannot use for fund-raising, transmit electronically. Available to researchers/scholars for on-site

Troy (cont'd)

viewing. May not borrow by mail. *Loan Period:* 7 days. *Total Yr Film Loan:* 1343. Produce films. Produce slide/cassettes, audio cassettes, video tapes, transparencies.

Film Collection   665t/668p. Approx 85t acquired annually. *Circ:* 16mm, 665t/668p; 8mm cartridge, 626t/p. *Pubns:* catalog, every 3 yrs ($.50); suppl, in yr catalog not published.

Other Film Serv   Obtain film from coop loan system (Capital Dist Library Council), film reference serv. Permanent viewing facility available for rent to community. *Equipment:* lend 16mm sound projector (21), 8mm reel projector (17), projection tables & stands (65), projection screens (80), slide projectors (10), audio/cassette players (15), slide/cassette projectors (9).

Other Media Collections   *Audio:* disc, 33⅓ rpm, 685t/c; tape, cassette, 652t. *Filmstrips:* sound sets, 681t/800c; silent sets, 294t/325c. *Slides:* single, 5000t; sets, 101t.

Budget & Expenditures   Total library budget $510,175 (FY 9/1/74-9/1/75). Total FY film budget $25,000. *Member:* EFLA.

Video Serv   *Est:* 1970. *Video Staff:* 2 f-t, 2 tech. *Video Use:* documentation of community/school events, to increase community's library use, community video access. Video serv available by appointment. Produce video tapes. Have production studio/space & separate control room.

Video Equipment/Facilities   *In-House Use Only:* recording deck (2), b&w, JVC450; playback deck (5), col, IVC700, 600, VCR100; editing deck; studio camera (2), col, IVC90; monitor (26), b&w/col, RCA, GE, Westinghouse; SEG (1), Shintron; keyer, Grass Valley; lighting (14); microphones (3); tripods (4); audio tape recorders (3). Have permanent viewing installation. Provide training in use of equipment to students.

Video Collection   Maintained by own production. Use/play ½" reel to reel. Tapes organized by division/department/instructor. *Collection, Color:* 1" reel, 250t/c. *Collection, B&W:* ½" reel, 36t/c.

Cable & CCTV   Have CCTV in inst, with 16 monitors. *Programming Sources:* tapes produced by inst.

Utica

P- MID-YORK LIBRARY SYSTEM, 1600 Lincoln Ave, 13502. *Tel:* (315) 735-8328. *Film Serv Est:* 1967. *In Charge:* Carleton E. Wood, Jr., AV Consultant. *AV Staff:* 4½ (1 prof, 3 cl, 1 tech). *Film Sel:* committee preview, staff recommendations, chief film librarian's decision. *Holdings:* black studies 2%, children's films 10%, feature films 6%, fine arts 4%.

Free-Loan Film Serv   *Eligibility:* civic groups, religious groups, indiv with library cards, prof groups, such as Community Action & others, such as member libraries. *Restrictions:* for indiv, only in Oneida, Herkimer & Madison Counties; for inst, only in Oneida, Herkimer & Madison Counties. Cannot use for fund-raising, transmit electronically. Available to researchers/scholars for on-site viewing. May not borrow by mail. *Loan Period:* 1 day. *Total Yr Film Loan:* 7473.

Film Rental Serv   *Eligibility:* educational org. *Restrictions:* only in Oneida, Herkimer & Madison Counties. Cannot use for fund-raising, transmit electronically. *Rental Period:* 1 day. *Total Yr Film Booking:* 2698.

Film Collection   1005t/1030p. Approx 100t acquired annually. *Circ:* 16mm, 1005t/1030p. *Pubns:* catalog, every 2 yrs ($2); suppl, no set policy.

Other Film Serv   Obtain film from coop loan system (N.Y. State Library), film reference serv, library film programs, annual film workshop. Permanent viewing facility.

Other Media Collections   *Audio:* disc, 33⅓ rpm, 7101t/11,048c. *Filmstrips:* sound sets, 221t/241c. *Slides:* sets, 73t/c.

Budget & Expenditures   Total library budget $100,000 (FY 1/1/75-1/1/76). Total FY film budget $22,000. *Member:* EFLA.

Watertown

P- NORTH COUNTRY LIBRARY SYSTEM, Box 192, 13601. *Tel:* (315) 782-5540. *Film Serv Est:* 1948. *In Charge:* Irma Epstein, Chief Clerk. *AV Staff:* 2½ (½ prof, 2 cl). *Film Sel:* committee preview. *Holdings:* children's films 30%.

Free-Loan Film Serv   *Eligibility:* educational inst, civic groups, indiv with library cards. *Restrictions:* for indiv, only in area of our 4 counties; for inst, only in area of our 4 counties. Cannot use for fund-raising. Public schools must pay $2 per film. Available to researchers/scholars for on-site viewing. May not borrow by mail. *Loan Period:* 7 days. *Total Yr Film Loan:* 1800.

Film Collection   1225t/1300p. Approx 130t acquired annually. *Circ:* 16mm, 1225t/1300p. *Pubns:* catalog, every 2 yrs; suppl, no set policy.

Other Film Serv   Obtain film from coop loan system (N.Y. State Library), film reference serv, library film programs. *Equipment:* lend 16mm sound projector (4).

Other Media Collections   *Audio:* disc, 33⅓ rpm, 1700t/2210c; 78rpm, 140t/160c.

Budget & Expenditures   Total library budget $134,000 (FY 1/1/74-1/1/75). Total FY film budget $32,460. *Member:* ALA, EFLA, N.Y. Library Assn.

West Point

C- UNITED STATES MILITARY ACADEMY, AV Section, USMA Library, 10996. *Tel:* (914) 938-2247. *Film Serv Est:* 1972. *In Charge:* A. Dean Hough, Media Specialist. *AV Staff:* 2½ (1½ prof, 1 tech). *Film Sel:* faculty/staff recommendations, chief film librarian's decision.

Free-Loan Film Serv   *Eligibility:* staff & students. *Restrictions:* for indiv, only in our inst. Cannot use for fund-raising, transmit electronically. Available to researchers/scholars for on-site viewing. May not borrow by mail. *Loan Period:* as needed. *Total Yr Film Loan:* 127.

Film Collection   130t/137p. *Circ:* 16mm, 130t/137p.

Other Film Serv   Film reference serv. Permanent viewing facility. *Equipment:* lend 16mm sound projector (1), projection screens (2).

Other Media Collections   *Audio:* disc, 33⅓ rpm, 5400t/5500c; tape, cassette, 233t/c; tape, reel, 200t/c. *Filmstrips:* sound, 4t/c; silent, 42t/c; sound sets, 21t/c. *Slides:* single, 6800t/7200c; sets, 11t/c.

Budget & Expenditures   Total library budget $221,000 (FY 7/1/74-7/1/75). No separate budget.

Video Serv   *Est:* 1975. *Video Staff:* 2 f-t, 1 p-t, 1 tech. *Video Use:* instruction. Video serv available on demand.

Video Equipment/Facilities   *In-House Use Only:* playback deck (8), ¾" col, Sony; monitor (8), col, Sony, Trinitron. Have permanent viewing installation.

Video Tape Loan/Rental/Sale Serv   *Serv Provided:* free loan. *Loan Eligibility:* staff & students. *Restrictions:* for indiv, only our inst. Cannot use for fund-raising, duplicate, air without permission. May not borrow by mail. *Loan Period:* as needed.

Video Collection   Maintained by purchase, own production. Use/play ¾" cassette. *Sources:* own productions. *Tape Sel:* faculty/staff recommendations. Tapes organized by production serial numbers. *Collection, Color:* ¾" cassette, 75t/c. *Collection, B&W:* ¾" cassette, 50t/c.

Cable & CCTV   Have CCTV in inst. *Programming Sources:* over-the-air commercial & public broadcasting, tapes produced by inst, tapes produced professionally.

North Carolina

Charlotte

C- CENTRAL PIEDMONT COMMUNITY COLLEGE, AV Center, Box 4009, 28204. *Tel:* (704) 373-6701. *Film Serv Est:* 1970. *In Charge:* Worth Campbell, Vice President Learning Resources. *Film Sel:* faculty/staff recommendations. Produce slides, cassettes, film loops, transparencies.

Film Collection 850t/p. Approx 100t acquired annually. *Circ:* 16mm, 850t; S8mm cartridge, 700t.

Other Film Serv Obtain film from other libraries, film reference serv.

Other Media Collections *Audio:* tape, cassette, 1000t; tape, reel, 250t. *Filmstrips:* silent, 500t; sound sets, 500t. *Slides:* sets, 300t.

Budget & Expenditures No separate budget. *Member:* Metrolina Library Assn.

Video Serv *Est:* 1974. *Video Staff:* 6 f-t, 4 p-t, 2 tech. *Video Use:* documentation of community/school events, in-service training, playback of professionally produced tapes, instructional materials production. Video serv available by appointment. Produce video tapes. Have production studio/space & separate control room.

Video Equipment/Facilities *In-House Use Only:* portapak (4), b&w/col, Sony; recording deck (25), ½″, ¾″, 1″ b&w/col, Sony, Concord, Panasonic; playback deck (30), ½″, ¾″ b&w/col, Sony, Concord; editing deck (3), ½″, 1″ col, Panasonic; studio camera (3), col, Shibaden; monitor (50), b&w/col, RCA, Concord, Bell, Setchell Carlson; SEG (4), Shibaden, Concord, Panasonic; keyer (1), Shintron; additional camera lenses (20); lighting (1); microphones (10); tripods (4); audio tape recorders (4). Have permanent & portable viewing installations. *Equipment Loan Period:* 1 week. Provide training in use of equipment to faculty. Have tape duplication serv.

Video Collection Maintained by purchase, rental, own production. Use/play ½″, 1″ reel to reel, ½″ cartridge, ¾″ cassette. *Sources:* commercial distributors. *Tape Sel:* preview, faculty/staff recommendations. *Special Collections:* in-house training tapes, films in video format. Tapes organized by accession number. *Collection, Color:* ½″ reel, 30t; ¾″ cassette, 25t. *Other Video Serv:* reference serv.

Cable & CCTV Have CCTV in inst, with 20 monitors. *Programming Sources:* tapes produced by inst, tapes produced professionally.

C- JOHNSON C. SMITH UNIVERSITY, James B. Duke Memorial Library, 100 Beatties Ford Rd, 28216. *Tel:* (704) 372-2370, ext 211, 212, 213. *Film Serv Est:* 1971. *In Charge:* Mildred Sanders, Librarian. *AV Staff:* 1 (1 prof, 1 tech). *Film Sel:* faculty/staff recommendations, chief film librarian's decision. *Holdings:* black studies 5%, social sciences 25%, teacher education 5%.

Free-Loan Film Serv *Eligibility:* staff & students, educational inst, indiv with library cards. *Restrictions:* for indiv, interlibrary loan; for inst, only in state. Cannot use for fund-raising, transmit electronically. Available to researchers/ scholars for on-site viewing. May borrow by mail. *Loan Period:* 3 days. *Total Yr Film Loan:* 114.

Film Collection 135t. Approx 15-25t acquired annually. *Circ:* 16mm, 235t; S8mm cartridge, 23t. *Pubns:* catalog, as needed; suppl, no set policy.

Other Film Serv Obtain film from coop loan system (Piedmont Univ. Center, N.C. Assn. of Independent Colleges & Universities). Permanent viewing facility available for rent to community. *Equipment:* lend 16mm sound projector (5), S8mm cartridge projector (3), S8mm reel projector (1), projection tables & stands (3), projection screens (3).

Other Media Collections *Audio:* disc, 33⅓ rpm, 429t; tape, cassette, 135t; tape, reel, 13t. *Filmstrips:* silent, 135t; sound sets, 103t; silent sets, 10t. *Slides:* single, 656t; sets, 33t. *Member:* N.C. Lib Assn.

Video Serv *Est:* 1970. *In Charge:* E. L. James, Jr., Coord, Media Communications. *Video Use:* to increase community's library use, in-service training, practical video/TV training courses, as art form, communications courses, speech & drama. Video serv available by appointment. Produce video tapes.

Video Equipment/Facilities *In-House Use Only:* playback deck (5), ½″ b&w, Shibaden; editing deck (1), ½″ b&w, Shibaden; studio camera (5), ½″ b&w, Shibaden, Craig; monitor (3), b&w, Shibaden; SEG (3), Shibaden, Craig; microphones (2); tripods (3). *For Loan:* portapak (1), ½″ b&w, Shibaden. *Equipment Loan Period:* depends on material. Provide training in use of equipment to faculty & students. Have tape duplication serv.

Video Collection Use/play ½″ reel to reel. *Other Video Serv:* programming, taping of other media, production workshops.

P- PUBLIC LIBRARY OF CHARLOTTE & MECKLENBURG COUNTY, Film and Sound Section, 310 North Tryon St, 28202. *Tel:* (704) 374-2912. *Film Serv Est:* 1942. *In Charge:* Carmen Lipe, Head, Film and Sound Section. *AV Staff:* 6 (1 prof, 4 cl, 1 tech). *Film Sel:* committee preview, staff recommendations, chief film librarian's decision.

Free-Loan Film Serv *Eligibility:* indiv with AV borrowing library cards. *Restrictions:* for indiv & inst, only in Mecklenburg County. Cannot use for fund-raising, transmit electronically. Available to researchers/scholars for on-site viewing. May not borrow by mail. *Loan Period:* 2 days. *Total Yr Film Loan:* 16,256.

Film Rental Serv *Eligibility:* no restrictions. *Restrictions:* only in neighboring counties.

Film Collection 1311t. Approx 75t acquired annually. *Circ:* 16mm, 884t/919p. *Pubns:* catalog, annual.

Other Film Serv Obtain film from coop loan system (N.C. State Library AV Service), film reference serv, library film programs. Permanent viewing facility available free to community. *Equipment:* lend 16mm sound projector (6), 8mm reel projector (1), S8mm reel projector, projection tables & stands, projection screens, carousel slide projectors (3); filmstrip projectors (2); overhead projectors (2); opaque projector (1); cassette players (4); cassette tape recorder (1); reel-to-reel tape recorder (1); portable record player (1); portable public address system (1).

Other Media Collections *Audio:* disc, 33⅓ rpm, 10,000c; tape, cassette, 20c. *Filmstrips:* sound, 160t; silent, 79t. *Slides:* sets, 152t.

Budget & Expenditures Total FY film budget $20,000 (FY 7/1/74-7/1/75). *Member:* ALA, N.C. Lib Assn, IFLA, SELA.

C- UNIVERSITY OF NORTH CAROLINA-CHARLOTTE, Learning Resources Center, 28223. *Tel:* (704) 597-2435. *Film Serv Est:* 1974. *In Charge:* Dorlan Mork, Dir, Learning Resources. *AV Staff:* 13 (4 prof, 2 cl, 2 tech). *Film Sel:* faculty/staff recommendations.

Free-Loan Film Serv *Eligibility:* staff & students. *Restrictions:* for indiv & inst, only in our institution. *Loan Period:* 1 day.

Film Collection 300t/p. Approx 50t acquired annually. *Circ:* 16mm, 300t/p. *Pubns:* catalog, every 2 yrs; suppl, no set policy.

Other Film Serv Rent film from distributors for patrons, obtain film from coop loan system. Permanent viewing facility. *Equipment:* lend S8mm camera (5), 16mm camera (1), 16mm sound projector (54), 8mm cartridge projector (10), 8mm reel projector (4), S8mm cartridge projector (4), S8mm reel projector (10), projection tables & stands (110), projection screens (85). *Member:* AECT, AFI, ALA, CUFC, EFLA, FLIC

Video Serv *Est:* 1975. *Video Use:* documentation of community/school events, in-service training, practical video/TV

Charlotte (cont'd)
training courses. Video serv available by appointment. Produce video tapes. Have production studio/space & separate control room.

Video Equipment/Facilities *In-House Use Only:* recording deck (10), ½", ¾" b&w/col; playback deck (10), ½", ¾" b&w/col; editing deck (1), ¾" b&w/col; studio camera (6), b&w; monitor (23), b&w/col; SEG (1), Concord; additional camera lenses (4); lighting (6); microphones (22); tripods (12); audio tape recorders (150). *For Loan:* portapak (8), ½" b&w, Panasonic, Concord; monitor (23), b&w/col; lighting (6); microphones (22); tripods (12); audio tape recorders (150). Have permanent & portable viewing installations. *Equipment Loan Period:* as needed. Provide training in use of equipment to faculty & students. Have tape duplication serv.

Video Tape Loan/Rental/Sale Serv *Serv Provided:* free loan. *Loan Eligibility:* org members, staff & students. *Restrictions:* for indiv & inst, only in our institution. May not borrow by mail. *Loan Period:* 7 days or as needed.

Video Collection Maintained by rental, own production. Use/play ½" reel to reel, ½" cartridge, ¾" cassette. *Sources:* commercial distributors. *Tape Sel:* faculty/staff recommendations. Tapes organized numerically. *Collection, B&W:* ½" reel, 60t/c; ¾" cassette, 20t/c. *Other Video Serv:* production workshops. *Pubns:* catalog.

Elizabeth City

C- ELIZABETH CITY STATE UNIVERSITY, G. R. Little Library, Parkview Dr, 27909. *Tel:* (919) 335-0551, ext 332. *Film Serv Est:* 1970.
Film Collection 2t. *Noncirc:* 16mm, 2t. Publish acquisitions list.
Other Media Collections *Audio:* tape, cassette, 10c; tape, reel, 15c. *Filmstrips:* sound, 240c; sound sets, 80c; silent sets, 10c. *Slides:* single, 2404c; sets, 12c.
Video Serv *Est:* 1970. *Video Use:* library related activities & student use. Video serv available as requested. Produce video tapes.
Video Equipment/Facilities *In-House Use Only:* studio camera (1), b&w; monitor (1), b&w; microphones (1); audio tape recorders (1).

Gastonia

S- SCHIELE MUSEUM OF NATURAL HISTORY & PLANE-TARIUM, Box 953, 28052. *Tel:* (704) 865-6131, 864-3962. *Film Serv Est:* 1961. *In Charge:* David R. Stultz, Curator of Education. *AV Staff:* 3 (3 prof). *Film Sel:* committee preview, staff recommendations. *Holdings:* fine arts 10%, science 65%, social sciences 15%, teacher education 10%, women.
Free-Loan Film Serv *Eligibility:* org members, staff & students, educational inst, civic & religious groups. *Restrictions:* for indiv, only in Gaston County; for inst, only in state. Cannot borrow for classroom use. Available to researchers/scholars for on-site viewing. *Loan Period:* 5 days. *Total Yr Film Loan:* 10. Produce 16mm b&w/col movies, 35mm b&w slides.
Film Collection 40t. Approx 3t acquired annually. *Circ:* 16mm, 2t. *Noncirc:* 16mm, 38t. Publish listing in newspapers.
Other Film Serv Obtain film from coop loan system (State Library, Southern Bell), obtain film from other libraries, film reference serv, library film programs. Permanent viewing facility.
Other Media Collections *Audio:* disc, 33⅓ rpm, 100t; tape, cassette, 10t; tape, reel, 25t. *Slides:* single, 2000t; sets, 14t.
Budget & Expenditures No separate budget. *Member:* N.C. Lib Assn.

Greensboro

P- GREENSBORO PUBLIC LIBRARY, Group Services Dept, Drawer X-4, 27402. *Tel:* (919) 373-2473. *Film Serv Est:* 1964. *In Charge:* Mary B. Welker, Group Services Librarian. *AV*

Staff: 3 (2 prof, 1 cl). *Film Sel:* published reviews, AV staff previews. *Holdings:* children's films 50%, feature films, travel.
Free-Loan Film Serv *Eligibility:* educational inst, civic groups, religious groups, indiv with adult library cards, prof groups. *Restrictions:* for indiv & inst, only in state. Available to researchers/scholars for on-site viewing. May not borrow by mail. *Loan Period:* as required. *Total Yr Film Loan:* 13,021.
Film Collection 300t/p. Approx 30t acquired annually. *Circ:* 16mm, 300t/p; 8mm reel, 250t/300p. *Pubns:* catalog, annual; suppl, no set policy.
Other Film Serv Obtain film from coop loan system (State Library), film reference serv, film fairs/festivals, library film programs. Permanent viewing facility available free to community. *Equipment:* rent 16mm sound projector (1), rent 8mm reel projector (3), filmstrip, slide, cassette player/recorder.
Other Media Collections *Audio:* disc, 33⅓ rpm, 10,000t; tape, cassette, 150t. *Filmstrips:* sound, 150t. *Slides:* sets, 75t.
Budget & Expenditures Total library budget $218,168 (FY 7/1/74-7/1/75). Total FY film budget $30,000. *Member:* N.C. Lib Assn.

Jacksonville

C- COASTAL CAROLINA COMMUNITY COLLEGE, Learning Resources Center, 222 Georgetown Rd, 28540. *Tel:* (919) 455-1221, ext 42. *Film Serv Est:* 1973. *In Charge:* Richard Martin, Media Coordinator. *AV Staff:* 1. *Film Sel:* faculty/staff recommendations, chief film librarian's decision.
Free-Loan Film Serv *Eligibility:* staff & students, educational inst, civic groups, religious groups, indiv with library cards. *Restrictions:* for indiv & inst, only in our county. Cannot use for fund-raising, borrow for classroom use. Available to researchers/scholars for on-site viewing. May not borrow by mail. *Loan Period:* 2 days. Produce video tapes & 35mm slide sets.
Film Collection 300t/p. Approx 10t acquired annually. *Circ:* 16mm, 300t. *Noncirc:* S8mm cartridge, 40t. *Pubns:* catalog, annual or as needed.
Other Film Serv Obtain film from coop loan system, obtain film from other libraries. Permanent viewing facility. *Equipment:* lend 16mm sound projector (14), 8mm cartridge projector (12), S8mm cartridge projector (2), projection screens (30).
Other Media Collections *Audio:* disc, 33⅓ rpm, 320t/c; tape, cassette, 400t/c; tape, reel, 50t/25c. *Filmstrips:* sound, 20t/c; silent, 10t/c; sound sets, 150t/c. *Slides:* single, 150t/c; sets, 120t/c.
Budget & Expenditures No separate budget. *Member:* N.C. Lib Assn, N.C. Resources Center.
Video Serv *Est:* 1972. *Video Staff:* 1 f-t. *Video Use:* documentation of community/school events, to increase community's library use. Video serv available by appointment. Produce video tapes. Have production studio/space & separate control room.
Video Equipment/Facilities *In-House Use Only:* portapak (2), ½" b&w/col, Panasonic; recording deck (6), ½", ¾" b&w/col, Panasonic; editing deck (2), ½"; studio camera (3), b&w/col, Panasonic; monitor (20), b&w/col, Panasonic, Sony; SEG (1), Panasonic; lighting (2); microphones (10); tripods (4); audio tape recorders (20). Have permanent & portable viewing installations. *Equipment Loan Period:* 1 day. Provide training in use of equipment to faculty & students. Have tape duplication serv.
Video Tape Loan/Rental/Sale Serv *Serv Provided:* free loan. *Loan Eligibility:* staff & students, educational inst, civic & religious groups, indiv with library cards, prof groups. *Restrictions:* for indiv & inst, only in our county. Cannot use for fund-raising, duplicate, air without permission. May not borrow by mail.
Video Collection Maintained by purchase, rental, own production, exchange/swap. Use/play ½" reel to reel, ½" cartridge, ¾" cassette. *Sources:* commercial distributors. *Tape Sel:* preview, faculty/staff recommendations, catalogs. *Special Collections:* in-house training tapes. Tapes organized numerically.

Collection, Color: ½″ reel, 20t/c; ¾″ cassette, 15t/c. *Collection, B&W:* ½″ reel, 125t/c; ½″ cartridge, 35t/c. *Other Video Serv:* programming.

Cable & CTTV Will receive serv of cable TV system. Have CCTV in inst, with 45 monitors. *Programming Sources:* over-the-air commercial & public broadcasting, tapes produced by inst, tapes produced professionally, tapes produced by community groups & indiv, rental tapes.

Louisburg

C- LOUISBURG COLLEGE, C. W. Robbins Library, Main St, 27549. *Tel:* (919) 496-2521, exts 289, 281, 279. *In Charge:* Don Richardson, Librarian. *Video Staff:* 1 f-t, 4 p-t. *Video Use:* community video access, in-service training, practical training courses, as art form, student media projects, classroom use. Video serv available by appointment. Produce video tapes. *For Loan:* portapak (2), ½″ b&w, Sony; recording deck (4), b&w; studio camera (6); monitor (6); SEG (1); tripods (4). Have portable viewing installation. Provide training in use of equipment to faculty & students.

Video Tape Loan/Rental/Sale Serv *Serv Provided:* free loan. *Loan Eligibility:* staff & students, civic & religious groups. *Restrictions:* for indiv & inst, none. May borrow by mail. *Loan Period:* according to need. *Total Yr Tape Loan:* 2.

Video Collection Maintained by own production, exchange/swap. Use/play ½″ reel to reel. *Sources:* exchange (WUNC-TV). *Tape Sel:* faculty/staff recommendations, own productions. Tapes organized by accession number. *Collection, B&W:* ¾″ cassette, 3t/c. *Pubns:* catalog.

Montreat

A- HISTORICAL FOUNDATION OF THE PRESBYTERIAN & REFORMED CHURCHES, Box 847, 28757. *Tel:* (704) 669-7061. *Film Serv Est:* 1928. *In Charge:* Kenneth Joseph Foreman, Jr., Executive Dir. *AV Staff:* 2 (1 prof). *Film Sel:* donations. *Holdings:* church history.

Film Collection 200t/p. Approx 20t acquired annually. *Noncirc:* 16mm, 180t/p; 8mm reel, 20t/p.

Other Media Collections *Audio:* disc 33⅓ rpm, 500t; tape, cassette, 1000t; tape, reel, 3500t. *Filmstrips:* sound, 200t; silent, 1t. *Slides:* single, 5000t. *Member:* ALA, N.C. Lib Assn, Western N.C. Lib Assn, ATLA.

New Bern

C- CRAVEN COMMUNITY COLLEGE, R. C. Godwin Memorial Library, Box 885, 28560. *Tel:* (919) 638-4131, ext 55. *Film Serv Est:* 1970. *Film Sel:* faculty/staff recommendations.

Free-Loan Film Serv *Eligibility:* staff & students, educational inst, civic & religious groups, indiv with library cards, prof groups, such as business & women's groups. *Restrictions:* for indiv, interlibrary loan; for inst, none. May borrow by mail. *Loan Period:* 1 day. *Total Yr Film Loan:* 1.

Film Collection 99t/p. *Circ:* 16mm, 99t/p; 8mm cartridge, 99t/142p.

Other Film Serv Obtain film from coop loan system (N.C. State Library). *Equipment:* lend S8mm camera (1), 16mm sound projector (12), 8mm reel projector (1), S8mm cartridge projector (7), projection tables & stands (16), projection screens (5), 35mm filmstrip projector (8), slide projector (13), record players (13), cassette recorders (22).

Other Media Collections *Audio:* disc, 33⅓ rpm, 347t; tape, cassette, 281t; tape, reel, 4t. *Filmstrips:* sound sets, 500t; silent sets, 29t. *Slides:* sets, 38t.

Budget & Expenditures Total library budget $12,000 (FY 7/1/74-7/1/75). No separate AV budget.

Video Serv *Est:* 1972. *In Charge:* Bill Ward, Media Technician. *Video Staff:* 1 tech. *Video Use:* documentation of community/school events, classroom instruction. Video serv available by appointment. Produce video tapes.

Video Equipment/Facilities *In-House Use Only:* portapak (1), ½″ b&w, Panasonic; recording deck (2), ½″ b&w, Panasonic; studio camera (2), ½″ b&w, Panasonic; monitor (1), ½″ b&w/col, Panasonic; SEG (1), Panasonic; microphones (2); tripods (1). Provide training in use of equipment to faculty.

Video Collection Maintained by own production. Use/play ½″ reel to reel. *Collection, B&W:* ¾″ cassette, 7t/c.

Raleigh

S- DEPT. OF HUMAN RESOURCES-DIVISION OF HEALTH SERVICES, The Film Library, 27602. *Tel:* (919) 829-3471. *Film Serv Est:* 1942. *In Charge:* Roger G. Whitley, Supervisor. *AV Staff:* 11 (1 prof, 4 cl, 6 tech). *Holdings:* animated films, career education, health, medicine, social sciences, teacher education.

Film Rental Serv *Eligibility:* no restrictions other than that no medical films are sent to schools or lay organizations. *Restrictions:* only in state. *Rental Period:* varies.

Film Collection 1100t. Approx 200t acquired annually. *Circ:* 16mm, 1100t/4500p. *Pubns:* catalog, annual; suppl, in yr catalog not published.

Other Film Serv Obtain film from other libraries, film fairs/festivals. Permanent viewing facility available free to community. *Equipment:* lend 16mm sound projector (175), projection screens (175).

Budget & Expenditures Total library budget $70,000 (FY 7/1/74-7/1/75). Total FY film budget $70,000.

P- WAKE COUNTY PUBLIC LIBRARIES, AV Dept, 104 Fayetteville St, 27601. *Tel:* (919) 833-2011. *Film Serv Est:* 1974. *In Charge:* Barry J. Mangum, Supervisor, AV Services. *AV Staff:* 4 (1 prof, 2½ cl, ½ tech). *Film Sel:* committee preview, chief film librarian's decision.

Free-Loan Film Serv *Eligibility:* indiv with library cards. *Restrictions:* for indiv, only in Wake County. Cannot use for fund-raising, transmit electronically. Available to researchers/scholars for on-site viewing. May not borrow by mail. *Loan Period:* 1-7 days.

Film Collection 140t/p. *Circ:* 16mm, 140t/p; S8mm cartridge, 40t/p. *Pubns:* catalog, annual; suppl, as needed.

Other Film Serv Obtain film from coop loan system (N.C. State Library), film fairs/festivals, library film programs. Permanent viewing facility. *Equipment:* lend 16mm sound projector (16), 8mm cartridge projector (6), 8mm reel projector (6), S8mm reel projector (6), projection tables & stands (4), projection screens (14), cassettes (12), lend phonographs (2).

Other Media Collections *Audio:* disc, 33⅓ rpm, 5000t; disc, tape, cassette, 200t; tape, reel, 50t. *Filmstrips:* sound, 90t; silent, 10t. *Slides:* single, 4000t; sets, 25t.

Budget & Expenditures Total library budget $200,000 (FY 7/1/74-7/1/75). Total FY film budget $18,000. *Member:* N.C. Library Assn.

Rocky Mount

C- NASH TECHNICAL INSTITUTE, Route 5, Box 255, 27801. *Tel:* (919) 443-4011, ext 244. *Film Serv Est:* 1968. *In Charge:* Geneva B. Chavis, Dean, Learning Resources Center. *AV Staff:* 1 (1 prof). *Film Sel:* faculty/staff recommendations. *Holdings:* automotive 2.6%, business 38.9%, cosmetology 5.2%, consumer affairs 6.5%, engineering 8%, experimental films 1%, instrumentation 3.9%, public health & safety 13%, science 7.8%, social sciences 1%, speech 1%, teacher education 1%.

Free-Loan Film Serv *Eligibility:* staff & students, educational inst, civic & religious groups, prof groups. *Restrictions:* for indiv & inst, only in our county & neighboring counties. Available to researchers/scholars for on-site viewing. *Loan Period:* 2 days. Produce slides, tapes, photographs.

Film Collection 77t. Approx 21t acquired annually. *Circ:* 16mm, 77t; 8mm reel, 105t. Print memo of new films. *Equipment:* lend 16mm sound projector (8), lend 8mm cartridge projector (4), lend projection tables & stands (9), lend projection screens (20).

Rocky Mount (cont'd)

Other Media Collections *Audio:* disc, 33⅓ rpm, 43t/c; tape, cassette, 1050t/1149c; tape, reel, 90c. *Filmstrips:* sound, 839c; silent, 740c. *Slides:* single, 3372c.

Budget & Expenditures No separate budget. *Member:* ALA, N.C. Lib Assn.

Video Serv *Est:* 1974. *In Charge:* Ron Capps, Dir, Evening Programs. *Video Staff:* 1 p-t. *Video Use:* classroom instruction. Video serv available on demand. Produce video tapes.

Video Equipment/Facilities *In-House Use Only:* studio camera (1); monitor (1); tripod (1); audio tape recorder (1).

Video Collection Maintained by own production. Use/play ¾" cassette. *Collection, Color:* ¾" cassette, 7t. Print memo of new videotapes.

Sanford

C- CENTRAL CAROLINA TECHNICAL INSTITUTE, Learning Resource Center, 1105 Kelly Dr, 27330. *Tel:* (919) 775-5401, ext 244. *In Charge:* William A. Myers, Media Facilitator. *AV Staff:* 1 (1 prof). *Film Sel:* faculty/staff recommendations. *Holdings:* career education 2%, driver education 12%, industrial arts 2%, math 5%, nursing 9%, safety 25%, science 2%, technical 20%.

Free-Loan Film Serv *Eligibility:* staff & students, educational inst, civic & religious groups, indiv with library cards, prof groups. *Restrictions:* for indiv, interlibrary loan, only in state; for inst, only in state. Available to researchers/scholars for on-site viewing. May borrow by mail. *Loan Period:* varies.

Film Collection 90t. Approx 5t acquired annually. *Circ:* 16mm, 90t; 8mm reel, 2t; S8mm cartridge, 30t.

Other Film Serv Obtain film from coop loan system, obtain film from other libraries. *Equipment:* lend S8mm camera, 16mm sound projector, 8mm reel projector, projection screens.

Other Media Collections *Audio:* disc, 33⅓ rpm, 300t; tape, cassette, 600c; tape, reel, 150c. *Filmstrips:* silent, 150t; sound sets, 274t. *Slides:* sets, 25t.

Budget & Expenditures No separate budget.

Video Serv *Est:* 1974. *In Charge:* William A. Myers, Media Facilitator. *Video Staff:* 1 f-t. *Video Use:* documentation of community/school events, in-service training. Video serv available on demand & by appointment. Produce video tapes.

Video Equipment/Facilities *In-House Use Only:* portapak (1), col, Shibaden; recording deck (1), col, Shibaden; playback deck (1), col, Shibaden; studio camera (1), col, Magnavox; monitor (1), col, Panasonic; lighting (3); microphones (1); tripods (1). Provide training in use of equipment to faculty & students.

Video Tape Loan/Rental/Sale Serv *Serv Provided:* swap with other inst. *Loan Eligibility:* staff & students.

Video Collection Maintained by own production. Use/play ½" reel to reel. *Tape Sel:* preview. *Collection, Color:* ½" reel, 3t. *Collection, B&W:* ½" reel, 18t.

Southern Pines

C- SANDHILLS COMMUNITY COLLEGE, AV Dept, Box 1379, 28387. *Tel:* (919) 692-6185, ext 24. *Film Serv Est:* 1965. *In Charge:* Wayne Livengood, AV Dir. *AV Staff:* 5 (2 prof, 1 cl, 2 tech). *Film Sel:* faculty/staff recommendations.

Free-Loan Film Serv *Eligibility:* staff & students, educational inst, civic groups, prof groups, & others, such as Rotary Clubs. *Restrictions:* for indiv, only in city; for inst, only in our county. Cannot use for noneducational purposes. Available to researchers/scholars for on-site viewing. May not borrow by mail. *Loan Period:* 2 days. *Total Yr Film Loan:* 50.

Film Collection 280t/p. Approx 12t acquired annually. *Circ:* 16mm, 280t/p. *Pubns:* catalog, annual.

Other Film Serv *Equipment:* lend 16mm sound projector (22), projection screens (5).

Other Media Collections *Audio:* disc, 33⅓ rpm, 500t; tape, cassette, 1200t. *Filmstrips:* sound, 600t; silent, 650t. *Slides:* single, 300t; sets, 100t.

Budget & Expenditures Total AV budget $7500 (FY 7/1/74-7/1/75). *Member:* EFLA.

Video Serv *Est:* 1973. *Video Use:* instruction. Video serv available by appointment. Produce video tapes.

Video Equipment/Facilities *In-House Use Only:* portapak (2), ¾" col, Sony; studio camera (2), b&w, Panasonic; monitor (12), b&w/col, GE; microphones (5); tripods (2); audio tape recorders (10). Provide training in use of equipment to faculty & students. Have tape duplication serv.

Video Collection Maintained by purchase, rental, own production. Use/play ¾" cassette. *Tape Sel:* faculty/staff recommendations. Tapes organized by subject. *Collection, Color:* ¾" cassette, 30t. *Other Video Serv:* taping of other media, production workshops.

Cable & CTTV Have CCTV in inst, with 6 monitors. *Programming Sources:* over-the-air commercial & public broadcasting.

Tarboro

C- EDGECOMBE COUNTY TECHNICAL INSTITUTE, Learning Resources Center, Box 550, 27886. *Tel:* (919) 823-5166, ext 25. *Film Serv Est:* 1972. *In Charge:* Dorothy M. Cherry, Technical Assistance. *AV Staff:* 1 (1 cl). *Film Sel:* faculty/staff recommendations. Produce slides, transparencies, 8mm films.

Film Collection 83t/p. Approx 10t acquired annually. *Circ:* 16mm, 33t; S8mm reel, 50t. Bibliographic list of holdings.

Other Film Serv Rent film from distributors for patrons, obtain film from coop loan system, obtain film from other libraries. *Equipment:* rent S8mm camera (2), 16mm sound projector (6), 8mm cartridge projector (3), projection screens (4).

Other Media Collections *Audio:* disc & tape, total 206t. *Filmstrips:* total 181t. *Slides:* total 111t.

Budget & Expenditures Total library budget $38,000 (FY 7/1/74-7/1/75). Total FY film budget $3000. *Member:* N.C. Library Assn, N.C. Learning Resources Assn.

Wilson

P- WILSON COUNTY PUBLIC LIBRARY, Nash & Jackson Sts., 27893. *Tel:* (919) 237-3818. *Film Serv Est:* 1952. *In Charge:* Mary Lou Rakow, Children's & AV Librarian. *Film Sel:* AV librarian previews. *Holdings:* children's films 90%.

Free-Loan Film Serv *Eligibility:* educational inst, civic & religious groups, indiv with library cards. *Restrictions:* for indiv & inst, only in Wilson County. Cannot use for fund-raising. Available to researchers/scholars for on-site viewing. May not borrow by mail. *Loan Period:* 16mm 1 day, 8mm 7 days. *Total Yr Film Loan:* 1041.

Film Collection 65t/p. Approx 5-12t acquired annually. *Circ:* 16mm, 15t/p; 8mm reel, 29t/p; S8mm reel, 21t/p.

Other Film Serv Obtain film from coop loan system (N.C. State Library Film Service, N.C. State Board of Health Film Library). *Equipment:* lend 16mm sound projector (1), 8mm cartridge projector (1), projection screens (1), cassette recorder/players (4), filmstrip projectors (4).

Other Media Collections *Audio:* disc, 33⅓ rpm, 2000t; disc, 78rpm, 160t; tape, cassette, 42t. *Filmstrips:* sound, 214t; sound sets, 43t; silent sets, 12t. *Slides:* sets, 6t.

Budget & Expenditures Total library budget $36,459.61 (FY 7/1/74-7/1/75). Total FY film budget $1500.

Winston-Salem

P- FORSYTH COUNTY PUBLIC LIBRARY, AV Dept, 660 W Fifth St, 27101. *Tel:* (919) 727-2556, ext 34. *Film Serv Est:* 1955. *In Charge:* Patrice Gaffney, Head, AV Dept. *AV Staff:* 3 (1 prof). *Film Sel:* committee preview. *Holdings:* children's films 45%.

Free-Loan Film Serv *Eligibility:* indiv with library cards. *Restrictions:* for indiv, interlibrary loan, only in region G of coop. system; for inst, only in region G of coop system. Cannot use for fund-raising, transmit electronically, use commercially. May borrow by mail. *Loan Period:* 1 day, 2 weeks if mailed to other libraries. *Total Yr Film Loan:* 7662.

Film Collection 558t/563p. Approx 80t acquired annually. *Circ:* 16mm, 558t/563p. *Noncirc:* S8mm cartridge, 75t. *Pubns:* catalog, annual.

Other Film Serv Obtain film from coop loan system (Piedmont Traid Council of Government Region G), obtain film from other libraries, library film programs. *Equipment:* lend 16mm sound projector (4).

Other Media Collections *Audio:* disc, 33⅓ rpm, 3500t/c.

Budget & Expenditures Total library budget $160,000 (FY 7/1/74-7/1/75). Total FY film budget $15,000. *Member:* ALA, N.C. Library Assn, Southeastern Library Assn.

Video Serv *Est:* 1972. *Video Staff:* 1 f-t. *Video Use:* documentation of community/school events, to increase community's library use, in-service training, public relations, publicity. Video serv available by appointment. Produce video tapes.

Video Equipment/Facilities *In-House Use Only:* portapak (1), ½″ b&w, Sony AV8400, AVC3400; recording deck (1), ½″ b&w, Sony 3600; editing deck (1), ½″ b&w/col, Shibaden 520D; studio camera (1), b&w, Sony 3200; monitor (3), b&w, Sony 1920, 115; additional camera lenses (1); lighting (4); microphones (3). Provide training in use of equipment to staff.

Video Collection Maintained by own production. Use/play ½″ reel to reel. *Collection, B&W:* ½″ reel, 1t/2c.

Cable & CCTV Receive serv of cable TV system. Produce programs for cablecasting.

North Dakota

Bismarck

S- NORTH DAKOTA STATE DEPARTMENT OF HEALTH, Health Education Loan Library, Capitol Bldg, 58505. *Tel:* (701) 224-2367. *Film Serv Est:* 1943. *In Charge:* Bernardine Cervinski, Dir of Health Education Div. *AV Staff:* 3 (1 prof, 1 cl, 1 tech). *Film Sel:* committee preview, staff recommendations. *Holdings:* health.
   Free-Loan Film Serv *Eligibility:* any individual or group. *Restrictions:* for indiv & inst, only in state. Cannot charge for viewing. May borrow by mail. *Loan Period:* 10 days.
   Film Collection 436t/483p. *Circ:* 16mm, 436t/483p. *Pubns:* catalog, every 2 yrs; suppl, no set policy.
   Budget & Expenditures No separate budget.

S- STATE LIBRARY COMMISSION, 58505. *Tel:* (701) 224-2490. *Film Serv Est:* 1974. *In Charge:* Cheryl Bailey, Head, Library Services. *AV Staff:* ½ tech. *Film Sel:* chief film librarian's decision. *Holdings:* management films, entertainment.
   Free-Loan Film Serv *Eligibility:* educational inst, civic groups, indiv with library cards, public libraries. *Restrictions:* for indiv & inst, only in state. Cannot use for fund-raising, transmit electronically. May borrow by mail. *Loan Period:* 7 days. *Total Yr Film Loan:* 958.
   Film Collection 515t/1010p. Approx 200t acquired annually. *Circ:* 16mm, 20t/p; S8mm cartridge, 495t/p. *Pubns:* catalog, annual ($2).
   Other Film Serv Obtain film from coop loan system (N. Dak. Network for Knowledge). Permanent viewing facility.
   Other Media Collections *Audio:* tape, cassette, 9000t/c. *Filmstrips:* sound sets, 1080t/c.
   Budget & Expenditures Total library budget $64,000 (FY 7/1/74-7/1/75). Total FY film budget $7500. *Member:* N. Dak. Library Assn.

P- VETERANS MEMORIAL PUBLIC LIBRARY, 520 Avenue "A" East, 58501. *Tel:* (701) 223-4267. *Film Serv Est:* 1970. *In Charge:* Nancy Ellingson, Circulation Dir. *Film Sel:* staff recommendations, published reviews. *Holdings:* social sciences.
   Free-Loan Film Serv *Eligibility:* indiv with library cards. *Restrictions:* for indiv & inst, none. Available to researchers/ scholars for on-site viewing. May borrow by mail. *Loan Period:* 10 days.
   Film Collection 74t.
   Other Film Serv Obtain film from coop loan system, film fairs/festivals, library film programs. *Equipment:* lend 16mm sound projector (1), projection screens (1).
   Other Media Collections *Audio:* disc, 78rpm, 500t/c; tape, cassette, 821t/c. *Filmstrips:* sound, 1t/c; silent, 128t/c. *Slides:* sets, 12t/c.

Crosby

P- DIVIDE COUNTY PUBLIC LIBRARY, 58730. *Tel:* (701) 965-6305. *Film Serv Est:* 1952. *In Charge:* Ruth Ralph, Dir. *Film Sel:* staff recommendations, chief film librarian's decision.
   Free-Loan Film Serv *Eligibility:* staff & students, civic & religious groups, indiv with library cards. *Restrictions:* for indiv, interlibrary loan; for inst, none. Available to researchers/scholars for on-site viewing.
   Film Collection 1400t. Approx 50t acquired annually. *Pubns:* catalog, every 3 yrs; suppl, in yr catalog not published.
   Other Film Serv Obtain film from other libraries. Permanent viewing facility available for rent to community. *Equipment:* lend 16mm sound projector (2), lend 8mm cartridge projector (1), 8mm reel projector (1), projection screens, filmstrip projectors (3).

Budget & Expenditures Total library budget $2500 (FY 7/1/74-7/1/75). Total FY film budget $200. *Member:* N. Dak. Library Assn, Mountain Plains Library Assn.

Fargo

P- FARGO PUBLIC LIBRARY, 102 Third St N, 58102. *Tel:* (701) 235-7567. *Film Serv Est:* 1968. *In Charge:* R. C. Waddington, Mgr. *AV Staff:* 2 (1 prof, 1 cl). *Film Sel:* chief film librarian's decision.
   Free-Loan Film Serv *Eligibility:* indiv with library cards. *Restrictions:* for indiv & inst, only in Cass County. Cannot use for fund-raising. Available to researchers/scholars for on-site viewing. May borrow by mail. *Loan Period:* 1-7 days.
   Film Collection 169t/178p. *Circ:* 16mm, 169t/178p. *Pubns:* catalog, annual.
   Other Film Serv Obtain film from other libraries, library film programs. Permanent viewing facility available for rent to community.
   Other Media Collections *Audio:* disc, 33⅓rpm, 5470c. *Filmstrips:* sound, 140c.
   Budget & Expenditures Total library budget $56,000 (FY 6/1/74-6/1/75). Total FY film budget $5500.

P- NORTH DAKOTA STATE FILM LIBRARY, Division of Independent Study, State University Station, 58102. *Tel:* (701) 237-8907. *Film Serv Est:* 1940. *In Charge:* Lillian M. Wadnizak, Film Library Manager. *AV Staff:* 6 (1 prof, 2 cl, 3 tech). *Film Sel:* committee preview, staff recommendations, chief film librarian's decision, published reviews.
   Free-Loan Film Serv *Eligibility:* anyone who requests films from the N. Dak. Wheat Commission for films they own that are housed in library.
   Film Rental Serv *Eligibility:* no restrictions. *Restrictions:* only in N. Dak., Minn., S. Dak., Mont. *Rental Period:* as requested by user. *Total Yr Film Booking:* 24,539.
   Film Collection 4000t/6000p. Approx 350t acquired annually. *Pubns:* catalog, every 2 yrs; suppl, in yr catalog not published.
   Other Film Serv Film reference serv. Permanent viewing facility.

Grand Forks

C- UNIVERSITY OF NORTH DAKOTA, Instructional Communications, Sayre Hall, 58202. *Tel:* (701) 777-2129. *In Charge:* Gary Redman, Admin Officer I. *AV Staff:* 2 cl.
   Free-Loan Film Serv *Eligibility:* staff & students, educational inst, civic & religious groups, prof groups. *Restrictions:* for indiv & inst, only in state. Available to researchers/scholars for on-site viewing. May borrow by mail. *Loan Period:* 3 days.
   Film Rental Serv *Eligibility:* no restrictions. *Restrictions:* only in state.
   Film Collection 350t/p. *Pubns:* catalog, every 2 yrs; suppl, no set policy.
   Other Film Serv Rent film from distributors for patrons, obtain film from other libraries. *Equipment:* lend/rent S8mm camera (1), 16mm sound projector (30), 8mm cartridge projector (2), 8mm reel projector (5), S8mm cartridge projector (2), projection screens (20).
   Budget & Expenditures No separate budget. *Member:* AECT.
   Video Serv *Est:* 1974. *In Charge:* Jack Mutzabaugh, Broadcasting Program Dir. *Tel:* (701) 777-4346. *Video Staff:* 2 f-t, 3 p-t, 1 tech. *Video Use:* documentation of community/school events, in-service training, practical video/TV training courses. Video serv available by appointment. Produce video tapes. Have production studio/space & separate control room.

Video Equipment/Facilities *In-House Use Only:* editing deck (1), ½" b&w/col, Sony 8650; studio camera (2), col, IVC 500A; monitor (5), col; SEG (1), INC; keyer (1), INC; lighting (25); microphones (9); tripods (2); audio tape recorders (2). *For Loan:* portapak (1), ½" b&w, Sony 2400; recording deck (4), ½" b&w, Sony 3600; playback deck (1), ¾" b&w/col, Sony VP 1000. Have permanent viewing installation. *Equipment Loan Period:* 3 days. Provide training in use of equipment to students. Have tape duplication serv.

Video Tape Loan/Rental/Sale Serv *Serv Provided:* free loan, sale (blank tapes). *Loan Eligibility:* staff & students. Cannot use for fund-raising, air without permission. May not borrow by mail.

Video Collection Maintained by own production. Use/play ½", 1" reel to reel, ¾" cassette. Tapes organized by subject. *Other Video Serv:* programming.

Cable & CCTV Receive serv of cable TV system. Produce programs for cablecasting. Serve as production facility for others. Run cable programs for special audiences. Have advisory/administrative role in cable system operation. Have CCTV in inst, with 18 monitors. *Programming Sources:* tapes produced by inst.

Jamestown

C- **JAMESTOWN COLLEGE,** Raugust Library, 58401. *Tel:* (701) 252-4331, ext 386. *Film Serv Est:* 1968. *AV Staff:* ½ prof. *Film Sel:* committee preview, faculty/staff recommendations.

Free-Loan Film Serv *Eligibility:* staff & students, educational inst, prof groups.

Film Collection *Circ:* 16mm, 37t; 8mm cartridge, 4t; S8mm reel, 10t.

Other Film Serv Rent film from distributors for patrons, obtain film from other libraries, film reference serv, film fairs/festivals, library film programs. Permanent viewing facility available for rent to community. *Equipment:* lend S8mm camera (1), 16mm sound projector (4), 8mm cartridge projector, S8mm cartridge projector (1).

Other Media Collections *Audio:* disc, 33⅓ rpm, 1100t; disc, 78rpm, 200t; tape, cassette, 127t; tape, reel, 120t. *Filmstrips:* silent, 38t; sound sets, 32t; silent sets, 5t. *Slides:* single, 6t; sets, 18t.

Budget & Expenditures No separate budget. *Member:* AECT, N. Dak. Library Assn.

Video Serv *Est:* 1972. *In Charge:* H. B. Kelly, Dir. *Video Use:* documentation of community/school events, to increase community's library use, community video access, in-service training, practical video/TV training courses. Video serv available on demand. Produce video tapes. Have production studio/space.

Video Equipment/Facilities *In-House Use Only:* studio camera (4), b&w, Sony, K&M; monitor (5), b&w; SEG (1), Sony SEG2; additional camera lenses (2); microphones (4); audio tape recorders (37). *For Loan:* portapak (1), b&w, Sony AV3400; recording deck (4), ¾", ½", 1" b&w; playback deck (4), ½", ¾", 1" b&w; lighting (3); tripods (2); audio tape recorders (37), tranceivers (4). *Equipment Loan Period:* no set policy. Have tape duplication serv.

Video Tape Loan/Rental/Sale Serv *Serv Provided:* free loan. *Loan Eligibility:* staff & students, educational inst, prof groups. *Restrictions:* cannot duplicate, air without permission.

Video Collection Use/play ½" reel to reel, ¾" cassette. *Sources:* commercial distributors, community productions. *Tape Sel:* preview, faculty/staff recommendations. *Special Collections:* films in video format. Tapes organized by Dewey Decimal. *Collection, B&W:* ½" reel, 25t; ¾" cassette, 1t.

Cable & CCTV Receive serv of cable TV system. Produce programs for cablecasting. Serve as production facility for others. Run cable programs for special audiences.

S- **NORTH DAKOTA STATE HOSPITAL,** Staff Library, 58401. *Tel:* (701) 252-2120, ext 396. *Film Serv Est:* 1962. *In Charge:* Laurie Reule, Librarian I. *AV Staff:* 1 (1 prof, 1 cl, 1 tech). *Film Sel:* committee preview. *Holdings:* medicine 85%, social sciences 15%.

Free-Loan Film Serv *Eligibility:* org members. *Restrictions:* for indiv, only in city. Cannot be used unless accompanied by a staff member. *Loan Period:* depending on need. *Total Yr Film Loan:* 25.

Film Collection 17t/18p. Approx 1t acquired annually. *Circ:* 16mm, 13t/12p.

Other Film Serv Obtain film from coop loan system (State Health Dept), obtain film from other libraries.

Budget & Expenditures Total library budget $23,000 (FY 7/1/74-7/1/75). Total FY film budget $400. *Member:* N. Dak. Library Assn, Medical Library Assn.

Ohio

Akron

C- THE UNIVERSITY OF AKRON, Bierce Library, 302 Buchtel
Ave, 44385. *Tel:* (216) 375-7248. *Video Serv Est:* 1961. *In
Charge:* Thomas T. Miles, Dir of Instruc Media. *Video
Staff:* 17 f-t, 130 p-t, 8 tech. *Video Use:* documentation of
community/school events, in-service training, practical
video/TV training courses, playback only of professionally produced tapes, as art form. Video serv available
on demand & by appointment. Produce video tapes. Have
production studio/space & separate control room.
   Video Equipment/Facilities *In-House Use Only:* recording & playback deck (35), ½″, ¾″, 1″, 2″ b&w/col, Sony,
RCA, Ampex; studio camera (7); monitor (15); SEG (2); keyer (3);
additional camera lenses (4); lighting; microphones (20); tripods
(6); audio tape recorders (100). Have permanent & portable
viewing installations. Provide training in use of equipment to
faculty & students. Have tape duplication serv.
   Video Collection Maintained by own production.
Use/play ½″, 1″, 2″ reel to reel, ¾″ cassette. *Sources:* commercial distributors. *Other Video Serv:* programming, taping of
other media, production workshops.
   Cable & CCTV Receive serv of cable TV system. Produce
programs for cablecasting. Have CCTV in inst, with 150
monitors. *Programming Sources:* tapes produced by inst.

Alliance

P- RODMAN PUBLIC LIBRARY, 215 E Broadway, 44601. *Tel:*
(216) 821-1410. *In Charge:* Wilda Feller, Film Librarian.
Member: Northern Ohio Film Circuit.

Archbold

P- McLAUGHLIN MEMORIAL PUBLIC LIBRARY, 301½
Stryker St, 43502. *Tel:* (419) 445-4781. *Film Serv Est:* 1975.
In Charge: Librarian. *AV Staff:* 1. *Film Sel:* chief film
librarian's decision. *Holdings:* cartoons, silent films.
   Free-Loan Film Serv *Eligibility:* indiv with library cards.
Cannot use for fund-raising. May borrow by mail. *Loan Period:*
3 days. *Total Yr Film Loan:* 208.
   Film Collection 30t. Approx 15t acquired annually. *Circ:*
S8mm cartridge, 30t.
   Other Film Serv Obtain film from coop loan system
(Norweld). *Equipment:* lend S8mm camera (1).
   Other Media Collections *Audio:* tape, cassette, 50t.

Bellefontaine

P- LOGAN COUNTY DISTRICT LIBRARY, 140 N Main,
43311. *Tel:* (513) 592-5986. *Film Serv Est:* 1972. *In Charge:*
Anita Morgan, Librarian. *AV Staff:* ¼ cl.
   Free-Loan Film Serv *Eligibility:* indiv with library cards.
Restrictions: for indiv, none. Cannot use for fund-raising. S8mm
free, 16mm $1 a day. May not borrow by mail. *Loan Period:* 3
days. *Total Yr Film Loan:* 108.
   Film Rental Serv *Eligibility:* no restrictions. *Restrictions:*
only in Logan County. *Rental Period:* 1 day. *Total Yr Film
Booking:* 610.
   Film Collection 95t/p. Approx 40t acquired annually. *Circ:*
16mm, 40t/p; S8mm reel, 45t/p. *Pubns:* publish catalog of 16mm
films in libraries in our circuit.
   Other Film Serv Obtain film from coop loan system
(Western Ohio Film Circuit).
   Budget & Expenditures Total library budget $19,664 (FY
1/1/74-1/1/75). Total circuit FY film budget $1200.

Canton

P- STARK COUNTY DISTRICT LIBRARY, 236 Third St, SW,
44702. *Tel:* (216) 452-0665, ext 54. *Film Serv Est:* 1948. *In
Charge:* Loretta Freed, Head, AV Dept. *AV Staff:* 4 (1 prof,
1 cl).
   Free-Loan Film Serv *Eligibility:* indiv with adult library
cards. *Restrictions:* for indiv, only in Stark County & neighboring counties. Cannot use for fund-raising, transmit electronically. May borrow by mail. *Loan Period:* 1 day. *Total Yr Film
Loan:* 5906.
   Film Collection 360t/p. Approx 25-30t acquired annually.
Circ: 16mm, 360t/p; 8mm reel, 436t/p. *Pubns:* catalog, as needed
($.50); suppl, annually.
   Other Film Serv Obtain film from coop loan system
(Northern Ohio Film Circuit), film reference serv, library film
programs, show films in nursing homes. *Equipment:* lend 16mm
camera (1), 16mm sound projector (5), 8mm reel projector (1),
projection tables & stands (1), projection screens (4).
   Other Media Collections *Audio:* disc, 33⅓ rpm, 7467t; disc,
78rpm, 531t; tape, cassette, 539t; tape, cartridge, 7t; tape, reel,
55t. *Filmstrips:* sound, 300t; silent, 124t; sound sets, 43t; silent
sets, 16t. *Slides:* single, 7495t; sets, 259t.
   Budget & Expenditures Total library budget $290,667.57
(FY 1/1/75-1/1/76). Total FY film budget $8000. *Member:* ALA,
EFLA, Ohio Library Assn.

Celina

P- DWYER-MERCER COUNTY DISTRICT LIBRARY, 303 N
Main St, 45822. *Tel:* (419) 586-2314, ext 1 or 2. *Film Serv
Est:* 1974. *In Charge:* A. Schneider, Librarian. *AV Staff:* ½
cl.
   Free-Loan Film Serv *Eligibility:* indiv with library cards.
Restrictions: for indiv, none. Cannot use for fund-raising.
Available to researchers/scholars for on-site viewing. May not
borrow by mail. *Loan Period:* 1-2 days. *Total Yr Film Loan:*
1500. *Pubns:* catalog, annual.
   Other Film Serv Obtain film from coop loan system
(Western Ohio Film Circuit). *Equipment:* lend/rent 16mm
camera (1), projection tables & stands (1), projection screens (1).
   Budget & Expenditures Total library budget $15,000. No
separate AV budget.

Chardon

P- GEAUGA COUNTY PUBLIC LIBRARY, 110 E Park St,
44024. *Tel:* (216) 285-7601. *Film Serv Est:* 1973. *In Charge:*
Stephen Harvey, Nonprint Librarian. *AV Staff:* 1 (1 prof).
Film Sel: staff recommendations.
   Free-Loan Film Serv *Eligibility:* indiv with library cards.
Restrictions: for indiv, only in Geauga County. Cannot use for
fund-raising, transmit electronically. May not borrow by mail.
Loan Period: 3-7 days.
   Film Collection 196t/241p. Approx 60t acquired annually.
Circ: 16mm, 100t/p; 8mm reel, 1t/p; S8mm reel, 95t/140p.
Pubns: catalog, as needed.
   Other Film Serv Library film programs.
   Other Media Collections *Audio:* disc, 33⅓ rpm, 1100t/
2300c; tape, cassette, 10t/30c. *Slides:* sets, 100t/c.
   Budget & Expenditures Total library budget $90,000 (FY
1/1/75-1/1/76). Total FY film budget $1500.

Cincinnati

P- PUBLIC LIBRARY OF CINCINNATI AND HAMILTON
COUNTY, Films & Recordings Center, 800 Vine St, 45202.
Tel: (513) 369-6924. *Film Serv Est:* 1947. *In Charge:* Janie

Pyle, Dept Head. *AV Staff:* 15 (4 prof, 9 cl, 2 tech). *Film Sel:* committee preview.

Free-Loan Film Serv *Eligibility:* educational inst, civic & religious groups, indiv with library cards. *Restrictions:* for indiv & inst, only in Hamilton County. Out-of-county must purchase fee card. Cannot use for fund-raising, transmit electronically. Available to researchers/scholars for on-site viewing. May not borrow by mail. *Loan Period:* 2 days. *Total Yr Film Loan:* 24,525.

Film Collection 1672t/2236p. Approx 75-100t acquired annually. *Circ:* 16mm, 1672t/2236p. *Pubns:* catalog, as needed ($2.50).

Other Film Serv Film reference serv, library film programs. Permanent viewing facility.

Other Media Collections *Audio:* disc, 33⅓ rpm, 22,241c; tape, cassette, 1631c. *Filmstrips:* total 1240c. *Slides:* single, 16,061c. *Member:* AFI, ALA, EFLA, FLIC.

Cleveland

P- CLEVELAND PUBLIC LIBRARY, AV Dept, 325 Superior Ave, 44114. *Tel:* (212) 241-1020, ext 178. *In Charge:* Arnold McClain, Head, AV Dept. *AV Staff:* 9 (2 prof, 3 cl, 4 tech). *Film Sel:* committee preview, chief film librarian's decision, published reviews.

Film Rental Serv *Eligibility:* no restrictions. *Restrictions:* only in Cuyahoga County. Cannot use for fund-raising, transmit electronically. *Rental Period:* 3 days. *Total Yr Film Booking:* 11,868.

Film Collection 2800t/3000p. Approx 175t acquired annually. *Circ:* 16mm, 2800t/3000p. *Pubns:* catalog, as needed ($2.25); suppl, no set policy.

Other Film Serv Film reference serv, library film programs. Permanent viewing facility.

Other Media Collections *Audio:* tape, cassette, 18t/c. *Filmstrips:* sound, 30t/p; silent, 400t/c; sound sets, 18t/c. *Slides:* single, 5000t/c; sets, 52t/c.

Budget & Expenditures Total FY film budget $27,500 (FY 1/1/74-1/1/75). *Member:* ALA, EFLA, FLIC, Ohio Library Assn.

P- CUYAHOGA COUNTY PUBLIC LIBRARY, AV Dept, 4510 Memphis Ave, 44144. *Tel:* (216) 398-1800, 26, 66, 67. *Film Serv Est:* 1953. *In Charge:* Leila Heasley, Head, AV Dept. *AV Staff:* 11 (3 prof, 4 cl, 4 tech). *Film Sel:* committee preview, staff recommendations, published reviews. *Holdings:* animated films, children's films, consumer affairs, dance, experimental films, feature films, fine arts, social sciences, women.

Free-Loan Film Serv *Eligibility:* all adults qualified to use library resources. *Restrictions:* for indiv, all who live, work or attend school in Cuyahoga County; for inst, only in Cuyahoga County. Cannot use for fund-raising, transmit electronically. Available to researchers/scholars for on-site viewing. May not borrow by mail. *Loan Period:* 3 days. *Total Yr Film Loan:* 20,475.

Film Collection 1816t/1930p. Approx 300t acquired annually. *Circ:* 16mm, 1770t/1884p; 8mm cartridge, 20t/p; S8mm cartridge, 26t/p. *Pubns:* catalog, every 3 yrs ($1.25); suppl, no set policy.

Other Film Serv Film reference serv, film fairs/festivals, library film programs. Permanent viewing facility available to community.

Other Media Collections *Audio:* disc, 33⅓ rpm, 34,557c; tape, cassette, 2093c. *Filmstrips:* sound, 2055c; silent, 4194c. *Slides:* sets, 8279c.

Budget & Expenditures Total library budget $2,124,637 (FY 1/1/75-1/1/76). Total FY film budget $150,000. *Member:* ALA, EFLA, FLIC, Ohio Library Assn.

C- DYKE COLLEGE, Library & Instructional Resource Center, 1375 E 6 St, 44146. *Tel:* (216) 696-9000, ext 43. *Video Serv Est:* 1975. *In Charge:* John Biros, Media Librarian. *Video Staff:* 2 f-t, 3 p-t, 1 tech. *Video Use:* playback of professionally produced tapes, playback of regular over-the-air commercial & public broadcasting. Video serv available on demand. Produce video tapes.

Video Equipment/Facilities *In-House Use Only:* portapak (1), ¾″ col, Panasonic; recording deck (2), ¾″ col, Panasonic; monitor (9), col, Sony; microphones (3); audio tape recorders (2). Have permanent viewing installation.

Video Tape Loan/Rental/Sale Serv *Serv Provided:* free loan. *Loan Eligibility:* educational inst. *Restrictions:* for inst, only in Cuyahoga, Summit, Lorain, Lake & Geauga counties. Cannot use for fund-raising, duplicate, air without permission. May not borrow by mail.

Video Collection Maintained by purchase, rental, exchange/swap. Use/play ¾″ cassette. *Sources:* commercial distributors, exchange, off-air retrieval. *Tape Sel:* preview, faculty/staff recommendations, published reviews, catalogs. Tapes organized by shelf-list. *Collection, Color:* ¾″ cassette, 3t. *Pubns:* catalog for faculty.

Cable & CCTV Have CCTV in inst, with 8 monitors. *Programming Sources:* over-the-air commercial & public broadcasting, tapes produced professionally.

Columbus

P- BEXLEY PUBLIC LIBRARY, 2411 E Main St, 43209. *Tel:* (614) 231-2784, ext 26. *In Charge:* Dorothy K. Morrisroe, Film Librarian. *AV Staff:* 4 (1 prof, 1 cl, 2 tech). *Film Sel:* chief film librarian's decision. *Holdings:* animated films 5%, children's films 50%.

Film Rental Serv *Eligibility:* no restrictions. *Restrictions:* only in our county. *Rental Period:* 1 day. *Total Yr Film Booking:* 6516.

Film Collection 800t/p. *Circ:* 16mm, 800t/p. *Pubns:* catalog, every 4 yrs ($1); suppl, no set policy.

Other Film Serv Library film programs. Permanent viewing facility available for rent to community.

Budget & Expenditures No separate budget. *Member:* Ohio Library Assn.

C- CAPITAL UNIVERSITY, Instructional Media Center, 43209. *Tel:* (614) 236-6508. *Film Serv Est:* 1970. *In Charge:* Theodore Fritz, Dir. *AV Staff:* 1 prof, 1 cl, 1 tech. *Film Sel:* faculty/staff recommendations, chief film librarian's decision.

Free-Loan Film Serv Available to researchers/scholars for on-site viewing. May not borrow by mail. *Loan Period:* 1 day. *Total Yr Film Loan:* 10.

Film Collection 30t/p. *Circ:* 16mm, 30t/p.

Other Film Serv Rent film from distributors for patrons, obtain film from other libraries, film reference serv, film fairs/festivals. Permanent viewing facility available for rent to community. *Equipment:* lend/rent S8mm camera, 16mm camera, 16mm sound projector, 8mm cartridge projector, 8mm reel projector.

Budget & Expenditures Total library budget $80,000. No separate AV budget. *Member:* AECT.

Video Serv *Est:* 1971. *Video Staff:* 3 f-t, 6 p-t, 1 tech. *Video Use:* in-service training, practical video/TV training courses. Video serv available by appointment. Produce video tapes. Have production studio/space & separate control room.

Video Equipment/Facilities *In-House Use Only:* portapak (1), ½″ b&w/col, Sony; recording deck (6), Panasonic; playback deck (1); studio camera (6); additional camera lenses (6); lighting (6); microphones (15); audio tape recorders (20). Have portable viewing installation. Provide training in use of equipment.

Video Tape Loan/Rental/Sale Serv *Serv Provided:* free loan, swap with other inst. *Loan Eligibility:* org members, staff & students. *Restrictions:* for indiv, only on campus. May not borrow by mail.

Video Collection Maintained by own production, exchange/swap. Use/play ½″ reel to reel, ¾″ cassette. *Sources:* commercial distributors. *Tape Sel:* faculty/staff recommendations. *Special Collections:* in-house training tapes. Tapes organized by title & numeric order. *Collection, Color:* ½″ reel, 6t; ¾″

Columbus (cont'd)
cassette, 2t. *Collection, B&W:* ½″ reel, 6t; ¾″ cassette, 2t. *Other Video Serv:* programming.
Cable & CCTV Will receive serv of cable TV system.

P- **COLUMBUS PUBLIC LIBRARY,** 96 S Grant Ave, 43215. *Tel:* (614) 461-6574. *Film Serv Est:* 1950. *In Charge:* Margaret Davies, Head, AV Div. *AV Staff:* 8 (1 prof, 6 cl, 1 tech). *Film Sel:* committee preview, chief film librarian's decision, published reviews. *Holdings:* animated films, black studies, children's films, women.
Film Rental Serv *Eligibility:* no restrictions. *Restrictions:* only in Franklin County. Cannot use for fund-raising, transmit electronically. *Rental Period:* 1 day.
Film Collection 2900t/3200p. Approx 350-400t acquired annually. *Circ:* 16mm, 2100p; 8mm & S8mm reel, 1075t; S8mm cartridge, 46p. *Pubns:* catalog, every 2 yrs ($2); suppl, every 3 months.
Other Film Serv Film reference serv, film fairs/festivals, library film programs, workshops, conferences. Permanent viewing facility available for rent to community. *Equipment:* rent 8mm & S8mm reel projector (10).
Other Media Collections *Audio:* disc, 33⅓ rpm, 12,056c; tape, cassette, 1000c. *Filmstrips:* silent, 1328c.
Budget & Expenditures Total library budget $619,800 (FY 1/1/75-1/1/76). Total FY film budget $45,000. *Member:* ALA, EFLA, Ohio Library Assn.
Video Serv *Est:* 1975. *In Charge:* Susan Mary Larson, Video Tape Specialist. *Video Staff:* 1 f-t. *Video Use:* documentation of community events, to increase community's library use, community video access, in-service training. Video serv available on demand & by appointment. Produce video tapes. Have production studio/space.
Video Equipment/Facilities *In-House Use Only:* recording deck (1), ¾″ col, Sony 1800; playback deck (6), ¾″ col, Panasonic NV2110; studio camera (2), col, Panasonic VW2300; monitor (2), Sony CUM1720, Panasonic WJ4500; SEG (1), Panasonic; keyer (1); lighting (9); microphones (5); tripods (2); audio tape recorders (2); multiplexor (1); tuner timer (1). Have portable viewing installation. Provide training in use of equipment to staff.
Video Collection Maintained by purchase, own production, exchange/swap. Use/play ¾″ cassette. *Sources:* public television library. *Tape Sel:* published reviews, catalogs. Tape organized by title. *Other Video Serv:* programming.
Cable & CCTV Receive serv of cable TV system. Produce programs for cablecasting. Inform public about cable system serv & facilities.

C- **COLUMBUS TECHNICAL INSTITUTE,** Educational Resources Center, 550 E Spring, 43215. *Tel:* (614) 221-6743, ext 256. *Film Serv Est:* 1973. *AV Staff:* 3 (2 prof, 1 tech). *Film Sel:* faculty/staff recommendations, published reviews.
Film Collection 171t/p. Approx 25t acquired annually. *Circ:* 16mm, 171t/p.
Other Film Serv Rent film from distributors for patrons. *Equipment:* lend S8mm camera (3), 16mm camera (1), 16mm sound projector (14), 8mm cartridge projector (2), 8mm reel projector (1), S8mm cartridge projector (3), S8mm reel projector (2), projection tables & stands (45), projection screens (110), S8mm sound cameras (1).
Other Media Collections *Audio:* disc, 33⅓ rpm, 63t/73c; tape, cassette, 228t/3304c. *Filmstrips:* silent, 146t/953c. *Slides:* single, 64t/5861c.
Budget & Expenditures Total library budget $22,700 (FY 7/1/75-7/1/76). No separate AV budget. *Member:* ALA, Ohio Library Assn, EMCO, American Film Institute.
Video Serv *Est:* 1973. *In Charge:* William C. Levan, Teleproduction Technician. *Video Staff:* 8 f-t, 7 p-t, 2 tech. *Video Use:* documentation of community/school events, to increase community's library use, community video access, in-service training. Video serv available by appointment. Produce video tapes. Have production studio/space & separate control room.
Video Equipment/Facilities *In-House Use Only:* recording deck (4), ½″, 1″ col, Sony EV320, UV340, AV8650, IVC600C;

editing deck (2), ¾″ col, Sony VO2850; studio camera (2), col, Sony DXC-5000 BP; monitor (30), col, Sony; SEG (1), Shintron; microphones (4); tripods (3); audio tape recorders (1). *For Loan:* portapak (2), ½″ b&w/col, Sony AV3400, AV8400; playback deck (2), ¾″ col, Sony VP2000. Have permanent viewing installation. *Equipment Loan Period:* no set policy. Provide training in use of equipment to faculty & students. Have tape duplication serv.
Video Tape Loan/Rental/Sale Serv *Serv Provided:* free loan, swap with other inst, sale. *Loan Eligibility:* educational inst, civic groups. *Restrictions:* for indiv & inst, none. Cannot use for fund-raising, air without permission. May borrow by mail.
Video Collection Maintained by purchase, rental, own production, exchange/swap. Use/play ½″, 1″ reel to reel, ¾″ cassette. *Sources:* commercial distributors, community productions, exchange (neighboring colleges). *Tape Sel:* preview, faculty/staff recommendations, published reviews, catalogs. Tapes organized by Dewey Decimal. *Collection, Color:* ½″ reel, 2t/c; 1″ reel, 10t/20c; ¾″ cassette, 15t/c. *Collection, B&W:* ½″ reel, 46t/c; 1″ reel, 5t/c. *Other Video Serv:* programming, reference serv, taping of other media.
Cable & CCTV Have CCTV in inst, with 30 monitors. *Programming Sources:* over-the-air commercial & public broadcasting, tapes produced by inst, tapes produced professionally, tapes produced by community groups & indiv.

P- **GRANDVIEW HEIGHTS PUBLIC LIBRARY,** AV Dept, 1685 W First Ave, 43212. *Tel:* (614) 486-2951. *Film Serv Est:* 1950. *AV Staff:* 3 tech. *Film Sel:* committee preview.
Free-Loan Film Serv *Eligibility:* indiv with library cards. *Restrictions:* for indiv, only in our county. Cannot use for fund-raising, transmit electronically. Available to researchers/ scholars for on-site viewing. May not borrow by mail. *Loan Period:* 2 days. *Total Yr Film Loan:* 17,929.
Film Collection 887t/895p. Approx 27t acquired annually. *Circ:* 16mm, 887t/895p. *Pubns:* catalog, every 2 yrs ($1); suppl, no set policy.
Other Film Serv library film programs. Permanent viewing facility available to community.
Other Media Collections *Audio:* disc, 33⅓ rpm, 5125t/5604c; tape, reel, 552t/572c.
Budget & Expenditures Total library budget $327,000 (FY 1/1/74-1/1/75). Total FY film budget $36,240.08. *Member:* EFLA, FLIC.

C- **THE OHIO STATE UNIVERSITY, DEPT. OF PHOTOGRAPHY & CINEMA,** The Film Library, 156 W 19th Ave, 43210. *Tel:* (614) 422-5966. *In Charge:* George Barber, Supervisor. *AV Staff:* 2 (1 prof, 1 cl). *Film Sel:* faculty/staff recommendations, chief film librarian's decision. *Holdings:* medicine, science.
Film Rental Serv *Eligibility:* no restrictions. *Restrictions:* only in U.S. *Rental Period:* 3 days. Sell films.
Film Collection Approx 5t acquired annually. *Pubns:* catalog, as needed; suppl, no set policy.
Other Film Serv Rent film from distributors for patrons, obtain film from coop loan system, obtain film from other libraries, film reference serv. Permanent viewing facility.
Budget & Expenditures Total library budget $35,000 (FY 7/1/74-7/1/75). No separate AV budget.

S- **STATE LIBRARY OF OHIO,** 65 S Front St, 43215. *Tel:* (614) 466-2693. *In Charge:* Jerry Wise, Media Specialist. *AV Staff:* 1 (1 prof). *Film Sel:* committee preview, staff recommendations. *Holdings:* library oriented films 100%.
Free-Loan Film Serv *Eligibility:* Ohio libraries. *Restrictions:* for inst, only in state. Available to researchers/ scholars for on-site viewing. May not borrow by mail. *Loan Period:* 3 days or special arrangement. *Total Yr Film Loan:* 36.
Film Collection 35t/40p. Approx 2t acquired annually.
Other Film Serv Obtain film from other libraries, film reference serv, library film programs. *Equipment:* lend 16mm sound projector (2), 8mm reel projector (1), projection screens (2).

Other Media Collections *Audio:* tape, cassette, 40t. *Filmstrips:* sound, 8t. *Slides:* single, 500t; sets, 10t.

Budget & Expenditures No separate AV budget. *Member:* ALA, Ohio Library Assn.

Video Serv *Est:* 1975. *Video Staff:* 1 f-t. *Video Use:* in-service training, practical video/TV training courses. Video serv available on demand & by appointment. Produce video tapes. Have production studio/space.

Video Equipment/Facilities *In-House Use Only:* deck cassette (1), ¾" col, Sony 8650; editing deck (1), ½" col, Sony 3650; monitor (2); lighting (1); microphones (3); tripods (1); audio tape recorders (3). *For Loan:* portapak (1), ½" b&w Sony. *Equipment Loan Period:* 1 day. Provide training in use of equipment to staff & anyone using equipment.

Video Tape Loan/Rental/Sale Serv *Serv Provided:* free loan, swap with other inst. *Loan Eligibility:* educational inst, & others, such as librarians in the state. *Restrictions:* for inst, none. May borrow by mail. *Loan Period:* 3 days. *Total Yr Tape Loan:* 16.

Video Collection Maintained by own production, exchange/swap. Use/play ½" reel to reel, ¾" cassette. *Sources:* exchange (ASLA Div of ALA). *Tape Sel:* preview, staff recommendations. *Special Collections:* in-house training tapes. Tapes organized by subject. *Collection, B&W:* ½" reel, 18t/c. *Other Video Serv:* production workshops.

Coshocton

P- COSHOCTON PUBLIC LIBRARY, 655 Main St, 43812. *Tel:* (614) 622-0956. *Film Serv Est:* 1950. *In Charge:* Jean Reddick, Film Clerk. *AV Staff:* ½ cl. *Film Sel:* Ohio Valley Film Circuit meetings.

Free-Loan Film Serv *Eligibility:* educational inst, civic & religious groups. *Restrictions:* for indiv, only in Coshocton County; for inst, only in Coshocton County & 2 neighboring libraries. Cannot use for fund-raising, transmit electronically. May not borrow by mail. *Loan Period:* 2 days. *Total Yr Film Loan:* 982.

Film Collection 16t/p. *Circ:* 16mm, 16t/p. *Pubns:* catalog, annual.

Other Film Serv Obtain film from coop loan system (Ohio Valley Film Circuit, Mid-eastern Ohio Library Organization).

Other Media Collections *Audio:* disc, 33⅓ rpm, 1268t/c. *Filmstrips:* sound, 108t/c. *Slides:* sets, 62t/c.

Budget & Expenditures Total library budget $35,000 (FY 1/1/75-1/1/76). Total FY film budget $1300. *Member:* Ohio Library Assn.

Dayton

P- DAYTON & MONTGOMERY COUNTY PUBLIC LIBRARY, Non-Print Media Center, 215 E Third St, 45402. *Tel:* (513) 224-1651, ext 42. *Film Serv Est:* 1951. *In Charge:* Theodore J. Nunn, Jr., Head, Non-Print Media Center. *AV Staff:* 8 (2 prof, 6 cl, 2 tech). *Film Sel:* committee preview. *Holdings:* general collection.

Free-Loan Film Serv *Eligibility:* indiv with library cards, any adult who lives, works or goes to school in Montgomery County (10¢ nonrefundable insurance per reel). *Restrictions:* for indiv, only in Montgomery County; for inst, only in Montgomery County. Cannot use for fund-raising, transmit electronically. Available to researchers/scholars for on-site viewing. May not borrow by mail. *Loan Period:* 1 day. *Total Yr Film Loan:* 21,320.

Film Collection 1660t/1700p. Approx 125t acquired annually. *Circ:* 16mm, 1660t/1700p; 8mm & S8mm reel, 2100t/2400p. *Pubns:* catalog, as needed ($.50); suppl, no set policy ($.50).

Other Film Serv Film fairs/festivals, library film programs, homebound service.

Other Media Collections *Audio:* disc, 33⅓ rpm, 28,806c; tape, cassette, 1947c. *Filmstrips:* sound, 1100c; silent, 70c. *Slides:* single, 17,700c.

Budget & Expenditures Total library budget $535,970 (FY 1/1/75-1/1/76). Total FY film budget $36,500. *Member:* ALA, EFLA, FLIC, Ohio Library Assn.

S- NATIONAL ASSOCIATION OF EDUCATIONAL BROADCASTERS, Teaching Materials Library, c/o Telecommunications, Wright State Univ, 45431. *Tel:* (513) 873-2885. *Film Serv Est:* 1965. *In Charge:* Clair R. Tettemer, Library Dir. *AV Staff:* 1 (1 prof). *Film Sel:* committee preview. *Holdings:* teachers education for use of TV in classroom, 100%.

Film Rental Serv *Eligibility:* no restrictions. *Restrictions:* only in U.S. Cannot transmit electronically without permission. *Rental Period:* 7 days. *Total Yr Film Booking:* 30. Sell films. Produce films.

Film Collection 8t/63p. *Circ:* 16mm, 8t/63p. *Pubns:* catalog, as needed. Publish teacher's manual.

Other Film Serv Obtain film from coop loan system (National Assn of Educational Broadcasting).

Budget & Expenditures Total budget $1950 (FY 7/1/74-7/1/75).

S- UNITED THEOLOGICAL SEMINARY, Communications Center, 1810 Harvard Blvd, 45406. *Tel:* (513) 278-5817, ext 275. *Video Serv Est:* 1970. *In Charge:* Aaron M. Sheaffer. *Video Staff:* 1 f-t, 3 p-t. *Video Use:* documentation of community/school events, in-service training, practical video/TV training courses, as art form. Video serv available on demand & by appointment. Produce video tapes. Have production studio/space & separate control room.

Video Equipment/Facilities *In-House Use Only:* recording deck (2), 1" col, IVC600; editing deck (1), ½" col, Shibaden 520DU; studio camera (2), b&w, Raytheon; monitor (8), b&w/col, Magnavox, RCA; SEG (1), Telemation; keyer (1); lighting (14); microphones (15); tripods (3); audio tape recorders (12). Provide training in use of equipment to students, pastors & laymen. Have tape duplication serv.

Video Tape Loan/Rental/Sale Serv *Serv Provided:* free loan, swap with other inst. *Loan Eligibility:* org members, staff & students, educational inst. *Restrictions:* for indiv, as negotiated. May borrow by mail.

Video Collection Maintained by exchange/swap. Use/play ½", 1" reel to reel. *Member:* Dayton/Miami Valley Consortium of Colleges & Universities. Tapes organized by topic & courses. *Other Video Serv:* production workshops.

Cable & CCTV Will receive serv of cable TV system. Have CCTV in inst, with 4 monitors. *Programming Sources:* tapes produced by inst.

C- WRIGHT STATE UNIVERSITY, Library, Media Equipment Distribution, Colonel Glenn Hwy, 45431. *Tel:* (513) 873-2760. *Film Serv Est:* 1966. *In Charge:* Ann White, Asst. Dean of the University Library. *AV Staff:* 13½ (4 prof, 3 cl, 6½ tech). *Film Sel:* faculty/staff recommendations. *Holdings:* children's films 20%, engineering 10%, fine arts 15%, science 10%, social sciences 5%, teacher education 40%.

Free-Loan Film Serv *Eligibility:* staff & students, educational inst, civic groups, religious groups, indiv with library cards, prof groups, such as medical assn & others, such as industry, public & school libraries. *Restrictions:* for indiv, interlibrary loan, only in state; for inst, only in state. Cannot transmit electronically. Available to researchers/scholars for on-site viewing. May not borrow by mail. *Loan Period:* as needed. *Total Yr Film Loan:* 1500. Produce slides, transparencies, audio tape, graphics for class & TV use. Slide/tape presentations, lettering, drymount, lamination.

Film Collection 1044t/1049p. Approx 70t acquired annually. *Circ:* 16mm, 1044t/1049p; 8mm & S8mm reel, 40t/p; 8mm & S8mm cartridge, 502t/p. *Pubns:* catalog, every 3 yrs; suppl, no set policy.

Other Film Serv Rent film from distributors for patrons, obtain film from coop loan system (Dayton-Miami Valley Consortium), obtain film from other libraries, film reference serv. Permanent viewing facility. *Equipment:* lend S8mm camera (25), 16mm camera (1), 16mm sound projector (46), 8mm cartridge projector (3), 8mm reel projector (3), S8mm cartridge projector (15), S8mm reel projector (16), projection tables & stands (80), projection screens (190), overhead projectors (76), video tape equipment (24).

Dayton (cont'd)

Other Media Collections *Audio:* disc, 33⅓ rpm, 1400t; disc, 45rpm, 6t; tape, cassette, 5000t; tape, reel, 500t. *Filmstrips:* total, 1454t. *Slides:* total, 4500t.

Budget & Expenditures Total library budget $440,546 (FY 7/1/74-7/1/75). Total FY AV budget $46,265. *Member:* AECT, ALA, Ohio Library Assn, Educational Media Council of Ohio, Ohio Assn of School Librarians, Academic Library Assn of Ohio, Inter-University Council of Media Directors.

Defiance

C- THE DEFIANCE COLLEGE, Anthony Wayne Library, 43512. *Tel:* (419) 784-4010, ext 134. *In Charge:* Maxie J. Lambright, Dir.

Film Serv Rent film from distributors for patrons, obtain film from other libraries. Permanent viewing facility available for rent to community. *Equipment:* lend S8mm camera (11), 16mm camera (1), 16mm sound projector (4), 8mm cartridge projector (2), S8mm cartridge projector (2), projection tables & stands (15), projection screens (4), slide projectors & 35mm cameras.

Other Media Collections *Audio:* disc, 78rpm, 2000t; tape, cassette, 200t; tape, reel, 275t. *Filmstrips:* silent, 3000t.

Budget & Expenditures Total library budget $44,989 (FY 7/1/74-7/1/75). No separate AV budget. *Member:* Ohio Library Assn, Educational Media Council of Ohio, Ohio Assn of School Librarians.

Video Serv *Video Use:* equipment loan only. Produce video tapes.

Video Equipment/Facilities *For Loan:* portapak (1), 1½″ b&w, Sony; editing deck (3), ½″ b&w, Sony; studio camera (3), b&w, Sony; monitor (5), b&w/col, Sony; lighting (1); microphones (4); audio tape recorders (3). *Equipment Loan Period:* 1 day. Provide training in use of equipment to faculty & students. Have tape duplication serv.

Video Collection Maintained by own production. Use/play ½″ reel to reel.

Cable & CCTV Receive serv of cable TV system. Produce programs for cablecasting. Run cable programs for special audiences.

Elyria

P- ELYRIA PUBLIC LIBRARY, 320 Washington Ave, 44035. *Tel:* (216) 323-5747. *Film Serv Est:* 1945. *In Charge:* Mary Ann Novak, AV Librarian. *AV Staff:* 1. *Film Sel:* committee preview.

Free-Loan Film Serv *Eligibility:* indiv with library cards, schools. *Restrictions:* for indiv, only in our county. Cannot use for fund-raising. Available to researchers/scholars for on-site viewing. May not borrow by mail. *Loan Period:* 1 day. *Total Yr Film Loan:* 3312.

Film Collection 100p, from circuit 963p. *Circ:* 8mm reel, 60p. *Pubns:* catalog, annual ($1).

Other Film Serv Obtain film from coop loan system (Western Reserve Film Circuit, Project Information Films, Northern Ohio Film Circuit). Permanent viewing facility available to community. *Equipment:* lend 16mm sound projector (3), 8mm reel projector (2), projection tables & stands (5), projection screens (3).

Other Media Collections *Audio:* disc, 33⅓ rpm, 2000t; disc, 45rpm, 50t; tape, cartridge, 10t. *Filmstrips:* silent, 60t. *Slides:* sets, 8t. *Member:* EFLA, FLIC.

Findlay

C- FINDLAY COLLEGE, Shafer Library, 1000 N Main, 45840. *Tel:* (419) 422-8313, ext 327. *In Charge:* Linda Lester, Public Services Librarian. *AV Staff:* ¼ prof.

Film Serv Obtain film from coop loan system (College Three). *Equipment:* lend S8mm camera, projection screens.

Other Media Collections *Audio:* total, 350t. *Filmstrips:* total, 105t. *Slides:* single, 100t.

Video Serv *Est:* 1974. *Video Use:* documentation of community/school events. Video serv available by appointment.

Video Equipment/Facilities *In-House Use Only:* recording deck (1), col, Sony TCV2110; monitor (1), col, Sony CVM1720. *For Loan:* portapak (2); recording deck (1), b&w, Sony AV5000; studio camera (1), b&w, Sony AVC3400; monitor (2), b&w, Sony CVM1720; additional camera lenses (1); audio tape recorders (1). *Equipment Loan Period:* 1 day. Provide training in use of equipment to faculty & students.

Video Tape Loan/Rental/Sale Serv *Serv Provided:* free loan. *Loan Eligibility:* staff & students. *Restrictions:* may not borrow by mail. *Other Video Serv:* production workshops.

Cable & CCTV Receive serv of cable TV system. Run cable programs for special audiences.

P- FINDLAY-HANCOCK COUNTY PUBLIC LIBRARY, 206 Broadway, 45840. *Tel:* (419) 422-1712. *Film Serv Est:* 1967. *In Charge:* Vanette M. Schwartz, AV Librarian. *AV Staff:* 1 (1 prof, ½ cl). *Film Sel:* committee preview. *Holdings:* children's films 12%.

Free-Loan Film Serv *Eligibility:* educational inst, civic & religious groups, indiv with library cards, prof groups, such as County Medical Assn. *Restrictions:* for indiv, only persons living or working in Hancock County; for inst, only in Hancock County. Cannot use for fund-raising, borrowers must be 18 years old or over. Available to researchers/scholars for on-site viewing. May not borrow by mail. *Loan Period:* 1 day. *Total Yr Film Loan:* 1250.

Film Rental Serv *Eligibility:* educational org, civic groups, patrons/public, religious & professional groups. *Restrictions:* only those living or working in Hancock County. Cannot use for fund-raising. *Rental Period:* 1 day. *Total Yr Film Booking:* 670.

Film Collection 105t/p. Approx 80t acquired annually. *Circ:* 16mm, 32t/p; 8mm reel, 26t/p; S8mm reel, 47t/p. *Pubns:* publish listings of 16mm films.

Other Film Serv Obtain film from coop loan system (NOR-WELD, Western Ohio Film Circuit), film reference serv, library film programs. *Equipment:* lend 16mm sound projector (1), 8mm reel projector (1), projection screens (1).

Other Media Collections *Audio:* disc, 33⅓ rpm, 1762t/c; tape, cassette, 48t/c; tape, cartridge, 58t/c. *Filmstrips:* sound, 44t/c; silent, 20t/c. *Slides:* sets, 89t/c.

Budget & Expenditures Total library budget $60,467.50 (FY 1/1/74-1/1/75). Total FY film budget $5000. *Member:* ALA, Ohio Library Assn.

Fostoria

P- KAUBISCH MEMORIAL LIBRARY, 205 Perry St, 44830. *Tel:* (419) 435-2813. *In Charge:* Doris Norris, Film Librarian. *Member:* Northern Ohio Film Circuit.

Fremont

P- BIRCHARD PUBLIC LIBRARY, 423 Crogham St, 43420. *Tel:* (419) 332-1121. *In Charge:* Richard Gooch. *Member:* Western Ohio Film Circuit.

Greenville

P- GREENVILLE PUBLIC LIBRARY, 520 Sycamore St, 45331. *Tel:* (513) 548-3915. *Film Serv Est:* 1969. *In Charge:* Susan Allen, Dir. *AV Staff:* 1 (1 prof). *Film Sel:* chief film librarian's decision, published reviews.

Film Rental Serv *Eligibility:* no restrictions. *Restrictions:* only in Darke County. *Rental Period:* as needed. *Total Yr Film Booking:* 2000.

Film Collection 10t/p. Approx 5t acquired annually. *Circ:* 16mm, 10t/p. *Pubns:* catalog, annual ($.50).

Other Film Serv Obtain film from coop loan system (Western Ohio Film Circuit), library film programs. *Equipment:* lend 16mm sound projector (1).

Other Media Collections *Audio:* disc, 33⅓ rpm, 10,000t/15,000c. *Filmstrips:* sound, 75t/c; silent, 25t/c.

Budget & Expenditures   Total library budget $33,000 (FY 1/1/75-1/1/76). Total FY film budget $6000. *Member:* ALA, Ohio Library Assn.

Hamilton

P- LANE PUBLIC LIBRARY, Film Dept, N Third & Buckeye Sts, 45011. *Tel:* (513) 894-7156. *In Charge:* Sharon Bradford, Reference Asst. *AV Staff:* 3 (3 tech). *Film Sel:* committee preview, staff recommendations, published reviews. *Holdings:* animated films, black studies, children's films, social sciences.
   Free-Loan Film Serv   *Eligibility:* educational inst, & others, such as Butler County Children's Home & The Juvenile Center. *Restrictions:* for inst, only in Butler County. Cannot use for fund-raising, transmit electronically. May not borrow by mail. *Loan Period:* 1 day. *Total Yr Film Loan:* 1531.
   Film Rental Serv   *Eligibility:* no restrictions. *Restrictions:* only in Butler County. Cannot use for fund-raising, transmit electronically. *Rental Period:* 1 day. *Total Yr Film Booking:* 896.
   Film Collection   167t/p. Approx 5t acquired annually. *Circ:* 16mm, 43t/p; 8mm reel, 47t/p; S8mm reel, 27t/p. *Pubns:* catalog, annual ($.75).
   Other Film Serv   Obtain film from coop loan system (Western Ohio Film Circuit).
   Other Media Collections   *Audio:* disc, 33⅓ rpm, 3830t; tape, cassette, 35t; tape, cartridge, 107t. *Filmstrips:* sound, 14t; silent, 28t; sound sets, 4t; silent sets, 4t.
   Budget & Expenditures   Total library budget $96,468 (FY 1/1/75-1/1/76). Total FY film budget $3800.
   Cable & CCTV   Receive serv of cable TV system. Have advisory/administrative role in cable system operation. Story hours for children.

Kent

C- KENT STATE UNIVERSITY, AV Serv Educational Film Rental Library, 215 Educational Bldg, 44242. *Tel:* (216) 672-2454. *Film Serv Est:* 1948. *In Charge:* Charles H. Hunger, Dir, AV Serv. *AV Staff:* 29 (6 prof, 14 cl, 9 tech). *Film Sel:* faculty/staff recommendations, chief film librarian's decision.
   Free-Loan Film Serv   *Eligibility:* staff & students. *Restrictions:* for indiv, only on campus. Cannot use for fundraising, transmit electronically. Available to researchers/scholars for on-site viewing. May not borrow by mail. *Loan Period:* 1-2 days or as requested. *Total Yr Film Loan:* 16,757.
   Film Rental Serv   *Eligibility:* no restrictions. *Restrictions:* only in eastern half of U.S. Cannot use for fund-raising, transmit electronically. *Rental Period:* 3-5 days. *Total Yr Film Booking:* 39,869. Produce slide programs, tapes, overhead transparencies etc, for instructional use only.
   Film Collection   7311t/8692p. Approx 500t acquired annually. *Circ:* 16mm, 7300t. *Noncirc:* 16mm, 11t. *Pubns:* catalog, every 3 yrs ($4); suppl in yr catalog not published. Publish Subject Area Catalog ($1).
   Other Film Serv   Rent film from distributors for patrons, obtain film from coop loan system, obtain film from other libraries, film reference serv, film fairs/festivals, library film programs. Permanent viewing facility available to community. *Equipment:* lend/rent 16mm sound projector (122), S8mm cartridge projector (15), S8mm reel projector (10), projection tables & stands (291), projection screens (425), large variety of misc equipment (715).
   Other Media Collections   *Audio:* tape, reel, 3500c.
   Budget & Expenditures   Total library budget $107,640 (FY 7/1/74-7/1/75). Total FY film budget $75,000. *Member:* AECT, CUFC, EFLA, Educational Media Council of Ohio, Inter-University Council of Media Directors.

Lima

P- LIMA PUBLIC LIBRARY, 650 W Market St, 45801. *Tel:* (419) 228-5113, ext 8. *Film Serv Est:* 1951. *In Charge:* Cathy Woodward, Head, AV Dept. *AV Staff:* 4 (1 cl). *Film Sel:* committee preview.
   Free-Loan Film Serv   *Eligibility:* indiv with library cards. *Restrictions:* for indiv, none. Cannot use for fund-raising. May not borrow by mail. *Loan Period:* 1 day. *Total Yr Film Loan:* 4591.
   Film Collection   600t/p. Approx 20t acquired annually. *Circ:* 16mm, 600t/p. *Pubns:* catalog, as needed ($1.25); suppl, no set policy.
   Other Film Serv   Obtain film from coop loan system (Western Ohio Film Circuit), library film programs. Permanent viewing facility available for rent to community.
   Other Media Collections   *Audio:* disc, 33⅓ rpm, 4000t/4300c. *Filmstrips:* sound, 300t/c; silent, 150t/c. *Slides:* sets, 83t/84c. *Member:* ALA, EFLA, Ohio Library Assn.

Lorain

P- LORAIN PUBLIC LIBRARY, 351 Sixth St, 44052. *Tel:* (216) 244-1192, ext 7. *Film Serv Est:* 1949. *In Charge:* Mary Conser, AV Librarian. *AV Staff:* 2 (1 prof, 1 cl). *Film Sel:* committee preview, staff recommendations. *Holdings:* children's films 13%, Spanish culture & language 21%.
   Free-Loan Film Serv   *Eligibility:* educational inst, civic & religious groups, indiv with library cards. *Restrictions:* for indiv & inst, only in Lorain County. Cannot use for fund-raising, transmit electronically. May not borrow by mail. *Loan Period:* 1 day. *Total Yr Film Loan:* 1836.
   Film Collection   374p. *Circ:* 16mm, 814t/p. *Pubns:* catalog, annual.
   Other Film Serv   Obtain film from coop loan system (Northern Ohio Film Circuit, Lorain & Melina County Film Circuit), film reference serv, film fairs/festivals, library film programs. Permanent viewing facility available for rent to community.
   Other Media Collections   *Audio:* disc, 33⅓ rpm, 6120t. *Filmstrips:* total, 62t. *Slides:* total, 2884t.
   Budget & Expenditures   Total library budget $88,493 (FY 1/1/74-1/1/75). Total FY film budget $9,697.70. *Member:* ALA, EFLA.

Louisville

P- LOUISVILLE PUBLIC LIBRARY, 700 Lincoln Ave, 44641. *Tel:* (216) 875-1696. *Film Serv Est:* 1954. *In Charge:* Elizabeth M. Chenot, AV Asst. *AV Staff:* 1 (1 tech). *Film Sel:* committee preview, staff recommendations.
   Free-Loan Film Serv   *Eligibility:* staff & students, educational inst, civic & religious groups, indiv with library cards. *Restrictions:* for indiv, interlibrary loan; for inst, none. May not borrow by mail. *Loan Period:* 1 day. *Total Yr Film Loan:* 1277.
   Film Collection   86p. Approx 7t acquired annually. *Circ:* 16mm, 66t; 8mm reel, 37t.
   Other Film Serv   Obtain film from coop loan system (Central Ohio Film Circuit, Mid-Eastern Ohio Library Org), obtain film from other libraries. *Equipment:* lend 16mm sound projector (1), 8mm reel projector (1), projection tables & stands (1), projection screens (1).
   Other Media Collections   *Audio:* disc, 33⅓ rpm, 3611t; disc, 45rpm, 75t; disc, 78rpm, 100t; tape, cassette, 109t; tape, reel, 10t. *Filmstrips:* silent, 173t; sound sets, 33t. *Slides:* single, 545t.
   Budget & Expenditures   Total library budget $137,838.68 (FY 1/1/75-1/1/76). Total FY film budget $2313.13. *Member:* Ohio Library Assn.

McConnelsville

P- KATE LOVE SIMPSON LIBRARY, 358 E Main St, 43756. *Tel:* (614) 962-2533. *AV Staff:* 1 (1 prof).
   Film Rental Serv   *Eligibility:* educational org, civic groups. *Restrictions:* only in Morgan County. *Rental Period:* flexible because of mailing.

McConnelsville (cont'd)
Other Film Serv Obtain film from other libraries. Permanent viewing facility available for rent to community. *Equipment:* lend 8mm reel projector (1), projection screens (1).
Other Media Collections *Audio:* 78rpm, 271c. *Filmstrips:* sound, 1082c.

Mansfield

P- MANSFIELD PUBLIC LIBRARY, 43 W Third St, 44902. *Tel:* (419) 524-1041. *Film Serv Est:* 1971. *In Charge:* Richard Allwardt, Assistant Dir. *Film Sel:* librarian's decision. *Holdings:* animated films 1%, children's films 2%, feature films 1%.
Free-Loan Film Serv *Eligibility:* indiv with library cards. *Restrictions:* for indiv, none. May not borrow by mail. *Total Yr Film Loan:* 3200.
Film Collection 286t/p. Approx 50t acquired annually. *Circ:* 286t/p.
Other Film Serv Rent film from distributors for patrons, obtain film from coop loan system (Kent State Univ Film Center), film reference serv. *Equipment:* lend 8mm reel projector (1).
Other Media Collections *Audio:* disc, 33⅓rpm, 1350t/1357c; tape, cassette, 30t/c.
Budget & Expenditures Total library budget $61,500 (FY 1/1/75-1/1/76). Total FY film budget $1000. *Member:* ALA, Ohio Library Assn, Ohio Library Trustee's Assn.

Massillon

P- MASSILLON PUBLIC LIBRARY, 208 Lincoln Way East, 44646. *Tel:* (216) 832-9831. *In Charge:* Johnnie Stenger, Film Librarian. *Member:* Northern Ohio Film Circuit.

Middletown

P- MIDDLETOWN PUBLIC LIBRARY, 1320 First Ave, 45042. *Tel:* (513) 424-1251. *In Charge:* Douglas Bean. *Member:* Western Ohio Film Circuit.

New Philadelphia

C- KENT STATE UNIVERSITY, Tuscarawas Campus Library, University Drive NE, 44663. *Tel:* (216) 339-3391, ext 56. *Video Serv Est:* 1974. *In Charge:* Lillian A. Hinds, Librarian. *Video Staff:* 2 p-t. *Video Use:* documentation of community/school events, teaching tool. Produce video tapes.
Video Equipment/Facilities *In-House Use Only:* portapak (1), b&w, Sony; recording deck (1), b&w, Sony AV3400; playback deck (1), b&w, Sony; studio camera (1), Sony AVC3400; monitor (1), Sony; microphones (1). Have portable viewing installation. Provide training in use of equipment to student operators.
Video Collection Maintained by own production. Use/play ¼″ reel to reel, ¾″ cassette. *Tape Sel:* faculty/staff recommendations. *Special Collections:* classroom use. *Collection, B&W:* ¾″ cassette, 18t.
Cable & CCTV Receive serv of cable TV system. Produce programs for cablecasting.

P- NEW PHILADELPHIA-TUSCARAWAS COUNTY DISTRICT LIBRARY, 121 Fair Ave NW, 44663. *Tel:* (216) 364-4474. *In Charge:* Thelma Murphy, Film Librarian. *Member:* Northern Ohio Film Circuit.

North Baltimore

P- NORTH BALTIMORE PUBLIC LIBRARY, 230 N Main St, 45872. *Tel:* (419) 257-6601. *Film Serv Est:* 1971. *In Charge:* Evelyn Basil, Film Librarian. *AV Staff:* 1 (1 prof). *Film Sel:* committee preview.

Free-Loan Film Serv *Eligibility:* indiv with library cards. *Restrictions:* for indiv, none. Available to researchers/scholars for on-site viewing. May not borrow by mail. *Loan Period:* 1 day.
Film Collection 650t/p. *Circ:* 16mm, 650t/p; 8mm reel, 980t/p. *Pubns:* catalog, annual.
Other Film Serv Obtain film from coop loan system (Northern Ohio Film Circuit, Norweld Film Collection, Kent State Univ Film Library), obtain film from other libraries, library film programs. Permanent viewing facility available for rent to community. *Equipment:* lend 8mm reel projector (2).
Other Media Collections *Audio:* total, 4951t/c. *Filmstrips:* total 924t/c. *Slides:* sets, 20t/c.
Budget & Expenditures Total library budget $32,000 (FY 1/1/74-1/1/75). Total FY film budget $1500.

Painesville

P- MORLEY LIBRARY, Lake County District, 184 Phelps St, 44077. *Tel:* (216) 352-3383. *In Charge:* Jeanne Prahl, AV Librarian. *Holdings:* Christmas.
Film Collection 150t.
Other Media Collections *Audio:* disc, 33⅓rpm, 2000t.
Budget & Expenditures Total FY AV budget $1600.

Perrysburg

C- MICHAEL J. OWENS TECHNICAL COLLEGE, Learning Resource Media Center, 30335 Oregon, 43551. *Tel:* (419) 666-0580, ext 251. *Film Serv Est:* 1972. *In Charge:* William Mears, Dir. *AV Staff:* 3 (2 prof, 1 tech). *Film Sel:* committee preview, faculty/staff recommendations. *Holdings:* engineering 25%, law 50%, medicine 20%, teacher education 5%.
Free-Loan Film Serv *Eligibility:* staff & students, & others, such as neighboring colleges. *Restrictions:* for indiv & inst, none. Available to researchers/scholars for on-site viewing. May borrow by mail. *Loan Period:* as needed.
Film Collection 250t/p. Approx 50t acquired annually. *Circ:* 16mm, 75t; 8mm cartridge 25t; S8mm cartridge, 150t. *Pubns:* catalog, annual.
Other Film Serv Obtain film from other libraries. *Equipment:* lend S8mm camera (1), 16mm sound projector (10), 8mm cartridge projector (20), 8mm reel projector, S8mm cartridge projector (1), S8mm reel projector (15), projection tables & stands (1), projection screens (15).
Other Media Collections *Audio:* disc, 33⅓rpm, 194t; tape, cassette, 387t. *Filmstrips:* silent, 4t; sound sets, 841t. *Slides:* sets, 45t.
Video Serv *Video Staff:* 2 p-t, 1 tech. *Video Use:* documentation of community/school events. Video serv available on demand. Produce video tapes.
Video Equipment/Facilities *For Loan:* portapak (1), b&w, Sony; recording deck (4), b&w/col, Sony 1200, Craig; monitor (4), b&w/col, Setchell Carlson, Sony; additional camera lenses (1); tripods (3). *Equipment Loan Period:* no set policy. Provide training in use of equipment to faculty & students.
Video Tape Loan/Rental/Sale Serv *Serv Provided:* free loan, swap with other inst, sale. *Loan Eligibility:* staff & students, civic groups. *Restrictions:* for indiv & inst, none. May borrow by mail. *Loan Period:* flexible.
Video Collection Maintained by purchase, own production. Use/play 1″ reel to reel, ¾″ cassette. *Sources:* own production. *Tape Sel:* preview, faculty/staff recommendations. Tapes organized by accession number. *Collection, Color:* ¾″ cassette, 25t. *Collection, B&W:* ¾″ cassette, 50t. *Pubns:* catalog.

Piqua

P- FLESH PUBLIC LIBRARY, 124 W Greene St, 45356. *Tel:* (513) 773-6753. *Film Serv Est:* 1951. *In Charge:* Wallace White, Dir. *AV Staff:* ½ cl. *Film Sel:* committee preview.
Film Rental Serv *Eligibility:* no restrictions. *Restrictions:* only in Miami County. *Rental Period:* 1 day. *Total Yr Film Booking:* 2240.

large

Film Collection 17t/p. *Circ:* 16mm, 17t/p. *Pubns:* catalog, annual ($.50).

Other Film Serv Obtain film from coop loan system (Western Ohio Film Circuit), film reference serv, film fairs/festivals, library film programs. Permanent viewing facility available for rent to community. *Equipment:* rent 16mm sound projector (1), projection screens (2).

Other Media Collections *Audio:* disc, 33⅓rpm, 2986t/3074c; tape, cassette, 12t/c.

Budget & Expenditures Total library budget $26,000 (FY 1/1/75-1/1/76). Total FY film budget $2500. *Member:* Ohio Library Assn.

Portsmouth

P- PORTSMOUTH PUBLIC LIBRARY, 1220 Gallia St, 45662. *Tel:* (614) 354-7506. *In Charge:* Betsy DeMent, Clerk. *AV Staff:* 1 cl. *Film Sel:* librarian's decision.

Free-Loan Film Serv *Eligibility:* educational inst, civic & religious groups, indiv with library cards, prof groups. *Restrictions:* for indiv & inst, only in our county. Cannot use for fund-raising, transmit electronically. Available to researchers/scholars for on-site viewing. May not borrow by mail. *Loan Period:* 1 day or weekend.

Film Collection 200p. *Pubns:* catalog, as needed.

Other Film Serv Obtain film from coop loan system (Central Ohio Film Circuit), library film programs.

Other Media Collections *Audio:* disc, 33⅓ rpm, 700t/c.

Budget & Expenditures Total library budget $36,000 (FY 1/1/75-1/1/76). Total FY film budget $1500. *Member:* Ohio Library Assn.

Ravenna

P- REED MEMORIAL LIBRARY, 167 E Main St, 44266. *Tel:* (216) 296-2827. *Film Serv Est:* 1974. *In Charge:* Bonnie McDaniel, Clerk. *AV Staff:* ½ (½ cl). *Film Sel:* committee preview, published reviews.

Free-Loan Film Serv *Eligibility:* indiv with adult library cards. *Restrictions:* for indiv, none. Available to researchers/scholars for on-site viewing. May not borrow by mail. *Loan Period:* 7 days. *Total Yr Film Loan:* 996.

Film Rental Serv *Eligibility:* educational org, civic groups, patrons/public (except students). *Restrictions:* only in Portage County. *Rental Period:* 1 day. *Total Yr Film Booking:* 821.

Film Collection *Circ:* 16mm, 10t/p; 8mm reel, 78t/p. *Pubns:* catalog, annual ($.75).

Other Film Serv Obtain film from coop loan system (Ohio Valley Film Circuit), obtain film from other libraries, library film programs. Permanent viewing facility available to community.

Other Media Collections *Audio:* disc, 33⅓rpm, 1419t; tape, cassette, 60t. *Filmstrips:* total, 124t.

Budget & Expenditures No separate AV budget. *Member:* ALA, Ohio Library Assn.

Sandusky

P- SANDUSKY PUBLIC LIBRARY, Columbus Ave and W Adams St, 44870. *Tel:* (419) 625-3834. *In Charge:* Louise Kuemmel, Film Librarian. *Member:* Northern Ohio Film Circuit.

Sidney

P- AMOS MEMORIAL PUBLIC LIBRARY, 230 E North St, 45365. *Tel:* (513) 492-8354. *In Charge:* Doris Stephens. *Member:* Western Ohio Film Circuit.

Springfield

P- WARDER PUBLIC LIBRARIES, 137 E High, 45501. *Tel:* (513) 323-8616. *In Charge:* Rose Castle, AV Asst. *AV Staff:* 2½ cl. *Film Sel:* staff recommendations.

Free-Loan Film Serv *Eligibility:* indiv with library cards (or out-of-district card, $2). *Restrictions:* for indiv, none. *Loan Period:* 1 day. *Total Yr Film Loan:* 6472.

Film Collection 420t/425p. Approx 45t acquired annually. *Circ:* 16mm, 285t/290p; S8mm reel, 135t/p. *Pubns:* catalog, annual ($1).

Other Film Serv Obtain film from coop loan system (Western Ohio Film Circuit), library film programs. *Equipment:* lend S8mm reel projector (3).

Other Media Collections *Audio:* disc, 78rpm, 7000t; tape, cassette, 200t.

Budget & Expenditures Total library budget $54,000 (FY 1/1/75-1/1/76). Total FY film budget $3000. *Member:* ALA, Ohio Library Assn.

Steubenville

P- PUBLIC LIBRARY OF STEUBENVILLE & JEFFERSON COUNTY, 407 S Fourth St, 43952. *Tel:* (614) 282-9782. *In Charge:* Cleo Rowe, Film Clerk. *AV Staff:* 2. *Film Sel:* staff recommendations. *Holdings:* career education 20%, children's films 80%.

Film Rental Serv *Eligibility:* no restrictions. *Restrictions:* none. Cannot use for fund-raising, transmit electronically. *Rental Period:* 1 day.

Other Film Serv Obtain film from coop loan system (Ohio Valley Film Circuit). *Equipment:* lend filmstrip projector.

Tiffin

P- TIFFIN PUBLIC LIBRARY, 77 Jefferson St, 44883. *Tel:* (419) 447-3751. *In Charge:* Joyce Miller. *Member:* Western Ohio Film Circuit.

Toledo

P- TOLEDO-LUCAS COUNTY PUBLIC LIBRARY, Film Service, 325 Michigan St, 43624. *Tel:* (419) 242-7361, ext 235, 236. *Film Serv Est:* 1948. *In Charge:* Barbara E. Schaich, Head, Film Serv. *AV Staff:* 7 (1 prof, 4 cl, 1 tech). *Film Sel:* committee preview, staff recommendations, chief film librarian's decision. *Holdings:* Canadian travel films 2%, coping skills 1½%, Ohio 1½%.

Free-Loan Film Serv *Eligibility:* indiv with library cards. *Restrictions:* for indiv, only in Lucas County (out-of-county library cards $10/yr). Cannot use for fund-raising, transmit electronically, borrow for classroom use. May not borrow by mail. *Loan Period:* 1 day. *Total Yr Film Loan:* 15,720.

Film Collection 1322t/1417p. Approx 50t acquired annually. *Circ:* 16mm, 1393t/1515p; 8mm reel, 335t/600p. *Noncirc:* 16mm, 1t/p. *Pubns:* catalog, as needed ($2.50); suppl, no set policy.

Other Film Serv Film reference serv, film fairs/festivals, library film programs, film catalogs on file.

Other Media Collections *Audio:* disc, 33⅓rpm, 11,625c; tape, cassette, 930c.

Budget & Expenditures Total library budget $543,780.54 (FY 1/1/75-1/1/76). Total FY film budget $32,000. *Member:* EFLA, FLIC.

University Heights

C- JOHN CARROLL UNIVERSITY, Grasselli Library, 44118. *Tel:* (216) 491-4231. *Film Serv Est:* 1961. *In Charge:* S. M. Randel. *AV Staff:* 1 (1 cl). *Film Sel:* faculty/staff recommendations.

Free-Loan Film Serv *Eligibility:* staff & students.

Film Collection 17t. *Circ:* 16mm, 17t.

Other Film Serv Obtain film from coop loan system (Cleveland Area Interlibrary Network). Permanent viewing facility.

Other Media Collections *Audio:* disc, 33⅓rpm, 1912c; tape, total, 168c. *Filmstrips:* total, 392c. *Slides:* total, 3338c.

University Heights (cont'd)

Budget & Expenditures   Total library budget $115,440 (FY 6/1/74-6/1/75). No separate AV budget. *Member:* ALA.

Urbana

P- CHAMPAIGN COUNTY LIBRARY, 160 W Market St, 43078. *Tel:* (513) 653-3811. *Film Serv Est:* 1957. *Film Sel:* published reviews.
   Film Rental Serv   *Eligibility:* no restrictions. *Restrictions:* only in Champaign County. *Rental Period:* 1 day. *Total Yr Film Booking:* 277.
   Film Collection   91t. *Circ:* 16mm, 28t; 8mm reel, 63t.
   Other Film Serv   Obtain film from coop loan system (Central Ohio Film Circuit). *Equipment:* rent 16mm sound projector (2).
   Other Media Collections   *Audio:* disc, 33⅓ rpm, 1045t.
   Budget & Expenditures   Total library budget $97,640.49 (FY 1/1/75-1/1/76). Total FY film budget $1400.

Versailles

P- WORCH MEMORIAL LIBRARY, 161 E Main St, 45380. *Tel:* (513) 526-3416. *In Charge:* Roberta Varner. *Member:* Western Ohio Film Circuit.

Westerville

C- OTTERBEIN COLLEGE, Main & Grove Sts, 43081. *Tel:* (614) 891-3291. *Video Serv Est:* 1968. *In Charge:* Ross A. Fleming, Dir, Learning Resource Center. *Video Staff:* 4 f-t, 1 p-t. *Video Use:* documentation of community/school events, in-service training, practical video/TV training courses, playback only of professionally produced tapes, as art form, student teaching. Video serv available by appointment. Produce video tapes. Have production studio/space & separate control room. Have permanent & portable viewing installations. Provide training in use of equipment to faculty & students.
   Video Collection   Maintained by purchase, rental, own production. Use/play ½″, 1″ reel to reel, ¾″ cassette. *Sources:* commercial distributors. *Tape Sel:* preview, faculty/staff recommendations, catalogs. *Special Collections:* in-house training tapes. Tapes organized by department. *Other Video Serv:* programming, production workshops. *Pubns:* catalog.

P- WESTERVILLE PUBLIC LIBRARY, Film Dept, 126 S State St, 43081. *Tel:* (614) 882-5225. *Film Serv Est:* 1970. *In Charge:* Jane Bradford, Head Librarian. *AV Staff:* 5 (5 cl). *Film Sel:* committee preview, staff recommendations, chief film librarian's decision, published reviews.
   Free-Loan Film Serv   *Eligibility:* indiv with library cards. *Restrictions:* for indiv, only in Franklin County, noncounty resident card $5 annually. Cannot use for fund-raising. Available to researchers/scholars for on-site viewing. May not borrow by mail. *Loan Period:* 1 day. *Total Yr Film Loan:* 18,720.
   Film Collection   750t/p. Approx 200t acquired annually. *Circ:* 16mm, 750t/p. *Pubns:* catalog, annual ($2); suppl, quarterly.
   Other Film Serv   Film fairs/festivals, library film programs. Permanent viewing facility.
   Budget & Expenditures   Total library budget $73,508.08 (FY 1/1/74-1/1/75). Total FY film budget $39,701.38.

Wooster

P- WAYNE COUNTY PUBLIC LIBRARY, 304 N Market, 44691. *Tel:* (216) 262-0916, Film Dept. 262-4087. *In Charge:* Elsie Hofstetter, Film Librarian. *Member:* Northern Ohio Film Circuit.

Xenia

P- GREENE COUNTY DISTRICT LIBRARY, 194 E Church St, 45385. *Tel:* (513) 376-2995. *Film Serv Est:* 1973. *In Charge:* Lillie Whitelow, Library Asst, Films & Periodicals. *AV Staff:* 1 (½ prof, ½ cl). *Film Sel:* library director's decision.
   Free-Loan Film Serv   *Eligibility:* educational inst, civic & religious groups, indiv with library cards, prof groups, & others, such as any community group. *Restrictions:* for indiv & inst, only in Greene County. Cannot use for fund-raising. May not borrow by mail. *Loan Period:* 16mm 1 day, 8mm 2 wks. *Total Yr Film Loan:* 1297.
   Film Collection   164t/184p. Approx 50t acquired annually. *Circ:* 16mm, 22t/p; 8mm reel, 142t/162p. *Pubns:* catalog, annual.
   Other Film Serv   Obtain film from coop loan system (Western Ohio Film Circuit), film fairs/festivals, library film programs. Permanent viewing facility available for rent to community. *Equipment:* lend 16mm sound projector (2), 8mm reel projector (1), projection screens (1), slide projectors (1).
   Other Media Collections   *Audio:* disc, 33⅓ rpm, 1200t/1750c. *Slides:* sets, 2t/c.
   Budget & Expenditures   Total library budget $86,000 (FY 1/1/75-1/1/76). Total FY film budget $5500. *Member:* Ohio Library Assn.

Yellow Springs

C- ANTIOCH COLLEGE, Antioch Video, 45387. *Tel:* (513) 767-7331, ext 494. *Video Serv Est:* 1965. *In Charge:* Robert H. Devine, Dir, Antioch Video. *Video Staff:* 2 f-t, 5 p-t. *Video Use:* documentation of community/school events, community video access, in-service training, practical video/TV training courses, playback only of professionally produced tapes, as art form, social analysis. Video serv available on demand & by appointment. Produce video tapes. Have production studio/space & separate control room.
   Video Equipment/Facilities   *In-House Use Only:* studio camera (4), b&w; monitor (15), b&w; SEG (1); microphones; tripods; audio tape recorders. *For Loan:* portapak (10), ½″ b&w, Sony AV3400, Panasonic 3082; recording, playback & editing decks (15), ½″, 1″ b&w/col, Sony 8600, 3600, 3650, 320F, Panasonic 3020, 3130, Shibaden 510. Have permanent & portable viewing installations. *Equipment Loan Period:* quarter semester. Provide training in use of equipment to faculty, students & community.
   Video Tape Loan/Rental/Sale Serv   *Serv Provided:* will copy free from library for anyone sending blank tape, sale. *Loan Eligibility:* staff & students. May borrow by mail. *Total Yr Tape Loan:* 200.
   Video Collection   Maintained by own production, exchange/swap. Use/play ½″, 1″ reel to reel. *Sources:* community productions, exchange (alternate media people), off the air. *Tape Sel:* own productions. Tapes organized by subject. *Collection, B&W:* ½″ reel, 500-600t. *Other Video Serv:* programming, reference serv, taping of other media, production workshops. *Pubns:* catalog. Publish materials on video.
   Cable & CCTV   Produce programs for cablecasting. Inform public about cable system serv & facilities. Serve as production facility for others. Run cable programs for special audiences. Communications Studies Center has advisory/consultant role in operation of several public access systems. Have CCTV in inst. *Programming Sources:* over-the-air commercial & public broadcasting, tapes produced by inst & by community groups & indiv.

Youngstown

P- PUBLIC LIBRARY OF YOUNGSTOWN AND MAHONING COUNTY, Project Outreach, 2815 Mahoning Ave, 44509. *Tel:* (216) 792-3869. *Film Serv Est:* 1972. *In Charge:* Elfreda

Chatman, Dir. *AV Staff:* 6 (3 prof, 3 cl). *Film Sel:* staff recommendations, published reviews. *Holdings:* animated films, black studies, children's films, feature films.

Free-Loan Film Serv *Eligibility:* civic & religious groups, of groups. *Restrictions:* for indiv & inst, only in Mahoning unty. Cannot use for fund-raising, borrow for classroom use. *an Period:* 1 day.

Film Collection 325p. Approx 20t acquired annually. *Pubns:* catalog, as needed.

Other Film Serv Obtain film from coop loan system (Youngstown Bd of Educ, Catholic Diocese), film fairs/festivals, library film programs. *Equipment:* lend 16mm sound projector, projection tables & stands, projection screens. *Member:* Ohio Library Assn.

Oklahoma

Altus

P- SOUTHERN PRAIRIE LIBRARY SYSTEM, PO Drawer U, 73521. *Tel:* (405) 477-1930. *Film Serv Est:* 1973. *In Charge:* Rama F. Widup, Dir. *AV Staff:* 1 (1 tech). *Film Sel:* rotating collection from Okla. Dept of Libraries.
Free-Loan Film Serv *Eligibility:* educational inst, civic & religious groups, prof groups. *Restrictions:* for inst, only in Jackson & Harmon counties. Cannot use for fund-raising, transmit electronically, borrow for classroom use. Available to researchers/scholars for on-site viewing. May borrow by mail. *Loan Period:* 1 day. *Total Yr Film Loan:* 921.
Film Collection 161t/193p. *Circ:* 16mm, 45t/p; 8mm reel, 51t/97p; S8mm reel, 32t/51p. *Pubns:* catalog, as needed.
Other Film Serv Obtain film from coop loan system (Okla. Dept of Libraries), library film programs. *Equipment:* lend 16mm sound projector (5), projection screens (3).
Other Media Collections *Slides:* sets, 3t.
Budget & Expenditures Total library budget $53,850 (FY 7/1/74-7/1/75). No separate AV budget. *Member:* Okla. Library Assn, South West Library Assn.

Ardmore

P- CHICKASAW LIBRARY SYSTEM, 22 Broadlawn Village, 73401. *Tel:* (405) 223-3164. *In Charge:* Margaret Finke, Film Librarian. *AV Staff:* 1 cl. *Film Sel:* committee preview.
Free-Loan Film Serv *Eligibility:* civic & religious groups, & others, such as business & nursing homes. *Restrictions:* for inst, only in Atoka, Carter, Coal, Johnston, Love & Murray counties. Cannot use for fund-raising, transmit electronically, borrow for classroom use. Available to researchers/scholars for on-site viewing. May borrow by mail. *Loan Period:* 1-7 days. *Total Yr Film Loan:* 607.
Film Collection 70t/p. Approx 3-4t acquired annually. *Circ:* 16mm, 80t; 8mm total, 150t/p.
Other Film Serv Obtain film from coop loan system (Okla. Dept of Libraries Film Circuit), library film programs. Permanent viewing facility available free to community. *Equipment:* lend/rent 16mm sound projector (12), lend 8mm reel projector (1), S8mm reel projector (1), projection screens (11), slide & filmstrip projectors (3), phonographs (6), cassette record-players (3).
Other Media Collections *Audio:* disc, 33⅓ rpm, 2400t; tape, cassette, 50t; tape, reel, 50t. *Filmstrips:* silent sets, 20t. *Slides:* single, 200t; sets, 15t.
Budget & Expenditures Total library budget $24,000 (FY 7/1/74-7/1/75). No separate AV budget.

Bartlesville

C- BARTLESVILLE WESLEYAN COLLEGE, Library, 2201 Silver Lake Rd, 74003. *Tel:* (918) 333-6151, ext 225. *In Charge:* Wendell D. Thompson, Librarian.
Video Tape Loan/Rental/Sale Serv *Serv Provided:* free loan. *Loan Eligibility:* staff.
Video Collection Maintained by rental.
Cable & CCTV Receive serv of cable TV system. Run cable programs for special audiences. Have CCTV in inst, with 2 monitors.

Claremore

C- CLAREMORE JUNIOR COLLEGE, 74017. *Tel:* (918) 341-7510, ext 278. *Film Serv Est:* 1967. *In Charge:* Jean Tanner, Librarian. *Film Sel:* faculty/staff recommendations, chief film librarian's decision.
Free-Loan Film Serv *Eligibility:* staff & students, educational inst, civic & religious groups, indiv with library cards.

Restrictions: for indiv, interlibrary loan, only in state; for inst, only in our county. Available to researchers/scholars for on-site viewing. May not borrow by mail. *Total Yr Film Loan:* 116.
Film Collection 69t. Permanent viewing facility available for rent to community.
Other Media Collections *Audio:* disc, 33⅓ rpm, 500t; disc, 45rpm, 20t; disc, 78rpm, 21t; tape, cassette, 174t. *Filmstrips:* silent, 499t. *Slides:* single, 960t.
Budget & Expenditures Total library budget $15,000 (FY 7/1/74-7/1/75). Total FY film budget $1000. *Member:* Okla. Library Assn.
Video Serv *Est:* 1976. *In Charge:* Mike Keller, AV Head. *Video Staff:* 1 f-t. *Video Use:* in-service training. Video serv available on demand. Produce video tapes. Have production studio/space. Have portable viewing installation. Provide training in use of equipment to faculty & students.

Enid

P- PUBLIC LIBRARY OF ENID AND GARFIELD COUNTY, 120 W Maine, Box 3337, 73701. *Tel:* (405) 234-6313.
Free-Loan Film Serv *Eligibility:* indiv with library cards. *Restrictions:* for indiv, only in Garfield County. *Loan Period:* 7 days.
Film Collection 48t. *Circ:* S8mm reel, 48t.
Other Film Serv Library film programs.
Other Media Collections *Audio:* disc, 78rpm, 1519t/c; tape, cassette, 200t/c. *Filmstrips:* sound, 20t/c; silent, 150t/c. *Slides:* single, 393t/c; sets, 45t/c.
Budget & Expenditures No separate AV budget.

Langston

C- LANGSTON UNIVERSITY, M. B. Tolson Black Heritage Center, 73050. *Tel:* (405) 466-2281, ext 348. *Film Serv Est:* 1971. *In Charge:* Denyvetta Fields, Curator. *Film Sel:* published reviews. *Holdings:* black studies 100%.
Free-Loan Film Serv *Eligibility:* staff & students, anyone from outside may use on the university premises. *Restrictions:* for indiv, only at the university. Cannot use for fund-raising, transmit electronically. Available to researchers/scholars for on-site viewing. May not borrow by mail. *Total Yr Film Loan:* 4. Produce slides.
Film Collection 25t. Approx 3-4t acquired annually. *Noncirc:* 16mm, 25t. Publish monthly acquisition list.
Other Film Serv Film reference serv, film fairs/festivals, library film programs. *Equipment:* lend projection tables & stands (2), projection screens (2).
Other Media Collections *Audio:* disc, 33⅓ rpm, 185t; tape, cassette, 187t; tape, reel, 2t. *Filmstrips:* sound, 215t; silent, 25t; sound sets, 10t. *Slides:* single, 1050t.
Budget & Expenditures Total library budget $25,000 (FY 7/1/74-7/1/75). Total FY film budget $6000. *Member:* ALA, Okla. Library Assn, Southwest Library Assn.

Miami

S- FIRST BAPTIST CHURCH, Media Center Servs, Box 1030, 74354. *In Charge:* Lillie Newberry, Dir.
Free-Loan Film Serv *Eligibility:* civic & religious groups. *Equipment:* lend 16mm sound projector (2), video tape recorder.

C- NORTHEASTERN OKLAHOMA A&M COLLEGE, Library, Second & I St, 74354. *Tel:* (918) 542-8441, ext 288, 220. *Video Serv Est:* 1973. *In Charge:* Robert Kilman, Dir, Library Instructional Media. *Video Staff:* 4 f-t, 6 p-t. *Video Use:* documentation of community/school events, document & playback student class performance. Video serv available by appointment. Produce video tapes.

Video Equipment/Facilities *In-House Use Only:* audio tape recorders (1). *For Loan:* portapak (6), ½″ b&w, Sony 3400; recording deck (3), ½″ b&w, Sony 3650; editing deck (1), ¾″ col, Sony VO1800; microphones (3); tripods (5). *Equipment Loan Period:* 3 days or 1 semester.

Video Tape Loan/Rental/Sale Serv *Serv Provided:* swap with other inst. *Loan Eligibility:* staff & students. *Restrictions:* for indiv, none.

Video Collection Maintained by own production, exchange/swap. Use/play ½″ reel to reel, ¾″ cassette. *Sources:* commercial distributors. *Tape Sel:* preview, faculty/staff recommendations. Tapes organized by Dewey Decimal.

Cable & CCTV Receive serv of cable TV system. Run cable programs for special audiences.

Norman

C- UNIVERSITY OF OKLAHOMA, Stovall Museum of Science and History, 1335 Asp, 73069. *Tel:* (405) 325-4711. *Film Serv Est:* 1971. *In Charge:* Marge Farwell, Dir of Education. *Film Sel:* committee preview, faculty/staff recommendations. *Holdings:* children's films, science, social sciences.

Free-Loan Film Serv *Eligibility:* staff & students, educational inst, civic & religious groups, prof groups. *Restrictions:* for indiv & inst, only in city. Available to researchers/scholars for on-site viewing. May not borrow by mail. *Loan Period:* varies. *Total Yr Film Loan:* 15. Permanent viewing facility available for rent to community. *Equipment:* audio tape recorders (2).

Oklahoma City

P- OKLAHOMA COUNTY LIBRARIES, Main Library, 131 NW Third, 73102. *Tel:* (405) 235-0571, ext 44. *In Charge:* Elsie Bell, Chief, Main Library. *AV Staff:* 4 (1 prof, 3 cl). *Film Sel:* committee preview.

Free-Loan Film Serv *Eligibility:* staff & students, educational inst, civic & religious groups, prof groups, & all groups & organizations in Okla. County. *Restrictions:* for indiv & inst, only in Oklahoma County. Cannot use for fund-raising, transmit electronically. A 75¢ insurance fee charged per reel. Available to researchers/scholars for on-site viewing. May not borrow by mail. *Loan Period:* 1 day. *Total Yr Film Loan:* 7599.

Film Collection 450t/490p. Approx 50t acquired annually. *Circ:* 16mm, 450t/480p; 8mm reel, 260t/p. *Noncirc:* 16mm, 8t. *Pubns:* catalog, as needed ($1); suppl, no set policy.

Other Film Serv Obtain film from coop loan system (Okla. State Film Library), film reference serv, library film programs. Permanent viewing facility available free to community.

Other Media Collections *Audio:* disc, 78rpm, 1726t; tape, cassette, 1662t. *Filmstrips:* sound sets, 358t/c.

Budget & Expenditures Total library budget $211,000 (FY 7/1/74-7/1/75). Total FY film budget $17,700. *Member:* ALA, Okla. Library Assn.

Video Equipment/Facilities *In-House Use Only:* recording deck, Sony 1600; playback deck, Sony VP1000; SEG, Sony. Have portable viewing installation. Provide training in use of equipment to staff. Have tape duplication serv.

Video Tape Loan/Rental/Sale Serv *Serv Provided & Restrictions:* not yet determined. Cannot duplicate, air without permission.

Video Collection Obtain tapes from local NBC affiliate. Use/play ¾″ cassette.

Sapulpa

S- LIBERTY GLASS COMPANY, Box 520, 74066. *Tel:* (918) 224-1440. *Film Serv Est:* 1935. *In Charge:* Judy Montgomery, Librarian. *AV Staff:* 1 (1 cl).

Free-Loan Film Serv *Eligibility:* staff & students, educational inst, civic groups, prof groups. *Restrictions:* for indiv & inst, none. Cannot use for fund-raising. *Loan Period:* 2 weeks. *Total Yr Film Loan:* 6.

Stillwater

C- OKLAHOMA STATE UNIVERSITY, AV Center-Film Center, 74074. *Tel:* (405) 372-6211, ext 7874. *Film Serv Est:* 1949. *In Charge:* Woodfin G. Harris, Dir, AV Center. *AV Staff:* 26 (9 prof, 11 cl, 6 tech). *Film Sel:* faculty/staff recommendations, chief film librarian's decision. *Holdings:* agriculture 10%, animated films 4%, black studies 2%, career education 5%, children's films 5%, consumer affairs 5%, engineering 5%, fine arts 8%, industrial arts 2%, law 2%, medicine 3%, science 20%, social sciences 16%, teacher education 6%, women 2%.

Film Rental Serv *Eligibility:* no restrictions. *Restrictions:* only in Okla., Kans., Col., N. Mex., Mo., Ark., La. Cannot transmit electronically. *Rental Period:* 2 days. *Total Yr Film Booking:* 13,000.

Film Collection 4200t/4500p. Approx 110t acquired annually. *Circ:* 16mm, 4200t/4500p. *Noncirc:* 16mm, 500t/525p. *Pubns:* catalog, every 2 yrs ($2); suppl, no set policy.

Other Film Serv Rent film from distributors for patrons, obtain film from coop loan system, obtain film from other libraries, film reference serv. Permanent viewing facility available for rent to community. *Equipment:* lend/rent S8mm camera (4), lend/rent 16mm sound projector (100), lend/rent 8mm cartridge projector · (45), lend/rent 8mm reel projector (10), lend/rent S8mm cartridge projector (15), lend/rent S8mm reel projector (5), lend/rent projection tables & stands (300), lend/rent projection screens (30).

Budget & Expenditures Total FY film budget $43,000 (FY 7/1/74-7/1/75). *Member:* AECT, CUFC, Okla. Assn for Education Communications & Technology.

Tulsa

P- TULSA CITY-COUNTY LIBRARY, Media Center, 400 Civic Center, 74103. *Tel:* (918) 581-5171. *Film Serv Est:* 1965. *In Charge:* Keith M. Edwards, Head, Media Center. *AV Staff:* 6 (4 prof, 1 cl, 1 tech). *Film Sel:* committee preview, chief film librarian's decision. *Holdings:* American Indian 5%, animated films 10%, black history 5%, children's films 20%, women.

Free-Loan Film Serv *Eligibility:* staff & students, educational inst, civic & religious groups, indiv with library cards, prof groups. *Restrictions:* for indiv & inst, only in Tulsa County. Cannot use for fund-raising, transmit electronically. Available to researchers/scholars for on-site viewing. May borrow by mail. *Loan Period:* 1-2 days.

Film Collection 900t/p. *Circ:* 16mm, 610t/p; 8mm reel, 200t/p. *Pubns:* catalog, every 2 yrs; suppl, in yr catalog not published.

Other Film Serv Rent film from distributors for patrons, obtain film from coop loan system (Okla. State Library), film reference serv, film fairs/festivals, library film programs. Permanent viewing facility available to community. *Equipment:* lend 16mm sound projector (11), 8mm reel projector (2), S8mm reel projector (2), projection tables & stands (7), projection screens (9), overhead projector & filmstrip projector.

Other Media Collections *Audio:* disc, 33⅓ rpm, 6000t; tape, cassette, 700t. *Filmstrips:* sound sets, 145t; silent sets, 15t. *Slides:* single, 120t.

Budget & Expenditures Total library budget $241,462 (FY 7/1/74-7/1/75). Total FY film budget $67,593. *Member:* AECT, ALA, EFLA, Okla. Library Assn.

Video Serv *Est:* 1974. *In Charge:* Tom Ledbetter, Manager Channel 24. *Tel:* (918) 581-5673. *Video Staff:* 3 f-t, 2 p-t, 1 tech. *Video Use:* documentation of community events, to increase community's library use. Video serv available by appointment. Produce video tapes. Have production studio/space & separate control room.

Video Equipment/Facilities *In-House Use Only:* portapak (1), ¼″ col, AKAI VTS150; recording deck (4), ½″, ¾″, 1″ col, Wollensak, IVC, Sony; editing deck (1), 1″ col, IVC870C; studio camera (3), ⅔″ col, Panasonic; monitor (5), b&w/col; SEG (1), Telemation; keyer (1), Telemation; lighting (40); microphones

Tulsa (cont'd)

(9); tripods (5); audio tape recorders (3). Provide training in use of equipment to volunteers in TV production.

Video Tape Loan/Rental/Sale Serv *Serv Provided:* free loan. *Loan Eligibility:* educational inst, civic groups. *Restrictions:* for inst, none. Cannot duplicate, air without permission. May borrow by mail. *Loan Period:* varies.

Video Collection Maintained by own production. Use/ play ½", ¼", 1" reel to reel, ¾" cassette. Tapes organized by subject. *Collection, Color:* ¾" cassette, 150t/c.

Cable & CCTV Receive serv of cable TV system. Produce programs for cablecasting. Run cable programs for special audiences. Have CCTV in inst, with 3 monitors. *Programming Sources:* tapes produced by inst.

Weatherford

C- SOUTHWESTERN OKLAHOMA STATE UNIVERSITY, Instructional Materials Center, 73096. *Tel:* (405) 772-6611, ext 5313. *In Charge:* David A. Gwinn, Dir. *AV Staff:* 2 (1 prof, 1 cl). *Film Sel:* committee preview, faculty/staff recommendations, chief film librarian's decision.

Film Rental Serv *Eligibility:* educational org. *Restrictions:* only in state. Cannot use for fund-raising, transmit electronically. *Rental Period:* 3 days. *Total Yr Film Booking:* 4621.

Film Collection 1200t/1250p. *Circ:* 16mm, 1200t/1250p. *Pubns:* catalog, as needed; suppl, no set policy.

Other Film Serv Film reference serv. Permanent viewing facility. *Member:* AECT.

Oregon

Albany

P- ALBANY PUBLIC LIBRARY, 1390 S Waverly Dr, 97321. *Tel:* (503) 926-8696. *Film Serv Est:* 1970. *Film Sel:* staff recommendations.

Free-Loan Film Serv *Eligibility:* indiv with library cards. *Restrictions:* for indiv & inst, only in city. Cannot use for fundraising. *Loan Period:* 1 day. *Total Yr Film Loan:* 750.

Film Collection 90t/p. Approx 15t acquired annually. *Circ:* 8mm reel, 60t/p; S8mm reel, 30t/p.

Other Film Serv Library film programs. Permanent viewing facility available for rent to community. *Equipment:* lend 16mm sound projector (1), 8mm reel projector (1), S8mm reel projector (1), projection screens (1).

Other Media Collections *Audio:* tape, cassette, 150t/c.

Budget & Expenditures Total library budget $18,000 (FY 7/1/74-7/1/75). No separate AV budget. *Member:* ALA.

Astoria

C- CLATSOP COMMUNITY COLLEGE, Library, 1680 Lexington Ave, 97103. *Tel:* (503) 325-0910, ext 262. *Video Serv Est:* 1967. *Video Use:* documentation of community/school events, community video access, practical video/TV training courses, as art form. Video serv available by appointment. Produce video tapes. Have production studio/space & separate control room.

Video Equipment/Facilities *In-House Use Only:* portapak (1), ½″ b&w, Sony; recording deck (3), 1″ b&w/col, Ampex 5000, 7000, 8500; playback deck (1), ¾″ col, Sony; editing deck (1), 1″ col, Ampex 5800; studio camera (3), b&w, Packard Bell; monitor (9), b&w, Sony, Conrac; SEG (1), Panasonic; additional camera lenses (2); lighting (13); microphones (12); tripods (3); audio tape recorders (6). Have permanent viewing installation. Provide training in use of equipment to students in TV program.

Video Collection Maintained by own production. Use/play ½″, 1″ reel to reel, ¾″ cassette. *Sources:* community productions. *Tape Sel:* preview, faculty/staff recommendations, catalogs. Tapes organized by subject & acquisition number. *Other Video Serv:* programming, taping of other media, production workshops. *Pubns:* catalog.

Cable & CCTV Receive serv of cable TV system. Produce programs for cablecasting. Inform public about cable system serv & facilities. Run cable programs for special audiences. Have CCTV in inst, with 8 rooms wired for portable TV sets. *Programming Sources:* over-the-air commercial & public broadcasting, tapes produced by inst & by community groups & indiv.

Eugene

P- EUGENE PUBLIC LIBRARY, Art-Music Room, 100 W 13 St, 97401. *Tel:* (503) 687-5450. *Film Serv Est:* 1970. *In Charge:* Mrs Svea Gold, Art-Music Librarian. *AV Staff:* 2¼ (1 prof, 1¼ cl). *Film Sel:* published reviews.

Free-Loan Film Serv *Eligibility:* indiv with library cards. *Restrictions:* for indiv & inst, only in city. *Loan Period:* 7 days. *Total Yr Film Loan:* 3551.

Film Collection 225t/250p. *Circ:* 16mm, 225t/250p.

Other Film Serv Library film programs. Permanent viewing facility.

Other Media Collections *Audio:* disc, 33⅓ rpm, 3000t/3129c.

Budget & Expenditures Total library budget $93,000 (FY 7/1/74-7/1/75). No separate AV budget.

Lake Oswego

S- LAKE OSWEGO UNITED METHODIST CHURCH, Video Library, 1855 S Shore Blvd, 97034. *Tel:* (503) 636-8423.

Video Serv Est: 1972. *In Charge:* Helen Lamb, Chairperson. *Video Staff:* 1 f-t, 12 p-t, 2 tech. *Video Use:* documentation of community events, community video access, inservice training, practical video/TV training courses, as art form. Video serv available on demand. Produce video tapes. Have production studio/space.

Video Equipment/Facilities *In-House Use Only:* studio camera (1), col, Shibaden. *For Loan:* recording deck (3), ¾″ col, Sony; playback deck (3), ¾″ col, Sony; editing deck (1), ¾″ col, JVC; studio camera (1), col, Shibaden; monitor (5), b&w/col; lighting (2); microphones (3); tripods (1); audio tape recorders (7). Have portable viewing installation. *Equipment Loan Period:* no set policy. Provide training in use to individuals or groups.

Video Tape Loan/Rental/Sale Serv *Serv Provided:* free loan, swap with other inst, rental. *Loan/Rental Eligibility:* educational inst, civic & religious groups. *Restrictions:* for indiv & inst, none. *Loan Period:* as needed. *Total Yr Tape Loan:* 25.

Video Collection Maintained by own production, exchange/swap. Use/play ¾″ cassette. *Sources:* community productions, exchange (CIRCT, CUE, other churches). *Member:* CIRCT, RAIN. *Tape Sel:* preview. *Special Collections:* in-house training tapes. Tapes organized by subject. *Collection, Color:* ¾″ cassette, 12t/18c. *Other Video Serv:* programming, production workshops. Publish text, *Videotape and Group Process: A Workbook* ($7.50).

Monmouth

C- OREGON COLLEGE OF EDUCATION, Educational Media Center, 97361. *Tel:* (503) 838-1220, ext 412. *Film Serv Est:* 1950. *In Charge:* Claude Smith, Dir, AV Serv & Productions. *AV Staff:* 7 (2 prof, 2½ cl, 2½ tech). *Film Sel:* faculty/staff recommendations. *Holdings:* Pacific Northwest 15%, psychology 15%.

Free-Loan Film Serv *Eligibility:* staff & students. *Restrictions:* for indiv, only on campus. Cannot transmit electronically. Available to researchers/scholars for on-site viewing. May not borrow by mail. *Loan Period:* based on need. *Total Yr Film Loan:* 700. Produce films & all forms of nonprint media.

Film Collection 200t/p. Approx 10t acquired annually. *Circ:* 16mm, 175t/p; 8mm reel, 50t/p. *Noncirc:* 16mm, 25t/p. *Pubns:* publish general announcements of new acquisitions.

Other Film Serv Rent film from distributors for patrons, obtain film from other libraries, film reference serv. Permanent viewing facility. *Equipment:* lend S8mm camera (3), 16mm camera (3), 16mm sound projector (24), 8mm cartridge projector (2), 8mm reel projector (2), S8mm cartridge projector (4), S8mm reel projector (2), projection tables & stands, projection screens.

Other Media Collections *Audio:* disc, 33⅓ rpm, 100t/c; tape cassette, 2000t. *Filmstrips:* sound sets, 25t/c; silent sets, 75t/c. *Slides:* sets, 25t/c.

Budget & Expenditures No separate AV budget.

Video Serv *Est:* 1958. *Video Staff:* 1 p-t, 2 tech. *Video Use:* documentation of community/school events, practical video/TV training courses, self-evaluation. Video serv available by appointment. Produce video tapes. Have production studio/space & separate control room.

Video Equipment/Facilities *In-House Use Only:* portapak (6), b&w, Sony; recording deck (4), b&w, Sony; studio camera (2), col, RCA TK15; monitor (8), b&w; SEG (2), Ball & Dage. *For Loan:* recording deck (4), b&w, Sony; monitor (2), b&w. Have permanent viewing installation. *Equipment Loan Period:* no set policy. Provide training in use of equipment to graduate level media specialists. Have tape duplication serv.

Video Tape Loan/Rental/Sale Serv *Serv Provided:* free loan. *Loan Eligibility:* staff & students. *Restrictions:* for indiv, only on campus. May not borrow by mail.

Video Collection Maintained by purchase, own production. Use/play ½″, 1″, 2″ reel to reel, ¾″ cassette. *Sources:* commercial distributors, exchange (other colleges). *Tape Sel:*

Monmouth (cont'd)
faculty/staff recommendations. Tapes organized by accession number. *Other Video Serv:* programming.

Cable & CCTV Receive serv of cable TV system. Run cable programs for special audiences. Have CCTV in inst, with monitors in classrooms & dormitory rooms. *Programming Sources:* over-the-air commercial & public broadcasting, tapes produced by inst, tapes produced professionally.

Portland

S- ARCHDIOCESE OF PORTLAND RADIO-TV COMMIS-SION, Co-Media, 2838 E Burnside, 97214. *Tel:* (503) 234-5334. *Video Serv Est:* 1969. *In Charge:* Leo Remington. *Video Staff:* 1 f-t. *Video Use:* documentation of community/school events, record of TV shows. Video serv available by appointment. Produce video tapes.

Video Equipment/Facilities *In-House Use Only:* portapak (1), ½″ b&w, Concord 460; recording deck (1), ½″ b&w, Shibaden SV5100; playback deck (1), ½″ b&w, Sony 2200; lighting (3); microphones (4); audio tape recorders (3). Have portable viewing installation. *Equipment Loan Period:* 1 week. Provide training in use of equipment to members requesting it.

Video Tape Loan/Rental/Sale Serv *Serv Provided:* rental. *Loan/Rental Eligibility:* org members, religious groups, & others, such as nonprofit organizations. *Restrictions:* for indiv, only in city; for inst, only in our diocese. May borrow by mail. *Loan Period:* according to need. *Total Yr Tape Loan:* 5.

Video Collection Maintained by own production. Use/play ½″ reel to reel, ¾″ cassette. Tapes organized alphabetically. *Collection, Color:* ¾″ cassette, 1t/c. *Collection, B&W:* ½″ reel, 35t/c.

S- BASSIST INSTITUTE, Library, 923 SW Taylor St, 97205. *Tel:* (503) 228-6528. *Film Serv Est:* 1967. *In Charge:* Marlys Eaton, Office Manager. *AV Staff:* 1 (½ prof, ½ cl). *Film Sel:* committee preview, faculty/staff recommendations. *Holdings:* career education 75%, fine arts 25%.

Film Rental Serv *Eligibility:* educational org, civic groups. *Restrictions:* only in U.S. & Canada. *Rental Period:* 7 days. *Total Yr Film Booking:* 1000. Sell films. Produce films & 35mm slides.

Film Collection 12t/350p. Approx 2t acquired annually. *Circ:* 16mm, 4t/330p. *Noncirc:* 16mm, 8t/20p.

Other Film Serv Rent film from distributors for patrons. Permanent viewing facility.

Other Media Collections *Slides:* single, 3600t.

Budget & Expenditures Total library budget $12,000 (FY 9/1/74-9/1/75). Total FY film budget $2000.

Video Serv *Est:* 1969. *In Charge:* Donald Bassist, Dir. *Video Staff:* 2 f-t, 6 p-t. *Video Use:* in-service training. Video serv available on demand. Produce video tapes. Have production studio/space.

Video Equipment/Facilities *In-House Use Only:* portapak (1), b&w, Craig; recording deck (1), b&w, Craig; studio camera (1), b&w, Craig; monitor (1), b&w; microphones (1); audio tape recorders (1). Have permanent viewing installation.

Video Collection Maintained by own production. Use/play ½″ reel to reel. *Tape Sel:* faculty/staff recommendations. *Special Collections:* in-house training tapes. Tapes organized by subject.

Cable & CCTV Have CCTV in inst, with 1 monitor. *Programming Sources:* over-the-air commercial & public broadcasting, tapes produced by inst, tapes produced professionally.

S- CENTER FOR INNOVATION AND RESEARCH IN CABLE TELEVISION, The Dekum Bldg, Rm 314, 519 SW Third, 97204. *Tel:* (503) 223-3419. *Video Serv Est:* 1975. *In Charge:* Charles Auch & Tom Kennedy, Co-Dirs. *Video Staff:* 5 f-t. *Video Use:* documentation of community events, community video access, practical video/TV training courses, as art form. Video serv available by appointment. Produce video tapes. Have production studio/space & separate control room.

Video Equipment/Facilities *For Loan:* portapak (3), ½″ b&w/col, Panasonic; editing deck (2), ½″ b&w/col, Panasonic; monitor (3), b&w, Panasonic, Sony; additional camera lenses (1); microphones (2); audio tape recorders (1). Have portable viewing installation. *Equipment Loan Period:* no set policy. Provide training in use of equipment to individuals, groups, agencies & institutional personnel. Have tape duplication serv.

Video Tape Loan/Rental/Sale Serv *Serv Provided:* free loan, swap with other inst. *Loan Eligibility:* organizations, individuals, groups, agencies & institutions within the community. *Restrictions:* for indiv & inst, only in our county. Cannot dub or air without permission. May borrow by mail. *Loan Period:* based on need.

Video Collection Maintained by own production, exchange/swap. Use/play ½″ reel to reel. *Sources:* community productions, exchange (other groups). *Tape Sel:* preview, gallery previews, catalogs. *Other Video Serv:* production workshops. *Pubns:* catalog.

Cable & CCTV Develop community programmed & operated cable channel. Serve as production facility for community. Have advisory & administrative role in community cable system operation. *Programming Sources:* tapes produced by inst, tapes produced by community groups. The Center is funded through a private foundation to explore & develop innovative uses of cable, closed circuit systems & video. Specific emphasis is on community use of small format TV as a communication tool. It also provides space for media-related activities.

C- CONCORDIA COLLEGE, Library-Educational Media Center, 2811 NE Holman, 97211. *Tel:* (503) 288-9371, ext 272. *Video Serv Est:* 1975. *In Charge:* Gary E. Lietke, Dir, Educ Med Ctr. *Video Staff:* 1 f-t, 3 p-t. *Video Use:* documentation of community/school events, in-service training, practical video/TV training courses, playback only of professionally produced tapes. Video serv available by appointment. Produce video tapes. Have production studio/space & separate control room.

Video Equipment/Facilities *In-House Use Only:* recording deck (1), ¾″ b&w/col, JVC CR6300U; playback deck (1), ¾″ b&w/col, JVC CP5000U; editing deck (1), ½″ b&w/col, Panasonic NV3160; studio camera (2), b&w, Panasonic; monitor (4), b&w/col, Sharp XR2194; SEG (1), Panasonic WJ545P; lighting (2); microphones (16); tripods (2); audio tape recorders (2). Have portable viewing installation. *Equipment Loan Period:* no set policy. Provide training in use of equipment to students.

Video Tape Loan/Rental/Sale Serv *Serv Provided:* free loan, swap with other inst. *Loan Eligibility:* org members, staff & students. *Restrictions:* for indiv & inst, none. Cannot air without permission. May borrow by mail. *Loan Period:* as requested.

Video Collection Maintained by purchase, rental, own production, exchange/swap. Use/play ½″ reel to reel, ¾″ cassette. *Tape Sel:* preview, faculty/staff recommendations, published reviews, catalogs. *Special Collections:* in-house training tapes. Tapes organized by subject. *Collection, Color:* ¾″ cassette, 2t/c. *Collection, B&W:* ¾″ cassette, 4t/c. *Other Video Serv:* production workshops. *Pubns:* catalog.

S- CREATIVE OUTLET, 201 SE 12 St, 97214. *Tel:* (503) 233-3654. *Video Serv Est:* 1973. *In Charge:* Ed Lyle, Dir. *Video Staff:* 3 f-t, 1 tech. *Video Use:* documentation of community events, to increase community's library use, community video access, in-service training, practical video/TV training courses, as art form. Video serv available by appointment. Produce video tapes. Have production studio/space & separate control room.

Video Equipment/Facilities *In-House Use Only:* editing deck (2), 1″ b&w, Panasonic 3020SD; studio camera (3), b&w, Panasonic 340B41; monitor (4), b&w; SEG (1), Panasonic 545P; lighting (4); microphones (7); tripods (4). *For Loan:* portapak (1), 1″ b&w, Panasonic 3082; recording deck (2), 1″ b&w, Panasonic 3020; editing deck (2), 1″ b&w, Panasonic 3020SD; monitor (4), b&w; microphones (7). Have portable viewing installation. *Equipment Loan Period:* 1 day. Provide training in use of equipment to students & paraprofessionals in drug & alcohol treatment programs. Have tape duplication serv.

Video Tape Loan/Rental/Sale Serv *Serv Provided:* free loan, swap with other inst, rental, sale. *Loan/Rental Eligibility:* staff & students, educational inst, civic & religious groups, prof groups, such as psychiatrists, teachers, mental health counselors & others, such as members of public. *Restrictions:* for indiv, only metropolitan area; for inst, only in Washington, Multnomah, Clackamas & Columbia Counties. Cannot air without permission, all use other than viewing must be reported. May borrow by mail. *Loan Period:* short as possible. *Total Yr Tape Loan:* 150-200.

Video Collection Maintained by own production, exchange/swap. Use/play ½″ reel to reel. *Sources:* galleries, community productions, exchange (alternative media, colleges & hospital media centers). *Member:* Regional Alcoholism Board. *Tape Sel:* preview, staff recommendations, gallery previews, published reviews, catalogs. *Special Collections:* in-house training tapes, video as art, films in video format. Tapes organized by subject. *Collection, B&W:* ½″ reel, 75t. *Other Video Serv:* taping of other media, production workshops. *Pubns:* catalog.

Cable & CCTV Produce programs for cablecasting. Inform public about cable system serv & facilities. Occasionally serve as production facility for others.

C- LEWIS & CLARK COLLEGE, Aubrey R. Watzek Library, 0615 SW Palatine Hill Rd, 97219. *Tel:* (503) 244-6161, ext 403. *In Charge:* Laurel Miller, Special Servs Librarian. *AV Staff:* 2 (1 prof, 1 tech). *Film Sel:* faculty/staff recommendations, chief film librarian's decision. *Holdings:* animated films 1%, career education 3%, children's films 1%, dance 2%, experimental films 1%, fine arts 5%, science 25%, social sciences 42%, teacher education 20%.

Free-Loan Film Serv *Eligibility:* org members. *Restrictions:* for indiv, only in city. Cannot transmit electronically. Available to researchers/scholars for on-site viewing. May not borrow by mail. *Loan Period:* 1 day. *Total Yr Film Loan:* 215.

Film Collection 170t/p. Approx 5t acquired annually. *Circ:* 16mm, 120t/p; S8mm cartridge, 50t. *Pubns:* catalog, as needed; suppl, no set policy.

Other Film Serv Rent film from distributors for patrons, obtain film from coop loan system (Northwest Assn of Private Colleges & Universities), obtain film from other libraries, film reference serv. Permanent viewing facility. *Equipment:* lend S8mm camera (1), 16mm sound projector (10), 8mm cartridge projector (2), 8mm reel projector (1), S8mm cartridge projector (2), S8mm reel projector (1), projection tables & stands, projection screens.

Other Media Collections *Audio:* disc, 33⅓ rpm, 1050t; tape, cassette, 500t; tape, reel, 1200t. *Filmstrips:* sound sets, 413t. *Slides:* sets, 1313t.

Budget & Expenditures Total library budget $101,000 (FY 7/1/75-7/1/76). No separate AV budget. *Member:* EFLA, Oreg. Library Assn, Oreg. Educational Media Assn.

Video Serv *Est:* 1965. *In Charge:* Stanley R. Clarke, AV Technician. *Video Staff:* 1 f-t, 13 p-t. *Video Use:* documentation of community/school events, practical video/TV training courses, as art form. Video serv available by appointment. Produce video tapes.

Video Equipment/Facilities *In-House Use Only:* recording deck (3), ½″ b&w, Sony 3600; studio camera (2), GE; monitor (30); additional camera lenses; microphones (60); tripods (10); audio tape recorders (50). *For Loan:* portapak (10), ¼″, ½″ b&w, Sony, AKAI, Panasonic; audio tape recorders (50). Have permanent viewing installation. *Equipment Loan Period:* no set policy. Provide training in use of equipment to faculty & students.

Video Tape Loan/Rental/Sale Serv *Serv Provided:* free loan, swap with other inst, rental. *Loan/Rental Eligibility:* staff & students, educational inst, religious groups. May not borrow by mail. *Total Yr Tape Loan:* 3.

Video Collection Maintained by purchase, own production, exchange/swap. Use/play ½″, ¼″ reel to reel. *Tape Sel:* faculty/staff recommendations. Tapes organized by accession number. *Collection, B&W:* ½″ reel, 8t/c.

P- MULTNOMAH COUNTY LIBRARY, Group Services Dept, 801 SW 10 Ave, 97205. *Tel:* (503) 223-7201, ext 43. *Film Serv Est:* 1948. *In Charge:* Ella Seely, Head, Group Servs Dept. *AV Staff:* 5 (1 prof, 3 cl, 1 tech). *Film Sel:* chief film librarian's decision. *Holdings:* animated films 20%, children's films 15%, experimental films 7%.

Free-Loan Film Serv *Eligibility:* indiv with library cards who register in Group Services Dept & pay $2 annual fee to cover minor damage to films. *Restrictions:* for indiv & inst, only in Multnomah County. Cannot use for fund-raising, transmit electronically. Available to researchers/scholars for on-site viewing. May not borrow by mail. *Loan Period:* 3 days. *Total Yr Film Loan:* 14,698.

Film Collection 1018t/1043p. *Circ:* 16mm, 1018t/1043p. *Noncirc:* 16mm, 25t/p. *Pubns:* publish Library Film Services brochure, a guide to film sources in the Portland area.

Other Film Serv Film reference serv, library film programs.

Other Media Collections *Audio:* disc, 33⅓ rpm, 16,017t/14,427c.

Budget & Expenditures Total film budget $15,500 (FY 6/1/74-6/1/75). *Member:* ALA, Oreg. Educational Media Assn.

S- NORTHWEST FILM STUDY CENTER, Portland Art Museum, SW Park & Madison Sts, 97205. *Tel:* (503) 226-2811, ext 60. *Film Serv Est:* 1971. *In Charge:* Dr. Robert M. Sitton, Dir. *AV Staff:* 12 (3 prof, 5 cl, 4 tech). *Film Sel:* director is programmer. *Holdings:* animated films.

Free-Loan Film Serv *Eligibility:* students enrolled in inst. Available to researchers/scholars for on-site viewing. May not borrow by mail.

Film Collection 35t. *Noncirc:* 16mm, 35t. *Pubns:* publish quarterly newspaper.

Other Film Serv Film reference serv, film fairs/festivals. Permanent viewing facility available for rent to community. *Equipment:* 16mm cameras (2), 8mm cameras with editors (6).

Other Media Collections *Audio:* tape, cassette. *Slides:* single.

Budget & Expenditures Total budget $80,000. Total FY film budget $25,000 in film rentals & purchases. *Member:* Assn of Specialized Film Exhibitors, AFI, NEA Regional Film Centers.

S- OREGON HISTORICAL SOCIETY, 1230 SW Park Ave, 97205. *Tel:* (503) 222-1741, ext 26. *Film Serv Est:* 1954. *In Charge:* Louis Clark Cook, Film Archivist. *AV Staff:* 1 (1 prof). *Film Sel:* staff recommendations, chief film librarian's decision. *Holdings:* documentary films, historical films, manuscript preservation films, TV news.

Free-Loan Film Serv *Eligibility:* prof groups, such as any affiliated historical agency or group & others, such as anyone contemplating purchase of a print. *Restrictions:* for indiv & inst, none. Cannot borrow for classroom use. Available to researchers/scholars for on-site viewing. May borrow by mail. *Loan Period:* 2 weeks. *Total Yr Film Loan:* 7.

Film Rental Serv *Eligibility:* no restrictions. *Restrictions:* none. *Rental Rate:* $7.50 per print. *Rental Period:* 2 weeks. Produce film, microfilm, slides, photographic reproductions.

Film Collection 500 motion pictures, 2500 TV news & documentaries. Approx 500-600t acquired annually.

Other Film Serv Obtain film from coop loan system (Oreg. Regional Union List of Serials), film fairs/festivals. Permanent viewing facility available for rent to community. *Equipment:* rent 16mm sound projector (1), projection screens (1).

Other Media Collections *Slides:* sets, 8t. *Member:* ALA.

Roseburg

P- DOUGLAS COUNTY LIBRARY, Film Dept, Courthouse, 97470. *Tel:* (503) 672-3311, ext 132. *Film Serv Est:* 1963. *In Charge:* Donna Wallace, Film Librarian. *AV Staff:* 1. *Film Sel:* chief film librarian's decision. *Holdings:* cartoons 33⅓%, comedy 33⅓%, documentaries 33⅓%.

Roseburg (cont'd)

Free-Loan Film Serv   *Eligibility:* indiv with library cards. *Restrictions:* for indiv & inst, only in Douglas County. Cannot use for fund-raising, transmit electronically, borrow for classroom use. Available to researchers/scholars for on-site viewing. May borrow by mail. *Loan Period:* 16mm overnight, 8mm 2 weeks. *Total Yr Film Loan:* 4460.

Film Collection   156t. Approx 15t acquired annually. *Pubns:* publish monthly list of 16mm films borrowed from Oreg. Div. of Continuing Education.

Other Film Serv   Obtain film from other libraries, film reference serv, film fairs/festivals, library film programs. Permanent viewing facility available to community. *Equipment:* lend 16mm sound projector (1), 8mm reel projector (1), S8mm reel projector (1), projection tables & stands (1), projection screens (1).

Other Media Collections   *Audio:* disc, 33⅓ rpm, 4361t; tape, cassette, 13t/c. *Member:* ALA.

Pennsylvania

Aliquippa

P- B. F. JONES MEMORIAL LIBRARY, 663 Franklin Ave, 15001. *Tel:* (412) 375-2900. *Film Serv Est:* 1970. *In Charge:* Mary Elizabeth Colombo, Head, Extension Services. *AV Staff:* ¹⁄₁₀. *Film Sel:* committee preview.

Free-Loan Film Serv *Eligibility:* indiv with library cards. *Restrictions:* for indiv, interlibrary loan, only in state; for inst, only in state. Cannot use for fund-raising. *Loan Period:* 1 day. *Total Yr Film Loan:* 340.

Film Collection 124t/125p. Approx 10t acquired annually. *Circ:* 16mm, 124t/125p. *Pubns:* catalog, annual; suppl, no set policy.

Other Film Serv Obtain film from coop loan system (Pa. Public Library Film Center, Pittsburgh Regional Library Center). *Equipment:* lend 16mm sound projector (3), 8mm reel projector (1), S8mm reel projector (1), projection screens (2).

Budget & Expenditures Total library budget $6000 (FY 1/1/75-1/1/76). Total FY film budget $750. *Member:* Pa. Library Assn.

Allentown

P- ALLENTOWN PUBLIC LIBRARY, 914 Hamilton Mall, 18101. *Tel:* (215) 434-4894. *Film Serv Est:* 1960. *In Charge:* Margaret Molesky. *AV Staff:* 2½ (1 prof, 1½ cl, 1 tech). *Film Sel:* committee preview, staff recommendations, chief film librarian's decision, published reviews.

Free-Loan Film Serv *Eligibility:* educational inst, civic groups, religious groups, indiv with library cards, prof groups, such as engineers, etc. *Restrictions:* for indiv, interlibrary loan, only in our library district; for inst, only our library district. Cannot use for fund-raising. Available to researchers/scholars for on-site viewing. May borrow by mail. *Loan Period:* 1-3 days. *Total Yr Film Loan:* 6686.

Film Collection 210t/p. Approx 30-40t acquired annually. *Circ:* 16mm, 210t/p. *Pubns:* catalog, every 2 yrs; suppl, in yr catalog not published.

Other Film Serv Obtain film from coop loan system (Pa. Film Library Center), obtain film from other libraries, film reference serv, library film programs. *Equipment:* lend 16mm sound projector (4), projection tables & stands (4), projection screens (2).

Other Media Collections *Audio:* disc, 33⅓ rpm, 6000t; tape, cassette, 3t. *Filmstrips:* sound sets, 46t. *Slides:* sets, 5t.

Budget & Expenditures Total library budget $75,000 (FY 7/1/74-7/1/75). Total FY film budget $10,000. *Member:* ALA, EFLA, FLIC, Pa. Library Assn.

Altoona

P- ALTOONA AREA PUBLIC LIBRARY, Media Center, 1130 Thirteenth Ave, 16601. *Tel:* (814) 946-1224. *Film Serv Est:* 1969. *In Charge:* Maxine Rhodes, Media Center Dir. *AV Staff:* 4 (2 cl, 2 tech). *Film Sel:* committee preview.

Free-Loan Film Serv *Eligibility:* indiv with library cards, & 12 local libraries in our district. *Restrictions:* for indiv & inst, only in Bedford, Huntingdon & Blair Counties. Cannot use for fund-raising, borrow for classroom use. Available to researchers/scholars for on-site viewing. May borrow by mail. *Loan Period:* 1 day. *Total Yr Film Loan:* 8433.

Film Collection 340t/p. Approx 25-50t acquired annually. *Circ:* 16mm, 350t; 8mm reel, 150t; S8mm reel, 139t. *Pubns:* catalog, every 2 yrs ($.50); suppl, in yr catalog not published.

Other Film Serv Obtain film from coop loan system (Altoona Area Public Library District Center), obtain film from other libraries, film fairs/festivals, library film programs. Permanent viewing facility. *Equipment:* lend S8mm camera (2), 16mm sound projector (5), 8mm reel projector (3), S8mm reel projector (2), projection screens (4).

Other Media Collections *Audio:* disc, 33⅓ rpm, 2890c; tape, cassette, 482c. *Filmstrips:* sound sets, 200c; silent sets, 189c. *Slides:* single, 1400c.

Budget & Expenditures Total library budget $61,550 (FY 7/1/74-7/1/75). Total FY film budget $3000. *Member:* EFLA, FLIC, Pa. Learning Resource Assn.

Video Serv *Est:* 1974. *Video Staff:* 4 f-t, 2 p-t, 2 tech. *Video Use:* documentation of community events, community video access, as art form. Video serv available on demand & by appointment. Produce video tapes. Have production studio/space.

Video Equipment/Facilities *In-House Use Only:* recording deck (1), col, Sony 1800; playback deck (1), col, Sony 1200; editing deck (1), ½″, Sony 8650; monitor (1), Sony; tripods (3); audio tape recorders (2). *For Loan:* portapak (2), ½″ b&w/col, Sony 8400; playback deck (1), col, Sony 1200; microphones (2); tripods (3); audio tape recorders (2). Have portable viewing installation. *Equipment Loan Period:* 1 day. Provide training in use of equipment to borrowers. Have tape duplication serv.

Video Tape Loan/Rental/Sale Serv *Serv Provided:* free loan. *Loan Eligibility:* indiv with library cards. *Restrictions:* for indiv, only in Bedford, Huntingdon & Blair Counties. Cannot use for fund-raising, duplicate, air without permission. May not borrow by mail. *Loan Period:* 1 day. *Total Yr Tape Loan:* 126.

Video Collection Maintained by purchase, own production. Use/play ¾″ cassette. *Sources:* commercial distributors. *Tape Sel:* published reviews. Tapes organized alphabetically. *Collection, Color:* ¾″ cassette, 58t/c. *Collection, B&W:* ¾″ cassette, 5t. *Other Video Serv:* production workshops.

Cable & CCTV Receive serv of cable TV system. Produce programs for cablecasting. Inform public about cable system serv & facilities. Serve as production facility for others. Run cable programs for special audiences. Have CCTV in inst. *Programming Sources:* over-the-air commercial & public broadcasting, tapes produced by inst, tapes produced professionally, tapes produced by community groups & indiv.

Beaver Falls

C- GENEVA COLLEGE, McCartney Library, 15010. *Tel:* (412) 846-5100, ext 314. *In Charge:* Mary Ann Soergel, AV Center Assistant. *AV Staff:* 1. *Film Sel:* faculty/staff recommendations.

Free-Loan Film Serv *Eligibility:* staff & students, educational inst, religious groups. *Restrictions:* for indiv, only in Beaver County; for inst, only in Beaver County. Cannot use for fund-raising, transmit electronically. Available to researchers/scholars for on-site viewing. May not borrow by mail. *Loan Period:* as needed. *Total Yr Film Loan:* 2.

Film Collection 35t/p. Approx 10t acquired annually. *Circ:* 16mm, 35t.

Other Film Serv Film reference serv. Permanent viewing facility available for rent to community. *Equipment:* lend 16mm sound projector (2), projection tables & stands (1), projection screens (2).

Other Media Collections *Audio:* disc, 33⅓ rpm, 2500t; tape, reel, 250t. *Filmstrips:* silent, 450t; sound sets, 25t. *Slides:* single, 7000t.

Budget & Expenditures Total library budget $44,000 (FY 7/1/74-7/1/75). No separate AV budget. *Member:* Pittsburgh Regional Library Center.

Bethlehem

P- BETHLEHEM PUBLIC LIBRARY, 11 W Church St, 18018. *Tel:* (215) 867-3761. *In Charge:* Philip Segal, AV Librarian. *AV Staff:* 3½ (1 prof, 1½ cl, 1 tech). *Film Sel:* committee preview. *Holdings:* animated films 8%, children's films 20%.

Bethlehem (cont'd)

Free-Loan Film Serv *Eligibility:* indiv groups & org with library cards. *Restrictions:* for indiv, only in city; for inst, only in city. Cannot use for fund-raising. Available to researchers/scholars for on-site viewing. May not borrow by mail. *Loan Period:* 1 day. *Total Yr Film Loan:* 8000.

Film Collection 350t/p. Approx 50-75t acquired annually. *Circ:* 16mm, 350t/p. *Noncirc:* 16mm, 1t/p. *Pubns:* catalog, annual ($.50); suppl, twice a yr.

Other Film Serv Obtain film from coop loan system (Pa. Public Libraries Film Center), film reference serv, film fairs/festivals, library film programs, show EFLA Blue Ribbon Films. *Equipment:* rent 16mm sound projector (4).

Other Media Collections *Audio:* disc, 33⅓ rpm, 7000c. *Slides:* single, 800t; sets, 15t.

Budget & Expenditures Total library budget $72,000 (FY 1/1/75-1/1/76). Total FY film budget $9500. *Member:* ALA, EFLA, Pa. Library Assn.

Chambersburg

P- CONOCOCHEAGUE DISTRICT LIBRARY, 102 N Main St, 17201. *Tel:* (717) 263-1054. *Film Serv Est:* 1972. *In Charge:* Judith Kern, Film Librarian. *AV Staff:* 1 (½ cl, ½ tech). *Film Sel:* committee preview, staff recommendations, chief film librarian's decision.

Free-Loan Film Serv *Eligibility:* educational inst, civic groups, religious groups, indiv with library cards. *Restrictions:* for indiv, only in tri-county area; for inst, only in tri-county area. Available to researchers/scholars for on-site viewing. May borrow by mail. *Loan Period:* 1 day. *Total Yr Film Loan:* 879.

Film Collection 100t/p. Approx 10t acquired annually. *Circ:* 16mm, 100t/p. *Pubns:* catalog, as needed; suppl, no set policy.

Other Film Serv Obtain film from coop loan system (Pa. Public Library Film Center), obtain film from other libraries, film fairs/festivals, library film programs. Permanent viewing facility available for rent to community.

Other Media Collections *Audio:* disc, 33⅓ rpm, 3369t/3198c; tape, cassette, 135t/c; tape, reel, 4t/c. *Filmstrips:* silent, 1t/c; silent sets, 8t/c. *Slides:* single, 480t/c; sets, 6t/c.

Budget & Expenditures Total library budget $21,000 (FY 1/1/75-1/1/76). Total FY film budget $6000. *Member:* ALA, Pa. Library Assn.

Clarks Summit

C- BAPTIST BIBLE COLLEGE OF PENNSYLVANIA, Instructional Materials Center, 18411. *Tel:* (717) 587-1172, ext 242. *Film Serv Est:* 1958. *In Charge:* Miriam Waggoner, Dir, Instructional Materials Center. *AV Staff:* 3½ (1 prof, 2 cl, 1 tech). *Film Sel:* committee preview, faculty/staff recommendations. *Holdings:* athletics, public speaking, religion.

Film Rental Serv *Eligibility:* no restrictions. *Restrictions:* only eastern U.S. Cannot use for fund-raising, transmit electronically. *Rental Period:* 1-3 days.

Film Collection *Circ:* 16mm, 2t/p; S8mm reel, 25t/p. *Pubns:* catalog, every 5 yrs ($1.50); suppl, no set policy.

Other Film Serv Rent film from distributors for patrons, obtain film from other libraries. Permanent viewing facility. *Equipment:* lend/rent 16mm sound projector (4), lend 8mm cartridge projector (3), lend S8mm cartridge projector (3), lend/rent projection screens (10), lend filmstrip/slide projectors, record players, tape players.

Other Media Collections *Audio:* disc, total, 71t; tape, cassette & reel, 691t. *Filmstrips:* sound sets, 1185t. *Slides:* sets, 53t.

Budget & Expenditures No separate AV budget. *Member:* ALA, Pa. Library Assn, Christian Librarians Fellowship, Church & Synagogue Library Assn.

Video Serv *Est:* 1972. *Video Staff:* 2 f-t, 3 p-t, 1 tech. *Video Use:* documentation of community/school events, in-service training, as art form, public speaking & homiletics classes.

Video serv available on demand. Produce video tapes. Have production studio/space & separate control room.

Video Equipment/Facilities *In-House Use Only:* recording deck (1), ½", Panasonic; playback deck (2), ½", Panasonic; editing deck (1), Panasonic; studio camera (2), Panasonic; monitor (4), Panasonic; SEG (1), Concord; additional camera lenses (2); lighting (4); microphones (12); tripods (2); audio tape recorders (6). Have portable viewing installation. Provide training in use of equipment to faculty & students.

Video Collection Maintained by own production. Use/play ½" reel to reel. *Tape Sel:* faculty/staff recommendations. Tapes organized by subject. *Collection, B&W:* ½" reel, 10t/c. *Other Video Serv:* production workshops.

Dallas

C- COLLEGE MISERICORDIA, Library, Lake St, 18612. *Tel:* (717) 675-2181, ext 325. *Film Serv Est:* 1966. *In Charge:* Myra Binau, Head Cataloger. *AV Staff:* 2 (1 prof, 1 cl). *Film Sel:* faculty/staff recommendations.

Free-Loan Film Serv *Eligibility:* staff & students, educational inst, indiv with library cards. *Restrictions:* for indiv, none; for inst, none. *Loan Period:* 3 days. *Total Yr Film Loan:* 163.

Other Film Serv Obtain film from coop loan system (Northeastern Pa. Bibliographic Center).

Other Media Collections *Audio:* disc, 33⅓ rpm, 1600t; tape, cassette, 837t; tape, reel, 264t. *Filmstrips:* silent, 900t. *Slides:* single, 2647t.

Budget & Expenditures Total library budget $53,000 (FY 7/1/75-7/1/76). *Member:* ALA, Pa. Library Assn.

Video Serv *Video Staff:* 2 f-t. Video serv available on demand.

Video Tape Loan/Rental/Sale Serv *Serv Provided:* free loan. *Loan Eligibility:* staff & students. *Restrictions:* for indiv & inst, none. May not borrow by mail. *Loan Period:* 3 days. *Total Yr Tape Loan:* 459.

Doylestown

P- BUCKS COUNTY FREE LIBRARY, Film Department, 50 N Main St, 18901. *Tel:* (215) 348-9081. *Film Serv Est:* 1968. *In Charge:* Linda T. Barr, Film Technician. *AV Staff:* (1 tech). *Film Sel:* committee preview.

Free-Loan Film Serv *Eligibility:* civic groups, religious groups, indiv with library cards. *Restrictions:* for indiv, interlibrary loan. Cannot use for fund-raising, transmit electronically. May not borrow by mail. *Loan Period:* 1 day. *Total Yr Film Loan:* 2059.

Film Collection 230t/232p. Approx 25t acquired annually. *Circ:* 16mm, 230t/232p. *Pubns:* catalog, as needed.

Other Film Serv Obtain film from coop loan system (Pa. Public Libraries Film Buying Consortium), obtain film from other libraries, library film programs.

Other Media Collections *Audio:* disc, 33⅓ rpm, 4023c. *Slides:* sets, 40c.

Budget & Expenditures Total library budget $102,000 (FY 1/1/74-1/1/75). Total FY film budget $4000. *Member:* EFLA.

Easton

P- EASTON AREA PUBLIC LIBRARY, Sixth & Church Sts, 18042. *Tel:* (215) 258-2917. *Film Serv Est:* 1968. *In Charge:* Ethel C. Drendall, Film Librarian. *AV Staff:* 1 (⅓ prof, ⅓ cl, ⅓ tech). *Film Sel:* committee preview.

Free-Loan Film Serv *Eligibility:* indiv with library cards, libraries in Pa. *Restrictions:* for indiv, only in Easton Dist & two neighboring districts. Cannot use for fund-raising, transmit electronically. May borrow by mail. *Loan Period:* 1 day. *Total Yr Film Loan:* 1885.

Film Collection 108t/109p. *Circ:* 16mm, 108t/109p. *Pubns:* catalog, as needed; suppl, no set policy.

Other Film Serv Obtain film from coop loan system (Pa. Public Libraries Film Center), film reference serv, film fairs/

festivals, library film programs. Permanent viewing facility available for rent to community. *Equipment:* rent 16mm sound projector (2), cassette player (1).
Other Media Collections *Audio:* disc, 33⅓ rpm, 2280t; tape, cassette, 122t. *Slides:* single, 100t.
Budget & Expenditures Total library budget $39,960 (FY 7/1/74-7/1/75). Total FY film budget $2969. *Member:* EFLA, Pa. Library Assn.

Edinboro

C- EDINBORO STATE COLLEGE, Hamilton Library, 16444. *Tel:* (814) 732-2273. *Film Serv Est:* 1966. *In Charge:* Barbara Grippe, Educational Media Librarian. *AV Staff:* 1 (½ prof, ½ cl). *Film Sel:* faculty/staff recommendations. *Holdings:* black studies 1%, children's films 2%, teacher education 97%.
Free-Loan Film Serv *Eligibility:* staff & students. *Restrictions:* for indiv, only on campus. Cannot transmit electronically. Available to researchers/scholars for on-site viewing. May not borrow by mail. *Loan Period:* 7 days. *Total Yr Film Loan:* 150. Produce 16mm films.
Film Collection 137t/140p. *Circ:* 16mm, 137t/140p. *Pubns:* catalog, as needed; suppl, no set policy.
Other Film Serv Obtain film from other libraries, film reference serv, film fairs/festivals, library film programs. Permanent viewing facility.
Other Media Collections *Audio:* disc, 33⅓ rpm, 6374t/c; tape, cassette, 911t/c; tape, reel, 496t/c. *Filmstrips:* sound, 1918t; silent, 1909t/c; sound sets, 613t/c; silent sets, 1909t/c. *Slides:* single, 1612t/c; sets, 42t/c.
Budget & Expenditures No separate AV budget. *Member:* Pa. Library Assn.
Video Serv *Est:* 1964. *In Charge:* Bob Wallace, Dir, Radio & TV Center. *Video Staff:* 2 f-t, 4 tech. *Video Use:* documentation of community/school events, in-service training, practical video/TV training courses, as art form, instruction, public relations. Video serv available by appointment. Produce video tapes. Have production studio/space & separate control room.
Video Equipment/Facilities *In-House Use Only:* editing deck (2), ½", 1" col, IVC 87CA, Panasonic 3130p; studio camera (6), b&w/col, Sarkes-Tarzian; SEG (3), Sony; lighting; microphones (4); audio tape recorders (4). *For Loan:* portapak (4), ½" b&w, Sony Videorover; recording deck (14), ½", ¾", 1" b&w/col, Sony AV500, AV3650, AV3600, Ucassette, EV210, Hitachi; playback deck (1), ¾" col, Sony U-matic. Have portable viewing installation. *Equipment Loan Period:* no set policy. Provide training in use of equipment to students & users. Have tape duplication serv.
Video Tape Loan/Rental Serv *Serv Provided:* free loan, rental. *Loan/Rental Eligibility:* staff & students, educational inst. *Restrictions:* for indiv & inst, none. Cannot use for fundraising, duplicate, air without permission. May borrow by mail. *Loan Period:* flexible. *Total Yr Tape Loan:* 30.
Video Collection Maintained by rental, own production, exchange/swap. Use/play ½", 1" reel to reel, ¾" cassette. *Sources:* commercial distributors. *Tape Sel:* preview, faculty/staff recommendations, gallery previews, published reviews, catalogs. *Special Collections:* in-house training tapes, video as art. Tapes organized by subject. *Colection, Color:* ½" reel, 30t/c; 1" reel, 15t/c. *Collection, B&W:* ½" reel, 10t/c. *Other Video Serv:* programming, production workshops.
Cable & CCTV Receive serv of cable TV system. Produce programs for cablecasting. Have CCTV in inst. *Programming Sources:* tapes produced by inst, tapes produced professionally & by students.

Erie

C- GANNON COLLEGE, Learning Resource Center, 109 W 6 St, 16501. *Tel:* (814) 456-7523, ext 350. *Video Serv Est:* 1973. *In Charge:* Rev. Thomas McSweeney, TV Dir. *Video Staff:* 2 f-t, 2 p-t. *Video Use:* in-service training, practical video/TV training courses, playback only of professionally produced

tapes, as art form. Video serv available on demand & by appointment. Produce video tapes. Have production studio/space & separate control room.
Video Equipment/Facilities *In-House Use Only:* portapak (1), ½" b&w, Sony; recording deck (1), 1" col, IVC; playback deck (5); editing deck (2), b&w/col, Sony, IVC; studio camera (3), Dage; SEG (1); keyer (1); additional camera lenses (2); lighting; microphones (7); tripods (3); audio tape recorders (1). *For Loan:* portapak (1), ½" b&w, Sony. Have permanent viewing installation. *Equipment Loan Period:* no set policy. Provide training in use of equipment to faculty & students. Have tape duplication serv.
Video Collection Maintained by purchase, own production. Use/play ½", 1" reel to reel, ¾" cassette. *Sources:* commercial distributors. *Tape Sel:* preview, faculty/staff recommendations. *Special Collections:* in-house training tapes, video as art, films in video format. Tapes organized by year taped. *Collection, Color:* 1" reel, 80t/c; ¾" cassette, 6t/c. *Collection, B&W:* ½" reel, 30t/c. *Other Video Serv:* programming, taping of other media, production workshops. *Pubns:* catalog.
Cable & CCTV Have CCTV in inst, with 35 monitors. *Programming Sources:* over-the-air commercial & public broadcasting, tapes produced by inst, tapes produced professionally & by community groups & indiv.

Huntingdon

C- JUNIATA COLLEGE, L. A. Beeghly Library, 16652. *Tel:* (814) 643-4310, ext 57. *Film Serv Est:* 1973. *In Charge:* Robert G. Sabin, Dir of Libraries. *AV Staff:* 1 (1 prof, 1 cl). *Film Sel:* faculty/staff recommendations. *Holdings:* fine arts 100%.
Free-Loan Film Serv *Eligibility:* staff & students. *Restrictions:* for indiv, only on campus. Available to researchers/scholars for on-site viewing. May not borrow by mail. *Loan Period:* 1 day. Produce films.
Film Collection *Circ:* 16mm, 60t; S8mm reel, 55t.
Other Film Serv Permanent viewing facility.
Other Media Collections *Audio:* disc, 33⅓ rpm, 350t; disc, 45rpm, tape, cassette, 85t; tape, reel, 400t.
Budget & Expenditures Total library budget $58,500 (FY 7/1/75-7/1/76). No separate budget. *Member:* ALA, Pa. Library Assn.
Video Serv *Video Staff:* 1 f-t. *Video Use:* documentation of community/school events, to increase community's library use, as art form. Video serv available on demand. Produce video tapes. Have production studio/space & separate control room.
Video Equipment/Facilities *In-House Use Only:* recording deck (1); playback deck (1); editing deck (2); studio camera (1); monitor (1); additional camera lenses (2); lighting (1); microphones (2); tripods (2); audio tape recorders (3). Have permanent viewing installation. Provide training in use of equipment to students assistants.
Video Collection Maintained by purchase, own production. *Tape Sel:* faculty/staff recommendations. *Special Collections:* video as art.
Cable & CCTV Have CCTV in inst, with several monitors. *Programming Sources:* over-the-air commercial & public broadcasting, tapes produced by inst, tapes produced professionally.

Indiana

C- INDIANA UNIVERSITY OF PENNSYLVANIA, Curriculum Materials Area, Rhodes R. Stabley Library, 15701. *Tel:* (412) 357-2343. *In Charge:* Edward G. Wolf, Coordinator, Curriculum Materials Area. *AV Staff:* 2 prof. *Film Sel:* faculty/staff recommendations, chief film librarian's decision, published reviews.
Free-Loan Film Serv *Eligibility:* staff & students, educational inst, indiv with library cards. *Restrictions:* for indiv, none; for inst, none. *Loan Period:* 3 wks.
Film Collection *Circ:* S8mm cartridge, 300t.
Other Film Serv Obtain film from coop loan system. Permanent viewing facility.

Indiana (cont'd)
Other Media Collections *Audio:* disc, 33⅓ rpm, 3500t; tape, cassette, 510t. *Filmstrips:* sound & silent, 7050t; sound & silent sets, 110t. *Slides:* single, 6900t; sets, 69t.
Budget & Expenditures Total library budget $5000 (FY 7/1/74-7/1/75). Total FY film budget $4000.

King of Prussia

S- REGIONAL RESOURCES CENTER FILM LIBRARY, 443 S Gulph Rd, 19406. *Tel:* (215) 265-7321. *Film Serv Est:* 1962. *In Charge:* Lucille Burbank, Media Specialist. *AV Staff:* 2 (2 prof). *Film Sel:* committee preview, staff recommendations. *Holdings:* animated films 1%, career education 5%, children's films 10%, fine arts 1%, science 1%, social sciences 3%, teacher education 85%.
Free-Loan Film Serv *Eligibility:* staff, students, educational inst, prof groups, such as educators in special schools & institutions. *Restrictions:* for indiv, only in 15 counties of eastern Pa; for inst, only in 15 counties of eastern Pa. Available to researchers/scholars for on-site viewing. May borrow by mail. *Loan Period:* 3 days. *Total Yr Film Loan:* 1228.
Film Collection 390t/390p. Approx 100t acquired annually. *Circ:* 16mm, 400t/p; 8mm & S8mm reel & cartridge, 125t/p. *Pubns:* catalog, every 2 yrs; suppl, no set policy.
Other Film Serv Film reference serv, film fairs/festivals, library film programs. Permanent viewing facility. *Equipment:* lend S8mm camera (1), 16mm camera, 16mm sound projector (2), 8mm cartridge projector (1), S8mm cartridge projector (1), S8mm reel projector, projection tables & stands (3), projection screens (2), slide projector (3).
Other Media Collections *Audio:* disc, 33⅓ rpm, 110t/110c; tape, cassette, 200t/c; tape, cartridge, 125t/c; tape, reel, 70t/c. *Filmstrips:* sound & silent sets, 600t/600c. *Slides:* sets, 5t/c.
Budget & Expenditures Total library budget $24,000 (FY 7/1/74-7/1/75). Total FY film budget $20,000.

Kutztown

C- KUTZTOWN STATE COLLEGE, AV Library, 19530. *Tel:* (215) 683-3511, ext 307. *Film Serv Est:* 1950. *In Charge:* Gerald D. Schaeffer, Chmn AV Dept. *AV Staff:* 4 (4 prof, 1 tech). *Film Sel:* faculty/staff recommendations. *Holdings:* animated films 5%, career education 1%, experimental films 3%, fine arts 5%, science 10%, social sciences 16%, teacher education 60%.
Free-Loan Film Serv *Eligibility:* staff & students, educational inst, civic groups, religious groups, indiv with library cards. *Restrictions:* for indiv, interlibrary loan; for inst, none. Cannot use for fund-raising, transmit electronically. Available to researchers/scholars for on-site viewing. May not borrow by mail. *Loan Period:* 7 days. *Total Yr Film Loan:* 3000.
Film Collection 2000t/p. *Circ:* 16mm, 1000t/p; 8mm reel, 10t; S8mm reel, 400t. *Noncirc:* 16mm, 1000t/p.
Other Film Serv Film reference serv. Permanent viewing facility. *Equipment:* lend S8mm camera, 16mm camera, 16mm sound projector, 8mm cartridge projector, 8mm reel projector, S8mm cartridge projector, S8mm reel projector, projection tables & stands, projection screens, tape recorder.
Other Media Collections *Audio:* disc, 33⅓ rpm, 2000t/c; disc, 78rpm, 200t/c; tape, cassette, 300t/c; tape, reel, 200t/c. *Filmstrips:* sound, 50t/c; silent, 4500t/c.
Budget & Expenditures No separate AV budget. *Member:* AECT, ALA, EFLA, Pa. Library Assn, Pa. School Library Assn.

Lewisburg

C- BUCKNELL UNIVERSITY, Media Services, 17837. *Tel:* (717) 524-1109. *Film Serv Est:* 1955: *In Charge:* Robert E. Dunkerly, Coordinator. *AV Staff:* 3 (1 prof, 1 cl, 1 tech). *Film Sel:* faculty/staff recommendations. *Holdings:* engineering 10%, Japanese studies 15%, teacher education 20%.

Film Rental Serv *Eligibility:* no restrictions. *Restrictions:* only in U.S. & territories. *Rental Period:* 3 days. *Total Yr Film Booking:* 50.
Film Collection 280t/294p. Approx 3t acquired annually. *Circ:* 16mm, 280t/294p. *Pubns:* catalog, every 3 yrs; suppl, no set policy.
Other Film Serv Rent film from distributors for patrons, obtain film from other libraries, film reference serv, library film programs. Permanent viewing facility available for rent to community. *Equipment:* lend S8mm camera (4), 16mm camera (1), 16mm sound projector (20), 8mm reel projector (2), S8mm reel projector (2), projection screens (12), speakers.
Other Media Collections *Audio:* tape, reel, 150c. *Filmstrips:* silent, 150c.
Budget & Expenditures No separate AV budget.
Video Serv *Est:* 1970. *Video Staff:* 1 f-t, 1 tech. *Video Use:* documentation of community/school events, practical video/TV training courses, as art form. Video serv available by appointment. Produce video tapes. Have production studio/space & separate control room.
Video Equipment/Facilities *In-House Use Only:* playback deck (1), 1″ col, Sony EV320; SEG (2); lighting; microphones; tripods; audio tape recorders. *For Loan:* recording deck (5), ½″ b&w/col, Sony 5000, 3600; studio camera (5), b&w, Sony AV3210DX. Have permanent viewing installation. *Equipment Loan Period:* no set policy. Provide training in use of equipment to faculty & students. Have tape duplication serv.
Video Collection Maintained by rental, own production. Use/play ½″, 1″ reel to reel. Tapes organized by subject. *Collection, Color:* ½″ reel, 8t/c. *Collection, B&W:* ½″ reel, 12t/c; 1″ reel, 50t/c.
Cable & CCTV Receive serv of cable TV system. Have CCTV in inst.

Media

C- DELAWARE COUNTY COMMUNITY COLLEGE, Film Library, Route 252, 19063. *Tel:* (215) 353-5400, ext 454. *Film Serv Est:* 1969. *In Charge:* Stephen Starcheski, Dir, Media Services. *AV Staff:* 8 (2 prof, 2 cl, 4 tech). *Film Sel:* faculty/staff recommendations. *Holdings:* career education 1%, consumer affairs 1%, feature films 1%, fine arts 17%, law 13%, medicine 7%, science 10%, social sciences 47%, women 3%.
Free-Loan Film Serv *Eligibility:* staff & students, educational inst, civic groups, religious groups, & others, such as members of film library coop. *Restrictions:* for indiv, only in Delaware County & nearby areas of Chester County; for inst, only in eastern half of Pa. Cannot use for fund-raising. Films must be shown in their entirety. Available to researchers/scholars for on-site viewing. May not borrow by mail. *Loan Period:* 3 days. *Total Yr Film Loan:* 50. Produce slides, filmstrips, video tape, audio tape, transparencies.
Film Collection 107t/p. Approx 6-10t acquired annually. *Circ:* 16mm, 74t/p. *Noncirc:* 16mm, 33t/p. *Pubns:* catalog, annual; suppl, as needed.
Other Film Serv Obtain film from coop loan system (Film Library Intercollegiate Cooperative), obtain film from other libraries. Permanent viewing facility. *Equipment:* lend S8mm camera (3), 16mm sound projector (15), S8mm cartridge projector (25), S8mm reel projector (3), projection tables & stands (50), varies projectors & recorders.
Other Media Collections *Audio:* disc, 33⅓ rpm, 1303c; tape, cassette, 495c; tape, reel, 306c. *Filmstrips:* sound, 60c; silent, 276c; sound sets, 372c; silent sets, 34c. *Slides:* single, 250c; sets, 30c.
Budget & Expenditures Total library budget $56,500 (FY 7/1/74-7/1/75). Total FY film budget $20,000. *Member:* AECT, Pa. Library Assn, Pa. Learning Resources Assn, Educational Media Assn of Southeastern Pa.
Video Serv *Est:* 1975. *Video Staff:* 7 f-t, 1 p-t, 2 tech. *Video Use:* documentation of community/school events, in-service training, practical video/TV training courses, as sales tool, playback only of professionally produced tapes, critique. Video

serv available by appointment. Produce video tapes. Have production studio/space & separate control room.

Video Equipment/Facilities *For Loan:* portapak (2), ½" b&w, Concord; recording deck (7), ½", ¾" col, Concord, Sony, JVC; playback deck (24), 1" col, IVC; editing deck (1), 1" col, IVC; studio camera (2), col, Shibaden; monitor (65), col, RCA; SEG (1), 3M; keyer (1), 3M; additional camera lenses (4); lighting (30); microphones (12); tripods (5); audio tape recorders (16). Have permanent viewing installation. *Equipment Loan Period:* no set policy. Provide training in use of equipment to faculty & students. Have tape duplication serv.

Video Tape Loan/Rental/Sale Serv *Serv Provided:* swap with other inst. *Loan Eligibility:* staff & students, educational inst, civic groups, religious groups, prof groups, such as AMA, ALA & others, such as law enforcement agencies, government agencies. *Restrictions:* for indiv & inst, only in Delaware County. Cannot use for fund-raising, duplicate, air without permission. May borrow by mail. *Loan Period:* 7 days. *Total Yr Tape Loan:* 23.

Video Collection Maintained by purchase, rental, own production, exchange/swap. Use/play ½", 1" reel to reel, ¾" cassette. *Sources:* commercial distributors, exchange (members of Film Library Intercollegiate Coop). *Member:* Film Library Intercollegiate Cooperative. *Tape Sel:* preview, faculty/staff recommendations. *Special Collections:* in-house training tapes, films in video format. Tapes organized by subject & LC system. *Collection, Color:* 1" reel, 61t/c; ¾" cassette, 190t/260c. *Collection, B&W:* ½" reel, 32t/c; 1" reel, 240t/c. *Other Video Serv:* production workshops.

Cable & CCTV Have CCTV in inst, with 65 monitors. *Programming Sources:* tapes produced by inst, tapes produced professionally, tapes produced by community groups & indiv, student produced programs, student information service utilizing an electronic character generator.

Monessen

P- MONESSEN PUBLIC LIBRARY, 326 Donner Ave, 15062. *Tel:* (412) 684-4750. *Film Serv Est:* 1963. *In Charge:* Joan McGee. *AV Staff:* 1 (1 cl). *Film Sel:* committee preview. *Holdings:* children's films 50%.

Free-Loan Film Serv *Eligibility:* civic groups, religious groups, indiv with library cards, libraries in our district. *Restrictions:* for indiv, only in our district; for inst, only in our district. Cannot transmit electronically, borrow for classroom use. May not borrow by mail. *Loan Period:* 1 day. *Total Yr Film Loan:* 562.

Film Collection 197t/200p. *Circ:* 16mm, 197t/200p; S8mm reel, 40t/p. *Pubns:* catalog, as needed; suppl, no set policy.

Other Film Serv Obtain film from other libraries, library film programs. Permanent viewing facility available to community.

Other Media Collections *Audio:* disc, 33⅓ rpm, 2675t.

Budget & Expenditures Total library budget $18,800 (FY 1/1/74-1/1/75). Total FY film budget $9687. *Member:* ALA, Pa. Library Assn.

Nanticoke

C- LUZERNE COUNTY COMMUNITY COLLEGE, Prospect St & Middle Rd, 18634. *Tel:* (717) 735-8300, ext 208. *Film Serv Est:* 1967. *In Charge:* Robert N. Cohee, Library Dir. *AV Staff:* 1 (1 tech). *Film Sel:* faculty/staff recommendations, preview. *Holdings:* science 20%, social sciences 80%.

Free-Loan Film Serv *Eligibility:* civic groups, religious groups, & film consortium members. *Restrictions:* for indiv, only in Luzerne County. May not borrow by mail. *Loan Period:* 4 days. *Total Yr Film Loan:* 45.

Film Collection 144t/p. Approx 10t acquired annually. *Circ:* 16mm, 144t/p.

Other Film Serv Rent film from distributors for patrons, obtain film from coop loan system (Film Library Intercollege Coop of Pa.), obtain film from other libraries. Permanent viewing facility. *Equipment:* lend 16mm sound projector (6), 8mm cartridge projector (1), 8mm reel projector (1).

Other Media Collections *Audio:* disc, 33⅓ rpm, 674c; tape, cassette, 528c. *Filmstrips:* sound, 683c. *Slides:* single, 5514c.

Budget & Expenditures Total library budget $46,000 (FY 7/1/74-7/1/75). Total FY film budget $2000.

Video Serv *Video Use:* in-service training, practical video/TV training courses, instruction. Video serv available on demand. Produce video tapes.

Video Equipment/Facilities *In-House Use Only:* portapak (1), ½" b&w, Sony.

Video Tape Loan Serv *Serv Provided:* swap with other inst. *Loan Eligibility:* staff & students, & others, such as film consortium members.

Video Collection Maintained by own production, exchange/swap. Use/play ½" reel to reel. *Member:* Film Library Inter-College Cooperative of Pa.

Norristown

P- MONTGOMERY COUNTY-NORRISTOWN PUBLIC LIBRARY, 542 DeKalb St, 19401. *Tel:* (215) 277-3355. *In Charge:* Stephen Landstreet, Film Librarian. *AV Staff:* 3 (1 prof). *Film Sel:* committee preview, chief film librarian's decision, published reviews. *Holdings:* agriculture 1%, animated films 12%, black studies 5%, children's films 40%, comedies, consumer affairs 1%, dance 2%, experimental films 11%, feature films 2%, fine arts 5%, historical documentaries, NASA, science 15%, social sciences 5%, women 2%.

Free-Loan Film Serv *Eligibility:* educational inst, indiv over 18 with library cards. *Restrictions:* for indiv, only in Montgomery County; for inst, only in Montgomery County. Cannot use for fund-raising, transmit electronically. May not borrow by mail. *Loan Period:* 2 days. *Total Yr Film Loan:* 4433.

Film Collection 262t/p. Approx 40-50t acquired annually. *Circ:* 16mm, 262t/p; 8mm reel, 175t/p; S8mm reel, 50t/p. *Pubns:* catalog, every 2 yrs.

Other Film Serv Obtain film from coop loan system (Tri-County Film Coop, Pa. Public Library Film Center), obtain film from other libraries, film reference serv, film fairs/festivals, library film programs. *Equipment:* lend 16mm sound projector (2), 8mm reel projector (1), projection screens (2).

Other Media Collections *Audio:* disc, 33⅓ rpm, 4600c; disc, 78rpm, 600c; tape, cassette, 761c; tape, cartridge, 7c; tape, reel, 1c. *Filmstrips:* silent, 121c. *Slides:* sets, 736c.

Budget & Expenditures Total library budget $113,000 (FY 1/1/74-1/1/75). Total FY film budget $10,000.

Philadelphia

S- ARCHDIOCESE OF PHILADELPHIA, Diocesan Media Center, Box 11188, 19136. *Tel:* (215) 332-2958. *Film Serv Est:* 1974. *In Charge:* Henry J. Coher, Coordinator-Diocesan Media Center. *AV Staff:* 9 (2 prof, 5 cl, 2 tech). *Film Sel:* staff recommendations. *Holdings:* animated films 10%, black studies 5%, children's films 10%, fine arts 10%, religion 35%, science 15%, social sciences 15%.

Film Rental Serv *Eligibility:* educational org. *Restrictions:* only in 5 counties of Archdiocese of Philadelphia. Cannot use for fund-raising. *Rental Period:* 4 days. *Total Yr Film Booking:* 27,465. Produce films. Produce slides, tapes, transparencies.

Film Collection 1650t/2740p. *Circ:* 16mm, 1600t/2400p. *Noncirc:* 16mm, 50t/340c. *Pubns:* catalog, annual ($3.10); suppl, semi-annually.

Other Film Serv Obtain film from coop loan system. Permanent viewing facility. *Equipment:* lend 16mm sound projector (24), projection screens (10), filmstrip projectors (20).

Other Media Collections *Filmstrips:* sound, 250t.

Budget & Expenditures Total library budget $65,000 (FY 7/1/74-7/1/75). Total FY film budget $65,000. *Member:* AECT, Pa. Learning Resources Assn.

Video Serv *Video Staff:* 9 f-t, 2 tech. *Video Use:* playback only of professionally produced tapes. Video serv available on demand. Provide training in use of equipment. Have tape duplication serv.

Philadelphia (cont'd)

Video Tape Loan/Rental/Sale Serv *Serv Provided:* rental. *Loan/Rental Eligibility:* educational inst. *Restrictions:* for inst, only in 5 counties of Archdiocese of Philadelphia. Cannot use for fund-raising, duplicate, air without permission. May not borrow by mail. *Total Yr Tape Loan:* 357.

Video Collection Maintained by purchase, rental. Use/play ½″ reel to reel. *Sources:* commercial distributors. *Tape Sel:* staff recommendations. Tapes organized by accession number. *Collection, Color:* ½″ reel, 54t/c. *Collection, B&W:* ½″ reel, 54t. *Pubns:* catalog.

C- COMMUNITY COLLEGE OF PHILADELPHIA, AV Services, 19107. *Tel:* (215) 972-7257. *Film Serv Est:* 1968. *In Charge:* George S. Beers, Instructional Development Specialist. *AV Staff:* 14 (3 prof, 2 cl, 9 tech). *Film Sel:* committee preview, faculty/staff recommendations, chief film librarian's decision. *Holdings:* animated films 20%, experimental films 20%, fine arts 10%, science 20%, social sciences 20%.

Free-Loan Film Serv *Eligibility:* staff & students, & others, such as members of film cooperative. May borrow by mail. *Loan Period:* up to 3 wks. *Total Yr Film Loan:* 4184.

Film Collection 2300t/p. Approx 400-500t acquired annually. *Circ:* 16mm, 750t/800p; S8mm reel, 1150t/p. *Pubns:* catalog, annual; suppl, no set policy.

Other Film Serv Rent film from distributors for patrons, obtain film from coop loan system (Film Library Intercollege Cooperative), film reference serv, film fairs/festivals, library film programs. Permanent viewing facility. *Equipment:* lend S8mm camera (2), 16mm sound projector (40), 8mm cartridge projector (2), 8mm reel projector (2), S8mm cartridge projector (2), S8mm reel projector (2), projection tables & stands (50), projection screens (100).

Other Media Collections *Audio:* disc, 33⅓ rpm, 4250t/c; tape, cassette, 8133t/c. *Filmstrips:* sound, 1000t/c; sound sets, 250t/c. *Slides:* single, 46,152t/c.

Budget & Expenditures No separate AV budget. *Member:* AECT, EFLA, Pa. Learning Resources Assn.

Video Serv *Video Staff:* 12 f-t, 4 p-t. *Video Use:* documentation of community/school events, in-service training, practical video/TV training courses, playback only of professionally produced tapes. Video serv available on demand & by appointment. Produce video tapes. Have production studio/space & separate control room.

Video Equipment/Facilities *In-House Use Only:* portapak (12), b&w/col, Sony; recording deck (8), ½″, ¾″ b&w/col, Sony; playback deck (2), ¾″ col, Sony; editing deck (1), ¾″ b&w, Sony; studio camera (8), b&w/col, Sony; monitor (12), col, Sony, Electrohome; SEG (2), Sony; keyer (1), American Data; microphones (20); tripods (10); audio tape recorders (200). Have permanent viewing installation. Provide training in use of equipment to video students & all users.

Video Tape Loan/Rental/Sale Serv *Serv Provided:* free loan, swap with other inst. *Loan Eligibility:* staff & students, & others, such as members of film cooperative. May borrow by mail. *Loan Period:* 3 wks. *Total Yr Tape Loan:* 130.

Video Collection Maintained by purchase, rental, own production, exchange/swap. Use/play ½″ reel to reel, ¾″ cassette. *Sources:* commercial distributors. *Member:* Film Library Inter-College Cooperative. *Tape Sel:* preview, faculty/staff recommendations. Tapes organized by subject & acquisition numbers. *Collection, Color:* ¾″ cassette, 110t/c. *Collection, B&W:* ½″ reel, 20t/c. *Other Video Serv:* production workshops. *Pubns:* catalog.

C- DREXEL UNIVERSITY, Instructional Systems, 32 & Chestnut Sts, 19104. *Tel:* (215) 895-2927.

Film Serv *Equipment:* lend S8mm camera, 16mm camera, 16mm sound projector, 8mm cartridge projector, 8mm reel projector, S8mm cartridge projector, S8mm reel projector, projection tables & stands, projection screens.

Video Serv *Est:* 1971. *In Charge:* John Gregory, Dir. *Video Staff:* 4 f-t, 3 p-t. *Video Use:* documentation of community/school events, to increase community's library use, in-service training, practical video/TV training courses, as art form. Video serv available by appointment. Produce video tapes. Have production studio/space & separate control room.

Video Equipment/Facilities *In-House Use Only:* portapak (5), ½″ b&w, Sony 3400; recording deck, ½″, ¾″, 1″ col, IVC, Sony; playback deck, ½″, ¾″, 1″ col, IVC, Sony; editing deck (5), col, Sony; studio camera (5), b&w, Telemation; monitor (25), various b&w/col, various; SEG (2), Telemation, Panasonic; additional camera lenses; lighting; microphones; tripods; audio tape recorders; portable camera/recorder (2). *For Loan:* portapak (5), ½″ b&w, Sony 3400; tripods; audio tape recorders. *Equipment Loan Period:* 1 day. Provide training in use of equipment to faculty, staff, & students. Have tape duplication serv.

Video Tape Loan/Sale Serv *Serv Provided:* free loan, swap with other inst, sale. *Loan Eligibility:* staff & students. *Restrictions:* only indiv affiliated with inst. Cannot use for fund-raising, duplicate, air without permission. May not borrow by mail.

Video Collection Maintained by purchase, own production. Use/play ½″, 1″ reel to reel, ¾″ cassette. *Sources:* commercial distributors, local TV station. *Special Collections:* in-house training tapes. *Collection, Color & B&W:* unspecified number.

Cable & CCTV Produce programs for cablecasting.

C- DREXEL UNIVERSITY, Library, Non-Print Section, 32 & Chestnut Sts, 19104. *Tel:* (215) 895-2764. *Film Serv Est:* 1973. *In Charge:* Robert R. Rhein, Head, Non-Print Section. *AV Staff:* 3-4 (1 cl). *Film Sel:* committee preview, faculty/staff recommendations, published reviews.

Free-Loan Film Serv *Eligibility:* org members, staff & students, indiv affiliated with inst. *Restrictions:* determined by agency with proprietary rights to film. May not borrow by mail. *Loan Period:* no set period. *Total Yr Film Loan:* 339.

Film Collection 175t/185p. Approx 4-5t acquired annually. *Circ:* 16mm, 150t/160p; 8mm reel, 1t/p; 8mm cartridge, 10t/p. *Noncirc:* 16mm, 1t/p; 8mm cartridge, 13t/p. *Pubns:* catalog, annual (free).

Other Film Serv Rent film from distributors for patrons. Permanent viewing facility.

Other Media Collections *Audio:* disc, 33⅓, 45, 78rpm, 1436t/1626c; tape, cassette, cartridge, reel to reel, 26t/39c. *Filmstrips:* sound, silent, sound & silent sets, 318t/325c. *Slides:* single, & sets 18,500t/23,000c.

Budget & Expenditures Total library expenditure $335,325 (FY 7/1/74-7/1/75). Total FY film budget $1200. *Member:* ALA, Pa. Library Assn.

Video Equipment/Facilities Have permanent viewing installations.

Video Collection Maintained by purchase, own production. Use/play ½″, 1″ reel to reel, ¾″ cassette. *Tape Sel:* preview, faculty/staff recommendations, published reviews, catalogs. Tapes organized by Library of Congress system. *Collection, B&W:* ¾″ cassette, 18t/342c. *Other Video Serv:* programming, production workshops. *Pubns:* catalog of non-print materials.

Cable & CCTV Produce programs for cablecasting.

P- THE FREE LIBRARY OF PHILADELPHIA, Films Department, Logan Square, 19103. *Tel:* (215) 686-5367. *Film Serv Est:* 1959. *In Charge:* Steven Mayover, Head. *AV Staff:* 6 (2 prof, 4 cl). *Film Sel:* committee preview, chief film librarian's decision. *Holdings:* Spanish language 3%.

Free-Loan Film Serv *Eligibility:* indiv with library cards, libraries in Delaware County. *Restrictions:* for indiv, only in city; for inst, only in Delaware County. *Loan Period:* 1 day. *Total Yr Film Loan:* 26,959.

Film Collection 1458t/1615p. Approx 100t acquired annually. *Circ:* 16mm, 1458t/1615p. *Pubns:* catalog, every 3 yrs.

Other Film Serv Obtain film from coop loan system (Pa. Public Libraries Film Center), library film programs. Permanent viewing facility available to community.

Other Media Collections *Audio:* disc, total, 52,552c; tape, total, 27,716c. *Filmstrips:* sound, 1745c. *Slides:* single, 1780c.

Budget & Expenditures Total library budget $1,800,000 (FY 7/1/74-7/1/75). Total FY film budget $47,341. *Member:* AFI, ALA, EFLA, FLIC.

Video Serv *Est:* 1973. *In Charge:* George M. Holloway, Head, Community Services. *Video Staff:* 1 p-t, 1 tech. *Video Use:* documentation of community events, to increase community's library use, in-service training, adult basic education classes. Video serv available by appointment. Produce video tapes. Have production studio/space.

Video Equipment/Facilities *In-House Use Only:* porta-pak (2), ½" b&w, Sony AV3400; recording deck (1), ½" b&w, Sony 3650; playback deck (1), ½" col, Panasonic NV 3130; editing deck (1), ½" b&w, Panasonic WV341P; monitor (5), b&w/col; microphones (4); tripods (3); video cassette recorder (1). Have portable viewing installation. Provide training in use of equipment to library staff.

Video Collection Maintained by own production. Use/play ½" reel to reel, ¾" cassette. *Tape Sel:* preview, own productions. *Collection, B&W:* ½" reel, 100t.

Cable & CCTV Receive serv of cable TV system. Produce programs for cablecasting. Have CCTV in inst, with 1 monitor.

C- PEIRCE JUNIOR COLLEGE, 1420 Pine St, 19102. *Tel:* (215) KI5-6400, ext 268. *Film Serv Est:* 1968. *In Charge:* James R. McAuliffe, Head Librarian. *AV Staff:* 1 (1 tech). *Film Sel:* faculty/staff recommendations. *Holdings:* humanities 20%, science 80%.

Film Collection 30t/p. Approx 1t acquired annually. *Non-circ:* 16mm, 4t/p; S8mm reel, 25t/c. Publish materials pertaining to collection.

Other Film Serv Rent film from distributors for patrons. *Equipment:* lend S8mm camera (1), 16mm sound projector (7), S8mm cartridge projector (1), S8mm reel projector (5), projection screens.

Other Media Collections *Audio:* disc, 33⅓ rpm, 600t/c; tape, cassette, 80t/c. *Filmstrips:* sound, 50t/c; silent, 20t/c. *Slides:* single, 2000t/c.

Budget & Expenditures Total FY film budget $1300.

Video Serv *Est:* 1975. *In Charge:* Pat Connor, AV Technician. *Video Staff:* 7 f-t, 1 tech. *Video Use:* documentation of community/school events, in-service training, rented tape playback. Video serv available by appointment. Produce video tapes. Have production studio/space.

Video Equipment/Facilities *In-House Use Only:* recording deck (1), ¾" col, Sony VO1600; playback deck (1); studio camera (2), b&w/col, Sony 3250; monitor (3), col, Zenith F470W, Sony KU1215; microphones (4); tripods (2); audio tape recorders (4). Have permanent viewing installation. Provide training in use of equipment to students. Have tape duplication serv.

Video Collection Maintained by own production. Use/play ¾" cassette. *Sources:* commercial distributors. *Tape Sel:* catalogs. *Special Collections:* films in video format. Tapes organized by title. *Collection, Color:* ¾" cassette, 10t/c. *Collection, B&W:* ¾" cassette, 30t/c.

Cable & CCTV Receive serv of cable TV system. Have CCTV in inst, with 3 monitors. *Programming Sources:* over-the-air commercial & public broadcasting, tapes produced by inst, tapes produced professionally.

S- UNITED CHURCH OF CHRIST, Office for AV, Stewardship Council, 1505 Race St, 19102. *Tel:* (215) LO8-5750, ext 77, 78. *Film Serv Est:* 1962. *In Charge:* Rev. William Wimer, Dir. *AV Staff:* 3½ (2 prof, 1 cl, ½ tech). *Film Sel:* committee preview, staff recommendations. *Holdings:* black studies 20%, children's films 5%, church, ecology, education, hunger & poverty, interpersonal relations, missions, social sciences 45%, women 20%.

Film Rental Serv *Eligibility:* no restrictions. *Restrictions:* none. *Rental Period:* 1 day. Produce films & filmstrips.

Film Collection 140t/560p. *Pubns:* catalog, annual.

Other Film Serv Film reference serv. Permanent viewing facility.

Budget & Expenditures No separate AV budget. *Member:* EFLA.

Pittsburgh

A- CARNEGIE INSTITUTE, Film Section, Museum of Art, 4400 Forbes Ave, 15213. *Tel:* (412) 622-3212. *Film Serv Est:*

1970. *In Charge:* William Judson, Curator. *AV Staff:* 3 (3 prof). *Film Sel:* staff recommendations. *Holdings:* experimental films 80%, fine arts.

Film Collection 50t/60p. Approx 10-20t acquired annually. *Noncirc:* 16mm, 50t/60p.

Other Film Serv Film reference serv, filmmakers travel sheet. Permanent viewing facility.

Budget & Expenditures Total FY film budget $85,000.

P- CARNEGIE LIBRARY OF PITTSBURGH, District Film Center, Allegheny Sq, 15212. *Tel:* (412) 321-1344. *Film Serv Est:* 1966. *In Charge:* Anne Meyer, Head. *AV Staff:* 5½ (½ prof, 3½ cl, 1½ tech). *Film Sel:* committee preview. *Holdings:* children's films 35%.

Free-Loan Film Serv *Eligibility:* civic groups, religious groups, indiv with library cards. *Restrictions:* for indiv, only in Allegheny County & part of Westmoreland County; for inst, only in Allegheny County & part of Westmoreland County. Cannot use for fund-raising, transmit electronically, borrow for classroom use. Available to researchers/scholars for on-site viewing. May borrow by mail. *Loan Period:* 1 day. *Total Yr Film Loan:* 11,663.

Film Collection 1158t/1439p. Approx 130t acquired annually. *Circ:* 16mm, 1158t/1439p. *Pubns:* catalog, every 3 yrs ($2.50); suppl, quarterly.

Other Film Serv Obtain film from coop loan system (Pa. Public Libraries Film Buying Consortium), film fairs/festivals, library film programs. Permanent viewing facility available to community.

Other Media Collections *Audio:* disc, 33⅓ rpm, 18,000c; tape, cassette, 639c. *Slides:* single, 95,000c.

Budget & Expenditures Total library budget $564,350 (FY 1/1/74-1/1/75). Total FY film budget $15,000. *Member:* ALA, EFLA, Pa. Library Assn.

C- CHATHAM COLLEGE, 15232. *Tel:* (412) 441-8200, ext 231. *In Charge:* Bruce Layton, Asst. Dir. Media Resources Center. *AV Staff:* 2 (1 prof, 1 cl). *Holdings:* women 100%.

Free-Loan Film Serv *Eligibility:* staff & students, & others, such as high schools, Chatham alumni. Available to researchers/scholars for on-site viewing. May not borrow by mail.

Film Collection 50t/p. *Noncirc:* 16mm, 50t/p.

Other Film Serv Rent film from distributors for patrons. Permanent viewing facility available for rent to community.

Budget & Expenditures No separate AV budget.

Video Serv *Est:* 1967. *Video Staff:* 1 f-t. *Video Use:* documentation of community/school events, in-service training, practical video/TV training courses, as art form. Video serv available by appointment. Produce video tapes. Have production studio/space.

Video Equipment/Facilities *In-House Use Only:* porta-pak (2), ½" b&w, Concord; recording deck (1), ½" b&w, Sony; playback deck (1), ½" b&w, Sony; editing deck (1), ½" col, Panasonic; studio camera (3), GBC, Sony; monitor (3), Sanyo; SEG (1), Panasonic; keyer (1), Sony; lighting (3); microphones (6); tripods (2); audio tape recorders (4). Have portable viewing installation. Provide training in use of equipment to faculty & students. Have tape duplication serv.

Video Collection Maintained by own production. Use/play ½" reel to reel. Tapes organized by department.

P- NORTHLAND PUBLIC LIBRARY, 120 Three Degree Rd, 15237. *Tel:* (412) 366-3350. *Film Serv Est:* 1969. *In Charge:* Laura Smith, Dir. *AV Staff:* 1 (1 cl). *Film Sel:* published reviews.

Free-Loan Film Serv *Eligibility:* indiv with library cards, & others, such as community groups. *Restrictions:* for indiv, only in our county; for inst, only in our county. May not borrow by mail. *Loan Period:* 1 day.

Film Collection 154t/204p. Approx 2t acquired annually. *Circ:* 16mm, 4t/p; 8mm reel, 100t; S8mm reel, 100t. Publish materials pertaining to collection.

Other Film Serv Rent film from distributors for patrons, obtain film from coop loan system (Carnegie Film Center), obtain film from other libraries, library film programs. *Equip-*

Pittsburgh (cont'd)
ment: lend Viewmaster projectors (10), viewmaster individual viewers (14).

Other Media Collections *Audio:* disc, 33⅓ rpm, 1700c.

Budget & Expenditures Total library budget $34,000 (FY 1/1/75-1/1/76). No separate budget. *Member:* ALA, Pa. Library Assn.

S- WESTINGHOUSE ELECTRIC CORPORATION, Nuclear Energy Systems Library, Box 355, 15230. *Tel:* (412) 373-4200. *Video Serv Est:* 1969. *In Charge:* M. Vasilakis, Library Manager. *Video Staff:* 12 f-t, 2 p-t. *Video Use:* documentation of community events, in-service training, as sales tool, playback of professionally produced tapes. Video serv available on demand. Produce video tapes. Have production studio/space & separate control room.

Video Equipment/Facilities *In-House Use Only:* playback deck (1), ¾″ col, Ampex 7800; studio camera (1), b&w, Raytheon; SEG (1), keyer (1), AVEX; additional camera lenses (3). *For Loan:* portapak (1), ½″ b&w, Sony 3400; recording deck (4), ½″ b&w/col, Sony 3650; editing deck (2), 1″ col, Ampex 5800; monitor (10), b&w, Sony, Panasonic, Magnavox; lighting (12); microphones (6); tripods (3). Have permanent & portable viewing installations. *Equipment Loan Period:* no set policy. Provide training in use of equipment to employees of this & other Westinghouse divisions. Have tape duplication serv.

Video Collection Maintained by purchase, rental, own production. Use/play ½″, 1″ reel to reel, ¾″ cassette. *Sources:* in-house production. *Tape Sel:* preview, catalogs. *Special Collections:* in-house training tapes. Tapes organized by subject & accession number.

Cable & CCTV Have CCTV in inst, with 10-12 monitors. *Programming Sources:* tapes produced by inst.

Pottsville

P- POTTSVILLE FREE PUBLIC LIBRARY, 3rd & Market St, 17901. *Tel:* (717) 622-8880, ext 7. *Film Serv Est:* 1961. *In Charge:* Joy Tomaino, Film Librarian. *AV Staff:* 2 (1 prof, ½ cl, ½ tech). *Film Sel:* committee preview, published reviews, state list of recommended films.

Free-Loan Film Serv *Eligibility:* educational inst, civic groups, religious groups, indiv with library cards, & others, such as clergymen, hospitals, any established group. *Restrictions:* for indiv, interlibrary loan; for inst, none. Cannot use for fundraising. Available to researchers/scholars for on-site viewing. May borrow by mail. *Loan Period:* 7 days. *Total Yr Film Loan:* 750.

Film Collection 148t/150p. Approx 8t acquired annually. *Circ:* 16mm, 148t/150p. *Pubns:* catalog, annual; suppl, no set policy.

Other Film Serv Rent film from distributors for patrons, obtain film from coop loan system (Pa. Public Library Film Buying Consortium), obtain film from other libraries. Permanent viewing facility. *Equipment:* lend 16mm sound projector (3), projection screens (4), filmstrips & slide projectors.

Other Media Collections *Audio:* disc, 33⅓ rpm, 1250t; disc, 45rpm, 1t; tape, cassette, 422t. *Filmstrips:* sound, 24t; silent, 1t. *Slides:* single, 1326t; sets, 5t.

Budget & Expenditures Total library budget $84,000 (FY 7/1/74-7/1/75). Total FY film budget $18,000. *Member:* ALA, EFLA, Pa. Library Assn.

Reading

C- ALBRIGHT COLLEGE, Library, 19604. *Tel:* (215) 921-2381. *Video Serv Est:* 1976. *In Charge:* G. Missonis, Asst Librarian. *Video Staff:* 1 f-t, 2 p-t. *Video Use:* speech classes. Video serv available by appointment. Produce video tapes. Have production studio/space & separate control room.

Video Equipment/Facilities *In-House Use Only:* recording deck (1), ½″ b&w, Sony 3400; editing deck (2), ½″ col, Panasonic NV3160; studio camera (2), col, Panasonic VW2300; monitor (1), col, Sony; SEG (1), Panasonic; lighting (2); tripods (3). *For Loan:* portapak (1), ¼″ b&w, AKAI. Have portable

viewing installation. Provide training in use of equipment to staff.

Video Collection Maintained by own production. Use/play ½″, ¼″ reel to reel.

Cable & CTTV Receive serv of cable TV system. Produce programs for cablecasting. Serve as production facility for others. Run cable programs for special audiences.

Rosemont

C- ROSEMONT COLLEGE, Gertrude Kistler Memorial Library, Education Resource Center, 19010. *Tel:* (215) LA7-0200, ext 257. *Film Serv Est:* 1969. *In Charge:* Sister Mary Dennis Lynch, Dir of Library Services. *AV Staff:* ¾ (½ prof, 1 cl). *Film Sel:* committee preview, faculty/staff recommendations.

Other Film Serv Rent film from distributors for patrons, obtain film from coop loan system (Tri-State College Library Cooperative). *Equipment:* lend S8mm camera (1), 16mm sound projector (4), 8mm cartridge projector (2), 8mm reel projector (1), projection tables & stands (4), projection screens (25).

Other Media Collections *Audio:* disc, 33⅓ rpm, 105t; disc, 45rpm, 150t; disc, 78rpm, 115t; tape, cassette, 89t; tape, reel, 13t. *Filmstrips:* sound, 33t; silent, 16t; sound sets, 10t. *Slides:* single, 167t; sets, 12t.

Budget & Expenditures Total library budget $94,920 (FY 7/1/75-7/1/76). No separate budget. *Member:* AECT, ALA, Pa. Library Assn, Catholic Library Assn.

Video Serv *Est:* 1973. *Video Staff:* 3 f-t, 5 p-t. *Video Use:* documentation of community/school events, in-service training, practical video/TV training courses, teacher training. Video serv available by appointment. Produce video tapes. Have production studio/space.

Video Equipment/Facilities *In-House Use Only:* portapak (1), b&w, Sony; recording deck (2), ½″ b&w; editing deck (1), b&w; studio camera (1), b&w; monitor (3), b&w; additional camera lenses (1); microphones (1); tripods (1). Have portable viewing installation. Provide training in use of equipment to teacher education students & resource center helpers. Have tape duplication serv.

Video Tape Loan Serv *Serv Provided:* free loan. *Loan Eligibility:* org members, staff. May not borrow by mail.

Video Collection Maintained by rental, own production. Use/play ½″ reel to reel. *Tape Sel:* faculty/staff recommendations. *Special Collections:* in-house training tapes. Tapes organized by subject.

Cable & CCTV Produce programs for cablecasting. Inform public about cable system serv & facilities. Serve as production facility for others. Run cable programs for special audiences. Have advisory/administrative role in cable system operation.

St. Davids

C- EASTERN COLLEGE, AV Department, McInnis Learning Center, 19087. *Tel:* (215) MU8-3300, ext 357, 314. *Film Serv Est:* 1970. *In Charge:* Bettie Ann Brigham, Dir, AV Dept. *AV Staff:* 1 (1 prof). *Film Sel:* faculty/staff recommendations. Produce video programs for own educational purposes.

Other Film Serv Rent film from distributors for patrons, obtain film from coop loan system (Tri-State Library Cooperative, Pa. State Univ.), obtain film from other libraries, film reference serv. Permanent viewing facility available for rent to community. *Equipment:* lend S8mm camera (4), 16mm sound projector (7), 8mm reel projector (3), S8mm reel projector (3), projection tables & stands (40), projection screens (10), overhead projectors (20).

Other Media Collections *Audio:* disc, 45rpm, 700t; disc, 78rpm, 100t; tape, cassette, 50t; tape, reel, 20t. *Filmstrips:* sound, 20t; silent, 30t; sound sets, 10t; silent sets, 13t. *Slides:* single, 638t; sets, 1270t.

Budget & Expenditures Total library budget $4000 (FY 7/1/74-7/1/75). Total FY film budget $1500. *Member:* ALA.

Video Serv *Video Staff:* 1 f-t, 7 p-t. *Video Use:* documentation of community/school events, in-service training, practical video/TV training courses, as sales tool, as art form. Video serv available by appointment. Produce video tapes. Have production studio/space & separate control room.

Video Equipment/Facilities *In-House Use Only:* recording deck (4), ½″ b&w/col, Sony 1600; playback deck (4), ½″ b&w/col, Sony 1600; studio camera (2), b&w, Sony; monitor (8), b&w/col, Sony, GE; SEG (1), Sony; additional camera lenses (2); lighting (4); microphones (4); tripods (4); audio tape recorders (45). Have portable viewing installation. *Equipment Loan Period:* no set policy. Provide training in use of equipment to faculty, students & elementary & secondary student teachers. Have tape duplication serv.

Video Tape Loan Serv *Serv Provided:* free loan, swap with other inst. *Loan Eligibility:* org members, staff & students.

Video Collection Maintained by purchase, rental, own production, exchange/swap. Use/play ½″ reel to reel, ¾″ cassette. *Sources:* commercial distributors, community productions. *Tape Sel:* preview, faculty/staff recommendations, published reviews. Tapes organized by subject & numerical. *Collection, Color:* ¾″ cassette, 183t. *Collection, B&W:* ½″ reel, 56t. *Other Video Serv:* taping of other media, production workshops. Publish materials on video.

Cable & CCTV Have CCTV in inst, with 8 monitors. *Programming Sources:* over-the-air commercial & public broadcasting, tapes produced professionally, tapes produced by community groups & indiv.

Slippery Rock

C- SLIPPERY ROCK STATE COLLEGE, Library, 16057. *Tel:* (412) 794-7251. *AV Staff:* 5 (2 prof, 1 cl, 2 tech). *Film Sel:* faculty/staff recommendations, dean's decision.

Free-Loan Film Serv *Eligibility:* staff & students, & others, such as high schools. *Restrictions:* for indiv, only in city; for inst, only in state. May borrow by mail. *Loan Period:* 7 days.

Film Collection 375t/p. Approx 10t acquired annually. *Circ:* 16mm, 375t/p; S8mm cartridge, 1412t/p. *Pubns:* catalog, as needed.

Other Film Serv Rent film from distributors for patrons, film reference serv, film fairs/festivals. *Equipment:* lend S8mm camera (2), 16mm camera (2), 16mm sound projector (78), 8mm reel projector (9), S8mm cartridge projector (20), S8mm reel projector (20), projection tables & stands (70), projection screens (20).

Other Media Collections *Audio:* disc, total, 6258t; tape, cassette, 3935t; tape, reel, 1077t. *Filmstrips:* sound & silent, 10,841t. *Slides:* single, 25,231t.

Budget & Expenditures No separate AV budget.

Video Serv *Est:* 1970. *In Charge:* George Price, Head, Instructional Support Service. *Video Staff:* 5 f-t, 1 p-t. *Video Use:* documentation of community/school events, in-service training, playback only of professionally produced tapes, image magnification, skill analysis, off-air recording. Video serv available on demand & by appointment. Produce video tapes. Have production studio/space & separate control room.

Video Equipment/Facilities *In-House Use Only:* editing deck (3), ½″, ¾″ b&w/col, Sony 3650; studio camera (2), b&w/col, Panasonic. *For Loan:* portapak (8), ½″, ¾″ b&w/col, Sony, Sanyo; monitor (15), b&w/col, Sony, Panasonic, Conrac; SEG (2), Sony, Panasonic; lighting (18); microphones (60); tripods (10); audio tape recorders (60). Have portable viewing installation. *Equipment Loan Period:* 7 days students, 1 semester faculty. Provide training in use of equipment to faculty & students. Have tape duplication serv.

Video Tape Loan Serv *Serv Provided:* free loan, swap with other inst. *Loan Eligibility:* staff & students. Cannot air without permission. May not borrow by mail.

Video Collection Maintained by own production. Use/play ½″ reel to reel, ½″ cartridge, ¾″ cassette. *Sources:* commercial distributors, locally produced shows. *Tape Sel:* faculty/staff recommendations, catalogs. Tapes organized by subject. *Collection, Color:* ¾″ cassette, 50t. *Collection, B&W:* ½″ reel, 50t. *Other Video Serv:* reference serv, taping of other media, production workshops.

University Park

C- THE PENNSYLVANIA STATE UNIVERSITY, AV Services, 17 Willard Bldg, 16802. *Tel:* (814) 865-6315. *Film Serv Est:* 1940. *In Charge:* T. M. Reeves, Dept Head. *Film Sel:* committee preview, faculty/staff recommendations, chief film librarian's decision. *Holdings:* anthropology, behavioral science, psychology.

Film Rental Serv *Eligibility:* educational org. *Restrictions:* only in U.S. & territories. Cannot copy, broadcast or use for closed circuit without permission of distributor. *Rental Period:* 1 day. Sell films.

Film Collection 9000t/14,000p. *Circ:* 16mm, 9000t/14,000p. *Pubns:* catalog, as needed; suppl, no set policy.

Other Film Serv Film reference serv. Permanent viewing facility.

Budget & Expenditures No separate AV budget. *Member:* EFLA.

Video Serv *Est:* 1975. *Video Staff:* 3 f-t. *Video Use:* rent & sell video productions. Video serv available by appointment.

Video Tape Loan/Rental/Sale Serv *Serv Provided:* rental, sale. *Loan/Rental Eligibility:* staff & students, educational inst, civic groups, prof groups. Cannot duplicate, air without permission. May borrow by mail.

Video Collection Maintained by purchase. Use/play ¾″ cassette. *Sources:* commercial distributors, community productions. *Tape Sel:* preview, faculty/staff recommendations. Tapes organized by subject. *Collection, Color:* ¾″ cassette, 50t. *Collection, B&W:* ¾″ cassette, 50t.

Cable & CCTV Have CCTV in inst.

Warren

P- WARREN LIBRARY ASSOCIATION, Box 489, 16365. *Tel:* (814) 723-4650. *Film Serv Est:* 1974. *In Charge:* District Extension Librarian. *AV Staff:* ½ (½ cl). *Film Sel:* committee preview, staff recommendations.

Free-Loan Film Serv *Eligibility:* residents (over 18 yrs of age) of 5-county Seneca Library Dist. *Restrictions:* for indiv, interlibrary loan; for inst, interlibrary loan. Cannot use for fund-raising, transmit electronically. Available to researchers/scholars for on-site viewing. May borrow by mail. *Loan Period:* 1 day. *Total Yr Film Loan:* 962.

Film Collection 124t/127p. *Circ:* 16mm, 125t/129p; 8mm reel, 383t. *Pubns:* catalog, as needed; suppl, no set policy.

Other Film Serv Obtain film from coop loan system (Inter-District Film Service), obtain film from other libraries, film reference serv, library film programs, program planning for film borrowers.

Other Media Collections *Audio:* disc, 33⅓ rpm, 2785c; tape, cassette, 323c. *Filmstrips:* sound & silent sets, 122t. *Slides:* sets, 4t.

Budget & Expenditures Total library budget $51,475 (FY 1/1/75-1/1/76). Total FY film budget $10,284. *Member:* ALA, Pa. Library Assn.

Wayne

P- MEMORIAL LIBRARY OF RADNOR TOWNSHIP, 110 W Lancaster Ave, 19087. *Tel:* (215) MU8-6475. *Film Serv Est:* 1966. *In Charge:* Marilyn Caltabiano, Library Dir.

Free-Loan Film Serv *Eligibility:* indiv with library cards. *Restrictions:* for indiv, only in Radnor Township. *Loan Period:* 3 weeks.

Film Collection 153t/p. Approx 24t acquired annually. *Circ:* 8mm reel, 103t/p; S8mm reel, 50t/p. Publish materials pertaining to collection.

Other Film Serv Obtain film from other libraries.

Budget & Expenditures Total library budget $21,750 (FY 1/1/75-1/1/76). Total FY film budget $350.

West Chester

S- CHESTER COUNTY INTERMEDIATE UNIT, Instructional Materials Service, West Chester State College, 19380. *Tel:* (215) 436-0242. *Film Serv Est:* 1959. *In Charge:* Lloyd C. Hall, Dir. *AV Staff:* 19 (1 prof, 14 cl). *Film Sel:* committee preview, staff recommendations, chief film librarian's decision, published reviews.

Film Rental Serv *Eligibility:* educational org. *Restrictions:* only in Chester County. Cannot use for fund-raising, transmit electronically. *Rental Period:* 3 days. *Total Yr Film Booking:* 76,880.

Film Collection 3360t/4600p. Approx 350t acquired annually. *Circ:* 16mm, 3360t/4600. *Pubns:* catalog, every 2 yrs; suppl, no set policy.

Other Film Serv *Equipment:* rent S8mm camera (5), 8mm reel projector (2).

Other Media Collections *Audio:* tape, cassette, 500t; tape, reel, 500t.

Budget & Expenditures Total library budget $202,000 (FY 7/1/74-7/1/75). Total FY film budget $95,000. *Member:* AECT, EFLA.

Video Serv *Video Staff:* 15 f-t, 8 p-t. *Video Use:* in-service training, classroom use. Video serv available for duplication from 250 masters.

Video Equipment/Facilities *In-House Use Only:* recording deck (3), 1″, 2″ col, Panasonic; SEG (1), Panasonic; audio tape recorders (1). Have tape duplication serv.

Video Collection Maintained by exchange/swap. Use/play ½″ reel to reel, ¾″ cassette. *Sources:* exchange (PDE Master Library). *Tape Sel:* preview, staff recommendations, catalogs. Tapes organized by subject. *Collection, Color:* ½″ reel, 250t/c. *Pubns:* catalog.

P- CHESTER COUNTY LIBRARY, AV Dept, 235 W Market St, 19380. *Tel:* (215) 696-8960, ext 22. *Film Serv Est:* 1967. *In Charge:* Hazelyn M. Weaver, AV Librarian. *AV Staff:* 1 (1 prof, ½ cl, ½ tech). *Film Sel:* committee preview, chief film librarian's decision.

Free-Loan Film Serv *Eligibility:* indiv over 18 with library cards. *Restrictions:* for indiv, only in Chester, Bucks & Montgomery counties. Cannot use for fund-raising, transmit electronically. Available to researchers/scholars for on-site viewing. May not borrow by mail. *Loan Period:* 1 day. *Total Yr Film Loan:* 2449.

Film Collection 140t/p. Approx 20t acquired annually. *Circ:* 16mm, 140t/p. *Pubns:* catalog, every 2 yrs; suppl, no set policy.

Other Film Serv Obtain film from coop loan system (Pa. Public Libraries Film Center, Tri-County Cooperative). *Equipment:* lend S8mm camera (1), 16mm sound projector (1), projection screens (1), rear projection screen (1).

Other Media Collections *Audio:* disc, 33⅓ rpm, 1046t; tape, cassette, 285t. *Slides:* sets, 43t.

Budget & Expenditures Total library budget $81,117 (FY 1/1/75-1/1/76). Total FY film budget $3000. *Member:* EFLA, Pa. Library Assn.

Wilkes Barre

P- OSTERHOUT FREE LIBRARY, 71 S Franklin St, 18701. *Tel:* (717) 823-0156. *Film Serv Est:* 1970. *In Charge:* Syma Rosenzweig, Film Librarian. *AV Staff:* 2 (1 prof, 1 cl). *Film Sel:* committee preview.

Free-Loan Film Serv *Eligibility:* residents of Luzerne County who are over 18 years old. *Restrictions:* for indiv, interlibrary loan, only in Luzerne County & adjacent counties. Cannot use for fund-raising, transmit electronically. May not borrow by mail. *Loan Period:* 1 day. *Total Yr Film Loan:* 3872.

Film Collection 308t/315p. Approx 15t acquired annually. *Circ:* 16mm, 283t/290p; S8mm cartridge, 25t/p. *Pubns:* catalog, as needed.

Other Film Serv Obtain film from coop loan system (Pa. State Library), obtain film from other libraries, film reference serv, film fairs/festivals, library film programs. *Equipment:* lend 16mm sound projector (8), S8mm cartridge projector (6), slide projectors (3), filmstrip projectors (3).

Other Media Collections *Audio:* disc, 33⅓ rpm, 4920t; tape, cassette, 439t. *Filmstrips:* sound sets, 11t. *Slides:* sets, 7t.

Budget & Expenditures Total library budget $61,000 (FY 1/1/75-1/1/76). Total FY film budget $6500. *Member:* ALA, EFLA, FLIC, Pa. Library Assn.

York

P- MARTIN MEMORIAL LIBRARY, 159 E Market St, 17401. *Tel:* (717) 843-3978. *In Charge:* Carol O. Commins, Film Librarian. *AV Staff:* 1½ (1 prof, ½ tech). *Film Sel:* committee preview.

Free-Loan Film Serv *Eligibility:* indiv with library cards. *Restrictions:* for indiv, only in York/Adams County. Cannot transmit electronically. May not borrow by mail. *Loan Period:* 3 days. *Total Yr Film Loan:* 1952.

Film Collection 191t/p. Approx 40t acquired annually. *Circ:* 16mm, 191t/p. *Pubns:* catalog, as needed; suppl, no set policy.

Other Film Serv Obtain film from coop loan system (Pa. Public Library Film Buying Consortium), obtain film from other libraries, film reference serv, film fairs/festivals, library film programs. Permanent viewing facility available for rent to community.

Other Media Collections *Audio:* disc, 33⅓ rpm, 4060c. *Filmstrips:* sound sets, 55c. *Slides:* sets, 6c.

Budget & Expenditures Total library budget $40,000 (FY 1/1/75-1/1/76). Total FY film budget $5000. *Member:* ALA, EFLA, Pa. Film Library Assn.

Rhode Island

Pawtucket

P- PAWTUCKET PUBLIC LIBRARY, 13 Summer St, 02860. *Tel:* (401) 722-8840.

Film Serv Obtain film from coop loan system (Warwick Film Coop). *Equipment:* lend 16mm sound projector (3), 8mm reel projector (1), S8mm reel projector (1), projection screens.

Other Media Collections *Audio:* tape, cassette, 90t/c.

Budget & Expenditures Total library budget $45,019 (FY 7/1/74-7/1/75). Total FY film budget $1700. *Member:* AECT, ALA.

Video Serv *Video Use:* documentation of community events, to increase community's library use, community video access, in-service training. Video serv available on demand. Produce video tapes. Have production studio/space.

Video Equipment/Facilities *In-House Use Only:* recording deck (1), ¾″ col, Wollensak VR210; monitor (1), col, Panasonic. *For Loan:* portapak (1), ½″ b&w, Sony AVC3450, AV3400; playback deck (1), ¾″, Wollensak VP205; microphones (5); tripods (1); audio tape recorders (5). Have portable viewing installation. *Equipment Loan Period:* no set policy. Provide training in use of equipment to staff, patrons, libraries. Have tape duplication serv.

Video Tape Loan/Rental/Sale Serv *Serv Provided:* swap with other inst. *Loan Eligibility:* anyone with administrative approval. *Restrictions:* for indiv, none. Cannot use for fund-raising, air without permission. May borrow by mail. *Loan Period:* 2 weeks.

Video Collection Maintained by own production, exchange/swap. Use/play ¾″ cassette. *Sources:* commercial distributors. *Collection, Color:* ¾″ cassette, 20t.

Providence

S- THE ELECTRON MOVERS, Research in the Electronic Arts, 128 N Main St, 02903. *Tel:* (401) 272-4305. *Video Serv Est:* 1974. *In Charge:* Bob Jungels, President. *Video Staff:* 3 f-t, 2 p-t, 1 tech. *Video Use:* documentation of community/school events, community video access, in-service training, practical video/TV training courses, as art form. Video serv available by appointment. Produce video tapes. Have production studio/space.

Video Equipment/Facilities *In-House Use Only:* portapak (1), ½″ b&w, Sony 3400; recording deck (3), ½″, ¾″ col, Panasonic; playback deck (1), ½″ b&w, Panasonic; editing deck (2), ½″ col, Panasonic 3130, 3140; studio camera (4), b&w, Sony; monitor (7), b&w; SEG (1), Panasonic; keyer (1); lighting (2); microphones (4); tripods (4); audio tape recorders (2). Have portable viewing installation. Provide training in use of equipment to teachers, students, schools, librarians. Have tape duplication serv.

Video Tape Loan/Rental/Sale Serv *Serv Provided:* free loan, swap with other inst, rental, sale. *Loan/Rental Eligibility:* staff & students, educational inst, prof groups, & others, such as artists & video artists. *Restrictions:* for indiv & inst, only in city.

Cannot use for fund-raising, duplicate, air without permission. May borrow by mail.

Video Collection Maintained by own production, exchange/swap. Use/play ½″ reel to reel, ¾″ cassette. *Sources:* exchange (with other groups). *Tape Sel:* preview. *Special Collections:* video as art. Tapes organized by artist. *Collection, Color:* ½″ reel, 15t. *Collection, B&W:* ½″ reel, 20t. *Other Video Serv:* reference serv, taping of other media, production workshops. *Pubns:* catalog.

Cable & CCTV Have CCTV in inst, with 4 monitors. *Programming Sources:* tapes produced by inst, tapes produced by community groups & indiv, live programming.

Warwick

P- RHODE ISLAND LIBRARY FILM COOPERATIVE, Warwick Public Library, 600 Sandy Lane, 02886. *Tel:* (401) 739-2278. *Film Serv Est:* 1967. *In Charge:* David Green, Dir. *AV Staff:* 4 (1 prof, 2 cl, 1 tech). *Film Sel:* committee preview, chief film librarian's decision.

Free-Loan Film Serv *Eligibility:* org members, civic & religious groups. *Restrictions:* for inst, only in state. R.I. Development Council films free to entire U.S. Cannot use for fund-raising, transmit electronically, borrow for classroom use. Available to researchers/scholars for on-site viewing. May not borrow by mail. *Loan Period:* 3-7 days. *Total Yr Film Loan:* 14,918.

Film Collection 913p. *Circ:* 16mm, 744t/914p. *Pubns:* catalog, every 2 yrs; suppl, in yr catalog not published.

Other Film Serv Film reference serv, film fairs/festivals. Permanent viewing facility. *Equipment:* lend 16mm sound projector (6), lend projection screens (4).

Budget & Expenditures Total FY film budget $46,300 (FY 7/1/74-7/1/75). *Member:* EFLA, FLIC, R.I. Library Assn.

P- WARWICK PUBLIC LIBRARY, 600 Sandy Lane, 02886. *Tel:* (401) 739-5440. *In Charge:* Bruce Macomber, AV/Fine Arts Specialist. *AV Staff:* 1¼ (¼ cl, 1 tech). *Film Sel:* published reviews.

Free-Loan Film Serv *Eligibility:* indiv with adult library cards. *Restrictions:* for indiv, only with cards in libraries in R.I. Western Interrelated System. *Loan Period:* 3 weeks. *Total Yr Film Loan:* 1002.

Film Collection 138t/150p. Approx 40t acquired annually. *Circ:* S8mm cartridge, 138t/150p. Publish brochures for teachers.

Other Film Serv Obtain film from coop loan system (R.I. Library Film Coop), library film programs. Permanent viewing facility available to community.

Other Media Collections *Audio:* disc, 33⅓ rpm, 500c; tape, cassette, 200c. *Filmstrips:* silent, 62c; sound sets, 35c. *Slides:* single, 1000c; sets, 33t/52c.

Budget & Expenditures Total library budget $70,000 (FY 2/1/75-2/1/76). No separate AV budget. *Member:* ALA, R.I. Library Assn.

South Carolina

Charleston

S- CHARLESTON MUSEUM, 121 Rutledge Ave, 29401. *Tel:* (803) 722-2996. *In Charge:* Daniel Johnson, Curator of Education. *Film Sel:* staff recommendations. *Holdings:* science 95%, social sciences 5%.

Film Collection 25t. Approx 1-2t acquired annually.

Other Film Serv Permanent viewing facility.

Other Media Collections *Audio:* disc, 33⅓ rpm, 10t; tape, reel, 8t. *Filmstrips:* silent, 15t. *Slides:* single, 150t.

Gaffney

C- LIMESTONE COLLEGE, A. J. Eastwood Library, 29340. *Tel:* (803) 489-7151, ext 179. *Video Serv Est:* 1972. *In Charge:* William Sutton, Assoc Prof Chem & Math. *Video Staff:* 1 p-t, 2 tech. *Video Use:* documentation of community/school events, in-service training. Video serv available by appointment. Produce video tapes.

Video Equipment/Facilities *In-House Use Only:* recording deck (1), ½″ b&w/col, Sony 3600; studio camera (1), b&w, GBC; monitor (1), b&w, Sony; additional camera lenses (1); microphones (1); tripods (1); audio tape recorders (6). Provide training in use of equipment to faculty & students.

Video Tape Rental Serv *Serv Provided:* rental. *Rental Eligibility:* staff. *Restrictions:* for indiv, none.

Video Collection Maintained by own production. Use/play ½″, ¼″ reel to reel. *Sources:* commercial distributors.

Cable & CCTV Receive serv of cable TV system.

Greenville

S- BOB JONES UNIVERSITY, Unusual Films, 29614. *Tel:* (803) 242-5100, ext 290. *Film Serv Est:* 1950. *In Charge:* Katherine Stenholm, Dir. *AV Staff:* 15 (6 prof, 4 cl, 5 tech). *Holdings:* feature films 20%, documentaries, religious sermons.

Film Rental Serv *Eligibility:* no restrictions. *Restrictions:* none. Cannot transmit electronically. *Rental Period:* 1 showing.

Film Collection 25t/1186p. *Circ:* 16mm, 20t/892p. *Noncirc:* 16mm, 5t/294c. *Pubns:* catalog, as needed. Publish souvenir booklets ($1).

Other Film Serv Permanent viewing facility available for rent to community.

P- GREENVILLE COUNTY LIBRARY, Art and AV Section, 300 College St, 29601. *Tel:* (803) 242-5000, ext 63. *Film Serv Est:* 1974. *In Charge:* Tom Gilson, Head, Arts and AV Section. *AV Staff:* 4 (1 prof). *Film Sel:* committee preview.

Free-Loan Film Serv *Eligibility:* civic & religious groups, & others, such as local clubs & organizations. *Restrictions:* for inst, only in Greenville County. Cannot use for fund-raising, transmit electronically, borrow for classroom use. May not borrow by mail. *Loan Period:* 1 day or weekend.

Film Collection 225t/p. Approx 70t acquired annually. *Circ:* 16mm, 225t/p; 8mm reel, 240t/310p.

Other Film Serv Obtain film from coop loan system (S.C. State Library). Permanent viewing facility available to community.

Budget & Expenditures Total library budget $354,770 (FY 7/1/75-7/1/76). Total FY film budget $15,000. *Member:* ALA, EFLA.

South Dakota

Mission

C- SINTE GLESKA COLLEGE, Library, Box 189, 57555. *Tel:* (605) 856-4550. *Film Serv Est:* 1972. *In Charge:* William H. McCloskey, Dir of Library Serv. *AV Staff:* 2 (2 prof, 2 tech). *Film Sel:* faculty/staff recommendations. *Holdings:* American Indians, 100%.

Free-Loan Film Serv *Eligibility:* available to anyone for charge of postage. *Restrictions:* for indiv & inst, only in state. Cannot use for fund-raising, borrow for classroom use. Available to researchers/scholars for on-site viewing. May borrow by mail. *Loan Period:* 10 days. *Total Yr Film Loan:* 521. Produce b&w/col slides, cassettes.

Film Collection 12t/13p. *Circ:* 16mm, 12t/13p. *Pubns:* catalog, as needed.

Other Film Serv Rent film from distributors for patrons, obtain film from coop loan system, film reference serv, film fairs/festivals, library film programs. Permanent viewing facility available for rent to community. *Equipment:* lend 16mm sound projector (4), projection tables & stands (1), projection screens (5), wide angle lens & cinescope lens (2).

Other Media Collections *Slides:* single, 6000t. *Member:* AECT.

Video Serv *Est:* 1974. *In Charge:* John R. Stewart, Media Dir. *Video Staff:* 1 f-t. *Video Use:* documentation of community/school events, to increase community's library use, community video access, in-service training, as art form, develop Indian learning materials & preserve tribal heritage. Video serv available on demand. Produce video tapes. Have production studio/space.

Video Equipment/Facilities *In-House Use Only:* portapak (1), ½'' b&w, Sony AV3400; recording deck (2), ½'' b&w, Sony CC2200; playback deck (2), ¾'' col, Sony VO1800; studio camera (1), b&w, Sony 3260. *For Loan:* monitor (3), b&w/col, Sony; additional camera lenses (1); microphones (5); tripods (4). Have permanent viewing installation. *Equipment Loan Period:* flexible. Provide training in use of equipment to students, Head Start aides & educators. Have tape duplication serv.

Video Tape Loan/Rental/Sale Serv *Serv Provided:* free loan, sale. *Loan Eligibility:* staff & students, educational inst, civic & religious groups, & others, such as community tribal Indian groups & neighboring schools. *Restrictions:* for indiv, only in state; for inst, only in state, out-of-state Indian schools. Cannot use for fund-raising, duplicate, air without permission, distort by deletion or editing of material. May borrow by mail. *Loan Period:* flexible.

Video Collection Maintained by own production, exchange/swap. Use/play ½'' reel to reel, ¾'' cassette. *Sources:* community productions, produce own video learning materials. *Tape Sel:* preview. *Special Collections:* in-house training tapes, video as art, own productions. Tapes organized by subject. *Collection, Color:* ½'' reel, 15t/c; ¾'' cassette, 4t/c. *Collection, B&W:* ½'' reel, 160t; ¾'' cassette, 2t/c. *Other Video Serv:* programming, taping of other media, production workshops, produce own broadcasts. *Pubns:* publish descriptive Indian print & nonprint catalog.

Pierre

S- SOUTH DAKOTA STATE LIBRARY, AV Services, 322 S Fort St, 57501. *Tel:* (605) 224-3131. *Film Serv Est:* 1969. *In Charge:* Ann E. Eichinger, Selector. *AV Staff:* 6½ (1 prof, 3½ cl, 2 tech). *Film Sel:* committee preview.

Free-Loan Film Serv *Eligibility:* any resident or library of S. Dak. *Restrictions:* for indiv & inst, only in state. Cannot use for fund-raising, transmit electronically, charge admission or to attract commercial trade. Available to researchers/scholars for on-site viewing. May borrow by mail. *Loan Period:* 1-7 days. *Total Yr Film Loan:* 13,571.

Film Collection 1120t/1240p. Approx 100-300t acquired annually. *Circ:* 16mm, 1120t/1240p. *Pubns:* catalog, as needed; suppl, in yr catalog not published.

Other Film Serv Film reference serv, library film programs. Permanent viewing facility.

Other Media Collections *Audio:* disc, 33⅓ rpm, 932c; tape, cassette, 314c; tape, reel, 293c. *Filmstrips:* silent, 1702c; sound sets, 980c. *Slides:* single, 3089.

Budget & Expenditures Total library budget $157,000 (FY 7/1/74-7/1/75). Total FY film budget $58,669. *Member:* ALA, EFLA, FLIC, S. Dak. Library Assn, Plains Library Assn.

Springfield

C- UNIVERSITY OF SOUTH DAKOTA AT SPRINGFIELD, Carl G. Lawrence Library, 57062. *Tel:* (605) 369-2296. *Film Serv Est:* 1946. *In Charge:* Joel T. Hanson, Dir. *Film Sel:* faculty/staff recommendations.

Free-Loan Film Serv *Eligibility:* staff & students, educational inst, civic groups, indiv with library cards. *Restrictions:* for indiv, interlibrary loan; for inst, none. Available to researchers/scholars for on-site viewing. May borrow by mail. *Loan Period:* 3 days. *Total Yr Film Loan:* 50.

Film Collection 200t/p. Approx 5t acquired annually. *Circ:* 16mm, 100t; 8mm cartridge, 100t.

Other Film Serv Obtain film from coop loan system (University of S. Dak.), obtain film from other libraries. *Equipment:* lend 16mm sound projector (3), 8mm cartridge projector (2), 8mm reel projector (1), S8mm cartridge projector (1), projection screens (3).

Budget & Expenditures Total library budget $58,000 (FY 7/1/74-7/1/75). Total FY film budget $5000.

Vermillion

C- UNIVERSITY OF SOUTH DAKOTA, Educational Media Center, 57069. *Tel:* (605) 677-5411. *Film Serv Est:* 1968. *In Charge:* Una Johnson, Supervisor. *AV Staff:* 4 (2 cl, 2 tech). *Film Sel:* faculty/staff recommendations. *Holdings:* children's films 60%.

Film Rental Serv *Eligibility:* educational org, civic groups. *Restrictions:* only in state. Cannot use for fund-raising, transmit electronically. *Rental Period:* 3 days.

Film Collection 2000t. *Pubns:* catalog, every 3 yrs; suppl, no set policy.

Tennessee

Chattanooga

C- UNIVERSITY OF TENNESSEE, Library at Chattanooga, Oak St, 37401. *Tel:* (615) 755-4705. *Video Serv Est:* 1962. *In Charge:* A. von Slagle, Head, AV Center. *Video Staff:* 1 f-t, 2 p-t, 10 tech. *Video Use:* documentation of community/school events, to increase community's library use, in-service training, practical video/TV training courses, as art form. Video serv available by appointment. Produce video tapes. Have production studio/space.

Video Equipment/Facilities *For Loan:* portapak (2), ½″; recording deck (4), ½″; playback deck (3), ½″, ¾″, 1″; editing deck (1), ½″; studio camera (5), ½″; monitor (6); SEG (1); keyer (1); additional camera lenses (6); lighting; microphones (12); tripods (8); audio tape recorders (53). Have permanent viewing installation. *Equipment Loan Period:* 1 day. Provide training in use of equipment to faculty & students.

Video Collection Maintained by exchange/swap. Use/play ½″, 1″ reel to reel, ¾″ cassette. *Sources:* community productions. *Tape Sel:* gallery previews. *Special Collections:* in-house training tapes. Tapes organized by LC system. *Other Video Serv:* reference serv, production workshops.

Jackson

C- JACKSON STATE COMMUNITY COLLEGE, Library, 38301. *Tel:* (901) 424-3520, ext 260. *Film Serv Est:* 1968. *In Charge:* Van H. Veatch, Library Dir. *AV Staff:* 1 (1 prof). *Film Sel:* faculty/staff recommendations. *Holdings:* black studies 7%, consumer affairs 23%, fine arts 26%, science 17%, social sciences 26%, women 1%.

Free-Loan Film Serv *Eligibility:* staff & students, educational inst, civic groups, & others, such as nurses, law enforcement agencies. *Restrictions:* for indiv & inst, only in Madison County. Available to researchers/scholars for on-site viewing. May not borrow by mail. *Loan Period:* 5 days. *Total Yr Film Loan:* 271.

Film Collection 149t/p. Approx 17t acquired annually. *Circ:* 16mm, 149t/p; S8mm reel, 33t/p.

Other Media Collections *Audio:* disc, 33⅓ rpm, 228t; tape, cassette, 385t; tape, reel, 52t. *Filmstrips:* silent, 162t. *Slides:* single, 3320c.

Budget & Expenditures Total library budget $39,379 (FY 7/1/74-7/1/75). Total FY film budget $6000. *Member:* ALA, Tenn. Library Assn.

Video Serv *Est:* 1969. *In Charge:* J. Charles Cooper, Dir of Instructional Media. *Video Staff:* 1 f-t. *Video Use:* practical video/TV training courses, in-house use by faculty. Video serv available on demand. Produce video tapes. Have production studio/space & separate control room.

Video Equipment/Facilities *In-House Use Only:* portapak (1), b&w, Concord 460; recording deck (6), b&w/col, Sony 3600, 3650, 8660; editing deck (1), b&w, Sony 3650; studio camera (5), 1″ b&w, Sony, GBC, Raytheon; monitor (15), b&w, Sony, Concord; SEG (1), Dynair; keyer (1), Dynair; additional camera lenses; lighting; microphones; tripods; audio tape recorders. Have permanent viewing installation. Provide training in use of equipment to students in TV production courses. Have tape duplication serv.

Video Tape Loan/Rental/Sale Serv *Serv Provided:* free loan. *Loan Eligibility:* staff & students. *Restrictions:* for indiv, only on campus. May not borrow by mail.

Video Collection Maintained by own production. Use/play ½″, 1″ reel to reel. *Sources:* own productions. Tapes organized numerically. *Collection, Color:* ½″ reel, 2t/c. *Collection, B&W:* ½″ reel, 45t/c; 1″ reel, 30t/c. *Other Video Serv:* classes in TV production.

Cable & CCTV Produce programs for cablecasting. Have CCTV in inst, with 10 monitors/receivers. *Programming Sources:* over-the-air commercial & public broadcasting, tapes produced by inst.

Jefferson City

C- CARSON-NEWMAN COLLEGE, Learning Resources Center, 37760. *Tel:* (615) 475-9061, ext 217, 247. *Video Serv Est:* 1972. *In Charge:* Jerome P. Harper, Dir, Comm Laboratory. *Video Staff:* 2 f-t, 6 p-t. *Video Use:* documentation of community/school events, to increase college's library use, practical video/TV training courses, playback only of professionally produced tapes. Video serv available by appointment. Produce video tapes. Have production studio/space & separate control room.

Video Equipment/Facilities *In-House Use Only:* studio camera (1), Sony AVC3260DX; monitor (2), Sony, Concord; SEG (2), Shintron; additional camera lenses. *For Loan:* portapak (5), ½″ b&w, Sony 3400; recording deck (3), ½″, ¾″ col, Sony 3650, VO1600, JVC CR6100U; microphones (5); tripods (2); audio tape recorders (10). Have permanent viewing installation. *Equipment Loan Period:* no set policy. Provide training in use of equipment to faculty & students. Have tape duplication serv.

Video Tape Loan/Rental/Sale Serv *Serv Provided:* swap with other inst. *Loan Eligibility:* staff & students. *Restrictions:* for indiv, none.

Video Collection Maintained by purchase, rental, own production, exchange/swap. Use/play ½″ reel to reel, ¾″ cassette. *Sources:* community productions, exchange (other libraries). *Member:* Mid-Appalachia College Council. *Tape Sel:* preview, faculty/staff recommendations, published reviews, catalogs. *Special Collections:* films in video format. Tapes organized by accession number, cross-referenced by subject & title.

Cable & CCTV Will receive serv of cable TV system. Have CCTV in inst, with 6 monitors. *Programming Sources:* over-the-air commercial & public broadcasting, tapes produced by inst, tapes produced professionally, tapes produced by community groups & indiv.

Johnson City

S- BROADSIDE VIDEO, SAVES Archives, Elm & Millard Sts, 37601. *Tel:* (615) 926-8191. *Video Serv Est:* 1973. *In Charge:* Dr. Richard Blaustein, Project Dir. *Video Staff:* 1 f-t, 3 p-t, 1 tech. *Video Use:* documentation of community events, practical video/TV training courses, documentation of regional folk culture. Video serv available by appointment. Produce video tapes. Have production studio/space & separate control room.

Video Equipment/Facilities *In-House Use Only:* portapak (9), ½″ b&w, Sony; recording deck (3), ½″ b&w, Sony; studio camera (2), b&w, Sony. Have portable viewing installation. Provide training in use of equipment to students & some civic club members. Have tape duplication serv.

Video Tape Loan/Rental/Sale Serv *Serv Provided:* swap with other inst, sale. *Loan Eligibility:* educational inst. May not borrow by mail.

Video Collection Maintained by own production, exchange/swap. Use/play ½″ reel to reel, ¾″ cassette. *Sources:* exchange (other video centers, folklorists, anthropologists). *Member:* Southern Video Network. *Tape Sel:* preview. Tapes organized by Human Relations Area Files (anthropological indexing system). *Collection, B&W:* ½″ reel, 25t/25c. *Other Video Serv:* programming, production workshops. *Pubns:* catalog. Publish materials on video.

Cable & CCTV Receive serv of cable TV system. Produce programs for cablecasting. Inform public about cable system serv & facilities.

C- EAST TENNESSEE STATE UNIVERSITY, Instructional Materials Center, Room 209, Education Building, 37601. *Tel:* (615) 929-4326. *Film Serv Est:* 1960. *In Charge:* James K. Vannoy, Dir of Instructional Materials Center. *AV Staff:* 12 (1 cl, 10 tech). *Film Sel:* committee preview, faculty/staff recommendations, chief film librarian's decision.
    Film Rental Serv *Eligibility:* educational org, civic groups. *Restrictions:* none. *Rental Period:* 3 days. *Total Yr Film Booking:* 50.
    Film Collection 650t/p. Approx 25t acquired annually. *Circ:* 16mm, 650t/p; 8mm cartridge, 45t/p; S8mm cartridge, 45t/p. *Pubns:* catalog, every 2 yrs; suppl, no set policy.
    Other Film Serv Rent film from distributors for patrons. Permanent viewing facility.
    Other Media Collections *Audio:* disc, total, 1600t/c; tape, cassette, 1300t/c; tape, reel, 277t/c. *Filmstrips:* total, 2200t/c. *Slides:* single, 6591t/c.
    Budget & Expenditures Total library budget $26,150 (FY 7/1/74-7/1/75). Total FY film budget, $15,000.

P- MAYNE WILLIAMS PUBLIC LIBRARY, 205 S Roan St, 37601. *Tel:* (615) 928-3532. *Film Serv Est:* 1974. *In Charge:* Robert F. Plotzke, Dir of Library Servs. *AV Staff:* 2 (1 prof, 1 cl). *Film Sel:* chief film librarian's decision, published reviews, patrons' requests. *Holdings:* children's films 39%.
    Free-Loan Film Serv *Eligibility:* educational inst, civic & religious groups, indiv with library cards, prof groups. *Restrictions:* for indiv & inst, only in Washington County. Available to researchers/scholars for on-site viewing. May not borrow by mail. *Loan Period:* 3 days. *Total Yr Film Loan:* 1347.
    Film Rental Serv *Eligibility:* educational org, civic groups. *Restrictions:* only in Washington County. Cannot use for fundraising, transmit electronically. *Rental Period:* 1 day.
    Film Collection 56t/p. Approx 20t acquired annually. *Circ:* S8mm reel, 56t/p.
    Other Film Serv Obtain film from coop loan system (Area Resource Center). *Equipment:* lend 16mm sound projector (1), 8mm reel projector (1), S8mm reel projector (1), projection screens (1), filmstrip/slide projector (1), lend cassette tape recorders (2).
    Other Media Collections *Audio:* disc, 33⅓ rpm, 170t/c; tape, cassette, 15t/c. *Filmstrips:* sound sets, 34t/c.
    Budget & Expenditures Total library budget $12,300 (FY 7/1/74-7/1/75). Total FY film budget $300. *Member:* ALA, Tenn. Library Assn., Southeastern Library Assn.

Kingsport

P- KINGSPORT PUBLIC LIBRARY, Broad & New Sts, 37660. *Tel:* (615) 245-3141. *In Charge:* June Presley, Film Librarian. *Film Sel:* staff recommendations, chief film librarian's decision, published reviews.
    Free-Loan Film Serv *Eligibility:* indiv with library cards. *Restrictions:* for indiv, none. Cannot use for fund-raising. Available to researchers/scholars for on-site viewing. May not borrow by mail. *Loan Period:* 1 day. *Total Yr Film Loan:* 1125.
    Film Collection 180t/p. Approx 10t acquired annually. *Circ:* 16mm, 181t/p; 8mm cartridge, 195t/p; S8mm cartridge, 30t/p. *Pubns:* catalog, as needed; suppl, no set policy.
    Other Film Serv Obtain film from coop loan system (Tenn. Film Circuit), obtain film from other libraries, library film programs. Permanent viewing facility.
    Other Media Collections *Audio:* disc, 33⅓ rpm, 1605t/c; tape, cassette, 44t. *Filmstrips:* sound, 130t/c; silent, 30t; sound sets, 199t.
    Budget & Expenditures Total library budget $35,500 (FY 7/1/74-7/1/75). Total FY film budget $3500. *Member:* ALA, Tenn. Library Assn.

Knoxville

C- KNOXVILLE COLLEGE, Alumni Library, 901 College St, 37921. *Tel:* (615) 546-0751, ext 281, 285. *Video Serv Est:*

1967. *In Charge:* Faye D. Kuehn, Media Specialist. *Video Staff:* 2 f-t. *Video Use:* documentation of community/school events, in-service training, as art form. Video serv available by appointment. Produce video tapes. Have production studio/space & separate control room.
    Video Equipment/Facilities *In-House Use Only:* portapak (1), b&w; recording deck (4), b&w/col, Sony; playback deck (4), b&w/col, Sony; studio camera (4), b&w, Sony, JVC; monitor (17), b&w/col, Setchell, Sony; SEG (1); lighting (8); tripods (3); audio tape recorders (33). *For Loan:* microphones (10). Have permanent & portable viewing installations. *Equipment Loan Period:* no set policy. Provide training in use of equipment to students, workers & coaches. Have tape duplication serv.
    Cable & CCTV Will receive serv of cable TV system. Have CCTV in inst, with 7 monitors. *Programming Sources:* over-the-air commercial & public broadcasting, tapes produced by inst, instructor-produced tapes for classroom information; student-produced tapes.

S- STUDENTS' MUSEUM, INC., Library, Box 6108, 37914. *Tel:* (615) 637-1121. *Film Serv Est:* 1970. *In Charge:* Edna Clark, Dir. *AV Staff:* 1 (1 prof). *Holdings:* children's films 90%, science 10%.
    Film Collection 44t/p. Approx 10t acquired annually.
    Other Media Collections *Audio:* disc, 33⅓ rpm, 10t; tape, cassette, 20t; tape, cartridge, 15t. *Slides:* single, 5000t.
    Budget & Expenditures Total library budget $200 (FY 7/1/74-7/1/75). Total FY film budget $100.
    Video Serv *Video Staff:* 3 f-t, 4 tech. *Video Use:* documentation of community events, community video access, practical video/TV training courses, as art form, to tape specialists & make available to groups. Video serv available by appointment. Produce video tapes. Have production studio/space.
    Video Equipment/Facilities *In-House Use Only:* studio camera (2), b&w, Panasonic; monitor (4), b&w, Panasonic; SEG (1), Panasonic; lighting (3); microphones (3); tripods (2); audio tape recorders (1). Have permanent viewing installation. Provide training in use of equipment to children.
    Video Collection Maintained by own production. Use/play ½″ reel to reel. *Sources:* commercial distributors. *Special Collections:* in-house training tapes, video as art. Tapes organized by subject. *Collection, B&W:* ½″ reel, 44t/c. Publish materials on video.
    Cable & CCTV Will receive serv of cable TV system. Have CCTV in inst, with 3 monitors. *Programming Sources:* tapes produced by inst.

C- THE UNIVERSITY OF TENNESSEE, Teaching Materials Center, R61 Communications & Ext Bldg, 37916. *Tel:* (615) 974-3236. *Film Serv Est:* 1939. *In Charge:* John T. Benton, Dir. *AV Staff:* 6 (1 prof, 4 cl, 1 tech). *Film Sel:* committee preview, faculty/staff recommendations. *Holdings:* black studies, business & management, career education, social sciences, teacher education.
    Free-Loan Film Serv *Eligibility:* staff & students. *Loan Period:* 2 days. *Total Yr Film Loan:* 8000.
    Film Rental Serv *Eligibility:* no restrictions. *Restrictions:* only in U.S. & territories. Cannot transmit electronically. *Rental Period:* 2 days.
    Film Collection 4500t/5000p. Approx 50-60t acquired annually. *Pubns:* catalog, every 3 yrs; suppl, no set policy.
    Other Film Serv Rent film from distributors for patrons, obtain film from other libraries, film reference serv. Permanent viewing facility. *Equipment:* lend 16mm sound projector, 8mm reel projector, S8mm reel projector, projection tables & stands, projection screens, slide, overhead & opaque projectors.
    Budget & Expenditures Total library budget $57,000 (FY 7/1/74-7/1/75). Total FY film budget $16,000. *Member:* AECT, CUFC.

Madisonville

C- HIWASSEE COLLEGE, Hardwick/Johnston Memorial Library, 37354. *Tel:* (615) 442-3343. *Video Serv Est:* 1968. *In*

Madisonville (cont'd)

Charge: Ken Yamada, Library Dir. *Video Staff:* 4 f-t, 3 p-t. *Video Use:* documentation of community/school events, to increase community's library use, ·community video access, in-service training, practical video/TV training courses, playback only of professionally produced tapes, instructional aid, entertainment, communication. Video serv available on demand & by appointment. Produce video tapes. Have production studio/space & separate control room.

Video Equipment/Facilities *In-House Use Only:* portapak (1), ½″ b&w, Sony; recording deck (1), ½″ b&w, Sony; editing deck (2), b&w/col, Sony; studio camera (3), b&w, Sony; monitor (15), b&w/col, Sony; SEG (1), Sony; additional camera lenses (2); microphones (8); tripods (3); audio tape recorders (3). Have permanent viewing installation. Provide training in use of equipment to library staff. Have tape duplication serv.

Video Collection Maintained by own production. Use/play ½″ reel to reel. *Sources:* local production. *Tape Sel:* faculty/staff recommendations. *Special Collections:* in-house training tapes, video as art. Tapes organized by Dewey Decimal. *Collection, B&W, Color:* ½″ reel, 400t/300c. *Other Video Serv:* programming, reference serv, taping of other media, production workshops.

Cable & CCTV Operates own cable TV system throughout campus including dormitories. Produce programs for cablecasting. Inform public about cable system serv & facilities. Serve as production facility for others. Run cable programs for special audiences. Have CCTV in inst, with 60 monitors. *Programming Sources:* over-the-air commercial & public broadcasting, tapes produced by inst, by community groups & indiv.

Memphis

P- MEMPHIS AND SHELBY COUNTY PUBLIC LIBRARY & INFORMATION CENTER, Films & Community TV Dept, 1850 Peabody Ave, 38104. *Tel:* (901) 528-2988. *Film Serv Est:* 1964. *In Charge:* Mary Helen Karpinski, Head, Films/Community TV Dept. *AV Staff:* 9 (2 prof, 1 cl, 6 tech). *Film Sel:* committee preview. *Holdings:* black studies, children's films, experimental films, feature films, fine arts.

Film Rental Serv *Eligibility:* educational org, civic groups, patrons/public. *Restrictions:* only in state. Cannot use for fundraising, transmit electronically. Must give library credit in all publicity. *Rental Period:* 2 days. *Total Yr Film Booking:* 16,135. Produce 35mm slides.

Film Collection 1102t/1391p. Approx 100t acquired annually. *Circ:* 16mm, 1220t/1572p; 8mm reel, 72t/99p. *Noncirc:* 16mm, 3t/p. *Pubns:* catalog, every 3 yrs ($1.75); suppl, no set policy ($.50).

Other Film Serv Obtain film from coop loan system (Tenn. Film Circuit), library film programs. Permanent viewing facility available to community.

Other Media Collections *Slides:* single, 4968c.

Budget & Expenditures Total library budget $715,733 (FY 7/1/74-7/1/75). Total FY film budget $38,500. *Member:* ALA, EFLA, FLIC, Mid-South AV Assn.

Video Serv *Est:* 1974. *Video Staff:* 9 f-t, 3 p-t, 6 tech. *Video Use:* documentation of community/school events, to increase community's library use, community video access, in-service training, practical video/TV training courses. Video serv available by appointment. Produce video tapes. Have production studio/space & separate control room.

Video Equipment/Facilities *In-House Use Only:* portapak (3), ½″ b&w/col, Sony AV3400, AV8400; recording deck (2), ½″, ¾″ col, Sony AV8650; playback deck (2), ½″, ¾″ b&w/col; editing deck (1), ½″ col, Sony AV8650; studio camera (5), b&w/col, Sony AVC3260, DXC 5000BP; monitor (9), b&w/col, RCA, Sony; SEG (1), Sony; keyer (1), Sony; additional camera lenses (1); lighting (18); microphones (6); tripods (6); audio tape recorders (8), filmchain (1); antenna distribution (1). *For Loan:* monitor (2), b&w/col, RCA, Sony. Have permanent viewing installation. *Equipment Loan Period:* no set policy. Provide training in use of equipment to faculty & students.

Video Tape Loan/Rental/Sale Serv *Serv Provided:* rental, sale. *Loan/Rental Eligibility:* civic groups, any community group with 10 people in audience. Cannot use for fundraising, duplicate, air without permission. May not borrow by mail. *Loan Period:* 2 days. *Total Yr Tape Loan:* 2.

Video Collection Maintained by own production. Tapes organized by title. *Other Video Serv:* production workshops.

Cable & CCTV Have CCTV in inst. *Programming Sources:* tapes produced by inst & by community groups & indiv.

C- MEMPHIS STATE UNIVERSITY, Learning Media Center, 38152. *Tel:* (901) 454-2098. *Film Serv Est:* 1972. *In Charge:* Earl Potter, Head. *AV Staff:* 4 (1 prof, 2 cl, 1 tech). *Film Sel:* faculty/staff recommendations.

Free-Loan Film Serv *Eligibility:* staff & students. *Restrictions:* for indiv, none. May only be used for university instruction. May not borrow by mail. *Loan Period:* 7 days. *Total Yr Film Loan:* 2000. Produce overhead transparencies, slides, cassettes.

Film Collection 600t/605p. Approx 25-50t acquired annually. *Circ:* 16mm, 400t; S8mm reel, 168t. *Pubns:* catalog.

Other Film Serv Rent film from distributors for patrons, obtain film from other libraries, film reference serv, film fairs/festivals, on preview. Permanent viewing facility. *Equipment:* lend 16mm sound projector (18), S8mm cartridge projector (8), S8mm reel projector (1), projection tables & stands (10), projection screens (5), variety of projectors & recorders.

Other Media Collections *Audio:* disc, 33⅓ rpm, 70t; tape, cassette, 300t. *Filmstrips:* silent, 30t; sound sets, 200t. *Slides:* sets, 57t.

Budget & Expenditures No separate budget.

Video Serv *Est:* 1975. *Video Staff:* 4 f-t, 6 p-t, 1 tech. *Video Use:* documentation of community/school events, in-service training, practical video/TV training courses, instructional support. Video serv available on demand & by appointment. Produce video tapes. Have production studio/space & separate control room.

Video Equipment/Facilities *For Loan:* portapak (5), b&w/col, Sony 3400; recording deck (3), b&w/col, Sony 3650; playback deck (2), b&w, Sony; editing deck (2), b&w/col, Sony; monitor (5), b&w/col, Sony; lighting (3); microphones (6); tripods (2); audio tape recorders (25). Have permanent viewing installation. *Equipment Loan Period:* no set policy. Provide training in use of equipment to anyone authorized to borrow. Have tape duplication serv.

Video Tape Loan/Rental/Sale Serv *Serv Provided:* free loan. *Loan Eligibility:* staff & students. *Restrictions:* for indiv, students must have approval by instructors. Cannot use for fund-raising, air without permission. May not borrow by mail. *Loan Period:* flexible.

Video Collection Maintained by purchase, rental, own production. Use/play ½″ reel to reel, ¾″ cassette. *Sources:* commercial distributors. *Tape Sel:* preview, faculty/staff recommendations. Tapes organized by subject & LC system. *Other Video Serv:* programming, reference serv, production workshops.

S- REAL TO REEL PRODUCTIONS, 2217 Sterick Bldg, 38103. *Tel:* (901) 525-3281. *Video Serv Est:* 1975. *In Charge:* Ann H. Rickey, Pres. *Video Staff:* 1 f-t, 4 tech. *Video Use:* community video access, as art form, commercial. Video serv available by appointment. Produce video tapes. Have production studio/space & separate control room.

Video Equipment/Facilities *In-House Use Only:* portapak (2), ½″ b&w/col, Sony DXC1600, Rover II; recording deck (2), 1½″ b&w/col, Sony 3600, JVC; editing deck (1), ½″ col, Sony 8650; studio camera (1), b&w, Sony 3210; monitor (2), b&w/col, JVC; additional camera lenses (3); microphones (3); tripods (3); audio tape recorders (2). *For Loan:* portapak (1), ½″ b&w, Sony DXC1600. Have permanent viewing installation. *Equipment Loan Period:* 1 day or weekend. Provide training in use of equipment to those borrowing.

Video Tape Loan/Rental/Sale Serv *Serv Provided:* sale, loan (planned).

Video Collection Maintained by own production. Use/play ½" reel to reel, ¾" cassette. *Sources:* own production. *Collection, Color:* ½" reel, 2t/c; ¾" cassette, 3t/c. *Collection, B&W:* ½" reel, 12t. *Other Video Serv:* programming, compiling library of books & periodicals on video.
    Cable & CCTV Will receive serv of cable TV system.

C- SHELBY STATE COMMUNITY COLLEGE, Library Services/Learning Resource Center, Box 4568, 38104. *Tel:* (901) 528-6743. *Film Serv Est:* 1972. *In Charge:* Joseph F. Lindenfeld, Dir. *Film Sel:* faculty/staff recommendations, chief film librarian's decision, published reviews.
    Free-Loan Film Serv *Eligibility:* staff & students, educational inst, indiv with library cards. *Restrictions:* for indiv & inst, only in city. Cannot transmit electronically. Available to researchers/scholars for on-site viewing. May not borrow by mail. *Loan Period:* 3 days. *Total Yr Film Loan:* 10.
    Film Collection 85t/p. Approx 10-15t acquired annually. *Circ:* 16mm, 30t/p; 8mm reel, 15t/p; 8mm cartridge, 40t/p.
    Other Film Serv Obtain film from other libraries (Memphis Public Library). Permanent viewing facility.
    Other Media Collections *Audio:* tape, cassette, 600t/800c. *Slides:* sets, 450t/500c.
    Budget & Expenditures Total library budget $125,000 (FY 7/1/74-7/1/75). Total FY film budget $3000. *Member:* AECT, ALA, Tenn. Library Assn.
    Video Serv *Video Use:* to increase community's library use. Video serv available on demand. Produce video tapes.
    Video Equipment/Facilities *In-House Use Only:* portapak (1), b&w, Sony; microphones (3); audio tape recorders (25). Have portable viewing installation. Provide training in use of equipment to faculty & staff.
    Video Tape Loan/Rental/Sale Serv *Serv Provided:* free loan. *Loan Eligibility:* staff & students, educational inst. *Restrictions:* for indiv & inst, only in city. Cannot duplicate, air without permission. May not borrow by mail.
    Video Collection Maintained by purchase, own production. Use/play ½" cartridge. *Sources:* commercial distributors. *Tape Sel:* preview, faculty/staff recommendations, published reviews. Tapes organized by Dewey Decimal. *Collection, Color:* ½" cartridge, 40t/60c. *Other Video Serv:* taping of other media.

Milligan College

C- MILLIGAN COLLEGE, Curriculum Center, Box M, 37643. *Tel:* (615) 929-0116, ext 54. *Film Serv Est:* 1966. *In Charge:* Paul Clark, Dir of Teacher Educ. *Film Sel:* faculty/staff recommendations. *Holdings:* fine arts 25%, social sciences 25%, teacher education 50%.
    Free-Loan Film Serv *Eligibility:* staff & students, educational inst, religious groups. *Restrictions:* for indiv, only in college.
    Film Collection 87t. *Circ:* 16mm, 87t.
    Other Film Serv Permanent viewing facility. *Equipment:* lend/rent 16mm sound projector (5), lend 8mm cartridge projector (1), projection screens (3).
    Other Media Collections *Audio:* disc, 33⅓ rpm, 292c; tape, cassette, 27c. *Filmstrips:* sound, 85c; silent, 255c; sound sets, 19c; silent sets, 5c. *Slides:* sets, 3c.
    Budget & Expenditures No separate budget.
    Video Serv *Video Use:* documentation of community/school events, in-service training. Produce video tapes.
    Video Equipment/Facilities *In-House Use Only:* portapak (1), b&w, Sony; playback & editing deck (4); studio camera (1); monitor (4), b&w, Sony, Admiral, Philco; additional camera lenses (3); lighting (1); microphones (1); tripods (3); audio tape recorders (8). Have portable viewing installation.
    Video Tape Loan/Rental/Sale Serv *Serv Provided:* free loan. *Loan Eligibility:* staff & students, educational inst. *Restrictions:* for indiv, on campus. May not borrow by mail.
    Cable & CCTV Receive serv of cable TV system. Have CCTV in inst. *Programming Sources:* tapes produced by inst.

Nashville

C- NASHVILLE STATE TECHNICAL INSTITUTE, Educational Resource Center, 120 White Bridge Rd, 37209. *Tel:* (615) 741-1229. *Film Serv Est:* 1970. *In Charge:* Duane Muir, AV Specialist. *AV Staff:* 2 (1 prof, 1 tech). *Film Sel:* faculty/staff recommendations.
    Free-Loan Film Serv *Eligibility:* educational inst, prof groups. *Restrictions:* for inst, none. *Loan Period:* 1 day. *Total Yr Film Loan:* 12. Produce slides.
    Film Collection 125t/p. Approx 25t acquired annually. *Circ:* 16mm, 125t/p. Publish materials pertaining to collection.
    Other Film Serv Permanent viewing facility available to community.
    Budget & Expenditures Total library budget $35,000 (FY 7/1/75-7/1/76). No separate AV budget. *Member:* ALA, Tenn. Library Assn.
    Video Serv *Video Staff:* 2 f-t, 1 tech. *Video Use:* documentation of community/school events, in-service training, playback only of professionally produced tapes. Video serv available on demand. Produce video tapes.
    Video Equipment/Facilities *In-House Use Only:* recording deck (2), ¾" col, Sony; playback deck (4), ¾" col, Sony. Provide training in use of equipment to faculty & students.
    Video Tape Loan/Rental/Sale Serv *Serv Provided:* free loan, swap with other inst. *Loan Eligibility:* staff & students, educational inst, civic & religious groups. *Restrictions:* for indiv & inst, none. May borrow by mail. *Loan Period:* 7 days. *Total Yr Tape Loan:* 4.
    Video Collection Maintained by purchase, own production. Use/play ¾" cassette. *Sources:* commercial distributors. *Tape Sel:* preview, faculty/staff recommendations. *Special Collections:* to support curriculum. Tapes organized by subject & LC system. *Collection, Color:* ¾" cassette, 120t/c. *Collection, B&W:* ¾" cassette, 116t.

P- PUBLIC LIBRARY OF NASHVILLE AND DAVIDSON COUNTY, 8th Ave North and Union St, 37203. *Tel:* (615) 244-4700. *In Charge:* H. E. Bivins, Multi-Media Coordinator. *AV Staff:* 5 (2 prof, 1 cl, 2 tech). *Film Sel:* chief film librarian's decision. *Holdings:* children's films 40%.
    Free-Loan Film Serv *Eligibility:* indiv with library cards. *Restrictions:* for indiv, only in city, middle Tenn. libraries in other counties; for inst, only in city. Cannot use for fund-raising, transmit electronically. Available to researchers/scholars for on-site viewing. May not borrow by mail. *Loan Period:* 1 day.
    Film Collection 900t/915p. Approx 40t acquired annually. *Circ:* 16mm, 900t/915p. *Pubns:* catalog, every 2 yrs.
    Other Film Serv Obtain film from coop loan system (Middle Tenn. Film Circuit), library film programs. Permanent viewing facility available to community.
    Other Media Collections *Audio:* disc, 33⅓ rpm, 23,000c; tape, cassette, 50c. *Filmstrips:* silent, 40c; sound sets, 10c. *Slides:* single, 200c. *Member:* ALA, EFLA, Tenn. Library Assn.
    Video Serv *Est:* 1975. *Video Staff:* 3 f-t. *Video Use:* documentation of community events, to increase community's library use, playback only of professionally produced tapes. Video serv available by appointment. Produce video tapes. Have production studio/space.
    Video Equipment/Facilities *In-House Use Only:* portapak (1), col, Sony; recording deck (2), col, Sony, JVC; playback deck (1), col, Sony; editing deck (1), col, JVC; monitor (3), col, Sony; audio tape recorders (2). Have portable viewing installation.
    Video Tape Loan/Rental/Sale Serv *Serv Provided:* free loan. *Loan Eligibility:* org members. *Restrictions:* for indiv, only in city. Cannot use for fund-raising, duplicate, air without permission. May not borrow by mail.
    Video Collection Maintained by purchase, own production. Use/play ¾" cassette. *Sources:* commercial distributors. *Tape Sel:* preview, published reviews, catalogs. Tapes organized by subject. *Collection, Color:* ¾" cassette, 35t.

C- TREVECCA NAZARENE COLLEGE, 333 Murfreesboro Rd, 37210. *Tel:* (615) 244-6000, ext 221. *Film Serv Est:* 1968. *In*

Nashville (cont'd)

> *Charge:* Carl Eby, AV Supervisor. *AV Staff:* 3 (1 prof). *Film Sel:* faculty/staff recommendations.
>
> **Free-Loan Film Serv** *Eligibility:* staff & students.
> **Film Collection** 5-10t. *Circ:* 16mm, 5-10p.
> **Other Film Serv** Rent film from distributors for patrons, obtain film from other libraries, film reference serv. Permanent viewing facility. *Equipment:* lend 16mm sound projector (7), 8mm cartridge projector (1), S8mm cartridge projector (1), projection tables & stands (15), projection screens (30).
> **Other Media Collections** *Audio:* disc, 33⅓ rpm, 1000c; tape, cassette, 50c; tape, reel, 50c. *Filmstrips:* silent, 600c; sound sets, 60c. *Slides:* sets, 20c.
> **Budget & Expenditures** Total library budget $4100 (FY 7/1/74-7/1/75). No separate AV budget. *Member:* AECT, ALA.
> **Video Serv** *Est:* 1970. *Video Staff:* 1 f-t, 4 p-t. *Video Use:* documentation of community/school events, in-service training, playback only of professionally produced tapes, teacher & ministerial training. Video serv available on demand & by appointment. Produce video tapes. Have production studio/ space.
> **Video Equipment/Facilities** *In-House Use Only:* recording deck (2); playback deck (2); monitor (2); lighting (2); microphones (5); tripods (2); audio tape recorders (5). Have portable viewing installation. Provide training in use of equipment to faculty & students.
> **Video Tape Loan/Rental/Sale Serv** *Serv Provided:* free loan. *Loan Eligibility:* org members, staff & students. *Restrictions:* for indiv, only on campus. May not borrow by mail.
> **Video Collection** Maintained by purchase, rental, own production. Use/play ½" reel to reel, ¾" cassette. *Tape Sel:* faculty/staff recommendations. Tapes organized by subject. *Collection, Color:* ¾" cassette, 5-10t.

Tullahoma

C- MOTLOW STATE COMMUNITY COLLEGE, Library-Learning Resources Center, 37388. *Tel:* (615) 455-8511, ext 226. *Film Serv Est:* 1970. *In Charge:* Harlan Stockton, Media Specialist. *AV Staff:* 2 (1 prof, 1 cl). *Film Sel:* faculty/staff recommendations.

> **Free-Loan Film Serv** *Eligibility:* org members. Cannot use for fund-raising, transmit electronically. Available to researchers/scholars for on-site viewing. May not borrow by mail. Produce slides, slide sets.
> **Film Collection** *Circ:* 16mm, 38t/p; 8mm reel, 28t/p; S8mm reel, 4t/p.
> **Other Film Serv** Obtain film from coop loan system (College Media Service), obtain film from other libraries. *Equipment:* lend 16mm sound projector (4), 8mm cartridge projector (3), projection tables & stands (8), projection screens (3).
> **Other Media Collections** *Audio:* disc, 33⅓rpm, 493t/c; tape, cassette, 412t/c; tape, reel, 3t/c. *Filmstrips:* sound, 177t; silent, 104t; sound sets, 142t; silent sets, 2t. *Slides:* sets, 54t.
> **Budget & Expenditures** Total library budget $48,838 (FY 7/1/74-7/1/75). No separate AV budget. *Member:* AECT.
> **Video Serv** *Video Use:* documentation of community/ school events, playback only of professionally produced tapes. Video serv available on demand. Produce video tapes.
> **Video Equipment/Facilities** *In-House Use Only:* portapak (1), col, Sony AV1800; recording deck (1), ½" col, Panasonic NV3130; studio camera (1), b&w, Panasonic; tripods (2). Provide training in use of equipment to staff.
> **Video Collection** Maintained by purchase, rental, own producton. Use/play ½" reel to reel, ¾" cassette. *Sources:* commercial distributors. *Tape Sel:* preview, faculty/staff recommendations, catalogs. Tapes organized by LC system. *Pubns:* catalog.

Texas

Abilene

P- ABILENE PUBLIC LIBRARY, AV Dept., 202 Cedar, 79601.
Tel: (915) 677-2474. *Film Serv Est:* 1958. *In Charge:* Sharon
Kay, Supervisor. *AV Staff:* 2 (2 prof). *Film Sel:* committee
preview, chief film librarian's decision. *Holdings:* animated films 20%, children's films 30%, dance 1%, experimental films 10%, feature films 2%, fine arts 20%, social
sciences 20%.
    Free-Loan Film Serv *Eligibility:* org members. *Restric-
tions:* for indiv, only MRC area libraries. Cannot use for fund-
raising, transmit electronically, borrow for classroom use.
Available to researchers/scholars for on-site viewing. May
borrow by mail. *Loan Period:* 1 day. *Total Yr Film Loan:* 2685.
    Film Collection 350t/p. Approx 12t acquired annually.
Circ: 16mm, 350t/p. *Pubns:* catalog, every 3 yr.
    Other Film Serv Obtain film from coop loan system (West
Texas Library Film Circuit). Permanent viewing facility available free to community.
    Other Media Collections *Audio:* disc, 33⅓ rpm, 12,000t.
    Budget & Expenditures Total library budget $61,779.55
(FY 10/1/74-10/1/75). No separate AV budget.

Alvin

C- ALVIN COMMUNITY COLLEGE, 3110 Mustang Rd, 77511.
Tel: (713) 331-6111, ext 213. *Video Serv Est:* 1972. *In
Charge:* J. A. Gebert, Media Dir. *Video Staff:* ½ p-t. *Video
Use:* documentation of community/school events. Video
serv available on demand. Produce video tapes.
    Video Equipment/Facilities *In-House Use Only:* porta-
pak (1), ½" b&w, Sony; recording deck (2), ¾" col, Wollensak,
JVC; playback deck (2), ¾" col, Wollensak, JVC; audio tape
recorders (20). Have portable viewing installation. *Equipment
Loa Period:* no set policy. Provide training in use of equipment
to faculty & students.
    Video Tape Loan/Rental/Sale Serv *Loan Eligibility:*
org members, staff & students, civic groups, indiv with library
cards.
    Video Collection Maintained by own production. Use/
play ¾" cassette. *Sources:* community productions. *Collection,
Color:* ¾" cassette, 75t. *Collection, B&W:* ¾" cassette, 25t.

Arlington

C- UNIVERSITY OF TEXAS AT ARLINGTON, Film Library,
AV Servs, 76019. *Tel:* (817) 273-3201. *Film Serv Est:* 1969.
In Charge: Elouise Knight, Head, AV Utilization Serv. *AV
Staff:* 5 (2 prof, 2 cl, 1 tech). *Film Sel:* faculty/staff recommendations.
    Film Rental Serv *Eligibility:* no restrictions. *Restrictions:*
only in U.S. Cannot transmit electronically. *Rental Period:* 1
day. *Total Yr Film Booking:* 2150.
    Film Collection 1374t/435p. *Circ:* 16mm, 1240t/410p; 8mm
reel, 408t; S8mm reel, 138t. *Noncirc:* 16mm, 134t/25p. *Pubns:*
catalog, as needed ($3.00); suppl, no set policy.
    Other Film Serv Rent film from distributors for faculty,
film reference serv. Permanent viewing facility. *Equipment:*
own S8mm camera, 16mm camera, 16mm sound projector, 8mm
cartridge projector, 8mm reel projector, S8mm cartridge projector, S8mm reel projector, projection tables & stands, projection
screens; lend only to our own campus.
    Other Media Collections *Audio:* disc, 33⅓ rpm, 993t; tape,
reel, 7892t. *Filmstrips:* silent, 962t; sound sets, 25t. *Slides:* single,
12,157t.
    Budget & Expenditures Total library budget $282,046. No
separate AV budget.

Austin

C- THE UNIVERSITY OF TEXAS AT AUSTIN, Visual Instruction Bureau Film Library, Drawer W, University
Station, 78712. *Tel:* (512) 471-3573. *Film Serv Est:* 1910. *In
Charge:* Jane Webb, Coord, Film Serv. *AV Staff:* 5 (1 prof, 3
cl, 2 tech). *Film Sel:* faculty/staff recommendations, chief
film librarian's decision. *Holdings:* agriculture, animated
films, black studies, career education, children's films,
dance, engineering, fine arts, industrial arts, medicine,
science, social sciences, teacher education, women.
    Film Rental Serv *Eligibility:* no restrictions. *Restrictions:*
none. Cannot transmit electronically. *Rental Period:* 5 days.
Total Yr Film Booking: 5,000.
    Film Collection 1000t/1500p. Approx 50t acquired annu-
ally. *Circ:* 16mm, 1000t/1500p. *Noncirc:* 16mm, 1800t/2300p.
Pubns: catalog, every 4 yr ($2.50); suppl, no set policy. Pub-
lish listings by subject, new acquisitions listings.
    Other Film Serv Rent film from distributors for patrons,
obtain film from coop loan system, obtain film from other
libraries, film reference serv. Permanent viewing facility available free to community. *Equipment:* rent S8mm camera (2),
16mm camera, 16mm sound projector (20), 8mm reel projector,
projection tables & stands (17), projection screens (20), overhead
opaque carousels, mikes, filmstrip projectors.
    Budget & Expenditures Total FY film budget $10,000.
Member: AECT, CUFC, EFLA.

Baytown

P- STERLING MUNICIPAL LIBRARY, Public Library Ave,
77520. *Tel:* (713) 427-7331. *Film Serv Est:* 1963. *In Charge:*
Mrs. Moore. *AV Staff:* 1 (½ prof, ¼ cl, ¼ tech). *Film Sel:*
committee preview, staff recommendations. *Holdings:* children's films 30%.
    Free-Loan Film Serv *Eligibility:* staff & students, educa-
tional inst, civic & religious groups, indiv with library cards.
Restrictions: for indiv, interlibrary loan; for inst, none. Cannot
use for fund-raising. Available to researchers/scholars for on-
site viewing. May borrow by mail. *Loan Period:* 1 day. *Total Yr
Film Loan:* 808.
    Film Collection 203t/p. Approx 15t acquired annually.
Circ: 16mm, 82t/p; 8mm reel, 121t/p. *Pubns:* catalog, every 2 yr;
suppl, no set policy. Publish materials pertaining to collection.
    Other Film Serv Obtain film from coop loan system (Hous-
ton Public Library Major Resource Center), obtain film from
other libraries, film reference serv, film fairs/festivals, library
film programs. Permanent viewing facility available free to
community. *Equipment:* lend 16mm sound projector (2), projection screens (3).
    Other Media Collections *Audio:* disc, 33⅓ rpm, 2020t;
tape, cassette, 97t/c. *Filmstrips:* sound & silent sets, 73t/c.
Slides: sets, 4t/c.
    Budget & Expenditures Total library budget $24,600 (FY
10/1/75-10/1/76). Total FY film budget $500. *Member:* ALA,
Texas State Library Assn.

Beaumont

P- BEAUMONT PUBLIC LIBRARY, Box 3827, 77704. *Tel:* (713)
838-0812, ext 23. *Film Serv Est:* 1939. *In Charge:* Helen
Davis, AV Librarian. *AV Staff:* 1½ (1½ cl). *Film Sel:*
committee preview.
    Free-Loan Film Serv *Eligibility:* indiv with library cards,
by payment, through interlibrary loan. *Restrictions:* for indiv &
inst, only in city. Cannot use for fund-raising, transmit electronically. Available to researchers/scholars for on-site viewing.
May borrow by mail. *Loan Period:* 1 day.

Beaumont (cont'd)

Film Collection 616t/625p. Approx 15-20t acquired annually. *Circ:* 16mm, 616t/625p; 8mm reel, 84t/p. *Pubns:* catalog, every 2 yr; suppl, no set policy. Publish pamphlets.

Other Film Serv Obtain film from coop loan system (Houston Public Library Major Resource Center), obtain film from other libraries, library film programs. Permanent viewing facility available for rent to community. *Equipment:* lend 16mm sound projector (4), 8mm reel projector (2), S8mm reel projector (1), projection tables & stands (1), projection screens (1), slide & filmstrip projectors (2).

Other Media Collections *Audio:* disc, 33⅓ rpm, 2500t/2400c; tape, cassette, 199t/c. *Filmstrips:* sound, 205t/c; sound sets, 25t/c.

Budget & Expenditures Total library budget $42,000 (FY 10/1/74-10/1/75). Total FY film budget $3500. *Member:* ALA, EFLA, FLIC, Texas State Library Assn.

Borger

P: HUTCHINSON COUNTY LIBRARY, 625 Weatherly, 79007. *Tel:* (806) 274-6221. *Film Serv Est:* c. 1950. *In Charge:* Barbara Smith. *AV Staff:* ½ (½ cl).

Free-Loan Film Serv *Eligibility:* educational inst, civic & religious groups, prof groups. *Restrictions:* for indiv & inst, only in county. May borrow by mail. *Loan Period:* 3 days.

Film Collection 173t. *Circ:* 16mm, 173t. *Pubns:* catalog, as needed.

Other Film Serv Obtain film from other libraries & major resource center, library film programs. Permanent viewing facility. *Equipment:* 16mm sound projector (1).

Budget & Expenditures Total library budget $11,000 (FY 1/1/75-1/1/76). No separate AV budget. *Member:* Texas State Library Assn.

Brownsville

C-P- TEXAS SOUTHMOST COLLEGE & CITY OF BROWNSVILLE, City-College Library, 1825 May St, 78520. *Tel:* (512) 546-7121, ext 47. *Film Serv Est:* 1973. *In Charge:* Gilbert Garza, Media Lab Superv. *AV Staff:* 2 (2 tech). *Film Sel:* faculty/staff recommendations, chief film librarian's decision. *Holdings:* fine arts 25%, science 75%.

Free-Loan Film Serv *Eligibility:* staff, indiv with library cards. *Restrictions:* for indiv, only in city. Cannot use for fundraising, transmit electronically. Available to researchers/scholars for on-site viewing. May not borrow by mail. *Loan Period:* 1 day.

Film Collection 80t. *Pubns:* Publish list of titles.

Other Film Serv Permanent viewing facility. *Equipment:* lend 16mm sound projector (6), 8mm cartridge projector (1), S8mm reel projector (1), projection tables & stands (18), projection screens (3), slide projector (4), filmstrip projector (8).

Other Media Collections *Audio:* tape, cassette, 500t/c; tape, reel, 100t/c. *Filmstrips:* sound, 300t/c; silent, 150t/c; sound sets, 150t/c. *Slides:* single, 750t/c; sets, 25t/c.

Budget & Expenditures Total library budget $26,260 (FY 9/1/74-9/1/75). No separate AV budget.

Video Serv *Video Staff:* 2 f-t, 4 p-t, 2 tech. *Video Use:* practical video/TV training courses, playback only of professionally produced tapes. Video serv available by appointment.

Video Equipment/Facilities *For Loan:* recording deck (1), ½″ b&w, Sony 3600; studio camera (1), b&w, Sony 3200; monitor (1), 19″ b&w, Toshiba. Have portable viewing installation. *Equipment Loan Period:* 2 days. Provide training in use of equipment to faculty & students.

Video Tape Loan/Rental/Sale Serv *Loan Eligibility:* staff. *Restrictions:* for indiv, only in city; for inst, none. Cannot use for fund-raising, duplicate, air without permission. May not borrow by mail.

Video Collection Maintained by purchase. Use/play ½″ reel to reel. *Tape Sel:* catalogs. *Collection, B&W:* ½″ reel, 2t/c. *Pubns:* catalog.

Commerce

C- EAST TEXAS STATE UNIVERSITY, 75428. *Tel:* (214) 468-6101. *Video Serv Est:* 1963. *In Charge:* Dr. Mary Wheeler, Dir, Instructional Television. *Video Staff:* 1 f-t, 4 p-t, 1 tech. *Video Use:* documentation of community/school events, in-service training, practical video/TV training courses. Video serv available by appointment. Produce video tapes. Have production studio/space & separate control room.

Video Equipment/Facilities *In-House Use Only:* portapak (1), ½″, b&w, Sony 3400; recording deck (17), ½″, ¾″, 1″, 2″ b&w/col, Ampex 420, 660B, 1500, 5000, 7500C, 7800, Panasonic 3020D, 8100, Shibaden 700, Wollensak; playback deck (1), ¾″ U-matic col, Panasonic NV2110; editing deck (2), ½″, 1″ b&w/col, Ampex 7800, Hitachi; studio camera (11), film/chain b&w/col, Ampex 326CC, Diamond STV-2, GPL-900, Shibaden FPC-1000A, HV-1100U; monitor (14), b&w/col, Conrac, Setchell-Carlson, Shibaden; SEG (3), Dynair VS-60A, 3M SEG 672; keyer (1), col, 3M SEG 672; additional camera lenses (6), lighting; microphones (23); tripods (17); audio tape recorders (5). Portable-type equipment sometimes loaned to faculty and/or students. Have permanent & portable viewing installations. *Equipment Loan Period:* no set policy. Provide training in use of equipment to faculty & students.

Video Tape Loan/Rental/Sale Serv *Loan Eligibility:* staff & students.

Video Collection Maintained by rental, own production, exchange/swap. Use/play ½″, 1″, 2″ reel to reel, ¾″ cassette. Tapes organized by subject.

Cable & CCTV Receive serv of cable TV system. Have CCTV in inst, with 80 monitors. *Programming Sources:* over-the-air commercial & public broadcasting, tapes produced by inst, tapes produced professionally.

Conroe

P- MONTGOMERY COUNTY LIBRARY, Box 579, 77301. *Tel:* (713) 756-4486. *Film Serv Est:* 1950. *Holdings:* career education, children's films, feature films, fine arts, industrial arts, science, social sciences.

Free-Loan Film Serv *Eligibility:* staff & students, educational inst, civic & religious groups, indiv with library cards, prof groups, & others. *Restrictions:* for indiv & inst, only in county. May borrow by mail. *Loan Period:* 7 days.

Film Collection 138t.

Other Film Serv Obtain film from coop loan system (Houston Public Library), obtain film from other libraries. *Equipment:* lend 16mm sound projector (2), projection tables & stands (1), projection screens (3), tripods (3) audio tape recorder (1).

Corpus Christi

P- LA RETAMA PUBLIC LIBRARY, (Corpus Christi Major Resource Center), Corpus Christi Area Library System Film Library, 505 N Mosquite, 78401. *Tel:* (512) 882-1937. *Film Serv Est:* 1969. *In Charge:* Anne E. Hollingsworth, Systems AV Librarian. *AV Staff:* 2 (1 prof, 1½ cl). *Film Sel:* committee preview, staff recommendations, chief film librarian's decision. *Holdings:* general, alcoholism, Mexican-American heritage.

Free-Loan Film Serv *Eligibility:* civic & religious groups, indiv with library cards, 26-county library system. *Restrictions:* for indiv, interlibrary loan, only in state; for inst, only in state, 26-county library system. Cannot use for fund-raising, transmit electronically, borrow for classroom use. Available to researchers/scholars for on-site viewing. May borrow by mail. *Loan Period:* 1 day. *Total Yr Film Loan:* 3606.

Film Collection 1141t. Approx 150t acquired annually. *Circ:* 16mm, 391t/381p; 8mm reel, 400t/320p; S8mm reel, 350t/275p. *Pubns:* catalog, annual; suppl, as needed.

Other Film Serv Obtain film from coop loan system, obtain film from other libraries, film reference serv, film fairs/festivals, library film programs. Permanent viewing facility available free to community. *Equipment:* in-house use only; 16mm sound projector (3), 8mm reel projector (1), S8mm reel projector (1), projection tables & stands (1), projection screens (2).

Budget & Expenditures Total library budget $106,205 (FY 10/1/74-10/1/75). Total FY film budget $80,000. *Member:* EFLA, Texas State Library Assn.

C- TEXAS A & I UNIVERSITY AT CORPUS CHRISTI, Box 6010, 78411. *Tel:* (512) 991-6810, ext 243. *Film Serv Est:* 1973. *AV Staff:* 2 (1 prof, 1 cl). *Film Sel:* faculty/staff recommendations. *Holdings:* medicine 30%, social sciences 30%, teacher education 30%.

Film Collection 25t. Approx 5t acquired annually.

Other Film Serv Rent film from distributors for patrons. Permanent viewing facility.

Other Media Collections *Audio:* disc, 33⅓ rpm, 1200c; tape, cassette, 91c; *Filmstrips:* sound, 12t; *Slides:* single, 500t; sets, 12t.

Budget & Expenditures Total library budget $177,000 (FY 10/1/74-10/1/75). Total FY film budget $500.

Video Serv *Est:* 1973. *Video Staff:* 2 f-t. *Video Use:* in-service training, practical video/TV training courses. Video serv available by appointment. Produce video tapes. Have production studio/space.

Video Equipment/Facilities *In-House Use Only:* porta-pak (2), b&w; studio camera (1), b&w; monitor (5), col; lighting (2); audio tape recorders (20).

Video Collection Maintained by purchase. Use/play 1″ reel to reel. *Sources:* commercial distributors, galleries. *Tape Sel:* faculty/staff recommendations. Tapes organized by accession number.

Cable & CCTV Receive serv of cable TV system.

Dallas

P- DALLAS PUBLIC LIBRARY, Film Library, 1954 Commerce St, 75201. *Tel:* (214) 748-9071, ext 255. *Film Serv Est:* 1942. *In Charge:* Masha R. Porte, Head, Film Library. *AV Staff:* 6¾ (2 prof, 3¾ cl, 1 tech). *Film Sel:* committee preview. *Holdings:* general collection.

Free-Loan Film Serv *Eligibility:* no restrictions. *Restrictions:* for indiv & inst, none. Cannot use for fund-raising, transmit electronically. May not borrow by mail. *Loan Period:* 1 day.

Film Rental Serv *Eligibility:* educational org, civic groups, patrons/public, individuals with library cards. *Restrictions:* only in Dallas County. Cannot use for fund-raising, transmit electronically. *Rental Period:* 1 day. *Total Yr Film Booking:* 17,600.

Film Collection 3170t/3200p. Approx 125t acquired annually. *Circ:* 16mm, 3170t/3200p. *Pubns:* catalog, as needed; suppl, no set policy.

Other Film Serv Film reference serv, film fairs/festivals, library film programs. Permanent viewing facility available free to community. *Equipment:* rent filmstrip/slide projector.

Other Media Collections *Audio:* disc, 33⅓ rpm, 11,622c; tape, cassette, 3942c. *Filmstrips:* sound sets, 680c.

Budget & Expenditures No separate budget. *Member:* AFI, ALA, EFLA, FLIC, Tex. Library Assn, Southwest Library Assn, National Microfilm Assn.

Video Serv *Video Use:* to increase community's library use, playback only of professionally produced tapes. Video serv available on demand.

Video Equipment/Facilities *In-House Use Only:* playback deck (4), ¾″ col, Sony VP1000; monitor (4), col, Sony CVM1225. Have portable viewing installation. Provide training in use of equipment to faculty.

Video Tape Loan/Rental/Sale Serv *Loan Eligibility:* org members. *Restrictions:* for indiv, only in city (inhouse use only); for inst, no set policy.

Video Collection Maintained by purchase. Use/play ¾″ cassette. *Sources:* commercial distributors. *Tape Sel:* preview, published reviews, catalogs. Tapes organized by Dewey Decimal. *Collection, Color:* ¾″ cassette, 95t/c.

Edinburg

P- HIDALGO COUNTY LIBRARY SYSTEM, P.L.A.N.E. Project (Public Library Action for Neighborhood Education Project), 1307 S. Closner Blvd, 78539. *Tel:* (512) 383-0532. *Video Serv Est:* 1975. *In Charge:* Beth Mann, Project Dir. *Video Staff:* 22 f-t, 2 tech. *Video Use:* documentation of community/school events, to increase community's library use, community video access, in-service training. Video serv available on demand and by appointment. Produce video tapes. Have production studio/space.

Video Equipment/Facilities *In-House Use Only:* recording deck (1), ¾″ col, Panasonic; playback deck (1), ¾″ col, U-Vision NV2125; monitor (2), b&w/col, Panasonic WV2300; lighting (3); microphones (3); tripods (1). *For Loan:* monitor (3), col, Panasonic WV2300; audio tape recorders (2). Have portable viewing installation. Provide training in use of equipment to project personnel. Have tape duplication serv.

Video Tape Loan/Rental/Sale Serv *Serv Provided:* free loan. *Loan Eligibility:* educational inst, civic groups, religious groups, indiv with library cards, prof groups, such as doctors & lawyers & others, such as any county resident. *Restrictions:* for indiv & inst, only in Hidalgo County. Cannot duplicate, air without permission. May not borrow by mail. *Loan Period:* 3 days. *Total Yr Tape Loan:* 50.

Video Collection Maintained by purchase, own production. Use/play ¾″ cassette. *Sources:* commercial distributors. *Tape Sel:* preview, faculty/staff recommendations, published reviews, catalogs. *Special Collections:* in-house training tapes, films in video format. Tapes organized by Dewey Decimal. *Collection, Color:* ½″ reel, 40t/c; ¼″ reel, 10t/c; ¾″ cassette, 150t/c. *Collection, B&W:* ½″ reel, 10t/c; ¼″ reel, 20t/c. *Other Video Serv:* programming, taping of other media. *Pubns:* catalog & monthly newsletter. Special presentations receive mass media attention.

Cable & CCTV Receive serv of cable TV system.

El Paso

P- EL PASO PUBLIC LIBRARY, 501 North Oregon St, 79901. *Tel:* (915) 543-6030. *Film Serv Est:* 1973. *In Charge:* Jacqueline L. Work, Asst. Reference Librarian-AV. *AV Staff:* 3 (1 prof, 1 cl, 1 tech). *Film Sel:* faculty/staff recommendations, chief film librarian's decision. *Holdings:* Southwest subjects (planned).

Free-Loan Film Serv *Eligibility:* educational inst, civic groups, religious groups, indiv with library cards, prof groups, such as police, drug counselors, parks & recreation personnel. *Restrictions:* for indiv, only in El Paso County; for inst, will service Trans Pecos system. Cannot transmit electronically, charge admission, must provide own equipment. May not borrow by mail. *Loan Period:* 1 day. *Total Yr Film Loan:* 2366.

Film Collection 663t/p. Approx 20-25t acquired annually. *Circ:* 16mm, 663t/p. *Pubns:* catalog (in preparation), every 5 yr; suppl, annual. Publish materials pertaining to collection. Publish monthly calendars & film flyers.

Other Film Serv Film reference serv, library film programs. Permanent viewing facility available free to community. *Equipment:* S8mm camera (1), 16mm sound projector (8), 8mm reel projector (1), projection tables & stands (7), projection screens (6).

Other Media Collections *Audio:* disc, 33⅓ rpm, 5100t; tape, cassette, 1055c. *Filmstrips:* sound, 40t; silent, 10t.

Budget & Expenditures Total library budget $895,000 (FY 9/1/74-9/1/75). Total FY film budget $2500. *Member:* Texas Library Assn, BRLA Border Library Assn.

Fort Worth

S- SOUTHWESTERN BAPTIST THEOLOGICAL SEMINARY, Fleming Library, Box 22,000-2E, 76122. *Tel:* (817) 923-1921. *Film Serv Est:* 1957. *In Charge:* Bob Trimble, AV Librarian. *AV Staff:* 9 (1 prof, 8 cl). *Film Sel:* faculty/staff

Fort Worth (cont'd)

recommendations. *Holdings:* biblical, Christian living, church history.

Free-Loan Film Serv *Eligibility:* staff & students. *Restrictions:* for indiv, within driving range of the city. Available to researchers/scholars for on-site viewing. May not borrow by mail. *Loan Period:* 4 days. *Total Yr Film Loan:* 613.

Other Media Collections *Audio:* disc, 33⅓ rpm, 4746t/4932c; tape, cassette, 4895t; tape, reel, 5934t. *Filmstrips:* sound, 1233c; silent, 513c. *Slides:* single, 24,892c; sets, 88c.

Budget & Expenditures Total library budget $56,000 (FY 8/1/74-8/1/75). Total FY film budget $2,000. *Member:* ALA, Tex. Library Assn, American Theological Library Assn, Southern Baptist Historical Society.

Video Serv *Est:* 1965. *In Charge:* Bill Langford, Coord of Media Servs. *Video Staff:* 5 f-t, 42 p-t, 5 tech. *Video Use:* documentation of community/school events, in-service training, for instruction in preaching, religious education. Video serv available on demand & by appointment. Produce video tapes. Have production studio/space & separate control room. Have permanent viewing installation. Provide training in use of equipment to inhouse technicians. Have tape duplication serv for audio-tapes only. May not borrow by mail.

Video Collection Maintained by own production. Use/play ½″ reel to reel, ½″ cartridge. Tapes organized by accession order.

C- TEXAS WESLEYAN COLLEGE, Box 3277, 76105. *Tel:* (817) 534-0251, ext 205. *Film Serv Est:* 1967. *In Charge:* Larry Kitchens, Dir of Media Serv. *AV Staff:* (3 prof, 20 cl, 4 tech). *Film Sel:* faculty/staff recommendations. *Holdings:* career education 1%, children's films 1%, experimental films 1%, feature films 5%, fine arts 1%, science 20%, social sciences 5%, teacher education 60%.

Film Collection 110t. Approx 5-10t acquired annually. *Circ:* 16mm, 63t/p; 8mm reel, 11t/p; S8mm cartridge, 73t/p.

Other Film Serv Rent film from distributors for patrons, obtain film from coop loan system, obtain film from other libraries, film reference serv. Permanent viewing facility.

Budget & Expenditures Total FY film budget $9000. *Member:* AECT, Tex. Assn of Education.

Video Serv *Est:* 1967. *Video Staff:* 3 f-t, 4 p-t. *Video Use:* documentation of community/school events. Video serv available on demand. Produce video tapes. Have production studio/space & separate control room.

Video Equipment/Facilities *In-House Use Only:* portapak (1), ½″ EIA-J b&w, Sony; recording deck (4), ½″ EIA-J b&w/col, Panasonic, Sony; studio camera (6), b&w, UMI, Sony; monitor (29), b&w/col, SC, Sony; SEG (1), USI; lighting (20); tripods (3); audio tape recorders (2). Have permanent viewing installation. Have tape duplication serv.

Video Tape Loan/Rental/Sale Serv *Serv Provided:* swap with other inst, sale. *Loan Eligibility:* staff, educational inst. *Restrictions:* for indiv & inst, none. Cannot duplicate. May borrow by mail. *Loan Period:* 7 days.

Video Collection Obtain tapes by purchase, own production. Use/play ½″, reel to reel. *Sources:* commercial distributors. *Tape Sel:* preview, faculty/staff recommendations, catalogs. *Collection, Color:* ½″ reel, 115t/121c. *Collection, B&W:* ½″ reel, 231t/c. *Other Video Serv:* production workshops.

Cable & CCTV Have CCTV in inst, with 22 monitors. *Programming Sources:* tapes produced by inst, tapes produced professionally.

Galveston

P- ROSENBERG LIBRARY, 2310 Sealy, 77550. *Tel:* (713) 763-8854. *Film Serv Est:* 1953. *In Charge:* Aubrey A. Jackson, Reference/Film Librarian. *AV Staff:* 1 (½ prof, ¼ cl, ¼ tech). *Film Sel:* committee preview.

Film Rental Serv *Eligibility:* no restrictions. *Restrictions:* only in state. Cannot use for fund-raising. *Rental Period:* 1 day. *Total Yr Film Booking:* 2500.

Film Collection 5t/5p. Approx 10-15t acquired annually. *Circ:* 16mm, 520t/522p; 8mm reel, 65t/68p; S8mm reel,

175t/178p. *Pubns:* catalog, as needed ($4.50); suppl, in yr catalog not published.

Other Film Serv Obtain film from coop loan system (Houston Public Library). Permanent viewing facility available for rent to community. *Equipment:* lend 16mm sound projector (1), projection screen (1).

Other Media Collections *Audio:* disc, 33⅓ rpm, 1960t/1985c; tape, cassette, 305t/305c. *Filmstrips:* silent, 270t/275c.

Budget & Expenditures Total library budget $48,000 (FY 10/1/74-10/1/75). Total FY film budget $2,000. *Member:* Tex. Library Assn.

Harlingen

C- TEXAS STATE TECHNICAL INSTITUTE, Instructional Media Center, Industrial Air Park, 78550. *Tel:* (512) 425-4922, ext 50. *Video Serv Est:* 1973. *In Charge:* Harlan B. Mumme, Jr., Dir of Media. *Video Staff:* 2 f-t, 6 p-t, 1 tech. *Video Use:* in-service training, production of technical/vocational education programs. Video serv available on demand. Produce video tapes. Have production studio/space & separate control room.

Video Equipment/Facilities *In-House Use Only:* recording/playback deck (4), ½″ b&w/col, Sony 8400, 8650, 3650; editing deck (3), ½″ b&w/col, Sony 3650, 8650; studio camera (3), ¾″ vidicon b&w/col, Panasonic WV341, IVC92; SEG (1), Sony; lighting (12); microphones (20); tripods (4). *For Loan:* audio tape recorders (34). Have permanent & portable viewing installations. Provide training in use of equipment to instructors & personnel. Have tape duplication serv.

Video Tape Loan Serv *Serv Provided:* free loan, swap with other inst. *Loan Eligibility:* staff, educational inst. *Restrictions:* for indiv, none; for inst, equipment—within four campuses, tape—no restrictions. Cannot use for fund-raising, must be used for instructional purposes only. May borrow by mail. *Loan Period:* 7 days. *Total Yr Tape Loan:* 68.

Video Collection Maintained by purchase, own production, exchange/swap. Use/play ½″ reel to reel. *Sources:* commercial distributors, exchange. *Tape Sel:* preview. Tapes organized by subject. *Collection, B&W:* ½″ reel, 128t/c. *Other Video Serv:* programming, taping of other media. *Pubns:* catalog.

Cable & CCTV Have CCTV in inst, with 38 monitors. *Programming Sources:* tapes produced by inst, tapes produced professionally.

Houston

P- HOUSTON PUBLIC LIBRARY, Film Library, 500 McKinney Ave, 77002. *Tel:* (713) 224-5441, ext 55. *Film Serv Est:* 1975. *In Charge:* Sue Pitre, Film Librarian. *AV Staff:* 2 (1 prof, 1 tech). *Film Sel:* committee preview, faculty/staff recommendations, chief film librarian's decision, previews. *Holdings:* minority studies 8%.

Free-Loan Film Serv *Eligibility:* civic groups, religious groups, indiv with library cards, prof groups, such as hospitals, oil companies. *Restrictions:* for indiv, only in city; for inst, only in city, 28 county area. Cannot use for fund-raising, transmit electronically, borrow for classroom use. May borrow by mail. *Loan Period:* 3 days. *Total Yr Film Loan:* 951.

Film Collection 500t/509p. Approx 100t acquired annually. *Circ:* 16mm, 500t/509p. *Pubns:* catalog, annual (free); suppl, no set policy (free). Publish rules & policy statement, free loan agencies, reserve forms.

Other Film Serv Library film programs. Permanent viewing facility.

Budget & Expenditures Total library budget $2,000,000 (FY 1/1/75-1/1/76). Total FY film budget $100,000 (LSCA grant to est film library). *Member:* Tex. Library Assn.

Hurst

C- TARRANT COUNTY JUNIOR COLLEGE SYSTEM, 828 Harwood Rd, 76053. *Tel:* (817) 281-7860, ext 485. *Film Serv*

Est: 1968. *In Charge:* Paul Vagt, District Dir of Learning Resources. *AV Staff:* (2 cl). *Film Sel:* faculty/staff recommendations.

Free-Loan Film Serv *Eligibility:* org members.

Film Collection 700t/775p. Approx 10-15t acquired annually. *Circ:* 16mm, 700t/775p. *Pubns:* catalog, quarterly.

Other Film Serv Obtain film from coop loan system, obtain film from other libraries, film reference serv. Permanent viewing facility available for faculty only.

Budget & Expenditures Total library budget $200,000 (FY 10/1/74-10/1/75). Total FY film budget $14,500. *Member:* AECT, ALA, EFLA, Tex. Library Assn, Tex. Assn for Educational Technol.

Video Serv *Est:* 1970. *Video Staff:* 2 f-t. *Video Use:* instruction. Video serv available on demand. Produce video tapes. Have production studio/space & separate control room.

Video Equipment/Facilities *In-House Use Only:* portapak (1), ½″ EIAJ b&w, Panasonic; recording deck (5), 1″ IVC col, Bell & Howell; playback deck (50), ¾″ col, JVC; editing deck (5); studio camera (8), b&w/col, Diamond, Panasonic; monitor (68), b&w/col, various; SEG (2), Shintron; keyer (2), 3M, Panasonic; lighting; microphones (18); tripods (8); audio tape recorders (200). Have viewing installation.

Video Tape Loan/Rental/Sale Serv *Loan Eligibility:* org members, staff. May borrow by mail.

Video Collection Maintained by purchase, own production. Use/play ¾″ cassette. *Sources:* commercial distributors. *Tape Sel:* faculty/staff recommendations.

Laredo

C- TEXAS A & I UNIVERSITY AT LAREDO, Learning Resource Center, Box 537, 78040. *Tel:* (512) 722-8001, ext 47. *Film Serv Est:* 1970. *In Charge:* Narcisco Vasquez III, Dir of AV. *AV Staff:* 4 (1 prof, 1 cl, 2 tech). *Film Sel:* faculty/staff recommendations. *Holdings:* teacher education 100%.

Free-Loan Film Serv *Eligibility:* staff. *Restrictions:* for indiv, interlibrary loan. Cannot use for fund-raising. May not borrow by mail.

Film Collection 20t/p. Approx 2t acquired annually. *Circ:* 16mm, 20t/p. Permanent viewing facility.

Other Media Collections *Audio:* disc, 33 rpm, 400t/c; tape, cassette, 150t/c; tape, reel, 30t/c. *Filmstrips:* sound, 200t/c; silent, 175t/c. *Slides:* sets, 6t/c.

Budget & Expenditures Total library budget $97,650 (FY 9/1/74-9/1/75). No separate AV budget. *Member:* ALA.

Video Serv *Est:* 1970. *Video Staff:* 2 f-t, 2 p-t, 2 tech. *Video Use:* teacher training aids. Video serv available by appointment. Produce video tapes. Have production studio/space.

Video Equipment/Facilities *In-House Use Only:* portapak (12), ½″ b&w, Sony 3400; studio camera (2), b&w, Sony AVC3200; monitor (12), 9″ b&w/col, Sony CVM9204; SEG (1), Sony; tripods (12); audio tape recorders (68). *For Loan:* portapak; monitor; tripods; audio tape recorders. Have permanent viewing installation. *Equipment Loan Period:* 2 days. Provide training in use of equipment to faculty & students.

Video Tape Loan/Rental/Sale Serv *Serv Provided:* free loan. *Loan Eligibility:* staff. *Restrictions:* for indiv, interlibrary loan; for inst, on request of president. Cannot use for fund-raising, air without permission. May not borrow by mail.

Video Collection Maintain by own production. Use/play ½″ reel to reel. *Sources:* commercial distributors. *Tape Sel:* faculty/staff recommendations. *Special Collections:* in-house training tapes. Tapes organized by subject. *Collection, Color:* ¾″ cassette, 20t/c. *Collection, B&W:* ½″ reel, 30t/c.

Marshall

C- WILEY COLLEGE, Thomas Winston Cole, Sr Library, 75670. *Tel:* (214) 938-8341, ext 70. *Video Serv Est:* 1974. *In Charge:* Mary L. Cleveland, Head Librarian. *Video Staff:* 1 f-t, 1 p-t, 3 tech. *Video Use:* documentation of community/school events, community video access, in-service training, playback only of professionally produced tapes, as art form. Video serv available by appointment. Produce video tapes.

Video Equipment/Facilities *In-House Use Only:* portapak (1), Sony; playback deck (1); editing deck (1); studio camera (1); monitor (1); additional camera lenses (2); lighting (2); microphones (2); tripods (2); audio tape recorders (1). Have portable viewing installation. *Equipment Loan Period:* 1 day. Provide training in use of equipment to student assistants.

Video Tape Loan/Rental/Sale Serv *Serv Provided:* free loan, swap with other inst, rental, sale. *Loan/Rental Eligibility:* org members, staff & students, educational inst, civic groups, religious groups. *Restrictions:* for indiv, interlibrary loan; for inst, none. Cannot use for fund-raising, air without permission. May borrow by mail. *Loan Period:* 7 days. *Total Yr Tape Loan:* 3.

Video Collection Maintained by purchase, own production. Use/play ½″, 2″ reel to reel. *Sources:* commercial distributors. *Tape Sel:* preview, faculty/staff recommendations, gallery previews, catalogs. *Special Collections:* in-house training tapes. Tapes organized by Dewey Decimal, subject, title. *Collection, Color:* ½″ reel, 3t/c; 1″ reel, 4t/c. *Collection, B&W:* ½″ reel, 3t/c; 1″ reel, 3t/c. *Other Video Serv:* production workshops. *Pubns:* catalog.

Midland

C- MIDLAND COLLEGE, 3600 North Garfield, 79701. *Tel:* (915) 684-7851, ext 210. *In Charge:* Dr. L. P. Coston, Dir of Learning Resources. *AV Staff:* 3 (1 prof, 1 cl, 1 tech). *Film Sel:* faculty/staff recommendations.

Film Collection 12t/p.

Other Film Serv Film reference serv, film fairs/festivals.

Other Media Collections *Audio:* disc, 33⅓ rpm, 50t/c; tape, cassette, 100t/c; tape, reel, 20t/c. *Slides:* single, 30t/c.

Budget & Expenditures Total library budget $50,000. No separate AV budget. *Member:* AECT.

Video Serv *Est:* 1975. *Video Staff:* 3 f-t. *Video Use:* documentation of community/school events, to increase community's library use, in-service training, practical video/TV training courses, playback only of professionally produced tapes, as art form. Video serv available by appointment. Produce video tapes. Have production studio/space & separate control room.

Video Equipment/Facilities *In-House Use Only:* recording deck (4), ½″, ¾″ col; playback deck (8); editing deck (2); monitor (8); SEG (1), ½″; microphones (10); tripods (30); audio tape recorders (40). Have permanent & portable viewing installations. provide training in use of equipment to faculty & students. Have tape duplication serv.

Video Tape Loan Serv *Loan Eligibility:* staff & students. *Restrictions:* for indiv, none. Cannot duplicate. May not borrow by mail.

Video Collection Maintained by purchase, rental, own production. Use/play ½″ reel to reel, ¾″ cassette. *Sources:* commercial distributors. *Tape Sel:* preview, faculty/staff recommendations. *Special Collections:* in-house training tapes. *Collection, Color:* ½″ reel, 20t/c; ¾″ cassette, 20t/c. *Other Video Serv:* production workshops. *Pubns:* catalog.

Richardson

P- NICHOLSON MEMORIAL LIBRARY, 900 Civic Center Drive, 75080. *Tel:* (214) 238-8251. *Film Serv Est:* 1970. *In Charge:* Phillip Barbosa, Media Librarian. *AV Staff:* 1 (1 prof). *Film Sel:* committee preview.

Film Collection 52t/p. *Circ:* 8mm cartridge, 173t/p. *Noncirc:* 16mm, 52/p.

Other Film Serv Obtain film from coop loan system (North Central Texas Film Coop), obtain film from other libraries, library film programs.

Other Media Collections *Audio:* disc, 33⅓ rpm, 638t/c. *Filmstrips:* sound sets, 43t/c.

Budget & Expenditures Total library budget $50,000 (FY 10/1/74-10/1/75). Total FY film budget $2867. *Member:* Tex. Library Assn.

Richardson (cont'd)

P- RICHARDSON PUBLIC LIBRARY, North Central Texas Film Coop, 900 Civic Center Drive, 75080. *Tel:* (214) 238-8251, ext 38. *Film Serv Est:* 1970. *AV Staff:* 3 (1 prof, 1 cl, 1 paraprof). *Film Sel:* committee preview. *Holdings:* animated films 40%, career education 2%, children's films 50%, dance, fine arts 2%, science 2%, women.

Free-Loan Film Serv *Eligibility:* civic groups, religious groups, indiv with library cards. *Restrictions:* for indiv & inst, film coop members. Cannot use for fund-raising, transmit electronically. Available to researchers/scholars for on-site viewing. May borrow by mail. *Loan Period:* 1 day. *Total Yr Film Loan:* 1680.

Film Collection 256t/p. *Circ:* 16mm, 81t/p; 8mm reel, 100t/p; S8mm reel, 169t/p.

Other Film Serv Obtain film from coop loan system (North Central Texas Film Coop), library film programs. Permanent viewing facility. *Equipment:* lend S8mm camera (2), 16mm sound projector (2), 8mm reel projector (2), S8mm reel projector (2), projection screens (3), overhead (1), slide projectors (2), filmstrip projectors (3).

Other Media Collections *Audio:* disc, 33⅓ rpm, 1387t/c; tape, cassette, 322t/322c. *Filmstrips:* sound, 55t/55c; sets, 6t/c.

Budget & Expenditures Total library budget $85,000 (FY 10/1/75-10/1/76). *Member:* ALA, Tex. Library Assn.

Video Serv *Est:* 1972. *Video Use:* documentation of community/school events, to increase community's library use. Video serv available to library members only. Produce video tapes. Have production space & separate control room.

Video Equipment/Facilities *In-House Use Only:* recording deck (1), Sony U-Matic; studio camera (1), col, Sony AVC3200DX; microphones (1); tripods (1). Have viewing installation.

Video Tape Loan Serv *Serv Provided:* swap with other inst. *Loan Eligibility:* educational inst, other libraries. *Restrictions:* for inst, North Central Tex. area. Cannot use for fund-raising, duplicate, air without permission. May not borrow by mail. *Loan Period:* flexible.

Video Collection Maintained by purchase, own production, exchange/swap. *Sources:* commercial distributors, exchange. *Tape Sel:* preview, faculty/staff recommendations. *Collection, Color:* ¾" cassette, 15t.

Cable & CCTV Have CCTV in inst, with 2 monitors. *Programming Sources:* tapes produced by inst, tapes produced professionally.

San Antonio

C- SAN ANTONIO COLLEGE, AV Serv Center, 1001 Howard St, 78284. *Tel:* (512) 734-7311, ext 257-259 or 250. *Film Serv Est:* 1967. *In Charge:* Don Drummond, AV Coord. *AV Staff:* 33¾ (3½ prof, 17½ cl, 13 tech). *Film Sel:* committee preview, faculty/staff recommendations.

Free-Loan Film Serv *Eligibility:* staff & students. *Restrictions:* for indiv, on-campus only; for inst, members of film coop. Available to researchers/scholars for on-site viewing. May not borrow by mail. *Loan Period:* flexible. *Total Yr Film Loan:* 1411.

Film Collection 582t/p. Approx 30-35t acquired annually. *Circ:* 16mm, 293t/p; 8mm & S8mm cartridge, 289t/p. *Pubns:* catalog, as needed; suppl, no set policy. Publish materials pertaining to collection. Publish occasional filmographies, part of series "Learning Resources Bulletins."

Other Film Serv Rent film from distributors for patrons, coop loan system (Council of Research and Academic Libraries CORAL of San Antonio), obtain film from other libraries, film reference serv, reference serv to faculty seeking specific titles or subjects.

Other Media Collections *Audio:* disc, 33⅓ rpm, 3085c; tape, cassette, 744c; tape, reel, 271c. *Filmstrips:* silent, 624c; sound sets, 545c. *Slides:* single, 4768c.

Budget & Expenditures Total library budget $215,000 (FY 9/1/75-9/1/76). Total FY film budget $12,000. *Member:* EFLA, Tex. Library Assn, Tex. Assn for Educational Technol.

Video Serv *Video Use:* classroom instruction. Video serv available by appointment to college instructors and classes only. Produce video tapes. Have production studio/space & separate control room.

Video Equipment/Facilities *In-House Use Only:* portapak (1), ½" b&w, AVC/AV Sony 3400; recording deck (4), ½", ¾" b&w/col, Sony 3600-JVC 6100; playback deck (1), ¾" col, JVC5000; studio camera (3), b&w, Ampex CC450, Sony AVC4600; SEG (2), Ampex AC125, 3M672; lighting (3); microphones (8); tripods (6); TV receivers (33), GE, Admiral, Panasonic, Setchell Carlson, Sony. Have viewing installation. Provide training in use of equipment to faculty & student assistants.

Video Tape Loan/Rental/Sale Serv *Loan Eligibility:* staff.

Video Collection Maintained by purchase, own production. Use/play ½" reel to reel, ¾" cassette. *Sources:* commercial distributors. *Tape Sel:* preview, faculty/staff recommendations. *Special Collections:* in-house training tapes, video as art, films in video format. Tapes organized by subject. *Collection, Color:* ¾" cassette, 17c. *Collection, B&W:* ½" reel, 75c. *Other Video Serv:* production workshops.

Cable & CCTV Have CCTV in inst, with 32 monitors. *Programming Sources:* tapes produced by inst, tapes produced professionally.

P- SAN ANTONIO PUBLIC LIBRARY, Art, Music & Films Dept, 203 S St. Mary's St, 78205. *Tel:* (512) 223-6851, ext 34. *Film Serv Est:* 1947. *In Charge:* Frances Smith, Head—Art, Music & Films. *Film Sel:* committee preview. *Holdings:* black studies 1%, children's films 40%, fine arts 1%, Spanish 4%.

Free-Loan Film Serv *Eligibility:* indiv with library cards. *Restrictions:* for inst, only in Bexar County. Cannot use for fund-raising, transmit electronically. *Loan Period:* 1 day. *Total Yr Film Loan:* 13,000.

Film Collection 850t/1000p. Approx 30t acquired annually. *Circ:* 8mm reel, 50t/p; S8mm reel, 60t/p. *Pubns:* catalog, every 2 yr ($.25); suppl, no set policy.

Other Media Collections *Audio:* disc, 33⅓ rpm, 3500t/4500c; tape, cassette, 225t. *Filmstrips:* silent, 110t; sound sets, 6t. *Slides:* single, 2200. No separate AV budget. *Member:* ALA, EFLA.

San Marcos

C- SOUTHWEST TEXAS STATE UNIVERSITY, AV Center, 600 LBJ Drive, 78666. *Tel:* (512) 245-2159. *Film Serv Est:* 1955. *In Charge:* William G. Henry, Jr., Dir, AV Center. *AV Staff:* 5 (2 prof, 2 cl, 1 tech). *Film Sel:* committee preview, faculty/staff recommendations. *Holdings:* black studies 5%, consumer affairs 10%, dance 1%, psychology/guidance 10%, science 20%, teacher education 54%.

Film Collection 456t/p. Approx 50t acquired annually. *Noncirc:* 16mm, 456t; 8mm cartridge, 50t. *Pubns:* catalog, as needed; suppl, no set policy. Publish list of new titles.

Other Film Serv Rent film from distributors for patrons, obtain film from coop loan system (Council of Research and Academic Libraries CORAL of San Antonio, Regional Service Center #13), obtain film from other libraries, film reference serv. *Equipment:* lend 16mm sound projector (30), 8mm cartridge projector (2), projection tables & stands (10), projection screens (10). *Member:* Tex. Assn for Educational Technol.

Video Serv *Est:* 1966. *In Charge:* Ted Harris, AV Tech. *Video Staff:* 1 f-t, 10 p-t, 1 tech. *Video Use:* in-service training, practical video/TV training courses. Video serv available on demand and by appointment. Produce video tapes. Have production studio/space & separate control room.

Video Equipment/Facilities *In-House Use Only:* portapak (1), ½" b&w, Sony; studio camera (10), b&w, Ampex, Shibaden; monitor (50), 21" b&w, Dage, GPL; SEG (1), S/C, Admiral; lighting (1); microphones (6); tripods (6); audio tape recorders (1); turntable (1). Have permanent & portable viewing installations. *Equipment Loan Period:* no set policy. Provide training in use of equipment. Have tape duplication serv.

Video Tape Loan/Rental/Sale Serve *Serv Provided:* swap with other inst. *Loan Eligibility:* org members, staff. Cannot air without permission. May not borrow by mail.

Video Collection Maintained by purchase, own production, exchange/swap. Use/play ½″, 1″, 2″ reel to reel, ¾″ cassette. *Sources:* commercial distributors. *Tape Sel:* preview, faculty/staff recommendations. *Special Collections:* in-house training tapes. Tapes organized by subject. *Collection, B&W:* ½″ reel, 50t; 1″ reel, 100t; 2″ reel, 100t; ¾″ cassette, 100t. *Other Video Serv:* programming, reference serv, taping of other media. *Pubns:* catalog.

Cable & CCTV Receive serv of cable TV system. Produce programs for cablecasting. Inform public about cable system serv & facilities. Serve as production facility for others. Run cable programs for special audiences. Have advisory/administrative role in cable system operation, serve as Board of Dirs, Tex. Microwave Project. Have CCTV in inst. *Programming Sources:* over-the-air commercial & public broadcasting, tapes produced by inst, tapes produced professionally.

Weslaco

P- WESLACO PUBLIC LIBRARY (PORTER DOSS MEMORIAL LIBRARY), 515 S Kansas St, 78596. *Tel:* (512) 968-2272. *Film Serv Est:* 1974. *In Charge:* Frances W. Isbell, Head Librarian. *AV Staff:* ½ (½ tech). *Film Sel:* faculty/staff recommendations. *Holdings:* children's films 30%, feature films 30%.

Free-Loan Film Serv *Eligibility:* civic groups, religious groups, indiv with library cards, prof groups. *Restrictions:* for indiv & inst, only in Hidalgo County. Cannot use for fundraising, transmit electronically, borrow for classroom use. Available to researchers/scholars for on-site viewing. May not borrow by mail. *Loan Period:* 1 day. *Total Yr Film Loan:* 432.

Film Collection 136t/p. Approx 20t acquired annually. *Circ:* 16mm, 77t/p; 8mm reel, 59t/p; S8mm reel, 6t/p. *Pubns:* catalog, as needed; suppl, no set policy.

Other Film Serv Obtain film from coop loan system (Corpus Christi Major Resource Area, Hidalgo County Library System), library film programs. *Equipment:* lend 16mm sound projector (2), 8mm reel projector (3), projection screens (1).

Budget & Expenditures Total library budget $3000 (FY 10/1/74-10/1/75). No separate AV budget. *Member:* Tex. Library Assn.

Utah

Logan

C- UTAH STATE UNIVERSITY, AV Servs, UMC 31, 84322. *Tel:* (801) 752-4100, ext 7954. *In Charge:* LaDell C. Hoth, AV Librarian. *AV Staff:* (2 prof, 2 cl). *Film Sel:* faculty/staff recommendations. *Holdings:* agriculture, animated films, black studies, career education, children's films, consumer affairs, dance, engineering, experimental films, feature films, fine arts, industrial arts, law, medicine, science, social sciences, teacher education, women.

Free-Loan Film Serv *Eligibility:* org members, staff, students enrolled in inst, educational inst, civic groups, religious groups, prof groups. *Restrictions:* for indiv & inst, only in member states ·of Region 6, Fish and Wildlife Serv (Utah, Mont., Wyo., Colo., Nebr., Kan., S. Dak., N. Dak., Iowa, Mo.) Cannot transmit electronically. Available to researchers/scholars for on-site viewing. May borrow by mail. *Loan Period:* 3 days. *Total Yr Film Loan:* 745.

Film Rental Serv *Eligibility:* no restrictions. *Restrictions:* only in Region 6, Fish & Wildlife Serv. Cannot transmit electronically. *Rental Period:* 3 days. *Total Yr Film Booking:* 3767.

Film Collection 1025t/1085p. Approx 20-30t acquired annually. *Circ:* 16mm, 1025t/1085p. *Pubns:* catalog, every 3 yr; suppl, in yr catalog not published.

Other Film Serv Rent film from distributors for faculty, obtain film from coop loan system, obtain film from other libraries. Permanent viewing facility. *Equipment:* lend/rent 16mm sound projector, 8mm cartridge projector (1), 8mm reel projector (6), projection screens (10), slide projectors, programmers.

Other Media Collections *Audio:* tape, 978c.

Budget & Expenditures Total library budget $26,025 (FY 7/1/74-7/1/75). Total FY film budget $12,500.

Video Serv *Video Use:* documentation of community/school events, to increase community's library use, in-service training. Video serv available on demand and by appointment. Produce video tapes. Have production studio/space & separate control room.

Video Equipment/Facilities *In-House Use Only:* porta-pak; recording deck; playback deck; editing deck; studio camera; monitor; SEG; keyer; synthesizer; additional camera lenses; lighting; microphones; tripods; audio tape recorders. *For Loan:* playback deck; audio tape recorders. Have permanent viewing installation.

Video Collection Maintained by own production. Use/play ½", 1" reel to reel, ¾" cassette. *Other Video Serv:* programming, taping of other media.

Cable & CCTV Receive serv of cable TV system. Produce programs for cablecasting. Inform public about cable system serv & facilities. Serve as production facility for others. Run cable programs for special audiences. Have CCTV in inst. *Programming Sources:* over-the-air commercial & public broadcasting, tapes produced by inst.

Ogden

C- WEBER STATE COLLEGE, Film Library, 3750 Harrison Blvd, 84408. *Tel:* (801) 399-5941, ext 473. *Film Serv Est:* 1968. *In Charge:* Barbara Buchanan, Film Librarian. *AV Staff:* 6 (6 cl). *Film Sel:* committee preview, faculty/staff recommendations. *Holdings:* agriculture 5%, black studies 10%, career education 5%, consumer affairs, dance, 5%, fine arts 15%, industrial arts 5%, medicine 5%, science 25%, social sciences 20%.

Free-Loan Film Serv *Eligibility:* faculty. *Restrictions:* for indiv, on-campus only. May not borrow by mail. *Total Yr Film Loan:* 11,662.

Film Collection 1400t. 50t acquired annually. *Circ:* 1400p. *Pubns:* catalog, annual.

Other Film Serv Film reference serv. *Equipment:* lend 16mm sound projector, 8mm cartridge projector, 8mm reel projector, S8mm cartridge projector, S8mm reel projector, projection tables & stands, projection screens, record players, filmstrip projectors, video units.

Other Media Collections *Audio:* tape, cassette, 1853t/2150c; tape, cartridge, 109t/c. *Filmstrips:* silent, 380t/c. *Slides:* single, 444t/c.

Budget & Expenditures Total library budget $163,000 (FY 7/1/74-7/1/75). Total FY film budget $4000. *Member:* AECT, ALA, Utah Library Assn.

Salt Lake City

P- SALT LAKE COUNTY LIBRARY SYSTEM, Whitmore Library, 2197 E 7000 S, 84121. *Tel:* (801) 943-7614. *Film Serv Est:* 1951. *In Charge:* Dale L. Jensen, AV Coord. *AV Staff:* 5 (1 prof, 3 cl, 1 tech). *Film Sel:* committee preview, faculty/staff recommendations, chief film librarian's decision, published reviews.

Free-Loan Film Serv *Eligibility:* prof groups. *Restrictions:* for inst, within interlibrary loan region. Available to researchers/scholars for on-site viewing. May borrow by mail. *Loan Period:* 3 days. *Total Yr Film Loan:* 15,000.

Film Rental Serv *Eligibility:* no restrictions. *Restrictions:* only in county. *Rental Period:* 3 days. *Total Yr Film Booking:* 15,000.

Film Collection 700t/1250p. Approx 50t acquired annually. *Circ:* 16mm, 700t/1250p. *Pubns:* catalog, every 2 yr ($.50); suppl, in yr catalog not published.

Other Film Serv Film fairs/festivals, library film programs. Permanent viewing facility available free to community. *Equipment:* rent 16mm sound projector (12), lend 8mm reel projector (6), S8mm reel projector (60), projection tables & stands (12), projection screens (24), tape recorders, record players, slide & filmstrip projectors, overhead, opaque.

Other Media Collections *Audio:* disc, 33⅓ rpm, 20,000c; tape, cassette, 6000c; tape, cartridge, 300c; tape, reel, 50c. *Filmstrips:* sound, 4800c; silent, 8000c.

Budget & Expenditures Total library budget $2,032,000 (FY 1/75-1/76). Total FY film budget $12,000. *Member:* AECT, AFI, ALA, EFLA, FLIC, Utah Library Assn, Mountain Plain Library Assn.

Video Serv *Est:* 1974. *Video Staff:* 1 f-t, 2 p-t, 1 tech. *Video Use:* to increase community's library use, in-service training, practical video/TV training courses, playback only of professionally produced tapes. Video serv available on demand and by appointment.

Video Equipment/Facilities *In-House Use Only:* recording deck (2), ¾" cassette/col, JVC6100; playback deck (5), ¾" cassette/col, JVC5000; studio camera (1), col, Panasonic; monitor (5), col, Sony. Have permanent viewing installations. *Equipment Loan Period:* no set policy. Provide training in use of equipment.

Video Collection Maintained by purchase, rental. Use/play ¾" cassette. *Sources:* commercial distributors. *Tape Sel:* preview, faculty/staff recommendations. *Special Collections:* in-house training tapes, films in video format. Tapes organized by subject. *Collection, Color:* ¾" cassette, 97t.

C- UNIVERSITY OF UTAH, Educational Media Center, 207 Milton Bennion Hall, 84112. *Tel:* (801) 581-6112. *Film Serv Est:* 1916. *In Charge:* Stephen H. Hess, Assistant Dir. *AV Staff:* 14 (2 prof, 8 cl, 5 tech). *Film Sel:* faculty/staff recommendations. *Holdings:* black studies 2%, career education 2%, children's films 20%, consumer affairs 2%, dance 15%, engineering 2%, experimental films 5%, fine arts 30%, law 3%, medicine 10%, science 20%, social sciences 25%, teacher education 15%, women 5%.

Film Rental Serv *Eligibility:* no restrictions. *Restrictions:* only in U.S. Cannot transmit electronically. *Rental Period:* 3, 5 days. *Total Yr Film Booking:* 25,000. Sell films. Produce films.

Film Collection 4200t/5000p. Approx 200t acquired annually. *Circ:* 16mm, 4200t/5000p. *Pubns:* catalog, every 2 yr; suppl, in yr catalog not published. Publish flyers announcing new acquisitions.

Other Film Serv Rent film from distributors for patrons, obtain film from coop loan system (Consortium of University Film Centers), obtain film from other libraries, film reference serv, library film programs. Permanent viewing facility. *Equipment:* rent 16mm sound projector (100), 8mm cartridge projector (2), 8mm reel projector (2), S8mm cartridge projector (2), S8mm reel projector (3), projection tables & stands (40), projection screens (40), tape recorders, overheads, opaque, record players.

Other Media Collections *Audio:* disc, 33⅓ rpm, 3000t/3500c; tape, reel, 3500t/c. *Filmstrips:* sound, 300t/c; silent, 900t/400c; sound sets, 40t/c; silent sets, 10t/c.

Budget & Expenditures Total library budget $24,000 (FY 7/1/74-7/1/75). Total FY film budget $24,000. *Member:* AECT.

Video Serv *Est:* 1973. *In Charge:* Ruth A. Frear, AV Librarian. *Video Staff:* 2 f-t, 5 p-t. *Video Use:* documentation of community/school events, to increase community's library use, curriculum support. Video serv available on demand and by appointment. Produce video tapes.

Video Equipment/Facilities *In-House Use Only:* recording deck (1), ¾″ U col, Sony; playback deck (10), ¾″ U, 1″ col, Sony VP-1000, JVC CP-5000U, Wollensak VP-205, Telemation TVP1010. Have permanent & portable viewing installations. Provide training in use of equipment to AV assistants.

Video Collection Maintained by purchase, own production. Use/play 1″ reel to reel, ¾″ cassette. *Sources:* commercial distributors. *Tape Sel:* preview, faculty/staff recommendations, published reviews, catalogs. *Special Collections:* curriculum support. Tapes organized by subject. *Collection, Color:* ¾″ cassette, 750t/800c. *Collection, B&W:* 1″ reel, 50t/c.

Cable & CCTV Receive serv of cable TV system. Produce programs for cablecasting. Inform public about cable system serv & facilities. Have CCTV in inst. *Programming Sources:* tapes produced by inst.

S- UTAH STATE LIBRARY COMMISSION, Film Library, 2150 S 300 West, Suite 16, 84115. *Tel:* (801) 533-5875. *Film Serv Est:* 1970. *In Charge:* Russell L. Davis, Dir. *Film Sel:* faculty/staff recommendations. *Holdings:* children's films 5%, educational films, health-oriented films, science 14%, travel.

Free-Loan Film Serv *Eligibility:* staff & students, educational inst, civic groups, prof groups, & others, such as travel clubs, TV, forest serv agencies, business. *Restrictions:* for indiv, only in state; for inst, only in state. Cannot use for fund-raising, special films for forest agencies only. Available to researchers/scholars for on-site viewing. May borrow by mail. *Loan Period:* differs depending on serv. *Total Yr Film Loan:* 9536.

Film Collection 1338t/1400p. Approx 25t acquired annually. *Circ:* 16mm, 1338t/1400p. *Pubns:* catalog, annual; suppl, no set policy.

Other Film Serv Film reference serv.

Other Media Collections *Audio:* disc, 33⅓ rpm, 20t/23c; disc, 78rpm, 3t; tape, cassette, 25t/c. *Filmstrips:* sound, 74t/75c; silent, 56t/60c; silent sets, 2t/c. *Slides:* single, 7t/10c; sets, 1t/6c.

Budget & Expenditures Total library budget $350,000 (FY 7/1/74-7/1/75). Total FY film budget $5000. *Member:* ALA.

Vermont

Burlington

C- UNIVERSITY OF VT, Film Library, University Media Serv, 05401. *Tel:* (802) 656-2970. *Film Serv Est:* 1943. *In Charge:* Marion DeThestrup, Film Librarian. *Film Sel:* faculty/staff recommendations, chief film librarian's decision, published reviews. *Holdings:* agriculture, animated films, black studies, career education, children's films, consumer affairs, engineering, experimental films, feature films, fine arts, industrial arts, medicine, science, social sciences, teacher education, women.
   Free-Loan Film Serv *Eligibility:* staff & students, educational inst, prof groups. *Restrictions:* for indiv, only in state. Cannot use for fund-raising, borrow for classroom use. Available to researchers/scholars for on-site viewing. May borrow by mail. *Loan Period:* 3 days.
   Film Rental Serv *Eligibility:* educational org. *Restrictions:* only in state. Cannot use for fund-raising. *Rental Period:* 3 days.
   Film Collection 2500t. *Pubns:* catalog, every 2 yr; suppl, in yr catalog not published.
   Other Film Serv Rent film from distributors for patrons. Obtain film from other libraries. Permanent viewing facility. *Equipment:* lend 16mm sound projector, 8mm cartridge projector, 8mm reel projector, S8mm reel projector, projection screens. *Member:* AECT.
   Video Serv *Est:* 1975. *In Charge:* Paul S Massie, Assistant Dir. *Video Staff:* 3 f-t. *Video Use:* documentation of community/school events, in-service training. Video serv available by appointment. Produce video tapes.
   Video Equipment/Facilities *In-House and Loan:* portapak (4), ½" b&w/col, Sony; recording/playback deck (3), ½" b&w, Panasonic; editing deck (1), ½" b&w, Panasonic; studio camera (3), ½" b&w, Panasonic; monitor (3), b&w/col, Panasonic; lighting (2); microphones (3). Have permanent viewing installation. Provide training in use of equipment to faculty & students. Have tape duplication serv.
   Video Tape Loan/Rental/Sale Serv *Loan/Rental Eligibility:* staff, students enrolled in inst. Cannot air without permission. May not borrow by mail.
   Video Collection Maintained by purchase, own production. Use/play ½" reel to reel, ¾" cassette. *Tape Sel:* preview, faculty/staff recommendations, catalogs. Tapes organized by Dewey Decimal. *Other Video Serv:* production workshops.

Cable & CCTV Receive serv of cable TV system. Have CCTV in inst. *Programming Sources:* over-the-air commercial & public broadcasting, tapes produced by community groups & indiv.

Montpelier

P- VERMONT DEPARTMENT OF LIBRARIES, 111 State St, 05602. *Tel:* (802) 828-3261. *Member:* North County Library Film Coop.

Plainfield

C- GODDARD COLLEGE, Learning Aids Center, 05667. *Tel:* (802) 454-8311, ext 286. *AV Staff:* 2 (1 cl, 1 tech). *Film Sel:* committee preview.
   Free-Loan Film Serv *Eligibility:* org members. *Restrictions:* for indiv, none. May borrow by mail. *Loan Period:* 1 day.
   Film Collection 82t/p. *Circ:* 16mm, 47t/p; 8mm reel, 21t/p; 8mm cartridge, 14t/p.
   Other Film Serv Film reference serv.
   Other Media Collections *Slides:* single, 2000t/c.
   Video Serv *Video Staff:* 2 f-t, 1 tech. *Video Use:* documentation of community/school events, as art form. Video serv available by appointment. Produce ½" b&w video tapes. Have production studio/space & separate control room.
   Video Equipment/Facilities *In-House Use Only:* playback deck (2), ½" b&w, Sony 3650; studio camera (3), ½" b&w, Panasonic 350P; SEG (1), Panasonic; keyer (1), Panasonic; additional camera lenses; lighting (5). *For Loan:* portapak (4), ½" b&w, Sony Rover II; monitor (9), b&w, various. *Equipment Loan Period:* 1 day. Provide training in use of equipment to faculty & students and staff.
   Video Tape Loan/Rental/Sale Serv *Serv Provided:* free loan, sale. *Loan Eligibility:* org members, students enrolled in inst. *Restrictions:* for indiv, none. Must be used for academic purposes. May not borrow by mail. *Loan Period:* indefinite.
   Video Collection Maintained by own production, exchange/swap. Use/play ½" reel to reel. *Sources:* exchange. *Other Video Serv:* programming, taping of other media.
   Cable & CCTV Will receive serv of cable TV system.

Virginia

Alexandria

P- ALEXANDRIA LIBRARY, Special Services Division, 815 King St, Suite 404, 22314. *Tel:* (703) 750-6354, 750-6439. *Film Serv Est:* 1956. *In Charge:* Frederic W. Boots, Division Head, Special Services. *AV Staff:* 5 (1 prof, 3 cl, 1 tech). *Film Sel:* committee preview, staff recommendations, chief film librarian's decision.

Free-Loan Film Serv *Eligibility:* indiv with library cards, member libraries of Suburban Washington Library Film Service. *Restrictions:* for indiv, only in city; & members of film coop. Cannot use for fund-raising, transmit electronically. Available to researchers/scholars for on-site viewing. May not borrow by mail. *Loan Period:* 3 days. *Total Yr Film Loan:* 20,613.

Film Collection 1103t/1142p. Approx 66t acquired annually. *Circ:* 16mm, 1103t/1142p. *Pubns:* catalog, every 2 yrs ($1.70); suppl, in yr catalog not published ($.35).

Other Film Serv Obtain film from coop loan system (Suburban Washington Library Film Service), film reference serv, library film programs. Permanent viewing facility available to community.

Other Media Collections *Audio:* disc, 33⅓ rpm, 4609t/11,399c.

Budget & Expenditures Total library budget $171,507 (FY 7/1/74-7/1/75). Total FY film budget $15,653. *Member:* EFLA.

Arlington

P- ARLINGTON COUNTY PUBLIC LIBRARY, Film Service, 1015 North Quincy St, 22201. *Tel:* (703) 527-4777, ext 43. *Film Serv Est:* 1954. *In Charge:* Lois A. Kane, Coordinator, Special Services. *AV Staff:* 3 (1 prof, 1 cl, 1 tech). *Film Sel:* committee preview, staff recommendations, chief film librarian's decision, patrons' suggestions. *Holdings:* animated films, black studies, career education, children's films, consumer affairs, dance, documentaries, experimental films, feature films, fine arts, health, history, nature, social problems, social sciences, women.

Free-Loan Film Serv *Eligibility:* civic groups, religious groups, indiv with library cards. Cannot use for fund-raising, transmit electronically, borrow for public school classroom use. Available to researchers/scholars for on-site viewing. May occasionally borrow by mail. *Loan Period:* 1 day. *Total Yr Film Loan:* 12,000.

Film Collection 675p. Approx 35t acquired annually. *Circ:* 16mm, 675p. *Pubns:* catalog, every 2 yrs ($2); suppl, in yr catalog not published ($.35).

Other Film Serv Obtain film from coop loan system (Suburban Washington Library Film Service), film reference serv, film fairs/festivals, library film programs. Permanent viewing facility available to community.

Other Media Collections *Audio:* disc, 33⅓ rpm, 3500c.

Budget & Expenditures Total library budget $220,000 (FY 7/1/75-7/1/76). Total FY film budget $8500. *Member:* ALA, EFLA, FLIC, Va. Library Assn, D.C. Library Assn.

Ashland

C- RANDOLPH-MACON COLLEGE, Walter Hines Page Library, 23005. *Tel:* (804) 798-8372, ext 256. *Film Serv Est:* 1973. *In Charge:* Flavia Owen, Librarian. *AV Staff:* 1 (1 cl). *Film Sel:* faculty/staff recommendations. *Holdings:* experimental films 2%, feature films 56%, religion, science 5%, social sciences 30%.

Free-Loan Film Serv *Eligibility:* staff & students, & non-educational members of film coop. *Restrictions:* for inst, only in state. Cannot use for fund-raising, transmit electronically. May borrow by mail. *Loan Period:* flexible. *Total Yr Film Loan:* 130.

Film Collection 45t/p. Approx 15t acquired annually. *Circ:* 16mm, 45t/p. *Pubns:* catalog, every 2 yrs; suppl, no set policy.

Other Film Serv Obtain film from coop loan system (Richmond Area Film Library Cooperative), obtain film from other libraries. Permanent viewing facility.

Other Media Collections *Audio:* disc, 33⅓ rpm, 1014c; tape, cassette, 33c.

Budget & Expenditures Total library budget $44,500 (FY 7/1/74-7/1/75). Total FY film budget $1000. *Member:* ALA, Va. Library Assn, Southeastern Library Assn.

Blacksburg

C- VIRGINIA POLYTECHNIC INSTITUTE & STATE UNIVERSITY, LRC Film Library, 4 Patton Hall, 24061. *Tel:* (703) 951-6718. *Film Serv Est:* 1971. *In Charge:* Carol Ness. *AV Staff:* 4 (2 prof, 1 cl, 1 tech). *Film Sel:* faculty/staff recommendations. *Holdings:* agriculture 25%, engineering 15%.

Free-Loan Film Serv *Eligibility:* staff, civic groups, local public schools. *Restrictions:* for indiv, none; for inst, none. May not borrow by mail. *Loan Period:* as needed. *Total Yr Film Loan:* 5000. Sell films. Produce films.

Film Collection 800t/900p. Approx 100t acquired annually. *Circ:* 16mm, 800t/900p. *Pubns:* catalog, every 2 yrs; suppl, in yr catalog not published.

Other Film Serv Rent film from distributors for patrons, obtain film from coop loan system (Va. Bureau of Teaching Materials). Permanent viewing facility. *Equipment:* lend 16mm sound projector, 8mm cartridge projector, 8mm reel projector, S8mm cartridge projector, S8mm reel projector, projection tables & stands, projection screens, tape recorders, overhead projectors, speakers, microphones.

Other Media Collections *Filmstrips:* sound, 40t/c. *Slides:* sets, 50t/c.

Budget & Expenditures No separate AV budget. *Member:* AECT, Va. Museum of Art.

Video Serv *Est:* 1971. *In Charge:* Robert F. Steffen, Assistant Dir. *Video Staff:* 8 f-t, 20 p-t, 4 tech. *Video Use:* practical video/TV training courses, support academic programs of 8 colleges. Video serv available on demand. Produce video tapes. Have production studio/space & separate control room.

Video Equipment/Facilities *In-House Use Only:* portapak (2), ½″, ¾″ b&w/col, Sony; recording deck (13), ½″, ¾″, 1″ b&w/col, IVC, Sony; playback deck (4), ¾″ col, Sony; editing deck (2), ¾″ col, Sony 2850; studio camera (6), col, IVC 500A, Sony DX1200; SEG (2), Richmond, Dynair; lighting (35); microphones (11); tripods (4); audio tape recorders (2). Have permanent & portable viewing installations. Provide training in use of equipment to faculty & students. Have tape duplication serv.

Video Tape Loan Serv *Serv Provided:* swap with other inst. *Loan Eligibility:* staff & students.

Video Collection Maintained by purchase, own production. Use/play ½″, 1″ reel to reel, ¾″ cassette. *Sources:* in-house production. *Tape Sel:* faculty/staff recommendations. Tapes organized by subject. *Collection, Color:* 1″ reel, 172t/c; ¾″ cassette, 450t/c. *Collection, B&W:* ½″ reel, 150t/c. *Other Video Serv:* programming, reference serv, taping of other media, production workshops, instructional development service in program design & production. *Pubns:* catalog.

Cable & CCTV Receive serv of cable TV system. Produce programs for cablecasting. Inform public about cable system serv & facilities. Have CCTV in inst, with 60 monitors & 3 projection systems. *Programming Sources:* over-the-air commercial & public broadcasting, tapes produced by inst, tapes produced professionally.

Bridgewater

C- BRIDGEWATER COLLEGE, Alexander Mack Memorial
Library, 22812. *Tel:* (703) 828-3928, ext 334. *Film Serv Est:*
1969. *In Charge:* Orland Wages, Librarian. *AV Staff:* ¼ (¼
prof, ½ cl). *Film Sel:* faculty/staff recommendations, chief
film librarian's decision. *Holdings:* black studies 5%, career
education 10%, fine arts 15%, science 25%, social sciences
25%, teacher education 10%.
  Free-Loan Film Serv *Eligibility:* staff & students, civic
groups. Cannot use for fund-raising, transmit electronically.
Available to researchers/scholars for on-site viewing. May not
borrow by mail. *Loan Period:* 1 day. *Total Yr Film Loan:* 25.
  Film Collection 20t/30p.
  Other Film Serv Rent film from distributors for patrons,
obtain film from Va. State Board of Education, obtain film
from other libraries. Permanent viewing facility.
  Other Media Collections *Audio:* disc, 33⅓ rpm, 3300t;
tape, cassette, 350t; tape, cartridge, 25t; tape, reel, 150t. *Filmstrips:* silent sets, 135t. *Slides:* single, 500t.
  Budget & Expenditures Total library budget $59,958 (FY
7/1/74-7/1/75). Total FY film budget $750.

Chester

P- CHESTERFIELD PUBLIC LIBRARY, Chester Branch,
12140 Harrowgate Rd, 23831. *Tel:* (804) 748-6049. Jene
Harrison Knoop, Dir. *Member:* Richmond Area Film Library Coop.

C- JOHN TYLER COMMUNITY COLLEGE, 13101 Jefferson
Davis Highway, 23831. *Tel:* (804) 748-6481, ext 251. *Film
Serv Est:* 1967. *In Charge:* Patti Jimison, Library Clerk.
Film Sel: faculty/staff recommendations & previews.
  Free-Loan Film Serv *Eligibility:* educational inst, any
member of community. *Restrictions:* for indiv, only in service
area of the college; for inst, only in state. Available to re-
searchers/scholars for on-site viewing. May borrow by mail.
Loan Period: 3 days. *Total Yr Film Loan:* 1248.
  Film Collection 257t/p. *Circ:* 16mm, 257t/p. *Pubns:* catalog, annual; suppl, no set policy.
  Other Film Serv Rent film from distributors for patrons,
obtain film from coop loan system (Richmond Area Libraries
Film Cooperative), obtain film from other libraries, library film
programs. Permanent viewing facility available to community.
Equipment: lend S8mm camera (1), 16mm sound projector (6),
8mm cartridge projector (1), 8mm reel projector (1), S8mm
cartridge projector (3), S8mm reel projector (2), projection tables
& stands (20), projection screens (20), filmstrip & slide projectors.
  Other Media Collections *Audio:* disc, 33⅓ rpm, 322t; tape,
cassette, 554t; tape, reel, 571t. *Filmstrips:* total, 384t. *Slides:*
single, 7473t.
  Budget & Expenditures Total library budget $42,404 (FY
7/1/74-7/1/75). No separate budget. *Member:* AECT, ALA, Va.
Library Assn.
  Video Serv *Video Staff:* 1 f-t. *Video Use:* documentation of
community/school events, in-service training, playback only of
professionally produced tapes, as art form, instructional purposes. Video serv available on demand. Produce video tapes.
Have production studio/space & separate control room.
  Video Equipment/Facilities *For Loan:* portapak (1), ½"
b&w, Panasonic NV3082; recording deck (2), ½", ¾" col, Wollensak, VR210; playback deck (3), ½", ¾" col, Panasonic NV3130,
NV340, JVC CP500U; studio camera (5), Sony, Ampex, Panasonic; monitor (19), b&w/col, Sony, Zenith; SEG (1), Sony;
additional camera lenses (7); lighting (5); audio tape recorders
(4). Have permanent viewing installation. *Equipment Loan
Period:* 2 days. Provide training in use of equipment to faculty.
  Video Tape Loan Serv *Serv Provided:* free loan, swap
with other inst. *Loan Eligibility:* staff & students, educational
inst, civic groups, religious groups, prof groups, members of
consortium. *Restrictions:* for indiv, interlibrary loan. Cannot
use for fund-raising, duplicate, air without permission. May
borrow by mail. *Loan Period:* 7 days. *Total Yr Tape Loan:* 5.

Video Collection Maintained by purchase, rental, own
production, exchange/swap. Use/play ¼" reel to reel, ¾"
cassette. *Sources:* commercial distributors, community productions, exchange. *Member:* Richmond Area Video Cooperative.
Tape Sel: preview, faculty/staff recommendations. Publish
materials on video.
  Cable & CCTV Have CCTV in inst, with 12 monitors.
Programming Sources: tapes produced by inst, tapes produced
professionally, tapes produced by community groups & indiv.

Hardy

S- BOOKER T. WASHINGTON NATIONAL MONUMENT,
Route 1, Box 195, 24101. *Tel:* (703) 721-2094. *Film Serv Est:*
1965. *In Charge:* Samuel H. Goodpasture, Park Technician. *Holdings:* black studies 100%.
  Free-Loan Film Serv *Eligibility:* educational inst, civic
groups. *Restrictions:* for inst, none. Cannot use for fund-raising,
transmit electronically. Available to researchers/scholars for
on-site viewing. May borrow by mail. *Loan Period:* 2 wks. *Total
Yr Film Loan:* 7.
  Film Collection 1t/12p.
  Other Film Serv Permanent viewing facility.
  Budget & Expenditures Total library budget $150 (FY
1/1/74-1/1/75). Total FY film budget $150.
  Video Serv *Video Use:* as interpretive tool. Video serv
available by appointment.
  Video Equipment/Facilities Have permanent viewing
installation. *Equipment Loan Period:* 2 wks.
  Video Tape Loan Serv *Serv Provided:* free loan, swap
with other inst. *Loan Eligibility:* educational inst, civic groups.
Restrictions: inst, none. Cannot use for fund-raising, duplicate,
air without permission. May borrow by mail. *Loan Period:* 2
wks. *Total Yr Tape Loan:* 7.

Harrisonburg

C- EASTERN MENNONITE COLLEGE, Learning Resources,
22801. *Tel:* (703) 433-2771, ext 219 or 148. *Film Serv Est:*
1959. *In Charge:* Milo D. Stahl, Dir of Learning Resources.
AV Staff: 4 (1 prof, 2 cl, 1 tech). *Film Sel:* committee
preview, faculty/staff recommendations.
  Free-Loan Film Serv *Eligibility:* staff & students. *Restrictions:* for indiv, only in city; for inst, only in city. Available to
researchers/scholars for on-site viewing. May borrow by mail.
Loan Period: flexible.
  Film Rental Serv *Eligibility:* no restrictions. *Restrictions:*
none. *Rental Period:* flexible. Produce films. Produce audio
tapes, slides & sound slide productions, transparencies, posters
etc.
  Film Collection 300t/p. Approx 10-20t acquired annually.
Circ: 8mm reel, 5t/p; 8mm cartridge, 15t/p; S8mm reel, 15t/p;
S8mm cartridge, 20t/24p. *Pubns:* catalog, as needed ($3); suppl,
no set policy ($1.50).
  Other Film Serv Rent film from distributors for patrons,
obtain film from other libraries, film reference serv, film fairs/
festivals. Permanent viewing facility available for rent to community. *Equipment:* rent 16mm sound projector (14), rent 8mm
cartridge projector (3), 8mm reel projector (1), S8mm cartridge
projector (8), S8mm reel projector (3), projection tables & stands
(15), projection screens (20), various media equipment.
  Other Media Collections *Audio:* disc, 33⅓ rpm, 380t/480c;
disc, 45rpm, 10t/c; disc, 78rpm, 10t/c; tape, cassette, 700t/c;
tape, reel, 480t/c. *Filmstrips:* sound, 280t/c; silent, 380t/400c.
Slides: single, 10,000c; sets, 55t/c.
  Budget & Expenditures Total FY film budget $4000. *Mem-
ber:* AECT, EFLA, Va. Library Assn, Valley Educational Media
Assn, Va. Educational Media Assn, National Assn of Educational Broadcasters.
  Video Serv *Est:* 1970. *Video Staff:* 4 f-t, 40 p-t, 10 tech.
Video Use: documentation of community/school events, community video access, in-service training, playback only of professionally produced tapes. Video serv available on demand &
by appointment. Produce video tapes.

Video Equipment/Facilities *In-House Use Only:* recording deck (5), ½″ b&w/col, Sony, Wollensak; playback deck (5), ½″ b&w/col, Sony, Wollensak; editing deck (1), ½″ b&w, Sony; studio camera (5), b&w, Sony, Shibaden; monitor (4), b&w/col, Panasonic, Sony. *For Loan:* monitor (4), b&w/col, Panasonic, Sony; additional camera lenses (3); microphones (20); tripods (3); audio tape recorders (30). Have permanent & portable viewing installations. *Equipment Loan Period:* rental charge per day. Provide training in use of equipment to faculty & students. Have tape duplication serv.

Video Tape Loan/Rental/Serv *Serv Provided:* free loan, rental. *Loan/Rental Eligibility:* staff & students (free), others (rental). *Restrictions:* for indiv & inst, only in city. May borrow by mail. *Loan Period:* negotiable.

Video Collection Maintained by purchase, rental, own production. Use/play ½″ reel to reel, ¾″ cassette. *Sources:* commercial distributors. *Tape Sel:* preview, faculty/staff recommendations, catalogs. Tapes organized by Dewey Decimal, special coding for nursing tapes. *Collection, Color:* ¾″ cassette, 121t/177t. *Collection, B&W:* ½″ reel, 68t/c. *Other Video Serv:* programming, reference serv. *Pubns:* catalog. Publish materials on video.

Cable & CCTV Receive serv of cable TV system. Inform public about cable system serv & facilities. Run cable programs for special audiences. Have CCTV in inst, with 14 monitors. *Programming Sources:* over-the-air commercial & public broadcasting, tapes produced by inst, tapes produced professionally.

Lexington

S- GEORGE C. MARSHALL RESEARCH FOUNDATION, Drawer 920, 24450. *Tel:* (703) 463-7103. *In Charge:* A. R. Crawford, Archivist & B. P. Vandegrift, Librarian. *Film Sel:* committee preview, gifts & donations. *Holdings:* Marshall, George C., Marshall Plan, military history.

Free-Loan Film Serv *Eligibility:* org members. Available to researchers/scholars for on-site viewing.

Film Collection 50t/p. *Circ:* 16mm, 48t/p.

Other Media Collections *Audio:* disc, 33⅓ rpm, 83t; tape, cassette, 24t; tape, reel, 200t. *Filmstrips:* sound, silent sets, 1t. *Slides:* single, 500t.

Budget & Expenditures No separate budget.

Lynchburg

C- LYNCHBURG COLLEGE, Library, 24504. *Tel:* (703) 845-9071, ext 271, 272. *Film Serv Est:* 1970. *In Charge:* Marjorie M. Freeman, Assistant Librarian for Media Services. *AV Staff:* 1 (½ prof, ½ cl). *Film Sel:* faculty/staff recommendations. *Holdings:* Asian studies 30%, biology 50%.

Free-Loan Film Serv *Eligibility:* staff & students. *Restrictions:* for indiv, only in classroom. Available to researchers/scholars for on-site viewing. May not borrow by mail. *Loan Period:* 7 days.

Film Collection 301t/p. Approx 12t acquired annually. *Circ:* 16mm, 121t; S8mm cartridge, 180t.

Other Film Serv Obtain film from coop loan system (Lynchburg Area Library Cooperative, Blue Ridge Tri-College Consortium), film reference serv. Permanent viewing facility. *Equipment:* lend 16mm sound projector (8), 8mm reel projector (1).

Other Media Collections *Audio:* disc, 33⅓ rpm, 2200t/2518c; disc, 78rpm, 650t/c; tape, cassette, 163t/c; tape, reel, 40t/c. *Filmstrips:* sound, 384t/c; silent, 1360t/c. *Slides:* single, 1216t/c.

Budget & Expenditures Total library budget $72,708 (FY 7/1/74-7/1/75). No separate budget. *Member:* ALA, Va. Library Assn.

Martinsburg

P- BLUE RIDGE REGIONAL LIBRARY 310 E Church St, 24112. *Tel:* (703) 632-7125. *In Charge:* Hazel S. Nickelston. **Free-Loan Film Serv** *Eligibility:* indiv with library cards.

Film Collection *Circ:* 16mm & 8mm.
Other Film Serv Obtain film from Va. State Library.

Petersburg

C- VIRGINIA STATE COLLEGE, Instructional Materials Lab, Box 27, 23803. *Tel:* (804) 526-5111, ext 465, 466. *Film Serv Est:* 1948. *In Charge:* Harry A. Johnson, Dir. *AV Staff:* 7 (4 prof, 1 cl, 2 tech). *Film Sel:* committee preview, faculty/staff recommendations. *Holdings:* agriculture, animated films, black studies, career education, children's films, fine arts, industrial arts.

Free-Loan Film Serv *Eligibility:* staff & students, educational inst, civic groups, religious groups, indiv with library cards. *Restrictions:* for indiv, interlibrary loan, only in state; for inst, only in state. Available to researchers/scholars for on-site viewing. May borrow by mail. *Loan Period:* 5 days.

Film Collection 450t/p. *Pubns:* catalog, every 3 yrs; suppl, no set policy.

Other Film Serv Obtain film from coop loan system (Richmond Area Film Library Coop), film reference serv, film fairs/festivals. Permanent viewing facility. *Equipment:* lend S8mm camera (1), 16mm camera (1), 16mm sound projector (15), 8mm cartridge projector (2), 8mm reel projector (3), S8mm cartridge projector (2), S8mm reel projector (3), projection tables & stands (10), projection screens (10).

Budget & Expenditures No separate AV budget. *Member:* AECT, ALA.

Video Serv *Est:* 1965. *Video Staff:* 7 f-t, 2 tech. *Video Use:* documentation of community/school events, in-service training, practical video/TV training courses. Video serv available on 24 hr request. Produce video tapes. Have production studio/space & separate control room.

Video Equipment/Facilities *In-House Use Only:* portapak (2), ½″ b&w, Sony 3700; recording deck (5), ½″ b&w, Sony 3600; playback deck (1), ½″ b&w, GE CV2100; editing deck (1), b&w, Sony 3200; studio camera (4), b&w, Sony CM142U; monitor (6), b&w; SEG (2); microphones (10); tripods (5). *For Loan:* portapak (2), ½″ b&w, Sony 3700; recording deck (5), ½″ b&w, Sony 3600; playback deck (1), ½″ b&w, GE CV2100; editing deck (1), b&w, Sony 3200; studio camera (4), b&w, Sony CM 142U; monitor (6), b&w; SEG (2); microphones (10); tripods (5). Have permanent & portable viewing installations. *Equipment Loan Period:* no set policy. Provide training in use of equipment to faculty & students.

Video Tape Loan Serv *Serv Provided:* free loan, swap with other inst. *Loan/Rental Eligibility:* staff & students, educational inst, civic groups, religious groups. *Restrictions:* for indiv & inst, none. May not borrow by mail. *Loan Period:* as needed.

Video Collection Maintained by purchase, exchange/swap. Use/play ½″ reel to reel, ¾″ cassette. *Sources:* locally produced. *Tape Sel:* faculty/staff recommendations. Tapes organized by computer code. *Collection, Color:* ½″ reel, 20t/c; ¾″ cassette, 6t/c. *Collection, B&W:* ½″ reel, 20t/c. *Pubns:* catalog.

Cable & CCTV Receive serv of cable TV system. Produce programs for cablecasting. Have CCTV in inst, with 9 monitors. *Programming Sources:* over-the-air commercial & public broadcasting, tapes produced professionally.

Portsmouth

C- TIDEWATER COMMUNITY COLLEGE, Frederick Campus, 23703. *Tel:* (804) 484-2121, ext 208, 209. *Film Serv Est:* 1968. *In Charge:* Marguerite B. Burgess, Coord, AV Servs. *AV Staff:* 4 (1 prof, 1 cl, 2 tech). *Film Sel:* committee preview, faculty/staff recommendations.

Free-Loan Film Serv *Eligibility:* staff & students, educational inst. *Restrictions:* for indiv, only in state; for inst, only in state. Available to researchers/scholars for on-site viewing. May borrow by mail. *Loan Period:* as needed.

Film Collection 300t/p. Approx 3-5t acquired annually. *Circ:* 16mm, 100t/p; 8mm reel, 1t/p; S8mm cartridge, 200t/p. *Pubns:* catalog, annual.

Other Film Serv Rent film from distributors for patrons, obtain film from other libraries. Permanent viewing facility.

Portsmouth (cont'd)
Equipment: lend 16mm sound projector (10), 8mm reel projector (1), S8mm cartridge projector (8), S8mm reel projector (1), projection screens (50).

Other Media Collections *Audio:* disc, 33⅓ rpm, 600t/c; tape, cassette, 300t/c; tape, reel, 100t/c. *Filmstrips:* sound, 50t/c; silent, 200t/c; sound sets, 100t/c; silent sets, 5t/c. *Slides:* single, 50t/c; sets, 30t/c.

Budget & Expenditures Total AV film budget $10,000. *Member:* ALA, EFLA, Va. Library Assn, Va. Educational Materials Assn.

Video Serv *Est:* 1972. *Video Staff:* 4 f-t, 2 p-t, 2 tech. *Video Use:* documentation of community/school events, in-service training, playback only of professionally produced tapes, educational. Video serv available by appointment. Produce video tapes.

Video Equipment/Facilities *For Loan:* portapak (1), ½″ b&w, JVC; recording deck (1), ¾″ col, Sony 1600; playback deck (1), ¾″ col, Sony 1200; studio camera (1), ¾″ b&w, Sony; monitor (3), col, Sony; microphones; tripods; audio tape recorders. *Equipment Loan Period:* no set policy. Provide training in use of equipment to faculty & students.

Video Tape Loan Serv *Serv Provided:* free loan, swap with other inst. *Loan Eligibility:* staff & students, educational inst, prof groups, such as city of Portsmouth. *Restrictions:* for indiv, only in Portsmouth, Chesapeake, Suffolk & Norfolk counties; for inst, only in city. Cannot duplicate. May not borrow by mail.

Video Collection Maintained by purchase, rental, own production. Use/play ½″ reel to reel, ¾″ cassette. *Sources:* commercial distributors. *Tape Sel:* published reviews, catalogs. Tapes organized by LC system.

Richmond

S- REYNOLDS METALS COMPANY, Executive Office Library, 6601 W Broad St, 23261. *Tel:* (804) 282-2311. *In Charge:* A. C. Fain, AV Dir. *Member:* Richmond Area Film Library Coop.

S- RICHMOND MEMORIAL HOSPITAL, 1300 Westwood Ave, 23227. *Tel:* (804) 359-6961. *In Charge:* Laura Murphy, Dir, School of Nursing. *Member:* Richmond Area Film Library Coop.

C- SARGEANT REYNOLDS COMMUNITY COLLEGE, Learning Resources Center, Library, 108 E Grace St, Box 6935, 23220. *Tel:* (804) 770-5734. *In Charge:* Diana K. Dixon, Dir. *Member:* Richmond Area Film Library Coop.

C- UNION THEOLOGICAL SEMINARY IN VIRGINIA, 3401 Brook Rd, 23227. *Tel:* (804) 355-0671, ext 68. *Film Serv Est:* 1950. *In Charge:* Eleanor Godfrey, Dir of Media Resources Dept. *AV Staff:* 5 (2 tech). *Film Sel:* faculty/staff recommendations. *Holdings:* television films 95%.

Film Rental Serv *Eligibility:* patrons/public. Cannot use for fund-raising, transmit electronically. *Rental Period:* 5 days. *Total Yr Film Booking:* 200. Produce slide programs.

Film Collection 250t/425p. Approx 2-3t acquired annually. *Circ:* 16mm, 250t/425p. *Noncirc:* 16mm, 1t/p. *Pubns:* catalog, every 2 yrs ($4); suppl, no set policy.

Other Film Serv Rent film from distributors for patrons, obtain film from coop loan system (Richmond Area Cooperative Film Library). Permanent viewing facility.

Other Media Collections *Audio:* tape, cassette, 18,000c; tape, cartridge, 3900t.

Budget & Expenditures Total library budget $64,983 (FY 6/1/74-6/1/75). Total FY film budget $1000.

Video Serv *In Charge:* John Coffman, Dir Media Services. *Video Staff:* 3 f-t, 1 p-t. *Video Use:* documentation of community/school events, to increase community's library use, practical video/TV training courses, playback only of professionally produced tapes, as art form, tape classes. Video serv available on demand. Produce video tapes. Have production studio/space & separate control room.

Video Equipment/Facilities *In-House Use Only:* recording deck (6), b&w/col, Sony AV3600, VD2500, Concord VCR 820; editing deck (1), Concord 820; studio camera (3), b&w, Concord TCM20; monitor (20), b&w, Sony, Concord; SEG (2), Concord, Shibaden; microphones (10); audio tape recorders (20); audio cassettes (14). *For Loan:* portapak (1), ½″ b&w, Concord 450T; audio tape recorders (20), audio cassettes (14). Have permanent & portable viewing installations. *Equipment Loan Period:* no set policy. Have tape duplication serv.

Video Tape Loan Serv *Serv Provided:* free loan. *Loan Eligibility:* staff & students. *Restrictions:* for indiv, only if one of our staff is present; for inst, only if operated by our staff. Cannot use for fund-raising, duplicate, air without permission. May borrow by mail.

Video Collection Maintained by purchase, own production. Use/play ½″ reel to reel, ¾″ cassette. *Sources:* commercial distributors, produce specific tapes for our classes. *Tape Sel:* preview, faculty/staff recommendations, catalogs. *Special Collections:* films in video format. Tapes organized by list. *Collection, Color:* ¾″ cassette, 4t/c. *Collection, B&W:* ½″ reel, 10t/c; ¾″ cassette, 6t/c. *Other Video Serv:* production workshops.

Cable & CCTV Have CCTV in inst, with 6 monitors. *Programming Sources:* tapes produced by inst, tapes produced professionally, classes in certain subjects taped for evaluation.

C- UNIVERSITY OF RICHMOND, Learning Resources Center, 23173. *Tel:* (804) 285-6314. *Film Serv Est:* 1972. *In Charge:* T. Goldman, Dir, Learning Resources Center. *AV Staff:* 1 (1 prof, 1 cl, 2 tech). *Film Sel:* faculty/staff recommendations. *Holdings:* experimental films 40%, feature films 50%.

Free-Loan Film Serv *Eligibility:* org members. Cannot transmit electronically, borrow for classroom use. Available to researchers/scholars for on-site viewing. May not borrow by mail. *Loan Period:* 5 days.

Film Collection 60t/p. Approx 10-15t acquired annually. *Circ:* 16mm, 60t/p; 8mm reel, 5t/p. *Pubns:* catalog, annual ($1); suppl, no set policy.

Other Film Serv Rent film from distributors for patrons, obtain film from coop loan system (Richmond Area Film Coop), obtain film from other libraries, film reference serv, film fairs/festivals. Permanent viewing facility.

Budget & Expenditures Total library budget $200,000 (FY 7/1/75-7/1/76). Total FY film budget $5000. *Member:* AECT, ALA, Va. Library Assn.

Video Serv *Est:* 1975. *Video Staff:* 1 f-t, 2 p-t. *Video Use:* documentation of community/school events, in-service training, practical video/TV training courses. Video serv available by appointment. Produce video tapes. Have production studio/space & separate control room.

Video Equipment/Facilities *In-House Use Only:* recording deck (3), ¾″ b&w, Sony VO1600; playback deck (3), ¾″ col, Sony VO1600; studio camera (2), b&w, Sony; microphones (2); tripods (2). Have portable viewing installation. Provide training in use of equipment to faculty & students.

Video Tape Loan Serv *Serv Provided:* free loan, swap with other inst. *Loan Eligibility:* staff & students, member of Richmond Area Coop. Cannot use for fund-raising, air without permission. May not borrow by mail. *Loan Period:* 7 days.

Video Collection Maintained by rental, own production, exchange/swap. Use/play ½″ reel to reel, ¾″ cassette. *Sources:* exchange (Richmond Area Film Cooperative). *Tape Sel:* faculty/staff recommendations, catalogs. Tapes organized by LC system. *Collection, Color:* ½″ reel, 2t/c; ¾″ cassette, 25t/c. *Collection, B&W:* ½″ reel, 2t/c; ¾″ cassette, 25t/c. *Other Video Serv:* taping of other media, production workshops.

S- VETERANS ADMINISTRATION HOSPITAL, 1201 Broad Rock Blvd, 23224. *Tel:* (804) 233-9631, ext 458. *In Charge:* Donna Kay Everett, AV Specialist. *Member:* Richmond Area Film Library Coop.

C- VIRGINIA COMMONWEALTH UNIVERSITY, AV Dept, 901 Park Ave, 23284. *Tel:* (804) 770-4834. *In Charge:* Willnette M. Dyer, Film Librarian. *Member:* Richmond Area Film Library Coop.

S- VIRGINIA MUSEUM OF FINE ARTS, Boulevard and Grove Ave, 23221. *Tel:* (804) 786-7440. *Video Serv Est:* 1970. *In Charge:* John P. Dworak, Communications Specialist. *Video Staff:* 1 f-t. *Video Use:* to increase community's library use, community video access, in-service training, as art form. Video serv available on demand. Produce video tapes. Have production studio/space.

Video Equipment/Facilities *In-House Use Only:* portapak (1), ¼" b&w, Sony AVC-3400; recording deck (2), ¾" col, Sony VO-1600; editing deck (1), ¾" col, JVC CR-6000U; studio camera (1), b&w, Sony AVC-3210; monitor (2), b&w/col, Sony, Panasonic; SEG (1), Sony; additional camera lenses (2); lighting (6); microphones (4); audio tape recorders (3). Have portable viewing installation. Provide training in use of equipment to museum staff. Have duplication serv.

Video Tape Loan/Rental/Sale Serv *Serv Provided:* free loan, swap with other inst. *Loan/Rental Eligibility:* org members, staff & students, educational inst, civic groups, religious groups, prof groups. *Restrictions:* for indiv & inst, only in state. Cannot duplicate, air without permission. May borrow by mail. *Loan Period:* 2 wks. *Total Yr Tape Loan:* 200.

Video Collection Maintained by own production, exchange/swap. Use/play ½" reel to reel, ¾" cassette. *Sources:* own production. Tapes organized by subject. *Collection, Color:* ¾" cassette, 45t. *Collection, B&W:* ½" reel, 30t; ¾" cassette, 15t. *Pubns:* catalog.

Cable & CCTV The Programs Division, working with the local PBS station and using their videotape equipment, has produced 14 ½-hr color productions on 2" tape. All programs have become part of the PBS network.

S- VIRGINIA STATE LIBRARY, Film Collection, 12th and Capitol St, 23219. *Tel:* (804) 786-2323. *Film Serv Est:* 1962. *In Charge:* William C. Luebke, Film Librarian. *AV Staff:* 5 (1 prof, 1 cl). *Film Sel:* committee preview.

Free-Loan Film Serv *Eligibility:* public libraries for their programs or to circulate to org & state inst within their community. *Restrictions:* for inst, only in state. Cannot use for fundraising, transmit electronically, borrow for classroom use. May not borrow by mail. *Loan Period:* 1 day. *Total Yr Film Loan:* 21,431.

Film Collection 2185t/3059p. Approx 339t acquired annually. *Circ:* 16mm, 2185t/3059p. *Pubns:* catalog, every 3 yrs ($2); suppl, in yr catalog not published ($1).

Other Film Serv Film reference serv, library film programs.

Budget & Expenditures Total library budget $203,252 (FY 7/1/74-7/1/75). Total FY film budget $99,852. *Member:* ALA, EFLA, Va. Library Assn.

C- VIRGINIA UNION UNIVERSITY, 1500 N Lombardy St, 23220. *Tel:* (804) 359-9331, ext 264. *In Charge:* Verdell Bradley, Librarian. *Member:* Richmond Area Film Library Coop.

Springfield

P- FAIRFAX COUNTY PUBLIC LIBRARY, Special Services, 5502 Port Royal Rd, 22151. *Tel:* (703) 451-7240. *Film Serv Est:* 1955. *In Charge:* Joseph E. Mersereau, Coordinator, Special Services. *AV Staff:* 8½ (1 prof, 7½ cl). *Film Sel:* committee preview.

Free-Loan Film Serv *Eligibility:* educational inst, civic groups, religious groups, indiv with library cards. *Restrictions:* for indiv, only in Fairfax County; for inst, only in Fairfax County. Cannot use for fund-raising, transmit electronically, borrow for public school classroom use. May not borrow by mail. *Loan Period:* 1 day. *Total Yr Film Loan:* 40,258.

Film Collection 1575t/1686p. Approx 200t acquired annually. *Circ:* 16mm, 1575t/1686p. *Pubns:* catalog, every 2 yrs ($1.70); suppl, no set policy.

Other Film Serv Obtain film from coop loan system (Suburban Washington Library Film Service), film reference serv, library film programs. *Equipment:* rent 16mm sound projector (12), projection screens (3).

Other Media Collections *Audio:* disc, 33⅓ rpm, 5359t/17,251c.

Budget & Expenditures Total library budget $933,621 (FY 7/1/74-7/1/75). Total FY film budget $48,000. *Member:* ALA, EFLA, FLIC, Va. Library Assn, Washington Film Council.

Virginia Beach

C- TIDEWATER COMMUNITY COLLEGE, Learning Laboratory, 1700 College Crescent, 23456. *Tel:* (804) 427-3070, ext 150. *Film Serv Est:* 1975. *In Charge:* Diane Heestand, Coordinator of Learning Lab. *AV Staff:* (3 prof, 3 cl). *Film Sel:* faculty/staff recommendations.

Free-Loan Film Serv *Eligibility:* staff & students, & others, such as members of community. *Restrictions:* for indiv, only in city; for inst, only in the college system. Cannot use for fundraising, transmit electronically. Available to researchers/scholars for on-site viewing. May not borrow by mail. *Loan Period:* 2 days.

Film Collection 35t/p. *Circ:* 16mm, 46t. *Noncirc:* 16mm, 14t.

Other Film Serv Obtain film from other libraries, film reference serv.

Other Media Collections *Audio:* disc, 33⅓ rpm, 164t; tape, cassette, 257t. *Filmstrips:* sound, 50t; silent, 6t; sound sets, 45t; silent sets, 17t. *Slides:* single, 47t; sets, 2t.

Budget & Expenditures Total library budget $54,930 (FY 7/1/75-7/1/76). Total AV film budget $10,000. *Member:* AECT, NAEB, CCAIT.

Video Serv *Video Staff:* 3 f-t, 1 p-t. *Video Use:* documentation of community/school events, community video access, practical video/TV training courses, playback only of professionally produced tapes. Video serv available on demand. Produce video tapes.

Video Equipment—Facilities *In-House Use Only:* recording deck (1), ¾" col, Wollensak; playback deck (10), ¾" col, Panasonic; studio camera (1), b&w. Provide training in use of equipment to faculty & students.

Video Tape Loan/Rental/Sale Serv *Serv Provided:* free loan, swap with other inst. *Loan Eligibility:* staff & students, & others, such as Tidewater residents. *Restrictions:* for indiv, only in city. Cannot use for fund-raising, duplicate, air without permission. May not borrow by mail. *Loan Period:* 2 days.

Video Collection Maintained by purchase, own production. Use/play ¾" cassette. *Sources:* commercial distributors, community productions. *Tape Sel:* preview, faculty/staff recommendations, catalogs. Tapes organized by acquisition number. *Collection, Color:* ¾" cassette, 137t. *Collection, B&W:* ¾" cassette, 95t. *Other Video Serv:* reference serv. Publish materials on video.

Washington

Aberdeen

C- GRAYS HARBOR COLLEGE, 98520. *Tel:* (206) 532-0920, ext 204. *In Charge:* Bonnie Kalinowski. *AV Staff:* 1 tech. Rent film from distributors for patrons.
Other Media Collections *Audio:* 78rpm, 500t; tape, cassette, 12t. *Filmstrips:* sound sets, 3t. *Slides:* sets, 2t.
Budget & Expenditures Total library budget $89,081 (FY 7/1/75-7/1/76). Total FY budget $4620. *Member:* Pacific Northwest Bibliographies Center.
Video Serv *Est:* 1971. *In Charge:* Don Cates, Asst Librarian. *Video Staff:* 1 p-t. *Video Use:* in-service training, practical video/TV training courses. Video serv available by appointment. Have production studio/space.
Video Equipment/Facilities *In-House Use Only:* studio camera (1), ½" b&w, Sony AV3600; monitor (1), b&w, Sony; microphones (4); tripods (1); audio tape recorders (12). Provide training in use of equipment to faculty & students.

Bellevue

C- BELLEVUE COMMUNITY COLLEGE, Library-Media Center, 3000-145th Place SE, 98007. *Tel:* (206) 641-2255. *Film Serv Est:* 1965. *In Charge:* Boyd Bolvin, Assoc Dean-L-MC. *AV Staff:* 2 (1½ cl, ½ tech). *Film Sel:* faculty/staff recommendations, chief film librarian's decision. *Holdings:* black studies 10%, fine arts 20%, medicine 10%, science 26%, social sciences 26%.
Film Rental Serv *Eligiblity:* educational org. *Restrictions:* only in state. *Rental Period:* 2 days. Sell films. Produce films. Produce video, slides, sound slides.
Film Collection 400t/p. Approx 6-8t acquired annually. *Pubns:* catalog, as needed; suppl, no set policy.
Other Film Serv Rent film from distributors for patrons, obtain film from coop loan system (C. C. Consortium), obtain film from other libraries. Permanent viewing facility available for rent to community. *Member:* AECT, ALA, Wash. Library Assn.
Video Serv *Est:* 1973. *In Charge:* Wayne Bitterman, Media Specialist. *Video Staff:* 1 f-t, 1 tech. *Video Use:* documentation of community/school events, practical video/TV training courses, instructional TV. Video serv available on demand & by appointment. Produce video tapes. Have production studio/space & separate control room.
Video Equipment/Facilities *In-House Use Only:* recording deck (3), b&w, Sony, Panasonic; playback deck (12), b&w/col, Sony, IVC, Panasonic; editing deck (2), b&w/col, Sony, Panasonic; studio camera (7), b&w/col, Norelco-TM; monitor (15), b&w/col; SEG (2); keyer (2); additional camera lenses (6); lighting (18); microphones (18); tripods (7); audio tape recorders (12), portable cameras (5). Have permanent & portable viewing installations. Provide training in use of equipment to faculty & students. Have tape duplication serv.
Video Tape Loan/Rental/Sale Serv *Serv Provided:* free loan, swap with other inst. *Loan Eligibility:* staff & students, non-profit groups (with producer permission). *Restrictions:* for indiv, only in college district; for inst, none. Cannot air without permission.
Video Collection Maintained by own production. Use/play ½", 1" reel to reel, ½" cartridge, ¾" cassette. *Sources:* exchange (colleges, CATV). Tapes organized by subject, name of producer. *Collection, Color:* ½" reel, 14t; 1" reel, 2t. *Collection, B&W:* ½" reel, 95t; 1" reel, 9t; ½" cartridge, 10c; ¾" cassette, 8c. *Other Video Serv:* programming, taping of other media, production workshops.
Cable & CCTV Receive serv of cable TV system. Run cable programs for special audiences. Have CCTV in inst, with 20 monitors. *Programming Sources:* over-the-air commercial & public broadcasting, tapes produced by inst, tapes produced by community groups & indiv. Have CATV channel. System is used as part of Media Technician program with students doing large part of production. New production facilities near completion for future production of more materials for instructors, dial access & CATV.

Bellingham

P- BELLINGHAM PUBLIC LIBRARY, Box 1197, 98225. *Tel:* (206) 676-6860. *Film Serv Est:* 1952. *In Charge:* Linda Hodge, AV Librarian. *AV Staff:* 1 (½ prof, ½ cl). *Film Sel:* committee preview.
Free-Loan Film Serv *Eligibility:* civic groups, religious groups, & others, such as residents of Whatcom County. *Restrictions:* for indiv, only in Whatcom County. Cannot use for fundraising. Teachers may borrow only 1 film at time; others up to 4 films. May borrow by mail occasionally. *Loan Period:* 1 day. *Total Yr Film Loan:* 3465.
Film Collection 240t/p. Approx 30-48t acquired annually. *Circ:* 16mm, 67t/p; 8mm reel, 140t/p; S8mm reel, 50t/p. *Pubns:* catalog, every 2 yrs; suppl, no set policy.
Other Film Serv Obtain film from coop loan system (Washington Library Film Circuit), film reference serv, library film programs. Permanent viewing facility available for rent to community.
Other Media Collections *Audio:* disc, 33⅓ rpm, 5085c; tape, cassette, 369t/c.
Budget & Expenditures Total library budget $66,488 (FY 1/1/75-1/1/76). Total FY film budget $2609. *Member:* Wash. Library Assn.

C- WESTERN WASHINGTON STATE COLLEGE, Educational Media/AV Center, Miller Hall 155, 98225. *Tel:* (206) 676-3300. *Film Serv Est:* 1950. *In Charge:* Corbin Ball, Media Coordinator. *AV Staff:* 10 (4 prof, 3 cl, 3 tech). *Film Sel:* faculty/staff recommendations, chief film librarian's decision, published reviews. *Holdings:* animated films 10%, black studies 5%, feature films 5%, fine arts 10%, science 10%, social sciences 30%, teacher education 30%.
Free-Loan Film Serv *Eligibility:* staff & students. *Restrictions:* for indiv, only on campus. Available to researchers/scholars for on-site viewing. May not borrow by mail.
Film Collection 500t/p. Approx 20t acquired annually. *Noncirc:* 16mm, 500t/p.
Other Film Serv Rent film from distributors for patrons, obtain film from other libraries, film reference serv. Permanent viewing facility. *Equipment:* lend/rent S8mm camera, 16mm sound projector, 8mm cartridge projector, 8mm reel projector, S8mm cartridge projector, S8mm reel projector, projection tables & stands, projection screens.
Budget & Expenditures Total library budget $20,000 (FY 9/22/74-9/22/75). Total FY film budget $13,000. *Member:* AECT.

Bremerton

P- KITSAP REGIONAL LIBRARY, 612-Fifth St, 98310. *Tel:* (206) 377-3955. *Film Serv Est:* 1972. *In Charge:* Elliott Swanson, Media Specialist. *AV Staff:* 2½ (1 prof). *Film Sel:* chief film librarian's decision.
Free-Loan Film Serv *Eligibility:* civic groups, indiv with library cards, & others, such as libraries with whom we have coop contract. *Restrictions:* for indiv & inst, only in bordering counties with coop agreements. Cannot use for fund-raising, transmit electronically. Some titles restricted for classroom use. Available to researchers/scholars for on-site viewing. May not borrow by mail. *Loan Period:* 1 day. *Total Yr Film Loan:* 8044.
Film Collection 100t. *Circ:* 16mm, 100t/p; S8mm & 8mm reel & cartridge, 350t. *Pubns:* catalog, as needed.

Other Film Serv Rent film from distributors for patrons, obtain film from coop loan system (Washington Library Film Circuit), obtain film from other libraries, film reference serv, film fairs/festivals, library film programs. *Equipment:* lend 16mm sound projector (1), 8mm reel projector (11), projection screens (5).

Other Media Collections *Audio:* disc, 33⅓ rpm, 4801t; 78rpm, 1t; tape, cassette, 640t. *Filmstrips:* silent, 100t.

Budget & Expenditures Total library budget $112,103 (FY 1/1/74-1/1/75). *Member:* Wash. Library Assn.

Cheney

C- EASTERN WASHINGTON STATE COLLEGE, Instructional Media Center, 99022. *Tel:* (509) 359-2265. *Film Serv Est:* 1968. *In Charge:* Jerry Donen, Dir, IMC. *AV Staff:* 20 (4 prof, 13 cl, 3 tech). *Film Sel:* faculty/staff recommendations, chief film librarian's decision.

Free-Loan Film Serv *Eligibility:* staff & students, educational inst. *Restrictions:* for indiv, only in our county. Available to researchers/scholars for on-site viewing. May not borrow by mail. Produce films. Produce sound slides.

Film Collection 300t/p. Approx 10t acquired annually.

Other Film Serv Rent film from distributors for patrons, obtain film from other libraries, film reference serv, film fairs/festivals, library film programs. Permanent viewing facility available for rent to community. *Equipment:* lend S8mm camera, 16mm camera, 16mm sound projector, 8mm cartridge projector, 8mm reel projector, S8mm cartridge projector, S8mm reel projector, projection tables & stands, projection screens.

Budget & Expenditures Total library budget $25,000 (FY 7/1/74-7/1/75). Total FY film budget $8000. *Member:* AECT.

Video Serv *Est:* 1968. *In Charge:* Bill Odell, TV Serv Coordinator. *Video Staff:* 2 f-t, 4 p-t. *Video Use:* documentation of community/school events, in-service training, practical video/TV training courses, playback only of professionally produced tapes, as art form. Video serv available on demand. Produce video tapes. Have production studio/space & separate control room.

Video Equipment/Facilities *In-House Use Only:* portapak (10), ½" b&w, Sony AV3400; recording deck (5), ½" b&w/col, Sony AV3600, AV8600; editing deck (1), b&w/col, Panasonic; studio camera (4), b&w/col, Sony, Telemation; monitor (10), col, Sony; SEG (1), Telemation; lighting (16); microphones (4). *For Loan:* portapak (10), ½" b&w, Sony AV3400; recording deck (5), ½" b&w/col, Sony AV3600, AV8600; monitor (10), col, Sony. Have permanent & portable viewing installations. *Equipment Loan Period:* 1-3 days. Provide training in use of equipment to faculty & students. Have tape duplication serv.

Video Collection Maintained by purchase, own production. Use/play ½", 1" reel to reel, ¾" cassette. *Tape Sel:* faculty/staff recommendation. *Special Collections:* specially produced PBS programs. Tapes organized by subject. *Collection, Color:* ¾" cassette, 45t. *Collection, B&W:* ½" reel, 95t; 1" reel, 20t; ¾" cassette, 25t.

Cable & CCTV Produce programs for cablecasting. Run cable programs for special audiences. Have advisory/administrative role in cable system operation. *Member:* Educational Consortium on Cable.

Longview

P- LONGVIEW PUBLIC LIBRARY, 1600 Louisiana St, 98632. *Tel:* (206) 423-2340, ext 21. *Film Serv Est:* 1951. *In Charge:* Jerry L. Ritchie, Film Clerk. *AV Staff:* 1 (1 cl). *Film Sel:* staff recommendations, chief film librarian's decision. *Holdings:* children's films 50%.

Free-Loan Film Serv *Eligibility:* indiv with library cards. *Restrictions:* for indiv, none. Cannot use for fund-raising, transmit electronically. Available to researchers/scholars for on-site viewing. May borrow by mail. *Loan Period:* 1 day. *Total Yr Film Loan:* 3691.

Film Collection 34t/p. Approx 7t acquired annually. *Circ:* 16mm, 34t/p; 8mm reel, 56t/57p; S8mm reel, 73t/p. Publish materials pertaining to collection.

Other Film Serv Obtain film from coop loan system (Washington State Film Circuit), obtain film from other libraries, film reference serv, library film programs. Permanent viewing facility available for rent to community. *Equipment:* lend 16mm sound projector (2), 8mm reel projector (2), S8mm reel projector (2), projection tables & stands (3), projection screens (4), filmstrip/slide projector (1).

Other Media Collections *Audio:* disc, 33⅓ rpm, 3316t/c; tape, cassette, 230t/c. *Filmstrips:* silent, 23t/c; sound sets, 10t/c. *Slides:* sets, 1t/c.

Budget & Expenditures Total library budget $49,918 (FY 1/1/74-1/1/75). Total FY film budget $1570. *Member:* ALA, EFLA, FLIC, Wash. Library Assn.

Mount Vernon

C- SKAGIT VALLEY COLLEGE, Library Media Center, 2405 College Way, 98273. *Tel:* (206) 424-1031, ext 111. *Video Serv Est:* 1971. *In Charge:* John King, Media Technician. *Video Staff:* 1 p-t, 1 tech. *Video Use:* documentation of community/school events, in-service training, practical video/TV training courses, as art form, class instruction. Video serv available by appointment. Produce video tapes. Have production studio/space & separate control room.

Video Equipment/Facilities *In-House Use Only:* lighting (10); microphones (5); tripods (4). *For Loan:* portapak (1), b&w, Sony 3400; playback deck (3), b&w/col, Sony 8600, 5000; editing deck (1), 1" b&w, Ampex EX6100; studio camera (5), b&w/col; microphones (5); audio tape recorders (30). Have permanent viewing installation. *Equipment Loan Period:* 2 days. Provide training in use of equipment to faculty & students.

Video Tape Loan/Rental/Sale Serv *Serv Provided:* free loan, swap with other inst. *Loan Eligibility:* staff & students, educational inst, civic groups, religious groups, indiv with library cards, prof groups, such as those meeting on campus. *Restrictions:* for indiv, only college district; for inst, only in area of Puget Sound Consortium. Cannot duplicate, air without permission. May borrow by mail. *Loan Period:* as needed.

Video Collection Maintained by own production, exchange/swap. Use/play ½", 1" reel to reel. *Sources:* exchange (Puget Sound Consortium). *Member:* Puget Sound Consortium of Community Colleges. *Tape Sel:* faculty/staff recommendations. Tapes organized by accession number. *Collection, Color:* ½" reel, 2t/c. *Collection, B&W:* ½" reel, 70t/90c; 1" reel, 12t/c. *Other Video Serv:* production workshops.

Cable & CCTV Receive serv of cable TV system.

Olympia

C- THE EVERGREEN STATE COLLEGE, Daniel J. Evans Library, 98505. *Tel:* (206) 866-6259. *Film Serv Est:* 1972. *In Charge:* Kaye Utsunomiya, Film Consultant. *AV Staff:* 17 (6 prof, 2 cl, 9 tech). *Film Sel:* faculty/staff evaluate & make recommendations, film consultant's decision. *Holdings:* animated films 5%, black studies 5%, dance 1%, engineering 3%, experimental films 3%, feature films 3%, fine arts 22%, science 33%, social sciences 10%, teacher education 3%, women 2%.

Free-Loan Film Serv *Eligibility:* staff & students, & others, such as residents of Thurston County. *Restrictions:* for indiv & inst, only in Thurston County. May borrow by mail. *Loan Period:* 1-7 days. *Total Yr Film Loan:* 2553.

Film Collection 175t/190p. Approx 30-35t acquired annually. *Circ:* 16mm, 175t/190p; S8mm reel, 475t/p. *Pubns:* catalog, as needed; suppl, in yr catalog not published.

Other Film Serv Obtain film from other libraries, film reference serv. Permanent viewing facility. *Equipment:* lend S8mm camera (36), 16mm camera (5), 16mm sound projector (10), 8mm cartridge projector (1), 8mm & S8mm reel projector (19), S8mm cartridge projector (1), projection tables & stands (40), projection screens (12), wide variety of misc equipment.

Other Media Collections *Audio:* tape, cassette, 8000t. *Slides:* single, 9000t.

Olympia (cont'd)

Budget & Expenditures Total library budget $347,643.25 (FY 7/1/74-7/1/75). Total FY film budget $11,211.

Video Serv *Est:* 1973. *In Charge:* Joyana Brown, Dean of Library. *Video Staff:* 42 f-t, 73 p-t, 10 tech. *Video Use:* documentation of community/school events, to increase community's library use, in-service training, playback only of professionally produced tapes, as art form, media education. Video serv available on demand & by appointment. Produce video tapes. Have production studio/space & separate control room.

Video Equipment/Facilities *In-House Use Only:* portapak (1), ½″ b&w, Sony AV-3400; recording & playback deck (6), ½″ b&w/col, Sony AV3600, 3650, 8600, 8650; editing deck (3), ½″, 1″ col, IVC 870, Sony 8650, RCA TIC44K; studio camera (4), b&w/col, RCA TIC44A, Telemation; monitor (20), b&w/col, Sony, RCA; SEG (4), Grass Valley, Panasonic; keyer (3), Grass Valley, Panasonic; lighting (45); microphones (33); tripods (4); audio tape recorders (4). *For Loan:* portapak (12), ½″ b&w, Sony AV-3400; recording & playback deck (11), ½″ b&w/col, Sony AV3600, 3650, 8600, 8650; monitor (38), b&w/col, Sony, RCA; SEG (1); keyer (1); lighting (20); microphones (42); tripods (11). Have permanent & portable viewing installations. *Equipment Loan Period:* no set policy. Provide training in use of equipment to faculty & students. Have tape duplication serv.

Video Tape Loan/Rental/Sale Serv *Serv Provided:* swap with other inst. *Loan Eligibility:* staff & students.

Video Collection Maintained by purchase, rental, own production, exchange/swap. Use/play ½″, 1″, 2″ reel to reel, ½″ cartridge, ¾″ cassette. *Sources:* student & staff productions. *Tape Sel:* preview, faculty/staff recommendations. Tapes organized by subject, title & author. *Other Video Serv:* programming, production workshops.

Cable & CCTV Have CCTV in inst. *Programming Sources:* over-the-air commercial & public broadcasting, tapes produced professionally.

P- **TIMBERLAND REGIONAL LIBRARY**, Olympia Public Library, 7th & Franklin, 98501. *Tel:* (206) 352-0595. *Film Serv Est:* 1971. *Film Sel:* committee preview, district staff preview. *Holdings:* animated films 10%, children's films 50%, experimental films 1%.

Free-Loan Film Serv *Eligibility:* civic groups, indiv with identification. *Restrictions:* for indiv, only in our 5-county library district; for inst, only in state. Cannot use for fund-raising, transmit electronically. Available to researchers/scholars for on-site viewing. May borrow by mail. *Loan Period:* 1 day. *Total Yr Film Loan:* 1086. Produce slides, videotapes.

Film Collection 157t/172p. *Circ:* 16mm, 157t/172p. *Noncirc:* 16mm, 17t/p. *Pubns:* catalog, annual; suppl, as needed.

Other Film Serv Obtain film from coop loan system (regional libraries of 5 counties), obtain film from other libraries, film reference serv, film fairs/festivals, library film programs. *Equipment:* lend 16mm sound projector (33), projection screens (30).

Other Media Collections *Audio:* tape, cassette, 16t. *Filmstrips:* sound, 127t; silent, 2t; sound sets, 25t; silent sets, 10t. *Slides:* single, 91t; sets, 2t.

Budget & Expenditures Total library budget $282,991 (FY 1/1/74-1/1/75). No separate AV budget. *Member:* ALA, Wash. Library Assn.

Video Serv *Est:* 1972. *In Charge:* Michael Hedges, Community Relations Officer. *Video Staff:* 1 f-t. *Video Use:* to increase community's library use. Video serv available by appointment. Produce video tapes. Have portable viewing installation. *Equipment Loan Period:* period of immediate need. Provide training in use of equipment to staff.

Video Tape Loan/Rental/Sale Serv *Serv Provided:* free loan, sale. *Loan Eligibility:* staff & students, civic groups, individuals with identification. *Restrictions:* for indiv & inst, none. Cannot use for fund-raising, duplicate, air without permission. May borrow by mail. *Loan Period:* flexible.

Video Collection Maintained by own production. Use/play ½″ reel to reel. *Collection, Color:* ½″ reel, 1t/2c. *Collection, B&W:* ½″ reel, 1t/c. *Other Video Serv:* production workshops. *Pubns:* catalog.

P- **WASHINGTON STATE LIBRARY**, Film Library, 98504. *Tel:* (206) 866-6470. *Film Serv Est:* 1968. *In Charge:* Jere Pennell, Coordinator. *AV Staff:* 13 (3 prof, 8 cl, 2 tech). *Film Sel:* committee preview. *Holdings:* agriculture 2%, career education 2%, consumer affairs 2%, law enforcement 12%, women 2%.

Free-Loan Film Serv *Eligibility:* any indiv or org in state of Wash. *Restrictions:* for indiv & inst, only in state, some titles internationally. Cannot use for fund-raising. Training films restricted to appropriate agency use. Available to researchers/scholars for on-site viewing. May borrow by mail. *Loan Period:* 5 days. *Total Yr Film Loan:* 38,683.

Film Collection 2153t/4402p. Approx 100-500t acquired annually. *Circ:* 16mm, 2119t/4265p; 8mm reel, 6t/p; S8mm reel, 6t/p; S8mm cartridge, 22t/125p. *Pubns:* catalog, as needed; suppl, no set policy.

Other Film Serv Rent film from distributors for patrons, obtain film from coop loan system (Washington Library Film Circuit), obtain film from other libraries, film reference serv. Permanent viewing facility available to community. *Equipment:* lend/rent S8mm camera, 16mm camera, 16mm sound projector, 8mm cartridge projector, 8mm reel projector, S8mm cartridge projector, S8mm reel projector, projection tables & stands, projection screens.

Other Media Collections *Audio:* tape, cassette, 600t/625c; tape, reel, 25t. *Filmstrips:* sound, 178t/198c; silent, 20t/22c. *Slides:* sets, 83t/103c.

Budget & Expenditures Total library budget $636,100 (FY 7/1/74-7/1/75). Total FY film budget $48,000. *Member:* AECT, ALA, EFLA, Wash. Library Assn, Pacific Northwest Library Assn.

Video Serv *Est:* 1973. *Video Staff:* 14 f-t. *Video Use:* documentation of community events, community video access, in-service training, playback only of professionally produced tapes, as art form. Video serv available by appointment. Produce video tapes. Have production studio/space & separate control room.

Video Equipment/Facilities *In-House Use Only:* recording deck (29), ½″, ¾″, 1″, 2″ b&w/col; playback deck (3); editing deck (10), ½″, 1″, 2″ b&w/col, RCA TK44; studio camera (4), b&w/col, Telemation; monitor (50), b&w/col, Telemation; SEG (6); keyer (6); additional camera lenses (18); lighting (200); microphones (200); tripods (20); audio tape recorders (200). *For Loan:* recording deck (29), ½″, ¾″, 1″, 2″ b&w/col; playback deck (3); studio camera (4), b&w/col, Telemation; monitor (50), b&w/col, Telemation; SEG (6); keyer (6); microphones (200); tripods (20); audio tape recorders (200). Have permanent viewing installation. *Equipment Loan Period:* 5 days. Provide training in use of equipment to faculty, students & state employees. Have tape duplication serv.

Video Tape Loan/Rental/Sale Serv *Serv Provided:* free loan, swap with other inst. *Loan Eligibility:* staff & students, educational inst, prof groups, such as those in health sciences & others, such as state & regional agencies. *Restrictions:* for indiv, only state or regionally affiliated; for inst, only in state. Cannot use for fund-raising, duplicate. Some titles restricted to special groups. May borrow by mail. *Loan Period:* 5 days. *Total Yr Tape Loan:* 2132.

Video Collection Maintained by own production. Use/play ½″, 1″, 2″ reel to reel, ¾″ cassette. *Special Collections:* in-house training tapes, video as art. Tapes organized by subject. *Collection, Color:* ½″ reel, 44t/83c; 1″ reel, 58t/158c; 2″ reel, 64t/225c; ¾″ cassette, 8t/16c. *Other Video Serv:* reference serv, taping of other media, production workshops. *Pubns:* catalog.

Cable & CCTV Have CCTV in inst, with 50 monitors. *Programming Sources:* student-produced tapes & live productions.

Port Angeles

P- **NORTH OLYMPIC LIBRARY SYSTEM**, 2210 Peabody, 98362. *Tel:* (206) 457-4464. *Film Serv Est:* 1971. *In Charge:* Marie Lorgen, AV Clerk. *AV Staff:* 1½ (1½ cl). *Film Sel:* staff recommendations, published reviews. *Holdings:* fisheries 10%, science 60%, sports 30%.

Free-Loan Film Serv *Eligibility:* indiv with library cards. *Restrictions:* for indiv, interlibrary loan; for inst, none. Cannot use for fund-raising, transmit electronically. May borrow by mail. *Loan Period:* 1 day. *Total Yr Film Loan:* 2424.

Film Collection 10t/p. *Circ:* 16mm, 10t/p; 8mm reel, 4t/p; S8mm cartridge, 23t/p.

Other Film Serv Obtain film from coop loan system (Wash. State Film Circuit, Wash. State Film Library), obtain film from other libraries. *Equipment:* lend 16mm sound projector (5), projection screens (4), slide projectors (3).

Other Media Collections *Audio:* disc, 33⅓ rpm, 1500t; tape, cassette, 650t; tape, cartridge, 25t. *Slides:* sets, 7t.

Budget & Expenditures Total library budget $92,550 (FY 1/1/75-1/1/76). No separate budget. *Member:* ALA, Wash. Library Assn, Pacific Northwest Library Assn.

Pullman

C- WASHINGTON STATE UNIVERSITY, Holland Library, AV Center, 99163. *Tel:* (509) 335-4535. *Video Serv Est:* 1968. *In Charge:* James W. Hardie, Coordinator Instructional Television. *Video Staff:* 3 f-t, 16 p-t, 1 tech. *Video Use:* in-service training, instructional purposes. Video serv available on demand & by appointment. Produce video tapes. Have production studio/space & separate control room.

Video Equipment/Facilities *In-House Use Only:* recording deck (18), ½″, ¾″, 1″ b&w/col, Sony EV310, IVC, Panasonic; playback deck (5), ¾″ col, Panasonic; editing deck (2), ¾″ col, Sony; studio camera (5), b&w/col, Sony, Panasonic; monitor (35), b&w/col, Sony, RCA, Trinitron; SEG (1) Panasonic; keyer (1), Panasonic; additional camera lenses (4); microphones (20); tripods (6); audio tape recorders (5). Have permanent & portable viewing installations. Provide training in use of equipment to students & employees. Have tape duplication serv.

Video Tape Loan/Rental/Sale Serv *Serv Provided:* free loan, swap with other inst, rental. *Loan/Rental Eligibility:* staff & students, educational inst (upon agreement). *Restrictions:* for indiv & inst, arrangements based on circumstances. Cannot use for fund-raising, duplicate, air without permission. May borrow by mail. *Loan Period:* negotiable. *Total Yr Tape Loan:* 12.

Video Collection Maintained by purchase, rental, own production. Use/play ½″, 1″ reel to reel, ¾″ cassette. *Sources:* commercial distributors, in-house production. *Tape Sel:* preview, faculty/staff recommendations, catalogs. *Special Collections:* films in video format, departments may purchase tapes from another university. Tapes organized by subject. *Collection, Color:* ¾″ cassette, 35t/c. *Other Video Serv:* programming, reference serv, production workshops. Publish materials on video.

Cable & CCTV Receive serv of cable TV system. Produce programs for cablecasting. Have CCTV in inst, with 50 monitors. *Programming Sources:* tapes produced by inst, tapes produced professionally, films & live instruction.

Seattle

S- CONTEMPORARY RESOURCES IN THE ARTS, 1525 10th Ave., 98122. *Tel:* (206) 324-5880. *Video Serv Est:* 1974. *In Charge:* Anne Focke, Dir. *Video Staff:* 1 f-t, 6 p-t. *Video Use:* documentation of our own events, playback only of professionally produced tapes, as art form, presentation & exhibition of artists' videotapes. Video serv available by invitation to exhibit. Produce video tapes. Have production studio/space.

Video Equipment/Facilities *In-House Use Only:* monitor (2), b&w, Magnavox. Have portable viewing installation. Provide training in use of equipment to students in video workshops.

Video Collection Maintained by rental, own production, exchange/swap. Use/play ½″ reel to reel, ¾″ cassette. *Sources:* galleries. *Tape Sel:* preview, gallery previews, published reviews, catalogs, according to artists' needs. *Special Collections:* video as art. *Other Video Serv:* reference serv, production workshops, periodicals & other literature on artists' video. Publish materials on video.

P- KING COUNTY LIBRARY SYSTEM, 300 Eighth Ave N, 98109. *Tel:* (206) 344-7457. *Film Serv Est:* 1962. *In Charge:* Ralph Huntzinger, Coordinator Nonbook Media Services. *AV Staff:* 4½ (1 prof, 2½ cl, 1 tech). *Film Sel:* committee preview, chief film librarian's decision. *Holdings:* Academy Award nominees in short subjects & documentaries.

Free-Loan Film Serv *Eligibility:* indiv with library cards, patrons from libraries in a cooperative system. *Restrictions:* for indiv & inst, only in King County or neighboring library system. Cannot use for fund-raising. Available to researchers/scholars for on-site viewing. May borrow by mail. *Loan Period:* within 1 day of last showing date. *Total Yr Film Loan:* 33,000.

Film Collection 700t/p. Approx 100t acquired annually. *Pubns:* catalog, as needed; suppl, no set policy.

Other Film Serv Obtain film from coop loan system (Wash. Library Film Circuit, Pudget Sound Cooperative), obtain film from other libraries, film reference serv, film fairs/festivals, library film programs. Permanent viewing facility. *Equipment:* lend 16mm sound projector (10), 8mm reel projector (3), S8mm reel projector (4), projection screens (6).

Budget & Expenditures Total library budget $747,000 (FY 1/1/74-1/1/75). Total FY film budget $60,000. *Member:* AECT, ALA, Wash. Library Assn, Wash. AECT.

S- THE MEDIA SHOP, 1505 Tenth Ave, 98122. *Tel:* (206) 322-8110. *Video Serv Est:* 1974. *In Charge:* E. Frank Blumer, Owner. *Video Staff:* 3 f-t, 4 p-t, 1 tech. *Video Use:* documentation of community/school events, in-service training, practical video/TV training courses, as art form. Video serv available on demand & by appointment. Produce video tapes. Have production studio/space & separate control room.

Video Equipment/Facilities *For Rent:* portapak (2), ½″ b&w, Sony 3400; recording, playback & editing deck (4), ¼″, ½″, ¾″, 1″ b&w, Sony, Panasonic; studio camera (2), b&w, Sony; monitor (5), b&w; SEG (1); additional camera lenses (2); lighting (3); microphones (6); tripods (5); audio tape recorders (2). Have permanent & portable viewing installations. *Equipment Rental Period:* no set policy. Provide training in use of equipment to faculty & public. Have tape duplication serv.

Video Tape Loan/Rental/Sale Serv *Serv Provided:* swap with other inst, rental, sale. *Loan/Rental Eligibility:* staff & students, educational inst, civic groups, religious groups, prof groups. *Restrictions:* for indiv & inst, none. May borrow by mail. *Loan Period:* no set policy.

Video Collection Maintained by own production, exchange/swap. Use/play ½″, ¼″, 1″ reel to reel, ¾″ cassette. *Sources:* commercial distributors, galleries, community productions, exchange. *Tape Sel:* preview, staff recommendations, gallery previews, published reviews, catalogs. *Special Collections:* all categories. Tapes organized by subject. *Other Video Serv:* programming, production workshops. Publish materials on video.

Cable & CCTV Receive serv of cable TV system. Produce programs for cablecasting. Inform public about cable system serv & facilities. Serve as production facility for others.

S- SEATTLE ART MUSEUM, Photograph & Slide Library, 14th & Prospect, 98112. *Tel:* (206) 447-4710. *Film Serv Est:* 1940. *In Charge:* Joan H. Nilsson. *AV Staff:* ½ (½ prof). *Film Sel:* staff recommendations. *Holdings:* fine arts 100%.

Film Collection Approx 3-4t acquired annually.

Other Film Serv Rent film from distributors for patrons, obtain film from other libraries. Permanent viewing facility.

Budget & Expenditures No separate AV budget.

Video Serv Under consideration.

S- SEATTLE ASSOCIATION FOR MEDIA ARTISTS, Library, 401 Prefontaine Bldg, 98104. *Tel:* (206) 624-8627. *Video Serv Est:* 1975. *In Charge:* Norie Sato, Executive Dir. *Video Use:* playback only of professionally produced tapes, as art form, education. *Other Video Serv:* reference serv, workshops for artists & students to incorporate video in art.

Seattle (cont'd)

C- SEATTLE PACIFIC COLLEGE, Weter Memorial Library, 98119. *Tel:* (206) 281-2228. *Film Serv Est:* 1970. *In Charge:* Carol Kruse, Coordinator of AV Services. *AV Staff:* 2 (1 prof, 1 cl). *Film Sel:* committee preview, faculty/staff recommendations. *Holdings:* medicine 90%, teacher education 10%. Produce videotape, 35mm slides & tape, overhead transparencies.

Film Collection 50t/p. Approx 9t acquired annually. *Circ:* 16mm, 35t/p; S8mm reel, 15t/p.

Other Film Serv Rent film from distributors for patrons, obtain film from coop loan system (Christian College Consortium, Northwest Assn of Private Colleges & Universities), obtain film from other libraries, film reference serv. Permanent viewing facility available for rent to community. *Equipment:* rent S8mm camera (1), 16mm sound projector (8), 8mm cartridge projector, 8mm reel projector (1), S8mm cartridge projector (1), S8mm reel projector (1), projection tables & stands (10), projection screens (20).

Budget & Expenditures Total library budget $65,000 (FY 9/1/74-9/1/75). No separate AV budget. *Member:* AECT, ALA, Wash. Library Assn, Wash. Assn for Educational Communications & Technology.

Video Serv *Video Staff:* 2 f-t, 1 p-t. *Video Use:* documentation of community/school events, in-service training, practical video/TV training courses, playback only of professionally produced tapes, as art form, teacher education. Video serv available on demand & by appointment. Produce video tapes. Have production studio/space & separate control room.

Video Equipment/Facilities *For Loan:* portapak (4), ½″ b&w, Sony AV3400; recording deck (2), ½″ b&w, Sony AV3600, 3650; editing deck (1), ½″ b&w, Sony AV3650; studio camera (2), b&w, Sony; monitor (10), 23″ b&w/col, RCA, Magnavox; SEG (1), SEG; lighting (10); microphones (10); tripods (5); audio tape recorders (25), video cassette-u-matic (1); recorder/player (1). Have permanent & portable viewing installations. *Equipment Loan Period:* 1 day. Provide training in use of equipment to students & users. Have tape duplication serv.

Video Tape Loan/Rental/Sale Serv *Serv Provided:* swap with other inst. *Loan Eligibility:* civic groups, religious groups, indiv with library cards. May not borrow by mail.

Video Collection Maintained by purchase, own production, exchange/swap. Use/play ½″ reel to reel, ¾″ cassette. *Sources:* commercial distributors, community productions, exchange (University of Wash.). *Tape Sel:* preview, faculty/staff recommendations. Tapes organized by Dewey Decimal. *Collection, Color:* ¾″ cassette, 5t/c. *Collection, B&W:* ½″ reel, 20t/c; ¾″ cassette, 20t/c. *Other Video Serv:* taping of other media, production workshops.

Cable & CCTV Receive serv of cable TV system. Inform public about cable system serv & facilities. Have CCTV in inst, with 25 monitors. *Programming Sources:* over-the-air commercial & public broadcasting, tapes produced by inst.

P- SEATTLE PUBLIC LIBRARY, Film Library, 1000 Fourth Ave, 98104. *Tel:* (206) 624-3800, ext 287. *Film Serv Est:* 1946. *In Charge:* Barbara Guptill, Head, Adult Education. *AV Staff:* 4 (2½, 2 cl). *Film Sel:* committee preview, chief film librarian's decision.

Free-Loan Film Serv *Eligibility:* indiv with library cards. *Restrictions:* for indiv, only in King County. Cannot use for fund-raising, transmit electronically. Available to researchers/scholars for on-site viewing. May not borrow by mail. *Loan Period:* 2 days. *Total Yr Film Loan:* 18,756.

Film Collection 1650t/2000p. *Circ:* 16mm, 1596t/1655p; 8mm reel, 54t/400p. *Pubns:* catalog, every 3 yrs; suppl, in yr catalog not published.

Other Film Serv Film reference serv, film fairs/festivals, library film programs. *Equipment:* lend 8mm reel projector (2), S8mm reel projector (2).

Budget & Expenditures Total library budget $29,303.28 (FY 1/1/75-1/1/76). Total FY film budget $25,889. *Member:* AECT, ALA, EFLA, Wash. Library Assn, Wash. AECT.

Video Serv *Est:* 1974. *Video Staff:* 1 p-t. *Video Use:* to increase community's library use, in-service training, practical video/TV training courses. Video serv available by appointment. Produce video tapes.

Video Equipment/Facilities *In-House Use Only:* recording deck (1), ¾″, Sony; playback deck (1), Sony; studio camera (1), b&w, Sony; monitor (1); tripods (1); audio tape recorders (1). Have portable viewing installation. Provide training in use of equipment to staff.

Video Collection Maintained by own production. Use/play ¾″ cassette. *Sources:* commercial distributors. *Collection, B&W:* ¾″ cassette, 10t.

C- SHORELINE COMMUNITY COLLEGE, 16101 Greenwood Ave N, 98036. *Tel:* (206) 546-4721. *In Charge:* G. R. Magelssen, Media Specialist. *AV Staff:* 1 (½ prof, ½ cl). *Film Sel:* faculty/staff recommendations.

Film Rental Serv *Eligibility:* educational org, civic groups, patrons/public. *Restrictions:* only in state. Cannot use for fundraising, transmit electronically. *Rental Period:* 2 days. *Total Yr Film Booking:* 4500.

Film Collection 540t/636p. Approx 50t acquired annually. *Circ:* 16mm, 540t/636p. *Pubns:* catalog, every 2 yrs; suppl, no set policy.

Other Film Serv Obtain film from coop loan system (Community College Library Cooperative).

Budget & Expenditures Total FY film budget $11,000.

C- UNIVERSITY OF WASHINGTON, AV Services, B54 Administration Bldg, 98195. *Tel:* (206) 543-2500. *In Charge:* Donald Riecks, Dir, AV Servs. *AV Staff:* 44. *Film Sel:* faculty/staff recommendations.

Film Rental Serv *Eligibility:* no restrictions. *Restrictions:* only in U.S. Cannot use for fund-raising, transmit electronically. *Rental Period:* 3 days. Sell films. Produce films.

Film Collection 2733t/3508p. Approx 225t acquired annually. *Circ:* 16mm, 1683t/2358p. *Noncirc:* 16mm, 1050t/1150p. *Pubns:* catalog, every 2 yrs ($2); suppl, in yr catalog not published ($1).

Other Film Serv Rent film from distributors for patrons, obtain film from other libraries, film reference serv, film fairs/festivals. Permanent viewing facility. *Equipment:* lend S8mm camera, 16mm camera, 16mm sound projector, 8mm cartridge projector, 8mm reel projector, S8mm cartridge projector, S8mm reel projector, projection tables & stands, projection screens.

Budget & Expenditures Total library budget $619,469 (FY 7/1/74-7/1/75). Total FY film budget $81,421. *Member:* AECT, CUFC, Wash. AECT.

C- UNIVERSITY OF WASHINGTON, Odegaard Undergraduate Library Media Center, DF-10, 98195. *Tel:* (206) 543-6051. *Film Serv Est:* 1972. *In Charge:* Harriett Marshall, Media Librarian. *AV Staff:* 10½ (2 prof, 1 cl, 3 tech). *Film Sel:* faculty/staff recommendations, chief film librarian's decision, published reviews. *Holdings:* early films, historical films, news reels, fine arts.

Free-Loan Film Serv *Eligibility:* staff & students, indiv with library cards. *Restrictions:* for indiv & inst, only in class or media center. Cannot use for fund-raising, transmit electronically. Available to researchers/scholars for on-site viewing, May not borrow by mail. *Loan Period:* class time only. Produce films. Produce TV tapes, slides & audio tapes.

Film Collection *Circ:* 8mm & S8mm reel, 141t; 8mm & S8mm cartridge, 35t. *Pubns:* catalog, annual.

Other Film Serv Rent film from distributors for patrons, obtain film from university AV services & depts, obtain film from other libraries, film reference serv, film fairs/festivals, library film programs. Permanent viewing facility. *Equipment:* lend S8mm camera (1), lend 16mm camera (1), lend 16mm sound projector (1), lend 8mm cartridge projector (1), lend 8mm reel projector (1), lend S8mm cartridge projector (2), lend projection screens (8).

Other Media Collections *Audio:* disc, total, 2678t; tape, total, 2098t. *Filmstrips:* total, 238t. *Slides:* single, 7315t.

Budget & Expenditures Total library budget $8000 (FY 7/1/74-7/1/75). Total FY film budget $1000. *Member:* AECT,

ALA, Wash. Library Assn, Pacific Northwest Library Assn, Music Library Assn, Assn of Recorded Sound Librarians.

Video Serv *Video Staff:* 10½ f-t, 4½ p-t, 3 tech. *Video Use:* documentation of community/school events, to increase community's library use, in-service training, practical video/TV training courses, as art form, educational tool. Video serv available on demand & by appointment. Produce video tapes. Have production studio/space & separate control room.

Video Equipment/Facilities *In-House Use Only:* recording deck (3), b&w/col, Sony; playback deck (5), col, Sony-u-matic; editing deck (1), b&w; studio camera (1), b&w, Sony; monitor (10), b&w/col, Sony; SEG (1); lighting; microphones (15); tripods (2); audio tape recorders (4). *For Loan:* portapak (1), b&w, Sony. Have permanent & portable viewing installations. *Equipment Loan Period:* 2-3 hrs. Provide training in use of equipment to faculty & students.

Video Tape Loan/Rental/Sale Serv *Serv Provided:* free loan. *Loan Eligibility:* org members, & others, such as libraries in state & some universities. *Restrictions:* for indiv, only in the center; for inst, only in state. Cannot use for fund-raising, duplicate, air without permission. May not borrow by mail.

Video Collection Maintained by purchase, own production. Use/play ½" reel to reel, ¾" cassette. *Sources:* commercial distributors, exchange (ALA, University of Toronto). *Tape Sel:* preview, faculty/staff recommendations, published reviews, catalogs. *Special Collections:* in-house training tapes, video as art, films in video format. Tapes organized by format & company. *Collection, Color & B&W:* ½" reel & ¾" cartridge, total, 563t. *Other Video Serv:* programming, reference serv, taping of other media, production workshops, instructions in camera, direction & scripts. *Pubns:* catalog. Publish materials on video.

Cable & CCTV Inform public about cable system serv & facilities. Run cable workshops. Have CCTV in inst, with 8 monitors. *Programming Sources:* over-the-air commercial & public broadcasting, tapes produced by inst, tapes produced professionally, tapes produced by community groups & indiv.

Spokane

S- EASTERN WASHINGTON STATE HISTORICAL SOCIETY, Joel E. Ferris Memorial Library, West 2316 First Ave, 99204. *Tel:* (509) 456-3931.

Film Serv Rent films for programs held in auditorium. Currently planning establishment of AV study center to house AV equipment, slides, filmstrips, oral history tapes, audio & video cassettes.

Other Media Collections *Audio:* disc, 33⅓ rpm, 20t; tape, cassette, 70t; tape, reel, 250t. *Filmstrips:* sound sets, 1t. *Slides:* single, 500t; sets, 2t.

Budget & Expenditures Total library budget $3500 (FY 7/1/74-7/1/75). *Member:* Pacific Northwest Library Assn, Wash. History Assn, Spokane History Assn.

Video Serv Still in planning stage with policies to be determined. *Est:* 1975. *In Charge:* Elinor C. Kelly, Librarian. *Video Staff:* 1 f-t, 2 p-t, 1 tech. *Video Use:* to increase community's library use, community video access. Video serv available by appointment.

Video Equipment/Facilities *In-House Use Only:* audio tape recorders (3). Have portable viewing installation.

Video Collection *Sources:* TV station records for library. *Special Collections:* TV programs. *Collection, Color:* 2" reel, 3t; ¾" cassette, 8t. *Other Video Serv:* reference & research serv.

Cable & CCTV Will receive serv of cable TV system.

C- SPOKANE COMMUNITY COLLEGE, E 3403 Mission, 99202. *Tel:* (509) 456-2498. *Film Serv Est:* 1967. *In Charge:* Verona Southern, Head Librarian. *AV Staff:* 1 (1 tech). *Film Sel:* committee preview, faculty/staff recommendations, chief film librarian's decision, published reviews. *Holdings:* agriculture, industrial arts, medicine.

Free-Loan Film Serv *Eligibility:* staff & students, educational inst. *Loan Period:* 3 days.

Film Rental Serv *Eligibility:* educational org, civic groups. *Restrictions:* only in our county. *Rental Period:* 4 days.

Film Collection 360t/365p. Approx 10-15t acquired annually. *Circ:* 16mm, 360t. *Pubns:* catalog, annual.

Other Film Serv Rent film from distributors for patrons, obtain film from other libraries, film reference serv.

Budget & Expenditures No separate AV budget. *Member:* AECT, ALA, Wash. Library Assn, Wash. AECT, WEST.

Video Serv *Est:* 1968. *Video Staff:* 1 tech. *Video Use:* documentation of community/school events, to increase community's library use, in-service training, playback only of professionally produced tapes. Video serv available by appointment. Produce video tapes. Have production studio/space & separate control room.

Video Equipment/Facilities *In-House Use Only:* portapak, ½" b&w/col, Sony; studio camera (2), b&w/col, Sony, Panasonic; monitor; SEG; keyer; additional camera lenses; lighting; microphones; tripods; audio tape recorders. Have portable viewing installation. Provide training in use of equipment to faculty & students. Have tape duplication serv.

Video Tape Loan/Rental/Sale Serv *Serv Provided:* swap with other inst. *Loan Eligibility:* staff & students, educational inst, civic groups, religious groups. *Restrictions:* for indiv, only campus or library district; for inst, only in library district. Cannot use for fund-raising, duplicate, air without permission. May borrow by mail. *Loan Period:* 7 days.

Video Collection Maintained by own production. Use/play ½" reel to reel, ¾" cassette. *Sources:* commercial distributors, in-house productions. *Tape Sel:* preview. *Special Collections:* films in video format. Tapes organized by subject. *Other Video Serv:* taping of other media.

Cable & CCTV Receive serv of cable TV system. Produce programs for cablecasting. Have advisory/administrative role in cable system operation. Have CCTV in inst. *Programming Sources:* tapes produced by inst.

C- SPOKANE FALLS COMMUNITY COLLEGE, Library/Media Services, 3410 Ft George Wright Dr, 99203. *Tel:* (509) 456-2860. *Film Serv Est:* 1966. *In Charge:* Diane Lloyd, Media Librarian. *AV Staff:* 4½ (½ prof, 1 cl, 3 tech). *Film Sel:* faculty/staff recommendations.

Free-Loan Film Serv *Eligibility:* staff & students. *Restrictions:* for indiv, none. Cannot use for fund-raising, transmit electronically. Available to researchers/scholars for on-site viewing. May not borrow by mail. *Loan Period:* 1 day. *Total Yr Film Loan:* 1123.

Film Rental Serv *Eligibility:* no restrictions. *Restrictions:* none. Cannot use for fund-raising, transmit electronically. May not rent by mail. *Rental Period:* 1 day. Produce video tapes.

Film Collection 734t/737p. Approx 40t acquired annually. *Circ:* 16mm, 734t/737p. *Pubns:* catalog, annual; suppl, mid-year.

Other Film Serv Rent film from distributors for patrons, obtain film from coop loan system (Community College Libraries Consortium), obtain film from other libraries, film reference serv, film fairs/festivals. Permanent viewing facility. *Equipment:* lend 16mm sound projector (1), 8mm reel projector (1), projection screens (4).

Other Media Collections *Audio:* disc, 33⅓ rpm, 563t/c; tape, cassette, 246t/c. *Filmstrips:* sound, 41t/c; silent, 28t/c. *Slides:* single, 25c; sets, 14c.

Budget & Expenditures Total FY (6/1/74-6/1/75) film budget $1800.

Video Serv *In Charge:* John Thompson, Dir, Media Services. *Video Staff:* 2 f-t, 1 p-t, 1 tech. *Video Use:* documentation of community/school events, in-service training, practical video/TV training courses, classroom instruction. Video serv available by appointment. Produce video tapes. Have production studio/space & separate control room.

Video Equipment/Facilities *In-House Use Only:* portapak (1), b&w, Sony AV3400; recording & playback deck (19), b&w/col, Sony AV2200, AV5000A, AV8600, JVC CR6000U, Panasonic NV2120; editing deck (2), col, Sony 2850; studio camera (2), col, Sony DXC1200; monitor (37), b&w/col, Sony, RCA XL-100; SEG (1), Panasonic; keyer (1), CBS; lighting (2); microphones (3); tripods (7). Have permanent & portable viewing installations. Provide training in use of equipment to faculty & students. Have tape duplication serv.

Spokane (cont'd)

Video Tape Loan/Rental/Sale Serv *Serv Provided:* swap with other inst. *Loan Eligibility:* staff & students.

Video Collection Maintained by purchase, rental, own production, exchange/swap. Use/play ½" reel to reel, ¾" cassette. *Sources:* commercial distributors, community productions, exchange, industrial organizations. *Tape Sel:* preview, faculty/staff recommendations. *Special Collections:* in-house training tapes, films in video format. Tapes organized by consecutive numbering. *Collection, Color:* ½" reel, 400t/c; 1" reel, 5t/c; ¾" cassette, 120t/c. *Collection, B&W:* ½" reel, 100t/c; 1" reel, 15t/c; ¾" cassette, 10t/c. *Other Video Serv:* programming, reference serv.

Cable & CCTV Receive serv of cable TV system. Produce programs for cablecasting. Inform public about cable system serv & facilities. Serve as production facility for others. Have advisory/administrative role in cable system operation to consortium. Have CCTV in inst, with 20 monitors. *Programming Source:* over-the-air commercial & public broadcasting, tapes produced by inst, tapes produced professionally, tapes produced by community groups & indiv.

P- **SPOKANE PUBLIC LIBRARY**, W 906 Main St, 99201. *Tel:* (509) 838-3361, ext 57, 58. *Film Serv Est:* 1952. *In Charge:* Janet Miller, Fine Arts Librarian. *AV Staff:* 1½ (1 cl, ½ tech). *Film Sel:* committee preview.

Free-Loan Film Serv *Eligibility:* educational inst, civic groups, religious groups, indiv with library cards, prof groups. *Restrictions:* for indiv & inst, only in state. Cannot transmit electronically, borrow for classroom use without permission of producer. May borrow by mail. *Loan Period:* 2 days. *Total Yr Film Loan:* 5820.

Film Collection 307t/309p. *Circ:* 16mm, 307t/309p. *Pubns:* catalog, as needed; suppl, no set policy.

Other Film Serv Obtain film from coop loan system (Wash. Library Film Circuit), film reference serv, library film programs. Permanent viewing facility.

Other Media Collections *Audio:* disc, total, 13,438c; tape, cassette, 1840c. *Filmstrips:* sound, 175c.

Budget & Expenditures Total library budget $154,200 (FY 1/1/75-1/1/76). Total FY film budget $6250.

Tacoma

S- **TACOMA ART MUSEUM**, 12th and Pacific Ave, 98402. *Tel:* (206) 272-4258. *Video Serv Est:* 1971. *In Charge:* J. W. Kowalek, Dir. *Video Staff:* 1 f-t, 1 tech. *Video Use:* community video access, in-service training, as art form, production of documentaries. Video serv available by appointment. Produce video tapes. Have production studio/space.

Video Equipment/Facilities *In-House Use Only:* portapak (1), b&w, Sony; recording deck (2), b&w, Sony; playback deck (2), b&w, Sony; editing deck (2), b&w, Sony; studio camera (1), b&w, Sony; monitor (3), b&w, Sony; microphones (2); tripods (2); audio tape recorders (2). Have permanent viewing installation. Provide training in use of equipment to staff.

Video Tape Loan/Rental/Sale Serv *Serv Provided:* free loan. *Loan Eligibility:* staff & students, educational inst, prof groups, such as other museums. Cannot use for fund-raising, duplicate, air without permission. May not borrow by mail.

Video Collection Maintained by own production. Use/play ½" reel to reel. *Special Collections:* video as art. Tapes organized by subject. *Collection, B&W:* ½" reel, 50t/c.

Cable & CCTV Receive serv of cable TV system.

C- **TACOMA COMMUNITY COLLEGE**, Pearl A. Wanamaker Learning Assistance Services, 5900 S 12 St, 98465. *Tel:* (206) 756-5089. *In Charge:* Nick Huddleston, Media Specialist. *Video Staff:* 2 f-t, ½ tech. *Video Use:* playback of commercial & locally produced tapes, instruction & analysis. Video serv available by appointment. Produce video tapes. Have production studio/space & separate control room.

Video Equipment/Facilities *In-House Use Only:* portapak (1), ½" b&w, Sony 3400; recording deck (3), ½" b&w/col, Sony 3600, 3650, Panasonic 3130; editing deck (2), b&w/col, Sony 3600, 3650; studio camera (4), Sony, Panasonic; monitor (20), b&w/col; SEG (1), Panasonic; additional camera lenses (1); lighting (6); microphones (6); tripods (3); audio tape recorders (3). Have portable viewing installation. Provide training in use of equipment to anyone who needs it. Have tape duplication serv.

Video Tape Loan/Rental/Sale Serv *Serv Provided:* swap with other inst. *Loan Eligibility:* staff & students.

Video Collection Maintained by own production, exchange/swap. Use/play ½" reel to reel, ¾" cassette. *Sources:* exchange (University of Wash.). *Tape Sel:* faculty/staff recommendations. Tapes organized by subject. *Collection, B&W:* ½" reel, 15t/c. *Other Video Serv:* taping of other media.

Cable & CCTV Receive serv of cable TV system. Have CCTV in inst, with 15 monitors. *Programming Sources:* live use & for testing.

Yakima

P- **YAKIMA VALLEY REGIONAL LIBRARY**, AV Department, 102 N Third St, 98901. *Tel:* (509) 452-8541, ext 35. *Film Serv Est:* 1951. *In Charge:* Karna Borders, Film Librarian in Charge. *AV Staff:* 2½ (1½ cl, 1 tech). *Film Sel:* committee preview, chief film librarian's & AV dept's decision. *Holdings:* agriculture 10%, children's films 40%, feature films 10%, industrial arts 10%, science 20%, social sciences 10%.

Free-Loan Film Serv *Eligibility:* indiv with adult library cards, other libraries in Yakima County pay $8 to use facilities. *Restrictions:* for indiv & inst, only in Yakima County. Cannot use for fund-raising, transmit electronically. Borrow for classroom use in special cases. May not borrow by mail. *Loan Period:* 1-2 days. *Total Yr Film Loan:* 10,820.

Film Collection 102p. Approx 15-25t acquired annually. *Circ:* 16mm, 182t/182p. Publish materials pertaining to collection.

Other Film Serv Obtain film from coop loan system (Wash. Library Film Circuit), library film programs. Permanent viewing facility available for rent to community. *Equipment:* lend slide projectors (3).

Other Media Collections *Audio:* disc, 33⅓ rpm, 7103c; tape, cassette, 100t/c. *Slides:* sets, 43t/c.

Budget & Expenditures Total library budget $113,885 (FY 1/1/75-1/1/76). Total FY film budget $6485. *Member:* FLIC, Wash. Library Assn.

West Virginia

Charleston

P- KANAWHA COUNTY PUBLIC LIBRARY, Film Library, 123 Capitol St, 25301. *Tel:* (304) 343-4646. *Film Serv Est:* 1975. *In Charge:* Brian Faust, AV Librarian. *AV Staff:* 2 (1 prof, 1 cl). *Film Sel:* recommendations made to film circuit.
Free-Loan Film Serv *Eligibility:* educational inst, civic groups, religious groups, indiv with library cards, prof groups. *Restrictions:* for indiv & inst, only in Kanawha County. Cannot use for fund-raising. Available to researchers/scholars for on-site viewing. *Loan Period:* 1 day.
Film Collection 500t/p. *Circ:* 16mm, 500t. *Pubns:* catalog, annual.
Other Film Serv Obtain film from coop loan system (Ohio Valley Regional Film Library). Permanent viewing facility available for rent to community.
Other Media Collections *Audio:* disc, 33⅓ rpm, 3000t. *Filmstrips:* sound, 100c.
Budget & Expenditures Total library budget $35,000 (FY 7/1/74-7/1/75). Total FY film budget $1600. *Member:* ALA, W. Va. Library Assn.

P- WEST VIRGINIA LIBRARY COMMISSION, Film Services, Science & Cultural Center, 25305. *Tel:* (304) 348-2041. *Film Serv Est:* 1976. *In Charge:* Steve Christo, Film Librarian. *AV Staff:* 1½ (1 prof, ½ cl). *Film Sel:* committee preview, staff recommendations, chief film librarian's decision. *Holdings:* Appalachian culture 5%.
Free-Loan Film Serv *Eligibility:* public libraries & state government agencies. *Restrictions:* for indiv & inst, only in state. Cannot use for fund-raising, transmit electronically, borrow for classroom use. Produce 35mm slides.
Film Collection 1000t. *Pubns:* catalog.
Other Film Serv Library film programs. Permanent viewing facility.
Other Media Collections *Audio:* disc, 33⅓ rpm, 5000t; tape, cassette, 5000t. *Slides:* single, 25,000t.
Budget & Expenditures Total library budget $610,000 (FY 7/1/74-7/1/75). Total FY film budget $355,000. *Member:* AECT, ALA, W. Va. Library Assn, W. Va. Educational Media Assn.
Video Serv To be est. in 1976. Receive servs of cable TV system.

Glenville

C- GLENVILLE STATE COLLEGE, Robert F. Kidd Library, 26351. *Tel:* (304) 462-7361, ext 291. *In Charge:* John W. Collins III, Media Librarian. *AV Staff:* 6 (3 prof, 2 cl, 1 tech). *Film Sel:* committee preview, faculty/staff recommendations, chief film librarian's decision, published reviews. *Holdings:* teacher education.
Free-Loan Film Serv *Eligibility:* staff & students, educational inst, civic groups, religious groups, indiv with library cards. *Restrictions:* for indiv, only in our county; for inst, only in state. Available to researchers/scholars for on-site viewing. *Loan Period:* 14 days. Produce video & audio tapes, slides, etc.
Film Collection 750t/p. *Circ:* 16mm, 100t/p; S8mm reel, 650t/p. *Pubns:* catalog.
Other Film Serv Rent film from distributors for patrons, obtain film from coop loan system (RESA), obtain film from other libraries, film reference serv. Permanent viewing facility available to community. *Equipment:* lend S8mm camera (4), lend 16mm camera (2), lend 16mm sound projector (2), lend 8mm cartridge projector (3), lend 8mm reel projector (2), lend S8mm cartridge projector (4), lend S8mm reel projector (2), lend projection tables & stands, lend projection screens.
Other Media Collections *Audio:* disc, 33⅓ rpm, 3000c; tape, cassette, 200c; tape, reel, 200c. *Filmstrips:* sound, 1000c; silent, 3000c. *Slides:* sets, 100c.

Budget & Expenditures (FY 9/1/75-9/1/76). Total FY film budget $4000. *Member:* AECT, ALA, W. Va. Library Assn.
Video Serv *In Charge:* Donald Phillips, Dir, Learning Materials Center. *Video Staff:* 3 f-t, 8 p-t. *Video Use:* documentation of community/school events, in-service training, practical video/TV training courses, playback only of professionally produced tapes. Video serv available by appointment. Produce video tapes. Have production studio/space & separate control room.
Video Equipment/Facilities *In-House Use Only:* monitor (12), b&w/col; SEG (1); additional camera lenses (3); microphones (10); tripods (5); audio tape recorders (25). *For Loan:* portapak (2), ½" b&w, Sony; recording deck (4), ½", ¾" b&w/col, Sony, JVC. Have permanent viewing installation. *Equipment Loan Period:* 1 day. Provide training in use of equipment to faculty & students. Have tape duplication serv.
Video Tape Loan/Rental/Sale Serv *Serv Provided:* free loan. *Loan Eligibility:* staff & students, educational inst, civic groups, religious groups, indiv with library cards. *Restrictions:* for indiv, only in our county; for inst, only in our county. Cannot use for fund-raising, duplicate, air without permission. May not borrow by mail.
Video Collection Maintained by purchase, own production. Use/play ½" reel to reel, ¾" cassette. *Sources:* commercial distributors. *Tape Sel:* preview, faculty/staff recommendations, published reviews, catalogs. Tapes organized by accession number. *Collection, Color:* ¾" cassette, 15t/c. *Other Video Serv:* programming, reference serv, taping of other media, production workshops.
Cable & CCTV Receive serv of cable TV system. Inform public about cable system serv & facilities. Run cable programs for special audiences. Have CCTV in inst, with 6 monitors. *Programming Sources:* tapes produced by inst, tapes produced professionally.

Morgantown

C- WEST VIRGINIA UNIVERSITY, AV Library, 9 Woodburn Hall, 26506. *Tel:* (304) 293-4019. *Film Serv Est:* 1974. *In Charge:* Mary S. Novak, AV Librarian. *AV Staff:* (2 prof, 3 cl, 3 tech). *Film Sel:* faculty/staff recommendations. *Holdings:* Appalachian films 10%.
Free-Loan Film Serv *Eligibility:* staff & students, educational inst, & others, such as university libraries. *Restrictions:* for indiv & inst, only in state. Available to researchers/scholars for on-site viewing. *Loan Period:* 3 days. *Total Yr Film Loan:* 833.
Film Collection 700t/p. Approx 100t acquired annually. *Circ:* 16mm, 650t/p; 8mm reel, 20t/p. *Noncirc:* 16mm, 30t/p. *Pubns:* catalog, annual; suppl, no set policy.
Other Film Serv Film reference serv, library film programs. Permanent viewing facility. *Equipment:* rent S8mm camera (2), 16mm sound projector (20), 8mm cartridge projector (4), 8mm reel projector (1), S8mm cartridge projector (2), S8mm reel projector (1), projection tables & stands, projection screens (10).
Other Media Collections *Audio:* tape, cassette, 100t; tape, reel, 50t. *Filmstrips:* silent, 350t. *Slides:* sets, 300t.
Budget & Expenditures No separate AV budget. *Member:* W. Va. Library Assn.
Video Serv *Est:* 1975. *Video Staff:* 4 f-t, 5 p-t, 3 tech. *Video Use:* documentation of community/school events, practical video/TV training courses, educational tool. Video serv available by appointment. Produce video tapes. Have production studio/space & separate control room.
Video Equipment/Facilities *In-House Use Only:* portapak (1), ½" b&w, Sony AV-3400; recording deck (1), 1" b&w, Ampex; playback deck (1), ¾" col, JVC; studio camera (2), 1" b&w, Ampex; monitor (3), b&w/col, Sony, Motorola; lighting (2); microphones (2); audio tape recorders (17). *For Loan:* portapak

Morgantown (cont'd)
(1), ½" b&w, Sony AV-3400; recording deck (1), 1" b&w, Ampex; playback deck (1), ¾" col, JVC; studio camera (2), 1" b&w, Ampex; monitor (3), b&w/col, Sony, Motorola; lighting (2); microphones (2); audio tape recorders (17). Have portable viewing installation. *Equipment Loan Period:* 1 day. Provide training in use of equipment to faculty & students.

Video Tape Loan/Rental/Sale Serv *Serv Provided:* free loan. *Loan Eligibility:* staff & students. *Restrictions:* for inst, only in state. Cannot air without permission. May borrow by mail. *Loan Period:* 3 days.

Video Collection Maintained by purchase, exchange/swap. Use/play ½", 1" reel to reel, ¾" cassette. *Sources:* commercial distributors, exchange. *Tape Sel:* faculty/staff recommendations. *Special Collections:* in-house training tapes. Tapes organized by accession number. *Collection, Color:* ½" reel, 1t/c; 1" reel, 100t/c; ¾" cassette, 50t/c. *Pubns:* catalog.

Cable & CCTV Have CCTV in inst. *Programming Sources:* tapes produced by inst.

Philippi

C- ALDERSON-BROADDUS COLLEGE, Pickett Library Media Center, 26416. *Tel:* (304) 457-1700, ext 258, 229. *Film Serv Est:* 1966. *In Charge:* Richard Hudson, Dir, Media Services. *AV Staff:* 8 (4 prof, 2 cl, 1 tech). *Film Sel:* faculty/staff recommendations. *Holdings:* children's films 1%, experimental films 1%, fine arts 5%, medicine 12%, science 1%, social sciences 50%, teacher education 34%.

Free-Loan Film Serv *Eligibility:* staff & students, educational inst, civic groups, religious groups, indiv with library cards, prof groups. *Restrictions:* for indiv & inst, only in Barbour County. Available to researchers/scholars for on-site viewing. May borrow by mail. *Loan Period:* 7 days. Produce films.

Film Collection 189t/192p. Approx 120t acquired annually. *Circ:* 16mm, 181t; 8mm reel, 128t; S8mm cartridge, 11t.

Other Film Serv Obtain film from coop loan system (Mountain State Film Circuit), film reference serv. *Equipment:* lend S8mm camera, 16mm sound projector, 8mm cartridge projector, 8mm reel projector, S8mm cartridge projector, S8mm reel projector, projection tables & stands, projection screens.

Other Media Collections *Audio:* disc, 33⅓ rpm, 1186t; tape, cassette, 382t; tape, cartridge, 4t; tape, reel, 190t. *Filmstrips:* sound sets, 658t; silent sets, 358t. *Slides:* sets, 80c.

Budget & Expenditures Total library budget $24,000 (FY 6/30/74-6/30/75). No separate AV budget. *Member:* AECT, ALA, W. Va. Library Assn, W. Va. Educational Media Assn, NAVA.

Video Serv *Est:* 1969. *Video Staff:* 8 f-t, 45 p-t, 1 tech. *Video Use:* documentation of community/school events, to increase community's library use, in-service training, practical video/TV training courses, playback of professionally produced tapes, as art form. Video serv available on demand & by appointment. Produce video tapes. Have production studio/space & separate control room.

Video Equipment/Facilities *In-House Use Only:* portapak (1), ½" b&w, Sony 3400; recording deck (6), ½" b&w/col, Sony 3600, 3650; playback deck (1), ½" col, Panasonic; editing deck (2), ¾" col, JVC; studio camera (2), b&w, Panasonic; monitor (6), 6" b&w, Panasonic; SEG (2), Telemation, Sony; keyer (1), Telemation; lighting; microphones (2); tripods (2). *For Loan:* portapak (1), ½" b&w, Sony 3400; recording deck (6), ½" b&w/col, Sony, 3600, 3650; SEG (2), Telemation, Sony. Have permanent & portable viewing installations. *Equipment Loan Period:* no set policy. Provide training in use of equipment to students.

Video Tape Loan/Rental/Sale Serv *Serv Provided:* free loan, swap with other inst. *Loan Eligibility:* staff & students, civic groups, religious groups, indiv with library cards, county residents, consortium. *Restrictions:* for indiv & inst, only in Barbour County. Cannot use for fund-raising, air without permission. May borrow by mail. *Loan Period:* 3 days.

Video Collection Maintained by purchase, own production, exchange/swap. Use/play ½" reel to reel, ¾" cassette.

Sources: commercial distributors. *Member:* Mountain State Film Circuit. *Tape Sel:* preview, faculty/staff recommendations. *Special Collections:* in-house training tapes. Tapes organized by accession number. *Collection, Color:* ½" reel, 44t/c; ¾" cassette, 38t/c. *Collection, B&W:* ½" reel, 174t/c. *Other Video Serv:* reference serv, production workshops.

Cable & CCTV Will receive serv of cable TV system. Have CCTV in inst, with 26 monitors. *Programming Sources:* over-the-air commercial & public broadcasting, tapes produced by inst, tapes produced professionally, tapes produced by community groups & indiv.

Princeton

P- PRINCETON-PUBLIC-MERCER MEMORIAL LIBRARY, 205 Center St, 24740. *Tel:* (304) 425-3324. *Film Serv Est:* 1975. *In Charge:* Jerry Flanagan, Dir. *AV Staff:* 1 (1 prof). *Film Sel:* chief film librarian's decision.

Other Film Serv Rent film from distributors for patrons, obtain film from other libraries, film fairs/festivals, library film programs. Permanent viewing facility available for rent to community.

Other Media Collections *Audio:* disc, 33⅓ rpm, 250t/c; tape, cassette, 40t/c; tape, cartridge, 10t.

Budget & Expenditures Total library budget $7000 (FY 7/1/74-7/1/75). No separate AV budget. *Member:* ALA, W. Va. Library Assn, South Eastern Library Assn.

Weirton

P- MARY H. WEIR PUBLIC LIBRARY, 3442 Main St, 26062. *Film Serv Est:* 1956. *In Charge:* Richard Badis, AV Clerk. *AV Staff:* ½ (½ cl, ½ tech). *Film Sel:* committee preview.

Film Rental Serv *Eligibility:* no restrictions. *Restrictions:* none. *Rental Period:* 1 day. *Total Yr Film Booking:* 933.

Film Collection 480t/500p. *Pubns:* catalog, annual (50¢).

Other Film Serv Obtain film from coop loan system (Ohio Valley Film Circuit). Permanent viewing facility available for rent to community.

Other Media Collections *Audio:* disc, 33⅓ rpm, 1156t.

Budget & Expenditures No separate AV budget.

West Liberty

C- WEST LIBERTY STATE COLLEGE, Media Resource Center, 26074. *Tel:* (304) 336-8037. *Film Serv Est:* 1971. *In Charge:* Laurence P. Williams, Media Resource Dir. *AV Staff:* 2 (1 prof, 1 cl). *Film Sel:* faculty/staff recommendations. *Holdings:* physical education, social sciences.

Film Collection 10t/p. Approx 2t acquired annually.

Other Film Serv Rent film from distributors for patrons, obtain film from coop loan system, obtain film from other libraries, film reference serv. Permanent viewing facility. *Equipment:* lend 16mm camera, 16mm sound projector, S8mm cartridge projector, projection tables & stands, projection screens.

Budget & Expenditures Total library budget $17,500 (FY 7/1/75-7/1/76). Total FY film budget $10,000.

Video Serv *Video Staff:* 2 f-t, 16 p-t. *Video Use:* documentation of community/school events, in-service training. Video serv available by appointment. Produce video tapes. Have production studio/space & separate control room.

Video Equipment/Facilities *For Loan:* portapak (3); recording deck (7); playback deck (7); editing deck (1); studio camera (5); monitor (11); SEG (1); keyer (1); additional camera lenses (2); microphones (25); tripods (5); audio tape recorders (35). Have portable viewing installation. *Equipment Loan Period:* 14 days. Provide training in use of equipment to faculty & students. Have tape duplication serv.

Video Tape Loan/Rental/Sale Serv *Serv Provided:* free loan, swap with other inst. *Loan Eligibility:* staff & students.

Video Collection Maintained by own production. Use/play ½", 1" reel to reel. Tapes organized by professor's name. *Other Video Serv:* taping of other media.

Wisconsin

Antigo

P- ANTIGO PUBLIC LIBRARY, 404 Superior St, 54409. *Tel:* (715) 623-5308. *Film Serv Est:* 1961.

Film Rental Serv *Eligibility:* no restrictions. *Restrictions:* only in Langlade County. *Rental Period:* 1 day. *Pubns:* catalog, annual.

Other Film Serv Rent film from distributors for patrons, obtain film from coop loan system (Wis. Valley Library Circuit), obtain film from other libraries, film reference serv, film fairs/festivals.

Other Media Collections *Audio:* disc, 33⅓ rpm, 197c; tape, cassette, 50c. *Filmstrips:* sound, 33c.

Budget & Expenditures Total library budget $12,330 (FY 1/1/75-1/1/76). Total FY film budget $600.

Appleton

C- FOX VALLEY TECHNICAL INSITITUE, 1825 N Bluemound Dr, 54911. *Tel:* (414) 739-8831, ext 233. *Film Serv Est:* 1971. *In Charge:* Henry Beno, Distribution Coordinator. *AV Staff:* 9 (4 prof, 2 cl, 3 tech). *Film Sel:* faculty/staff recommendations. *Holdings:* agriculture 10%, career education 15%, industrial arts 45%, law 10%, social sciences 20%, teacher education 10%.

Free-Loan Film Serv *Eligibility:* staff & students. *Restrictions:* for indiv & inst, only in 5 county district. Available to researchers/scholars for on-site viewing. May not borrow by mail. *Loan Period:* 3 days. *Total Yr Film Loan:* 25.

Film Collection 263t/p. Approx 25-30t acquired annually. *Circ:* 16mm, 112t/p; S8mm reel, 151t/p.

Other Film Serv Permanent viewing facility.

Other Media Collections *Audio:* disc, 33⅓ rpm, 300t; tape, cassette, 850t/c; tape, reel, 150t/c. *Filmstrips:* sound sets, 300t; silent sets, 100t. *Slides:* single, 1500t; sets, 350t.

Budget & Expenditures Total library budget $47,348 (FY 7/1/74-7/1/75). Total FY film budget $24,597. *Member:* AECT, ALA, Wis. Library Assn.

Video Serv *In Charge:* L. E. Schuff, ERC Supervisor. *Video Staff:* 6 f-t, 17 p-t, 1 tech. *Video Use:* in-service training, practical video/TV training courses. Video serv available on demand. Produce video tapes. Have production studio/space & separate control room.

Video Equipment/Facilities *In-House Use Only:* portapak (1), ½″ b&w, Sony AV3400; recording deck (2), 1″ col, IVC800; playback deck (22), ¾″ col, Sony VP1000; editing deck (1), 1″ col, IVC870; studio camera (2), col, Shibaden FP1000; monitor (6), b&w, Ball; SEG (1), Telemation; keyer (1); lighting (40); microphones (8); tripods (2); audio tape recorders (1). Have permanent & portable viewing installations. Provide training in use of equipment to faculty & students.

Video Tape Loan/Rental/Sale Serv *Serv Provided:* free loan, swap with other inst. *Loan Eligibility:* org members. *Restrictions:* for indiv, only in Calumet, Winnebago, Outagomie, Waupaca & Waushara Counties. Cannot use for fundraising. May not borrow by mail.

Video Collection Maintained by purchase, rental, own production, exchange/swap. Use/play ½″, 1″ reel to reel, ¾″ cassette. *Sources:* commercial distributors. *Tape Sel:* preview, faculty/staff recommendations, catalogs. *Special Collections:* in-house training tapes, films in video format. Tapes organized by accession number. *Collection, Color:* ½″ reel, 10t/c; 1″ reel, 65t/c; ¾″ cassette, 540t/c. *Collection, B&W:* ½″ reel, 30t/c. *Other Video Serv:* taping of other media, production workshops. *Pubns:* catalog.

Cable & CCTV Have CCTV in inst, with 12 monitors. *Programming Sources:* over-the-air commercial & public broadcasting, tapes produced by inst, tapes produced professionally.

Baraboo

S- CIRCUS WORLD MUSEUM, Library, 53913. *Tel:* (608) 356-8341. *Film Serv Est:* 1971. *In Charge:* Robert L. Parkinson, Librarian. *AV Staff:* ½ (1 prof, ½ tech). *Film Sel:* chief film librarian's decision. *Holdings:* circus 100%.

Film Rental Serv *Eligibility:* educational org, civic groups. *Restrictions:* only in U.S. & territories. Cannot rent for more than 2 showings. *Rental Rate:* $2 per film. *Rental Period:* 7 days. *Total Yr Film Booking:* 70.

Film Collection 200p. *Circ:* 16mm, 200p. Publish materials pertaining to collection.

Other Film Serv Permanent viewing facility available for rent to community.

Budget & Expenditures No separate AV budget.

Beloit

P- BELOIT PUBLIC LIBRARY, 409 Pleasant St, 53511. *Tel:* (608) 362-8974. *Film Serv Est:* 1962. *In Charge:* Peggy Zanbow, Reference Librarian. *AV Staff:* ½. *Film Sel:* chief film librairan's decision.

Free-Loan Film Serv *Eligibility:* indiv with library cards. *Restrictions:* for indiv, only in Rock County. Cannot transmit electronically. Available to researchers/scholars for on-site viewing. May not borrow by mail. *Loan Period:* 1 day.

Film Collection 85t/p. Approx 5t acquired annually. *Circ:* 16mm, 85t/p. *Pubns:* catalog, annual.

Other Film Serv Rent film from distributors for patrons, obtain film from coop loan system (Wis. Reference & Loan Library, Wis. Public Library Film Circuit), obtain film from other libraries, film reference serv, film fairs/festivals, library film programs. Permanent viewing facility available to community.

Other Media Collections *Audio:* disc, 33⅓ rpm, 2772t.

Budget & Expenditures Total library budget $34,282 (FY 1/1/75-1/1/76). Total FY film budget $1800.

Burlington

P- BURLINGTON PUBLIC LIBRARY, 301 N Pine, 53105. *Tel:* (414) 763-3663. *Film Serv Est:* 1951. *In Charge:* Grace Lofgren, Dir. *Film Sel:* through film circuit.

Film Rental Serv *Eligibility:* educational org, civic groups, patrons/public. *Restrictions:* only in city & contracting cities. *Rental Period:* 1 day.

Film Collection *Circ:* 16mm, 3t/p; 8mm & S8mm reel, 55t/p. *Pubns:* catalog, annual.

Other Film Serv Obtain film from coop loan system (Wis. Library Film Circuit). *Equipment:* rent 16mm sound projector (2), 8mm reel projector (1), S8mm reel projector (1), projection screens (1).

Other Media Collections *Audio:* disc, 33⅓ rpm, 900t.

Budget & Expenditures Total library budget $6900 (FY 1/1/74-1/1/75). Total FY film budget $600.

Cleveland

C- LAKESHORE TECHNICAL INSTITUTE, Educational Resources Center, 1290 North Ave, 53015. *Tel:* (414) 693-8211, ext 149. *Film Serv Est:* 1967. *In Charge:* Charles Ma, Media Specialist. *AV Staff:* 3 (1 prof, 2 cl, 2 tech). *Film Sel:* faculty/staff recommendations, published reviews. *Holdings:* career education 85%, consumer affairs 1%, engineering 5%, industrial arts 2%, medicine 4%, social sciences 2%, women 1%.

Free-Loan Film Serv *Eligibility:* staff & students, educational inst, civic groups, religious groups. *Restrictions:* for indiv

Cleveland (cont'd)
& inst, only in our tax area. Cannot transmit electronically
May borrow by mail. *Loan Period:* 4 days. *Total Yr Film Loan:*
150.
  Film Collection 178t/p. Approx 24t acquired annually.
Circ: 16mm, 153t/p. *Noncirc:* 16mm, 25t/p; S8mm reel, 25t/p.
Pubns: catalog, annual.
  Other Film Serv Permanent viewing facility available for
rent to community. *Equipment:* lend 16mm sound projector (2),
8mm cartridge projector (4), S8mm reel projector (3), projection
tables & stands (6), projection screens (6).
  Other Media Collections *Audio, Filmstrips, Slides:* total
2022.
  Budget & Expenditures Total library budget $5924 (FY
7/1/75-7/1/76). No separate AV budget.
  Video Serv *Est:* 1976. *Video Staff:* 1 f-t, 2 tech. *Video Use:*
documentation of community/school events, to increase community's library use, community video access, in-service training, practical video/TV training courses, as sales tool, instructional tool. Video serv available on demand. Produce video
tapes. Have production studio/space & separate control room.
  Video Equipment/Facilities *For Loan:* portapak (1), ½″
b&w, Sony; recording deck (7), ¾″ col, Sony; playback deck (1),
1″ col, Sony; editing deck (1), col, Sony; studio camera (2), col,
Sony; monitor (10), col, Sony; SEG (1); keyer (1); additional
camera lenses (3); lighting; microphones (10); tripods (5); audio
tape recorders (50). Have permanent viewing installation.
Equipment Loan Period: 6 days. Provide training in use of
equipment to faculty & students. Have tape duplication serv.
  Video Tape Loan/Rental/Sale Serv *Serv Provided:* free
loan, swap with other inst. *Loan Eligibility:* staff & students,
educational inst, civic groups, religious groups, indiv with
library cards, prof groups, members of community. *Restrictions:*
for indiv & inst, only in our tax area. Cannot duplicate. May
borrow by mail. *Total Yr Tape Loan:* 15.
  Video Collection Maintained by purchase, own production. Use/play ¾″ cassette. *Sources:* commercial distributors.
Tape Sel: preview, faculty/staff recommendations, published
reviews, catalogs. *Special Collections:* in-house training tapes.
Tapes organized by LC system. *Collection, Color:* ¾″ cassette,
775t. *Collection, B&W:* ¾″ cassette, 25t. *Other Video Serv:*
programming, taping of other media. *Pubns:* catalog.
  Cable & CCTV Have CCTV in inst, with 50 monitors.
Programming Sources: over-the-air commercial & public broadcasting, tapes produced by inst, tapes produced professionally,
central studio which shows tapes in any school classroom or
shop.

Eau Claire

C- UNIVERSITY OF WISCONSIN-EAU CLAIRE, William
    D. McIntyre Library, Park and Garfield Ave, 54701. *Tel:*
    (715) 836-5820. *In Charge:* Cleo Powers, IMC Librarian.
    Film Sel: committee preview, faculty/staff recommenda-
    tions, chief film librarian's decision.
  Free-Loan Film Serv *Eligibility:* staff & students. *Restric-
tions:* for indiv, classroom only. Available to researchers/schol-
ars for on-site viewing. May not borrow by mail. *Loan Period:* 2-
7 days. *Total Yr Film Loan:* 1114.
  Film Collection *Circ:* 16mm, 297t; 8mm cartridge, 25t;
S8mm cartridge, 161t.
  Other Film Serv Permanent viewing facility.
  Budget & Expenditures Total FY film budget $3000. (FY
7/1/74-7/1/75).
  Video Serv *Est:* 1973. *Video Staff:* 4 f-t. *Video Use:* playback of professionally produced tapes, playback of tapes produced on campus. Video serv available on demand.
  Video Equipment/Facilities *In-House Use Only:* recording deck (3), ½″ b&w, Sony AV3600; playback deck (5), ¾″ col,
Sony-U-matic. Have permanent & portable viewing installations. Provide training in use of equipment to faculty & students.
  Video Tape Loan/Rental/Sale Serv *Serv Provided:* free
loan. *Loan Eligibility:* staff & students. *Restrictions:* for indiv,

only on campus. May not borrow by mail. *Total Yr Tape Loan:*
2108.
  Video Collection Maintained by purchase. Use/play ½″
reel to reel, ¾″ cassette. *Sources:* commercial distributors, locally produced by Media Development Center. *Tape Sel:* preview, faculty/staff recommendations, published reviews, catalogs. Tapes organized by accession number. *Collection, Color:*
¾″ cassette, 10t. *Collection, B&W:* ¾″ cassette, 23t.
  Cable & CCTV Receive serv of cable TV system.

Green Bay

P- BROWN COUNTY LIBRARY, 515 Pine St, 54301. *Tel:* (414)
    432-0311, ext 52. *In Charge:* Ruth Kuhs, AV Librarian. *AV
    Staff:* 6½ (2 prof, 4½ cl). *Film Sel:* staff recommendations,
    chief film librarian's decision. *Holdings:* children's films
    20%, fine arts 20%, sports 20%.
  Free-Loan Film Serv *Eligibility:* indiv with adult library
cards. *Restrictions:* for indiv, interlibrary loan. Cannot use for
fund-raising. Available to researchers/scholars for on-site viewing. *Total Yr Film Loan:* 5087.
  Film Collection 464t/474p. Approx 86t acquired annually.
Circ: 16mm, 350t; 8mm cartridge, 124t. *Pubns:* catalog, annual
(50¢); suppl, no set policy.
  Other Film Serv Obtain film from coop loan system (Wis.
Film Circuit), obtain film from other libraries, film reference
serv, film fairs/festivals, library film programs, headquarters
for Nicolet area film circuit. Permanent viewing facility available to community. *Equipment:* lend projection screens.
  Other Media Collections *Audio:* disc, 33⅓ rpm, 2200t;
tape, cassette, 250t. *Filmstrips:* sound, 5000t/5500c; silent,
3000t/3500c.
  Budget & Expenditures Total FY film budget $4700 (FY
1/1/75-1/1/76). *Member:* FLIC, Wis. Library Assn.

Lake Geneva

P- LAKE GENEVA PUBLIC LIBRARY, 918 Main St, 53147.
    Tel: (414) 248-8311. *Film Serv Est:* 1950. *In Charge:* Flor-
    ence Netzel, Film Librarian. *AV Staff:* 2. *Film Sel:* commit-
    tee preview. *Holdings:* children's films 50%, Christmas
    50%.
  Film Rental Serv *Eligibility:* patrons/public. *Restrictions:*
only in Walworth County. *Rental Period:* 1 day. *Total Yr Film
Booking:* 207.
  Film Collection 31t/p. Approx 1t acquired annually.
Pubns: catalog, as needed.
  Other Film Serv Rent film from distributors for patrons,
obtain film from coop loan system (Wis. Library Film Circuit,
Walworth County Library Services), obtain film from other
libraries. Permanent viewing facility.
  Other Media Collections *Audio:* disc, 33⅓ rpm, 1374t;
tape, cassette, 22t. *Filmstrips:* silent, 104t.
  Budget & Expenditures No separate AV budget. *Member:*
ALA, Wis. Library Assn.

Madison

P- MADISON PUBLIC LIBRARY, 201 W Mifflin, 53703. *Tel:*
    (608) 266-6323. *Film Serv Est:* 1966. *In Charge:* Vada C.
    Mayfield, AV Librarian. *AV Staff:* 1 (½ prof, 1 cl). *Film Sel:*
    committee preview. *Holdings:* children's films 22%.
  Free-Loan Film Serv *Eligibility:* indiv with library cards.
Restrictions: for indiv, only in South Central & Southwest
Library Systems. Cannot use for fund-raising, transmit elec-
tronically, borrow for classroom use. Available to researchers/
scholars for on-site viewing. May borrow by mail. *Loan Period:*
3 days. *Total Yr Film Loan:* 6332.
  Film Collection 358t/425p. Approx 50t acquired annually.
Circ: 16mm, 358t/425p; S8mm reel, 250t/350p. *Pubns:* catalog,
annual; suppl, no set policy.

Other Film Serv Obtain film from coop loan system (Wis. Libraries Film Circuit), film reference serv, library film programs. *Equipment:* lend 16mm sound projector, S8mm reel projector, projection screens.
Other Media Collections *Audio:* disc, 33⅓ rpm, 10,000 t/14,000c; tape, cassette, 150c; tape, reel, 70c.
Budget & Expenditures Total library budget $340,238. Total FY film budget $23,000. *Member:* Wis. Library Assn.

C- UNIVERSITY OF WISCONSIN, Bureau of AV Instruction, Box 2093, 53701. *Tel:* (608) 262-1644. *Film Serv Est:* 1914. *In Charge:* Hal Richle, Dir. *AV Staff:* 40 (7 prof, 30 cl, 3 tech). *Film Sel:* faculty/staff recommendations, chief film librarian's decision.
Film Rental Serv *Eligibility:* no restrictions. *Restrictions:* only in Wis. & bordering states. Cannot use for fund-raising, transmit electronically. *Rental Period:* 5 days. *Total Yr Film Booking:* 91,767. Sell films.
Film Collection 7000t/15,000p. *Circ:* 16mm, 7000t/15,000p. *Pubns:* catalog, every 2 yrs; suppl, in yr catalog not published.
Other Film Serv Rent film from distributors for patrons, obtain film from other libraries, film reference serv. Permanent viewing facility. *Equipment:* rent 16mm sound projector, 8mm cartridge projector, 8mm reel projector, S8mm cartridge projector, S8mm reel projector, projection tables & stands, projection screens.
Budget & Expenditures Total library budget $155,000. Total FY film budget $155,000. *Member:* AECT, CUFC, EFLA.

P- WISCONSIN DEPT OF PUBLIC INSTRUCTION, Div for Library Services, Reference and Loan Library, Box 1437, 53701. *Tel:* (608) 266-1081. *Film Serv Est:* 1972. *In Charge:* Willeen Tretheway, AV Services Librarian. *AV Staff:* 1¾ (¾ prof, 1 tech). *Film Sel:* committee preview, staff recommendations, chief film librarian's decision. *Holdings:* library science 90%, Wisconsin 10%.
Free-Loan Film Serv *Eligibility:* indiv, Wis. libraries, state employees for work-related use. *Restrictions:* for indiv, interlibrary loan, only in state; for inst, only in state. Cannot use for fund-raising. All loans subject to provisions of our *Manual.* Available to researchers/scholars for on-site viewing. May borrow by mail. *Loan Period:* flexible. *Total Yr Film Loan:* 240.
Film Collection 59t. Approx 2t acquired annually. *Circ:* 16mm, 37t/41p. *Noncirc:* 16mm, 22t/p. *Pubns:* catalog, as needed; suppl, no set policy.
Other Film Serv Film reference serv. Permanent viewing facility.
Other Media Collections *Audio:* disc, 33⅓ rpm, 5800t; tape, cassette, 600t. *Filmstrips & Slides:* total, 430.
Budget & Expenditures Total library budget $590,664 (FY 7/1/74-7/1/75). No separate AV budget. *Member:* ALA, Wis. Library Assn, Special Libraries Assn, Music Library Assn.
Video Serv *Video Staff:* 1½ f-t, 1 p-t, 1 tech. *Video Use:* to increase community's libraries use. Video serv available on demand. Produce video tapes.
Video Equipment/Facilities *In-House Use Only:* playback deck (2), Sony VP1000, VP1200; monitor (1), Sony Trinitron. *For Loan:* playback deck (2), Sony VP1000, VP1200; monitor (1), Sony Trinitron. Have portable viewing installation. *Equipment Loan Period:* no set policy. Provide training in use of equipment.
Video Tape Loan/Rental/Sale Serv *Serv Provided:* free loan. *Loan Eligibility:* indiv, libraries in Wis., state employees. *Restrictions:* for indiv, interlibrary loan, only in state; for inst, only in state. Cannot use for fund-raising, duplicate, air without permission. All tapes subject to provisions in our *Manual.* May borrow by mail. Loan Period: flexible. *Total Yr Tape Loan:* 724.
Video Collection Maintained by purchase. Use/play ¾" cassette. *Sources:* commercial distributors. *Tape Sel:* preview, staff recommendations, published reviews, catalogs. Tapes organized by accession number. *Collection, Color:* 2" reel, 1t/c; ¾" cassette, 112t/c. *Collection, B&W:* ½" reel, 1t/c; ¾" cassette, 23t/c. *Pubns:* catalog.

Manitowoc

P- MANITOWOC PUBLIC LIBRARY, 808 Hamilton St, 54220. *Tel:* (414) 682-6861. *Film Serv Est:* 1974. *In Charge:* Barbara F. Kelly, Dir. *AV Staff:* ½. *Film Sel:* committee preview, staff recommendations, chief film librarian's decision, published reviews.
Free-Loan Film Serv *Eligibility:* anyone in our tax area. *Restrictions:* for indiv & inst, only in our county. *Loan Period:* 1 day. *Total Yr Film Loan:* 4129.
Film Collection 150t. *Circ:* 16mm, 150t. *Pubns:* catalog, annual.
Other Film Serv Obtain film from coop loan system (Wis. Library Film Circuit), obtain film from other libraries, library film programs. Permanent viewing facility.
Other Media Collections *Audio:* disc, 33⅓ rpm, 3607c; tape, cassette, 520c. *Filmstrips:* total, 1294c. *Slides:* total, 472c.
Budget & Expenditures Total library budget $73,000. Total FY film budget $11,000. *Member:* ALA, FLIC.

Menomonie

C- UNIVERSITY OF WISCONSIN-STOUT, Pierce Library, 54751. *Tel:* (715) 232-1215. *In Charge:* M. E. Schultze, Circulation Associate. *Film Sel:* committee preview, faculty/staff recommendations. *Holdings:* home economics 25%, industrial arts 25%, teacher education 15%.
Free-Loan Film Serv *Eligibility:* staff & students. *Restrictions:* for indiv & inst, none. Cannot transmit electronically. Available to researchers/scholars for on-site viewing. May not borrow by mail. *Loan Period:* 3 days. *Total Yr Film Loan:* 6001. Sell films. Produce films.
Film Collection 883t/910p. Approx 50t acquired annually. *Circ:* 16mm, 883t/910p; S8mm cartridge, 50t/p. *Pubns:* catalog, annual.
Other Film Serv Rent film from distributors for patrons. Permanent viewing facility. *Equipment:* lend 16mm sound projector, 8mm cartridge projector, 8mm reel projector (1), S8mm cartridge projector (1), S8mm reel projector (2), projection tables & stands, projection screens (14), variety of other equipment.
Other Media Collections *Audio:* tape, cassette, 843t/853c. *Filmstrips:* total, 221c. *Slides:* single, 26c; kits 571c.
Budget & Expenditures Total library budget $204,051 (FY 7/1/74-7/1/75). No separate budget. *Member:* AECT, ALA, EFLA, Wis. Library Assn.
Video Serv *Est:* 1968. *In Charge:* Greg Schubert, Teleproduction Mgr. *Video Staff:* 4 f-t, 5 p-t, 3 tech. *Video Use:* documentation of community/school events, in-service training, practical video/TV training courses, playback only of professionally produced tapes. Video serv available by appointment. Produce video tapes. Have production studio/space & separate control room.
Video Equipment/Facilities *In-House Use Only:* portapak (4), ½" b&w, Sony; recording deck (48), ½", ¾" b&w/col, Sony; editing deck (2), ½" col, Sony 8650; studio camera (2), col, RCA TK630; monitor (19), col, Nasco, Sony; SEG (10), SEG. *For Loan:* portapak (2), ½" b&w, Sony; recording deck (2), ½", ¾" b&w/col, Sony; monitor (1), col, Nasco. Have permanent & portable viewing installations. *Equipment Loan Period:* no set policy. Provide training in use of equipment to faculty & students. Have tape duplication serv.
Video Tape Loan/Rental/Sale Serv *Serv Provided:* free loan. *Loan Eligibility:* staff & students. *Restrictions:* Cannot duplicate, air without permission. May not borrow by mail.
Video Collection Maintained by purchase, own production. Use/play ½", 2" reel to reel, ¾" cassette. *Sources:* commercial distributors, community productions. *Tape Sel:* preview, faculty/staff recommendations. Tapes organized by LC system. *Other Video Serv:* production workshops. *Pubns:* catalog.
Cable & CCTV Receive serv of cable TV system. Have CCTV in inst, with 200 monitors. *Programming Sources:* over-the-air commercial & public broadcasting, tapes produced by inst, tapes produced by community groups & indiv, commercially produced programs for which we have CCTV clearance.

Merrill

P- T. B. SCOTT FREE LIBRARY, 54452. *Tel:* (715) 536-7191. *Film Serv Est:* 1965. *In Charge:* Leora Young, AV Librarian. *AV Staff:* ¼ (¼ prof).

Free-Loan Film Serv *Eligibility:* educational inst, civic groups, religious groups, indiv with library cards. *Restrictions:* for indiv, none; for inst, none. May borrow by mail. *Loan Period:* 2-7 days. *Total Yr Film Loan:* 169.

Film Collection 5t/9p. *Circ:* 16mm, 4t/8p; 8mm reel, 1t/p.

Other Film Serv Obtain film from coop loan system (Wis. Valley Library Service). Permanent viewing facility available to community. *Equipment:* lend 16mm sound projector (1), projection screens (1).

Other Media Collections *Audio:* disc, 33⅓ rpm, 900t; tape, cassette, 610t. *Filmstrips:* sound, 75t; silent, 1390t; sound sets, 3t. *Slides:* sets, 1t.

Budget & Expenditures Total library budget $20,597 (FY 1/1/75-1/1/76). No separate AV budget. *Member:* ALA, Wis. Library Assn.

Milwaukee

S- INPUT: COMMUNITY VIDEO CENTER, 1015 W Mitchell St, 53204. *Tel:* (414) 645-8116. *Video Serv Est:* 1972. *In Charge:* Kate Hudgens, Joan McManus, Mary Ann Onorato. *Video Staff:* 3 f-t, 3 p-t. *Video Use:* documentation of community/school events, community video access, community education & awareness on social issues. Video serv available on demand & by appointment. Produce video tapes. Have production studio/space.

Video Equipment/Facilities *In-House Use Only:* recording deck (1), ½" b&w, Concord 820; editing deck (1), ½" col, Panasonic 3130; studio camera (2), ½" b&w, Panasonic 314; monitor (4), b&w; SEG (1), Panasonic; keyer (1), SEG; mike mixer (1). *For Loan:* portapak (2), ½" b&w, Panasonic 3082; playback deck (1), ½" b&w, Concord 310; monitor (4); microphones (3); tripods (2). Have portable viewing installation. *Equipment Loan Period:* no set policy. Provide training in use of equipment to students, residents & community groups. Have tape duplication serv.

Video Tape Loan/Rental/Sale Serv *Serv Provided:* free loan, swap with other inst, rental. *Loan/Rental Eligibility:* students, area residents, community groups. *Restrictions:* for indiv & inst, only in city.

Video Collection Maintained by own production, exchange/swap. Use/play ½" reel to reel. *Sources:* community productions, exchange, in-house productions. Tapes organized by subject. *Collection, B&W:* ½" reel, 75t/c. *Other Video Serv:* production workshops. Publish *Citizen's Handbook on Cable Television* (50¢), *Video Manual.*

S- MILWAUKEE ART CENTER, Film Rental Resource Library, 750 N Lincoln Memorial Dr, 53202. *Tel:* (414) 271-9508, ext 271. *In Charge:* John Thurman, Asst Curator, Multi Media. *AV Staff:* 2 (1 prof, 1 tech). *Film Sel:* staff recommendations. *Holdings:* animated films 10%, children's films 100%, experimental films 10%, fine arts 50%.

Film Rental Serv *Eligibility:* no restrictions. *Restrictions:* none. Cannot use for fund-raising. *Rental Period:* 1 day. Produce filmstrips, slide instructional packages.

Film Collection 15t/20p. Approx 2-3t acquired annually. *Circ:* 16mm, 13t. *Noncirc:* 16mm, 2t/p. *Pubns:* catalog, annual.

Other Film Serv Rent film from distributors for patrons, film fairs/festivals, library film programs. Permanent viewing facility available for rent to community. *Equipment:* rent S8mm camera (2), 16mm sound projector (3), 8mm reel projector (1), S8mm reel projector (1), projection tables & stands (6), projection screens (3), slide projectors (25), tape recorders (5).

Other Media Collections *Audio:* tape, reel, 70t/c. *Filmstrips:* sound, 5t/c; silent, 5t/c; silent sets, 20t/c. *Slides:* sets, 45t/c.

Budget & Expenditures (FY 1/1/75-1/1/76). Total FY film budget $2600.

Video Serv *Est:* 1975. *Video Staff:* 1 f-t. *Video Use:* documentation of community events, to increase community's library use, community video access, in-service training, as sales tool, playback only of professionally produced tapes, as art form. Video serv available by appointment.

Video Equipment/Facilities *In-House Use Only:* recording deck (1), ¾" col, JVC CR6300U; studio camera (1), 15" col, Hitachi Shibaden; microphones (5); audio tape recorders (3). Have portable viewing installation. Have tape duplication serv.

Video Collection Maintained by purchase. Use/play ¾" cassette. *Sources:* community productions, artists. *Tape Sel:* pertinence to Art Center's activities. *Special Collections:* video as art, films in video format, Center's archival use. *Collection, Color:* ¾" cassette, 10t/c.

P- MILWAUKEE COUNTY FEDERATED LIBRARY SYSTEM, 814 W Wisconsin Ave, 53233. *Tel:* (414) 278-3000. *Film Serv Est:* 1976. *In Charge:* Edward G. Cessna, Multi-Media Librarian. *AV Staff:* 2 (1 prof, 1 cl). *Film Sel:* committee preview.

Free-Loan Film Serv *Eligibility:* indiv with library cards. *Restrictions:* for indiv & inst, only in Milwaukee County in community which is a system member. Cannot use for fund-raising, transmit electronically. May not borrow by mail. *Loan Period:* 1 day.

Film Collection 220t/p. *Circ:* 16mm, 220t/p. *Pubns:* catalog, as needed.

Other Media Collections *Audio:* tape, cassette, 2000t/2500c. *Filmstrips:* sound, 300t/350c.

Budget & Expenditures Total library budget $294,000 (FY 1/1/75-1/1/76). Total FY film budget $180,000. *Member:* AECT, EFLA.

Video Serv *Video Staff:* 2 f-t. *Video Use:* to increase community's library use. Video serv available on demand & by appointment. Have production studio/space.

Video Equipment/Facilities *In-House Use Only:* recording deck (9), ¾", Sony VO1800; playback deck (18), ¾", Sony VP1200; studio camera (2), b&w, Panasonic WV-341P; monitor (27), 19" col, Panasonic; microphones (2); tripods (2). Have portable viewing installation. Provide training in use of equipment to staff.

Video Tape Loan/Rental/Sale Serv *Serv Provided:* free loan. *Loan Eligibility:* indiv with library cards. *Restrictions:* for indiv, only in library; for inst, only residents of Milwaukee County. Cannot use for fund-raising, duplicate, air without permission. May not borrow by mail.

Video Collection Maintained by purchase. Use/play ¾" cassette. *Sources:* commercial distributors, community productions. *Tape Sel:* preview, staff recommendations. Tapes organized by Dewey Decimal. *Collection, Color:* ¾" cassette, 450t/550c. *Collection, B&W:* ¾" cassette, 100t/130c. *Pubns:* catalog.

S- MILWAUKEE PUBLIC MUSEUM, AV Center, 815 N Seventh St, 53233. *Tel:* (414) 278-2727. *In Charge:* Sharon Kayne Chaplock, Dir. *AV Staff:* 16 (3 prof, 5 cl, 8 tech). *Film Sel:* committee preview, staff recommendations, recommendations of resource people. *Holdings:* agriculture 1%, black studies 2%, consumer affairs 1%, dance 1%, experimental films 1%, fine arts 2%, industrial arts 1%, language arts 25%, science 35%, social sciences 29%, teacher education 1%, women 1%.

Free-Loan Film Serv *Eligibility:* staff, educational inst, civic groups, religious groups, indiv with library cards, prof groups. *Restrictions:* for indiv & inst, only in city. Cannot transmit electronically. Available to researchers/scholars for on-site viewing. May borrow by mail. *Loan Period:* flexible. *Total Yr Film Loan:* 131,248.

Film Rental Serv *Eligibility:* educational org, civic groups. *Restrictions:* only in Milwaukee County. Cannot use for fund-raising, transmit electronically. *Rental Period:* 1 day plus mailing time. *Total Yr Film Booking:* 907. Produce films. Produce slides, videotapes.

Film Collection 6912t/16,000p. Approx 700t acquired annually. *Circ:* 16mm, 6912t/15,872p. *Noncirc:* 16mm, 50t/52p. *Pubns:* catalog, every 2 yrs ($3.50); suppl, no set policy ($1.50).

Other Film Serv Film fairs/festivals, library film programs. Permanent viewing facility.

Other Media Collections *Audio:* disc, 33⅓ rpm, 122t/125c. *Filmstrips:* silent, 2452t/3518c; sound sets, 275t/279c. *Slides:* sets, 114t/c, glass slides, 75,000t/c.

Budget & Expenditures Total library budget $62,000 (FY 1/1/75-1/1/76). Total FY film budget $60,400. *Member:* AECT, Wis. AV Assn, Southeastern Wis. AV Assn.

C- UNIVERSITY OF WISCONSIN-MILWAUKEE, Library, Media Resource Center, Box 604, 53201. *Tel:* (414) 963-4673. *Film Serv Est:* 1968. *In Charge:* Wendy Young, Supervisor. *AV Staff:* 2 (1 prof, 1 cl). *Film Sel:* committee preview, faculty/staff recommendations, chief film librarian's decision.

Free-Loan Film Serv *Eligibility:* staff & students. *Restrictions:* for indiv, only on campus. Cannot use for fund-raising, transmit electronically. Available to researchers/scholars for on-site viewing. May not borrow by mail. *Loan Period:* class length. *Total Yr Film Loan:* 700.

Film Collection 179t/180p. *Circ:* 16mm, 179t/180p; S8mm reel, 23t. *Pubns:* catalog, as needed; suppl, no set policy.

Other Film Serv Rent film from distributors for patrons, obtain film from other libraries, film reference serv. Permanent viewing facility. *Equipment:* lend S8mm camera (10), 16mm sound projector (45), S8mm cartridge projector (3), projection tables & stands (30), projection screens (20), recorders (20), overhead projectors (30).

Other Media Collections *Audio:* disc, 33⅓ rpm, 5000t; tape, cassette, 125t; tape, reel, 600t. *Filmstrips:* sound, 25t; silent, 1629t; sound sets, 100t. *Slides:* sets, 55t.

Budget & Expenditures Total library budget $718,001 (FY 7/1/75-7/1/76). Total FY film budget $25,244. *Member:* ALA, EFLA.

Video Serv *Est:* 1974. *Video Staff:* 2 f-t, 1 p-t. *Video Use:* playback only of professionally produced tapes. Video serv available by appointment.

Video Equipment/Facilities *In-House Use Only:* portapak (1), ½" b&w, Sony AV-AVC; recording deck (4), ½" b&w/col, Sony 3400; playback deck (1), ¾" col, Sony 3610; camera (3), b&w, Sony AV1200; monitor (20), b&w/col, Sony, RCA; microphones (10); audio tape recorders (25). *For Loan:* portapak (1), ½" b&w, Sony AV-AVC; recording deck (4), ½" b&w/col, Sony 3400; camera (3), b&w, Sony AV1200; monitor (20), b&w/col, Sony, RCA; microphones (10); audio tape recorders (25). Have portable viewing installation. *Equipment Loan Period:* 3 hr class period. Provide training in use of equipment to faculty & students.

Video Tape Loan/Rental/Sale Serv *Serv Provided:* free loan. *Loan Eligibility:* staff & students. *Restrictions:* for indiv, only on campus. Cannot use for fund-raising, duplicate, air without permission. May not borrow by mail. *Total Yr Tape Loan:* 20.

Video Collection Maintained by purchase, rental. Use/ play ½", 1", 2" reel to reel, ¾" cassette. *Sources:* commercial distributors, community productions, WHA-TV Univ Wis.-Madison. *Tape Sel:* preview, faculty/staff recommendations, catalogs. *Special Collections:* original productions. Tapes organized by format & accession number. *Collection, Color:* ½" reel, 4t/7c; 1" reel, 1t/c; 2" reel, 1t/c; ¾" cassette, 24t/c. *Pubns:* catalog.

Cable & CCTV Have CCTV in inst, with 70 monitors. *Programming Sources:* tapes produced by inst, tapes produced professionally.

Oshkosh

P- OSHKOSH PUBLIC LIBRARY, 106 Washington Ave, 54901. *Tel:* (414) 424-0473. *Film Serv Est:* 1965. *In Charge:* Gloria Hoegh, Head, Circulation Services. *AV Staff:* 1 (½ prof, ½ cl). *Film Sel:* chief film librarian's decision, published reviews. *Holdings:* feature films 20%.

Free-Loan Film Serv *Eligibility:* civic groups, religious groups, indiv with library cards, prof groups, & others, such as social service agencies. *Restrictions:* for indiv & inst, only in our county. Cannot use for fund-raising. Available to researchers/ scholars for on-site viewing. May not borrow by mail. *Loan Period:* 7 days. *Total Yr Film Loan:* 1463.

Film Collection 554t/567p. Approx 150t acquired annually. *Circ:* 8mm & S8mm reel, 554t/567p. *Pubns:* catalog, as needed ($3); suppl, no set policy.

Other Film Serv Library film programs. Permanent viewing facility. *Equipment:* rent projection screens (1), dual 8mm silent projectors (7).

Other Media Collections *Audio:* disc, 33⅓ rpm, 8221c; tape, cassette, 1524c. *Filmstrips:* silent sets, 127c.

Budget & Expenditures Total library budget $102,000 (FY 1/1/75-1/1/76). Total FY film budget $3800.

C- UNIVERSITY OF WISCONSIN-OSHKOSH, Educational Materials Center of Polk Library, 800 Algoma Blvd, 54901. *Tel:* (414) 424-3346. *Film Serv Est:* 1962. *In Charge:* Sally Teresinski, Librarian. *AV Staff:* 1 prof. *Film Sel:* faculty/staff recommendations. *Holdings:* animated films, black studies, career education, children's films, dance, experimental films, fine arts, law, medicine, science, social sciences, teacher education, women.

Free-Loan Film Serv *Eligibility:* staff & students, indiv with library cards. *Restrictions:* for indiv, only on campus. Cannot use for fund-raising. Available to researchers/scholars for on-site viewing. May not borrow by mail. *Total Yr Film Loan:* 6481.

Film Rental Serv *Eligibility:* only this university. Cannot use for fund-raising, transmit electronically. *Rental Period:* varies. *Total Yr Film Booking:* 600.

Film Collection 996t. Approx 50t acquired annually. *Circ:* 16mm, 652t/p; S8mm & 8mm reel & cartridge, 334t. Publish materials pertaining to collection.

Other Film Serv Rent film from distributors for patrons. Permanent viewing facility.

Other Media Collections *Audio:* disc, total, 1027c; tape, reel, 930c. *Filmstrips:* silent sets, 2346c. *Slides:* sets, 4398c.

Budget & Expenditures Total library budget $190,000 (FY 7/1/74-7/1/75). Total FY film budget $12,000. *Member:* Wis. Library Assn, Wis. AV Assn.

Racine

S- RACINE TELECABLE, 53406. *Tel:* (414) 632-3131. *Video Serv Est:* 1973. *In Charge:* Dean Teeselink, Program Manager. *Video Staff:* 5 f-t, 20 p-t, ½ tech. *Video Use:* playback only of professionally produced tapes. Video serv available by appointment. Produce video tapes. Have production studio/space & separate control room.

Video Equipment/Facilities *In-House Use Only:* portapak (2), ½" b&w/col, Sony 8400; recording deck (7), ¾" col, Sony 1800; editing deck (1), 1" col, IVC870; studio camera (2), col, Sony 5000B; monitor (7), b&w/col, Sony, TM, RCA; lighting (20); microphones (9); audio tape recorders (5), film chain (1). Provide training in use of equipment to high school & college students.

Video Tape Loan/Rental/Sale Serv *Serv Provided:* swap with other inst. *Loan Eligibility:* org members.

Video Collection Maintained by purchase, rental, own production, exchange/swap. Use/play ½", 1" reel to reel, ¾" cassette. *Sources:* commercial distributors, galleries. *Tape Sel:* preview, catalogs. *Special Collections:* in-house training tapes, video as art, films in video format.

Shawano

P- SHAWANO CITY-COUNTY PUBLIC LIBRARY, 128 S Sawyer St, 54166. *Tel:* (715) 526-3829. *Film Serv Est:* 1955. *In Charge:* Evan Cooper, Head, AV Services. *AV Staff:* 1. *Film Sel:* committee preview, published reviews.

Shawano (cont'd)

Free-Loan Film Serv *Eligibility:* educational inst, civic groups, religious groups, indiv with library cards, prof groups, such as teachers, doctors. *Restrictions:* for indiv & inst, only in Shawano & Menominee Counties. Cannot transmit electronically. Available to researchers/scholars for on-site viewing. May borrow by mail. *Loan Period:* 4 days. *Total Yr Film Loan:* 300.

Film Rental Serv *Eligibility:* no restrictions. *Restrictions:* only in Shawano & Menominee Counties. Cannot transmit electronically. *Rental Period:* 4 days. *Total Yr Film Booking:* 300.

Film Collection 75t/p. Approx 10t acquired annually. *Circ:* 16mm, 38t/p; 8mm cartridge, 62t/p. *Pubns:* catalog, annual; suppl, no set policy.

Other Film Serv Rent film from distributors for patrons, obtain film from coop loan system (Wis. Library Film Circuit, Nicolet Library System), obtain film from other libraries, film reference serv, library film programs. Permanent viewing facility available for rent to community. *Equipment:* rent 8mm reel projector (1), S8mm cartridge projector (1), projection screens (1).

Budget & Expenditures Total library budget $118,236 (FY 1/1/75-1/1/76). Total FY film budget $1000. *Member:* Wis. Library Assn.

Sheboygan

C- LAKELAND COLLEGE, Community Memorial Library, 53081. *Tel:* (414) 565-1238. *In Charge:* Jo Lynn Drudge, Dir of Library. *AV Staff:* 2 (1 prof, 1 cl).

Other Film Serv *Equipment:* lend 16mm sound projector (2), projection tables & stands (1), projection screens (1).

Other Media Collections *Audio:* disc, total, 2000t; tape, total, 75t. *Filmstrips:* total, 746t.

Budget & Expenditures Total library budget $38,212 (FY 7/1/74-7/1/75). No separate AV budget. *Member:* ALA.

Video Serv *Video Staff:* 2 f-t. *Video Use:* documentation of community/school events, in-service training. Video serv available by appointment. Produce video tapes.

Video Equipment/Facilities *For Loan:* portapak (1), b&w, Sony 8400. Have permanent & portable viewing installations.

Video Collection Maintained by own production.

Cable & CCTV Have CCTV in inst, with 1 monitor. *Programming Sources:* over-the-air commercial & public broadcasting, tapes produced by inst.

Superior

P- SUPERIOR PUBLIC LIBRARY, 1204 Hammond Ave, 54880. *Tel:* (715) 394-0252. *Film Serv Est:* 1974. *In Charge:* Barbara Knotts, Reference Librarian. *AV Staff:* 2 (1 prof, ½ cl, ½ tech). *Film Sel:* staff recommendations, chief film librarian's decision.

Free-Loan Film Serv *Eligibility:* any person or group in NW Wis. Cannot use for fund-raising, transmit electronically. May borrow by mail. *Loan Period:* 2-5 days. *Total Yr Film Loan:* 2878.

Film Collection 250t/p. *Circ:* 16mm, 250t/p; 8mm reel, 126t/p. *Pubns:* catalog, bi-annual.

Other Film Serv Obtain film from coop loan system (Wis. Library Film Circuit), film reference serv, library film programs. *Equipment:* lend 16mm sound projector (2), 8mm reel projector (3), projection screens (1), slide projector (1).

Other Media Collections *Audio:* disc, 33⅓ rpm, 1250t/c; tape, cassette, 4t/c. *Filmstrips:* sound, 3t/c; sound sets, 12t/c. *Slides:* sets, 1t/3c.

Budget & Expenditures Total library budget $40,000 (FY 1/1/74-1/1/75). No separate AV budget. *Member:* Wis. Library Assn.

C- UNIVERSITY OF WISCONSIN-SUPERIOR, Film Library, AV Services, 54880. *Tel:* (715) 392-8101, ext 340. *Film Serv*

Est: 1968. *In Charge:* John R. Cumming, Dir, AV Services. *AV Staff:* 4 (1 prof, ½ cl, 2½ tech). *Film Sel:* faculty/staff recommendations. *Holdings:* science 40%.

Film Rental Serv *Eligibility:* no restrictions. *Restrictions:* only in U.S. & territories. Cannot use for fund-raising, transmit electronically. *Rental Period:* 5 days. *Total Yr Film Booking:* 200. Produce still photography, graphics, audio, multi-media instruction.

Film Collection 540t/550p. Approx 60-70t acquired annually. *Circ:* 16mm, 540t/550p. *Pubns:* catalog, every 2 yrs.

Other Film Serv Rent film from distributors for patrons, obtain film from coop loan system (Lake Superior Assn of Colleges & Universities), obtain film from other libraries, film reference serv. Permanent viewing facility.

Other Media Collections *Audio:* tape, cassette, 50t/c.

Budget & Expenditures No separate AV budget. *Member:* AECT.

Wauwatosa

P- WAUWATOSA PUBLIC LIBRARY, 7635 W North Ave, 53213. *Tel:* (414) 258-5700. *In Charge:* John Gettelman, Coord, AV Servs. *AV Staff:* 1 (1 prof).

Free-Loan Film Serv *Eligibility:* indiv with library cards. *Restrictions:* for inst, only Milwaukee County Library System members. *Loan Period:* 7 days.

Film Collection *Circ:* 8mm reel, 583t.

Other Film Serv Obtain film from Milwaukee County Federated Library System, library film programs. Permanent viewing facility.

Other Media Collections *Audio:* disc, 33⅓ rpm, 3711c; tape, cassette, 696c; tape, cartridge, 371c. *Filmstrips:* sound, 168c.

Budget & Expenditures Total library budget $58,518 (FY 1/1/74-1/1/75). Total FY AV budget $9500. *Member:* Wis. Library Assn.

Video Serv In development. Policy yet to be established. *Video Staff:* 1 f-t, 1 p-t. *Video Use:* to increase community's library use, in-service training. Video serv available by appointment. Produce video tapes. Have production studio/space.

Video Equipment/Facilities *In-House Use Only:* recording deck (1), ¾", Sony VO-1800; playback deck (1), ¾", Sony VP 1200; studio camera (1), col, Hitachi FP-1500; monitor (2), col, RCA JJ970W; lighting (3); microphones (3); tripods (1); audio tape recorders (12). Have permanent viewing installation. *Member:* Milwaukee County Federated Library System. *Other Video Serv:* reference serv. *Pubns:* catalog.

Cable & CCTV Receive serv of cable TV system. Produce programs for cablecasting.

West Allis

P- WEST ALLIS PUBLIC LIBRARY, 1508 S 75th St, 53214. *Tel:* (414) 476-6550. *Film Serv Est:* 1953. *In Charge:* Susan Rahn, Head, Adult Services. *AV Staff:* 1½ (1 prof, ½ cl). *Film Sel:* committee preview. *Holdings:* children's films 33%.

Free-Loan Film Serv *Eligibility:* indiv with library cards. *Restrictions:* for indiv, only in Milwaukee County. May not borrow by mail. *Loan Period:* 1 day. *Total Yr Film Loan:* 3611.

Film Collection 257t/p. Approx 8-9t acquired annually. *Circ:* 16mm, 257t; 8mm reel, 202t; S8mm reel, 162t. *Pubns:* catalog, annual.

Other Film Serv Obtain film from Milwaukee County Federated Library System, Wis. Film Library Circuit.

Other Media Collections *Audio:* disc, total, 3483t; tape, total, 1402c.

Budget & Expenditures No separate AV budget. *Member:* Wis. Library Assn.

Video Serv *Est:* 1976. *Video Use:* to increase community's library use. Video serv available on demand & by appointment.

Video Equipment/Facilities *In-House Use Only:* playback deck (3), ¾" col, Sony VP-1200. Have portable viewing installation. Provide training in use of equipment to library staff. *Member:* Milwaukee County Federated Library System. *Pubns:* catalog.

Whitewater

C- UNIVERSITY OF WISCONSIN-WHITEWATER, Instructional Media Services, 53190. *Tel:* (414) 472-1012. *Film Serv Est:* 1966. *In Charge:* Jerome Johnson, Coordinator. *AV Staff:* 5½ (2½ prof, 2 cl, 1 tech). *Film Sel:* faculty/staff recommendations.

Free-Loan Film Serv *Eligibility:* staff & students. *Restrictions:* for indiv, classroom use only. Cannot use for fund-raising, transmit electronically. Available to researchers/scholars for on-site viewing. May not borrow by mail. *Loan Period:* 7 days. *Total Yr Film Loan:* 495. Produce slide-tape presentations.

Film Collection 236t/p. Approx 0-8t acquired annually. *Circ:* 16mm, 236t/p. *Pubns:* catalog, as needed; suppl, no set policy.

Other Film Serv Rent film from distributors for patrons, obtain film from other libraries, film reference serv. Permanent viewing facility. *Equipment:* lend/rent S8mm camera (2), 16mm sound projector (48), 8mm cartridge projector (10), S8mm cartridge projector (14), S8mm reel projector (14), projection tables & stands (200), projection screens (20).

Budget & Expenditures Total FY (7/1/74-7/1/75) film budget $1200.

Video Serv *Est:* 1970. *In Charge:* Douglas Weber, Electronics Technician. *Video Staff:* 5 p-t, 1 tech. *Video Use:* in-service training, practical video/TV training courses, playback only of professionally produced tapes. Video serv available by appointment. Produce video tapes. Have production studio/space & separate control room.

Video Equipment/Facilities *In-House Use Only:* editing deck (1), ½" b&w, Sony AV-3650; studio camera (2), b&w, Sony AVC-4600. *For Loan:* portapak (9), ½" b&w, Sony AV3400; recording deck (27), ½" b&w, Sony AV-3600; monitor (42); SEG (1), Sony; lighting (1); microphones (47); tripods (93); audio tape recorders (268). Have portable viewing installation. *Equipment Loan Period:* no set policy. Provide training in use of equipment to faculty & students. Have tape duplication serv.

Video Tape Loan/Rental/Sale Serv *Serv Provided:* free loan. *Loan Eligibility:* staff & students. *Restrictions:* for indiv, instructional use only. Cannot use for fund-raising. May not borrow by mail.

Video Collection Maintained by own production, receive free. Use/play ½" reel to reel, ¾" cassette. *Sources:* receive free with purchase of blank tape. Tapes organized by in-house numbering system. *Other Video Serv:* reference serv, production workshops.

Wyoming

Casper

P- NATRONA COUNTY PUBLIC LIBRARY, 307 E Second St, 82601. *Tel:* (307) 234-1553. *Film Serv Est:* 1970. *In Charge:* Chris Jones, TV Coord. *Film Sel:* chief film librarian's decision. *Holdings:* children's films 80%, comedy, silent classics.

Free-Loan Film Serv *Eligibility:* indiv with library cards. *Restrictions:* for indiv, only in Natrona County. *Loan Period:* 7-14 days. *Total Yr Film Loan:* 600-800.

Film Collection Approx 12t acquired annually. *Circ:* S8mm reel, 147t.

Other Film Serv Permanent viewing facility available to community. *Equipment:* lend 16mm sound projector (2), S8mm reel projector (2), projection screens (1), slide projector (1).

Other Media Collections *Audio:* disc, 33⅓ rpm, 1425c; tape, cassette, 126c.

Budget & Expenditures Total library budget $19,499.49 (FY 7/1/74-7/1/75). Total FY film budget $500. *Member:* ALA, Wyo. Library Assn, Mountain Plains Library Assn.

Video Serv *Video Staff:* 3 p-t. *Video Use:* documentation of community events, to increase community's library use, community video access, in-service training, practical video/TV training courses. Video serv available by appointment. Produce video tapes. Have production studio/space & separate control room.

Video Equipment/Facilities *In-House Use Only:* recording deck (5), ½", ¾", 1" col, Sony, Concord; playback deck (5), ½", ¾", 1" col, Sony, Concord; editing deck (2), ½", 1" col, Sony, Concord; studio camera (2), col, Shibaden, Sony; monitor (8), b&w/col, Sony, Panasonic; SEG (2), Shibaden; keyer (1), Shibaden; lighting (16); microphones (8); tripods (3); audio tape recorders (2). *For Loan:* portapak (1), ½" b&w, Panasnoic. Have permanent viewing installation. *Equipment Loan Period:* 1 day. Provide training in use of equipment to patrons using equipment. Have tape duplication serv.

Video Tape Loan/Rental/Sale Serv *Serv Provided:* swap with other inst, rental, sale. *Loan/Rental Eligibility:* staff & students, educational inst, civic groups, religious groups, indiv with library cards. *Restrictions:* for indiv & inst, only in Natrona County. Cannot use for fund-raising. May borrow by mail. *Loan Period:* interlibrary loan period.

Video Collection Maintained by own production, exchange/swap. Use/play ½", 1" reel to reel, ½" cartridge, ¾" cassette. *Sources:* own production. *Special Collections:* in-house training tapes, films in video format, local history, children's programs, book reviews. *Collection, Color:* ½" reel, 200t. *Other Video Serv:* programming, reference serv, taping of other media, production workshops, lending portapak. *Pubns:* catalog.

Cable & CCTV Receive serv of cable TV system. Produce programs for cablecasting. Inform public about cable system serv & facilities. Serve as production facility for others. Run cable programs for special audiences. Have CCTV in inst, with 6 monitors. *Programming Sources:* over-the-air commercial & public broadcasting, tapes produced by inst, tapes produced professionally, security.

Cheyenne

P- CITIZENS COMMUNITY ACCESS TELEVISION, Laramie County Library System, 2800 Central Ave, 82001. *Tel:* (307) 634-3561, ext 26. *Video Serv Est:* 1975. *In Charge:* Timothy M. Lahiff, Dir of TV. *Video Staff:* 2 f-t, 1 tech. *Video Use:* to increase community's library use, community video access. Video serv available by appointment. Produce video tapes. Have production studio/space.

Video Equipment/Facilities *In-House Use Only:* portapak (1), ½" b&w, Panasonic WV-3082; recording deck (3), ½" col, Panasonic NV3130; editing deck (1), ½" col, Panasonic TC3130; studio camera (3), b&w, Panasonic WV341P, 350P; monitor (3),

b&w, Panasonic; SEG (1), Panasonic; additional camera lenses (10); lighting (10); microphones (6); tripods (6); audio tape recorders (1). Have portable viewing installations. Provide training in use of equipment to interested volunteers.

Video Tape Loan/Rental/Sale Serv *Serv Provided:* free loan. *Loan Eligibility:* civic groups, religious groups, indiv with library cards. *Restrictions:* for indiv, only in county; for inst, none. Cannot use for fund-raising, duplicate, air without permission. May borrow by mail. Loan Period: 7 days.

Video Collection Maintained by own production. Use/play ½" reel to reel. *Sources:* community productions, exchange University of Wyo. *Tape Sel:* preview. Tapes organized by subject. *Collection, B&W:* ½" reel, 30t/c.

Cable & CCTV Receive serv of cable TV system. Produce programs for cablecasting. Inform public about cable system serv & facilities. Serve as production facility for others. Run cable programs for special audiences. Have CCTV in inst, with 3 monitors. *Programming Sources:* tapes produced by inst, tapes produced by community groups & indiv.

P- LARAMIE COUNTY LIBRARY SYSTEM, AV Department, 2800 Central Ave, 82001. *Tel:* (307) 634-3561, ext. 6. *In Charge:* Bard Ferrall, Head-AV Dept. *AV Staff:* (2 prof, 2 cl). *Film Sel:* chief film librarian's decision.

Free-Loan Film Serv *Eligibility:* educational inst, civic groups, religious groups, indiv with adult library cards. *Restrictions:* for indiv & inst, only in Laramie County. Cannot transmit electronically. Available to researchers/scholars for on-site viewing. May not borrow by mail. *Loan Period:* 16mm 1 day, 8mm 1 wk. Produce video tapes.

Film Collection 45t/p. Approx 5t acquired annually. *Circ:* 16mm, 15t/p; 8mm reel, 30t/p.

Other Film Serv Permanent viewing facility available to community. *Equipment:* lend 16mm sound projector, 8mm cartridge projector, 8mm reel projector, S8mm cartridge projector, S8mm reel projector, projection screens, filmstrip projectors & viewers.

Other Media Collections *Audio:* disc, 33⅓ rpm, 1500t; tape, cassette, 150t. *Filmstrips:* silent, 100t/c; sound sets, 100t/c.

Budget & Expenditures No separate AV budget.

Lander

P- FREMONT PUBLIC LIBRARY, 451 N Second St, 82520. *Tel:* (307) 332-5194. *Film Serv Est:* 1973. *In Charge:* William Heuer, Dir of Libraries. *AV Staff:* 1 cl. *Film Sel:* chief film librarian's decision. *Holdings:* entertainment.

Free-Loan Film Serv *Eligibility:* indiv with library cards, & others, such as service org. *Restrictions:* for indiv, only in our county; for inst, only in state. *Loan Period:* 7 days. *Total Yr Film Loan:* 75.

Film Collection 75t/p. *Circ:* 8mm reel, 30t/p; S8mm reel, 45t/p.

Other Film Serv Obtain film from Wyo. State Library. *Equipment:* lend 8mm reel projector (4), S8mm reel projector (4), projection screens (4).

Other Media Collections *Audio:* disc, 33⅓ rpm, 2000t; tape, cassette, 150t.

Budget & Expenditures Total library budget $28,000 (FY 7/1/74-7/1/75). Total FY film budget $200. *Member:* ALA.

Laramie

C- UNIVERSITY OF WYOMING, AV Services, Box 3273—University Station, 82071. *Tel:* (307) 766-3184. *Film Serv Est:* 1942. *In Charge:* Kay Graves, Manager. *AV Staff:* 3 (2 cl, 1 tech). *Film Sel:* committee preview, faculty/staff recommendations, chief film librarian's decision.

Free-Loan Film Serv *Eligibility:* staff. *Restrictions:* for indiv, only in state. Available to researchers/scholars for on-site viewing. May not borrow by mail. *Loan Period:* 3 days. *Total Yr Film Loan:* 265.

Film Rental Serv *Eligibility:* no restrictions. *Restrictions:* none. *Rental Period:* 3 days. *Total Yr Film Booking:* 4471.

Film Collection 2500t/2600p. Approx 30t acquired annually. *Circ:* 16mm, 2500t/2600p. *Pubns:* catalog, every 2 yrs ($2); suppl, no set policy.

Other Film Serv Rent film from distributors for patrons, obtain film from coop loan system (Mountain Plains Educational Media Council), obtain film from other libraries, film reference serv. Permanent viewing facility. *Equipment:* lend/rent S8mm camera (1), 16mm camera (1), 16mm sound projector (14), 8mm cartridge projector (1), 8mm reel projector (3), S8mm cartridge projector (1), S8mm reel projector, projection screens (11), variety of equipment.

Budget & Expenditures Total film budget $14,000 (FY 7/1/74-7/1/75). *Member:* Wyo. Assn for Educational Communications & Technology.

Sheridan

P- SHERIDAN COUNTY FULMER PUBLIC LIBRARY, 320 N Brooks, Box 1039, 82801. *Tel:* (307) 674-8585. *Film Serv Est:* 1970. *In Charge:* Karen Woinoski. *AV Staff:* 1. *Film Sel:* committee preview. *Holdings:* Wyoming.

Free-Loan Film Serv *Eligibility:* educational inst, civic groups, religious groups, indiv with library cards, prof groups. *Restrictions:* for indiv, interlibrary loan, only in Sheridan County; for inst, only in state. Cannot use for fund-raising, transmit electronically. Available to researchers/scholars for on-site viewing. *Loan Period:* 3 days. *Total Yr Film Loan:* 1163.

Film Collection 150t/p. Approx 20t acquired annually. *Circ:* 16mm, 90t. *Pubns:* catalog.

Other Film Serv Obtain film from other libraries, library film programs. Permanent viewing facility.

Other Media Collections *Audio:* tape, cassette, 50t. *Filmstrips:* silent, 540t; sound sets, 25t. *Slides:* sets, 15t.

Budget & Expenditures Total library budget $20,500 (FY 7/1/74-7/1/75). Total FY film budget $8500. *Member:* ALA, Wyo. Library Assn.

CANADA

Alberta

Calgary

P- CALGARY PUBLIC LIBRARY, Film & Record Section—
Fine Arts Dept, 616 Macleod Trail SE, T2G 2M2. *Tel:* (403)
268-5283. *Film Serv Est:* 1947. *In Charge:* June I
Newnham, Head Fine Arts Dept. *AV Staff:* 4 (1 prof, 4 cl).
Film Sel: committee preview, chief film librarian's deci-
sion.
Film Rental Serv *Eligibility:* patrons/public. *Restrictions:*
only in city. *Rental Period:* 1 day. *Total Yr Film Booking:* 8612.
Film Collection 1450t. Approx 75t acquired annually. *Circ:*
16mm, 1430p; S8mm 155p. *Pubns:* catalog, as needed; suppl, no
set policy.
Other Film Serv Library film programs, headquarters for
S Central Alta. Film Federation. Permanent viewing facility
available for rent to community.
Other Media Collections *Audio:* 9654c.
Budget & Expenditures Total library budget $547,000
approx (FY 1/1/75-1/1/76). Total FY film budget $10,000. *Mem-
ber:* Canadian Library Assn, Library Assn of Alta.

S- GLENBOW—ALBERTA INSTITUTE, Ninth Ave & First,
SE, T2G 0P3. *Tel:* (403) 264-8300. *Film Serv Est:* 1961. *In
Charge:* Hugh A. Dempsey, Dir. *AV Staff:* ½ prof. *Film Sel:*
staff recommendations. *Holdings:* art 10%, history 30%,
native peoples 60%.
Film Rental Serv *Eligibility:* native & anthropological
groups. *Restrictions:* none. Cannot use for fund-raising, transmit electronically. Cannot use where admission fees are
charged. *Rental Period:* 2 weeks. Produce films.
Film Collection 100t. Approx 12t acquired annually.
Other Film Serv Obtain film from other libraries, film
fairs/festivals, library film programs. Permanent viewing facility.

C- SOUTHERN ALBERTA INSTITUTE OF TECHNOLOGY,
Learning Resources Centre, 1301 16 Ave NW, T2M 0L4.
Tel: (403) 284-8647. *In Charge:* Frederick Ryan, Head of
Learning Resources Centre. *Film Sel:* committee preview,
faculty/staff recommendations, chief film librarian's decision.
Free-Loan Film Serv *Eligibility:* org members. *Restrictions:* for indiv, none. Available to researchers/scholars for on-
site viewing. Produce films. Produce slides, graphics.
Film Collection 600t. Approx 50t acquired annually.
Pubns: catalog, annual. Publish materials pertaining to collection. Publish media catalog.
Other Film Serv Rent film from distributors for patrons,
obtain film from other libraries, film reference serv, library film
programs. Permanent viewing facility.
Video Serv *Video Use:* documentation of community/
school events, in-service training, practical video/TV training
courses, playback of professionally produced tapes. Video serv
available on demand & by appointment. Produce video tapes.
Have production studio/space & separate control room.
Video Equipment/Facilities Have permanent & portable
viewing installations.
Video Tape Loan/Rental/Sale Serv *Serv Provided:*
swap with other inst. *Loan Eligibility:* org members.

Video Collection Maintained by purchase, rental, own
production, exchange/swap. *Tape Sel:* preview, faculty/staff
recommendations. Tapes organized by Dewey Decimal, subject,
accession numbers. *Collection:* 600t. *Pubns:* catalog.
Cable & CCTV Receive serv of cable TV system. Produce
programs for cablecasting. Serve as production facility for
others. Have advisory/administrative role in cable system
operation. Have CCTV in inst. *Programming Sources:* tapes
produced by inst.

C- UNIVERSITY OF CALGARY, Dept of Communications
Media, 2920 24 Ave NW, T2N 1N4. *Tel:* (403) 284-5285.
Video Serv Est: 1968. *In Charge:* David Harvie, Supervisor,
Program Development & Production Serv. *Video Staff:* 8
f-t. *Video Use:* documentation of community/school
events, in-service training, playback only of professionally
produced tapes, teaching. Video serv available on demand
& by appointment. Produce video tapes. Have production
studio/space & separate control room.
Video Equipment/Facilities *In-House Use Only:* portapak (8), ½" b&w, Sony; recording deck (15); playback deck;
editing deck, b&w/col, Ampex/Sony; studio camera (5),
b&w/col, Philco, Sony; SEG (2), Fernseh; keyer (2), Richmond
Hill; additional camera lenses (1); lighting (1); microphones (1);
tripods (1); audio tape recorders (1). Have permanent & portable
viewing installations. *Equipment Loan Period:* 7 days. Provide
training in use of equipment to students. Have tape duplication
serv.
Video Tape Loan/Rental/Sale Serv *Serv Provided:*
rental, sale. *Loan/Rental Eligibility:* org members, staff, students enrolled in inst, staff & students. *Restrictions:* for indiv,
university use only; for inst, university use only. Cannot duplicate, air without permission.
Video Collection Maintained by purchase, own production. Use/play ½", 1", 2" reel to reel, ¾" cassette. *Sources:*
commercial distributors, dept produced. *Tape Sel:* preview,
catalogs. Tapes organized by subject. *Collection, B&W:* ½" reel,
40t/c; 1" reel, 20t/c; 2" reel, 20t/c; ¾" cassette, 40t/c. *Other
Video Serv:* programming, reference serv, taping of other media,
production workshops. *Pubns:* will begin by Spring, 1976.
Cable & CCTV Receive serv of cable TV system. Produce
programs for cablecasting. Run cable programs for special
audiences. Have advisory/administrative role in cable system
operation. Own cable channel. Have CCTV in inst, with approx
50 monitors. *Programming Sources:* over-the-air commercial &
public broadcasting, tapes produced by inst.

College Heights

C- CANADIAN UNION COLLEGE LIBRARY, Box 460,
T0C 0Z0. *Tel:* (403) 782-3871. *In Charge:* Reuben S. Buhler,
Librarian. *Film Sel:* faculty/staff recommendations.
Film Collection 10t. *Noncirc:* 16mm, 10t.
Other Film Serv Obtain film from coop loan system (Univ.
of Alta., National Film Board, AV Branch), library film pro-
grams. *Equipment:* lend 16mm sound projector (3), projection
tables & stands (2), projection screens (5).
Other Media Collections *Audio:* disc, 33⅓ rpm, 35c; tape,
cassette, 40c. *Filmstrips:* silent sets, 15c. *Slides:* sets, 5c.

College Heights (cont.)
Budget & Expenditures No separate budget. *Member:* Alta. Library Assn.

Edmonton

S- CHARLES CAMSELL HOSPITAL LIBRARY, 12815-115 Ave, T5M 3A4. *Tel:* (403) 452-8770. *Video Staff:* 1 f-t. *Video Use:* in-service training, playback of professionally produced tapes. Video serv available by qualified staff members. Produce video tapes. Have production studio/space.
Video Equipment/Facilities Have portable viewing installation. Provide training in use of equipment to students in nursing education.
Video Tape Loan/Rental/Sale Serv *Loan Eligibility:* org members, staff & students.
Video Collection Use/play ½" reel to reel. *Tape Sel:* preview.
Cable & CCTV Receive serv of cable TV system.

P- EDMONTON PUBLIC LIBRARY, Seven Sir Winston Churchill Square, T5J 2U4. *Tel:* (403) 429-5351, ext 231. *Film Serv Est:* 1956. *In Charge:* Val Tougas, Supervisor. *AV Staff:* 7. *Film Sel:* committee preview, published reviews from film news, previews, booklist, Landers. *Holdings:* animated films 30%, children's films 30%, dance 5%, experimental films 28%, fine arts 30%.
Free-Loan Film Serv *Eligibility:* charitable inst, hospitals, nursing homes. *Restrictions:* for inst, only in province. Cannot use for fund-raising, transmit electronically. May not borrow by mail. *Loan Period:* 3 days.
Film Rental Serv *Eligibility:* patrons/public. *Restrictions:* only in province. Cannot use for fund-raising, transmit electronically. *Rental Period:* 3 days. *Total Yr Film Booking:* 3500.
Film Collection 300t/p. Approx 50t acquired annually. *Circ:* 16mm, 300t/p. *Pubns:* catalog, annual; suppl, in yr catalog not published.
Other Film Serv Library film programs. *Equipment:* rent 8mm reel projector (1), S8mm reel projector (2).
Other Media Collections *Audio:* disc, 33⅓ rpm, 9000t/10,000c; tape, cassette, 1000t/1200c. *Filmstrips:* silent, 100t/c; sound sets, 30t/c.
Budget & Expenditures Total library budget $405,405 (FY 1/1/75-1/1/76). Total FY film budget $12,000.

C- UNIVERSITY OF ALBERTA, Educational Media Division, Faculty of Ext, Room 132, Corbett Hall, T6G 2G4. *In Charge:* Jim Shaw, Supervisor. *AV Staff:* (1 prof, 8 cl, 1 tech). *Film Sel:* faculty/staff recommendations, chief film librarian's decision, demands of faculty members & public.
Free-Loan Film Serv *Eligibility:* org members, staff. *Restrictions:* cannot use for fund-raising, transmit electronically. Available to researchers/scholars for on-site viewing. May borrow by mail.
Film Rental Serv *Eligibility:* no restrictions, educational org, civic groups, patrons/public. *Restrictions:* only in Canada. Cannot use for fund-raising, transmit electronically. *Total Yr Film Booking:* 1247.
Film Collection 4000t/500p. *Circ:* 16mm, 4500t/p. *Pubns:* catalog, as needed ($3).
Other Film Serv Rent film from distributors for patrons, obtain film from other libraries. Permanent viewing facility. *Equipment:* lend S8mm camera (5), lend/rent 16mm sound projector (20), lend/rent 8mm cartridge projector (1), lend/rent S8mm reel projector (4), lend/rent projection tables & stands (12), lend/rent projection screens (19).
Other Media Collections *Audio:* disc, 33⅓ rpm, 3200t; tape, cassette, 2500t; tape, reel, 2500t.
Budget & Expenditures Total FY film budget $30,000 (FY 4/75-4/76). *Member:* EFLA.

Lethbridge

P- LETHBRIDGE PUBLIC LIBRARY, Audio-Visual Serv, 810 Fifth Ave, T1J 4C4. *Tel:* (403) 329-3233, ext 8. *Film Serv*

Est: 1948. *In Charge:* Duncan Rand, Chief Librarian. *AV Staff:* 2 (1 cl, 1 tech). *Film Sel:* committee preview, chief film librarian's decision, published reviews.
Film Rental Serv *Eligibility:* no restrictions. *Restrictions:* only in region (Southern Alta.). Cannot transmit electronically. *Rental Period:* 3 days.
Film Collection 825t. Approx 25-30t acquired annually. *Circ:* 16mm, 825t/p. *Pubns:* catalog, annual (50¢); suppl, in yr catalog not published.
Other Film Serv Obtain film from other libraries, film fairs/festivals, library film programs, projectionist training. Permanent viewing facility available for rent to community. *Equipment:* rent 16mm camera, 16mm sound projector (6), projection screens (6), overhead projector (1), 35mm slide projector (1).
Other Media Collections *Audio:* disc, total, 2035t; tape, cassette, 100t.
Budget & Expenditures Total library budget $63,000 (FY 1/1/75-1/1/76). Total FY film budget $8000. *Member:* Library Assn of Alta., Canadian Library Assn.

British Columbia

Abbotsford

P- FRASER VALLEY REGIONAL LIBRARY, Film Department, 2469 Montrose Ave, V2S 3T2. *Tel:* (604) 759-7141, ext 5. *Film Serv Est:* 1958. *In Charge:* Mrs. R. Vander Meulen, Head, Film Dept. *AV Staff:* 3 (3 cl). *Film Sel:* previews, chief film librarian's decision. *Holdings:* agriculture 1%, animated films 9%, Canadian industry 4%, Canada—The land 17%, children's films 10%, experimental films 5%, feature films ½%, fine arts 7%, health-medicine 6%, science 10%, social sciences 11½%, sports & recreation 8%, women 1%, world affairs 10%.
Free-Loan Film Serv *Eligibility:* senior citizen's groups, homes for handicapped. *Restrictions:* only in regional serving area (lower mainland, Fraser Valley, Upper Fraser Valley).
Film Rental Serv *Eligibility:* no restrictions, educational org, civic groups, patrons/public. *Restrictions:* only in region (as above). Cannot use for fund-raising, transmit electronically. *Rental Period:* 7 days. *Total Yr Film Booking:* 10,036.
Film Collection 900t/1200p. Approx 80t acquired annually. *Circ:* 16mm, 880t/1180p; S8mm reel, 300t/p. *Noncirc:* 16mm, 20t/p. *Pubns:* catalog, annual.
Other Film Serv Film reference serv, library film programs. *Equipment:* 16mm sound projector (12), projection screens (9).
Budget & Expenditures Total library budget $315,000 (FY 1/1/74-1/1/75). Total FY film budget $10,000. *Member:* ALA.

Burnaby

C- SIMON FRASER UNIVERSITY, AV Centre, V5A 1S6. *Tel:* (604) 291-4311. *Video Serv Est:* 1971. *In Charge:* Wayne Carr, Coord. *Video Staff:* 4 f-t, 2 tech. *Video Use:* documentation of community/school events, community video access, in-service training, as art form, production of programs to support teaching & research. Video serv available on demand & by appointment. Produce video tapes. Have production studio/space & separate control room.
Video Equipment/Facilities *In-House Use Only:* portapak (2), ½" b&w, Sony 8400; recording deck (6), 1", ½", ¾" b&w/col, Nec, Sony 3650, Sony 320; editing deck (4), 1", ½" col, Sony 8650, Sony 320; studio camera (6), b&w, Phillips, GBC; monitor (26), 12", 26" b&w/col, Sony, Conrac, Setchel; SEG (1), Viscount; keyer (1), Viscount; synthesizer (2); additional camera lenses (4); lighting (30); microphones (12); tripods (5); audio tape recorders (3). Have permanent & portable viewing installations.

Equipment Loan Period: no set policy. Provide training in use of equipment to students. Have tape duplication serv.

Video Tape Loan/Rental/Sale Serv *Serv Provided:* free loan, swap with other inst. *Loan Eligibility:* org members, staff & students, educational inst. *Restrictions:* cannot use for fund-raising, duplicate, air without permission. May not borrow by mail.

Video Collection Maintained by own production. Use/play ½", 1", reel to reel, ¾" cassette. *Sources:* exchange (B. C. Media Exchange Coop). *Member:* B. C. Media Exchange Coop. *Special Collections:* in-house training tapes, video as art. Tapes organized by subject. *Collection, Color:* ½" reel, 15t; 1" reel, 6t; ¾" cassette, 26t. *Collection, B&W:* ½" reel, 200t; 1" reel, 150t. *Other Video Serv:* programming, reference serv, taping of other media.

Cable & CCTV Receive serv of cable TV system. Produce programs for cablecasting. Serve as production facility for others. Have CCTV in inst, with 8 monitors. *Programming Sources:* tapes produced by inst, tapes produced professionally.

Castlegar

C- SELKIRK COLLEGE, Film Library, Box 1200, V1N 3J1. *Tel:* (604) 365-7292, ext 266. *Film Serv Est:* 1965. *In Charge:* Ken Cazakoff, Film Library Assistant. *AV Staff:* 3 (3 prof, 1 cl, 2 tech). *Film Sel:* faculty/staff recommendations. *Holdings:* general education.

Free-Loan Film Serv *Eligibility:* anyone. *Restrictions:* for indiv, only certain school districts; for inst, only in state. Cannot use for fund-raising, borrow for classroom use. Available to researchers/scholars for on-site viewing. May borrow by mail. *Loan Period:* 14 days. *Total Yr Film Loan:* 3000.

Film Collection 700t/p. Approx 25t acquired annually. *Pubns:* catalog, every 3 yrs; suppl, each yr.

Other Film Serv Obtain film from other libraries, film reference serv, film fairs/festivals, library film programs. Permanent viewing facility available for rent to community. *Equipment:* lend S8mm camera, lend 16mm camera, lend/rent 16mm sound projector, lend 8mm cartridge projector, lend 8mm reel projector, lend S8mm cartridge projector, lend S8mm reel projector, lend projection screens, carrousel & filmstrips.

Budget & Expenditures Total library budget $5000 (FY 6/74-6/75). Total FY film budget $3000. *Member:* EFLA.

Dawson Creek

P- LIBRARY DEVELOPMENT COMMISSION, PEACE RIVER BRANCH, 1017—105 Ave. *Tel:* (604) 782-2814. *Film Serv Est:* 1974. *In Charge:* James L. O'Hare, Branch Librarian. *AV Staff:* (1 prof, 1 cl, 1 tech). *Film Sel:* chief film librarian's decision.

Free-Loan Film Serv *Eligibility:* only to libraries. *Restrictions:* for indiv & inst, only Peace River—Liard regional district. Cannot use for fund-raising, transmit electronically. Available to researchers/scholars for on-site viewing. May borrow by mail. *Loan Period:* as needed.

Film Collection 74t/75p. Approx 50t acquired annually. *Circ:* 16mm, 50t/p; S8mm reel, 24t/25p. *Pubns:* catalog, as needed; suppl, no set policy.

Other Film Serv Obtain film from coop loan system (Peace River Associated Libraries).

Budget & Expenditures Total library budget $85,000 (FY 4/74-4/75). Total FY film budget $5000. *Member:* B. C. Library Assn, Canadian Library Assn.

Essondale

S- RIVERVIEW HOSPITAL, Industrial Division, AV Section, V0M 1J0. *Tel:* (604) 521-1911, ext 281. *In Charge:* W. R. Masterson, Photographer. *AV Staff:* 2 (1 cl, 1 tech). *Film Sel:* staff recommendations. *Holdings:* mental health.

Free-Loan Film Serv *Eligibility:* staff, educational inst, civic groups, religious groups, prof groups. *Restrictions:* for inst, only in province. Cannot use for fund-raising, transmit electronically. Available to researchers/scholars for on-site viewing.

May borrow by mail. *Loan Period:* as needed. *Total Yr Film Loan:* 825.

Film Collection 600t/p. *Circ:* 16mm, 600t/p. *Pubns:* catalog, as needed; suppl, no set policy.

Other Film Serv Obtain film from other libraries. *Equipment:* lend 16mm sound projector (1), projection screens (2).

Budget & Expenditures No separate budget.

Video Serv *In Charge:* O. R. Vidal, Communications Tech. *Video Staff:* 2 tech. *Video Use:* in-service training, patient therapy. Video serv available by appointment. Produce video tapes.

Video Equipment/Facilities *In-House Use Only:* portapak (1), ½" b&w/col, Sony 8400; editing deck (1), ½" b&w/col, Sony 8650; studio camera (1), b&w, AVC3250; monitor (1), 12" b&w, Sony; SEG (1), Electrohome; lighting (6); microphones (2); tripods (2); audio tape recorders. Have portable viewing installation. *Equipment Loan Period:* no set policy. Provide training in use of equipment to staff.

Video Collection Use/play ½" reel to reel. *Other Video Serv:* will start tape library.

Cable & CCTV Receive serv of cable TV system.

Kelowna

P- OKANAGAN REGIONAL LIBRARY, Film Dept—Kelowna Branch, 480 Queensway, V1Y 6S7. *Tel:* (604) 762-2800. *In Charge:* Kathryn Feeney, Film Librarian. *AV Staff:* 2 (1 cl). *Film Sel:* chief film librarian's decision.

Film Rental Serv *Eligibility:* no restrictions. *Restrictions:* only in region (Golden to Princeton). *Rental Period:* as needed. *Total Yr Film Booking:* 4563.

Film Collection 737t/753p. Approx 25t acquired annually. *Circ:* 16mm, 737t/750p. *Noncirc:* 16mm, 3t/p. *Pubns:* catalog, every 2 yrs; suppl, in yr catalog not published.

Other Film Serv Obtain film from other libraries, film reference serv, library film programs. Permanent viewing facility. *Equipment:* rent S8mm camera (1), 16mm sound projector (6), projection screens (8).

Other Media Collections *Filmstrips:* sound, 2t/c; sound sets, 6t/c.

Budget & Expenditures Total FY film budget $6000 (FY 1/1/75-1/1/76).

Nanaimo

C- MALASPINA COLLEGE, Learning Resource Center, 375 Kennedy St, V9R 2J3. *Tel:* (604) 753-3245, ext 269. *Film Serv Est:* 1972. *In Charge:* K. Rumsby, AV Coord. *AV Staff:* 4 (1 prof, 2 cl, 1 tech). *Film Sel:* faculty/staff recommendations, chief film librarian's decision. *Holdings:* experimental films 10%, fine arts 20%, science 20%, social sciences 50%.

Film Collection 30t/p. Approx 5t acquired annually. *Noncirc:* 16mm, 30t/p; S8mm cartridge, 3t/p.

Other Film Serv Rent film from distributors for patrons, obtain film from other libraries, film reference serv, film society. *Equipment:* lend/rent S8mm camera (2), 16mm sound projector (12), S8mm cartridge projector (1), S8mm reel projector (1), lend projection tables & stands (24), lend/rent projection screens (4).

Other Media Collections *Audio:* disc, 33⅓ rpm, 988c; tape, cassette, reel, 477c. *Filmstrips:* silent, 62c; sound sets, 33c. *Slides:* single, 1301c; sets, 880c.

Budget & Expenditures Total library budget $37,000 (FY 4/1/75-4/1/76). No separate AV budget.

Video Serv *Est:* 1972. *In Charge:* K. Rumsby, AV Coord. *Video Staff:* 3 f-t, 1 p-t, 1 tech. *Video Use:* documentation of community/school events, to increase community's library use, community video access, in-service training. Video serv available by appointment. Produce video tapes.

Video Equipment/Facilities *In-House Use Only:* recording deck (3), ½", ¾" col; playback deck (3), ½", ¾" col; studio camera (1), b&w, Sanyo; monitor (14), b&w/col, Sony Electrohome. *For Loan:* portapak (2), ½" b&w, Sony; monitor (14), b&w/col, Sony Electrohome; additional camera lenses (3); lighting (6); microphones (20); tripods (8); audio tape recorders (20).

Nanaimo (cont.)

Have portable viewing installation. *Equipment Loan Period:* 1 day. Provide training in use of equipment to faculty. Have tape duplication serv.

Video Tape Loan/Rental/Sale Serv *Serv Provided:* swap with other inst. *Loan Eligibility:* staff & students.

Video Collection Maintained by purchase, rental, own production, exchange/swap. Use/play ½" reel to reel, ¾" cassette. *Sources:* commercial distributors, exchange. *Tape Sel:* faculty/staff recommendations. Tapes organized by Library of Congress system. *Collection, Color:* ½" reel, 10t/c; ¾" cassette, 120t/c. *Collection, B&W:* ½" reel, 80t/c; ¾" cassette, 10t/c. *Other Video Serv:* programming.

Cable & CCTV Receive serv of cable TV system. Produce programs for cablecasting. Serve as production facility for others. Run cable programs for special audiences. Have CCTV in inst, with 10 monitors. *Programming Sources:* over-the-air commercial & public broadcasting, tapes produced by inst, tapes produced professionally, tapes produced by community groups & indiv.

Port Alberni

S- ALBERNI CABLE TELEVISION LTD, 735 Third Ave N. *Tel:* (604) 723-7042. *Video Serv In Charge:* Gunther H. Smuda, Program Dir. *Video Staff:* 1 f-t. *Video Use:* community video access. Video serv available for community programming. Produce video tapes. Have production studio/space & separate control room.

Video Equipment/Facilities *In-House Use Only:* portapak (2), ½" b&w, Sony; playback deck (3), ½" b&w, Sony 3650; editing deck (1), ½" b&w/col, Sony 8650; studio camera (4), b&w, Sony; monitor (4), b&w/col, Sony; SEG (1). *For Loan:* portapak (2), ½" b&w, Sony.

Video Collection Own production. Use/play ½" reel to reel, ¾" cassette. *Sources:* community productions. *Tape Sel:* preview, discussion with other dir. *Other Video Serv:* local programming.

Cable & CCTV Receive serv of cable TV system. Produce programs for cablecasting. Inform public about cable system serv & facilities. Serve as production facility for others. Run cable programs for special audiences. Have advisory/administrative role in cable system operation.

Vancouver

S- CINEMATHEQUE PACIFIQUE, 1616 West Third Ave, V6J 1K2. *Tel:* (604) 732-5322. *Film Serv Est:* 1972. *In Charge:* Kirk Tougas, Dir. *AV Staff:* 2 (3 prof, 1 cl, 4 tech). *Film Sel:* committee preview, chief film librarian's decision. *Holdings:* animated films 10%, experimental films 10%, feature films 50%, film classics, films produced in B.C., third world films.

Film Rental Serv *Eligibility:* no restrictions. *Restrictions:* only in province. Cannot use for fund-raising, transmit electronically. *Rental Period:* 1 day. Sell films.

Film Collection 450t/500p. Approx 50t acquired annually. *Circ:* 16mm, 50t/p. *Noncirc:* 16mm, 400t/450p. *Pubns:* catalog, annual; suppl, no set policy.

Other Film Serv Rent film from distributors for patrons, obtain film from other libraries, film reference serv, film fairs/festivals, library film programs. Permanent viewing facility available for rent to community. *Member:* Canadian Film Institute, Cinematheque Quebecoise.

C- UNIVERSITY OF BRITISH COLUMBIA, Instructional Media Centre, V6T 1W5. *Tel:* (604) 228-4771, ext 7, 5. *Film Serv Est:* 1945. *In Charge:* Gwyn Bartram, Film Librarian. *AV Staff:* 7 (3 cl, 4 tech). *Film Sel:* committee preview, faculty/staff recommendations, film librarian's decision.

Film Rental Serv *Eligibility:* some films only to specific groups. *Restrictions:* only in province. *Rental Period:* 1 day.

Film Collection 1400t/p. Approx 50t acquired annually. *Pubns:* catalog, every 2 yrs ($1.50); supp, no set policy.

Other Film Serv Rent film from distributors for patrons, obtain film from coop loan system (Media Exchange Coop), obtain film from other libraries. Permanent viewing facility. *Equipment:* rent S8mm camera (5), 16mm sound projector (15), 8mm cartridge projector (2), 8mm reel projector (2), S8mm cartridge projector (2), S8mm reel projector (2), projection tables & stands (2), projection screens (12), overheads & opaques (9), tape recorders (26), record players (5), slide & filmstrip projectors (18), public address (40).

Victoria

P- GREATER VICTORIA PUBLIC LIBRARY, Audio Visual Serv, 794 Yates St, V8W 1L4. *Tel:* (604) 382-7241, ext 01. *Film Serv Est:* 1940. *In Charge:* Cheryl Osborn, AV Librarian. *AV Staff:* 4 (1 prof, 3 cl). *Film Sel:* chief film librarian's decision, preview with resource individuals. *Holdings:* agriculture, animated films, career education, children's films, consumer affairs, dance, experimental films, fine arts, general audience material, industrial arts, medicine, science, social sciences, women.

Film Rental Serv *Eligibility:* members only. *Restrictions:* only in city. Cannot use for fund-raising, transmit electronically. *Rental Period:* 2 days.

Film Collection 400t. *Circ:* 16mm, 400t; 8mm reel, 150t. *Pubns:* publish a title listing containing b&w, col, duration information.

Other Film Serv Obtain film from other libraries, film reference serv, film fairs/festivals, library film programs. Permanent viewing facility. *Equipment:* rent 16mm sound projector (5), projection screens (11), speaker (1), 35mm projector (3).

Other Media Collections *Audio:* disc, 33⅓ rpm, 5650t; tape, cassette, 621t; tape, talking book 190t. *Filmstrips:* silent, 85t. *Slides:* single, 62t.

Manitoba

Thompson

P- THOMPSON PUBLIC LIBRARY, 81 Thompson Drive North, R8N 0C3. *Tel:* (204) 677-3717. *Equipment:* lend projection screens (1), slide projector (1).

Winnipeg

P- TRANSCONA PUBLIC LIBRARY, 111 Victoria Ave West, R2C 1S6. *Film Serv Est:* 1973. *In Charge:* Heather Graham, Assistant Librarian. *AV Staff:* 1 prof. *Film Sel:* committee preview, chief film librarian's decision.

Film Collection 10t/p. Approx 5t acquired annually.

Other Film Serv Library film programs.

Other Media Collections *Audio:* disc, 33⅓ rpm, 1200t/1c. *Filmstrips:* sound, 48t/1c. *Slides:* single, 500t/1c.

Budget & Expenditures Total library budget $37,000 (FY 1/1/75-1/1/76). Total FY film budget $2000.

C- UNIVERSITY OF MANITOBA, Education Library, 230 Education Bldg, R3T 2N2. *Tel:* (204) 474-9422. *In Charge:* Doreen Shanks, Head, Education Library. *AV Staff:* ½ cl. *Film Sel:* faculty/staff recommendations.

Free-Loan Film Serv *Eligibility:* staff & students. *Restrictions:* for indiv, only in city. May not borrow by mail. *Loan Period:* 7 days.

Film Collection 52t.

Other Media Collections *Audio:* disc, 33⅓ rpm, 4200c; tape, cassette, 1800c. *Slides:* single, 1315c; sets, 5c.

Budget & Expenditures No separate AV budget.

Video Serv *Video Use:* in-service training, playback only of professionally produced tapes. Video serv available on demand.

Video Tape Loan/Rental/Sale Serv *Serv Provided:* free loan. *Loan Eligibility:* staff & students. *Restrictions:* for indiv, only in city. May not borrow by mail. *Loan Period:* 7 days.

Video Collection Maintained by purchase. *Sources:* commercial distributors. *Tape Sel:* faculty/staff recommendations. *Special Collections:* in-house training tapes. *Collection, B&W:* ½″ reel, 192t; 1″ reel, 8t.

New Brunswick

Sackville

C- MOUNT ALLISON UNIVERSITY, Ralph Pickard Bell Library, E0A 3C0. *Tel:* (506) 536-2040. *Film Serv Est:* 1970. *In Charge:* Brian Morrell, Reference Librarian. *Film Sel:* faculty/staff recommendations.

Free-Loan Film Serv *Eligibility:* staff & students, civic groups, prof groups. *Restrictions:* for indiv, & inst, only within this inst. Available to researchers/scholars for on-site viewing. May not borrow by mail.

Film Collection 160t. *Noncirc:* 16mm, 160t. *Pubn:* publish materials pertaining to collection. Publish biennially an AV holdings list which includes film holdings. Permanent viewing facility.

Other Media Collections *Audio:* disc, 33⅓ rpm, 3551c; tape, cassette, 227c.

Budget & Expenditures No separate budget. *Member:* ALA.

Northwest Territories

Frobisher Bay

S- ADULT EDUCATION CENTRE, Box 730, X0A 0H0. *Tel:* (819) 979-5221. *Video Serv Est:* 1972. *In Charge:* W. T. Hoggarth, Adult Educator. *Video Staff:* 1 f-t. *Video Use:* documentation of community events, community video access, in-service training, inter-settlement communications. Video serv available on demand. Produce video tapes. Have production studio/space & separate control room.

Video Equipment/Facilities *For Loan:* portapak (1), ½″ b&w, Sony 3400; recording deck (1), ½″ b&w, Sony 3610; editing deck (1), ½″ b&w, Sony 3650; studio camera (1), ½″ b&w, Sony 3200; monitor (3), b&w, Sony; microphones (2); tripods (2); audio tape recorders (3). Have permanent & portable viewing installations. *Equipment Loan Period:* no set policy. Provide training in use of equipment to faculty, students, community group members. Have tape duplication serv.

Video Tape Loan/Rental/Sale Serv *Serv Provided:* free loan, swap with other inst. *Loan Eligibility:* staff & students, educational inst, civic groups, religious groups, prof groups, such as hunters & trappers assn. *Restrictions:* for indiv, & inst, only in Eastern Arctic. May borrow by mail.

Video Collection Maintained by own production, exchange/swap. Use/play ½″, reel to reel. *Sources:* community productions, exchange (government agencies, native organizations). *Tape Sel:* by Northern content. *Collection, B&W:* ½″ reel, 20t. *Other Video Serv:* programming, taping of other media.

Nova Scotia

Amherst

P- CUMBERLAND REGIONAL LIBRARY, Box 220, Ratchford St. *Tel:* (902) 667-2135. *Film Serv Est:* 1970. *In Charge:* Beverly True, Chief Librarian. *Film Sel:* committee preview.

Film Rental Serv *Eligibility:* no restrictions. *Restrictions:* only in region (Cumberland County, N.S.). Cannot use for fundraising. *Rental Rate:* $1. *Rental Period:* 7 days. *Total Yr Film Booking:* 190.

Film Collection 94t/p. Approx 7-10t acquired annually. *Circ:* 16mm, 94t/p. *Pubns:* catalog, as needed; suppl, no set policy.

Other Film Serv Library film programs. Permanent viewing facility.

Other Media Collections *Audio:* disc, 33⅓ rpm, 934t.

Budget & Expenditures Total library budget $17,500 (FY 1/1/75-1/1/76). No separate AV budget.

Halifax

S- NOVA SCOTIA COLLEGE OF ART AND DESIGN, 5163 Duke St. *Tel:* (902) 422-7381. *Video Serv Est:* 1970. *In Charge:* Fred McFadzem, Dir, AV Serv. *Video Staff:* 2 f-t, 1 p-t. *Video Use:* documentation of community/school events, practical video/TV training courses, as art form. Video serv available on demand internally & by appointment externally. Produce video tapes. Have production studio/space & separate control room.

Video Equipment/Facilities *In-House Use Only:* portapak (5), ½″ b&w, Sony AV3400, 8400; recording deck (6), ½″ b&w, Sony 3600, VR1600; editing deck (3), ½″ b&w, Sony 3650; studio camera (3), ½″ b&w, Sony 4200; monitor (10), 9″, 1″, 23″ b&w, Sony, Electrohome; SEG (1), Sony; additional camera lenses (1); microphones (15); tripods (10); audio tape recorders (25), 35mm camera, 8mm & 16mm film cameras, 16mm projectors. Have permanent viewing installation. *Equipment Loan Period:* 1-2 days internally only. Provide training in use of equipment to faculty staff & students. Have tape duplication serv.

Video Tape Loan/Rental/Sale Serv *Serv Provided:* swap with other inst. *Loan Eligibility:* staff & students. *Restrictions:* only by college community. Cannot use without permission of artist. May not borrow by mail.

Video Collection Maintained by own production. Use/play ½″ reel to reel, ¾″ cassette. *Tape Sel:* faculty/staff request. *Special Collections:* video as art. Tapes organized by subject. *Collection, B&W:* ½″ reel, 40t; ¾″ cassette, 20t.

S- NOVA SCOTIA PROVINCIAL LIBRARY, AV Services, 5250 Spring Garden Rd, B3J 1E8. *Tel:* (902) 422-6481, ext 28. *Film Serv Est:* 1937. *In Charge:* J. G. McDonald, Supervisor. *AV Staff:* 10 (2 prof, 4 cl, 4 tech). *Film Sel:* committee preview, published reviews. *Holdings:* government dept films.

Free-Loan Film Serv *Eligibility:* educational inst, & others, such as schools within province. *Restrictions:* for indiv & inst, only in province. Cannot transmit electronically. May borrow by mail. *Loan Period:* 7-14 days. *Total Yr Film Loan:* 40,000.

Film Collection 3000t/4000p. Approx 150-200t acquired annually. *Circ:* 16mm, 3000t/4000p. *Pubns:* catalog, every 3 yrs; suppl, in yr catalog not published.

Other Film Serv Permanent viewing facility. *Equipment:* lend S8mm camera (2), 16mm sound projector (5), 8mm cartridge projector (1), S8mm cartridge projector (2), S8mm reel projector (1), projection tables & stands (3), projection screens (5).

Other Media Collections *Audio:* tape, cassette, 750c; tape, reel, 1000c.

Budget & Expenditures Total library budget $168,000 (FY 4/1/75-4/1/76). No separate AV budget. *Member:* AECT, Assn for Media Technol in Education in Canada.

Halifax (cont.)

Video Serv *Est:* 1975. *Video Use:* duplication, educational television programming. Video serv available on demand.

Video Equipment/Facilities *In-House Use Only:* portapak (1), ½" b&w, Sony 3400; recording deck (3), ¾" col, Sony VO1600; playback deck (1), ¾" col, Sony VP1200; deck (2), ½" col, Sony 8600. *For Loan:* portapk (1), ½" b&w, Sony 3400; playback deck (1), ¾" col, Sony VP1200. Have permanent viewing installation. Have tape duplication serv. *Loan Eligibility:* educational inst. *Restrictions:* for indiv, none. Copies of tapes provided for use in schools.

Video Collection Use/play ½" reel to reel, ¾" cassette. *Collection, Color:* ¾" cassette, 20t/c. *Collection, B&W:* ¾" cassette, 20t/c.

Cable & CCTV Receive serv of cable TV system.

C- NOVA SCOTIA TECHNICAL COLLEGE LIBRARY, Box 1000, B3J 2X4. *Tel:* (902) 429-8300, ext 270. *Video Serv Est:* 1974. *In Charge:* M. R. Hussain, Librarian. *Video Staff:* 1 p-t. *Video Use:* as sales tool, playback only of professionally produced tapes. Video serv available on demand & by appointment.

Video Equipment/Facilities *In-House Use Only:* playback deck (3), ¾"; studio camera (3), col. Have portable viewing installation. *Equipment Loan Period:* no set policy. Provide training in use of equipment.

Video Collection Maintained by purchase. Use/play ¾" cassette. *Sources:* commercial distributors, corporations that provide free copies of their tapes. *Tape Sel:* faculty/staff recommendations, published reviews, catalogs. Tapes organized by title. *Collection, Color:* ¾" cassette, 10t/1c. *Collection, B&W:* ¾" cassette, 24t/1c.

C- SAINT MARY'S UNIVERSITY LIBRARY, Inglis and Robie Sts, B3H 3C3. *Tel:* (902) 422-7361, ext 218. *Video Serv Est:* 1975. *In Charge:* Bob Atkinson, Non-Book Librarian. *Video Staff:* 1 f-t, 4 p-t, 1 tech. *Video Use:* documentation of community/school events, to increase community's library use. Video serv available on demand & by appointment. Have production studio/space.

Video Equipment/Facilities *In-House Use Only:* portapak (1), ½" b&w, Sony 3650; recording & playback deck (1), ¾" col, Sony VO1800; studio camera (1), b&w, Sony AVC3260DX; monitor (1), 12" b&w, Sony; microphones (2); tripods (1); audio tape recorders, graphic frequency equalizer (1). Have portable viewing installation. *Equipment Loan Period:* no set policy. Provide training in use of equipment to faculty & students. Have tape duplication serv.

Video Tape Loan/Rental/Sale Serv *Serv Provided:* free loan, swap with other inst. *Loan Eligibility:* staff & students, educational inst. *Restrictions:* for indiv, only in city; for inst, only in city. Cannot use for fund-raising, air without permission. May not borrow by mail.

Video Collection Maintained by purchase, own production. Use/play ½" reel to reel, ¾" cassette. *Sources:* commercial distributors. *Tape Sel:* published reviews, catalogs. *Special Collections:* films in video format. Tapes organized by subject. *Other Video Serv:* taping of other media, production workshops.

Sydney

C- CANADA MINISTRY OF TRANSPORT, CANADIAN COAST GUARD COLLEGE, Box 4500, B1P 6L1. *Tel:* (902) 539-2115, ext 229. *Film Serv Est:* 1965. *In Charge:* Valerie Smith, Assistant Librarian. *Film Sel:* faculty/staff recommendations. *Holdings:* engineering 60%, industrial arts 5%, science 30%, social sciences 5%.

Free-Loan Film Serv *Eligibility:* staff & students, & others, such as support staff. *Restrictions:* for indiv, & inst, only in college. Cannot use for fund-raising, transmit electronically. Available to researchers/scholars for on-site viewing. May not borrow by mail. *Loan Period:* 1 month. *Total Yr Film Loan:* 250.

Film Collection 200t/250p. Approx 20t acquired annually. *Circ:* 16mm, 200t/250p. *Pubn:* publish materials pertaining to collection. New films are included with new books. -

Other Film Serv Obtain film from coop laon system (National Film Board of Canada), obtain film from other libraries.

Other Media Collections *Audio:* disc, 33⅓ rpm, 45t. *Filmstrips:* sound sets, 1t/1c.

Budget & Expenditures Total FY film budget $5000. (FY 4/1/74-4/1/75). *Member:* Canadian Library Assn.

Ontario

Ajax

P- AJAX PUBLIC LIBRARY, 65 Harwood Ave South, L1S 2H8. *Tel:* (416) 683-6911. *Film Serv Est:* 1957. *In Charge:* Jean Tomlinson, Film Dept Head. *AV Staff:* 1 cl. *Film Sel:* chief film librarian's decision.

Free-Loan Film Serv *Eligibility:* indiv with library cards, & any local taxpaying business employee. *Restrictions:* for indiv, interlibrary loan. Cannot use for fund-raising, transmit electronically. Available to researchers/scholars for on-site viewing. May not borrow by mail. *Loan Period:* 1 day. *Total Yr Film Loan:* 1486.

Film Collection 157t/p. Approx 15t acquired annually. *Circ:* 16mm, 72t; 8mm reel, 46t; S8mm reel, 39t.

Other Film Serv Rent film from distributors for patrons, obtain film from coop loan system (Film Federation of Eastern Ont.), obtain film from other libraries, library film programs. Permanent viewing facility available for rent to community. *Equipment:* lend 16mm sound projector (4), S8mm reel projector (2), projection screens (3), filmstrip projectors (2).

Other Media Collections *Filmstrips:* sound, 1t; silent, 29t; silent sets, 25t.

Budget & Expenditures Total library budget $33,300 (FY 1/1/75-1/1/76). Total FY film budget $3500. *Member:* Ont. Film Assn.

Barrie

P- GEORGIAN BAY REGIONAL LIBRARY SYSTEM, 30 Morrow Rd, L4N 3V8. *Tel:* (705) 726-8251. *Film Serv Est:* 1969. *In Charge:* Marie B. Deane, AV Coord. *AV Staff:* 3 (1 prof, 2 cl, 1 tech). *Film Sel:* staff recommendations, chief film librarian's decision.

Free-Loan Film Serv *Eligibility:* educational inst, civic groups, religious groups, indiv with library cards. Cannot use for fund-raising, transmit electronically. Available to researchers/scholars for on-site viewing. *Loan Period:* 1 day. *Total Yr Film Loan:* 30,000.

Film Collection 1800t/2000p. Approx 120t acquired annually. *Circ:* 16mm, 1800t/2000p; 8mm reel, 300t/600p; S8mm reel, 200t/400p. *Pubns:* catalog, every 2 yrs; suppl, in alternate yr.

Other Film Serv Rent film from distributors for patrons, obtain film from other libraries, film reference serv, film fairs/festivals, library film programs. Permanent viewing facility available for rent to community. *Equipment:* lend S8mm camera (2), 16mm sound projector (50), 8mm reel projector (2), S8mm reel projector (1), projection screens (25).

Other Media Collections Tape, cassette, 500t/600c. *Member:* EFLA, FLIC, Canadian Film Inst, Canadian Library Assn, Ont. Film Assn, Ont. Library Assn.

Video Serv *Est:* 1975. *Video Use:* to increase community's library use, in-service training, playback only of professionally produced tapes. Video serv available on demand. Produce video tapes.

Video Equipment/Facilities *In-House Use Only:* recording deck (1), ¾" b&w, Sony VP1800; playback deck (4), ¾" b&w, Sony VP1200; studio camera (1), b&w, Sony AVC3210; monitor (5), col, Sony Trinitron; microphones (1); tripods (1); audio tape recorders (5). Have portable viewing installation. *Equipment Loan Period:* no set policy. Provide training in use of equipment to faculty.

Video Tape Loan/Rental/Sale Serv *Serv Provided:* free loan in library only. *Loan Eligibility:* educational inst, civic groups, religious groups, indiv with library cards, prof groups. *Restrictions:* cannot use for fund-raising, duplicate.

Video Collection Maintained by purchase. Use/play ¾″ cassette. *Sources:* commercial distributors. *Tape Sel:* preview, catalogs. *Special Collections:* films in video format. Tapes organized by subject. *Collection, Color:* ¾″ cassette, 400t. *Other Video Serv:* catalogue of videotapes available.

Cable & CCTV Produce programs for cablecasting. Inform public about cable system serv & facilities.

Belleville

P- LAKE ONTARIO REGIONAL LIBRARY SYSTEM, Belleville (Corby) Public Library, 223 Pinnacle St, K8N 3A7. *Tel:* (613) 968-8240. *Film Serv Est:* 1970. *In Charge:* Olive Delaney, AV Librarian. *AV Staff:* 1½ (½ prof, ¼ cl, 1 tech). *Film Sel:* committee preview. *Holdings:* children's films 25%, consumer affairs 5%, fine arts 8%.

Free-Loan Film Serv *Eligibility:* org members & other regional library systems. *Restrictions:* for indiv & inst, none. Cannot use for fund-raising, transmit electronically. May borrow by mail. *Loan Period:* 1 day. *Total Yr Film Loan:* 3634.

Film Rental Serv *Eligibility:* educational org. Cannot use for fund-raising. *Rental Period:* 1 day. *Total Yr Film Booking:* 3634. Produce films.

Film Collection 660t. Approx 29t acquired annually. *Circ:* 8mm reel, 660t/p. *Pubns:* catalog, as needed ($5); suppl, no set policy.

Other Film Serv Rent film from distributors for patrons, obtain film from coop loan system (regional library systems of Ont.), obtain film from other libraries, library film programs. Permanent viewing facility available for rent to community. *Equipment:* rent 16mm camera (4), projection screens (1).

Other Media Collections *Audio:* disc, 33⅓ rpm, 31t/1c; tape, cassette, 53t/1c. *Filmstrips:* silent, 10t/1c. *Slides:* single, 48t/1c.

Budget & Expenditures Total library budget $12,000 (FY 1974-1975). No separate AV budget.

Video Serv *Est:* 1970. *In Charge:* Olive Delaney, AV Librarian. *Video Staff:* ½ f-t, 1 p-t, ¼ tech. *Video Use:* playback only of professionally produced tapes, as art form. Video serv available by appointment.

Video Tape Loan/Rental/Sale Serv *Serv Provided:* free loan. *Loan Eligibility:* org members, educational inst. *Restrictions:* for indiv, only in counties of regional system; for inst, none. Cannot use for fund-raising, duplicate, air without permission. May borrow by mail. *Loan Period:* 1 day. *Total Yr Tape Loan:* 50.

Video Collection Maintained by purchase. Use/play ¾″ cassette. *Sources:* exchange. *Member:* Regional Library Systems of Ont. *Tape Sel:* catalogs, library committee. *Special Collections:* educational tapes, "how-to" tapes. Tapes organized by Dewey Decimal. *Collection, Color:* ¾″ cassette, 58t/c. *Collection, B&W:* ¾″ cassette, 57t/c. *Other Video Serv:* catalog. *Pubns:* publish book mark bibliographies.

C- LOYALIST COLLEGE OF APPLIED ARTS & TECHNOLOGY, Anderson Resource Centre, Box 4200, K8N 5B9. *Tel:* (613) 962-9501, ext 249. *Film Serv Est:* 1972. *In Charge:* M. McConnell, Head of Resource Centre. *AV Staff:* 4½ (1 prof, ½ cl, 3 tech). *Film Sel:* faculty/staff recommendations, chief film librarian's decision.

Free-Loan Film Serv *Eligibility:* staff & students, educational inst, prof groups, such as hospitals, & others, such as clubs & organizations. *Restrictions:* for indiv & inst, only in province. Cannot use for fund-raising, internal college bookings have first priority. Available to researchers/scholars for on-site viewing. May borrow by mail. *Loan Period:* 1 day. *Total Yr Film Loan:* 305.

Film Rental Serv *Eligibility:* only our own faculty. *Restrictions:* no foreign countries. Cannot use for fund-raising. *Rental Period:* as needed. Produce films. Produce video tape, slides, audio-cassettes, transparencies, signs, photo prints.

Film Collection *Circ:* 16mm, 206t/209p. *Pubns:* publish annotated subject lists.

Other Film Serv Rent film from distributors for patrons, obtain film from coop loan system (College Bibliocentre), film reference serv, library film programs. Permanent viewing facility. *Equipment:* lend/rent 16mm sound projector (24), 8mm cartridge projector (16), 8mm reel projector (5), S8mm reel projector (20), projection tables & stands (10), lend/rent projection screens, video cassette units (9), television receivers (15).

Other Media Collections *Audio:* disc & tape 481t/c. *Filmstrips:* sound & silent 251t/c. *Slides:* single & sets, 3544t/c.

Budget & Expenditures Total library budget $69,916 (FY 4/1/74-4/1/75). Total FY film budget $24,535. *Member:* Canadian Library Assn., Ont. Library Assn.

Video Serv *Video Use:* documentation of community/school events, playback only of professionally produced tapes. Video serv available by appointment. Produce video tapes.

Video Equipment/Facilities *In-House Use Only:* playback deck (9), ½″, ¾″, 1″ b&w/col, Ampex; audio tape recorders (1); cassette decks (3). *For Loan:* portapak (1), Sony EV3400; recording deck (7), ½″, ¾″, 1″ b&w/col, Sony UV1600; playback deck (9), ½″, ¾″, 1″ b&w/col, Sony; monitor (30), b&w/col, Electrohome, Sony; SEG (1), Sony; lighting (1); microphones (6); tripods (5); audio tape recorders. Have portable viewing installation. *Equipment Loan Period:* no set policy. Provide training in use of equipment to anyone. Have tape duplication serv.

Video Tape Loan/Rental/Sale Serv *Serv Provided:* free loan. *Loan Eligibility:* staff. *Restrictions:* for inst, only in province. Cannot use for fund-raising, duplicate. May not borrow by mail. *Loan Period:* 7 days.

Video Collection Maintained by purchase, rental, own production, exchange/swap. Use/play ½″, 1″ reel to reel, ¾″ cassette. *Sources:* Ont. Educational Communication Assn. *Tape Sel:* faculty/staff recommendations, gallery previews. *Special Collections:* in-house training tapes. Tapes organized by MV & Accessions Numbering. *Collection, Color:* 71t. *Other Video Serv:* reference serv, catalog. *Pubns:* publish annotated lists.

Cable & CCTV Receive serv of cable TV system. Produce programs for cablecasting. Serve as production facility for others. Run cable programs for special audiences. Have CCTV in inst, with 20 monitors.

Bramalea

P- CITY OF BRAMPTON PUBLIC LIBRARY & ART GALLERY, Chinguacousy Branch, 150 Central Park Drive, L6T 1B4. *Tel:* (416) 457-9612, ext 49. *Film Serv Est:* 1969. *In Charge:* Anne Bibby, AV Coord. *AV Staff:* 4 (3 cl, 1 tech). *Film Sel:* committee preview, staff recommendations, individual previewing.

Free-Loan Film Serv *Eligibility:* staff & students, civic groups, religious groups, indiv with library cards. *Restrictions:* for indiv, only in state; for inst, at discretion of lending library. Cannot use for fund-raising, transmit electronically, borrow for classroom use. May not borrow by mail. *Loan Period:* 1 day. *Total Yr Film Loan:* 13,000.

Film Collection 800t/100p. Approx 70t acquired annually. *Circ:* 16mm, 900t/p; 8mm & S8mm reel & cartridge, 645t. *Pubns:* catalog, annual; suppl, annual. Publish press releases of titles of interest.

Other Film Serv Obtain film from coop loan system (Central Ont. Regional Library System), obtain film from other libraries, film reference serv, library film programs. Permanent viewing facility. *Equipment:* rent 16mm sound projector (12), lend S8mm reel projector (2).

Budget & Expenditures Total FY film budget $16,000 (FY 1/75-1/76). *Member:* EFLA.

Video Serv *Est:* 1972. *Video Staff:* 3 f-t, 2 p-t, 1 tech. *Video Use:* to increase community's library use, in-service training, playback only of professionally produced tapes. Video serv available on demand. Produce video tapes.

Video Equipment/Facilities *In-House Use Only:* portapak (1), ½″ b&w, Sony; recording deck (1); playback deck (1); monitor (4); microphones (6); tripods (2); audio tape recorders (1); receivers (9). Have permanent viewing installation. *Equipment*

Bramalea (cont.)
Loan Period: 1 day. Provide training in use of equipment to anyone.

Video Tape Loan/Rental/Sale Serv *Serv Provided:* free loan. *Loan Eligibility:* staff & students, civic groups, religious groups, prof groups, such as family serv, regional planning dept. Cannot use for fund-raising, duplicate, air without permission. May not borrow by mail. *Loan Period:* 1 day. *Total Yr Tape Loan:* 553.

Video Collection Maintained by purchase, own production. Use/play ½" reel to reel. *Sources:* Ont. Educational Communications Authority. *Tape Sel:* preview. *Special Collections:* language learning. Tapes organized by title. *Collection, Color & B&W:* 322t/c. *Other Video Serv:* programming, catalog. *Pubns:* publish press releases on titles of interest.

Cable & CCTV Receive serv of cable TV system. Inform public about cable system serv & facilities. Run cable programs for special audiences. Have CCTV in inst, with 13 monitors. *Programming Sources:* tapes produced by inst, tapes produced professionally.

Brantford

P- BRANTFORD PUBLIC LIBRARY, 73 George St, N3T 2Y3. *Tel:* (519) 753-3404. *Film Serv Est:* 1948. *In Charge:* Margaret Zahra, Film Librarian. *AV Staff:* 2 (2 tech). *Film Sel:* committee preview, chief film librarian's decision.

Film Rental Serv *Eligibility:* no restrictions. *Restrictions:* only in region (Brant, Wentworth, Halton Counties). *Rental Period:* 1 day. *Total Yr Film Booking:* 3798.

Film Collection 300t/p. Approx 20t acquired annually. *Circ:* 16mm, 300t/p. *Pubns:* catalog, as needed ($1); suppl, as needed.

Other Film Serv Obtain film from coop loan system (S Central Regional Libraries System), film fairs/festivals, library film programs. *Equipment:* lend/rent 16mm sound projector (3), projection tables & stands (3), projection screens (3).

Other Media Collections *Audio:* disc, 33⅓ rpm, 3250t; disc, 45rpm, 2t; disc, 78rpm, 46t. *Filmstrips:* silent sets, 176t.

Budget & Expenditures Total library budget $491,438 (FY 1/1/75-1/1/76). Total FY film budget $8759. *Member:* Ont. Film Assn, Ont. Library Assn.

Burlington

P- BURLINGTON PUBLIC LIBRARY, 2331 New St, L7R 1J4. *Tel:* (416) 639-3611, ext 53. *Film Serv Est:* 1970. *In Charge:* Christine Hoyland, Film Librarian. *AV Staff:* 2 (1 cl, 1 tech). *Film Sel:* committee preview.

Free-Loan Film Serv *Eligibility:* staff & students, educational inst, civic groups, religious groups, indiv with library cards, & others, such as businessmen. *Restrictions:* for indiv, only in region; for inst, interlibrary loan. Cannot use for fund-raising, transmit electronically. Available to researchers/scholars for on-site viewing. May not borrow by mail. *Loan Period:* 1 day. *Total Yr Film Loan:* 12,857.

Film Collection 400t/p. Approx 50t acquired annually. *Circ:* 16mm, 400t/p. *Noncirc:* 16mm, 12t/p.

Other Film Serv Obtain film from coop loan system (S Central Regional Library System), obtain film from other libraries, film reference serv, film fairs/festivals, library film programs. Permanent viewing facility available for rent to community. *Equipment:* rent 16mm sound projector (4), projection screens (3).

Budget & Expenditures Total FY film budget $10,000 (FY 1/1/75-1/1/76). *Member:* Ont. Film Assn.

Video Serv *In Charge:* Justin Haraschuk, Head, AV Dept. *Video Staff:* 2 f-t, 2 p-t. *Video Use:* to increase community's library use, in-service training. Video serv available on demand. Produce video tapes. Have production studio/space.

Video Equipment/Facilities *In-House Use Only:* recording deck (1), ½" b&w, Sony TAV3610; playback deck (1), ¾" col, Sony VP1200; monitor, 12" col, Sony; microphones (1). Have portable viewing installation.

Video Tape Loan/Rental/Sale Serv *Restrictions:* for indiv & inst, interlibrary loan. May not borrow by mail.

Video Collection Maintained by purchase, rental, own production. Use/play ½" reel to reel, ¾" cassette. *Sources:* Ont. Educational Communications Authority. *Member:* S Central Regional Library System. *Tape Sel:* preview, faculty/staff recommendations, published reviews, catalogs. *Special Collections:* in-house training tapes. Tapes organized by subject. *Collection, Color:* ¾" cassette, 5t/1c. *Collection, B&W:* ½" reel, 8t/1c. *Other Video Serv:* programming, catalog.

Cable & CCTV Receive serv of cable TV system. Produce programs for cablecasting. Have CCTV in inst, with 1 monitor. *Programming Sources:* tapes produced by inst, tapes produced professionally.

Chatham

P- CHATHAM PUBLIC LIBRARY, 120 Queen St, N7M 2G6. *Tel:* (519) 354-2940, ext 7. *Film Serv Est:* 1940 approx. *In Charge:* Rose Austin, Film Librarian. *AV Staff:* 2 (2 cl). *Film Sel:* staff recommendations.

Free-Loan Film Serv *Eligibility:* no restrictions. *Restrictions:* for indiv, none; for inst, only in region. Cannot use for fund-raising, transmit electronically. Available to researchers/scholars for on-site viewing. May borrow by mail. *Loan Period:* 2 days. *Total Yr Film Loan:* 6279.

Film Collection 1637t/1737p. Approx 25-50t acquired annually. *Circ:* 16mm, 1637t/1737p; 8mm reel, 750t/802p. *Pubns:* catalog, as needed ($2); suppl, no set policy (50¢).

Other Film Serv Obtain film from coop loan system (Southwestern Regional Library System), obtain film from other libraries, library film programs. *Equipment:* rent 16mm sound projector (7), 8mm reel projector (5), S8mm reel projector (1), filmstrip projectors (2).

Other Media Collections *Audio:* disc, 33⅓ rpm, 4499t/4536.

Budget & Expenditures No separate budget.

Video Serv *Est:* 1975. *In Charge:* Isabel Cimolino, AV Librarian. *Video Staff:* 2 f-t, 3 p-t. *Video Use:* to increase community's library use, playback only of professionally produced tapes, complement other library material. Video serv available on demand & by appointment.

Video Equipment/Facilities *In-House Use Only:* audio tape recorders (1); tape players (3). Have portable viewing installation.

Video Tape Loan/Rental/Sale Serv *Serv Provided:* free loan, swap with other inst, rental. *Loan/Rental Eligibility:* all residents of Southwestern Ont. who are library members. *Restrictions:* for indiv, none; for inst, only in city. Cannot use for fund-raising, duplicate. *Total Yr Tape Loan:* 105.

Video Collection Use/play ¾" cassette. *Sources:* commercial distributors, regional coord. *Member:* Southwestern Regional Library System. *Tape Sel:* regional coord. Tapes organized by accession numbers. *Pubns:* publish stencils.

Cable & CCTV Will receive serv of cable TV system.

Cornwall

P- SIMON FRASER CENTENNIAL LIBRARY, Box 939, K6H 5V1. *Tel:* (613) 932-4797. *Film Serv Est:* 1972. *In Charge:* I. Howells, Head, Library Serv. *AV Staff:* 3 (1 prof, 2 cl). *Film Sel:* chief film librarian's decision.

Free-Loan Film Serv *Eligibility:* educational inst, civic groups, religious groups, indiv with library cards, prof groups. *Restrictions:* for indiv & inst, only in Stormont, Dundas, Glengarry Counties. Cannot transmit electronically. May not borrow by mail. *Loan Period:* 1 day. *Total Yr Film Loan:* 2483.

Film Rental Serv *Eligibility:* no restrictions. *Restrictions:* only in Stormont, Dundas, Glengarry Counties. Cannot transmit electronically. *Rental Period:* 1 day. *Total Yr Film Booking:* 197.

Film Collection 226t. *Circ:* 16mm, 39t; 8mm reel, 187t. *Pubns:* catalog, as needed; suppl, no set policy.

Other Film Serv Obtain film from coop loan system (Eastern Ont. Regional Library System), library film programs.

Equipment: rent 16mm sound projector (2), 8mm cartridge projector (1), 8mm reel projector (2), S8mm cartridge projector (1), S8mm reel projector (2), projection screens (1).

Other Media Collections *Audio:* disc, 33⅓ rpm, 3102t; tape, cassette, 68t; tape, cartridge, 60t.

Budget & Expenditures Total library budget $41,000 (FY 1/75-1/76). No separate AV budget.

Video Serv *Est:* 1975. *Video Staff:* 3 f-t. *Video Use:* to increase community's library use, community video access. Playback only of professionally produced tapes, as art form. Video serv available on demand.

Video Equipment/Facilities *For Loan:* playback deck (1), ¾″ col, Sony VP1000. *Equipment Loan Period:* 1 day. Provide training in use of equipment to public.

Video Tape Loan/Rental/Sale Serv *Serv Provided:* free loan. *Loan Eligibility:* staff & students, educational inst, civic groups, religious groups, indiv with library cards, prof groups. *Restrictions:* for inst, only in Stormont, Dundas, Glengarry Counties. Cannot duplicate, air without permission. May not borrow by mail.

Video Collection Maintained by purchase. Use/play ¾″ cassette. *Sources:* commercial distributors. *Tape Sel:* catalogs. Tapes organized by subject. *Collection, Color:* ¾″ cassette, 57t/c. *Collection, B&W:* ¾″ cassette, 9t/c.

Don Mills

S- CANADIAN DENTAL ASSN, 1875 Leslie St. *Tel:* (416) 444-7347. *Film Serv Est:* 1970. *Film Sel:* committee preview. *Holdings:* dental education.

Free-Loan Film Serv *Eligibility:* prof groups, such as universities, faculties, study groups. *Restrictions:* for indiv & inst, only in own county. Cannot transmit electronically. May borrow by mail. *Loan Period:* as needed. *Total Yr Film Loan:* 218.

Film Collection 10t/70p. *Circ:* 16mm, 10t/70p. *Pubns:* catalog, annual. Publish promotion serv.

Budget & Expenditures Total FY film budget $1500 (FY 1/1/75-1/1/76).

Downsview

C- YORK UNIVERSITY, Dept of Instructional Aid Resources, 4700 Keele St, MJ3 2R2 *Tel:* (416) 667-3411. *Video Serv Est:* 1967. *In Charge:* David A. Homer, Dir. *Video Use:* community video access, practical video/TV training courses, playback only of professionally produced tapes. Video serv available by appointment. Produce video tapes. Have production studio/space & separate control room.

Video Equipment/Facilities *In-House Use Only:* portapak (5), ½″ b&w, Sony 3400; recording, playback & editing deck (24), ½″, ¾″, 1″, 2″ b&w/col, Sony, Ampex; studio camera (3), b&w, Marconi MK4; monitor (80), b&w, Conrac, Electrohome; SEG & keyer (2), Richmond Hill; lighting (50); microphones (16); tripods (6); audio tape recorders (3). Have permanent & portable viewing installations. *Equipment Loan Period:* 1 day.

Video Tape Loan/Rental/Sale Serv *Serv Provided:* swap with other inst, rental. *Loan/Rental Eligibility:* org members. *Restrictions:* for indiv, only on campus. Cannot use for fund-raising, duplicate, air without permission. May borrow by mail.

Video Collection Maintained by purchase, rental, own production. Use/play ½″, 1″, 2″ reel to reel, ¾″ cassette. *Sources:* Ont. Educational Communication Authority, other universities. *Tape Sel:* faculty/staff recommendations. Tapes organized by subject. *Collection, Color:* 2″ reel, 1t. *Collection, B&W:* 1″ reel, 300t. *Other Video Serv:* production workshops.

Dundas

P- DUNDAS PUBLIC LIBRARY, AV Dept, 18 Ogilvie St, L9H 2S2. *Tel:* (416) 627-3507. *Film Serv Est:* 1968. *In Charge:* Juliette Allan, Head, AV Dept. *AV Staff:* 2 (1 prof, 1 cl). *Film Sel:* previews.

Free-Loan Film Serv *Eligibility:* indiv with library cards. *Restrictions:* for indiv, only in region. Cannot use for fund-raising, transmit electronically. Available to researchers/scholars for on-site viewing. May not borrow by mail. *Loan Period:* 1 day. *Total Yr Film Loan:* 2017.

Film Collection 161t/p. Approx 20t acquired annually. *Circ:* 16mm, 161t/p; 8mm reel, 100t/p; S8mm reel, 50t/p. *Pubns:* catalog, every 2 yrs ($2); suppl, in yr catalog not published. Publish special subject listings.

Other Film Serv Rent film from distributors for patrons, obtain film from other libraries, film reference serv, film fairs/festivals, library film programs. Permanent viewing facility available for rent to community. *Equipment:* lend 16mm sound projector (2), lend projection screens (1); 35mm slide (1).

Budget & Expenditures Total FY film budget $5900 (FY 1/1/75-1/1/76). *Member:* FLIC, Canadian Film Inst, Ont. Film Assn.

Etobicoke

P- ETOBICOKE PUBLIC LIBRARY, Richview Headquarters, Box 501, M9C 4V5. *Tel:* (416) 248-5681. Three branches with film departments: Richview; New Toronto, 110 11 St, M8V 3G5, *Tel:* 259-3971; Albion, 1515 Albion Rd, M9V 1B2, *Tel:* 741-7734. Figures given in entry reflect combined total. *Film Serv Est:* Richview—1966, New Toronto—1957, Albion—1973. *AV Staff:* 9 (2½ prof, 6 cl, 1 tech). *Film Sel:* committee preview. *Holdings:* children's films 20%.

Free-Loan Film Serv *Eligibility:* indiv with library cards. *Restrictions:* for indiv & inst, only within Metropolitan Toronto. Cannot use for fund-raising, transmit electronically. Available to researchers/scholars for on-site viewing. May not borrow by mail. *Loan Period:* 1 day. *Total Yr Film Loan:* 19,708 (1-7/75).

Film Collection 780t/p. Approx 130t acquired annually. *Circ:* 16mm, 780t/p. *Pubns:* film catalog published by Metro Toronto AV Services includes films owned by libraries within Metro Toronto.

Other Film Serv Obtain film from coop loan system (Metro Toronto AVS) & from other libraries, film reference serv, film fairs/festivals, library film programs. Permanent viewing facility available for rent to community. *Equipment:* rent 16mm sound projector (26), lend/rent projection screens, rent slide projector.

Other Media Collections *Audio:* disc, 33⅓ rpm, 24,911c; tape, cassette, 2901c. *Filmstrips:* sound & silent, 1009c. *Slides:* single, 4000.

Budget & Expenditures Total library budget $537,252 (FY 1/74-1/75). Total FY film budget $40,500. *Member:* EFLA, Ontario Film Assn.

Goderich

P- HURON COUNTY PUBLIC LIBRARY, 60 Lighthouse St, N7A 4A4. *Tel:* (519) 524-7751. *Film Serv Est:* 1971. *In Charge:* Grace MacDonald, Secretary. *AV Staff:* 1 (1 tech). *Film Sel:* by regional system. *Holdings:* general interest collection.

Free-Loan Film Serv *Eligibility:* org members. *Restrictions:* for inst, only in Huron County. *Loan Period:* 1 day.

Film Rental Serv *Eligibility:* no restrictions. *Restrictions:* only in Huron County. Cannot transmit electronically. *Rental Period:* 5 days. *Total Yr Film Booking:* 735.

Film Collection 214t/215p. Approx 10t acquired annually. *Circ:* 16mm, 214t/215p.

Other Film Serv Rent film from distributors for patrons, obtain film from coop loan system (Midwestern Regional Library System), obtain film from other libraries, library film programs. *Equipment:* rent 16mm sound projector (2), projection screens (2).

Guelph

C- UNIVERSITY OF GUELPH, Media Resources Centre, McLaughlin Library, N1G 2W1. *Tel:* (519) 824-4120, ext

Guelph (cont.)

2426. *Film Serv Est:* 1973. *In Charge:* Virginia Gillham, Head, Documentation & Media Resources. *AV Staff:* 3 (1 cl, 2 tech). *Film Sel:* committee preview, faculty/staff recommendations. *Holdings:* beginning 1976, Depository for National Film Board of Canada Archival collection.

Free-Loan Film Serv *Eligibility:* staff & students, educational inst, & others, such as industrial organizations, public libraries. *Restrictions:* for inst, none. Cannot use for fundraising, transmit electronically, borrow for classroom use. Cannot lend to individuals. Available to researchers/scholars for on-site viewing. May borrow by mail. *Loan Period:* as needed. *Total Yr Film Loan:* 1304.

Film Collection 400t/p. Approx 100t acquired annually. *Circ:* 16mm, 400t/p. *Pubns:* catalog, as needed.

Other Film Serv Rent film from distributors for patrons, obtain film from coop loan system (Ont. University Library Coop System), obtain film from other libraries, film reference serv, faculty previews. Permanent viewing facility.

Other Media Collections *Audio:* disc, 33⅓ rpm, 2000t/c.

Budget & Expenditures No separate budget.

Video Serv *Est:* 1967. *In Charge:* Don McIntosh, Coord. *Video Staff:* 4 f-t, 3 p-t, 2 tech. *Video Use:* documentation of community/school events, in-service training, practical video/TV training courses, as art form. Video serv available on demand & by appointment. Produce video tapes. Have production studio/space & separate control room.

Video Equipment/Facilities *In-House Use Only:* portapak (2), ½″ b&w, Sony 3400; recording deck (13), ½″, 1″ b&w, Sony 3650, 320; playback deck (5), ¾″ col, Sony VP1200; editing deck (1), 1″ b&w, Sony; studio camera (3), b&w; monitor, b&w, Electrohome; SEG & keyer (1), Richmond Hill; lighting (15); microphones (10); tripods (4); audio tape recorders (3). Have permanent viewing installation. *Equipment Loan Period:* 3 days. Provide training in use of equipment to faculty & students. Have tape duplication serv.

Video Tape Loan/Rental/Sale Serv *Serv Provided:* free loan, sale. *Loan/Rental Eligibility:* org members, staff, students enrolled in inst. *Restrictions:* for indiv & inst, only own members. May borrow by mail.

Video Collection Maintained by purchase, own production. Use/play ½″, 1″ reel to reel, ¾″ cassette. *Sources:* commercial distributors. *Tape Sel:* faculty/staff recommendations, catalogs. *Collection, B&W:* ½″ reel, 100t/1c; ¾″ cassette, 10t/1c. *Other Video Serv:* programming, taping of other media, production workshops.

Cable & CCTV Receive serv of cable TV system. Produce programs for cablecasting. Have CCTV in inst, with 10 monitors. *Programming Sources:* tapes produced by inst, tapes produced professionally.

Hamilton

P- HAMILTON PUBLIC LIBRARY, AV Serv, 55 Main St W, L8P 1H5. *Tel:* (416) 529-8111, ext 46, 47, 57. *In Charge:* Josephine Cuneo, Supervisor. *AV Staff:* 8 (1 prof, 6 cl, 1 tech). *Film Sel:* chief film librarian's decision.

Film Rental Serv *Eligibility:* patrons/public. *Restrictions:* only in region (S Central). Cannot use for fund-raising, transmit electronically. *Rental Period:* 1 day.

Film Collection 1060p. Approx 150t acquired annually. *Circ:* 16mm, 1060p; 8mm reel, 175p; S8mm reel, 300p.

Other Film Serv Obtain film from coop loan system (S Central Regional Library System), obtain film from other libraries, film reference serv, library film programs. Permanent viewing facility. *Equipment:* rent 16mm sound projector (6), rent projection screens (4).

Other Media Collections *Audio:* disc, 33⅓ rpm, 3000c.

Budget & Expenditures Total FY film budget $99,000 (FY 1/1/75-1/1/76). *Member:* Ont. Film Assn, Ont. Library Assn.

Video Serv *Est:* 1972. *Video Staff:* 8 f-t, 1 tech. *Video Use:* documentation of community/school events, in-service training, playback of professionally produced tapes, library programs. Video serv available for in-house use only. Produce video tapes.

Video Equipment/Facilities *In-House Use Only:* portapak (1), ½″ b&w, Sony AV3400; recording & playback deck (1), ½″ col, Sony AV8600; monitor (1), 11″ b&w, Sony; tripods (1); color monitor (1). Have portable viewing installation. *Equipment Loan Period:* provide training in use of equipment to library personnel.

Video Tape Loan/Rental/Sale Serv May not borrow by mail.

Video Collection Maintained by purchase, own production. Use/play ½″ reel to reel. *Sources:* educational networks. *Special Collections:* in-house training tapes. Tapes organized by subject. *Collection, Color:* ½″ reel, 107t. *Collection, B&W:* ½″ reel, 5t. *Other Video Serv:* programming.

Cable & CCTV Receive serv of cable TV system. Run cable programs for special audiences.

C- MOHAWK COLLEGE, Library Resource Centre, 135 Fennell Ave West, L8N 3T2. *Tel:* (416) 389-4461, ext 467. *Film Serv Est:* 1969. *In Charge:* Helen Shaver, Resource Centre Supervisor. *AV Staff:* 1 prof, 4 cl. *Film Sel:* faculty/staff recommendations.

Free-Loan Film Serv *Eligibility:* staff & students, educational inst, civic groups, religious groups, prof groups. *Restrictions:* for indiv, only in city. Cannot use for fund-raising. Available to researchers/scholars for on-site viewing. May not borrow by mail. *Loan Period:* no set policy. *Total Yr Film Loan:* 800.

Film Collection 540t. Approx 50-100t acquired annually. *Circ:* 16mm, 505t; 8mm reel, 4t; S8mm reel, 37t. *Pubns:* catalog, every 2 yrs; suppl, in yr catalog not published.

Other Film Serv Rent film from distributors for patrons, obtain film from other libraries.

Other Media Collections *Audio:* disc, 33⅓ rpm, 900t; tape, cassette, 1000t. *Filmstrips:* sound, 150t; silent, 75t. *Slides:* single, 1000t; sets, 25t.

Budget & Expenditures Total library budget $80,000 (FY 3/31/74-3/31/75). Total FY film budget $17,000.

Video Serv *Est:* 1970. *Video Staff:* 5 f-t. *Video Use:* documentation of community/school events, playback only of professionally produced tapes. Video serv available on demand. Produce video tapes. Have production studio/space.

Video Equipment/Facilities *In-House Use Only:* playback deck (3), col, Sony KV1710; monitor (3), col, Sony. *For Loan:* audio tape recorders (25). Have permanent & portable viewing installations.

Video Tape Loan/Rental/Sale Serv *Serv Provided:* free loan. *Loan Eligibility:* org members, staff & students. May not borrow by mail. *Total Yr Tape Loan:* 300.

Video Collection Maintained by purchase, own production. Use/play ¾″ cassette. *Sources:* commercial distributors. *Tape Sel:* faculty/staff recommendations. Tapes organized by Accession order. *Collection, Color:* ¾″ cassette, 300t. *Collection, B&W:* ¾″ cassette, 200t.

Kingston

C- QUEEN'S UNIVERSITY, Faculty of Education, Duncan McArthur Hall, K7L 5C4. *Tel:* (613) 547-5831. *Film Serv Est:* 1968. *In Charge:* F. Johnston, Coord. *AV Staff:* 7 (1 cl, 6 tech). *Film Sel:* faculty/staff recommendations. *Holdings:* teacher education 60%.

Free-Loan Film Serv *Eligibility:* staff & students. *Restrictions:* available to researchers/scholars for on-site viewing. May not borrow by mail. *Loan Period:* 1 day. *Total Yr Film Loan:* 3000.

Film Collection 348t/350p. Approx 8-10t acquired annually. *Circ:* 16mm, 325t; 8mm reel, 25t. *Pubns:* catalog, every 2 yrs; suppl, in yr catalog not published.

Other Film Serv Rent film from distributors for patrons, obtain film from other libraries. Permanent viewing facility available for rent to community. *Equipment:* lend S8mm camera (12), 16mm sound projector (15), 8mm reel projector (7), S8mm cartridge projector (8), S8mm reel projector (7), projection tables & stands (30), projection screens (40).

Other Media Collections *Audio:* disc, 33⅓ rpm, 1200t/1250c; disc, 45rpm, 20t/20c; tape, cassette, 335t/340c; tape, reel, 60t/60c. *Filmstrips:* silent, 2000t/2200c; sound sets, 400t/400c. *Slides:* single, 2400t/2500c; sets, 30t/30c.

Budget & Expenditures Total FY film budget $2500 (FY 7/1/74-7/1/75). *Member:* AMTEC.

Video Serv *Est:* 1968. *Video Staff:* 7 f-t, 3-4 p-t, 6 tech. *Video Use:* documentation of community/school events, in-service training, practical video/TV training courses. Video serv available on demand & by appointment. Produce video tapes. Have production studio/space & separate control room.

Video Equipment/Facilities *In-House Use Only:* portapak (2), 3000 b&w, Sony; recording deck (15), 3000, Sony; editing deck (1), 3000 b&w, Sony; studio camera (3); monitor (20), b&w/col, Electrohome; SEG (3), Sony, Richmond; lighting; microphones (15); tripods (15); audio tape recorders (10). Have permanent & portable viewing installations. *Equipment Loan Period:* no set policy. Provide training in use of equipment to faculty & students. Have tape duplication serv.

Video Tape Loan/Rental/Sale Serv *Loan Eligibility:* staff & students. *Restrictions:* may not borrow by mail. *Total Yr Tape Loan:* 200.

Video Collection Maintained by purchase, own production. Use/play ½", 1" reel to reel. *Sources:* commercial distributors. *Tape Sel:* faculty/staff recommendations, catalogs. *Special Collections:* in-house training tapes. Tapes organized by subject. *Collection, B&W:* ½" reel, 30t; 1" reel, 150t. *Other Video Serv:* programming, taping of other media, production workshops.

Cable & CCTV Have CCTV in inst, with 25 monitors. *Programming Sources:* tapes produced by inst, tapes produced professionally.

C- ST. LAWRENCE COLLEGE OF APPLIED ARTS & TECHNOLOGY, Learning Resources Centre, Box 6000, K7A 5A6. *Tel:* (613) 544-5400, ext 126, 251. *Film Serv Est:* 1973. *In Charge:* James Doran, Supervisor Educational Media Serv. *AV Staff:* 8 (2 prof, 1 cl, 5 tech). *Film Sel:* committee preview.

Free-Loan Film Serv *Eligibility:* staff & students, educational inst. *Restrictions:* for indiv, none; for inst, only in city. Cannot use for fund-raising, transmit electronically. Available to researchers/scholars for on-site viewing. May borrow by mail. *Loan Period:* as needed. *Total Yr Film Loan:* 349.

Film Collection 26t/p. Approx 5t acquired annually. *Circ:* 16mm, 26t.

Other Film Serv Rent film from distributors for patrons, obtain film from coop loan system (Assn for Media & Technol in Education in Canada), obtain film from other libraries. *Equipment:* lend S8mm camera (3), 16mm sound projector (10), S8mm cartridge projector (2), S8mm reel projector (2), projection screens (50).

Other Media Collections *Audio:* disc, 33⅓ rpm, 93t/c; tape, cassette, 871t/c; tape, reel, 63t/c. *Filmstrips:* silent, 70t. *Slides:* single, 8000t.

Budget & Expenditures Total library budget $140,000 (FY 4/1/74-4/1/75). Total FY film budget $4588.

Video Serv *Est:* 1970. *In Charge:* James Doran, Supervisor. *Video Staff:* 1 p-t, 6 tech. *Video Use:* documentation of community/school events, to increase community's library use, community video access, in-service training. Video serv available on demand. Produce video tapes. Have production studio/space & separate control room.

Video Equipment/Facilities *In-House Use Only:* portapak (1), ½" b&w, Sony 5000; recording deck (12), ½" b&w, Sony 3600; playback deck (6), ½" b&w, Panasonic; editing deck (2), ½" col, Sony 8650; monitor (24), b&w/col; SEG (1), Sony; microphones (12); tripods (6); audio tape recorders (200). *For Loan:* recording deck (12), ½" b&w, Sony 3600; playback deck (6), ½" b&w, Panasonic; monitor (24), b&w/col; microphones (12); tripods (6); audio tape recorders (200). Have portable viewing installation. *Equipment Loan Period:* 1-2 days. Provide training in use of equipment to faculty & students.

Video Tape Loan/Rental/Sale Serv *Serv Provided:* swap with other inst, sale. *Loan Eligibility:* staff & students,

educational inst, civic groups, religious groups, indiv with library cards. *Restrictions:* for indiv, interlibrary loan; for inst, none. Cannot use for fund-raising, duplicate, air without permission. *Total Yr Tape Loan:* 1378.

Video Collection Maintained by purchase, own production, exchange/swap. Use/play ½" reel to reel. *Sources:* commercial distributors, exchange (educational inst). *Tape Sel:* preview, faculty/staff recommendations. Tapes organized by subject. *Collection, B&W:* ½" reel, 176t/c. *Other Video Serv:* taping of other media, production workshops.

Cable & CCTV Produce programs for cablecast at cable studios.

Kitchener

P- KITCHENER PUBLIC LIBRARY, 85 Queen St North, N2H 2H1. *Tel:* (519) 743-0271, ext 56. *Film Serv Est:* 1944. *In Charge:* Carmen Lichtenheldt, Head of Film & Video Services. *AV Staff:* 4 (1 tech). *Film Sel:* committee preview, staff recommendations, preview by dept head.

Film Rental Serv *Eligibility:* no restrictions. *Restrictions:* only in province. Cannot use for fund-raising, transmit electronically. *Rental Period:* 3 days. *Total Yr Film Booking:* 20,194.

Film Collection 1029t/1112p. Approx 100t acquired annually. *Circ:* 16mm, 1029t/1112p. *Pubns:* catalog, every 3 yrs ($3); suppl, in yr catalog not published.

Other Film Serv Obtain film from coop loan system (National Film Board), obtain film from other libraries, film reference serv, film fairs/festivals, library film programs. Permanent viewing facility available for rent to community. *Equipment:* rent 16mm sound projector (8), projection screens (5).

Other Media Collections *Audio:* disc, 6500t; tape, 485t.

Budget & Expenditures Total library budget $256,372 (FY 1/1/75-1/1/76). Total FY film budget $19,000. *Member:* ALA.

Video Serv *Est:* 1974. *Video Staff:* 4 f-t, 1 tech. *Video Use:* to increase community's library use, in-service training. Video serv available on demand. Produce video tapes.

Video Equipment/Facilities *In-House Use Only:* recording deck (1), ¾" col, Sony; playback deck (2), ¾" col, Sony; monitor (1), 12" col, Sony; microphones (3); tripods (1); audio tape recorders (1); receivers (3). *For Loan:* cassettes (35). Have portable viewing installation.

Video Tape Loan/Rental/Sale Serv May not borrow by mail.

Video Collection Maintained by purchase. Use/play ¾" cassette. *Sources:* community productions. *Tape Sel:* faculty/staff recommendations, catalogs. Tapes organized by title. *Collection, Color:* ¾" cassette, 135t. *Other Video Serv* catalog.

Cable & CCTV Receive serv of cable TV system. Produce programs for cablecasting. *Programming Sources:* over-the-air commercial & public broadcasting.

S- KITCHENER WATERLOO ART GALLERY, 43 Benton St, N2G 3H1. *Tel:* (519) 745-6671.

Film Serv Rent film from distributors for patrons, obtain film from coop loan system (Ont. Assn of Art Galleries), obtain film from other libraries. Permanent viewing facility available for rent to community.

Other Media Collections *Slides:* single, 300c; sets, 8c.

Budget & Expenditures Total library budget $200 (FY 4/74-4/75). No separate AV budget.

Video Serv *Video Use:* as art form. Have production studio/space & separate control room.

Video Collection *Sources:* galleries, community productions. *Other Video Serv:* production workshops.

Cable & CCTV Receive serv of cable TV system. Produce programs for cablecasting.

Lindsay

P- LINDSAY PUBLIC LIBRARY, 190 Kent St. W, K9V 2Y6. *Tel:* (705) 324-5632. *Film Serv Est:* 1968. *In Charge:* Moti

Lindsay (cont.)

Tahiliani, Chief Librarian. *AV Staff:* 1 tech. *Film Sel:* chief film librarian's decision.

Free-Loan Film Serv *Eligibility:* educational inst. *Restrictions:* for indiv & inst, only in Victoria County. Cannot use outside school programming. May borrow by mail. *Loan Period:* 5 days. *Total Yr Film Loan:* 7458.

Film Rental Serv *Eligibility:* no restrictions. *Restrictions:* only in Victoria County. Fee will be charged if film is damaged. *Rental Period:* 1 day. *Total Yr Film Booking:* 7458.

Film Collection 600t/p. Approx 20t acquired annually. *Circ:* 16mm, 600t/p. *Pubns:* catalog, every 3 yrs; suppl, in yr catalog not published.

Other Film Serv Rent film from distributors for patrons, obtain film from coop loan system (Lake Ontario Regional Library System). Permanent viewing facility available for rent to community. *Equipment:* rent 16mm sound projector (4), 8mm reel projector (1), S8mm reel projector (1), projection screens (4); cassette player (1); slide projector (1); speakers (1).

Other Media Collections *Audio:* tape, cassette, 77c; tape, reel, 208c.

Budget & Expenditures Total library budget $1000 (FY 1974-1975). No separate AV budget.

Video Serv *Video Staff:* 1 tech. *Video Use:* to increase community's library use, educational inst. Video serv available on demand.

London

P- LAKE ERIE REGIONAL LIBRARY SYSTEM, 380 Saskatoon St, N5W 4R3. *Film Serv Est:* 1963. *In Charge:* Shirley Edgar, Coord Information Serv. *AV Staff:* 3 (2 cl, 1 tech). *Film Sel:* committee preview, chief film librarian's decision.

Free-Loan Film Serv *Eligibility:* indiv with library cards. *Restrictions:* for indiv & inst, only members of libraries. Cannot transmit electronically. Available to researchers/scholars for on-site viewing. May borrow by mail. *Loan Period:* 3 days.

Film Collection 2000t. *Pubns:* catalog, every 2 yrs ($2); suppl, in yr catalog not published ($1).

Other Film Serv Obtain film from coop loan system, film reference serv, library film programs. Permanent viewing facility. *Equipment:* lend 16mm sound projector (2). *Member:* OECA.

Video Serv *Est:* 1974. *In Charge:* Shirley Edgar, Coord, Informative Serv. *Video Use:* to increase community's library use, general entertainment. Video serv available on demand.

Video Equipment/Facilities *In-House Use Only:* portapak (1), col; recording deck (1), col, Sony; playback deck (3), Sony. Have portable viewing installation. *Equipment Loan Period:* no set policy.

Video Tape Loan/Rental/Sale Serv *Serv Provided:* free loan, swap with other inst. *Loan Eligibility:* org members. *Restrictions:* for indiv, interlibrary loan; for inst, none. Cannot air without permission. May borrow by mail. *Loan Period:* 28 days.

Video Collection Maintained by purchase. Use/play ¾" cassette. *Sources:* commercial distributors. *Tape Sel:* preview, catalogs. Tapes organized by computer catalog. *Collection, Color:* ¾" cassette, 20t. *Collection, B&W:* ¾" cassette, 150t. *Other Video Serv:* reference serv, catalog.

C- UNIVERSITY OF WESTERN ONTARIO, Teaching Aids/Resource Centre, 1137 Western Rd, N6A 3K7. *Tel:* (519) 679-3902. *Video Serv Est:* 1967. *In Charge:* C. M. Heddington, Dir, Teaching Aids Centre. *Video Staff:* 2 p-t, 3 tech. *Video Use:* documentation of community/school events, in-service training, playback only of professionally produced tapes, as art form, microteaching. Video serv available by appointment. Produce video tapes. Have production studio/space.

Video Equipment/Facilities *In-House Use Only:* recording deck (8), ½" b&w, Sony 3400; playback deck (8), ½" b&w, Sony 3600, 3650; editing deck (1), ½" col, Sony 8650; studio camera (1), ½" col, Hitachi VS530; monitor (2), 1" b&w, Sony;

SEG (5), Sony; additional camera lenses (6); lighting (6); microphones (6); audio tape recorders (150). Have permanent & portable viewing installations. *Equipment Loan Period:* 1 day. Provide training in use of equipment to faculty & student teachers. Have tape duplication serv.

Video Tape Loan/Rental/Sale Serv *Loan Eligibility:* org members, students enrolled in inst, staff & students, educational inst, & others, such as special schools. *Restrictions:* for indiv, only in city. Cannot use for fund-raising, duplicate, air without permission. May not borrow by mail.

Video Collection Maintained by purchase, rental, own production, exchange/swap. Use/play ½", 1" reel to reel. *Sources:* commercial distributors. *Tape Sel:* preview, faculty/staff recommendations, catalogs. *Special Collections:* in-house training tapes. Tapes organized by subject.

Cable & CCTV Receive serv of cable TV system. Have CCTV in inst, with 34 monitors. *Programming Sources:* over-the-air commercial & public broadcasting, tapes produced by inst.

Midland

P- MIDLAND PUBLIC LIBRARY, Film Dept, 320 King St, L4R 3M6. *Tel:* (705) 526-5811. *Film Serv Est:* 1967. *In Charge:* Eileen D. Boden, Deputy Librarian. *Holdings:* general interest films 60%.

Free-Loan Film Serv *Eligibility:* indiv with library cards. *Restrictions:* for indiv & inst interlibrary loan. Cannot use for fund-raising, transmit electronically. Available to researchers/scholars for on-site viewing. May borrow by mail. *Loan Period:* 1 day. *Total Yr Film Loan:* 508.

Film Collection 60t/p. Approx 2-3t acquired annually.

Other Film Serv Rent film from coop loan system (Georgian Bay Regional Library Service), obtain film from other libraries, film reference serv. Permanent viewing facility. *Equipment:* rent 16mm sound projector (3), projection screens (3).

Video Serv *Est:* 1975. *In Charge:* C. G. MacKenzie, Reference Librarian. *Video Staff:* 1 f-t, 1 p-t, 1 tech. *Video Use:* to increase community's library use, community video access, playback only of professionally produced tapes. Video serv available by appointment.

Video Equipment/Facilities Have portable viewing installation. *Equipment Loan Period:* may not borrow. Provide training in use of equipment to group leaders. Have tape duplication serv.

Video Collection Use/play ¾" cassette. *Sources:* regional system. *Member:* Georgian Bay Regional Library System. *Tape Sel:* staff requests, catalogs. Tapes organized by subject. *Other Video Serv:* reference serv. *Pubns:* catalog.

Mississauga

P- MISSISSAUGA PUBLIC LIBRARY, AV Dept, 110 Dundas West L5B. *Tel:* (416) 279-7002. *Film Serv Est:* 1965. *In Charge:* Ann Eddie, Head, AV Dept. *AV Staff:* 7 (2 prof, 2 cl, 3 tech). *Film Sel:* committee preview.

Free-Loan Film Serv *Eligibility:* indiv with library cards. *Restrictions:* for indiv & inst, only in city. Cannot use for fund-raising, transmit electronically, borrow for classroom use. Available to researchers/scholars for on-site viewing. May not borrow by mail. *Loan Period:* 1 day. *Total Yr Film Loan:* 13,738.

Film Collection 696t/p. Approx 150t acquired annually. *Circ:* 16mm, 696t/p. *Noncirc:* 16mm, 2t/p. *Pubns:* catalog, annual ($3.50); suppl, 6 months after catalog.

Other Film Serv Obtain film from coop loan system (Central Ont. Regional Library System), obtain film from other libraries, film reference serv, library film programs. Permanent viewing facility available for rent to community. *Equipment:* rent 16mm sound projector (14), projection screens (5).

Other Media Collections *Audio:* tape, cassette, 3676c.

Budget & Expenditures Total FY film budget $40,000 (FY 1/1/75-1/1/76). *Member:* ALA, EFLA, Ont. Film Assn.

Newmarket

P- NEWMARKET PUBLIC LIBRARY, 438 Park Ave, L3Y 1W1. *Tel:* (416) 895-5196. *Film Serv Est:* 1960. *In Charge:* Mrs. J. Lindsay, AV Technician. *AV Staff:* 2. *Film Sel:* committee preview. *Holdings:* animated films 20%, children's films 30%.

Free-Loan Film Serv *Eligibility:* indiv with library cards. *Restrictions:* for indiv, interlibrary loan; for inst, only in city. Cannot borrow for classroom use. Available to researchers/scholars for on-site viewing. May not borrow by mail. *Loan Period:* 1 day. *Total Yr Film Loan:* 680.

Film Collection 200t/p. Approx 20-30t acquired annually. *Pubns:* catalog, annual; suppl, no set policy. Publish flyers.

Other Film Serv Obtain film from coop loan system (Central Ont. Regional Library System), obtain film from other libraries, library film programs. *Equipment:* lend 16mm sound projector (5), 8mm reel projector (2), projection screens (3).

Other Media Collections *Audio:* tape, cassette, 250c.

Budget & Expenditures Total library budget $55,756 (FY 1/1/75-1/1/76). Total FY film budget $5500. *Member:* ALA, Canadian Library Assn, Ont. Library Assn.

North Bay

P- NORTH BAY & DISTRICT FILM COUNCIL, North Bay Public Library, 271 Worthington St, East, P1B 1H1. *Tel:* (705) 474-4830, ext 25. *Film Serv Est:* 1961-62. *In Charge:* Florence Sanders, AV Dept. *AV Staff:* 1. *Film Sel:* committee preview. *Holdings:* general interest films.

Film Rental Serv *Eligibility:* no restrictions. *Restrictions:* only in city. Cannot transmit electronically. *Rental Period:* 1-2 days.

Film Collection 800t/p. Approx 8-12t acquired annually. *Circ:* 16mm, 800t/p; S8mm reel, 60t/p. *Pubns:* catalog, annual.

Other Film Serv Obtain film from coop loan system (Northern Ont. Film Federation), obtain film from other libraries, film reference serv. *Equipment:* lend/rent 16mm sound projector (5), S8mm reel projector (4), projection screens (6).

Other Media Collections *Audio:* disc, 33⅓ rpm, 368t/c; tape, cassette, 266t/c.

Budget & Expenditures No separate budget. *Member:* Ont. Film Assn.

Video Serv *Est:* 1975. *Video Staff:* 1 f-t. *Video Use:* to increase community's library use, as art form. Video serv available on demand & by appointment.

Video Equipment/Facilities Have portable viewing installation. *Equipment Loan Period:* 1 day.

Video Tape Loan/Rental/Sale Serv *Serv Provided:* free loan. *Loan Eligibility:* civic groups, religious groups, indiv with library cards. *Restrictions:* for indiv & inst, only in city. May borrow by mail. *Loan Period:* 7 days.

Video Collection Maintained by exchange/swap. Use/play ½″ reel to reel. *Member:* Northern Ont. Film Federation. *Collection, Color:* ½″ reel, 40t/c; ¼″ reel, 40t/c.

Oakville

P- OAKVILLE PUBLIC LIBRARY, 120 Navy St, L6J 2Z4. *Tel:* (416) 845-3405, ext 0, 22. *In Charge:* Patricia Wiebe, Coord AV Serv. *AV Staff:* 2 (1 cl, 1 tech). *Film Sel:* committee preview.

Film Rental Serv *Eligibility:* patrons/public. *Restrictions:* only in region (other regions by ILLO). Cannot use for fund-raising, transmit electronically. *Rental Period:* 1 day. *Total Yr Film Booking:* 8497.

Film Collection 250t/p. Approx 20t acquired annually. *Circ:* 16mm, 250t/p; 8mm reel, 50t. *Pubns:* catalog, every 2 yr ($2); suppl, in yr catalog not published.

Other Film Serv Rent film from distributors for patrons, obtain film from other libraries, film reference serv, library film programs. Permanent viewing facility available for rent to community. *Equipment:* rent 16mm sound projector (2), 8mm reel projector (2), S8mm reel projector (2), projection screens (2).

Other Media Collections *Audio:* disc, 33⅓ rpm, 300t/c; tape, cassette, 250t/c.

Budget & Expenditures Total FY film budget $6000 (FY 1/75-1/76). *Member:* Ont. Film Assn.

Video Serv *Est:* 1975. *Video Staff:* 2 f-t, 4 p-t, 1 tech. *Video Use:* community video access, playback only of professionally produced tapes. Video serv available on demand & by appointment. Produce video tapes (at community cable station).

Video Equipment/Facilities *In-House Use Only:* recording deck (1), ¾″ col, Sony; playback deck (1), ¾″ col, Sony; monitor (1), Sony; 1 Sony timer. Have portable viewing installation. *Equipment Loan Period:* no set policy. Provide training in use of equipment.

Video Tape Loan/Rental/Sale Serv *Serv Provided:* swap with other inst. *Restrictions:* for indiv, interlibrary loan; for inst, only in SCL region. Cannot use for fund-raising, duplicate, air without permission, remove from library. *Loan Period:* as long as required.

Video Collection Maintained by purchase, exchange/swap. Use/play ¾″ cassette. *Sources:* commercial distributors, exchange (loan only by regional libraries). *Tape Sel:* preview, published reviews, catalogs. Tapes organized by subject. *Collection, Color:* ¾″ cassette, 125t/c. *Other Video Serv:* production workshops. *Pubns:* catalog.

Cable & CCTV Receive serv of cable TV system. Produce programs for cablecasting.

Orillia

P- ORILLIA PUBLIC LIBRARY, 36 Mississaga St, W, L3V 3A6. *Tel:* (705) 325-2338. *In Charge:* Olive Doughty, Head, Film Dept. *AV Staff:* 2 (1 cl, 1 tech). *Film Sel:* chief film librarian's decision.

Free-Loan Film Serv *Eligibility:* indiv with library cards. *Restrictions:* city residents & surrounding townships. Cannot use for fund-raising, transmit electronically. Available to researchers/scholars for on-site viewing. *Loan Period:* 1 day. *Total Yr Film Loan:* 3273.

Film Collection 172t/p. Approx 9t acquired annually. *Circ:* 8mm cartridge, 38t/p. *Pubns:* catalog, every 2 yr; suppl, in yr catalog not published.

Other Film Serv Rent film from distributors for patrons, obtain film from coop loan system (Georgian Bay Regional Library System), film reference serv, library film programs. *Equipment:* lend 16mm sound projector, projection screen.

Other Media Collections *Audio:* disc, 33⅓ rpm, 360t/361c; tape, cassette, 63t/c. *Slides:* sets, 3t/c.

Budget & Expenditures Total library budget $28,174 (FY 1/74-1/75). Total FY film budget $1000. *Member:* ALA, Ont. Library Assn, Canadian Library Assn.

Video Serv *Est:* 1975. *In Charge:* Edna Steeper, Head, Circulation Dept. *Video Use:* playback only of professionally produced tapes. Video serv available on demand.

Video Equipment/Facilities *In-House Use Only:* playback deck (1), cassette, col, Sony VP1200; monitor (1), col, Sony; audio tape recorders (1). Have portable viewing installation. Provide training in use of equipment.

Video Collection Maintained by purchase. Use/play ¾″ cassette. *Sources:* commercial distributors. *Member:* Georgian Bay Regional Library System. *Tape Sel:* catalogs. *Special Collections:* films in video format. Tapes organized alphabetically. *Collection, Color:* ¾″ cassette, 56t. *Other Video Serv:* catalog of videotapes available.

Cable & CCTV Produce programs for cablecasting.

Oshawa

P- OSHAWA PUBLIC LIBRARY, Film Servs—McLaughlin Building, 65 Bagot St, L1H 1N2. *Tel:* (416) 723-2725. *Film Serv Est:* 1946. *In Charge:* Isia Scott, AV Specialist. *AV Staff:* 4 (2 cl). *Film Sel:* committee preview, chief film librarian's decision.

Free-Loan Film Serv *Eligibility:* civic groups, religious groups, indiv with library cards. *Restrictions:* for indiv, none; interlibrary loan. Cannot use for fund-raising, transmit elec-

Oshawa (cont.)
tronically. Available to researchers/scholars for on-site viewing. May borrow by mail. *Loan Period:* 1 day or special arrangement. *Total Yr Film Loan:* 26,679.

Film Collection 1000t. Approx 100t acquired annually. *Circ:* 16mm, 1000p; 8mm reel, 107p; S8mm reel, 182p. *Pubns:* catalog, every 2 yr ($1); suppl, no set policy. Publish materials pertaining to collection.

Other Film Serv Obtain film from coop loan system (Central Ont. Regional Library System), film reference serv, film fairs/festivals, library film programs. Permanent viewing facility available for rent to community. *Equipment:* rent 16mm sound projector, 8mm reel projector, S8mm reel projector, projection screens.

Other Media Collections *Audio:* 5890c; tape, cassette, 543c; tape, reel, 34c. *Filmstrips:* silent, 339c. *Slides:* sets, 22c.

Budget & Expenditures Total library budget $171,000. (FY 1/74-1/75). Total FY film budget $27,000. *Member:* EFLA, Ont. Film Assn, Canadian Music Library Assn.

S- **THE ROBERT McLAUGHLIN GALLERY**, Civic Center. *Tel:* (416) 576-3000. *Film Serv Est:* 1975. *In Charge:* Gisele Pageau, Public Relations, Dir. *AV Staff:* 1. *Film Sel:* interviews with Canadian artists. *Holdings:* fine arts 100%.

Free-Loan Film Serv *Eligibility:* indiv with library cards, & others in very special circumstances. *Restrictions:* for indiv & inst, only in city. Cannot use for fund-raising. Available to researchers/scholars for on-site viewing. May not borrow by mail. *Loan Period:* 7 days. *Pubns:* catalog.

Other Film Serv Obtain film from other libraries, film reference serv.

Video Serv *Est:* 1975. *Video Staff:* 1 f-t. *Video Use:* as art form. Video serv available by appointment. Produce video tapes.

Video Equipment/Facilities Have portable viewing installation. *Equipment Loan Period:* 7 days.

Video Tape Loan/Rental/Sale Serv *Serv Provided:* free loan. *Loan Eligibility:* indiv with library cards, prof groups, such as artists & others, such as those directly involved in art. *Restrictions:* for indiv & inst, only in city. Cannot use for fund-raising, duplicate. May not borrow by mail. *Loan Period:* 7 days.

Video Collection Maintained by own production. *Sources:* galleries. *Tape Sel:* gallery previews. *Special Collections:* video as art. Tapes organized alphabetically. *Other Video Serv:* special events at gallery.

Cable & CCTV Receive serv of cable TV system. *Programming Sources:* tapes produced by community groups & indiv.

Ottawa

P- **EASTERN ONTARIO REGIONAL LIBRARY SYSTEM**, 120 Metcalfe St, K1P 5M2. *Tel:* (613) 236-0301, ext 219. *Video Serv Est:* 1975. *In Charge:* Albert Parsons, AV Coord. *Video Staff:* 1 f-t. *Video Use:* to increase community's library use, community video access, as art form. Video serv available on demand.

Video Equipment/Facilities *In-House Use Only:* playback deck (5), col; editing deck (1), col; monitor (6), col; audio tape recorders (1). Have permanent viewing installation. *Equipment Loan Period:* no set policy. Provide training in use of equipment to library personnel, public.

Video Tape Loan/Rental/Sale Serv *Serv Provided:* swap with other inst. *Restrictions:* for indiv, interlibrary loan, only in Eastern Ont.

Video Collection Maintained by purchase, exchange/swap. Use/play ¾″ cassette. *Sources:* commercial distributors. *Tape Sel:* catalogs. *Special Collections:* films in video format. *Collection, Color:* ¾″ cassette, 275t. *Collection, B&W:* ¾″ cassette, 25t.

Cable & CCTV Receive serv of cable TV system. Inform public about cable system serv & facilities.

A- **NATIONAL GALLERY OF CANADA**, Elgin & Slater. K1A 0M8. *Tel:* (613) 992-4636. *In Charge:* Michael Pan-

tazzi, Head of Education Serv. *Film Sel:* committee preview. *Holdings:* fine arts 100%.

Film Rental Serv *Eligibility:* art galleries, adult study groups, universities. *Restrictions:* no foreign countries. New films & new prints acquired by the National Gallery are automatically turned over to Canadian Film Institute, 1762 Carling Ave, Ottawa, for distribution. Rental charged does not revert to the National Gallery but to the CFI. *Rental Period:* as long as is needed—occasionally for months. Fund the production of films on art, about one each year, in two versions, French and English. Production is carried out by the National Film Board, another Government agency.

Film Collection 400t/12c. Approx 6t acquired annually. *Circ:* 16mm, 400t/12c. *Noncirc:* 16mm, 3t. *Pubns:* catalog, annual.

Other Film Serv Permanent viewing facility available for rent to community. *Equipment:* 16mm sound projector (2), projection table/stand (1). In 1963 the Canadian Centre for Films on Art, 150 Kent St, Ottawa, was created to coordinate the many films on art collections in the country. Jointly funded by the National Gallery of Canada, the National Film Board, & the Canada Council, it serves as an information center which advises the National Gallery on purchase of films, offers free services to those needing advice on programming, & publishes annually a catalog of films on art available in Canada. The catalog appears every second year in English & every other year in French & is distributed free of charge.

Budget & Expenditures Total library budget $5000 (FY 4/75-4/76). Total FY film budget $5000. Two budgets are maintained: one remains in the National Gallery & is spent on renting films which are shown free of charge in the Gallery's 470-seat auditorium (screen approx 500 films per year), & the other is spent on acquisition of either new films or new prints given to CFI for distribution. *Member:* National Museums of Canada.

P- **OTTAWA PUBLIC LIBRARY FILM SERVS**, 120 Metcalfe St, K1P 5M2. *Tel:* (613) 236-0301, ext 265. *Film Serv Est:* 1950's. *In Charge:* William J. Wallis, AV Librarian. *AV Staff:* 3 (1 prof, 2 cl). *Film Sel:* committee preview, chief film librarian's decision. *Holdings:* children's films 40%.

Film Rental Serv *Eligibility:* no restrictions. *Restrictions:* only in region (Eastern Ontario Regional System). Cannot use for fund-raising, transmit electronically. *Rental Period:* 7 days. *Total Yr Film Booking:* 18,283.

Film Collection 500t/p. Approx 100t acquired annually. *Circ:* 16mm, 500t. *Pubns:* catalog, as needed; suppl, no set policy, (free).

Other Film Serv Obtain film from other libraries, film reference serv, library film programs. *Equipment:* rent 16mm sound projector (4), 8mm reel projector (1), S8mm reel projector (1), projection screens (6).

Other Media Collections *Audio:* 7000t. *Filmstrips:* silent, 400t; sound sets, 100t.

Budget & Expenditures Total library budget $531,000 (FY 1/1/75-1/1/76). Total FY film budget $20,000.

C- **OTTAWA UNIVERSITY**, Resource Library, Morisset Library, 65 Hastey, K1N 9A5. *Tel:* (613) 231-2374/2375. *Film Serv Est:* 1969. *In Charge:* Raynald Brassard, Manager. *AV Staff:* 7. *Film Sel:* committee preview, faculty/staff recommendations, chief film librarian's decision. *Holdings:* animated films 3%, communications & media 3%, experimental films 4%, feature films 10%, fine arts 7%, management 3%, medicine 11%, physical education 8%, science 14%, social sciences 11%.

Free-Loan Film Serv *Eligibility:* educational inst on reciprocity basis. *Restrictions:* for indiv, interlibrary loan; for inst in Canada on reciprocity basis. Cannot use for fund-raising. Available to researchers/scholars for on-site viewing. May borrow by mail. *Loan Period:* 5 days. *Total Yr Film Loan:* 3500.

Film Collection 755t/p. Approx 15t acquired annually. *Circ:* 16mm, 600t/p; S8mm cartridge, 157t/p. *Noncirc:* 16mm, 1t/1p. *Pubns:* catalog (unit cost); as needed.

Other Film Serv Rent film from distributors for patrons, obtain film from other libraries, film reference serv, film fairs/festivals. Permanent viewing facility available for rent to community.

Other Media Collections *Audio:* tape, cassette, 150t/c; tape, reel, 101t/c. *Filmstrips:* silent, 30t/c; sound sets, 32t/c; silent sets, approx 50,000t. *Slides:* sets, 17t.

Owen Sound

P- OWEN SOUND PUBLIC LIBRARY, 824 First Ave E, N4K 2H4. *Tel:* (519) 376-6623. *Film Serv Est:* 1969. *In Charge:* Marguerite Mercer, Film Librarian. *AV Staff:* 1. *Film Sel:* chief film librarian's decision. *Holdings:* agriculture 3%, animated films 15%, black studies 1%, children's films 25%, consumer affairs 1%, dance 5%, experimental films 6%, fine arts 8%, industrial arts 3%, science 12%, social sciences 21%.

Free-Loan Film Serv *Eligibility:* educational inst, prof groups, & others in Georgian Bay Regional Library System. *Restrictions:* for indiv, interlibrary loan in 4 counties; for inst, only in Georgian Bay Regional Library System. May not borrow by mail. *Loan Period:* 1 day. *Total Yr Film Loan:* 4573.

Film Collection 400t/p. *Circ:* 16mm, 400t/p; 8mm reel, 50t/p. *Pubns:* catalog, every 2 yrs; suppl, no set policy.

Other Film Serv Obtain film from coop loan system (Georgian Bay Regional Library System), obtain film from other libraries, film reference serv, film fairs/festivals, library film programs. Permanent viewing facility available for rent to community. *Equipment:* rent 16mm sound projector (8), projection screens, slide projectors.

Pembroke

P- PEMBROKE PUBLIC LIBRARY, 237 Victoria St, K8A 6X3. *Tel:* (613) 732-8844. *Film Serv Est:* 1968. *In Charge:* Brian Hobbs, AV Librarian. *AV Staff:* 3. *Film Sel:* chief film librarian's decision. *Holdings:* agriculture 5%, animated films 15%, black studies 2%, career education 1%, children's films 10%, consumer affairs 5%, experimental films 10%, feature films 10%, fine arts 10%, medicine 10%, science 10%, social sciences 10%, women 2%.

Film Rental Serv *Eligibility:* no restrictions. *Restrictions:* members of libraries in Ont. & Que. school boards. *Rental Period:* 7 days. *Total Yr Film Booking:* 2500.

Film Collection 650t/600p. Approx 50-70t acquired annually. *Circ:* 16mm, 575t/580p; 8mm reel, 60t/p; S8mm reel, 85t/p. *Pubns:* catalog, as needed (free); suppl, no set policy.

Other Film Serv Obtain film from coop loan system (Film Federation of Eastern Ont.), obtain film from other libraries, film fairs/festivals. Permanent viewing facility available. *Equipment:* rent 16mm sound projector (6), 8mm reel projector (4), S8mm reel projector, rent projection tables & stands, projection screens, 35mm slide projector (1).

Other Media Collections *Audio:* disc, 33⅓ rpm, 1226t/1300c. *Filmstrips:* sound, 46t/c. silent, 190t/c.

Budget & Expenditures Total library budget $20,000 (FY 1/75-1/76). Total FY film budget $5000. *Member:* Eastern Ont. Library System.

Peterborough

P- PETERBOROUGH PUBLIC LIBRARY, 510 George St North, K9H 3R8. *Tel:* (705) 745-5831. *In Charge:* Gladys Mansell, Film Librarian. *AV Staff:* 1 (1 tech). *Film Sel:* chief film librarian's decision.

Film Rental Serv *Eligibility:* no restrictions. *Restrictions:* only in Lake Ont. Regional Library Serv. Cannot use for fund-raising, transmit electronically. *Rental Rate:* $10 annual or $1 per film. *Rental Period:* 1 day. *Total Yr Film Booking:* 3926.

Film Collection 501t/507p. Approx 30t acquired annually. *Circ:* 16mm, 456t/462p; 8mm reel, 30t/p; S8mm reel, 15t/p. *Pubns:* catalog, as needed (free); suppl, in yr catalog not published (free).

Other Film Serv Obtain film from coop loan system (Lake Ont. Regional Library Serv), obtain film from other libraries, library film programs. *Equipment:* rent projection screens (3), filmstrip projector, slide projector.

Other Media Collections *Audio:* 1000t/c.

Budget & Expenditures Total FY film budget $2800 (FY 1/1/75-1/1/76). *Member:* FLIC.

C- SIR SANDFORD FLEMING COLLEGE OF APP. ARTS & TECHNOLOGY LIBRARY, Brealey Drive, K9J 7B1. *Tel:* (705) 743-5610, ext 268, 269. *Film Serv Est:* 1968. *AV Staff:* 4 (1 prof, 1 cl, 3 tech). *Film Sel:* committee preview, faculty/staff recommendations, chief film librarian's decision, published reviews.

Free-Loan Film Serv *Eligibility:* staff & students, educational inst, civic groups. *Restrictions:* for indiv, only in Province of Ont. Cannot use for fund-raising. Available to researchers/scholars for on-site viewing. *Loan Period:* depends on need & availability.

Film Rental Serv *Eligibility:* faculty. *Restrictions:* no foreign countries. Cannot use for fund-raising, transmit electronically. *Total Yr Film Booking:* 1132.

Film Collection 240t. Approx 15t acquired annually. *Circ:* 16mm, 240t. *Pubns:* computer printout annual (free); suppl, no set policy.

Other Film Serv Rent film from distributors for patrons, obtain film from coop loan system (College Bibliocentre), obtain film from other libraries, film reference serv, library film programs. Permanent viewing facility. *Equipment:* lend 16mm sound projector, projection screens.

Other Media Collections *Audio:* tape, cassette, 250c. *Filmstrips:* silent, 400c. *Slides:* single, 6000c; sets, 268c.

Budget & Expenditures Total library budget $51,000 (FY 4/1/74-4/1/75). No separate AV budget.

Video Serv *Est:* 1970. *In Charge:* T. E. W. Robson, Manager AV Servs. *Video Staff:* 5 f-t, 3 p-t, 4 tech. *Video Use:* documentation of community/school events, in-service training. Video serv available on demand. Produce video tapes. Have production studio/space & separate control room.

Video Equipment/Facilities *In-House Use Only:* portapak (1), ½" b&w, Sony; recording deck (2), ½" b&w/col, 3650-5000; studio camera (2), b&w, Sony 3200; monitor (several), b&w/col; SEG (1); lighting (2); microphones (4); tripods (3); audio tape recorders (several). Have permanent & portable viewing installations.

Video Tape Loan/Rental/Sale Serv *Serv Provided:* free loan, swap with other inst, sale. *Loan Eligibility:* staff, students enrolled in inst, educational inst, civic groups. *Restrictions:* for inst, only in city. Cannot use for fund-raising, duplicate.

Video Collection Obtain tapes by purchase, rental, own production, exchange/swap. Use/play ½", 1", ¾" cassette. *Sources:* commercial distributors. *Member:* OEPA. *Tape Sel:* preview, faculty/staff recommendations. Tapes organized by subject & numerical listing. *Collection, B&W:* 1" reel, 250t; ¾" cassette, 200t.

Cable & CCTV Receive serv of cable TV system. Produce programs for cablecasting, community servs only. Have CCTV in inst. *Programming Sources:* over-the-air commercial & public broadcasting, tapes produced by inst, tapes produced professionally, tapes produced by community groups & indiv.

Port Colborne

P- PORT COLBORNE PUBLIC LIBRARY, 310 King St, L3K 4H1. *Tel:* (416) 834-6512. *Film Serv Est:* 1960. *In Charge:* Bette Kalailieff, Film Librarian. *AV Staff:* 2. *Film Sel:* committee preview, faculty/staff recommendations, published reviews. *Holdings:* children's films 50%.

Free-Loan Film Serv *Eligibility:* educational inst, civic groups, religious groups, indiv with library cards, prof groups, such as public health clinics & others, such as industries. *Restrictions:* for indiv, interlibrary loan, for inst, only in city. Cannot use for fund-raising, transmit electronically. May not borrow by mail. *Loan Period:* 1 day.

Port Colborne (cont.)

Film Collection 247t/247p. Approx 20t acquired annually. *Circ:* 16mm, 147t/p; 8mm reel, 65t/p; S8mm cartridge, 27t/p. *Pubns:* catalog, annual ($1.50); suppl, (free).

Other Film Serv Rent film from distributors for patrons, obtain film from coop loan system (Niagara Regional Library System), obtain film from other libraries, film reference serv, library film programs. Permanent viewing facility available for rent to community. *Equipment:* rent 16mm sound projector (4), 8mm reel projector (3), S8mm reel projector (1), projection screens (5), slide projector (1).

Other Media Collections *Audio:* 624t; tape, cassette, 50t. *Slides:* single, 310c; sets, 7c.

Budget & Expenditures Total library budget $3500 (FY 1/1/75-1/1/76). Total FY film budget $2500. *Member:* Ont. Film Assn.

Rexdale

P- ALBION LIBRARY, 1515 Albion Rd, M9V 1B7. *Tel:* (416) 741-7734. *Video Serv Est:* 1975. *In Charge:* Cathy Richardson, Head, AV Dept. *Video Staff:* 3 f-t, 1 tech. *Video Use:* to increase community's library use. Video serv available on demand & by appointment.

Video Equipment/Facilities *In-House Use Only:* recording deck (1), ¾″ col, Sony VO-1600; audio tape recorders (2). Have portable viewing installation. *Equipment Loan:* provide training in use of equipment to library patrons for in library use.

Video Collection Maintained by purchase. Use/play ¾″ cassette. *Sources:* Ont. Educational Communications Authority. *Tape Sel:* catalogs. Tapes organized by Dewey Decimal. *Collection, Color:* ¾″ cassette, 103t/c. *Collection, B&W:* ¾″ cassette, 20t/c.

Cable & CCTV Will receive serv of cable TV system.

C- HUMBER COLLEGE OF APPLIED ARTS & TECHNOLOGY, Instructional Materials Center, M9W 5L7. *Tel:* (416) 676-1200, ext 207. *Video Serv Est:* 1969. *In Charge:* A. Hiscoke, Chairman, IMC. *Video Staff:* 22 f-t, 3 p-t, 17 tech. *Video Use:* documentation of community/school events, in-service training, as art form, distribution & dubbing center. Video serv available on booking basis. Produce video tapes. Have production studio/space & separate control room.

Video Equipment/Facilities *In-House Use Only:* editing deck (6), ½″, 1″ b&w/col, Amp, Sony, Pan; tripods (3). *For Loan:* portapak (7), ½″ b&w/col, Sony, Panasonic; recording deck (20), ½″, 1″ b&w/col, Amp, Sony, Pan; playback deck (5), ½″, 1″ b&w/col, Amp, Sony, Pan; studio camera (3), Vid b&w, Ampex 327; monitor (30), b&w/col, Sony/Electonic; SEG (2); keyer (1); lighting (25); microphones (25); tripods (3); audio tape recorders (100). Have permanent viewing installation. *Equipment Loan Period:* 3 days. Provide training in use of equipment to faculty & students. Have tape duplication serv.

Video Tape Loan/Rental/Sale Serv *Serv Provided:* free loan, swap with other inst. *Loan Eligibility:* staff & students, educational inst. *Restrictions:* for indiv, only in city; for inst, none. Cannot use for fund-raising, duplicate, air without permission. May borrow by mail. *Loan Period:* 7 days. *Total Yr Tape Loan:* 200.

Video Collection Maintained by purchase, rental, own production, exchange/swap. Use/play ½″, 1″ reel to reel, ½″ cartridge, ¾″ cassette. *Tape Sel:* preview, faculty/staff recommendations, catalog. Tapes organized by subject, alphabetically. *Collection, Color:* ½″ reel, 600t. *Collection, B&W:* ½″ reel, 300t. *Other Video Serv:* programming, production workshops, catalog of video tapes available.

Cable & CCTV Produce programs for cablecasting. Have CCTV in inst, with 35 monitors.

Richmond Hill

P- RICHMOND HILL PUBLIC LIBRARY, 24 Wright St. *Tel:* (416) 884-0130. *Film Serv Est:* 1969. *In Charge:* Suzanne Buxton, AV Specialist. *AV Staff:* 2 (2 prof, 1 p-t cl, 1 p-t

tech). *Film Sel:* committee preview, chief film librarian's decision. *Holdings:* children's animated films 50%, comedy, feature films 2%, fine arts 7%, nature, social sciences 30%, sports, travel, women 3%.

Free-Loan Film Serv *Eligibility:* civic groups, religious groups, indiv with library cards, prof groups, such as doctors, social workers, business persons. *Restrictions:* for indiv, interlibrary loan, must be 18 yrs old. Cannot use for fund-raising, borrow for classroom use. Available to researchers/scholars for on-site viewing. May borrow by mail. *Loan Period:* 1 day. *Total Yr Film Loan:* 6000.

Film Collection 350t/p. Approx 30-50t acquired annually. *Pubns:* catalog, annual (free). Publish materials pertaining to collection.

Other Film Serv Obtain film from coop loan system, obtain film from other libraries, film reference serv, film fairs/festivals, library film programs. Permanent viewing facility available for rent to community. *Equipment:* rent 16mm sound projector, 8mm reel projector, S8mm reel projector, projection screens.

Other Media Collections *Audio:* disc, 33⅓ rpm, 600t; tape, cassette, 160t.

Budget & Expenditures Total FY film budget $10,000 (FY 1/75-1/76). *Member:* Ont. Film Assn.

St. Catharines

P- NIAGARA REGIONAL LIBRARY SYSTEM, St. Catharines Public Library, 59 Church St, L2R 3C3. *Tel:* (416) 684-8410. *Film Serv Est:* 1940's. *In Charge:* Margaret Tocque. *AV Staff:* 4 (3 cl, 1 tech). *Film Sel:* committee preview.

Free-Loan Film Serv *Restrictions:* for indiv, interlibrary loan, only in Niagara Regional System; for inst, only in Niagara Regional System. Cannot use for fund-raising, transmit electronically. Available to researchers/scholars for on-site viewing. May borrow by mail. *Loan Period:* 1 day. *Total Yr Film Loan:* 37,000.

Film Collection 850t. Approx 40-50t acquired annually. *Pubns:* catalog, annual; suppl, every 2 yrs.

Other Film Serv Rent film from distributors for patrons, obtain film from coop loan system, obtain film from other libraries, film reference serv, library film programs. Permanent viewing facility. *Equipment:* rent 16mm sound projector (4), 8mm cartridge projector (1), 8mm reel projector, projection screens (8), slide projector.

Other Media Collections *Audio:* disc, 33⅓ rpm, 6000t; tape, cassette, 400t. *Slides:* sets, 20t.

Budget & Expenditures Total FY film budget $15,000 (FY 1/75-1/76).

Sarnia

C- LAMBTON COLLEGE, Resource Centre, Box 969, N7T 6W6. *Tel:* (519) 542-7751, ext 261. *Film Serv Est:* 1967. *In Charge:* Margaret Turner, Librarian. *AV Staff:* 2 (2 tech). *Film Sel:* committee preview, faculty/staff recommendations.

Film Collection 310t. Approx 2-3t acquired annually. *Noncirc:* 16mm, 63t; S8mm reel, 247.

Other Film Serv Rent film from distributors for patrons, obtain film from other libraries.

Other Media Collections *Audio:* 500c. *Filmstrips:* sound, 305t. *Slides:* 1827c. *Member:* ALA.

Video Serv *Est:* 1969. *In Charge:* B. C. Allen, Supervisor, AV/TV Servs. *Video Staff:* 2 f-t, 2 p-t, 1 tech. *Video Use:* documentation of community/school events, practical video/TV training courses, as sales tool, teaching. Produce video tapes. Have production studio/space & separate control room.

Video Equipment/Facilities portapak (4), EIAJ b&w, Sony; recording deck (11), b&w/col, IVC, Sony, Pan; playback deck (2); editing deck (1), col, TRI, EAS; studio camera (8), b&w/col, Sony, IVC; SEG (4); additional camera lenses (6); microphones (30); tripods (15); audio tape recorders (10). Have permanent & portable viewing installations. *Equipment Loan Period:* provide training in use of equipment to faculty & students. Have tape duplication serv.

Video Collection Maintained by purchase, own production. Use/play ½", 1" reel to reel, ½" cartridge, ¾" cassette. *Sources:* commercial distributors. *Tape Sel:* preview, faculty/staff recommendations, published reviews, catalogs. Tapes organized by subject, accession. *Collection, Color:* ½" reel, 15t/1c; ½" cartridge, 7t/1c; ¾" cassette, 15t/1c. *Collection, B&W:* ½" reel, 101t/1c; ¾" cassette, 9t/1c. *Other Video Serv:* programming, taping of other media, production workshops.

Cable & CCTV Receive serv of cable TV system. Produce programs for cablecasting. Serve as production facility for others. Have CCTV in inst, with 12 monitors. *Programming Sources:* tapes produced by inst, tapes produced professionally, tapes produced by community groups & indiv.

Scarborough

C- CENTENNIAL COLLEGE OF APPLIED ARTS AND TECHNOLOGY, Centennial College—Resource Centre, 651 Warden Ave, M1L 3Z6. *Tel:* (416) 694-3241, ext 291. *In Charge:* Nancy Broomfield, AV Library Technician. *AV Staff:* 2½ (½ prof, 2 cl/tech). *Film Sel:* faculty/staff recommendations, chief film librarian's decision.

Free-Loan Film Serv *Eligibility:* staff & students, educational inst, civic groups, religious groups, & others, such as companies offering continuing education courses. *Restrictions:* for indiv & inst, none; only in Canada. Available to researchers/scholars for on-site viewing. May not borrow by mail. *Loan Period:* 1 day. *Total Yr Film Loan:* 1809.

Film Collection 600t. Approx 6t acquired annually. *Circ:* 16mm, 600t; 8mm reel, 2t; S8mm cartridge, 148t. *Pubns:* catalog, as needed (free); suppl, no set policy. Publish materials pertaining to collection. Publish newsletters regarding new acquisitions & films available for preview.

Other Film Serv Rent film from distributors for patrons, obtain film from other libraries, film reference serv. Permanent viewing facility. *Equipment:* lend 16mm sound projector.

Other Media Collections *Audio:* 1556c; tape, 1988c. *Filmstrips:* silent, 155t; silent sets, 379t. *Slides:* sets, 184t.

Budget & Expenditures Total library budget $71,695 (FY 4/1/75-4/1/76). No separate AV budget. *Member:* ALA, EFLA, Ont. Library Assn, Canadian Library Assn.

Video Serv *Est:* 1970. *In Charge:* Judy Downs, Librarian. *Video Staff:* 7 f-t, 1 p-t, 7 tech. *Video Use:* documentation of community/school events, playback only of professionally produced tapes. Video serv available by appointment.

Video Equipment/Facilities *In-House Use Only:* portapak (4), ½" b&w, Sony; recording deck (4), ½", ¾" col, Sony 5000A; playback deck (6), ½", ¾" col, Sony; editing deck (3), ½" b&w, Sony; studio camera (3), ½" b&w, Sony, Shibaden; monitor (1), Conrac; lighting (4); microphones (10); tripods (6); audio tape recorders (3). Have permanent viewing installation. *Equipment Loan Period:* 1 day. 24 hour notice required. Provide training in use of equipment.

Video Collection Maintained by purchase, own production. Use/play ½" reel to reel, ¾" cassette. *Sources:* commercial distributors. *Tape Sel:* preview, faculty/staff recommendations, cat. *Special Collections:* in-house training tapes. Tapes organized by accession number. *Collection, Color:* ½" reel, 700t/c; ¾" cassette, 300t/c. *Other Video Serv:* taping of other media, production workshops. *Pubns:* catalog.

Cable & CCTV Receive serv of cable TV system. Run cable programs for special audiences. Have CCTV in inst, with 60 monitors. *Programming Sources:* over-the-air commercial & public broadcasting, tapes produced by inst.

P- SCARBOROUGH PUBLIC LIBRARY, Albert Campbell District Library, 496 Birchmount Rd, M1K 1N8. *Tel:* (416) 698-1191. *In Charge:* Kathryn Elder, AV Librarian. *AV Staff:* 5 (1 prof, 3 cl, 1 tech). *Film Sel:* committee preview.

Free-Loan Film Serv *Eligibility:* educational inst, civic groups, religious groups, indiv with library cards, prof groups, & others, such as businesses, hospitals, government dept, social/welfare agencies. *Restrictions:* for indiv & inst, only in Metropolitan Toronto. Cannot use for fund-raising, transmit electroni-

cally. Available to researchers/scholars for on-site viewing. May not borrow by mail. *Loan Period:* 1 day. *Total Yr Film Loan:* 26,500.

Film Collection 905t/915p. Approx 75t acquired annually. *Circ:* 16mm, 905t/915p. *Pubns:* publish a description of film lending serv.

Other Film Serv Obtain film from coop loan system (Metropolitan Toronto Library Board), film reference serv, film fairs/festivals, library film programs. Permanent viewing facility available for rent to community. *Equipment:* lend/rent S8mm camera, lend/rent 16mm camera, lend 16mm sound projector (16), S8mm reel projector (4), projection screens (6).

Budget & Expenditures Total FY film budget $13,000 (FY 1/1/75-1/1/76). *Member:* EFLA, FLIC.

Video Serv *Video Use:* documentation of community/school events, to increase community's library use, in-service training. Video serv available on demand. Produce video tapes.

Video Equipment/Facilities *In-House Use Only:* portapak (1), ½" b&w, Sony 3400; recording deck (2), ½" b&w, Sony 3650; monitor (7), b&w, Sony; SEG (1), Admiral; keyer (1), Electrohome; microphones (5). Have portable viewing installation. Provide training in use of equipment to faculty & students.

Video Collection Maintained by purchase, own production. Use/play ½" reel to reel. *Tape Sel:* preview. Tapes organized by accession number. *Collection, B&W:* ½" reel, 70t/140c. *Other Video Serv:* programming, production workshops, catalog of video tapes available.

Cable & CCTV Receive serv of cable TV system. Produce programs for cablecasting. Inform public about cable system serv & facilities. Run cable programs for special audiences. Have CCTV in inst. *Programming Sources:* over-the-air commercial & public broadcasting, tapes produced by inst, tapes produced professionally.

Stratford

P- STRATFORD PUBLIC LIBRARY, AV Services, 19 St. Andrew's St, N5A 1A2. *Tel:* (519) 271-0220, ext 06. *In Charge:* Brian McKone, AV Librarian. *AV Staff:* 2 (1 prof, 1 cl, 1 tech). *Film Sel:* committee preview.

Film Rental Serv *Eligibility:* no restrictions. *Restrictions:* only in region (Perth, Waterloo, Wellington & Huron Counties). Cannot use for fund-raising, transmit electronically. *Rental Period:* 3 days. *Total Yr Film Booking:* 500.

Film Collection 265t/265p. Approx 25-30t acquired annually. *Circ:* 16mm, 265t/265p; 8mm cartridge, 85t/85p. *Pubns:* catalog, every 2 yr (free); suppl, no set policy (free).

Other Film Serv Obtain film from coop loan system (Regional Library System), film reference serv, library film programs. Permanent viewing facility available for rent to community. *Equipment:* rent S8mm camera (1), rent 16mm sound projector (7), rent 8mm reel projector (3), rent S8mm reel projector (3), rent projection screens, tape recorder, opaque projectors, transparency projectors, slide & film strip projectors, public address system.

Other Media Collections *Audio:* 750t/1c.

Video Serv *Est:* proposed Jan 1976. Information following submitted prior to that date. *Video Staff:* 1 f-t, 3 p-t. *Video Use:* to increase community's library use. Video serv available by appointment. Produce video tapes. Have production studio/space.

Video Equipment/Facilities *In-House Use Only:* ¾" equipment to be purchased. Have permanent viewing installation. *Equipment Loan Period:* no loan planned.

Video Tape Loan/Rental/Sale Serv *Serv Provided:* swap with other inst. *Loan Eligibility:* org members. *Restrictions:* for inst, regional libraries only. Cannot use for fund-raising, air without permission. May not borrow by mail.

Video Collection Planned for 1976. Use/play ¾" cassette. *Sources:* commercial distributors, exchange (regional libraries). *Member:* Midwestern Regional Library System. *Tape Sel:* preview, catalogs. *Special Collections:* films in video format. *Other Video Serv:* taping of other media.

Sudbury

P- SUDBURY PUBLIC LIBRARY, Sudbury & District Film Council, 74 MacKenzie St, P3C 4X8. *Tel:* (705) 673-1155, ext 32. *Film Serv Est:* 1948. *In Charge:* Mrs. R. Tremblay, Head, AV. *AV Staff:* 1 (1 cl). *Film Sel:* committee preview, National Film Board.
　　Film Rental Serv *Eligibility:* no restrictions. Cannot use for fund-raising, transmit electronically. *Rental Period:* 1 day. *Total Yr Film Booking:* 707.
　　Film Collection 172t/p. *Circ:* 16mm, 172t/p.
　　Other Film Serv Rent film from distributors for patrons, obtain film from coop loan system (Northern Ontario Film Federation), obtain film from other libraries, film reference serv, library film programs. Permanent viewing facility available for rent to community. *Equipment:* rent 16mm sound projector (7), rent projection screens (6).
　　Video Serv *Est:* 1975. *Video Use:* to increase community's library use. Video serv available on demand.
　　Video Equipment/Facilities *In-House Use Only:* deck (1), cassette col. Have portable viewing installation. *Equipment Loan Period:* 7 days.
　　Video Tape Loan/Rental/Sale Serv *Serv Provided:* free loan, swap with other inst. *Loan Eligibility:* indiv with library cards. *Restrictions:* only in city. Cannot duplicate. May not borrow by mail. *Loan Period:* 7 days. *Total Yr Tape Loan:* 26.
　　Video Collection Maintained by purchase, exchange/swap. Use/play ¾″ cassette. *Sources:* commercial distributors, exchange (Regional Headquarters). *Member:* North Central Regional Library System. *Tape Sel:* published reviews. Tapes organized by Dewey Decimal. *Collection, Color:* ¾″ cassette, 79t/c. *Collection, B&W:* ¾″ cassette, 18t/c. *Pubns:* catalog.

Thunder Bay

S- MONITOR NORTH, 324 John St. *Tel:* (807) 344-9156. *Video Serv Est:* 1973. *In Charge:* L. G. Stiller. *Video Staff:* 2 f-t. *Video Use:* documentation of community/school events, to increase community's library use, community video access, in-service training, political & social issues. Video serv available on demand. Produce video tapes.
　　Video Equipment/Facilities *In-House Use Only:* recording deck (2), ½″ b&w, Sony 3650; editing deck (1), ½″ b&w/col, Sony 8650. *For Loan:* portapak (4), ½″ b&w, Sony 3600; playback deck (1), ½″ b&w, Sony 3600; monitor (3), b&w, Sony; lighting (2); microphones (5); tripods (4); audio tape recorders (5). Have portable viewing installation. *Equipment Loan Period:* no set policy. Provide training in use of equipment. Have tape duplication serv.
　　Video Tape Loan/Rental/Sale Serv *Serv Provided:* free loan, swap with other inst. *Loan Eligibility:* org members, staff, staff & students, educational inst, civic groups, religious groups, indiv with library cards, prof groups. *Restrictions:* none. Cannot use for fund-raising. May borrow by mail. *Loan Period:* varies with need.
　　Video Collection Maintained by own production, exchange/swap. Use/play ½″ reel to reel. *Sources:* community productions, exchange (Government, Education, National Film Board). *Tape Sel:* preview, faculty/staff recommendations, published reviews, catalogs, personal contact. *Special Collections:* organizing, political & social process. Tapes organized alphabetically. *Collection, B&W:* ½″ reel, 42t/30c. *Other Video Serv:* reference serv, production workshops.
　　Cable & CCTV Receive serv of cable TV system. Produce programs for cablecasting. Inform public about cable system serv & facilities. Serve as production facility for others. Run cable programs for special audiences.

Toronto

S- ADDICTION RESEARCH FOUNDATION, 33 Russell St, M5S 2S1. *Tel:* (416) 595-6144. *Film Serv Est:* 1972. *In Charge:* R. J. Hall, Librarian. *AV Staff:* 1 (1 cl). *Film Sel:* committee preview. *Holdings:* alcoholism, drug addiction.

Free-Loan Film Serv *Eligibility:* residents of Ont. *Restrictions:* for indiv & inst, only in state. Available to researchers/scholars for on-site viewing. May borrow by mail. *Loan Period:* as arranged. *Total Yr Film Loan:* 1476.
　　Film Rental Serv Sell films. Produce films.
　　Film Collection 120t/243p. Approx 8t acquired annually. *Circ:* 16mm, 120t/243p. *Pubns:* catalog, annual (free).
　　Other Film Serv Permanent viewing facility.
　　Other Media Collections *Audio:* tape, cassette, 60t/c.
　　Budget & Expenditures Total library budget $26,654 (FY 4/1/74-4/1/75). Total FY film budget $2747.

S- ART GALLERY OF ONTARIO, Audio-Visual Library, Orange Park, M5T 1G4. *Tel:* (416) 361-0414, ext 260. *In Charge:* Susan Arthur, AV Librarian. *AV Staff:* (4 prof, 1 cl, 1 tech). *Film Sel:* staff recommendations, chief film librarian's decision. *Holdings:* fine arts 100%.
　　Film Collection 54t/55p. Approx 2-3t acquired annually. *Noncirc:* 16mm, 54t/55p.
　　Other Film Serv Gallery film programs. Permanent viewing facility.
　　Other Media Collections *Audio:* 3t/6c; tape, 85t/c. *Filmstrips:* sound sets, 14t/16c. *Slides:* 34,000c. *Member:* FLIC.
　　Video Serv *Est:* 1975. *Video Staff:* 5 f-t, 2 p-t. *Video Use:* documentation of community/school events, in-service training, as art form. Video serv available by appointment. Produce video tapes. Have production studio/space.
　　Video Equipment/Facilities *In-House Use Only:* portapak (1), ½″ col, Sony 8400; recording deck (4), ½″ b&w/col, Panasonic, Sony 1800; playback deck (1), ¾″ col, Sony 1200; editing deck (2), ½″ col, Panasonic; studio camera (3), b&w, Sony; monitor (4), b&w, Electrohome; SEG (1), Sony; microphones (10); tripods (2); audio tape recorders (2); Super 8mm cameras (3).
　　Video Collection Maintained by purchase. Use/play ½″ reel to reel, ¾″ cassette. *Sources:* galleries, artists. *Tape Sel:* faculty/staff recommendations. Tapes organized by artists name. *Other Video Serv:* publish catalog of 1974-75 Videoscope exhibition.
　　Cable & CCTV Receive serv of cable TV system. Have CCTV in inst. *Programming Sources:* tapes produced by inst, tapes produced professionally, tapes produced by community groups, indiv, artists.

S- ART—OFFICIAL, INC, Art Metropole, 241 Yonge St, M5B 1N8. *Tel:* (416) 368-7787. *Video Serv Est:* 1974. *In Charge:* Peggy Gale, Video Manager. *Video Staff:* 1 f-t. *Video Use:* as art form. Video serv available on demand.
　　Video Equipment/Facilities *In-House Use Only:* recording deck (1), ½″ col, Sony AV 8600; playback deck (1), ¾″ col, Panasonic; monitor (1), col, Sony. Have portable viewing installation. Have tape duplication serv.
　　Video Tape Loan/Rental/Sale Serv *Serv Provided:* rental, sale. Cannot duplicate, air without permission. May borrow by mail. *Loan Period:* as requested.
　　Video Collection Maintained by purchase, exchange/swap. Use/play ½″ reel to reel, ¾″ cassette. *Sources:* commercial distributors, artists, galleries. *Tape Sel:* preview, personal contact. *Special Collections:* video as art. Tapes organized by artists name. *Other Video Serv:* programming, reference serv, cooperation in artists' productions, performances, exhibitions. *Pubns:* catalog. Publish materials on video.
　　Cable & CCTV Receive serv of cable TV system. Produce programs for cablecasting. Have CCTV in inst, with 1 monitor.

P- BOROUGH OF YORK PUBLIC LIBRARY, Film Library, 1745 Eglinton Ave West, M6E 2H4. *Tel:* (416) 781-5208. *Film Serv Est:* 1968. *In Charge:* Ms C. To, AV Librarian. *AV Staff:* 2 (1 prof, 1 cl). *Film Sel:* committee preview.
　　Free-Loan Film Serv *Eligibility:* indiv with library cards over 18 yr of age. *Restrictions:* for indiv, only in city. Cannot use for fund-raising, transmit electronically. May not borrow by mail. *Loan Period:* 7 days super 8mm, 1 day 16mm.
　　Film Collection 400t/p. Approx 50t acquired annually. *Circ:* 16mm, 300t/p; S8mm reel, 100t/p. *Pubns:* catalog, annual; suppl, no set policy. Publish film programs.

Other Film Serv Obtain film from coop loan system (AV Servs of Metropolitan Toronto Public Library), obtain film from other libraries, film reference serv, library film programs. Permanent viewing facility available for rent to community. *Equipment:* rent 16mm sound projector (2), projection screens (3).

Other Media Collections *Audio:* disc, 33⅓ rpm, 5655c; tape, cassette, 1025c. *Filmstrips:* sound, silent, 110c.

Budget & Expenditures Total library budget $221,500 (FY 1/75-1/76). Total FY film budget $10,300. *Member:* EFLA.

P- CHURCH OF THE HOLY TRINITY, Trinity Video, 10 Trinity Square, M5G 1B1. *Tel:* (416) 362-4523. *Video Serv Est:* 1972. *In Charge:* Bill George, Coord. *Video Staff:* 1 f-t, 4 p-t, 1 tech. *Video Use:* documentation of community/school events, community video access, as art form. Video serv available by appointment. Produce video tapes. Have production studio/space & separate control room.

Video Equipment/Facilities *For Loan:* portapak (1), ½″ b&w, Sony 3400; editing deck (2), ½″ b&w, Sony 3650; studio camera (3), b&w, Sony 3200; monitor (3), 11″ b&w, Sony; SEG (1), Sony; lighting (3); tripods (3). Have portable viewing installations. *Equipment Loan Period:* 3 days. Provide training in use of equipment ($30 minimum charge). Have duplication serv.

Video Tape Loan/Rental/Sale Serv *Serv Provided:* free loan, swap with other inst, rental, sale. *Loan/Rental Eligibility:* civic groups, religious groups, & others. *Restrictions:* none. May borrow by mail. *Loan Period:* 1 month. *Total Yr Tape Loan:* 20.

Video Collection Maintained by own production, exchange/swap. Use/play ½″ reel to reel. *Sources:* community productions, exchange, independent producers. *Tape Sel:* preview. Tapes organized by Dewey Decimal. *Collection, B&W:* ½″ reel, 100t. *Other Video Serv:* programming, reference serv, production workshops.

Cable & CCTV Receive serv of cable TV system. Produce programs for cablecasting. Serve as production facility for others.

P- METROPOLITAN TORONTO LIBRARY BOARD, Audio Visual Services, 559 Ave Rd, M4V 2J7. *Tel:* (416) 962-3901. *Film Serv Est:* 1968. *In Charge:* Laura Murray, Coord. *AV Staff:* 8 (2 prof). *Film Sel:* committee preview.

Free-Loan Film Serv *Eligibility:* film libraries of the city/5 boroughs public library systems of Metropolitan Toronto. *Restrictions:* cannot use for fund-raising, transmit electronically. Available to researchers/scholars for on-site viewing by appointment. May not borrow by mail. *Total Yr Film Loan:* 44,399.

Film Collection 3620t/4260p. Approx 500t acquired annually. *Circ:* 16mm, 3620t/4260p. *Noncirc:* 16mm, 40t/p. *Pubns:* catalog, annual ($15); suppl, no set policy (free). Publish materials pertaining to collection.

Other Film Serv Film reference serv, film fairs/festivals, library film programs. Permanent viewing facility. *Equipment:* lend S8mm camera (5), 16mm sound projector (8), 8mm reel projector (1), S8mm reel projector (1), lend/rent projection tables & stands (5), projection screens (6), opaque projector, overhead projector, slide projector.

Budget & Expenditures Total AV budget $200,000 (FY 1/1/75-1/1/76). *Member:* AECT, ALA, EFLA, FLIC, Ontario Film Assn, Canadian Film Institute, Canadian Library Assn.

Video Serv *Est:* 1972. *In Charge:* Bruce Fairley, Head, Production/Equipment Dept. *Video Staff:* 2 f-t, 1 tech. *Video Use:* documentation of community/school events, to increase community's library use, in-service training, as sales tool playback only of professionally produced tapes. Video serv available by appointment. Produce video tapes.

Video Equipment/Facilities *In-House Use Only:* recording deck (2), ¾″ col, Sony VO2850; playback deck (1), ¾″ col, Sony VP1000; editing deck (1), ¾″ col, RM400. *For Loan:* portapak (5), ¾″, ½″ b&w/col, Sony, AV/AVC; playback deck (2), ¾″ col, Sony VP1000; monitor (8), b&w/col, Sony; lighting (5); microphones (6); tripods (9); audio tape recorders (4), microphone mixer. *Equipment Loan Period:* no set policy. Provide training in use of equipment.

Video Tape Loan/Rental/Sale Serv *Serv Provided:* free loan. *Loan Eligibility:* public library systems of Metropolitan Toronto. *Restrictions:* for inst, only in city. Cannot use for fundraising, duplicate, air without permission.

Video Collection Maintained by purchase, own production. Use/play ½″ reel to reel, ¾″ cassette. *Sources:* commercial distributors, in house productions. *Tape Sel:* preview. *Special Collections:* in-house training tapes. *Collection, Color:* ¾″ cassette, 76t/c. *Collection, B&W:* ½″ reel, 12t/c. *Other Video Serv:* programming, production workshops.

Cable & CCTV Will receive serv of cable TV system.

A- ONTARIO SCIENCE CENTRE, Ontario Film Institute, 770 Don Mills Rd. *Tel:* (416) 429-4100, ext 122-134. *Film Serv Est:* 1969. *In Charge:* Gerald Pratley, Dir, OFI. *AV Staff:* 4 (3 prof, 1 cl). *Film Sel:* chief film librarian's decision.

Film Collection 100t/p. Approx 10t acquired annually. Publish monthly film showing brochure.

Other Film Serv Rent film from distributors for patrons, obtain film from coop loan system, obtain film from other libraries, film reference serv, film fairs/festivals. Permanent viewing facility available for rent to community.

Budget & Expenditures Total library budget $5000 (FY 4/1/74-4/1/75). No separate AV budget. *Member:* AFI, EFLA, British Film Institute, Canadian Film Institute.

S- ROYAL ASTRONOMICAL SOCIETY OF CANADA, 252 College St, M5T 1R7. *Tel:* (416) 923-3784. *Film Serv Est:* 1955. *In Charge:* Harlan Creighton, National Librarian. *AV Staff:* 1 (1 prof). *Film Sel:* committee preview, faculty/staff recommendations. *Holdings:* astronomy 100%.

Free-Loan Film Serv *Eligibility:* org members, & others at discretion of librarian. *Restrictions:* only in Canada. *Loan Period:* 7 days. *Total Yr Film Loan:* 5.

Film Collection 10t/11p. Approx 1t acquired annually. *Circ:* 16mm, 10t/11p. *Noncirc:* S8mm reel, 1t/p. *Pubns:* catalog, as needed (free); suppl, no set policy (free).

Other Media Collections *Filmstrips:* sound, 10t/11c. *Slides:* single, 400t.

Budget & Expenditures Total library budget $600 (FY 1/74-1/75). No separate AV budget.

C- RYERSON POLYTECHNICAL INSTITUTE, Ryerson Media Library, 350 Victoria St, M5B 1E8. *Tel:* (416) 595-5099. *In Charge:* T. Stipanovich, Supervisor, Media Library. *AV Staff:* 4 (2 prof, 2 cl). *Film Sel:* faculty/staff recommendations, chief film librarian's decision. *Holdings:* career education 10%, engineering 10%, experimental films 10%, feature films 5%, fine arts 15%, industrial arts 15%, medicine 10%, science 5%, social sciences 15%, teacher education 5%.

Free-Loan Film Serv *Eligibility:* staff & students, educational inst. *Restrictions:* for indiv, only within the institution; for inst, those with reciprocal lending policies. Cannot use for fund-raising, transmit electronically. Available to researchers/scholars for on-site viewing. May not borrow by mail. *Loan Period:* 1 day. *Total Yr Film Loan:* 700.

Film Collection 600t/p. Approx 50t acquired annually. *Circ:* 16mm, 600t/p. *Noncirc:* 16mm, 4t. *Pubns:* catalog, annual; suppl, bi-monthly (free).

Other Film Serv Rent film from distributors for patrons, obtain film from coop loan system, obtain film from other libraries, film reference serv, film fairs/festivals, library film programs. Permanent viewing facility available for rent to community. *Equipment:* lend/rent S8mm camera (5), 16mm sound projector (40), 8mm cartridge projector (4), 8mm reel projector (4), S8mm cartridge projector (5), S8mm reel projector (100), projection screens (7), cassette recorders (15), cassette players (12).

Other Media Collections *Audio:* disc, 33⅓ rpm, 500t; tape, cassette, 800t; tape, reel, 25t. *Filmstrips:* silent, 50t. *Member:* AECT.

Video Serv *Est:* 1969. *In Charge:* J. L. Phidd, Coord, Media Centre. *Video Staff:* 11 f-t, 12 p-t, 18 tech. *Video Use:* documentation of community/school events, in-service training, practical

Toronto (cont.)
video/TV training courses. Produce video tapes. Have production studio/space & separate control room.

Video Equipment/Facilities *In-House Use Only:* recording deck (5), ¾″, 1″ col, Sony VO1600, VR1000, IVC600, IVC800, IVC825; playback deck (24), ¾″ col, Pan NV2125, 2120; editing deck (5), 1″ col, IVC870; studio camera (9), b&w/c; SEG (2); lighting (35); microphones (16); tripods (6); audio tape recorders (2). *For Loan:* recording deck (11), ½″, ¾″, 1″ col, Sony 8600, VO1600, VR1000, IVC600, 800, 825; playback deck (4), ¾″ col, Pan NV2125, 2120; editing deck (2), ½″, 1 col, Pan NV3130, IVC870; studio camera (2), b&w/c; lighting (5); tripods (3). Have permanent viewing installation. *Equipment Loan Period:* no set policy. Provide training in use of equipment to faculty & students. Have tape duplication serv.

Video Tape Loan/Rental/Sale Serv *Serv Provided:* free loan, swap with other inst. *Loan Eligiblity:* staff & students, prof groups. *Restrictions:* for inst with reciprocal agreements. Cannot use for fund-raising, duplicate, air without permission. May not borrow by mail. *Total Yr Tape Loan:* 67.

Video Collection Maintained by purchase, own production. Use/play ¾″ cassette. *Sources:* commercial distributors, own productions. *Tape Sel:* faculty/staff recommendations, catalogs. *Special Collections:* in-house training tapes, video as art, films in video format. Tapes organized by title. *Collection, Color:* ¾″ cassette, 85t/c. *Collection, B&W:* ¾″ cassette, 65t/c. *Other Video Serv:* taping of other media, production workshops.

Cable & CCTV Receive serv of cable TV system. Produce programs for cablecasting. Have CCTV in inst. *Programming Sources:* over-the-air commercial & public broadcasting, tapes produced by inst.

S- A SPACE GALLERY, 85 St. Nicholas St. *Tel:* (416) 964-3627. *Video Serv In Charge:* Elke Hayden, Coord. *Video Staff:* 1 f-t. *Video Use:* as art form. Video serv available by appointment. Produce video tapes. Have production studio/space.

Video Equipment/Facilities *In-House Use Only:* portapak (1), ½″ b&w, Sony; recording deck (1), ½″ b&w, Sony; playback deck (2), ½″ b&w, Sony; monitor (3), b&w/col, Sony; microphones (3); tripods (1); audio tape recorders (1), cassette (1). Have permanent viewing installation.

Video Tape Loan/Rental/Sale Serv *Serv Provided:* swap with other inst. *Loan Eligibility:* galleries or related art institutions. Cannot duplicate, air without permission. May not borrow by mail.

Video Collection Maintained by purchase, rental, own production, exchange/swap. Use/play ½″ reel to reel, ¾″ cassette. *Sources:* exchange (Video Inn, Western Front), artists & producers. *Special Collections:* video as art, documentation of art related events. Tapes organized by simplified card & number coding. *Collection, Color:* ½″ reel, 20t/1c; ¾″ cassette, 5t/1c. *Collection, B&W:* ½″ reel, 80t/1c; ¾″ cassette, 10t/1c. *Other Video Serv:* programming, reference serv, taping of other media. *Pubns:* catalog.

P- TORONTO PUBLIC LIBRARIES, Film Dept, 40 Orchard View Blvd, M4R 1B9. *Tel:* (416) 484-8250. *Film Serv Est:* 1972. *In Charge:* Tony Metie, AV Librarian. *AV Staff:* 6 (1 prof). *Film Sel:* committee preview.

Free-Loan Film Serv *Eligibility:* indiv with library cards. *Restrictions:* for indiv & inst, only in city. Cannot borrow for classroom use. Available to researchers/scholars for on-site viewing. May not borrow by mail. *Loan Period:* 1 day. *Total Yr Film Loan:* 18,386.

Film Collection 915p. Approx 150t acquired annually. *Circ:* 16mm, 915p; 8mm—S8mm 166p. *Pubns:* catalog, annual ($15); suppl. Publish special film lists.

Other Film Serv Obtain film from other libraries, library film programs. Permanent viewing facility available for rent to community. *Equipment:* rent 16mm sound projector (9), rent projection screens (1).

Budget & Expenditures Total library budget $864,000 (FY 12/1/75-12/1/76). Total FY film budget $35,000.

Video Serv *Est:* 1972. *Video Use:* to increase community's library use, in-service training, practical video/TV training

courses. Video serv available on demand & by appointment. Produce video tapes. Have production studio/space & separate control room.

Video Equipment/Facilities *In-House Use Only:* portapak (1), ½″ b&w, Sony 3400; playback deck (2), ¾″ col, Sony VT1000; editing deck (1), 1″ b&w/col, Sony EV320; studio camera (2), 1″ b&w, Sony DXC2000; monitor (5), b&w; lighting (4); microphones (10); tripods (2); audio tape recorders (12), lighting grids (70). Have permanent viewing installation. *Equipment Loan Period:* no set policy. Provide training in use of equipment to staff members & community.

Video Collection Use/play ¾″ cassette. *Sources:* commercial distributors. *Tape Sel:* preview. *Collection, Color:* ¾″ cassette, 90t/90c. *Other Video Serv:* production workshops.

Cable & CCTV Have CCTV in inst, with 2 monitors. *Programming Sources:* tapes produced professionally.

C- UNIVERSITY OF TORONTO, AV Library, Media Centre, 121 St. George St, M5S 1A1. *Tel:* (416) 928-6522. *Video Serv Est:* 1970. *In Charge:* Liz Avison, Supervisor. *Video Staff:* 4 f-t, 1 p-t. *Video Use:* documentation of community/school events, playback only of professionally produced tapes. Video serv available on demand & by appointment. Produce video tapes. Have production studio/space & separate control room.

Video Equipment/Facilities *For Loan:* portapak, b&w/col; recording deck, b&w/col; playback deck, b&w/col; editing deck, b&w/col; studio camera, b&w/col; monitor, b&w/col; additional camera lenses; lighting; microphones; tripods; audio tape recorders. Have permanent & portable viewing installations. *Equipment Loan Period:* provide training in use of equipment to faculty & students. Have tape duplication serv.

Video Tape Loan/Rental/Sale Serv *Serv Provided:* free loan, swap with other inst, rental, sale. *Loan/Rental Eligibility:* staff & students, educational inst. Cannot duplicate, air without permission. May borrow by mail. *Loan Period:* 5 days. *Total Yr Tape Loan:* 300.

Video Collection Maintained by purchase, rental, own production, exchange/swap. Use/play ½″ reel to reel, ¾″ cassette. *Sources:* commercial distributors, exchange (University Media Centres in Ont.). *Member:* Higher Education Learning Program Survey (HELPS). *Tape Sel:* preview, faculty/staff recommendations, catalogs. Tapes organized by accession. *Collection, Color:* ½″ reel, 200t; ¾″ cassette, 450t. *Other Video Serv:* programming, taping of other media, production workshops.

Cable & CCTV Receive serv of cable TV system. Produce programs for cablecasting. Serve as production facility for others. Have advisory/administrative role in cable system operation. Have CCTV in inst. *Programming Sources:* tapes produced by inst, tapes produced professionally.

S- VISUS FOUNDATION, 155A George St, M5A 2M8. *Tel:* (416) 869-1589. *Video Serv Est:* 1973. *Video Staff:* 3 f-t. *Video Use:* documentation of dance. Produce video tapes. Have production studio/space & separate control room.

Video Equipment/Facilities *In-House Use Only:* editing deck, ½″ col, Pan 3130; microphones (1); tripods (1); colourizer (1). Have portable viewing installation. *Equipment Loan Period:* provide training in use of equipment to dancers. Have tape duplication serv.

Video Tape Loan/Rental/Sale Serv *Serv Provided:* loan, rental, sale.

Video Collection Maintained by own production. Use/play ½″ reel to reel, ¾″ cassette. Tapes organized by subject. *Collection, Color:* ½″ reel, 2t. *Collection, B&W:* ½″ reel, 7t. *Pubns:* catalog.

Trenton

P- TRENTON MEMORIAL PUBLIC LIBRARY, 18 Albert St, K8V 4S3. *Tel:* (613) 392-3655.

Film Serv Obtain film from coop loan system (Lake Ontario Regional Public Library System). *Equipment:* rent 16mm sound projector (1).

Welland

P- WELLAND PUBLIC LIBRARY, AV Dept, 140 King St, L3B 3J3. *Tel:* (416) 734-6210. *Film Serv Est:* 1954. *In Charge:* Anne McIntosh, Head, AV Dept. *AV Staff:* 3 (1 prof, 2 cl). *Film Sel:* committee preview.
 Free-Loan Film Serv *Eligibility:* educational inst, civic groups, religious groups, indiv with library cards. *Restrictions:* for indiv & inst, within our regional library system. Cannot use for fund-raising, transmit electronically. Available to researchers/scholars for on-site viewing. May not borrow by mail. *Loan Period:* 1 day. *Total Yr Film Loan:* 2150.
 Film Collection 230t/p. Approx 10t acquired annually. *Circ:* 16mm, 230t/p. *Pubns:* catalog, annual (free).
 Other Film Serv Obtain film from coop loan system (Niagara Regional Library System), obtain film from other libraries. Permanent viewing facility. *Equipment:* rent 16mm sound projector (5), 8mm reel projector (2), S8mm reel projector (1), opaque projector (1), transparency projector (1), slide projector (2), film strip projector (3).
 Other Media Collections *Audio:* disc, 33⅓ rpm, 1100t/1c; tape, cassette, 200t/1c. *Filmstrips:* silent, 150t/1c; sound sets, 20t/1c.
 Budget & Expenditures Total library budget $42,450 (FY 1/75-1/76). Total FY film budget $5500. *Member:* Ont. Film Assn, Ont. Library Assn, Canadian Library Assn.
 Video Serv *Est:* 1975. *Video Staff:* 3 f-t, 1 p-t. *Video Use:* to increase community's library use, community video access. Video serv available on demand.
 Video Equipment/Facilities *In-House Use Only:* recording deck (1), ¾″ col, Sony VO1600; playback deck (1), ¾″ col, Sony VP1000. Have permanent viewing installation. *Equipment Loan Period:* no set policy. Provide training in use of equipment to staff members.
 Video Tape Loan/Rental/Sale Serv *Serv Provided:* free loan. *Loan Eligibility:* educational inst, civic groups, religious groups, indiv with library cards. *Restrictions:* for indiv & inst, within regional library system. Cannot duplicate, air without permission. May not borrow by mail.
 Video Collection Maintained by purchase. Use/play ¾″ cassette. *Sources:* exchange. *Tape Sel:* published reviews, catalogs. Tapes organized by Dewey Decimal. *Collection, Color:* ¾″ cassette, 300t/c. *Collection, B&W:* ¾″ cassette, 30t/c. *Pubns:* catalog.
 Cable & CCTV Receive serv of cable TV system. Have CCTV in inst, with 6 monitors. *Programming Sources:* over-the-air commercial & public broadcasting, tapes produced professionally, tapes produced by community groups & indiv.

Willowdale

P- NORTH YORK PUBLIC LIBRARY, Fairview Area Branch, 35 Fairview Mall Dr, M2J 4S4. *In Charge:* Janet MacDonald, AV Librarian. *AV Staff:* 11 (2 prof, 8 cl, 1 tech). *Film Sel:* AV Librarian.
 Free-Loan Film Serv *Eligibility:* indiv with library cards over 18 yrs of age. *Restrictions:* only in city. Cannot use for fund-raising, transmit electronically. Available to researchers/scholars for on-site viewing. May not borrow by mail. *Loan Period:* 1 day. *Total Yr Film Loan:* 2386.
 Film Collection 880t/900p. Approx 125t acquired annually. *Circ:* 16mm, 880t/900p. *Pubns:* catalog, annual ($15); suppl, quarterly. Publish materials pertaining to collection.
 Other Film Serv Obtain film from coop loan system (Metropolitan Toronto Boroughs & City Libraries), film reference serv, library film programs. Permanent viewing facility available for rent to community. *Equipment:* rent 16mm sound projector (13), 8mm reel projector (2), S8mm reel projector (2), projection screens (6), opaque projector (1), slide projector (1), filmstrip projector (1).
 Other Media Collections *Audio:* disc, 33⅓ rpm, 5000t/10c; tape, cassette, 1000t/5c. *Filmstrips:* sound, 5t/1c; silent, 138t/1c. *Slides:* single, 997t; sets, 12t/1c.
 Budget & Expenditures Total library budget $1,200,000 (FY 1/1/75-1/1/76). Total FY film budget $52,000. *Member:*

ALA, EFLA, FLIC, Ont. Film Assn, Ont. Library Assn, Canadian Library Assn.

Windsor

C- ST. CLAIR COLLEGE OF APPLIED ARTS AND TECHNOLOGY, St. Clair College Library Resource Centre, 2000 Talbot Rd, N9A 6S4. *Tel:* (519) 966-1656, ext 286. *Film Serv Est:* 1971. *In Charge:* Lea Simms, Library Technician. *AV Staff:* 1 tech. *Film Sel:* committee preview, faculty/staff recommendations.
 Free-Loan Film Serv *Eligibility:* staff & students. May not borrow by mail. *Loan Period:* 7 days. *Total Yr Film Loan:* 1257.
 Film Collection 429t. *Circ:* 16mm, 260t; S8mm cartridge, 169t. *Pubns:* catalog, every 3 yr (free).
 Other Film Serv Rent film from distributors for patrons, obtain film from coop loan system (Modern Talking Pictures Assn Films), obtain film from other libraries, film reference serv.
 Other Media Collections *Audio:* disc, 33⅓ rpm, 800t; tape, cassette, 348t. *Filmstrips:* silent, 269t; sound sets, 124t. *Slides:* sets, 178t.
 Budget & Expenditures Total library budget $51,000 (FY 4/1/74-4/1/75). No separate AV budget.
 Video Serv *Est:* 1970. *In Charge:* A. Rae, Senior Technician. *Video Staff:* 2 f-t, 2 tech. *Video Use:* documentation of community/school events, in-service training, practical video/TV training courses. Video serv available by appointment. Produce video tapes. Have production studio/space & separate control room.
 Video Equipment/Facilities *In-House Use Only:* portapak (2), ½″ b&w, Sony AV3400; recording deck (33), ½″, ¾″ b&w/col, Sony AV3600, VO1800; editing deck (5), 1″ b&w, Sony EV320F, AV3650; studio camera (3), 1″ b&w, Shebaden PP107; monitor (3), b&w/col, Electrohome, Sylvania; SEG (1); keyer (1); additional camera lenses (3); lighting (2); microphones; tripods; audio tape recorders. Have permanent & portable viewing installations. *Equipment Loan Period:* up to 4 weeks. Provide training in use of equipment to faculty & students. Have tape duplication serv.
 Video Tape Loan/Rental/Sale Serv *Serv Provided:* free loan, swap with other inst. *Loan Eligibility:* org members, staff, educational inst, civic groups, & others, such as nonprofit serv groups. *Restrictions:* for indiv, only in Essex County. May not borrow by mail.
 Video Collection Maintained by purchase, own production, exchange/swap. Use/play ½″, 1″ reel to reel, ¾″ cassette. *Sources:* commercial distributors. *Tape Sel:* faculty/staff recommendations, published reviews, catalogs. *Special Collections:* in-house training tapes, films in video format. Tapes organized by accession number.
 Cable & CCTV Serve as production facility for others. Have CCTV in inst, with 12 monitors. *Programming Sources:* over-the-air commercial & public broadcasting, tapes produced by inst, tapes produced professionally.

P- SOUTHWESTERN REGIONAL LIBRARY SYSTEM, 850 Ouellette Ave, N9A 4M9. *Tel:* (519) 258-2533. *Film Serv Est:* 1967. *In Charge:* Mary Agnes Fuerth, Film Librarian. *AV Staff:* 10 (1 prof, 9 cl). *Film Sel:* committee preview. *Holdings:* agriculture, animated films, black studies, children's films, consumer affairs, dance, experimental films, fine arts, medicine, science, social sciences, teacher education, women.
 Free-Loan Film Serv *Eligibility:* org members, staff & students, educational inst, civic groups, religious groups, indiv with library cards, prof groups. *Restrictions:* for indiv & inst, only in Essex, Kent & Lambton County; for inst, only interregional loan for library programming. Cannot use for fundraising, transmit electronically. Available to researchers/scholars for on-site viewing. May not borrow by mail. *Loan Period:* 1 day or by special arrangement. *Total Yr Film Loan:* 22,371.
 Film Collection 1530t/2155p. Approx 100t acquired annually. *Circ:* 16mm, 1530t/2155p; 8mm reel, 877t/2631p. *Noncirc:*

Windsor (cont.)
16mm, 1530t/2155p. *Pubns:* catalog, every 2 yr ($2); suppl, in yr catalog not published ($1). Publish materials pertaining to collection.

Other Film Serv Obtain film from other libraries, film reference serv, library film programs. Permanent viewing facility available to community. *Equipment:* lend 8mm reel projector.

Other Media Collections *Audio:* disc, 33⅓ rpm, 680t/ 2050c; tape, cassette, 70t/c.

Budget & Expenditures Total library budget $141,000 (FY 1/1/74-1/1/75). Total FY film budget $30,000. *Member:* Ont. Library Assn, Ont. Film Assn, Canadian Film Institute.

Video Serv *Est:* 1974. *In Charge:* Howard Ford, Coord Regional Servs. *Video Use:* documentation of community/ school events, to increase community's library use, in-service training, playback only of professionally produced tapes. Video serv available on demand. Produce video tapes. Have production studio/space & separate control room.

Video Equipment/Facilities *In-House Use Only:* recording deck (1), U-Matic col, Sony 2850; playback deck (5), U-Matic, col, Sony VP1000; studio camera (1), b&w, Pan WV341P; monitor (1), col, Electrohome; additional camera lenses (1); microphones (1); tripods (1). Have portable viewing installation. *Equipment Loan Period:* provide training in use of equipment to staff.

Video Tape Loan/Rental/Sale Serv *Loan Eligibility:* org members. *Restrictions:* for inst, only in our region. Cannot use for fund-raising, air without permission. May not borrow by mail. *Loan Period:* unlimited.

Video Collection Maintained by purchase, own production. Use/play ¾" cassette. *Sources:* commercial distributors, galleries, in house productions. *Tape Sel:* preview, catalogs. Tapes organized by title & series. *Collection, Color:* ¾" cassette, 681t/c. *Collection, B&W:* ¾" cassette, 152t/c. *Pubns:* catalog.

S- UNIVERSITY OF WINDSOR, Faculty of Law, Community Law Program, N9B 3P4. *Tel:* (519) 254-4155. *Video Serv Est:* 1973. *In Charge:* Ellie Airey, Program Coord. *Video Staff:* 1 f-t. *Video Use:* community legal education. Video serv available by appointment. Produce video tapes.

Video Equipment/Facilities *In-House Use Only:* recording deck (1), ¾" col; playback deck (1). Have portable viewing installation.

Video Tape Loan/Rental/Sale Serv *Serv Provided:* free loan, swap with other inst. *Loan Eligibility:* org members, staff, students enrolled in inst, staff & students, educational inst, civic groups, religious groups, prof groups, such as legal education groups. *Restrictions:* for indiv & inst, none. May not borrow by mail. *Loan Period:* 7 days. *Total Yr Tape Loan:* 100.

Video Collection Maintained by purchase, own production, exchange/swap. Use/play ½" reel to reel, ¾" cassette. *Tape Sel:* preview, faculty/staff recommendations. *Special Collections:* public legal education. Tapes organized by subject. *Collection, Color:* ½" reel, 20t/40c; ¾" cassette, 35t.

Cable & CCTV Produce programs for cablecasting. Have CCTV in inst, with 10 monitors. *Programming Sources:* over-the-air commercial & public broadcasting, tapes produced by inst, tapes produced professionally, tapes produced by community groups & indiv.

Prince Edward Island

Charlottetown

S- CONFEDERATION CENTRE ART GALLERY & MUSEUM, Box 1000. *Tel:* (902) 892-2464, ext 143. *In Charge:* Norman Osborne, Ext Officer. *Film Sel:* staff recommendations. *Holdings:* fine arts 90%.

Free-Loan Film Serv *Eligibility:* staff & students, educational inst, civic groups, religious groups, prof groups. *Restrictions:* for indiv & inst, none. Available to researchers/scholars for on-site viewing. *Loan Period:* 7 days. *Total Yr Film Loan:* 6.

Film Collection 25t. 5t acquired annually.

Other Film Serv Film reference serv, film fairs/festivals, library film programs. Permanent viewing facility. *Equipment:* lend S8mm reel projector, projection tables & stands, projection screens.

Budget & Expenditures No separate AV budget. *Member:* ALA.

Video Serv *Est:* 1975. *Video Staff:* 3 f-t. *Video Use:* documentation of community/school events, as art form. Video serv available by appointment. Produce video tapes.

Video Equipment/Facilities *In-House Use Only:* recording deck (1), col, Sony; playback deck (1); col, Sony; editing deck (1), Sony; studio camera (1), col; microphones (1); tripods (1); audio tape recorders (1).

Video Tape Loan/Rental/Sale Serv *Serv Provided:* swap with other inst. *Loan Eligibility:* staff & students, educational inst. *Restrictions:* for inst, none. May not borrow by mail.

Video Collection Maintained by purchase, own production. *Sources:* galleries. *Tape Sel:* faculty/staff recommendations, gallery previews. *Special Collections:* video as art. Tapes organized by subject.

S- GOVERNMENT OF P.E.I., Dept. of Education Media Centre, 202 Richmond St, C1A 1J2. *Tel:* (902) 894-3786. *In Charge:* W. A. Ledwell, Chief Educational Media. *AV Staff:* 4 (4 tech). *Film Sel:* committee preview, staff recommendations. *Holdings:* agriculture 10%, animated films 10%, children's films 30%, consumer affairs 1%, engineering 5%, experimental films 5%, feature films 2%, fine arts 2%, industrial arts 1%, law 1%, medicine 10%, science 10%, social sciences 30%, teacher education 2%, women 1%.

Free-Loan Film Serv *Eligibility:* educational inst, civic groups, religious groups, indiv with library cards. *Restrictions:* for indiv & inst, only in our province. Cannot transmit electronically. Available to researchers/scholars for on-site viewing. May borrow by mail. *Loan Period:* 7 days. *Total Yr Film Loan:* 12,830.

Film Collection 2400t/p. Approx 250t acquired annually. *Circ:* 16mm, 2400t/p. *Noncirc:* 16mm, 20t/p. *Pubns:* catalog, as needed (free); suppl, no set policy (free).

Other Film Serv Obtain film from coop loan system (National Film Board). Permanent viewing facility available to community. *Equipment:* lend 16mm sound projector (5), projection screens (5), filmstrip projector (4), slide projector (2), overhead projector (1), opaque projector (1), record player (1), filmstrip & cassette projector.

Other Media Collections *Filmstrips:* sound, 10t/c; silent, 2500t/c; sound sets, 60t/c; silent sets, 10t/c. *Slides:* single, 15t/c.

Budget & Expenditures Total library budget $27,000 (FY 4/1/74-4/1/75). No separate AV budget. *Member:* ALA.

S- GOVERNMENT OF P.E.I., Dept. of Public Works, Audio Visual Service Centre, Box 2000, Provincial Administration Building, C1A 7N8. *Tel:* (902) 892-7431. ext 65. *Video Serv Est:* 1973. *In Charge:* Douglas Murray, Dir AV Servs. *Video Staff:* 6 f-t, 1 tech. *Video Use:* documentation of community/school events, community video access, inservice training, practical video/TV training courses, playback only of professionally produced tapes, as art form. Video serv available on demand & by appointment. Produce video tapes. Have production studio/space & separate control room.

Video Equipment/Facilities *In-House Use Only:* editing deck (2), Sony 2850; studio camera (3), b&w/col, Sony; monitor (7), col, Sony; SEG (1), Sony; lighting (4); microphones (20); tripods (6); audio tape recorders (25). *For Loan:* portapak (3), b&w, Sony 3400; recording deck (10), Sony 1800, 1600; playback deck (4), VP1000. Have permanent viewing installation. *Equipment Loan Period:* no set policy. Provide training in use of equipment to faculty & students. Have tape duplication serv.

Video Tape Loan/Rental/Sale Serv *Serv Provided:* free loan, swap with other inst. *Loan Eligibility:* all government dept.

Video Collection Maintained by own production, exchange/swap. Use/play ½" reel to reel, ¾" cassette. *Sources:* commercial distributors, exchange. *Tape Sel:* staff recommendations. *Special Collections:* in-house training tapes. *Other Video Serv:* production workshops. *Pubns:* catalog.

Quebec

Hull

P- BIBLIOTHÈQUE CENTRALE DE PRÊT DE L'OUTAOU-AIS, Cinémathèque Régionale du Nord de l'Outaouais, Chemin Freeman, C.P. 30, Succ. A, Hull, J8Y 6M7. *Tel:* (819) 770-2877. *In Charge:* Claire Castrillo. *AV Staff:* 1¼ (1 cl, ¼ tech). *Film Sel:* staff recommendations. *Holdings:* history of film.

Free-Loan Film Serv *Eligibility:* civic groups, religious groups, indiv with library cards. *Restrictions:* for indiv, only Outaouais & Larentides region. Available to researchers/scholars for on-site viewing. May borrow by mail. *Total Yr Film Loan:* 4718.

Film Rental Serv *Eligibility:* educational org, those not served by an affiliated library. *Restrictions:* Outaouais & Laurentides. Cannot transmit electronically.

Film Collection 1352t/p. Approx 10t acquired annually. *Circ:* 16mm, 1276t; 8mm reel, 76t. *Pubns:* catalog, as needed (free); suppl (free).

Other Film Serv Rent film from distributors for patrons, film fairs/festivals, library film programs. Permanent viewing facility. *Equipment:* lend 16mm sound projector (2), projection screens (1).

Other Media Collections *Audio:* disc, 33⅓ rpm, 1200t/c.

Budget & Expenditures Total library budget $162,000 (FY 4/74-4/75). Total FY film budget $8500. *Member:* Canadian Assn of Museums, ASTED, AAM.

P- BIBLIOTHÈQUE MUNICIPALE DE HULL, 39 Leduc, J8X 3A3. *Tel:* (819) 777-4341. *Film Serv Est:* 1975. *In Charge:* Denis Boyer, Dir. *AV Staff:* 1 p-t. *Film Sel:* chief film librarian's decision. *Holdings:* animated films 50%, children's films 40%, sports 10%.

Film Collection 75t. Approx 75t acquired annually. *Non-circ:* S8mm cartridge, 75t/p.

Other Film Serv Obtain film from other libraries. Permanent viewing facility.

Other Media Collections *Audio:* disc, 33⅓ rpm, 15,000t; disc, 45rpm, 35,000t; disc, 78rpm, 1500t; tape, cassette, 500t. *Slides:* single, 2000t; sets, 75t.

Budget & Expenditures Total library budget $60,000 (FY 1/1/75-1/1/76). Total FY film budget $1000.

Montreal

P- BIBLIOTHÈQUE DE LA VILLE DE MONTRÉAL, Cinematheque de la Ville de Montréal/Montreal Film Library, 2207 rue Montcalm, H2L 3H8. *Tel:* (514) 872-3680. *Film Serv Est:* 1947. *In Charge:* Lise D. Bourassa, Chef de la Documentation Audio-Visuelle. *AV Staff:* 10 (2 prof, 3 cl, 5 tech). *Film Sel:* committee preview, chief film librarian's decision.

Film Rental Serv *Eligibility:* no restrictions. *Restrictions:* only in region (Montreal). Cannot use for fund raising, transmit electronically. *Rental Period:* 7 days. *Total Yr Film Booking:* 24,031.

Film Collection 3842t/4038p. Approx 250t acquired annually. *Pubns:* catalog, as needed ($1); suppl, in yr catalog not published (free).

Other Film Serv Film reference serv, library film programs. Permanent viewing facility. *Equipment:* rent 16mm sound projector (10), 8mm reel projector (1), projection screens (11).

Other Media Collections *Filmstrips:* silent, 1480t/c. *Slides:* single, 18,681t/c.

Budget & Expenditures Total FY film budget $40,000 (FY 5/1/74-5/1/75). *Member:* ALA, Ont. Film Assn.

C- McGILL UNIVERSITY, Undergraduate Library Audio Visual Centre, 3459 McTavish St, H3A 1Y1. *Tel:* (514) 392-6776, ext 27. *Video Serv Est:* 1971. *In Charge:* Daniel Phelan, AV Reference Librarian. *Video Staff:* 3 f-t, 10 p-t. *Video Use:* playback only of professionally produced tapes. Video serv available on demand.

Video Equipment/Facilities *In-House Use Only:* playback deck (16), ¾", Sony U-Matic; monitor (30), b&w/col, Sony, Trinitron. Have permanent installations.

Video Collection Maintained by purchase. Use/play ¾" cassette. *Sources:* commercial distributors, galleries, in house productions, exchange. *Tape Sel:* preview, faculty/staff recommendations, published reviews, catalogs. Tapes organized by subject. *Collection, Color:* ¾" cassette, 13t/c. *Collection, B&W:* ¾" cassette, 200t/c.

Cable & CCTV Serve as production facility for others. Run cable programs for special audiences. Have CCTV in inst, with 30 monitors. *Programming Sources:* over-the-air commercial & public broadcasting, tapes produced by inst.

A- MUSÉE D'ART CONTEMPORAIN, Cité du Havre, H3C 3R4. *Tel:* (514) 873-2878. *In Charge:* Louise Letocha, Education Dept Dir. *Holdings:* animated films 1%, fine arts 99%.

Film Collection 30t/p. Approx 5t acquired annually. *Non-circ:* 16mm, 25t; 8mm reel, 5t.

Video Serv *Video Use:* as art form, documentation of art. Video serv available by appointment. Produce video tapes. Have production studio/space.

Video Equipment/Facilities *In-House Use Only:* portapak (1), b&w, Sony 3400; studio camera (2), b&w, Sony; monitor (6), b&w/col, RCA, Shibaden; lighting (1); microphones (3); tripods (2); audio tape recorders (2). Have portable viewing installation.

Video Tape Loan/Rental/Sale Serv *Serv Provided:* free loan. *Loan Eligibility:* educational inst. *Restrictions:* cannot use for fund-raising, duplicate. May borrow by mail. *Loan Period:* 7 days.

Video Collection Maintained by own production. Use/play ½" reel to reel, ¾" cassette. *Special Collections:* video as art. *Collection, Color:* ¾" cassette, 5t. *Collection, B&W:* ½" reel, 18t/c.

Cable & CCTV Have CCTV in inst, with 4 monitors. *Programming Sources:* tapes produced by inst.

S- ORDER OF NURSES OF QUEBEC, Hersey-Upton Library, 4200 Dorchester Blvd, H3Z 1V4. *Tel:* (514) 935-2501, ext 53. *Film Serv Est:* 1973. *In Charge:* France Doyon, Library Dir. *AV Staff:* 1 (1 cl). *Film Sel:* committee preview. *Holdings:* nursing.

Film Rental Serv *Eligibility:* educational org, ONQ mem. *Restrictions:* only in region (P.Q.). *Rental Period:* 7 days. *Total Yr Film Booking:* 240.

Film Collection 7t/2p. *Circ:* 16mm, 7t/2p. *Pubns:* catalog, as needed (free).

Other Film Serv Film reference serv. Permanent viewing facility.

Other Media Collections *Audio:* tape, cassette, 2t/c; tape, reel, 36t/3c. *Filmstrips:* sound sets, 2t/10c. *Slides:* sets, 3t/c.

Budget & Expenditures No separate AV budget.

Pointe Claire

P- POINTE CLAIRE PUBLIC LIBRARY, 484 St Louis, H9R 4V1. *Tel:* (514) 695-0222. *Film Serv Est:* 1975. *In Charge:* Rosemary Kozak, Adult Servs Librarian. *AV Staff:* 1. *Film Sel:* committee preview, published reviews.
Free-Loan Film Serv *Eligibility:* indiv with library cards. *Restrictions:* cannot use for fund-raising. Available to researchers/scholars for on-site viewing. May borrow by mail. *Loan Period:* 2 days.
Film Collection 178t/p. Approx 50-100t acquired annually. *Circ:* 16mm, 100t; 8mm-S8mm reel, 78t. *Pubns:* catalog, annual ($0.50); suppl, no set policy.
Other Film Serv Library film programs. *Equipment:* rent S8mm camera, 16mm sound projector (2), 8mm reel projector (2), S8mm reel projector.
Other Media Collections *Audio:* disc, 33⅓ rpm, 2000t.
Budget & Expenditures Total FY film budget $10,000. *Member:* Canadian Library Assn, Quebec Library Assn, ASTED.

Quebec

C- BIBLIOTHÈQUE GÉNÉRALE CINÉMATHÈQUE, Université Laval Bibliothèque Générale, G1K 7P4. *Tel:* (418) 656-3252. *In Charge:* Gary Ross, Dir. *AV Staff:* 9 (2 prof, 5 cl, 2 tech). *Film Sel:* committee preview, faculty/staff recommendations, chief film librarian's decision.
Film Rental Serv *Eligibility:* no restrictions. *Restrictions:* only in region (P.Q.). Cannot use for fund-raising, transmit electronically. *Rental Period:* 5 days. *Total Yr Film Booking:* 9435.
Film Collection 2700t. Approx 150-175t acquired annually. *Circ:* 16mm, 1900t/2276p; 8mm—S8mm reel, 817p. *Noncirc:* 16mm, 120t. *Pubns:* catalog, every 2 yr ($2); suppl, in yr catalog not published (free).
Other Film Serv Rent film from distributors for patrons, obtain film from other libraries, film reference serv, film fairs/festivals, library film programs. Permanent viewing facility available to community.
Other Media Collections *Audio:* disc, 33⅓ rpm, 8000t/c. *Filmstrips:* silent, 300t/c. *Slides:* single, 85,000t/c; sets, 100t/c.
Budget & Expenditures Total library budget $3,691,591 (FY 6/1/74-6/1/75). Total FY film budget $218,045. *Member:* EFLA.

C- UNIVERSITY LAVAL, Service de L'Audio Visuel, Section Diffusion Loc. 0446. Pav. de Koninck, G1K 7P4. *Tel:* (418) 656-3986. *Video Serv Est:* 1967. *In Charge:* Paul Premont, Adjoint AV Dir. *Video Staff:* 67 f-t, 10 p-t, 25 tech. *Video Use:* documentation of community/school events, to increase community's library use, community video access, in-service training, practical video/TV training courses. Video serv available on demand. Produce video tapes. Have production studio/space & separate control room.
Video Equipment/Facilities *In-House Use Only:* recording deck (13); playback deck (13); studio camera (7), b&w; monitor (87), b&w, Conrac; SEG (2), Richmond Hill; keyer (1), Richmond Hill; additional camera lenses (6); lighting (52); microphones (18); tripods (9); audio tape recorders (20). *For Loan:* portapak (5); studio camera (2), b&w; monitor (16), b&w, Conrac; SEG (1), Richmond Hill; lighting (3); microphones (14); tripods (15); audio tape recorders (49). Have permanent & portable viewing installations. *Equipment Loan Period:* 2-3 days. Provide training in use of equipment to faculty & students. Have tape duplication serv.
Video Tape Loan/Rental/Sale Serv *Serv Provided:* free loan. *Loan Eligibility:* staff & students, educational inst, prof groups, such as Red Cross, government, cultural agencies. *Restrictions:* for indiv & inst, none. Cannot air without permission. May not borrow by mail. *Loan Period:* 30 days. *Total Yr Tape Loan:* 15.
Video Collection Maintained by own production. Use/play ½" reel to reel. *Sources:* commercial distributors. *Tape Sel:* faculty/staff recommendations. *Special Collections:* in-house training tapes. *Collection, B&W:* ½" reel, 25t.
Cable & CCTV Have advisory role in cable system operation. Have CCTV in inst, with 90 monitors. *Programming Sources:* tapes produced by inst.

Rouyn

C- COLLÈGE DU NORD-OUEST, Bibliothèque, Dept. Audio-vidéothèque, C.P. 8000, J9X 5M5. *Tel:* (819) 762-0931, ext 133. *Film Serv Est:* 1972. *In Charge:* Gisèle Neas-Caron, Bibliotechniciènne. *AV Staff:* 2 (1 cl, 1 tech). *Film Sel:* staff recommendations, chief film librarian's decision.
Other Media Collections *Audio:* disc, 33⅓ rpm, 443t/652c; tape, cassette, 142t/340c; tape, reel, 174t/259c. *Filmstrips:* silent, 784t/943c. *Slides:* single, 3129t/15,453c; sets, 125t/131c.
Budget & Expenditures Total library budget $17,000 (FY 7/75-7/76). No separate AV budget.
Video Serv *Est:* 1972. *Video Staff:* 2 f-t, 1 tech. *Video Use:* documentation of community/school events. Video serv available on demand. Produce video tapes. Have production studio/space.
Video Equipment/Facilities *In-House Use Only:* monitor (1), b&w, Sony. Have permanent viewing installation. *Equipment Loan Period:* provide training in use of equipment. Have tape duplication serv.
Video Collection Maintained by purchase, rental, own production. Use/play ½", 1" reel to reel. *Collection, B&W:* ½" reel, 373c.

Saint Jean

P- BIBLIOTHÈQUE MUNICIPALE DU SAINT JEAN, Cinematheque Municipale, 203 Jacques Cartier. *Tel:* (514) 347-1305. *Film Serv Est:* 1949. *In Charge:* Yudn Payette, AV Technicien. *AV Staff:* 2 (2 tech). *Film Sel:* chief film librarian's decision upon recommendation. *Holdings:* local history.
Free-Loan Film Serv *Eligibility:* org members. *Restrictions:* cannot transmit electronically. Available to researchers/scholars for on-site viewing. May borrow by mail. *Loan Period:* as required.
Film Rental Serv *Restrictions:* only in region (Haut Richelein). *Rental Period:* as required.
Film Collection 1200t/p. Approx 30-40t acquired annually. *Noncirc:* 16mm, 10t/p. *Pubns:* catalog, every 5 yr; suppl, no set policy (free).
Other Film Serv Rent film from distributors for patrons, library film programs. Permanent viewing facility available for rent to community. *Equipment:* rent S8mm camera, 16mm sound projector, 8mm reel projector, S8mm reel projector, projection tables & stands, projection screens, record players, loud speaker, tape recorder.
Other Media Collections *Filmstrips:* silent, 600t. *Slides:* sets, 100t.
Budget & Expenditures Total library budget $18,300 (FY 1/1/75-1/1/76). Total FY film budget $5300. *Member:* Canadian Library Assn, Quebec Library Assn, ASTED.

Sherbrooke

C- UNIVERSITE DE SHERBROOKE, Cinematheque-Universite de Sherbrooke, Pavillon Marie-Victorin, J1K 2R1. *Tel:* (819) 565-5458. *Film Serv Est:* 1965. *AV Staff:* 2 (1 cl, 1 tech). *Film Sel:* faculty/staff recommendations. *Holdings:* agriculture 1%, animated films 10%, children's films 20%, dance 1%, engineering 10%, experimental films 10%, fine arts 10%, law 1%, medicine 10%, science 10%, sports 15%, teacher education 2%.
Free-Loan Film Serv *Eligibility:* org members, students enrolled in inst. *Restrictions:* cannot transmit electronically. Available to researchers/scholars for on-site viewing. May borrow by mail. *Loan Period:* 7 days.

Film Rental Serv *Eligibility:* no restrictions. *Restrictions:* only in state. Cannot transmit electronically. *Rental Period:* 7 days.

Film Collection 725t/800p. Approx 75t acquired annually. *Pubns:* catalog, annual; every 5 yr ($3); suppl, in yr catalog not published (free). Publish materials pertaining to collection.

Other Film Serv Obtain film from coop loan system, obtain film from other libraries. Permanent viewing facility.

Budget & Expenditures Total library budget $25,265 (FY 6/1/75-6/1/76). No separate AV budget. *Member:* EFLA.

Saskatchewan

Regina

P- REGINA PUBLIC LIBRARY, AV Service Film Dept, 2311 12th Ave. *Tel:* (306) 523-7621, ext 253. *Film Serv Est:* 1949. *In Charge:* Gary Deane, AV Coord. *AV Staff:* 4 (1 prof, 2 cl, 1 tech). *Film Sel:* committee preview, staff recommendations. *Holdings:* agriculture 2%, animated films 15%, children's films 20%, comedy 7%, consumer affairs 3%, dance 2%, experimental films 3%, feature films 5%, fine arts 15%, medicine 1%, science 8%, social sciences 15%, women 4%.

Free-Loan Film Serv *Eligibility:* staff & students, educational inst, civic groups, religious groups, indiv with library cards, prof groups. *Restrictions:* for indiv, interlibrary loan, only in state; for inst, only in state. Cannot use for fund-raising. Available to researchers/scholars for on-site viewing. May not borrow by mail. *Loan Period:* 3 days, extended loan if required. *Total Yr Film Loan:* 5000.

Film Collection 1200t/p. *Circ:* 16mm, 800t/p; 8mm reel, 400t/p. *Pubns:* catalog, annual (free). Publish materials pertaining to collection.

Other Film Serv Obtain film from other libraries, film reference serv, film fairs/festivals, library film programs. Permanent viewing facility available for rent to community. *Equipment:* 16mm sound projector (10), projection screens (6).

Other Media Collections *Audio:* disc, 33⅓ rpm, 9000t/9500c; tape, cassette, 300t/c.

Budget & Expenditures Total FY film budget $20,000 (FY 1/1/75-1/1/76). *Member:* EFLA.

Saskatoon

P- SASKATOON PUBLIC LIBRARY, 311-23 St E, S7K 0J6. *Tel:* (306) 652-7313, ext 236, 237. *In Charge:* Frances Daw Bergles, Fine and Performing Arts Librarian. *AV Staff:* 7 (2½ prof, 1½ cl, 3 tech). *Film Sel:* staff recommendations, chief film librarian's decision, published reviews.

Free-Loan Film Serv *Eligibility:* educational inst, civic groups, religious groups, indiv with library cards, community. *Restrictions:* for indiv & inst, only in province. Cannot use for commercial profit. Available to researchers/scholars for on-site viewing. May borrow by mail. *Loan Period:* 1 day. *Total Yr Film Loan:* 7086.

Film Collection 515t/523p. *Circ:* 16mm, 347t/349p; 8mm reel, 168t/174p. *Pubns:* catalog, as needed; suppl, no set policy (free). Publish materials pertaining to collection.

Other Film Serv Obtain film from coop loan system (Saskatchewan Library System), obtain film from other libraries, film reference serv, film fairs/festivals, library film programs. Permanent viewing facility available to community. *Equipment:* rent 16mm sound projector (3), projection screens, slide projector.

Budget & Expenditures Total library budget $226,600 (FY 1/1/75-1/1/76). Total FY film budget $15,000. *Member:* EFLA, Saskatchewan Library Assn.

C- UNIVERSITY OF SASKATCHEWAN, Film Library, D.A.V.S. U of S, S7N 0W0. *Tel:* (306) 343-5773. *Film Serv Est:* 1945. *In Charge:* G. M. Clothier, Film Librarian. *AV Staff:* 2 (1 prof, 1 cl). *Film Sel:* faculty/staff recommendations, chief film librarian's decision. *Holdings:* agriculture 15%, animated films 5%, children's films 5%, fine arts 5%, medicine 15%, science 20%, social sciences 20%, teacher education 25%.

Free-Loan Film Serv *Eligibility:* staff & students. *Loan Period:* 2 days.

Film Rental Serv *Restrictions:* only in region (province of Sask.). *Rental Period:* 2 days. *Total Yr Film Booking:* Sell films. Produce films.

Film Collection 1000t/p. Approx 10-30t acquired annually. *Circ:* 16mm, 1000t/p. *Pubns:* catalog, every 2 yr (free); suppl, in yr catalog not published (free).

Other Film Serv Obtain film from other libraries, film reference serv. Permanent viewing facility available for rent to community. *Equipment:* lend S8mm camera (2), 16mm sound projector (20), 8mm cartridge projector (1), 8mm reel projector (1), S8mm cartridge projector (5), S8mm reel projector (5), projection tables & stands (50), projection screens (50).

Other Media Collections *Slides:* sets, 50t/c.

Budget & Expenditures No separate AV budget.

Video Serv *Est:* 1970. *Video Staff:* 2 f-t, 2 p-t. *Video Use:* in-service training, university classes. Video serv available on demand. Produce video tapes. Have production studio/space & separate control room.

Video Equipment/Facilities *In-House Use Only:* studio camera (20); monitor (100); SEG (1); keyer (2); microphones (20). *For Loan:* portapak (2), ½" b&w, Sony; recording deck (10), ¾" col, Sony, Pan; playback deck (4), 1" b&w; studio camera (20), b&w/col; monitor (100); audio tape recorders (130). Have portable viewing installations. *Equipment Loan Period:* no set policy. Provide training in use of equipment. Have tape duplication serv.

Video Tape Loan/Rental/Sale Serv *Serv Provided:* free loan. *Loan Eligibility:* org members, staff & students. *Restrictions:* for indiv on campus only. May not borrow by mail. *Total Yr Tape Loan:* 230.

Video Collection Maintained by own production. *Tape Sel:* faculty/staff recommendations. Tapes organized by Dewey Decimal.

Yukon Territory

Whitehorse

P- GOVERNMENT OF THE YUKON TERRITORY, Library Services Branch, Box 2703, Y1A 2C6. *Tel:* (403) 667-5240. *Film Serv Est:* 1966. *In Charge:* Mrs. Rusty Reid, Media Librarian. *AV Staff:* 3 (2 cl, 1 tech). *Film Sel:* staff recommendations, chief film librarian's decision.

Free-Loan Film Serv *Eligibility:* residents, schools, org. *Restrictions:* for indiv & inst, only in Yuk. Territory. Cannot use for fund-raising, transmit electronically. Available to researchers/scholars for on-site viewing. May borrow by mail. *Loan Period:* up to 6 weeks. *Total Yr Film Loan:* 11,179.

Film Collection 1000t/1100p. Approx 20t acquired annually. *Circ:* 16mm, 1000t/1100p. *Noncirc:* 16mm, 100t; S8mm reel, 1t. *Pubns:* catalog, every 2 yr; suppl, no set policy.

Other Film Serv Obtain film from other libraries, film reference serv, film fairs/festivals, library film programs. Permanent viewing facility. *Equipment:* rent 16mm sound projector (6), 8mm reel projector (1), S8mm reel projector (1), projection screens (5), filmstrip projector.

Other Media Collections *Audio:* 600c.

Budget & Expenditures Total FY film budget $10,000 (FY 4/1/75-4/1/76).

INDEX OF LIBRARIES

This index lists the institutions included in this directory in alphabetical order by first word of the institution name. The asterisk denotes an institution having video services.

Abilene Public Library, Abilene, Tex.
*Ace Space Company (Spaceco), Crested Butte, Colo.
*Adams Library, Chelmsford, Mass.
*Adams State College, Alamosa, Colo.
Addiction Research Foundation, Toronto, Ont., Canada
*Adelphi University, Garden City, N.Y.
Adrian Public Library, Adrian, Mich.
*Adult Education Centre, Frobisher Bay, N.W.T., Canada
*Aims Community College, Greeley, Colo.
Air University, Maxwell Air Force Base, Ala.
Ajax Public Library, Ajax, Ont., Canada
A. K. Smiley Public Library, Redlands, Calif.
Alabama Public Library Service, Montgomery, Ala.
Alameda County Library System, Hayward, Calif.
Alaska State Library, Juneau, Alaska
*Alaska State Museum, Juneau, Alaska
*Albany Dougherty Public Library, Albany, Ga.
Albany Public Library, Albany, Oreg.
*Alberni Cable Television Ltd., Port Alberni, B.C., Canada
Albert Lea Public Library, Albert Lea, Minn.
*Albion Library, Rexdale, Ont., Canada
*Albright College, Reading, Pa.
*Alderson-Broaddus College, Philippi, W. Va.
Alemeda Free Library, Alemeda, Calif.
Alexandria Library, Alexandria, Va.
Alexandria Public Library, Alexandria, Minn.
*Alice Lloyd College, Pippa Passes, Ky.
Allegan Public Library, Allegan, Mich.
Allentown Public Library, Allentown, Pa.
*Alma College, Alma, Mich.
Altedena Library District, Altedena, Calif.
Alternate Media Center. See New York University
*Altoona Area Public Library, Altoona, Pa.
*Alvin Community College, Alvin, Tex.
American Society of Association Executives, Washington, D.C.
Amos Memorial Public Library, Sidney, Ohio
Anaheim Public Library, Anaheim, Calif.
Anchorage Public Libraries, Anchorage, Alaska
Andalusia Public Library, Andalusia, Ala.
Anderson-Anderson, Stony Creek Township Public Library, Anderson, Ind.
Andrews University, Berrian Springs, Mich.
*Angstrom Productions, Inc., New York, N.Y.
Anoka County Library, Blaine, Minn.
Anoka County Library, Fridley, Minn.
*Anoka-Ramsey Community College, Coon Rapids, Minn.
Antigo Public Library, Antigo, Wis.
*Antioch College, Yellow Springs, Ohio
Arcadia Public Library, Arcadia, Calif.
*Archdiocese of Philadelphia, Philadelphia, Pa.
*Archdiocese of Portland Radio-TV Commission, Portland, Oreg.
Arizona Department of Library, Archives, & Public Records, Tempe, Ariz.
Arizona State University, Tempe, Ariz.
Arlington County Public Library, Arlington, Va.
Arrowhead Regional Library System, Virginia, Minn.
*Art Gallery of Ontario, Toronto, Ont., Canada

*Art—Official Inc, Toronto, Ont., Canada
*Asbury College, Wilmore, Ky.
Atchison County Library, Rock Port, Mo.
Atlanta Film Library. See Georgia State Department of Education
Auburn Community College, Auburn, N.Y.
*Auburn Public Library, Auburn, Mass.
Auburn University, Auburn, Ala.
Augusta Regional Library, Augusta, Ga.
Aurora Public Library, Aurora, Colo.
Austin-Mower County Library, Austin, Minn.
Azusa Public Library, Azusa, Calif.

Baldwin Public Library, Birmingham, Mich.
*Baptist Bible College of Pennsylvania, Carks Summit, Pa.
*Barnard College, New York, N.Y.
Barry-Lawrence Regional Library, Monett, Mo.
*Bartlesville Wesleyan College, Bartlesville, Okla.
*Barton County Community College, Great Bend, Kans.
*Bassist Institute, Portland, Oreg.
Bay County Library System, Bay City, Mich.
Beaumont Public Library, Beaumont, Tex.
Bedford Public Library, Bedford, Ind.
*Bellarmine College, Louisville, Ky.
*Bellevue Community College, Bellevue, Wash.
Bellingham Public Library, Bellingham, Wash.
Bellville Public Library, Bellville, N.J.
Beloit Public Library, Beloit, Wis.
Bemidji Public Library, Bemidji, Minn.
*Berea College, Berea, Ky.
*Bergen Community Museum, Paramus, N.J.
Bergenfield Free Public Library, Bergenfield, N.J.
*Berkeley Heights Public Library, Berkeley Heights, N.J.
Berne Public Library, Berne, Ind.
Bethlehem Public Library, Bethlehem, Pa.
Beverly Hills Public Library, Beverly Hills, Calif.
Bexley Public Library, Columbus, Ohio
B. F. Jones Memorial Library Aliquippa, Pa.
Bibliothèque centrale de prêt de l'Outaouvais, Hull, P.Q., Canada
Bibliothèque de la Ville de Montréal, Montréal, P.Q., Canada
Bibliothèque Municipale de Hull, Hull, P.Q., Canada
Bibliothèque Municipale de Saint Jean, Saint Jean, P.Q., Canada
*Billings Public Library, Billings, Mont.
Binghamton Public Library, Binghamton, N.Y.
Birchard Public Library, Fremont, Ohio
*Black Hawk College, Moline, Ill.
*Bloomfield College, Bloomfield, N.J.
Bloomfield Public Library, Bloomfield, N.J.
Bloomfield Township Public Library, Bloomfield Hills, Mich.
Blue Ridge Regional Library, Martinsburg, Va.
Blue Water Library Federation, St. Clair County Library, Port Huron, Mich.
Bluffton-Wells County Public Library, Bluffton, Ind.
Bob Jones University, Greenville, S.C.

*Booker T. Washington National Monument, Hardy, Va.
Boonslick Regional Library, Sedalia, Mo.
Borough of York Public Library, Toronto, Ont., Canada
*Boston Public Library, Boston, Mass.
Bowling Green Public Library, Bowling Green, Ky.
*Brainerd Community College, Brainerd, Minn.
*Brampton Public Library & Art Gallery, Bramalea, Ont., Canada
Brantford Public Library, Brantford, Ont., Canada
Bremen Public Library, Bremen, Ind.
Brewer State Junior College, Fayette, Ala.
Bridgewater College, Bridgewater, Va.
*Bridgewater State College, Bridgewater, Mass.
*Bridgeport Public Library, Bridgeport, Conn.
*Brigham Young University—Hawaii Campus, Laie, Hawaii
Brighton Public Library, Brighton, Mich.
Bristol Public Library, Bristol, Conn.
*Broadside Video, Johnson City, Tenn.
Brooklyn Public Library, Brooklyn, N.Y.
*Broward Community College, Fort Lauderdale, Fla.
Brown County Library, Green Bay, Wis.
Bruggemeyer Memorial Library, Monterey Park, Calif.
*Brunswick-Glynn County Regional Library, Brunswick, Ga.
Buckham Memorial Library, Faribault, Minn.
*Bucknell University, Lewisburg, Pa.
Bucks County Free Library, Doylestown, Pa.
*Buffalo & Erie County Public Library, Buffalo, N.Y.
*Burlington County Library, Mount Holly, N.J.
*Burlington Public Library, Burlington, Ont., Canada
Burlington Public Library, Burlington, Wis.
Bur Oak Library System Joliet, Ill.
*Butte Community College District, Oroville, Calif.

*Cabrillo College, Aptos, Calif.
Calcasieu Parish Public Library, Lake Charles, La.
Calgary Public Library, Calgary, Alta., Canada
*California Baptist College, Riverside, Calif.
*California Institute of the Arts, Valencia, Calif.
*California State College Bakersfield, Bakersfield, Calif.
California State College, Dominguez Hills, Calif.
*California State University Long Beach Library, Long Beach, Calif.
California State University, Sacramento, Calif.
*Calvin College, Grand Rapids, Mich.
*Camden County College, Blackwood, N.J.
Camden County Library, Camden, N.J.
Camden Public Library, Camden, N.J.
*Campbellsville College, Campbellsville, Ky.
Canada Ministry of Transport, Sydney, N.S., Canada
Canadian Dental Association, Don Mills, Ont., Canada

Canadian Union College, College Heights, Alta., Canada

Cape Girardeau Public Library, Cape Girardeau, Mo.

*Capital University Columbus, Ohio

*Carlsbad City Library, Carlsbad, Calif.

Carnegie Institute, Pittsburgh, Pa.

Carnegie Library of Pittsburgh, Pittsburgh, Pa.

*Carson-Newman College, Jefferson City, Tenn.

Carver County Library, Chaska, Minn.

Cass County Library, Cassopolis, Mich.

Cass County Library, Harrisonville, Mo.

Cass County Public Library, Logansport, Ind.

*Castelli-Sonnabend Tapes & Films, Inc., New York, N.Y.

Cattermole Memorial Library, Fort Madison, Iowa

*Cecil Community College, Northeast, Md.

*Cedar Falls Public Library, Cedar Falls, Iowa

*Cedar Rapids Public Library, Cedar Rapids, Iowa

*Centennial College of Applied Arts & Technology, Scarborough, Ont., Canada

Center Cinema Co-op, Chicago, Ill.

*Center for Innovation & Research in Cable Television, Portland, Oreg.

*Central Carolina Technical Institute, Sanford, N.C.

*Central Florida Community College, Ocala, Fla.

*Central Massachusetts Regional Library System, Worcester, Mass.

Central Missouri State University, Warrensburg, Mo.

*Central Piedmont Community College, Charlotte, N.C.

Cerritos Public Library, Cerritos, Calif.

*Chabot College, Hayward, Calif.

*Chaminade College of Honolulu, Honolulu, Hawaii

Champaign County Library, Urbana, Ohio

Champaign Public Library, Champaign, Ill.

*Charles Camsell Hospital, Edmonton, Alta., Canada

Charleston Museum, Charleston, S.C.

*Chatham College, Pittsburgh, Pa.

*Chatham Public Library, Chatham, Ont., Canada

*Chautauqua-Cattaraugus Library System, Jamestown, N.Y.

Cheboygan Public Library, Cheboygan, Mich.

Cherry Hill Free Public Library, Cherry Hill, N.J.

*Chester County Intermediate Unit, West Chester, Pa.

Chester County Library, West Chester, Pa.

Chesterfield Public Library, Chester, Va.

Chicago Public Library, Chicago, Ill.

*Chicago State University, Chicago, Ill.

Chickasaw Library System, Ardmore, Okla.

*Children's Hospital-University Affiliated Program, Los Angeles, Calif.

*Chipola Junior College, Marianna, Fla.

Chippewa County Library, Montevideo, Minn.

Christian Church Services, Office of Communication, Indianapolis, Ind.

Christian County Library, Ozark, Mo.

*Chula Vista Public Library, Chula Vista, Calif.

*Church of the Holy Trinity, Toronto, Ont., Canada

Cinémathèque Pacifique, Vancouver, B.C., Canada

Circus World Museum, Baraboo, Wis.

*Citrus College, Azusa, Calif.

*City University of New York, Manhattan Community College, New York, N.Y.

*City University of New York, New York Community College, Brooklyn, N.Y.

*Claremore Junior College, Claremore, Okla.

Clark County Library District, Las Vegas, Nev.

*Clatsop Community College, Astoria, Oreg.

Cleveland Public Library, Cleveland, Ohio

*Clinton Community College, Clinton, Iowa

Clinton Public Library, Clinton, Iowa

*Coastal Carolina Community College, Jacksonville, N.C.

*Cochise College, Douglas, Ariz.

*Colby College, Waterville, Maine

*Collège du Nord-Ouest, Rouyn, P.Q., Canada

*College Misericordia, Dallas, Pa.

*College of DuPage, Glen Ellyn, Ill.

*College of St. Benedict, St. Joseph, Minn.

*College of Saint Elizabeth, Convent Station, N.J.

*College of St. Thomas, St. Paul, Minn.

*College of San Mateo, San Mateo, Calif.

*College of the Desert, Palm Desert, Calif.

*College of the Redwoods, Eureka, Calif.

Colorado State Library, Denver, Colo.

*Columbia-Greene Community College, Hudson, N.Y.

*Columbia University, New York, N.Y.

*Columbus Public Library, Columbus, Ohio

*Columbus Technical Institute, Columbus, Ohio

Commerce Public Library, Commerce, Calif.

*Community College of Baltimore, Baltimore, Md.

*Community College of Denver, Denver, Colo.

*Community College of Philadelphia, Philadelphia, Pa.

*Concordia College, Portland, Oreg.

*Concordia Seminary, St. Louis, Mo.

*Concordia Teachers College, River Forest, Ill.

*Concordia Theological Seminary, Fort Wayne, Ind.

*Confederation Centre Art Gallery & Museum, Charlottetown, P.E.I., Canada

Connecticut College, New London, Conn.

Connersville Public Library, Connersville, Ind.

Conococheague District Library, Chambersburg, Pa.

*Contemporary Resources in the Arts, Seattle, Wash.

*Contra Costa County Library, Pleasant Hill, Calif.

Cornell University, Ithaca, N.Y.

Corning Museum of Glass, Corning, N.Y.

*Cornwall Public Library, Cornwall-on-Hudson, N.Y.

Coshocton Public Library, Coshocton, Ohio

*Cosumnes River College, Sacramento, Calif.

*Cranbrook Academy of Art, Bloomfield Hills, Mich.

*Craven Community College, New Bern, N.C.

Crawfordsville Public Library, Crawfordsville, Ind.

*Creative Outlet, Portland, Oreg.

Cromaine Public Library, Hartland, Mich.

*Crow River Regional Library, Willmar, Minn.

Culver Public Library, Culver, Ind.

*Cumberland County College, Vineland, N.J.

Cumberland County Library, Bridgeton, N.J.

Cumberland Regional Library, Amherst, N.S., Canada

*Current River Regional Library, Van Buren, Mo.

Currier Gallery of Art, Manchester, N.H.

Cuyahoga County Public Library, Cleveland, Ohio

Dakota County Library System, Burnsville, Minn.

Dakota-Scott Regional Library, St. Paul, Minn.

*Dallas Public Library, Dallas, Tex.

*Danbury Public Library, Danbury, Conn.

Daniel Boone Regional Library, Columbia, Mo.

Dartmouth College, Hanover, N.H.

*Daviess County Library, Gallatin, Mo.

Dayton & Montgomery County Public Library, Dayton, Ohio

Dearborn Department of Libraries, Dearborn, Mich.

Decatur Public Library, Decatur, Ind.

*Defiance College, Defiance, Ohio

*Dekalb Community College-South Campus, Decatur, Ga.

Dekalb Library System, Decatur, Ga.

*Delaware County Community College, Media, Pa.

*Delaware Technical & Community College, Georgetown, Del.

*Denver Public Library, Denver, Colo.

Des Moines Public Library, Des Moines, Iowa

Detroit Public Library, Detroit, Mich.

Divide County Public Library, Crosby, N. Dak.

Douglas County Library, Roseburg, Oreg.

Dowagiac Public Library, Dowagiac, Mich.

*Drew University, Madison, N.J.

*Drexel University, Instructional Systems, Philadelphia, Pa.

*Drexel University, Library, Non-Print Section, Philadelphia, Pa.

*Duluth Public Library, Duluth, Minn.

*Dundalk Community College, Baltimore, Md.

Dundas Public Library, Dundas, Ont., Canada

Dunklin County Library, Kennett, Mo.

Dwight D. Eisenhower Library, Totowa Borough, N.J.

Dwyer-Mercer County District Library, Celina, Ohio

*Dyke College, Cleveland, Ohio

*Earlham College, Richmond, Ind.

East Central Regional Library, Cambridge, Minn.

East Chicago Public Library, East Chicago, Ind.

*East Islip Public Library, East Islip, N.Y.

East Orange Public Library, East Orange, N.J.

East Tennessee State University, Johnson City, Tenn.

*East Texas State University, Commerce, Tex.

*Eastern College, St. Davids, Pa.

*Eastern Illinois University, Charleston, Ill.

*Eastern Mennonite College, Harrisonburg, Va.

*Eastern Michigan University, Ypsilanti, Mich.

*Eastern Montana College, Billings, Mont.

*Eastern Ontario Regional Library System, Ottawa, Ont., Canada

Eastern Peninsula Library System, Sault Ste. Marie, Mich.

*Eastern Washington State College, Cheney, Wash.

*Eastern Washington State Historical Society, Spokane, Wash.

Easton Area Public Library, Easton, Pa.

Eckhart Public Library, Auburn, Ind.

Edgecombe County Technical Institute, Tarboro, N.C.

*Edinboro State College, Edinboro, Pa.

Edmonton Public Library, Edmonton, Alta., Canada

Edwin Bemis Public Library, Littleton, Colo.

*The Electron Movers, Providence, R.I.

*Electronic Arts Intermix, Inc., New York, N.Y.

*Elizabeth City State University, Elizabeth City, N.C.

*Elizabethtown Community College, Elizabethtown, Ky.

Elk Grove Village Public Library, Elk Grove, Ill.

Elkhart Public Library, Elkhart, Ind.

*Elko County Library, Elko, Nev.

Elizabeth Public Library, Elizabeth, N.J.

*Ellsworth Community College, Iowa Falls, Iowa

*Elmira College, Elmira, N.Y.

El Paso Public Library, El Paso, Tex.

Elyria Public Library Elyria, Ohio

*Emporia Kansas State College, Emporia, Kans.

Escondido Public Library, Escondido, Calif.

*Etobicoke Public Library, Etobicoke, Ont., Canada

Eugene Public Library, Eugene, Oreg.

Evanston Public Library, Evanston, Ill.

Evansville Public Library & Vanderburgh County Public Library, Evansville, Ind.

*Evergreen State College, Olympia, Wash.

*Everson Museum of Art, Syracuse, N.Y.

Spokane Public Library, Spokane, Wash.
Stanford University, Stanford, Calif.
*Stanislaus County Free Library, Modesto,
Calif.
Stark County District Library, Canton, Ohio
Starved Rock Library System, Ottawa, Ill.
*State Library of Ohio, Columbus, Ohio
*State University of New York, Agricultural
and Technical College, Farmingdale, N.Y.
State University of New York at Buffalo,
Buffalo, N.Y.
State University of New York at Stony Brook,
Stony Brook, N.Y.
*State University of New York, College at
Cortland, Cortland, N.Y.
*State University of New York, College at
Potsdam, Potsdam, N.Y.
Sterling College, Sterling, Kans.
*Sterling Municipal Library, Baytown, Tex.
*Stevens Institute of Technology, Hoboken,
N.J.
Stoneham Public Library, Stoneham, Mass.
*Stratford Public Library, Stratford, Ont.,
Canada
*Students' Museum, Inc., Knoxville, Tenn.
Sturgis Public Library, Sturgis, Mich.
*Sudbury Public Library, Sudbury, Ont.,
Canada
*Sue Bennett College, London, Ky.
Suffolk Cooperative Library System, Bellport,
N.Y.
Suomi College Library, Hancock, Mich.
Superior Public Library, Superior, Wis.
Sussex County Library, Newton, N.J.
Syracuse University, Syracuse, N.Y.

*Tacoma Art Museum, Tacoma, Wash.
*Tacoma Community College, Tacoma, Wash.
*Tallahassee Community College Library,
Tallahassee, Fla.
*Tampa College, St. Petersburg, Fla.
*Tarrant County Junior College System, Hurst,
Tex.
Taylor University, Upland, Ind.
T. B. Scott Free Library, Merrill, Wis.
Teachers College Library, New York, N.Y.
*Tennessee Valley Authority, Golden Pond, Ky.
Terrebonne Parish Library, Houma, La.
*Texas A & I University at Corpus Christi,
Corpus Christi, Tex.
*Texas A & I University at Laredo, Laredo, Tex.
Texas County Library, Houston, Mo.
*Texas Southmost College & City of
Brownsville City-College Library,
Brownsville, Tex.
*Texas State Technical Institute, Harlingen,
Tex.
*Texas Wesleyan College, Fort Worth, Tex.
Thomas Jefferson Library System, Jefferson
City, Mo.
Thomas More College, Fort Mitchell, Ky.
Thompson Public Library, Thompson, Man.,
Canada
*Three Rivers Community College, Poplar
Bluff, Mo.
*Tidewater Community College, Portsmouth,
Va.
*Tidewater Community College, Virginia
Beach, Va.
Tiffin Public Library, Tiffin, Ohio
*Timberland Regional Library, Olympia, Wash.
Tipton County Public Library, Tipton, Ind.
Toledo-Lucas County Public Library, Toledo,
Ohio
*Tompkins County Public Library, Ithaca, N.Y.
Topeka Public Library, Topeka, Kans.
*Toronto Public Libraries, Toronto, Ont.,
Canada
Town & Country Regional Library, Neosho,
Mo.
*Trails Regional Library, Warrensburg, Mo.
Transcona Public Library, Winnipeg, Man.,
Canada

Traverse City Public Library, Traverse City,
Mich.
Traverse Des Sioux Regional Library,
Mankato, Minn.
Trenton Memorial Public Library, Trenton,
Ont., Canada
Trenton Public Library, Trenton, N.J.
*Trenton State College, Trenton, N.J.
*Trevecca Nazarene College, Nashville, Tenn.
*Tri-County Regional Library, Rome, Ga.
Troy Public Library, Troy, Mich.
Troy State University, Troy, Ala.
*Tucson Public Library, Tucson, Ariz.
Tufts Library, Weymouth, Mass.
*Tulsa City-County Library, Tulsa, Okla.
Tunxis Community College, Farmington,
Conn.

*Union Theological Seminary in Virginia,
Richmond, Va.
Union County Public Library, Liberty, Ind.
United Church of Christ, Philadelphia, Pa.
United States Golf Association Library, Far
Hills, N.J.
*United States International University, San
Diego, Calif.
*United States Military Academy, West Point,
N.Y.
*United Theological Seminary, Dayton, Ohio
Université de Sherbrooke, Sherbrooke, P.Q.,
Canada
Université Laval, Bibliothèque Générale,
Quebec, P.Q., Canada
*University of Akron, Akron, Ohio
*University of Alabama, University, Ala.
*University of Alaska, Fairbanks, Alaska
University of Alberta, Edmonton, Alta.,
Canada
University of Albuquerque, Center for
Learning & Information Resources,
Albuquerque, N. Mex.
University of Arizona, Tucson, Ariz.
University of British Columbia, Vancouver,
B.C., Canada
*University of Calgary, Calgary, Alta., Canada
University of California Art Museum,
Berkeley, Calif.
*University of California, Berkeley Campus,
Berkeley, Calif.
University of California, Extension Media
Center, Berkeley, Calif.
*University of California, Santa Cruz, Calif.
University of California, UCLA Medical
Center, Los Angeles, Calif.
University of Colorado, Boulder, Colo.
*University of Connecticut, Storrs, Conn.
*University of Delaware, Newark, Del.
*University of Detroit, Detroit, Mich.
*University of Florida, Gainesville, Fla.
*University of Guelph, Guelph, Ont., Canada
*University of Hawaii, Instructional Resources
Service Center, Honolulu, Hawaii
University of Hawaii Library, AV Services,
Honolulu, Hawaii.
University of Hawaii, Lihue, Hawaii
*University of Illinois at Urbana-Champaign,
Urbana, Ill.
University of Illinois, Champaign, Ill.
*University of Idaho, Moscow, Idaho
University of Iowa, Media Library, Iowa City,
Iowa
*University of Iowa, TV Unit, Iowa City, Iowa
University of Kansas, Lawrence, Kans.
*University of Kentucky, Lexington, Ky.
University Laval, Service de l'Audiovisuel,
Quebec, P.Q., Canada
*University of Maine, Augusta, Maine
University of Maine, Orono, Maine
*University of Manitoba, Winnipeg, Man.,
Canada
*University of Maryland, College Park, Md.
University of Michigan, AV Education Center,
Ann Arbor, Mich.

*University of Michigan, School of Dentistry,
Ann Arbor, Mich.
*University of Michigan, TV Center, Ann
Arbor, Mich.
University of Michigan, Undergraduate
Library, Ann Arbor, Mich.
University of Minnesota, Minneapolis, Minn.
University of Minnesota, St. Paul, Minn.
University of Missouri-Columbia, Columbia,
Mo.
*University of Missouri, Rolla, Mo.
University of Nebraska, Instructional Media
Center, Lincoln, Nebr.
University of Nebraska, Sheldon Film
Theater, Lincoln, Nebr.
University of New Hampshire, Durham,
N.H.
*University of New Mexico, Health Sciences
Library, Albuquerque, N. Mex.
*University of New Mexico, Instructional
Media Service, Albuquerque, N. Mex.
*University of New Orleans, New Orleans, La.
*University of North Carolina-Charlotte,
Charlotte, N.C.
*University of Northern Iowa, Cedar Falls,
Iowa
*University of North Dakota, Grand Forks, N.
Dak.
University of Oklahoma, Norman, Okla.
*University of Richmond, Richmond, Va.
*University of Rochester, Rochester, N.Y.
*University of Santa Clara, Santa Clara, Calif.
*University of Saskatchewan, Saskatoon,
Sask., Canada
*University of South Alabama, Mobile, Ala.
University of South Dakota, Vermillion, S.
Dak.
University of South Dakota at Springfield,
Springfield, S. Dak.
University of South Florida, Film Library,
Tampa, Fla.
*University of South Florida, Learning
Laboratory, Tampa, Fla.
*University of Southern California, Los
Angeles, Calif.
*University of Southern Mississippi,
Hattiesburg, Miss.
University of Southwestern Louisiana,
Lafayette, La.
*University of Tennessee, Chattanooga, Tenn.
University of Tennessee, Knoxville, Tenn.
University of Texas at Arlington, Arlington,
Tex.
University of Texas at Austin, Austin, Tex.
*University of Toronto, Toronto, Ont., Canada
*University of Utah, Salt Lake City, Utah
*University of Vermont, Burlington, Vt.
University of Washington, AV Services,
Seattle, Wash.
*University of Washington, Odegaard
Undergraduate Library Media Center,
Seattle, Wash.
*University of Western Ontario, London, Ont.,
Canada
*University of Windsor, Windsor, Ont., Canada
*University of Wisconsin-Eau Claire, Eau
Claire, Wis.
University of Wisconsin, Madison, Wis.
*University of Wisconsin-Milwaukee,
Milwaukee, Wis.
University of Wisconsin-Oshkosh, Oshkosh,
Wis.
*University of Wisconsin-Stout, Menomonie,
Wis.
University of Wisconsin-Superior, Superior,
Wis.
*University of Wisconsin-Whitewater,
Whitewater, Wis.
University of Wyoming, Laramie, Wyo.
Upsala College, East Orange, N.J.
Utah State Library Commission, Salt Lake
City, Utah
*Utah State University, Logan, Utah
*University Student Telecommunications
Corp., Minneapolis, Minn.

INDEX OF SPECIAL COLLECTIONS

Within the body of most entries contained in the text of this volume, film collections have been identified in terms of the percentage of films held by category, or subject, compared to total holdings. Those institutions which indicated category or subject holdings representing 20 percent or more of a total collection appear here under their appropriate headings. For a more specific breakdown of kinds of films maintained in a collection, see individual entries.

CONSUMER AFFAIRS

CRIME & CRIMINAL JUSTICE

DANCE

DUNSTAN, GATEWOOD, COLLECTION

ENGINEERING

ERNST, LOUISE, COLLECTION

EROTICA & STAG FILMS

EXPERIMENTAL FILMS

FEATURE FILMS

FINE ARTS

FOREIGN CULTURES

HEALTH & SAFETY

HOLIDAYS

HOME ECONOMICS

HUMANITIES

SPORTS

Brown County Library, Green Bay, Wis.
National Baseball Hall of Fame & Museum, Inc., Cooperstown, N.Y.
North Olympic Library System, Port Angeles, Wash.
Suomi College, Hancock, Mich.
United States Gold Association Library, Far Hills, N.J.
University of Albuquerque, Center for Learning & Information Resources, Albuquerque, N. Mex.

TEACHER EDUCATION

Alderson-Broaddus College, Philippi, W. Va.
Bucknell University, Lewisburg, Pa.
California State College Bakersfield, Bakersfield, Calif.
Calvin College, Grand Rapids, Mich.
Chicago State University, Chicago, Ill.
Concordia Teachers College, River Forest, Ill.
Edinboro State College, Edinboro, Pa.
Elmira College, Elmira, N.Y.
Emporia Kansas State College, Emporia, Kans.
Friends University, Wichita, Kans.
Glenville State College, Glenville, W. Va.
Illinois State University, Educational Media Service Center, Normal, Ill.
Kutztown State College, Kutztown, Pa.
Northern Illinois University, Dekalb, Ill.
Lewis & Clark College, Portland, Oreg.
Milligan College, Milligan College, Tenn.
National Association of Educational Broadcasters, Dayton, Ohio
New York State Department of Education, Albany, N.Y.
New York University, Film Library, New York, N.Y.
Oakland University, Rochester, Mich.
Queen's University, Kingston, Ont., Canada
Regional Resources Center Film Library, King of Prussia, Pa.
Southwest Texas State University, San Marcos, Tex.
Texas A & I University at Corpus Christi, Corpus Christi, Tex.
Texas A & I University at Laredo, Laredo, Tex.
Texas Wesleyan College, Fort Worth, Tex.
University of Saskatchewan, Saskatoon, Sask., Canada
Western Washington State College, Bellingham, Wash.
Wright State University, Dayton, Ohio

TELEVISION

The Library of Congress, Washington, D.C.
Union Theological Seminary in Virginia, Richmond, Va.
Wesleyan University, Middletown, Conn.

TRAVEL

Binghamton Public Library, Binghamton, N.Y.
Brunswick-Glynn County Regional Library, Brunswick, Ga.
Mishawaka Public Library, Mishawaka, Ind.

TRUMAN, HARRY S.

National Archives and Records Service, Independence, Mo.

WOMEN

Chatham College, Pittsburgh, Pa.
United Church of Christ, Philadelphia, Pa.

WORLD WAR II FILMS

The Library of Congress, Washington, D.C.

WYOMING

Sheridan County Fulmer Public Library, Sheridan, Wyo.

FILM CIRCUITS AND COOPERATIVES

In questionnairing libraries throughout North America in the compilation of this volume, it is apparent that, because of the high cost of film service to the smaller library, there is a heavy reliance on membership in cooperative arrangements in order to meet the film demands of patrons and groups. For purposes of creating this section, we have used the following definitions dealing with such cooperative arrangements which appear in Dr. George Rehrauer's *The Film User's Handbook* (Bowker): A *cooperative* consists of several libraries joined together to provide film service; methods include acquisition, rental, circuit, or central pool. A *circuit* is a group of libraries that routes packets of films on a scheduled basis. A member library has custody of each packet for a specific, uniform period of time and then arranges delivery of it to the next member. The *packet* usually includes six or more films placed together as a unit package that is circulated in round-robin fashion among member libraries of a circuit. The *central pool* is a film collection retained in one location which serves as the administrative center. Films from the collection are booked for specific periods by member libraries. After use the films are returned directly to the center.

California

FILM COUNCIL FILM CIRCUIT, 4819 Regalo Rd, Woodland Hills 93164. *Tel:* (213) 348-8767. *In Charge:* William J. & Iris A. Speed, Co-admins.
Film Holdings: 380t/p. *Membership Total:* 13. *Membership Criteria & Audience Served:* Any public library applying for & being accepted by the governing commission. The Circuit was organized in 1958. *Initial Fee:* $1200. *Yearly Assessment:* $1400. *General Meetings:* Held annually at a member library. *Preview-Selection Committee Meetings:* Monthly. *Pubns:* Catalog.

PUBLIC LIBRARY FILM CIRCUIT, c/o Pomona Public Library, 625 S Garey Ave, Box 2271, Pomona 91766. *Tel:* (714) 620-2033. *In Charge:* Gregory B. Shapton, AV Superv. (admin changes annually).
Film Holdings: 425t/428p. *Membership Total:* 14. *Membership Criteria & Audience Served:* Membership restricted to public libraries. Audience consists of general public. *Initial Fee:* $2500. *Yearly Assessment:* $1200. *Budget:* $17,704.86 (7/1/75-6/30/76). *General Meetings:* Held monthly. Rotate among member libraries. *Preview-Selection Committee Meetings:* Monthly. *Pubns:* Catalog.

SOUTHERN CALIFORNIA FILM CIRCUIT, 4819 Regalo Rd, Woodland Hills 93164. *Tel:* (213) 348-8767. *In Charge:* William J. & Iris A. Speed, Co-Admins.
Film Holdings: 450t/p. *Membership Total:* 12. *Membership Criteria & Audience Served:* Any. public library applying & being accepted by the governing commission. Membership has traditionally been restricted to 12. This year the commission voted to increase membership to 13. Circuit has been in continuous operation since October 1951. *Initial Fee:* $1200. *Yearly Assessment:* $1400. *General Meetings:* Held annually at a member library. *Preview-Selection Committee Meetings:* Monthly. *Pubns:* Catalog.

Connecticut

CONNECTICUT FILM CIRCUIT, c/o Russell Library, 119 Broad St, Middletown 06457. *Tel:* (203) 347-2528, ext 22. *In Charge:* Linda Rusczek, Admin.
Film Holdings: Approx 420t/p. *Membership Total:* 12. *Membership Criteria & Audience Served:* Public libraries and public

library patrons. Each member library sets own regulations. Film inspection required. *Initial Fee:* Varies. *Yearly Assessment:* $1200. *Budget:* $14,000 (7/1-6/30). *General Meetings:* Held monthly at various member libraries. *Preview-Selection Committee Meetings:* Monthly.

EASTERN CONNECTICUT FILM CIRCUIT, c/o Public Library of New London, 63 Huntington St, New London 06320. *Tel:* (203) 447-1411. *In Charge:* Elizabeth Whitten, Admin.
Film Holdings: 165t. *Membership Total:* 13.

FAIRFIELD COUNTY FILM CIRCUIT, Stamford's Public (Ferguson Memorial) Library, 96 Broad St, Stamford 06901. *Tel:* (203) 325-4354. *In Charge:* W. Gage Smith, Admin.
Film Holdings: 12 feature films. *Membership Total:* 6.

FILM COOPERATIVE OF CONNECTICUT, Seymour Public Library, 46 Church St, Seymour 06483. *Tel:* (203) 888-5558. *In Charge:* Open.
Film Holdings: 500t. *Membership Total:* 22. *Membership Criteria & Audience Served:* Public libraries. No films may be used for classroom use and no admission charged for use of films. *Initial Fee:* According to population served (.065 per capita). *Yearly Assessment:* According to population. *Budget:* $27,821 (includes $13,000 state grant for purchase of films with ethnic heritage theme for children in hospitals). *General Meetings:* Held quarterly at Seymour Public Library headquarters. *Preview-Selection Committee Meetings:* Monthly. *Pubns:* Catalog of sponsored films, *The Loop* (newspaper).

TOWN AND GOWN FILM CIRCUIT, Village Library, 71 Main St, Farmington 06032. *Tel:* (203) 677-1529. *In Charge:* Barbara Gibson, Admin.
Film Holdings: 175t. *Membership Total:* 8.

Indiana

INDIANA LIBRARY FILM SERVICE, 2201 Godman Ave, Muncie 47303. *Tel:* (317) 289-4271. *In Charge:* Suzanne Kieffer, Exec Sec.
Film Holdings: 750t/770p. *Membership Total:* 35. *Membership Criteria & Audience Served:* Members are Indiana public libraries. Audiences are public library patrons. *Initial Fee:* Twice annual fee or $6000. *Yearly Assessment:* $700-$1300, depending on population served. *Budget:* $39,000 (1976 calendar yr). Film Service also contractually administrates Library Flicks. *General Meetings:* Held twice a year; location varies. *Preview-Selection Committee Meetings:* Annually. *Pubns:* Catalog plus catalog for federally funded film program serving all Indiana public libraries. (This program has holdings of about 600 prints.)

LIBRARY FLICKS LIBRARY SERVICES AUTHORITY, 2201 Godman Ave, Muncie 47303. *Tel:* (317) 289-4271. *In Charge:* Suzanne Kieffer, Exec Sec.
Film Holdings: 40-film initial collection purchased in 1976. *Membership Total:* 8. *Membership Criteria & Audience Served:* Members are Indiana public libraries with audience of public library patrons. *Initial Fee:* $2000. *Yearly Assessment:* $1000. *Budget:* $13,000. *General Meetings:* Held annually. *Preview-Selection Committee Meetings:* As required. *Pubns:* Catalog.

Iowa

FILMS FOR IOWA LIBRARY MEDIA SERVICES, INC, 321 Main, Davenport 52801 *Tel:* (319) 323-7511. *In Charge:* Jacqueline Logan, Exec Admin.
Film Holdings: 575t/p. *Membership Total:* 21. *Membership Criteria & Audience Served:* Public libraries of Iowa. Have packets which circulate & a feature film collection. *Initial Fee:* $2100. *Yearly Assessment:* $1800. *Budget:* $27,800 (4/1/76-3/31/77). *General Meetings:* Held annually. *Pubns:* Catalog, newsletter.

Massachusetts

MASSACHUSETTS FILM & MEDIA SERVICE COOPERATIVE, Fitchburg State College, Fitchburg 01440. *Tel:* (617) 345-0166. *In Charge:* Paul E. McKenna, Jr, Coord.
Film Holdings: Approx. 4000t/5500p. *Membership Criteria & Audience Served:* Membership open to institutions of public higher education, public schools, private schools, public libraries, hospitals, community agencies, government agencies, other governmental agencies with the Commonwealth of Massachusetts at a minimum of $200 per year. *Initial Fee:* $200. *Yearly Assessment:* $72 per $200. *General Meetings:* Held 6 times yearly at Fitchburg State College. *Preview-Selection Committee Meetings:* Presently working on revision of policy. *Pubns:* Catalog.

Michigan

MICHIGAN LIBRARY FILM CIRCUIT, INC, 735 E Michigan Ave, Lansing 48933. *Tel:* (517) 373-1579. *In Charge:* A. Michael Deller, Pres (Bloomfield Twp PL, 1099 Lone Pine Rd, Bloomfield Hills, MI 48013).
Film Holdings: 800t/860p. *Membership Total:* 35. *Membership Criteria & Audience Served:* Must be a public library. Audience consists of the general public, individuals, & clubs, groups such as Scouts, community action centers & inst such as hospitals, convalescent homes, churches. *Initial Fee:* $750. *Yearly Assessment:* $750. *Budget:* $50,000 (7/1-6/30). *General Meetings:* Held once a year at various locations. *Preview-Selection Committee Meetings:* 7 times or more. *Pubns:* Catalog.

SOUTHEAST MICHIGAN REGIONAL FILM LIBRARY, c/o Raisin Valley Library System, 3700 S Custer Rd, Monroe 48161. *Tel:* (313) 241-5277. *WATS:* 1-800-572-6575. *In Charge:* Bernard A. Margolis, Dir.
Membership Total: 6 public library systems in SE Michigan (all of the public libraries in the 8 counties of Wayne, Oakland, Macomb, Livingston, Washtenaw, Monroe, Lenawee & Jackson. *Membership Criteria & Audience Served:* Funded under LSCA 1, the Southeast Michigan Regional Film Library serves a population of close to five million public library patrons with popular film materials available free from the members of the participating system libraries. *Budget:* $100,000 (7/1/75-6/30/76). *General Meetings:* Held quarterly, usually at library headquarters. *Preview-Selection Committee Meetings:* Individually & continually. *Pubns:* Catalog, request forms, etc.

Minnesota

MINNESOTA LIBRARY FILM CIRCUIT, c/o Office of Public Libraries, 301 Hanover Bldg, 480 Cedar St, St Paul 55101. *Tel:* (612) 296-2821. *TWX:* 910-563-3571. *In Charge:* Nowell Leitzke, Film Circuit Coord.
Film Holdings: 1665t/1915p. *Membership Total:* 35. *Membership Criteria & Audience Served:* Membership is open to any public library in Minn., subject to acceptance by majority vote of the membership, and subject to the payment of dues. The Circuit serves as a supportive resource for public library film collections; it does not purchase films that would be of use primarily to schools. *Initial Fee:* $1600. *Yearly Assessment:* $1000. *Budget:* $66,000 (1/1/76-1/1/77). *General Meetings:* Held once a year at Minneapolis Public Library. *Preview-Selection Committee Meetings:* Quarterly. *Pubns:* Catalog.

Mississippi

MISSISSIPPI LIBRARY COMMISSION, Box 3260, Jackson 39207. *Tel:* (601) 354-6369. *In Charge:* Gerald Buchanan, Asst Dir for Library Operations.
Film Holdings: 282t/286p. *Membership Criteria & Audience Served:* Films are available for public use statewide through public & academic libraries. *Budget:* $25,000 (7/1/76-6/30/76). *Preview-Selection Committee Meetings:* Weekly. *Pubns:* Catalog.

Missouri

MISSOURI LIBRARIES FILM COOPERATIVE, 15616 E 24 Highway, Independence 64050. *Tel:* (816) 833-4234. *In Charge:* Mrs. Mary MacPherson, Admin.
Film Holdings: 2892t/3986p. *Membership Total:* 36. *Membership Criteria & Audience Served:* Membership at present is limited to public libraries. Audiences include nursing homes, scouts, churches, men's groups, preschools (schools may use package films only), home users, practically any type of organization, etc. *Yearly Assessment:* Fees are based on a budget figure set by the executive board & approved by the membership. This is calculated on a percentage basis, ½ on each library's assessed valuation to the total, and ½ on the library's population to the total membership population. *Budget:* $60,000 (7/1/75-6/30/76). *General Meetings:* Held annually in Independence of Kansas City, Mo. *Preview-Selection Committee Meetings:* Not a committee; membership meets annually & divides into room groups (5 in 1976). *Pubns:* Two catalogs, one Spot Booking Catalog & one Package Catalog (with scheduling calendar & programs).

New Hampshire

NORTH COUNTRY LIBRARIES FILM COOPERATIVE, 42 Al's Ave, Suncook 03275. *Tel:* (603) 485-9076. *In Charge:* Carol A. Brown, Coord.
Film Holdings: 890t/20p. *Membership Total:* 3. *Membership Criteria & Audience Served:* Equal commitments for film purchases. Audience consists of public libraries programs, community organizations, residents in state inst. *Budget:* $700 (7/1/75-6/30/76). *General Meetings:* Held monthly in rotation around Maine, New Hampshire, Vermont. *Preview-Selection Committee Meetings:* Monthly. *Pubns:* Catalog, occasional lists by subject.

New Jersey

GARDEN STATE LIBRARY FILM CIRCUIT, Irvington Public Library, Irvington 07111. *Tel:* (201) 372-6400, ext 25. *In Charge:* Jim Thomas, Pres.
Film Holdings: Approx. 800t/950p. *Membership Total:* 19. *Membership Criteria & Audience Served:* The GSLFC serves the patrons of the member libraries—including teachers. Approx. 35% of the Circuit's prints are children's films. *Initial Fee:* Not set. *Yearly Assessment:* $1500. *Budget:* $28,500 (calendar year). *General Meetings:* Held monthly at N.J. State Library, Trenton. *Pubns:* Catalog.

NEW JERSEY LIBRARY FILM CIRCUIT, Somerset County Library, County Administration Bldg, Somerville 08876. *Tel:* (201) 725-4700, ext 234. *In Charge:* Mrs. Elizabeth G. MacConnell, AV Librarian.
Film Holdings: 612t/600p. *Membership Total:* 12. *Membership Criteria & Audience Served:* Must be a public library in N.J. interested in furthering the use of motion picture film, pay $500 entrance fee (put in the insurance fund), must have film inspection equipment in the library, pay $1500 yearly, share in the work of running the Circuit. Audience served is the public library community or anyone with a public library card. *Initial Fee:* $500 plus automatic inspection equipment. *Yearly Assessment:* $1500. *Budget:* $1800 (9/1/75-8/31/76). *General Meetings:* Rotate monthly, at various libraries. *Preview-Selection Committee Meetings:* Monthly. *Pubns:* Catalog.

New York

NASSAU COUNTY COOPERATIVE FILM CIRCUIT, c/o
Film Circuit Chairman, 280 Central Ave, Lawrence 11559.
Tel: (516) CE9-3262. *In Charge:* Martin Landweber, Coop
Film Circuit Chairman.
Film Holdings: 270t/p. *Membership Total:* 9. *Membership Criteria & Audience Served:* General audience appropriate to that
library's community. Criteria is based on the library being
served by the NLS, and that the library member has the
facilities to inspect, maintain & care for the films while in its
possession. Responsibility for damage rests with the library
that has the film for that period. *Initial Fee:* $1000. *Yearly
Assessment:* $1000. *General Meetings:* Held once a year. Location varies. *Preview-Selection Committee Meetings:* Members
preview their own films for the circuit. *Pubns:* Catalog.

Ohio

CENTRAL OHIO FILM CIRCUIT, Louisville Public Library,
Louisville 44641. *Tel:* (216) 875-1696. *In Charge:* Mary
Louise Lowe, Circuit Sec.
Film Holdings: 405t/p. *Membership Total:* 12. *Membership
Criteria & Audience Served:* Generally only criteria is desire to
extend film service to patronage and the ability to pay. The
audience served can be any individual, group, or service offered
by a public library. *Yearly Assessment:* $1250. *Budget:* $15,000
(7/1/76-7/1/77). *General Meetings:* Held annually in libraries of
membership. *Preview-Selection Committee Meetings:* Handled
through correspondence & phone calls after individual previewing. *Pubns:* Catalog.

NORTHERN OHIO FILM CIRCUIT, Elyria Public Library,
Elyria 44035. *Tel:* (216) 323-5747. *In Charge:* Gary B.
Pummell, Admin.
Film Holdings: 700p. *Membership Total:* 10. *Membership Criteria & Audience Served:* Any new member must be voted upon by
the present membership. The Northern Ohio Film Circuit serves
a population of over 1,000,000 people in northern Ohio. This
does not include Cleveland or Cuyahoga County. Any adult
possessing a library card with special registration for film use
may borrow films. *Yearly Assessment:* $1500 plus 25¢ per
showing. *Budget:* $29,000 (7/1/75-6/30/76). *General Meetings:*
Held one or two times per year at various libraries. *Preview-Selection Committee Meetings:* At least four times per year.
Pubns: Catalog.

NORWELD (NORTHWEST LIBRARY DISTRICT), PO Box
828, Bowling Green 43402. *Tel:* (419) 353-5721. *In Charge:*
Richard C. Pritsky, Project Dir.
Film Holdings: 16mm—95t/p. S8mm—750t/1200p. *Membership
Total:* 34 public libraries plus 17 branches. 16mm film program
(Central Pool)—29 public libraries. S8mm film circuit—29 libraries plus 13 branches. *Membership Criteria & Audience
Served:* NORWELD is a multi-county coop library project
funded for a large part by federal (LSCA) funds. The two film
programs are just one side of the operation. Full membership is
open to any public library in the 13-county NW Ohio area. The
16mm film program began in July 1975. $25,000 has been spent
to purchase films. Except to obtain about 115 films by the end of
1976. The S8mm film circuit began in 1974. By June 1976, will
have 42 outlets (libraries & branches) on the circuit, each with a
collection of 30 S8mm films rotated monthly. Membership fees
range in 1976 from approx. $260 to $800, based on operating
budget size. *Initial Fee:* Varies. *Yearly Assessment:* Varies.
Budget: $125,000 (1/1/76-12/31/76). *General Meetings:* Held
twice yearly. *Preview-Selection Committee Meetings:* As
needed. *Pubns:* Catalog.

WESTERN OHIO FILM CIRCUIT, 650 W Market St, Lima
45801. *Tel:* (419) 228-5113, ext 8. *In Charge:* Cathy Woodward, Admin.
Film Holdings: 492t. *Membership Total:* 12. *Membership Criteria & Audience Served:* There are no specific requirements for
membership. The audience served is a vast one ranging from

church & civic groups to schools to home entertainments. *Initial
Fee:* $1000. *Yearly Assessment:* $750 plus 30¢ per showing.
General Meetings: Held annually at Lima Public Library, Lima.
Preview-Selection Committee Meetings: Each member previews
a subject area and sends recommendations to admin. *Pubns:*
Catalog.

Pennsylvania

PENNSYLVANIA PUBLIC LIBRARIES FILM CENTER,
4501 Ethel St, Harrisburg 17101. *Tel:* (717) 232-7556. *TWX:*
510-650-4919. *In Charge:* Dean Blair, Coord.
Film Holdings: 1275t/1821p. *Membership Total:* 600. *Membership Criteria & Audience Served:* Serve patrons of public libraries throughout the Commonwealth of Pennsylvania. Service is free. *Budget:* $85,000 (7/1/76-6/30/77). *Pubns:* Catalog.

TRI-COUNTY FILM COOPERATIVE, c/o Montgomery
County-Norristown Public Library, 542 DeKalb St, Norristown 19401. *Tel:* (215) 277-3355. *TWX:* 510-660-0158. *In
Charge:* Stephen Landstreet, Head of AV.
Membership Total: 3. *Membership Criteria & Audience Served:*
As a coop, make available entire collections to the general
public of three library districts (which correspond exactly to
Bucks, Chester, & Montgomery Counties). In addition to Montgomery County-Norristown Public Library, the Cooperative
includes the film libraries of Bucks County Free Library, 50 N
Main St, Doylestown 18901 (*Tel:* 215-348-9081) and Chester
County District Library Center, 235 W Market St, West Chester
19380 (*Tel:* 215-696-8960). *Budget:* $10,000 (1/75-12/75). *General
Meetings:* Held sporadically at the three libraries. *Preview-Selection Committee Meetings:* Preview independently. *Pubns:*
Catalog.

TRI-STATE COLLEGE LIBRARY COOPERATIVE FILM
LIBRARY, c/o Widener College, Wolfgram Memorial Library Media Center, Chester 19013. *Tel:* (215) 876-5551, ext
268. *In Charge:* Henrietta S. Bruce, Chairperson, Media
Librarian.
Film Holdings: 162t/p. *Total Membership:* 19. *Membership
Criteria & Audience Served:* Those members of the Tri-State
College Library Cooperative who also opt for membership in the
Film Library. The library is set up to support the academic
curriculum. *Yearly Assessment:* $25. *Budget:* $1500 (7/1/75-
6/30/76). *General Meetings:* Annually, rotating among member
libraries. *Preview-Selection Committee Meetings:* 3 or 4 times
per year. *Pubns:* Catalog, updates of new acquisitions.

Rhode Island

RHODE ISLAND LIBRARY FILM COOPERATIVE, Warwick
Public Library, 600 Sandy Lane, Warwick 02886. *Tel:* (401)
739-2278. *In Charge:* David Green, Dir.
Film Holdings: 744t/914p. *Pubns:* Catalog.

Virginia

RICHMOND AREA FILM LIBRARY COOPERATIVE, c/o
Virginia Commonwealth University, AV Dept, 901 Park
Ave, Richmond 23284. *Tel:* (804) 770-4834. *In Charge:*
Gerard B. McCabe, Dir of University Libraries.
Film Holdings: 1500t/1600p. *Membership Total:* 12. *Membership Criteria & Audience Served:* Must be located in Greater
Richmond metropolitan area. Serve academic, public & special
libraries. *Budget:* $13,500 (7/1/75-6/30/76). *General Meetings:*
Held once a year on a rotating basis. *Pubns:* Catalog.

Washington

WASHINGTON LIBRARY FILM CIRCUIT, Washington State
Library, Olympia 98504. *Tel:* (206) 866-6471. *In Charge:*
Jere Pennell, Exec Dir.

Washington (cont'd)
Film Holdings: 1211t/1422p. *Membership Total:* 38. *Membership Criteria & Audience Served:* Any public library in the State who can meet the membership requirements may join: first, a formal request to the Director. Prospective member must have $3,900 to pay for a new packet & equipment. Yearly dues of $1725. Definite commitment in terms of manpower for operation of packet. Instruction to librarians & film clerks. Workshops. Storage area. $50 a year for supplies. A reserve fund for film damage. The audience served is the public of Washington state. *Budget:* $65,550. *General Meetings:* Held periodically all around the state. *Preview-Selection Committee Meetings:* Year-round film previews by members. *Pubns:* Catalog, MEMOs.

ADDENDUM

Information on the following libraries arrived too late to be included as an entry in proper geographic order within the text of the directory.

California

P- COVINA PUBLIC LIBRARY, 234 N Second St, Covina 91722. *Tel:* (213) 967-3935. *In Charge:* Mary Stolz, Film Librarian. *Member:* Public Library Film Circuit.

P- DOWNEY CITY LIBRARY, 8490 E Third St, Downey 90241. *Tel:* (213) 923-3256. *In Charge:* Betty Davis, Film Librarian. *Member:* Public Library Film Circuit.

P- GLENDORA LIBRARY AND CULTURAL CENTER, 140 S Glendora Ave, Glendora 91740. *Tel:* (213) 963-4168. *In Charge:* Sandy Sheffer, Film Librarian. *Member:* Public Library Film Circuit.

P- SANTA FE SPRINGS CITY LIBRARY, 11700 Telegraph Rd, Santa Fe Springs 90670. *Tel:* (213) 868-7738. *In Charge:* Mary Austin, Film Librarian. *Member:* Public Library Film Circuit.

Iowa

P- CENTRAL REGIONAL LIBRARY SYSTEM, 4235 Fleur Dr, Des Moines 50315. *Tel:* (515) 287-3102. *In Charge:* Marjorie Humby, Admin. *Member:* Films for Iowa Library Media Servs.

P- EAST CENTRAL REGIONAL LIBRARY SYSTEM, 1500 Second Ave, SE, Suite 203, Cedar Rapids 52400. *Tel:* (319) 365-0521. *In Charge:* Mrs. Nelle Neafie, Admin. *Member:* Films for Iowa Library Media Servs.

P- MUSSER PUBLIC LIBRARY, 304 Iowa Ave, Muscatine 52761. *Tel:* (319) 263-3065. *In Charge:* Dorothy Bemis, Acting Dir. *Member:* Films for Iowa Library Media Servs.

P- NORTHEASTERN REGIONAL LIBRARY SYSTEM, 619 Mulberry St, Waterloo 50703. *Tel:* (319) 233-1200. *In Charge:* Mrs. Beverly Lind, Admin. *Member:* Films for Iowa Library Media Servs.

P- OTTUMWA PUBLIC LIBRARY, 129 N Court, Ottumwa 52501. *Tel:* (515) 682-7563. *In Charge:* Dennis Davis, Dir. *Member:* Films for Iowa Library Media Servs.

P- SOUTHEASTERN REGIONAL LIBRARY SYSTEM, 321 Main, Davenport 52801. *Tel:* (319) 324-0019. *In Charge:* Marie Lindquist, Admin. *Member:* Films for Iowa Library Media Servs.

P- WATERLOO PUBLIC LIBRARY, Fifth & Mulberry Sts, Waterloo 50703. *Tel:* (319) 291-4496. *In Charge:* Michael Phipps, Dir. *Member:* Films for Iowa Library Media Servs.

P- WEST DES MOINES PUBLIC LIBRARY, 1105 Grand Ave, West Des Moines 50265. *Tel:* (515) 274-2544. *In Charge:* Mrs. Miriam E. Hansen, Dir. *Member:* Films for Iowa Library Media Servs.

Maryland

P- ENOCH PRATT FREE LIBRARY, AV Dept, 400 Cathedral St, Baltimore 21201. *Tel:* (301) 396-4616. *Film Serv Est:* 1949. *In Charge:* Helen W. Cyr, Head, AV Dept. *AV Staff:* 12 (2 prof, 8 cl, 2 tech). *Film Sel:* chief film librarian's decision.

Free-Loan Film Serv *Eligibility:* institutions, schools, churches, civic organizations, religious groups, & indiv on an indiv library card from any public library in Md. *Restrictions:* for indiv & inst, only in state. Cannot use for fund-raising, transmit electronically, 4 films not to exceed 90 minutes of running time. Available to researchers/scholars for on-site viewing. *Loan Period:* Baltimore city, 1 day, Mon thru Fri, or weekend, Fri to Mon. County, 7-10 days. *Total Yr Film Loan:* 23,443.

Film Collection 2611t/3899p. Approx 300t acquired annually. *Circ:* 16mm, 2258t/3171p; 8mm reel, 353t/728p. *Noncirc:* 16mm, 10t/8p. *Pubns:* catalog, every 3 yrs ($2.50); suppl, 2 yearly issues after complete catalog. Publish quarterly list of films, filmstrips, and 2"x2" slides; special lists, e.g., Black Man in Films.

Other Film Serv Film reference serv, film fairs/festivals, library film programs. Permanent viewing facility available for rent to community.

Other Media Collections *Filmstrips:* sound sets, 313t/517c; silent sets, 165t/185c. *Slides:* sets, 500t/559c.

Budget & Expenditures Total library budget $737,591 (FY 7/1/74-7/1/75). *Member:* AFI, ALA, EFLA, FLIC.

Video Serv *Est:* 1975. *Video Use:* documentation of community/school events, in-service training, as art form. Video serv available on demand. Produce video tapes.

Video Equipment/Facilities *In-House Use Only:* portapak (2), ½" reel b&w, Panasonic NV3082; recording & editing deck (1), ½" reel col, Panasonic NV3130; playback deck (4), ¾" cassette col, Sony VP1000; editing deck (1), ½" reel col, JVC; monitors (4); microphones (4); tripods (2); audio tape recorders (12). Have portable viewing installation (monitor & playback deck & headphones on table). Provide training in use of equipment to library staff.

Video Collection Maintained by purchase. Use/play ¾" cassette. *Sources:* commercial distributors, local Public Broadcasting System. *Tape Sel:* published reviews, communication with staff of local Public Broadcasting station. Tapes organized by title shelved alphabetically. *Other Video Serv:* programming, reference serv, production workshops. *Pubns:* catalog listing of video collection.

Mississippi

P- JACKSON METROPOLITAN LIBRARY, 301 N State St, Jackson 39201. *Tel:* (601) 352-3677, ext 14. *Film Serv Est:* 1973. *In Charge:* Earl Terrell Blackmon, AV Coord. *AV Staff:* 2 (1 prof). *Film Sel:* committee preview. *Holdings:* general collection.

Free-Loan Film Serv *Eligibility:* org members, indiv with library cards, & others, such as members of Miss. Film Coop. *Restrictions:* for indiv, only in state. Cannot use for fund-raising, transmit electronically. Available to researchers/scholars for on-site viewing. May borrow by mail. *Loan Period:* 2 days. *Total Yr Film Loan:* 1000.

Film Rental Serv *Eligibility:* no restrictions. *Restrictions:* only in state. Cannot use for fund-raising, transmit electronically. *Rental Period:* 2 days. *Total Yr Film Booking:* 10,000 (based on number of times shown).

Film Collection 1000t/p. Approx 500t acquired annually. *Circ:* 16mm, 1000t/p. *Pubns:* catalog, as needed ($1.00); suppl, every few months.

Other Film Serv Film fairs/festivals, library film programs. Permanent viewing facility available free to community. *Member:* ALA, Miss. Film Coop, Miss. Library Assn.

Video Serv *Est:* 1972. *Video Staff:* 2 f-t, 2 p-t. *Video Use:* to increase community's library use. Video serv available on demand.

Video Equipment/Facilities *In-House Use Only:* Sony TV & tape player, b&w or col. Have portable viewing installation (2 Sony players). *Equipment Loan Period:* one-half hour per person in library if another is waiting. Provide training in use of video equipment to aides & viewing public.

Video Tape Loan/Rental/Sale Serv *Serv Provided:* free-loan. *Loan Eligibility:* indiv with library cards. *Restrictions:* for indiv, interlibrary loan & to members of Film Coop; for inst, within 6-county system & Film Coop. Cannot use for fund-raising. *Loan Period:* 2 days.

Video Collection Maintained by purchase. Use/play ¾″ cassette. *Sources:* ETV, special Watch a Book experimental program from Bloomington, Ind. Tapes organized alphabetically. *Collection:* Approx 200. *Pubns:* 16mm film & video cassette catalog.

Cable & CCTV Have CCTV in inst, with 2 monitors. *Programming Sources:* over-the-air commercial & public broadcasting, ETV, & The Public TV Library, Bloomington, Ind.

New York

P- NEW YORK PUBLIC LIBRARY, Donnell Library Center, Film Library, 20 W 53 St, New York 10019. *Tel:* (212) 790-6418. *Film Serv Est:* 1958. *In Charge:* William Sloan, Film Librarian. *AV Staff:* 8 (3 prof, 4 cl, 1 tech). *Film Sel:* committee previews, chief film librarian's decision. *Holdings:* animated film 10%, black studies 10%, children's films 33%, experimental films 5%, feature films 3%, social documentary 60%, women 5%.

Free-Loan Film Serv *Eligibility:* civic groups, religious groups, indiv with library cards, prof groups, such as day care centers, hospitals. *Restrictions:* for indiv & inst, only in city. Cannot use for fund-raising, transmit electronically, borrow for classroom use. Available to researchers/scholars for on-site viewing. May not borrow by mail. *Loan Period:* 2 days or over a weekend. *Total Yr Film Loan:* 38,000.

Film Collection 3500t/4000p. Approx 300t acquired annually. *Circ:* 16mm, 3500t/4000p. *Pubns:* catalog, every 3 yrs ($5.00); suppl, no set policy ($2.00).

Other Film Serv Obtain film from coop loan system (NY State Library). Permanent viewing facility available for rent to community.

Other Media Collections Video tapes, 50t/c.

Budget & Expenditures Total film budget $72,500 (FY 7/1/75-7/1/76) *Member:* AECT, AFI, ALA, EFLA, FLIC, NY State Library Assn.

Ohio

P- TUSCARAWAS COUNTY PUBLIC LIBRARY, 121 Fair, NW, New Philadelphia 44663. *Tel:* (216) 364-4474. *Film Serv Est:* 1953. *In Charge:* Cathy Spears, AV Specialist. *AV Staff:* 1. *Film Sel:* committee preview & Northern Ohio Film Circuit. *Holdings:* business & industrial collection 90%, holiday films 10%.

Free-Loan Film Serv *Eligibility:* no restrictions ($1.00 service fee). *Restrictions:* only in county (for Circuit). Cannot use for fund-raising. *Loan Period:* 1 day. *Total Film Loan:* 262 loans, 1540 showings (1/1/75-7/1/75).

Film Collection 87t. *Circ:* 16mm, 34t/p; 8mm reel, 53t. Figures do not include 444 regional films from Ohio Film Circuit or 284 8mm films from Mideastern Ohio Library Organization (MOLO).

Other Film Serv Obtain film from cooperative loan system (Northern Ohio Film Service).

Other Media Collections *Audio:* disc, 33⅓ rpm, 900t/p; tape, cassette, 20c. *Filmstrips,* silent, 50.

Budget & Expenditures Total library budget $23,000 (FY 1/1/75-12/31/75). Total AV budget $3000.